Michael B. Gerrard, Editor

✔ KU-735-652

Global Climate Change and U.S. Law

For updates: http://www.abanet.org/abapubs/globalclimate

ABA
Defending Liberty
Pursuing Justice

ABA SECTION OF
ENVIRONMENT
ENERGY AND RESOURCES

American Bar Association
Section of Environment, Energy, and Resources

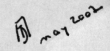

may 2002

Cover and interior design by Cathy Zaccarine.

The materials contained herein represent the opinions and views of the authors and/or the editors, and should not be construed to be the views or opinions of the law firms or companies with whom such persons are in partnership with, associated with, or employed by, nor of the American Bar Association or the Section of Environment, Energy, and Resources, unless adopted pursuant to the bylaws of the Association.

Nothing contained in this book is to be considered as the rendering of legal advice for specific cases, and readers are responsible for obtaining such advice from their own legal counsel. This book and any forms and agreements herein are intended for educational and informational purposes only.

11 09 08 07 07 5 4 3 2 1

Cataloging-in-Publication data is on file with the Library of Congress

Global climate change / Michael B. Gerrard, editor.

ISBN-13: 978-1-59031-816-4

Discounts are available for books ordered in bulk. Special consideration is given to state bars, CLE programs, and other bar-related organizations. Inquire at Book Publishing, ABA Publishing, American Bar Association, 321 North Clark Street, Chicago, Illinois 60610.

www.ababooks.org

Summary Table of Contents

Contents

Chapter Four
The Impact of the Kyoto Protocol on U.S. Business 101
Donald M. Goldberg and Angela Delfino

Chapter Seven
Consideration of Climate Change in Facility Permitting **259**
Laura H. Kosloff and Mark C. Trexler

Chapter Ten
State Initiatives **343**
David Hodas

Chapter Eleven
The State Response to Climate Change: 50-State Survey **371**
Pace Law School Center for Environmental Legal Studies

Acknowledgments

As I served as an officer and then chair of the American Bar Association's Section of Environment, Energy and Resources (SEER), it became clear that the issue of climate change was having an increasingly pervasive impact on many aspects of environmental law. Even in the absence of a federal regulatory scheme, activity was bursting forth at the regional, state and local levels, and in administrative agencies, legislatures and courts. This book is an attempt to capture the state of U.S. law on the subject. It is current through August 2006 but reflects a few developments through November 2006.

Many people contributed to the preparation of this book. Most important are the authors of the individual chapters, who all devoted considerable time to putting together extraordinarily useful analyses, and some of whom also peer-reviewed others' chapters. Brock Adler and Nancy Ketcham-Colwill also generously peer-reviewed several chapters. Thanks also go to Sam Kalen, chair of SEER's Book Publications Committee; Rick Paszkiet and Amelia Stone of ABA Publishing; Dolia Christoffersen, my terrific secretary; and my colleagues at Arnold & Porter LLP. My family — Barbara, David, William — continue to provide wonderful (and needed) love and support.

Each chapter in this book represents the views of each chapter author in his or her individual capacity. It does not necessarily reflect the views of the authors' firms, employers, or clients, nor of the editor or the authors of the other chapters, nor of the American Bar Association or SEER. This book does not provide legal advice, which should be sought from the reader's own lawyers.

Michael B. Gerrard
New York, N.Y.
November 2006

About the Authors

Joel Beauvais is an associate with the Washington, D.C. office of Latham & Watkins LLP. He is a member of the firm's Environment, Land and Resources and Litigation Departments. Mr. Beauvais served from 2003 to 2004 as a law clerk to the Hon. Harry T. Edwards of the United States Court of Appeals for the D.C. Circuit and during the October 2004 term as a law clerk to the Hon. Sandra Day O'Connor, Associate Justice of the United States Supreme Court. Mr. Beauvais graduated *summa cum laude* from the New York University School of Law in 2002, and from 2002 to 2003 was a Postgraduate Fellow at the NYU School of Law Center for Environmental and Land Use Law.

Andrew S. Bergman is an attorney with Porter, Wright, Morris & Arthur in Columbus, Ohio. He specializes in environmental law and is a member of the firm's Environmental Markets Practice Area. He is also an adjunct professor at Ohio State University's School of Public Health, teaching environmental law and policy. He received a bachelor's degree from Grinnell College, a master's degree from the Humphrey Institute of Public Affairs at the University of Minnesota, and a law degree from the University of Minnesota Law School.

Kyle Danish is a member of the law firm of Van Ness Feldman, P.C., in the Washington, D.C. office. He advises a range of private and nonprofit clients on environmental and energy matters, with a special focus on corporate climate strategy and emissions trading-related transactions. Mr. Danish is also an adjunct faculty member at American University's Washington College of Law.

Angela Delfino is an associate in the Environmental Law Group at the London offices of LeBoeuf, Lamb, Greene & MacRae. Her academic career includes time spent at the University of Lisbon, LMU in Munich, UCL in London, and the New York University School of Law. She worked for PLMJ law firm in Lisbon, the Directorate-General Environment of the European Commission in Brussels, and the Center for International Environmental Law in Washington, D.C.

John C. Dernbach is professor of law at Widener University in Harrisburg, Pennsylvania. He recently returned to teaching after directing the Policy Office at the Pennsylvania Department of Environmental Protection for two and a half years. He is the editor of *Stumbling Toward Sustainability* (Environmental Law Institute 2002) and co-authored an amicus brief to the U.S. Supreme Court on behalf of 18 prominent climate scientists in *Massachusetts v. Environmental Protection Agency*. Professor Dernbach chairs the ABA Committee on Sustainable Development, Ecosystems, and Climate Change. He is a member of the Roundtable on Science and Technology for Sustainability of the National Academy of Sciences and also is a member of the IUCN Commission on Environmental Law. He graduated *cum laude* from the University of Michigan Law School in 1978 and *summa cum laude* from the University of Wisconsin-Eau Claire in 1975.

Michael B. Gerrard is a partner in the New York office of Arnold & Porter LLP, where he heads the environmental practice group. He has practiced environmental law in New York since 1979, concentrating in litigation, project development, and transactions, and handling numerous trials and appellate arguments. He was the 2004-2005 chair of the American Bar Association's Section of Environment, Energy and Resources. He has also taught environmental law as an adjunct professor at Columbia Law School and the Yale School of Forestry and Environmental Studies. He is the author or editor of seven books, two of which were named Best Law Book of the Year by the Association of American Publishers—*Environmental Law Practice Guide* (12 volumes) and *Brownfields Law and Practice* (4 volumes). His other books concern environmental justice, facility siting, and environmental impact review.

Donald M. Goldberg helped found the Center for International Environmental Law in 1989 and currently directs its Climate Change Program. Mr. Goldberg was the first NGO representative on the U.S. delegation to the international climate negotiations and the first NGO representative to the Global Environment Facility. He helped organize the Alliance of Low-Lying Island States. He headed an evaluation of "joint implementation" forest projects and an EPA-funded study of compliance with the Kyoto Protocol, which contributed to several key elements of the Protocol's Marrakesh Accords. Mr. Goldberg has been developing "action targets" with the World Resources Institute and assisting the Inuit Circumpolar Conference to bring a global warming-based human rights lawsuit against the United States. He is co-chair and vice-chair, ABA Committee on Climate Change and Sustainable Development, and adjunct professor, American University Washington College of Law.

Gary Guzy is senior vice president and national practice leader, Emerging Environmental Risk, at Marsh USA Inc. He develops new solutions for clients in responding to emerging environmental risks and trends, spearheading Marsh's efforts in the climate-change arena. He was the general counsel of the U.S. Environmental Protection Agency from 1998 to 2001. He has also served as counselor to the administrator at EPA and as the agency's deputy general counsel, as well as having been a senior attorney at the U.S. Department of Justice. Mr. Guzy practiced environmental law in the private sector as a partner with the law firm of Foley Hoag LLP. He began his legal career as a judicial clerk to Judge Elbert P. Tuttle of the U.S. Court of Appeals for the Eleventh Circuit.

David J. Hayes is the global chair of the Environment, Land & Resources Department at Latham & Watkins. Mr. Hayes is resident in the Washington, D.C. office, where his practice focuses on counseling, litigation, and transactions involving environmental, energy, and natural resources matters. He served as the Deputy Secretary of the Interior during the second term of the Clinton Administration; he is the former chairman of the board of the Environmental Law Institute; and he is a current board member of American Rivers, RESOLVE, and the Natural Heritage Institute. Mr. Hayes is a graduate of Stanford Law School and the University of Notre Dame, and he is chair of Stanford Law School's Board of Visitors.

J. Kevin Healy received his law degree from Fordham University School of Law in 1973. He served in the Enforcement Division of the U.S. Environmental Protection Agency, Region II, and as the general counsel of the New York City Department of Environmental Protection. As a member of the law firm Bryan Cave, LLP, he represents corporations and public entities in a wide variety of environmental matters. Mr. Healy has served as co-chair of the Global Climate Change Subcommittee of the New York State Bar Association Environmental Law Section since 1992 and was a member of Governor Pataki's Climate Change Task Force.

Michael E. Heintz is an associate with Porter Wright Morris & Arthur, LLP in Columbus, Ohio. He specializes in environmental law and economic development issues and is a member of the Environmental Markets practice area at Porter Wright. He received a bachelor's degree in environmental science from Purdue University and his law degree and master's degree in environmental science from Indiana University.

Dennis D. Hirsch is associate dean and professor at Capital University Law School. Dean Hirsch directs the Environmental Law Concentration Program at Capital and teaches courses in the areas of environmental law and property law. He is also counsel to the firm at Porter, Wright, Morris & Arthur in Columbus, Ohio, where he specializes in environmental law and is a member of the firm's Environmental Markets practice area. He received his B.A. from Columbia University and his J.D. from Yale Law School.

David R. Hodas is professor of law at Widener University School of Law (Delaware). He earned a B.A. *cum laude and with departmental honors* from Williams College in 1973; a J.D. *cum laude* from Boston University School of Law in 1976; and an LL.M. in environmental law from Pace University School of Law in 1989, where he was the Feldshuh Fellow. Professor Hodas is a member of the editorial board of *Natural Resources and Environment*, is a former chair and vice-chair of the Sustainable Development, Ecosystems and Climate Change Committee of the ABA Section of Environment, Energy, and Resources, is a member of the Environmental Law Commission of the IUCN—The World Conservation Union and its Energy Law and Climate Change Specialists Group, and served on the American Bar Association's Standing Committee on Environmental Law from 2001 to 2006.

Tom Kerr is a senior analyst at the International Energy Agency (IEA), where he manages policy and data analysis aimed at advancing clean energy, including work on combined heat and power, energy efficiency, transportation, carbon capture and storage, and energy research and development. Prior to this, he was chief of the U.S. Environmental Protection Agency's Energy Supply and Industry Branch, a group that promotes clean energy solutions to avoid the risk of climate change. The Branch included partnership efforts to encourage corporate renewable energy purchasing and to facilitate clean, efficient combined heat and power projects, as well as Climate Leaders, a partnership that promoted corporate commitments to reduce and report greenhouse gas emissions.

Laura H. Kosloff is senior counsel at EcoSecurities Consulting Ltd., an energy and environmental policy consulting firm based in Portland, Oregon, specializing in strategic and project-related climate change services to the private sector. Ms. Kosloff works on greenhouse gas mitigation project development, corporate strategic advice, and development of emissions-trading programs. She has provided policy development support in forestry and climate change, early action crediting, and state and local climate change policies and measures, and has developed legal agreements addressing legal issues associated with the long-term reliability of GHG mitigation projects. She was previously a trial attorney in the Environmental Section at the U.S. Department of Justice. Ms. Kosloff holds a J.D. degree from the University of California at Davis and a B.A. in Environmental Science from Antioch College.

Bradford C. Mank is the James B. Helmer, Jr. Professor of Law at University of Cincinnati. He teaches environmental law, international environmental law, and administrative law. He practiced environmental law with a private law firm in Hartford and as an assistant attorney general for the state of Connecticut. He earned his B.A. at Harvard University and his J.D. at Yale Law School.

Roberta F. Mann is professor of law at Widener University School of Law in Wilmington, Delaware. She is a *cum laude* graduate of the Arizona State University School of Law and obtained her LL.M. in taxation with distinction from the Georgetown University Law Center. She serves as the chair of the A.B.A. Tax Section Committee on Individual and Family Taxation. Her research interests focus on the intersection of tax policy and environmental policy, and she has written about the effect of tax policy on sprawl, climate change, and transportation choice.

Jonathan Martel is a partner at Arnold & Porter LLP. His practice concentrates on air emissions matters, environmental litigation and counseling. Mr. Martel's recent work includes representation of electric utilities, consumer products, automotive, nonroad equipment, and other diversified manufacturers in Clean Air Act regulatory, permitting, and enforcement matters, as well as other environmental litigation and regulatory matters. He rejoined Arnold & Porter's Washington, D.C. office in 1994 after serving for three years at the Office of General Counsel of the U.S. Environmental Protection Agency.

Alan S. Miller is a principal project officer in the International Finance Corporation, Department of Environment and Social Development. His responsibilities include coordination of climate change policies and oversight of clean energy and other environmentally beneficial projects funded by the Global Environment Facility. He is a member of the summer faculty at the Vermont Law School and co-author of a leading environmental law textbook, *Environmental Regulation: Law, Science and Policy* (New York: Aspen Publishing, 5th ed., 2006).

Matthew Morreale is an associate at Cravath, Swaine & Moore LLP. His practice focuses on addressing environmental risks in connection with business transactions, including mergers and acquisitions, public and private offerings of securities, and acquisition and other financing matters, as well as advising clients on environmental regulatory matters. He is an adjunct professor at the Benjamin N. Cardozo School of Law, where he teaches environmental concerns in corporate transactions. He also was the senior articles and notes editor of the *Columbia Journal of Environmental Law* and now serves on its board of directors.

Lee Paddock is director of Environmental Law Programs at Pace University School of Law. He is chair of the ABA SEER Committee on Innovations, Management Systems and Trading and serves as a senior consultant to the National Academy of Public Administration. Mr. Paddock was director of Environmental Policy for the Minnesota Attorney General's Office from 1986 to 1999.

Jeffrey A. Smith is the partner in charge of the environmental practice group at Cravath, Swaine & Moore LLP. His practice encompasses environmental matters arising in financings, underwritings, and mergers and acquisitions, nationally and internationally, in all industries. Mr. Smith also provides day-to-day counseling on disclosure obligations and board responsibilities relating to environmental issues and advice on environmental litigation. He currently serves as chairman of the ABA's Special Committee on Environmental Disclosure. Mr. Smith received an A.B., *cum laude*, from Harvard University in 1974 and a J.D. from the University of Pennsylvania Law School in 1981.

Eleanor Stein is an administrative law judge at the New York State Public Service Commission, where she presided over New York's Renewable Portfolio Standard proceeding. For the last two years Judge Stein was visiting associate professor at Albany Law School, teaching, among other courses, transnational environmental law with a focus on catastrophic climate change. Recently she has served as the Virtual Guest Lecturer in Environmental Law at Mercer University Law School.

Kerri L. Stelcen is a law clerk at Arnold & Porter LLP in Washington, D.C. She will receive her J.D. from George Washington University School of Law in May 2007.

Mark C. Trexler is director of EcoSecurities Consulting Ltd. and is involved in corporate strategic planning, GHG market forecasting, mitigation project development, and the development of emissions-trading programs. Dr. Trexler has published extensively on climate change mitigation and has served as a lead author for the Intergovernmental Panel on Climate Change. Prior to joining EcoSecurities Consulting Ltd., Dr. Trexler established TC+ES and worked at the World Resources Institute in Washington, D.C., where he managed technical analysis of the very first carbon mitigation projects pursued by U.S. companies. He also has been involved in the siting of facilities generating more than 2,000 MWs of power and has worked on a range of energy policy issues, including technology R&D and efficiency standards. Dr. Trexler earned his M.P.P. in 1982 and his Ph.D. in 1990 from the Graduate School of Public Policy at the University of California, Berkeley, and his B.A. in 1978 from Antioch College.

Glossary*

Additionality: "Environmental additionality" requires that emission reductions represent a physical reduction or avoidance of emissions over those that would have occurred under a business-as-usual scenario. "Financial additionality" means projects will only earn credit if funds additional to existing official development assistance commitments are specifically dedicated to achieve the greenhouse gas reductions. Source: hhtp://www.co2e.com/common/glossary.asp.

Afforestation: Planting of new forests on lands that have not been recently forested. Source: http://www.pewclimate.org/global-warming-basics/full_glossary/terms_a.cfm

Annex I Parties: The 40 countries plus the European Economic Community listed in Annex I of the United Nations Framework Convention on Climate Change that agreed to try to limit their GHG emissions: Australia, Austria, Belarus, Belgium, Bulgaria, Canada, Croatia, Czech Republic, Denmark, European Economic Community, Estonia, Finland, France, Germany, Greece, Hungary, Iceland, Italy, Japan, Latvia, Liechtenstein, Lithuania, Luxembourg, Monaco, The Netherlands, New Zealand, Norway, Poland, Portugal, Romania, Russian Federation, Slovakia, Slovenia, Spain, Sweden, Switzerland, Turkey, Ukraine, and the United States. Source: http://www.pewclimate.org/global-warming-basics/full_glossary/terms_a.cfm

Annex B Parties: Parties to the Kyoto Protocol that have taken on binding emissions reduction commitments. The list is identical to the Annex I Parties listed in the Convention except that it does not include Belarus or Turkey. Source: http://www.pewclimate.org/global-warming-basics/full_glossary/terms_a.cfm

Annex B entities: Private entities domiciled in Annex B Party countries.

Assigned Amount: The amount to which an Annex I Party (with a commitment inscribed in Annex B of the Kyoto Protocol) must reduce its emissions over the five-year commitment period. Source: http://unfccc.int/kyoto_mechanisms/items/2998.php

Berlin Mandate: The Berlin Mandate is the decision reached at the first session of the Conference of the Parties to the Framework Convention in 1995 in Berlin that the commitments made by Annex I countries were inadequate and thus needed to be strengthened.

Best Available Control Technology (BACT): An emission limitation under the Clean Air Act based on the maximum degree of emission reduction (considering energy,

---

* The glossary was prepared by Mackenzie Schoonmaker, Pace Law School and Yale School of Forestry and Environmental Studies (Class of 2007).

environmental, and economic impacts) achievable through application of production processes and available methods, systems, and techniques.
Source: http://www.epa.gov/OCEPAterms/bterms.html

Biodiesel: A fuel consisting of mono-alkyl esters of long-chain fatty acids derived from vegetable oils or animal fats, designated B100, and meeting the requirements of ASTM D 6751. Biodiesel is typically produced by a reaction of a vegetable oil or animal fat with an alcohol, such as methanol or ethanol, in the presence of a catalyst to yield mono-alkyl esters and glycerin, which is removed.
Source: http://www.biodiesel.org/resources/definitions/

Biomass: Living and recently living biological material that can be used as fuel or for industrial production. Examples include crop waste and sawmill wood waste.

Carbon adders: An expected future price for carbon dioxide that is assumed when comparing investment options. Carbon adders are a means of accounting for possible future costs of mitigating greenhouse gas emissions.
Source: http://www.pewclimate.org/states.cfm?ID=57

Carbon intensity: The ratio of carbon emissions to economic activity.

Certified Emission Reductions: Units earned by Annex I investors for participation in eligible Clean Development Mechanism projects under the Kyoto Protocol.

Clean Development Mechanism: An arrangement under the Kyoto Protocol allowing Annex I countries to invest in emission-reducing projects in developing countries as an alternative to what is generally considered more costly emission reductions in their own countries.
Source: http://en.wikipedia.org/wiki/Clean_Development_Mechanism

Clean renewable energy bond: A tax credit bond under the Energy Policy Act of 2005 that serves as an incentive for producing electricity from renewable energy sources.
Source: http://www.appanet.org/files/PDFs/CREB.pdf

Conference of the Parties: All the governments that are parties to the Framework Convention.

Corporate Average Fuel Economy: The sales weighted average fuel economy, expressed in miles per gallon, of a manufacturer's fleet of passenger cars or light trucks with a gross vehicle weight rating of 8,500 lbs. or less, manufactured for sale in the United States, for any given model year.
Source: http://www.nhtsa.dot.gov/cars/rules/cafe/overview.htm

Deforestation: The loss of forest cover.

Designated operational entity: The entity designated by the Conference of the Parties as qualified to validate proposed Clean Development Mechanism project activities as well as verify and certify reductions in anthropogenic emissions by sources of greenhouse gases.
Source: http://www.cincs.org/glossary.html

Emission Reduction Units: Units of greenhouse gas reductions that have been generated in developed countries via the joint implementation mechanism under the Kyoto Protocol.

Flexible Mechanisms: The emissions-trading system, joint implementation, and Clean Development Mechanism under Kyoto Protocol.

Framework Convention: United Nations Framework Convention on Climate Change.

Global Warming Potential: A system of multipliers devised to enable comparison of warming effects of different gases.
Source: http://www.pewclimate.org/global-warming-basics/full_glossary/terms_d.cfm

Green building: The practice of reducing building impacts on human health and the environment through better siting, design, construction, operation, maintenance, and removal. Key elements are sustainable site development, water savings, energy efficiency, materials selection, and indoor environmental quality.

Green pricing: Programs in which electricity users are charged a premium for electricity produced from renewable sources.
Source: http://www.repartners.org/greenpower.htm

Integrated gasification combined-cycle: A power generation process that uses a combined-cycle format with a gas turbine driven by combusted syngas, and exhaust gases comprised of heat exchanged with water/steam to generate superheated steam to drive a steam turbine. This method separates the carbon dioxide so that it can be sequestered.
Source: http://www.iea-coal.org.uk/content/default.asp?PageId=74

Joint Implementation: One of the three market mechanisms established by the Kyoto Protocol. Joint Implementation occurs when an Annex B country invests in an emissions reduction or sink enhancement project in another Annex B country to earn emission reduction units.
Source: http://www.pewclimate.org/global-warming-basics/full_glossary/terms_j.cfm

Land use, land use change, forestry (LULUCF): Land uses and land-use changes can act either as sinks or as emission sources. It is estimated that approximately one-fifth of global emissions result from LULUCF activities. The Kyoto Protocol allows Parties to receive emissions credit for certain LULUCF activities that reduce net emissions.
Source: http://www.pewclimate.org/global-warming-basics/full_glossary/terms_j.cfm

Leadership in Energy and Environmental Design (LEED): A voluntary, consensus-based national standard, promulgated by the United States Green Building Council, for developing "green buildings."

Marrakesh Accords: A set of agreements reached at the Conference of the Parties 7 meeting in 2001 on the rules of meeting the targets set out in the Kyoto Protocol.

Millennium Development Goals (MDGs): The MDGs are a set of goals that the world's governments agreed to that promote poverty reduction, education, maternal health and gender equality, and aim at combating child mortality, AIDS and other diseases. Source: http://www.undp.org/mdg

National Allocation Plan: Under the European Union greenhouse gas allowance trading scheme, each member state has to establish a national allocation plan for each trading period. In this allocation the member state decides the total number of allowances to be created for the period and the distribution of these allowances to individual plants.

National Ambient Air Quality Standards: Pollutant concentration limits established by the United States Environmental Protection Agency pursuant to the Clean Air Act.

New Source Performance Standards: Standards issued by the United States Environmental Protection Agency pursuant to the Clean Air Act to dictate the level of pollution that a new stationary source may produce.

New source review: Clean Air Act requirement that certain stationary sources of air pollution obtain permits before they start construction or are significantly modified.

Nonattainment new source review: Clean Air Act permits that are required for new major sources or major sources making a major modification in a nonattainment area (i.e., an area that does not meet the relevant National Ambient Air Quality Standard).

Prevention of Significant Deterioration: Clean Air Act requirements that apply to new major sources or major modifications at existing sources for pollutants where the location of the source is in attainment or unclassifiable with the National Ambient Air Quality Standards.

Project Design Document: A project-specific document required under the Clean Development Mechanism rules.

Public Benefit Funds: State-established funds that are dedicated to supporting energy efficiency and renewable energy projects.

Reforestation: Replanting of forests on lands that have recently been harvested. Source: http://www.pewclimate.org/global-warming-basics/full_glossary/terms_j.cfm

Renewables: Renewable energy sources, which include energy obtained from geothermal, wind, photovoltaic, solar, and biomass. Source: http://www.pewclimate.org/global-warming-basics/full_glossary/terms_j.cfm

Renewable Portfolio Standard: Policy that ensures that a minimum amount of renewable energy is included in the portfolio of electricity resources serving a state or country. Source: http://www.awea.org/policy/rpsbrief.html

Removal Units: Credits arising from emissions reductions created by countries by means of projects that reduce emissions according to Article 3 of the Kyoto Protocol. Source: http://knowledge.allianz.com/en/globalissues/climate_change/climate_emissions_trading/glossary_emissions_trading.html

Sequestration: Keeping carbon dioxide out of the atmosphere, either through biological processes (e.g., trees) or by injecting it into geological formations.

Supplementarity: The requirement of the Kyoto Protocol that Annex I parties may not meet their emission targets entirely through use of emissions trading and other flexibility mechanisms, but must also have adequate domestic energy and other policies.

Acronyms

AAU:	Assigned Amount Units
BACT:	Best available (pollution) control technology
BAU:	Business as usual
CAA:	Clean Air Act
CAFE:	Corporate Average Fuel Economy
CARB:	California Air Resources Board
CCS:	Carbon capture and storage
CDM:	Clean Development Mechanism
CER:	Certified Emission Reduction
CFCs:	Chlorofluorocarbons
CH_4:	Methane
CO_2:	Carbon dioxide
COP:	Conference of the Parties (to UNFCCC)
COP/MOP:	Conference of the Parties serving as the Meeting of Parties to the Kyoto Protocol
CREB:	Clean renewable energy bond
CCX:	Chicago Climate Exchange
CTE:	Committee on Trade and Environment
DOE:	Designated operational entity
DOE :	U.S. Department of Energy
ECAs:	Export credit agencies
EPA:	U.S. Environmental Protection Agency
EPAct:	Energy Policy Act of 2006
EPCA:	Energy Policy and Conservation Act of 1975
ERU:	Emissions Reduction Unit
EU ETS:	European Union Emissions Trading Scheme
FASB:	Federal Accounting Standards Board
FERC:	U.S. Federal Energy Regulatory Commission
FTC:	U.S. Federal Trade Commission
G-8:	Group of Eight industrialized nations (Canada, France, Germany, Italy, Japan, Russia, United Kingdom and the United States)
GAAP:	Generally Accepted Accounting Principles
GATS:	General Agreement on Trade in Services
GATT:	General Agreement on Tariffs and Trade
GEF:	Global Environment Facility
GHG:	Greenhouse gas
GWP:	Global warming potential
HFCs:	Hydrofluorocarbons
IBRD:	International Bank for Reconstruction and Development
IDA:	International Development Association

IEA:	International Energy Agency
IET:	International Emission Trading program of Kyoto Protocol
IFC:	International Finance Agency
IFIs:	International financial institutions
IGCC:	Integrated gasification combined-cycle
IPCC:	Intergovernmental Panel on Climate Change
ISO:	Independent system operator
ISO:	International Organization for Standardization
JI:	Joint Implementation
lCER:	Long-term certified emissions reductions
LEED:	Leadership in Energy and Environmental Design
LULUCF:	Land use, land use change, forestry
MD&A:	Management's Discussion and Analysis
MDG:	Millenium Development Goals
MEAs:	Multilateral environmental agreements
MVICSA:	Motor Vehicle Information and Cost Savings Act
NAAQS:	National Ambient Air Quality Standards
NAP:	National Allocation Plan
NASA:	U.S. National Aeronautics and Space Administration
NEG-ECP:	Conference of New England Governors and Eastern Canadian Premiers
NEPA:	National Environmental Policy Act
NFIP:	National Flood Insurance Program
NGO:	Non-governmental organization
NHTSA:	National Highway Traffic Safety Administration
NNSR:	Nonattainment new source review
NO_x:	Nitrogen oxide
NRC:	National Research Council
NRC:	U.S. Nuclear Regulatory Commission
NSR:	New source review
NSPS:	New Source Performance Standards
ODA:	Official development assistance
OECD:	Organization for Economic Co-operation and Development
PDD:	Project Design Document
PFCs:	Perfluorocarbons
PSD:	Prevention of Significant Deterioration
RGGI:	Regional Greenhouse Gas Initiative
RMUs:	Removal Units
SAB 92:	SEC Staff Accounting Bulletin No. 1992
SEC:	U.S. Securities and Exchange Commission
SF_6:	Sulfur hexafluoride
SO_2:	Sulfur dioxide
tCER:	Temporary certified emissions reductions
'33 Act:	Securities Act of 1933

'34 Act: Securities and Exchange Act of 1934
UNCLOS: United Nations Convention on the Law of the Sea
UNDP: United Nations Development Programme
UNEP: United Nations Environment Programme
UNFCCC: United Nations Framework Convention on Climate Change
WB: World Bank
WGA: Western Governors' Association
WRI: World Resources Institute
WTO: World Trade Organization

chapter one
Introduction and Overview

Michael B. Gerrard

I. Plan of the Book

The United States Congress has enacted, and the President has signed, no laws that explicitly require public entities or private companies to mitigate their impact on the global climate. Nonetheless, several laws have the effect of requiring or encouraging mitigation, and many more are now under active consideration. Some of these laws are federal; more are state or local. International law also has a major influence.

This book aims to cover comprehensively the state of U.S. law as it relates to global climate change. It is up-to-date as of mid-2006, and also reports on some developments later in 2006. An accompanying Web site, www.abanet.org/abapubs/globalclimate, will report on subsequent legal events in this very fast-moving field.

Part I of this book lays out the international and national legal framework. The principal international agreement on the subject, the Kyoto Protocol, has entered into force. Though the United States has not signed it and is therefore not bound by it, the Protocol is already affecting U.S. companies that operate abroad, and many observers believe that before the decade ends the U.S. will have negotiated a re-entry into the international climate change control system. This anticipation is powerfully influencing many domestic actions. Meanwhile, as also discussed in Part I, the U.S. courts have been asked to decide whether existing statutes, and the common law, can be used to advance—or impede—efforts to control climate change.

In the absence of a mandatory federal program, the states—acting both individually and as part of regional organizations—are adopting their own programs. So are many municipalities. Part II surveys these efforts.

Corporations find themselves in the middle of these debates. As described in Part III, the legal and scientific uncertainties surrounding climate change combine to create serious issues of disclosure and of corporate governance. The insurance industry is playing

Above is a photograph of Muir Glacier taken on August 13, 1941, by glaciologist William O. Field; below, a photograph taken from the same vantage on August 31, 2004, by geologist Bruce F. Molnia of the United States Geological Survey. According to Molnia, between 1941 and 2004 the glacier retreated more than twelve kilometers (seven miles) and thinned by more than 800 meters (875 yards).

Source: National Snow and Ice Data Center , W. O. Field, B. F. Molnia

an especially active role. Various governmental subsidies, mostly in the form of tax relief, are available to help companies advance alternative sources of energy.

Part IV concerns the legal aspects of various efforts now under way to reduce climate change. These include a wide variety of voluntary programs (some organized by the government, some purely private); emissions trading programs; and carbon sequestration.

This introductory chapter attempts to summarize the factual and scientific background that is necessary to understand the rest of the book. It relies primarily on governmental statistics and other official sources; when matters are the subject of serious controversy, it says so. This chapter discusses global temperature trends, the relevance of the greenhouse effect to these trends, the nature of greenhouse gases and the activities that generate them, and the environmental impacts of these phenomena. It then describes some of the solutions that have been proposed to mitigate climate change, and the various projections as to what the future may bring.

After this scientific introduction, this chapter presents a brief summary of the rest of the book, with references to the chapters where details may be found. Thus the reader who does not have the time to read the book cover-to-cover will be directed to the particular chapters of interest.

II. The Factual Context

A. Global Temperatures and the Greenhouse Effect

According to NASA, 2005 was the warmest year in over a century, but was about the same as 1998, the second warmest year.[1] The other three warmest years in the past century were 2002, 2003 and 2004.[2]

In 1998 and 1999, Michael Mann and colleagues published a study that concluded that the Northern Hemisphere was warmer during the late 20th century than at any other time during the past millennium.[3] This study presented what became known as the "hockey stick" chart, because it showed a fairly steady, slightly upward temperature line over the last centuries that ended with a sharp upward spike in temperatures in recent decades. This depiction became controversial, and Congress asked the National Research Council (NRC) to assess Mann's conclusions. In June 2006 the NRC concluded "with a high level of confidence that global mean surface temperature was higher during the last few decades of the 20th century than during any comparable period during the preceding four centuries." It said, with less confidence, that there is some evidence that temperatures in many locations were higher during the past 25 years than during any period of comparable length since A.D. 900.[4]

The past century has also seen other changes to the global climate. The most authoritative summary was adopted in September 2001 at a plenary session of the Intergovernmental Panel on Climate Change (IPCC),* a body created in 1988 by two United Nations agencies—the World Meteorological Organization and the U.N. Environment Programme. Among the IPCC's conclusions was that during the 20th century the duration of ice cover of rivers and lakes very likely decreased by about two weeks in mid- and high latitudes of the Northern Hemisphere; that Arctic sea-ice likely thinned by 40% in recent decades in late summer to early autumn; that non-polar glaciers experienced widespread retreat; that permafrost thawed, warmed, and degraded in parts of the polar, sub-polar, and mountainous regions; that El Niño events became more frequent, persistent, and intense; that plant and animal ranges shifted poleward and up in elevation for

Exhibit 1-1
Variation of the Earth's Surface Temperature, Year 1000 to Year 2100

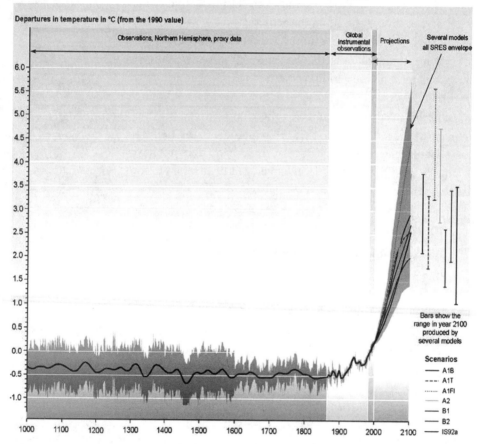

Source: Intergovernmental Panel on Climate Change (2001)

---

* As this book was going to press in February 2007, the IPCC released the first volume of its latest assessment. The new report mostly affirmed and expanded upon the conclusions of the IPCC's 2001 report, but with a great deal more confidence in the results, and based on much more data. See www.ipcc.ch.

plants, insects, birds and fish; and that global mean sea level increased at an average annual rate of 1-2 millimeters. Moreover, the IPCC found that hot days likely increased, cold/frost days likely decreased, heavy precipitation events likely increased at mid- and high northern latitudes, and droughts likely increased in a few areas.[5]

The same IPCC report recounted increasing concentrations of several key gases in the atmosphere, For example, between the pre-industrial period (1750) and 2000, carbon dioxide increased from 280 parts per million (ppm) to 368 ppm in 2000; methane increased from 700 ppb (parts per billion) to 1,750 ppb, and nitrous oxide increased from 270 ppb to 316 ppb.[6] One striking data set (known as the Keeling Curve) was compiled by NASA at the Mauna Loa Observatory in Hawaii; it shows a steady upward climb in carbon dioxide levels every year since observations began in 1958.

The IPCC further concluded that these increases in temperature and pollution levels were largely caused by human activities.[7] This is not an especially controversial conclusion. Nor is it widely disputed that the principal mechanism is through alteration of the natural "greenhouse effect." Solar radiation passes through the atmosphere, is absorbed by the earth's surface, and warms it. Some of this energy is converted into heat, causing the emission of infrared radiation back into the atmosphere. Some of the infrared radiation passes through the atmosphere and is lost in space. However, the accumulation of certain gases in the atmosphere traps some of the infrared radiation and prevents it from escaping. Instead, the greenhouse gases absorb and re-radiate the heat. This warms the surface of the earth. The more greenhouse gases in the atmosphere, the more warming of the earth.

B. Greenhouse Gases

The most important greenhouse gas (GHG) is carbon dioxide. It is emitted in by far the greatest quantities. However, there are other GHGs, and pound-for-pound they are more potent than carbon dioxide in that they trap more energy. This potency is expressed as global warming potential (GWP). The other principal GHGs are methane, which has a GWP of 23 (meaning it is 23 times more potent than carbon dioxide on a ton-for-ton basis); nitrous oxide, with a GWP of 296; various types of hydrofluorocarbons, with GWPs ranging from 120 to 12,000; various perfluorocarbons, with GWPs ranging from 5,700 to 11,900; and sulfur hexafluoride, with a GWP of 22,200.[8]

Two physical characteristics of all these GHGs are especially important. First, once emitted into the atmosphere, they travel around the globe; thus a ton of carbon dioxide that is emitted over New York has the same effect on global warming as a ton emitted over Paris, Shanghai or Honolulu. Second, most types of GHGs circling the globe remain in the atmosphere for many decades;[9] thus their emissions have a cumulative impact. This is unlike many other air pollutants, which have primarily local or regional effects, and which degrade or are washed back to earth within weeks or months.

Different countries emit far different quantities of GHGs. When all of the principal GHGs are combined, taking account of their respective GWPs, and expressed in million metric tons of carbon dioxide equivalent ($MtCO_2e$), the countries with the largest emissions in 2000 are shown in Exhibit 1-2.

Exhibit 1-2
Top GHG Emitting Countries[10] (CO_2, CH_4, N_2O, HFCs, PFCs, SF_6)—2000

	Country	$MtCO_2e$	% of World GHGs
1	United States	6,928	20.6
2	China	4,938	14.7
3	EU-25	4,725	14.0
4	Russia	1,915	5.7
5	India	1,884	5.6
6	Japan	1,317	3.9
7	Germany	1,009	3.0
8	Brazil	851	2.5
9	Canada	680	2.0
10	United Kingdom	654	1.9
11	Italy	531	1.6
12	South Korea	521	1.5
13	France	513	1.5
14	Mexico	512	1.5
15	Indonesia	503	1.5
16	Australia	491	1.5
17	Ukraine	482	1.4
18	Iran	480	1.4
19	South Africa	417	1.2
20	Spain	381	1.1
21	Poland	381	1.1
22	Turkey	355	1.1
23	Saudi Arabia	341	1.0
24	Argentina	289	0.9
25	Pakistan	285	0.8
	Top 25	**27,915**	**83**
	Rest of world	**5,751**	**17**
	Developed	**17,355**	**52**
	Developing	**16,310**	**48**

These figures for 2000 are not representative of what came before or what is projected for the future. In 2000, the combined GHG emissions of China and India added to about the same as the total for the United States. In 1990, China and India were 57% of the U.S. total. Under a 2004 projection from the U.S. government, China alone is expected to surpass the United States before 2020, and in 2025, China and India together are expected to contribute 133% as much CO_2 as the U.S.[11] However, the International Energy Agency projected in late 2006 that China would overtake U.S. carbon dioxide emissions before 2010.[12]

C. U.S. Emissions

When GWP is considered, the total U.S. emissions of GHGs in 2004 in carbon dioxide equivalents is shown in Exhibit 1-3.

Exhibit 1-3
U.S. Emissions of GHGs[13]

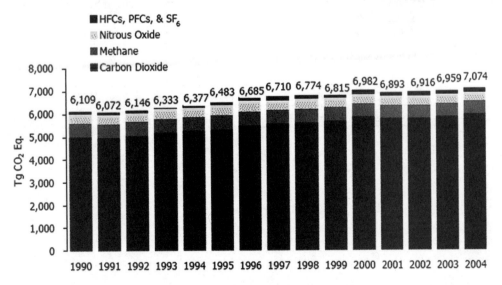

Source: U.S. Energy Information Administration

Since 84% of the total U.S. emissions (as measured in global warming potential) are from carbon dioxide, the sources of carbon dioxide emissions deserve special attention. Exhibit 1-4 shows the sources of carbon dioxide emissions from energy and industry in 1990 and 2004.

Exhibit 1-4
U.S. Carbon Dioxide Emissions from Energy and Industry[14]
Million Metric Tons Carbon Dioxide

Fuel Type or Process	1990	2004
Energy Consumption		
Petroleum	2,179.6	2,595.2
Coal	1,783.5	2,090.0
Natural Gas	1,027.2	1,203.4
Renewables	6.2	11.4
Energy Subtotal	**4,996.6**	**5,899.9**
Nonfuel Use Emissions	**98.1**	**114.3**
Nonfuel Use Sequestration	**251.2**	**316.6**
Adjustments to Energy		
U.S. Territories	31.1	61.7
Military Bunker Fuels	-13.6	-9.2
International Bunker Fuels	-100.1	-84.4
Total Energy Adjustments	**-82.6**	**-31.9**
Adjusted Energy Subtotal	**4,914.0**	**5,868.0**
Other Sources		
Natural Gas Flaring	9.1	5.9
Carbon Dioxide in Natural Gas	14.0	17.8
Cement Production	33.3	44.8
Other Industrial	26.8	28.7
Waste Combustion	5.1	7.8
Total Other Sources	**88.3**	**105.0**
Total	**5,002.3**	**5,973.0**

When broken down by end-use sector, the figures are as shown in Exhibit 1-5.

Exhibit 1-5
U.S. Carbon Dioxide Emissions from Energy Consumption[15]
Million Metric Tons Carbon Dioxide

End-Use Sector	1990	2004
Residential	953.7	1,212.0
Commercial	780.7	1,024.2
Industrial	1,692.2	1,730.2
Transportation	1,569.9	1,933.7
Total	**4,996.6**	**5,899.9**
Electric Power	1,803.1	2,298.6

The above table highlights the importance of two particular activities to the U.S. emissions picture—electricity generation and transportation. The generation of electricity created 39% of all the carbon dioxide from energy consumption in 2004. Carbon dioxide from electricity generation increased 28% from 1990 to 2004. During this period, the amount of carbon dioxide from the burning of natural gas increased 67%, from the burning of coal increased 25%, and from the burning of petroleum declined 4%.[16]

The transportation sector accounted for 33% of total U.S. energy-related carbon dioxide emissions in 2004. Almost all of this—98%—is from the consumption of petroleum products. Specifically, 60% of total transportation sector emissions involve gasoline (automobiles and light trucks), 22% is diesel fuel (heavy trucks, locomotives, ships), and 12% is jet fuel. Carbon dioxide emissions from petroleum use for transportation was 24% higher in 2004 than in 1990.[17]

Exhibit 1-6
2004 Key Categories

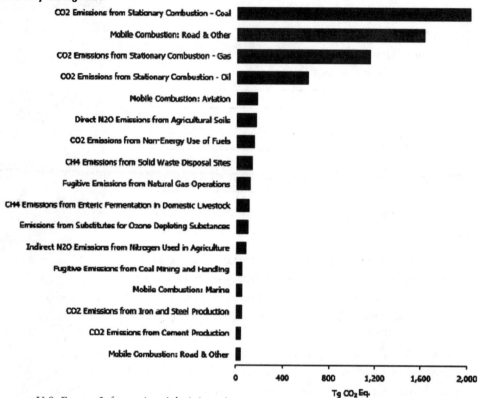

Source: U.S. Energy Information Administration

As shown in Exhibit 1-7, 10 states account for half of all U.S. carbon dioxide emissions from fossil fuel combustion.

Exhibit 1-7
Carbon Dioxide Emissions from Fossil Fuel Combustion, 2001[18]
Million Metric Tons (MMT)

Rank	State	CO_2 Emissions (MMT)	% Change, 1990-2001
1	TX	668.5	178
2	CA	368.7	85
3	PA	258.0	4
4	OH	249.5	20
5	FL	235.6	347
6	IL	224.7	21
7	IN	223.8	79
8	NY	207.6	-0.2
9	MI	189.1	46
10	LA	183.0	128

Several factors account for the wide variation in percent changes shown above for emissions growth over the last two decades. The two high-emitting states with the highest percentage increases, Texas and Florida, both saw substantial increases in vehicle travel due to population growth and spread-out land development. Additionally, Texas increased its emissions from coal by 138%, and Florida by 64%, between 1990 and 2001, while New York, the only one of these states to have a decrease in carbon dioxide emissions, reduced its emissions from coal by 35% (largely by converting electric power plants from coal to oil or natural gas).[19]

The largest anthropogenic source of U.S. *methane* emissions is energy production—mostly from coal mines and from petroleum and natural gas systems. Waste management (primarily landfills) and agriculture (mostly from domesticated animals) are also significant sources of methane.[20] *Nitrous oxide* comes chiefly from agricultural activities, especially nitrogen fertilization and, to a lesser extent, the management of animal waste. Motor vehicles and certain industrial processes are also significant sources of nitrous oxide.[21] The other GHG gases—hydrofluorocarbons, perfluorocarbons, and sulfur hexafluoride—are used in numerous applications, such as solvents, refrigerants, firefighting, aerosol propellants, aluminum and semiconductor production, and in electrical equipment.[22]

D. Environmental Impacts

Virtually every weekly issue of the peer-reviewed journals *Science* and *Nature*, and many more specialized publications, report on new studies showing the adverse effects of global climate change. Global warming skeptics believe that many of these reports are overblown, or based on weak evidence, or ignore positive impacts; other observers believe that these studies understate a dire situation, and that when considered together they paint a picture of a planet rushing toward an irreversible tipping point. This book, written by lawyers, not scientists, does not attempt to settle these debates, though the remnants of the debates of course have important influence over the actions of decision-makers in the legal sphere—judges, legislators, and government executives. As noted above, a fairly reliable common denominator is the reports of the IPCC. Its 2001 assessment reached the following conclusions. (Where the IPCC stated the degree of confidence it has in its views, that is stated here.)

Direction of impact—"Projected climate change will have beneficial and adverse effects on both environmental and socio-economic systems, but the larger the changes and rate of change in climate, the more the adverse effects predominate."[23] The IPCC found, with medium confidence, "[w]hile beneficial effects can be identified for some regions and sectors for small amounts of climate change, these are expected to diminish as the magnitude of climate change increases. In contrast, many identified adverse effects are expected to increase in both extent and severity with the degree of climate change."

Human health effects—"Overall, climate change is projected to increase threats to human health, particularly in lower- income populations, predominantly within tropical/subtropical countries."[24] Some of the effects are direct; though there is reduced cold stress in temperate countries, there is also increased heat stress, and loss of life in floods and storms. Indirect effects include changes in the ranges of disease vectors such as mosquitoes, water-borne pathogens, and food availability and quality (medium to high confidence).[25]

Species diversity—"Ecological productivity and biodiversity will be altered by climate change and sea-level rise, with an increased risk of extinction of some vulnerable species (high to medium confidence)."[26] The IPCC said it expected "[s]ignificant disruptions of ecosystems from disturbances such as fire, drought, pest infestation, invasion of species, storms, and coral bleaching events."

Agricultural productivity—In some temperature areas, potential yields of cereal crops increase with small increases in temperature "but decrease with larger temperature changes (medium to low confidence). In most tropical and subtropical regions, potential yields are projected to decrease for most projected increases in temperature (medium confidence)."[27]

Water supply—"Climate change will exacerbate water shortages in many water-scarce areas of the world."[28] Higher water temperatures would degrade freshwater quality generally (high confidence), but increased flows may offset this in some regions.

Extreme weather—"Models project that increasing atmospheric concentrations of greenhouse gases result in changes in frequency, intensity, and duration of extreme events, such as more hot days, heat waves, heavy precipitation events, and fewer cold days."[29] This could lead to increased risks of flood and droughts, "and predominantly adverse impacts on ecological systems, socio-economic sectors, and human health."

As a further indication of the international scientific consensus on these issues, in June 2005 the heads of the national science academies of 11 leading nations issued a joint statement endorsing the IPCC conclusions and declaring that "a lack of full scientific certainty about some aspects of climate change is not a reason for delaying an immediate response that will, at a reasonable cost, prevent dangerous anthropogenic interference with the climate system." The signatory science academies were those of the United States, Brazil, Canada, China, France, Germany, India, Italy, Japan, Russia and the United Kingdom.[30]

E. Projecting the Future

In June 2006 the U.S. Energy Information Administration (EIA), part of the Department of Energy, published its *International Energy Outlook 2006*. It projected future worldwide carbon dioxide emissions based on a reference case that did not assume implementation of the Kyoto Protocol. The reference case projections are shown in Exhibit 1-8.

Exhibit 1-8
World Carbon Dioxide Emissions[31]
Million Metric Tons

Year	Projection
1990	21,223
2003	25,028
2010	30,362
2015	33,663
2020	36,748
2025	40,045
2030	43,676

Thus EIA foresees more than a doubling of carbon dioxide emissions between 1990 and 2030. The EIA added that the Kyoto Protocol would only decrease worldwide emissions very slightly (from 43,676 MMT to about 43,000 MMT in 2030), largely because the largest emitters of carbon—especially the United States and China—were assumed not to participate in Kyoto's mandatory reductions (though even if the U.S. did participate, emissions would still grow drastically).

The IPCC projected future levels of carbon dioxide in the atmosphere, and future temperatures, to the year 2100 using a variety of scenarios. The projections varied widely and are subject to considerable uncertainty and controversy. However, even the most optimistic scenarios yielded radically higher carbon dioxide levels and temperatures than now exist (see Exhibit 1-8). One of the reasons is that "[i]nertia is a widespread inherent characteristic of the interacting climate, ecological, and socio-economic systems. Thus some impacts of anthropogenic climate change may be slow to become apparent, and some could be irreversible if climate change is not limited in both rate and magnitude before associated thresholds, whose positions may be poorly known, are crossed."[32] For example, according to the IPCC, surface air temperatures would continue to rise for a century or more, while sea level would continue to rise for

Exhibit 1-9

Past and Future Carbon Dioxide Emissions

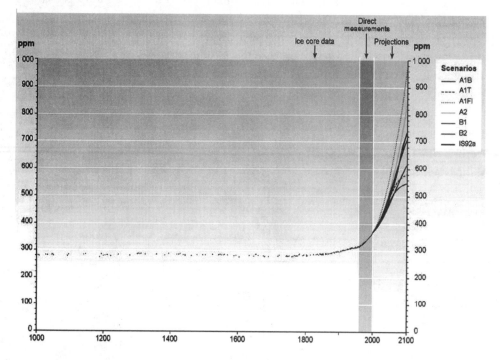

Source: Intergovernmental Panel on Climate Change (2001)

many centuries, after carbon dioxide emissions are stabilized. (As just noted, carbon dioxide emissions appear to be on their way to at least doubling, not stabilizing.)

A report released by the U.K. government in October 2006 stated that the current stock of greenhouse gases in the atmosphere is equivalent to around 430 parts per million (ppm) carbon dioxide, compared with only 280 ppm before the Industrial Revolution. According to the report, even if the annual flow of emissions did not increase beyond current rates, the level would reach 550 ppm by 2050; current rates of development could lead to a 550 ppm level as early as 2035. The report went on to say that stabilizing at or below a 550 ppm level would require global emissions to be around 25% below current levels by 2050. That level would lead to severe adverse environmental impacts. To stabilize at 450 ppm and thereby make the adverse effects less severe, global emissions would need to peak in the next 10 years and then fall at more than 5% per year, reaching 70% below current levels by 2050.[33]

F. Possible Solutions

Methods to control GHG emissions generally fall into three categories: energy efficiency and conservation, energy sources, and carbon sequestration. Most readers will already be very familiar with the first two of these categories, while the third is not as well known, so it requires greater discussion.

Energy efficiency and conservation—Carbon dioxide emissions from vehicles are inversely proportional to fuel economy. Given the importance of the transportation sector in emissions, more stringent vehicle fuel economy standards are high on all lists of ways to reduce GHGs. So are more use of energy-saving technologies, such as hybrid vehicles, and less use of heavy and energy-inefficient vehicles, such as sport utility vehicles (SUVs). Also frequently discussed, but requiring more decentralized effort over a much longer period of time, is changing land use patterns to reduce vehicle miles traveled by passenger vehicles and to increase trips by mass transit, bicycles and walking.

In the residential and commercial sectors, much effort is now being directed toward construction of "green buildings" that minimize the use of energy in heating, cooling, lighting, and other operations. Energy efficiency is also being pursued in home appliances and office equipment. Likewise, increased efficiency of many industrial operations has the potential to yield major reductions in GHG emissions.

Energy sources—The use of renewable, low-carbon sources of energy, such as wind, solar and biomass, is widely embraced, at least in theory. The substitution of natural gas for coal is generally popular, provided natural gas supplies are adequate. On the other hand, there continues to be major controversy over the idea of generating more electricity from nuclear power. An increasing number of environmentalists who have traditionally opposed nuclear power are growing to accept it more if the security and waste issues are resolved.

Carbon sequestration—This emerging concept falls into two categories: biological sequestration and carbon capture and storage (CCS).[34]

Biological sequestration uses the natural function of plants to take up carbon dioxide through photosynthesis. A portion of the carbon is then stored in plant biomass and in soil organic matter. The amount of carbon dioxide stored in natural systems can be increased through forest conservation and management, reforestation, agricultural practices that increase levels of soil organic matter, and conserving or creating certain kinds of wetlands. However, stored carbon can be released back into the atmosphere as a result of fires, decomposition, and land use changes. Storage through biological sequestration is also very difficult to measure.

CCS uses engineered systems to capture carbon dioxide before it is emitted into the atmosphere, and then injects it into reservoirs for long-term storage. Much attention is now going to integrated gasification combined cycle, an emerging technology that helps capture carbon dioxide from power plants. Carbon-capture technologies are also being developed for other industries, such as cement manufacture, oil refining, ammonia production, and iron and steel manufacture. Once the carbon dioxide is captured, it can be transported (usually by pipeline) to underground geologic formations; this may have the side benefit of enhancing oil and gas recovery from certain formations. The injection of carbon dioxide into the bottom of the oceans has also been proposed, but this raises environmental as well as legal concerns.

Possible programs—All agree that no one or two of the above measures will be nearly enough to stabilize GHG emissions; a combination of many approaches will be needed. In one well-known effort to describe a comprehensive program, two professors at Princeton University, Robert H. Socolow and Stephen W. Pacala, have listed 15 actions that could each, when phased in over 50 years, prevent the release of 25 billion tons of carbon. If seven of them were carried out, emissions would be frozen at their current levels for the next 50 years and then reduced by about half over the following 50 years.[35] These are the listed measures:

Exhibit 1-10
Greenhouse Gas Emissions Flow, 2004
(million metric tons of carbon dioxide-equivalent)

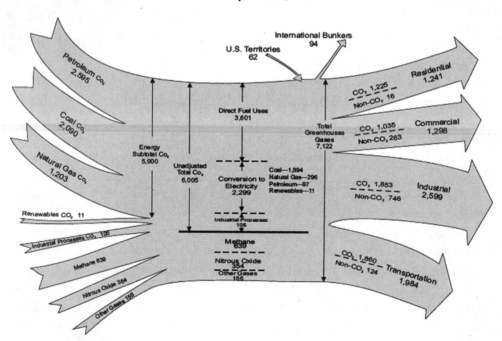

Source: Energy Information Administration, Emissions of Greenhouse Gases in the United States 2004.

End-user efficiency and conservation
1. Increase fuel economy of two billion cars from 30 to 60 mpg.
2. Drive two billion cars 5,000 rather than 10,000 miles/year (at 30 mpg).
3. Cut electricity use in homes, offices and stores by 25%.

Power generation
4. Raise efficiency at 1,600 large coal-fired plants from 40% to 60%.
5. Replace 1,400 large coal-fired plants with gas-powered plants.

Carbon capture and storage
6. Install CCS at 800 large coal-fired power plants.
7. Install CCS at coal plants that produce hydrogen for 1.5 billion vehicles.
8. Install CCS at coal-to-syngas plants.

Alternative energy sources
9. Add twice today's nuclear output to displace coal.
10. Increase wind power 40-fold to displace coal.
11. Increase solar power 700-fold to displace coal.
12. Increase wind power 80-fold to make hydrogen for cars.
13. Drive two billion cars on ethanol, using one-sixth of world cropland.

Agriculture and forestry
14. Stop all deforestation.
15. Expand conservation tillage to 100% of cropland.

III. The Legal Context

Now that the basic factual setting has been set forth, the legal situation will be briefly summarized. Considerable detail on all items discussed below will be found in the referenced chapters in this book.

A. International Context[36]

The international agreement underlying this field is the United Nations Framework Convention on Climate Change (UNFCCC). It was opened for signature at the United Nations Conference on Environment and Development in Rio de Janeiro in 1992. The United States Senate ratified it on October 7, 1992, and President George H.W. Bush signed it less than a week later. It came into force in 1994 and now has 189 parties.

The UNFCCC states that developed and developing countries have "common but differentiated responsibilities and respective capabilities." It established a Conference of the Parties (COP)—a legislative-like body that meets annually and is charged with devising ways to implement the UNFCCC's goals. At the COP meeting in Kyoto, Japan, in 1997, the Kyoto Protocol was negotiated. The United States actively participated in these negotiations, and Vice President Al Gore played a central role.

The Kyoto Protocol sets binding emissions limitations on the developed countries that have signed it. These limitations must be met during the period 2008–2012. They are set as designated percentage reductions from a 1990 baseline of each country's emissions. Different countries must meet different percentages; the figure for the United States was to be 7% below 1990 emissions. All in all, the Kyoto Protocol aimed to reduce emissions about 30% below what would have occurred under "business as usual." The six principal types of GHGs are covered—carbon dioxide, methane, nitrous oxide, hydrofluorocarbons, perfluorocarbons, and sulfur hexafluoride—though everything is expressed in the form of "carbon dioxide equivalent" tons of GHG emissions.

> **. . . the Kyoto Protocol is very flexible in the ways that countries could meet their emission reduction mandates.**

Recognizing the difficulty of lowering emissions at a time when they would otherwise be increasing, the Kyoto Protocol is very flexible in the ways that countries could meet their emission reduction mandates. Each country makes its own decisions on how to reduce emissions. Developed country signatories could trade emissions among themselves. Thus if Country A can reduce its GHG emissions by 100 tons at a lower cost than Country B can achieve the same emissions reduction, the two countries can enter into a transaction whereby Country B pays Country A a sum they agree upon; Country A spends the money on the emissions reduction, and Country B gets credit for an emissions reduction.

Two additional forms of flexibility under the Kyoto Protocol are "Joint Implementation," in which a developed country invests in an emission-reducing project in another developed country, and the "Clean Development Mechanism," in which a developed country invests in a project in a developing country. There are special provisions for countries "undergoing the process of transition to a market economy"—that is, the former Soviet-bloc nations. Countries are also allowed to band together and be treated as a unit; thus the European Union has developed its own system within the overall Kyoto structure, with each country having its own emissions reduction mandate, and with a vigorous emissions trading program among European Union countries.

Another separate international law regime that affects climate change is the international development assistance arena, which is attempting to introduce less-polluting energy technologies to developing countries. The World Bank, the Global Environment Facility, and other international financial institutions are participating, with financial assistance from developing countries.[37]

B. U.S. Policy[38]

Though the Clinton Administration negotiated the Kyoto Protocol, it did not have support in the Senate for ratification. During the Kyoto talks, the Senate, by a vote of 95-0, passed a resolution sponsored by Senators Robert Byrd and Chuck Hagel directing the government not to enter into any agreements under the UNFCCC that would "mandate new commitments to limit or reduce greenhouse gas emissions for the Annex I [developed country] Parties, unless the protocol or other agreement also mandates new specific scheduled commitments to limit or reduce greenhouse gas emissions for Developing Country Parties within the same compliance period." The Kyoto Protocol did not meet this standard.

On March 13, 2001, less than two months after taking office, President George W. Bush expressly repudiated the Kyoto Protocol, primarily on the grounds that it exempts China and India from compliance, and would cause serious harm to the U.S. economy. Nonetheless, the Kyoto Protocol entered into force in February 2005 when it was ratified by Russia. The United States and Australia are the only major industrialized countries that are not parties. Thus they are not bound by the Kyoto Protocol, though the rest of the developed world is actively participating.

President Bush's policy has been to encourage voluntary reductions in GHG emissions. In May 2001 he established a policy of reducing the GHG intensity of the U.S. economy by 18% by 2012, meaning that less GHG would be emitted for each unit of economic activity. However, the U.S. economy has been growing at a faster rate than 18% over 11 years, and thus total U.S. GHG emissions continue to grow under this policy.

The United States has numerous programs to inventory GHGs (one of the requirements of the UNFCCC) and to conduct research in climate change and the technologies to control it. There are tax incentives for renewable energy and energy efficiency (as well as for conventional fossil energy).[39] Another Bush Administration initiative is the Asia-Pacific Partnership on Clean Development and Climate. It includes the U.S., South Korea, India, China, Australia and New Zealand, which collectively account for approximately half of global GHG emissions. This program provides a voluntary framework for international cooperation to facilitate development and transfer of clean technologies and practices among the partner countries.[40]

C. Clean Air Act and Motor Vehicle Emissions[41]

Vigorous legal activity has swirled around the role of the Clean Air Act (CAA). The three key questions posed to date—all very much still open—are:

- What authority does the CAA confer on the U.S. Environmental Protection Agency (EPA) to regulate climate change?
- If EPA does possess such authority, does it have a mandatory duty under the CAA to act?
- Does the CAA preempt state authority to regulate motor vehicle emissions of GHGs?

During the Clinton Administration, two successive EPA general counsels opined that EPA does have the authority under the CAA to regulate GHGs as "air pollutants." Their successor under President George W. Bush took the opposite view.

While a global problem would seem to require at least national action, the federal government has declined to take regulatory action.

In 1999, several nongovernmental organizations petitioned EPA to regulate certain GHG emissions from new motor vehicles. This petition wound its way through the EPA process and was denied in 2003. The denial was challenged, and the U.S. Court of Appeals for the District of Columbia upheld the denial in a split decision.[42] The U.S. Supreme Court has granted certiorari and heard argument on November 29, 2006. The resulting decision is likely to be extremely important.

Separate lawsuits and administrative proceedings are also pending on whether the CAA obligates EPA to regulate carbon dioxide from stationary sources such as electric power plants, and whether technology to capture carbon dioxide from power plants and sequester it geologically must be considered as part of Best Available Control Technology assessments.

A separate federal law, the Energy Policy and Conservation Act of 1975, established the Corporate Average Fuel Economy (CAFE) program. Fuel economy is directly related to carbon dioxide emissions; in fact EPA measures carbon dioxide emissions from vehicles to determine their compliance with the CAFE standards. In 2002 the California Assembly required adoption of state regulations to reduce GHG emissions from motor vehicles. This law was challenged by the auto industry on the grounds that it is preempted by the CAA and the Energy Policy and Conservation Act, and suffers various other deficiencies. This lawsuit is being actively litigated.

D. Litigation[43]

Numerous lawsuits have been filed to address global climate change. They fall into three broad categories.

The first category is administrative law claims that existing statutes require agencies to take (or not take) certain actions. The Clean Air Act and motor vehicle cases just discussed fall within this classification. So does pending litigation under the National Environmental Policy Act and threatened cases under the Endangered Species Act.

The second category is civil claims. Several lawsuits are pending claiming that GHG emissions are a public nuisance or otherwise actionable at common law. One of these cases claims that climate change contributed to the severity of Hurricane Katrina, and that major emitters of GHGs are therefore liable for the weather damage.

The third category is public international law claims. Petitions have been filed with several international commissions concerning the adverse effects of climate change on indigenous peoples or protected places.

These actions tend to face several related problems. Who has standing to assert injuries that affect the entire planet? Who is liable for injuries that were created by millions of entities? What is the proper role of the courts, as opposed to the executive and legislative branches, in addressing climate change? What kind of relief can be ordered by the courts? Most of the answers rendered by the courts to these questions so far have not been favorable to the plaintiffs, but definitive rulings are yet to come.

E. Regional, State and Local Efforts

The hostility of the U.S. government toward the Kyoto Protocol, starting with the Byrd-Hagel Resolution of 1997 and culminating with President Bush's action in 2001, created a chaotic situation that is, if anything, intensifying. Scientific and public opinion appear to be solidifying that human activity is contributing to climate changes that are having lasting negative impacts. While a global problem would seem to require at least national action, the federal government has declined to take regulatory action. States and cities, individually and collectively, have rushed into this vacuum. It would be charitable to call the resulting legal structure a patchwork quilt, because that suggests a two-dimensional object, albeit one with gaps and ragged edges. Instead we now have a construct of three or even four dimensions—since it exists in time as well as space—that continues to morph. Indeed, one of the purposes of this book is to present a snapshot of these emerging authorities.

Some of these efforts to fill the federal vacuum are regional. A total of six multi-state organizations are addressing climate change issues.[44] The most advanced of these is the northeastern states' Regional Greenhouse Gas Initiative (RGGI). Its members are Connecticut, Delaware, Maine, New Hampshire, New Jersey, New York and Vermont; Maryland will also be joining. Collectively the member states are such large emitters that they would count as the sixth-largest country in the world by volume of GHG emissions in 2000. RGGI aims initially at carbon dioxide from electric power plants that have a capacity of at least 25 MW, though other sources and gases may be targeted in the future. Mandatory emission reduction targets will take effect on January 1, 2009. Meeting these targets will be aided by a cap-and-trade system and will be governed by a complex set of rules that in some ways resemble those of the European Union's Emissions Trading System. Governor Arnold Schwarzenegger has announced that California may attempt to join RGGI.

Even more activity is occurring at the state level.[45] Most of the 50 states have adopted some sort of law or policy that has an impact on climate change issues. Some do so explicitly, and others are aimed at the energy policies that underlie most carbon dioxide emissions, as well as agricultural, forestry and waste management practices. A few states have adopted enforceable statewide limits on GHG emissions from power plants. Even more have programs to inventory and report on emissions. Some states have adopted energy-efficiency standards for appliances and for government buildings (though often before the advent of concern over climate change). One especially notable law was adopted by California in September 2006, requiring that carbon dioxide emissions be cut to 1990 levels by 2020, including the carbon dioxide emitted by out-of-state electricity generation for transmission into the state—still well short of the Kyoto Protocol formula that the United States achieve an emission level 7% below 1990 levels by 2012. Industry groups have promised to challenge the California law in court.

One of the most important categories of state programs is renewable portfolio standards (RPSs), which require that a certain percentage of the electricity that utilities sell to retail customers be generated by renewable sources. There are wide variations in terms of what kinds of renewable sources qualify, and the targets, deadlines, and program designs. These programs largely arose from the deregulation of the electric utility industry (an event that also led to the creation of regional transmission organizations, which happen to facilitate regional GHG control programs). Renewable energy and conservation are also aided by public benefit funds, which derive from small fees or surcharges on electricity rates. RPSs were not adopted to control climate change, but often have climate change benefits.

Cities are also taking action.[46] Municipal governments are themselves GHG generators through their sewage treatment plants; solid waste landfills; fleets of police cars, garbage trucks, fire engines, and maintenance vehicles; and school, office, and social service buildings. Many cities are reducing their own emissions and utilizing their considerable purchasing power to specify clean appliances, vehicles, and electricity. Some are using their zoning and building code powers to influence private construction. Through the U.S. Mayors Climate Protection Agreement, some cities have agreed to reduce their emissions to Kyoto levels. The Clinton Foundation is leading other efforts by some of the world's largest cities.

F. Voluntary Programs and Corporate Actions

While opposing mandatory GHG reductions, the Bush Administration has encouraged voluntary programs. Federal efforts have focused on enhancing the scheme for voluntary reporting of GHG emissions; encouraging key industry sectors to reduce their emissions intensity; and encouraging individual companies to reduce their emissions through a variety of programs.[47] A key issue is the lack of consistent standards in many voluntary programs.

Several nongovernmental organizations (NGOs) have formed partnerships with companies and trade associations, and some corporations have adopted their own GHG management strategies. The principal elements of these strategies generally include performing a corporate-wide GHG inventory; developing a management plan to ensure the accuracy of the inventory; setting and working to achieve GHG reduction targets; and communicating their activities to employees, shareholders, and the public.

Companies see a variety of benefits in undertaking such programs. They hope to reduce their energy costs; to develop good relations with government agencies and NGOs; to enhance their public image; to become familiar with clean energy and climate mitigation technologies; and possibly to receive credit for their activities in a future regulatory scheme.

However, this country's rejection of the Kyoto Protocol puts U.S. companies at a distinct disadvantage in regard to the business opportunities that are created by controlling and adapting to climate change.[48] U.S. companies that operate in countries that have bound themselves to the Kyoto Protocol (the "Annex B" countries) clearly must meet those countries' emissions limitations, but they get no credit under Kyoto for emissions reductions they achieve in the United States. They hope they will receive credit later on, but they have no assurance they will. They find a limited U.S. market for any climate-friendly products or services they develop, for there is no federal mandate to purchase such items. U.S. companies also find that the regulatory uncertainty makes it difficult for them to commit to major capital expenditures whose necessity could be affected by future climate mitigation laws. Nonetheless, in the permitting processes for several industrial facilities, especially coal-fired power plants, applicants have agreed to undertake GHG mitigation measures.[49]

The regulatory uncertainty also creates challenges for lawyers who advise public companies on their disclosure obligations. Regulation S-K of the Securities and Exchange Commission requires disclosure of the material effects that the costs of environmental compliance may have on capital expenditures; material legal proceedings; and the company's overall financial conditions. Many corporations are struggling with what they should say about climate-related risks, though quite a few examples of such disclosures are now available.[50] Closely tied to these issues is consideration of the fiduciary responsibilities of corporate directors to take action with respect to climate change.[51]

> **The pressures of public opinion and scientific consensus, coupled with concerns over continued reliance on foreign sources of oil, are driving many state legislatures and city councils to take action.**

The insurance industry is in many ways in the front lines of this uncertainty. Sea-level rise, extreme weather events, and other possible consequences of climate change have the potential of leading to enormous claims by policyholders. Several large insurance companies have been actively studying climate risks, advocating regulatory actions, and selling specialized insurance products to cover these risks.[52]

G. Outlook for the Future

The current situation in the United States with respect to regulation of climate change is unstable. Opinion polls show that the American public is increasingly convinced that vigorous governmental action is needed. Dire predictions about the future of the climate are constantly seen in the news and entertainment media, including television and theatrical movies. The pressures of public opinion and scientific consensus, coupled with concerns over continued reliance on foreign sources of oil, are driving many state legislatures and city councils to take action. Thus companies are faced with an ever more bewildering array of incentives and mandates.

It is always perilous to make political predictions, but there is unquestionably a reasonable chance that whoever becomes the President of the United States in January 2009—whether a Democrat or a Republican—will favor reengagement of the U.S. in the international system of climate change control. The countries that are participating in the Kyoto Protocol are already considering what to do after the end of the first Kyoto commitment period in 2012. Thus a convergence of U.S. policy and the post-2012 Kyoto world is widely anticipated.

Numerous climate change bills have been introduced by leading members of the Senate and the House from both parties. These bills vary in the number of air pollutants they would cover, the timing and magnitude of emissions reductions they mandate, the mechanisms they would use to achieve these reductions, and the sectors of the economy they would regulate.[53] Almost all of them involve some form of emission trading, since that has proven in the past to be an effective way to encourage the lowest-cost methods of reducing pollution (e.g., with sulfur dioxide).[54]

Whatever legal mechanisms emerge, it is very likely that they will strongly encourage, if not mandate, wind, solar, biomass, and other renewable sources of energy, and more energy-efficient vehicles, appliances, buildings, and industrial processes. Somewhat less likely, but still probable, are the expansion of carbon capture and storage, other ways to utilize coal while minimizing climate impacts, and the construction of more nuclear power plants.

Since even the fastest plausible stabilization of GHG emissions will not prevent the climate situation from getting worse before it gets better, there will also be considerable activity for decades to come in adapting to higher sea levels; increased flooding, droughts, and other extreme weather events; and changed agricultural and settlement patterns.

Much of the global community's efforts will necessarily be focused on the most rapidly growing economies, especially those of China and India, since growth of GHG emissions from those countries can swiftly wipe out any gains achieved domestically by the developed countries, and also because it will generally be less expensive pound for pound to reduce emissions in China and India than in North America, Europe and Japan. Thus many advanced technologies and the people needed to install and operate them, will have a locus in China and India.

In all of the above, lawyers will have major roles. They will negotiate and document the transactions for the development and transfer of technologies and for the emissions trades. They will advise companies and governments on the rapidly changing regulatory schemes. They will litigate the inevitable disputes. It is hoped that this book will assist them in carrying out all these tasks.

Endnotes

1. Goddard Institute for Space Studies, National Aeronautics and Space Administration, *GISS Surface Temperature Analysis—Global Temperature Trends: 2005 Summation*, data.giss.nasa.gov/gistemp/2005 (December 2005).

2. Goddard Institute for Space Studies, National Aeronautics and Space Administration, *2005 Warmest Year in Over a Century*, www.nasa.gov/vision/earth/environment/2005_warmest.html (2006).

3. Michael E. Mann et al., *Northern hemisphere temperatures during the past millennium: Inferences, uncertainties, and limitations*, 26 GEOPHYSICAL RESEARCH LETTERS 759 (1999).

4. NATIONAL ACADEMY OF SCIENCE, SURFACE TEMPERATURE RECONSTRUCTIONS FOR THE LAST 2,000 YEARS (2006).

5. Intergovernmental Panel on Climate Change, *Climate Change 2001: Synthesis Report—Summary for Policymakers* 5-6 (2001) (hereinafter "IPCC 2001").

6. IPCC 2001 at 5.

7. *Id.* at 4-5.

8. U.S. Energy Information Administration, *Emissions of Greenhouse Gases in the United States 2004* (December 2005) (hereafter "EIA 2004") at 12 based on IPCC Third Assessment Report.

9. EIA 2004 at 13.

10. KEVIN A. BAUMERT ET AL., NAVIGATING THE NUMBERS: GREENHOUSE GAS DATA AND INTERNATIONAL CLIMATE POLICY 12 (World Resources Institute 2005).

11. Calculated from EIA 2004 at 4.

12. INTERNATIONAL ENERGY AGENCY, WORLD ENERGY OUTLOOK 2006 (November 2006).

13. EIA 2004 at x.

14. *Id.* at 29.

15. *Id.* at 30.

16. *Id.* at 22.

17. *Id.* at 22, 31.

18. U.S. PIRG EDUCATION FUND, THE CARBON BOOM: NATIONAL AND STATE TRENDS IN GLOBAL WARMING POLLUTION SINCE 1960 (June 2006), Appx. A, B.

19. *Id.* at 14, Appx. E.

20. EIA 2004 at 35-43.

21. *Id.* at 53-65.

22. *Id.* at 67-74.

23. IPCC 2001 at 9.

24. *Id.* at 9.

25. *See also* Anthony J. McMichael et al., *Climate change and human health: present and future risks,* 367 LANCET 859 (2006); Jonathan A. Patz, *Impact of regional climate change on human health,* 438 NATURE 310 (2005); CENTER FOR HEALTH AND THE GLOBAL ENVIRONMENT, HARVARD MEDICAL SCHOOL, CLIMATE CHANGE FUTURES: HEALTH, ECOLOGICAL AND ECONOMIC DIMENSIONS (2005).

26. IPCC 2001 at 9.

27. *Id.* at 12.

28. *Id.* at 12.

29. *Id.* at 14.

30. *Joint science academies' statement: Global response to climate change* (June 2005).

31. U.S. ENERGY INFORMATION ADMINISTRATION, INTERNATIONAL ENERGY OUTLOOK *2006* (June 2006), Ch. 7, Table 12.

32. IPCC 2001 at 16.

33. Stern Review, *The Economics of Climate Change* (HM Treasury, October 30, 2006), at iii, xi.

34. Chapter 19 *infra.*

35. Robert H. Socolow & Stephen W. Pacala, *A Plan to Keep Carbon in Check,* 295 SCI. AM. No. 3 at 50 (September 2006); S. Pacala & R. Socolow, *Stabilization Wedges: Solving the Climate Problem for the Next 50 Years With Current Technologies,* 305 SCI. 968 (August 13, 2004). *See also* TONY DUTZIK & EMILY FIGDOR, RISING TO THE CHALLENGE: SIX STEPS TO CUT GLOBAL WARMING POLLUTION IN THE UNITED STATES (U.S. PIRG Education Fund 2006).

36. Chapter 2 *infra.*

37. Chapter 8 *infra.*

38. Chapters 3, 4 *infra.*

39. Chapter 16 *infra*.
40. Chapter 2 *infra*.
41. Chapter 5 *infra*.
42. Massachusetts v. EPA, 415 F.3d 50 (D.C. Cir. 2005), *cert. granted*, 126 S. Ct. 2960 (2006).
43. Chapter 6 *infra*.
44. Chapter 9 *infra*.
45. Chapter 10 *infra* (overview of state efforts); Chapter 11 *infra* (50-state survey).
46. Chapter 12 *infra*.
47. Chapter 17 *infra*.
48. Chapter 4 *infra*.
49. Chapter 7 *infra*.
50. Chapter 13 *infra*.
51. Chapter 14 *infra*.
52. Chapter 15 *infra*.
53. Chapter 3 *infra*.
54. Chapter 18 *infra*.

Part One

International and National Framework

chapter two

The International Regime

Kyle W. Danish

I. Introduction

Efforts to construct an international regime to address global climate change have been under way since 1990. A high water mark in the evolution of this regime was the entry into force in February 2005 of the Kyoto Protocol to the United Nations Framework Convention on Climate Change.[1] However, the Kyoto Protocol will not be the final word on the issue. Its emission limits cover only a fraction of the world's greenhouse gas emissions and those limits expire in 2012.

The current international climate change regime comprises a network of agreements and mechanisms.[2] Some of these agreements are "nested" in the sense that one unfolds from another. For example, the Kyoto Protocol is an outgrowth of and is formally linked to the United Nations Framework Convention on Climate Change.[3] The United States is a party to the Framework Convention, but opted not to join to the Protocol. The European Union Emissions Trading Scheme is a part of the European Union's strategy for compliance with the Kyoto Protocol, but could continue to exist after the expiration of the Protocol's 2008-2012 "commitment period." Standing parallel to these initiatives is the Asia-Pacific Partnership on Clean Development and Climate, which is a multilateral, not legally binding program. The Asia-Pacific Partnership is not formally linked to the Framework Convention or to the Protocol.

Addressing climate change presents unique challenges for international law, which already is complicated to negotiate and difficult to enforce. The climate change issue has a truly global reach, exceeding the ability of any one country to fully address. Ultimately, mitigating climate change risks will require engagement of the major countries of the developing world. While industrialized countries bear a greater historical responsibility, annual emissions from developing countries are expected to start exceeding those of industrialized countries within the next two decades.[4] Yet, different countries place very different priorities on the issue, and climate change raises complicated issues of equity.

The success of international efforts to address environmental issues such as depletion of atmospheric ozone have turned out to have only modest precedental value for climate change, in no small part because of the far greater impact of climate policies on national economies. While ozone-related laws and policies affect a rather specialized industry, climate policies potentially reach all activities that burn fossil fuels and therefore go to the heart of each country's economy. Governments are understandably cautious about making commitments to limit greenhouse gas emissions and sensitive as to whether their trade competitors will commit to undertake comparable efforts.

Climate change presents other challenges for international cooperation. The nature of the issue is such that it will require a very long-term response under conditions of scientific uncertainty. Yet, countries have varying capacities to administer policies and have different views on what are appropriate policies in the first instance. For example, some governments, such as the U.S. administration of President George W. Bush, have questioned the emissions "cap" approach of the Kyoto Protocol and have advocated technology promotion and transfer policies as an alternative. The United States has opted not to be a party to the Protocol, and the possibility that the United States will join the Protocol before 2012 is increasingly remote irrespective of the party that occupies the Oval Office.

These challenges aside, the Kyoto Protocol has broken new ground in international law. The Protocol has spawned an international market in emissions trading, which generated upwards of $10 billion in transactions in 2005.[5] It also has a more robust compliance system than most other international agreements.

The long-term evolution of the Protocol, however, remains in question. The "first commitment period" of the Protocol expires in 2012 and it is unclear what will follow. A vigorous international discussion is under way about what kind of international climate change policy architecture can accommodate the United States and major developing-country emitters, especially China and India.

This chapter will provide an overview of the different treaties, rules, and institutions that constitute the existing international climate change regime, including a review of the negotiating history that has brought the regime to it current status. The chapter also will look ahead, outlining some of the proposals for international cooperation to address climate change "beyond Kyoto."

II. The United Nations Framework Convention on Climate Change

The foundation for the international climate change regime is the United Nations Framework Convention on Climate Change, a treaty with practically global participation by governments. The Framework Convention was the first chapter in the evolution of the regime and has served as a kind of constitution-like document guiding intergovernmental cooperation on climate change. The Kyoto Protocol is a direct and formal outgrowth of the Framework Convention.

A. Negotiating History

Outlining the history of the Framework Convention also provides an opportunity to introduce an influential institution in the evolution of the international climate change regime: the Intergovernmental Panel on Climate Change (IPCC). Formed in 1988 by the World Meteorological Organization and the United Nations Environment Programme, the mission of the IPCC has been to convene scientists and other experts to publish reports assessing the state of the science on climate change, as well as to evaluate climate change–related economic, technical, and other issues. The IPCC has issued three comprehensive "Assessment Reports" since its establishment. The IPCC's First Assessment Report, published in 1990, identified significant uncertainties about climate change, but characterized the phenomenon as a matter of substantial international concern.[6] Later in the same year, the United Nations General Assembly initiated negotiations on what later became the Framework Convention.

> **The Framework Convention provides that the "ultimate objective" is . . . "stabilization of greenhouse gas concentrations in the atmosphere at a level that would prevent dangerous interference with the climate system."**

The Framework Convention was opened for signature at the 1992 United Nations Conference on Environment and Development in Rio de Janeiro, also known as the "Earth Summit." It garnered a sufficient number of ratifications to enter into force in 1994 and now has 189 parties, including the United States.[7]

B. Structure and Objective

The Framework Convention does not establish binding limits on GHG emissions for any countries. Rather, true to its name, it forms a framework for further action and cooperation on the issue of climate change. This framework comprises principles, information requirements, and institutions. In this way, the Framework Convention has served as a kind of constitution for international action on climate change.[8]

The Framework Convention provides that the "ultimate objective" of the treaty and any of its "related legal instruments," which include the Kyoto Protocol, is "stabilization of greenhouse gas concentrations in the atmosphere at a level that would prevent dangerous interference with the climate system." This objective is notably general; it does not identify a particular quantitative goal.

C. Principles

Article 3 of the Framework Convention sets forth a series of guiding "principles" that have provided important signposts and negotiating points in further discussions and negotiations. A number of these principles attempt to balance the aims of environmental protection and economic development. They also address the general division of burdens between developed and developing country parties.

One of the Article 3 principles is the so-called "precautionary principle," which provides that where there are "threats of serious or irreversible damage, lack of full scientific certainty should not be used as a reason for postponing [precautionary] measures."[9] However, such measures should be "cost-effective so as to ensure global benefits at the lowest cost."[10] Furthermore, the parties have a "right to, and should promote sustainable development," taking into account "that economic development is essential for adopting measures to address climate change."[11]

A fundamental and recurring theme in the Framework Convention is that developed and developing country parties have "common but differentiated responsibilities and respective capabilities."[12] The Framework Convention generally reflects a view that developed countries bear a greater historical responsibility for the accumulation of greenhouse gas emissions and have greater capacity to take action. For this reason, a critical principle of the Framework Convention is that "the developed country Parties should take the lead in combating climate change and the adverse effects thereof."[13]

Furthermore, the parties are to give "full consideration" to the "specific needs and special circumstances of developing country parties, especially those that are particularly vulnerable to the adverse effects of climate change."[14]

D. Commitments

Consistent with these principles, the Framework Convention divides the parties into two main groups: the Annex I countries, which comprise primarily developed countries, and the non-Annex I countries, which comprise primarily developing countries.[15] In setting forth commitments under the treaty, the Framework Convention makes certain commitments general to all parties, but also assigns certain additional commitments to the Annex I parties.

Thus, the Framework Convention provides that all parties will develop and submit national inventories of emissions by sources and removals by sinks,[16] implement national plans that include measures to mitigate climate change,[17] promote and cooperate in technology transfer,[18] and promote and cooperate in scientific research on climate change.[19] Each party is required to submit "national communications" reporting on its progress in meeting these various commitments.[20]

However, the Framework Convention also outlines certain commitments only for "developed countries and other Parties included in Annex I." The European Union and certain other parties had pressed to establish a binding emissions limit for the Annex I countries. In the face of resistance from the United States and others, the resulting commitment for Annex I parties became more hortatory in character. Article 4.2 obliges

Annex I parties to adopt national policies to mitigate climate change and to report on the progress of these policies "with the aim of" returning emissions to their 1990 levels.[21] This became a "soft" commitment; it was neither enforced nor, for the most part, achieved. The 1990 emissions "baseline," however, would become a touchstone for development of binding emissions limits under the Kyoto Protocol.

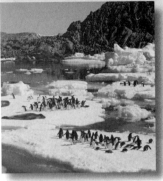

The Convention also states that the extent to which developing-country parties effectively implement their commitments will depend on the level of assistance from developed countries.[22] To this end, the Convention obliges developed countries to provide new and additional financial resources to developing countries,[23] to assist "particularly vulnerable" developing countries with costs of adaptation,[24] and to transfer mitigation technologies to developing countries.[25]

E. Institutions

The Framework Convention establishes a set of institutions to govern further cooperation among the parties. The most important of these institutions is the "Conference of the Parties" or "COP." A kind of super-legislature for the climate change regime, the COP consists of all of the governments that are parties to the Framework Convention. It has responsibilities for reviewing implementation of the Framework Convention, receiving information submitted by the parties, and considering the need for new measures or commitments.[26] In particular, article 4.2 obliges the COP to review at its first meeting the "adequacy" of the Convention. The COP also can adopt amendments or new protocols to the Framework Convention.[27]

With the exception of procedures for amendments or protocols, the parties have never developed particular voting rules for the COP. Accordingly, the COP generally acts on a consensus basis.

The COP convenes annually in numbered meetings; the inaugural meeting was "COP-1," held in Berlin. A professional staff supports the COP. Referred to as the Framework Convention "secretariat," this staff has its offices in Bonn, Germany.[28]

The COP has two subcommittees, the Subsidiary Body on Scientific and Technical Implementation (SBSTA) and the Subsidiary Body on Implementation.[29] The former has responsibility for providing the COP with information on scientific and technical matters related to the Framework Convention; the latter assists the COP with assessment and review of implementation of the Framework Convention. In addition to these COP-related institutions, the Convention designates a "financial mechanism" to assist in transfer of financial resources from developed to developing countries.[30]

To date, the Global Environment Facility—an agency managed jointly by the United Nations Environment Programme, the United Nations Development Programme, and the World Bank—has served as the Convention's financial mechanism.

III. The Kyoto Protocol

The Kyoto Protocol is the current apogee of international efforts to address global climate change and a significant milestone in the evolution of international environmental law generally.

A. Negotiating History

The origins of the Kyoto Protocol can be found in COP-1 in Berlin in 1995. At that meeting, the parties to the Framework Convention collectively determined that a more forceful international response to the threat of climate change was needed.[31] This determination led to the "Berlin Mandate," a commitment to develop a protocol with binding emission limits.[32] Consistent with the principle of "common but differentiated responsibilities," it was agreed that such limits should apply only to the developed-country parties.

Subsequent negotiations resulted in the Kyoto Protocol, which was adopted by the parties at COP-3 at Kyoto in 1997. The Protocol outlined emission limits for the Convention's Annex I parties and described a series of "mechanisms" to promote compliance with those limits. However, it was also agreed that many key details about the Protocol had yet to be resolved. Accordingly, negotiations continued on a more elaborated "rulebook" for the Protocol. At COP-4, held in Buenos Aires, the parties adopted a "Plan of Action" to guide further discussions on the development of the Kyoto rulebook.

During this period of discussions, the United States government was negotiating under a cloud of uncertainty. Around the time of the Kyoto meetings in 1997, the U.S. Senate had passed a near-unanimous resolution directing the government not to enter into any protocols or other agreements under the Convention that would "mandate new commitments to limit or reduce greenhouse gas emissions for the Annex I Parties, unless the protocol or other agreement also mandates new specific scheduled commitments to limit or reduce greenhouse gas emissions for Developing Country Parties within the same compliance period."[33]

Negotiations surrounding the Protocol reached a crisis point at COP-6, which was held in November 2000 in The Hague. After nearly reaching a compromise, the negotiations collapsed. A key point of division was the issue of how to account for emission removals resulting from forestry. The European Union opposed a formulation proposed by the United States and certain other countries. In the view of the European Union, the U.S. proposal allowed the United States and other countries with significant forestland to credit themselves too much for removals that would occur merely from natural growth—that is, without additional effort.

The collapse of negotiations in The Hague was followed by the election of George W. Bush. The Bush Administration quickly repudiated the Protocol, asserting that it "fails to establish a long-term goal based on science, poses serious and unnecessary risks to the United States and world economies, and is ineffective in addressing climate change because it excludes major parts of the world."[34]

The exit of the United States from the Protocol created a crisis in the negotiations because the Protocol rules for entry into force were designed to privilege the position of the United States and Russia.

The exit of the United States from the Protocol created a crisis in the negotiations because the Protocol rules for entry into force were designed to privilege the position of the United States and Russia. Article 25 of the Protocol provides that the Protocol can enter into force only if it is ratified by not less than 55 parties to the Convention, incorporating Annex I parties accounting for at least 55 percent of the total carbon dioxide emissions in 1990 of Annex I parties. In effect, this formula allowed the Protocol to enter into force only if the United States or Russia (or both) ratified—and if practically all other Annex I countries ratified. The United States' repudiation (followed by Australia) meant that Russia became the keystone for the Protocol's entry into force.

In the end, continued negotiations through the restarted COP-6 in Bonn—referred to as "COP-6*bis*"—and COP-7 in Marrakesh allowed the Protocol to reach the finish line. Negotiations at COP-7 in 2001 produced the "Marrakesh Accords," the detailed rulebook that provides flesh to the skeletal structure of the Protocol. The Marrakesh Accords elaborated key procedures and rules for the trading mechanisms, the compliance systems, and other key elements of the Protocol, thereby setting the stage for ratifications.

The Protocol finally received a sufficient number of ratifications to enter into force in February 2005 after Russia ratified. November of that same year saw a parallel session of the COP (COP-11) and the first meeting of Parties to the Protocol (COP/MOP-1).

B. Overview of the Protocol's Structure

The Protocol sets forth binding emission limits for its developed-country parties for the period 2008–2012. Parties effectively have full discretion in developing national measures to meet their limits. Furthermore, they can take advantage of certain "flexible mechanisms," which offer market-based approaches for achieving emission reductions across borders. The Protocol is buttressed by a compliance system that combines facilitative systems with harder enforcement mechanisms.

In most instances, references to rules and guidelines under the "Protocol" should be read as references to a body of rules and guidelines that includes the Protocol and the Marrakesh Accords. A detailed rulebook, the Marrakesh Accords embodies the COP's further decisions and elaborations of the Protocol.

The Protocol also has added a new body to the institutional infrastructure of the climate change regime: the "Conference of the Parties serving as the meeting of Parties to the Protocol" or COP/MOP. Until the Protocol entered into force in 2005, the COP made critical binding decisions to elaborate the modalities of the Protocol; now the COP/MOP will serve as the supreme governing body for the Protocol.

As a non-party, the United States has no obligations under the Protocol, nor does it participate in the COP/MOP.

C. Emission Limits

The central element of the Protocol is its binding quantified emission limitation and reduction commitments, which are established by Article 3 and inscribed in Annex B. These Article 3 commitments apply, for the most part, only to those parties to the Protocol that are Annex I parties under the Framework Convention.[35] The commitments vary on a party-by-party basis.

The commitments are calculated—with some variations—with reference to each party's 1990 emissions level. Each Annex I party must meet its commitment as an annual average during the period 2008–2012, which is referred to as the "first commitment period." For example, Japan agreed to limit its annual average emissions during 2008–2012 to a level that is 6% below its 1990 emissions. This corresponds to a certain amount of total allowable emissions for the first commitment period, which is referred to as Japan's "Assigned Amount." Collectively, the Assigned Amounts of the Annex I parties correspond to a 5.2% reduction below their 1990 emissions levels.

D. Basket of Greenhouse Gases

Each Annex I party's commitment applies on the basis of a "basket" of six GHGs: carbon dioxide (CO_2), methane (CH_4), nitrous oxide (N_2O), hydrofluorocarbons (HFCs), perfluorocarbons (PFCs), and sulfur hexafluoride (SF_6).[36] The Intergovernmental Panel on Climate Change has determined the global warming potential of each of these types of GHGs relative to carbon dioxide.[37] Adopting this approach, the Protocol expresses each party's limit in the form of a certain amount of "carbon dioxide equivalent" tons of GHG emissions. In addition, for HFCs, PFCs, and SF_6, the Protocol allows the use of 1995 as a base year, which has the effect of easing the stringency of requirements for those GHGs because, for most countries, emissions of those GHGs were higher in 1995 than in 1990.[38]

As a whole, the "basket" approach allows each Annex I party a degree of flexibility in determining a cost-effective combination of reductions of different types of GHGs.

E. Consideration of Russia and Economies in Transition

The Protocol provides former Soviet-bloc countries, referred to in the treaty as parties "undergoing the process of transition to a market economy," with certain additional flexibility. Under certain circumstances, these parties may use a base period other than 1990 for their emission commitments.[39]

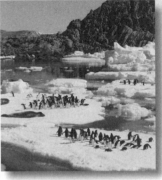

Russia also has a significant and somewhat controversial accommodation under the Protocol. Russia's Annex B commitment limits the country to its emissions level in 1990. However, because of the collapse of the Russian economy in the 1990s, the country's emissions are below its 1990 level and are projected to stay below that level through 2012. Accordingly, Russia has significant headroom between its projected emissions and its Assigned Amount. This headroom not only eases Russia's compliance burden, but also—because of the Protocol's emissions trading mechanisms—provides Russia with a potential surplus of credits it can trade to others and therefore a likely financial windfall. The Russian surplus, among other concessions, was critical to securing the country's participation in the Protocol. However, some critics refer to the surplus as "hot air," deriding the arrangement as effectively watering down the overall environmental effectiveness of the treaty. They note that Annex I countries can avoid implementing "real" emission reductions in their own countries by purchasing surplus credits from Russia, but because those credits would not result from "new" emission reductions, the net effect would be to reduce the amount of reductions that would occur otherwise.[40]

F. Commitment Period Approach

One of the elements of the treaty designed to provide for cost-effective compliance is the commitment period approach. Instead of a single fixed-year limit, the Protocol's emission commitments apply as an annual average to be achieved over a five-year period. This approach responds to the concern that a country's GHG emissions could rise or fall in any particular year because of difficult-to-control factors. Carbon dioxide emissions, for example, come from sources throughout a country's energy sector and therefore are sensitive to the level of overall economic activity and the vagaries of business cycle. Similarly, annual fluctuations in weather could affect the extent to which a country operates its power plants, with resulting fluctuations in emissions. The commitment period approach makes a government's efforts to mitigate its emissions less vulnerable to such factors.

G. European Union "Bubble"

Article 4 of the Protocol provides that two or more Annex I parties may agree to fulfill their Article 3 commitments jointly, in which case they become subject to a summed Assigned Amount, rather than their individual commitments. The European Union opted to take advantage of this provision, replacing each member state's Annex B commitment with a collective commitment. The European Union (EU) separately negotiated a burden-sharing agreement that re-distributes the emission commitments under the Protocol among the EU member states.[41]

Under the EU burden-sharing agreement, member states with relatively fast-growing economies have relatively more lenient emissions commitments. For example, Ireland and Spain are permitted to increase their emissions from 1990 levels by 15% and 27% respectively; by comparison, each is required under the Protocol to reduce its emissions 8% below 1990 levels.[42] Germany, on the other hand, has agreed to reduce its emissions 21% below 1990 levels under the burden-sharing agreement, as compared to 8% under the Protocol.

H. Accounting for Land Use, Land Use Change, and Forestry

Forests store substantial amounts of carbon; they are significant "sinks." Activities that lead to deforestation, or even clearing of agricultural land and disturbance of soils, result in substantial releases of carbon dioxide. For these reasons, issues related to land use, land use change, and forestry—or "LULUCF" in the parlance of Protocol negotiators—have been a significant topic of discussion at the COPs.

Notwithstanding the general benefits of focusing on LULUCF for purposes of climate change mitigation, LULUCF has been a controversial and complicated area for at least two reasons. First, data on emissions and removals associated with LULUCF activities—particularly forest conservation and agriculture-based activities—are less certain and reliable than the data associated with industrial and power generation activities.

Second, most LULUCF activities have a distinct characteristic of "non-permanence." While activities that reduce emissions in the energy sectors effectively reduce those emissions indefinitely, emissions reduced or sequestered through LULUCF activities are reversible; a planted forest can be cut or burned down. Policies addressing LULUCF activities necessarily must account for this reversibility risk.

Third, some governments and NGOs hold the view that LULUCF activities distract from the kinds of investments in cleaner energy technologies that ultimately will be needed to address climate change. The European Union, for example, opposed the efforts of Canada, Russia, Australia, and the United States (when it was an active participant in the negotiations) to rely on management of their substantial forestland—or merely the natural growth of those forests—to meet their commitments.

The Protocol and the Marrakesh Accords embody a complicated set of compromises on these issues. First, the Protocol provides that, in meeting their Article 3 commitments, Annex I countries may only take into account a finite set of relatively easily-measured activities: "net changes in greenhouse gas emissions by sources and removals by sinks resulting from direct human-induced land-use change and forestry activities, limited to afforestation, reforestation, and deforestation since 1990."[43] The Protocol did not resolve whether forest management activities other than afforestation and reforestation could count. The Protocol also left open the treatment of agricultural activities, including revegetation, cropland management, and grazing-land management.

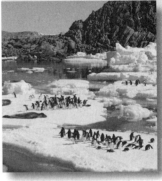

At COP-6*bis* in Bonn, the Kyoto parties further expanded, albeit subject to limits, the categories of LULUCF activities that could be used to fulfill an Annex I party's commitment. The Bonn decisions allowed an Annex I party, at its option, to take into account agricultural LULUCF activities, provided that the activities are "human-induced," were implemented after 1990, and achieve net sequestration benefits. An Annex I party also may opt to use forest management under similar limits, except that the Bonn agreement capped forest management at a level of approximately 83 million tons of carbon annually and established a formula for apportioning the rights to these tons to Annex I parties (other than the United States). During the negotiation of the Marrakesh Accords, Russia obtained a near doubling of its forest management apportionment, a concession that may have been needed to secure its ratification and the entry into force of the Protocol.[44]

Annex I parties that opt to use LULUCF activities to meet their commitments must issue certain credits for tons sequestered by these activities, referred to as Removal Units or RMUs. Annex I parties may add RMUs to their Assigned Amount or trade them through the Kyoto flexible mechanisms. However, the Marrakesh Accords prohibit the banking of surplus RMUs for future commitment periods.[45]

Finally, the parties established certain limits to LULUCF-related projects under the Clean Development Mechanism. These are outlined in greater detail in the discussion of the Clean Development Mechanism on page 44.

I. National Policies and Measures

Central to the Protocol's structure is an understanding that Annex I parties are free to determine what combination of policies and measures they will develop to meet their quantified commitments. During the negotiations surrounding the Protocol, the governments debated whether the treaty should prescribe particular national policies. The final document, however, leaves national policies largely to the discretion of the parties. Article 2.1 provides that each Annex I party, in meeting its Article 3 commitment, shall "implement and/or further elaborate policies and measures in accordance with its national circumstances." It goes on to delineate a list of preferred examples of such policies, including enhancement of energy efficiency, enhancement of sinks and reservoirs of GHGs, and increased use of renewable energy. In all, however, Article 2 is more hortatory than obligatory in form.

J. The Flexible Mechanisms[46]

Perhaps the most important international environmental law innovation of the Kyoto Protocol is its establishment and significant reliance on market-based instruments, often referred to as the "flexible mechanisms." These mechanisms are the Article 17 International Emissions Trading system, Article 6 Joint Implementation, and the Article 12 Clean Development Mechanism. Each provides a pathway through which an Annex I government, and entities regulated by that government, can meet the Article 3 commitments by investing in emission reduction or sequestration opportunities in other countries. As explained below, the accounting mechanisms of the Protocol allow Annex I parties to add credits acquired through the flexible mechanisms to their Assigned Amounts and thereby use them to offset their emissions. Detailed rules for the flexible mechanisms can be found in the Marrakesh Accords.

> Perhaps the most important international environmental law innovation of the Kyoto Protocol is its establishment and significant reliance on market-based instruments, often referred to as the "flexible mechanisms."

The rationale for the flexible mechanisms is straightforward. All emissions of GHG have an identical impact on the atmosphere regardless of their source; in other words, a ton of carbon dioxide emitted from the clearing of a forest in Ghana has the same impact as a ton of carbon dioxide emitted from a power plant in Germany. On other hand, the cost of achieving emission reductions varies substantially from country to country. In particular, mitigation costs are in many instances lower in developing countries. The three flexible mechanisms exploit these characteristics of the climate change issue by providing what has been referred to as "where" flexibility. In theory, an environmental program with "where" flexibility can ensure that reductions will be implemented wherever they can be achieved at lowest cost, achieving an effect that approximates a situation in which the world were governed by a single omniscient policy maker.

It is important to recognize that, in addition to the flexible mechanisms, the Protocol has other features and mechanisms that promote other kinds of flexibility and cost-effectiveness. For example, the Protocol also provides "what" flexibility. As discussed above, it does not prescribe what types of measures Annex I governments must adopt to meet their commitments, but rather allows them to use their discretion. This "what" flexibility promotes cost-effectiveness in that different countries will find that different combinations of, for example, renewable energy programs or energy-efficiency measures will make more sense under their individual national circumstances. Similarly, the "basket" approach for the various types of GHGs allows, for example, a country with a sizable industry in HFCs to focus a relatively greater portion of its mitigation efforts in that area.

The Protocol also provides for temporal or "when" flexibility, which also promotes cost-effectiveness. One element of the Protocol's "when" flexibility is the commitment period approach, which allows Annex I parties to manage the timing of their mitigation efforts. With the commitment period approach, for example, a party can adopt a compliance strategy in which it invests in emission reduction technologies and projects at the beginning of the period that pay off in lower emissions at the end of the period.

Another element of "when" flexibility embodied in the Protocol is the ability of Annex I parties to "bank" surplus Assigned Amount. Article 3.13 provides that if an Annex I party's Assigned Amount exceeds its emissions at the end of the first commitment period, it may carry over the additional Assigned Amount to a subsequent commitment period.[47]

1. Article 17 International Emissions Trading

As discussed above, each Annex I party's Article 3 commitment translates into an "Assigned Amount," an allowable amount of GHG emissions over the five-year commitment period. The Protocol further provides that a party's Assigned Amount can be subdivided into "Assigned Amount Units" or AAUs, with each AAU corresponding to the right to emit one carbon dioxide

equivalent ton of GHG emissions. Article 17 directs the COP to develop rules under which parties with commitments under Annex B can trade AAUs with one another. The rules for Article 17 international emissions trading are elaborated in the Marrakesh Accords.[48]

The Article 17 trading system is very similar to the Sulfur Dioxide Emissions Program established under Title IV of the Clean Air Act.[49] Under each program, the regulated entities are required to hold certain permits to cover their emissions. Under the Protocol, the regulated entities are national governments, while the Title IV system regulates power plants. Under the Protocol, the permits are AAUs; the Title IV system uses "allowances." Each program allocates a certain amount of permits to its regulated entities and allows the entities to trade them freely.

The concept of emissions trading was controversial during the Protocol's negotiations. Some countries, particularly the member states of the European Union, viewed trading with skepticism. This skepticism is reflected in the provision in Article 17 that states that any trading "shall be supplemental to domestic actions" for the purpose of meeting Article 3 commitments. Elaborating this "supplementarity" requirement became a recurrent focus of post-Kyoto negotiations. For some time, the European Union pushed for a quantitative limit on the extent to which a party could rely on trading. Ultimately, however, the parties to the Protocol rejected such an approach. Now, the supplementarity concept remains more as an exhortation not to rely exclusively on emissions trading, rather than an obligatory limit.[50]

Another concern identified during the Protocol negotiations was that the Article 17 system could create a risk of "overselling." Because Annex I parties would have their full allotment of AAUs from the very beginning of the commitment period, a party might sell off in the early years of the commitment period AAUs that it ultimately would need for compliance purposes at the end of the period. Such overselling could result from good-faith mismanagement or by bad-faith rent seeking. In any event, it was far from certain that the Protocol's compliance system could prevent such overselling, both because the mechanisms for gathering information on a party's emissions would lag behind selling activity and because the penalties for noncompliance might not be great enough to exceed the potential financial gains from overselling.[51]

For these reasons, the Bonn agreements established a requirement that each Annex I party hold onto a portion of its AAUs in a "commitment period" reserve. The required portion is the lower of 90 percent of a party's Assigned Amount or the equivalent of five times its most recent annual emissions inventory (which reflects the view that the most recent inventory is a reasonable if conservative predictor of actual emissions during the commitment period).[52] The Marrakesh Accords provide that an Annex I party may not engage in trades that would bring its holdings of AAUs or other Kyoto credits below the level of the commitment period reserve. The result is that most countries cannot trade more than 10 percent of their Assigned Amounts. The commitment period reserve requirement also reduced the amount of "hot air" that Russia can sell; Russia can sell only the difference between its Assigned Amount and its actual recent emissions.

The decision of the United States not to become a party to the Kyoto Protocol removed a major source of projected demand for AAUs. As a result, concerns about overselling have diminished. Indeed, some economists now believe that the countries with potential "hot air" AAUs, principally Russia and the Ukraine, have greater incentives to limit their sales of AAUs in order to obtain a higher price.[53]

2. Article 6 Joint Implementation

The Protocol also establishes a form of emissions trading among Annex I countries that revolves around projects that reduce or remove emissions, referred to as "Joint Implementation" or JI.

In a JI transaction, an Annex I party enters into a transaction respecting an emissions abatement project in the country of another Annex I party, presumably because the abatement costs are lower in the host country than in the purchasing country. The host Annex I party then transfers a corresponding portion of its Assigned Amount to the purchasing Annex I party in the form of "Emission Reduction Units" or ERUs. The purchasing Annex I party can add these ERUs to its Assigned Amount.

Article 6 provides certain basic rules for JI transactions, including that the project must have the approval of the Annex I parties involved and the project must achieve emission reductions or removals "additional to any that would otherwise occur." Article 6 also allows an Annex I party to authorize "legal entities," *i.e.*, companies or other persons, to participate in JI projects.[54] ERUs may be earned only for reductions or removals occurring during the 2008–2012 commitment period.

The requirement that the project achieve mitigation results "additional to any that would otherwise occur" is a central, complicated, and controversial touchstone for project-based emissions trading—both for JI and for the Clean Development Mechanism. At the heart of the so-called "additionality" requirement is the view that credits should not go to reductions that would have occurred even without the intervention of an investing Annex I party or legal entity. After all, whenever an Annex I party can earn Emission Reduction Units, this absolves the party of achieving a corresponding amount of emission reductions through activities in its own country. Accordingly, if Emission Reduction Units were awarded for reductions that would have occurred anyway, then the ERUs would effectively "inflate" the Protocol's overall emissions cap.

In the first instance, the JI mechanism has a built-in incentive structure that avoids crediting non-additional projects; presumably, an Annex I government should be loathe to part with some of its Assigned Amount for a project that does not achieve additional reductions or removals. By doing so, it would increase the difficulty of complying with its Article 3 commitment. However, many of the parties to the Protocol believed that until Annex I governments have complied with certain compliance-related obligations, they should not be able to approve JI projects on their own. The relevant obligations are established by Articles 5 and 7 of the Protocol and include establishing a national system for calculating emissions by sources and removals by sinks, developing a national registry for tracking holdings of credits, and submitting an annual emissions inventory.

Accordingly, the COP decided on a two-track process for JI projects.[55] If an Annex I government has met its Article 5 and Article 7 requirements, it may proceed under Track 1, which allows the government to approve a JI project without external review. If an Annex I government has not yet met the Article 5 and Article 7 requirements, however, it must proceed under Track 2. Track 2 establishes a third-party international reviewer—the Joint Implementation Supervisory Committee—which has responsibility for determining whether proposed projects meet additionality requirements. The Committee consists of members from governments that are parties to the Protocol.

In addition, the Committee is expected to develop methodologies and other guidance to facilitate expedited project reviews, using modalities developed for the Clean Development Mechanism as appropriate (these modalities are discussed in greater detail in the section that follows).

Annex I governments that qualify for Track 1 status still may opt to use the Track 2 process. One rationale for using the Track 2 process instead of Track 1 is that it is a cost-saving alternative to establishing a separate national administrative apparatus for reviewing and verifying JI projects. A second rationale is to increase the credibility of the country's projects in the marketplace—because a project approved under Track 1 procedures can lose its ability to generate ERUs if the host country falls out of compliance with its Article 5 and Article 7 requirements.

3. Article 12 Clean Development Mechanism

a. Introduction

A significant innovation of the Kyoto Protocol is the establishment of the Clean Development Mechanism or CDM. Through the CDM, Annex I governments (and companies or other persons authorized by them) can purchase "Certified Emission Reductions" generated by emission reduction projects in non-Annex I countries.

Like Joint Implementation, the CDM provides for project-based emissions trading. However, under the CDM, the host countries are non-Annex I parties. In this way, the CDM has been the primary mechanism for involvement of developing countries during the Kyoto Protocol's first commitment period. Because of a perceived abundance of low-cost mitigation project opportunities in developing countries, many experts believe that Annex I parties are likely to rely on CDM projects as a significant strategy for compliance with their Article 3 commitments.

The CDM brings into sharp relief the issue identified by the JI with respect to self-certification by host countries. Non-Annex I parties do not have Article 3 commitments. Accordingly, a non-Annex I government does not have any incentive to ensure that a project implemented in its country achieves reductions that are additional to those that would occur without "carbon finance." Therefore, all CDM projects are subject to a third-party verification process similar to the JI Track 2 process. This process is administered by the CDM Executive Board, a body of officials serving in their personal capacity, but who typically also hold environmental positions in government.

b. Basic Requirements

Article 12 of the Protocol outlines the fundamental elements and requirements for the CDM. As with other parts of the Protocol, these elements and requirements have received further elaboration in the Marrakesh Accords and subsequent decisions at the COP/MOP.

CDM projects, like JI projects, are required to achieve reductions in emissions that are "additional to any that would occur in the absence of the certified project activity."[56] In addition, participation in each project must be voluntary and approved by each Kyoto party involved.[57] Governments have established "Designated National

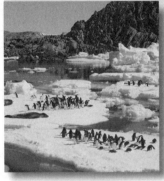

Authoritie s" to approve projects and project participants. Article 12 al; o provides that participation in CDM project activities may i nvolve private or public entities.[58]

Unlik e JI, Article 12 adds an overlying "purpose" for CDM projects t hat is additional to climate change mitigation: to assist non- Annex I parties in "achieving sustainable development."[59] The determination of whether a project contributes to achievin g sustainable development has been left to host country Designa ted National Authorities.

Arti cle 12 also directs the CDM to collect a "share of the proceed s" from each CDM project activity to cover the CDM's admini; trative expenses and to provide financial assistance to aid dev eloping country parties that are particularly vulnerable to the ; adverse effects of climate change in meeting the costs of adapta tion.[60] The "share of the proceeds" levy on a CDM project is prop ortional to its size.[61]

W hile the JI mechanism cannot generate ERUs until 2008, the CI)M has a "prompt start" provision, which provides that the CJ DM may award CERs for reductions achieved from the year 2 :000.[62] The COP/MOP has decided that a project will be eligib le to earn retroactive CERs for the years 2000–2006 if the proje ct has been "registered" by the CDM Executive Board (a proce ss discussed in greater detail below) and otherwise meets certai n other conditions by no later than December 31, 2006.[63]

c. The CDM Project Cycle

At th e heart of the Clean Development Mechanism is its project approval cycle.[64] The cycle is a process through which the CDM Executive Board approves a project and then issues CERs for that project.

I Note that the CDM Executive Board has taken a number of steps to facilitate and expe dite the project cycle—and, indeed, to avoid a full project-by-project review whenever possible. One of the steps taken by the Executive Board has been to accredit a num ber of private companies to serve as project reviewers; these accredited companies are l known as "Designated Operational Entities" or DOEs. DOEs have the primary resp onsibility for (1) validating that a proposed CDM project meets all relevant requir ements and (2) periodically verifying that a registered project has generated reduction s. A second expediting strategy adopted by the Executive Board has been to build up a library of standard emissions baseline methodologies for certain types of commonly implemented projects. The Executive Board has encouraged project participa nts to use these pre-approved methodologies. New proposed methodologies go before a subcommittee of the Executive Board, referred to as the Methodology Panel.

With this overview, the discussion that follows outlines the various steps in the project cycle. The first step is for the project participant(s) to develop a Project Design Document, for which there is a specific template. The Project Design Document contains critical information about the project, including whether it has earned host country approval from the Designated National Authority (including the confirmation that the project contributes to sustainable development), information about environmental impacts and stakeholder comments, and plans for annual monitoring of the project's emission reduction results. The Project Design Document describes the project's baseline, including whether the project participant is using a standard methodology or proposing a new methodology, and sets forth the case for the project's additionality. In addition, the project participant uses the Project Design Document to request a crediting period for the project. The project participant has two choices for a crediting period: (1) a single ten-year period or (2) a seven-year period with the option of two renewals (for a total of up to 21 years.)

A DOE reviews the Project Design Document. If the DOE determines that the project meets the CDM rules and that the countries involved are parties to the Protocol and otherwise meet eligibility requirements, then the DOE transmits a "validation" report for the project to the Executive Board. If the Executive Board agrees with the recommendations of the DOE, it "registers" the project. A registered project is eligible to receive CERs.

The project participant must implement the monitoring systems set forth in the approved PDD. When the project participant seeks to receive CERs, it must prepare a monitoring report calculating the emission reductions achieved since the previous report. The participant must retain a second DOE, different from the one responsible for the validation of the project, to verify these results. The DOE delivers its verification report to the Executive Board.

If the Executive Board concurs with the DOE's verification, it will issue CERs into specified accounts in the national registry or registries requested by the project participant. In other words, issuance of CERs is on a *post hoc* basis; it occurs only after a demonstration that the project has achieved reductions.

d. Non-Standard Projects

The CDM has special rules for certain categories of projects, including "small-scale" projects and LULUCF projects.

Recognizing that the burdens of the standard CDM project approval process might exceed the resources of the developers of small projects, the CDM Executive Board has developed a set of streamlined procedures for approval of "small-scale" projects.[65] Eligible project categories include certain types of renewable energy projects and certain types of energy efficiency projects.

Also, reflecting concerns about the environmental integrity of LULUCF activities, the COP has put in place for the first commitment period a variety of restrictions on forestry projects under the CDM.[66] First, only two types of forestry-related projects can earn CERs: afforestation and reforestation projects. Second, forestry-related CDM projects have a different crediting period from other CDM projects; the project participant must choose either a single crediting period of 30 years or a series of three renewable crediting periods of 20 years each (for a total of up to 60 years). This longer crediting period reflects, among other things, the fact that the uptake of carbon resulting from a LULUCF project can take a long period of time.

The CDM Executive Board also issues unique CERs for forestry projects: either "tCERs" or "lCERs." These credits were developed in recognition of the fact that forestry-related projects have a unique "non-permanence" risk. Unlike other types of emission reduction projects, an LULUCF project can generate removals for several years, but then release all of its carbon into the atmosphere as a result of fire or disease, thereby effectively eliminating all of the climate-related benefits achieved in the prior years. The two types of LULUCF credits are designed to avoid awarding permanent credits for projects that are vulnerable to this kind of reversal. One option for a forestry project participant is to request tCERs, which expire at the end of the commitment period and therefore can be used only in the period in which they were issued. In the subsequent commitment period, the participant can request additional tCERs upon a demonstration that the project is still viable. The other option is to request lCERs. Unlike tCERs, lCERs do not expire at the end of the commitment period. However, the rules provide that if, in any year, the project

has released carbon for which lCERs previously have been issued, then the project participant must replace the previously issued lCERs with AAUs, ERUs, CERs, or RMUs.

Finally, Annex I parties are subject to a first commitment period cap on their use of CERs from forestry projects; each party's cap equals 1% of its base-year emissions multiplied by five.

e. Criticisms of the CDM

Because of the prompt start provision, the CDM began operation in advance of other elements of the Protocol. The cumbersome performance of the CDM in its early years generated criticism.

To many observers, the project approval cycle proved lengthy and bureaucratic. The International Emissions Trading Association (IETA) has estimated that to meet expected demand, there will have to be upwards of 200 CDM projects registered each year and 300 baseline methodologies approved in total to cover the various types of projects.[67] Yet, as of late 2005, the Executive Board had registered only 13 projects and approved only 23 methodologies. IETA has put the blame on the CDM's cumbersome, multistep bureaucratic processes. In addition, IETA and others have expressed frustrations with the Executive Board's implementation of the additionality test, asserting that the test is too stringent and turns away too many high-quality, environmentally sound projects.

COP/MOP-1 introduced a package of reforms for the CDM, including an increase in funding. It is hoped that this combination of reforms and funding, plus an increasing foundation of approved baseline methodologies, will open up clogged pipelines of proposed CDM projects and speed approvals.

K. Compliance

The Kyoto Protocol compliance system is more robust than that of any other international environmental agreement and has introduced a number of innovations to international law generally.[68] The participating governments generally have seen rigorous compliance enforcement as central to ensuring the viability of and confidence in the emissions trading market. The Protocol's compliance system includes mechanisms to generate information about performance, mechanisms to facilitate compliance, and mechanisms to deter noncompliance through penalties.

The fundamental measure of compliance under the Protocol is the obligation of each Annex I party to hold a sufficient combination of AAUs, ERUs, CERs, tCERs, lCERs, and RMUs at the end of the commitment period to cover its emissions. To this end, the Protocol establishes a number of mechanisms to generate information about holdings of credits and emissions. Article 5 of the Protocol requires Annex I parties to develop national systems for estimating emissions by sources and removals by sinks. Article 7 requires each Annex I party to submit an annual emissions inventory that provides information necessary to determine progress toward compliance with its Article 3 commitment.

> **The Kyoto Protocol compliance system is more robust than that of any other international environmental agreement and has introduced a number of innovations to international law generally.**

The Marrakesh Accords include further guidelines on the development of systems and inventories required under Articles 5 and 7. In addition, the Marrakesh Accords add the further requirement that Annex I parties develop a national registry that can provide, at all times, an accounting of holdings of Kyoto credits and can also serve as a mechanism to record transactions of these credits. The parties may set up subaccounts within their national registries for companies and other private entities that are participating in the international emissions trading market. The national registries will link to an International Transactions Log. The International Transactions Log is intended to serve as the mechanism through which transactions occur; it is expected to become operational in mid-2007.

In acknowledgment of the importance of the Article 5 and 7 obligations to ensuring ultimate compliance with the Protocol, the parties have made fulfillment of these obligations a condition to an Annex I party's participation in the flexible mechanisms.[69]

To evaluate compliance, Article 8 of the Protocol calls for the establishment of

Expert Review Teams. These teams are empowered to audit information submitted by Annex I parties pursuant to Article 5 and Article 7.

Claims of noncompliance come before the Compliance Committee.[70] The Compliance Committee consists of two bodies: the Facilitative Branch and the Enforcement Branch, each consisting of delegates appointed by the parties. The Facilitative Branch, consistent with its name, has assistance and early warning functions and aims to prevent noncompliance before it occurs. It can direct financial and technical assistance to parties. The Enforcement Branch, by contrast, has quasi-judicial functions. It assesses compliance by Annex I parties with respect to reporting requirements and Article 3 emission-reduction commitments. The Enforcement Branch is empowered to determine that Annex I parties are ineligible to participate in the flexible mechanisms and can apply adjustments to emission inventories in response to information provided by Expert Review Teams. Under certain circumstances, a party may appeal a decision of the Enforcement Branch to the COP/MOP.

An Annex I party that fails to fulfill its Article 3 commitment—*i.e.*, because its emissions exceed its holdings of credits—is subject to a penalty. The violating party's second commitment period Assigned Amount will be reduced by a number of credits sufficient to restore it to compliance—plus a penalty interest rate of 30%. The hope is that this penalty will be sufficient to deter willful noncompliance. Yet, its deterrent effect

will be diminished if the negotiation and adoption of Assigned Amounts for a second commitment period extends into the first commitment period.

L. National Programs for Meeting Kyoto Commitments

Annex I parties to the Kyoto Protocol have developed or are developing a variety of different national programs to meet their Article 3 commitments. A particularly noteworthy program is the cap-and-trade program established by the European Union member states to help contribute to compliance with their "bubble" commitment: the European Union Emissions Trading Scheme or EU ETS.

The 25 EU member states developed the EU ETS as a cap-and-trade program, which will operate over two phases.[71] The first phase runs from 2005 to 2007, and the second phase runs for the duration of the first commitment period, 2008 to 2012. During the first phase, each member state must include in the program all of its "installations" in the following sectors: (1) energy (electricity and refineries with direct emissions); (2) production and processing of iron and steel; (3) minerals (cement, glass, and ceramic production); and (4) pulp and paper. Approximately 12,000 installations are covered in the first phase. In addition, Phase I will cover only emissions of carbon dioxide—the covered sectors represent 46 percent of the EU's carbon dioxide emissions. In Phase II, the EU might extend the ETS to cover other sectors and other greenhouse gases.

Before each phase, each member state must establish a "National Allocation Plan" (NAP). The NAP process involves two determinations. First, the government must determine what portion of its cap under the EU Kyoto burden-sharing agreement will be given to installations subject to the EU ETS and what portion will be reserved for uncovered sectors, such as transportation. Once a government has determined this "cap within the cap," it then must determine allocations of "EU Allowances" for each of its covered installations. NAPs are subject to review and approval by the European Commission.

Finally, entities regulated under the EU ETS may use CERs and ERUs for compliance, subject to certain restrictions.

In the years before the onset of the first commitment period, the EU ETS has been a powerful engine for the development of a global emissions trading market, generating US$8.2 billion in transactions in 2005.[72]

Furthermore, the EU ETS may continue on after the terminus of the Kyoto Protocol's 2008–2012 commitment period. EU officials have advocated a "unilateral" post-2012 cap for the European Union—in other words, a cap that would apply irrespective of the outcome of talks occurring under the aegis of the UNFCCC.[73]

IV. The Future of the International Climate Regime

Article 3.9 of the Protocol provides that the COP/MOP shall initiate no later than 2005 the consideration of commitments for subsequent commitment periods—but only with respect to Annex I countries. Article 9 provides that a broader review of the Protocol should take place starting at the second meeting of the COP/MOP; such a review presumably could include consideration of commitments for non-Annex I parties.

At the COP-11/MOP-1 meeting, the parties to the Protocol agreed to launch an *ad hoc* working group to consider post-2012 commitments for Annex I parties. The group is called the Ad Hoc Working Group on Further Commitments for Annex I Parties under the Kyoto Protocol. They also consented to extending an invitation to all parties to submit their views on how an Article 9 review should proceed. At the same time, pressed by the United States and other large developing countries, the COP agreed on an initiative aimed at enhancing long-term cooperation on climate change through the Framework Convention, including cooperation with regard to technology.[74] This second process—referred to as the Dialogue on Long-Term Cooperation Action to Address Climate Change by Enhancing the Implementation of the Convention—is not taking the form of a negotiation. Instead, it is a two-year series of workshops, which will examine a range of issues and themes. Both groups met for the first time at the second meeting of the parties to the Kyoto Protocol (MOP-2) and the twelfth meeting of the

Conference of the Parties to the UNFCCC (COP-12), held in Nairobi from November 6 to November 17, 2006.

The launching of these parallel consultation processes reflects the wide differences of opinion on where the international climate change regime should go after 2012, and an acknowledgment that it will be difficult for Annex I parties to adopt further emission reduction commitments without corresponding commitments from the United States and major-emitting developing countries. At the Nairobi meetings, the ad hoc working group stated that stabilizing concentrations would require a reduction in global GHG emissions "well below half of levels in 2000," a target that likely would be impossible to achieve without significant effort from developing countries.[75]

A. Sources of Skepticism about the Kyoto Protocol

Negotiations on possible commitments after 2012 will need to contend with the range of criticisms that have emerged about the Kyoto Protocol's architecture. One criticism is that the Protocol's emission targets do not conform to the most cost-effective approach to addressing the problem. According to many experts, reducing the risk of global climate change ultimately will require very steep reductions in emissions, but the optimally cost-effective path to achieving these reductions involves starting with relatively modest commitments and then imposing more stringent commitments over time. In this light, the Protocol's model is "too much, too soon," imposing sharp, near-term reductions that force costly premature retirements of capital stock while leaving uncertain the long-term path of reductions.[76]

Indeed, critics of the Protocol often assert that few Annex I countries are on track to meet their Article 3 commitments and that for several countries, compliance appears increasingly out of reach.[77] In 2006, the government of Canada announced that it expected to miss its target.[78]

Another fundamental criticism of the Protocol is that it does not extend commitments to developing countries, including major emitters such as China and India, even though—as discussed above—the emissions from developing countries are expected to surpass those of industrialized countries in the next two decades.

To be sure, the Protocol's architects assert that its structure is consistent with the Framework Convention's principle of "common but differentiated responsibilities." According to this view, the first commitment period necessarily had to impose commitments only on Annex I parties in order to lay the foundation for key developing countries to adopt limits in the subsequent commitment period. The text of the Protocol, however, does not make any such bargain explicit, much less enforceable.

Moreover, there is some question as to whether the Protocol's initial architecture of absolute emissions caps can be feasibly extended to developing countries. One issue is political; developing countries are reluctant to accept fixed limits on their emissions, lest they effectively amount to limits on their economic growth. The second issue is administrative; many developing country governments lack the capacity to develop an economy-wide regulatory program that could achieve a precise numerical limit on emissions.

Indeed, the Bush Administration and like-minded critics of the Protocol argue that an emissions targets approach is fundamentally flawed. They assert that the key elements of the problem—the ultimate need for possibly substantial reductions in emissions and the imperative of involving developing countries—point away from an emissions targets approach toward a technology-based program. In their view, the aim should be to promote the development of a new generation of clean energy technologies and to ensure that such technologies can be transferred to fast-growing developing countries. They argue that the Protocol's near-term emissions targets are a costly and inequitable distraction from this technology-based path. Others, however, have made the point that technological development and deployment will not be possible without both the "push" of government promotion and the "pull" of a regulatory-based or tax-based price on emissions.[79]

> ... there is some question as to whether the Protocol's initial architecture of absolute emissions caps can be feasibly extended to developing countries.

B. Possible Future Paths

Proposals for future directions of international efforts on climate change are multiplying rapidly.

In 2004, the Pew Center on Global Climate Change published a report that reviewed over 40 different proposals.[80] The Pew Center report identifies several elements of climate policy design along which the proposals vary.

For example, while the majority of proposals assume the continued negotiation of commitments by governments under the auspices of the Framework Convention, a few would abandon the Framework Convention and the Protocol for some other form and forum. For instance, some proposals would bring together a more limited number of major-emitting and like-minded countries. Part of the theory behind the approaches that propose an alternative forum is the difficulty of making progress under the Framework Convention's United Nations "mega-conference" approach.

Similarly, there are different proposals as to how to develop commitments to mitigate GHG emissions. While some proposals would maintain the top-down approach of multilateral negotiation of national commitments, other proposals would encourage countries to make pledges of particular domestic measures.

In addition, experts have come forward with various approaches to the design of commitments. Some propose extending the Protocol's quantitative emission targets,

but with variations. For example, alternative emission targets could be indexed to economic growth, *e.g.*, "intensity" targets, which are expressed in terms of emissions per unit GDP. Such targets could be appropriate for developing countries because they would allow emissions to increase along with economic growth, albeit at a slower pace. Also possible are "action targets," in which a country would commit to achieve a certain percentage of reductions for each ton it emits. For example, a country could pledge to cut 5% of a ton of GHG emissions for each ton emitted. This approach also would allow for economic growth while ensuring continuous effort to mitigate emissions.[81]

Other designs would replace or supplement the emissions targets approach with harmonized domestic policies and measures, which could take the form of coordinated carbon taxes, energy-efficiency standards, or technology policies.

Many proposals address the question of how to share the burdens of climate change mitigation equitably among countries. These proposals accept the Framework Convention's principle of "common but differentiated responsibilities," but would replace the "Annex I" and "non-Annex I" categories. The proposals advance a broad variety of alternative criteria for differentiation among countries, including per capita GDP, per capita emissions, emissions per unit GDP, population, and historical emissions. The proposals also reflect various approaches to differentiating the form, stringency, and timing of commitments for different countries.

C. Asia-Pacific Partnership on Clean Development and Climate

The Asia-Pacific Partnership on Clean Development and Climate represents a possible alternative or parallel path for international cooperation to address global climate change.[82] An initiative of the Bush Administration, the Partnership includes the United States, South Korea, India, China, Australia, and New Zealand. Collectively, these countries account for approximately half of global GHG emissions, and the contribution of India and China is growing rapidly with each year.[83]

The non-legally-binding Charter for the Partnership provides that its purposes include creating a voluntary framework for international cooperation to facilitate the development and transfer of clean technologies and practices among the partner countries.[84] The Charter further provides that the purposes of the Partnership are to be consistent with the principles of the Framework Convention and "are intended to complement but not replace the Kyoto Protocol."[85] The Charter also declares, however, that while the Partners have come together to advance clean development and climate objectives, they recognize that "development and poverty eradication are urgent and overriding goals internationally."[86]

Structurally, the Partnership eschews the binding quantitative emissions targets approach of the Protocol in favor of a series of working groups that will explore opportunities related to transfer and deployment of advanced clean energy technologies. At its inaugural meeting in July 2005, the Partnership established eight public/private-sector "Task Forces" covering (1) cleaner fossil energy; (2) renewable energy and distributed generation; (3) power generation and transmission; (4) steel; (5) aluminum; (6) cement; (7) coal mining; and (8) buildings and appliances. The Partnership directed each Task Force to review the current status of its thematic area, share knowledge of experience and good practices, systematically roadmap existing and emerging technologies, and develop an action plan that identifies opportunities for cooperation and goals.[87]

V. Conclusion

The international climate change regime is a multifaceted complex of institutions, legal rules, voluntary systems, and commercial transactions. At the core of the regime is the Kyoto Protocol, an innovative and complicated system of national obligations and market-based mechanisms. The Protocol has spawned the European Union Emissions Trading Scheme, which is itself an international climate change regime. Together, the Protocol and the EU ETS also have given rise to a multibillion-dollar global market in emission reduction credit transactions.

Yet, the half-life of both the Protocol and the EU ETS is uncertain. The international climate change regime faces an important benchmark in 2012, when the Protocol's first—or perhaps only—commitment period officially expires. Accordingly, the task of crafting an international climate change regime that equitably and efficiently meets the long-term challenge of global climate change will continue.

Endnotes

1. 31 I.L.M. (1998) (hereinafter "Kyoto Protocol" or the "Protocol").

2. Because of their multifaceted character, the various international laws and institutions addressing climate change aptly fit the definition of what international relations scholars refer to as a "regime," *i.e.*, a "persistent and connected set[s] of rules (formal and informal) that prescribe[s] behavioural roles, constrain activity, and shape expectations" in a particular issue area. ROBERT O. KEOHANE, INTERNATIONAL INSTITUTIONS AND STATE POWER at 3. For an extensive and detailed analysis of the international climate change regime, *see* FARHANA YAMIN & JOANNA DEPLEDGE, THE INTERNATIONAL CLIMATE CHANGE REGIME: A GUIDE TO RULES, INSTITUTIONS, AND PROCEDURES (2004).

3. 31 I.L.M. 849 (1992) (hereinafter the "Framework Convention" or the UNFCCC).

4. *See, e.g.,* INTERGOVERNMENTAL PANEL ON CLIMATE CHANGE, SPECIAL REPORT ON EMISSIONS SCENARIOS (Nakicenovic, Nebojsa & Rob Swart eds.) (2000).

5. THE WORLD BANK AND THE INTERNATIONAL EMISSIONS TRADING ASSOCIATION, STATE AND TRENDS OF THE CARBON MARKET 2006 (May 2006).

6. INTERGOVERNMENTAL PANEL ON CLIMATE CHANGE, SCIENTIFIC ASSESSMENT OF CLIMATE CHANGE—REPORT OF WORKING GROUP 1 (J.T. Houghton, G.J. Jenkins & J.J. Ephraums eds.) (1990).

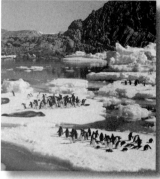

7.   For a listing of ratifications, *see* http://unfccc.int/essential_background/convention/status_of_ratification/items/2631.php (listing ratifications as of June 12, 2006).

8.   For a scholarly discussion of how the UNFCCC establishes a regime framework for further action, *see* Daniel Bodansky, *The Emerging Climate Change Regime*, 20 Ann. Rev. of Energy and Env't 425 (1995).

9.   Framework Convention, art. 3.

10.   *Id.*

11.   *Id.*, art. 3.4.

12.   *Id.*, art. 3.1.

13.   *Id.*

14.   *Id.*, art. 3.2.

15.   The Framework Convention includes another categorization that recognizes those former Soviet bloc countries that, at the time of the treaty's entry into force, were considered "economies in transition." The Framework Convention establishes an Annex II, which includes all of the developed countries that are not economies in transition.

16.   *Id.*, art. 4.1(a).

17.   *Id.*, art. 4.1(b).

18.   *Id.*, art. 4.1(c).

19.   *Id.*, art. 4.1(g).

20.   *Id.*, art. 12.

21.   *Id.*, art. 4.2(a) and (b).

22.   *Id.*, art. 4.7.

23.   *Id.*, art. 4.3.

24.   *Id.*, art. 4.4.

25.   *Id.*, art. 4.5.

26.   *Id.*, art. 7.

27.   *See id.*, arts. 15-17.

28.   *Id.*, art. 8.

29.   *See id.*, arts. 9 and 10.

30.   *Id.*, art. 11.

31.   The Berlin meeting coincided with the publication of the Intergovernmental Panel on Climate Change's *Second Assessment Report*, which outlined a stronger basis for concern about the risks of human-induced climate change. *See generally* Climate Change 1995: The Science of Climate Change: Contribution of Working Group I to the Second Assessment of the Intergovernmental Panel on Climate Change (J.T. Houghton, et al., eds.) (1995).

32.   *See* Report of the Conference of the Parties on its First Session, Held at Berlin From 28 March to 7 April 1995, FCCC/CP/1995/7 Add. 1 (June 1995).

33.   S. 98, 105th Cong. 1st Session, 143 Cong. Rec. S8138 (1997). See Chapter 3 for a more detailed discussion.

34.   Analysis of the Kyoto Protocol, U.S. Global Climate Change Policy Book (February 2002), *available at* http://www.whitehouse.gov/news/releases/2002/02/climatechange.html.

35.   There are some differences between the list of countries in Annex B and the original list of Annex I of the Framework Convention. The Czech Republic, the Slovak Republic, Slovenia and Croatia are all listed in Annex B but are not listed in Annex I of the Framework Convention. Conversely, Belarus and Turkey are listed in Annex I of the Framework Convention but not included in Annex B because they were not parties

to the UNFCCC when the Protocol was adopted. Kazakhstan has declared that it wishes to be bound by the commitments of Annex I Parties under the UNFCCC and has become an Annex I Party under the Protocol. However, it had not made this declaration when the Protocol was adopted, so Kazakhstan does not have an emissions target listed for it in Annex B.

36. *See* Protocol Annex A.

37. *See* Intergovernmental Panel on Climate Change, Climate Change 2001: the Scientific Basis (2001), at 6.1.2.

38. Protocol, art. 3.8.

39. *Id.*, art. 3.5.

40. For a critical viewpoint on the "hot air" issue, *see, e.g.*, David M. Driesen, *Free Lunch or Cheap Fix?: the Emissions Trading Idea and the Climate Change Convention*, 26 B.C. Envtl. Aff. L. Rev. 1, 60-61 (1998).

41. Council Decision 2002/358/EC of 25 April 2002 concerning the approval, on behalf of the European Community, of the Kyoto Protocol to the United Nations Framework Convention on Climate Change and the joint fulfilment of commitments thereunder *OJ L 130, 15.5.2002 P. 0001-0003.*

42. *See* Climate Action Network Europe, Burden Sharing Agreement of the EU, *available at* http://www.climnet.org/resources/euburden.htm.

43. Protocol, art. 3.3.

44. David A. Wirth, *Current Developments: The Sixth Session (Part Two) and Seventh Session of the Conference of the Parties to the Framework Convention on Climate Change*, 96 AJIL 648, 654 (2002).

45. Decision 19/CP.7, FCCC/CP/2001/13/Add.2, at par. 16. This constraint might not be particularly meaningful, since a party that holds both RMUs and AAUs can use its RMUs first and bank its AAUs. Personal communication with Erik Haites, Margaree Consultants (September 2006).

46. *See also* Chapter 18 of this volume for more detailed discussions of the Kyoto flexible mechanisms.

47. Note, however, that there are limits to banking of other types of Kyoto Protocol credits. An Annex I party may bank Certified Emission Reductions and Emission Reduction Units up to only 2.5 percent of its Assigned Amount. Parties may not bank Removal Units. However, as noted *supra*, these restrictions might be essentially symbolic because a Party with surplus Kyoto credits can submit its non-bankable credits first and bank its AAUs.

48. *See* Decision 18/CP.7, FCCC/CP/2001/13/Add.2.

49. 42 U.S.C. §§ 7401-7671q (1998).

50. *See* Decision 9/CMP.1, FCCC/FCCC/KP/CMP/2005/8/Add.2, at p. 65 (requiring each Annex I Party only to "provide information on how its use of the mechanisms is supplemental to domestic action," and "how its domestic action thus constitutes a significant element of the effort" to meet its Article 3 commitment).

51. Robert R. Nordhaus et al., *International Emissions Trading Rules as a Compliance Tool: What Is Necessary, Effective and Workable?* 30 ELR 10837, 10841-44 (2000).

52. Decision 11/CMP.1, FCCC/CMP/2005/8/Add.2, Annex.

53. Personal communication with Erik Haites, Margaree Consultants (September 2006).

54. Protocol, art. 6.1(a)-(d).

55. *See* Decision 9/CMP.1 (Guidelines for Implementation of Article 6 of the Kyoto Protocol), FCCC/KP/CMP/2005/8/Add.2.

56. Protocol, art. 12.5(c).

57. *Id.*, art. 12.5(a).

58. *Id.*, art. 12.9.

59. *Id.*, art. 12.2.

60. *Id.*, art. 12.8.

61. For a discussion of how the "share of the proceeds" is calculated, *see* International Emissions Trading Association, *IETA's Guidance Note Through the CDM Project Approval Process* (v. 2.0, May 2006), *available at* www.ieta.org, at para. 2.6.8.

62. Protocol, art. 12.10.

63. *See* Decision 7/CMP.1, FCCC/KP/CMP/2005/8/Add.1, at p. 94.

64. *See generally* Decision 3/CMP.1, FCCC/KP/CMP/2005/8/Add.1, at pp. 14-20. Decision 17/CP.7, Annex.

65. *See generally* Decision 4/CMP.1, FCCC/KP/CMP/2005/8/Add.1, Annex II.

66. *See generally* Decision 5/CMP.1. FCCC/KP/CMP/2005/8/Add.1.

67. International Emissions Trading Association, IETA Position on the CDM for COP 11 and COP/MOP (Sept. 19, 2005), *available at* www.ieta.org, at pp. 7-8.

68. Wirth, *Current Developments, supra* note 44, at 655.

69. Decision 2/CMP.1, FCCC/KP/CMP/2005/8/Add.1, at para. 5.

70. *See generally* Decision 25/CMP.1, FCCC/KP/CMP/2005/8/Add.3.

71. *See generally* Directive 2003/87/EC of the European Parliament and of the Council of Oct. 13, 2003, establishing a scheme for greenhouse gas emission allowance trading within the Community and amending Council Directive 96/61/EC, *available at* http://europa.eu.int/comm/environment/climat/emission/implementation_en. htm.

72. State and Trends of the Carbon Market, *supra* note 5, at 1.

73. *See, e.g., Top EC Environmental Official Backs 'Unilateral' Post-2012 CO_2 Cap*, Platts Emissions Daily (Oct. 20, 2006).

74. *Summary of the Eleventh Conference of the Parties to the United Nations Framework Convention on Climate Change and the First Conference of the Parties Serving as the Meeting of Parties to the Kyoto Protocol, 28 November–10 December 2005*, Earth Negotiations Bull. Vol. 12 (Dec. 12, 2005), at p. 14.

75. Pew Center on Global Climate Change, *Summary of the Twelfth Session of the Conference of the Parties to the UN Framework Convention on Climate Change and Second Meeting of the Parties Serving to the Kyoto Protocol* (November 2006), *available at* http://www.pewclimate.org/what_s_being_done/in_the_world/cop12/index.cfm. Advanced unedited versions of the Nairobi decisions are available at http://unfccc.int/meetings/cop 12/items/3754.php.

76. *See, e.g.,* Robert Stavins, *Can an Effective Global Climate Treaty Be Based on Sound Science, Rational Economics, and Pragmatic Politics? Resources for the Future Discussion Paper 04-28* (May 2004), *available at* www.rff.org/Documents/RFF-DP-04-28.pdf, at pp. 8-9. Note, however, that the withdrawal of the United States—which was expected to be a major source of demand for Kyoto units—might reduce the price of "hot air" AAUs, CERs, and ERUs sufficiently to lower the overall compliance costs associated with the 2008-2012 commitment period.

77. *See, e.g., EU Way Off Course for Meeting Kyoto Targets: Latest Figures*, Agence France Press (June 22, 2006).

78. *Interpreting Smoke Signals: Canada*, The Economist (July 22, 2006)).

79. *See, e.g.*, Congressional Budget Office, *Evaluating the Role of R&D in Reducing Carbon Dioxide Emissions* (September 2006), *available at* http://www.cbo.gov.

80. Daniel Bodansky, International Climate Efforts Beyond 2012: A Survey of Approaches, Pew Center on Global Climate Change (Dec. 2004).

81. Donald Goldberg & Kevin Baumert, *Action Targets: A New Form of GHG Commitment*, 10 Joint Implementation Quarterly 8 (Oct. 2004).

82. *See Charter for the Asia-Pacific Partnership on Clean Development and Climate, agreed at the Inaugural Ministerial Meeting, Sydney, 11-12 January 2006, available at* www.asiapacificpartnership.org/charter.pdf (hereinafter the "Partnership").

83. "U.S. Agrees to Climate Deal with Asia," *BBC News* (July 28, 2005).

84. Charter, at par. 2.1.1.

85. *Id.*, preamble.

86. *Id.*, at par. 1.

87. Asia-Pacific Partnership on Clean Development and Climate, *Inaugural Ministerial Meeting Communiqué, available at* www.asiapacificpartnership.org/communique. pdf.

chapter three

U.S. Policy

John C. Dernbach

United States government policy concerning climate change can broadly be divided into two categories. The first category consists of laws and policies that expressly address climate change, most of which were adopted with at least the knowledge that they might have some effect on greenhouse gas emissions or on the ability of the United States to respond to climate change. In most cases, these laws and policies were adopted with the intention of making some progress toward understanding or mitigating climate change. Most of these laws are not regulatory.

The second category is based on laws and policies that were adopted for purposes other than climate change mitigation, or at least whose primary purpose is not to address climate change. Perhaps the majority of these laws and policies were adopted before climate change became a prominent issue. These laws nonetheless have an effect—both positive and negative—on net greenhouse gas emissions, adaptation to changing climate, and other aspects of climate change mitigation. These are the background or baseline on which U.S. law and policy to intentionally and constructively address climate change is being built. Some of these laws and policies are being applied in ways that attempt to mitigate climate change. Others are being implemented in a manner that has the incidental effect of helping to increase greenhouse gas emissions and in other ways worsen climate change. Still, these laws have been amended, if at all, in ways that keep their basic purpose and architecture in place.

This chapter surveys both categories of U.S. law and policy relating to climate change. The timing of the major international agreements that address climate change—the 1992 United Nations Framework Convention on Climate Change and the 1997 Kyoto Protocol—provides a kind of rough dividing line between these two categories. As a result, the chapter begins with a discussion of U.S. participation (or not) in each of these agreements. (The substance of these and related agreements is addressed in Chapter 2.) The chapter then discusses the background or baseline laws that the United States brings to this issue, particularly laws relating to energy production. The next part addresses the new law and policy of climate change. It focuses on emissions reporting, scientific research, policies and measures to reduce greenhouse gas emissions, public education, and adaptation. The chapter concludes by looking ahead to likely federal legislation to reduce greenhouse gas emissions by examining bills that are now being discussed as well as two recent reports on energy policy and climate change.[1] Issues relating to this topic are evolving rapidly; the daily news is a necessary supplement to this chapter.

I. U.S. Participation (or Not) in Major International Agreements

A. Ratification of Framework Convention on Climate Change

The United States participated actively in the negotiations that led to the United Nations Framework Convention on Climate Change[2] (Framework Convention), and played a major role in shaping it. The negotiations, which took place in five sessions between February 1991 and May 1992, involved two key issues of importance—then and now—to the United States. The first issue was whether there should be a binding target and timetable. The European Community and many U.S. environmental groups advocated a proposal that would cap carbon dioxide emissions in 2000 at 1990 levels. The first Bush Administration vigorously opposed this proposal, advocating instead that each country develop and implement national plans to reduce greenhouse gas emissions.[3] As a result, under the final text of the Convention, developed countries ("Annex I countries") agreed only to the "aim" of reducing their greenhouse gas emissions to 1990 levels by 2000.[4] The final text also required all parties to establish, implement, and periodically update national programs to mitigate climate change.[5]

The second issue concerned technology transfer and financial assistance for developing countries. According to the Senate Foreign Relations Committee, developing countries sought "transfer of environmentally sound technologies on preferential and noncommercial terms and a financial mechanism that would give them more power than they currently have in the multilateral development banks."[6] The United States, and most developed countries, resisted this approach. Consequently, the technology transfer and financial assistance provisions of the Convention do not provide for preferential access or access on noncommercial terms.[7]

The United States signed the Convention on June 12, 1992, at the United Nations Conference on Environment and Development in Rio de Janeiro. Under the U.S. Constitution, the President has the power to ratify treaties, subject to the "advice and consent" of two-thirds of the Senate.[8] When a treaty contains significant provisions that would bind the United States under international law, the advice and consent of the Senate is often linked to the adoption of legislation that would implement the treaty. Such legislation prevents the United States from being subject to an international law obligation that it has no domestic authority to carry out. In this case, however, the Senate's advice and consent was not conditioned upon any implementing legislation. In its report, the Foreign Relations Committee emphasized the absence of quantitative limitations in the Convention, and stated that ratification of the Convention would not subject the United States to legally enforceable obligations.[9] The Senate gave its advice and consent on October 7, 1992.[10] Less than a week later, on October 13, President George H.W. Bush signed the instrument of ratification and transmitted it to the Convention Secretariat.[11]

> **The United States was the fourth country to ratify the Convention. The Framework Convention took effect in 1994 and now has 185 additional parties, for a total of 189.**

The United States was the fourth country to ratify the Convention.[12] The Framework Convention took effect in 1994 and now has 185 additional parties, for a total of 189.[13] In 2001, President George W. Bush specifically reaffirmed U.S. commitment to the Convention.[14]

B. Refusal to Ratify Kyoto Protocol

The Framework Convention treats developed countries and developing countries differently. As the Convention's preamble states, developed countries have contributed "the largest share of historical and current global emissions of greenhouse gases, and have higher *per capita* emissions levels than developing countries."[15] Thus, in ratifying the Framework Convention, developed countries agreed to adopt policies and measures that will demonstrate that they "are taking the lead" in addressing climate change.[16] The Convention also contains a commitment to review the adequacy of developed country commitments, including the "aim" commitment, at the first session of the conference of the parties.[17] The initial annual meetings of the conference of the parties saw growing consensus that developed countries should agree to targets and timetables for the reduction of their greenhouse gas emissions.

In 1997, it appeared that there might be an agreement on this issue at the upcoming annual meeting of the conference of the parties to be held in Kyoto, Japan, in December. In July of that year, the Senate, by a vote of 95–0, passed a resolution sponsored by Senators Robert Byrd (D.-W.Va.) and Chuck Hagel (R.-Neb.). The Byrd-Hagel resolution expressed the sense of the Senate that the United States should not sign any protocol to the Climate Convention unless the protocol met several key conditions.[18] According to the resolution, the protocol must not "mandate new commitments to limit or reduce greenhouse gas emissions" for developed countries unless it also "mandates new specific scheduled commitments to limit or reduce greenhouse gas emissions for Developing Country Parties within the same compliance period."[19] In addition, the protocol should not "result in serious harm to the economy of the United States."[20] The resolution's preamble suggests that the Senate's core concern was with binding greenhouse gas emission limits on developed countries (including the United States) if developing countries are not also subject to binding limits. The "disparity of treatment," the preamble states, "could result in serious harm to the United States economy, including significant job loss, trade disadvantages, increased energy and consumer costs, or any combination thereof."[21] The resolution did not address the issue of developed country leadership, as expressed in the Convention.

At the Kyoto meeting, the parties agreed to a protocol containing binding greenhouse gas emission limits for developed countries.[22] Under the Kyoto Protocol, developed countries agreed to reduce their net greenhouse gas emissions by at least 5% from 1990 levels by 2008–2012.[23] No comparable commitment was included for developing countries. The Protocol contains somewhat different commitments for individual developed countries; the U.S. commitment is 7% below 1990 levels.[24] Greenhouse gas emissions in the United States are now projected to be more than 25% higher in 2012 than they were in 1990. Thus, the Kyoto target is about 30% below projected "business as usual" emissions.[25]

In some respects, the United States achieved much of what it sought in the Kyoto Protocol, most prominently in the form of several mechanisms for increased flexibility in meeting emissions reduction targets, including emissions trading.[26] Because of its positive experience in emissions trading under the 1990 Clean Air Act Amendments (described below), the United States championed such mechanisms as a way of reducing the overall cost of addressing climate change. On the other hand, the absence of binding commitments by developing countries squarely contradicted the Byrd-Hagel resolution. The Protocol was intended to be legally binding under international law, and thus required ratification. It was difficult to see how two-thirds of the Senate would provide its advice and consent under these circumstances. Apparently, U.S. negotiators committed to a 7% reduction below 1990 levels in Kyoto—a greater reduction than its earlier proposal of simply returning to 1990 levels—in order to "at the very least, open the door to reduction obligations for developing countries."[27] However, language in the draft protocol that would have allowed developing countries to voluntarily agree to greenhouse gas emission limits was removed near the end of negotiations after China and other developing countries objected.[28] In any event, the Clinton Administration did not attempt to seek the advice and consent of the Senate on the Kyoto Protocol.

On March 13, 2001, less than two months after taking office, President George W. Bush expressly repudiated the Kyoto Protocol.[29] Referring to the Byrd-Hagel resolution, he said he opposed the Protocol "because it exempts 80 percent of the world, including major population centers such as China and India, from compliance, and would cause serious harm to the U.S. economy." He also said the Administration "takes the issue of global climate change very seriously," and that he would work with "our friends and allies . . . to develop technologies, market incentives, and other creative ways to address global climate change."[30]

On February 16, 2005, following Russia's ratification, the Kyoto Protocol went into effect.[31] Among major developed countries, only the United States and Australia are not parties.

C. Negotiations on Post-Kyoto Commitments

As already noted, the reductions agreed to by developed country parties to the Kyoto Protocol are to be achieved by 2008–2012. A question left open in the Kyoto Protocol is what greenhouse gas reduction commitments, if any, should be made for the period after 2012. The Protocol provides that discussions of subsequent commitment periods must begin by 2005, and that commitments for subsequent periods are to be treated as amendments to the Protocol.[32] After a meeting in Bonn in May 2006, it appeared that developed countries would agree to a subsequent commitment period.[33] The United States did not participate in that meeting because it refuses to participate in any talks that could lead a second round of commitments on greenhouse gas reductions. The United States has, however, participated in more general talks on future cooperation as a party to the Framework Convention.[34]

II. Background or Baseline Law

This background or baseline law is composed largely of energy and environmental law. Significantly, the law of climate change in the United States is evolving at the intersection of these two areas of law. For at least the past several decades, environmental law and energy law have been overlapping but largely separate domains. While Congress is the primary federal lawmaker in both domains, energy and environment are covered by different statutes that have different purposes. They also involve different administrative agencies at both the federal and state level. For energy, these agencies are mainly the Federal Energy Regulatory Commission and the Department of Energy at the federal level, and public utility or public service commissions at the state level. For environment, these agencies are chiefly the Environmental Protection Agency (EPA), the Army Corps of Engineers, and the Fish and Wildlife Service at the federal level, and various environmental and natural resource agencies at the state level. This presents a challenge and an opportunity for practitioners, most of whom have been active in one domain but not the other. This background or baseline law includes environmental laws that are discussed in other chapters, including the Clean Air Act (Chapter 5), the National Environmental Policy Act (Chapter 6), and facility permitting requirements (Chapter 7). It also includes corporate disclosure and governance requirements (Chapters 13 and 14), insurance law (Chapter 15), and subsidies, tax policy, and technological innovation laws (Chapter 16).

A. Energy Law

Even before the United States began considering policies to understand, monitor, or reduce greenhouse gas emissions, it already had a body of policy that had a significant effect on such emissions. Much of that policy was, and is, anchored in U.S. energy policy. Virtually all emissions of the dominant greenhouse gas, carbon dioxide, are from fossil fuel emissions.[35]

1. Energy Law—A Very Brief Overview

The traditional purposes of U.S. energy policy have been to supply plentiful energy at low prices and with appropriate environmental and public health protections. Energy law plays a significant role in economic development. Energy law itself is divided according to the type or source of energy. Thus, there are largely separate bodies of law for nuclear energy, coal, oil, natural gas, electricity, hydropower, and alternative energy sources.[36] Still, several themes cut across most or all of these bodies of law. Much of this law involves regulation of production to avoid adverse public health, public safety, economic, and environmental effects. This protection is accomplished through permits, licenses, leases, or other governmental approvals along with attendant performance standards.

Another feature of energy law has been government control over prices. Because consumers often do not have realistic choices about who provides a particular form of energy, price regulation has been used to protect consumers against monopolistic practices. In the past several decades, faith in the market and other factors have led to some lessening of price regulation at the state and federal level.[37]

A third feature is federal subsidies, mostly in support of production. Although the overall effect of energy laws and policies on U.S. greenhouse gas emissions does not seem to have been assessed in any comprehensive manner, it appears that energy law has had the effect of increasing greenhouse gas emissions. Fossil fuel subsidies, for instance, have made it more difficult for alternative energy sources and energy efficiency to compete effectively in the market.[38] (Subsidies are covered in greater detail in Chapter 16.) Other policies, including highway policy, have had the same effect.

While a detailed analysis of energy law is beyond the scope of this chapter, energy law is inextricably linked with climate change for several reasons. To begin with, different sources of energy have different impacts on greenhouse gas emissions. Thus, laws and policies that encourage, or discourage, the production of energy from certain sources

... laws and policies that encourage, or discourage, the production of energy from certain sources will have more effect on greenhouse gas emissions than laws and policies directed at other sources.

will have more effect on greenhouse gas emissions than laws and policies directed at other sources. More generally, climate change forces a recalculation of the costs and benefits of each form of energy production in light of greenhouse gas impacts and may affect the desirability of particular forms of energy, or the circumstances under which they are produced. For example, there is growing federal interest in, and support for, integrated coal gasification combined-cycle power plants and other advanced technologies that lower carbon dioxide emissions from coal combustion and provide opportunities to sequester any carbon that is produced. Renewed interest in nuclear energy, which does not directly produce greenhouse gas, is another example. In addition, the means chosen to address climate change may or may not be consistent with the traditional purposes of energy policy—particularly keeping prices low or encouraging the production of certain forms of energy. For instance, a frequently discussed legal tool for addressing greenhouse gas emissions—a tax on carbon, BTUs, or petroleum—appears to fly in the face of the goal of keeping energy prices low (although some would argue that such a tax would reduce demand and thus reduce prices).

Domestic energy issues are also inextricably linked to a set of international policies relating to energy security and climate change. Most obvious is the oft-stated U.S. desire to be independent of, or at least less dependent on, foreign oil and natural gas supplies. Although coal burning now produces more greenhouse gases than any other fuel, coal is also abundant in the United States. As a result, the use of coal gasification is seen as a way of reducing dependence on foreign energy supplies. A question also persists about U.S. leadership on climate change. The United States is the largest energy producer and consumer in the world, accounting for about one-fourth of the world's annual energy use, as well as the world's largest emitter of greenhouse gases.[39] These are not simply interesting facts; they also provide a point of departure for considering what U.S. leadership, or failure to lead, can mean internationally.

2. National Energy Policy—2001

In May 2001, President George W. Bush's National Energy Policy Development Group, a group of federal officials headed by Vice President Dick Cheney, issued a National Energy Policy.[40] The Policy describes "our nation's energy crisis" in terms of a "fundamental imbalance between supply and demand." Energy production, it said, is not keeping pace with energy demand, and energy consumption is expected to grow by 32 percent by 2020.[41] The Policy contains recommendations for each major facet of U.S. energy policy—protecting and increasing domestic energy supplies, reducing the impacts of high energy prices, improving environmental protection, modernizing energy efficiency and conservation, increasing renewable and alternative energy, strengthening and enhancing energy infrastructure, and strengthening global alliances on energy and security.[42] Many of these recommendations, including those for renewable energy and energy efficiency, indirectly mitigate climate change to some degree. Thus, for example, the report recommended a variety of actions to improve technology for energy efficiency, to provide tax credits for hybrid and fuel cell vehicles, and to streamline permitting for power plants that produce both heat and electricity.[43] Only one recommendation specifically referred to climate change. The Policy recommended that federal agencies support continued research on global climate change and that they continue to identify cost-effective approaches to address it.[44]

The National Energy Policy spawned at least two legal challenges. Judicial Watch and the Sierra Club filed a lawsuit alleging that a number of private parties associated with various energy industries were *de facto* members of the National Energy Policy Development Group, and that the Group was therefore an advisory committee under the Federal Advisory Committee Act. As a result, plaintiffs claimed, they were entitled under that Act to see the documents on which the Group relied. In 2005, the U.S. Court of Appeals for the District of Columbia Circuit ruled that these private persons were not given a vote or a veto in the Group's decisions, and consequently, the plaintiffs were not entitled to the relief they sought.[45] The same court held, in a separate lawsuit, that government agencies were not required under the Freedom of Information Act to release documents on which the Group relied.[46]

According to the Bush Administration, many of the Policy's recommendations have already been implemented to some degree.[47] In accordance with the Policy, for example, President Bush issued an Executive Order directing federal agencies to prepare an energy impact statement prior to taking any action that could adversely and significantly affect energy supplies, distribution, or use.[48]

3. Energy Policy Act of 2005

The National Energy Policy also contained a number of legislative recommendations. Many, but not all, of them were enacted in some form in the Energy Policy Act of 2005.[49] The Act contains a great variety of provisions across 18 titles (or subchapters) and 441 pages. The subtitle on climate change has two sections.[50] There are also longer subtitles on energy efficiency, renewable energy, hydrogen, ethanol, and nuclear power, all of which could be said to address climate change. The Act contains additional subtitles on oil and gas production, coal (including provisions for clean power projects), electricity, and research and development. The diverse provisions of the Act vary in their significance; some are described in more detail later in this chapter and others are described in Chapter 16. Still, this Act and the National Energy Policy make it unmistakably clear that U.S. energy policy and climate policy are inextricably linked.

B. Energy Efficiency

Energy efficiency can reduce greenhouse gas emissions by reducing the amount of energy that is used. By definition, energy efficiency involves doing the same amount of work, or producing the same amount of goods or services, with less energy.[51] U.S. energy consumption more than tripled between 1949 and 2004, increasing from 31.98 to 99.74 quadrillion BTUs.[52] Gross Domestic Product (measured in 2000 dollars) rose by an even greater margin in the same period, from $1.6 to $10.8 trillion. That energy consumption only tripled in this period is due to considerable gains in energy efficiency. Energy intensity—energy consumption per dollar of GDP (measured again in 2000 dollars)—declined from 19.57 to 9.20 thousand BTUs per dollar between 1949 and 2004.[53]

The United States has a range of laws in place that are intended to increase the efficiency with which the country uses

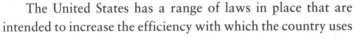

energy. Many of these laws were adopted after the Organization of the Petroleum Exporting Countries (OPEC) oil embargo in 1973–74, before climate change was a prominent issue. While these laws were not intended to reduce greenhouse gas emissions, they are being administered with an understanding that more efficient use of energy has such an effect. At the national level, the greatest energy savings have been achieved for motor vehicles and appliances.[54] (Automobile efficiency standards are discussed in Chapter 5.)

The Energy Policy and Conservation Act of 1975, as amended most recently by the Energy Policy Act of 2005,[55] requires the Department of Energy to adopt testing procedures for the standardized determination of energy efficiency, energy use, or estimated annual operating cost for particular products.[56] The Federal Trade Commission is required to adopt labeling rules based on energy use stating the estimated annual operating cost of the particular product and the range of annual estimated operating cost for such products.[57] These rules are intended to inform consumers about a product's energy use and costs at the time of purchase. The Act also establishes energy-efficiency standards for certain consumer products and authorizes the Department of Energy to set new or amended energy and water conservation standards for a variety of consumer products other than automobiles.[58] (Water conservation furthers energy efficiency to the extent that it reduces the amount of water that needs to be pumped, heated or cooled.)

New or amended standards are to be based on the "maximum improvement in energy efficiency, or, in the case of showerheads, faucets, water closets, or urinals, water efficiency, which the Secretary determines is technologically feasible and economically justified."[59] As a consequence, standards have been established (and often subsequently made more stringent) for new refrigerators, refrigerator-freezers, freezers, central air conditioners and central air-conditioning heat pumps, water heaters, furnaces, dishwashers, clothes washers, clothes dryers, general service fluorescent lamps and incandescent reflector lamps, fluorescent lamp ballasts, washing machines, clothes dryers, faucets, showerheads, ceiling fans, and ceiling fan light kits.[60] In general, federal standards for a particular product preempt state standards for the same product, unless the state files a petition with the Department of Energy and convinces the agency that the state's interests are substantially different from, or greater than, those in the United States generally, and that the state regulation is preferable or necessary based on "costs, benefits, burdens, and reliability of energy or water savings."[61]

A somewhat similar set of testing, labeling, and standard-setting requirements exists for commercial and industrial equipment.[62] The Department of Energy has adopted efficiency standards for electric motors and a variety of other equipment.[63]

Primarily because of these standards, significant improvements in efficiency were achieved between 1972 and 2001. Gas furnaces became 25% more efficient, central air conditioners became 40% more efficient, and refrigerators became more than 75% more efficient.[64] Because of the great improvement in energy efficiency, the refrigerator is the poster child for the effectiveness of national appliance efficiency standards. In the early 1970s, refrigerators alone were the largest energy user in most homes, consuming as much electricity as was produced by 30 large coal-fired power plants.[65] Although it appears possible to build refrigerators that are 50% more efficient than the currently applicable 2001 standard, the improvement in refrigerator efficiency has been so great that it is possible to envision a point at which "refrigerators will use so little energy that it may well make sense to focus attention on other products."[66]

Although this statute was not adopted to reduce greenhouse gas emissions, it has had that effect. Residential appliance efficiency standards are projected to reduce annual carbon emissions between 1990 and 2010 by an amount equal to 4% of 1990 U.S. carbon emissions, and at a net savings to the U.S. economy.[67] Greenhouse gas reduction benefits are often cited in preambles to rulemakings for more stringent standards. For example, the central air-conditioning and heat pump standards, adopted in 2002, are projected to prevent 24 million metric tons of carbon dioxide emissions from 2006 to 2030.[68] Similarly, the efficiency standards for residential water heaters, adopted in 2001, are projected to prevent 152 million metric tons of carbon dioxide emissions by 2020.[69]

The Energy Policy Act of 2005 requires new or more stringent standards for a variety of products[70] as well as commercial and industrial equipment.[71] The Act also instructs the Federal Trade Commission to consider improvements to product labeling.[72] Some of its energy-efficiency provisions cover subjects other than appliance and equipment standards. For instance, by fiscal year 2015, federal agencies are to reduce energy consumption in federal buildings by 20 percent from fiscal year 2003 levels.[73] Daylight Saving Time was extended by a month in the spring and a month in the fall.[74]

C. Renewable Energy

Much of the law of renewable energy is in the form of federal tax incentives (Chapter 16), federal research and development funding, and state permitting requirements (Chapter 7). The Energy Policy Act of 2005 contains additional requirements relating to renewable energy. The Act requires EPA to establish regulations requiring the volume of renewable fuel sold or introduced into commerce in the United States annually to increase from 4.0 billion gallons in 2006 to 7.5 billion gallons in 2012.[75] According to a clarifying rule adopted by EPA at the end of 2005, the 2006 requirement works out to 2.78 percent by volume of the gasoline sold or introduced into commerce.[76]

Under the Act, renewable fuels include cellulosic biomass ethanol, waste-derived ethanol, and biodiesel.[77] Ethanol production was already projected to exceed 4.0 billion gallons in 2006, and thus there was little concern about meeting the initial target.[78] In addition, dual-fueled vehicles in the federal fleet are now required, in general, to be operated using only alternative fuels.[79]

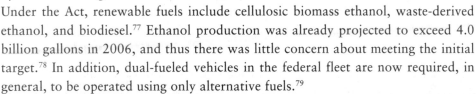

In principle, the use of renewable fuels or biofuels is preferable to the use of fossil fuel from a greenhouse gas perspective because fossil fuel combustion puts carbon dioxide into the atmosphere that had been stored for millions of years. Biofuel combustion, by contrast, returns carbon dioxide to the atmosphere that plants such as corn or soybeans removed from the atmosphere only a short time before. But the *net* greenhouse gas benefit of ethanol, after taking into account the energy (much from fossil fuel) required to produce it, has emerged as an important question. According to a recent study: "Relative to the fossil fuels they displace, greenhouse gas emissions are reduced 12 percent by the production and combustion of ethanol and 41 percent by biodiesel."[80] Neither biofuel can be derived from corn and soybeans in substantial amounts without affecting food supplies, but the energy and environmental benefits of such fuels would be greater if they were made from waste biomass or grown on marginal land.[81]

The Energy Policy Act of 2005 requires the Secretary of Energy to publish an annual report "describing the available amount and characteristics" of U.S. renewable energy resources as well as other information that would be useful in developing those resources.[82] Landfill gas, livestock methane, and ocean energy ("including tidal, wave, current, and thermal") were included as renewable energy. The Act amended the definition of renewable energy contained in multiple other places in the U.S. Code to include these energy sources.[83] Congress also took steps to facilitate leasing of federal lands for geothermal energy production. Among other things, the Act requires the Departments of Agriculture and the Interior to establish a coordinated leasing procedure, create a five-year program for geothermal leasing in the National Forest System, and end the backlog in pending applications.[84]

D. Other Laws

Virtually every sector in the economy has some effect on greenhouse gas emissions. As a consequence, a variety of other (non-energy-related) existing laws can influence greenhouse gas emissions, or can be interpreted or applied to address climate change. Still, some laws have greater impact than others. Three are illustrative. Federal transportation laws affect greenhouse gas emissions in a variety of ways—by both encouraging more driving and by directing, to greater and greater degrees, that transportation systems be planned to incorporate alternatives to driving.[85] Federal agricultural laws that encourage soil conservation, including the Conservation Reserve Program, also have the benefit of encouraging the storage of carbon in those soils.[86] A federal waste management rule requires municipal waste landfills to capture their methane emissions. Methane is a potent greenhouse gas (trapping about 21 times more heat per molecule than carbon dioxide), and this rule has had resulted in lower methane emissions.[87]

III. Laws and Policies Intended to Address Climate Change

The United States has laws and policies and practices in place that address, to some degree, most of the obligations contained in the Framework Convention. The most specific and detailed of these laws concern scientific research. Under the Global Climate Protection Act of 1987, EPA was given responsibility for developing and coordinating U.S. domestic policy, and the State Department was given responsibility for diplomatic and international efforts.[88] Thus, unless another statute assigns responsibility for a particular task to another agency, EPA and the State Department have the lead in their respective spheres.

A. National Emissions Reporting

Parties to the Framework Convention agreed to develop and make publicly available, on a periodic basis, "national inventories of anthropogenic emissions by sources and removals by sinks of all greenhouse gases not controlled by the Montreal Protocol."[89] This inventory is also to be provided to the Conference of the Parties.[90] In the Energy Policy Act of 1992, Congress directed the preparation of an annual inventory of aggregate greenhouse gas emissions.[91] Six greenhouse gases were considered significant enough to be included in the Kyoto Protocol. These are carbon dioxide, methane, nitrous oxide, hydrofluorocarbons, perfluorocarbons, and sulfur hexafluoride.[92] The United States reports emissions of these gases though it has not ratified the Kyoto Protocol.[93] Chapter 1 contains a description of the U.S. inventory.

B. Scientific Research

Parties to the Framework Convention agreed to "[p]romote and cooperate" in "research, systematic observation and development of data archives" to better understand the climate system.[94] To that end, they agreed to support and develop international and intergovernmental efforts to improve data collection, systematic observation, and "national scientific and technical research capacities and capabilities."[95] U.S. policy concerning science can be broadly divided into two categories—what this country's leaders say the existing science means, and how the United States is proceeding with additional research.

> **Parties to the Framework Convention agreed to "[p]romote and cooperate" in "research, systematic observation and development of data archives" to better understand the climate system.**

1. The 2001 National Academy of Sciences Report

In May 2001, shortly after President George W. Bush repudiated the Kyoto Protocol, the Administration asked the National Academy of Sciences for an assessment of the state of climate change science. The Administration's request asked for identification of the "greatest certainties and uncertainties."[96] The Academy responded with a succinct summary of the research by a panel that included at least one prominent skeptic, Prof. Richard Lindzen of MIT. The report begins:

> Greenhouse gases are accumulating in Earth's atmosphere as a result of human activities, causing surface air temperatures and subsurface ocean temperatures to rise. Temperatures are, in fact, rising. The changes observed over the last several decades are likely mostly due to human activities, but we cannot rule out that some significant part of these changes is also a reflection of natural variability. Human-induced warming and associated sea level rise are expected to continue through the 21st century. Secondary effects are sug-

gested by computer model simulations and basic physical reasoning. These include increases in rainfall rates and increased susceptibility of semi-arid regions to drought. The impacts of these changes will be critically dependent on the magnitude of the warming and the rate at which it occurs.[97]

The Academy's report observed that concentrations of carbon dioxide had increased from about 280 parts per million by volume (ppmv) at the time of the Industrial Revolution to about 370 ppmv at present, and are increasing by about 1.5 ppmv annually. "Human activities are responsible for the increase," the report said, adding that carbon dioxide levels in the atmosphere are higher now than they have been any time in the past 400,000 years.[98]

The Academy said it generally agreed with the scientific assessment provided by the 2001 report of the Intergovernmental Panel on Climate Change (IPCC).[99] The IPCC is the internationally recognized body of climate scientists that analyzes peer-reviewed published articles and studies on climate change, and publishes periodic reports synthesizing the available literature.[100] IPCC atmospheric temperature scenarios for 2100 range from an average of 2.5 to 10.4 degrees Fahrenheit above 1990 levels. Acknowledging the "wide range" between the upper and lower estimates, the Academy said this range was due to different projections of the sensitivity of climate to increasing greenhouse gases and to different assumptions about future greenhouse gas concentrations.[101] Reducing these uncertainties, the report said, will require "a vigorous, ongoing program of basic research."[102]

Higher carbon dioxide concentrations will likely benefit agriculture and forestry in the short term, but there are also significant risks of drought, greater wind and flood damage in coastal areas, and greater heat stress and smog-induced respiratory disease. Because models only forecast impacts by the end of the century, even though they indicate rising sea levels and temperatures after 2100, the Academy said, these models "may well underestimate the magnitude of the eventual impacts."[103]

The President's immediate response to the Academy report was to acknowledge some of the certainties—average surface temperatures are increasing—and emphasize the uncertainties. "We do not know how much our climate could, or will change in the future," he said. "We do not know how fast change will occur, or even how some of our actions could impact it."[104] Nonetheless, he said, we "recognize our responsibility and will meet it."[105] The United States has also used the uncertainties described in the 2001 NRC report to justify its scientific research program.[106]

In May 2002, when the State Department filed the most recent U.S. national report under the Framework Convention, it included the foreword and executive summary of the 2001 NAS report in an appendix.[107] It also summarized the science in a way that tracks the 2001 report:

Greenhouse gases are accumulating in Earth's atmosphere as a result of human activities, causing global mean surface air temperature and subsurface ocean temperatures to rise. While the changes observed over the last several decades are likely due mostly to human activities, we cannot rule out that some significant part is also a reflection of natural variability.[108]

At a press briefing shortly after this report was released, President Bush was asked whether he planned any new initiative on global warming based on this conclusion. He replied:

> No, I've laid out that very comprehensive initiative. I read the report put out by a—put out by the bureaucracy. I do not support the Kyoto treaty. The Kyoto treaty would severely damage the United States economy, and I don't accept that. I accept the alternative we put out, that we can grow our economy and, at the same time, through technologies, improve our environment.[109]

2. Research and Systematic Observation

Parties to the Framework Convention, including the United States, agreed to promote and support scientific research and observation that is intended "to further the understanding and to reduce or eliminate the remaining uncertainties regarding the causes, effects, magnitude and timing of climate change.[110] Parties also agreed to support intergovernmental and international scientific efforts.[111] The United States has a well-developed and reasonably well-funded scientific research and observation program, and has adopted a climate change research strategy. This program is considered by many to be the best in the world.[112]

The United States has two statutes directly addressing scientific research on climate change. The first, the National Climate Program Act,[113] was adopted in 1978, 14 years before the United States ratified the Framework Convention. Recognizing the importance of weather and climate to human security and well-being, and also recognizing that the United States "lacks a well-defined and coordinated" climate research and assessment program, Congress established a National Climate Program "to understand and respond to natural and man-induced climate processes and their implications."[114] The Act created a National Climate Program Office in the Department of Commerce to coordinate interagency climate activities, and directed the development and implementation of five-year interagency plans establishing goals and priorities for the Program. The act also directed the Program to include "assessments of the effect of climate change on the natural environment, agricultural production, energy supply and demand, land and water resources, transportation, human health and national security."[115]

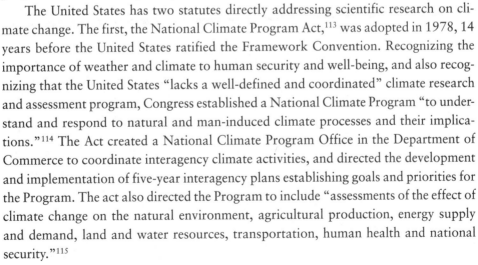

The Global Change Research Act of 1990[116] includes but is not limited to climate change research. "Global change" is defined by the Act as "changes in the global environment (including alterations in climate, land productivity, oceans or other water resources, atmospheric chemistry, and ecological systems) that may alter the capacity of the Earth to sustain life."[117] Congress found that a variety of human activities as well as growing human population "are contributing to processes of global change that may significantly alter the Earth habitat within a few human generations," and identified global warming and the release of stratospheric ozone-depleting chemicals as two of these change-inducing activities.[118] The legislation is intended to provide for "development and coordination of a comprehensive and integrated United States research program" to "understand, assess, predict, and respond to human-induced and natural processes of global change."[119] It requires the creation of an interagency Committee on Earth and Environmental Sciences which, among other things, is to develop a National Global Change Research Plan. The Plan is to establish, for a 10-year period, "the goals and priorities for Federal global change research which most effectively advance scientific understanding of global change and provide usable information on which to base policy decisions relating to global change."[120] The work of the National Climate Program under the National Climate Program Act is to be considered in this effort.[121]

In 2002, President George W. Bush created the U.S. Climate Change Science Program to integrate activities under these two statutes. In 2003, at the conclusion of a drafting and review process that began in the late 1990s, the Climate Change Science Program and the Subcommittee on Global Change Research issued the first 10-year strategic plan for climate change science.[122] The strategy, which focuses on research "conducted, sponsored, or applied" by 13 U.S. government agencies, is intended to guide the development and application of knowledge concerning climate change.[123]

The strategic plan has five goals: improving knowledge of the earth's climate system, improving quantification of the forces changing the earth's climate, reducing uncertainty about future projections, understanding the adaptability of natural and human systems to climate change, and improving our ability to manage the "risks and opportunities" of climate change.[124] These goals are to be achieved by planning, sponsoring, and conducting scientific research; by improving observations and data management systems; by improving science resources for decision-making; and by publicly communicating the results of these efforts.[125] For each goal, the strategy contains a list of priority work products, a statement of their significance, and a projected completion date.

One of the work products identified in connection with the third goal, reducing future uncertainties, is a better understanding of the risks of abrupt climate change. Because abrupt climate changes have occurred in the past, the strategy says, we need to learn more about the possibility for future abrupt changes. The projected completion date is two to four years (between 2005 and 2007).[126] For each of these work products, the strategy also assesses the state of knowledge, identifies research needs, and provides a detailed work plan. On abrupt climate change, the strategy points out that changes of up to 30 degrees Fahrenheit and a doubling or halving of precipitation have in the past occurred in a matter of years and lasted for centuries.[127] Because most of the previous modeling has assumed a more or less gradual warming, the potential for such abrupt changes is important, particularly in light of the rapid warming that has occurred in the Arctic over the past several decades. The "causes and mechanisms" of past abrupt changes are not well understood, and we do not have a good idea how to model for future abrupt changes.[128] A research agenda to address these and other issues is detailed in the strategy.[129] The strategy also covers a variety of cross-cutting issues, such as public communication, decision support, international cooperation, and modeling strategy.

The National Research Council (NRC) of the National Academy of Sciences evaluated the draft strategy[130] as well as the final strategy.[131] In its review of the final strategy, the NRC said it "includes the elements of a strategic management framework that could permit it to effectively guide research on climate and associated global changes over the next decades," and urged its implementation "with urgency."[132] The NRC added that the government's scientific research program could be, or appear to be, "influenced by political considerations." It therefore urged the adoption of an independent oversight mechanism to ensure the "scientific credibility" of this effort.[133]

Research supported by this strategy appears to be closing gaps in our scientific understanding. The reliability of climate models and the reality of human-caused global warming had been called into question by apparent discrepancies between surface temperatures and temperatures recorded higher in the atmosphere by instruments contained in satellites and balloons. A careful analysis of the data, however, turned up errors showing that the discrepancy does not exist, at least in nontropical latitudes. This research is one of the specific work products identified in the strategy.[134]

In addition to its domestic climate science agenda, the United States is a member of the Group on Earth Observations (GEO), whose membership is comprised of 63 other countries, the European Commission, and 43 international organizations.[135] GEO "is leading a worldwide effort to build a Global Earth Observation System of Systems (GEOSS) over the next 10 years."[136] The premise is that existing earth observation systems are fragmented and incomplete. While the United States supports a variety of observation systems, it reported in 2002 that it had "no comprehensive system designed to observe climate change and climate variability"; that much data was obtained for other purposes, including weather forecasting or providing public information; and that such data "are usually limited in their spatial and temporal extent."[137] GEOSS is intended to remedy such limitations by building on existing national, regional, and other observation systems to obtain coordinated, integrated, and comprehensive observation and measurement of agriculture, biodiversity, climate, disasters, ecosystems, energy, weather, and other factors. Such information is intended, among other things, to assist in "[u]nderstanding, assessing, predicting, mitigating, and adapting to climate variability and change."[138] The United States is contributing to GEOSS through the Integrated Earth Observation System (IEOS), which is an effort to collect, synthesize, manage, and disseminate a wide variety of data. In 2005, the United States issued a strategic plan for the development and implementation of IEOS.[139]

> ... there is no U.S. policy currently in place to directly reduce greenhouse gas emissions, and no rule of domestic or international law requiring the United States to reduce greenhouse gas emissions by a particular amount by a particular time.

Every year, the Climate Change Science Program and the Subcommittee on Global Change Research publish a report entitled *Our Changing Planet*. This report is issued in response to a requirement in the 1990 Global Change Research Act for the submission to Congress of an annual report on efforts under the statute, including activities, achievements, and expenditures.[140] The report for fiscal year 2006 describes progress in implementing the strategic plan for climate science, advances in modeling capability, and international efforts in scientific cooperation.[141] As described in the annual *Our Changing Planet* reports and elsewhere, annual federal science funding increased slightly between 1993 and 2004—from $1.82 billion to $1.98 billion in inflation-adjusted dollars.[142]

C. Policies and Measures to Reduce Emissions

Repudiation of the Kyoto Protocol means that there is no U.S. policy currently in place to directly reduce greenhouse gas emissions, and no rule of domestic or international law requiring the United States to reduce greenhouse gas emissions by a particular amount by a particular time. Nor is there any overall nonbinding goal for reduction of net greenhouse gas emissions. The United States nonetheless has some laws and policies in place that are intended to reduce emissions.

Developed-country parties to the Framework Convention, including the United States, agreed to "adopt national policies and take corresponding measures on the mitigation of climate change," including limits on greenhouse gas emissions.[143] Each developed country also agreed to provide the Conference of the Parties, on a periodic basis, with "a detailed description of the policies and measures that it has adopted to implement" the Convention.[144] Such reports are submitted periodically; the most recent report from the United States was issued in 2002.[145] The U.S. report identifies 59 policies and measures or categories of policies and measures that it is employing to

address climate change. These policies and measures are predominantly voluntary, research, and information oriented; only six are identified as regulatory.[146] Among the laws and policies being employed by the United States are the energy-efficiency and renewable energy measures described above. Another is the Bush Administration's greenhouse gas intensity goal.

Considerable improvements in energy efficiency occur on an annual basis. A commonly used measure for improvements in energy efficiency is energy intensity. Energy intensity is measured by energy use per dollar of GDP (measured in 2000 dollars to keep the measure constant over time). Between 1972 and 2000, energy intensity declined at an average annual rate of about 2 percent per year.[147] Reductions in energy intensity are caused by technological improvements, product substitutions, economic restructuring, and other factors, and have been occurring in the United States over the past several decades. In its *Annual Energy Outlook 2005*, the Energy Information Administration projected a 1.6% annual decline in energy intensity for the next several decades. One year later, in its *Annual Energy Outlook 2006*, it projected energy intensity to decline at an average annual rate of 1.8% from 2004 until 2030.[148] Higher energy prices, and consequent lower energy consumption, provide most of the reason.[149]

In May 2001, President Bush established a policy of reducing the greenhouse gas intensity of the U.S. economy by 18% by 2012, which is projected to prevent the emission of 500 million tons of carbon.[150] This policy works out to a 1.96% annual reduction.[151] Greenhouse gas intensity is closely related to energy intensity. The Administration claimed that this would be an improvement over the 1.4% annual improvement that was then projected for the same period.[152]

In the Energy Policy Act of 2005, Congress directed that a newly created Committee on Climate Change Technology submit to the President in 18 months (Feb. 2007) a "national strategy to promote the deployment and commercialization of greenhouse gas intensity-reducing technologies and practices."[153] The Committee is also required to develop recommendations for the removal of barriers to the development and deployment of such technologies and practices.[154]

As described in Chapter 17, the Bush Administration has also organized a number of voluntary programs around achievement of this goal. In July 2006, for example, EPA and the Department of Energy announced a National Action Plan for Energy Efficiency.[155] Its stated goal is "to create a sustainable, aggressive national commitment to energy efficiency through gas and electric utilities, utility regulators, and partner organizations."[156] The plan, which is directed at the generation, distribution, and use of electricity, contains five recommendations for achieving this goal: recognition of energy efficiency as a "high-priority energy resource," long-term commitment to energy efficiency, communication of its benefits, stable and sufficient program funding, and providing utilities with appropriate incentives.[157]

D. Education, Training, and Public Awareness

Parties to the Framework Convention agreed to "[p]romote and cooperate in education, training and public awareness related to climate change."[158] These efforts are to include development and implementation of educational, training, and public awareness programs as well as "public access to information on climate change and its effects."[159] The national and regional assessments described below were intended to help carry out these commitments. In addition, the Department of Energy, EPA, the National Aeronautics and Space Administration, the National Oceanic and Atmospheric Administration, the U.S. Global Change Research Information Office, the U.S. Global Change Research Program, and the U.S. Geological Survey provide considerable information through a variety of Web sites.[160] EPA also provides information and assistance to state and local governments through its State and Local Climate Change Program.[161] The U.S. government's goal in these and other education, training, and public awareness efforts "is to create an informed populace."[162]

E. Adaptation to Climate Change Impacts

The two most certain effects of climate change are increased surface temperatures and rising sea levels. Most observers believe that these changes have already begun and are likely to continue even if serious efforts are made to mitigate climate change. Accordingly, adaptation is a necessary part of any national effort to address climate change.

In 2001, the U.S. Global Change Research Program published *Climate Change Impacts on the United States: The Potential Consequences of Climate Variability and Change,* an assessment of U.S. effects.[163] This report contains an assessment of the likely impact of climate change on each region of the United States (Northeast, Southeast, Midwest, Great Plains, West, Pacific Northwest, Alaska, islands, and native peoples and homelands) as well as a variety of economic sectors (agriculture, water, human health, coastal areas and marine resources, and forests). For example, even if there is no increase in the number or intensity of storms in the Southeast, rising sea levels and coastal erosion will increase the damage caused by hurricanes that make landfall.[164] With financial support from the federal government, a number of other reports on possible regional impacts were also published.[165] A regional assessment for the Gulf Coast published in 2003 said that warmer sea temperatures from climate change could lead to more intense hurricanes, with greater storm surges and flooding, and greater impacts on public safety and ecosystems.[166]

The purpose of these assessments was to provide state, local, and regional decision-makers with useful information about the likely effects of climate change. This work has received much less attention and funding under the George W. Bush Administration, however. In its report on the final climate change science strategy, the National Research Council noted that the strategy ignored the contributions of the 2001 report, *Potential Consequences of Climate Variability and Change*.[167] Since 2003, new or updated regional assessments have been produced predominantly by states (e.g., California) or by nongovernmental organizations (e.g., *Union of Concerned Scientists for the northeast*).[168]

In 2003, EPA published for comment its *Draft Report on the Environment*, which it described as "its first-ever national picture of the U.S. environment."[169] The EPA report attempted to explain "what is happening, why is it happening, and what are the effects."[170] The draft report covered five broad categories: air, water, land, human health, and ecological conditions. For each category, it described conditions, trends, and what is not known. For instance, it stated that much is known about water conditions at local, state, regional, and tribal levels, but that "we do not have enough information to provide a comprehensive picture at the national level."[171] The draft report was silent, however, on climate change.[172] Although the report was identified as a draft, no final version of that report was issued.

EPA is now preparing a new report on the environment for 2007. The report will be issued in three parts—a public document that is intended to communicate information and trends in an understandable way, a technical document that provides scientific and technical background, and an interactive Web site.[173] Work on the technical document is well under way; a peer review process for selection of air indicators, for instance, was initiated in 2005.[174] Two of the proposed air indicators in the technical document are atmospheric concentrations of greenhouse gas emissions and U.S. greenhouse gas emissions.[175]

Sea-level rise is of particular interest in light of flooding and storm damage from recent hurricanes. The United States has sponsored, conducted, or collected considerable research about the likely effects of sea-level rise,[176] including maps of the land on the Atlantic and Gulf coasts that are most likely to be affected.[177] A 1991 report by U.S. governmental officials, academic experts, and others predicted that a one-meter (three-foot) rise in sea levels would inundate 14,000 square miles in the United States. Some 6,000–7,000 miles of developed land, the report said, could be protected for $1,000–$2,000 annually for a typical coastal lot.[178] The estimated total cost of a one-meter sea-level rise, not including future development or significant environmental effects, was estimated to be $270 billion–$475 billion. The environmental consequences, moreover, would be significant.[179] Rising sea levels raise a thicket of property, land use, planning, and regulatory issues for coastal property owners that lawyers and policy makers have only begun to understand.[180] The federal government has available a variety of options for addressing the property, environmental, and other consequences of sea-level rise.[181]

IV. Looking Ahead

The next several years may or may not produce significant change in U.S. national policy on climate change. This is particularly true of one of the least well-developed parts of that policy—measures to reduce greenhouse gas emissions. If they do, those changes are likely to be influenced by national reports and recommendations on this issue as well as bills being discussed in Congress in 2006.

A. Recent Reports on Energy and Climate Change

A great many reports or papers have been issued over the past several years on U.S. energy and climate policy. Two of particular interest and importance here are a report by the National Commission on Energy Policy (NCEP) and a paper by Robert Nordhaus and Kyle Danish on options for designing a greenhouse gas regulatory program.

The NCEP report, *Ending the Energy Stalemate: A Bipartisan Strategy to Meet America's Energy Challenges*, was issued in 2004.[182] The NCEP was made up of 16 members with diverse expertise and co-chaired by Prof. John Holdren of Harvard University and William Reilly, founding partner of Aqua International Partners and former EPA Administrator. As its title suggests, the NCEP sought to "establish a constructive center in the often-polarized debate about energy."[183] For climate change, the Commission recommends that the United States adopt, beginning in 2010, "an annual emissions target that reflects a 2.4 percent per year reduction in the average greenhouse gas emissions intensity of the economy."[184] According to the Commission, this cap would cause U.S. greenhouse gas emissions in 2020 to be 6% to 11% below "business as usual" levels.[185] The cap would be administered through the annual issuance, by the U.S. government, of permits or allowances for greenhouse gas emissions. Allowance trading would be permitted. Most allowances "would be issued at no cost to existing emitters, but a small pool, 5 percent at the outset, would be auctioned to accommodate new entrants, stimulate the market in emissions permits, and fund research and development of new technologies."[186] To provide a safety valve on costs, the government would also be authorized to issue additional permits or allowances at a price of $7 per ton of carbon dioxide equivalent.[187] This safety valve functions as a cost cap. By comparison, carbon dioxide credits closed at $4.50 per ton in the Chicago Climate Exchange on July 28, 2006.[188] The NCEP also recommended that Congress review the program every five years beginning in 2015 "and evaluate whether emissions control progress by major trading partners and competitors (including developing countries such as China and India) supports its continuation." Based on that evaluation, the United States would decide whether to strengthen the program or "suspend further escalation of program requirements."[189]

The Commission also recommended, among other things, that the federal government strengthen and expand efficiency standards for appliances and equipment, and that it expand federal research on energy efficiency and renewable energy technologies and practices.[190] Other recommendations include expanding natural gas supplies, making advance coal technologies more available, removing obstacles to the greater use of nuclear energy, reducing barriers to siting of energy infrastructure, and protecting such infrastructure from terrorism and accidents.[191]

The Commission also recommended . . . that the federal government strengthen and expand efficiency standards for appliance and equipment, and that it expand federal research on energy efficiency and renewable energy technologies and practices.

The paper by Robert Nordhaus and Kyle Danish assesses options for designing a mandatory greenhouse gas reduction program in the United States.[192] Nordhaus and Danish do not analyze whether to set a target or what the target should be; rather, they evaluate different program designs for meeting whatever target is chosen.[193] Nordhaus and Danish identify three types of approaches that could be employed—a cap-and-trade approach, a greenhouse gas tax, and a "sectoral hybrid" approach. The latter represents the direction, they say, in which U.S. policy is most likely to evolve.[194]

The cap-and-trade approach builds on U.S. experience with the acid rain provisions of the 1990 Clean Air Act amendments, which imposed emissions reductions on coal-fired electric power plants.[195] This legislation is considered to be successful model because it required, and achieved, roughly a 50% reduction in sulfur dioxide emissions from covered power plants and a smaller reduction in nitrogen oxide emissions, at a fraction of the cost that many feared. The reduction was achieved through a set of legal requirements that are referred to as a trading or cap-and-trade program. To begin with, the law capped overall emissions from these plants at a certain level. Then it created a set of plant-specific emission reduction requirements and timetables that applied to all power plants. EPA was obliged to adopt regulations creating a second and more stringent set of plant-specific requirements. In these two steps, the overall cap was to be achieved by 2000. Each operator was allowed to decide how to meet its individual emission reduction requirement. One method it could choose is trading.

The factual premise of trading, as explained in greater detail in Chapter 18, is that emissions reductions have different costs at different power plants. In a conventional program, each operator might be required to reduce its emissions by an equivalent amount. But in a trading program, operators with lower costs can reduce more than required and offer to sell or trade their excess reductions to other operators in the form of "allowances," each equal to one ton of pollutant emissions. Operators with greater costs can consider and accept such offers, particularly if the cost of acquiring allowances is less than the cost of employing conventional controls. Trading is a key feature in such systems, but the emissions caps and the operator's freedom to choose a method of compliance provide the necessary legal structure to make trading possible and meaningful.

In reviewing cap-and-trade options, Nordhaus and Danish distinguish between "downstream" and "upstream" options. A "downstream" approach involves the direct regulation of emitters. The 1990 Clean Air Act amendments, for instance, represent "downstream" regulation of coal-fired power plants. A pure "downstream" approach in the United States would be impossible because it would include direct regulation of each of 200 million cars and 100 million commercial and residential buildings.[196] An "upstream" approach, by contrast, would capture such sources through direct regulation of, for example, upstream gasoline and home-heating fuel refiners or suppliers. Under such an approach, caps would be imposed on upstream suppliers, and the economic effect of such caps would run downstream to individual cars and buildings. While theoretically attractive as a cost-effective and administratively manageable approach, a pure upstream program is largely untried.[197] Still another approach to cap-and-trade would establish a "downstream" cap-and-trade system that would apply only to large stationary sources such as power plants or industrial facilities. A problem with such an approach is its lack of comprehensiveness and the distorting economic effects partial regulation could create.[198]

A greenhouse gas tax is attractive because it would be comprehensive and because it would reach all sources regardless of their size. It is not clear in advance, however, how much greenhouse gas emissions reduction would be achieved. The public reaction to recent high oil prices indicates that the effect may be easier to measure afterwards than it is to predict in advance. Despite considerable speculation about how the public would react, a review of the data at the end of 2005 showed that the number of miles driven during the summer of 2005 increased, but at a slower rate.[199] An additional problem is political acceptability; "Americans are reflexively opposed both to tax programs and to gasoline price increases," and a greenhouse gas tax "combines both."[200]

The most likely (although not necessarily the most cost-effective) approach is the "sectoral hybrid" approach, which employs both a large-source cap-and-trade program and product efficiency standards such as those for automobiles and appliances.[201] This approach would build on existing experience and would, if designed properly, reach most of the economy. Efficiency standards, however, do not discourage the amount of use (and consequently energy) to which a product is put. There may also be problems with double counting of emissions reductions. Thus, Nordhaus and Danish conclude, such problems will need to be overcome if this approach is used.[202]

A considerable amount of other work has been done to identify and explain options for energy and climate policy. For instance, Amory Lovins and others issued an ambitious road map in 2004, *Winning the Oil Endgame*, for "[s]aving half the oil America uses, [and] substituting cheaper alternatives for the other half," by 2025.[203] In addition, the Aspen Institute has conducted a policy dialogue on climate change legislation and published papers resulting from that dialogue.[204]

B. Congressional Proposals

More bills are being introduced in climate change with each session of Congress. Although the most ambitious of these bills have yet to be adopted, the growing number of bills appears to reflect growing awareness of the issue. Many observers believe that it is just a matter of time until Congress adopts comprehensive legislation to address climate change. They are supported in their view by the Senate's adoption, on June 22, 2005, of the following resolution during the debate on legislation that ultimately became the Energy Policy Act of 2005:[205]

Congress finds that—

1.   greenhouse gases accumulating in the atmosphere are causing average temperatures to rise at a rate outside the range of natural variability and are posing a substantial risk of rising sea-levels, altered patterns of atmospheric and oceanic circulation, and increased frequency and severity of floods and droughts;
2.   there is a growing scientific consensus that human activity is a substantial cause of greenhouse gas accumulation in the atmosphere; and
3.   mandatory steps will be required to slow or stop the growth of greenhouse gas emissions into the atmosphere.

It is the sense of the Senate that Congress should enact a comprehensive and effective national program of mandatory, market-based limits and incentives on emissions of greenhouse gases that slow, stop, and reverse the growth of such emissions at a rate and in a manner that—

1.   will not significantly harm the United States economy; and
2.   will encourage comparable action by other nations that are major trading partners and key contributors to global emissions.

At least four major approaches were under consideration in 2006. Subsequent legislative proposals will draw on the ideas reflected in those approaches. One focuses on electric power plants and another is more comprehensive. A third approach, which in early summer of 2006 had not yet resulted in introduced legislation, is based on a set of questions on program design that were publicly circulated for comment. A fourth would set significant reduction goals for greenhouse gas emissions.

Much of the debate on power plant legislation masks what appears to be substantial agreement on some key premises. There is substantial agreement that sulfur dioxide and nitrogen oxide, the two pollutants addressed in the cap-and-trade part of the 1990 Clean Air legislation described above, ought to be subject to another round of reductions. There is also substantial agreement on the need to reduce a third pollutant, mercury, about which considerable toxicity data has developed and become publicly known since 1990.[206] There is considerable disagreement, however, on whether to add a fourth pollutant, carbon dioxide.

The Bush Administration position is reflected in the proposed Clear Skies Act, which was originally introduced in 2002 but which was reintroduced in 2005 by Senator James Inhofe, then chair of the Senate Environment and Public Works Committee.[207] This legislation would require coal-fired power plants to reduce their emissions of sulfur dioxide, nitrogen oxide, and mercury by about 70% by 2018.[208] The legislation would employ a cap-and-trade approach that is substantially similar to that in the 1990 Clean Air legislation. The bill also contains incentives for the use of "clean coal technology," which it defines as any technology that makes substantial reductions in sulfur dioxide and nitrogen oxide emissions and was not in widespread use in 1990. These incentives include exemption of some plants from new source performance standards as well as a more streamlined approval process.[209]

On March 9, 2005, the Senate Environment and Public Works Committee voted 9–9 to report out this bill. The tie vote defeated the proposed legislation. With the exception of Republican Lincoln Chafee (Rhode Island), who voted against the bill, the vote was along party lines, with Republican senators voting for the bill and Democratic senators—and Independent James Jeffords (Vermont)—voting against it. Among other things, the senators opposing the bill sought steeper emission reductions and the inclusion of carbon dioxide.[210]

Other proposed power plant legislation focuses on four pollutants, including carbon dioxide. In March 2006, Republican Senator Thomas Carper (Delaware) and seven other senators introduced a bill that would more strictly regulate sulfur dioxide, nitrogen oxide, and mercury from power plants and would also impose controls on carbon dioxide.[211] This bill, which was described as a "new and improved" version of earlier four-pollutant legislation, would by 2015 reduce emissions of mercury by 90 percent, nitrogen oxide by 68 percent, and sulfur dioxide by 82 percent.[212] The bill would also cap carbon dioxide emissions from affected coal-fired power plants at 2001 levels by 2015.[213] Power plants that emit more than their limit of sulfur dioxide, nitrogen oxide, and carbon dioxide may acquire allowances from power plants that have

achieved greater reductions than required; trading is not authorized for mercury.[214]

A more comprehensive approach to climate change is contained in legislation introduced in 2005 by Senators John
McCain and Joseph Lieberman.[215] This legislation is directed
at all six greenhouse gases covered under the Kyoto Protocol.
Instead of focusing only on electric power plants, this legislation applies to any entity in the electric, commercial, or industrial sectors of the economy that emits from any facility more
than 10,000 metric tons of greenhouse gases per year. It would
also apply to any refiner or importer of petroleum products
used in transportation that, when combusted, will emit more
than 10,000 metric tons of greenhouse gases per year, and to
any producer or importer of greenhouse gases (including
hydrofluorocarbons, perfluorocarbons, or sulfur hexafluoride)
that, when used, will emit more than 10,000 metric tons of
greenhouse gases per year.[216] These sectors represent about 85%
of U.S. greenhouse gas emissions. Under the legislation, these
sectors would, by 2010, be required to reduce their emissions
to 2000 levels.[217] As in the 1990 Clean Air legislation, emissions trading would be permitted in the form of allowances.
Some allowances would be auctioned. Unlike the NCEP proposal, though, there is no safety valve or cost cap. The bill
contains detailed provisions for monitoring and tracking greenhouse gas emissions and reductions and for using allowances
from other countries. The 2005 bill adds a subtitle providing
that money generated from the emissions trading auction be
used for the development and deployment of innovative energy technologies.[218] A
proposal to incorporate this legislation into energy policy legislation was defeated in
a 38–60 Senate floor vote in 2005.[219] In 2003, an earlier form of the bill was killed in
the Senate by a vote of 43–55.[220]

Senators Pete Domenici and Jeff Bingaman, then chair and ranking minority member
of the Senate Energy and Natural Resources Committee, have taken still another approach. In early 2006, they published for public comment a "white paper" that was
intended "to lay out some of the key questions and design elements of a national
greenhouse gas program in order to facilitate discussion and the development of consensus around a specific bill."[221] The white paper uses the Senate's June 22, 2005,
resolution on climate change as a starting point. The paper raises four questions:[222]

1. Who is regulated and where?
2. Should the costs of regulation be mitigated for any sector of the economy, through
   the allocation of allowances without cost? Or, should allowances be distributed

by means of an auction? If allowances are allocated, what are the criteria for and method of such allocation?

3. Should a U.S. system be designed to eventually allow for trading with other greenhouse gas cap-and-trade systems being put in place around the world, such as the Canadian Large Final Emitter system or the European Union emissions trading system?

4. If a key element of the proposed U.S. system is to "encourage comparable action by other nations that are major trading partners and key contributors to global emissions," should the design concepts in the NCEP plan (*i.e., to take some action and then make further steps contingent on a review of what these other nations do)* be part of a mandatory market-based program? If so, how?

In addition to receiving written submissions answering these questions, the Environment and Natural Resources Committee held a conference on April 6, 2006, to hear testimony.[223] Senators Domenici and Bingaman subsequently published a short summary of "key areas where there appears to be a narrowing of disagreement and in some cases an emerging consensus."[224] Senators Domenici and Bingaman said they intend to use the answers they receive to draft comprehensive legislation on climate change. They explained the emerging consensus as follows:

> In both the written submissions and comments at the workshop, many participants and respondents expressed the view that the risks associated with a changing climate justified the adoption of mandatory limits on greenhouse gas emissions. While opinions varied on the stringency of initial limits, there was support for the notion that a program should begin modestly and strengthen gradually over time. Consistent with the success of the acid rain program and other market-based approaches, most participants supported a market-based approach that would set a "forward price" on greenhouse gas emissions in order to provide both the flexibility and incentive needed to accelerate technology development and deployment.[225]

The apparent consensus on specific issues, according to the senators, is as follows:

> **Economy-wide approach:** In general, there was agreement on the need for economy-wide action to address the wide diversity of sources of GHGs. Many participants argued that an economy-wide program is the most equitable and efficient approach.
>
> **Upstream or hybrid point of regulation:** Most participants supported either an entirely upstream or a hybrid approach for point of regulation . . . .
>
> **Offsets and set-asides:** There was general agreement about the benefits of emission reduction projects at sources outside of a cap on GHG emissions. However, there was some disagreement about how to ensure the environmental integrity of these types of projects . . . .

Links to other trading programs: Ultimately, GHG emissions cannot be reduced absent an effort that includes meaningful participation from all nations with significant GHG emissions. An emission reduction program in the United States could be designed to leave open the possibility of trading with GHG systems in other countries. Most panelists at the conference agreed that linking to other domestic emissions trading programs is theoretically more efficient . . . .

> **Ultimately, GHG emissions cannot be reduced absent an effort that includes meaningful participation from all nations with significant GHG emissions.**

Developing country action: Many participants agreed that an important component of a U.S. GHG program should encourage major trading partners and large emitters of GHGs to take actions that are comparable to those taken by the U.S. Panelists noted that ultimately, action by major developing countries like China and India is critical to address climate change. There was also discussion of the competitive implications if the United States takes action to address climate change and other major trading partners do not. Not all, but many panelists said that the United States should not wait for developing countries to act . . . .

Allowance distribution: . . . . Based on the discussion at the conference, we believe the following principles for allocation are emerging:

- Allowances should be allocated in a manner that recognizes and roughly addresses the disparate costs imposed by the program.
- Allowances should not be allocated solely to regulated entities because such entities do not solely bear the costs of the emissions trading program.
- A portion of the allowances should be auctioned (or used for "set-aside" programs), with revenues used to advance climate-related policy goals and other public purposes.
- Over time, an allowance distribution approach should transition from approaches that attempt to fairly compensate sectors for past investments in carbon-intensive technologies to approaches that create incentives for energy efficiency and lower-carbon technologies. In practice, this means a gradual transition over an extended period of time from a largely free allocation of allowances to the use of an auction as the predominant method for distribution of allowances.[226]

On July 20, 2006, Senator James Jeffords introduced a bill that would require greenhouse gas reductions from 1990 levels over a 40-year period.[227] The bill has 11 co-sponsors.[228] Among other things, the proposed legislation is intended to ensure that U.S. greenhouse gas emissions in 2050 are 80% below 1990 levels.[229] Within two years after the effective date of this legislation, EPA would be required to adopt rules requiring that greenhouse gas emissions in 2020 are no higher than they were in 1990. For each of the three decades between 2020 and 2050, EPA would adopt regulations achieving one-third of the 80% reduction.[230] The legislation proposes a variety of approaches to achieve this reduction, including specified carbon dioxide emission limits on motor vehicles, emission limits for many electric generating units that are as stringent as those for new combined-cycle natural gas generating plants, and much greater use of renewable energy, energy efficiency, and carbon sequestration.[231]

V. Conclusion

The United States is the world's largest consumer and producer of energy, and the world's largest emitter of greenhouse gases. Despite a diverse array of programs, greenhouse gas emissions continue to increase. Thanks in part to an impressive U.S. scientific research program, the remaining gaps in our understanding are growing smaller. Those who follow climate change see more legal activity every year, and have little reason to believe this trend will change. In 2005, the Committee on Sustainable Development, Ecosystems, and Climate Change of the ABA Section on Environment, Energy, and Resources began holding an annual national conference for lawyers on climate change. As this issue becomes more important to Americans, it is likely to become more important to clients, and thus to their lawyers.

Endnotes

1.   This chapter does not evaluate whether the United States is complying with its various commitments under the Framework Convention. For an evaluation, see Donald A. Brown, *Climate Change, in* STUMBLING TOWARD SUSTAINABILITY 273 (John C. Dernbach ed. 2002).

2.   *United Nations Framework Convention on Climate Change,* U.N. Doc. A/AC.237/18 (1992), *reprinted in* 31 I.L.M. 849 (1992) [hereinafter Framework Convention].

3.   EXEC. REP. NO. 102-55, 102d Cong., 1st Sess., at 10–11 (1992).

4.   Framework Convention, *supra* note 2, art. 4.2(a) & (b).

5.   *Id.* art. 4.1(b).

6.   EXEC. REP. NO. 102-55, *supra* note 3 at 11.

7.   *Id.*

8.   U.S. CONST. art. 2, § 2, ¶ 2.

9.   The Senate Foreign Relations Committee made clear that its approval was based on the absence of targets and timetables for reduction of greenhouse gas emissions. EXEC. REP. NO. 102-55, *supra* note 3, at 14.

10.   138 CONG. REC. S17150, S17156 (daily ed. Oct. 7, 1992) (reporting Senate approval of ratification of the resolution).

11.   United States Instrument of Ratification, United Nations Framework Convention on Climate Change (Oct. 13, 1992) (copy on file with author).

12.   United Nations Framework Convention on Climate Change: Status of Ratification (last modified on May 24, 2004), http://unfccc.int/resource/conv/ratlist.pdf.

13. *Id.*

14. George W. Bush, President Bush Discusses Global Climate Change (June 11, 2001), http://www.whitehouse.gov/news/releases/2001/06/20010611-2.html (last visited June 14, 2006).

15. Framework Convention, *supra* note 2, preamble para. 3. In the preamble, parties also recognize the "special difficulties" of developing countries, including their need for access to new technologies to address climate change *Id.* ¶¶ 20 & 22.

16. *Id.* art. 4.2(a).

17. *Id.* art. 4.2(d).

18. S. Res. 98, 105th Cong., 1st Sess. (July 22, 1997); 143 Cong Rec. S8138 (daily ed. July 25, 1997).

19. *Id.* § 1(1) (A). During debate on the resolution, Senator Byrd stated several times that it did not mean developing country commitments would have to be the same as developed country commitments. 143 Cong. Rec. S8117 (daily ed. July 25, 1997). "While countries have different levels of development, each must make unique and binding commitments of a pace and kind consistent with their industrialization." *Id.* at S8131.

20. S. Res. 98, *supra* note 18, § (1)(B).

21. *Id.* preamble.

22. Kyoto Protocol to the United Nations Framework Convention on Climate Change, Dec. 10, 1997, U.N. Doc. FCCC/CP/197/L.7/Add. 1, art. 3.1 & Annex B, *reprinted in* 37 I.L.M. 22 (1998).

23. *Id.* art. 3.1. The Annex I or developed countries also agreed to make "demonstrable progress" by 2005 in meeting their commitments. *Id.* art. 3.2

24. *Id.* Annex B.

25. Nat'l Comm'n on Energy Pol'y, Ending the Energy Stalemate: A Bipartisan Strategy to Meet America's Energy Challenges 25 (2004).

26. Amy Royden, *U.S. Climate Change Policy Under President Clinton: A Look Back*, 32 Golden Gate U. L. Rev. 415, 440–45 (2002).

27. Michael R. Molitor, *The United Nations Climate Change Agreements, in* The Global Environment: Institutions, Law, and Policy 210, 227–28 (Norman J. Vig & Regina S. Axelrod eds. 1999).

28. *Id.*

29. Letter from President George W. Bush to Senators Hagel, Helms, Craig, and Roberts (March 13, 2001), http://www.whitehouse.gov/news/releases/2001/03/20010314.html.

30. *Id.*

31. The Protocol could not become effective until countries accounting for 55% of the carbon dioxide generated by "Annex I" industrialized nations had ratified it. Kyoto Protocol, *supra* note 22, art. 24.1. After the United States declined to ratify the Protocol, the Protocol could only become effective if Russia ratified it.

32. Kyoto Protocol, *supra* note 22, art. 3, ¶ 9.

33. Dean Scott, *Kyoto Parties End Meetings With Consensus for Avoiding 'Gap' in Post-2012 Reductions*, 37 Env't Rep. (BNA) No. 22, at 1154 (June 2, 2006).

34. *Id.*

35. Environmental Protection Agency, Inventory of U.S. Greenhouse Gas Emissions and Sinks: 1990–2004 at ES-4–5 (2006), http://yosemite.epa.gov/oar/globalwarming.nsf/UniqueKeyLookup/RAMR6MBLP4/$File/06ES.pdf.

36. For an overview, see JOSEPH P. TOMAINA & RICHARD D. CUDAHY, ENERGY LAW IN A NUTSHELL (2004).

37. Alan S. Miller, *Energy Policy from Nixon to Clinton: From Grand Provider to Grand Facilitator*, 25 ENVTL. L. 715 (1995).

38. Doug Koplow & John Dernbach, *Federal Fossil Fuel Subsidies and Greenhouse Gas Emissions: A Case Study of Increasing Transparency for Fiscal Policy*, 26 ANNUAL REVIEW OF ENERGY & ENV'T 361 (2001).

39. U.S. Dep't of State, U.S. Climate Action Report—2002: Third National Communication of the United States of America Under the United Nations Framework Convention on Climate Change 14 (2002), http://yosemite.epa.gov/oar/globalwarming.nsf/UniqueKeyLookup/SHSU5BWHU6/$File/uscar.pdf [hereinafter Climate Action Report 2002]. George W. Bush, President Bush Discusses Global Climate Change (June 11, 2001), http://www. whitehouse.gov/news/releases/2001/06/20010611-2.html (last visited June 25, 2006).

40. NATIONAL ENERGY POLICY DEVELOPMENT GROUP, NATIONAL ENERGY POLICY (2001), http://www.whitehouse.gov/energy/National-Energy-Policy.pdf.

41. *Id.* at viii & 1-1.

42. *Id.* at app. 1.

43. *Id.* at 4-11 & 4-12.

44. *Id.* at 8-16.

45. *In re* Cheney, 406 F.3d 723 (D.C. Cir. 2005).

46. Judicial Watch, Inc. v. Dep't of Energy, 412 F.3d 125 (D.C. Cir. 2005).

47. U.S. Dep't of Energy, National Energy Policy: Status Report on Implementation of NEP Recommendations (2005), http://www.energy.gov/media/NEP_Implementation_Report.pdf.

48. NATIONAL ENERGY POLICY, *supra* note 40 at 1-14; Executive Order 13,211, 66 Fed. Reg. 28,355 (May 22, 2001).

49. Pub. L. No. 109-58, 119 Stat. 594, compiled in scattered sections of U.S. Code.

50. §§ 1610 & 1611, Energy Policy Act of 2005, 42 U.S.C. § 13389 & 22 U.S.C. §§ 7901–7908. Both concern greenhouse gas intensity, which is defined to mean "the ratio of greenhouse gas emissions to economic output." One section requires a study of technologies for reducing greenhouse gas intensity and the other directs that the goal of reducing greenhouse gas intensity in developing countries be integrated into U.S. foreign assistance.

51. NATIONAL ENERGY POLICY, *supra* note 40, at 1-3. *See also* NAT'L COMM'N ON ENERGY POL'Y, *supra* note 25, at 30 (defining energy efficiency as "doing more with less, as opposed to suffering hardships or closing businesses"). *See also* 42 U.S.C. § 6291(5) (defining energy efficiency as "the ratio of the useful output of services from a consumer product to the energy use of such product)." Conservation, a broader term, involves the use of less energy. NATIONAL ENERGY POLICY, *supra* note 40, at 1-3.

52. U.S. DEP'T OF ENERGY, ENERGY INFORMATION ADMINISTRATION, ENERGY CONSUMPTION, EXPENDITURES, AND EMISSIONS INDICATORS, 1949–2004, http://www.eia.doe.gov/emeu/aer/txt/ptb0105.html.

53. *Id.*

54. Steven Nadel, *Appliance and Equipment Efficiency Standards*, 27 ANN. REV. ENERGY & ENVT. 159, 170 (2002).

55. 42 U.S.C. §§ 6291–6309.

56. 42 U.S.C. § 6293. For showerheads, faucets, water closets and urinals, the test procedures are required to cover water use. *Id.* § 6293(b).

57. *Id.* § 6294(c)(1).

58. 42 U.S.C. § 6295.

59. *Id.* § 6295(o)(2)(A).

60. 10 C.F.R. § 430.32. There are also water conservation standards for water closets and urinals, which do not ordinarily involve heating or cooling of water. *Id.* § 430.32(q) & (r).

61. 42 U.S.C. § 6297(d)(1).

62. 42 U.S.C. §§ 6311-6317.

63. 10 C.F.R. Part 431.

64. Nadel, *supra* note 54, at 168.

65. NATIONAL COMM'N ON ENERGY POLICY, *supra* note 25, at 32.

66. Nadel, *supra* note 54, at 188.

67. Jonathan G. Koomey et al., *Projected Regional Impacts of Appliance Efficiency Standards for the U.S. Residential Sector* (1998), http://enduse.lbl.gov/info/LBNL-39511.pdf.

68. Energy Conservation Program for Consumer Products; Central Air Conditioners and Heat Pumps Energy Conservation Standards, 67 Fed. Reg. 36,368, 363,777 (2002).

69. Energy Conservation Program for Consumer Products: Energy Conservation Standards for Water Heaters, 66 Fed. Reg. 4,474, 4,475 (2001).

70. Energy Policy Act of 2005 § 135; 42 U.S.C. §§ 6291–6297.

71. *Id.* § 136; 42 U.S.C. § 6311–6316.

72. *Id.* § 137; 42 U.S.C. § 6294(a)(2)(F).

73. *Id.* § 102(a)(1); 42 U.S.C. § 8253(a)(1).

74. *Id.* § 110; 15 U.S.C. § 260a(a).

75. *Id.* § 1501; 42 U.S.C. § 7545.

76. Regulation of Fuels and Fuel Additives: Renewable Fuel Standard Requirements for 2006, 70 Fed. Reg. 77,325 (Dec. 30, 2005) (to be codified at 40 C.F.R. Part 80).

77. Energy Policy Act of 2005 § 1501(a); 42 U.S.C. § 7545.

78. 70 Fed. Reg. at 77,327.

79. Energy Policy Act of 2005 § 701; 42 U.S.C. § 6374(a)(3)(E).

80. Jason Hill et al., *Environmental, Economic, and Energetic Costs and Benefits of Biodiesel and Ethanol Biofuels*, 103 PROC. NAT'L ACAD. SCI. 11,206 (2006).

81. *Id.*

82. Energy Policy Act of 2005 § 201; 42 U.S.C. § 15851.

83. *Id.* § 202; 42 U.S.C. § 13317.

84. *Id.* § 225; 42 U.S.C. § 15871.

85. F. Kaid Benfield & Michael Replogle, *Transportation, in* STUMBLING TOWARD SUSTAINABILITY, *supra* note 2, at 647.

86. U.S. Climate Action Report—2002, *supra* note 39, at 59–60.

87. *Id.* at 60–61.

88. 15 U.S.C. § 2901 (see note).

89. Framework Convention, *supra* note 2, art. 4(1)(a).

90. *Id.* art. 12.1(b).

91. 42 U.S.C. § 13385(a).

92. Kyoto Protocol, *supra* note 22, Annex A.

93. INVENTORY OF U.S. GREENHOUSE GAS EMISSIONS AND SINKS: 1990–2004, *supra* note 35.

94. Framework Convention, *supra* note 2, art. 4.1(g).

95. *Id.* art. 5.

96. Letter from John M. Bridgeland and Gary Edson to Bruce Alberts (May 11,

2001), *reprinted in* COMMITTEE ON THE SCIENCE OF CLIMATE CHANGE, NATIONAL RESEARCH COUNCIL, CLIMATE CHANGE SCIENCE: AN ANALYSIS OF SOME KEY QUESTIONS 27 (2001).

97. *Id.* at 1.

98. *Id.* at 2. Methane, which is a much more potent greenhouse gas than carbon dioxide, also exists in higher atmospheric concentrations now than in the past 400,000 years. *Id.*

99. *Id.* at 1.

100. Intergovernmental Panel on Climate Change, About IPCC, http://www.ipcc.ch/about/about.htm (last visited July 27, 2006).

101. CLIMATE CHANGE SCIENCE, *supra* note 96, at 2.

102. *Id.* at 4.

103. *Id.*

104. President Bush Discusses Global Climate Change, *supra* note 14.

105. *Id.*

106. U.S. Climate Action Report—2002, *supra* note 39, at 138–39.

107. *Id.* at 249–55. For an assessment of U.S. compliance with the Framework Convention, *see* Brown, *supra* note 1.

108. U.S. Climate Action Report—2002, *supra* note 39, at 4.

1090. President George W. Bush, Remarks by the President to the Travel Pool (June 4, 2002), http://www.whitehouse.gov/news/releases/2002/06/20020604-16.html (last visited June 26, 2006).

110. Framework Convention, supra note 2, art. 4.1(g).

111. *Id.* at art. 5.

112. *See, e.g.,* ELIZABETH KOLBERT, FIELD NOTES FROM A CATASTROPHE: MAN, NATURE AND CLIMATE CHANGE 161 (2006) ("In the [past] half century . . . the United States has contributed more than any other nation to the advancement of climate science . . . ."); Brown, supra note 1, at 281 ("Without doubt, the United States should get very high marks in complying with its obligations under the UNFCCC regarding research and systematic observation.").

113. 15 U.S.C. §§ 2901–2908.

114. *Id.* §§ 2901(1) & (5), 2902, & 2904(a).

115. *Id.* § 2904(b)-(d).

116. 15 U.S.C. §§ 2931–2961.

117. 15 U.S.C. § 2921(3).

118. *Id.* § 2931(a)(1)-(3).

119. *Id.* § 2931(b).

120. *Id.* § 2934(b)(1).

121. *Id.* § 2938.

122. CLIMATE CHANGE SCIENCE PROGRAM AND THE SUBCOMMITTEE ON GLOBAL CHANGE RESEARCH, STRATEGIC PLAN FOR THE U.S. CLIMATE CHANGE SCIENCE PROGRAM (2003), http://www.climatescience.gov/Library/stratplan2003/final/ccspstratplan2003-all.pdf. The Subcommittee runs the Global Change Research Program.

123. *Id.* at 1.

124. *Id.* at 3-4.

125. *Id.* at 4-7.

126. *Id.* at 19.

127. *Id.* at 47 (citing COMMITTEE ON ABRUPT CLIMATE CHANGE, NATIONAL RESEARCH COUNCIL, ABRUPT CLIMATE CHANGE: INEVITABLE SURPRISES (2002).

128. *Id.* at 48.

129. Another work product is an assessment of the impact of climate change on long-range U.S. energy production and use. Dean Scott, *Energy Department Begins First Appraisal of Effects on U.S. Energy Production, Use,* 37 Env't Rep. (BNA) No. 17, at 888

(April 28, 2006). *See also* U.S. CLIMATE CHANGE SCIENCE PROGRAM, EFFECTS OF CLIMATE CHANGE ON ENERGY PRODUCTION AND USE IN THE UNITED STATES, http://www.climatescience.gov/Library/sap/sap4-5/default.htm.

130. NATIONAL RESEARCH COUNCIL, PLANNING CLIMATE AND GLOBAL CHANGE RESEARCH: A REVIEW OF THE DRAFT U.S. CLIMATE CHANGE PROGRAM STRATEGIC PLAN (2003).

131. NATIONAL RESEARCH COUNCIL, IMPLEMENTING CLIMATE AND GLOBAL CHANGE RESERARCH: A REVIEW OF THE FINAL U.S. CLIMATE CHANGE SCIENCE PROGRAM STRATEGIC PLAN (2004).

132. *Id.* at 1.

133. *Id.* at 3.

134. U.S. CLIMATE CHANGE SCIENCE PROGRAM, TEMPERATURE TRENDS IN THE LOWER ATMOSPHERE: STEPS FOR UNDERSTANDING AND RECONCILING DIFFERENCES (2006), http://www. climatescience.gov/Library/sap/sap1-1/finalreport/sap1-1-final-all.pdf.

135. GROUP ON EARTH OBSERVATIONS, ABOUT GEO, http://www.earthobservations.org/about/about_GEO.html (last visited June 12, 2006).

136. *Id.*

137. U.S. Climate Action Report—2002, *supra* note 39, at 145.

138. GROUP ON EARTH OBSERVATIONS, THE GLOBAL EARTH OBSERVATION SYSTEM OF SYSTEMS (GEOSS) 10-YEAR IMPLEMENTATION PLAN (2005), http://www.earthobservations.org/docs/10-Year%20Implementation%20Plan.pdf.

139. INTERAGENCY WORKING GROUP ON EARTH OBSERVATIONS, NSTC COMMITTEE ON ENVIRONMENT AND NATURAL RESOURCES, STRATEGIC PLAN FOR THE U.S. INTEGRATED EARTH OBSERVATION System (2005), http://usgeo.gov/docs/EOCStrategic_Plan.pdf.

140. 15 U.S.C. § 2937.

141. CLIMATE CHANGE SCIENCE PROGRAM AND SUBCOMMITTEE ON GLOBAL CHANGE RESEARCH, OUR CHANGING PLANET: THE U.S. CLIMATE CHANGE SCIENCE PROGRAM FOR FISCAL YEAR 2006 (2005), http://www.usgcrp.gov/usgcrp/Library/ocp2006/ocp2006.pdf.

142. U.S. GOV'T ACCOUNTABILITY OFFICE, CLIMATE CHANGE: FEDERAL REPORTS ON CLIMATE CHANGE FUNDING SHOULD BE CLEARER AND MORE COMPLETE 15 (2005), http://www.gao.gov/new.items/d05461.pdf (summarizing data).

143. Framework Convention, *supra* note 2, art. 4.2(a).

144. *Id.* art. 12.2(a).

145. U.S. Climate Action Report—2002, *supra* note 39.

146. *Id.* at 164-222. Each of the policies and measures is labeled by type, and often a particular measure is of more than one type. The policies and measures are of the following types: economic (7), voluntary (26), regulatory (6), research (26), outreach (7), information (25), education (13), and technical assistance (3). *Id.*

147. Lynn Price & Mark D. Levine, *Production and Consumption of Energy, in* STUMBLING TOWARD SUSTAINABILITY 79, 87 (John C. Dernbach ed. 2002).

148. U.S. DEP'T OF ENERGY, ENERGY INFORMATION ADMINISTRATION, ANNUAL ENERGY OUTLOOK 2006 WITH PROJECTIONS TO 2030, at 65 (2006), http://www.eia.doe.gov/oiaf/aeo/index.html [hereinafter ANNUAL ENERGY OUTLOOK 2006].

149. *Id.* at 6.

150. Status Report, *supra* note 47, at 34.

151. S. Pacala & R. Socolow, *Stabilization Wedges: Solving the Climate Problem for*

the Next 50 Years with Current Technologies, 305 SCIENCE 968, 969 (Aug. 13, 2004).
152. The 1.4% figure is slightly lower than the annual intensity reductions forecast during the same period. In 2002, a 1.5% annual energy intensity reduction was projected for 2002–2020. U.S. DEP'T OF ENERGY, ENERGY INFORMATION ADMINISTRATION, ANNUAL ENERGY OUTLOOK 2002 WITH PROJECTIONS TO 2020: OVERVIEW (2002), http://www.eia.doe.gov/oiaf/archive/aeo02/index.html. The projected energy intensity reduction one year earlier, in 2001, was 1.6%. U.S. DEP'T OF ENERGY, ENERGY INFORMATION ADMINISTRATION, ANNUAL ENERGY OUTLOOK 2002 WITH PROJECTIONS TO 2020 at 5 (2001), http://tonto.eia.doe.gov/FTPROOT/forecasting/0383(2001).pdf.
153. Energy Policy Act of 2005 § 1610(a) & (b), 42 U.S.C. § 13389(a) & (b).
154. *Id.* § 13389(g)(1).
155. U.S. DEP'T OF ENERGY & EPA, NATIONAL ACTION PLAN FOR ENERGY EFFICIENCY (2006), http://www.epa.gov/cleanenergy/pdf/ActionPlanReport_PrePublication_073106.pdf.
156. EPA, NATIONAL ACTION PLAN FOR ENERGY EFFICIENCY, http://www.epa.gov/cleanenergy/actionplan/eeactionplan.htm (last visited August 1, 2006).
157. NATIONAL ACTION PLAN FOR ENERGY EFFICIENCY, *supra* note 155, at 8.
158. Framework Convention, *supra* note 2, art. 4.1(i).
159. *Id.* art. 6.
160. U.S. Climate Action Report—2002, *supra* note 39, at 151 (listing key Web sites).
161. *Id.* at 153; U.S. ENVTL. PROTECTION AGENCY, STATE AND LOCAL OUTREACH KIT, http://yosemite.epa.gov/oar/globalwarming.nsf/content/ResourceCenterPublicationsOutreachMaterialStateKit.html (last visited June 13, 2006).
162. U.S. Climate Action Report—2002, *supra* note 39, at 7.
163. The report was published in shorter and longer versions. The longer version is U.S. National Assessment Synthesis Team Global Climate Change Research Program, *Climate Change Impacts on the United States: The Potential Consequence of Climate Variability and Change, Foundation* (2001), *available at* http://www.gcrio.org/NationalAssessment/foundation.html [Foundation]. The shorter version is National Assessment Synthesis Team, U.S. Global Climate Change Research Program, *Climate Change Impacts on the United States: The Potential Consequences of Climate Variability and Change, Overview (2000), available at* http://www.gcrio.org/NationalAssessment/overpdf/overview.html. *See also* Stewart Cohen & Kathleen Miller, *North America,* in INTERGOVERNMENTAL PANEL ON CLIMATE CHANGE 2002: IMPACTS, ADAPTION, AND VULNERABILITY 735 (James J. McCarthy et al. eds. 2001) (assessing climate change impacts on North America, including United States). For a more recent assessment, see CAMILLE PARMESAN & HECTOR GALBRAITH, OBSERVED IMPACTS OF GLOBAL CLIMATE CHANGE IN THE U.S. (2004), http://www.pewclimate.org/docUploads/final%5FObsImpact%2Epdf.
164. Foundation, *supra* note 163, at 22.
165. *See, e.g.,* MID-ATLANTIC REGIONAL ASSESSMENT TEAM, PENN STATE UNIVERSITY, PREPARING FOR A CHANGING CLIMATE: MID-ATLANTIC OVERVIEW (2000); ZHU H. NING ET AL., PREPARING FOR A CHANGING CLIMATE: THE POTENTIAL CONSEQUENCES OF CLIMATE VARIABILITY AND CHANGE—GULF COAST REGION (2003), http://www.usgcrp.gov/usgcrp/Library/nationalassessment/gulfcoast/gulfcoast-brief.pdf.
166. *Id.* at 33, 62.
167. REVIEW OF THE FINAL U.S. CLIMATE CHANGE SCIENCE PROGRAM STRATEGIC PLAN, *supra* note 131, at 29–30.
168. CALIFORNIA APPLICATIONS PROGRAM AND THE CALIFORNIA CLIMATE CHANGE CENTER, CLIMATE INFORMATION FOR CALIFORNIA DECISION MAKERS, http://meteora.ucsd.edu/cap/caphome.html (last visited July 27, 2006); UNION OF CONCERNED SCIENTISTS, CLIMATE CHANGE IN THE U.S. NORTHEAST: A REPORT OF THE NORTHEAST CLIMATE IMPACTS ASSESSMENT (2006), http://www. climatechoices.org/assets/documents/climatechoices/NECIA_

climate_report_final.pdf.

169. U.S. Environmental Protection Agency, Draft Report on the Environment 2003, at i (2003) (hereinafter Draft Report]; U.S. Environmental Protection Agency, Draft Report on the Environment 2003, Technical Document (2003) [hereinafter Technical Document].

170. Draft Report, *supra* note 169, at ix.

171. *Id.* at ii, iii.

172. Technical Document, *supra* note 170, at 1-38 ("This report does not attempt to address the complexities of this issue."). Media reports said the omission was the result of White House review. *See, e.g.*, Elizabeth Shogren, *Editing Flap Over EPA's Report on Environment; Whitman cut section on climate because only language White House agreed on was 'pablum,'* L.A. Times, June 20, 2003, at 16.

173. U.S. Envtl. Protection Agency, EPA Report on the Environment (2005), http://www.epa.gov/indicate/ (last visited June 27, 2006).

174. U.S. Envtl. Protection Agency, Charge to the Peer Reviewers: Air and Other Relevant Indicators for the U.S. Environmental Protection Agency's 2007 *Report on the Environment* Technical Document (May 20, 2005), http://www.epa.gov/ncea/ROEIndicators/pdfs/AirCharge_PublicPR.pdf.

175. U.S. Envtl. Protection Agency, Proposed Indicators for 2007 Report on the Environment (ROE 2007) (2005), http://www.epa.gov/ncea/ROEIndicators/#chapter1 (last visited June 27, 2006).

176. Environmental Protection Agency, Sea Level Rise Reports, http://yosemite.epa.gov/OAR/globalwarming.nsf/content/ResourceCenterPublicationsSeaLevelRiseIndex. html#now (last visited June 12, 2006).

177. Environmental Protection Agency, Maps of Lands Vulnerable to Sea Level Rise, http://yosemite.epa.gov/OAR/globalwarming.nsf/content/ResourceCenterPublications SLRMaps.html (last visited June 12, 2006).

178. James G. Titus et al., *Greenhouse Effect and Sea Level Rise: The Cost of Holding Back the Sea*, 19 Coastal Mgmt. 171 (1991), http://yosemite.epa.gov/OAR/globalwarming.nsf/UniqueKeyLookup/SHSU5BPPAL/$File/cost_of_holding.pdf.

179. *Id.*

180. For an overview, *see* James G. Titus, *Rising Seas, Coastal Erosion, and the Takings Clause: How to Save Wetlands and Beaches Without Hurting Property Owners*, 57 Md. L. Rev. 1279 (1998).

181. James G. Titus, *Does the U.S. Government Realize that the Sea Is Rising? How to Restructure Federal Programs so that Wetlands and Beaches Survive*, 30 Golden Gate U. L. Rev. 717 (2000).

182. Nat'l Comm'n on Energy Pol'y, *supra* note 25. The Commission was established by the William and Flora Hewlett Foundation and other foundation partners.

183. *Id.* at vi.

184. *Id.* at x.

185. *Id.* at 22.

186. *Id.* at x.

187. *Id.* at 23.

188. Chicago Climate Exchange, *Welcome to the Chicago Climate Exchange*, http://www.chicagoclimatex.com/ (last visited July 28, 2006).

189. Nat'l Comm'n on Energy Pol'y, *supra* note 25, at x.

190. *Id.* at 37 & 69.

191. *Id.* at iv-v.

192. Robert R. Nordhaus & Kyle W. Danish, *Assessing the Options for Designing a Mandatory U.S. Greenhouse Gas Reduction Program*, 32 B.C. ENVTL. AFF. L. REV. 97 (2005) [*Assessing the Options*]. The paper also appears, in substantially the same form, as ROBERT R. NORDHAUS & KYLE W. DANISH, DESIGNING A MANDATORY GREENHOUSE GAS REDUCTION PROGRAM FOR THE U.S. (2003), http://www.pewclimate.org/docUploads/USGas%2Epdf.

193. *Assessing the Options*, *supra* note 192, at 111.

194. *Id.* at 163.

195. 42 U.S.C. §§ 7651–7651o.

196. ELECTRIC POWER RESEARCH INSTITUTE, UPSTREAM AND DOWNSTREAM APPROACHES TO CARBON DIOXIDE REGULATION (2005), http://www.epriweb.com/public/000000000001007762.pdf.

197. *Assessing the Options*, *supra* note 193, at 159–61.

198. *Id.* at 161.

199. Tom Vanden Brook & Paul Overberg, *High Gas Prices Alter Driving Habits*, USA TODAY (Dec. 8, 2005), http://www.usatoday.com/news/nation/2005-12-08-gas-prices_x.htm (conclusion based on analysis of Federal Highway Administration data).

200. *Assessing the Options*, *supra* note 192, at 148.

201. *Id.* at 110 & 163.

202. *Id.* at 161–63.

203. AMORY B. LOVINS ET AL., WINNING THE OIL ENDGAME: INNOVATION FOR PROFITS, JOBS, AND SECURITY (2004), http://www.rmi.org/images/other/WtOE/WtOEg_72dpi.pdf.

204. A CLIMATE POLICY FRAMEWORK: BALANCING POLICY AND POLITICS (John A. Riggs ed. 2004).

205. 151 CONG. REC. S6980, S7033 (daily ed. June 22, 2005)), *quoted in* PETE V. DOMENICI & JEFF BINGAMAN, DESIGN ELEMENTS OF A MANDATORY MARKET-BASED GREENHOUSE GAS REGULATORY SYSTEM (Feb. 2006) 1, http://energy.senate.gov/public/_files/ClimateChangeWhitePaper.doc.

206. There is nonetheless disagreement about whether mercury should be subject to trading. Opponents argue that mercury is more toxic than sulfur dioxide and nitrogen oxide, that it is deposited in the vicinity of power plants, and that a trading program would allow the development or continuation of local "hot spots" with greater mercury concentrations where power plant operators can afford to purchase allowances rather than control their own emissions.

207. S. 131, 109th Cong. (2005). Sen. George Voinovich (Ohio) is the lone co-sponsor.

208. U.S. Environmental Protection Act, Clear Skies Act of 2003, http://www.epa.gov/air/clearskies/fact2003.html (last visited June 15, 2006). The 2005 bill is essentially the same as the 2003 proposal.

209. S. 131, *supra* note 207, § 408.

210. Steve Cook, *Tie Vote in Senate Environment Committee Kills President's Clear Skies Bill in Congress*, Daily Env't Rep. (BNA) No. 46, at A-2 (March 10, 2005).

211. S. 2724, 109th Cong. (2006). The other six sponsors were Republicans Lamar Alexander (Tennessee), Lincoln Chafee (Rhode Island), Lindsey Graham (South Carolina), and Judd Gregg (New Hampshire), and Democrats Christopher Dodd (Connecticut), Diane Feinstein (California), and Mary Landrieu (Louisiana). A companion bill was also introduced in the House, H.R. 1873, 190th Cong. (2006).

212. Press Release, Sen. Tom Carper, Senator Carper, Others Introduce "New and Improved" Bipartisan Clean Air Bill (May 3, 2006), http://carper.senate.gov/test/release.cfm?type= press&id=255083.

213. S. 2724 § 3.

214. *Id.* §§ 3 & 5.

215. Climate Stewardship and Innovation Act of 2005, S. 1151, 109th Cong. (2005). The other two sponsors are Republican Olympia Snowe (Maine) and Democrat Barack Obama (Illinois) *See also* S. 342, 109th Cong. (2005) and H.R. 759, 109th Cong. (2005) (similar bills).

216. *Id.* § 3 (definition of covered entity).

217. Press Release, Sen. Joe Lieberman, Climate Stewardship and Innovation Act of 2005—Summary (May 26, 2005), http:// lieberman.senate.gov/newsroom/release. cfm?id=238307.

218. Press Release, Sen. John McCain, McCain, Lieberman Add New Technologies Provision to Global Warming Bill (May 26, 2005), http://mccain.senate.gov/index.cfm?fuseaction= Newscenter.ViewPressRelease&Content_id=1576.

219. Pamela Najor, *Senate Rejects Effort to Force U.S. Cuts in Greenhouse Gas Emissions on 38–60 Vote*, Daily Env't Rep. (BNA) No. 120, at A-1 (June 23, 2005).

220. Pamela Najor, *McCain Plans to Offer Bill to Cut Emissions of Greenhouse Gases as Energy Amendment*, 36 Daily Env't Rep. (BNA) No. 24, at 1229 (June 27, 2005).

221. DESIGN ELEMENTS, *supra* note 205, at 1.

222. *Id.* at 3, 6, 13 & 14.

223. Climate Change, Conference before the Senate Comm. on Energy and Natural Resources, S. Hrg. No. 190-420 (2006), http://frwebgate.access.gpo.gov/cgi-bin/getdoc.cgi?dbname= 109_senate_hearings& docid=f:28095.pdf.

224. Pete V. Domenici and Jeff Bingaman, Chairman and Ranking Member Statement: Climate Conference (2006), http:// energy.senate.gov/public/_files/JointStatementon ClimateConference.pdf.

225. *Id.* at 1.

226. *Id.* at 2-4.

227. S. 3698, 109th Cong. (2006).

228. The other sponsors, all Democrats, were Daniel Akaka (Hawaii), Barbara Boxer (California), Christopher Dodd (Connecticut), Russell Feingold (Wisconsin), Daniel Inouye (Hawaii), Edward Kennedy (Massachusetts), Frank Lautenberg (New Jersey), Patrick Leahy (Vermont), Robert Menendez (New Jersey), Jack Reed (Rhode Island), and Paul Sarbanes (Maryland).

229. S. 3698, § 702(2).

230. *Id.* § 704

231. *Id.* §§ 710–714.

chapter four

The Impact of the Kyoto Protocol on U.S. Business

Donald M. Goldberg
*and Angela Delfino**

I. Introduction

This chapter assesses the impacts of the Kyoto Protocol to the United Nations Framework on Climate Change (UNFCCC)[1] on U.S. business. Although the United States was very involved in the negotiation of the Kyoto Protocol, and, as a result, the Protocol reflects many U.S. ideas, President Bush decided not to ratify the Protocol.[2] Even if the President had been in favor of ratification, it is unlikely that the U.S. Congress would have given its consent.[3]

From the standpoint of international law, the Kyoto Protocol will not affect U.S. business directly, but rather through the implementing laws and regulations that parties to the Protocol adopt. Because most parties have not yet fully drafted these laws and regulations, it is difficult to assess the actual impacts of the Protocol on U.S. business. The most evolved national system of implementation to date is the European Union's (EU) Emissions Trading Scheme, which is discussed in detail below. Two other schemes being developed in Canada and Japan are described in less detail, mainly to provide examples of other approaches. But because the details of these systems remain to be developed, the chapter draws its specific examples from the EU system.

Because the Kyoto Protocol and its implementing laws are not fully formed, an inquiry into its effect on U.S. business is a highly speculative enterprise. We will never

*   The authors would like to thank Jillian Button, Amanda Noonan Heyman, and James Swetz for their invaluable contributions to this chapter.

know what would have happened in the absence of the Kyoto Protocol. Given the scientific consensus that now exists about global warming, however, it is likely that the world would have eventually have responded, with or without a Kyoto Protocol.

. . . we know the climate is changing and we know businesses are taking actions that should result in fewer GHG emissions. As to the cause-and-effect relationship between these two observations, we can only speculate.

A second problem is that we know that many businesses have already taken actions that have had, or will have, the effect of lowering their greenhouse gas (GHG) emissions. Some have made their production processes more efficient, saving energy in the process. Others have reduced their carbon emissions by switching fuels and energy sources or invested in emissions offsets through such activities as planting or restoring forests. We cannot always say precisely what motivated these changes. Although many companies have said their actions were a response to climate change,[4] they may have taken many of the same actions for other reasons, such as reducing fuel costs.

Even more difficult is predicting what businesses will do in the future. Many businesses have already announced actions they intend to take, but they may be responding to state regulations that in many cases are already planned, or to demands from shareholders or consumers. These regulations and demands may themselves be related to the existence of the Kyoto Protocol, but it is difficult to say precisely what the link is, even if we assume one exists.

A third problem is that it is difficult to say what the Kyoto Protocol will look like in the future (or whether there will even be a Kyoto Protocol in the future). In the past few years, several international meetings have been held to discuss future rules of the Kyoto Protocol, particularly those that will apply in the second commitment period, from 2013 to 2017.[5] During this period other agreements have also been discussed or adopted. Some experts view these as potential alternatives to the Kyoto Protocol.[6]

The point should be clear: we know the climate is changing and we know businesses are taking actions that should result in fewer GHG emissions. As to the cause-and-effect relationship between these two observations, we can only speculate.[7]

The Kyoto Protocol is an experiment. Nothing really similar predates it. From an environmental perspective, it has elements in common with the Montreal Protocol, the international treaty to phase out ozone-depleting substances.[8] While the Montreal Protocol is widely considered to have been a success, many doubts have been raised about the Kyoto Protocol, which is far more complex. Uncertainty about how Kyoto parties will implement the Protocol, the absence of the United States—the world's largest GHG emitter—from the Protocol regime, the limited role assigned to developing countries, and the provision of excess emissions allowances to Russia and other countries "with economies in transition" all increase uncertainty about how effective it will be, or even what it will look like in the future.

For many questions, the best we can do as lawyers is to provide educated guesses. Economic analysis would be helpful but is beyond the scope of this chapter. Many aspects of the Protocol could affect the competitive balance between parties, non-parties, and parties with limited commitments. With so many novel and untested elements in play, even economists would find the predictive capabilities of their tools stretched thin.

Finally, it should be noted that although the present U.S. Administration has decided not to ratify the Protocol, much of its design reflects U.S. ideas and experience. Emissions trading, extended (five-year) commitment periods, and the "basket of gases" approach[9] were all U.S. ideas. As the United States begins to take climate change more seriously, which is something that has already begun to happen at the state and local levels, these ideas may be integrated into U.S. regulatory systems. On the other hand, thinking in the United States and elsewhere about how best to regulate GHG emissions has evolved, and the international and domestic regimes that finally emerge to solve the problem of climate change may bear little resemblance to the ones we think we know today.

The Bush Administration rejected the Kyoto Protocol on the grounds that it would harm the U.S. economy and would be ineffective in any event because large-emitting developing countries, such as China, India, and Brazil, were also refusing to take on commitments to reduce emissions.[10] A critical, albeit unanswerable, question is whether the United States might ratify the Kyoto Protocol sometime in the future and, if so, whether it would leave the structure largely undisturbed or, more likely, seek to rewrite it to reflect more recent U.S. thinking.

Several sources provide insight into current thinking in the United States about the structure of either a domestic or international emissions control system. (This issue is addressed in Chapter 3 of this book.) The Administration has adopted a voluntary approach for major U.S. emitters based on improving the nation's GHG intensity, *i.e.*, its emissions per dollar of GDP. The goal—to reduce GHG intensity 18% by 2010—is quite modest (some say it is essentially business-as-usual). The Administration is also investing substantial resources in additional scientific research, development and deployment of new technologies, and bilateral agreements with major developing countries.[11]

The U.S. Congress has introduced several bills aimed at addressing global warming over the past few years. These include the Climate Stewardship Act introduced in both the Senate and the House and the Keep America Competitive Global Warming Policy Act.[12] None of these approaches is entirely consistent with the Kyoto Protocol. This is important, because any disjuncture between the U.S. approach and that of the parties to the Kyoto Protocol could result in a less efficient and effective global system.

The perceived ineffectiveness of the Administration's voluntary approach and the failure of Congress thus far to adopt anything stronger (although, as noted above, attempts continue to be made) have led a number of states and municipalities to create local, state, and multistate emissions control regimes.[13] The utility of such regimes is likely to be limited, however, as other states have made it clear they do not intend to self-regulate GHGs, giving rise to significant concerns among regulating states and municipalities about possible negative effects on the competitiveness of their industries.[14] Moreover, a "patchwork" of municipal, state, and regional programs could be difficult to administer and even more difficult to comply with.

This chapter will begin with a discussion of some of the domestic regulatory regimes that are emerging in Kyoto countries. We focus on the EU and its emissions trading system (ETS) because it is the most developed system to date. We then discuss how these regimes are likely to affect U.S. firms and their operations in the EU and in the United States. Next, we discuss some transitional issues, including possible forms that future domestic regulation, adopted partly in response to Kyoto, might take. Finally, we will attempt to draw some conclusions about how U.S. firms might alter their future operations to meet the looming crisis of climate change.

II. Regulatory Regimes Emerging in Kyoto Countries

We now examine the regulatory regimes being developed by three Kyoto Protocol Annex B Parties: the European Union, Japan, and Canada. We focus on the EU and its emissions trading system because it is the most developed system to date. This raises an important caveat: it is quite likely that by the time this treatise is published, some of what we report will have become outdated as a result of new scientific findings, political decisions, new industry and other stakeholder initiatives, new plans, new ideas, new regulations, and new effects. Although our descriptions and opinions will necessarily be incomplete, we hope they will still be helpful.

A. The EU Emissions Trading Scheme

On January 1, 2005, six weeks before the Kyoto Protocol entered into force, the EU Emissions Trading Scheme (EU ETS) became operational, creating the world's largest emissions trading system, with approximately 11,500 industrial emitters. The ETS scheme (also discussed in Chapters 2 and 17 of this book) introduces a new environmental instrument, "the tradable emissions allowance," which is now an important new tradable commodity. Briefly, the ETS limits total EU emissions to a certain agreed level (the "cap"). Allowances equal to the number of tons of emissions allowed under the cap are then distributed to EU governments, which allocate them to their domestic emitters, with each emitter receiving allowances equal to a predetermined quota. Emitters are permitted to trade allowances among themselves, which in theory will allow the market to determine the most efficient allocation of allowances and emissions. The EU ETS was created and is regulated at the EU level by the Emissions Trading Directive.[15]

Although other greenhouse gases are covered by the current Emission Trading Directive,[16] carbon dioxide (CO_2) is its primary target, and CO_2 will be the only tradable GHG emission until 2008,[17] at which time other activities and installations may be included. Until 2008, the Directive is limited to certain industries: energy activities,[18] production and processing of ferrous metals,[19] mineral industry (cement, glass and ceramics),[20] and pulp and paper industrial plants. In implementing the Directive, EU Member States may choose capacity limits below, but not above, those in the Emission Trading Directive.

Additionally, the Directive regulates the emissions allocation procedure. It stipulates that at least 95 percent of the allowances will be allocated free of charge for the first three-year period (2005-2008) and 90 percent for the second five-year period (2008-2012).[21] Each Member State must draw up a national plan in accordance with Annex III of the Directive, indicating the number of allowances the Member State intends to allocate and which facilities will receive allocations. This method of distribution, sometimes called "grandfathering," is intended to reduce the cost incurred by industry in adapting to the EU ETS. Grandfathering represents a strong incentive for the acceptance of the scheme by many industry sectors.[22]

The Directive also speaks to penalties for noncompliance, although each Member State has determined its own sanctions. If operators fail to surrender the quantity of allowances equal to the emissions from their installations during the previous year, they will be required to pay an excess emissions penalty of •100 for each ton of CO_2 equivalent.[23] Payment of the penalty does not release the operator from the obligation to surrender an amount of allowances equal to the excess emissions.

Since the scheme is regulated by Directive, EU law requires that, in furtherance of the general obligation framed in the Directive, each Member State must transpose and implement the ETS scheme as described above. However, the Directive leaves many decisions, including the number of allowances to be allocated to each regulated facility, up to the individual Member State. Many commentators have stated that the economic and environmental effectiveness of the scheme will depend on how these allocations are made and, in particular, how uniform the allocations will be. Many analyses of the ETS system have already been performed, and more are currently under way.

In addition to the ETS, the EU has committed itself to continue international efforts to move the Kyoto process forward in a way that includes broader participation by all major emitters, including developing countries like China and India. The

EU's broader climate change strategy includes developing new policy areas; promoting, developing, and deploying low-emission technologies; using flexible market-based instruments; and creating adaptation policies.[24] Simultaneously, the EU plans to continually monitor the success of the ETS, and may revise the system before 2008 by adding new sectors and additional GHGs to the scheme. In addition, a legislative proposal on aviation emissions is under preparation following a recommendation by the Commission.[25]

B. The Canadian Plan

To comply with the Kyoto Protocol, Canada has committed to reduce its GHG emissions to 6% below 1990 levels during the first commitment period, 2008 to 2012. Canada's Climate Change Plan, released in April 2005, aims to reduce emissions by approximately 240 megatons of CO_2 equivalent annually during this period.[26] In order to reach this overall target, Canadian private-sector entities will use a domestic emissions trading system.

The four most significant components of Canada's domestic emissions trading system are the Large Final Emitters System, the Offset System, the Climate Fund, and the Partnership Fund.[27] The Large Final Emitters System, which has yet to be translated into regulations, covers approximately 700 companies in the oil, gas, thermal electricity, mining, and manufacturing sectors. Companies in these sectors may utilize a number of approaches to meet their obligations, including upgrading facilities to achieve in-house reductions, purchasing emissions reductions from other large final emitters (LFEs), investing in domestic offset credits, and purchasing international Kyoto units (provided that these represent emission reductions that have been verified in accordance with Kyoto mechanisms). Taken together, these options will allow the more than 700 LFEs in Canada to achieve reductions of approximately 36 megatons of CO_2 equivalent.

The Offset System for GHG emissions aims to establish a market incentive to identify and develop projects that reduce emissions or enhance removals not covered by the proposed framework establishing targets for emissions reductions for LFEs. Such reductions or enhancements result in credits that can be used for compliance with the Large Final Emitters System and for other purposes, such as the increased cost savings from allowing entities with potential GHG reductions or removals not covered by the proposed framework to participate in the trading program by supplying offset credits.[28] In addition, Canada envisions that the government would be prepared to exchange Kyoto compliance units for offset credits as appropriate so that they could be sold internationally.

The Climate Fund, with an initial capitalization of $1 billion Canadian, is a permanent institution to purchase, on behalf of the government of Canada, GHG emissions reduction and removal credits generated in Canada and abroad.

The Partnership Fund aims to execute new agreements and improve existing ones with provinces and territories, to find strategic investments on the basis of mutual priorities, and to finance, on a cost-sharing basis, major technology and infrastructure investments identified in collaboration with provinces and territories. Investments could include, for example, clean coal, phasing out coal-fired power plants, CO_2 capture and storage pipelines, and extension of the East-West electricity power grid.

The design of the Canadian Program is still in a fairly early stage, and U.S. industry should pay close attention to further developments within the largest U.S. trading partner.[29] Furthermore, some climate change decisions previously made by the Canadian government may be revisited by the new, more conservative government.[30]

C. The Japanese System

In 2005 the Japanese Ministry of the Environment selected 34 companies and corporate groups to participate in the country's new Voluntary Emissions Trading Scheme.[31] Under this scheme, the Japanese Government will subsidize the installation cost of CO_2 emissions reduction equipment for participating companies.[32] In exchange for the subsidies, the participants must commit to a certain level of CO_2 emissions reductions,[33] which can also be achieved through CO_2 emission allowance trading. If the stipulated reduction targets are not met, participating companies must reimburse the government for the subsidy expenditure.[34]

The main objective of the Japanese scheme is to achieve a cost-effective and substantial reduction in GHG emissions levels and to accumulate knowledge and experience relating to emissions trading at the national level.[35] Although the system is presently just a voluntary pilot scheme, Japan is committed to the Kyoto Protocol and will create a mandatory emissions trading scheme in the future. Japan's intention to utilize emissions trading in order to fully implement its Kyoto commitments should be taken seriously by potential investors, especially in the medium and long term. With respect to near-term prospective business opportunities, U.S. businesses should also consider the possibility of participating in the Voluntary Emissions Trading Scheme to gain access to short-term subsidies available from the Japanese government.

III. The Effects of Regulatory Regimes in Kyoto Countries on U.S Businesses

This section discusses the types of effects that domestic implementing regulations in Kyoto countries could have on U.S. business. For the most part, we limit our discussion to regimes in Annex B countries. Annex B countries are the Kyoto parties that have committed to limiting or reducing their emissions under Annex B of the Protocol. For specific examples of the effects of domestic regulation, we discuss the EU ETS, as this is the only system detailed enough to make meaningful analysis possible.[36]

The types of direct impacts we discuss include compliance with domestic GHG control regulations, the ability of U.S. companies to compete in overseas (and in some cases domestic) markets for GHG control technologies and other green goods and services, and the ability to use and profit from the emissions trading mechanisms set up under both the Protocol itself and national systems developed by Annex B countries to implement the Protocol.

We also look at some indirect impacts: the ability of U.S. businesses to plan in an uncertain regulatory environment, their lack of political influence in shaping emerging international and domestic regulatory regimes, and consumer and investor attitudes toward the U.S. corporate response to climate change (or the perceived lack thereof).

Although economic analysis is beyond the scope of this chapter, it is well known that the U.S. Administration rejected the Kyoto Protocol at least partly on economic grounds.[37] A closer look reveals that non-participation in the Kyoto regime (the Protocol and its domestic and international implementing rules) may also create disadvantages, in some cases increasing costs or causing companies to forgo formidable opportunities related to the trading of emissions and other investment opportunities brought about by the Kyoto Protocol.

The Kyoto Protocol only regulates behavior of states parties (i.e., governments, not firms). Each Annex B government can decide for itself how to regulate entities operating within its borders, and national regulations to implement Kyoto may differ considerably from one Annex B country to another. Because each Annex B Party may decide for itself how to implement its Kyoto obligations, U.S. companies with multiple overseas facilities may be subject to a plethora of different Kyoto-related requirements. Of course, prior to Kyoto, they already were faced with different regulatory regimes in different countries, but Kyoto compliance adds a new level of complexity for companies operating or transacting in multiple overseas markets.

Some of the analysis that follows may raise issues concerning the interplay between international and domestic regulation and international trade and investment law. The connection between the Kyoto Protocol and WTO Agreements is discussed in Chapter 8 and, hence, is not discussed at length here. To a large extent, however, the regulation of climate change and the relationship between climate change and international trade rules cannot be made entirely clear, as measures being adopted by Kyoto parties are a work in progress. A comprehensive analysis of WTO consistency will have to await their completion and then must be determined on a case-by-case basis.

A. Direct Impacts on U.S. Businesses Operating in Annex B Countries

1. Compliance with Annex B GHG Control Regulations

There is little doubt that U.S. firms with operations in Annex B countries will have to comply in substance with domestic rules for implementation of the Kyoto Protocol. The EU ETS provisions, for example, make no distinction between domestic facilities and foreign-owned facilities. This is largely due to the fact that Kyoto Protocol emissions-accounting rules are geographically based. Emissions are attributed to the country in which they occur, regardless of who owns the emitting facility or purchases goods or services from the facility.

This fact in itself does not seem to raise any particular issues beyond those of complying with more than one regulatory system, something that is routine for multinationals. Climate change and the Kyoto Protocol, however, may make the situation more complicated because of the inherent and designed-in characteristics of emissions trading systems. In particular, emissions trading schemes are often designed to comprise a multiplicity of relationships between regulatory entities and companies, and, in the particular case of EU ETS, among Member States and the Commission. As a result, U.S.-owned firms may find they have fewer options and less flexibility in meeting those rules than do their domestic Annex B counterparts.

Parent companies located in Annex B countries may be able to comply with existing GHG emissions regulations more easily and cheaply than their U.S. counterparts if they have subsidiaries in different sectors or if their processes of production are vertically integrated. Annex B companies (and to a lesser extent, U.S. firms) that have some old plants and some modern plants or that are in the process of modernizing also may have options that are not available to companies that do not intend to modernize their Annex B facilities. Current EU ETS rules, which do not permit companies to utilize allowances from countries that are not Kyoto parties, create a clear advantage for companies concentrated in Europe or other Annex B countries and that do not have their production dispersed between Annex B countries and the United States. For example, Annex B companies may have more opportunities for internal (intra-firm) trading of emissions allowances than U.S. firms with few facilities operating in Annex B countries (or none at all). This may present a particular disadvantage for U.S.-owned facilities, as reductions achieved in the United States cannot be used to comply with the Kyoto Protocol.

U.S. companies located in Annex B countries might seek to avoid or minimize the impact of GHG control regulations by, for example, conducting high-emitting activities (such as manufacturing) at home but locating low-emitting ones (such as assembly) in an Annex B country. EU rules, as they currently stand, would not prevent this, but future rules could be envisioned to discourage such behavior. For example, an Annex B country might treat such a split production process as though the emissions associated with the entire process occurred within its borders, thus requiring companies to hold allowances for all their emissions, whether the emissions occur domestically or in the United States. This might entail imputing emissions to imported components and requiring the U.S. assembly or sales facility to obtain allowances to cover those emissions. This type of emission accounting could be analogized to a GHG-related tax or other measure imposed at the border, which may be permitted by the rules of the WTO, provided the importing country has in place a domestic measure of equal or greater stringency.[38]

> **The Kyoto Protocol creates incentives for the development of new markets for what are called "green goods". . . products that are the result of cleaner, more efficient production methods or that operate in a way that allows better environmental outcomes.**

As time goes on, and the Kyoto Protocol controls become more stringent, Annex B countries will be forced to tighten their domestic regulation accordingly. Incremental tightening of the domestic regime can already be observed in EU states. Despite difficulties already apparent in the first phase of the EU emissions control regime (2005-2007),[39] a second, Kyoto-compliant phase is scheduled to begin in 2008, and proposals to add more regulated sectors are being discussed. For example, on July 4, 2006, the European Parliament, on the recommendation of the EU Commission and the Council of Ministers, supported a proposal by the Parliament's Environmental Committee to extend the EU ETS scheme to include civil aviation.[40] Although clear rules have not been adopted in respect of the geographical scope of the measures under consideration, it appears likely that all airlines will be required to comply with any adopted provisions within the geographical area of application of the system, regardless of nationality.[41]

2. Competing in Markets for GHG Control Technologies and Green Goods

The Kyoto Protocol creates incentives for the development of new markets for what are called "green goods." Green goods are products that are the result of cleaner, more efficient production methods or that operate in a way that allows better environmental outcomes. Green goods include the control technology necessary to achieve certain levels of emissions-reduction or efficiency standards that allow for lower energy consumption. These could include such things as renewable energy technologies (wind turbines, solar panels, geothermal technologies, etc.), more efficient energy-consuming products (electric motors, boilers, and appliances), and products that help conserve energy passively (including thermal-pane windows, insulation, and other green building products).

If the market for green goods and services is stronger in Europe and other Annex B countries than it is in the United States, or if Annex B countries prohibit the sale of some non-green products altogether, U.S. companies may be at a disadvantage, especially if their major market is the United States. If U.S firms decide to serve their less environmentally demanding domestic market exclusively and forgo more costly opportunities in Annex B countries, they could find themselves "behind the curve" when green technologies are widely accepted, as they almost surely will be. Their foreign competitors will gradually become more efficient and innovative and eventually may be able to lock in their access to cleaner technologies markets, much as Asian and other countries have done with certain consumer electronics and are now doing with cars.[42] If U.S. firms decide, in the future, to get "back into the game," they could find it is expensive to enter the race long after it has started.

U.S. companies face another risk. To prevent their own companies from facing excessive start-up costs as they make the transition to greener products and services, it is not unlikely that Annex B Kyoto parties will provide subsidies. This may already be happening, as EU states provide free emissions allowances to their regulated industries, as discussed below.

3. Ability to Use and Profit from Emissions Trading and Other Market Mechanisms

Emissions trading and other "market mechanisms" can increase economic efficiency, saving firms money by reducing the cost of complying with GHG emissions reduction requirements. In addition, firms that can reduce their emissions cheaply can make money by selling these reductions to companies with higher reduction costs. Such reductions could become quite valuable as controls on emissions become more stringent.

First, as discussed in the previous section, firms that have most or all of their operations located in Annex B countries will have more opportunities for internal (intra-firm) trading. Thus, it is likely that they will have strategic opportunities to reduce the overall costs of meeting their emissions obligations that will not be available to companies that have only a small part of their operations based in Annex B countries and must buy needed allowances from other companies.

Second, U.S.-owned facilities that seek to meet Annex B emissions obligations by obtaining low-cost emissions reduction units (ERUs) through joint implementation (JI)[43] or certified emissions reductions (CERs) through the clean development mechanism[44] (CDM) may also face hurdles. These companies will need to obtain the approval of the Annex B country "involved," as well as the approval of the non-Annex I Kyoto host country, to participate in a CDM project.[45] While arbitrary withholding of such approval may raise WTO questions, restricted or conditional approval could withstand WTO scrutiny if the environmental rationale is clear. Strict reliance on WTO rules to overcome such governmental resistance could prove misplaced, especially since the Protocol is unequivocal about the need for government approval but virtually silent on the criteria by which governments may provide or withhold their approval.[46]

Third, U.S.-owned facilities in Annex B countries would face an even larger problem if Annex B governments refuse to provide them with accounts in their Kyoto registries. The Kyoto Protocol requires all Annex B countries to create national registries to account for their national emissions and to enable trading with other Annex B countries.[47] Firms that wish to engage in trading must establish accounts within those national registries. Under the rules of the Kyoto Protocol, however, the establishment of such private accounts is entirely at the discretion of the government.[48] The WTO and other international trade rules notwithstanding, the Kyoto Protocol does not obligate Annex B countries to treat all emitters the same with respect to national registries. Thus, in theory at least, U.S.-owned emitters in Annex B countries could be prevented from participating in Kyoto trading altogether.

B. Direct Impacts on U.S. Businesses Operating in the United States

1. Compliance with Annex B GHG Control Regulations

U.S. firms seeking to sell their goods or services into Annex B markets may be affected by, if not required to fully comply with, Annex B greenhouse gas control regulations. No doubt, their products will have to meet the same efficiency and other performance standards as products manufactured in Annex B countries. In addition, as noted above, unless prohibited by the WTO, some Annex B countries may restrict or regulate imports based on "embodied" GHGs (*i.e.*, GHGs emitted during the production process). Furthermore, green subsidies (including freely allocated allowances) that may be available to companies in Annex B countries may not be available to U.S. firms.[49] This also could depend on WTO rules and rulings.

2. Competing in Markets for GHG Control Technologies and Green Goods

It seems unlikely that Annex B countries would attempt to prohibit the importation or sale of GHG control technologies or green goods produced by U.S. companies simply because they are manufactured partly or entirely in the United States. Furthermore, such restrictions would almost certainly raise difficulties with respect to WTO rules. Nevertheless, there are several reasons why U.S. companies may have difficulty marketing GHG control technologies and other green products in Annex B countries. Some reasons are discussed below in this section, while others are discussed below in the section on indirect impacts.

One problem facing U.S. companies is that, until the United States adopts stringent emissions control regulations, U.S. companies presumably will not find a similar (or equal) demand for such products in their home market. Thus, they may be forced to simultaneously meet demand for inexpensive "brown" goods at home and more expensive "green" goods in Annex B countries. This may discourage U.S. companies from being leaders in the development of such goods and technologies, leaving them ill-equipped to serve the carbon-constrained markets of the future.

U.S. firms also may face future difficulties in meeting eco-labeling requirements and government procurement specifications. While this does not seem to be a problem at the present time, future Annex B governments may adopt eco-labeling requirements or specifications for goods and services purchased by the government itself or by its contractors. These requirements could be a powerful tool to promote U.S. ratification or compliance with the Kyoto Protocol and are unlikely to run afoul of WTO rules.[50]

An additional problem, similar to the one noted above, and which may not be unique to U.S. firms, is the difficulty of serving many different Annex B markets. Although EU Member States are somewhat restricted by their Trading Directive, they still possess a lot of latitude in choosing their implementing regulations. Thus, different Annex B countries may have different specifications, requiring different types of green goods and technologies. In subsequent phases, however, the European Union is likely to seek more consistency among its Member States. In principle, adjusting to a range of different and possibly conflicting regulatory restrictions is standard operating procedure for companies with many overseas operations, though the problem may be more extreme in the Kyoto context, since implementing regu-

lations will be new and untested in the early phases of the Protocol, with little opportunity for harmonization.

3. Ability to Benefit from Emissions Trading and Other Market Mechanisms

Companies in Annex B countries that can reduce their emissions relatively cheaply will be able to sell their excess allowances to other Annex B companies or countries. It is unlikely, however, that U.S. firms that have or are able to create cheap opportunities for reducing their emissions will be able to market those reductions to firms or governments in Annex B countries, as reductions generated in the United States could not be used to meet commitments under the Kyoto Protocol. U.S. businesses will face an additional disadvantage if Annex B countries choose to "grandfather" allowances, as the EU has.

Of course, as domestic emissions trading markets spring up in the United States, as is already happening in some states and regions, U.S. firms located in those states and regions will be able to sell reductions within their own markets. However, potential sellers will have a smaller market in which to sell reductions, and hence may not be able to demand as high a price as they could get if the United States were a Kyoto party.

A potentially more significant problem, mentioned above, is that Annex B governments presumably could refuse to provide U.S. firms with accounts in their Kyoto registries. Thus, in theory at least, U.S. companies could be prevented from participating in Kyoto trading altogether. At present, the EU ETS specifically authorizes trading only with other Annex B countries, although it is not completely clear that this prohibits trading with the United States. The same problem could arise with respect to JI. Because JI projects also reduce the emissions that must be reported by the Annex B country hosting the project, the transfer of ERUs must be accompanied by a parallel transfer of AAUs.[51]

Annex B governments, arguably, could create other barriers to participation by U.S. firms in JI projects by imposing taxes or implementing unfavorable legislation. While such barriers might violate WTO rules or internationally agreed rules on investment, it is difficult to predict the outcome until the specific domestic rules have been adopted and adjudicated in the appropriate international forum.[52] It is not obvious, however, that the WTO or other international investment rules would prevail over rules established to further the goals of the Kyoto Protocol.

The CDM, somewhat like JI, provides the opportunity for governments and private firms to finance projects that reduce greenhouse gas emissions in developing countries that are Kyoto parties and receive certified emissions reductions (CERs) in return.[53] CERs, once created, must be transferred directly into the account of the firm or government that is designated by the project agreement to receive them. This could create an accounting problem similar to one identified above. Such accounts must be housed within an Annex B country's registry. Since the Kyoto rules leave the decision about which entities may have accounts within their registries entirely to the discretion of each Annex B party,[54] it is possible that U.S. firms that finance CDM projects would not have accounts to receive the resulting CERs.

While U.S. firms might be able to circumvent such limitations by making deals with firms that do have such accounts, the cost attached to such deal-making will be borne by U.S. firms but not by Annex B firms. U.S. firms with Annex B facilities may not encounter this problem, as their Annex B facility may have the same right as domestic firms to establish an account in the registry of the country in which it is located. On the other hand, Annex B countries may view the establishment of such accounts as a privilege to be accorded only to firms belonging to countries that have accepted all the strictures of the Kyoto Protocol.

If ownership and resale of CERs, as well as AAUs, ERUs, and RMUs, pose special difficulties for U.S. firms, then investing in such projects may not be worthwhile. Even if these difficulties may be circumvented, for example, by striking deals with firms or governments that have Annex B accounts, the extra effort and expense this would entail would place the U.S. firm at a disadvantage relative to its Annex B competitor. As Kyoto emissions targets become more ambitious, and the value of CERs increases, this disadvantage may become significant enough to make participation in CDM projects prohibitively expensive for U.S. firms. Such costs may also limit the ability of U.S. firms to market goods or services to CDM projects if, for example, Annex B firms are able to receive CERs or equity positions in the projects themselves as partial or full payment for providing such goods and services, while U.S. firms may not.

C. Indirect Impacts on U.S. Business

It is often assumed that, all other things being equal, companies in Annex B countries that are saddled with the cost of implementing Kyoto will be at a disadvantage vis-à-vis their competitors in the United States. As the discussion above shows, however, U.S. facilities operating both in the United States and in Annex B countries will not necessarily enjoy a competitive advantage, and in fact may even find themselves at a disadvantage.

This section discusses other problems that U.S. firms may face, no matter where they are situated, as a result of the decision by the United States not to participate in Kyoto. These may be thought of as the "indirect effects" of the Kyoto Protocol.[55] These include abilities of U.S. businesses to plan in an uncertain regulatory environment, lack of political influence in shaping emerging international and domestic regulatory regimes, and consumer and investor attitudes toward the U.S. corporate response to climate change (or the perceived lack thereof).

1. Regulatory Uncertainty

To a much greater extent than their Kyoto competitors, U.S. firms face an uncertain regulatory future. This includes uncertainty regarding the nature, scope, and timing of potential federal regulations, and the multiple and sometimes contradictory legislative approaches emerging at the state and municipal levels. As a result, business decisions for U.S. firms may be more costly and risky than similar decisions faced by Annex B firms, especially where long-term strategic planning and foreign investment are concerned.[56]

On the one hand, firms may not be adequately preparing for the possibility of regulation and compliance in the most cost-effective manner. On the other, firms may incur unnecessary costs if they guess wrong in trying to anticipate and prepare for a future regulatory scenario and the instruments that it will adopt. Geography amplifies this uncertainty, as many companies make the difficult choice of either pursuing different policies in different places, which is likely to be inefficient and expensive, or bearing the costs of making Kyoto-equivalent improvements in the United States.[57]

2. Lack of Political Influence

A similar problem that could also create a significant potential disadvantage for U.S. firms is that they will likely have less influence than their Annex B competitors on the process of developing Kyoto rules, both at the international and domestic levels. The United States cannot participate directly in Kyoto Protocol negotiations, where Kyoto rules are made. Similarly, U.S. firms may have less say than their domestic counterparts in shaping domestic regulations for implementing Kyoto rules. For industries that rely on overseas sales, the inability to have their concerns considered on par with their competitors might be a substantial impediment.

As has already been noted, each Annex B government can decide for itself how to regulate entities operating within its borders, and national regulations to implement Kyoto may differ considerably from one Annex B country to another. Because each Annex B Party may decide for itself how to implement its Kyoto obligations, U.S. companies, particularly those with multiple overseas facilities, may be subject to a plethora of different Kyoto-related requirements. Having limited influence in the development of these rules could only exacerbate this problem.

3. Consumer and Investor Attitudes

Consumer preference, especially in Annex B countries, could give Annex B companies an additional competitive advantage. As consumers become more aware of the dangers of global warming, they may grow increasingly reluctant to purchase goods from countries that do not have stringent GHG emissions controls. Moreover, performance specifications of goods manufactured and sold by U.S. companies for the U.S. market may not meet the more rigorous needs of consumers in Annex B countries. Energy-efficiency standards for appliances and other goods are likely to become more stringent over time in Kyoto countries, possibly forcing U.S. firms to redesign their overseas products to meet Kyoto-based specifications, while continuing to market cheaper, less efficient products at home.

Compliance with standards equivalent to those required by the Kyoto Protocol could help a firm improve its reputation and enhance its brand value, not to mention its shareholder value. It is even possible that, as the problem of global warming grows more severe and Kyoto-compliant countries strengthen their efforts to respond, citizens of Kyoto countries might boycott products from non-Kyoto or non-Annex B countries, as has already happened in the area of genetically modified organisms.[58] Investors, too, are finding green companies and products more attractive. Sustainability indexes and stock markets providing information on environmental internal policies and associated risks are now a reality, as discussed in Chapter 17.

IV. Transitional Issues

In this section we consider how the approach of the United States to regulating GHG emissions might change in the future, how different options available to U.S. policymakers could interact with the regulatory regimes of Kyoto Protocol parties, and the effects on U.S. businesses that might result. The types of options we consider for U.S regulation fall into three categories: domestic regulation at the state and regional levels, domestic regulation at the federal level, and regulation pursuant to international agreements. We should note that, while the Constitution prohibits states from entering into agreements with other countries,[59] certain elements of state systems could be linked to non-U.S. systems, for example, in the area of emissions trading.

At the federal level, each of the options we consider could be implemented independently by the United States, or it could be tied to systems in other countries through international agreements. In other words, any permutation of these two categories is possible. We analyze the effects on U.S. businesses of regulatory changes at the state, regional, federal and international levels utilizing the same set of issues as in part 5: direct impacts, including compliance with Annex B regulations, markets for green goods and services, and emissions trading; and indirect impacts, including regulatory uncertainty, political clout, and public attitudes.

A. State/Regional Regulations

As a threshold matter, it should be noted that principles of federalism do not permit state laws controlling GHG gas emissions to conflict with federal laws. They may, however, expand on federal laws—for example, by adding to the number of covered sectors—unless it is clear that Congress intended to preempt the entire field of GHG regulation.[60] Currently, federal law does not regulate GHG emissions, though, as noted above, the U.S. Administration has put in place voluntary programs. Thus, within some limits that are beyond the scope of this chapter, states presumably are free to regulate emissions as they see fit. Many approaches to GHG regulation have been considered at both the state and federal level, and several of these are discussed below in the section on federal regulation. In this section, we consider only one type of state regulation: mandatory emissions limits and trading (cap-and-trade) along the lines of the Northeast Regional Greenhouse Gas Initiative.[61] Chapter 10 of this book describes the kinds of actions that states have taken, and Chapter 11 provides a 50-state survey.

1. Compliance with Annex B Emissions Regulations

The adoption by a state or group of states of a mandatory cap-and-trade program could lessen the impact of Annex B emissions regulations on emissions-intensive U.S. products if Annex B countries decide to distinguish between products imported from states with cap-and-trade (or other equally effective) programs from products produced in states lacking such programs. The basis for the distinction would be the amount of GHGs presumed to have been emitted in manufacturing the product. Such a distinction poses a host of questions, however, that would make implementation difficult. Does the state program entail equally stringent reduction, compliance and enforcement measures? Can it be determined that the product in question is entirely from a regulated state, or does it include parts or labor from unregulated states? Does the WTO permit its members to distinguish between products from cap-and-trade states and "like" products from states that choose not to regulate GHG emissions? The difficulties countries would face in trying to answer these questions make it unlikely that products from states with cap-and-trade programs would receive more favorable treatment in Annex B countries than products from states that fail to regulate emissions.

> **Companies in states that adopt mandatory GHG cap-and-trade programs might benefit somewhat in marketing green goods and services in Kyoto countries as a result of experience gained in meeting their own state's requirements.**

2. Markets for Green Goods and Services

Companies in states that adopt mandatory GHG cap-and-trade programs might benefit somewhat in marketing green goods and services in Kyoto countries as a result of experience gained in meeting their own state's requirements. For example, new power plant designs developed to meet emissions reduction requirements in the electric power sector might be more marketable in Annex B countries or developing countries hosting CDM projects than older, conventional designs. On the other hand, this benefit would be available to any company, regardless of its location, that has redesigned its products to meet requirements in regulated states. It is unlikely that the importing country could confer some special benefit that would be unavailable to companies in states that fail to regulate emissions without running afoul of WTO rules.[62]

3. Emissions Trading and Other Market Mechanisms

Although states may not enter into agreements with foreign countries, it would be possible for a state to explicitly link certain aspects of its trading program to similar trading programs in other countries. For example, state regulations could recognize allowances or credits purchased from other countries, regardless of whether those countries are parties to the Kyoto Protocol. This likely would require those countries to have monitoring and compliance systems that are as stringent as state systems, but this should not be a problem for Annex B countries, since Kyoto monitoring and compliance systems are relatively stringent, and some parties, such as the EU, have even stricter requirements than those mandated by Kyoto.

In addition to having the ability to purchase allowances and credits from other countries, some companies will want to be able to resell those units. Sales to other U.S. companies should be straightforward and will be governed by state or federal law only. If the intent is eventually to use those units for purposes of compliance with the Protocol, however, the transaction may be more complicated.

The simplest way to purchase a unit out of another country's system would be to pay a company in that country, or the government itself, to cancel or retire a unit. This would also ensure that the unit is not counted twice, once in the purchasing state and again in the selling country. Once a specific Kyoto unit is cancelled or retired, however, it cannot be reactivated; that is, it can no longer be used for purposes of Kyoto compliance. Thus, a U.S. company using cancellation or retirement to purchase a Kyoto unit will not be able to resell that unit to any entity that intends to use it to meet its obligations under the Protocol.

A different approach that would permit such resale would be for the purchasing entity to establish an account in the national registry of a Kyoto party and have the purchased unit transferred into that account. Kyoto units retain their character as such (i.e., can be used for compliance with the Protocol) as long as they do not leave the Kyoto system. This means they must always be located in an account in the registry of a Kyoto party. Such accounts are discretionary; a party can withhold permission to establish an account within its registry. It is reasonable to suppose that parties will be more willing to accord this privilege to companies in states with mandatory emissions reduction programs. This may be especially important for carbon brokers, such as the Chicago Climate Exchange (CCX).[63]

As we have already noted, Kyoto parties probably will not purchase allowances or credits generated in the United States, as those units could not be used to meet Kyoto commitments. On the other hand, some countries might provide limited or full recognition of allowances or credits generated in states with mandatory reduction programs (for purposes of domestic compliance only) to induce U.S. states to begin to regulate their emissions. Several EU ETS participants have already expressed interest in such linkage with state or regional trading programs.[64] The Protocol would have to be amended, however, for these Annex B countries to use such allowances or credits to meet their Kyoto commitments.

B. Federal Regulations

In part 3 we analyzed some of the possible effects of the Kyoto Protocol on U.S. business if the United States remains opposed to mandatory federal controls on its greenhouse gas emissions. The effects of the Protocol on U.S. business could be quite different, however, if the United States were to adopt mandatory federal emissions regulations some time in the future, even if it remains outside the Protocol. There have been many different proposals for mandatory U.S. regulations. In this section we discuss several of these proposals—cap-and-trade with allowances allocated for free, cap-and-trade with auctioned allowances, and cap-and-trade with a "safety valve."[65] We also briefly consider a relatively new proposed approach called action targets.[66]

We focus on cap-and-trade because it is included to varying degrees in most of the proposals for federal regulation. It is also the approach taken by the Kyoto Protocol for regulating emissions from industrialized (Annex B) countries.[67] Although many Annex B countries are still formulating their programs to implement the Protocol, it appears likely that all will utilize some form of domestic trading. The most developed of these national programs, as well as the largest, is the EU ETS, which in many respects mirrors the Kyoto Protocol.

To put any of these approaches into action, many questions would have to be addressed: What sectors would it cover? Could other sectors opt-in? Would regulation occur upstream or downstream? Would all regulated sectors receive equal treatment or would some be regulated more stringently than others? Would all gases be included? How would removals of carbon from the atmosphere (e.g., through growing forests) be handled?, and many more. It is beyond the scope of this paper to consider all of these variations. Unless we specify otherwise, assume that all scenarios discussed below are economy-wide, all sectors are regulated equally, and all activities and gases are included.

It should also be pointed out that all these approaches have an important feature in common: they are all "market mechanisms," meaning they all utilize market principles to minimize the aggregate cost of reducing emissions. This is important, because the decision was made early in the negotiation of the UN Framework Convention on Climate Change that a market approach would be utilized to reduce compliance costs. Not only would a domestic market-based approach reduce compliance costs in the United States, but, to the extent the U.S. approach can be linked to the Kyoto Protocol, it can also save Kyoto parties money, while providing additional savings in the United States. Generally speaking, the more gases, sectors, geographic area, and regulated entities a market system covers, the more efficient and cost-effective it will be.

1. Cap-and-Trade with Allowances Allocated for Free

This approach has the most in common with the EU ETS, which requires Member States to freely allocate 90% of their allowances to regulated entities during the commitment period. It is also similar to the Protocol itself, in that the Protocol allocates assigned amounts to the parties at no cost. The most common method of allocation is "grandfathering," that is, allocating allowances on the basis of historical emissions. This is the approach currently taken by the Kyoto Protocol and the EU ETS, though for both systems proposals have been made to allocate allowances based on other considerations, such as "benchmark" performance standards at the national level and population at the international level.

a. Compliance with Annex B Emissions Regulations

Because free allocation of allowances is essentially the approach taken in the EU ETS and the Kyoto Protocol itself, effects on U.S. business likely would result more from domestic regulation than from Annex B rules aimed at leveling the playing field or coercing the United States to join the Protocol. Of course, the sectors covered, the stringency of the cuts, and other details of the U.S. regulatory program ultimately would determine the similarity and compatibility of the U.S. system with the EU ETS and other Annex B approaches. If the systems diverge significantly in these details, impacts on U.S. business from Annex B regulation could still be significant.

For example, U.S. products in sectors not subject to U.S. emissions controls might be taxed at the border when they are imported into Annex B countries. On the other hand, if the overall U.S system achieved a level of abatement that was in line with the efforts of Annex B parties, there would be little justification for targeting unregulated U.S. products in this manner. The EU might argue that it adjusts its border taxes to match the cost of allowances required to manufacture domestic "like products," but this argument would raise several problems. First, most of the allowances required by EU products in regulated sectors are allocated for free, so EU manufacturers are not required to pay the full costs of allowances. This fact could give rise to a WTO challenge based on the WTO requirement that taxes imposed at the border may not exceed the tax imposed on domestic like products.[68]

A second problem is that it would be unnecessarily provocative, from a trade standpoint. If the United States failed to regulate certain products that are regulated in some Annex B countries, it would have to regulate other products more stringently than similar products in those countries to achieve comparable levels of abatement. The United States likely would react by imposing similar trade measures on products produced in Annex B countries. In fact, it was decided early in the negotiation of the Framework Convention that each party could pick its own measures for implementing its emissions commitments. There would be little reason to violate that principle merely because the United States has decided to implement Kyoto-type emissions cuts without actually joining the Protocol.

b. Markets for Green Goods and Services

Were the United States to adopt emissions controls comparable in stringency to controls in Annex B countries, there is little reason to expect that green U.S. goods and services would receive differential treatment in Annex B countries. Of course, sectors that are not regulated in the United States may not stimulate the same level of innovation as would occur in comparable sectors in Annex B countries that choose to regulate them, but this would cut both ways, giving a potential advantage to U.S. products designed to meet the needs of sectors that are regulated in the United States but not in some other Annex B countries. Less direct effects, like consumer preference, likely would not be significant.

c. Emissions Trading and Other Market Mechanisms

With respect to emissions trading and other market mechanisms, the closer the U.S. approach is to approaches in Annex B countries, the more compatible the systems are likely to be, and the less reason for restricting trading between the systems. Nevertheless, Annex B countries would still be prohibited by the rules of the Protocol from utilizing U.S.-generated allowances or credits to meet their commitments under the Protocol. Changing this restriction would require an amendment of the Protocol, but accomplishing such an amendment may be relatively straightforward, especially if it is done in conjunction with negotiation and adoption of the second commitment period, which requires an amendment in any event.

Kyoto Parties may, on the other hand, be reluctant to adopt such an amendment for several reasons. First, they probably would insist that the U.S. reduction commitment equal their own in its level of stringency. Second, they would be concerned that the U.S. approach to monitoring, compliance and enforcement is as effective as their own. Third, a great deal of time and effort was spent devising the Kyoto system for registering and tracking trades, and presumably the United States would not be a part of that system. Fourth, and most important, they probably would be concerned about setting a precedent for the Kyoto Protocol by, in effect, allowing the United States to be a partial party to the Protocol, picking and choosing which elements of the Protocol it will comply with and which elements it rejects.

2. Cap-and-Trade with Allowances Auctioned

This approach differs from the one just discussed only in that allowances, rather than being allocated to emitters for free on the basis of historical emissions, technology benchmarks, or other criteria, would be auctioned periodically to the highest bidder. An advantage of this approach is that it allows new companies to enter into the market on equal footing with established companies. Allocations based on historical emissions are disadvantageous to new firms, as they have no historical emissions on which to base an allocation. On the other hand, allocations based on technology benchmarks could give new companies an advantage, as they would have the opportunity to utilize cleaner, more efficient technology from the start, whereas existing companies with older, less efficient technology would be forced to purchase additional allowances or invest in expensive retrofits.

Auctioning would also provide a revenue stream to the government that could be used to offset other types of taxes, such as taxes on income and capital formation. Many economists have observed that shifting the tax burden in this fashion would be good for the economy. Such a revenue stream could be used for many other purposes: to assist in the transition to a low-carbon or zero-carbon economy, for example, by retraining coal miners and by providing assistance to low-income families saddled with higher energy costs. Some have even proposed lump-sum annual transfer of auction proceeds to U.S. citizens.[69]

a. Compliance with Annex B Emissions Regulations

From the perspective of an Annex B country, whether the United States chooses to allocate or auction allowances probably would make little difference. Auctioning, however, could place U.S. companies at a competitive disadvantage, vis-à-vis companies in Annex B countries that choose to allocate. One of the stated reasons for allocating allowances in the EU ETS is to relieve companies of some or all of the costs of compliance.[70] Thus it seems unlikely that U.S. companies would agree to a cap-and-trade system in which most or all allowances are auctioned.

b. Markets for Green Goods and Services

It is unlikely that the decision to auction rather than allocate allowances would have any effect on marketing of green U.S. goods and services in Kyoto countries.

c. Emissions Trading and Other Market Mechanisms

Kyoto parties that allocate most of their allowances, such as the European Union and its members, should have little reason to care whether the United States disseminates allowances by means of auctions, allocations, or some combination of the two. If anything, they should prefer that the United States auction allowances, since that gives companies in countries that allocate an advantage over their U.S. competitors, as noted above. Thus, they may be more willing to allow full trading with U.S. companies.

3. Cap-and-Trade with a "Safety Valve"

As described above, a safety valve is a predetermined price at which the government will sell as many allowances as an emitter desires to buy. Thus the market price of allowances can never exceed the safety valve price. In fact, once the price of allowances reaches the safety valve level, the system effectively converts to a GHG tax, unless and until the price for allowances subsequently drops below the safety valve price.

a. Compliance with Annex B Emissions Regulations

Annex B countries' response to a U.S. cap-and-trade program, and their efforts to devise regulations that would have the effect of reducing U.S. emissions or at least leveling the playing field, probably would be determined, in large measure, by the price at which the safety valve was set. A high price might be viewed as little more than insurance for the United States that compliance costs would not be excessive, in which case, if the U.S. cap itself was sufficiently stringent, Annex B countries might respond much as they would to a conventional U.S. cap-and-trade program, that is, one that had no safety valve. But if the safety valve price were perceived as being too low, Annex B countries might view the U.S. effort as insufficient, and take the types of measures discussed in part 3 to induce stronger action by the United States.

> **... how much U.S. companies are able to benefit from emissions trading could be linked directly to the level at which the safety valve price is set.**

b. Markets for Green Goods and Services

The extent to which Annex B countries would treat green U.S. goods and services more favorably than in the scenario discussed in part 3 might depend on the safety valve price; a high price would provide less incentive for Annex B countries to attempt to restrict sales within their borders. A low price, on the other hand, would provide little incentive for Annex B countries to behave differently toward U.S. goods and services than they would in the no-regulation scenario discussed in part 3. A low safety valve price also would provide less motivation for development in the United States of emissions reduction strategies and technologies, leaving U.S. companies behind the curve compared to the Annex B competitors, as also discussed in part 3.

c. Emissions Trading and Other Market Mechanisms

Similar to the issues discussed above, how much U.S. companies are able to benefit from emissions trading could be linked directly to the level at which the safety valve price is set. Some commentators believe that the European Union will not engage in full-scale trading with the United States or seek the necessary rules changes in the Kyoto Protocol if the U.S. system includes a safety valve, out of concern that their own systems would be weakened if allowance prices hit safety valve levels. The fear would be that if Annex B companies could buy U.S. allowances for compliance purposes, then their own systems could be "infected" by the safety valve. If the price of allowances in their own markets rose above the safety valve price, their companies would simply turn to the United States as a limitless source of allowances at the safety valve price. On the other hand, if the safety valve price was set at a sufficiently high level, other Annex B countries may choose to disregard it or even adopt their own safety valve to afford their own companies the same financial protection as that given to their U.S. competitors.

4. Action Targets

Action targets are a new form of market mechanism. They are similar to the cap-and-trade mechanisms discussed above in that they allow trading, but differ in that they utilize emission reductions, or cuts, rather than caps. (For this reason, the designers of this system sometime refer to it as "cut-and-trade.")

The system works as follows: Rather than setting an emissions target, or cap, for a given period, a country adopting action targets would set a target for the number of reductions it will achieve during that period. While it is beyond the scope of this paper to discuss the pros and cons of action targets, its two major advantages, according to its designers, are that it would: (1) make the level of effort a country would have to exert to achieve its target more predictable,[71] and (2) have a smaller impact on consumer prices for a given level of reductions.[72]

a. Compliance with Annex B Emissions Regulations

Action targets are sufficiently different from cap-and-trade that it is difficult to assess how they would be treated by the EU and other Annex B parties that adopt cap-and-trade schemes. Action targets are designed to be compatible with cap-and-trade, and there is no inherent characteristic of action targets that would inhibit integration with other market mechanisms. The EU, however, has tended to be wary of reduction-based systems, such as the clean development mechanism, and may be reluctant to accept credits resulting from U.S. action targets. Furthermore, the use of such credits for Kyoto compliance would require amendment of the Protocol. On the other hand, the EU and other parties recognize the need to incorporate reduction-based credits into their domestic systems in order to gain the participation of developing countries, and such systems are already integrated into the Kyoto Protocol through Articles 6 and 12.

Given the importance of the United States to solving the problem of climate change, most Annex B countries likely would welcome a U.S. approach based on action targets if both the target and the system for counting and verifying reductions are sufficiently stringent. The ultimate measure of success of action targets or any other system will be emissions trends. If U.S. emission reductions meet expectations, there is little reason for other parties to throw up barriers, and if they did, international trade rules might be used to remove those barriers.

b. Market for Green Goods and Services

Like all market mechanisms, action targets are designed to provide regulatory incentives to companies to reduce their emissions. Under action targets, U.S. firms will have the same need for renewable energy and energy-efficient products as they would under cap-and-trade. In other words, if the scheme succeeds as its designers predict, action targets will push U.S. firms to be as competitive in the market for green goods and services as their Annex B counterparts.

c. Emissions Trading and Other Market Mechanisms

As noted above, some countries, notably those of the EU, have expressed reservations about utilizing reduction-based credits, but this reluctance is likely to melt away if such systems prove effective in bending emissions trajectories downward. Indeed, its designers believe action targets will remove some of the political barriers to adopting the steep reductions needed to solve the problem of climate change, so the scheme may, in the long run, prove to be more effective than cap-and-trade and other conventional schemes for reducing emissions. If this proves to be the case—and emissions inventories will tell the tale—action targets should integrate fully with cap-and-trade and other market mechanisms, as its designers intend.

V. Conclusion

Under international law, the Kyoto Protocol will not affect U.S. business directly, but rather through the implementing laws and regulations that parties to the Protocol adopt. Because most parties have not yet fully drafted these laws and regulations, any assessment of impacts of the Protocol on U.S. business is necessarily speculative. At present, the only national system that is sufficiently developed to provide a concrete basis for analysis is the EU ETS. The schemes being developed in Canada and Japan are still too much in flux to provide useful guidance.

While many businesses have taken actions that have had, or will have, the effect of lowering their GHG emissions, it is difficult to know what motivated those actions. Although many companies have claimed they acted in response to climate change, they may have taken the same or similar actions for other reasons, such as reducing fuel costs. It is even more difficult to predict what businesses will do in the future.

A third problem is that it is difficult to envision the Kyoto Protocol of the future. The Protocol is an experiment, and many doubts have been raised about its chances for success. Businesses in the United States and elsewhere will be reluctant to respond to the Kyoto regime, given the uncertainty of its future prospects. The abstention of the United States and the limited and unpredictable role of developing countries and countries with economies in transition contribute to this air of uncertainty, making predictions about business impacts little more than educated guesses.

Although the United States ultimately decided not to ratify the Protocol, much of its design reflects U.S. ideas and experience. Emissions trading, extended commitment periods, and the "basket of gases" approach were all U.S. ideas. Thinking in the United States about how best to regulate GHG emissions has evolved, however, and it may select a different path for the future. Other countries may choose to follow the U.S. lead.

Nevertheless, for the present the Kyoto Protocol is the sole international vehicle for building a mandatory regime for controlling GHGs, and U.S. businesses that ignore it do so at their peril. Any approach that might succeed Kyoto likely would be evolutionary rather than revolutionary, and undoubtedly would retain many of Kyoto's characteristics. In any event, U.S.-owned facilities located in Annex B countries will be required to comply with domestic regulations, whether or not they were adopted to implement Kyoto, and for a number of reasons may find compliance is made more difficult by the U.S. government's decision to remain outside the Protocol. In particular, they may not be able to take full advantage of the Protocol's trading rules, as reductions generated in the United States cannot be counted for purposes of Kyoto compliance. They may also find that their parent companies are "out of synch" with markets in Kyoto countries, making it increasingly more difficult for U.S. foreign subsidiaries to compete with their domestic counterparts, for example, in markets for green goods and services.

> **. . . for the present the Kyoto Protocol is the sole international vehicle for building a mandatory regime for controlling GHGs, and U.S. businesses that ignore it do so at their peril.**

Other problems may confront U.S. companies as the Kyoto regime develops and markets in Annex B countries and elsewhere evolve in response to the changing regulatory environment. U.S. companies are likely to find that their own decision-making will become increasingly more difficult if uncertainty about U.S. emissions controls continues. Their competitors, through their national legislatures, will shape the future regulatory environment in ways that they cannot. Perhaps the greatest risk to U.S. firms is that consumers in foreign countries, and possibly even in the United States, will turn away from companies that are perceived not to be good stewards of the climate.

Eventually, the United States must develop domestic emissions controls, and it will need to be mindful of the existing international regime, whether that regime is Kyoto or something new. The United States may have opportunities to improve upon current approaches, but whatever emerges must be compatible with Kyoto or its successor, as well as with the domestic regimes that implement the international one. Despite Kyoto's possible flaws, its underlying fundamental logic remains sound: climate change is a global problem, and solving it will require a market-based regime that is internationally coherent, if not uniform.

Endnotes

1.   *See* Kyoto Protocol to the United Nations Framework on Climate Change, Dec. 11, 1997, 37 I.L.M. 22 [hereinafter Kyoto Protocol].

2.   *See* Letter to Members of the Senate on the Kyoto Protocol on Climate Change, 1 PUB. PAPERS 235, 235 (Mar. 13, 2001).

3.   Although U.S. treaties are ratified by the President, ratification requires consent of two-thirds of the Senate. Practically speaking, it also requires acceptance by the House, which must consent to any implementing legislation.

4.   Beginning in the late 1990s, many businesses began to take action to reduce greenhouse-gas emissions. *See* John Carey, *Global Warming*, BUS. WK., Aug. 16, 2004, *available at* http://www.businessweek.com/magazine/content/04_33/b3896001_mz001.htm).

5.   In May 2006, several UN-sponsored conferences were held in Bonn, Germany, to discuss climate negotiations for the period following the end of the first commitment period of the Kyoto Protocol. For further news, articles and press releases, visit the United Nations Framework Convention on Climate Change's Web site, http://unfccc.int/press/items/2794.php (last visited Oct. 19, 2006). *See also* Chapter 2 of this book.

6.   *See, e.g.*, the Asia-Pacific Partnership on Clean Development and Climate, Inaugural Ministerial Meeting, January 2006, http://www.dfat.gov.au/environment/climate/ap6/ (last visited Oct. 19, 2006).

7.   For a comprehensive overview of potential implications of the Kyoto Protocol on U.S. businesses, *see* DANIEL BODANSKY, PEW CENTER ON GLOBAL CLIMATE CHANGE, IMPLICATIONS FOR U.S. COMPANIES OF KYOTO'S ENTRY INTO FORCE WITHOUT THE UNITED STATES 1-8 (2002).

8.   The Montreal Protocol was originally signed in 1987 and substantially amended in 1990 and 1992. Montreal Protocol on Substances that Deplete the Ozone Layer, Sept. 16, 1987, 26 I.L.M. 1541 (1987).

9.   The Kyoto Protocol regulates six gases listed in Annex A of the Kyoto Protocol and include: carbon dioxide (CO_2), methane (CH_4), nitrous oxide (N_2O), hydrofluorocarbons (HFCs), perfluorocarbons (PFCs), and sulphur hexafluoride (SF_6). At the urging of the United States, the Protocol permits each party to decide on the amount of each gas it will reduce. The Protocol targets determine the total amount of reduction of the six gases based on their "GHG potential," which involves a complex scientific determination of their potency and residency time in the atmosphere. *See supra* note 2, Annex A; *see also* Chapter 2 of this book.

10.   Letter, *supra* note 3, at 235.

11.   *See, e.g.*, *Climate Change Review from the President's Council on Environmental Quality*, http://www.whitehouse.gov/news/releases/2001/06/climatechange.pdf (last visited Oct. 19, 2006).

12.   *See, e.g.*, Climate Stewardship Act, S. 139, 108th Cong. (2003); Keep America Competitive Global Warming Policy Act, H.R. 5049, 109th Cong. (2006).

13.   *See, e.g.*, the U.S. Mayors Climate Protection Agreement, the Regional Greenhouse Gas Initiative (RGGI), the Western Governors' Association: Clean and Diversified Energy Initiative, the West Coast Governors' (WGA) Global Warming Initiative: Powering the Plains, the New England Governors: Climate Change Action Plan conducted in conjunction with the Eastern Canadian Premiers (NEG-ECP), and the South-

west Climate Change Initiative. *See infra*, Part 4, Section A.3, of this chapter and Chapter 9 for more discussion of regional initiatives.

14. *See, e.g.*, RANDY L. LOFTIS, AM. SOC'Y OF LANDSCAPE ARCHITECTS, TEXAS COOL TO CONFRONT GLOBAL WARMING (2006), http://www.texasasla.org/index.php?option=com_content&task=view&id=94&Itemid=113.

15. *See* Council Directive 2003/87, 2003 O.J. (L 275) 32 (EC) (establishing a scheme for emission allowance trading within the Community and amending the original Emissions Trading Directive, Council Directive 96/61, 1996 O.J. (L 257) 26 (EC); *see also* Council Directive 2004/101, 2004 O.J. (L 338) 18 (EC) (establishing a scheme for greenhouse gas emission allowance trading within the Community, in respect of the Kyoto Protocol's project mechanisms and amending Council Directive 2003/87, 2003 O.J. (L 275) 32 (EC). Other relevant instruments include Council Directive 2004/8, 2004 O.J. (L 52) 50 (EC), on the promotion of cogeneration based on a useful heat demand in the internal energy market and amending Council Directive 92/42, 1992 O.J. (L 167) 17 (EC).

16. Kyoto Protocol, *supra* note 2.

17. Under Article 24 of the Emissions Trading Directive, this is further dependent on the discretion of the individual Member States and on approval by the European Commission.

18. This includes combustion installations with a rated thermal input exceeding 20 MW, mineral oil refineries and coke ovens in accordance with the Emissions Trading Directive. *See also* Commission Communication on Further Guidance on Allocation Plans for the 2008 to 2012 Period of the European Union Emission Trading Scheme, at 20, COM (2005) 703 final (Dec. 22, 2005), *available at* http://europa.eu.int/comm/environment/climat/pdf/nap_2_ guidance_en.pdf. (defining "combustion installation" to include all combustion processes, *i.e.*, oxidation of fuels, and comprises a stationary technical unit that burns fuel for the production of an energy product, which could be electricity, heat or mechanical power).

19. Metal ore roasting or sintering installations and those for the production of pig iron or steel with a capacity exceeding 2.5 tons per hour. *Id.* at 36.

20. Of a certain capacity. *Id.* at 27.

21. *See* Emissions Trading Directive, Council Directive 96/61, 1996 O.J. (L 257) 26 (EC).

22. The effects of this method of allocation have been analyzed by different scholars in comparison to auctioning. For the discussion of advantages, disadvantages and pernicious effects, *see, e.g.*, Svante Mandell, *The Choice of Multiple or Single Auctions in Emissions Trading*, 5:1 CLIMATE POL'Y 97, 102 (2005); Boemare & Quirion, *Implementing Greenhouse Gas Trading in Europe: Lessons from Economic Literature and International Experiences*, 43 ECOLOGICAL ECONOMICS 213, 222 (2002); Bent Mortensen, *The EU Emissions Trading Directive*, EUR. ENVTL. L. REV. 275, 281 (2004).

23. *See* Emissions Trading Directive, *supra* note 21, at 37 (art. 16).

24. *See* Commission Communication on Winning the Battle Against Global Climate Change, at 8, 9, COM (2005) 35 final (Feb. 2, 2005), *available at* http://eur-lex.europa.eu/LexUriServ/site/en/com/2005/com2005_0035en01.pdf.

25. *See* Commission Communication on Reducing the Climate Change Impact of Aviation, at 4, COM (2005) 459 final (Sep. 27, 2005), *available at* http://europa.eu.int/eur-lex/lex/LexUriServ/site/en/com/2005/com2005_0459en01.pdf (defining plans to reduce the greenhouse gas emissions of the aviation sector). Additional initiatives for 2006 include the presentation of an Energy Efficiency Plan to assist in reducing energy dependency, promote growth and fight climate change, Commission Communication: Green Paper on Energy or Doing More with Less, at 17, COM (2005) 265 final (June 22, 2005), *available at* http://europa.eu.int//comm/energy/efficiency/doc/2005_06_green_paper_text_en.pdf; the publication of Communications on Clean Coal Technologies, to stimulate technological development, Commission Communication: 2005 Environmental Policy Review, COM (2006) 70 final (Feb. 16, 2006), *available at* http://eur-lex.europa.eu/LexUriServ/site/en/com/2006/com2006_0070en01.pdf, and a strategy proposing policies beyond 2010, Commission Communication: An EU Strategy for Biofuels, at 16, COM (2006) at 34 final (Feb. 2, 2006), *available at* http://eur-lex.europa.eu/LexUriServ/site/en/com/2006/com2006_0034en01.pdf. The Second Phase of the European Climate Change Program (ECCP) will start defining policy in the household, industrial, commercial and transport sectors as well as adaptation policies. Press Release, European Comm'n, Climate Change: Start of the Second European Climate Change Programme (Oct. 21, 2005), *available at* http://europa.eu/rapid/pressReleasesAction.do?reference=IP/05/155&format=HTML&aged=1&language=EN&guiLanguage=en.

26. The Plan provides for Government of Canada investments in the order of $10 billion between now and 2012 to fully realize the anticipated reductions of about 240 megatons of CO_2 equivalent. It also commits the Government of Canada to annual assessments of climate change initiatives and investments. First, there are investments to date that will address one-third of the total reduction (80 Mt). Second, the Plan defines a strategy for a further 100 Mt reduction. And finally, it outlines a number of current and potential actions that should enable Canada to address the remaining 60 Mt reduction.

27. Canadian Gov't, Project Green, Moving Forward on Climate Change. A Plan for Honoring Our Kyoto Commitment (2005), *available at* http://www. climatechange connection.org/pdfs_ccc/report_e.pdf.

28. An offset is a "credit" awarded for net GHG reductions or removals achieved by a registered offset project during 2008-2012, as verified through the offset review process.

29. *See* Canada-U.S. Trade Relationship, http://www.buyusa.gov/canada/en/traderelationsusacanada.html (last visited Oct. 20, 2006).

30. Canadian Gov't, *supra* note 27.

31. *See* Tomonori Sudo, Inst. for Global Envt'l Strategies, Japanese Voluntary Emissions Trading Scheme (VETS): Overview and Analysis 5 (2006), *available at* http://www.epa.gov/ies/documents/Workshops/Sudo.pdf. The participants were chosen among applicants who responded to an open invitation by the Japanese government and were screened based on their cost-effectiveness for the program.

32. The government's budget for the subsidy is 2,596,340,000 yen or about $23.6 million. *Id.* at 11.

33. The total of emissions promised by the schemes' participants for the fiscal year of 2006 is 276,380 tons, which represents 21% of their average annual CO_2 emissions in the base years 2002-2004. *Id.*

34. *Id.* at 12.

35. *Id.* at 2-3.

36. The analysis of EU law is necessarily incomplete. As previously mentioned, the Directive establishing the EU ETS provides only for general principles and obliga-

tions, its implementation being dependent on Member States' actions. Hence, our analysis is necessarily general because it cannot describe the 25 Member States' legislation, especially taking into consideration that the measures adopted have in many cases not been fully harmonized. Therefore, in fact, the effects on U.S. industry will depend not only on the design of the second phase of the scheme, which is claimed and hoped to be more harmonized, but also on the legislation put in force by each Member State.

37. Letter, *supra* note 2, at 235.

38. *See* General Agreement on Tariffs and Trade, Art. III, *available at* http://www.wto.org/english/docs_e/legal_e/gatt47_01_e.htm.

39. *See, e.g., Terminating Greenhouse Gases,* THE ECONOMIST, Oct. 19, 2006; *Slow collapse seen for EU allowance prices,* CARBON FINANCE, May 2006.

40. *See* Commission Communication on Reducing the Climate Change Impact of Aviation, at 4, COM (2005) 459 final (Sept. 27, 2005), *available at* http://europa.eu.int/eur-lex/lex/LexUriServ/site/en/com/2005/com2005_0459en01.pdf.

41. *Id.*

42. Kyle W. Danish, *The Effect of the Kyoto Protocol on U.S. Companies,* 36:4 TRENDS (2005), *available at* http://www.vnf.com/content/articles/trends0405.pdf.

43. Kyoto Protocol, *supra* note 2, art. 6.

44. *Id.* at art. 12.

45. *Id.* at art. 12, ¶ 5(a).

46. *Id.*

47. *Id. at* art. 7.4.

48. *See* FCCC/CP/2001/13/Add.2, Decision 19/CP.7, Annex II.A., ¶ 21(b).

49. While, at first glance, allocating allowances for free may appear to do no more than help offset compliance costs, economists have shown that such "grandfathering" can result in a windfall to firms receiving free allowances.

50. Government Procurement Agreement art. V, Apr. 15, 1994. Unlike most WTO agreements, the Agreement on Government Procurement does not require every WTO member to participate, and only a handful of developing countries do so at the moment. Furthermore, it only applies to goods and services that a Member Country chooses to "list" when it joins the agreement.

51. Decision 11/CMP.1, U.N. Doc. FCCC/KP/CMP/2005/8/Add.2 (March 30, 2005).

52. At this stage, it is not even clear where such conflicts might be adjudicated. Questions pertaining to conflicts that may arise between the Kyoto Protocol and other treaties, and how those conflicts could be resolved, are addressed elsewhere in this book.

53. Kyoto Protocol, *supra* note 2, art. 12.

54. Dec. 3/CMP.1, Appendix D, U.N. Doc. FCCC/KP/CMP/2005/8/Add.1 (March 30, 2005).

55. Danish, *supra* note 42.

56. According to Robert W. Fri, *Resources for the Future, Business Planning in a Post-Kyoto World: For U.S. Firms, Which End Is Up?,* 159 RESOURCES 16, 16 (2005), *available at* http://www.rff.org/rff/News/Features/loader.cfm?url=/commonspot/security/

getfile. cfm&PageID=18458, different designs of a control strategy make a huge difference in future costs—by a factor of five or more.

57. According to Stuart Eizenstat and Rubén Kraiem, *In Green Company*, FOREIGN POLICY, September/October 2005, U.S. corporations have nearly USD $1 trillion in direct investments in the EU and the U.S. industrial presence in Canada is estimated at USD $200 billion. Moreover, Canada is still the largest single U.S. trading partner.

58. This has important trade implications. On this see the pending *EC—Measures Affecting the Approval and Marketing of Biotech Products* Case, WT/DS291/INTERIM, WT/DS292/INTERIM and WT/DS293/INTERIM. For a good summary on the controversy and consumer issues surrounding the facts of this case, see Nicholas Perdikis, *EU-US Trade in Genetically Modified Goods: a Trade Dispute in the Making*, in THE WTO AND THE REGULATION OF INTERNATIONAL TRADE—RECENT TRADE DISPUTES BETWEEN THE EUROPEAN UNION AND THE UNITED STATES 215 (Nicholas Perdikis & Robert Read eds. 2005), and Mark Pollack & Gregory Schaffer, *The Challenge of Reconciling Regulatory Differences: Food Safety and GMOs in the Transatlantic Relationship*, in TRANSATLANTIC GOVERNANCE IN THE GLOBAL ECONOMY 153 (Mark Pollack & Gregory Schaffer eds., 2001). For a comprehensive work on the differences between EU and U.S. environmental policies, *see* GREEN GIANTS? ENVIRONMENTAL POLICIES IN THE US AND THE EU (Norman J. Vig & Michael G. Faure eds., 2004).

59. *See* U.S. CONST. art. I, § 10 ("No state shall enter into any treaty, alliance, or confederation . . . .").

60. *See, e.g.*, Barnett Bank of Marion County, N.A. v. Nelson, 517 U.S. 25, 30 (1994) (in determining whether a federal statute preempts a state statute, the critical question to be asked is whether Congress intended such preemption); *see also* U.S. CONST. art. VI, cl. 2.

61. *See* Regional Greenhouse Gas Initiative (RGGI), discussed in chs. 9, 18 *infra*.

62. This may fall under the GATT principle of most favored nation, which prevents WTO Members from distinguishing between products based solely on their place of origin, unless there is a sufficient justification to trigger the environmental exceptions contained in Art. XX.

63. *See* http://www.chicagoclimatex.com/ (last visited Oct. 25, 2006). The CCX is North America's only GHG emissions registry, reduction and trading system for all six GHGs identified in the Kyoto Protocol.

64. *See* VIVIAN E. THOMSON, EARLY OBSERVATIONS ON THE EUROPEAN UNION'S GREENHOUSE GAS EMISSION TRADING SCHEME: INSIGHTS FOR UNITED STATES POLICYMAKERS 18 (2006), *available at* http://www.earthscape.org/r1/ES17152/PCGCC_European_ Trading_0406.pdf.

65. A safety valve is a predetermined price beyond which abatement costs would not be permitted to rise. To prevent the cost of allowances from exceeding that level, the government would make additional allowances available to regulated entities at a predetermined price, in effect converting the program from a cap-and-trade approach to a carbon tax.

66. Kevin A. Baumert & Donald M. Goldberg, *Action Targets: A New Approach to International Greenhouse Gas Controls*, 5 CLIMATE POL'Y 567, 567-580 (2006).

67. Developing countries may utilize a voluntary, credit-based system called the clean development mechanism (CDM) to reduce their emissions quantitatively under Kyoto Protocol. The CDM is similar, in many respects, to action targets.

68. General Agreement on Tariffs and Trade, art. III, ¶ 1, Oct. 30, 1947.

69. *See, e.g.*, PETER BARNES, WHO OWNS THE SKY?: OUR COMMON ASSETS AND THE FUTURE OF CAPITALISM (2001).

70. *See* THOMSON, *supra* note 64, at 18.

71. *See* Baumert, *supra* note 66, 567-80.

72. Donald M. Goldberg, Danielle Rosengarten & Taylor Ferrell, *Cut and Trade: A Better Model for Addressing Climate Change* (2006) (on file with author).

chapter five

Clean Air Regulation

Jonathan S. Martel and Kerri L. Stelcen

I. Introduction and Overview

In the absence of statutory or regulatory action, proponents of regulations directed toward global climate change have both sought to force action at the federal level and pursued independent state action. This has involved efforts to force federal action to address emissions of greenhouse gases as pollutants under the Clean Air Act and to tighten fuel economy requirements (which effectively reduces carbon dioxide emissions) for passenger cars under the Energy Policy and Conservation Act. This chapter discusses those efforts.

A. The Clean Air Act

The applicability of the Clean Air Act (CAA) to greenhouse gas emissions has been a focus of debate and litigation, as proponents of greenhouse gas regulation have sought to force federal action through these provisions. At the same time, Clean Air Act provisions preempting state regulation of emissions from motor vehicles have been at issue in litigation seeking to block state regulation of greenhouse gases from such vehicles. Most of these provisions were implemented as part of the 1970 and 1977 amendments to the CAA, when climate change was not an issue specifically contemplated by Congress in its deliberations over this statute. Although the 1990 amendments included provisions aimed at gathering information about greenhouse gases (GHGs), these were accompanied by express provisos that the GHG provisions were not to be interpreted as conferring regulatory authority. Congress has not otherwise modified these general provisions.

Section II begins with a discussion of the structure and history of the CAA. Following this overarching review, Section II addresses the CAA provisions that have been the subject of federal and state action. From these discussions, two primary issues arise:

1. *EPA Authority.* What authority does the CAA confer to regulate climate change, should the EPA wish to exercise it? If the EPA indeed possesses such authority, does it have a mandatory duty under the CAA to act?
2. *Preemption.* Does the CAA preempt state authority to regulate motor vehicle emissions of GHGs?

B. The 1975 Energy Policy and Conservation Act

The motor vehicle fuel economy laws contained in the Energy Policy and Conservation Act (EPCA) do, in effect, regulate GHG emissions from motor vehicles, since carbon dioxide is a direct surrogate for fuel economy; indeed, carbon dioxide emissions are the basis by which EPA measures fuel economy under the EPCA.

Section III describes the structure of the corporate average fuel economy (CAFE) program under the EPCA, as well as how this program is implemented by the National Highway Traffic and Safety Administration (NHTSA) and EPA. As this discussion demonstrates, two primary issues arise under the program:

1. *Stringency.* Should the stringency of the CAFE requirements be increased to force greater fuel efficiency?
2. *Preemption.* To what extent does the CAFE law preempt state regulation of GHGs from motor vehicles?

II. The Clean Air Act

A. Statutory History and Structure

1. The Clean Air Act—pre-1970

The Clean Air Act of 1970 is often viewed as the start of federal air pollution control in the United States. In fact, air pollution received its first formal identification as a national problem in the Air Pollution Control Act of 1955 (APCA), which mandated federal research programs to investigate the health and welfare effects of air pollution.[1] Eight years later, the APCA was replaced by the Clean Air Act of 1963 (1963 CAA), which focused on improving air pollution conditions at the state and local levels by granting $95 million over a three-year period to state and local governments and air pollution agencies to conduct research and create control programs.[2] The 1963 CAA also recognized the dangers of motor vehicle exhaust and stationary source emissions and encouraged the development of emissions standards.[3] Motor

vehicle emissions standards were eventually established by a 1965 amendment to the 1963 CAA;[4] a 1966 amendment further expanded state and local programs.[5] The 1967 Air Quality Act established air quality control regions as a means of monitoring ambient air; it also established both national emissions standards for stationary sources and a fixed timetable for state implementation plans (SIPs).[6] A 1969 amendment extended authorization for research on low-emissions fuels and automobiles.[7]

2. 1970 Amendments

The 1963 CAA was entirely rewritten in 1970 (1970 CAA).[8] The 1970 CAA treated air pollution as a matter of primarily state responsibility, adopting a cooperative federalism approach to address the perceived failures of prior guidance to the states. The focus was on pollutants identified as having direct human health effects that were a local or regional problem for which the states would continue to have primary responsibility to address. EPA's role was to establish national standards and guidelines and step in where states failed to act. Section 109 of the 1970 CAA required the EPA to publish national ambient air quality standards (NAAQS) for pollutants including carbon monoxide, nitrogen oxides, sulfur oxides, photochemical oxidants, hydrocarbons, and particulate matter.[9] Emphasizing the local nature of the air pollution of concern, areas within each state were to be classified as either in "attainment" or "nonattainment" of these standards, based on readings from a

monitoring network. The NAAQS were then to be provided to the states, along with specific deadlines for the states to develop SIPs that met these standards.[10] To develop SIPs, the states had to create an inventory of emissions contributing to local exceedance of the NAAQS and then develop regulatory measures that, when combined with EPA's nationally applicable standards, would reduce that inventory sufficiently to ensure compliance with the NAAQS. EPA's national emissions standards under the 1970 CAA included new source performance standards (NSPS) that strictly regulated the emissions of a new source entering an area,[11] a provision to establish such standards for hazardous air pollutants,[12] and nationally uniform emissions standards applicable to motor vehicles.[13] In addition to these general provisions, the 1970 CAA featured a general mandate to "protect and enhance" air quality,[14] and the Court of Appeals for the D.C. Circuit interpreted that mandate to require a program to prevent significant deterioration of air quality in areas attaining the NAAQS.[15]

3. 1977 Amendments

The 1970 CAA was amended in 1977.[16] In general, the 1977 amendments established a more prescriptive cooperative federalism program for clean air regulation, effectively elaborating and refining the primary programs from the 1970 law that focused on local air quality. The amendments required the EPA to conduct both a national review of overall air quality every five years[17] and extended the deadline for states that had not yet complied with the NAAQS and motor vehicle emissions requirements of the 1970 CAA.[18] Additionally, the 1977 amendments codified a prevention of significant deterioration (PSD) program for areas that had attained NAAQS to insure that air quality did not degrade in those areas.[19] The newly codified PSD program required classification of attainment areas to govern the extent of degradation that would be allowed, reserving pristine parks and wilderness areas as "class I" for which very stringent local standards apply.[20] These amendments also established new source review (NSR), a pre-construction permitting program that served to (1) ensure that air quality is not "significantly degraded from the addition of new and modified factories, industrial boilers, and power plants";[21] and (2) "assure" citizens that any new or modified industrial source in their area will be "as clean as possible" and that advancements in "pollution control occur concurrently with industrial expansion."[22]

4. 1990 Amendments

Following more than a decade of near inactivity on the matter, Congress in 1990 passed major amendments to the CAA.[23] Again, the 1990 Amendments added substantial refinements to the pre-existing law, adding more specific requirements for SIPs aimed at bringing local areas into attainment of the NAAQS and adopting a new Title V operating permit program; new requirements for fuels, motor vehicles and nonroad engines; and a technology-based program to address hazardous air pollutants. While the 1990 amendments did not include any significant changes to the general definition of "air pollutant," nor to NSPS, PSD, NSR and motor vehicle emissions control authority,[24] several provisions indicate that climate change and global environmental changes had entered Congress's radar screen.

a. *Title VI*

Congress added Title VI[25] to the CAA as a means of implementing the United States' international treaty obligations under the Montreal Protocol, which addressed protection of stratospheric ozone.[26] Consistent with the Montreal Protocol, the new program divided ozone-depleting substances into two classes; EPA was required to phase out each substance according to the timetable for its class. Title VI also recognized these stratospheric ozone-depleting substances as GHGs.[27] Title VI required EPA to list all regulated substances, along with their ozone depletion potential, atmospheric lifetimes and global-warming potentials.[28] However, this provision explicitly states that it "shall not be construed to be the basis of any additional regulation under [the CAA]."[29]

Finally, Title VI established the Significant New Alternatives Policy (SNAP) program, which authorizes EPA to develop a program for evaluating alternatives to ozone-depleting substances.[30]

i. SNAP

Pursuant to its authority under the SNAP program, EPA recently proposed designating two substances—carbon dioxide and hydrofluorocarbon—as acceptable substitutes for ozone-depleting substances to be used as refrigerants in new motor vehicle air conditioners.[31] The draft rule, issued on September 21, 2006, conditions the use of these substances on the employment of "engineering devices or mitigation strategies . . . so that in the event of a leak, the resulting concentrations of refrigerant in the free space and vehicle occupant breathing zone within the interior car compartment are maintained at safe levels."[32]

EPA's proposal appears to be designed to encourage the use of "more benign alternatives to the current refrigerant."[33] EPA noted that its determination was made after "assess[ing] the impact of [carbon dioxide and hydrofluorocarbon] on human health and the environment," although "the global warming potential of [carbon dioxide and hydrofluorocarbon] was not a determinative factor" in the analysis.[34] EPA nonetheless stated that the global-warming potential for carbon dioxide and hydrofluorocarbon is "well below that of previously accepted substitutes in this sector."[35]

b. Collection of GHG Information

Section 821 of the 1990 amendments—*Information Gathering on Greenhouse Gases Contributing to Global Climate Change*—also touched on matters related to climate change, requiring measurement of carbon dioxide emissions for utilities subject to permitting under Title V.[36] These measurements were required to be reported directly to EPA, whereupon they would be made available to the public.[37] Section 821 was not codified, however.

B. Are GHGs "Air Pollutants"?

A seminal debate is ongoing as to whether GHGs are air pollutants within the meaning of the CAA and, thus, within the regulatory jurisdiction of the EPA.

1. Cannon Memorandum

In a 1998 memorandum to then-EPA Administrator Carol Browner during the first Clinton Administration, then-EPA General Counsel Jonathan Cannon asserted that

GHGs[38] were air pollutants.[39] Cannon based this assertion on the language of section 302(g) of the CAA, which defines "air pollutant" as "any physical, chemical, biological, or radioactive substance or matter that is emitted into or otherwise enters the ambient air."[40] Cannon wrote that since sulfur dioxide, nitrogen oxide, carbon dioxide and mercury from "electric power generation are each a 'physical [and] chemical . . . substance which is emitted into . . . the ambient air,' . . . each is an air pollutant within the meaning of the [CAA]."[41] Cannon wrote that since the EPA's regulatory authority extended to air pollutants, it extended to these GHGs.[42] Cannon, however, distinguished this general statement of authority from an "EPA determination that a particular air pollutant meets the specific criteria for EPA action under a particular provision of the [CAA]."[43] He noted that several CAA provisions potentially applicable to the GHGs in question required a "determination by the Administrator regarding the air pollutants' actual or potential harmful effects on public health, welfare or environment."[44] Cannon noted that EPA already regulated sulfur dioxide, nitrogen oxide and mercury based on determinations by Congress that those substances had a negative effect on public health.[45] However, no such determination had been made with respect to carbon dioxide emissions.[46] Thus, according to Cannon, even though carbon dioxide emissions were within the scope of EPA's authority to regulate, EPA had made no determination to exercise that authority under specific criteria provided under any provision of the CAA.[47]

2. Guzy Statements

Gary Guzy succeeded Cannon as General Counsel in November 1998.[48] In congressional testimony, Guzy agreed with Cannon's conclusion that carbon dioxide fell within the CAA definition of "air pollutant," despite the fact that carbon dioxide has both natural and man-made sources.[49] Guzy also shared Cannon's opinion that carbon dioxide may be regulated under the CAA to the extent that the criteria of any of the CAA's specific regulatory provisions are met.[50] Guzy asserted that there was no "statutory ambiguity" as to this question, given that the CAA clearly defines air pollutant and provides EPA with the authority to regulate air pollutants.[51] Guzy also reiterated Cannon's point that EPA had not yet determined that carbon dioxide met the criteria for regulation under a specific provision of the CAA.[52] Guzy testified that Cannon's opinion—which Guzy "endorse[d]"—"simply clarifie[d] . . . that [carbon dioxide] is in the class of compounds that could be subject to several of the [CAA's] regulatory approaches."[53] Thus, Guzy submitted that "many of the concerns raised about the statutory authority to address [carbon dioxide] relate more to factual and scientific, rather than legal, questions regarding whether and how the criteria for regulation under the [CAA] could be satisfied."[54]

3. Fabricant Memorandum

Following the election of President George W. Bush, Robert Fabricant succeeded Guzy as General Counsel of EPA in 2001.[55] In a 2003 memorandum, Fabricant withdrew

Cannon's 1998 memorandum as "no longer representing the views of the EPA's General Counsel," concluding that the CAA did not authorize EPA to regulate to address global climate change, thereby precluding GHGs from being considered "air pollutants subject to the CAA's regulatory provisions for any contribution they may make to global climate change."[56] Fabricant criticized the Cannon Memorandum's interpretation of the term "air pollutant" as overbroad, arguing that under Cannon's definition, "virtually anything entering the ambient air [is a pollutant] regardless of whether it pollutes the air."[57] Fabricant reached this conclusion after considering the history, text and structure of the CAA in the context of other congressional actions addressing global climate change and in light of Supreme Court precedent.

a. *Brown & Williamson*

Fabricant argued that the change in EPA's position was supported by the Supreme Court's decision in *FDA v. Brown & Williamson Tobacco Corp.*[58] In *Brown & Williamson*, the Court invalidated the FDA's assertion of authority to regulate tobacco products under the Food, Drug and Cosmetic Act (FDCA).[59] The Court acknowledged that the FDCA contained broad language granting the FDA authority to regulate drugs and devices, but found that in certain "extraordinary" cases, "there may be reason to hesitate" before concluding that an agency has an "implicit delegation from Congress to fill in the statutory gaps."[60] In such situations, the Court explained, it examines the agency's authority in light of the language, structure and history of the statute to determine whether the specific regulation is authorized.[61] Fabricant argued that the FDA's assertion of the right to regulate tobacco under the FDCA was analogous to the EPA's assertion of the right to regulate GHGs and that a *Brown & Williamson* analysis of the CAA's language, structure and history demonstrate that the CAA does not authorize regulation to address climate change.[62]

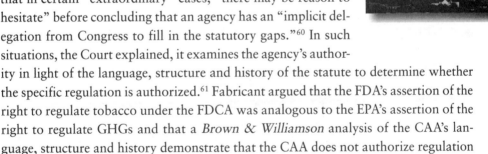

b. *Legislative History*

Fabricant also wrote that whether binding emission limitations on GHGs should be set forth in the CAA was debated by Congress during the development of the 1990 Amendments.[63] In fact, Fabricant wrote, "a Senate committee included in its bill to amend the CAA a provision requiring EPA to set [carbon dioxide] emission standards for motor vehicles," but the provision was removed from the bill before the full Senate voted.[64] Additionally, Fabricant discussed "other congressional actions" in which Congress spoke directly on the issue of climate change—for example, the Global Climate Protection Act of 1987, in which Congress "directed the Secretary of State to coordinate U.S. negotiations concerning climate change" and the EPA to "develop and propose to Congress a coordinated national policy on the issue."[65] Fabricant argued that actions such as these demonstrate that Congress meant to "develop a foundation for considering whether future legislative action was warranted and, if so, what that action should be," rather than to authorize a federal agency to take any regulatory action.[66]

c. Text

Fabricant wrote that, while three provisions[67] of the CAA discuss matters related to global climate change, none of these actually authorizes regulation; in fact, two of them "expressly preclude their use for authorizing regulation."[68] According to Fabricant, only the research and development provision of the CAA, section 103(g), specifically mentioned carbon dioxide emissions, and the "legislative history of that section indicates that Congress was focused on seeking a sound scientific basis on which to make future decisions on global climate change," rather than on regulating under the CAA.[69] Moreover, Fabricant pointed out that section 103(g) was eventually revised in conference to include the term "nonregulatory" to describe the "'strategies and technologies' the subsection was intended to promote."[70]

Finally, Fabricant noted that Congress included in the CAA provisions addressing stratospheric ozone depletion; these provisions contained "express authorization for the EPA to regulate" a global atmospheric issue.[71] This, Fabricant argued, demonstrated that where Congress wishes to grant regulatory authority on atmospheric issues, it does so not under the CAA's general regulatory provisions, but via specific provisions that expressly grant regulatory authority. Fabricant concluded that Congress's decision not to include such express authorization with respect to GHG emissions indicates that EPA may not regulate them.

d. Structure

Fabricant discussed whether the NAAQS system, a "key" structural component of the CAA,[72] could effectively address global climate change. He wrote that "unique and basic aspects of the presence of key GHGs in the atmosphere [made] the NAAQS system fundamentally ill-suited to address[] global climate change."[73] Fabricant wrote that GHGs, particularly carbon dioxide, generally stay in the earth's atmosphere for extended periods of time, resulting in a "vast global atmospheric pool that is fairly consistent in concentration everywhere" along the earth's surface.[74] Given this even dispersal of carbon dioxide, Fabricant wrote, states would have little control over their respective atmospheric carbon dioxide conditions and, thus, over whether they meet the NAAQS for carbon dioxide.[75] The NAAQS structure, argued Fabricant, is therefore "fundamentally inadequate" for addressing carbon dioxide.[76] Because implementation of NAAQS is a "basic underlying premise of the CAA regime," Fabricant concluded that no general CAA provision could authorize it to regulate GHGs.[77]

4. EPA Advisory Panel

Notwithstanding the position taken in the Fabricant Memorandum, an EPA advisory panel recently asked the agency to consider the issue of climate change with respect to its impact on other air quality problems. In a May 2006 meeting, the air quality management subcommittee of the Clean Air Act Advisory Committee finalized recommendations that the EPA evaluate the impact of climate change on air quality, including studying how global warming could worsen air pollution problems such as ozone.[78] The subcommittee, which is comprised of representatives from the EPA, state and local agencies, tribes, industry, and environmental and research organizations,[79] made several specific recommendations:

1. EPA should "assist states and localities in quantifying the potential for [GHG] co-benefits and disbenefits of emissions reduction measures primarily designed to address ozone, PM2.5, regional haze and air toxics."[80]

2. EPA should "undertake a comprehensive assessment of the implications climate change will have on future air quality objectives. The assessment should include estimation of the potential increases in the average and high temperatures during ozone season and the impacts of such increases on ozone formation. The assessment should estimate the air quality impact of secondary effects of temperature increases, such as wildfires, heat island effect, increased electric use, decreased hydroelectric generation and others. The assessment should include an estimation of any additional costs associated with potential mitigation or transition measures."[81]

3. EPA should "renew its efforts to assist states in the development of annual [GHG] emission inventories. . . . EPA should also provide additional technical assistance to [s]tates so they may effectively evaluate [GHG reduction strategies in conjunction with the development of their air quality management plans."[82]

The subcommittee's recommendations must be approved by the full Clean Air Act Advisory Committee before they can be submitted to the EPA.[83] However, that these steps were proposed at all is significant. The auto industry apparently objected to the subcommittee's recommendations.[84]

C. Regulation of Motor Vehicle GHGs Under Section 202

1. October 1999 Petition

On October 20, 1999, the International Center for Technology Assessment (ICTA), in conjunction with several other organizations, petitioned EPA to regulate certain GHG emissions from new motor vehicles pursuant to the EPA's "mandatory authority" under section 202(a)(1) of the CAA.[85, 86] The Clinton Administration did not rule on the matter; after a 2001 comment period, the Bush Administration denied the ICTA's petition on September 8, 2003.[87] In its notice of denial, issued in conjunction with the Fabricant Memorandum, the EPA concluded that it "[could] not and [should] not regulate GHG emissions from U.S. motor vehicles under the CAA" based on several factors:[88]

1. The EPA found that it lacked authority to so regulate under the CAA.[89] This portion of the notice of denial essentially reiterates the analysis presented by Fabricant in his memorandum, quoting Fabricant at length.[90]

2. The EPA noted that even if GHGs were air pollutants subject to regulation under the CAA, such regulation would inevitably interfere with fuel economy standards implemented by the Department of Transportation (DOT).[91] EPA explained that the only presently available method of reducing motor vehicle emissions was to improve fuel economy, and Congress had already "created a detailed set of mandatory emissions standards" governing that matter in the form of the Energy Policy and Conservation Act (EPCA). Thus, Congress intended fuel economy to be governed by the DOT alone, and "any EPA effort to set [emissions] standards under the CAA would either abrogate EPCA's regime (if the standards were effectively more stringent than the applicable [DOT] standard) or be meaningless (if they were effectively less stringent)."[92]

3. EPA determined that, even if it found that the CAA did confer authority upon the Administrator to regulate motor vehicle emissions, section 202(a) did not impose a "mandatory duty" on the Administrator to "exercise her judgment" on the issue.[93] Rather, according to the Agency, section 202(a)(1) provided the Administrator with "*discretionary* authority to address emissions."[94] "While section 202(a)(1) uses the word 'shall,' it does not *require* the Administrator to act . . . and it conditions authority to act on a discretionary exercise of the Administrator's judgment regarding whether . . . emissions cause or contribute to air pollution . . . ."[95]

4. The EPA wrote that, "[b]eyond issues of authority and interference with fuel economy standards," it disagreed with the ICTA's suggested approach for addressing global climate change.[96] EPA wrote that no "causal linkage" between GHGs in the atmosphere and climate change could be "unequivocally established."[97] EPA indicated that it would adhere to President Bush's policy for addressing global climate change, which emphasized research and "international cooperation."[98]

2. ICTA Challenge to Denial

In 2005, the ICTA and the other petitioners challenged the EPA's denial in the Court of Appeals for the D.C. Circuit.[99] In *Massachusetts v. EPA*, the court held that EPA's denial of the petition was proper.[100] Writing for the majority, Judge Randolph first addressed EPA's contention that the petitioners lacked standing under Article III to challenge the denial because they failed to adequately demonstrate that (1) their injuries were caused by EPA's denial and (2) their injuries could be redressed by a decision by the court in their favor.[101] The court concluded that the standing issues in the case were intertwined with the merits and that the case law[102] provided several options for addressing this overlap, the best of which was simply to proceed to the merits of EPA's decision, where the issue of standing would necessarily be addressed.[103]

The court of appeals then "assume[d] *arguendo* that EPA [had] statutory authority to regulate [GHGs] from new motor vehicles" and considered only whether the EPA "properly declined to exercise that authority."[104] The court found instructive with respect to EPA authority under section 202 the court's 1976 decision in *Ethyl Corp. v. EPA*,[105] in which the court held that the EPA Administrator has "considerable discretion" to make a judgment about whether to regulate, and his decision whether or not to do so may be based on scientific evidence as well as policy judgments.[106] The court concluded that EPA's analysis, as articulated in the notice of denial, was "entirely consistent with" *Ethyl Corp.* and, therefore, EPA's denial was proper.[107] The court

did not, however, reach the issue of whether GHGs qualify as "air pollutants" under the CAA.

Judge Sentelle concurred in the judgment but dissented in part. He found that EPA correctly asserted that the petitioners lacked standing because they alleged only a "generalized public harm"[108] posed by EPA's denial rather than a "distinct risk to a particularized interest"[109] of the petitioners.

Judge Tatel dissented, having found that at least one of the petitioners—the Commonwealth of Massachusetts—satisfied the standing requirement, and that to reach the merits, the court need only determine that one petitioner had standing.[110] Tatel concluded that the CAA "plainly cover[ed] GHGs emitted from motor vehicles"[111] and that the EPA in its denial "failed to provide a statutorily-based justification for refusing to make an endangerment finding."[112] For example, Judge Tatel characterized the NAAQS "unworkability argument" as "unwieldy." [113, 114] He wrote that "[e]ven assuming that the states' limited ability to meet [carbon dioxide] NAAQS render[ed] these provision unworkable as to carbon dioxide, . . . the absurd-results canon would justify at most an exception limited to the particular unworkable provision, i.e., the NAAQS provision."[115] This rule "allows an agency to establish that seemingly clear statutory language does not reflect the unambiguously expressed intent of Congress."[116] Judge Tatel further noted that EPA acknowledged in its denial of the ICTA petition that the regulation of carbon dioxide emissions from automobiles is "perfectly feasible."[117]

In December 2005, the court of appeals denied the petitioners' petition for rehearing by a 2-1 vote;[118] the court also denied, by a 4-3 vote, the petitioners' petition for a rehearing en banc.[119] On March 2, 2006, the petitioners petitioned the United States Supreme Court to review the D.C. Circuit's decision, arguing that the decision was "an extreme departure from [the Supreme Court's] precedents on statutory interpretation," since the EPA "rewrote [section 202(a)(1) of the CAA] to justify its decision."[120] The petitioners also cited a need for the Court to review EPA's interpretation of *FDA v. Brown & Williamson*, arguing that the Court should correct EPA's "overreading" of that case: "*Brown & Williamson* is not a blank check to avoid regulating in politically controversial settings."[121] The Supreme Court granted certiorari on June 26, 2006, on the following questions: (1) whether the EPA Administrator may decline to issue emission standards for motor vehicles based on policy considerations not enumerated in Section 202(a)(1); and (2) whether the EPA Administrator has authority to regulate carbon dioxide and other air pollutants associated with climate change under section 202(a)(1).[122] The Court heard oral arguments on November 29, 2006; a decision is expected by late spring, 2007.

D. EPA Listing of GHGs as "Criteria" Air Pollutants and Established NAAQS

On January 30, 2003, the attorneys general of Massachusetts, Connecticut and Maine filed notice of intent to sue EPA, announcing their intent to compel EPA to list carbon dioxide as a criteria air pollutant, pursuant to section 108 of the CAA.[123] These states based their claim on two grounds: (1) EPA had previously acknowledged, in the Cannon Memorandum and the Guzy comments, carbon dioxide as an "air pollutant" under section 302(g);[124, 125] and (2) EPA had recognized that carbon dioxide met the elements of section 108.[126] The notice also cited a State Department document that discussed "specific examples of adverse impacts to weather and public health . . . and health effects due to air pollution and extreme weather events"; the report also stated that the fact that "carbon dioxide emissions result from numerous or diverse mobile or stationary sources" was an "indisputable fact."[127]

These states filed suit on June 4, 2003, in federal district court in Hartford, Connecticut, claiming that EPA's failure to list carbon dioxide as a criteria pollutant was, among other things, "unlawfully denying residents of each of the Plaintiff States the benefits due them under the [CAA]."[128] On August 28, 2003, citing both its decision to deny the ICTA petition and the Fabricant Memorandum supporting that decision, EPA moved to dismiss the suit on the grounds that (1) EPA's authority to revise the list of criteria air pollutants under section 108 was discretionary, and (2) EPA had not made any of the threshold determinations required for the addition of carbon dioxide to the list of criteria for air pollutants.[129] Because EPA's legal authority to regulate carbon dioxide was a "threshold question" in the suit, the states voluntarily terminated their suit without prejudice on September 3, 2003.[130]

E. New Source Construction

1. NSPS—Section 111 Challenges

The issue of regulation of GHGs also has arisen in the context of citizens' petitions regarding New Source Performance Standards (NSPS). In order to control the emission of air pollutants by newly constructed sources, the CAA directs the EPA to set NSPS for categories of new or modified stationary sources that the Administrator determines cause or contribute significantly to air pollution that may reasonably be anticipated to endanger public health or welfare.[131] Under this program, EPA establishes emissions performance standards for each category reflecting the best system of emissions reduction that has been adequately demonstrated, taking into account cost and any non-air-quality health and environmental impacts and energy requirements.

> **... the CAA directs the EPA to set NSPS for categories of new or modified stationary sources that the Administrator determines cause or contribute significantly to air pollution that may reasonably be anticipated to endanger public health or welfare.**

a. Our Children's Earth Foundation and Sierra Club

On August 27, 2002, a group of environmental organizations noticed their intent to file a citizens' suit against EPA, seeking to compel EPA under section 111 of the CAA[132] to review and revise NSPS for sulfur dioxide and nitrogen oxide as well as the non-nitrous oxide provisions relating to fossil fuel-fired steam-generating units and stationary turbines.[133] On February 21, 2003, the plaintiffs filed suit in federal district court in San Francisco, California.[134] In addition to targeting particulate matter, sulfur dioxide and nitrogen oxides, the complaint suggested that EPA may be required to establish an NSPS for carbon dioxide.[135] On May 23, 2003, the Attorneys General of nine states filed an amici curiae brief, later accepted by the court, seeking to include carbon dioxide as a pollutant subject to promulgation of NSPS.[136]

In September 2003, the government notified the court of the EPA's denial of the ICTA petition, and indicated that the court's order in the NSPS case should exclude any requirement to restate the EPA's already announced position that it lacked authority to regulate GHGs to address global climate change.[137] On November 12, 2003, the parties filed a proposed consent decree for the court's review and approval, indicating that EPA must (1) revise NSPS for sulfur dioxide, and (2) either revise NSPS for nitrogen oxides and particulate matter or determine that review or revision of these pollutants was inappropriate.[138] On February 6, 2004, the parties filed a joint motion to enter the proposed consent decree, entered by the court on February 9.[139]

Pursuant to the terms of the consent decree, EPA proposed amendments to the NSPS on February 28, 2005.[140, 141] Following a comment period, EPA issued its final amendments on February 27, 2006.[142] EPA's final rule contained three notable elements. First, EPA reduced emissions limits for nitrogen oxides, sulfur dioxide and particulate matter.[143] Second, EPA rejected requests by several commenters to set emissions limits based on the availability of a power plant technology called Integrated Gasification Combined Cycle.[144] IGCC is a technology that involves conversion of coal to gas streams prior to combustion, and has been identified as providing the potential to segregate and sequester carbon dioxide.[145] Finally, EPA rejected commenters' request for the establishment of NSPS for carbon dioxide, reiterating its position from *Massachusetts v. EPA*, discussed in section II.C.2, *supra*, that the EPA "does not presently have the authority to set NSPS to regulate [carbon dioxide] or other [GHGs] that contribute to global climate change."[146]

b. Attorneys General

On February 20, 2003, the attorneys general of several states announced their intent to file a citizens' suit against EPA for violating its "mandatory duty" under section 111 of the CAA to review and revise the NSPS for fossil fuel-fired electric-generating units.[147] The petitioners wrote:

> The existing standards for sulfur dioxide and particulate matter fail to reflect the technological advances that have occurred in the past two decades as well as the current information regarding the environmental harm posed by those pollutants. In addition, we believe that [the NSPS] is inadequate in that it does not contain a standard for emissions of carbon dioxide, a pollutant that causes global warming with its attendant adverse health and environmental impacts. In this regard, recent information confirms that:
>
> 1. Carbon dioxide emissions from power plants in the United States are significant contributors to global warming;
> 2. Global warming and other aspects of climate change will significantly endanger public health and welfare; and
> 3. Demonstrated, effective technology exists to significantly reduce carbon dioxide emissions from electric utility generating systems.
>
> Thus, power plant carbon dioxide emissions meet all the conditions set forth in the Act for inclusion within an NSPS. We therefore call on EPA to add

limitations for carbon dioxide emissions when it revises [the NSPS].[148]

On April 27, 2006, the attorneys general of 10 states sued the EPA for failing to adopt stronger emission standards for new power plants.[149] The lawsuit, filed in the Court of Appeals for the D.C. Circuit, alleges that the EPA's February 2006 rulemaking (issued pursuant to the *Our Children's Earth Foundation* consent decree (discussed in section II.E.1.a, *supra*)) was deficient in two "fundamental" respects:

First, EPA refused to regulate carbon dioxide, despite overwhelming research and scientific consensus that carbon dioxide contributes to global warming and thus harms "public health and welfare." EPA's claim that it does not have the authority to regulate carbon dioxide emissions is contrary to the plain language of the Clean Air Act.

Second, EPA failed to set adequate standards for sulfur dioxide and nitrogen oxides, power plant pollutants that contribute to soot, smog, acid rain and higher levels of respiratory disease. The law dictates that the emission safeguards be set at levels that require use of the best demonstrated technology, but EPA is setting weak standards that can be met through less effective technologies.[150]

2. Consideration of GHGs in PSD and NNSR

As discussed in section II.A.3, *supra*, the 1977 amendments to the CAA implemented both the PSD and NSR programs. The PSD program is focused on avoiding degradation in air quality in areas that meet the NAAQS, with particularly stringent limits on air quality degradation in "class I" areas, including national parks and wilderness areas.[151] For construction in an attainment area, a new major plant (or an existing plant wishing to make a major modification or addition) is required to obtain a pre-construction PSD permit, which includes an air quality impacts review and a requirement to install Best Available Control Technology (BACT).[152] In areas not meeting the NAAQS, a new major plant (or an existing plant wishing to make a major modification or addition) must obtain a nonattainment NSR (NNSR) permit, which includes a requirement to offset emissions and to install emissions control technology qualified as achieving the lowest achievable emissions rate (LAER).[153] Regulation of GHGs has also been debated in the context of both PSD and NNSR, particularly in connection with (1) lawsuits alleging violation of the permitting programs, and (2) consideration of alternative designs for coal-fired power plants, such as IGCC coal gasification technology, that offer the potential to separate and sequester carbon dioxide emissions.

a. Northwest Environmental Defense Center v. Owens Corning

In June 2006, the U.S. District Court for the District of Oregon considered a claim by several environmental groups that Owens Corning violated the PSD provisions of the CAA when it began construction of a foam insulation plant without obtaining a permit, and argued that the plant would increase emissions of GHGs and thereby cause them harm.[154] The court rejected Owens Corning's claim that the plaintiff organizations lacked standing to bring the lawsuit.[155] The court concluded that the plaintiffs had satisfied both the "constitutional" and the "prudential" elements of standing;[156] analysis of both of these elements required the court to discuss regulation of GHGs.

With respect to the three constitutional elements of a standing claim, the court first found that the plaintiffs had demonstrated "injury in fact" in the form of a procedural injury. That is, the court found that the plaintiffs had established that the PSD procedures were designed to protect a concrete interest, and that Owens Corning's construction of the facility threatened these interests.[157] The court held that "Congress established [the PSD program] to protect the very kinds of interests asserted" by the plaintiffs, and that Owens Corning's conduct would "allegedly threaten those interests, releasing a significant quantity of pollutants into the atmosphere in a densely populated metropolitan region where many members of the [p]laintiff organizations live, work, commute, or recreate."[158] Second, the court found that GHG emissions from Owens Corning's facility were forecasted to have both direct and indirect impacts on the plaintiffs' environment.[159] The court also found that the plaintiffs had articulated a "causal connection" between the alleged injury and the conduct complained of (i.e., violation of the PSD requirements),[160] noting that plaintiffs in cases such as these need only "assert that emissions from [the] [d]efendant's facility will contribute to the pollution that threatens [the] [p]laintiffs' interests."[161] Finally, the court found that the plaintiffs satisfied the redressability element of a standing claim—that is, it was likely that their injury would be redressed by an injunction.[162] The court noted that the plaintiffs were "not obligated to show that the permit request would be denied," nor that the design of Owens Corning's facility would be altered as a result of the litigation.[163] Rather, the court held, the plaintiffs were only required to show that if they prevailed, the defendant's conduct could not continue unless Owens Corning complied with the PSD requirements, which "are intended to protect the public health and the public's right to participate in the review process."[164]

The court also discussed regulation of GHGs in determining that the plaintiffs satisfied the three prudential aspects of standing: (1) plaintiff must assert his own legal rights, not those of third parties; (2) federal courts must "refrain[ ] from adjudicating 'abstract questions of wide public significance' which amount to 'generalized grievances,' pervasively shared and most appropriately addressed in the representative branches"; and (3) the plaintiff must "fall within 'the zone of interests to be protected or regulated by the statute or constitutional guarantee in question.'"[165] The court found that the first two elements were "not seriously in dispute," and that, assuming the "zone of interest" requirement applied, it was "plainly satisfied" because the CAA was

"intended to protect the interests advanced by [the] [p]laintiffs here, and Congress expressly provided for citizen suits to enforce its provisions."[166] The court noted that the procedural and substantive requirements articulated in the PSD section of the CAA were designed to address the "ills" of emissions into the atmosphere.[167]

b. New Electric Utility Construction and IGCC

As discussed in Gregory Foote's article, discussed further in section II.E.2.c, *infra*, integrated coal gasification combined cycle (IGCC) is a production technology with potentially lower emissions of pollutants than traditional pulverized coal combustion. IGCC is at least 10% more thermally efficient than older processes; it produces the same amount of electricity with less fuel.[168] This thermal efficiency reduces all pollutants (including carbon dioxide) by that same amount, compared to traditional combustion.[169] Unlike pulverized coal, IGCC can also be configured in a way that can separately capture carbon dioxide emissions at a reasonable cost, making it possible to store nearly all of the carbon dioxide emissions in geologic formations in coming years.[170]

IGCC is not widely used because it is perceived as being more expensive than traditional technologies and has not been sufficiently demonstrated for larger plants.[171] However, Foote argued, states have failed to include important factors in their cost analysis, if they have considered IGCC at all.[172] Among these factors, he argued, are an attendant reduction in carbon dioxide emissions and the fact that IGCC enables use of mercury controls at a fraction of the cost of conventional plants.[173] Further, Foote urged, states have failed to consider the risks posed if utilities continue to build new coal-fired plants that last for more than 50 years without taking into account the likelihood that carbon dioxide restrictions will be established early in the existence of those plants, thereby encumbering citizens with unexpected costs for outmoded plants.[174]

i. State Consideration of IGCC

Several state environmental agencies have ruled that IGCC is required to be considered in a BACT analysis. For example, in *Sierra Club v. Environmental and Public Protection Cabinet & Thoroughbred Generating Co., LLC*, petitioners challenged a Title V operating and PSD construction permit for the construction of a coal-fired power plant issued by Kentucky's Division for Air Quality (DAQ) to Thoroughbred Generating Company (Thoroughbred).[175] Petitioners argued that the DAQ's BACT determinations with respect to Thoroughbred's proposal contained several errors, including a failure to consider IGCC.[176] Thoroughbred and the DAQ argued that consideration of IGCC was discretionary because it would have amounted to a redefinition of the source, which, the DAQ maintained, was not required for a BACT analysis.[177, 178]

Hearing Officer Janet Thompson ruled that the DAQ's determination was erroneous, as the DAQ "[c]learly . . . had authority to require [Thoroughbred] to do a BACT analysis on . . . IGCC."[179] Citing the Foote article, Thompson wrote:

> [I]t would be contrary to the CAA for a permitting agency not to be able to consider a redefinition of the source in response to commenters who are proposing alternatives. In exercising its discretion to consider IGCC . . ., it was incumbent on DAQ to consider the persuasive value of those alternatives. I conclude that a remand is appropriate to require DAQ to exercise its discretion to consider IGCC given the considerable evidence adduced as to the validity of IGCC.[180]

Similarly, Montana[181] and Illinois[182] require coal-fired power plant applicants to evaluate the use of IGCC as part of meeting the BACT demonstration. Wisconsin, on the other hand, does not require consideration of IGCC.[183]

c. Academic Literature

As noted in section II.E.2.c, *supra*, in July 2004, the Environmental Law Institute published an article by Gregory Foote, an assistant general counsel at EPA who was then working on a detail at the Center for International Environmental Law, which discussed ways in which the CAA can be used to limit carbon dioxide emissions from new coal-fired power plants.[184] Foote noted that U.S. emissions of carbon dioxide were expected to rise thirty percent in the next twenty years, largely as a result of planned coal-fired power plants.[185] Against this background, Foote outlined the CAA's PSD program, noting that it requires states to undertake an environmental impact analysis and consider energy efficiency, renewable energy, and other reasonable alternatives before deciding to allow any new power plants.[186] In discussing the required environmental impact analysis under this program, Foote argued that states are required to take into account emissions of GHGs such as carbon dioxide.[187] Foote wrote that once a state has conducted this analysis for a proposed coal-fired plant, the state may reject a new plant in favor of a less-polluting alternative.[188] Alternatively, Foote wrote, if the state decides to proceed with the coal-fired plant, the state is required to construct using the best available pollution control technology (BACT), which he contended must also take climate change impacts into account.[189]

Foote focused in particular on considering IGCC as BACT.[190] Because even IGCC would not satisfactorily resolve the problem of carbon dioxide emissions, Foote further recommended that states require "offsets," or GHG reductions from other sources of emissions.[191]

d. Environmental Appeals Board Decisions

In a 1986 decision, the EPA's Environmental Appeals Board discussed the permissibility of considering unregulated pollutants (such as GHGs) in making a BACT decision.[192] In *In re North County Resource Recovery Associates*, the Board considered a citizens' petition for review of a PSD permit that had been granted to a California facility in 1985.[193] The Board determined that Region IX of the EPA had adequately addressed all of the citizens' concerns, with the exception of Region IX's assertion that the EPA lacked authority to consider pollutants not regulated by the CAA when making a PSD determination.[194] The Board noted that this contention was correct if narrowly construed to mean that EPA "lacks the authority to impose limitations or other restrictions directly on the emission of unregulated pollutants." However, the Board determined that such an assertion is "overly broad . . . if it is meant as a limitation on EPA's authority to evaluate, for example, the environmental impact of *unregulated* pollutants in the course of making a BACT determination for *regulated* pollutants."[195] The Board noted that unregulated pollutants generally do not form part of the BACT analysis, since by statute and regulation BACT is defined as an emissions limitation for a regulated pollutant, but an exception applies whenever choosing one control technology over another, for a regulated pollutant has the incidental effect of increasing or decreasing emissions of unregulated pollutants.[196] Since such an incidental effect would inevitably have an environmental impact, the Board determined that the environmental impact of unregulated pollutants under such circumstances is relevant to the selection of an appropriate control technology for regulated pollutants.[197]

As Foote wrote in his NSR article, discussed in section II.E.2.b and c, *supra*, subsequent Environmental Appeals Board decisions have adopted this view.[198]

e. Page Letter

In a December 2005 letter to an energy consulting firm, EPA again elaborated on the required components of a BACT analysis. Stephen Page, director of the EPA's Office of Air Quality, Planning and Standards, responded to a request for the EPA's position on whether a BACT analysis for proposed coal-fired power plants must include an evaluation of alternative designs such as IGCC.[199] Page began his analysis by citing the portions of the CAA's PSD permitting process that addressed alternative designs and production processes.[200] Page stated that the EPA's view is that in creating these categories of processes, Congress intended to distinguish between "'production processes and all available methods, systems and techniques'" that are potentially applicable to a particular type of facility and should be considered in the analysis of BACT, from "'alternatives' to the proposed source that would wholly replace the proposed facility with a different type of facility"; such "alternatives" are not required as part of a BACT analysis.[201] Page acknowledged that this distinction was often difficult to make—particularly with respect to coal gasification—because the definition of BACT listed "innovative fuel combustion techniques" as an example of production processes or methods to be considered in the BACT analysis.[202] Applying this distinction, Page concluded that "applying the IGCC technology would fundamentally change the scope of [the construction of a coal-fired power plant] and redefine the basic design of the proposed source," and therefore, where an applicant seeks to construct such a plant, the IGCC process is not required as part of the BACT analysis.[203]

However, Page noted that under Section 165(a)(2), the permitting authority must allow an "opportunity for interested persons . . . to appear and submit written or oral presentations on the air quality impact of such source, *alternatives thereto*, control technology requirements, and other appropriate considerations."[204] The EPA had not previously drawn this distinction between analysis of alternatives to a source under Section 165(a)(2) and BACT, and has not promulgated policy or guidance giving content to the alternatives analysis.[205] In a March 7, 2006 brief to the EPA Environmental Appeals Board, however, the EPA addressed what it envisions such "alternatives" consideration to require.[206] In the *Prairie State Generation* case, the EPA was asked by the Board to address whether the Illinois EPA, in considering a permit for a new coal-fired plant, was required to consider low-sulfur coal and other alternatives to the proposed source. The EPA, consistent with its IGCC letter, maintained that the "proposed facility" referenced in section 165(a)(4) refers to the specific facility proposed by the applicant, which has certain design characteristics, and not some differently designed facility that is fundamentally different. EPA pointed to its historical approach in which it has found that "the BACT review should not be used to frustrate an applicant's ability to construct a particular type of facility in order to meet objectives that may be independent of environmental protection."[207] The EPA argued that requiring Prairie State to fire low-sulfur coal would fundamentally redesign the scope of the project, where the facility was planned and sited to burn fuel from a mine close to the plant.

The EPA went on, however, in its *Prairie State* brief to interpret section 165(a)(2), for what appears to be the first time, to require the permitting authority "to provide a reasoned response to comments identifying alternatives to the proposed source and raising other appropriate considerations."[208] The EPA noted that the statute requires a public hearing and an opportunity to comment on alternatives and other appropriate considerations, and concluded that the requirement to respond to such comments is "inherent" in the requirement to provide an opportunity to make the comments. Although this might suggest an opening to require a reasoned consideration of IGCC, the EPA also appeared to have an eye on that issue in its *Prairie State* brief, limiting the scope of the requirement in two important respects. First, the EPA explained that the permitting authority has discretion to modify the PSD permit based on comments raising alternatives or other appropriate considerations, "but this is a highly discretionary matter," suggesting that the permitting authority's obligation is satisfied by a "reasoned explanation for why it has elected not to exercise its discretion."[209] Second, the EPA noted that the permitting authority was "not obligated to respond to comments addressing matters outside the scope of the [Clean Air] Act, such as the need for a particular facility."[210] This comment might also encompass the EPA's current position that greenhouse gas emissions are outside the scope of the Clean Air Act.[211]

The EPA recently indicated that it may issue a rule to codify the opinions set forth in the Page letter. In an April 4, 2006, submission to Senator James Jeffords, then ranking member of the Committee on the Environment and Public Works, the EPA stated that it is "considering the possibility of adopting this interpretation through rulemaking."[212] The submission, authored by William Wehrum, the EPA's Acting Assistant Administrator for Air and Radiation, consisted of responses to questions posed by Senator Jeffords following a February 9, 2006 hearing on the effect of clean air regulations on natural gas prices.[213] Wehrum also stated that current EPA Administrator Stephen Johnson "concurred with" the Page letter, and that Wehrum played a "substantive role" in developing the agency's position in the letter.[214]

Following the issuance of the Page letter, several environmental advocacy groups filed petitions for judicial review in the D.C. Circuit.[215] The petitioners claimed that the Page letter had no binding legal effect, given that it was addressed to a private party; was not promulgated as a formal regulation under the CAA; and was not subjected to public notice and comment before it was issued.[216] In a September 12, 2006, letter to the petitioners, EPA stated that it "intends to establish a process that will foster a dialogue among a balanced array of interested stakeholder groups on the deployment of advanced coal technology and result in policy recommendations to EPA on this topic."[217] Following EPA's letter, in October 2006 the parties filed a proposed settlement agreement in the D.C. Circuit in which EPA agreed and stipulated that the Page letter "is not final agency action and creates no rights, duties, obligations, nor any other legally binding effects on EPA, the states, tribes, any regulated entity or any person."[218]

f. "Redefining the Source"—Additional Case Law

Several Environmental Appeals Board decisions have considered the general issue addressed in the Page letter—whether NSR proceedings should be limited to the specific configuration of fuel and production process presented by the permit applicant, that is, whether there are any limits on the consideration of alternatives:

- *In re Pennsauken County, New Jersey Resource Recovery Facility*[219]: In this 1988 case, the Board ruled that BACT permit conditions are imposed on the source *as the applicant has defined it.*[220] The Board noted that, although BACT conditions may affect the viability of the proposed facility as envisioned by the applicant, the conditions themselves are not intended to "redefine the source."[221]
- *In re Hibbing Taconite Co.*[222]: Decided a year after *Pennsauken County*, this case involved a permit for the modification of a gas-burning boiler to switch to petroleum coke.[223] In determining that the permitting agency failed to justify its rejection of continued use of gas (since the plant's prior history showed that gas was a viable alternative), the Board concluded that requiring the company to stay with its current method would not "redefine the source."[224]
- *In re Kendall New Century Development*[225]: More recently, in this 2003 case, the Board ruled that "redefinition of the source is not always prohibited."[226] However, the Board noted that the petitioner bears a heavy burden in such cases: to obtain a review of a permit issuer's decision not to conduct a broader BACT, the petitioner must show a good reason for curtailing the permit-issuer's discretion, or that the issuer abused this discretion.[227]

F. Preemption of State GHG Controls on Motor Vehicles Under Section 209

States are generally preempted from establishing their own motor vehicle tailpipe emissions standards by section 209(a) of the CAA.[228] Section 209(b), however, provides for waiver of section 209(a) for any state that adopted motor vehicle emissions standards prior to March 30, 1966, so long as the state has determined that its standards are "at least as protective of public health and welfare as applicable federal standards."[229] California is the only state that is qualified to seek and receive a waiver under section 209(b),[230] since it was the only state to enact emissions standards prior to March 30, 1966.[231] Section 177 allows other states to enact emissions standards if they are "identical to the California standards and do not, in effect, compel manufacturers to make a 'third car' (i.e., a car that is different from the type required by the California or federal standards)."[232]

The Energy Policy and Conservation Act (EPCA), the federal fuel economy law, also contains an express preemptive provision that applies nationwide, including in California. On March 29, 2006, the NHTSA issued a final rule that reformed the structure of the corporate average fuel economy program for light trucks for model years 2008-2011 and addressed the relationship between fuel economy and carbon dioxide emissions. The rule concluded that:

> In mandating federal fuel economy standards under EPCA, Congress has expressly preempted any state laws or regulations relating to fuel economy standards. A State requirement limiting [carbon dioxide] emissions is such a law or regulation because it has the direct effect of regulating fuel consumption. [Carbon dioxide] emissions are directly linked to fuel consumption because [carbon dioxide] is the ultimate end product of burning gasoline. Moreover, because

there is but one pool of technologies for reducing tailpipe [carbon dioxide] emissions and increasing fuel economy available now and for the foreseeable future, regulation of [carbon dioxide] emissions and fuel consumption are inextricably linked. It is therefore NHTSA's conclusion that such regulation is expressly preempted.[233]

Additional aspects of the NHTSA's final rule are discussed in section III.B.2, *infra*.

III. The 1975 Energy Policy and Conservation Act

A. Statutory History and Structure

1. Legislative History

The Corporate Average Fuel Economy (CAFE) standards were first authorized under subchapter V of the Motor Vehicle Information and Cost Savings Act (MVICSA), part of the EPCA.[234] The EPCA, enacted largely in response to the OPEC oil embargo of 1973-74,[235] had both short- and long-term components. In the short term, the EPCA was designed to reduce vulnerability to energy price increases and to insure fair allocation in the event of supply disruption.[236] In the long term, the EPCA was designed to decrease dependence on imports and to enhance national security and efficient energy use while insuring energy supply at reasonable cost.[237] Climate change does not appear to have been on Congress's radar at the time, as "[n]either reductions in [GHGs], nor environmental protection more generally, are mentioned as relevant factors in establishing the fuel economy standard";[238] and, further, the EPCA's history "appears devoid of any reference to environmental considerations."[239] Although the CAFE statute has been renumbered, and some of its wording has been changed, there have been no substantive changes since the EPCA was enacted.[240]

> **In the long term, the EPCA was designed to decrease dependence on imports and to enhance national security and efficient energy use while insuring energy supply at reasonable cost.**

2. Structure

a. *Section 502*

Section 502 of the EPCA requires the Secretary of Transportation to promulgate rules establishing maximum feasible average fuel economy standards for automobiles.[241] The Secretary is authorized to exempt a manufacturer from these standards if the manufacturer makes a proper application and the Secretary "finds that the applicable standard under [section 502] is more stringent than the maximum feasible average fuel economy level that the manufacturer can achieve,"[242] and the Secretary "prescribes by regulation an alternative average fuel economy standard for the passenger automobiles manufactured by the exempted manufacturer that the Secretary decides is the maximum feasible average fuel economy level for the manufacturers to which the alternative standard applies."[243] Additionally, section 502 provides that the Secretary may develop and prescribe alternative standards for alternative-fueled vehicles.[244]

b. EPA Role

Sections 503 and 506 of the EPCA charge the EPA Administrator with determining test procedures and calculating fuel economy,[245] and with implementing fuel economy labeling requirements.[246] Section 503 states that "[t]o the extent practicable, fuel economy tests shall be carried out with emissions tests under section 206 of [the CAA]."[247] The EPA calculates corporate average fuel economy for each manufacturer's automobiles, separating domestic and imported fleets for each manufacturer with separate calculations for each category.[248]

The EPA recently proposed changes to its current testing procedures for the fuel economy estimates that appear on the window stickers of vehicles.[249] This information "provide[s] consumers with a basis on which to compare the fuel economy of different vehicles, and . . . a reasonable estimate of the range of fuel economy they can expect to achieve."[250] These were last revised in 1985.[251] Under the proposed rule changes, the new tests will account for three current "real-world" driving conditions: (1) driving with air conditioning in use; (2) high-speed and rapid-acceleration driving; and (3) operation of vehicles in cold temperatures.[252] These changes would take effect beginning with model years 2008.[253] According to the EPA, under the new rules, the city mpg estimates for most vehicles would decrease by 10% to 20% from today's labels, while the highway mpg estimates would generally drop 5% to 15%.[254]

Importantly, these changes would not impact the methods used in the CAFE program, as section 503 of the EPCA requires that the CAFE values be determined from the EPA test procedures in place as of 1975.[255] This means that any changes implemented by the EPA to its test procedures for window stickers "must leave in place the existing tests used for CAFE determination," while "the proposed test methods for determining the new fuel economy label estimates would be incorporated in sections of the regulations that are entirely separate from the CAFE regulations."[256]

B. CAFE Today

1. Current Regulations

CAFE requires each automobile manufacturer or importer to meet average fuel economy standards, expressed in miles per gallon (mpg), for the fleet of new vehicles it manufactures or imports in each model year.[257] There are separate standards for passenger automobiles—currently 27.5 mpg[258]—and "light-duty trucks" (including sport utility vehicles (SUVs) and minivans)—currently 20.7 mpg.[259] CAFE provides for favorable special treatment of alternative fuel vehicles.[260] Thus, standards for trucks and SUVs are far less stringent than those for cars. CAFE applies only to new vehicles; it does not regulate in-use consumption of fuel,[261] meaning that increased stringency "improve[s] on-the-road fuel economy only to the extent that new vehicles replace less efficient existing vehicles."[262] Additionally, compliance with CAFE is determined separately for vehicles manufactured in the United States, Canada, or Mexico, and those manufactured elsewhere but used in the United States.[263]

CAFE also provides a credit system: where the average fuel economy of either a manufacturer's passenger car or light truck fleet for a particular model year exceeds the established standard, the manufacturer earns "credits."[264] These credits may be applied to any three consecutive model years immediately prior to (carry back-credits) or subsequent to (carry-forward credits) the model year in which the credits are earned.[265] Credits cannot be passed between manufacturers or between fleets—for example, from domestic passenger cars to light trucks.[266, 267]

2. Stringency

The emergence of the issue of global climate change has prompted consideration of whether the CAFE requirements should be tightened to force greater fuel efficiency, thereby lowering GHG emissions.[268] Proponents of this approach point out that while the program initially made a significant contribution to moderating fuel use,[269] its impact has abated because the CAFE standards were frozen by Congress through much of the 1990s,[270] when sales of trucks, SUVs and minivans increased substantially.[271]

In 2001, Congress requested that the National Academy of Sciences, together with the Department of Transportation, conduct a study to evaluate the effectiveness of the CAFE standards.[272] In response to that request, the National Academy of Sciences established the Committee on the Effectiveness and Impact of CAFE Standards.[273] In its 2002 final report, the Committee noted that CAFE had undoubtedly contributed to improved fuel economy but suggested that making CAFE standards more stringent was not the most effective measure:

> Raising CAFE standards would reduce future fuel consumption below what it otherwise would be; however, other policies could accomplish the same end at lower cost, provide more flexibility to manufacturers, or address inequities arising from the present system. Possible alternatives that appear to the committee to be superior to the current CAFE structure include tradable credits for

fuel economy improvements, feebates, higher fuel taxes, standards based on vehicle attributes (for example, vehicle weight, size, or payload), or some combination of these. . . .

Such a system would create incentives to reduce the variance in vehicle weights between large and small vehicles, thus providing for overall vehicle safety. It has the potential to increase fuel economy with fewer negative effects on both safety and consumer choice.[274]

Following consideration of the Committee's report and comment periods on the issue of fuel efficiency reform, the DOT proposed a reform of the CAFE program for light trucks, including minivans, pickup trucks and SUVs.[275] Under the plan, announced in August 2005, by 2011 all manufacturers will be required to comply with a "reformed" CAFE standard, under which fuel economy standards will be "restructured so that they are based on a measure of vehicle size called 'footprint,' the product of multiplying a vehicle's wheelbase by its track width."[276] The vehicles are to be divided into six footprint categories, with a target level of average fuel economy proposed for each—smaller footprint light trucks expected to achieve more fuel economy and larger ones, less.[277]

The NHTSA issued a final rule implementing these reforms on March 29, 2006.[278] In response to the NHTSA's final rule, however, 10 states and the District of Columbia filed a lawsuit in the United States Court of Appeals for the Ninth Circuit.[279] The lawsuit alleges that, in issuing the final rule, the NHTSA failed to meet the requirements of the EPCA because the NHTSA "failed to consider alternative approaches that would have promoted energy conservation, made meaningful contributions to increased fuel economy and encouraged technological innovation."[280] The lawsuit further alleges that the NHTSA failed to "consider the environmental consequences of its proposed overhaul of light truck standards, failed to consider the changes in the environment since . . . the 1980s, and failed to evaluate the impact of carbon dioxide emissions despite identifying the threat of carbon dioxide and global climate change as new information concerning the environment."[281]

Additionally, on May 23, 2006, the Sierra Club filed a lawsuit in the Ninth Circuit.[282] The Sierra Club has advanced claims similar to those set forth by the states, arguing that the NHTSA has "failed to follow the law by setting fuel economy standards below the technically feasible level."[283] The Sierra Club argues that the new standards could raise CAFE standards for SUVs, pickup trucks, and other light trucks by 1.8 miles per gallon by 2011 at best, and may actually erode the fuel economy of new vehicles sold in the United States and increase our dependence on oil. Sierra Club urged that this action is clearly much less than is both economically feasible and possible with existing technology—a violation of the law's "maximum feasible" provision.[284]

In addition to the administration's proposed changes, some members of Congress have recently signaled their willingness to become involved in CAFE reform. At a February 2006 energy-efficiency briefing, Kevin Carroll, majority staff director for the House

Science Energy Subcommittee, stated that while the most "'economically efficient' way to reduce oil consumption would be through taxation," such a policy would prove too unpopular.[285] On the other hand, overhauling CAFE might be more successful: "A lot of people say, 'Well, it's CAFE, it's an old hat, people don't like it.' But people like taxes even less. I'm not sure that kicking the rulemaking over to the executive branch is really what the Congress should do. . . . Congress should take . . . responsibility and set the rules."[286]

C. Preemption of State GHG Controls Under the EPCA
1. Section 509

Under section 509 of the EPCA, a state cannot "adopt or enforce a law or regulation relating to fuel economy standards or average fuel economy standards."[287] Further, section 509(b) provides that a state cannot "adopt or enforce" a regulation not identical to federal regulations concerning disclosure of fuel economy or fuel costs.[288] Thus, the federal government is essentially vested with the "exclusive authority to determine and enforce" fuel economy standards.[289]

2. Statutes and Regulations in Question
a. Maryland

In 1992, Maryland attempted to implement a "fee-bate" program for automobile fuel efficiency. Under the legislation, passenger cars with a model year of 1993 or 1994 with a fuel economy of less than 21 mpg were taxed $100; after 1995, cars with a fuel economy of less than 27 mpg were taxed $50 for every mile they fell below the 27 mpg mark.[290] Conversely, those cars with a fuel economy of more than 35 mpg were awarded a credit of $50 per mpg above the 27 mpg mark.[291] The legislation also contained a labeling/disclosure provision requiring that motor vehicle dealers "prominently display on a vehicle offered for sale a notice on a form prescribed [by the state] to inform consumers of the fuel efficiency surcharge and . . . credit program."[292]

In a June 8, 1992 letter, the chief counsel of the National Highway Traffic Safety Administration (NHTSA) concluded that the Maryland legislation was preempted by the CAFE program and could therefore not be enforced.[293] The NHTSA determined that the legislation was "related to" federal fuel economy standards and was thus preempted.[294] This determination was apparently influenced by the Supreme Court's decision in *Morales v. Transworld Airlines, Inc.*,[295] in which the Court considered the phrase in the context of ERISA. The Court held that "the ordinary meaning of ["relating to"] is a broad one—'to stand in some relation; to have bearing or concern; to pertain; refer; to bring into association with or connection with,' and the words thus express a broad pre-emptive purpose."[296] The NHTSA wrote:

While the Maryland program does not purport to require automobile manufacturers to achieve any particular average fuel economy level, it clearly "has a connection with" and a "reference to" fuel economy standards. Indeed, the Supreme Court has held that State laws are preempted by the "relate to" language of ERISA "even if the law is not specifically designed to affect such benefit plans, or the effect is only indirect."[297]

In a June 24, 1992, opinion letter to the Maryland Motor Vehicle Administration, Maryland Attorney General J. Joseph Curran wrote that while he believed the NHTSA "overall assessment" to be "too broad," he nevertheless agreed that the labeling requirement was preempted because it was not identical to the federal disclosure requirement, as mandated by section 509(b) of the MVISCA.[298, 299] While Curran defended the tax and credit provisions of the legislation, he advised against its enforcement because he determined that the labeling/disclosure requirement was not severable under Maryland law.[300] Curran noted, however, that if the General Assembly took steps to correct the labeling provision by "eliminat[ing] any reference to 'fuel economy,'"[301] his office would defend the validity of the legislation if it was challenged in court.[302]

Despite this qualification, however, the program was never implemented, and the issue of preemption was never adjudicated.[303]

b. California

i. Pavley Amendment

On July 1, 2002, the California Assembly enacted Bill 1493, authored by Assemblywoman Fran Pavley (the "Pavley Amendment"); the bill was signed into law by then-Governor Gray Davis on July 22, 2002.[304] The Pavley Amendment required the California Air Resources Board (CARB) to "develop and adopt regulations that achieve the maximum feasible and cost-effective reduction of [GHG] emissions from motor vehicles" by January 1, 2005.[305] The regulations applied only to motor vehicles with model years 2009 and later, and were not to be effective until January 1, 2006.[306] CARB was granted "widespread latitude to craft the regulations, [but] the legislature . . . prohibited [CARB] from reducing [GHG] emissions by imposing fees or taxes; banning any vehicle category . . . or reducing vehicle weights, speed limits or vehicle miles traveled."[307] The regulations were adopted in August 2005.[308]

The Pavley Amendment would probably violate the CAA absent California's unique status; California is the only state eligible to receive waivers from preemption pursuant to section 209 of the CAA.[309] CARB requested a waiver of preemption from the EPA on December 21, 2005; the request is pending.[310] The EPA has not yet indicated how the NHTSA's recent conclusion in its final rule that states are preempted from regulating fuel economy standards, discussed in section III.B.2, *supra*, will affect its decision on California's request. However, the EPA noted that it plans to issue a notice in the *Federal Register* announcing a public hearing on the waiver request, although it is unclear whether the notice will propose to deny the waiver.[311]

In a September 26, 2006, letter to EPA Administrator Stephen L. Johnson, 104 members of the House of Representatives—representing 27 states and the Virgin Islands—urged the EPA to grant California's waiver request.[312] The representatives stated that the EPA has "routinely granted California's waiver requests over [forty] times in the last three decades," and that "[t]here is no basis for EPA to treat [the latest] request differently."[313]

ii. Central Valley Chrysler-Jeep, Inc. v. Witherspoon

On February 16, 2005, 10 automobile dealers, together with the Alliance of Automobile Manufacturers, filed an amended complaint against CARB Executive Officer Catherine Witherspoon in the U.S. District Court for the Eastern District of California.[314] Pursuant to the Supremacy Clause of the U.S. Constitution and 42 U.S.C. § 1983, the plaintiffs sought (1) a declaratory judgment that the Pavley Amendment violated federal law[315] and (2) a permanent injunction enjoining CARB from implementing or enforcing the Pavley Amendment.[316] Specifically, the plaintiffs argued that the Pavley Amendment:

- was preempted under section 509 of the EPCA because it is "inconsistent with NHTSA's determination of the 'maximum feasible' [CAFE] standards for cars and light-duty trucks";[317]
- was preempted under section 209 of the CAA;[318] and
- violated the "authoritative determination" by the EPA in its September 8, 2003 Notice of Proposed Rulemaking that "regulation of carbon dioxide and [GHGs] to address global climate change is not authorized by section 202(a)" of the CAA.[319]

In addition to these statutory arguments, the plaintiffs cited safety concerns[320] and claimed that the Pavley Amendment "will require motor vehicles to attain substantially higher fuel economy than required by federal regulation, at higher retail prices to the consumer, and with much higher costs and burdens on the industry."[321] Further, the plaintiffs argued that the Pavley Amendment will "raise vehicle prices, and those price increases will slow the rate at which newer gasoline-powered vehicles replace older vehicles in California."[322] Since these older vehicles have higher emissions of pollutants, the plaintiffs claimed that the Pavley Amendment created more air pollution because it delayed the "essential" process of replacing older vehicles with newer ones "as rapidly as possible."[323] The plaintiffs also challenged the effectiveness of the Pavley Amendment, noting that CARB did not claim that the regulations would "result in any reduction in ambient temperatures in California"; such a claim was scientifically unsustainable because the level of GHG emissions in the atmosphere is "largely determined by the level of industrial activity . . . occurring on a global basis, and that activity is beyond the control of the California regulatory process."[324]

On June 1, 2006, California filed a motion for judgment on the pleadings, contending that each of the plaintiffs' causes of action had failed to state a claim upon which relief could be granted;[325] the court heard the motion on September 11, 2006.[326] In a September 25, 2006 opinion, Judge Anthony Ishii denied California's motion.[327] With respect to each of the plaintiffs' claims, Judge Ishii found that:

- Both the language of the EPCA and the NHTSA's interpretation of the EPCA's objectives support the plaintiffs' contention that "the objectives of the CAFE program are maximizing fuel economy, avoiding economic harm to the automobile industry, maintaining consumer choice, and ensuring vehicle safety."[328] Further, Judge Ishii wrote that the NHTSA has "echo[ed]" the plaintiffs' position that imposition of the Pavley Amendment would create a conflicting standard that "risk[s] serious adverse economic consequences for motor vehicle manufacturers generally and unduly limit[s] choices for consumers."[329] Judge Ishii concluded that, given the NHTSA's position and the lack of evidence of congressional intent to "permit California regulations that stand as an obstacle to the EPCA's objectives," the plaintiffs' claim of EPCA preemption could go forward.[330]
- EPA has not waived preemption under section 209 of the CAA, and nothing in the record "justifie[d] granting judgment on the pleadings by speculating that the EPA will make a future factual finding that favors" California.[331]

In January 2007, Judge Ishii postponed the trial pending the outcome of the Supreme Court's decision in *Massachusetts v. EPA*.

iii. Discovery Issues

A recent ruling in the *Witherspoon* litigation may impact discovery disputes in climate change litigation, and particularly cases challenging state attempts to regulate GHGs. In April 2006, California served a demand for the plaintiffs' documents on the science of global warming, the vehicle manufacturers' knowledge of global warming, and their domestic and foreign activities with respect to the issue of global warming.[332] The plaintiffs refused to produce these documents, arguing that the requests were "overbroad, unduly burdensome, and in no way . . . 'reasonably calculated to lead to the discovery of admissible evidence.'"[333] California moved to compel production.[334]

In a July 7, 2006 ruling, the district court denied California's motion. First, the court found that the discovery had no relevance to the plaintiffs' claims that the Pavley Amendment was preempted by federal law.[335] Its only plausible relevance, the court found, was to the plaintiffs' claim that the Pavley Amendment violated the dormant Commerce Clause—that is, the Pavley Amendment is unconstitutional because its burden on interstate commerce exceeds the local benefits.[336] California argued that the plaintiffs' knowledge of global warming is relevant to this "burden" analysis, because plaintiffs should have foreseen laws like the Pavley Amendment in light of their knowledge of vehicles' contribution to global warming.[337] The court rejected this argument, finding that the foreseeability of a regulation, and what the plaintiffs knew or had been "saying internally" about climate change, are irrelevant to the burden analysis under the dormant Commerce Clause.[338]

c. Oregon

i. Clean Cars Program

In 2003, Oregon Governor Ted Kulongoski appointed an advisory group composed of representatives from business, agricultural, ranching, academic, energy and environmental backgrounds to study the impact of global warming on the state.[339] The Oregon Advisory Council on Global Warming issued a report that, among other items, recommended stricter vehicle emission standards.[340] Based on this report, the governor proposed a Clean Cars program, under which Oregon would permanently adopt California's emissions standards for automobiles and light trucks beginning in model year 2009.[341] Oregon's Environmental Quality Commission temporarily adopted the standards in December 2005; under Oregon law, the Commission has 180 days to permanently adopt them.[342]

ii. Ferrioli v. Oregon Department of Environmental Quality

Oregon State Senator Ted Ferrioli, together with two other lawmakers, several automobile dealers and the Alliance of Automobile Manufacturers, filed suit in September 2005 against the Oregon Department of Environmental Quality and the Oregon Environmental Quality Commission.[343] The plaintiffs challenged the Clean Cars program on state law grounds, claiming that Governor Kulongoski impermissibly vetoed a provision in the Department of Environmental Quality's budget, inserted by legislators during the 2005 session, barring the agency from investing resources to adopt the California standards.[344] The plaintiffs claimed that the governor may use his authority to delete a particular spending program from appropriations bills, but not to delete a "legislative condition" imposed on a particular program.[345] The state argued that the Oregon constitution authorizes the governor to line-item veto a "single item" from a budget bill, but does not limit what kind of item that can be.[346]

On March 23, 2006, a state circuit judge rejected the plaintiffs' claims, finding that the vetoed provision was not tied to a specific amount of money.[347] Rather, the court held, the single-sentence item simply said that the Department of Environmental Quality may not expend any funds to adopt rules that impose the California standards.[348] The court noted that "[u]nder the plaintiffs' theory, the governor must veto the entire appropriation bill in order to get to the objectionable item," and that Oregon's line item veto law "was passed to prevent that outcome."[349]

d. Maine

i. Amendment to Chapter 127

A 2003 Maine law required the state's Department of Environmental Protection (Maine DEP) to develop and submit a Climate Action Plan for the state.[350] As part of this plan, the DEP was directed to conduct an annual state GHG emissions inventory.[351] Following a 2005 inventory which revealed that transportation accounted for nearly half of Maine's total carbon dioxide emissions, the Maine DEP issued a public notice stating its intent to adopt amendments to its motor vehicle emissions standards, contained in Chapter 127 of its agency rules.[352] The amendments required Maine to adopt California's GHG emission standards for new motor vehicles beginning with model year 2009.[353] Following a comment period, the amendments were permanently adopted on December 19, 2005.[354]

ii. Alliance of Automobile Manufacturers v. Maine

Shortly after the Maine DEP adopted the amendments to Chapter 127, the Alliance of Automobile Manufacturers sought review of the action in the Kennebec County Superior Court.[355] The plaintiffs claimed that (1) the Maine DEP failed to adequately consider submissions made by the plaintiffs during the comment period;[356] (2) the amendments represented a significant agency action that should be reviewed by the Maine legislature prior to adoption;[357] and (3) adoption of the amendments was generally "arbitrary and capricious."[358] The plaintiffs requested that the amendments be stayed until their comments were reviewed and sought a declaration that the Maine DEP must obtain legislative review.[359] The plaintiffs further sought an order invalidating the amendments.[360]

On February 3, 2006, the court denied the plaintiffs' request for a stay both on procedural grounds and because they failed to demonstrate that irreparable harm would result if the rule remained in place while the lawsuit goes forward.[361]

e. Vermont

i. Amendments to the Air Pollution Control Regulations

In November 2005, the Vermont Department of Environmental Conservation (Vermont DEC) amended its Air Pollution Control Regulations to include more stringent GHG emissions standards for new motor vehicles, incorporating by reference the California standards under the Pavley Amendment.[362] The amendments, which became effective on November 22, 2005, set forth different standards for four classifications of vehicles and established near- and mid-term standards for GHG emissions that apply to model years 2009 and later.[363] There was some precedent for this, as Vermont was one of the early states—"following closely on New York's and Massachusetts' heels in 1998"—to adopt California's standards for other pollutants such as sulfur dioxide.[364]

ii. Green Mountain Chrysler Plymouth Dodge Jeep v. Torti

On November 18, 2005, several Vermont car dealerships, together with the Alliance of Automobile Manufacturers and General Motors and DaimlerChrysler, filed an action in federal district court for declaratory and injunctive relief, pursuant to the Supremacy Clause, against the Vermont DEC.[365] The plaintiffs argued that the amendments would "force Vermont citizens to pay thousands of dollars more for new vehicles than residents of most other [s]tates in the nation—but will do nothing concrete to improve air quality or the health of Vermont residents."[366] The complaint alleged that the amendments were preempted by the both section 509 of the EPCA and section 209 of the CAA.[367] In the alternative, the plaintiffs alleged that the amendments were an "undue burden on the automobile industry and its customers" under the CAA:

> [The Vermont amendments] require[] manufacturers to ensure that the mix of vehicles sold in Vermont meets specific average [carbon dioxide] levels on a multi-year basis. This element of the Vermont regulation is on its face identical to the requirements of [the Pavley Amendment].

> Although nominally identical to the California regulation, as applied in Vermont [the amendments] will directly or indirectly force some manufacturers to restrict or limit the sale of some vehicles that would be legal for sale in California, and that could be sold in California in compliance with [the Pavley Amendment]. This will be necessary because, for some manufacturers, the mix of various types of vehicles sold in Vermont differs substantially from the mix of vehicles sold in California. Manufacturers will be forced to limit the availability of some of their California product offerings in Vermont, to the detriment of Vermont dealers, consumers, and themselves.[368]

The plaintiffs further argued that the amendments violate U.S. foreign policy,[369] the dormant Commerce Clause,[370] and section 1 of the Sherman Antitrust Act.[371]

This lawsuit is pending.

iii. Association of International Automobile Manufacturers v. Torti

Also on November 18, 2005, the Association of International Automobile Manufacturers filed a complaint against the Vermont DEC in district court.[372] As with the

Green Mountain plaintiffs, the plaintiffs here asserted that the amendments were preempted by both section 509 of the MVICA[373] and section 209 of the CAA.[374] The plaintiffs sought a declaratory judgment that the amendments violated federal law and preliminary and permanent injunctions enjoining the Vermont DEC from implementing the amendments.[375]

This lawsuit is pending.

f. New York

i. Amendment to the New York Statutes

The New York State Department of Environmental Conservation (New York DEC) amended its emissions standards for motor vehicles on December 22, 2005, to incorporate the modifications California made via the Pavley Amendment.[376]

ii. Alliance of Automobile Manufacturers v. Sheehan

On August 5, 2005, the Alliance of Automobile Manufacturers, together with several car dealerships, filed a petition in New York Supreme Court (Albany County), pursuant to Article 78 of the New York Civil Practice Law and Rules, to annul the New York DEC's Negative Declaration.[377] The petitioners also sought an injunction barring the New York DEC from implementing the new standards.[378] The petition stated two causes of action: (1) that the New York DEC failed to comply with the procedural mandates of the State Environmental Quality Review Act (SEQRA);[379] and (2) that the New York DEC failed to take a "hard look" at the adverse environmental impacts of the amendments, as required by SEQRA.[380]

With respect to the first cause of action, the petitioners noted that SEQRA requires state agencies to "determine whether the actions they directly undertake, fund or approve may have a significant impact on the environment, and if it is determined that the action may have a significant adverse impact, prepare or request an environmental impact statement."[381] The petitioners further noted that SEQRA requires the New York DEC in undertaking an action to:

1. properly define the proposed action;
2. identify all potential adverse environmental impacts that may result from the action;
3. thoroughly analyze the relevant impacts; and
4. provide a reasoned elaboration for the basis of its significance determination with reference to any supporting documentation (the "hard look").[382]

The petitioners argued that the New York DEC violated SEQRA by failing to classify its action as a "Type I" action,[383] or one that "carries with it the presumption that it is likely to have a significant adverse impact on the environment and may require" an Environmental Impact Statement (EIS),[384] for example, "the adoption by any agency of a comprehensive resource management plan."[385] Instead, the New

York DEC classified the amendments as an "unlisted" action and, pursuant to SEQRA regulations, prepared a "short" Environmental Assessment Form (EAF) indicating that the rule did not exceed the Type I threshold.[386] The petitioners claimed that the amendment was a Type I action, thus requiring a more detailed "full" EAF, because it amounts to a "comprehensive resource management plan."[387]

The petitioners also argued that the short EAF was erroneous because the New York DEC "improperly failed to identify *any* potential adverse impacts," such as the two identified by the petitioners—the fleet turnover and rebound effects.[388, 389] The petitioners further claimed that the New York DEC failed to include in the EAF the requisite "hard look," or a "reasoned elaboration" to support its conclusion that the amendments had no potential for causing significant adverse environmental impact.[390]

On May 19, 2006, the petitioners dropped their lawsuit, explaining that they "reviewed their strategy and decided that this particular action doesn't fit in with the approach we're pursuing."[391] The petitioners did, however, note that they had not made any decisions as to whether they would pursue the matter in federal court.[392] To date, no federal suit has been filed.

IV. Conclusion

Congress did not adopt either the Clean Air Act or the fuel economy requirements of the Energy Policy and Conservation Act with climate change in mind. Rather, Congress's intent was both broader in the case of the Clean Air Act (to provide a general framework for addressing air pollution) and narrower in the case of the fuel economy laws (to promote energy conservation and independence). With the advent of global climate change as a matter of policy and increasing political concern, a political stalemate has developed on national efforts to set goals and establish measures to control emissions of greenhouse gases for purposes of mitigating global climate change, and legal maneuvering has intensified as to whether these existing statutes should be utilized to control emissions of greenhouse gases and whether they in fact preempt such action by the states. With the current Administration's stance against a national regulatory effort, the Clean Air Act battle has focused on forcing further action. With a different Administration, that battle might well shift to contesting whether the Clean Air Act provides a valid basis for such action. In any case, in the long run it is fair to view such battles as skirmishes in the ongoing broader political debate over what should be the appropriate goals and measures that we should be adopting as a nation to address this issue. Assuming current trends continue toward reaching political consensus that national action is warranted, such goals and measures will be clarified either in these statutes or in a separate stand-alone law that establishes a coherent strategy and program.

Endnotes

1. Air Pollution Control Act of 1955, Pub. L. No. 84-159, 69 Stat. 322.
2. Clean Air Act of 1963, Pub. L. No. 88-206, 77 Stat. 392.
3. *Id.*
4. Motor Vehicle Air Pollution Control Act of 1965, Pub. L. No. 89-272, 79 Stat. 992.
5. Act of Oct. 15, 1966, Pub. L. No. 89-675, 80 Stat. 954-55.
6. Air Quality Act of 1967, Pub. L. No. 90-148, 81 Stat. 485.
7. Act of Dec. 5, 1969, Pub. L. No. 91-137, 83 Stat. 283.
8. Clean Air Act of 1970, Pub. L. No. 91-604, 84 Stat. 1676-1713 (codified at 42 U.S.C. §§ 7401- 7671q (2000)).
9. 42 U.S.C. § 7409.
10. 42 U.S.C. §§ 7409-10.
11. 42 U.S.C. § 7429.
12. 42 U.S.C. § 7412.
13. 42 U.S.C. § 7521.
14. 42 U.S.C. § 7401(b)(1).
15. *See* Sierra Club v. EPA, 540 F.2d 1114, 1124-27 (D.C. Cir. 1976) ("It would fly in the face of overwhelming evidence of legislative intent to hold that the Clean Air Act does not contain a requirement of prevention of significant deterioration.").
16. Act to Amend the Clean Air Act, Pub. L. No. 95-95, 91 Stat. 685 (1977).
17. *Id.*
18. *Id.*
19. *Id.*
20. *Id.*
21. In areas with unhealthy air, NSR assures that new emissions do not slow progress toward cleaner air; in areas with clean air, especially pristine areas like national parks, NSR assures that new emissions do not significantly worsen air quality. *See* EPA, *New Source Review (NSR), available at* http://www.epa.gov/nsr/ (last visited May 26, 2006).
22. EPA, *New Source Review (NSR), available at* http://www.epa.gov/nsr/ (last visited May 26, 2006).
23. Act to Amend the Clean Air Act, Pub. L. No. 101-549, 104 Stat. 2399 (1990).
24. *Id.*
25. Title VI was codified at 42 U.S.C. §§ 7671-7671p (2000).
26. *See, e.g.,* Katya Jestin, *International Efforts to Abate the Depletion of the Ozone Layer,* 7 GEO. INT'L ENVTL. L. REV. 829, 837-38 (1995).
27. EPA, *Overview: The Clean Air Act Amendments of 1990, available at* http://www.epa.gov/oar/caa/overview.txt (last visited May 26, 2006).
28. 42 U.S.C. § 7671a(e); *see also* EPA, *Overview: The Clean Air Act Amendments of 1990, available at* http://www.epa.gov/oar/caa/overview.txt (last visited May 26, 2006).
29. 42 U.S.C. § 7671a(e).
30. *See generally* 42 U.S.C. § 7671k(a).
31. Protection of Stratospheric Ozone: Listing of Substitutes in the Motor Vehicle Air Conditioning Sector Under the SNAP Program, 71 Fed. Reg. 55,140, 55,141 (Sept. 21, 2006).

32. Protection of Stratospheric Ozone: Listing of Substitutes in the Motor Vehicle Air Conditioning Sector Under the SNAP Program, 71 Fed. Reg. at 55,142.

33. New Refrigerant Plan Highlights Plaintiffs' Case in CO_2 Suit, InsideEPA (Oct. 5, 2006) (on file with author).

34. Protection of Stratospheric Ozone: Listing of Substitutes in the Motor Vehicle Air Conditioning Sector Under the SNAP Program, 71 Fed. Reg. at 55,142.

35. *Id.*

36. Act to Amend the Clean Air Act, § 821, Pub. L. No. 101-549, 104 Stat. 2399 (1990).

37. *Id.*

38. Memorandum from Jonathan Z. Cannon, General Counsel, EPA, to Carol M. Browner, Administrator, EPA 1 (Apr. 10, 1998), *available at* http://www.law.umaryland.edu/environment/casebook/documents/EPACO2memo1.pdf (last visited May 26, 2006) [hereinafter "Cannon Mem."]. Specifically, Cannon discussed sulfur dioxide, nitrogen oxide, carbon dioxide and mercury.

39. *See* Cannon Mem., *supra* note 38, at 1-2. Cannon's memorandum was a response to Congressman Tom DeLay's request to Browner for a legal opinion on whether the CAA granted the EPA the power to regulate carbon dioxide emissions from electric power plants. DeLay's question apparently arose in the context of proposed legislation addressing the restructuring of the electric utility industry.

40. 42 U.S.C. § 7602(g).

41. Cannon Mem., *supra* note 38, at 2.

42. *Id.*, at 3.

43. *Id.*

44. *Id.*

45. *Id.*, at 3-4.

46. *Id.*, at 4.

47. *Id.*, at 5.

48. Press Release, The White House, President Names Gary Guzy as General Counsel at the EPA (Nov. 17, 1998), *available at* http://www.clintonfoundation.org/legacy/111798-president-names-gary-guzy-as-general-counsel-at-the-epa.htm (last visited May 26, 2006).

49. *Is CO₂ a Pollutant and Does EPA Have the Power to Regulate It?: Joint Hearing of the Subcomm. on National Economic Growth, Natural Resources and Regulatory Affairs of the H. Comm. on Government Reform and the Subcomm. on Energy and Environment of the H. Comm. on Science*, 106th Cong. (1999) (testimony of Gary S. Guzy, General Counsel, EPA), *available at* http://www.epa.gov/ocirpage/hearings/testimony/106_1999_2000/100699gg.htm (last visited May 26, 2006) [hereinafter "Guzy Test"].

50. *See* Guzy Test, *supra* note 49.

51. *Id.*

52. *Id.* ("EPA has not made any of the Act's threshold findings that would lead to regulation of CO2 emissions from electric utilities or, indeed, from any source.").

53. *Id.*

54. *Id.*

55.   EPA, EPA History – Office of General Counsel, http://www.epa.gov/history/admin/ogc/index.htm (last visited May 26, 2006).

56.   Memorandum from Robert E. Fabricant, General Counsel, EPA, to Marianne L. Horinko, Acting Administrator, EPA 1 (Aug. 28, 2003), *available at* http://www.epa.gov/airlinks/co2_ general_counsel_
opinion.pdf (last visited May 26, 2006) [hereinafter "Fabricant Mem."].

57.   Fabricant Mem., *supra* note 56, at 10 n.9.

58.   529 U.S. 120 (2000).

59.   529 U.S. at 126.

60.   529 U.S. at 159.

61.   Fabricant Mem., *supra* note 56, at 9.

62.   *Id.*, at 4, 9-10.

63.   *Id.*, at 5.

64.   *Id.*

65.   *Id.*, at 8.

66.   *Id.*

67.   *Id.*, at 5. Fabricant referred to uncodified section 821 of the 1990 Amendments, section 602 and section 103(g), which called for development of non-regulatory measures for prevention of multiple air pollutants.

68.   *Id.*, at 5. Fabricant referred to sections 103(g) and 602 of the 1990 Amendments.

69.   *Id.*

70.   *Id.*, at 6 (*citing* H.R. Conf. Rep. No. 101-952 at 349 (1990)).

71.   *Id.*

72.   *Id.*, at 7.

73.   *Id.*

74.   *Id.*

75.   *Id.*, at 7-8.

76.   *Id.*, at 7.

77.   *Id.*, at 7-8.

78.   *See* Meeting Materials, Air Quality Management Subcommittee of the Clean Air Act Advisory Committee, May 18-19, 2006, *available at* http://www.epa.gov/air/caaac/aqm/200605_meeting_ materials.pdf (last visited August 9, 2006) [hereinafter "AQMS Meeting Materials"].

79.   *See* EPA Clean Air Act Advisory Committee, Air Quality Management Subcommittee, http://www.epa.gov/air/caaac/aqm.html#membership (last visited Aug. 9, 2006).

80.   AQMS Meeting Materials, *supra* note 78, at 27.

81.   *Id.*

82.   *Id.*

83.   *See* EPA Clean Air Act Advisory Committee, Air Quality Management Subcommittee, http://www.epa.gov/air/caaac/aqm. html#membership (last visited August 9, 2006).

84.   *See* EnergyWashingtonWeek, Honda Breaks With Auto Industry in Call For Emissions Trading Waiver, Apr. 13, 2006, *available at* http://www.sustainablebusiness.com/news/sbnews.cfm?id=9456 (noting that, at an April 4, 2006 meeting of the full Clean Air Act Advisory Committee, Greg Dana of the Alliance of Automobile Manufacturers informed meeting participants that "[m]any in the industry and our lawyers told me they don't want any discussion of greenhouse gas activities" in the committee").

85.   Control of Emissions from New Highway Vehicles and Engines, 68 Fed. Reg. 52,922, 52,923 (EPA Sept. 8, 2003) (notice of denial of petition for rulemaking).

86.   Section 202(a)(1) provides that the EPA Administrator "shall by regulation prescribe . . . in accordance with the provisions of [section 202], standards applicable to the emission of any air pollutant from any class or classes of new motor vehicle . . .

which in his judgment cause, or contribute to, air pollution which may reasonably be anticipated to endanger public health or welfare." 42 U.S.C. § 7521(a)(1).

87. Control of Emissions from New Highway Vehicles and Engines, 68 Fed. Reg. at 52,925.

88. *Id.*

89. *Id.*

90. *Id.*

91. *Id.*

92. *Id.*

93. *Id.*

94. *Id.* (emphasis added).

95. *Id.* (emphasis added).

96. *Id.*, at 52,929-30.

97. *Id.*, at 52,930.

98. *Id.*, at 52,933.

99. Section 307(b)(1) of the CAA provides the Court of Appeals for the D.C. Circuit with exclusive jurisdiction over final actions taken by the Administrator. *See* 42 U.S.C. 7607(b)(1).

100. Massachusetts v. EPA, 415 F.3d 50 (D.C. Cir. 2005).

101. *Id.*, at 54.

102. The court referred to *Lujan v. Defenders of Wildlife,* 504 U.S. 555, 560 (1992) and *Steel Co. v. Citizens for a Better Environment,* 523 U.S. 83, 97 (1998).

103. Massachusetts v. EPA, 415 F.3d at 55-56.

104. *Id.*, at 56.

105. Ethyl Corp. v. EPA, 541 F.2d 1 (D.C. Cir. 1976).

106. Massachusetts v. EPA, 415 F.3d at 57-58 (*citing* Ethyl Corp., 541 F.2d at 20, 26).

107. *Id.*, at 58.

108. *Id.*, at 59.

109. *Id.*, at 60 (*quoting* Fla. Audubon Soc'y v. Bentsen, 94 F.3d 658, 664 (D.C. Cir. 1996).

110. *Id.*, at 64.

111. *Id.*, at 67.

112. *Id.*, at 80-82.

113. *See* § II.C.2, *supra.*

114. Massachusetts v. EPA, 415 F.3d at 69-70.

115. *Id.*, at 70.

116. Mova Pharm., 140 F.3d at 1068 (*citing* Chevron U.S.A., Inc. v. Natural Res. Defense Council, Inc., 467 U.S. 837, 842 (1984)).

117. Massachusetts v. EPA, 415 F.3d at 70 (*citing* Control of Emissions from New Highway Vehicles and Engines, 68 Fed. Reg. at 52,929 (noting that "improving fuel economy" is a "practical way of reducing . . . tailpipe emissions" and that other technologies for reduction may develop in the future)).

118. *See* Petition for Writ of Certiorari at 11, Massachusetts v. EPA, No. 05-1120 (Mar. 22, 2006).

119. *See* Massachusetts v. EPA, 466 F.3d 66, 67 (D.C. Cir. 2005).

120. Petition for Writ of Certiorari at 4, 12, Massachusetts v. EPA, No. 05-1120 (Mar. 22, 2006).

121. Petition for Writ of Certiorari at 4, 16-22, Massachusetts v. EPA, No. 05-1120 (Mar. 22, 2006).

122. Massachusetts v. EPA, 126 S. Ct. 2960 (2006); *see also* United States Supreme Court Docket, No. 05-1120, *available at* http://www.supremecourtus.gov/docket/05-1120.htm (last visited August 9, 2006).

123. Section 108 charges the EPA Administrator with establishing a list of air pollutants "reasonably . . . anticipated to endanger public health or welfare," created by "numerous or diverse mobile or stationary sources." 42 U.S.C. § 7408(a)(1).

124. *See* Richard W. Thackeray, Jr., *Struggling for Air: The Kyoto Protocol, Citizens' Suits Under the Clean Air Act, and the United States' Options for Addressing Global Climate Change*, 14 IND. INT'L & COMP. L. REV. 855, 888 (2004) (*citing* Notice of Intent to Sue Under Clean Air Act § 7604, Massachusetts v. Whitman, Jan. 30, 2003).

125. The states cited both the Cannon Memorandum and Guzy's October 1999 testimony before Congress. *See* Complaint ¶¶ 34-35, Massachusetts v. Whitman, No. 3:03-CV-984 (D. Conn. June 4, 2003), *available at* http://www.ago.state.ma.us/filelibrary/108%20complaint%2006-04-03.pdf (last visited May 26, 2006).

126. Thackeray, Jr., *Struggling for Air*, *supra* note 124, at 888-89 (*citing* Notice of Intent to Sue Under Clean Air Act § 7604, Massachusetts v. Whitman, Jan. 30, 2003).

127. Complaint ¶¶ 55-58, Massachusetts v. Whitman (*citing* United States Dep't of State, *United States Climate Action Report – 2002* (May 2002), *available at* http://unfccc.int/resource/docs/natc/usnc3.pdf (last visited Feb. 7, 2006)) (last visited May 26, 2006).

128. Complaint ¶ 123, Massachusetts v. Whitman.

129. *See* Press Release, Office of the Massachusetts Attorney General, AG Reilly to Challenge EPA Ruling That Refuses to Regulate Greenhouse Gases From Cars (Aug. 28, 2003), *available at* http://www.ago.state.ma.us/sp.cfm?pageid=986&id=1068 (last visited May 26, 2006); *see also* Fabricant Mem., *supra* note 56.

130. *See* Office of the Massachusetts Attorney General, Climate Change (Global Warming), http://www.ago.state.ma.us/sp.cfm?pageid=1234 (last visited May 26, 2006).

131. *See* 42 U.S.C. § 7411 (b)(1)(B).

132. Section 111 of the CAA provides: "The Administrator shall, at least every [eight] years, review and, if appropriate, revise [NSPS] following the procedure required by this subsection for promulgation of such standards. Notwithstanding the requirements of the previous sentence, the Administrator need not review any such standard if the Administrator determines that such review is not appropriate in light of readily available information on the efficacy of such standard." 42 U.S.C. § 7411(b)(1)(B).

133. Complaint ¶¶ 1, 4, Our Children's Earth Found. v. EPA, No. C 03-0770 (N.D. Cal. Feb. 21, 2003,) *available at* http://www.ocefoundation.org/NSPS%20Complaint%20Final.pdf (last visited May 26, 2006).

134. *See generally* Complaint, Our Children's Earth Found.

135. Complaint ¶¶ 22-34, Our Children's Earth Found.

136. These were California, Maine, Massachusetts, Connecticut, New York, New Jersey, Rhode Island, Washington and New Hampshire. Peter Glaser, *"Greenhouse Gas" Debate Enters the Courthouse*, 24 No. 9 ANDREWS ENVTL. LITIG. REP. (Wash. Legal Found.) 11 (Dec. 5, 2003).

137. *See* Darren Samuelsohn, *Clean Air: Enviros, EPA Settle Pollution Lawsuit for New Power Plants*, GREENWIRE, Nov. 13, 2003.

138. Proposed Consent Decree ¶¶ 5-6, Our Children's Earth Found. v. EPA, No. C 03-0770 (N.D. Cal. Nov. 12, 2003), *available at* http://www.ocefoundation.org/10-3-03OCE-SCNSPS Decreefinal.pdf (last visited May 26, 2006).

139. *See* Our Children's Earth Foundation, *Enforcement: Completed Cases*, http://www.ocefoundation.org/litigation.html (last visited May 26, 2006).

140. *See* 70 Fed. Reg. 9706 (Feb. 28, 2005).

141. Proposed Consent Decree ¶¶ 5-6, Our Children's Earth Found.

142. *See* 71 Fed. Reg. 9866 (Feb. 27, 2006).

143. *See* 71 Fed. Reg. at 9867.

144. *See* 71 Fed. Reg. at 9869, 9871.

145. Center for International Environmental Law, *CIEL Attorney Publishes Article Suggesting Legal Tools to Limit CO2 Emissions from New Coal-Fired Power Plants*, *available at* http://www.ciel.org/Climate/CO2_Foote_11May04.html) (last visited May 26, 2006) [hereinafter "CIEL Analysis"]. *See also* Chapter 19, *infra*.

146. *See* 71 Fed. Reg. at 9869.

147. Letter from Attorneys General of New York, Connecticut, Maine, Massachusetts, New Jersey, Rhode Island and Washington to Christine Todd Whitman, Commissioner, EPA 1-2 (Feb. 20, 2003), *available at* http://www.oag.state.ny.us/press/2003/feb/whitman_letter.pdf (last visited May 26, 2006) [hereinafter "Attorneys General Letter"].

148. Attorneys General Letter, *supra* note 147, at 1-2.

149. Press Release, Office of the Attorney General of New York, States Sue EPA for Violating Clean Air Act and Refusing to Act on Global Warming, Apr. 27, 2006, *available at* http://www.oag.state.ny.us/press/2006/apr/apr27a_06.html (last visited May 26, 2006).

150. Press Release, Office of the Attorney General of New York, States Sue EPA for Violating Clean Air Act and Refusing to Act on Global Warming, *available at* http://www.oag.state.ny.us/press/2006/apr/apr27a_06.html (last visited May 26, 2006).

151. *See* Act to Amend the Clean Air Act, Pub. L. No. 95-95, 91 Stat. 685 (1977).

152. 42 U.S.C. § 7475(a)(4).

153. 42 U.S.C. § 7502(3).

154. Nw. Envtl. Def. Ctr. v. Owens Corning Corp., 434 F. Supp. 2d 957, 961-62 (D. Or. 2006).

155. *Nw. Envtl. Def. Ctr.*, 434 F. Supp. 2d at 962.

156. *Id.*, at 962 (*citing* Warth v. Seldin, 422 U.S. 490, 498 (1975)).

157. *Id.*, at 964 (citations omitted).

158. *Id.*, at 964.

159. *Id.*, at 965.

160. *Id.*, at 967.

161. *Id.*, at 967-68.

162. *Id.*, at 968.

163. *Id.*

164. *Id.*

165. *Id.* (*quoting* Valley Forge Christian Coll. v. Ams. United for Separation of Church & State, 454 U.S. 464, 474-75 (1982)).

166. *Id.*, at 969.

167. *Id.*, at 970.

168. *See* CIEL Analysis, *supra* note 145.

169. *Id.; see also* EPA, *Multipollutant Emission Control Technology Options for Coal-fired Power Plants* 3-84 (2005), *available at* http://www.epa.gov/airmarkets/articles/

multireport2005.pdf (last visited May 26, 2006) [hereinafter *"Multipollutant Emission Control Technology Options"*].

170. *See* CIEL Analysis, *supra* note 145; *see also* EPA, *Multipollutant Emission Control Technology Options*, *supra* note 169, at 3-84.

171. EPA, *Multipollutant Emission Control Technology Options*, *supra* note 169, at 3-83.

172. Gregory B. Foote, *Considering Alternatives: The Case for Limiting CO2.*
Emissions from New Power Plants Through New Source Review, 34 ENVTL. L. REP. (Envtl. Law Inst.) 10,642, 10,665-66 (2004), *available at* http://www.ciel.org/Publications/CO2_Foote_11May04.pdf (last visited May 26, 2006).

173. Foote, *Considering Alternatives*, *supra* note 172, at 10,665-66.

174. *Id.*, at 10,666-67

175. Hr'g Officer's Report and Recommended Sec'y's Order at 6-7, *Sierra Club v. Envtl. & Pub. Prot. Cabinet & Thoroughbred Generating Co., LLC*, File Nos. DAQ-26003-037 and DAQ-26048-037 (Ky. Envtl. & Pub. Prot. Cabinet Aug. 9, 2005), *available at* http://www.sierraclub.org/environmentallaw/lawsuits/docs/2005-08-09-thoroughbred-ky-decision.pdf (last visited May 26, 2006) [hereinafter "Sierra Club Report & Order"].

176. Sierra Club Report & Order, *supra* note 175, ¶¶ 311-12.

177. *Id.* ¶¶ 378-79.

178. The DAQ and Thoroughbred cited *In re* Pennsauken County, N.J. Res. Recovery Facility for this proposition. *See* Sierra Club Report & Order, *supra* note 175, ¶ 382.

179. Sierra Club Report & Order, *supra* note 175, ¶¶ 413-14.

180. *Id.* ¶ 415.

181. *See* Montana Dep't of Environmental Quality, *Montana Top-Down Best Available Control Technology (BACT) Analysis Process And Procedures Manual* 8 (2004), *available at* http://deq.mt.gov/ber/2004_Agendas/2004JANUARY/MT_BACT_Manual_Final_Draft_12-17-03.pdf (last visited May 26, 2006).

182. *See* Renee Cipriano, Director, Illinois EPA, Director's Viewpoint, *Mercury Reduction is a Priority*, *available at* http://www.epa.state.il.us/environmental-progress/v29/n1/directors-viewpoint.html (last visited May 26, 2006).

183. *See* Clean Wis., Inc. v. Pub. Serv. Comm'n of Wis., 2005 WI 93, ¶¶ 192-93, 282 Wis.2d 250, 377, ¶¶ 192-93, 700 N.W.2d 768, 830, ¶¶ 192-93 (Wis. 2005) (rejecting environmental group's claim that IGCC should have been considered as part of the BACT analysis for grant of permit).

184. Foote, *Considering Alternatives*, *supra* note 172, at 10,642.

185. *Id.*

186. *Id.*, at 10,643-51.

187. *Id.*, at 10,648.

188. *Id.*, at 10,650-51.

189. *Id.*, at 10,651.

190. *Id.*, at 10,647, 10,659-61.

191. *Id.*, at 10,667-68.

192. *In re* N. County Res. Recovery Assocs., 2 E.A.D. 229 (EPA Envtl. App. Bd. 1986).

193. *Id.*

194. *Id.*

195. *Id.*

196. *Id.* (emphasis added).

197. *Id.*

198. Foote, *Considering Alternatives*, *supra* note 172, at 10649 n.71 (*citing In re* Steel Dynamics, Inc., 9 E.A.D. 165 (Envtl. App. Bd. 2000) (*citing In re* North County as characterizing "statutory and regulatory definitions of BACT as requiring consider-

ation of environmental impacts); *In re* Genesee Power Station, 4 E.A.D. 832 (EPA Envtl. App. Bd. 1993) (definition of BACT provides for consideration of the environmental consequences of choosing one control technology over another)).

199. Letter from Stephen D. Page, Director, EPA Office of Air Quality, Planning and Standards, to Paul Plath, Senior Partner, E3 Consulting, LLC 1 (Dec. 13, 2005) (on file with author) [hereinafter "Page Letter"].

200. Page Letter, *supra* note 199, at 1-2. Page cited sections 165(a)(2) (requiring the permitting authority to allow an "opportunity for interested persons . . . to appear and submit write or oral presentations on the air quality impact of such source, *alternatives thereto*, control technology requirements, and other appropriate considerations) and 165(a)(4) (requiring that a proposed facility subject to PSD apply BACT). Page then noted that BACT is defined under section 169(3) as "an emission limitation based on the maximum degree of reduction . . . which the permitting authority . . . determines is achievable for such facility through application of production processes and available methods, systems and techniques."

201. Page Letter, *supra* note 199, at 2.

202. *Id.*

203. *Id.*, at 2-3.

204. *Id.*, at 1 (emphasis in EPA letter, added to statutory text).

205. EPA, Draft New Source Review Manual (1990), *available at* http://www.epa.gov/nsr/publications.html (last visited May 26, 2006) (drawing no distinction between the alternatives analysis and analysis).

206. *In re* Prairie State Generation Company, PSD Appeal No. 05-05 (EPA Brief filed March 7, 2006) [hereinafter "Prairie State Br."].

207. Prairie State Br., *supra* note 206, at 6.

208. *Id.*, at 15.

209. *Id.*

210. *Id.*

211. *See, e.g.*, Fabricant Mem., *supra* note 56.

212. *EPA Eyes Rulemaking to Codify Memo Rejecting IGCC in Air Permits*, CLEAN AIR REPORT, May 4, 2006.

213. *EPA Eyes Rulemaking to Codify Memo Rejecting IGCC in Air Permits*, CLEAN AIR REPORT, May 4, 2006; *see also Impact of Clean Air Regulations on Natural Gas Prices: Hearing Before the S. Comm. on Environment & Public Works*, 109th Cong. (2006) (statement of Sen. Jeffords), *available at* http://www.senate.gov/comm/environment_and _public_works/general/hearing_statements.cfm?id=251443 (last visited May 26, 2006).

214. *EPA Eyes Rulemaking to Codify Memo Rejecting IGCC in Air Permits*, CLEAN AIR REPORT, MAY 4, 2006.

215. Natural Res. Def. Council v. EPA, No. 06-1059 (consolidated with Nos. 06-1062 and 06-1063) (D.C. Cir. 2006).

216. Settlement Agreement at 1-2, Natural Res. Def. Council v. EPA, No. 06-1059 (consolidated with Nos. 06-1062 and 06-1063) (D.C. Cir. 2006).

217. Settlement Agreement at 2, Natural Res. Def. Council v. EPA, No. 06-1059 (consolidated with Nos. 06-1062 and 06-1063) (D.C. Cir. 2006).

218. *Id.*

219. 2 E.A.D. 667 (EPA Envtl. App. Bd. 1988).

220. *In re* Pennsauken County, N.J. Res. Recovery Facility, 2 E.A.D. 667 (emphasis added).

221. *Id.*

222. 2 E.A.D. 838 (EPA Envtl. App. Bd. 1988).

223. In re Hibbing Taconite Co., 2 E.A.D. 838.

224. *Id.*

225. PSD Appeal No. 03-01, 2003 EPA LEXIS 3 (EPA Envtl. App. Bd. Apr. 29, 2003).

226. *In re* Kendall New Century Dev., 2003 EPA LEXIS 3, at *30 n.14.

227. *Id.*

228. Section 209(a) reads: "No State or any political subdivision thereof shall adopt or attempt to enforce any standard relating to the control of emissions from new motor vehicles or new motor vehicle engines subject to this part. No State shall require certification, inspection, or any other approval relating to the control of emissions from any new motor vehicle or new motor vehicle engine as condition precedent to the initial retail sale, titling (if any), or registration of such motor vehicle, motor vehicle engine, or equipment." 42 U.S.C. § 7543(a).

229. 42 U.S.C. § 7543(b)(1).

230. The EPA must grant the waiver unless it finds that: (1) the determination of the state is arbitrary and capricious; (2) the state does not need the state standards to meet a compelling need; and (3) the state standards and accompanying enforcement procedures are not consistent with section 202(a). 42 U.S.C. § 7543(b)(1)(A)-(C).

231. *See, e.g.*, Rachel L. Chanin, *California's Authority to Regulate Mobile Source Greenhouse Gas Emissions*, 58 N.Y.U. ANN. SURV. AM. L. 699, 712 & n.79 (2003) [hereinafter "*California's Authority to Regulate*"].

232. *See* DAVID WOOLEY & ELIZABETH MORSS, CLEAN AIR HANDBOOK § 2:11 (2005) (*citing* 42 U.S.C. § 7507).

233. Average Fuel Economy Standards for Light Trucks Model Years 2008-2011, 71 Fed. Reg. 17,566-01, 17,654-01 (NHTSA Apr. 6, 2006) (final rule).

234. Pub. L. No. 94-163, § 301, 89 Stat. 871, 902 (1975) (current version codified at 49 U.S.C. §§ 32901-19).

235. *See* H.R. REP. No. 94-340, at 1 (1975), *as reprinted in* 1975 U.S.C.C.A.N. 1762, 1763-64; *see also* Chanin, *California's Authority to Regulate Mobile Source Greenhouse Gas Emissions, supra* note 231, at 734.

236. *See* H.R. REP. No. 94-340, at 1 (1975), *as reprinted in* 1975 U.S.C.C.A.N. 1762, 1763.

237. *Id.*

238. Chanin, *California's Authority to Regulate, supra* note 231, at 735.

239. *Id.*

240. *Id.*, at 734 n.168 (*citing* Appellant's Opening Brief at 30-31, Cent. Valley Chrysler-Plymouth v. Cal. Air Res. Bd., No. 02-16395 (9th Cir. Aug. 21, 2002) (No. 02-16395)).

241. 49 U.S.C. § 32902(a)-(c).

242. 49 U.S.C. § 32902(d)(1)(A).

243. 49 U.S.C. § 32902(d)(1)(B).

244. 49 U.S.C. § 32902(d)(2).

245. 49 U.S.C. § 32904(c).

246. 49 U.S.C. § 32908(b).

247. 49 U.S.C. § 32904(c).

248. Dep't of Transportation, Nat'l Highway Transp. & Safety Admin., CAFE Overview, http://www.nhtsa.dot.gov/cars/rules/cafe/overview.htm (last visited May 26, 2006).

249. *See* Fuel Economy Labeling of Motor Vehicles: Revisions to Improve Calculation of Fuel Economy Estimates, 71 Fed. Reg. 5426 (proposed Feb. 1, 2006).

250. 71 Fed. Reg. at 542.

251. *See* Regulatory Announcement, EPA, Office of Transportation and Air Quality, *EPA Proposes New Test Methods for Fuel Economy Window Stickers* 1 (Jan. 2006), *available at* http://www.epa.gov/fueleconomy/420f06009.pdf (last visited May 26, 2006).

252. *See id.,* at 1-2.

253. 71 Fed. Reg. at 5426.

254. *Id.*

255. 71 Fed. Reg. at 5428.

256. *Id.*

257. *See generally* 49 U.S.C. § 32902.

258. 49 U.S.C. § 32902(b).

259. Dep't of Transportation, Nat'l Highway Transp. & Safety Admin., CAFE Overview, http://www.nhtsa.dot.gov/cars/rules/cafe/overview.htm (last visited May 26, 2006).

260. The fuel economy of dedicated alternative fuel vehicles is determined by dividing its fuel economy in equivalent mpg of gasoline or diesel fuel by 0.15. For dual-fuel vehicles, the rating is the average of the fuel economy on gasoline or diesel and the fuel economy on the alternative fuel vehicle divided by 0.15. 49 U.S.C. § 32908(b)(3).

261. Robert R. Nordhaus & Kyle W. Danish, *Assessing the Options for Designing a Mandatory U.S. Greenhouse Gas Reduction Program,* 32 B.C. Envtl. Aff. L. Rev. 97, 105 (2005) [hereinafter *"Assessing the Options"*].

262. Nordhaus & Danish, *Assessing the Options, supra* note 261, at 105.

263. National Research Council, Transportation Research Board, Report, *Effectiveness and Impact of Corporate Average Fuel Economy (CAFE) Standards* 15 (2002), *available at* http://www.nhtsa.dot.gov/cars/rules/CAFE/docs/162944_web.pdf (last visited May. 26, 2006) [hereinafter *"Impact of CAFE Standards"*].

264. *See* 49 U.S.C. § 32903(a)-(b). The amount of credit earned is determined by multiplying the tenths of a mile per gallon by which the manufacturer exceeded the CAFE standard in that model year by the number of vehicles they manufactured in that year. 49 U.S.C. § 32903(c).

265. 49 U.S.C. § 32903(a)(1)-(2).

266. 49 U.S.C. § 32903(e).

267. Several limitations are established for CAFE credits for dual fuel vehicles. For model years 1993-2004, the maximum CAFE increase attributable to dual-fueled vehicles in a manufacturer's passenger car or light truck fleet is 1.2 mpg. 49 U.S.C. § 32906(a)(1).

268. National Research Council, Transportation Research Board, *Impact of CAFE Standards, supra* note 263, at 13-14.

269. Nordhaus & Danish, *Assessing the Options, supra* note 261, at 106.

270. National Research Council, *Impact of CAFE Standards, supra* note 259, at 1 ("Provisions in DOT's annual appropriations bills for fiscal years 1996 through 2001 prohibited the agency from changing or even studying CAFE standards.").

271. National Research Council, Transportation Research Board, *Impact of CAFE Standards, supra* note 263, at 18-19.

272. H.R. REP. No. 106-940, 146 CONG. REC. H8922, H8926 (2000).

273. National Research Council, Transportation Research Board, *Impact of CAFE Standards, supra* note 263, at 1.

274. National Research Council, Transportation Research Board, *Impact of CAFE Standards, supra* note 263, at 4-5 (citations omitted).

275. Average Fuel Economy Standards for Light Trucks, 70 Fed. Reg. 51,414, 51,420-23 (proposed Aug. 30, 2005).

276. *Id.,* at 51,414.

277. *Id.*

278. Average Fuel Economy Standards for Light Trucks Model Years 2008-2011, 71 Fed. Reg. 17,566-01 (NHTSA Apr. 6, 2006) (final rule).

279. *See* Press Release, Office of the New York Attorney General, State and City Sue for Better Fuel Efficiency Standards (May 2, 2006), *available at* http://www.oag.state.ny.us/press/2006/may/may02a_06.html (last visited May 26, 2006).

280. *See id.*

281. *See id.*

282. *See* Press Release, Sierra Club, Lawsuit, Website Take on Bush Administration Over Fuel Economy Standards, *available at* http://www.sierraclub.org/pressroom/releases/pr2006-05-23.asp (last visited May 26, 2006).

283. *Id.*

284. *See id.*

285. Lucy Kafanov, *Senior Boehlert Aide Says CAFE Movement Possible,* ENV'T & ENERGY DAILY, Feb. 15, 2006.

286. *Id.*

287. 49 U.S.C. § 32919(a).

288. 49 U.S.C. § 32919(b). The federal regulations are set forth at 49 U.S.C. § 32908.

289. Chanin, *California's Authority to Regulate, supra* note 227, at 733.

290. Md. Code Ann., Transp. § 13-818(c)(i)-(ii) (1992).

291. Md. Code Ann., Transp. § 13-818(c)(iii).

292. Md. Code Ann., Transp. § 13-818(f).

293. Vehicle Laws – Taxation – Environment – Preemption – Validity of "Gas Guzzler Law," 77 Op. Md. Att'y Gen. 222, 1999 WL 524661, at *1 (Op. No. 92-020 June 24, 1992) [hereinafter "Md. Gas Guzzler Law Mem."].

294. Md. Gas Guzzler Law Mem., *supra* note 293, at *4.

295. 504 U.S. 374 (1992).

296. *Morales,* 504 U.S. at 383 (*quoting* BLACK'S LAW DICTIONARY 1158 (5th ed. 1979)

297. Chanin, *California's Authority to Regulate, supra* note 231, at 749 (*quoting* Letter from Paul Jackson Rice, Chief Counsel of the NHTSA, to Joseph T. Curran, Jr., Attorney General of the State of Maryland 2 (June 8, 1992)).

298. Md. Gas Guzzler Law Mem., *supra* note 293, at *1, 3-4.

299. Curran wrote: "For example, the federal label shows separate 'City MPG' and 'Highway MPG' figures; [the Maryland legislation] mandates disclosure of a single 'fuel economy rating.' As NHTSA points out . . . these differing versions of information on the same topic – 'fuel economy' . . . potentially give rise to consumer confusion." Md. Gas Guzzler Law Mem., *supra* note 293, at *4.

300. Md. Gas Guzzler Law Mem., *supra* note 293, at *6-7.

301. *Id.,* at *4.

302. *Id.,* at *7.

303. Chanin, *California's Authority to Regulate, supra* note 231, at 751.

304. *See* Press Release, Office of the Governor of the State of California, Governor Davis Signs Historic Global Warming Bill (July 22, 2002), *available at* http://www.governor.ca.gov/state/govsite/
gov_homepage.jsp (last visited Mar. 26, 2006).

305. CAL. HEALTH & SAFETY CODE § 43018.5(a) (West 2003).

306. CAL. HEALTH & SAFETY CODE § 43018.5(b)(1).

307. Ann E. Carlson, *Federalism, Preemption, and Greenhouse Gas Emissions*, 27 ENVIRONS ENVTL. L. & POL'Y J. 281, 292 (2003) (*citing* CAL. HEALTH & SAFETY CODE § 43018.5(d)(1)-(5)).

308. *See* California Air Resources Board, Regulatory Documents for the Greenhouse Gas Emissions from Motor Vehicles, *available at* http://www.arb.ca.gov/regact/grnhsgas/grnhsgas.htm (last visited May 26, 2006).

309. Ann E. Carlson, *supra* note 307 at 281, 293 (2003); *see also* 42 U.S.C. § 7543(b)(1).

310. *See* Letter from Catherine Witherspoon, Executive Officer, CARB, to Stephen L. Johnson, Administrator, EPA (Dec. 21, 2005), *available at* http://www.arb.ca.gov/cc/docs/waiver.pdf (last visited May 26, 2006).

311. *See CAFE Rule Suggests EPA Likely to Deny California Greenhouse Waiver*, CLEAN AIR REPORT (Apr. 6, 2006), *available at* 2006 WLNR 5705082.

312. Letter from Rep. Henry A. Waxman, et al. to Hon. Stephen L. Johnson, Administrator, EPA (Sept. 26, 2006) (on file with author).

313. *Id.*

314. First Amended Complaint at 2, Cent. Valley Chrysler-Jeep, Inc. v. Witherspoon, No. CV-F-04-6663 (E.D. Cal. Feb. 16, 2005) [hereinafter "Witherspoon Compl."].

315. In addition to violations of the MVICSA and the CAA, the plaintiffs argued that the Pavley Amendment violated federal antitrust law; conflicted with "national control of foreign policy matters"; and created a burden on interstate commerce. *See* Witherspoon Compl., *supra* note 314, at 43-47.

316. *See id.*, at 47.

317. *Id.*, at 39-40.

318. *Id.*, at 41.

319. *Id.*

320. "NHTSA and other safety organizations have recognized that increases in fuel economy standards can result in reductions in the weight of the motor vehicle fleet as a whole because . . . reducing the weight of a given vehicle model can be used to reduce its fuel consumption. Reductions in vehicle weight can also reduce vehicle crashworthiness." Witherspoon Compl., *supra* note 314, at 29.

321. Witherspoon Compl., *supra* note 314, at 25-26.

322. *Id.*, at 39.

323. *Id.*

324. *Id.*

325. In July 2006, the district court denied California's request to postpone the trial until after the Supreme Court reaches a decision in *Massachusetts v. EPA*. *See* United States District Court for the Eastern District of California, Court Calendar, *available at* http://www.caed.uscourts.gov/caed/staticOther/page_455.htm (last visited August 9, 2006).

326. Cent. Valley Chrysler-Jeep, Inc. v. Witherspoon, No. CV-F-04-6663, 2006 WL 2734359 (E.D. Cal. Sept. 25, 2006).

327. *Witherspoon*, 2006 WL 2734359, at *23.

328. *Id.*, at *6.

329. *Id.*, at *7 (*quoting* Average Fuel Economy Standards for Light Trucks Model Years 2008-2011, 71 Fed. Reg. 17,566-01, 17,654-01 (NHTSA Apr. 6, 2006) (final rule)).

330. *Id.*,, at *11.

331. *Id.*, at *11-12.

332. Cent. Valley Chrysler-Jeep, Inc. v. Witherspoon, No. CV-F-04-6663, 2006 WL 1883363, at *1 (E.D. Cal. July 7, 2006).

333. *Witherspoon*, 2006 WL 1883363, at *1.

334. *Id.*

335. *Id.*, at *5.

336. *Id.* (*citing* Nat'l Audubon Soc'y, Inc. v. Davis, 307 F.3d 835, 837 (9th Cir. 2002)).

337. *Id.*, at *5-6.

338. *Id.*, at *7-8.

339. *See* Office of Governor Ted Kulongoski, Remarks by Governor Kulongoski to the Oregon Environmental Quality Commission (Dec. 22, 2005), *available at* http://governor.oregon.gov/Gov/speech/speech_122205.shtml (last visited May 26, 2006) [hereinafter "Kulongoski Remarks"].

340. *See* Kulongoski Remarks, *supra* note 339.

341. *Id.*

342. William McCall, *Oregon Panel Backs Tight Emissions Lid*, VANCOUVER COLUMBIAN, Dec. 23, 2005, at C2.

343. *See* Press Release, Sen. Ted Ferrioli, Ferrioli Files Suit to Protect Oregonians (Sept. 14, 2005), *available at* http://www.leg. state.or.us/press_releases/ferrioli_091405.pdf (last visited Mar. 22, 2006); *see also* William McCall, *Oregon Panel Backs Tight Emissions Lid*, VANCOUVER COLUMBIAN, Dec. 23, 2005, at C2.

344. Brad Cain, *Auto Industry, GOP Ask Judge to Block Oregon Emissions Cuts*, VANCOUVER COLUMBIAN, Nov. 8, 2005, at C2.

345. *See* Plaintiffs' Response to Defendant's Motion for Summary Judgment at 15-17, Ferrioli v. Or. Dep't of Envtl. Quality, No. 05C18514 (Or. Cir. Ct. Nov. 2, 2005).

346. *See* Plaintiffs' Response to Defendant's Motion for Summary Judgment at 15-17, Ferrioli v. Or. Dep't of Envtl. Quality.

347. Ferrioli v. Ore. Dep't of Envtl. Quality, No. 05C18514 (Or. Cir. Ct. May 23, 2006); *see also* Tom Alkire, *Judge Approves Governor's Line-Item Veto*, Daily Env't Rep. (BNA) No. 59, at A-4 (Mar. 28, 2006).

348. Tom Alkire, *Judge Approves Governor's Line-Item Veto*, Daily Env't Rep. (BNA) No. 59, at A-4 (Mar. 28, 2006).

349. *Id.*

350. Maine Dep't of Environmental Protection, *Maine Climate Action Plan 2004* iii, *available at* http://maineghg.raabassociates. org/Articles/MaineClimateActionPlan2004 Volume%201.pdf (last visited May 26, 2006).

351. *Id.*

352. *See* Memorandum from Lynne Cayting, Maine Department of Environmental Protection, Bureau of Air Quality, to Board of Environmental Protection 3 (Dec. 1, 2005), *available at* http://www.maine.gov/dep/air/regulations/recentlyadopted.htm (last visited May 26, 2006).

353. 06-096 ME. CODE R. ch. 127, § 4 (2005).

354. Notice of Agency Rulemaking Adoption, Chapter 127 New Motor Vehicle Emis-

sion Standards (Dec. 19, 2005), *available at* http://www.maine.gov/dep/air/regulations/recentlyadopted. htm (last visited May 26, 2006).

355. *See* Complaint ¶ 10, Alliance of Auto. Mfrs. v. Me. Bd. of Envtl. Prot. (filed Dec. 29, 2005) [hereinafter "AAM Compl."].

356. AAM Compl., *supra* note 355, ¶¶ 28-33.

357. *See id.* ¶¶ 34-38.

358. *See id.* ¶¶ 40-41.

359. *See id.* ¶ 41.

360. *See id.*

361. *Automakers Lose Legal Bid to Postpone Emissions Rule*, PORTLAND PRESS HERALD, Feb. 9, 2006, at B2.

362. *See* Vt. Air Pollution Control Reg. §§ 5-1101-09; *see also* Incorporation by Reference Statement, *available at* http://www.anr.state.vt.us/air/docs/Incorporation%20by%20Reference.pdf (last visited May 26, 2006).

363. Vt. Air Pollution Control Reg. §§ 5-1103.

364. David Gram, *Gearing Up for a Fight – Vermont, New York Weigh Tougher Standards for Car Emissions*, BUFFALO NEWS, Aug. 14, 2005, at I6.

365. *See generally* Complaint, Green Mountain Chrysler Plymouth Dodge Jeep v. Torti, No. 2:04-CV-302 (D. Vt. filed Nov. 18, 2005) [hereinafter "Green Mountain Compl."].

366. Green Mountain Compl., *supra* note 365, ¶ 4.

367. *Id.* ¶¶ 95-110.

368. *Id.* ¶¶ 112-13.

369. *Id.* ¶¶ 119-24.

370. *Id.* ¶¶ 125-30.

371. *Id.* ¶¶ 131-38.

372. *See generally* Complaint, Ass'n of Int'l Auto. Mfrs. v. Torti, No. 2:05-CV-304 (D. Vt. filed Nov. 18, 2006) [hereinafter "AIA Compl."].

373. *See* AIA Compl., *supra* note 372, ¶¶ 53-61.

374. *Id.* ¶¶ 62-69.

375. *Id.* ¶¶ 60-61, 68-69.

376. *See* New York State Department of Environmental Conservation, Division of Air Resources, Proposed, Emergency, and Recently Adopted Regulations Pertaining to Air Pollution, *available at* http://www.dec.state.ny.us/website/dar/air_regs.html (last visited May 26, 2006).

377. *See generally* Verified Petition, Alliance of Auto. Mfrs. v. Sheehan (N.Y. Sup. Ct. filed Aug. 5, 2005) [hereinafter "Sheehan Pet."].

378. Sheehan Pet., *supra* note 377, ¶ 2.

379. *See id.* ¶¶ 57-69.

380. *See id.* ¶¶ 70-72.

381. *Id.* ¶ 40 (*quoting* 6 NYCRR § 617.1(c)).

382. *Id.* ¶ 44 (*quoting* 6 NYCRR § 617.7(b)).

383. *Id.* ¶ 77.

384. *Id.* ¶ 46 (*quoting* 6 NYCRR § 617.4(a)(1)).

385. *Id.* (*quoting* 6 NYCRR § 617.4(b)(1)).

386. *Id.* ¶¶ 57-58.

387. *Id.* ¶ 60.

388. *Id.* ¶ 61.

389. The petitioners cited an analysis apparently provided to the New York DEC by Sierra Research and NERA Economic Consulting, which stated that "[I]mplementation of the proposed [amendments] in New York [would] increase ozone-forming emissions, in part due to rebound and fleet turnover effects. . . . [T]he study concludes that the increase could be at least 10 tons per day in . . . 2020." Sheehan Pet., *supra* note 377, ¶ 72.

390. *Id.* ¶ 63.

391. Danny Hakim, *Automakers Drop Lawsuit on New York's Emissions Rule*, N.Y. TIMES, May 19, 2006, at B2 (*quoting* Gloria Bergquist, spokeswoman for the Alliance of Automobile Manufacturers).

392. *Id.*

chapter six

Civil Remedies

Bradford C. Mank

I. Introduction

Chapter 6 examines how a plaintiff might file a lawsuit in a state or federal court to sue either a private party or the government that is allegedly directly or indirectly responsible for the release of greenhouse gases (GHGs) that likely exacerbate global warming. Section II reviews whether a plaintiff can demonstrate standing, even though proving that GHGs cause

global warming raises complex causation questions, her injuries are likely the same as those of many other people, and any viable remedies raise the political question doctrine. Section III examines how a plaintiff might prove causation in different types of tort, nuisance and product liability actions against private defendants, and possible remedies, including damages and injunctions. In global warming suits, there are likely complex preemption and displacement issues depending upon whether the suit is based on federal or state common law. Section IV discusses whether a plaintiff may sue the federal government under the National Environmental Policy Act (NEPA) to require study of global warming issues before a federal project or action can be taken; similar suits could be filed in the many states that have little NEPAs or executive orders requiring environmental assessments. Section V discusses whether a plaintiff may sue the federal government under the Endangered Species Act to require the government to protect species and their critical habitat threatened or endangered by global warming. Section VI briefly discusses whether global warming raises environmental justice policy issues by causing disproportionate impacts on Native Alaskans and racial minorities.

Section VII discusses whether a plaintiff may file a claim relating to global warming against the United States in various international human rights commissions. Finally, Section VIII discusses whether a plaintiff may file a claim relating to global warming under the Alien Tort Statute. Almost every global warming case raises novel legal and factual issues. It is very difficult for a plaintiff to win any type of global warming suit, but it is likely that many such suits will be filed over the next several years until appellate courts and ultimately the Supreme Court start setting clear precedent in this important area.

II. Standing

A. Introduction

The Constitution does not specifically require that a plaintiff have standing to file suit in federal courts, but Article III indirectly places limits on the federal judicial power by stating that the "judicial Power shall extend to all Cases ... [and] ... Controversies," thus excluding advisory opinions.[1] Since 1944, the Supreme Court has interpreted Article III's limitation of judicial decisions to cases and controversies as implying that federal courts should require plaintiffs to meet certain standing criteria to ensure that the plaintiff has a genuine interest and stake in a case.[2] For standing in an Article III court, the Court currently requires a plaintiff to show "[(1)][she] has suffered 'an injury in fact' that is (a) concrete and particularized and (b) actual or imminent, not conjectural or hypothetical; (2) the injury is fairly traceable to the challenged action of the defendant; and (3) it is likely, as opposed to merely speculative, that the injury will be redressed by a favorable decision."[3] A plaintiff has the burden of establishing all three elements.[4] In its 2001 decision, *Friends of the Earth, Inc. v. Laidlaw Environmental Services (TOC), Inc.* (Laidlaw), the Court stated that a plaintiff does not have to prove an actual injury to the environment, but must demonstrate "reasonable concerns" that the defendant's discharges directly affected plaintiff's recreational, aesthetic and economic interests.[5]

> **It is very difficult for a plaintiff to win any type of global warming suit, but it is likely that many such suits will be filed over the next several years . . .**

In applying the broad principles in the three-part standing test, a judge to some extent has to decide whether the facts alleged by the plaintiff are sufficiently serious to justify a court hearing the case. In *Korsinsky v. EPA*, the plaintiff filed a public nuisance action against EPA and New York state environmental agencies alleging that they were responsible for substantial carbon dioxide emissions and that they should adopt the plaintiff's invention to eliminate those emissions, for which he was seeking a patent.[6] The U.S. District Court for the Southern District of New York dismissed the case for lack of standing where the plaintiff alleged that his chronic sinus condition made him more vulnerable to illness from environmental harms resulting from global warming, including an increased risk of illness from drinking contaminated drinking water; in an unpublished opinion, the Second Circuit affirmed the dismissal for lack of standing.[7] The District Court concluded, "Such allegations fall more within the realm of the hypothetical and conjectural than the actual or imminent and therefore are insufficient for purposes of standing." In a footnote, the District Court distinguished the facts in this case from a prior case where the Second Circuit had found standing because the plaintiff had alleged that he was at a moderately elevated risk of contracting a deadly disease that had no cure or treatment, stating, "Here, by contrast, plaintiff alleges nothing more than an increase in risk over a long period of time of aggravating a chronic condition similar to allergies."[8] Additionally, even if the plaintiff could prove his second allegation that he suffered a mental illness from fear of global warming, the District Court found "[T]he requested relief in this case — that defendants be held liable for contributions to global warming, enjoined from contributing further and required to use plaintiff's invention—simply would not redress plaintiff's alleged mental injury stemming from knowledge of the general dangers of pollution."[9]

All three parts of the Article III standing test raise questions in the context of a global warming suit. First, are the injuries allegedly caused by global warming too speculative and uncertain to be a "concrete" injury-in-fact?[10] Because the Arctic is warming more rapidly than more temperate areas, an Alaskan resident might have a stronger basis than others for arguing that she is suffering specific injuries from global warming causing the melting of permafrost, which is discussed in sections VI and VII.[11] Second, is the scientific evidence sufficient to prove that

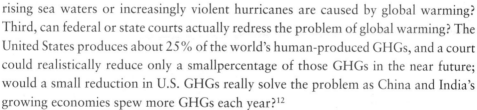

rising sea waters or increasingly violent hurricanes are caused by global warming? Third, can federal or state courts actually redress the problem of global warming? The United States produces about 25% of the world's human-produced GHGs, and a court could realistically reduce only a smallpercentage of those GHGs in the near future; would a small reduction in U.S. GHGs really solve the problem as China and India's growing economies spew more GHGs each year?[12]

Even if a plaintiff meets the three-part standing test, courts under the prudential standing doctrine may still bar a suit if it would impose excessive burdens on the court system or if the issue is better resolved by the political branches of government.[13] In cases involving generalized, abstract injuries that affect the public as a whole, such as misuse of taxpayer funds, the courts have often invoked the prudential standing or political question doctrine to reject such suits. In *Duke Power Co. v. Carolina Environmental Study Group, Inc.*, the Supreme Court stated in 1978 that a court could deny standing if a suit would raise "general prudential concerns 'about the proper—and properly limited—role of the courts in a democratic society.'"[14] The *Duke Power* Court concluded,

"Thus, we have declined to grant standing where the harm asserted amounts only to a generalized grievance shared by a large number of citizens in a substantially equal measure." But in its 1975 decision in *Warth v. Seldin*, the Court held that a plaintiff may be able to satisfy Article III standing requirements "even if it is an injury shared by a large class of other possible litigants."[15] In its 1998 decision in *Federal Election Commission v. Akins*, which granted standing to voters to challenge a Federal Election Commission final decision even though the plaintiffs' lack of access to certain information was the same as other voters, the Court clarified its apparently conflicting decisions about whether plaintiffs who suffer common injuries are entitled to standing, stating that the Court denied standing for widely shared, generalized injuries only if the harm is both widely shared and also of "an abstract and indefinite nature—for example, harm to the 'common concern for obedience to law.'"[16]

In global warming cases, it is unclear whether courts will reject suits because of *Duke Power's* concern that the complex and difficult policy issues raised are better suited to resolution by the political branches or will allow such suits following *Akins* even if plaintiffs have injuries from global warming similar to many others.[17] In the *Korsinsky* decision, which is discussed above, the district court also dismissed the case because it concluded that the plaintiff's second allegation, "that he has developed some form of mental illness from knowledge of the dangers of pollution over the years, is also insufficient to confer standing."[18] The court explained, "If we interpret plaintiff's allegation to mean that he has some continuing apprehension from the dangers of pollution, then it is clearly a generalized grievance, which is insufficient to confer standing." Courts would likely be more sympathetic to a plaintiff alleging more serious injuries even if many others are experiencing those same injuries.

Some lower courts have held that a plaintiff must establish a "geographical nexus" between where the injury occurs and her location, especially in procedural rights cases where the alleged procedural error must affect land or the environment reasonably near to where the plaintiff lives or uses land for recreation.[19] The Supreme Court has not used the term "geographical nexus," but has emphasized that the proximity of a plaintiff to the location of alleged harm is a significant factor in deciding whether the plaintiff has a concrete injury necessary for standing.[20]

There is a split in the circuits about how much evidence of injury and proof of causation a plaintiff must show to have standing in cases involving the National Environmental Policy Act of 1969 (NEPA) in general, and global warming in particular.[21] The District of Columbia Circuit has demanded substantial proof that a plaintiff has specific, personally distinct injuries from a pollutant and that the polluter caused injuries to that specific plaintiff rather than to the world in general. The District of Columbia Circuit's approach to standing raises substantial barriers to global warming suits. On the other hand, the Ninth Circuit and probably the Tenth Circuit have recognized standing where plaintiffs have alleged fairly general injuries such as rising sea levels, even though the polluter may be contributing only a relatively small percentage of the total harm, and even if the pollutant is harming a broad area and not just the plaintiffs. With its liberal approach to standing in NEPA and other procedural rights cases, the Ninth Circuit appears to be the best circuit for plaintiff suits and the Tenth Circuit would also be a favorable circuit.

B. The Shift in the District of Columbia Circuit to a Stricter Standing Test

1. City of Los Angeles v. NHTSA

In a 1990 lawsuit, *City of Los Angeles v. National Highway Traffic Safety Administration*, the Natural Resources Defense Council (NRDC) complained that the National Highway Traffic Safety Administration (NHTSA) "should have prepared an [environmental impact statement (EIS)] in order to consider the adverse climatic effects of the increase in fossil fuel consumption that would result from setting a Corporate Average Fuel Economy (CAFE) standard lower than 27.5 mpg" because the less stringent standard would result in greater fuel usage and GHG emissions by 1989 model year cars, which would allegedly "lead to a global increase in temperatures, causing a rise in sea level and a decrease in snow cover that would damage the shoreline, forests, and agriculture of California."[22] According to NRDC, global warming resulting from less stringent CAFE standards would injure the economic and recreational interests of its members in California. Two of the three members of the D.C. Circuit panel concluded that the NRDC had standing to challenge the failure of the NHTSA to con-

sider the impacts of global warming when it decided that it was not necessary to prepare an EIS under NEPA in setting CAFE standards for model year 1989 at 26.5 miles per gallon (mpg), one mpg below the presumptive level of 27.5 set by Congress.[23] The majority concluded that an agency's failure to prepare an EIS causes injury to a plaintiff if the agency fails to assess a "reasonable risk" that environmental damage could occur in the plaintiff's geographical location.[24] Following a two-part test used in the Ninth Circuit for standing in NEPA cases, the court first required a plaintiff to demonstrate that the "agency's failure to prepare an EIS . . . 'creates a risk that serious environmental harms will be overlooked.'"[25] The second part of the test requires a plaintiff to prove that he "'has a sufficient geographical nexus to the site of the challenged project that he may be expected to suffer whatever environmental consequences the project might have.'"

Chief Judge Wald, with Judge Ruth Bader Ginsburg concurring, concluded that the NRDC plaintiffs had demonstrated an injury under the two-part standing test because NHTSA's "failure to prepare an EIS explaining the effects of the rollbacks on global warming present[ed] the risk of overlooking an environmental injury that will personally affect its members."[26] Judge Wald concluded that the plaintiffs had demonstrated a "geographical nexus" between their alleged injuries and global warming by showing that their members living in coastal and agricultural locations would be harmed by a warmer climate's effect on coastal and agricultural resources even though "the effects of a change in global atmosphere would obviously be felt throughout this country, and indeed, the world." The causation prong of the standing test was met because "no one disputes the causal link between carbon dioxide and global warming" and the agency decision to reduce the fuel economy standard would increase these emissions. To meet the causation and redressability requirements, "NRDC had only to show some likelihood that a full EIS would influence [the agency's] decision."

Judge D.H. Ginsburg dissented from the majority's conclusion that NRDC had standing for its global warming claim. Although acknowledging that NRDC's "allegations make out injury indeed," he contended that "NRDC has failed to explain how that injury can be traced causally to the challenged decision and how the relief it seeks could redress the harm it foresees."[27] He contended that the causation requirements for both traceability and redressability required NRDC to allege and then prove that NHTSA's decision to reduce the CAFE standard from 27.5 mpg to 26.5 mpg would have an "identifiable," "marginal impact" on global warming, and not simply to assert that fossil fuel emissions cause global warming. Because the "NRDC failed to allege that a 1.0 mpg reduction would produce any marginal effect on the probability, the severity, or the imminence of global warming," he concluded that it did not have standing to raise any global warming issues. He criticized the majority's relaxed approach to causation that allowed NRDC to simply allege that fossil fuel emissions cause global warming and that CAFE standards are a part of the overall problem because under the majority's standing methodology, "the standing requirement would, as a practical matter, have been eliminated for anyone with the wit to shout 'global warming' in a crowded courthouse."

The judges in the majority explicitly rejected Judge D.H. Ginsburg's strict approach to causation because it "confuses the standing determination with the assessment of [the] case on the merits."[28] Quoting *Duke Power*, they questioned Judge Ginsburg's strict causation test by observing that "to meet the causal nexus, petitioners need only show that the alleged injury is 'fairly traceable' to the proposed action." To avoid conflating standing with assessing the merits, they warned "that where, as here, the relevant harms are probablistic and systemic, with widespread impact, courts must be especially careful not to manipulate the causation requirements of standing so as to prevent the anticipated regulatory beneficiaries from gaining access to court." The majority rejected the judges's demand for precise causal proof because such a demanding standard would cause courts to exclude all but the simplest evidence in environmental cases, would result in courts ignoring "virtually any contributory cause to the complex calculus of environmental harm . . . as too small to supply the causal nexus required for standing, and would call into question cases where we have found standing in the past." Furthermore, because the appropriate causation standard was "some likelihood" that preparing an EIS would influence the ultimate decision, the majority concluded that the proper redressability standard is not whether changing the CAFE decision would reduce global warming, but whether "an EIS would redress its asserted injury, i.e., that any serious effects in global warming will not be overlooked." See Chapter 5 for a discussion of substantive issues relating to CAFE standards.

2. *Florida Audubon* Overrules *City of Los Angeles*

In 1996, in *Florida Audubon Society v. Bentsen* (*Florida Audubon*), the D.C. Circuit in an en banc decision overruled *City of Los Angeles* and essentially adopted the standing approach in Judge D.H. Ginsburg's dissenting opinion in that case.[29] In *Florida Audubon*, the plaintiffs were environmental groups challenging the refusal of the Treasury Department and the Internal Revenue Service (IRS) to prepare an EIS on the environmental impacts of a tax credit for ethyl-tertiary butyl ether (ETBE), a fuel additive derived from plant-based ethanol.[30] The plaintiffs contended that the tax credit for ETBE would increase production of corn, sugar cane, and sugar beets that are the natural sources for the ethanol and its derivative ETBE, and that increased production of these crops would in turn harm neighboring wildlife areas that the plaintiffs used for recreation and aesthetic enjoyment.

> **The plaintiffs contended that . . . increased production of these crops would . . . harm neighboring wildlife areas that the plaintiffs used for recreation and aesthetic enjoyment.**

The *Florida Audubon* majority adopted a four-part test for procedural rights plaintiffs who challenge an agency's failure to follow a procedural statute such as NEPA that is far more restrictive than the two-part test of *City of Los Angeles*. The first part of the *Florida Audubon* standard requires that the procedural rights plaintiff have a particularized injury and demonstrate that "everyone else" is not injured, so that the injury is not too general for judicial action.[31] Going beyond standing precedent, however, the *Florida Audubon* court also stated that the D.C. Circuit would apply "even more exacting scrutiny" in reviewing standing for a plaintiff alleging an injury from broad rulemaking than in the case of a plaintiff challenging a governmental action at a particular site. Additionally, to prove that an injury is particularized and personal, rather than general, a plaintiff must present evidence addressing the "geographical nexus" between the governmental action and the location of the injury to the plaintiff—a requirement that also implicates the second part of the test.

The second part of the *Florida Audubon* standing test requires that plaintiffs demonstrate they are suffering an injury in fact as a result of a governmental action that affects "a particularized environmental interest of theirs that will suffer demonstrably increased risk."[32] In the ETBE case before it, the court stated that the plaintiffs must show "whether the tax credit promulgated by the defendant is substantially likely to cause that demonstrable increase in risk to their particularized interest." The Florida Audubon court explicitly adopted Judge D.H. Ginsburg's test in his *City of Los Angeles* dissenting opinion that, to demonstrate a requisite injury in fact for standing purposes, a plaintiff "must show" that the EIS failure creates a "demonstrable risk not previously measurable (or the demonstrable increase of an existing risk) of serious environmental impacts that imperil [plaintiff's] particularized interests." In response to Judge Rogers's dissenting opinion, the majority acknowledged that, under its new "demonstrable risk" or "demonstrable increase" test for standing, "a plaintiff seeking to challenge a governmental action with alleged diverse environmental impacts may have some difficulty meeting this standard," but contended that its approach was consistent with the Supreme Court's standing precedent. Even if the second part of the *Florida Audubon* standing test was consistent with Supreme Court precedent in 1996, the second part is arguably inconsistent with the Supreme Court's subsequent 2001 standing decision in *Laidlaw*, which simply requires a plaintiff to demonstrate "reasonable concerns" about the impacts of a pollutant.

The third part of the *Florida Audubon* test mandates that the demonstrable particularized injury be fairly traceable to the agency action, or in other words, appropriately requires a plaintiff to present evidence that the government's action or omission caused the particular harm alleged to have injured the plaintiff.[33] In the fourth part of its standing test, the *Florida Audubon* majority required a procedural rights plaintiff to show that it is "substantially probable" that the agency action will cause the demonstrable injury alleged by the plaintiff.[34] This "substantial probability" standard is arguably inconsistent with the spirit of footnote seven in the Supreme Court's 1992 decision in *Lujan v. Defenders of Wildlife* (*Defenders*), which implied that a plaintiff with a threatened concrete injury can challenge an agency's failure to follow mandatory statutory procedures even if there is no guarantee that correcting the procedural error will change the substantive result.[35] Additionally, the "substantial probability" standard is arguably inconsistent with the subsequent *Laidlaw* decision's "reasonable concerns" test.

Applying the four-part test, the majority determined that the plaintiffs had failed to prove that the tax credit would necessarily cause the farmers near the wilderness areas to increase their crop production and thereby cause harm to wilderness areas used by the plaintiffs.[36] Even though members of Congress predicted in the statute's legislative history that the tax credit would increase agricultural production in the United States, the majority found too many "uncertain links in a causal chain" to be sure that the tax credit would cause increased production among the farmers neighboring the plaintiffs. Because the plaintiffs could not prove increased crop production would take place in areas near them, the court concluded that the plaintiffs had "not demonstrated such a geographical nexus to any asserted environmental injury." Accordingly, the court held that the plaintiffs had failed to establish an injury to their interests, which is a necessary requirement for standing, and therefore did not have standing to sue.

Judge Buckley concurred in the result, but not with the reasoning of the majority. Agreeing with the dissent that the majority's opinion "imposes an unduly heavy burden on appellants," Judge Buckley argued that the court's opinion would require plaintiffs to perform the research expected of the government in writing an EIS simply to meet the four-part standing test.[37] Judge Rogers's dissenting opinion, which was joined by Chief Judge Edwards and Judges Wald and Tatel, argued that the majority's new test for standing in procedural rights cases "imposes so heavy an evidentiary burden on appellants to establish standing that it will be virtually impossible to bring a NEPA challenge to rulemakings with diffuse impacts."[38] Both Judge Buckley and Judge Rogers preferred retaining the two-part test in *City of Los Angeles*.[39]

3. *Massachusetts v. EPA*

The next major decision on standing in the global warming context came nearly a decade later, in 2005. In *Massachusetts v. EPA*, 12 states, with Massachusetts as lead petitioner, joined 14 environmental groups and five governmental entities in challenging EPA's denial of a petition to regulate GHGs from vehicle emissions and an EPA general counsel memorandum concluding that EPA lacks authority under the Clean Air Act (CAA) to regulate GHGs.[40] The EPA argued that the petitioners had not "'adequately demonstrated' two elements of standing: 'that their alleged injuries were caused by EPA's decision not to regulate emissions of greenhouse gases from mobile sources' and that their injuries 'can be redressed by a decision in their favor' by this court."[41] To demonstrate that they met the injury, causation and redressability standing elements, the petitioners obtained numerous affidavits from scientists and property owners that alleged that global warming was likely to cause significant economic harm to the petitioners and their citizens by causing increasing flooding and filed two affidavits from a climatologist and an engineer alleging that reducing vehicle emissions would reduce these harms. The three judges on the D.C. Circuit panel sharply disagreed about whether the plaintiffs had meet the causation and redressability portions of standing.

Although courts normally decide whether a plaintiff has standing before considering the merits, Judge Randolph concluded that Supreme Court precedent allowed the court to decide the merits of the case without first deciding whether the petitioners had standing because the merits of the case and standing overlapped to a considerable extent.[42] He acknowledged that the petitioners' affidavits and declarations supported each element of standing sufficiently to withstand a motion for summary judgment, but he contended that *Lujan* required even stronger evidence for standing when a defendant submits evidence that controverts the petitioners' evidence. Because some of the EPA's evidence contradicted the petitioners' claim that GHGs from new vehicles will significantly increase global warming, Judge Randolph concluded that the most appropriate way to resolve the contentious evidentiary issues concerning standing was to decide the case on the merits. On the merits, he concluded that even if the EPA had the authority under the CAA to regulate GHGs, it had the discretion not to regulate GHG emissions from motor vehicles because the EPA's denial of the rulemaking petition was based on "policy" considerations, including scientific uncertainties regarding climate change and endangerment to public health.[43] When an agency makes a policy judgment at the frontiers of science, as in this case, Judge Randolph determined that a court must give deference to its discretionary policy judgment. He did not address whether the EPA has the authority under the CAA to regulate GHGs. Judge Randolph's opinion represents the opinion of the panel.

Judge Sentelle dissented in part and concurred in the judgment.[44] He argued that courts were required to decide standing questions before reaching the merits and that the petitioners did not have standing. Because global warming affects the public at large, Judge Sentelle contended that "[h]ere, as in *Florida Audubon*, the alleged harm is not particularized, not specific, and in my view, not justiciable." He maintained that the broad policy issues and generalized grievances raised by global warming should be resolved in the executive branch and the Congress.

Judge Tatel, in his dissenting opinion, argued that at least Massachusetts had made sufficient particularized allegations about the harm to its coastline from rising ocean waters caused by global warming to meet Article III standing requirements.[45] He thought the petitioners had produced strong evidence that GHGs increased global warming, that global warming was causing or threatened to cause serious environmental harms such as rising sea levels, and that reducing vehicle emissions would help to reduce those harms. Thus, he concluded that the petitioners had demonstrated causation and that a favorable ruling would redress those harms and that at least Massachusetts had met standing requirements. On the merits, Judge Tatel concluded that "EPA has both misinterpreted the scope of its statutory authority and failed to provide a statutorily based justification for refusing to make an endangerment finding. I would thus grant the petitions for review."[46]

On June 26, 2006, the Supreme Court granted the petitioners a writ of certiorari on two issues: "(1) whether the Administrator of the Environmental Protection Agency has authority to regulate air pollutants associated with climate change under section

202(a)(1) of the Clean Air Act, 42 U.S.C. 7521(a)(1); and (2) whether the EPA Administrator may decline to issue emission standards for motor vehicles based on policy considerations not enumerated in section 202(a)(1) of the Clean Air Act."[47] On August 31, 2006, the petitioners filed their brief in the case, and numerous amicus curiae, including former EPA Administrators Carol M. Browner, William K. Reilly, Douglas M. Costle and Russell E. Train, filed briefs supporting the petitioners.[48] Although standing is not one of the two certified issues, the Supreme Court is likely to address standing because it is a jurisdictional issue that must be resolved by a court before it proceeds to the merits.

4. *NRDC v. EPA*

In *NRDC v. EPA*, the plaintiff NRDC brought a petition for review of a final rule issued by EPA under the 1987 "Montreal Protocol" treaty exempting in 2005 certain "critical uses" of the otherwise banned methyl bromide, a chemical with many beneficial uses that also destroys stratospheric ozone.[49] The Montreal Protocol phases out and eventually bans chemicals that destroy stratospheric ozone, which performs an essential function in preserving life by absorbing most dangerous ultraviolet radiation from the sun so that high levels never reach the surface of the earth.

In its first decision, the D.C. Circuit in an opinion by Judge Randolph held that NRDC did not have standing to petition the court to review the final rule because the annualized risk to members of the NRDC was so remote as to be hypothetical, following the reasoning in *Florida Audubon*.[50] After the NRDC successfully petitioned for a rehearing, the D.C. Circuit in an opinion also written by Judge Randolph found that its prior decision had failed to consider data showing that two to four members of the NRDC's nearly half a million members would develop skin cancer during their lifetimes as a result of EPA's rule and concluded that this injury was sufficient to give the NRDC standing.[51] On the merits, the D.C. Circuit rejected the NRDC's argument that the EPA's rule violates the express terms of decisions by parties to the Montreal Protocol interpreting the scope of the methyl bromide exception. The court suggested that the Constitution does not allow American courts to be bound by the decisions of an international body interpreting a treaty because the Senate has never ratified those decisions even if the Treaty authorizes those decisions, and concluded that the Protocol did not intend the decisions to be binding on parties, but that the decisions were simply post-ratification side agreements meant to guide the political negotiations of the parties in implementing the treaty. In a concurring opinion, Judge Edwards agreed with the result of the case, but also argued that the Supreme Court had never decided whether American courts might be bound by a decision of an international tribunal if a treaty ratified by the Senate specifically provided that decisions of such a panel were binding on parties to the treaty.

C. The Ninth and Tenth Circuits Reject Florida Audubon

1. *Committee to Save Rio Hondo v. Lucero*

In 1996, the Tenth Circuit in *Committee to Save the Rio Hondo v. Lucero (Rio Hondo)* expressly disagreed with *Florida Audubon's* "substantial probability" causation standard, and argued that the D.C. Circuit's approach to causation was inconsistent with *Defenders* and congressional intent underlying NEPA.[52] The *Rio Hondo* court interpreted *Defenders* as making it relatively easy for procedural rights plaintiffs to achieve standing if they have a concrete injury. In particular, the Tenth Circuit observed that footnote seven in *Defenders* relaxed the immediacy standard for procedural rights plaintiffs because NEPA reviews are often conducted years before a project is actually built. The Tenth Circuit also concluded that the causation requirements in Defenders for procedural rights plaintiffs are relatively relaxed as long as a plaintiff has a concrete injury. "To establish causation, a plaintiff need only show its increased risk is fairly traceable to the agency's failure to comply with the National Environmental Policy Act." In determining causation in a NEPA case, the Tenth Circuit argued that the proper analysis is whether the agency's alleged failure to prepare an EIS in accordance with NEPA increases the risk of harm to the plaintiff and not whether there is a substantial probability that the action will actually harm the plaintiff. The *Rio Hondo* court concluded that the burdensome evidentiary requirements in *Florida Audubon's* "substantial probability" test for standing were contrary to NEPA's intent to require federal agencies to examine the environmental impacts of their actions because that test inappropriately placed the burden on the plaintiffs to prove those harms.

2. *Citizens for Better Forestry v. U.S.D.A.*

In 2003, the Ninth Circuit in *Citizens for Better Forestry v. United States Dept. of Agriculture* (*Citizens for Better Forestry*) explicitly rejected *Florida Audubon's* standing test and held that plaintiffs in NEPA cases do not have to prove immediacy in light of footnote seven in *Defenders*.[53] Based on that footnote, the Ninth Circuit stated, "Once a plaintiff has established an injury in fact under NEPA, the causation and redressability requirements are relaxed." In the Ninth Circuit, plaintiffs "need only establish 'the reasonable probability of the challenged action's threat to [their] concrete interest.'"

3. *Covington v. Jefferson County*: Judge Gould's Concurring Opinion

In *Covington v. Jefferson County*, the Ninth Circuit held that the plaintiffs, property owners who lived across the street from a county landfill, had standing to bring citizen suits under both the CAA and the Resource Conservation and Recovery Act (RCRA) for local injuries allegedly caused by the defendants, a county and a district health department, from the improper disposal of ozone-destroying chemicals at a landfill owned by Jefferson County and operated by the district health department.[54] In a concurring opinion, Judge Gould concluded that the plaintiffs had standing to sue based on the global impacts on stratospheric ozone resulting from the defendants' alleged mishandling of CFCs.[55] Reviewing standing precedent, he observed that some courts, especially in taxpayer suits, had suggested that a plaintiff may not assert standing if an alleged injury harms all persons equally, or in other words, "'that injury to all is injury to none.'" On the whole, however, Judge Gould determined that the Supreme Court's most recent standing cases, especially *Akins* and *Laidlaw*, have allowed a plaintiff to achieve standing resulting from general injury if the injury to the plaintiff is sufficiently concrete. Judge Gould concluded that the risk to the plaintiffs of skin cancer, cataracts, and suppressed immune systems was sufficiently concrete to justify Article III standing even though the defendants' allegedly improper treatment of CFCs only contributed a small amount to a global problem. Although skeptical that allowing standing for global pollution injuries would trigger an avalanche of litigation, even Judge Gould acknowledged that if so many global pollution suits were filed that it became burdensome for courts to decide them all, a court might for prudential reasons limit suits alleging such harms to cases where the plaintiffs, like the Covingtons, have suffered

relatively direct injuries. The District of Columbia Circuit, however, would likely have rejected Judge Gould's standing argument because it is not "substantially probable" that the plaintiffs would suffer skin cancer, cataracts or suppressed immune systems from the chemicals released at the site.

4. Owens Corning

In 2005, the Northwest Environmental Defense Center, the Sierra Club and the Oregon Center for Environmental Health filed a citizens' suit under the CAA alleging that the Oregon Department of Environmental Quality violated the CAA and the State Implementation Plan for the State of Oregon by failing to require Owens Corning Corp. (Owens Corning) to submit a complete permit application, including all information underlying Owens Corning's emissions estimates, for the construction and operation of a new polystyrene foam insulation board manufacturing plant in Gresham, Oregon, by failing to release this information to the public for review, and by acting on an incomplete permit application.[56] The plant would have the potential to emit at least

250 tons per year of HCFC-142b, which is a potent global warming agent. On June 8, 2006, after all the parties consented to have him hear the case, Magistrate Judge John Jelkerks issued an opinion denying the defendant's motion to dismiss for lack of standing. Owens Corning argued that the plaintiffs had only generalized injuries and therefore they did not have standing. Citing Judge Gould's concurring opinion in *Covington*, Judge Jelkerks rejected the view that injury to all means standing for none because under that theory no one would have standing to prevent harm "to the Grand Canyon or Yellowstone National Park, or threats to the giant sequoias and blue whales, as the loss of those treasures would be felt by everyone." The same day that he denied the defendant's motion to dismiss for lack of standing, Judge Jelkerks approved a settlement between the plaintiffs and defendants in which Owens Corning denied any wrongdoing, agreed that if it built the plant it would do so without using HCFC-142b or similar ozone-damaging substances, agreed to spend $300,000 on a low-energy classroom at Portland's da Vinci Arts Middle School and other renewable energy initiatives, and agreed to pay the plaintiffs' attorney fees.[57]

5. *Friends of the Earth v. Watson*

In *Friends of the Earth v. Watson*, the plaintiffs sued the Overseas Private Investment Corporation ("OPIC"), an independent government corporation that offers insurance and loan guarantees for projects in developing countries, and the Export-Import Bank of the United States ("Ex-Im"), an independent governmental agency and wholly-owned government corporation that provides financing support for exports from the United States, for failing to perform environmental assessments under NEPA and the Administrative Procedure Act regarding the impact of their loans on building projects in foreign countries that contribute to global warming.[58] A federal district court in the Ninth Circuit denied the defendants' motion for summary judgment on standing, rejecting the defendant's argument that Ex-Im's and OPIC's role with respect to the projects that produce the greenhouse gas emissions is too limited and attenuated to justify standing. The court stated, "When, as here, a plaintiff seeks to challenge a procedural violation, some uncertainty about redressability and causality is allowed." The court continued: "Moreover, such plaintiffs need not present proof that the challenged federal project will have particular environmental effects." Quoting *Citizens for Better Forestry*, the district court stated: "Instead, the 'asserted injury is that environmental consequences might be overlooked' as a result of deficiencies in the government's analysis under environmental statutes. Thus, Plaintiffs only need to demonstrate that 'it is reasonably probable that the challenged action will threaten their concrete interests.'"[59] Rejecting the defendants' assertion that most of the projects would have been built without their assistance, the court concluded that the plaintiffs had "submit[ed] evidence demonstrating a stronger link between the agencies' assistance and the energy-related projects." The court also rejected the defendants' claim that the suit was improper because the plaintiffs were challenging the agencies' day-to-day program, but instead found that it was proper to challenge the cumulative

GHG impacts of several projects assisted by the defendants. Thus, the plaintiffs met the test for standing. This case is discussed in more detail in Chapter 8 on international financing.

6. Challenge to NHTSA CAFE Standards for Light Trucks and SUVs

In May 2006, 10 states, the District of Columbia and New York City, with California as lead plaintiff, sued NHTSA in the Ninth Circuit challenging its new rule setting CAFE mileage standards for light trucks, including sport utility vehicles (SUVs), as failing to consider the environmental benefits of improved fuel economy standards, including reducing global warming, under NEPA and the Energy Policy and Conservation Act (EPCA).[60] Additionally, in May 2006, the Sierra Club sued the NHTSA in the Ninth Circuit challenging that same new CAFE rule, but made a different legal argument that the cost-benefit analysis used by NHTSA is unlawful because it failed to consider the benefits of reducing CO_2.[61] Some attorneys believe that California's NEPA challenge has a greater chance of success than the Sierra Club's cost-benefit challenge.[62]

D. Parens Patriae Standing: Should Standing Rules Be Different for Public Officials?

Many of the standing cases involving environmental issues have been citizen suits, but state attorneys general (AGs) have played an increasingly active role in global warming cases.[63] In the *Massachusetts* case, 12 state AGs filed suit.[64] In *Connecticut v. American Electric Power*, eight state AGs, with Connecticut as lead plaintiff, filed a public nuisance suit in federal district court in Manhattan against five large utilities.[65] The district court dismissed the case under the political question doctrine, as is discussed in Section II.E, and did not address standing.[66]

Especially in public nuisance cases, should different standing rules apply to suits brought by state attorneys general or other public officials?[67] Since 1901, in transboundary suits where pollution from one state harms another state, state AGs may bring public nuisance suits under the Supreme Court's original jurisdiction.[68] Early transboundary suits did not refer to standing because the Supreme Court did not explicitly refer to standing requirements until 1944, and it is only since the 1970s that the Court began to formulate its current three-part standing test.[69] More recently, the Court has developed a doctrine of parens patriae standing or "quasi sovereign" interests to justify suits by states in a number of areas, including transboundary cases.[70] The Court has never decided whether standing requirements in parens patriae cases are different for states than for ordinary citizens, although it implied in one case that states must meet standing requirements similar to ordinary citizens when the Court stated that such suits "must be sufficiently concrete to create an actual controversy between the State and the defendant" and must "survive the standing requirements of Article III."[71]

E. Political Question Doctrine: *Connecticut v. American Electric Power*

In *Connecticut*, Federal District Court Judge Loretta A. Preska held that the complex policy questions regarding the problem of global warming were better suited to resolution by the political branches and were non-justiciable political questions beyond the limits of the court's jurisdiction.[72] She declined to address whether the plaintiffs had standing because "determining causation and redressability in the context of alleged global warming would require me to make judgments that could have an impact on the other branches' responses to what is plainly a political question. Accordingly, because the issue of Plaintiffs' standing is so intertwined with the merits and because the federal courts lack jurisdiction over this patently political question, I do not address the question of Plaintiffs' standing."[73] Next she argued that there were no workable judicial standards to resolve the issues in the case and, therefore, such issues had to be resolved by the political branches. She contended that the court would have to make legislative policy judgments in many areas of national and international policy if it allowed the suit. She asserted that determining relief in the case would inappropriately require the court to:

> **In *Connecticut*, Federal District Court Judge Loretta A. Preska held that the complex policy questions regarding the problem of global warming were better suited to resolution by the political branches and were non-justiciable political questions beyond the limits of the court's jurisdiction.**

(1) determine the appropriate level at which to cap the carbon dioxide emissions of these Defendants; (2) determine the appropriatepercentage reduction to impose upon Defendants; (3) create a schedule to implement those reductions; (4) determine and balance the implications of such relief on the United States' ongoing negotiations with other nations concerning global climate change; (5) assess and measure available alternative energy resources; and (6) determine and balance the implications of such relief on the United States' energy sufficiency and thus its national security—all without an "initial policy determination" having been made by the elected branches.[74]

She concluded "[b]ecause resolution of the issues presented here requires identification and balancing of economic, environmental, foreign policy, and national security interests . . . these actions present non-justiciable political questions that are consigned to the political branches, not the Judiciary."[75] Accordingly, she granted the defendants' motion to dismiss the case. The plaintiffs have appealed to the Second Circuit.

F. A Cloudy View of Standing

There has been considerable disagreement about whether plaintiffs alleging harm from climate change can meet standing requirements. Some judges, especially in the District of Columbia
Circuit, reject standing because they argue that the plaintiffs'
injuries are the same general injuries affecting all other citizens
and that such injuries are better addressed by the political
branches, that the science of climate change is still not fully
understood, that such suits fail to meet the causation and
redressability elements of standing because each government
action has only a small marginal impact on climate change and
the impact of a favorable judicial decision on the worldwide
problem is uncertain, or that the issue involves complicated policy
issues that are more appropriately resolved by the political
branches. Conversely, other judges, especially in the Ninth Circuit, argue that standing is appropriate because plaintiffs are
suffering concrete injuries from impacts such as rising sea levels
and diminished snow melt, that there is strong evidence that
manmade GHGs are causing global warming, and that judicial
action will at least force government officials to study their impacts on climate change.

Although standing is not one of the two certified issues in
Massachusetts, the Supreme Court is likely to address standing
because it is a jurisdictional issue that must be resolved by a
court before it proceeds to the merits. The following speculates
on how the various justices may vote on the standing issue in
Massachusetts based on their past votes or legal commentary.[76] Even if it does not
accurately predict the result in *Massachusetts*, the following shows some of the rough
divisions on standing issues by the various current members of the Court. Based on
their majority vote in *Defenders*, and dissents in *Akins* and *Laidlaw*, Justice Scalia
along with Justice Thomas will likely argue that petitioners do not have standing
because their injuries are generalized and the issues are best resolved by the political
branches. Although they have only recently joined the Court and their views on standing are not known for certain, Chief Justice Roberts in a law review article that praised
the reasoning in *Defenders* and Justice Alito, who joined a Third Circuit decision
requiring environmental plaintiffs to prove actual harm to the environment, which
Laidlaw subsequently rejected, suggested that they have a relatively narrow view of
standing that is closer to Justice Scalia's. By contrast, Justices Stevens, Souter, Ginsburg
and Breyer took a broad view of standing in *Akins* and *Laidlaw*. Justice Kennedy, who
concurred in *Defenders*, joined the majority in *Akins* and concurred in *Laidlaw*, is
likely the key swing vote in this case, as he was so often during the 2005-2006 term of
the Court.

III. Tort, Nuisance Actions, and Product Liability Actions
A. Causation, Potential Defendants, and Liability for Damages
1. Generic and Specific Causation

In most tort suits, a plaintiff must prove proximate causation between the defendant's activities and the alleged injury. In a simple negligence or battery action, a plaintiff may easily prove specific causation between the defendant's actions in touching, hitting or cutting the plaintiff and any resulting damages to the plaintiff. In many toxic tort cases, however, plaintiffs must use statistical or probabilistic methodologies to establish general causation that it is more probable than not that the defendant's actions caused the harm suffered by the defendant despite the presence of other possibilities[77]—for example, that the plaintiff's stomach cancer was caused by the defendant's dumping of chemical A into a river and the plaintiff's drinking of that river water, although there are many other possible causes. Similarly, climate scientists use computer models to demonstrate general probabilistic associations between increased GHG emissions and recent increases in temperatures on the earth, as well as the likelihood of future GHG or temperature increases.

In toxic tort cases, some courts have held that mere evidence of general causation through statistical associations found in epidemiological studies are inadequate proof of whether a substance caused a plaintiff's injuries.[78] These courts have demanded additional evidence of specific causation, such as "supporting scientific evidence, statistical evidence, expert testimony, or further epidemiological evidence that a causal link is probable." If courts demand more specific evidence of causation, it would be more difficult for climate change plaintiffs to meet that burden.[79]

In climate change litigation, it may be possible to prove generic causation, but more difficult to prove specific causation.[80] As is discussed more fully in chapter one, there is plenty of general evidence that rising concentrations of CO_2 and GHGs are probably responsible for most of the global warming at least since 1980 and perhaps since the 1860s, when society first began accurately measuring temperatures.[81] The significant increase in CO_2 and other GHGs since 1850, when industrialization became widespread in Western Europe and the Eastern United States, and especially since 1980, is highly correlated with rising temperatures. The amount of supporting scientific evidence of rising temperatures, rising sea levels and melting glaciers and permafrost has grown dramatically in recent years. In its 2001 report, the United Nations' appointed scientific task force on global warming, the Intergovernmental Panel on Climate Change (IPCC), concluded: "In the light of new evidence and taking into account the remaining uncertainties, most of the observed warming over the last 50 years is likely to have been due to the increase in greenhouse gas concentrations."[82] There is a minority of scientists who argue that global warming may be caused by natural climatic or solar variations, but the proportion of scientists arguing that global warming is not significantly affected by human activities is rapidly diminishing.

By contrast, proving specific causation between GHGs and climate change is more difficult because the impacts involve intensification of existing climatic phenomenon, such as more frequent storms, rather than the creation of unique "signature diseases," such as asbestosis, which is caused only by exposure to asbestos, or clear cell adenocarcinoma, which is caused only by the drug DES.[83] Because climate is affected by several factors interacting in complex ways, it is difficult for scientists to tease out what percentage of any climate change is affected by GHGs, and it is even more difficult to determine what percentage is affected by a specific polluter or group of polluters, such as U.S. utilities. Climate is a chaotic system affected by natural fluctuations in frequency and severity, so it is difficult to determine to what extent human activities, such as producing GHGs, affect those frequencies or variations.

It is easier for states or governments to prove causation from climate change because they can base their claims on a larger geographic area where it is easier to measure the impacts of global warming than on smaller geographic areas.[84] For example, Judge Tatel argued in his dissenting opinion in *Massachusetts* that there was strong evidence regarding rising sea levels in the Boston area.[85] Similarly, there is strong scientific evidence of rising sea levels in New York City.[86] Thus, coastal states or cities may be able to prove climate change causes rising sea levels in their political jurisdiction. As is discussed in sections VI and VII below, Alaskans can point to the most tangible evidence of warming as rapidly rising temperatures in the Arctic melt per-

mafrost and erode coastal villages.[87] For coastal states or cities, especially in Alaska, there may be enough evidence that global warming and GHGs cause rising sea levels and melting permafrost. In addressing the merits, a defendant would undoubtedly emphasize the many scientific uncertainties about global warming and argue that any alleged harms are the result of natural climatic variations.

a. Specific Causation—Proving Global Warming Caused Hurricane Katrina: *Comer v. Murphy Oil*

In *Comer v. Nationwide Mutual Insurance*, lead plaintiffs Ned and Brenda Comber, as well as three other married couples, in September 2005 filed suit in the U.S. District Court for the Southern District of Mississippi alleging that they suffered severe damage to their homes from Hurricane Katrina and further alleged that these damages were worsened by global warming that was caused, in part, by emissions from oil produced by five named and an unknown number of unnamed energy companies.[88] After the plaintiffs filed their Second Amended Complaint, in a memorandum opinion addressing various procedural issues, Senior Judge Senter observed that the plaintiffs' claims that individual oil and chemical companies caused global warming that in turn intensified Hurricane Katrina raised "daunting evidentiary problems," but he allowed the plaintiffs to proceed with their case until he addressed the defendants' motion for summary judgment at a later date.[89]

In April 2006, the plaintiffs filed, with permission of the Court, a Third Amended Class Action Complaint that sought to address the concerns raised in Judge Senter's memorandum opinion.[90] The Third Amended Complaint named an Oil Company Defendants class consisting of seven named oil companies, the American Petroleum Institute, which is an industry trade association, and an unknown number of unnamed oil companies operating in Mississippi.[91] The Third Amended Complaint also named a Coal Company Defendants class consisting of 31 named utilities and coal-mining companies. The Third Amended Complaint alleges that the Oil Company and Coal Company Defendant classes produce GHGs through their mining, drilling, production and consumption activities and that the "Earth's climate has 'demonstrably changed' as a result of Defendants' greenhouse gas emissions."[92] It alleges that "[d]efendants' emissions have also substantially increased frequency and intensity of storms known as hurricanes, effectively doubling the frequency of category four and five hurricanes over the past thirty years." The Third Amended Complaint alleges that "Defendants' Actions Were a Proximate and Direct Cause of the Increase in the Destructive Capacity of Hurricane Katrina" and that "[p]rior to striking the Mississippi Gulf Coast, Hurricane Katrina had developed into a cyclonic storm of unprecedented strength and destruction, fueled and intensified by the warm waters and warm environmental conditions present in the Atlantic Ocean, Caribbean Sea, and the Gulf of Mexico, all of which were a direct and proximate result of the defendants' greenhouse gas emissions."[93]

In their Third Amended Complaint, the plaintiffs try to address the concerns raised about such suits, stating:

> This case presents discrete and justiciable questions (whether Defendants' emissions of greenhouse gases caused damage to Plaintiffs' property, and, if so, the extent of those damages). There are manageable standards for resolving the controversy (common law claims of nuisance, unjust enrichment, negligence, civil conspiracy, and intentional torts including fraudulent misrepresentation and concealment and trespass, with all such causes of action being cognizable under the laws of the State of Mississippi and appropriate legal regimes imported by the applicable choice of law rules). These issues are neither textually committed to a coordinate political department nor do they implicate the primary authority of the executive or legislative branch. . . . Plaintiffs do not ask this Court to regulate Global Warming or change national global warming policy. Instead, Plaintiffs seek legal redress for the damages caused by these Defendants.[94]

The Third Amended Complaint also alleged that the Oil company defendants had engaged in a civil conspiracy, alleging:

> The API and other Oil Company Defendants have engaged in concerted financial activity—far in excess of $1 million—in furtherance of a tortious civil conspiracy to "reposition global warming as theory rather than fact." In addition, "from 2001 to 2003, ExxonMobil [alone] donated more than $6.5 million to organizations that attack mainstream climate science and oppose greenhouse-gas controls." All of this activity has been part of a concerted and tortious effort to intentionally decrease public awareness and divert public policy activity away from the real dangers associated with Global Warming and the known need to restrict the emission of greenhouse gases.[95]

Furthermore, the plaintiffs alleged that the defendants' misleading statements about global warming constituted fraudulent misrepresentation and concealment because "[a]t the time Defendants made these materially false statements, the public and State and Federal Governments did not know that Defendants' statements were false."[96] The plaintiffs alleged the following injuries:

> As a direct and proximate result of the activities of the Defendants (including their production of environmentally harmful by-products), there has been a marked increase in global temperature which, in turn, produced the conditions whereby a storm of the strength and size of Hurricane Katrina would inevitably form and strike the Mississippi Gulf Coast resulting in extensive death, injury and destruction.[97]

The plaintiffs sought damages for loss of property, loss of business income, disruption of the "normal course of their lives," loss of loved ones, and mental anguish and emotional distress.[98] The plaintiffs also sought punitive damages for alleged "willful indifference, extreme recklessness, gross negligence and an illegal conspiracy to prevent dissemination of scientific information regarding the specific hazards created by Global Warming." The plaintiffs in their Third Amended Complaint also made global warming claims against three chemical companies and a chemical industry trade association for producing halocarbons, including chlorofluorocarbons (CFCs), which are powerful and long-lasting heat-trapping chemicals that contribute to global warming.[99] Furthermore, the plaintiffs sought to have the suit certified under Federal Rule of Civil Procedure 23 as a class action both for a class of plaintiffs consisting of all Mississippi residents or property owners harmed by Hurricane Katrina and for the three classes of oil company, coal company and chemical company defendants."[100]

On June 30, the oil company defendant class, the coal company defendant class and the chemical company defendant class filed separate motions to dismiss under Rule 12(b) of the Rules of Civil Procedure.[101] The main arguments in their memoranda are that the suit should be dismissed because it involves non-justiciable political questions, that the suit is preempted under federal law because it would interfere with the ability of the federal government to carry out its existing energy and other policies regulating these industries, that the plaintiffs' lack standing because their injuries are a generalized grievance common to all people, that Mississippi's regulation of the defendants' national and international activities would violate the constitutional prohibition on extraterritorial regulation, that liability for past GHG emissions would violate due process, and that the plaintiffs' conclusory state tort law claims failed to sufficiently allege facts to meet the elements of a tort claim. such as proving proximate causation. On August 21, 2006, the plaintiffs filed memoranda opposing these motions to dismiss.[102] On September 19, 2006, Senior Judge Senter transferred the case to federal District Judge Guirola of the Southern District of Mississippi.[103]

> ... a recent study found that rising sea surface temperatures were the primary factor in the increase in Category 4 and 5 hurricanes ...

The *Comer* suit is a difficult case because it is uncertain whether global warming caused or worsened a specific event such as Katrina even if increases in GHGs probably increase weather extremes. There is a scientific controversy about whether global warming increases the frequency or intensity of hurricanes. For example, a recent study found that rising sea surface temperatures were the primary factor in the increase in Category 4 and 5 hurricanes, the strongest storms with winds over 130 miles per hour, from 10 per year during the 1970s to 18 per year since 1990, but that study did not establish to what extent human-produced GHGs as opposed to natural warming influences caused the increase in hurricanes.[104] Proving that global warming caused a specific storm such as Katrina is even more difficult. Additionally, as is discussed below, there are difficult causation issues in proving that oil and chemicals produced by classes of American companies were the specific and substantial cause of either global warming in general or a specific event such as Katrina.

2. Proximate Causation and the Substantiality Requirement

According to the *Restatement (Second) of Torts*, an actor's activities are the legal cause of another's harm if the conduct is a "substantial factor" in causing that harm.[105] The *Restatement* defines "substantial" to mean that a defendant's activities "ha[ve] such an effect in producing the harm as to lead responsible men to regard it as a cause, using that word in the popular sense, in which there always lurks the idea of responsibility."[106] A defendant may be liable even if a third party is also a substantial factor as long as the defendant's responsibility is not diluted or made insignificant by that other party.[107] Accordingly, "substantial cause" is similar to the question of "proximate causation," which also requires proof of substantiality.[108] Both "proximate causation" and substantiality are concerned with the degree of a defendant's connection with and impact on a plaintiff's injuries.[109] The proposed *Restatement (Third) of Torts*, however, has criticized the substantial factor test as difficult to apply and has argued for a return to the classic "but for" test, stating that the "essential requirement, recognized in both Torts Restatements, is that the party's tortious conduct be a necessary condition . . . for the occurrence of the plaintiff's harm."[110]

Because oil, chemical and transportation companies produce products that will emit GHGs when consumers use their products as intended, there is an argument that the companies rather than the consumers are the proximate cause of releasing enormous quantities of GHGs; similarly, utilities are arguably the responsible cause of GHGs even though consumers benefit from using electricity.[111] It was foreseeable for these companies that their products or power generation would cause enormous emissions of GHGs and therefore they are a substantial cause of global warming. In his dissenting opinion in *Massachusetts,* Judge Tatel argued that there was strong scientific evidence that CO_2 and other GHGs caused global warming, that pollution from vehicles was a significant source of GHGs and, more specifically, that global warming was causing rising sea levels in Massachusetts.[112] Though he did not use the terms "proximate causation" or "substantiality,"

Judge Tatel's analysis would clearly support finding substantial and proximate causation. On the other hand, because they only emit about 2% to 2.5% of the CO_2 created worldwide by people and the requested relief of an annual reduction of 3% would only decrease worldwide emissions of CO_2 by less than one-tenth of 1%, the defendant utilities in *Connecticut* argued that they are such a small source of GHGs that they are not the cause of global warming, nor can they solve global warming caused by sources from many nations.[113]

Some commentators have advocated using a market share approach in global warming cases against the utility or energy industries.[114] In a few cases, including DES cases where a drug taken by pregnant women caused serious birth defects, courts have imposed damages on companies within an industry based on their market share or enterprise liability even though the plaintiffs could not prove which defendants within the industry caused their individual injuries because the suits were filed long after the alleged harms took place.[115] Courts have been reluctant to expand the market share or similar theories of liability because liability in such cases stretches traditional understanding of individual responsibility and there are often complicated factual questions concerning how to measure an industry's responsibility.[116] For instance, in cases where plaintiffs have sued gun manufacturers for the use of their guns by criminals, critics of such suits have argued in part that market share liability should not be used in such cases because the responsibility of the defendants is small and difficult to measure because of the responsibility of criminals for those harms and the class of plaintiffs potentially harmed by firearm violence is so large and hard to define.[117]

3. Potential Types of Defendants

Traditional tort law typically focused on a single defendant or small number of defendants who were allegedly responsible for certain tortious conduct, such as a battery or negligence that violated the plaintiff's rights and caused specific injuries to the plaintiff.[118] Modern tort law sometimes allows aggregative torts in which large groups of plaintiffs allege that an entire industry has caused them harm. In several cases, plaintiffs, including states or local governments, have sued the asbestos,[119] tobacco,[120] firearms,[121] and lead paint industries.[122] States were successful in suing the tobacco industry for the cost of tobacco-related health-care expenditures because of evidence that the industry had misled the public about the amounts and addictiveness of nicotine in their products.[123] Cities have been less successful in suing the firearms industry for the use of guns by criminals because the causal connection between industry practices and the use of firearms in crimes is not as clear.[124]

As is discussed in the *Comer* case, section II.A.1.a above, the most likely defendants in a climate change public nuisance action would be companies developing, producing, refining and distributing fossil fuels—energy companies; utilities that burn fossil fuels: or transportation manufacturers whose products burn fossil fuels because their activities contribute to the overwhelming majority of CO_2 emisions—98%, and other GHGs—81%. In September 2006, California sued the six largest car manufacturers for public nuisance under federal and California law seeking damages from past, present and future emissions.[125] The complaint alleges that these emissions currently amount to 9% of the CO_2 emissions in the world and more than 30% in California. The complaint asks the court to hold the defendants liable for damages, including future harm, caused by their ongoing, substantial contribution to the public nuisance of global warming. The complaint alleges that global warming has already injured California:

> California is responding to the ongoing impacts and the inevitable additional future impacts of global warming. The State is spending millions of dollars on planning, monitoring, and infrastructure changes to address a large spectrum of current and anticipated impacts, including reduced snow pack, coastal and beach erosion, increased ozone pollution, sea water intrusion into Sacramento Bay-Delta drinking supplies, response to impacts on wildlife, including endangered species and fish, wildfire risks, and the long-term need to monitor ongoing and inevitable impacts. California has already begun to expend money and other resources to address the declining snow pack and earlier melting of the snow pack in order to avert future water shortages and flooding.

Addressing the future effects of global warming, the complaint alleges, "will certainly cost millions more." Another possible defendant would be chemical companies manufacturing halocarbons. Because individual consumers only contribute to a tiny portion of the problem and it would be impossible to sue millions of consumers, it is arguable that the large transportation, energy and chemical industries are more logical defendants than consumers.

The *Comer* suit alleges that the oil company defendants engaged in a civil conspiracy to mislead the public, state governments and the federal government about the dangers of global warming.[126] At this early stage in global warming litigation where there has been little discovery of industry documents, it is questionable whether there is sufficient evidence that utilities, transportation or energy companies fraudulently misled the public about the effect of their activities on global warming. Utilities, transportation and energy companies are more sympathetic defendants than the tobacco industry. On the other hand, as evidence of global warming mounts, there will be growing political and social pressure on these industries to do something about global warming, and judges or juries in the future may have greater expectations about what is a reasonable standard of care for these industries in reducing GHGs.

4. Equitable Defense of "Unclean Hands"

Because all potential plaintiffs in climate change suits have contributed to the problem of GHGs by benefiting from fossil fuels, defendants could raise the equitable defense of "unclean hands."[127] The "'unclean hands' doctrine 'closes the door of a court of equity to one tainted with inequitableness or bad faith relative to the matter in which he seeks relief, however improper may have been the behavior of the defendant.'"[128] The Supreme Court in federal common law interstate nuisance cases has considered whether the plaintiff's own conduct has contributed to the causation of harm of which the plaintiff complains and applied the unclean hands doctrine to bar equitable relief.[129] Because most of the states that have brought climate change suits have adopted legislation encouraging or requiring reductions in GHGs, state plaintiffs may be able to claim that they have at least partially washed their hands from responsibility for creating GHGs.[130] The unclean hands doctrine does not affect plaintiffs seeking damages only.

5. Liability for and Apportionment of Damages

According to the *Restatement (Second) of Torts*, when multiple actors cause a harm, if there is a reasonable basis for dividing the harm according to each defendant's contribution, each is liable only for that portion of the total harm that each has caused.[131] As is discussed in section III.A.2, a court might also consider the controversial market share or enterprise theory of liability. According to traditional tort law, if the harm is an indivisible harm, all parties that are legal causes of the harm are jointly and severally liable for the entire harm.[132] Because the harms caused by utilities, energy companies, and transportation companies are arguably indivisible because current science cannot untangle their cumulative impacts, courts could hold such companies jointly and severally liable for global warming, but that doctrine is problematic in the context of global warming cases where there are so many different sources of the problem.[133] Because the majority of GHGs are emitted by sources outside the United States and any reductions in the U.S. raise enormous social and economic concerns, courts may follow *Connecticut* in concluding that the problem is a political question better left to the political branches, as is discussed in section II.E. If the issue of apportionment of damages is reached, American courts could apportion damages based on each firm or industry's contribution to an industry's GHG emissions or could order firms or industries to reduce GHGs by a certain percentage in the future, but any court attempting to apportion damages or order changes in industry practices would face enormous issues of jurisdiction, preemption, and the political question doctrine.[134]

6. Damages and Injunctions in Tort and Nuisance Suits

Plaintiffs in tort suits may seek either injunctive relief or monetary damages.[135] Usually, a court will grant injunctive relief only if damages cannot adequately redress the injury, but courts are more likely to enjoin the interfering activity when a nuisance affects public health or causes other serious harms to the public good. In specifying the remedy sought, a sensible strategy for plaintiffs would be to ask for reductions in emissions over a number of years rather than a complete shutdown of America's fossil fuel economy. For example, in *Connecticut* the eight state AGs suggested that the utilities reduce CO_2 emissions by a recommended amount of 3% each year for at least 10 years, although they left the final decision to the district court's determination, and they did not seek damages.[136] Because they only emit about 2% to 2.5% of the CO_2 created worldwide by people and the requested relief of an annual reduction of 3% would only reduce decrease worldwide emissions of CO_2 by less than one-tenth of 1%, the utilities have argued that American courts cannot redress the problem of global warming, but that only international treaties can afford real relief.[137]

Although a court in theory could adopt the percentage reduction scheme sought by the state AGs in *Connecticut*, one may question how the plaintiffs arrived at a 3% annual reduction other than picking a number out of the air or, more positively, an attempt to pick a number that sounds realistic. Thus, defendants will undoubtedly raise the issue of whether there are any workable judicial standards for a court to use other than a judge attempting to usurp executive or legislative authority, as Judge Sentelle argued in his concurring and dissenting opinion in *Massachusetts*.[138]

B. Preemption and Displacement

1. Can Plaintiffs Sue Under the Federal Common Law?

A plaintiff filing a public nuisance or other type of tort claim must sue under either the federal common law or state common law, but not both.[139] The federal common law of interstate nuisance is based on the Constitution's grant of original jurisdiction to the Supreme Court for "[c]ontroversies between two or more States" and "between a State and Citizens of another State."[140] Suing under federal common law would potentially allow a plaintiff to sue defendants on a national or at least regional basis using one uniform standard, and therefore would usually offer many advantages compared to a state common law action. The key question is whether a plaintiff may bring a federal common law public nuisance suit regarding global warming or whether the Clean Air Act (CAA) displaces such suits. Commentators have disagreed about whether the CAA is a comprehensive scheme like the CWA that displaces federal common law or is somewhat less comprehensive and thus does not necessarily displace federal common law.[141]

In *City of Milwaukee v. Illinois (Milwaukee II)*,[142] the Supreme Court held that the Clean Water Act of 1972 (CWA), which was enacted after the original suit was filed, displaced the federal common law of water pollution, which the Court had recognized before the 1972 Act. The Court has never addressed whether the CAA displaces the federal common law of

air pollution.[143] Before the 1970 CAA, the Court in 1907 had implicitly recognized a federal common law of air pollution in an original action brought by Georgia against a Tennessee air pollution source, although the Court did not explicitly use the term "federal common law."[144] *Milwaukee II* did not provide a clear test for when a federal statute displaces federal common law.[145] It is unclear whether *Milwaukee II* adopted a "field displacement" approach that the CWA is a comprehensive statute that displaces the entire field of any possible federal common law action. Alternatively, the case may have adopted a "conflict displacement" approach that would bar federal common law actions only if they conflict with a specific provision of the statute.

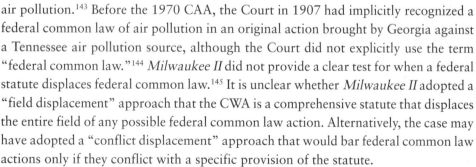

Courts have not clearly answered whether the CAA is a comprehensive scheme that displaces the field of federal common law or is a somewhat less comprehensive statute than the CWA and thus only displaces federal common law where there is a conflict between the suit and the statute.[146] In *New England Legal Foundation v. Castle*, the Second Circuit held that the Clean Air Act preempted a common law claim based on air pollution from a facility with a Clean Air Act permit, but it withheld judgment on "whether the Clean Air Act totally preempt[ed] federal common law nuisance actions based on the emission of chemical pollutants into the air."[147] Two federal district court decisions from 1982 and 1984, respectively, found that the CAA was a comprehensive statute and that any common law actions were displaced by the statute, but these cases did not squarely address the issue of whether displacement still applies if the CAA does not regulate a type of pollution at all.[148] Unlike the CWA, which prohibits every pollutant discharged from a point source into navigable waters, plaintiffs in a global warming suit would argue that the CAA does not cover every air pollutant and most notably does not regulate GHGs.[149] Defendants in a global warming case would argue that the CAA is a comprehensive statute that displaces the entire field of federal common law and that any public nuisance suit is barred.[150] By contrast, plaintiffs would argue a conflict displacement thesis that because the CAA does not regulate GHGs, there is no conflict in allowing a federal common law public nuisance suit regarding global warming.

In *Massachusetts*, the EPA argued that it did not have the authority under the CAA to regulate carbon dioxide or GHGs, but that Congress, when enacting the 1990 Amendments to the Act, wanted the agency to only study the problem and then allow Congress to decide the appropriate policies.[151] The EPA also stated that it would not regulate GHGs at this time, even if had the authority to do so, because there were too many uncertainties about climate change. In *Massachusetts*, Judge Randolph agreed with the EPA that it had the discretion not to regulate GHGs because of the uncertainties; he did not address whether the agency had the authority to regulate them.[152] By contrast, Judge Tatel in his dissenting opinion argued that the EPA did have the authority to regulate them.[153] If the EPA does not have the authority to regulate CO_2 or GHGs, the law regarding displacement is unclear about whether the CAA would nevertheless still displace a federal common law public nuisance suit concerning global warming.[154] If the EPA does not have the authority to regulate CO_2 or GHGs, a plaintiff would have a stronger, but still uncertain, argument for a federal common law public nuisance suit concerning global warming.

If the EPA does not have the authority to regulate CO_2 or GHGs, a plaintiff would have a stronger, but still uncertain, argument for a federal common law public nuisance suit concerning global warming.

2. State Common Law

It is more likely that a plaintiff can file a state common law action based on the law of the source state. Federal law may preempt state common law actions in three relatively narrow circumstances: when (1) it is the "clear and manifest purpose of Congress,"[155] (2) the federal law is "sufficiently comprehensive to make reasonable the inference that Congress 'left no room' for supplementary state regulation,"[156] or (3) a state law "actually conflicts with a . . . federal statute"[157] so that it "stands as an obstacle to the accomplishment and execution of the full purposes and objectives of Congress."[158] In *International Paper Co. v. Ouellette*, the U.S. Supreme Court held that the CWA preempted state nuisance actions based on the law of the receiving state because making sources with CWA permits subject to the laws of multiple receiving states would undermine Congress's goal of making the permit a single clear guide for the regulated source.[159] The Court, however, also held that a plaintiff could bring a transboundary nuisance action for water pollution based on the source state's nuisance law.[160] Subjecting a permitted source to the source state's nuisance laws did not undermine the CWA's goal of uniformity. Where there is diversity of citizenship, the Court also stated that a plaintiff may sue in federal district court in the receiving state.[161] On remand, the district court applied the source state rule to the plaintiffs' air claims and concluded that the same concerns about uniformity for the CWA applied as well to the CAA.[162] Thus, a plaintiff filing a public nuisance action under a source state's tort law probably can bring suit against public utilities in another state, assuming that there is diversity of citizenship and jurisdiction lies in federal district court.[163] Because the CAA does not regulate CO_2 or GHGs, at least according to the EPA, there is an even stronger argument that the CAA does not conflict with or preempt source state nuisance suits.

As is discussed in more detail in Chapter 5, the CAA may preempt both state and federal common law claims against automobile or fuel manufacturers because Congress has spoken directly to the issue of automobile emissions and fuels.[164] Under section 209 of the CAA, "no State or any political subdivision thereof shall adopt or attempt to enforce any standard relating to the control of emissions from new motor vehicles or new motor vehicle engines."[165] The Supreme Court has held that "Congress has largely pre-empted the field with regard to 'emissions from new motor vehicles' and motor vehicle fuels and fuel additives."[166] There are, however, some exceptions to this rule of preemption if a lawsuit's purpose is different from the primary concerns of the CAA.[167] For example, state-law litigation over MTBE, a fuel additive, has not been preempted because the plaintiffs' claims were about groundwater contamination, not emissions controls.[168] In that case, the contamination concern was not "intertwined" with the primary concerns of the CAA, including air pollution and "protection of our air resources."[169] As is discussed in more detail in Chapter 5, in *Central Valley Chrysler-Jeep, Inc., et al. v. Catharine E. Witherspoon*, a California district court concluded that California Assembly Bill 1493, which authorizes the state's Air Resources Board to regulate CO_2 emissions from all cars sold in the state beginning in 2009, is preempted under Section 209 unless the EPA issues a waiver and therefore denied the Air Resources Board's motion for judgment on the pleadings.[170]

3. Dormant Foreign Affairs Preemption

Because global warming is an international problem with strong foreign policy implications, a "dormant foreign policy preemption" might preempt at least some types of actions by State attorneys general or private plaintiffs if they would interfere with the President's foreign policy negotiating authority.[171] The United States has ratified the United Nations Framework Convention on Climate Change,[172] which requires the United States to cooperate with other nations in seeking international solutions to the problem of climate change, although the United States refused to agree to the binding reductions in the Kyoto Treaty.[173] Arguably, climate change litigation could result in binding reductions that would interfere with the President's ability to use the promise of the same reductions as a bargaining chip in future negotiations.[174] In *Zschernig v. Miller*, the Supreme Court established a quasi-dormant foreign policy preemption when it preempted an Oregon statute that allowed aliens to inherit property only if the alien's own country assured Oregon courts that the foreign country extended equivalent rights to American citizens.[175] The Court concluded that the factual inquiries by Oregon courts impermissibly involved them in negotiating with foreign governments. In light of *Zschernig*, state AGs may not enter into direct negotiations with foreign governments regarding GHG reductions.[176]

The question that remains unanswered by courts is whether climate change suits in which American plaintiffs seek to impose GHG limits on American corporate defendants are foreclosed because arguably they could interfere with the conduct of foreign policy by the President of the United States. The Supreme Court has stated that state governments may not enact a statute that cuts off state purchases from firms doing business in Burma[177] or requires insurance companies to disclose a list of policies issued by affiliated companies to holocaust survivors[178] because such state laws take away bargaining chips from the President in any future negotiations with the affected foreign governments.[179] What is unanswered by the courts is whether state regulations on domestic companies for domestic activities that could affect foreign governments are subject to similar foreign policy restrictions. In *Central Valley Chrysler-Jeep*, as is discussed in Chapter 5, automobile manufacturers have challenged California Assembly Bill 1493, which authorizes the state's Air Resources Board to regulate CO_2 emissions from all cars sold in the state beginning in 2009, and the district court in a preliminary decision has found that the plaintiffs have stated a valid claim in raising the foreign affairs preemption defense in that case even though there is no explicit statute or executive order barring state regulation of GHGs, stating:

> Nothing in the Supreme Court's foreign policy preemption jurisprudence forecloses the possibility of preemption of a generally applicable law that interferes with foreign policy. The focus is on whether the practical effect of the state law is to disturb foreign relations or impair a proper exercise of presidential authority. *See Crosby*, 530 U.S. at 375, 120 S.Ct. 2288; *Zschernig*, 389 U.S. at 440, 88 S.Ct. 664. Plaintiffs have demonstrated that current Executive Branch policy is

to negotiate with other nations to reach agreements regarding greenhouse gas emissions reductions. They have alleged that the California regulations, by unilaterally reducing such emissions, potentially undercut the Executive's ability to pursue such agreements. Accordingly, Plaintiffs have stated a claim for preemption of the regulations based on foreign policy.[180]

By contrast, global warming plaintiffs will likely argue that state laws regulating domestic firms are traditional subjects of state sovereignty and thus are quite different from state statutes that affect foreign countries or businesses. Professor Merrill argues:

> I think the dormant foreign policy preemption argument should fail. A suit brought by legal officers of American States against American defendants in an American court under a cause of action based on American common law is not preempted simply because a favorable outcome in the action might have reverberations or ramifications for the conduct of American foreign policy. The preemption argument should fail as long as the case remains grounded in federal common law, because the *Zschernig* doctrine is probably best understood as preempting only applications of state law.[181]

C. General Principles of Public Nuisance Law

A public nuisance suit is the tort best suited to address transboundary pollution affecting the public at large.[182] Although the line between what is a private and a public nuisance is not precise, public nuisances must affect a "right common to the general public," such as affecting the public at large or public lands, while a private nuisance affects only a limited number of private citizens.[183] Global warming is a paradigmatic example of a public nuisance. Under the common law, only public officials could bring public nuisance actions, but some states now allow private citizens to bring such suits if they can prove that they have suffered injuries different from the public at large.[184] A private citizen filing a public nuisance action about global warming would have to prove, for example, that harm to it from melting permafrost is different from the injuries suffered by most Americans; courts might well differ about whether Alaskan natives suffer injuries that are sufficiently different to allow them to bring a public nuisance action.[185] Public officials have an easier burden in public nuisance actions because it is presumed that they are representing the public interest.[186] Thus, state AGs or municipal attorneys may be the best plaintiffs in global warming public nuisance suits.

Most states follow the *Restatement (Second) of Torts'* definition of a public nuisance as "an unreasonable interference with a right common to the general public."[187]

It states that conduct is unreasonable if it involves a "significant interference" with "public health, safety, or convenience." The *Restatement* does not explain how severe the interference must be to qualify as "significant," and does not discuss whether only harms are to be considered in determining the significance of a nuisance or whether a court would weigh the harms only after considering an activity's benefits.[188] Courts generally require evidence that the defendant is causing a continuing harm, or has caused a permanent or long-lasting impact.[189] The comments in the *Restatement*'s public nuisance section make a cross-reference to the discussion of unreasonableness in its private nuisance section.[190] The private nuisance section uses two alternative tests for deciding when the interference is "unreasonable." The first test contains an implicit cost-benefit analysis that asks whether "the gravity of the harm outweighs the utility of the actor's conduct."[191] The second test implies a strict liability approach to serious harms, defining conduct unreasonable when it causes harm that is "serious" or "severe" and compensation of all victims of the harm would be feasible.[192] The *Restatement* does not define either "serious" or "severe," and does not explain whether the harm is to be measured in isolation or net of benefits.[193] Some courts have emphasized the first test, others the second test.[194] Some courts consider a third factor of whether the defendants failed "to take reasonable actions within their control that would eliminate, ameliorate, or minimize the harm."[195]

Under the first test for public nuisances, defendants would argue that the benefits of using fossil fuels for the American far outweigh any possible harms; this is essentially President Bush's position. Under the second test, plaintiffs could attempt to demonstrate that the harms are serious and that the defendants are capable of paying some sort of damages, or, more likely, that the court should require the defendants to spend certain sums, such as apercentage of their profits, to reduce emissions or develop less harmful alternative sources of energy.[196]

D. Product Liability

A product liability claim requires a plaintiff to show that a product has a defect that makes it unreasonably dangerous, that this defect existed when the product left the defendant's control, and that the defect proximately caused plaintiff's injuries.[197] Depending on state law, a plaintiff might use either a strict liability or a negligence theory of liability. There are three types of defects that can cause an unreasonably dangerous product: (1) warning defects, (2) manufacturing defects, and (3) design defects, but manufacturing defects claims are not relevant to global warming suits. A warning defect results when it is foreseeable that a product may cause harm, but the manufacturer fails to warn users of that risk. A design defect claim alleges that the harm results from the faulty design of the product. In all types of defect cases, a plaintiff must prove that the defendant's product caused her injuries, which raises many of the complex causation issues discussed in section III.A.

In theory, a plaintiff could bring a product liability suit suing transportation manufacturers or utilities alleging that vehicles or power plants using fossil fuels are defectively designed, or that the manufacturers had a duty to warn the public about the risks of GHGs from these products.[198] For example, a plaintiff could argue that she would have chosen solar or wind power for energy if a coal-burning utility had warned her of the risks of GHGs and global warming, or that a car manufacturer could have designed a more gas-efficient car.[199] As a practical matter, such product liability suits are unlikely to succeed today because there arguably have not been practical alternatives to such vehicles or power plants, so design changes would have been impractical and warnings futile.[200] Plaintiffs could argue that technologies for lighter and more efficient vehicles have been deliberately ignored by car manufacturers so that they could make more profits by selling fuel-inefficient vehicles such as SUVs, even though manufacturers knew at least for several years about the dangers of GHGs.[201] Defendant manufacturers would likely argue that their designs were "state of the art," and therefore that their designs are not defective.[202] Because of technological advances such as hybrid cars and coal gasification, there may be a heavier burden in the future on manufacturers to minimize GHGs to avoid future product liability suits.

IV. National Environmental Policy Act

NEPA requires that federal agencies "include in every recommendation or report on proposals for legislation and other major federal actions significantly affecting the quality of the human environment, a detailed statement by the responsible official on the environmental impact of the proposed action."[203] The statement requirement is fulfilled when agencies prepare an environmental impact statement (EIS), which is required only if the project has "significant" environmental impacts.[204] An agency first prepares an environmental assessment (EA), typically a short report, to determine if the project will create significant environmental impacts.[205] Agencies find significant impacts requiring an EIS in less than 1% of federal actions—approximately 400 to 500 EISs out of a total of 50,000 EAs; for the remaining 99% of all assessments, an agency makes a finding of no significant impact (FONSI), which ends the assessment process.[206] Similar suits could be filed in the many states that have little NEPAs or executive orders requiring environmental assessments.[207]

NEPA serves the dual purposes of (1) "injecting environmental considerations into the federal agency's decisionmaking process" and (2) "informing the public that the agency has considered environmental concerns in its decisionmaking process."[208] An agency must consider any significant environmental impacts of the proposed action, reasonable alternatives to the proposed plan, and discuss why it selected the proposal rather than the alternatives.[209]

The statute has only procedural requirements, and judicial review is limited to determining whether the agency adequately evaluated a proposal's environmental impacts.[210] A court may not reject an EA or EIS because the judge believes that the agency's decision to build a project is unwise. For instance, the agency must adequately discuss ways to mitigate the impacts of the proposed action, but is not required to actually implement mitigation techniques, except in the rare case where the agency's own internal NEPA regulations clearly mandate that it conduct mitigation.[211] An agency must consider and discuss reasonable alternatives to a proposed project or action but does not have to select the least environmentally damaging alternative.[212] Because NEPA does not provide for a private right of action, citizens must sue under the Administrative Procedure Act (APA) to challenge a federal agency's alleged failure to comply with NEPA.[213] A plaintiff has the burden of proving that an agency's decision not to discuss an allegedly significant environmental issue or alternative, or to issue a FONSI instead of preparing an EIS, was "arbitrary, capricious, an abuse of discretion, or otherwise not in accordance with law."[214]

A. The District of Columbia Circuit and NEPA: City of Los Angeles v. NHTSA

Judges D.H. Ginsburg and Ruth Bader Ginsburg concluded on the merits that NHTSA's preparation of a shorter EA document addressing the impacts on global warming rather than a fuller EIS was not arbitrary and capricious, although a "close question," according to Judge Ruth Bader Ginsburg.[215] On the merits, both judges concluded that NHTSA's conclusion that a one-mile per gallon change in the CAFE standard would not cause significant enough environmental impacts to justify the time and expense of preparing an EIS was reasonable, not arbitrary and capricious, because that small increase was unlikely to have a significant impact on the environment.[216] Chief Judge Wald dissented from the disposition on the merits, arguing that the court should remand the case to the NHTSA for further explanation of the agency's conclusion that the 1987-88 CAFE standards would not have an environmental impact significant enough to require an EIS.[217] She, however, would have left the current 26.5 mpg standard in place pending completion of a cumulative EIS covering the entire CAFE program, which the NHTSA had begun to prepare in 1990. This case demonstrates that injury sufficient to achieve standing is not always significant enough to require an agency to prepare an EIS.

Both because she now sits on the Supreme Court, which presumably magnifies the importance of her decisions as a circuit judge, and because she generally votes with environmentalists,[218] Justice Ruth Bader Ginsburg's conclusion in *City of Los Angeles* that the agency's decision not to prepare an EIS on global warming issues was acceptable suggests that NEPA plaintiffs arguing that an agency should prepare an EIS concerning global warming impacts face a substantial burden in showing that impacts from a particular project are significant. Since any single project is likely to have only a small impact on total world emissions, an agency can almost always argue that the impacts are not significant. Because an agency's decision not to prepare an EIS may be rejected by a court only if that decision is "arbitrary and capricious," NEPA plaintiffs effectively bear the burden of proving that the impacts are significant. Where separate projects pursued by an agency have cumulative impacts, NEPA requires an agency to assess such impacts on a cumulative basis.[219] Following the approach used in *Friends of the Earth v. Watson*, a NEPA plaintiff's best strategy in some global warming cases might be to argue that separate agency projects have significant impacts on global warming when their cumulative impacts are added together, although the plaintiff would need to establish standing for each project and may not simply challenge an agency's day-to-day program.[220]

B. The Ninth Circuit and NEPA

1. *Border Power Plant Working Group v. Dep't of Energy*

Pursuant to the Ninth Circuit's broad approach to NEPA cases, in *Border Power Plant Working Group v. Dep't of Energy*, a federal district court in California in 2003 concluded that an environmental assessment (EA) prepared by federal agencies, including the Department of Energy (DOE), was inadequate because it did not disclose or consider the significance of the environmental impacts of CO_2 emissions, but also held that the agencies did not have to consider the human health impacts of CO_2.[221] The EA had evaluated the proposed issuance of presidential permits and federal rights of way allowing two utilities to build electricity transmission lines to connect new power plants in Mexico with the power grid in southern California. In response to the plaintiffs' contention that the EA was inadequate because it did not consider the environmental impacts of CO_2 emissions, the court stated, "Because these emissions have potential environmental impacts and were indicated by the record, the Court finds that the EA's failure to disclose and analyze their significance is counter to NEPA."[222] Unfortunately, the court did not provide a fuller explanation of its reasoning regarding why the agencies should have included a discussion of CO_2 impacts in the EA. The court found that the plaintiffs had standing because they lived near the transmission lines and power plants at issue, but did not specifically address whether the plaintiffs had standing regarding their CO_2 claim.[223]

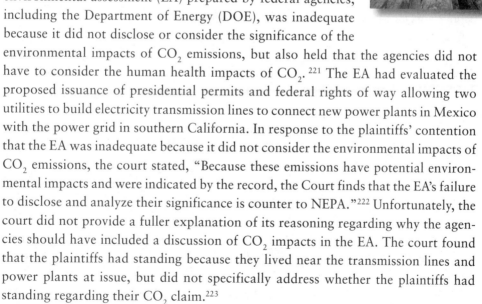

2. Friends of the Earth v. Watson

Although it addressed only standing issues and has not yet addressed the merits of the NEPA case, the *Friends of the Earth v. Watson* decision took an approach to NEPA that appears favorable to the plaintiffs in the case.[224] The court rejected defendants' assertion that most of the projects would have been built without their assistance and determined that the plaintiffs had "submit[ed] evidence demonstrating a stronger link between the agencies' assistance and the energy-related projects." The court's standing decision suggests that it could consider the cumulative impacts of several energy-related projects rather than individual projects alone when it addresses NEPA on the merits, although it is important to emphasize that the court's standing decision does not bind its future decision on the merits. If it has a choice of forum, a plaintiff in a global warming suit should sue in the Ninth Circuit.

C. The Eighth Circuit and NEPA: *Mid States Coalition for Progress v. Surface Transportation Board*

In *Mid States Coalition for Progress v. Surface Transportation Board,* the petitioners challenged the final decision of the federal Surface Transportation Board (STB), which is part of the U.S. Department of Transportation, to approve the Dakota, Minnesota & Eastern Railroad Corporation's plan to construct roughly 280 miles of new rail to reach the coal mines of Wyoming's Powder River Basin and to upgrade 600 miles of existing rail in Minnesota and South Dakota.[225] The petitioners argued that the STB violated NEPA by failing in its Final EIS (FEIS) to consider whether increased access to coal would increase coal consumption relative to other fuels, which would increase air emissions of several air pollutants including carbon dioxide.[226] In 2003, the Eighth Circuit rejected the STB's conclusion that the potential air impacts of burning low-sulfur coal were too speculative and too far removed from the Board's approval of the construction and operation of the new rail line for the Board to be required to consider them in its NEPA analysis. The court stated that "when the *nature* of the effect is reasonably foreseeable but its *extent* is not, . . the agency may not simply ignore the effect."[227] The court found "that it would be irresponsible for the Board to approve a project of this scope without first examining the effects that may occur as a result of the reasonably foreseeable increase in coal consumption."[228] The Eighth Circuit remanded the case back to the STB to prepare a Supplemental EIS (SEIS) to address the air issue and various noise issues. The *Mid States* decision is a valuable precedent for global warming plaintiffs in NEPA cases to require consideration of climate change issues.

On remand, in 2005, the STB's Section of Environmental Analysis issued the SEIS, which used a computer model to estimate the increase in national air emissions that may occur as a result of the reasonably foreseeable increase in coal consumption caused by the new rail line.[229] The SEIS found that there would be a minimal 1% increase in national air emissions from the new rail line, including carbon dioxide emissions, because alternative rail lines would otherwise deliver about the same amount of coal even if the new line is not built. The SEIS concluded that there was no need to mitigate the small amount of air impacts. In February 2006, the STB issued a final decision approving the construction of the new rail line and agreeing with the SEIS's finding that there was no need to mitigate any air impacts. In July 2006, the petitioners filed a brief in the Eighth Circuit challenging the STB's new approval of the rail line and arguing that the SEIS's findings failed to comply with NEPA because the revised analysis does not address the CO_2 from the coal and ignores the significant climate impacts if the project increases national use of coal by up to 10%.[230]

V. Endangered Species Act

On February 9, 2006, the U.S. Fish and Wildlife Service (FWS) announced in the *Federal Register* that it found that a revised petition filed on December 27, 2005, by the Center for Biological Diversity and other environmental groups proposing to list the polar bear (*Ursus maritimus*) as a threatened species under the Endangered Species Act of 1973 presented substantial scientific or commercial information indicating that the petitioned action of listing the polar bear may be warranted.[231] As a result, the FWS initiated a status review of the polar bear to determine if listing under the Act is warranted. Under section 4(b)(3)(B) of the Act, FWS is required to make a finding as to whether listing the polar bear is warranted by December 27, 2006. To ensure that the status review is comprehensive, the FWS announced a 60-day public notice-and-comment period to solicit scientific and commercial information regarding polar bears. The notice specifically requested "[i]nformation on the effects of climate change

and sea ice change on the distribution and abundance of polar bears and their principal prey over the short- and long-term." On May 17, 2006, the FWS reopened the public comment period until June 16, 2006, "in response to requests we received from the public regarding their intent to provide the Service with additional information, including information from other polar bear range states (e.g., Canada and Russia) on the worldwide status of polar bears and to ensure that all interested parties have an opportunity to submit comment and information to us concerning the status of polar bears."[232]

If it lists the polar bear as threatened, FWS has one year from that listing date to decide how much land must be designated as critical habitat for the bear. The designation of critical habitat could be even more important than listing the polar bear as threatened. In the past, designating critical habitat, for example, meant that timber companies could not cut down trees where spotted owls lived. Protecting the critical habitat of polar bears, however, would raise more difficult issues, such as whether the FWS could stop energy companies or utilities from emitting GHGs that harm the Arctic environment in which polar bears live.

VI. Environmental Justice

There is evidence that low-income and racial minorities in some areas of the United States are exposed to higher levels of pollution than the average American, although some studies have found no significant income or racial disparities.[233] Beginning in the 1980s and 1990s, a grassroots environmental justice (EJ) movement developed in many low-income and minority communities, and in 1994 they achieved their most notable political victory when President Clinton signed Executive Order 12898 (E.O. 12898), which requires federal agencies to conduct research to assess whether their programs cause pollution inequities and to establish policies to reduce any unfair pollution burdens on low-income and minority communities.[234]

Due to criticism that EJ policies may give low-income and minority communities a higher priority in pollution reduction than other Americans, the Bush Administration has proposed redefining EJ as the fair treatment and meaningful involvement of all people regardless of race, color, national origin, or income with respect to the development, implementation, and enforcement of environmental laws, regulations and policies. A Draft Policy states, "Environmental justice is achieved when everyone, regardless of race, culture or income enjoys the same degree of protection from environmental and health hazards and equal access to the decision-making process to have a healthy environment in which to live, learn and work."[235] Many EJ activists believe that the proposed redefinition of EJ will harm low-income and minority communities. To allay fears in minority communities about EJ, on November 4, 2005, EPA Administrator Stephen Johnson issued a memorandum, "Reaffirming the U.S. EPA's Commitment to Environmental Justice," that directed EPA's senior managers "to more fully and effectively integrate environmental justice into all EPA policies, programs, and activities" and that "EPA will continue to implement its programs and activities to ensure that they do not adversely affect populations with critical environmental and public health issues, including minority and low-income communities."[236]

Serious barriers exist to suing the government or industry for alleged EJ inequities. E.O. 12898 contains no private right of action to sue in federal court, although administrative judges in the EPA and some other federal agencies may consider the Order.[237] Before 2001, many EJ activists filed suits under Title VI of the 1964 Civil Rights Act, which prohibits federal grant recipients such as state or local governments from discriminatory policies or actions.[238] Plaintiffs usually relied on the EPA's Title VI regulations prohibiting forbidding recipients of agency funds from engaging in practices or actions causing disparate impacts against racial or ethnic minorities.[239] In 2001, however, the Supreme Court in *Alexander v. Sandoval* held that the Title VI disparate impact regulations were not enforceable in private rights of action and that plaintiffs in Title VI cases must prove intentional discrimination.[240] A person or group that believes it is being harmed by disparate discriminatory policies or actions by an EPA grant recipient may still file an administrative complaint with the agency. In deciding Title VI complaints, the EPA has never found a recipient to be guilty of discrimination, but it has sometimes negotiated consent decrees or settlements in which recipients promise to modify allegedly discriminatory practices without admitting that they have actually committed discriminatory acts.[241]

Global warming may impose more severe impacts on Native Alaskans and racial minorities than the rest of the American population. Rapidly rising temperatures and melting permafrost are causing flooding and erosion problems in 184 of 213 Alaskan Native villages, with about 20 villages suffering severe damage that could threaten their destruction.[242] The media has extensively reported that Hurricane Katrina caused far more damage in low-lying areas of New Orleans where the population was predominantly poor and African-American, while more affluent, mostly white residents living in upland areas were far less affected.[243] That raises the question of whether minorities and low-income populations in the future will be more vulnerable to hurricanes, flooding or tornadoes that could be increased in severity by global warming. For instance, residents of mobile home parks are more likely to be poor, and their homes are more vulnerable to strong winds.

Even though global warming may be causing additional hardships to vulnerable racial minorities and low-income populations, proving that climate change has caused specific harms to these groups is often difficult. As is further discussed below in section VII, Alaskan Natives would have the strongest factual claims about harm from global warming because climate change is occurring far more rapidly in Arctic regions than in the continental United States.

VII. Human Rights Claims

Some plaintiffs have turned to international human rights commissions to sue the United States to force it to take action to reduce GHGs. The U.S. government is extremely unlikely to acknowledge that such commissions have jurisdiction over it, and thus such suits are likely to be symbolic actions that place some political pressure on the U.S. to appear that it is taking responsibility for its GHG emissions.

A. Inuit Circumpolar Conference Claim to Inter-American Human Rights Commission

The term "Inuit" refers to all the indigenous peoples in all the Arctic regions, but is often used to refer to the indigenous peoples in Canada and Alaska in particular. On December 7, 2005, Sheila Watt-Cloutier, an Inuit woman and elected chair of the Inuit Circumpolar Conference (ICC), filed a petition with the Inter-American Human Rights

Commission (IAHRC), which is an independent seven-member body of the Organization of American States (OAS), alleging human rights violations by the United States government against the Inuit people of the United States and Canada.[244] The IACHR can issue findings, recommendations and rulings, but it is not a court, and member states must voluntarily accept its recommendations or rulings.[245] The United States is a member of the OAS. The Inuit have standing with the OAS through Canada. The petition relies on scientific evidence in the 2004 Arctic Climate Impact Assessment (ACIA), which was prepared over a four-year period by more than 300 scientists from 15 countries and six indigenous peoples' organizations. The ACIA found that the Arctic has already suffered significant harm from global warming and that continued warming over the next 100 years by an average of 6 degrees Celsius could destroy many species such as the polar bear, walrus, and some seal species, as well as the entire Inuit way of life.[246] For example, thinning sea ice means that the Inuit in many cases can no longer safely hunt seals because of the risk of falling through the ice, and the thinning ice also allows stronger storm surges to harm coastal areas, increasing erosion already accelerated by melting permafrost. The petition focuses on the United States because it is by far the largest emitter of greenhouse gases and has refused to adopt mandatory measures to reduce GHG emissions.

The petition asks the Commission to hold hearings in Alaska and northern Canada to investigate the harm caused to the Inuit by global warming. The petition argues that the impact in the Arctic of human-induced climate change infringes upon the environmental, subsistence and other human rights of the Inuit. Specifically, the petition asks the Commission to declare the United States in violation of their rights in the 1948 American Declaration of the Rights and Duties of Man, which is the foundational document on human rights for the OAS, *inter alia*, of life, liberty and security; freedom to live and move within one's territorial home; the inviolability of the home, of health, of culture; and to own and enjoy property.[247] The Declaration originally did not create any binding legal obligations, but the Inter-American Court on Human Rights, an independent quasi-judicial body of the OAS, has recognized that it now creates binding obligation on members of the OAS, at least to the extent that they submit to the Inter-American Court's or IAHRC's jurisdiction.[248] The petition argues that the rights in the Declaration be interpreted in light of the United States' treaty obligations in the UN Framework Convention on Climate Change. The petition urges the Commission to recommend that the United States adopt mandatory limits to its emissions of GHGs. Additionally, the petition requests that the Commission declare that the United States has an obligation to work with Inuit to develop a plan to help the Inuit adapt to unavoidable impacts of climate change and consider the impact of its

> **The ACIA found that . . . continued warming over the next 100 years by an average of 6 degrees Celsius could destroy many species such as the polar bear, walrus, and some seal species, as well as the entire Inuit way of life.**

emissions on the Arctic and Inuit before approving all major government actions.

The Commission has not yet accepted the petition. The Inuit Petition is potentially a great tool for educating the public about harms from GHGs to the Arctic, but the petition will have little or no direct legal impact. Neither the OAS nor the IAHRC can enforce any measures against the United States without its voluntary consent. The United States has already stated that it will not be bound by any rulings by the OAS or IAHRC on global warming.[249] A favorable IAHRC ruling on the Inuit petition, however, could provide the evidentiary basis for future class-action lawsuits against the United States government, as well as private firms, in either international courts or in American courts, although whether the Inuit people could actually win an enforceable judgment in such a suit is highly uncertain.[250]

B. Waterton Glacier Petition

On February 16, 2006, the International Environmental Law Project at Lewis & Clark Law School filed a petition with the United Nations' World Heritage Committee, which is a committee falling within the jurisdiction of the United Nations Educational, Scientific, and Cultural Organization, to list Waterton-Glacier International Peace Park as a "World Heritage Site in Danger" because of climate change, pursuant to its authority under Article 11, paragraph 4 of the Convention Concerning the Protection of the World Cultural and Natural Heritage (World Heritage Convention).[251] Article 11, Paragraph 4 states as follows:

> The Committee shall establish, keep up to date and publish, whenever circumstances shall so require, under the title of "List of World Heritage in Danger," a list of the property appearing in the World Heritage List for the conservation of which major operations are necessary and for which assistance has been requested under this Convention. This list shall contain an estimate of the cost of such operations. The list may include only such property forming part of the cultural and natural heritage as is threatened by serious and specific dangers, such as the threat of disappearance caused by accelerated deterioration, large- scale public or private projects or rapid urban or tourist development projects; destruction caused by changes in the use or ownership of the land; major alterations due to unknown causes; abandonment for any reason whatsoever; the outbreak or the threat of an armed conflict; calamities and cataclysms; serious fires, earthquakes, landslides; volcanic eruptions; changes in water level, floods and tidal waves. The Committee may at any time, in case

of urgent need, make a new entry in the List of World Heritage in Danger and publicize such entry immediately.[252]

In 1932, Canada and the United States combined Waterton National Park in Alberta, Canada, and Glacier National Park in northwestern Montana to create the first International Peace Park, although each nation continued to manage the parks separately as they had before the theoretical merger. In 1995, the UN listed the park as a World Heritage site, but not as a site in danger.[253] Because of rising temperatures, about 80% of the park's glaciers that existed in 1850 have disappeared, and the remaining 20% will disappear by 2030 if nothing is done to stop global warming.[254]

The petition seeks not just the listing of the site, but also that the Committee impose "corrective measures" to reduce GHGs by all parties to the Convention and especially the United States. The petition seeks very broad corrective measures, including: (1) "a plan to reduce reliance on coal to produce electricity through the promotion of alternative energy sources, like wind power"; (2) "a cap-and-trade program for carbon dioxide emissions"; (3) "transportation sector reductions, including increases in fuel efficiency standards, regulation of tail-pipe emissions, and increased reliance on non-petroleum-based fuels, like ethanol and biodiesel"; and (4) "programs aimed at achieving greater energy efficiency through appliance efficiency standards."[255] The proposed corrective measures are far beyond any previous measures by the Committee or United Nations to address climate change or any other environmental issue.

In March 2006, a panel of the Committee met in Paris to discuss the petition.[256] The Bush Administration filed a memorandum in opposition to the petition that argues that climate change is not caused solely by human actions and, therefore, that even if all human-caused GHGs were eliminated, it is not certain that climate change would stop.[257] The Bush Administration contends that the Committee's role is solely to conduct research and provide advice, and that the Committee lacks the authority to impose any policy changes. The Committee has not yet acted on the petition. Because global temperatures would continue to rise for several decades even if the amount of GHGs in the world's atmosphere stopped increasing today, the park faces a grim future even if the listing is successful.

VIII. Alien Tort Statute

A. General Principles

The first Congress enacted the Alien Tort Statute (ATS)[258] as part of the Judiciary Act of 1789.[259] The original language of the ATS gave the district courts "cognizance, concurrent with the court of the several States, or circuit courts, as the case may be, of all causes where an alien sues for a tort only in violation of the law of nations or a treaty of the United States."[260] As amended, the ATS currently provides that "the district courts shall have original jurisdiction over any civil action by an alien for a tort only, committed in violation of the law of nations or a treaty of the United States."[261] Before 2004, a majority of lower courts interpreted the ATS to create a cause of action for an alien seeking damages for tort-like injuries caused by a violation of the law of nations.[262] In 2004, however, the Supreme Court in *Sosa v. Alvarez-Machain* held that the ATS is a jurisdictional statute that was not intended to automatically confer new causes of action every time that there is a change in international law, but only allows suits for rules of international law that are as fundamental as those recognized as causes of action in 1789, as is discussed in section VIII.A.2.[263]

There are many unresolved issues relating to ATS claims in general, and the legal uncertainties about environmental ATS suits are substantial. Although an ATS claim must be based on a "clear and unambiguous" right in international law, there are often no clear international standards for deciding whether particular behavior constitutes a violation or to determine the types of damages available.[264] To fill any gaps in international law, courts face unresolved choice of law questions about whether to use federal common law, state law, general principles of international law, or the domestic law of the nation where the violation occurred to resolve substantive law or damages issues. Additionally, there are difficult questions about under which circumstances private parties may be liable, including conduct that is undertaken "under the color of state authority" or corporate business activities in a foreign nation that "aid and abet" human rights violations committed by foreign governments or paramilitary groups.[265]

When an ATS claim is based on wholly foreign acts by non-U.S. citizens, the defendant must have sufficient contacts with the forum state to give rise to personal jurisdiction under the "minimum contacts" test.[266] Furthermore, in cases involving wholly foreign actions by non-U.S. citizens, defendants usually seek to dismiss the case based on the doctrine of forum non conveniens (FNC), which requires U.S. courts to assess whether a foreign court would be an adequate forum to resolve the case, which is discussed in sections VIII.B.2 and B.4. Additionally, defendants may seek dismissal based on the act of state, international comity or political question doctrines, which is discussed in sections VIII.B.4.

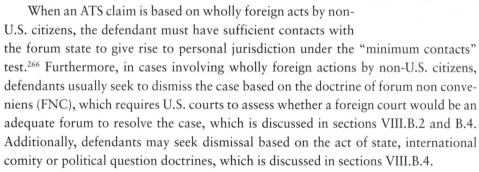

1. *Filartiga v. Pena-Irala*

Until 1980, the ATS had been used successfully only twice. It was generally rejected or ignored by courts and appeared to only be a historical anachronism buried in the federal statute books.[267] In 1980, however, in *Filartiga v. Pena-Irala*, a Paraguayan family brought suit under the ATS against a former Paraguayan police chief for inflicting torture that resulted in the death of a family member of the plaintiffs.[268] The Second Circuit held that the plaintiffs could sue the defendant under the ATS because torture violates the law of nations and therefore is actionable under the ATS.[269] The court held that the ATS was not limited to rights recognized in 1789, stating, "[I[t is clear that courts must interpret international law not as it was in 1789, but as it has evolved and exists among the nations of the world today."[270] The *Filartiga* decision, however, stated that evolving norms of international law are enforceable under the ATS only if they are "universal," definable, and obligatory under the "law of nations."[271] The court stated, "The requirement that a rule command the 'general assent of civilized nations' to become binding upon them all is a stringent one."[272] *Filartiga* stated that the law of nations "may be ascertained by consulting the works of jurists, writing professedly on public law; or by the general usage and practice of nations; or by judicial decisions recognizing and enforcing that law."[273]

Before the Court's 2004 *Sosa* decision, lower courts struggled to apply *Filartiga's* "'general assent of civilized nations'" standard.[274] Before 2004, what was most controversial about *Filartiga* was to what extent American courts should recognize new rights and duties that have developed in international law since 1789.[275] Lower courts and commentators frequently interpreted *Filartiga* to mandate that a plaintiff demonstrate a violation of customary international law, which is shown by widely adopted state practices and norms that are widely recognized as *opinio juris* (mandatory legal obligations).[276] Most courts before 2004 interpreted the "law of nations" requirement more narrowly than how most international law experts define customary international law, to demand that a plaintiff demonstrate three factors: (1) that no state condones the act at issue and there is a "universal" norm against it; (2) that there are workable criteria to define whether a particular act constitutes a prohibited act that violates the norm; and (3) the prohibition against the act is consistently applied against every actor.[277] By contrast, rejecting almost entirely the *Filartiga* decision, in his concurring opinion in *Tel-Oren v. Libyan Arab Republic,* Judge Bork advocated the "originalist" approach that claims under the ATS are limited to those torts that violated the "law of nations" when Congress enacted the legislation in 1789.[278] At that time in history, the ATS would have reached only claims of piracy and prize claims involving seizures of ships, offenses against ambassadors and violations of safe conduct.[279]

2. *Sosa v. Alvarez-Machain*

In 2004, the Supreme Court in *Sosa* finally addressed when courts may import customary international law norms into the ATS.[280] In *Sosa*, the United States indicted Mexican national Humberto Alvarez-Machain for the torture and murder of a Drug Enforcement Agency (DEA) agent. Mexico refused to extradite Alvarez-Machain to the United States.[281] Mexican nationals hired by the DEA abducted Alvarez-Machain, briefly detained him for less than a day and brought him to the United States, where federal officers arrested him. After being tried and acquitted, Alvarez-Machain returned to his home in Mexico and filed a civil suit under the ATS against Sosa, a Mexican citizen involved in the abduction, and a Federal Tort Claims Act[282] suit against several DEA agents and the U.S. government. The Ninth Circuit, sitting en banc, held that the plaintiff could sue under the ATS because there is a "clear and universally recognized norm" prohibiting arbitrary arrest and detention, and also allowed suit under the FTCA.[283]

The Supreme Court reversed the court of appeals. The *Sosa* Court held that the FTCA's exception for "[a]ny claim arising in a foreign country" barred all claims based on any injury suffered in a foreign country, regardless of where the tortious act or omission occurred.[284] Furthermore, the Court held that the defendant's proposed reliance on norm of protection against arbitrary arrest was not sufficiently and universally recognized in international law to serve as a fundamental norm of customary international law recognized as creating a cause of action under the ATS, at least where he was illegally detained for less than one day.

The *Sosa* Court adopted a relatively narrow interpretation of the ATS, but refused to adopt the "originalist" approach that the statute is limited to only those norms that existed in 1789.[285] The Court unanimously agreed that the ATS's text "is in terms *only* jurisdictional."[286] Although its text would suggest that the ATS does not create any causes of action, the Court interpreted Congress's original intent in 1789 as authorizing the ATS to incorporate a limited number of common law causes of action based on the small number of international-law violations with a potential for personal liability that existed in 1789, such as offenses against ambassadors, violations of safe conduct, and

possibly claims of piracy and prize claims involving seizures of ships.[287] Although the ATS did not preclude all new causes of action arising out of evolving international norms, the Court concluded that the limited nature of jurisdiction in the 1789 statute suggests that "there are good reasons for a restrained conception of the discretion a federal court should exercise in considering a new cause of action of this kind. Accordingly, we think courts should require any claim based on the present-day law of nations to rest on a norm of international character accepted by the civilized world and defined with a specificity comparable to the features of the 18th-century paradigms we have recognized."[288] Disagreeing with the Ninth Circuit, the Court concluded that Alvarez-Machain's claim did not meet that standard because there is no clear and universally recognized norm of international law prohibiting arbitrary arrest and a brief detention lasting less than one day. The Court observed that a prolonged arbitrary detention might violate customary international law, but it did not decide that question.

The justices were divided about more whether the ATS allows federal courts to incorporate new norms of international law into the ATS or whether the statute is limited to those norms in 1789, or perhaps those adopted before 1938. Rejecting the argument in Justice Scalia's concurring opinion that, after the Court's 1938 decision in *Erie Railroad Co. v. Tompkins,*[289] federal courts no longer have common law-making authority and hence cannot adopt new norms of evolving international law, Justice Souter's majority opinion concluded "that the door is still ajar subject to vigilant doorkeeping, and thus open to a narrow class of international norms today."[290] By contrast Justice Scalia, joined by Justice Thomas and Chief Justice Rehnquist, disagreed with allowing federal courts to selectively incorporate new norms into the ATS because, in his view, "the judicial lawmaking role it invites would commit the Federal Judiciary to a task it is neither authorized nor suited to perform."[291]

Sosa did not shut the door to all new claims of emerging international law norms, and thus environmental ATS plaintiffs still have an opportunity to pursue their claims.[292] Even under Justice Souter's majority approach, however, plaintiffs in ATS cases face a heavy burden in trying to sue based on new norms, such as an argument that global warming offends emerging norms of protecting Earth's environmental health. In deciding which new international norms are so fundamental that they deserve recognition under the ATS, federal courts have only recognized a small number of norms prohibiting the very worst forms of human rights abuses: torture, genocide, slavery, crimes against humanity, and war crimes.[293] It is questionable whether most federal judges will characterize polluters who contribute to global warming as criminals similar to those committing torture or war crimes. As is discussed in section VIII.B.6 below, environmental ATS claims that allege violations of specific treaty provisions to which the United States or a foreign government is a party are more likely to succeed than global warming claims based on customary international law.

3. Private Versus State Actors

The *Sosa* decision indicated that the Supreme Court will usually reject ATS claims against a private party that is acting as an agent for a foreign sovereign, unless the agent is committing severe crimes against humanity, such as torture or war crimes.[294] *Sosa* did not address to what extent plaintiffs may sue non-state actors under the ATS for actions that are not connected with the actions of state actors. In *Kadic v. Karadzic,* the Second Circuit held that non-state actors were within the reach of the ATS. The court stated, "We do not agree that the law of nations, as understood in the modern era, confines its reach to state action. Instead, we hold that certain forms of conduct violate the law of nations whether undertaken by those acting under the auspices of a state or only as private individuals."[295] The court used torture, piracy, slave trading, genocide, war crimes, and violations of international humanitarian law as examples of conduct for which there is an individual, as opposed to solely state, responsibility. In addition, the court recognized the well-settled rule that non-state actors acting in close concert or cooperation with a state are held to be acting as a state and, therefore, subject to the same standards of conduct as a state. In *Beanal v. Freeport-McMoRan, Inc.*, the Federal District Court for Eastern Louisiana announced a four-part test to determine if a private party is acting in such close concert with a sovereign government to be considered a "state actor." The court stated that only one of the following parts need be met to treat a private party as a state actor: (a) the presence of a nexus between the state's and the defendant's conduct, (b) the state and the defendant operate in a symbiotic relationship, (c) the defendant participated in joint action with the state or its agents, or (d) the defendant performed a public function traditionally conducted by the public sector.[296] The Supreme Court has not addressed when private parties may be treated as quasi-state actors under the ATS.

B. Environmental Claims and the ATS

The argument for recognizing environmental ATS claims is that environmental harms can result in significant human injuries that violate fundamental norms of international law.[297] One theory is that environmental harms are significant human rights abuses when multi-national corporations (MNCs) in developing countries harm environmental quality or destroy natural resources that poor "local people depend on for their subsistence, without providing meaningful local benefits."[298] Second, some commentators argue that a polluter that severely damages the environment itself, even absent direct economic or physical harms to human beings, has violated international human rights norms because there is a fundamental human right to live in a clean and healthy environment.[299]

1. *Amlon Metals, Inc. v. FMC Corp.*

In *Amlon Metals, Inc. v. FMC Corp.*, a court for the first time directly addressed an environmental claim under the ATS.[300] The plaintiffs sued FMC under the ATS for fraudulently transporting hazardous materials that contained far more toxicity than the non-hazardous material promised in the contract between the plaintiffs and the defendant.[301] The plaintiffs argued that the fraudulent sale violated Principle 21 of the 1972 Stockholm Declaration of Principles, which grants states the "sovereign right to exploit their own resources pursuant to their own environmental policies, and the responsibility to ensure that activities within their jurisdiction or control do not cause damage to the environment of other States or of areas beyond the limits of national jurisdiction," and the *Restatement (Third) of the Foreign Relations Law of the United States (Restatement).*[302] The District Court for the Southern District of New York held that the environmental claims were insufficient to establish a violation of international law. The court found that the Stockholm Principles do not "set forth any specific proscriptions, but rather refer only in a general sense to the responsibility of nations to insure that activities within their jurisdiction do not cause damage to the environment beyond their borders."[303] The court determined that the *Restatement* possibly reflected American views on environmental law, but not "universally recognized principles of international law." Accordingly, under *Filartiga*, the court concluded that the plaintiff failed to demonstrate universal recognition in international law of a prohibition against fraudulently shipping hazardous materials.[304] The court dismissed the ATS claim for failure to state a claim upon which relief could be granted.

2. *Aguinda v. Texaco*

In *Aguinda v. Texaco*, the plaintiffs sued a multinational oil corporation, Texaco, for significant environmental destruction, including intentional release of toxins into the environment, damage to pristine rainforests, and destruction of streams and aquifers.[305] The plaintiffs sought to certify a class of over 30,000 Ecuadorians whose environment was damaged by the oil company's practices in Ecuador. In a preliminary decision in 1994, the Federal District Court for the Southern District of New York, in an opinion by Judge Broderick, defined the law of nations as "customary in nature, to be defined by the usages, solemn commitments and clearly articulated principles of the international community." Judge Broderick appeared to accept a broad view of states' responsibility for preventing environmental damage.

> Although many authorities are relevant, perhaps the most pertinent in the present case is the Rio Declaration on Environment and Development (1992). Principle 2 on the first page of the document recognizes that states have "the sovereign right to exploit their own resources pursuant to their own environmental and developmental policies," but also have "the responsibility to ensure that activities within their jurisdiction or control do not cause damage to the environment of other States or areas beyond the limits of national jurisdiction."[306]

Observing that the alleged pollution would likely violate American law, he suggested that the defendant's actions could amount to a violation of the ATS "if there were established misuse of hazardous waste of sufficient magnitude to amount to a violation of international law." But he also cautioned that "[n]ot all conduct which may be harmful to the environment, and not all violations of environmental laws, constitute violations of the law of nations." He also had reservations about interfering with the decisions of other nations. Responding to motions by Texaco and the government of Ecuador to dismiss the case because it should be resolved in Ecuador's courts, Judge Broderick delayed deciding the case on the merits and instead sought to determine if Ecuador's courts would accept the case.

After Judge Broderick's death, in 1996, the district court, in a decision by Judge Rakoff, dismissed the action on three separate grounds: (1) FNC, (2) international comity, and (3) failure to join two indispensable parties—the Republic of Ecuador and its state-owned oil company, Petroecuador.[307] In dismissing the case, Judge Rakoff opined in dicta that "[i]n short, plaintiffs' imaginative view of this Court's power must face the reality that United States district courts are courts of limited jurisdiction. While their power within those limits is substantial, it does not include a general writ to right the world's wrongs."[308] The Second Circuit reversed and remanded the dismissal because Judge Rakoff had erred in granting the dismissals absent an agreement by appellee Texaco to submit to the jurisdiction of the courts in Ecuador.[309] After defendant Texaco agreed to accept Ecuador's jurisdiction, on remand the district court granted defendant's motion to dismiss on the grounds of FNC.[310] Judge Rakoff in dicta argued that "federal courts should exercise extreme caution when adjudicating environmental claims under international law to insure that environmental policies of the United States do not displace environmental policies of other governments."[311] The Second Circuit then affirmed the decision to dismiss the case on grounds of FNC.[312] The *Aguinda* decision demonstrates the importance of FNC in determining whether U.S. courts will take jurisdiction over an ATS case or will instead require that it be decided in a foreign court.

3. *Beanal v. Freeport-McMoRan, Inc.*

In *Beanal v. Freeport-McMoRan, Inc.,* the plaintiff sued Freeport under the ATS for torture, cultural genocide of his Amungme tribe, and environmental torts allegedly resulting from the defendant's mining activities in Tamika, Irian Jaya, Indonesia.[313] The environmental claims alleging that the defendant's mining practices caused destruction, pollution, alteration, and contamination of natural waterways, as well as surface and groundwater sources, deforestation, and destruction and alteration of physical surroundings are the closest analogy to a global warming claim, but they involve the different problem of internal pollution in one nation rather than the transboundary issues of global warming. Because international law recognizes transboundary pollution as an issue potentially within its domain but generally treats internal pollution as an issue for national governments, Beanal's environmental claims were arguably weaker claims under international law than a serious transboundary pollution issue such as global warming.

In an April 1997 opinion, the district court stated that the initial claim of "cultural genocide" not only requires specific intent, but also requires the destruction of a group, not a culture.[314] The court also stated that the plaintiff could in theory allege facts that, if true, would constitute genocide, including torture. The court also indicated that extreme environmental injuries might constitute genocide, but only if the defendant specifically intended to cause such destruction. The court dismissed the first amended complaint without prejudice, and allowed the plaintiff to re-file a second amended complaint that more specifically pled his allegations of cultural genocide. After the plaintiff filed a second amended complaint, in August 1997, the district court granted the defendant's motion to strike that complaint and dismissed the complaint because the plaintiff had pled too conclusively and again failed to plead his allegations with sufficient specificity, especially on the issues of genocide and state action.[315] In March 1998, the district court granted Freeport's motion to strike Beanal's third amended complaint and dismissed his claims with prejudice.[316] Despite the plaintiff's failure to file a satisfactory complaint, the district court's initial decision suggested that claims for environmental human rights violations might be filed under the ATS if pled with sufficient specificity.[317]

On appeal, the Fifth Circuit affirmed the decision of the district court to dismiss the complaint with prejudice.[318] The Fifth Circuit appeared to be skeptical of environmental claims under the ATS. The court observed that the "sources of international law cited by Beanal and the amici merely refer to a general sense of environmental responsibility and state abstract rights and liberties devoid of articulable or discernable standards and regulations to identify practices that constitute international environmental abuses or torts."[319] The court also stated that "federal courts should exercise extreme caution when adjudicating environmental claims under international law to insure that environmental policies of the United States do not displace environmental policies of other governments . . . especially when the alleged environmental torts and abuses occur within the sovereign's borders and do not affect neighboring countries." The Fifth Circuit's opinion was arguably more hostile to future environmental claims under the ATS than the district court's decision.

4. *Sarei v. Rio Tinto PLC*

In *Sarei v. Rio Tinto PLC*, the plaintiffs, citizens of Papua New Guinea (PNG), alleged, *inter alia*, that defendant Rio Tinto's mining operations destroyed their island's environment and harmed the health of its people.[320] The defendant allegedly dumped tailings from the mine into the Kawerong-Jaba river system, resulting in the destruction of the river valley, rainforests, and thousands of acres. Furthermore, the tailings polluted the local bay and killed fish, a major food source for the local population. The mining operation also caused significant air pollution, which allegedly caused respiratory infections and asthma among the local population.

The plaintiffs alleged that these environmental harms violated the law of nations and caused human rights violations infringing upon a "right to life" and "right to health" recognized in international law.[321] The U.S. District Court for Central California held that neither the "right to life" nor the "right to health" was sufficiently specific to form the basis for an ATS claim.[322] Furthermore, the court found "that nations [did not] universally recognize [that such rights] can be violated by perpetrating environmental harm."[323] The court determined that some of the international conventions[324] relied upon by the plaintiff did not specifically address environmental harm, and those conventions that did address environmental harm did not provide "specific proscriptions" establishing mandatory international law.[325] The court agreed with earlier ATS decisions that had held that "allegations of environmental harm do not state a claim under the law of nations."[326]

The plaintiffs also argued that environmental harm alone violated the international law norms of sustainable development, which requires states to avoid serious and irreversible environmental or human health impacts from development actions, and the United Nations Convention on the Law of the Sea (UNCLOS), which prohibits some types of marine pollution.[327] The court found the principle of sustainable development far too broad to create a cause of action under the ATS because even the plaintiffs' expert could not identify the limits of that "right."[328] Although it observed that the United States was not a party to the UNCLOS treaty, the court found that UNCLOS was now a part of customary international law, and therefore concluded that the plaintiffs' UNCLOS claim was

cognizable under the ATS.[329] The court also found that the plaintiffs' war crimes and crimes against humanity allegations presented cognizable ATS claims, but those issues are beyond the scope of this chapter.[330]

The court next addressed whether it had jurisdiction over the cognizable ATS claims. The court declined to dismiss on FNC grounds and send the case to a PNG forum, finding that "the private interests favor retaining jurisdiction, and the public interests are neutral."[331] The court suggested that the ATS expresses a policy preference for deciding international law issues in American courts, especially if the plaintiff is a lawful U.S. resident.[332] "The court believes such a result is particularly appropriate given that the case is brought under the ATCA and alleges violations of international law. *See Wiwa [v. Royal Dutch Petroleum Co.*, 226 F.3d 88, 106-08 (2d Cir. 2000)] (holding that "the policy expressed in the [Torture Victim Prevention Act] favoring adjudication of claims in violation of international prohibitions on torture" weighed against dismissing the action on forum non conveniens grounds)."[333]

Because the defendant's mining activities were pursuant to an agreement between its subsidiary and the PNG government, which constituted the acts of a foreign sovereign, the court concluded that it must dismiss the environmental and racial discrimination claims based on the act of state doctrine.[334] The court also cited international comity as an alternative justification for dismissing the environmental and racial discrimination claims because of compensation remedies in PNG law.[335] Additionally, the court invoked the political question doctrine to dismiss all claims, including plaintiffs' war crimes and crimes against humanity claims, because federal courts' involvement in the case would interfere with foreign relations between the U.S. government and PNG.[336]

On appeal, after rearguing the case in light of the Supreme Court's *Sosa* decision, the Ninth Circuit affirmed the district court's conclusion that the UNCLOS claim could provide a basis for an ATS claim because ratification of the Convention by 149 nations was sufficient to make UNCLOS part of customary international law.[337] The Ninth Circuit reversed the district court's dismissal of all claims as nonjusticiable political questions because the court of appeals did not believe that sufficiently serious adverse political consequences would result from litigating the issues in the case, despite the State Department's Statement of Interest (SOI) advocating that the court should dismiss the case.[338] The Ninth Circuit reversed the district court's dismissal of the racial discrimination claim on act of state grounds because the court of appeals concluded that international law does not recognize alleged acts of racial discrimination as constituting official sovereign acts because the prohibition against racial discrimination is a jus cogens norm that states may not violate without repercussion.[339] The Ninth Circuit agreed with the district court that PNG's actions to exploit its natural resources were official sovereign acts. The court of appeals observed that "although UNCLOS codifies norms of customary international law . . . it is not yet clear" whether UNCLOS norms are widely recognized jus cogens norms that may not be violated by a state. The Ninth Circuit vacated the district court's dismissal of the UNCLOS claims on act of state grounds and remanded the case to the district court for reconsideration of the SOI and any new factual developments concerning the PNG's attitude toward the suit because the court of appeals concluded that the district court had relied too heavily upon the State Department's SOI to justify the dismissal of the case.[340] Although finding that the district court's dismissal of the racial discrimination claim and UNCLOS claims on comity grounds was within its discretion, the Ninth Circuit, nevertheless, vacated the comity portion of the decision so the district court could reconsider the comity grounds in light of the Ninth Circuit's rejection of the lower court's overreliance on the State Department's SOI and also so that the district court could consider any new factual information about whether the PNG government's past opposition to the suit had changed.[341] The Ninth Circuit affirmed the district court's conclusion that the ATS does not contain a requirement that plaintiffs exhaust any local remedies in PNG before suing in federal court.[342] In his dissenting opinion, Judge Bybee argued that the ATS and general principles of international law required plaintiffs to exhaust any local remedies in PNG before suing in federal court.[343]

5. *Flores v. Southern Peru Copper*

In *Flores v. Southern Peru Copper*, Peruvian residents brought an ATS claim alleging that pollution from defendant's copper mining, refining, and smelting operations violated both the plaintiffs' individual human rights and international environmental law because of the injuries to the local environment.[344] Plaintiffs first claimed that the air pollution from the defendant's mining and smelting operations caused plaintiffs' or their decedents' severe lung disease in violation of their "right to life," "right to health" and right to "sustainable development" under the Universal Declaration of Human Rights, the International Covenant on Economic, Social and Cultural Rights, and the Rio Declaration on Environment and Development.[345] The plaintiffs argued these declarations and conventions constituted fundamental customary international law creating rights to life and health. The U.S. District Court for the Southern District of New York held that plaintiffs had failed to establish subject matter jurisdiction or to state a claim under the ATS because they had not "demonstrated that high levels of environmental pollution within a nation's borders, causing harm to human life, health, and development, violate 'well-established, universally recognized norms of international law.'"[346] The district court also dismissed the case because Peru was an adequate alternative forum, and, therefore, dismissal was warranted under the FNC doctrine.[347]

On appeal, the Second Circuit affirmed the district court's dismissal, concluding that the alleged rights relied upon by the plaintiffs were "boundless and indeterminate . . . , expressing virtuous goals understandably expressed at a level of abstraction needed to secure the adherence of States that disagree on many of the particulars regarding how actually to achieve them."[348] The Second Circuit held that "vague" and "amorphous" statements in international declarations and conventions do not establish customary international law cognizable under the ATS. The Second Circuit also rejected the plaintiffs' second claim alleging that "egregious" intra-national pollution from the mining activities violated customary international environmental law because intra-national pollution, even if severe, is generally a concern of that particular nation alone and not a "mutual concern" of the international community at large.[349] The court did not address transboundary pollution because the plaintiffs did not allege that any of the pollution had an effect outside of Peru, but Judge Cabranes' "mutual concern" analysis suggests that transboundary pollution is a more appropriate subject of customary international law than intra-national pollution, although courts would have to face the difficult question of whether there are specific enforceable standards for transboundary pollution.[350] Due to its conclusion that the plaintiffs failed to state a claim under the ATS, the Second Circuit did not address the district court's dismissal under the FNC doctrine.[351]

6. Future Environmental Human Rights Claims After *Sosa*

No plaintiff has yet won a purely environmental or an environmental human rights claim under the ATS. Some language in the district court's decision in *Beanal* and Judge Broderick's initial decision in *Aguinda* suggested that an environmental plaintiff could establish a cognizable ATS claim, but even these decisions set a very high standard of proof. The Second Circuit's *Flores* decision and the Fifth Circuit's *Beanal* decision, as well as the district court decisions in *Amlon* and *Sarei* and Judge Rakoff's dicta in *Aguinda*, suggest that most international environmental declarations and conventions are too vague to be enforceable under the ATS. The Ninth Circuit in *Sarei*, however, recognized UNCLOS as establishing customary international law against some forms of marine pollution.

After *Sosa* limited ATS claims to international norms that are as widely recognized today as the prohibition against piracy was in 1789, it is likely that most courts will follow the Second and Fifth Circuit's critical reaction to environment claims under the ATS.[352] Nevertheless, the Ninth Circuit in *Sarei* concluded that the plaintiffs' UNCLOS claim was cognizable under *Sosa*'s standards, although the court of appeals acknowledged that this claim was more controversial than the racial discrimination, war crimes and crimes against humanity claims in *Sarei*.[353] After *Sosa*, environmental human rights claims alleging transboundary pollution or violations of treaty obligations have a better chance of succeeding under the ATS than claims that allege purely intra-national environmental harms.[354] If the United States or possibly a foreign nation violated a specific and particularized provision in an environmental treaty to which it is a party, a plaintiff would have a stronger chance of winning an ATS claim, but many environmental treaties contain generalized language rather than specific provisions that clearly delineate when a state is in violation.[355]

> **. . . the district court decisions in *Amlon* and *Sarei* and Judge Rakoff's dicta in *Aguinda* suggest that most international environmental declarations and conventions are too vague to be enforceable under the ATS.**

Additionally, as *Aguinda* demonstrates, even if a plaintiff can establish a cognizable environmental human rights claim under the ATS, there is a significant possibility that a court will dismiss the case on FNC grounds if a foreign court is at least plausibly capable of hearing the case.[356] Furthermore, in *Sarei*, the district court invoked the act of state, international comity, and political question grounds as additional reasons for dismissing an ATS case where the defendant had contracted with a foreign sovereign or its agents to conduct activities that resulted in pollution, although on appeal the Ninth Circuit reversed, vacated, and remanded the case for reconsideration.[357] The *Sosa* decision suggested that the Supreme Court may reject ATS claims against a private party that is acting as an agent for a foreign sovereign, unless the agent is committing severe crimes against humanity, such as torture or war crimes.[358] It is not clear whether other courts will follow the *Sarei* decision, in which the Ninth Circuit took a relatively narrow reading of *Sosa*'s impact on environmental claims.

IX. Conclusion

As section II discusses, standing doctrine poses several difficulties for climate change plaintiffs. Standing doctrine is better suited to a simple car accident, where there are clear injuries caused by one or at most a handful of defendants, than to a transboundary pollution problem caused by thousands or millions of actors that results in generalized global warming harms to most of humanity. It remains uncertain whether courts will allow plaintiffs who receive generalized injuries similar to many others to sue. The District of Columbia and Ninth Circuits, as well as probably the Tenth Circuit, have disagreed concerning the extent to which a plaintiff must demonstrate specific and particularized evidence of injury. Additionally, what remedies should a court impose if finds that defendant utility or energy companies contribute to global warming? For example, injunctive remedies might require courts to engage in the difficult public policy issues of determining what percentage utilities should reduce their emissions over the next 10 years. Similarly, a court attempting to calculate damages would face complex problems in measuring the financial harm of global warming as well as difficult philosophical questions, such as whether it is appropriate to make a utility pay for the harms caused by its historical emissions, even before global warming was widely recognized as an international problem in the 1990s.

The political question doctrine is a serious barrier to both domestic public nuisance suits and ATS suits. The political question doctrine may be especially pertinent when plaintiffs seek injunctive remedies that would require judges to adopt policies to reduce GHGs, but perhaps is also an issue where plaintiffs seek enormous damages that could seriously impact major industries. Judge Preska in *Connecticut* and Judge Sentelle concurring in *Massachusetts* noted that the complexities of both causation and remedies in global warming suits raised too many difficult policy questions for the courts and argued that the political branches should decide these questions. Any solution to solve global warming would have enormous economic consequences and require substantial investments in new technology. Thus, there is a strong argument that only the political branches can solve the problem through legislation and international treaties rather than litigation. The district court in *Sarei*, in an ATS case, thought that a suit against an agent of a foreign government raised too many foreign policy questions and likewise should be dismissed under the political question doctrine. The political question doctrine is a serious obstacle to global warming suits, although not the only barrier.

As is discussed in section III, the plaintiffs in any climate change suit face substantial difficulties in proving that either private firms or government entities caused global warming because of the GHGs released from fossil fuel emissions. As demonstrated by the *Massachusetts* decision in section II.3, defendants can still challenge whether human-generated GHGs cause global warming, although the scientific evidence for a linkage between the two is growing stronger. Even though there is wide scientific agreement that GHGs cause most global warming, it is difficult to prove the contribution of specific defendants to the problem in a specific location. It will be difficult for the *Comer* plaintiffs to prove that energy companies caused or worsened Hurricane Katrina, even though many scientists believe that global warming exacerbates weather extremes. State, municipal or private plaintiffs that can demonstrate rising sea levels in their jurisdiction or melting permafrost probably have the strongest evidence of causation. If the political question defense is rejected, industry can argue that there are no practical alternatives to using fossil fuels for the majority of our energy and transportation needs, although environmentalists would counter-argue that vehicle manufacturers or utilities have failed for a number of years to pursue potential alternatives.

As is discussed in section IV, in the Eighth and Ninth Circuits, as well as probably the Tenth Circuit, plaintiffs have a reasonably good chance of arguing that the government has a duty under NEPA to examine policies or projects that cause significant GHG emissions. Following its four-part standing text, however, the District of Columbia Circuit demands that plaintiffs demonstrate that a project will cause specific and particularized injuries before the government must write an EA or EIS. A plaintiff in the District of Columbia Circuit must practically conduct its own environmental assessment to prove that the government should perform an EA or EIS. On the merits of a NEPA claim, the *Los Angeles* court demanded that plaintiffs demonstrate that a government policy would have a significant impact on worldwide global warming before the District of Columbia Circuit would order the government to perform an EIS. Even if a plaintiff forces the government to conduct an EA or EIS concerning global warming, the government is under no duty to take action because NEPA is a purely procedural statute, except in the rare case where the agency's own internal NEPA regulations clearly mandate that it conduct mitigation.[359]

As is discussed in section V, under the Endangered Species Act, the FWS may list species threatened by global warming, such as the polar bear, as threatened or endangered species and also list the critical habitat of the species for protection. It is unclear, however, how the ESA's listing and critical habitat provisions will work in the context of a global transboundary problem. If the FWS lists the polar bear's Arctic habitat as critical habitat, does the FWS have the authority to regulate GHGs that cause melting in Arctic areas?

As is discussed in section VII, human rights claims before the IAHRC or United Nations are likely to have only symbolic and political value, because the United States will almost certainly refuse to recognize the jurisdiction of international human rights or cultural commissions.

As is discussed in section VIII, an ATS suit could in theory have tangible consequences for private firms that release GHGs in foreign countries and have sufficient minimum contacts to create jurisdiction in American courts. After *Sosa*, winning an ATS environmental claim will be difficult. Also, many courts have used the FNC doctrine to dismiss cases that could be brought in foreign courts instead of American courts, although the *Sarei* decision argued that the ATS has a policy preference in favor of adjudicating such claims. If the United States violated a specific provision of a treaty to which it is a party, an ATS plaintiff is more likely to succeed in its suit, but many environmental treaties contain language too vague and generalized for a successful ATS suit.

Any global warming suit brought in American courts faces heavy odds. Suits that have only procedural consequences, such as writing an EIS or listing an endangered species, have a better chance of success than substantive suits that would require an industry to pay damages or restructure its operations to reduce GHGs. Any major solutions to global warming are more likely to come from the political branches than the courts. Nevertheless, plaintiffs are likely to continue to file climate change suits as a way to influence the political debate about reducing GHGs.

Endnotes

1. U.S. Const. art. III. A more in-depth discussion of the standing issues is contained in my article, Bradford C. Mank©, *Standing and Global Warming: Is Injury to All Injury to None?*, 35 Envtl. L. 1-84 (2005). The standing and NEPA sections of this chapter borrows heavily from that article.
2. Stark v. Wickard, 321 U.S. 288, 310 (1944); Mank, *supra* note 1, at 22.
3. Lujan v. Defenders of Wildlife (Defenders), 504 U.S. 555, 560-61 (1992); Mank, *supra* note 1, at 23-24.
4. *Defenders*, 504 U.S. at 561; Mank, *supra* note 1, at 24.
5. 528 U.S. 167, 181, 183-84 (2000) ("The affiant members' reasonable concerns about the effects of those discharges directly affected those affiants' recreational, aesthetic, and economic interests.").
6. 2005 U.S. Dist. LEXIS 21778 (S.D.N.Y. Sept. 29, 2005), at 2-3, *aff'd*, 2006 U.S. App. LEXIS (2d Cir. Aug. 10, 2006) (unpublished opinion).
7. *Id.* at 6-8.
8. *Id.* at 8 n.5 (distinguishing Baur v. Veneman, 352 F.3d 625, 634-37 (2d Cir. 2003)).
9. *Id.* at 9.

10. Thomas W. Merrill, *Global Warming as a Public Nuisance*, 30 COLUM. J. ENVTL. L. 293, 296-97 (2005).

11. David A. Grossman, *Warming Up to a Not-So-Radical Idea: Tort-Based Climate Change Litigation*, 28 COLUM. J. ENVTL. L. 1, 14-16, 18-20, 22, 40, 53-54 (2003); Mank, *supra* note 1, at 6, 11, 15-16, 77-84.

12. Merrill, *supra* note 10, at 297-98.

13. Mank, *supra* note 1, at 21-22.

14. 438 U.S. 59, 80 (1978) (quoting Warth v. Seldin, 422 U.S. 490, 498 (1975)); *see generally* DaimlerChrysler v. Cuno, 126 S. Ct. 1854 (2006) (denying standing in tax-payer suit in part because plaintiffs' alleged injuries were generalized grievances).

15. 422 U.S. 490, 501 (1975).

16. 524 U.S. 11 (1998); Mank, *supra* note 1, at 37-40.

17. Mank, *supra* note 1, at 37-40; Merrill, *supra* note 10, at 298.

18. 2005 U.S. Dist. LEXIS 21778 (S.D.N.Y. Sept. 29, 2005), at 9.

19. *See, e.g., Florida Audubon*, 94 F.3d 658, 667 n.4 (D.C. Cir. 1996) (en banc) ("As the 'geographic nexus' test at issue here was in fact intended to ensure that a plaintiff's injury met this first criterion of being particularized and personal, an analysis of that test that does not actually require the plaintiff to demonstrate that such particularity must be invalid."); City of Evanston v. Reg'l Transp. Auth., 825 F.2d 1121, 1126, *cert. denied*, 484 U.S. 1005 (7th Cir. 1987) (holding that plaintiffs did not prove standing under NEPA because they did "not sufficiently allege where they lived in relation to the property"); City of Davis v. Coleman, 521 F.2d 661, 671 (9th Cir. 1975) ("The procedural injury implicit in agency failure to prepare an EIS . . . is itself a sufficient 'injury in fact' to support standing, provided this injury is alleged by a plaintiff having a sufficient geographical nexus to the site of the challenged project that he may be expected to suffer whatever environmental consequences the project may have."); Mank, *supra* note 1, at 24-25.

20. *See Defenders*, 504 U.S. 555, 567 n.3 (1992) ("The dissent may be correct that the geographic remoteness . . . does not 'necessarily' prevent such a finding—but it assuredly does so when no further facts have been brought forward."); *id.* at 572 n.7 (rejecting "standing for persons who have no concrete interests affected—persons who live (and propose to live) at the other end of the country from [the environmental impact]"); Mank, *supra* note 1, at 25.

21. Mank, *supra* note 1, at 7-8, 45-63.

22. 912 F.2d 478, 483 (D.C. Cir. 1990) (per curiam) (Ginsburg, D.H., J., Opinion for the Court on the failure to issue an EIS for Model Years 1987-1988 and dissenting on NRDC standing), overruled by *Florida Audubon*, 94 F.3d 658 (D.C. Cir. 1996) (en banc); Mank, *supra* note 1, at 48.

23. *City of Los Angeles*, 912 F.2d at 482-83, 494-98; Mank, *supra* note 1, at 48-51.

24. *City of Los Angeles*, 912 F.2d at 492 (Wald, C.J., Opinion for the Court on NRDC standing and dissenting on the failure to issue an EIS for Model Years 1987-1988).

25. *Id.* at 492 (quoting City of Davis v. Coleman, 521 F.2d 661, 671 (9th Cir. 1975)).

26. *Id.* at 494-98; Mank, *supra* note 1, at 49.

27. *City of Los Angeles*, 912 F.2d at 483-84 (Ginsburg, D.H., J., Opinion for the Court on the failure to issue an EIS for Model Years 1987-1988 and dissenting on NRDC standing); Mank, *supra* note 1, at 49-50.

28. *City of Los Angeles*, 912 F.2d at 495-99 (Wald. C.J., Opinion for the Court on NRDC standing and dissenting on the failure to issue an EIS for Model Years 1987-1988); Mank, *supra* note 1, at 50-51.

29. 94 F.3d 658 (D.C. Cir. 1996) (en banc); Mank, *supra* note 1, at 51-56.

30. *Florida Audubon*, 94 F.3d at 662; Mank, *supra* note 1, at 51-52.

31. *Florida Audubon*, 94 F.3d at 667 & n.4; Mank, *supra* note 1, at 52-53.

32. *Florida Audubon*, 94 F.3d at 665-66; Mank, *supra* note 1, at 53.

33. *Florida Audubon*, 94 F.3d at 666; Mank, *supra* note 1, at 54.

34. *Florida Audubon*, 94 F.3d at 672; Mank, *supra* note 1, at 54.

35. Lujan v. Defenders of Wildlife (Defenders), 504 U.S. 555, 572 n.7 (1992); Mank, *supra* note 1, at 35-37, 54, 60-63.

36. *Florida Audubon*, 94 F.3d at 668-70; Mank, *supra* note 1, at 54-55.

37. *Florida Audubon*, 94 F.3d at 672 (Buckley, J., concurring); Mank, *supra* note 1, at 55.

38. *Florida Audubon*, 94 F.3d at 674 (Rogers, J., dissenting); Mank, *supra* note 1, at 55-56.

39. *Florida Audubon*, 94 F.3d at 672 (Buckley, J., concurring); *Florida Audubon*, 94 F.3d at 674 (Rogers, J., dissenting); Mank, *supra* note 1, at 55-56.

40. Massachusetts v. EPA, 415 F.3d 50, 53-54 (D.C. Cir.), *reh'g en banc denied*, 433 F.3d 66 (2005), *cert. granted*, 126 S. Ct. 2960 (June 26, 2006) (No. 05-1120); Mank, *supra* note 1, at 8-9, 63-76.

41. *Id.* at 54 (quoting Brief for Respondent at 16).

42. *Id.* at 55-59 (Randolph, J., opinion of court) (citing Steel Co. aka Chicago Steel & Pickling Co. v. Citizens for a Better Environment, 523 U.S. 83, 97 n.2 (1998)).

43. *Id.* at 56-58.

44. *Id.* at 59-61 (Sentelle, J., dissenting in part and concurring in the judgment).

45. *Id.* at 61-67 (Tatel, J., dissenting).

46. *Id.* at 67-82 (Tatel, J., dissenting).

47. 126 S. Ct. 2960 (June 26, 2006) (No. 05-1120).

48. Commonwealth of Mass. v. Envtl. Prot. Agency (No. 05-1120), 2006 WL 2563378; Brief of Former EPA Administrators Carol M. Browner, William K. Reilly, Douglas M. Costle and Russell E. Train as Amici Curiae in Support of Petitioners (Aug. 31, 2006), 2006 WL 2569575.

49. 440 F.3d 476 (D.C. Cir. 2006), *opinion withdrawn* by 464 F.3d 1 (D.C. Cir. 2006); Montreal Protocol on Substances that Deplete the Ozone Layer, Sept. 16, 1987, S. Treaty Doc. No. 100-10, 1522 U.N.T.S. 29 ("Montreal Protocol"); Clean Air Act Amendments of 1990, Pub. L. No. 101-549, tit. VI, 104 Stat. 2399, 2648 (implementing Montreal Protocol); 42 U.S.C. § 7671c(h) (requiring EPA to "promulgate rules for reductions in, and terminate the production, importation, and consumption of, methyl bromide under a schedule that is in accordance with, but not more stringent than, the phaseout schedule of the Montreal Protocol Treaty as in effect on October 21, 1998"); *see* EPA, Protection of Stratospheric Ozone: Process for Exempting Critical Uses From the Phaseout of Methyl Bromide, Final Rule, 69 Fed. Reg. 76,982, 76,990 (2004) (exempting certain "critical uses" of methyl bromide for 2005).

50. 440 F.3d at 483-84, *opinion withdrawn* by 464 F.3d 1 (D.C. Cir. 2006).

51. 464 F.3d 1 (D.C. Cir. 2006).

52. 102 F.3d 445, 447 n.2, 449 n.4, 451-52 (10th Cir. 1996); Mank, *supra* note 1, at 56-59.

53. 341 F.3d 961, 972-75 (9th Cir. 2003); Mank, *supra* note 1, at 59.

54. 358 F.3d 626 (9th Cir. 2004); Mank, *supra* note 1, at 6, 40-41.

55. *Covington*, 358 F.3d at 650-55 (Gould, J., concurring); Mank, *supra* note 1, at 6-7, 40-45

56. Northwest Environmental Defense Center et al., Sixty-day notice of violations of Clean Air Act and Oregon State Implementation Plan (Aug. 10, 2005), at http://www.lclark.edu/org/nedc/objects/OwensCorningNOI.pdf.

57. Northwest Environmental Defense Center v. Owens Corning Corp., 434 F. Supp. 2d 957, 964-71 (D. Ore. 2006) (denying defendant's motion to dismiss for lack of standing); Michael Milstein, *School, groups benefit in Owens deal*, THE OREGONIAN, June 9, 2006 (discussing settlement), http://www.oregonlive.com/search/index.ssf?/base/business/1149821721263810.xml?oregonian?fng&coll=7&thispage=1. Because a judge deciding a motion to dismiss assumes that the plaintiffs' allegations are true, he did not address whether the plaintiffs could prove their allegations that the HCFC-142b would increase global warming and thereby cause rising sea levels in Oregon.

58. 2005 WL 2035596 at 1-6, 35 Envtl. L. Rep. 20,179 (N.D. Cal., Aug. 23, 2005).

59. *Id.* at 2 (quoting Citizens for Better Forestry v. U.S. Dept. of Agric., 341 F.3d 961, 969-71 (9th Cir. 2003). The *Watson* court rejected the defendants' reliance on *Center for Biological Diversity v. Abraham*, 218 F. Supp. 2d 1143, 1155 (N.D. Cal. 2002), which had held that the plaintiffs' claim that the federal government's failure to purchase sufficient alternative fuel vehicles had caused them injuries from increased global warming as "too general, too unsubstantiated, too unlikely to be caused by defendants' conduct, and/or too unlikely to be redressed by the relief sought to confer standing," *id.*, because that case was decided before the Ninth Circuit's decision in *Citizens for Better Forestry. Watson*, 2005 WL 2035596 at 3 n.3.

60. California v. NHTSA (9th Cir. May 2, 2006) (challenging NHTSA, *Fuel economy standards: Light trucks; 2008-2011 model years*, 71 Fed. Reg. 17,566 (April 6, 2006)), *available at* http://ag.ca.gov/newsalerts/cms06/06-046_0a.pdf ; Danny Hakim, *10 States, in Challenge to U.S., Plan suit to Force Better Mileage Rules for SUVs*, N.Y. TIMES, May 2, 2006; Office of Attorney General, State of California, Press Release, Attorney General Lockyer Challenges Federal Fuel Standards for Failing to Increase Fuel Efficiency, Curb Global Warming Emissions (May 2, 2006), *available at* http://ag.ca.gov/newsalerts/release.php?id=1299.

61. Sierra Club, Press Release, Lawsuit, Website Take on Bush Administration Over Fuel Economy Standards, May 23, 2006, *at* http://www.sierraclub.org/pressroom/releases/pr2006-05-23.asp.

62. *Sierra Club Files First-Time Suit on CO₂ Cost-Benefit Test in CAFE Rule*, May 24, 2006, Envtl. Pol'y Alert, insideepa.com (subscription required).

63. Merrill, *supra* note 10.

64. Massachusetts v. EPA, 415 F.3d 50 (D.C. Cir.), *reh'g en banc denied*, 433 F.3d 66 (2005), *cert. granted*, 126 S. Ct. 2960 (June 26, 2006) (No. 05-1120); Mank, *supra* note 1, at 8-9.

65. Connecticut v. Am. Elec. Power, 406 F. Supp. 2d 265 (S.D.N.Y. 2005); Mank, *supra* note 1, at 9-10; Merrill, *supra* note 10, at 297. Arguably, there are six corporations because American Electric Power Service Corporation is technically separate from but a subsidiary of American Electric Power Company, Inc. Connecticut v. Am. Elec. Power Co., 2004 WL 1685122, at 1.

66. *Id.* at 271-74 & n.6.

67. Merrill, *supra* note 10, at 299-300.

68. Missouri v. Illinois, 180 U.S. 208 (1901); Merrill, *supra* note 10, at 303 & n.44 (listing cases).

69. Merrill, *supra* note 10, at 305-06.

70. Alfred L. Snapp & Son, Inc. v. Puerto Rico *ex rel.* Barez, 458 U.S. 592, 600-02 (1982); Merrill, *supra* note 10, at 303-04.

71. *Alfred L. Snapp & Son, Inc.*, 458 U.S. at 602; *id.* at 611 (Brennan, J., concurring) (stating "at the very least, the prerogative of a State to bring suits in federal court should be commensurate with the ability of private organizations"); Merrill, *supra* note 10, at 304-05.

72. *Connecticut*, at 271-74.

73. *Id.* at 271 n.6.

74. *Id.* at 272-73.

75. *Id.* at 274.

76. *See generally* Erwin Chemerinsky, *The Kennedy Court: October Term 2005*, 9 Green Bag 2d 335 (2006) (arguing Justice Kennedy was the key swing vote during the October Term 2005); Amy L. Major, *Foxes Guarding the Henhouse: How to Protect Environmental Standing From a Conservative Supreme Court*, 36 Envtl. L. Rep. 10,698 (Sept. 2006) (arguing Chief Justice Roberts and Justice Alito are likely to join with Justices Scalia and Thomas in taking narrow view of standing, especially concerning environmental plaintiffs); John G. Roberts Jr., *Article III Limits on Statutory Standing*, 42 Duke L.J. 1219 (1993); Public Interest Research Group of N.J., Inc. v. Magnesium Elektron, Inc., 123 F.3d 111 (3d Cir. 1997) (Judge Alito joined majority) (denying standing because plaintiff's evidence failed to prove that defendant's pollution had caused actual harm to the waterways that plaintiffs used for swimming and fishing).

77. Grossman, *supra* note 11, at 22.

78. *Id.* at 23.

79. *Id.* at 24.

80. Benjamin P. Harper, Note: *Climate Change Litigation: The Federal Common Law of Interstate Nuisance and Federalism Concerns*, 40 Ga. L. Rev. 661, 684-85 (2006).

81. Grossman, *supra* note 11, at 24-25; Mank, *supra* note 1, at 3, 12-16

82. Working Group I, Intergovernmental Panel on Climate Change (IPCC), Climate Change 2001: The Scientific Basis 61 (2001) [hereinafter *Climate Change 2001: The Scientific Basis*], *available at* http://www.grida.no/climate/ipcc tar/wg1/index.htm.

83. Grossman, *supra* note 11, at 24.

84. *Id.* at 24-25.

85. Massachusetts v. EPA, 415 F.3d 50, 61-67 (D.C. Cir.) (Tatel, J., dissenting), *reh'g en banc denied*, 433 F.3d 66 (2005), *cert. granted*, 126 S. Ct. 2960 (June 26, 2006) (No. 05-1120).

86. Mark Clayton, *In Hot Pursuit of Polluters*, Christian Sci. Monitor, Aug. 19, 2004, at 15 (quoting "'Climate change and sea-level rise, particularly with respect to New York City and the surrounding region, is fairly well understood,' says William Solecki, professor of geography at City University of New York and a project co-leader on a 2001 study that charted expected sea-level impacts. 'We know the region is already undergoing sea-level rise.'"), *available at* 2004 WLNR 1664979.

87. Grossman, *supra* note 11, at 14-16, 18-20, 22, 40, 53-54; Mank, *supra* note 1, at 6, 11, 15-16, 77-84.

88. Joseph Cox was the lead plaintiff in the original complaint filed on September 20, 2005, but the court dismissed him from the case and he was not a named plaintiff

in the amended complaint. Joseph B. Cox v. Nationwide Mutual Ins. Co., Complaint (No. 1:05-cv-436-LG-RHW (S.D. Miss., filed Sept. 20, 2005); Ned Comer v. Nationwide Mutual Ins. Co., Amended Complaint No. 1:05CV436-LG-RHW (S.D. Miss., filed Sept. 30, 2005). The plaintiffs in the fiirst amended complaint had sued Nationwide Mutual Insurance Co. and six other named insurance companies, as well as unnamed insurance companies, in a class action alleging that the defendant insurance companies had wrongfully denied coverage to the plaintiffs by claiming that flooding, which is excluded in the insurance policies, rather than wind damage from Hurricane Katrina, caused the damage to the plaintiffs' homes. Id. at 2-10. The issue of the liability of insurance companies for global warming is discussed in Chapter 15. The plaintiffs also named three mortgage companies, as well as unnamed mortgage companies, in a class action, alleging the defendants failed to obtain necessary insurance on plaintiffs' homes and therefore that the defendant class of mortgage companies has waived any right to collecting the remainder of the mortgages on plaintiffs' homes. Id. at 14-18. On February 23, 2006, Senior Judge Senter dismissed the insurance companies and mortgage companies from the case with leave to file a separate action against them because the plaintiffs' contractual claims against them were quite distinct from the tort-based global warming claims. Memorandum Opinion, Comer v. Nationwide Mutual Insurance, No. 1:05CV436-LG-RHW, at 2-6 (S.D. Miss. Feb. 23, 2006) (Senter, Senior Judge).

89. Id. at 2-6.

90. Ned Comer v. Murphy Oil, Third Amended Complaint, No. 1:05-cv-00436-LTS-RHW (S.D. Miss. April 18, 2006).

91. The seven named oil company defendants were Murphy Oil, USA; Universal Oil Products (UOP); Shell Oil Corp.; Chevron/Texaco Corp.; ExxonMobil Corp., BP; and ConocoPhillips Co. Id. at 2-4.

92. Id. at 7-10.

93. Id. at 10-11.

94. Id. at 11-12.

95. Id. at 15.

96. Id. at 18-19.

97. Id. at 19-20.

98. Id. at 20.

99. The three chemical companies named by the plaintiffs were: Dow Chemical Co.; E.I. Du Pont de Nemours & Co.; and Honeywell, International, Inc. Id. at 20-22.

100. Id. at 22-26.

101. (1) Murphy Oil et al. [Oil Company Defendants], Joint Motion to Dismiss; (2) Dow Chemical Co., Inc. & E.I. Du Pont de Nemours & Co. [Chemical Company Defendants], Motion to Dismiss the Third Amended Class Action Complaint (June 30, 2006); (3) Coal Companies' Motion to Dismiss for Lack of Subject Matter Jurisdiction and Failure to State a Claim, in Ned Comer v. Murphy Oil, No. 1:05-cv-00436-LTS-RHW (S.D. Miss. June 30, 2006).

102. Memorandum in Opposition to Joint Motion to Dismiss; Memorandum in Opposition to Motion to Dismiss the Third Amended Class Action Complaint; Memorandum in Opposition to Motion to Dismiss for Lack of Subject Matter Jurisdiction and Failure to State a Claim, in Ned Comer v. Murphy Oil, No. 1:05-cv-00436-LTS-RHW (S.D. Miss. Aug. 21, 2006). In late September 2006, the Oil Company Defendants and Coal Company Defendants each filed reply briefs responding to the Plaintiffs' memoranda in opposition. Docket Sheet, Ned Comer v. Murphy Oil, No. 1:05-cv-00436-LTS-RHW.

103. Order, Ned Comer v. Murphy Oil, No. 1:05-cv-00436-LTS-RHW (S.D. Miss. Sept. 19, 2006) (Senter, Senior Judge).

104. Ker Than, *Warmer Seas Creating Stronger Hurricanes, Study Confirms*, March 16, 2006, *at* http://www.livescience.com; *see also* Thom Akeman, *Global warming behind record 2005 storms: experts*, Reuters, April 24, 2006 (reporting "The record Atlantic hurricane season last year can be attributed to global warming, several top experts, including a leading U.S. government storm researcher, said on [April 24, 2006].").

105. RESTATEMENT (SECOND) OF TORTS § 431 (1965); *see also id.* at § 834 ("One is subject to liability for a nuisance caused by an activity, not only when he carries on the activity but also when he participates to a substantial extent in carrying it on."); RESTATEMENT (THIRD) OF TORTS: PRODUCTS LIABILITY § 16(a) (1998) ("When a product is defective at the time of commercial sale or other distribution and the defect is a substantial factor in increasing the plaintiff's harm beyond that which would have resulted from other causes, the product seller is subject to liability for the increased harm."); Shetterly v. Raymark Indus., 117 F.3d 776, 780 (4th Cir. 1997) ("In order to sustain an action against Raymark for asbestos-related injuries, Plaintiffs must prove that Raymark products were a substantial causative factor in their injuries.") (internal quotation marks and citations omitted); Grossman, *supra* note 11, at 25 & n.119.

106. RESTATEMENT, *supra* note 105, at § 431 cmt. a (1965); *see also id.* at § 433; Grossman, *supra* note 11, at 25.

107. RESTATEMENT, *supra* note 105, at § 433 cmt. d (1965); *see also id.* at § 439; Grossman, *supra* note 11, at 25 & n.120.

108. *See* Laborers Local 17 Health & Benefit Fund v. Philip Morris, Inc., 191 F.3d 229, 235-36 (2d Cir. 1999), *cert. denied*, 528 U.S. 1080 (2000) (noting that critical elements of proximate cause are direct injury, defendant's acts being substantial cause of injury, and plaintiff's injury being reasonably foreseeable); Grossman, *supra* note 11, at 25-26 & n.121.

109. *See* City of Bloomington, Ind. v. Westinghouse Elec. Corp., 891 F.2d 611, 614 (7th Cir. 1989) (holding Monsanto not to be liable for nuisance because "Westinghouse was in control of the product purchased and was solely responsible for the nuisance it created."); *In re* Methyl Tertiary Butyl Ether ("MTBE") Prod. Liab. Litig., MDL No. 1358, Master File No. 00 Civ. 1898 (SAS), 2001 U.S. Dist. LEXIS 12192, at 95-96 (S.D.N.Y. Aug. 20, 2001) (holding defendant may be liable even if third parties contribute to harm if defendant has some control over harm to plaintiff by choosing to engage in harmful conduct); Grossman, *supra* note 11, at 26 & n.122.

110. *See* RESTATEMENT (THIRD) OF TORTS: LIABILITY FOR PHYSICAL HARM: BASIC PRINCIPLES (Tentative Draft No. 2, Mar. 25, 2002), § 26, at 39-40, 56-64 (discussing factual causation issues in torts), *id.* at § 26 rep.'s notes cmt. j., at 39 (Tentative Draft No. 2, 2002) (claiming substantial factor test has "prove[n] confusing and [is] being misused"); John D. Rue, *Returning to the Roots of the Bramble Bush: The "But For" Test Regains Primacy in Causal Analysis in the American Law Institute's Proposed Restatement (Third) of Torts*, 71 FORDHAM L. REV. 2679, 2681-82 (2003).

111. Grossman, *supra* note 11, at 27.

112. Massachusetts v. EPA, 415 F.3d 50, 61-67 (D.C. Cir.) (Tatel, J., dissenting), *reh'g en banc denied*, 433 F.3d 66 (2005), *cert. granted*, 126 S. Ct. 2960 (June 26, 2006) (No. 05-1120).

113. Daniel V. Mumford, Note: *Curbing Carbon Dioxide Emissions Through the Rebirth of Public Nuisance Laws—Environmental Legislation by the Courts*, 30 Wm. & Mary Envtl. L. & Pol'y Rev. 195, 204-05 (2005).

114. Grossman, *supra* note 11, at 33, 44 n.238, 59 (discussing use of market share approach to liability in global warming suits).

115. Sindell v. Abbot Labs., 607 P.2d 924 (Cal. 1980); Conley v. Boyle Drug Co., 570 So. 2d 275 (Fla. 1990); Smith v. Cutter Biological, Inc., 823 P.2d 717 (Haw. 1991); Hymowitz v. Eli Lilly & Co., 539 N.E.2d 1069 (N.Y. 1989); Martin v. Abbot Labs., 689 P.2d 368 (Wash. 1984); Collins v. Eli Lilly Co., 342 N.W.2d 37 (Wis. 1984) (finding liability proportional to the risk created, as measured by market share).

116. The following cases rejected market share liability. *See, e.g.,* Hamilton v. Beretta U.S.A. Corp., 264 F.3d 21 (2d Cir. 2001) (gun manufacturers); Santiago v. Sherwin-Williams Co., 794 F. Supp. 29 (D. Mass. 1992) (lead paint pigmentation); N.Y. Tel. Co. v. AAER Sprayed Insulations, Inc., 250 A.D.2d 49 (N.Y. App. Div. 1998) (asbestos).

117. Aaron Twerski & Anthony J. Sebok, *Liability Without Cause? Further Ruminations on Cause-in-Fact as Applied to Handgun Liability*, 32 Conn. L. Rev. 1379, 1401 (2000).

118. James A. Henderson, *The Lawlessness of Aggregative Torts*, 34 Hofstra L. Rev. 329 (2006).

119. Detroit Bd. of Educ. v. Celotex Corp., 493 N.W.2d 513 (Mich. App. 1992).

120. Texas v. Am. Tobacco Co., 14 F. Supp. 2d 956 (E.D. Tex. 1997).

121. City of Gary v. Smith & Wesson Corp., 801 N.E.2d 1222 (Ind. 2003).

122. City of St. Louis v. Lead Indus. Ass'n, No. 002-0245 (Mo. Cir. Ct. Nov. 20, 2002).

123. Henderson, *supra* note 118, at 331-32.

124. City of Philadelphia v. Beretta U.S.A. Corp., 277 F.3d 415 (3d Cir. 2002); City of Chicago v. Beretta U.S.A. Corp., 821 N.E.2d 1099 (Ill. 2004); Henderson, *supra* note118, at 332; *but see City of Gary*, 801 N.E.2d at 1222, 1231-32.

125. The defendants are General Motors Corp.; Toyota Motor NorthAmerica, Inc.; Ford Motor Co.; Honda NorthAmerica, Inc.; Chrysler Motors Corp.; and Nissan NorthAmerica, Inc. People of the State of California *ex rel.* Bill Lockyer, Attorney General v. General Motors Corp., (Sept. 20, N.D. Calif.), http://ag.ca.gov/newsalerts/cms06/06-082_0a.pdf; Grossman, *supra* note 11, at 28-31 (2000 GHG data).

126. *See supra* notes 95-96 and accompanying text.

127. Harper, *supra* note 80, at 685-87.

128. ABF Freight Sys., Inc. v. NLRB, 510 U.S. 317, 329- 30 (1994) (quoting Precision Instrument Mfg. Co. v. Auto. Maint. Mach. Co., 324 U.S. 806, 814 (1945)); Harper, *supra* note 80, at 685-86.

129. Missouri v. Illinois, 200 U.S. 496, 522 (1906); Harper, *supra* note 80, at 686.

130. Harper, *supra* note 80, at 687-88.

131. Restatement, *supra* note 105, at § 881 (1979); *see also* Restatement (Third) of Torts: Products Liability § 16(a), (b) (1998); Grossman, *supra* note 11, at 31-33.

132. Restatement, *supra* note 105, at §§ 875, 879 (1979); *see also* Restatement (Third) of Torts: Products Liability § 16(c) (1998); Grossman, *supra* note 11, at 31-32.

133. Grossman, *supra* note 11, at 31-32.

134. *Id.* at 32-33.

135. Mumford, *supra* note 113, at 207.

136. Connecticut v. Am. Elec. Power, 04 Civ. 5669 (LAP), 2005 U.S. Dist. LEXIS 19964 (S.D.N.Y., Sept. 15, 2005); Mank, *supra* note 1, at 9-10; Merrill, *supra* note 10, at 294; Mumford, *supra* note 113, at 196.

137. Mumford, *supra* note 113, at 204-05.

138. Massachusetts v. EPA, 415 F.3d 50, 59-61 (D.C. Cir.) (Sentelle, J., dissenting in part and concurring in the judgment), *reh'g en banc denied*, 433 F.3d 66 (2005), *cert. granted*, 126 S. Ct. 2960 (June 26, 2006) (No. 05-1120).

139. City of Milwaukee v. Illinois (Milwaukee II), 451 U.S. 304, 314 n.7 (1981).

140. U.S. CONST. art. III, § 2; Missouri v. Illinois, 200 U.S. 496, 519 (1906) ("The Constitution extends the judicial power of the United States to controversies between two or more states, and between a state and citizens of another state, and gives this court original jurisdiction in cases in which a state shall be a party."); Harper, *supra* note 80, at 673-74.

141. Merrill, *supra* note 10, at 311-19 (arguing that CAA is a comprehensive statute that displaces federal common law).

142. 451 U.S. 304 (1981).

143. Merrill, *supra* note 10, at 311-19; Harper, *supra* note 80, at 679-81.

144. Georgia v. Tennessee Copper Co., 206 U.S. 230 (1907) (granting injunction to prevent discharge of noxious gases from the defendant's plant in Tennessee that had caused air pollution in Georgia); Merrill, *supra* note 10, at 308-10; Harper, *supra* note 80, at 676.

145. Merrill, *supra* note 10, at 311-19.

146. *Compare* Grossman, *supra* note 11, at 33-37 (arguing CAA is not a comprehensive statute because it does not regulate either carbon dioxide emissions or climate change and thus that the CAA does not "preempt a federal common law climate change tort claim") *with* Merrill, *supra* note 10, at 311-19 (arguing that CAA is a comprehensive statute that displaces federal common law); *see also* Harper, *supra* note 80, at 682 ("Although the similarities between the Clean Air and Clean Water Acts suggest they should be treated the same for preemption purposes, there are significant differences between the two Acts that might lead to different results.").

147. New Eng. Legal Found. v. Costle, 666 F.2d 30, 32 (2d Cir. 1981) (following Milwaukee II); Harper, *supra* note 80, at 682.

148. Reeger v. Mill Service, Inc., 593 F. Supp. 360 (W.D. Pa. 1984); United States v. Kin-Buc, Inc., 532 F. Supp. 699 (D. N.J. 1982); Harper, *supra* note 80, at 682.

149. Grossman, *supra* note 11, at 35-37 ("Not only are carbon dioxide emissions unregulated by the CAA, therefore, but climate change itself is outside the scope of the statute. As such, it does not seem that the CAA would preempt a federal common law climate change tort claim.").

150. Merrill, *supra* note 10, at 311-19 (arguing that CAA is a comprehensive statute that displaces federal common law).

151. Massachusetts v. EPA, 415 F.3d 50, 53-54 (D.C. Cir.), *reh'g en banc denied*, 433 F.3d 66 (2005), *cert. granted*, 126 S. Ct. 2960 (June 26, 2006) (No. 05-1120); Mank, *supra* note 1, at 8-9, 63-76.

152. *Massachusetts*, 415 F.3d at 57-61 (Randolph, J., opinion of the Court).

153. *Id.* at 67-82 (Tatel, J., dissenting).

154. Merrill, *supra* note 10, at 311-19.

155. Rice v. Santa Fe Elevator Corp., 331 U.S. 218, 230 (1947); Grossman, *supra* note 11, at 37.

156. Hillsborough County v. Automated Med. Lab., Inc., 471 U.S. 707, 713 (1985); Grossman, *supra* note 11, at 37.

157. Ray v. Atlantic Richfield Co., 435 U.S. 151, 158 (1978); Grossman, *supra* note 11, at 37.

158. Hillsborough County, 471 U.S. at 713; Grossman, *supra* note 11, at 37.

159. 479 U.S. 481, 491-97 (1987).

160. *Id.* at 497-99.

161. *Id.* at 499-500.

162. Ouellette v. Int'l Paper Co., 666 F. Supp. 58, 62 (D. Vt. 1987).

163. Grossman, *supra* note 11, at 37-38.

164. *But see* Grossman, *supra* note 11, at 38-39 (arguing that state regulation of CO₂ and other GHGs is not preempted under CAA because GHGs are not really air pollutants in the usual sense of the CAA in that they do not harm human breathing or directly cause air pollution, but affect the atmosphere indirectly through the greenhouse effect of trapping heat in the atmosphere).

165. 42 U.S.C. 7543 (2001); *see also id.* 7545(c)(4)(A).

166. Washington v. General Motors Corp., 406 U.S. 109, 114 (1972); *see also* American Auto. Mfrs. Ass'n v. Cahill, 152 F.3d 196, 198 (2d Cir. 1998).

167. Grossman, *supra* note 11, at 38-39.

168. *In re* Methyl Tertiary Butyl Ether ("MTBE") Prod. Liab. Litig., MDL No. 1358, Master File No. 00 Civ. 1898 (SAS), 2001 U.S. Dist. LEXIS 12192, at 46-48 (S.D.N.Y. Aug. 20, 2001).

169. *Id.* at 51; Grossman, *supra* note 11, at 39.

170. Central Valley Chrysler-Jeep, Inc., et al. v. Catharine E. Witherspoon, 2006 WL 2734359 (E.D. Cal. Sept. 25, 2006) (No. CV F 04 6663 AWI LJO), at 12.

171. Merrill, *supra* note 10, at 319-28; Note, *Foreign Affairs Preemption and State Regulation of Greenhouse Gas Emissions*, 119 HARV. L. REV. 1877 (2006).

172. United Nations Framework Convention on Climate Change, May 9, 1992, 31 I.L.M. 849 (1992); Merrill, *supra* note 10, at 320.

173. Kyoto Protocol to the United Nations Framework Convention on Climate Change, Dec. 10, 1997, 37 I.L.M. 32. *See also* Text of March 13, 2001 Letter from President Bush to Senators Hagel, Helms, Craig, and Roberts, *available at* http://www.whitehouse.gov/news/releases/2001/03/20010314.html (last visited Feb. 28, 2006).

174. Merrill, *supra* note 10, at 320-21.

175. 389 U.S. 429 (1968).

176. Merrill, *supra* note 10, at 321.

177. Crosby v. National Foreign Trade Council, 530 U.S. 363, 377-81 (2000).

178. Am. Ins. Ass'n v. Garamendi, 539 U.S. 396, 401, 405-06, 424-25 (2003).

179. Merrill, *supra* note 10, at 322-23.

180. Central Valley Chrysler-Jeep, Inc., et al. v. Catharine E. Witherspoon, 2006 WL 2734359 (E.D. Cal. Sept. 25, 2006) (No. CV F 04 6663 AWI LJO) at 12-19.

181. Merrill, *supra* note 10, at 325-28; *accord* Note, *supra* note 241.

182. Grossman, *supra* note 11, at 53-57.

183. RESTATEMENT, *supra* note 105, at 821B; Grossman, *supra* note 11, at 52.

184. RESTATEMENT, *supra* note 105, at 821B cmt. a, 821C(1); Grossman, *supra* note 11, at 55.

185. Grossman, *supra* note 11, at 14-16, 18-20, 22, 40, 53-54; Mank, *supra* note 1, at 6, 11, 15-16, 77-84.

186. Grossman, *supra* note 11, at 55.

187. RESTATEMENT, *supra* note 105 at 821B; Grossman, *supra* note 11, at 53.

188. Merrill, *supra* note 10, at 329.

189. Grossman, *supra* note 11, at 54.

190. Restatement, *supra* note 105 at 821B cmt. a (stating that statutes prohibiting public nuisances "usually have been interpreted to carry over this rule [applying to private nuisances] from the common law"); Merrill, *supra* note 10, at 329; Mumford, *supra* note 113, at 207.

191. Restatement, *supra* note 105 at 826(a).

192. *Id.* at 826(b); 829A; Merrill, *supra* note 10, at 329.

193. Merrill, *supra* note 10, at 329.

194. *Id.* at 329; *see generally* Henry E. Smith, *Exclusion and Property Rules in the Law of Nuisance*, 90 Va. L. Rev. 965 (2004).

195. David Kairys, *The Governmental Handgun Cases and the Elements and Underlying Policies of Public Nuisance Law*, 32 Conn. L. Rev. 1175, 1177 & n.7 (2000); Grossman, *supra* note 11, at 54-55.

196. Grossman, *supra* note 11, at 58-59.

197. *Id.* at 39-40.

198. *Id.* at 39-42; *see generally* Restatement (Third) of Products Liability §§ 2(b) (1998) (stating a product is defective in design "when the foreseeable risks of harm posed by the product could have been reduced or avoided by the adoption of a reasonable alternative design . . . and the omission of the alternative design renders the product not reasonably safe"), 2(c) (stating a product has a warning defect "when the foreseeable risks of harm posed by the product could have been reduced or avoided by the provision of reasonable instructions or warnings by the seller [or manufacturer] and the omission of the instructions or warnings renders the product not reasonably safe").

199. Grossman, *supra* note 11, at 42-46.

200. *Id.* at 42-52.

201. *Id.* at 46, 51.

202. *Id.* at 49-50.

203. 42 U.S.C. § 4332(2)(C) (2000).

204. *See* Robertson v. Methow Valley Citizens Council, 490 U.S. 332, 349 (1989); 40 C.F.R. § 1502.1-.25 (2004); Mank, *supra* note 1, at 45-46.

205. 40 C.F.R. § 1501.4 (2004).

206. See 40 C.F.R. §§ 1501.4(e), 1508.13 (2004); Mank, *supra* note 1, at 46.

207. Matt Weiser, *Levee suit cites global warming: Officials who OK'd Delta homes illegally failed to consider sea level rise, groups say,* Sacramento Bee (Cal.), Aug. 18, 2006) (discussing suit arguing flood-control officials violated the California Environmental Quality Act by failing to examine how sea level rise will affect proposed levee modifications in San Joaquin County); *see generally* Daniel R. Mandelker, NEPA Law and Litigation §§ 12:1-12:2 (2d ed. 2001 & update 2006) (listing and discussing states with mini-NEPA statutes or requiring environmental assessments through executive orders or other legal methods); Stephen M. Johnson, *NEPA and SEPAs in the Quest for Environmental Justice*, 30 Loy. L.A. L. Rev. 565 (1997) (same); Jeffrey L. Carmichael, Note, *The Indiana Environmental Policy Act: Casting a New Role for a Forgotten Statute*, 70 Ind. L.J. 613, 622-36 (1995) (same).

208. Catron County Bd. of Comm'rs v. U.S. Fish & Wildlife Serv., 75 F.3d 1429, 1434 (10th Cir. 1996); Mank, *supra* note 1, at 46.

209. 42 U.S.C. § 4332(2)(C)(iii) (2000) (requiring EA/EIS to consider "alternatives to the proposed action"); 40 C.F.R. § 1502.14 (2004) (same); 40 § C.F.R. § 1505.2 (stating agency has duty in its record of decision to discuss why it selected its proposal

instead of alternatives); Vermont Yankee Nuclear Power Corp. v. Natural Res. Def. Council, 435 U.S. 519, 551 (1978) (requiring the agency to evaluate "reasonable" alternatives in an EIS, but not "uncommon or unknown" alternatives); Mank, *supra* note 1, at 46.

210. *Robertson*, 490 U.S. at 350 ("NEPA itself does not mandate particular results, but simply prescribes the necessary process."); Mank, *supra* note 1, at 47.

211. *See* 40 C.F.R. § 1502.16(h) (2004) (requiring the agency to discuss mitigation methods); *Robertson*, 490 U.S. at 352-53 (holding that the agency has a duty in an EIS to discuss mitigation measures, but is not required to implement them); Mank, *supra* note 1, at 47. An agency may be bound in some circumstances to implement mitigation measures that it has publicly promised to adopt. Mank, *supra* note 1, at 47 n.322. Some agencies have adopted internal NEPA regulations that may require them to mitigate some types of impacts. In *Robertson*, the Ninth Circuit held that the Forest Service's own regulations required the development of a "complete mitigation plan." 490 U.S. at 357 (citing 833 F.2d at 814 & n.3, 819 & n.14); Marion D. Miller, Note, *The National Environmental Policy Act and Judicial Review After* Robertson v. Methow Valley Citizens Council *and* Marsh v. Oregon Natural Resources Council, 18 ECOLOGY L.Q. 223, 243-46. Applying the *Seminole Rock* doctrine that courts should reject an agency's interpretation of its own regulations only if that interpretation is "plainly erroneous or inconsistent with the regulation," the Supreme Court, however, concluded that Ninth Circuit failed to give sufficient deference to the Forest Service's determination that it had complied with its own regulations regarding mitigation measures. *Robertson*, 490 U.S. at 358-59 (citing Bowles v. Seminole Rock & Sand Co., 325 U.S. 410, 414 (1945)); Miller, *supra*, at 244-45; *see also* Auer v. Robbins, 519 U.S. 452, 461 (1997) (holding that an agency's interpretation of its own regulation is entitled to deference). Following *Robertson*, a plaintiff has a heavy burden in convincing a court that an agency's regulations require it to implement mitigation measures if the agency interprets its regulations not to require such mitigation. That burden is likely to be even greater in a global warming case in which a plaintiff seeks to compel an unwilling agency to impose broad mitigation measures that would involve significant costs and impacts on the national economy.

212. Mank, *supra* note 1, at 47.

213. 5 U.S.C. § 702 (2000); Mank, *supra* note 1, at 47.

214. See 5 U.S.C. § 706(2)(A) (2000); Mank, *supra* note 1, at 47.

215. *City of Los Angeles*, 912 F.2d at 482 (per curiam), 484-90 (Ginsburg, D.H., J., Opinion for the Court on the failure to issue an EIS for Model Years 1987-1988 and dissenting on NRDC standing); *id.* at 504 (Ginsburg, Ruth B., J., concurring); Mank, *supra* note 1, at 48.

216. *City of Los Angeles*, 912 F.2d at 484-90 (Ginsburg, D.H., J., Opinion for the Court on the failure to issue an EIS for Model Years 1987-1988 and dissenting on NRDC standing); *id.* at 504 (Ginsburg, Ruth B., J., concurring).

217. *Id.* at 482 (per curiam), 490-91, 499-504 (Wald, C.J., Opinion for the Court on NRDC standing and dissenting on the failure to issue an EIS for Model Years 1987-1988).

218. *See, e.g.*, Friends of the Earth, Inc. v. Laidlaw Envtl. Servs. (TOC), Inc., 528 U.S. 167 (2000) (Justice Ginsburg wrote the majority opinion).

219. 40 C.F.R. § 1508.7.

220. Friends of the Earth v. Watson, 2005 WL 2035596 at 1-6 (arguing defendants provided loans or insurance for numerous projects that have significant cumulative impact on global warming), 35 Envtl. L. Rep. 20,179 (N.D. Cal., Aug. 23, 2005); Jennifer Woodward, *Turning Down the Heat: What United States Laws Can Do to Help Ease Global Warming*, 39 AM. U. L. REV. 203, 225 (1989) (suggesting plaintiffs raise challenges based on cumulative impacts).

221. Border Power Plant Working Group v. Dep't of Energy, 260 F. Supp. 2d 997, 1008-11, 1028-29, 1033 (S.D. Cal. 2003); Mank, *supra* note 1, at 59.

222. *Border Power Plant Working Group*, 260 F. Supp. 2d at 1029.

223. *Id.* at 1010-11.

224. *See supra* notes 57-58 and accompanying text.

225. 345 F.3d 520 (8th Cir. 2003).

226. *Id.* at 548-50.

227. *Id.* at 549 (emphasis in original).

228. *Id.* at 550.

229. Surface Transp. Board, Decision, Dakota, Minnesota & Eastern RR Corp. Const. into the Powder River Basin, STB Fin. Docket No. 33407, No. 36665 (Feb. 13, 2006), at 1-6, 10-17, *available at* http://www.stb.dot.gov/decisions/readingroom.nsf/ UNID/53FE263777B8A00485257116004C24D7/$file/36665.pdf.

230. *Activists Say Revised NEPA Review Fails to Address Climate Impacts*, INSIDE EPA, July 14, 2006, *available at* www.insideepa.com (subscription required), LEXIS Allnews or Westlaw 2006 WLNR 12051682.

231. Dept. of Interior, U.S. Fish & Wildlife Service (FWS), Endangered and Threatened Wildlife and Plants; Petition to List the Polar Bear as Threatened, 71 Fed. Reg. 6745 (2006); 16 U.S.C. § 1533 (b)(3)(B).

232. Dept. of Interior, U.S. Fish & Wildlife Service (FWS), Endangered and Threatened Wildlife and Plants; Petition to List the Polar Bear as Threatened, 71 Fed. Reg. 28,653-54 (2006).

233. CLIFFORD RECHTSCHAFFEN & EILEEN GAUNA, ENVIRONMENTAL JUSTICE 55-85 (2002) (summarizing various studies).

234. *See* Executive Order 12898, Federal Actions to Address Environmental Justice in Minority Populations and Low-Income Populations, 59 Fed. Reg. 7629 (1994), 3 C.F.R. § 859, *reprinted in* 42 U.S.C. § 4321; RECHTSCHAFFEN & GAUNA, *supra* note 233, at 3-4, 391-404; Bradford C. Mank, *Executive Order 12,898*, Chapter 4, in ENVIRONMENTAL JUSTICE (Michael B. Gerrard & Sheila Foster eds., 2d ed. 2006). Other chapters in that same book offer a wealth of valuable information about the definition of EJ.

235. EPA, Environmental Justice Strategic Plan Framework and Outline, 70 Fed. Reg. 36,167 (June 22, 2005) (announcing availability of draft strategic plan framework and outline on EPA Web site); Environmental Justice Strategic Plan (June 16, 2005 Working Draft) at 2, available at http://www.epa.gov/compliance/resources/publications/ data/planning/strategicplan/ej/outline-strategicplan-publiccomment.pdf.

236. http://www.epa.gov/Compliance/resources/policies/ej/admin-ej-commit-letter-110305.pdf.

237. Executive Order 12898, *supra* note 234, at § 6-609; Mank, *supra* note 234.

238. Civil Rights Act of 1964, Pub. L. No. 88-352, §§ 601-605, 78 Stat. 241, 252-53, 42 U.S.C. § 2000d; Bradford C. Mank, *Title VI*, Chapter 2, in ENVIRONMENTAL JUSTICE (Michael B. Gerrard & Sheila Foster eds., 2d ed. 2006).

239. 40 C.F.R. § 7.35(b) (prohibiting use of discriminatory program criteria), (c) (prohibiting location of facility that has discriminatory effect); RECHTSCHAFFEN & GAUNA, *supra* note 233, at 351-89; Mank, *supra* note 238.

240. 532 U.S. 275, 287-88 (2001).

241. RECHTSCHAFFEN & GAUNA, *supra* note 233, at 351-89; Mank, *supra* note 238.

242. Mank, *supra* note 1, at 15-16.

243. Susan Cutter et al., *The Long Road Home: Race, Class, and Recovery from Hurricane Katrina*, 48 ENV'T 9, 10-18 (March 2006).

244. Petition to the Inter-American Commission on Human Rights Seeking Relief from Violations Resulting from Global Warming Caused by Acts and Omissions of the United States, http://www.earthjustice.org/news/documents/12-05/ FINALPetitionICC.pdf; Center for Int'l Envtl. Law, Inuit File Petition with Inter-American Commission on Human Rights, www.ciel.org/Climate/ICC_Petition_7Dec05.html; Earthjustice, Press Release, Inuit Human Rights Petition Filed over Climate Change, *available at* http://www.earthjustice.org/news/display.html?ID=1086; Donald Goldberg & Martin Wagner, *Human Rights Litigation to Protect the Peoples of the Arctic*, 98 AM. SOC'Y INT'L L. PROC. 227 (2004); Erika M. Zimmerman, Student Essay, *Valuing Traditional Ecological Knowledge: Incorporating the Experiences of Indigenous People into Global Climate Change Policies*, 13 N.Y.U. ENVTL. L. J. 803, 837-41 (2005). The IACHR is based in Washington, D.C., and consists of seven members appointed by the Organization of American States' (OAS) General Assembly; its members act independently and do not represent any particular country. INTER-AMERICAN COMMISSION ON HUMAN RIGHTS, WHAT IS THE IACHR?, http://www.cidh.oas.org/what.htm.

245. James C. Chen & Joanne Rotondi, *Raising the Heat: Climate Change Litigation in the United States*, SUSTAINABLE DEVELOPMENT, ECOSYSTEMS & CLIMATE CHANGE COMMITTEE NEWSLETTER, Vol. 8, No. 2, April 2005, at 7.

246. Arctic Climate Impact Assessment, www.acia.uaf.edu. and http://amap.no/acia.

247. *See, e.g.*, American Declaration of the Rights and Duties of Man, May 2, 1948, O.A.S. Official Rec., Res. XXX, adopted by the Ninth International Conference of American States (1948), *reprinted in* Basic Documents Pertaining to Human Rights in the Inter-American System, OAS/Ser.L/V/I.4 Rev. 9 (2003), *available at* http:// www.cidh.org/Basicos/Basic.htm at art. I ("[e]very human being has the right to life, liberty and the security of his person"); art. VIII ("the right to fix his residence within the territory of the state of which he is a national, to move about freely within such territory, and not to leave it except by his own will"); art. IX ("the right to the inviolability of his home"); art. XI ("Every person has the right to the preservation of his health through sanitary and social measures relating to food, clothing, housing and medical care, to the extent permitted by public and community resources."); art. XIII ("Every person has the right to take part in the cultural life of the community, to enjoy the arts, and to participate in the benefits that result from intellectual progress, especially scientific discoveries."); art. XXIII ("own such private property as meets the essential needs of decent living and helps to maintain the dignity of the individual and of the home"; "[e]veryone has the right to the use and enjoyment of his property").

248. *See* Inter-Am. Court H.R., Advisory Opinion OC-10/89, Interpretation of the American Declaration of the Rights and Duties of Man Within the Framework of Article 64 of the American Convention on Human Rights, July 14, 1989, Ser. A. No. 10, at ¶¶ 35, 45 (1989); Inuit Petition, *supra* note 244, at 70*.

249. Andrew C. Revkin, *Eskimos Seek to Recast Global Warming as a Rights Issue*, N.Y. TIMES, Dec 15, 2004, *available at* http://www.nytimes.com/2004/12/15/international/americas/15climate.html (subscription required).

250. Chen & Rotondi, *supra* note 245, at 7; Zimmerman, *supra* note 244, at 840-41.

251. Petition to the World Heritage Committee Requesting Inclusion of Waterton-Glacier International Peace Park on the List of World Heritage in Danger as a Result of Climate Change and for Protective Measures and Actions (Feb. 16, 2006), *available at* http://law.lclark.edu/org/ielp/glacierpetition.html. Previously, in November 2004, foreign nongovernmental organizations and individuals had filed petitions with the Committee requesting that Belize's Barrier Reef (Belize Petition), Peru's Huarascan

National Park (Peru Petition), and Nepal's Sagarmatha (Everest) National Park (Nepal Petition) be placed on the List of World Heritage in Danger because of harms from climate change. Hari M. Osofsky, *The Geography of Climate Change Litigation: Implications for Transnational Regulatory Governance*, 83 WASH. U. L. REV. 1789, 1846 & n.257 (listing petitions). They had earlier filed a September 2004 report with the Committee on climate change's impact on the Great Barrier Reef in Australia (Australia Report) that discussed Australia's obligations under the World Heritage Convention. *Id.* & n.258. In July 2005, at its 29th session, the Committee responded to the petitions and report by recognizing that "the impacts of climate change are affecting many and are likely to affect many more World Heritage properties, both natural and cultural in the years to come," calling upon "all States Parties to seriously consider the potential impacts of climate change within their management planning," and asking that the World Heritage Centre establish "a broad working group of experts" to prepare a report on these issues for its 30th session. *Id.* & n.259 (quoting U.N. Educ., Scientific & Cultural Org. World Heritage Comm., Decisions of the 29th Session of the World Heritage Committee (Durban 2005), Decision 29 COM 7B.a (Sept. 9, 2005), *available at* http://whc.unesco.org/archive/2005/whc05-29com-22e.pdf , pp. 36-37.

252. Art. 11, para. 4, Convention Concerning the Protection of the World Cultural and Natural Heritage (adopted Nov. 16, 1972), http://whc.unesco.org/pg.cfm?cid=182. Everglades National Park is the only one of the 34 properties on the list that is located in the United States.

253 Waterton-Glacier Petition, *supra* note 251, at vii-viii, 1-2.

254. *Id.* at viii; Stephan Kaufman, *Glaciers Melting in Montana Park* (CBS News, March 13, 2006) (reporting "Dr. Daniel Fagre, a federal research scientist based at Glacier National Park in Montana, says that in 1850, the park had 150 glaciers. Today, because of global warming, there are only 27 left, with estimates that all the glaciers in the park will be gone by the year 2030"), *available at* http://www.cbsnews.com/stories/2006/03/13/tech/main1391827.shtml.

255. *Id.* at vii-viii, 21-26.

256. CBS News/Associated Press, *Glaciers Melting in Montana Park*, March 13, 2006 (reporting by CBS News correspondent Stephan Kaufman), *available at* http://www.cbsnews.com/stories/2006/03/13/tech/main1391827.shtml.

257. *Bush administration opposes expanded protection for World Heritage sites*, GREENWIRE, March 21, 2006 (available by subscription or on LEXIS); Friends of the Earth, Press Release, *USA opposing world heritage action on climate change*, March 16, 2006, *available at* http://www.foei.org/media/2006/0316climate.html.

258. Sometimes referred to as the Alien Tort Claims Act (ATCA). *See* Curtis A. Bradley, *The Alien Tort Statute and Article III*, 42 VA. J. INT'L L. 587 (2002) (characterizing the reference of the ATS as the Alien Tort Claims Act as "less accurate").

259. The Judiciary Act of 1789, ch. 20, § 9, 1 Stat. 73, 77 (Sept. 24, 1789).

260. *Id.* § 9(b).

261. 28 U.S.C. § 1350.

262. *See, e.g.*, Flores v. S. Peru Copper, 343 F.3d 140, 150-60 (2d Cir. 2003); Beanal v. Freeport-McMoran, 197 F.3d 161, 165 (5th Cir. 1999); Paul E. Hagen & Anthony L. Michaels, *The Alien Tort Statute: A Primer on Liability for Multinational Corporations*, SK046 ALI-ABA 121, 124 (May 5-6, 2005).

263. *See, e.g.*, Sosa v. Alvarez-Machain, 542 U.S. 692 (2004); James Boeving, Essay, *Half Full . . . or Completely Empty?: Environmental Alien Tort Claims Post Sosa v. Alvarez-Machain*, 18 GEO. INT'L ENVTL. L. REV. 109 & n.1 (2005).

264. Hagen & Michaels, *supra* note 262, at 129-30.

265. *Id.* at 130-31.

266. *Id.* at 131.

267. The two successful cases were *Adra v. Clift*, 195 F. Supp. 857 (D. Md. 1961) (upholding jurisdiction in a child custody suit involving an alien in violation of international law for holding a falsified passport) and *Bolchos v. Darrell*, 3 F. Cas. 810 (D. S.C. 1795) (No. 1,607) (finding an alternative basis of jurisdiction under the ATS over a suit to determine title to slaves on board an enemy vessel taken as a prize of war on the high seas). *Contra Anh v. Levi*, 586 F.2d 625 (6th Cir. 1978) (rejecting attempts to use the ATS as a jurisdictional nexus); Benjamins v. British European Airways, 572 F.2d 913 (2d Cir. 1978) (denying jurisdiction); Maxon v. the Fanny, 17 F. Cas. 942 (D.C. Pa. 1793) (denying jurisdiction); Boeving, *supra* note 263, at 110 n.6

268. 630 F.2d 876, 878 (2d Cir. 1980); Boeving, *supra* note 263, at 110.

269. *Id.* at 880 ("We find that an act of torture committed by a state official against one held in detention violates established norms of the international law of human rights, and hence the law of nations."); *id.* at 887 (finding that the ATS simply authorizes suits in "the federal courts for adjudication of the rights already recognized by international law").

270. *Id.* at 881.

271. *Id.*; Rosemary Reed, *Rising Seas and Disappearing Islands: Can Island Inhabitants Seek Redress Under the Alien Tort Claims Act?*, 11 PAC. RIM L. & POL'Y J. 399, 406 (2002).

272. *Filartiga*, 630 F.2d at 881.

273. *Id.* at 880.

274. *See, e.g.*, Forti v. Suarez-Mason, 672 F. Supp. 1531 (N.D. Cal. 1987); Eastman-Kodak Co. v. Kavlin, 978 F. Supp. 1078 (S.D. Fla. 1997); Xuncax v. Gramajo, 886 F. Supp. 162 (D. Mass. 1995); Beanal v. Freeport-McMoRan, Inc., 969 F. Supp. 362 (E.D. La. 1997); Reed, *supra* note 271, at 409-10.

275. Boeving, *supra* note 263, at 110-11.

276. *See, e.g.*, Flores v. S. Peru Copper, 343 F.3d 140, 154, 160 (2d Cir. 2003); Boeving, *supra* note 263, at 116 & nn.41-42.

277. *Flores*, 343 F.3d at 154-55 ("In determining what offenses violate customary international law, courts must proceed with extraordinary care and restraint."); *Beanal*, 969 F. Supp. 362, 370 (E.D. La. 1997); Boeving, *supra* note 263, at 116.

278. 726 F.2d 774, 798-827 (D.C. Cir. 1989) (Bork, J., concurring).

279. Boeving, *supra* note 263, at 111 n.14.

280. 542 U.S. 692 (2004).

281. *Id.* at 732-33.

282. 28 U.S.C.S. §§ 1346(b)(1), 2671 et seq.

283. Alvarez-Machain v. United States, 331 F.3d 604 (9th Cir. Cal. 2003) (en banc).

284. Sosa v. Alvarez-Machain (quoting 28 U.S.C.S. § 2680(k)).

285. *See* Boeving, *supra* note 263, at 131.

286. *Sosa*, 542 U.S. at 741 (emphasis added); Boeving, *supra* note 263, at 131.

287. *Sosa*, 542 U.S. at 741, 745-48, 755; Boeving, *supra* note 263, at 131-32.

288. *Sosa*, 542 U.S. at 749; Boeving, *supra* note 263, at 131-32.

289. 304 U.S. 64 (1938).

290. *Sosa*, 542 U.S. at 752.

291. *Id.* at 757-58 (Scalia, J., concurring); Boeving, *supra* note 263, at 132.

292. Boeving, *supra* note 263, at 133-36, 144-47.

293. *Sosa*, 542 U.S. at 762 (Breyer, J., concurring in part and concurring in the judgment) ("Today international law will sometimes similarly reflect not only substantive agreement as to certain universally condemned behavior but also procedural agreement that universal jurisdiction exists to prosecute a subset of that behavior. . . .That subset includes torture, genocide, crimes against humanity, and war crimes."); Kadic v. Karadzic, 70 F.3d 232, 239-46 (2d Cir. 1995) (same); Boeving, *supra* note 263, at 129 n.146 ("It is also useful to note that the ATS cases that have survived a motion to dismiss have involved serious human rights abuses, such as torture, slavery, or genocide . . .").

294. *Sosa*, 542 U.S. at 750 (stating American courts will usually reject ATS claims alleging "a limit on the power of foreign governments over their own citizens, and to hold that a foreign government or its agent has transgressed those limits."); Boeving, *supra* note 263, at 136.

295. 70 F.3d 232, 239-46 (2d Cir. 1995).

296. 969 F. Supp. 362, 377-79 (E.D. La. 1997); Reed, *supra* note 271, at 407.

297. Boeving, *supra* note 263, at 114-15.

298. Richard L. Herz, *Making Development Accountable to Human Rights and Environmental Protection*, 94 Am. Soc'y of Int'l Law Proc. 216, 217 (2000).

299. *See* Boeving, *supra* note 263, at 115; John Alan Cohan, *Environmental Rights of Indigenous Peoples Under the Alien Tort Claims Act, the Public Trust Doctrine and Corporate Ethics, and Environmental Dispute Resolution*, 20 UCLA J. Envtl. L. & Pol'y 133, 155 (2002); Lauren A. Mowery, *Earth Rights, Human Rights: Can International Environmental Human Rights Affect Corporate Accountability?*, 13 Fordham Envtl. L.J. 343 (2002); Prudence Taylor, *From Environmental to Ecological Human Rights: A New Dynamic in International Law*, 10 Geo. Int'l Envtl. L. Rev. 309, 350, 364 (1998).

300. 775 F. Supp. 668 (S.D.N.Y. 1991).

301. The plaintiffs also sued under the Resource Conservation and Recovery Act (RCRA), but that topic is beyond the scope of this chapter.

302. *Amlon Metals*, 775 F. Supp. at 671; Report of the United Nations Conference on the Human Environment, Declaration of Principles, June 16, 1972, princ. 21, U.N. Doc. A/CONF.48/14, *reprinted in* 11 I.L.M. 1416 (1972)); Restatement (Third) of the Foreign Relations Law of the United States § 602(2) (1987); Boeving, *supra* note 263, at 118-19.

303. *Amlon Metals*, 775 F. Supp. at 671.

304. Reed, *supra* note 271, at 408.

305. 1994 U.S. Dist. LEXIS 4718 (S.D.N.Y. Apr. 11, 1994).

306. United Nations Conference on Environment and Development, Rio Declaration on Environment and Development, June 14, 1992, princ. 2, U.N. Doc. A/CONF.151/5/Rev.1, *reprinted in* 31 I.L.M. 874 [hereinafter Rio Declaration].

307. Aquinda v. Texaco, Inc., 945 F. Supp. 625 (S.D.N.Y. 1996).

308. *Id.* at 628.

309. Jota v. Texaco, 157 F.3d 153 (2d Cir. 1998).

310. Aguinda v. Texaco, 142 F. Supp. 2d 534 (S.D.N.Y. 2001).

311. *Id.* at 552-53 (quoting *Beanal II*, 197 F.3d at 167*).

312. Aguinda v. Texaco, 303 F.3d 470 (2d Cir. 2002).

313. Beanal v. Freeport-McMoran, 969 F. Supp. 362, 366-70 (E.D. La. 1997) [hereinafter *Beanal I*]; Boeving, *supra* note 263, at 120-22; Reed, *supra* note 271, at 409.

314. *Beanal I*, 969 F. Supp. at 372-73; Boeving, *supra* note 263, at 120-21.

315. Beanal v. Freeport-McMoran, 1997 U.S. Dist. LEXIS 12001 (E.D. La. 1997) [hereinafter *Beanal II*].

316. Beanal v. Freeport-McMoran, 197 F.3d 161, 163-64 (5th Cir. 1999) [hereinafter *Beanal III*].

317. Reed, *supra* note 271, at 409.

318. *Beanal III*, 197 F.3d at 165-69.

319. *Id.* at 167.

320. Sarei v. Rio Tinto PLC, 221 F. Supp. 2d 1116, 1116-24 (C.D. Cal. 2002), *aff'd in part, rev'd in part and remanded*, 2006 U.S. App. LEXIS 20174 (9th Cir. 2006); Boeving, *supra* note 263, at 123-26.

321. *Sarei*, 221 F. Supp. 2d at 1156-59; Boeving, *supra* note 263, at 124.

322. *Sarei*, 221 F. Supp. 2d at 1158; Boeving, *supra* note 263, at 124.

323. *Sarei*, 221 F. Supp. 2d at 1158 (citing Aguinda v. Texaco, Inc., 1994 U.S. Dist. LEXIS 4718 (S.D.N.Y. Apr. 11, 1994) (Broderick, J.) ("Not all conduct which may be harmful to the environment, and not all violations of environmental laws, constitute violations of the law of nations."); Boeving, *supra* note 263, at 124.

324. The plaintiffs relied on the International Covenant on Civil and Political Rights, Dec. 19, 1966, 999 U.N.T.S. 171 [hereinafter ICCPR]; Universal Declaration of Human Rights, G.A. Res. 217A, U.N. GAOR, 3d Sess., U.N. Doc. A/810 (1948), *available at* http://www.unhchr.ch/udhr/lang/eng.pdf [hereinafter Universal Declaration]; American Declaration on the Rights and Duties of Man, O.A.S. Res. XXX, Ninth International Conference of American States, O.A.S. Doc. OEA/Ser. L/I.4 Rev. (1965) [hereinafter American Declaration]; American Convention on Human Rights, Nov. 22, 1969, 1144 U.N.T.S. 123 [hereinafter American Convention]; African Charter of Human and Peoples' Rights, June 27, 1981, 1520 U.N.T.S. 217; European Convention for the Protection of Human Rights and Fundamental Freedoms, Nov. 4, 1950, 312 U.N.T.S. 221; and the Charter of Fundamental Rights of the European Union, 2000 O.J. (C 362) 1. *See Sarei*, 221 F. Supp. 2d at 1156; Boeving, *supra* note 263, at 124 n.106.

325. *Sarei*, 221 F. Supp. 2d at 1158-59; Boeving, *supra* note 263, at 124-25.

326. *Sarei*, 221 F. Supp. 2d at 1159 (citing Beanal v. Freeport-McMoran, 197 F.3d 161, 167 (5th Cir. 1999)); Boeving, *supra* note 263, at 125.

327. *Sarei*, 221 F. Supp. 2d at 1158; Boeving, *supra* note 263, at 125; United Nations Convention on the Law of the Sea, *opened for signature* Dec. 10, 1982, 21 I.L.M. 1261 [hereinafter UNCLOS].

328. *See Sarei*, 221 F. Supp. 2d at 1160-61; Boeving, *supra* note 263, at 125. The plaintiff's expert acknowledged that sustainable development may be "too broad a concept to be legally meaningful." *Sarei*, 221 F. Supp. 2d at 1160.

329. *See Sarei*, 221 F. Supp. 2d at 1161; Boeving, *supra* note 263, at 125.

330. *Sarei*, 221 F. Supp. 2d at 1125-51 (holding plaintiffs can bring war crime and crimes against humanity claims under ATS against defendant Rio Tinto PLC); Boeving, *supra* note 263, at 123-24.

331. *Sarei*, 221 F. Supp. 2d at 1175; Boeving, *supra* note 263, at 125.

332. *Id.*; Hagen & Michaels, *supra* note 262, at 131.

333. *Sarei,* 221 F. Supp. 2d at 1175.

334. *Sarei,* 221 F. Supp. 2d at 1183-88; Boeving, *supra* note 263, at 125.

335. *Sarei,* 221 F. Supp. 2d at 1199-1206; Boeving, *supra* note 263, at 126 n.118.

336. *Sarei,* 221 F. Supp. 2d at 1193-99; Boeving, *supra* note 263, at 126 n.117.

337. Sarei v. Rio Tinto PLC, 2006 U.S. App. LEXIS 20174 (9th Cir. 2006), at 14-16. The Ninth Circuit also affirmed the district court's determination that the plaintiffs' war crimes and crimes against humanity allegations presented cognizable ATS claims, although those issues are beyond the scope of this chapter. *Id.* at 13-15.

338. *Id.* at 27-33.

339. *Id.* at 37

340. *Id.* at 38-40.

341. *Id.* at 41-47.

342. *Id.* at 48-78.

343. *Id.* at 80-148.

344. Flores v. Southern Peru Copper, 253 F. Supp. 2d 510 (S.D.N.Y.2002) [hereinafter [*Flores I*] , aff'd, 414 F.3d 233 (2d Cir. 2003) [*Flores II*]; Boeving, *supra* note 263, at 126-28.

345. International Covenant on Economic, Social and Cultural Rights, *opened for signature* Dec. 19, 1966, 993 U.N.T.S. 3 [hereinafter ICESCR]. "The State Parties to the present Covenant recognize the right of everyone to the enjoyment of the highest attainable standard of physical and mental health." *Id.* art. 12; *Rio Declaration, supra* note 228, at princ. I. ("Human beings are . . . entitled to a healthy and productive life in harmony with nature."); Universal Declaration, *supra* note 245, at art. 25 ("Everyone has the right to a standard of living adequate for the health and well-being of himself and of his family. . .").

346. *Flores I,* 253 F. Supp. 2d at 525 (quoting Filarartiga v. Pena-Irala, 630 F.2d 876, 888 (2d Cir. 1980)).

347. *Id.* at 525-44.

348. *Flores II,* 414 F.3d at 255.

349. *Id.* at 248-66.

350. *Id.* at 255 n.29 ("Because plaintiffs do not allege that defendants' conduct had an effect outside the borders of Peru, we need not consider the customary international law status of transnational pollution. *See* note 6, *ante* (quoting the provision of the Restatement (Third) addressing transnational pollution).").

351. *Flores II,* 414 F.3d at 266.

352. Boeving, *supra* note 263, at 133-34 (stating "though the [*Sosa*] Court did not provide specific parameters, it seems fair to say that it narrowed the scope of permissible claims somewhat . . .").

353. Sarei v. Rio Tinto PLC, 2006 U.S. App. LEXIS 20174 (9th Cir. 2006), at 13-16.

354. *Id.* at 134-35 (stating "[I]t seems doubtful that purely environmental damage will become part of the law of nations anytime soon. Therefore, [the *Sosa*] decision signals to environmental plaintiffs that the human rights proxy approach is the most viable alternative and perhaps only route through which to pursue their claims.").

355. *Id.* at 135-37 (arguing ATS claims based on treaty violations by the United States "may prove to be the most useful route for future environmental plaintiffs," but acknowledging that many treaties contain vague and general provisions that are likely unenforceable under the ATS).

356. *See supra* notes 307, 312, and accompanying text.

357. *See supra* notes 334-43 and accompanying text.

358. *Sosa,* 542 U.S. at 750 (stating American courts will usually reject ATS claims alleging "a limit on the power of foreign governments over their own citizens, and to hold that a foreign government or its agent has transgressed those limits"); Boeving, *supra* note 263, at 135.

359. *See supra* note 211 and accompanying text.

chapter seven

Consideration of Climate Change in Facility Permitting

Laura H. Kosloff and Mark C. Trexler

I. Introduction

Growing public and policy concern over climate change has the potential to influence a wide variety of facility and other permitting processes. Approximately two-thirds of U.S. greenhouse gas emissions, encompassing sources from power plants to landfills to industrial and residential installations, are from facilities subject to siting or permitting rules, mostly at the state level. This influence will be felt from two directions:

- As part of climate greenhouse gas (GHG) emissions reduction efforts through climate change strategies.
- As part of efforts to adapt to the impacts of climate change. Numerous permitting procedures are directed at facilities that could be affected by the impacts of climate change, from sea-level rise to flooding risk to water availability for industrial or residential development. Adapting to climate change could result in building prohibitions in sensitive areas, promote tougher building standards against natural disasters, and force adoption of stricter water conservation and recycling.

It is still early, however, in the development of these two influences, particularly the latter. While insurance companies are beginning to adjust insurance coverages and exposures in light of recent payouts for natural disasters, there is no evidence that climate change adaptation has yet found its way into facility permitting. As part of writing this chapter, the authors conducted an e-mail survey of several hundred state officials looking for examples of ways in which climate change might affect siting procedures from the standpoint of adapting to the impacts of climate change. While it is to be expected that climate change considerations will enter into facility siting decisions of all kinds at some point, no examples of such changed permitting procedures could be found to have occurred as of the writing of this chapter.

Climate change concerns are already having a noticeable impact on the permitting of facilities with greenhouse gas emissions, particularly in the power sector.

Any discussion of climate change and law needs to distinguish between rules and regulations undertaken to reduce GHG emissions, on the one hand, and rules and regulations that have the effect of reducing GHG emissions, but were not enacted to that end, on the other hand. Renewable energy, for example, generally will displace fossil fuel generation at the margin. Indeed, almost all renewable energy policy and mandates could be attributed to climate change mitigation objectives, and one could generate long lists of "climate legislation" as a result. In reality, there are many motivations behind renewable energy development and deployment. While beneficial from the standpoint of CO_2 emissions, it is a stretch to attribute today's renewables energy legislation to climate change concerns. The same can be said for the myriad of programs, rules, and regulations that promote energy efficiency. While these programs will have the effect of reducing GHG emissions from what they might otherwise have been, we don't consider it appropriate to consider energy efficiency mandates as primarily a manifestation of climate change concerns. Thus, this chapter does not address the law surrounding renewable energy and energy efficiency, although it can be hard to distinguish in some cases between the motivations for pursuing such programs. As climate change policy accelerates, for example, renewables and energy efficiency will no doubt form important components of a portfolio of public policy measures (see Chapters 10 and 11).

Climate change concerns are already having a noticeable impact on the permitting of facilities with greenhouse gas emissions, particularly in the power sector. Although still limited in the context of the hundreds of power plants on the drawing boards around the country, climate change concerns are manifesting themselves more often. This chapter reviews how early-stage GHG emissions reduction efforts have been and are being pursued through the facility-permitting processes of electricity generation and, to a lesser extent, industrial facilities, including:

- Companies making facility-specific voluntary emissions reduction commitments largely outside the regulatory or siting process;
- The influencing of facility-specific technology choices in anticipation of future emissions reduction mandates, including through carbon adders;

- Companies negotiating voluntary settlements with intervenors in administrative proceedings to prevent climate change from becoming a contested part of the facility siting process;
- Provisions in state law mandating GHG emissions mitigation as part of the siting process; and
- Intervenors challenging the siting of power or industrial facilities.

Because the influence of climate change on facility siting is still so limited, we have chosen to organize the examples by the five categories described above.

II. Climate Change as an Influence on Facility Permitting

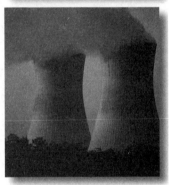

As noted above, many factors affect facility-specific decisions. Generally speaking, the influence of climate change on facility siting still has relatively little to do with established law, either through statutory mandate or case law. As such, the examples provided here will have limited lifetimes, and are profiled here to help set the stage for understanding the future manifestations of the climate issue, rather than presenting specific guidance based on established law.

Facility-level mitigation dates back to 1989, when AES Corp. first decided to offset the emissions of a coal-fired power plant under construction in Connecticut. Working with the World Resources Institute, a nonprofit environmental think-tank in Washington, D.C., AES selected and funded its first offset project in 1989, an agroforestry project in Guatemala. AES later pursued two additional offset projects in Paraguay and in the Amazon Basin, spending a total of more than $6 million to offset the emissions of several coal-fired plants built by AES around the United States. The offset purchases did not play a role in the regulatory siting of the facilities, but the company pioneered facility-specific mitigation.

Since AES's early efforts, voluntary mitigation efforts tended to be pursued at the utility level, rather than at the facility level. Numerous utilities have undertaken voluntary mitigation offset efforts for public relations reasons, "coming up the learning curve," and strategic risk management reasons.[1]

The choice of technology in developing new power facilities has major implications for the GHG emissions of the facility and for the potential long-term liability of those emissions under climate change mandates. Building a natural gas plant instead of a coal plant, for example, can reduce GHG emissions by more than 50%. Nuclear energy plants and renewable energy technologies can go even further toward reducing GHG emissions associated with meeting the country's energy needs.

Climate change concerns are likely to have very different impacts on different technology decisions:

A. Nuclear Facilities

In recent years, the issues of energy, environment, and security have increasingly become linked. This is especially key in the context of nuclear energy development, which has always been intertwined with security concerns. The nuclear energy industry has been looking to these issues and, more specifically, concerns about global climate change, as a key element in its rebirth. There is no evidence yet of this taking concrete form, although studies are under way. In connection with this, in December 2004, the National Commission on Energy Policy issued a report on energy, environment, and security that recommended that government "improve the prospects for the expansion of nuclear energy" because of society's interest "in abating climate-change risks by expanding the share of no-carbon and low-carbon energy options in the electricity-generating mix."[2]

B. Coal Gasification

The technology innovation most commonly cited when it comes to climate change mitigation is coal gasification. Integrated gasification combined-cycle (IGCC) technology holds the promise of being able to strip out and bury carbon dioxide in abandoned gas fields, deep aquifers, and other geologic formations. Many utilities are actively considering IGCC as an alternative to pulverized or even super-critical coal plants as a preferred means to meet future load. Given limited field experience, however, concern remains regarding the economics and performance of IGCC plants. Most utilities are reluctant to pay the higher up-front costs associated with the IGCC technology. Key interest groups in California, however, are suggesting that the state should allow only IGCC-generated coal-fired power to be imported into California as part of its climate change strategy. In April 2006, California Governor Schwarzenegger and Wyoming Governor Freudenthal signed a memorandum of understanding on development of clean coal technology.[3] A joint task force has been formed and will work with U.S. DOE to help develop a commercial-scale IGCC coal plant with carbon sequestration in Wyoming.[4]

Companies that have sought to move forward with the IGCC technology have not necessarily fared well. An example is Wisconsin Energy Corporation's proposal to build an IGCC facility as one of two new facilities needed to meet new load in the state. The Wisconsin Public Service Commission denied the WEC proposal, treating the question in a single paragraph of a 72-page decision, with no mention at all of the potential environmental benefits of IGCC.[5] This setback is not deterring other companies, however. Xcel Energy recently announced plans to develop an IGCC facility in Colorado.[6]

FutureGen is a $1 billion initiative to build the world's first integrated sequestration and hydrogen production research power plant; it would be the world's first coal-fueled, near-zero emissions power plant. The commercial-scale plant is intended to prove the technical and economic feasibility of producing low-cost electricity and hydrogen from coal while nearly eliminating emissions, and will be operated as a research facility.[7] The backers of FutureGen intend to address climate change concerns regarding the use of coal. Most of the CO_2 generated from the FutureGen plant will be permanently stored in deep geologic formations; this technology is intended to virtually eliminate GHG concerns associated with the plant.[8] However, it remains untested.

In May 2006, seven states submitted proposals to host the FutureGen plant. In July 2006, four sites in Texas and Illinois were chosen for review. Current debates include whether the states have sufficient rules for addressing possible liability stemming from the underground storage of CO_2 in the event that the CO_2 escapes.[9] A final decision is not expected until late 2007.

C. Traditional Coal-Fired Facilities

Dozens of coal-fired power plants are on the drawing boards in the United States, perhaps a hundred. Climate change concerns may affect the speed with which such plants are being pursued. Sempra Energy, for example, recently announced it was giving up on plans to build coal-fired power plants in Idaho and Nevada as a result of strong opposition.

In Texas, recent reports suggest up to 16 new coal-fired plants could be built just in the next five or six years. The Texas Commission on Environmental Quality issued draft permits for six of these plants to the Dallas-based utility TXU in October 2006. Multiple environmental organizations and the mayors of major cities have announced they will challenge the siting of new coal plants, with GHG emissions being a significant factor in their opposition.[10]

In Idaho, then-Governor Dirk Kempthorne signed H.B. No. 791 in April 2006.[11] The new law imposes a two-year moratorium on the building or permitting of certain coal-fired power plants. Although a concern for climate change as a result of high CO_2 emissions from coal power plants was not the direct reason for this decision, the legislature acknowledged that some coal plants might have a negative impact on the environment and economy, and these effects need to be understood.

D. Carbon Adders as a Means of Promoting New Technologies

One of the mechanisms being used at the state level to promote change in technology choice for future generation purposes is carbon adders. These are values that regulators assign to certain technologies for use by utilities when evaluating technology choices for future generations. In Colorado, for example, the Colorado Public Utility Commission approved a carbon adder as part of a settlement with environmental groups allowing the proposed Comanche 3 coal-fired generating unit to move through the Commission approval process. The carbon adder was set at $9 per ton of CO_2 emissions beginning in 2010 and escalates at 2.5% annually.[12]

In California, in April 2004, the California Public Utilities Commission (CPUC) filed R.04-04-003, an Order Instituting Rulemaking to Promote Policy and Program Coordination and Integration in Electric Utility Resource Planning. The CPUC directed the state's investor-owned utilities (IOUs) to begin considering the GHG emissions associated with the resource options in their long-term plans. Assuming that GHG emissions will be constrained in the future, forcing IOUs to purchase allowances for every ton of emissions, the CPUC adopted a "climate risk adder." In Decision 04-12-048, the CPUC set the range of GHG adder values between $8 and $25 per ton of CO_2.[13] For every ton of GHG emissions associated with a megawatt-hour (MWh) of production from a fossil resource, the IOUs will add $8 to the bid price of the resource when modeling the economics of the facility.[14] The risk adder is an analytic tool only, changing the relative costs of resource options when compared against each other. It is intended to affect which bids are selected, not the price of those bids. No cost will be passed through to rate payers.

Agencies began negotiating greenhouse gas provisions with utilities in the early 1990s. In 1992, Tenaska, Inc., an independent power producer headquartered in Omaha, Nebraska, agreed in a power sales agreement with the Bonneville Power Administration (BPA) to spend $1 million to partially offset the CO_2 emissions of the natural gas-fired power plant it was building for BPA near Tacoma, Washington. BPA had asked bidders in its original request for proposals to accept all CO_2 risk associated with the planned power plant, but none of the bidders were willing to do so. Tenaska's negotiated contract with BPA represented the first time that a power purchase agreement incorporated a requirement for CO_2 mitigation in the United States. Tenaska pursued carbon offset forestry projects in eastern Washington and in Costa Rica.[15]

Voluntary agreements have continued more recently. In one recent example, EPCOR Utilities, Inc. and TransAlta Corp. in Alberta, Canada, created a joint venture for development of a 450 MW coal-fired power plant, Genesee 3, which began operation in 2005.[16] Originally, EPCOR and TransAlta both intended to construct independent facilities. EPCOR "sweetened" its siting application by committing to net CO_2 reductions of approximately 50 percent, effectively bringing the plant's emissions down to combined-cycle gas turbine (CCGT) levels. In response, TransAlta made the same commitment. Collapse of the energy sector in 2002 made the future of the proposed facilities uncertain, later leading to a joint venture proposal for one facility.[17]

The Alberta Energy and Utilities Board wrote the CO_2 mitigation commitment into the proposed facility's permit issued in 2003. The permit requires that net CO_2-equivalent emissions from the coal-fired facility shall not exceed those of a CCGT power plant of an equivalent size. This will require mitigation of approximately 1.6 million tons per year, with responsibility equally split between the two companies. The companies have agreed to use reductions that are certifiable, verifiable, and real.

In another example, Xcel Energy has made a voluntary mitigation commitment as part of a new coal-fired facility being built in Colorado. A coalition of environmental and energy advocacy groups came to an agreement with Xcel concerning its least-cost plan; in exchange for the NGOs removing their opposition to construction of Xcel's new coal-fired power plant, Xcel Energy agreed to take various pollution mitigation actions, including CO_2 emissions reductions.[18] In consideration of the potential of future costs due to GHG regulation (e.g., CO_2 taxes or allowance costs) during the 30-year planning period of the least-cost plan, the parties to the settlement agreed that all evaluations of resources acquired under the least-cost plan should include "imputation of CO_2 costs of $9/ton beginning in 2010 and escalating at 2.5% per year beginning in 2011 and continuing over the planning life of the resource."[19]

State emissions reduction mandates date back to 1997, but remain limited.

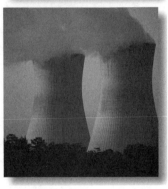

1. Oregon CO_2 Standard

Oregon's statute requiring CO_2 mitigation for all new natural gas-fired power plants built within the state was the first such statute in the United States. In 1997, Oregon's legislature enacted a CO_2 standard requiring that new natural gas power plants reduce emissions by 17% below the commercially prevailing "state of the art" level through a combination of cogeneration efficiencies and offsets (to an equivalent of 0.70 lbs CO_2 per kilowatt-hour (kWh).[20] Developers could meet the standard by developing their own CO_2 mitigation portfolios of carbon-offset projects, or by paying a fee per ton of CO_2 produced to a state-sanctioned nongovernmental organization (currently limited to the Climate Trust) that invests the funds in offset projects.

The Oregon Energy Facility Siting Council has updated the standard periodically as more efficient plants are built. The standard now applies to other large energy facilities (non-generating) in addition to power plants and currently is set at 0.675 lb. CO_2/kWh for base-load gas plants and non-base-load plants, and 0.504 lb. CO_2/horsepower hour for non-generating facilities. While the standard for base-load gas plants applies only to natural gas–fired plants, the standards for non-base-load plants and non-generating facilities apply to all fuels. The fee per ton of CO_2 has increased, but the rules stipulate that it may not increase by more than 50% every two years. It was first set at $0.57 per ton, but is now $0.85 per ton.

Nine facilities, including two power plants, have been required to meet the standard since 1997. All have followed the "monetary path" by which project developers simply write a check to the Climate Trust.[21] This is partially an artifact of the values built into the legislation. While companies can now buy their way out of the obligation at $0.85 per ton, it would be almost impossible for a company to propose a portfolio on its own with these economics.[22]

2. Washington CO_2 Standard

Largely as a result of the Oregon CO_2 standard, the Washington State Energy Facility Site Evaluation Council (EFSEC) began to pressure energy projects in Washington to make mitigation commitments in the late 1990s and early 2000s. These included:

- EFSEC required the Satsop Combustion Turbine Project to mitigate facility CO_2 emissions exceeding 0.675 lb/kWh, at a rate of $0.57 per ton of CO_2 to be paid to an approved organization for CO_2 mitigation projects. The per-ton fee corresponds to the original per-ton fee set in Oregon's CO_2 standard in 1997, which has since been increased to $0.85/ton. In addition, the plant must pay 7.5% of administrative costs. These payments will be made annually for the first 30 years of the facility's operational lifetime, or until it is retired.[23] However, there is no construction activity taking place regarding this facility.[24]
- Sumas Energy 2 Generation Facility was required to pay $0.57 per ton of CO_2 to mitigate 2-5% of the emissions expected over the plant's 30-year lifetime. The arrangement was that once the plant opened, the $8.04 million payment would be made in five annual installments.[25] The project was approved by the governor of Washington in August 2004. However, later the same year, the Canadian National Energy Board denied a permit to construct the proposed transmission line from the U.S./Canadian border to a British Columbia substation. The Supreme Court of Canada upheld this denial in early 2006. In March 2006, the company requested that EFSEC terminate the Site Certification Agreement (SCA), which EFSEC did in April 2006.[26]
- The Chehalis Generation Facility was required to acquire offsets to mitigate 8% of its overall GHG emissions. The company was allowed to purchase the offsets from a recognized third party, or to develop and implement GHG projects itself.[27] Commercial operation of the Chehalis facility began in October 2003.[28]
- The Wallula Power Project was required to make a $6 million payment to nonprofit and tribal organizations helping to develop renewable energy resources and projects or organizations involved with habitat restoration programs in the region. Although EFSEC issues the site certificate for the project in 2002, no construction is currently planned for this project.[29]

In 2004, Washington became the second state to implement mandatory mitigation requirements for new power plants.[30] The law covers new power plants 25 megawatts and larger. The law applies to existing power plants if they boost their carbon dioxide emissions 15% or more. New fossil fuel–fired power plants in Washington will need to mitigate 20% of their output of CO_2 emissions. If Washington plants choose to pay a third party to implement offset projects, they will have to pay $1.60 per ton CO_2.

3. California Statewide GHG Cap

In June 2005, California Governor Schwarzenegger signed an executive order established GHG reduction targets for California.[31] The targets are to reduce GHG emissions to 2000 emission levels by 2010 (11% reduction); to 1990 levels by 2020 (25% reduction); and to 80% below 1990 levels by 2050. In April 2006, the California Climate Action Team released its recommendations to meet California's reduction targets to the governor and the California legislature,[32] and in September 2006, the state enacted the Global Warming Solutions Act of 2006 (commonly referred to as AB 32), which will implement a statewide cap on GHG emissions.[33]

4. Other States

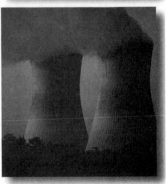

Other states are considering emissions reduction mandates. The most well-known of these mandates is the Regional Greenhouse Gas Initiative (RGGI) in the Northeast. Seven states signed the RGGI MOU in late 2005; one additional state also announced its intent to join RGGI. The states issued a Model Rule for implementing RGGI in August 2006.[34] Massachusetts has its own limits on several existing power plants, and also requires new power plants with a capacity of more than 100 MW to offset 1% of their CO_2 emissions for at least 20 years at $1.50 per ton.

E. Intervenors Challenging the Siting of Power or Industrial Facilities

Challenges to facility siting cases can occur through informal challenges through the press and through advocacy, or through formal siting or legal challenges.

Some environmental groups are strongly opposed to construction of new coal-fired power plants. The Sierra Club, for example, has adopted a policy to challenge any new power plants until more stringent rules for air pollution and global warming are imposed. The Sierra Club is challenging the Missouri Department of Natural Resources' approval to construct an 850 MW coal-fired plant, Iatan II, in Missouri by Kansas City Power & Light.[35] Although CO_2 emissions are not the only concern the

Sierra Club has, the Club points out that the plant will release eight million tons of CO_2 without any possibility of reduction in the future.[36]

Liquefied natural gas (LNG) siting is also likely to become a particularly contentious topic. From a climate change perspective, it could be argued that increased supplies of natural gas will make it easier to displace coal-fired generation and even oil imports. But opposition to LNG facilities is increasing, and it is unclear how climate change considerations will affect the siting of LNG facilities; will it inhibit LNG facility siting (due to direct and indirect CO_2 emissions) or encourage siting (due to displacement of coal-fired emissions)? LNG opponents argue that LNG is a major source of greenhouse gases and contributes to global warming. Organizations opposing additional LNG terminal construction argue that LNG production, transportation, and use emits 18% to 40% more greenhouse gases than domestic natural gas.[37] Environmental organizations have argued that an LNG terminal could release at least 23 million tons of GHGs into the atmosphere annually.[38]

In a lawsuit filed in August 2005, the Ratepayers for Affordable Clean Energy (RACE) challenged the California CPUC's plan to boost natural gas supplies through increased LNG imports. RACE charged that the CPUC violated the California Environmental Quality Act's (CEQA's) requirements that state agencies conduct an environmental impact report before undertaking any project that will impact the environment; the suit argued that the CPUC did not do so before authorizing California natural-gas utilities to enter into long-term contracts with suppliers of imported LNG. Petitioners argued that the CPUC should have held an evidentiary hearing to determine whether the projections it received from the utilities about growing demand for natural gas in California over the next decade were accurate. RACE alleged that it requested a hearing because the federal government and others have projected that demand for natural gas will not increase significantly during that period; the utilities making the projections are financially affiliated with the LNG suppliers; the CPUC committed to employing efficiency measures and renewable energy sources before resorting to fossil fuel in order to meet demand; and California rate payers will pay for construction and operation of the LNG facilities even though there is enough domestic supply of natural gas to meet objective projections.[39] On May 11, 2006, the California court of appeal denied the petition.[40]

With renewables, climate change considerations can be used to help overcome other objections to particular facilities. NIMBY ("not in my back yard") considerations, however, can be a more immediate concern for environmental constituencies. The Cape Wind project is an example of this. This project would be the first offshore wind farm in the United States, in which 130 wind turbines would generate up to 420 MW of energy. According to the project's draft environmental impact statement, "the project provides an opportunity, and an example of how to achieve a significant annual and long-term reduction of greenhouse gases emitted by existing or new fossil fuel plants to help stem global warming processes and inhibit their associated environmental effect."[41] Despite favorable regulatory review, significant opposition exists to the

project, including from Massachusetts Governor Mitt Romney and Senator Edward Kennedy. Opponents argue that the project would hurt birds, scenic views, and tourism. The 2005 Energy Policy Act transferred regulatory authority for offshore energy projects from the Army Corps of Engineers to the Department of Interior's Mineral Management Service (MMS). Cape Wind had expected to obtain approval quickly from the Corps, but transfer of authority to the MMS seems to have delayed the project. Cape Wind Associates now plans to complete the project by 2010.[42]

Energy production is not the only sector in which climate change is beginning to lead to opposition to facility siting. Some insulation products, for example, while covered by the Montreal Protocol's ban on hydrofluorocarbons (HFCs), have the potential to emit relatively large amounts of GHGs that are not covered by the Montreal Protocol. One such HFC is HCFC-142b,

which has a global warming potential of 2400.[43] In 2005, environmental groups sued Owens Corning Corp. in connection with the construction of a polystyrene foam board insulation plant in Gresham, Oregon. Plaintiffs contended that Owens Corning's facility would have the potential to emit more than 250 tons per year of harmful gases, without having obtained a required preconstruction permit, in violation of

. . . it is unclear how climate change considerations will affect the siting of LNG facilities; will it inhibit LNG facility siting . . . or encourage siting . .

section 165(a) of the Clean Air Act.[44] They further contended that the unpermitted construction violated Part C of Title I of the Act,[45] as well as New Source Review provisions of the Oregon state implementation plan.[46] In November 2005, U.S. EPA announced its plan to ban the use of HCFC-142b in the foam sector under the Significant New Alternative Policy Program under section 612 of the Clean Air Act.[47] The Owens Corning permit was put on hold while the company considered its options.[48]

In May 2006, Owens Corning announced it would not pursue the plant.[49] On May 17, 2006, the federal magistrate judge denied the company's motion to dismiss; a decision was issued on June 9, 2006.[50] Owens Corning had argued, among other things, that the environmental plaintiffs lacked standing to bring suit based on injuries that could result from the facility's HCFC-142b emissions. The court ruled that the plaintiffs did have standing to sue for these global problems. On the issue of whether plaintiffs had suffered injury-in-fact, the court observed:

Defendant does not suggest, however, that the harm described in the complaint is entirely without any credible scientific basis nor—at this stage of the proceedings—are Plaintiffs required to prove their contentions. The enactment by Congress of laws governing these emissions, and the participation by the United States in related international agreements, also weigh against any suggestion that the threatened harm is entirely chimerical.[51]

The court concluded that Congress established the Clean Air Act preconstruction review and permit requirements to protect the kinds of interests asserted by plaintiffs; that is, the "release of a significant quantity of pollutants into the atmosphere in a densely populated metropolitan region where many members of the plaintiff organizations live, work, commute, or recreate."[52]

The court also held that plaintiffs had demonstrated that the injury was "fairly traceable" to the company's activities; Owens Corning had commenced construction, intended to operate the facility, and was the entity responsible for Clean Air Act violations arising from facility activities. To satisfy the "fairly traceable" requirement, a plaintiff need not show to a scientific certainty that the defendant's emissions are the sole source of the threatened harm; they need only assert that the facility's emissions will contribute to the pollution that threatens plaintiffs' interests.[53] The court also held the plaintiffs had shown redressability. If the plaintiffs prevail, the company would not be able to operate the plant until it complied with legal requirements. Imposition of civil penalties would assist in redressing the injury by deterring future violations. Also, plaintiffs need not show that the entire problem of global warming will be cured if they were to prevail.[54]

The court rejected the company's argument that prudential limitations precluded standing. The complaint falls within the "zone of interests to be protected or regulated by the statute or constitutional guarantee in question."[55] The Clean Air Act was intended to protect the interests advanced by plaintiffs, and Congress expressly provided for citizen suits to enforce its provisions. The court concluded that "[a]t issue here is nothing more than whether the courts will enforce the Congressional mandate set forth in the Clean Air Act and its enabling regulations."[56]

Instead of continuing the litigation, the company settled by agreeing to spend $300,000 on an energy-efficient classroom project; $125,000 for a solar classroom project; and $50,000 for public education and outreach work on alternative energy sources.[57] The settlement allows the company to proceed with the Gresham plant as long as it does not use HCFC-142b.

Challenges are also being filed for actions being taken to help fund energy facilities in other countries. The National Environmental Policy Act (NEPA) requires federal agencies to consider the impacts to the environment of all proposals for major federal actions, although climate change is not specifically mentioned. In *Friends of the Earth v. Watson*, several environmental groups and two U.S. cities argued that the Export-Import Bank (EIB) and the Overseas Private Investment Corporation (OPIC),

two U.S. agencies, unlawfully funded fossil-fuel projects abroad. The suit alleged that OPIC and EIB illegally provided financing and insurance for oil fields, pipelines, and coal-fired power plants without assessing their contribution to global warming or their impact on the U.S. environment as required by NEPA. The government argued that (1) the plaintiffs lacked standing; (2) OPIC and EIB had not taken any action subjecting them to judicial review; and (3) OPIC is exempt from complying with NEPA.

In August 2005, the federal court held that: (1) the plaintiffs had sufficiently demonstrated standing; (2) final agency actions had occurred; (3) OPIC's statute does not preclude judicial review; and (4) environmental procedures in OPIC's statute do not displace NEPA.[58] Substantive findings specific to climate change remain to be made.

III. Looking to the Future

This chapter has illustrated that efforts to regulate GHG emissions through facility permitting rules and processes remain quite rare, while efforts to adapt to climate change through facility-siting rules and procedures are virtually nonexistent. There is little question that emissions reduction mandates will be material to power generators and electricity rate payers in the future, assuming that climate change policy continues to develop. Today's trading price under the European Union's Emissions Trading Scheme—which has reached more than \$35/ton of CO_2-equivalent—is the equivalent of adding approximately 2-3 cents per kilowatt-hour to the cost of conventional coal-fired electricity in the United States. Such a CO_2 value, combined with stringent emissions reduction mandates, would radically change the economics of power generation in the United States.

Companies would be well-served, however, to take the prospect of such developments in the future seriously. Today, more than 450 power projects with a capacity over 100 MW have been proposed in this country to start operation by 2010. Almost 20% of these plants would be coal-fired.[59] Many of these projects no doubt are intended to serve the same load growth, or replace the same retiring plants; it is likely that only a fraction of the list will be built. It is increasingly likely, however, that GHG mitigation requirements will affect many of these new projects, as more states will impose limitations on GHG emissions from new plants over the next few years.

For one thing, climate change is more widely accepted as a material business issue. It is not difficult to see why.[60] First, the scientific community has repeatedly concluded that climate-change concerns are significant. Thus, it is becoming much harder for a company to downplay the issue politically. Scientists around the world strongly advocate taking action to limit GHG emissions as a means of avoiding the doubling, tripling, or even quadrupling of GHG concentrations in the atmosphere.

Second, the United States—still the largest emitter of GHGs—can expect persistent international pressure to participate in meaningful international climate-change mitigation efforts. Companies of all sizes and in many sectors are following international developments closely to gauge the direction of these efforts.

Third, U.S. state and local governments are becoming increasingly frustrated with the lack of national action and are moving forward on their own. The growing trend toward state and local climate-change programs is requiring companies to follow climate-change policies and measures at multiple levels of government. There is little doubt that GHG emissions-reduction mandates will ultimately move to the national level. Many companies already advocate just such a move.

Many ordinary business decisions—ranging from design of a manufacturing facility to disposal of a company's final product—affect CO_2 emissions. The most straightforward approach companies can take is to maximize the energy efficiency of their products and operations. Efficiency improvements—and thus actions taken to reduce GHG emissions—will often also benefit a company's bottom line.

All of this is relevant to facility-permitting processes. As climate change policy evolves, governments increasingly will focus on power plants in their efforts to curb CO_2 reductions. The power sector with its centralized emissions sources has always been an obvious target for air pollution control efforts; this will not change as the focus of these efforts expands to include greenhouse gases. As a result, climate change concerns will increasingly manifest themselves in the facility-siting arena.

Owners and operators should be concerned about the impacts of new mitigation requirements and with staying competitive in a deregulated marketplace. Given what appears to be a trend toward the targeting of power plant emissions even in the absence of federal policy, power project developers would be well-advised to consider the GHG emissions of proposed projects and how those emissions could play into the siting process. Not only does it make sense to think of this as a risk management strategy, but project developers should also recognize that the growing concern over climate change provides an opportunity for them to differentiate their proposals if they can develop innovative and cost-effective ways of doing so. Siting boards and environmental organizations might view such an approach favorably.

Endnotes

1.   Trexler, M.C. & O. Smith, *Mandatory and Voluntary Climate Change Initiatives: Strategic Options for Companies*, PROC. OF THE 12TH ANNUAL FALL MEETING, ABA SEC. OF ENVIRONMENT, ENERGY AND RESOURCES (San Antonio, Texas, Oct. 6-10, 2004).
2.   NATIONAL COMMISSION ON ENERGY POLICY, ENDING THE ENERGY STALEMATE: A BIPARTISAN STRATEGY TO MEET AMERICA'S ENERGY CHALLENGES (DEC. 2004).
3.   Memorandum of Understanding Between the Governors' Offices of California and Wyoming, http://www.frontierline.org/summit/WY_CA_MOU.pdf.
4.   The 2005 Energy Policy Act authorized $200 million each fiscal year for clean coal research. Section 413 of the Energy Policy Act provides for federal support for a

Western Integrated Coal Gasification Demonstration Project at an elevation common to Wyoming, and the President's 2007 budget for the U.S. Department of Energy includes $54 million for advanced gasification combined-cycle technology. *See* http://www.wyia.info/announce.htm.

5. Mary Anne Sullivan, *Voluntary Plans Will Not Cut Greenhouse Gas Emission in the Electricity Sector*, Sustainable Dev. L. & Pol'y J., Winter 2006, at 47.

6. The company plans to file an application with the Colorado Public Utilities Commission for approval of the project in late 2007. Press Release, Xcel Energy increases commitment to IGCC, Aug. 15, 2006, *available at* http://www.xcelenergy.com/XLWEB/CDA/0,3080,1-1-1_15531_26314-28427-0_0_0-0,00.html; press release, Western Governors Laud Efforts to Expand IGCC Technology Development in the West, Aug. 16, 2006, *available at* http://www.westgov.org/wga/press/igcc8-16-06.htm.

7. The FutureGen Alliance is an international nonprofit consortium that includes some of the largest coal producers in the world. The FutureGen Alliance is partnering with the U.S. Department of Energy to design and construct the FutureGen plant. FutureGen Alliance, http://www.futuregenalliance.org/. *See also* U.S. Dep't of Energy, FutureGen: Tomorrow's Pollution-Free Power Plant, http://www.fossil.energy.gov/programs/powersystems/futuregen/.

8. FutureGen Alliance, http://www.futuregenalliance.org/benefits.stm.

9. *Illinois' Lack of CO_2 Liability Rules Creates Hurdle in Bid for FutureGen*, Inside Washington, July 27, 2006.

10. *See, e.g.*, Randy Lee Loftis, *Permits Issued for Coal Plants: State's Step Begins Public Review Process for TXU's Plan to Build 11 Facilities*, Dallas Morning News, Oct. 19, 2006, *available at* http://www.dallasnews.com/sharedcontent/dws/dn/latestnews/stories/101906dnbustxu.4f7f30e5.html; Daniel Mottola, *Texas Coal Rush Update*, Austin Chron., Oct. 13, 2006, *available at* http://www.austinchronicle.com/gyrobase/Issue/story?oid=oid%3A410276; Catherine Komp, *Texas Utility Admits Coal Plants Will Increase Some Pollutants*, The New Standard, Aug. 23, 2006, *available at* http://newstandardnews.net/content/index.cfm/items/3574.

11. Governor Kempthorne became Secretary of the Interior in May 2006.

12. Colo. Pub. Utilities Comm'n, In the Matter of the Application of Public Service Company of Colorado for a Certificate of Public Convenience and Necessity for the Comanche Unit 3 Generation Facility: Order Approving Settlement (Dec. 17, 2004), at 30.

13. Cal. Pub. Utilities Comm'n, Decision 04-12-048, Opinion Adopting Pacific Gas & Electric Company, Southern California Edison Company, and San Diego Gas & Electric Company's Long-Term Procurement Plans, Dec. 16, 2004, at § VIII.F.3, *available at* http://www.cpuc.ca.gov/Published/Final_decision/43224.htm.

14. Dan Adler, California Public Utility Commission, *Renewable Energy and Climate Change: Regulatory and Policy Issues*, Presentation at California Climate Action Registry Annual Conference, Berkeley, Calif., April 18-20, 2005, *available at* http://www.climateregistry.org/docs/EVENTS/Conference%202005/Adler_Renewable.pdf.

15. TREXLER & ASSOCIATES, INC., TENASKA EASTERN WASHINGTON REFORESTATION PROJECT: 1996 PROGRESS REPORT (1996); TREXLER & ASSOCIATES, INC., ESQUINAS CARBON OFFSET LAND CONSERVATION INITIATIVE (ECOLAND): A USIJI PROJECT PROPOSAL (1994).

16. EPCOR, Press Release, Genesee 3, Canada's Most Advanced Coal-Fired Unit, Declared Operational (March 1, 2005), *available at* http://www.epcor.ca/About/Media+Room/News+Releases/2005archive/Mar0105.htm (last visited May 25, 2006).

17. EPCOR, Press Release, TransAlta Purchases Half of EPCOR Genesee Phase 3 Project in Alberta; EPCOR and TransAlta Also Sign Option Agreement for Alberta and Ontario, Jan. 13, 2003, *available at* http://www.epcor.ca/Media+Room/News+Releases/2003+Archives/January1303.htm.

18. Xcel Energy, Colorado Least-Cost Plan Settlement Fact Sheet, *available at* http://www.xcelenergy.com/docs/corpcomm/COLeastCostSettlementFactSheet.pdf.

19. COLO. PUB. UTILITIES COMM'N, COMPREHENSIVE SETTLEMENT AGREEMENT IN THE MATTER OF THE APPLICATION OF PUBLIC SERVICE COMPANY OF COLORADO FOR APPROVAL OF ITS 2003 LEAST-COST RESOURCE PLAN, No. 04A-214E, Dec. 3, 2004, at 15, *available at* http://www.xcelenergy.com/docs/corpcomm/SettlementAgreementFinalDraftclean20041203.pdf.

20. OR. REV. STAT. § 469.503 (2003).

21. The Climate Trust invests the offset funds it receives from power plants regulated under the Oregon statute into various projects that are intended to reduce CO_2 levels. Projects to date include building energy-efficiency programs, wind power financing, domestic riparian reforestation, rainforest restoration, and truck-stop electrification. *See* http://www.climatetrust.org/programs_powerplant.php (last visited July 13, 2006).

22. The statute and the monetary values arose out of a 1996 contested case administrative proceeding that evaluated the ability of three proposed power plants to mitigate their CO_2 (and other) emissions as compared to each other. Following the lengthy proceeding, the legislature enacted the CO_2 standard for future proposed power plants in the state and included a monetary value. OR. REV. STAT. § 469.503 (2003). However, standards for offset projects are considerably stricter now than they were in 1996, and offsets cost more than $0.85/ton of CO_2 on the open GHG market.

23. Duke Energy Grays Harbor, LLC, Satsop Combustion Turbine GHG Mitigation Plan (June 2003), *available at* http://www.efsec.wa.gov/Satsop/SatsopGHGPlan.pdf.

24. Ongoing maintenance at the facility preserves assets. State of Washington, Energy Facility Site Evaluation Council, Satsop Combustion Turbine Project, http://www.efsec.wa.gov/satsop.shtml (last visited Oct. 31, 2006).

25. Washington State Energy Facility Site Evaluation Council, Draft Site Certification Agreement Between the State of Washington and Sumas Energy 2, Inc. (2002), *available at* http://www.efsec.wa.gov/Sumas2/Recommendation/se2sca5-24-02.pdf.

26. State of Washington, Energy Facility Site Evaluation Council, Resolution 316, Sumas 2 Generation Facility Termination of Site Certification Agreement, *available at* http://www.efsec.wa.gov/FILES/resolutions/SE2%20Resolution%20316%20final.pdf.

27. Chehalis Power Generating Limited Partnership, Greenhouse Gas Offset Strategy and Plan: Chehalis Generation Facility (Sept. 2002), *available at* http://www.efsec.wa.gov/Chehalis/GHG/ChehalisGHGPlan.pdf.

28. State of Washington, Energy Facility Site Evaluation Council, Chehalis Generation Facility, http://www.efsec.wa.gov/cgf.shtml.

29. State of Washington, Energy Facility Site Evaluation Council, Wallula Power Project, http://www.efsec.wa.gov/wallula.shtml.

30. WASH. REV. CODE ch. 80.70 (2006).

31. State of California, Office of the Governor, Executive Order S-3-05, June 1, 2005, *available at* http://www.dot.ca.gov/hq/energy/ExecOrderS-3-05.htm (last visited May 31, 2006).

32. Cal. Envtl. Protection Agency, Climate Action Team Report to the Governor and Legislature, March 2006, *available at* http://www.climatechange.ca.gov/climate_action_team/reports/index.html (last visited May 31, 2006).

33. Cal. Health & Safety Code Div. 25.5, § 38500 et seq. (Sept. 2006).

34. Regional Greenhouse Gas Initiative Model Rule, Aug. 15, 2006, *available at* http://www.rggi.org/docs/model_rule_8_15_06.pdf.

35. Karen Dillon, *Environmentalists Taking on Utilities: Coal Plants' Renaissance Pits Energy vs. Pollution*, Kansas City Star, April 11, 2006, *available at* http://www.contracostatimes.com/mld/cctimes/news/nation/14312879.htm (last visited May 24, 2006).

36. *See* http://www.sierraclub.org/environmentallaw/lawsuits/viewCase.asp?id=309.

37. Press Release, Schwarzenegger Can't Fight Global Warming with More Fossil Fuels, Activists Say (April 11, 2006), *available at* http://www.commondreams.org/news2006/0411-09.htm (last visited May 25, 2006).

38. Han Laetz, *Lawyers File 143-page Objection to Malibu LNG Project*, Malibu Times, May 17, 2006, *available at* http://www.malibutimes.com/articles/2006/05/17/news/news2.txt (last visited May 18, 2006).

39. Ratepayers for Affordable Clean Energy v. Cal. Pub. Utilities Comm'n, No. D046994, Cal. Ct. App. 4th Dist., Div. 1, filed Aug. 15, 2005. Text of petition is *available at* http://lngwatch.com/race/pr_RACEvsCPUC.htm (last visited April 27, 2006).

40. Ratepayers for Affordable Clean Energy v. Cal. Pub. Utilities Comm'n, No. 046994, Cal. Ct. of App. 4th Dist., Div. 1, May 11, 2006. The court stated that the petition was denied because petitioner had failed to present a convincing argument for annulment of the CPUC's decision, citing *Pac. Bell v. Pub. Utilities Comm'n* (2000), 79 Cal. App. 4th 269, 272. Docket history can be found at http://appellatecases.courtinfo.ca.gov/search/case/dockets.cfm?dist=41&doc_id=45184&doc_no=D046994.

41. U.S. Army Corps of Engineers, Cape Wind Energy Project Draft Environmental Impact Statement (2004).

42. Cape Wind Associates, http://www.capewind.org/.

43. Intergovernmental Panel on Climate Change, Climate Change 2001: The Scientific Basis—Contribution of Working Group I to the Third Assessment Report of the Intergovernmental Panel on Climate Change, at 388-89 (2001).

44. 42 U.S.C. § 7475(a).

45. 42 U.S.C. §§ 7470-7479.

46. Or. Admin. Code §§ 340-224-0010 to 340-224-0100.

47. 70 Fed. Reg. 67,120 (Nov. 4, 2005).

48. George Davis, Ore. Dep't of Envtl. Quality, e-mail to Yuri Nakamoto, Trexler Climate + Energy Services, Inc., May 2, 2006.

49. Catherine Trevison, *Owens Corning Backs Out of Gresham Plant*, OREGONIAN, May 9, 2006, *available at* http://www.oregonlive.com/search/index.ssf?/base/metro_east_news/1147141519321570.xml?oregonian?fng&coll=7 (last visited June 5, 2006).

50. Nw. Envt'l Defense Ctr. v. Owens Corning Corp., 434 F. Supp. 2d 957 (D. Or. June 8, 2006). The court's decision replaced its Findings and Recommendation dated May 17, 2006. *Id.* at 1. The court noted that although Owens Corning had agreed to halt construction pending resolution of the dispute regarding its air permit, the case was not moot:

> At a minimum, the parties still dispute whether construction was undertaken without one or more required permits, whether Defendant's facility is subject to those permit requirements, whether civil penalties should be imposed, and, if so, the amount and disposition of those penalties.

Id. at 4-5.

51. *Id.* at 10-11. In a footnote, the court rejected the decision in *Natural Resources Defense Council v. Environmental Protection Agency*, 440 F.3d 476 (D.C. Cir. 2006), holding that the probability of a person being harmed by ozone depletion is so remote that it cannot support standing. The *Owens Corning* court concluded that:

> [S]ince Congress has determined that emissions into the atmosphere can pose a threat to human health and warrant regulation, it does not seem appropriate for the court to second-guess that Congressional determination under the cloak of a standing inquiry. In addition, it is likely that the evidence of harm to Oregon from ozone depletion and global warming would at least be sufficient to create a material factual dispute. *Cf.* Friends of the Earth, Inc. v. Watson, 2005 WL 2035596 at 3 (N.D. Calif. 2005).

Id. at 11 n.3.

52. *Id.* at 12.

53. *Id.* at 18-19.

54. *Id.* at 20-21.

55. *Id.* at 21, Valley Forge Christian Coll. v. Americans United for Separation of Church & State, Inc., 454 U.S. 464, 474-75 (1982) (citations omitted).

56. *Id.* at 25. The court distinguished *Conn. v. Am. Elec. Power Co.*, 406 F. Supp. 2d 265 (S.D.N.Y. 2005), noting it was not being asked to decide whether global warming is a serious threat.

57. Michael Milstein, *Schools, Groups Benefit in Owens Deal*, OREGONIAN, June 9, 2006, *available at* http://www.oregonlive.com/business/oregonian/index.ssf?/base/business/1149821721263810.xml&coll=7&thispage=1 (last visited July 24, 2006).

58. 2005 WL 2035596, 35 Envtl. L. Rep. 20,179 (N.D. Cal. Aug. 23, 2005) (No. C 02-4106 JSW); *see also* Chapter 6, *supra*.

59. J.J. Dooley & R.T. Dahowski, *Examining Planned U.S. Power Plant Capacity Additions in the Context of Climate Change*, Joint Global Change Research Inst. (Pac. Nw. Nat'l Lab. and Univ. of Md.), http://www.globalchange.umd.edu/publications/PNNL-SA-36829.pdf (2002).

60. M. Trexler & J. Pienovi, *Going for the Green: Best Actions in Approaching Climate Change*, NATURAL GAS & ELEC., April 2006, at 14 (filed Aug. 15, 2005). Text of petition is *available at* http://lngwatch.com/race/pr_RACEvsCPUC.htm (last visited April 27, 2006).

chapter eight

International Trade and Development

Alan S. Miller

I. Overview

Globalization has become one of the most significant forces shaping economic growth and development worldwide, and in turn the international rules and institutions dealing with international trade and development are likely to have a significant impact on the evolving international regime for climate change. The relationship between these two very different systems raises many issues; both systems are undergoing considerable change, the principles and political leadership are highly distinct, and until recently there was little effort to bring the two communities together. The subject will therefore most likely undergo considerable additional evolution in the near future.

This chapter provides an overview of the linkages among international trade, development, and climate change. Part I reviews the issues arising from trade and the environment, including the basic principles and institutions shaping the agenda. This Part then focuses more specifically on the implications of this relationship for the future evolution of climate change regulation and responses, with a brief description of the evolving trade regime, its institutions, and the potential opportunities possible from a more integrated approach. Part II reviews the role of development assistance, beginning with a description of the relationship between energy and development, and then describing the role of the World Bank and other international financial institutions (IFIs), with a focus on programs such as the Global Environment Facility that target climate change. Part III reviews some emerging domestic and international adjudications related to climate change, a field likely to grow in the future.

II. A Brief Introduction to International Institutions Central to Trade, Development, and the Environment

Some familiarity with the major institutions involved in trade and development provides a useful context for the issues discussed in this chapter. The World Trade Organization, or WTO, is the overseer of international agreements and negotiations to lower trade barriers. It was created in 1995 as the successor to the General Agreement on Tariffs and Trade (GATT) established after World War II.[1] The WTO system includes panels established to review trade disputes as well as to manage trade negotiations, or "rounds," targeted to reduce trade barriers in specific economic sectors. The recent Doha Round is framed around reduction of agricultural subsidies and tariffs, a politically difficult but environmentally important objective.[2] The WTO is managed by an executive director, currently Pascal Lamy, and has a staff of over 600 based in Geneva, Switzerland. Several potential conflicts between the international regimes for trade and climate change are discussed below, although to date these issues remain largely conjecture.

The World Bank was established by international agreement in Bretton Woods on July 1, 1944, as a source of multilateral financing for the reconstruction of Europe. In subsequent decades, the Bank evolved into the premier source of financing for development.[3] In the fiscal year ending July 1, 2006, the Bank made loans of over $20 billion for 245 projects in developing countries worldwide. An increasing share of lending has been for social and development-related objectives, including improving health systems, access to education, and post-disaster reconstruction.

The World Bank Group actually comprises several legally and financially distinct financial entities; the government lending programs encompassed by what is commonly termed the World Bank include the International Bank for Reconstruction and Development (IBRD) and the International Development Association. Both make sovereign guaranteed loans to governments, but IDA provides no-interest terms and some grants to the poorest countries. The International Finance Corporation (IFC) was created in 1956 to address the need for private-sector financing; as of June 2005 its portfolio was $19.3 billion for its own account and another $5.3 billion held for loan syndications.[4] The Multilateral Investment Guarantee was added in 1988 to address the need for political risk insurance.[5]

The World Bank and other international financial institutions have to date had a relatively limited direct role in addressing climate change, as the UN Framework Convention on Climate Convention does not obligate developing countries to reduce their emissions. Two important exceptions have been the implementation of projects financed by the Global Environment Facility (GEF) and the creation of a carbon finance program with support from several donor governments. These programs, dis-

cussed below, have given the World Bank limited resources to address the incremental costs of projects that reduce greenhouse gas emissions. The GEF is a source of multilateral financing for projects with global environmental benefits, including climate change and biodiversity.[6] Funding is primarily channeled through several "implementing agencies," the WB, UN Development Programme (UNDP), and UN Environment Programme (UNEP). Both the World Bank and IFC have programs supporting the growth of the carbon market; the former now manages more than $1 billion in donor funds for the acquisition of carbon credits,[7] while the latter has introduced financial products to address the project risks associated with carbon reduction investments.[8]

The World Bank has recently undertaken to prepare proposals for a potentially significantly expanded role in climate change in response to a request from the G8.

The World Bank has recently undertaken to prepare proposals for a potentially significantly expanded role in climate change in response to a request from the G8. The G8 process began in 1975 as an annual meeting of six heads of state from leading industrialized countries: the U.S., U.K., Germany, France, Italy, and Japan.[9] Canada was asked to join the following year and Russia in 1996. Each year the heads of state gather, in a location that rotates among the eight, to address the most pressing international foreign policy, economic, and other issues of shared concern. At the Gleneagles G8 Summit in 2005, the parties adopted a Climate Change Communique calling on the World Bank to engage with major developing countries and to prepare proposals for responding to climate change.[10] This request and the subsequent response of the World Bank are also discussed below.

The export credit agencies (ECAs) are another set of international institutions with significant influence on exports and financing for large energy projects in developing countries. The ECAs have taken on increasing importance as private commercial flows have expanded and the demand for protection from political and financial risks has grown correspondingly. While these functions are partly served by the World Bank and regional banks, the ECAs are bilateral organizations created to promote exports of domestic companies.[11] These agencies typically provide direct or indirect subsidies such as below-interest loan terms, extended repayment periods, and insurance against country risk, and are frequently involved in support of energy-intensive projects. The environmental consequences of their operations have been the subject of focus by the G8.[12]

A. Economic Growth and Pollution: Theory and Practice

One of the most important issues in development studies concerns the relationship between economic growth and pollution. If, as some economists hypothesize, pollution declines as countries achieve some minimum level of development and thereafter become more affluent, environmental problems might be to some extent self-correcting—increasing at first with infrastructure and investments necessary to meet basic human needs, but then declining as income rises past a certain point. This concept is generally referred to as the "Kuznets curve" after the economist and Nobel laureate Simon Kuznets, who found such a relationship between income growth and inequality (with the latter rising at first, then declining with increasing per capita income).[13] There is some logic behind extending this hypothesis to environmental quality; beyond some basic level of development, economies shift toward services and less pollution-intensive activities (the "composition effect"). Increasing income is also often associated with greater environmental awareness and demands for pollution control.

Two Princeton economists, Gene Grossman and Alan Krueger, applied this reasoning to test the relationship between air pollution and economic growth in research in the early 1990s.[14] They looked at income growth and several conventional air pollutants and found evidence of a reduction in pollution intensity (emissions per capita) of between $3,000 and $5,000 per capita income in 1985 dollars.[15] Subsequent research has found some significant limitations on the "environmental Kuznets curve."[16] Of most relevance to climate change, there is no evidence that carbon emissions generally decrease with income. This is not necessarily contrary to the theory, in that carbon emissions are linked to climate change but not directly to local environmental problems, and thus are less likely to decline in response to increasing environmental awareness. Second, the turning point for reducing local pollution appears to be much higher than estimated—closer to $13,000 per capita—and thus not within reach for most developing countries for decades. For example, the relevant per capita income figures for India and China are between a quarter and half this level, respectively, on a purchasing power parity basis.[17]

On the other hand, the fear that free trade may lead to "pollution havens"—the movement of polluting industries to locations with lax environmental standards—may also be overstated. The empirical evidence shows that low environmental standards are rarely a significant factor in industrial location decisions.[18] The end result serves to reinforce the importance of effective legal and regulatory regimes without which "trade-led growth will also lead to increases in environmental degradation."[19]

B. The UNFCC and Trade Regimes: Conflicts and Synergies

Another set of issues arises from the potential conflict between the institutions and evolving sets of rules dealing with, respectively, international trade and climate change.[20] As Charnovitz notes, "To date multilateral efforts to liberalize trade and to prevent global warming have proceeded largely on separate paths. Increasingly, however, these parallel regimes—one defined by the Agreement Establishing the World Trade

Organization (WTO) and its annexes, the other by the UN Framework Convention on Climate Change (UNFCCC) and its Kyoto Protocol—are likely to come into closer contact as climate policies lead to significant economic effects."[21]

The potential significance of the interaction between these two regimes is reflected in language in the Convention as well as some discussion in the 2001 IPCC report. Article 3.5 of the Convention states:

> Parties shall co-operate to promote a supportive and open international economic system that would lead to sustainable economic growth and development in all Parties . . . Measures taken to combat climate change, including unilateral ones, should not constitute a means of arbitrary or unjustifiable discrimination or a disguised restriction on international trade.

Article 2.3 of the Kyoto Protocol similarly exhorts parties to "strive to implement policies and measures . . . in such a way as to minimize adverse effects . . . on international trade."

In a section titled "Conflicts with International Environmental Regulation and Trade Law," the 2001 report of the Intergovernmental Panel on Climate Change (IPCC) on Mitigation summarizes several potential sources of conflict while noting the absence of trade claims—so far—against measures enacted in widely subscribed multilateral environmental agreements.[22] The policies most likely to be subject to review under WTO provisions, according to the IPCC, are trade-related mea-

sures adopted to regulate importation of polluting practices, particularly restrictions on goods based on the energy or polluting processes used to produce goods, as opposed to the performance of the final product or service (e.g., a regulation on cars based on the energy used in manufacturing, as opposed to energy consumption in use).[23]

In addition to the debate about the allegedly beneficial environmental effects of income growth discussed above, there are several more direct effects of expanded trade that may promote the objectives of the climate regime.[24] The argument for a positive view is based primarily on the environmentally harmful effect of subsidies and trade barriers as applied to natural resources. As summarized by Sampson, "Trade liberalization leads to a more efficient use of resources; a more efficient relative price structure (trade restrictions themselves are market distortions); more resources available for environmental management programs because of growth in real income; and an increase in the availability of environment-related goods and services through market liberalization."[25]

There is little doubt that, worldwide and particularly in many developing countries, energy subsidies contribute significantly to the waste of energy and generation of substantial emissions. Global subsidies to the power sector were estimated to exceed $200 billion per year in 2002, and, according to the IPCC, removing energy subsidies would reduce global CO_2 emissions between 4% and 18%.[26] Unfortunately, there does not appear to be any short-term interest in taking up the elimination of energy subsidies as a focus for expanding the trade regime, perhaps because the major industrialized countries would also be forced to confront vested political interests.[27]

In addition to the likely reductions in GHG emissions from removing subsidies and market-distorting policies, the potential exists for trade rules to directly reinforce the objectives of the UNFCCC. Some countries ratified the Montreal Protocol on Substances that Deplete the Ozone Layer because it included trade sanctions that made it impossible for non-parties to obtain chemicals (CFCs) essential for refrigeration, air conditioning, and manufacturing components for computers and electronics. The Protocol required all parties who manufactured these chemicals to stop their exports to non-parties by July 1, 1990, leaving most developing countries with little choice but to ratify. The Protocol also regulated trade of some valuable export commodities: "The Parties, in their third meeting in 1991, made a list of products containing CFCs that now could not be imported by non-Parties to the Protocol. Thus even countries like South Korea, who made their own [CFCs] but who had a large export market of goods with CFCs like automobiles with air conditioners were forced to ratify the Protocol."[28]

Frankel gives three additional examples of potential "win-win" outcomes from linking trade and environment.[29] One is the political leverage attainable through trade negotiations with countries otherwise reluctant to agree to multilateral environmental agreements ("MEAs"). The prime example is Russia, which agreed to ratify the Kyoto Protocol in return for EU support for its acceptance by the WTO. As Russia's participation was essential to bring the Kyoto Protocol into effect, this trade was of enormous importance for the climate regime. A second example is the potential for negotiation of more favorable trade terms for environmental goods and services (e.g., renewable energy equipment). Liberalization of trade in environmental goods and services is on the agenda for negotiation, and proposals have been to include removal of trade barriers to clean energy.[30] Frankel's third example is the prospect of an international ban on subsidies to fossil fuels—politically unlikely, but theoretically possible.[31]

An important caveat is that ratification is not the same as compliance, and as the Montreal Protocol experience indicates, trade sanctions can create significant economic incentives for cheating. Several elements in the Montreal Protocol created significant incentives for smuggling of CFCs. Whereas significant reductions in CFC use were required by industrialized country parties and imports were barred, the available substitutes were at least initially much more expensive. The United States also imposed taxes on CFC use to hasten the phase-out process, further increasing prices and incentives for illegal imports. Meanwhile, developing countries were allowed a longer

transition period and thus continued production and imports. To further complicate matters, imports of recycled CFCs were permitted, so that customs officials were required to inspect chemical shipments to verify compliance. A major black market developed in the port of Miami, leading to the observation that for a time CFCs were second only to cocaine as the focus of smugglers into that city.

For several years in the mid-1990s, Russia was a major supplier of contraband CFCs passed through European companies and imported into the United States with labels indicating a South American destination, when the shipments instead entered the black market. The magnitude of the problem led to the creation of a special task force on CFC smuggling, bringing together staff and expertise from the Justice Department, Environmental Protection Agency, FBI, the Customs Service, and the IRS. Some large violators received extended jail time. A shutdown in Russian production led to a shift in supply from China, sometimes headed for India and other developing countries where some CFC use was still permitted. The problem was gradually brought under control as the phase-out reduced demand for CFCs and document labeling, tracking systems, and enforcement capabilities improved with experience.[32]

While the linkages between trade and environment have been recognized for decades, the issue achieved much greater prominence in the 1990s following several highly publicized trade decisions by WTO panels reviewing challenges to U.S. restrictions on imports of tuna based on harvesting methods judged to be adverse to dolphins, and similarly restricting imports of shrimp based on fishing methods found to be harmful to sea turtles.[33] These decisions addressed a key tenet of the GATT framework, a prohibition on policies that discriminate between domestic and imported goods on the basis of the process by which a product was made, if they are "like goods." This issue might arise, for example, if regulations restricted importation of products based on the embodied carbon content.

The publicity associated with these controversies led to the creation of a Committee on Trade and Environment (CTE) following the Uruguay Round of trade negotiations in 1994. Subsequently, at the Doha Ministerial Conference in 2001, the CTE was directed to begin negotiations on several specific issues, including fisheries subsidies, the relationship between WTO rules and multilateral environmental agreements (MEAs), and trade in environmental goods and services.[34] Pascal Lamy, the WTO Director General, described the significance of the mandate (Paragraph 51 of the Doha Ministerial Declaration) to consider the developmental and environmental aspects of ongoing trade negotiations in a speech in October 2005:

In paragraph 51, Ministers instructed us to change our frame of mind. In other words, to no longer compartmentalize our work; discussing environmental and developmental issues in isolation of the rest of what we do. These are issues that permeate all areas of the WTO. In fact, it is through the lens of Paragraph 51 that we must now begin to look at the rest of the WTO. We must remember that sustainable development is the end goal of this institution. It is enshrined in page 1, paragraph 1, of the Agreement that establishes the WTO.[35]

Another set of issues arises from the use of trade sanctions within multilateral agreements, as opposed to domestic regulations. For example, as discussed above, the Montreal Protocol restricts Parties from importing CFCs and other regulated chemicals from nonparties, and further restricts exports by developing-country parties as of January 1993.[36] The Convention on International Trade in Endangered Species—as its name implies—is primarily focused on the creation of a detailed system for regulating trade in order to protect endangered species.[37] As Charnovitz notes,

> [T]he underlying assumption is that it will matter to the WTO dispute resolution system whether the contested action arises from a multilateral obligation. A recurrent theme in the trade-and-environment debate over the past 13 years has been the desirability of approaching global environmental problems through multilateral cooperation. Therefore, it seems likely that in adjudicating the GATT environmental exceptions, a dispute panel would be sympathetic to a defense based on a parallel obligation under a climate treaty.[38]

So far, this issue is academic in the context of climate change in that neither trade sanctions nor trade controls have been incorporated in the UNFCCC or Kyoto Protocol. In the case of the Montreal Protocol, its trade sanctions were never challenged by nonparties, perhaps because its membership was sufficiently inclusive.[39] According to one of the principal negotiators of the Montreal Protocol, the inclusion of the trade provisions was sanctioned by a GATT representative under exceptions for standards "necessary to protect human, animal, or plant life or health" or "relating to the conservation or exhaustion of natural resources."[40] The Protocol allowed for the possible imposition of restrictions on trade in products made with but not containing CFCs—a potentially more difficult case under GATT rules—but this provision was never implemented.[41]

A further possible area of uncertainty is associated with the potential use of pollution taxes. WTO rules allow the use of compensating charges or "border adjustments" to equalize taxes imposed on domestic production. According to many authorities, border adjustments are not allowable for taxes on inputs such as energy fully consumed during production, in contrast with taxes on fuels and other final products or goods "physically incorporated" into final products.[42] Other authorities disagree, arguing that this theory is based on a mistaken reading of the original tax provisions of the GATT as well as more recent Uruguay Round provisions relating to subsidies that allow the rebate of taxes on energy used in production processes.[43] Some experts also posit potential conflicts with national emission-trading rules if carbon credits take a form that can be considered "securities" and if trading is only open to Annex I parties.[44]

The relationship between the WTO and the climate regime, despite the few practical concerns to date, is the subject of a rapidly growing literature.[45] The prospects for achieving greater clarity, or more likely some effective basis for avoiding conflict between the WTO and MEAs, remain the subject of considerable debate. Many authorities take a pragmatic view and interpret recent rulings as calling for primarily rules of reason: measures must be flexible in specifying how the environmental objective is to be achieved; efforts should be made to achieve a multilateral agreement; and reasonable periods must be provided affected states to come into compliance.[46]

In contrast, many environmental groups question whether a meaningful rapprochement can ever come about given the fundamental difference in perspectives between the two systems. They would keep the environment out of the WTO.[47] Others see a chilling effect in a continued lack of clarity and posit that some effort to further define principles is necessary.[48] Still others would place most emphasis on reform of process and procedures to provide greater transparency and public confidence in the decisions and principles emerging from the trade system, recognizing that anticipating the range of future conflicts is not possible.[49]

III. Energy for Development

A. Energy, Development, and Climate Change: Meeting the Millennium Development Goals While Minimizing the Increase in GHG

The Millennium Development Goals (MDGs) were adopted in September 2000 at the United Nations Millennium Summit as a set of measurable targets for promoting development in the world's poorest nations.[50] Eight specific goals were set for attainment by 2015, including halving extreme poverty and hunger, achieving universal primary education, reducing under-five mortality by two-thirds, reversing the spread of disease, especially HIV/AIDS and malaria, and ensuring environmental sustainability. The MDGs have given structure and specificity to global poverty alleviation efforts, with measurable indicators and reporting on an annual basis.[51]

There is no MDG on energy per se, but there is widespread understanding that access to energy services is essential to their achievement.[52] Cleaner fuels and cookstoves can reduce diseases associated with smoke, lower child mortality rates, and improve maternal health. Cleaner fuels and improvements in the efficiency of energy use can reduce the time and transport burden required to collect fuelwood and dung—work disproportionately imposed on women—increasing opportunities for education and income generation. The availability of electricity is associated with greater availability of medicines and health services, clean water and sanitation, and machinery that supports income-generating activities.

Recent economic progress in many parts of the world has been directly linked to an increase in access to modern energy services, particularly electricity . . .

Recent economic progress in many parts of the world has been directly linked to an increase in access to modern energy services, particularly electricity, relative to the growth in population, with the most noticeable progress in East Asia.[53] India and the broader South Asia region are also beginning to show promising signs of progress as well. However, Sub-Saharan Africa continues to lag behind; the number of people without access to electricity has been increasing, and by all accounts most likely will continue to do so in the decades to come. South Africa is a significant exception, as a well-managed electrification program succeeded in significantly reducing costs while increasing the number of households connected from 36 percent in 1990 to 67 percent in 2000.[54]

The UN Millennium Project was initiated to bring realism to MDG efforts by supporting preparation of practical plans to define the necessary measures and quantify the costs of achieving the goals on a country basis. One result was a study estimating the costs of meeting three energy goals for Kenya by 2015, each linked to meeting the MDGs: providing improved cooking fuels based on LPG stoves and sustainable forestry/more efficient cookstoves; extending the grid to urban and peri-urban areas; and providing electricity to rural schools, clinics, and community centers.[55] The total cost for all three objectives was $443 million per year, or about $12.70 per capita per year—a manageable amount if subsidized by donors, but too much if the entire cost is imposed on the poor.

From the perspective of development institutions like the World Bank, the extension of access to modern energy services to the poor is a primary objective, as discussed below. For this reason, it is likely to remain important to bridge discussions of energy for development with the transition to a lower-carbon energy system in the large, rapidly growing, carbon-intensive developing country economies—particularly China and India. Fortunately, however, compelling analysis indicates that the two objectives are not in conflict; providing modern energy services essential for addressing global poverty need not result in a significant increase in global CO_2 emissions. Robert Socolow, an energy expert at Princeton University, has calculated the increased

GHG emissions that would result if a basic level of modern energy services could somehow be provided immediately for the estimated 1.6 billion persons without access to electricity and the 2.6 billion people without clean cooking fuel—a technically feasible and socially desirable scenario, but without any imminent prospect of attainment. His analysis shows that despite their large numbers, the low rate of consumption per person would produce only a very modest increase in global CO_2 emissions.[56]

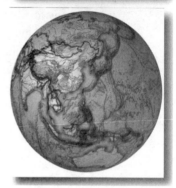

Currently, rapid economic growth in the two most populated and coal-intensive countries is resulting in a rapid increase in GHG emissions. According to projections by the International Energy Agency, in a business-as usual-scenario, emissions from developing countries are projected to more than double between 2002 and 2030 (from 8.2 to 18.4 Gt CO_2)—much of this due to combustion of coal and other fossil fuels for electricity. China is now the world's largest coal consumer, while India ranks third (behind the United States). As coal prices are only weakly related to oil prices—unlike those for natural gas—the run-up in oil prices in 2006 is expected to further increase the relative role of coal in fueling global energy consumption.[57] Business-as-usual scenarios by the U.S. Energy Information Administration project an increase in coal consumption within the industrialized (OECD) countries from 2,476 million short tons (MST) in 2003 to 3,436 in 2030, whereas consumption in China and India increases over the same period from 1,962 MST to 5,532—a steady increase of about 166 GW between 2003 and 2010 (versus 12 in the OECD), 216 GW between 2011 and 2020 (versus 184 in the OECD), and 305 GW between 2021 and 2030 (versus 218 in the OECD).[58] Growth in Chinese fossil fuel consumption has exceeded most forecasts, and the most recent analysis indicates China may surpass the United States as the largest emitter of GHG emissions in 2009, nearly a decade ahead of previous predictions.[59]

Even in the short term, the expected growth in coal generation is impressive; by 2012—the end of the Kyoto Protocol commitment period—the three largest coal-producing nations, China, the United States, and India, collectively plan to build more than 800 new coal plants with combined cumulative emissions exceeding 2.5 billion tons of CO_2.[60] By 2012, emissions from these plants—if all are built—would be five times the total reductions required by the Kyoto Protocol.[61] Yet reducing the rate of growth in developing-country emissions confronts the pressing need for increasing energy use to alleviate poverty and promote sustainable development.

B. The Rise of Private Financial Flows Versus Official Development Assistance

One of the most important trends relevant to meeting the energy needs of developing countries in recent years has been the rising dominance of private sources of finance relative to public development assistance. As of 1985, official financial transfers were more than 10 times total private flows to developing countries.[62] By 2002, private financial flows increased nearly tenfold to exceed $380 billion versus official flows of less than $180 billion.[63] As one recent study concludes, while it goes too far to speak of the "privatization" of foreign aid, "Private finance is now the biggest show in town. . . . [M]oney from overseas is reaching the private sector in far greater amounts than a couple of decades ago, a large share of it remittances from migrant workers. Also very large are investment flows, which increasingly take the form of equity rather than debt finance, probably because direct investment has more attractive risk-sharing properties."[64]

Private investments tend to be more volatile than aid and also concentrate in the most commercially promising environments. In the late 1990s, for example, private flows dropped due to several factors.[65] One was that privatization transactions resulted in large but one-time investments, particularly in Brazil. A more general consideration was the declining appeal of the investment environment resulting from fiscal problems in several large countries in Asia and South America. More recently, declining equity markets in industrial countries and corporate-level problems affecting some major energy companies and international investors caused reduced investment.

Official development assistance (ODA) has increased only modestly in recent years but remains important for several reasons. While private investment is relatively concentrated geographically in more prosperous middle-income countries, ODA is critical for low-income countries, as a source of support for sector reforms necessary to attract capital to energy markets, and also to help commercialize investments in environmentally promising but initially higher-cost new technologies. As noted above, the G8 countries have recently asked the World Bank and other international financial institutions (IFIs) to play a leading role in facilitating a dialogue with large, rapidly growing developing countries about possible cooperation to reduce their growth in GHG emissions. In undertaking this role, these institutions will need to provide a range of services in addition to financing, including supporting institutional and governance reforms, assistance in developing locally appropriate policies, and creating a favorable investment climate (discussed below).

The availability of financing, whether from public or private sources, is critical for the energy sector due to its capital intensity. Power plants, oil refineries, and transmission systems are among the most capital-intensive projects in any economy. Renewable energy systems are almost entirely capital cost, as once put into operation they have no fuel cost (excluding biomass systems) and minimal maintenance costs. Energy-efficiency investments also typically require the payment of some modest initially higher capital cost in return for reduced operating (fuel) costs over time. The cost and availability of capital is therefore key to making clean energy services available for development, and insofar as the climate regime can help direct more capital to such services, it can have a major positive impact.[66]

The terms and availability of financing are particularly important for developing countries with limited credit and a wide range of investment needs. There are few estimates of capital requirements specifically for clean energy in developing country applications, although such studies have been done at varying levels of detail for the United States and other industrialized countries.[67] These analyses recognize that demand and supply-side investments are fungible, and accordingly require detailed modeling to allow an assessment of the lowest-cost societal options over time. However, by any measure it is evident that capital requirements for energy-related investments will be very large. The IEA estimates that between 1997 and 2020, developing countries will need to invest $1.7 trillion, or an average of $75 billion per year, in power plants alone.[68] Oil and gas production can be equally costly, albeit more geographically limited. In Russia, the oil sector requires an annual investment of $5 billion to $7 billion; in Nigeria, the estimate is $35 billion over five years.[69] On average, 1% to 1.5% of GDP is invested in energy worldwide, or around $290 billion to $430 billion a year, with much higher levels in many developing countries.[70]

From a global perspective, these percentages are consistent with historic norms and, while relatively large, are not infeasible. However, the challenge in raising these funds is changing with the increasing share of energy-related capital required by developing countries due to their higher growth rates. The total current investment in energy infrastructure in the OECD and developing countries is about equal. However, according to the International Energy Agency (IEA), to support projected economic growth to 2030, investment in energy infrastructure will have to increase by more than 50 percent in developing countries while remaining roughly constant in the OECD.[71]

C. The Role of the World Bank and Other International Financial Institutions

Prior to the early 1990s, the World Bank and other IFIs dedicated about a fourth of their annual financial commitments to the energy sector.[72] This percentage has declined to about 10%; in the case of the World Bank, from about $3.7 billion in 1990 to about $1.4 billion in 2001 and $1.9 billion in FY 2005. This trend reflected several broader influences on the energy sector. One was the emphasis given to the liberalization and privatization of infrastructure services as an alternative to traditional state-owned monopolies, previously the focus of substantial support. This policy change to some extent mirrored that taking place in industrialized countries, where competition and regulatory reform had become powerful forces. An additional rationale for promoting this reform in developing countries is that state-owned enterprises in many developing countries are often poorly managed and financially weak or insolvent, as tariffs were kept below cost recovery in order to attract political support from particular constituencies.

An example of the Bank effort to achieve policy reform was in Cote d'Ivoire, where in the mid-1990s the government agreed to give management of electricity to a private operator. The World Bank had applied considerable pressure through conditions for release of an energy sector loan and provided technical assistance as the basis for the change in management. Bank-supported reforms have been implemented in many other countries, particularly in Central America, parts of South America, and Eastern Europe.[73]

The role of the World Bank in what has been termed "policy lending" or conditionalities—requirements for the adoption of specific policies as a condition for loans—has been a source of controversy. As an institution guided largely by economic principles, the Bank was very influenced by new concepts of deregulation, unbundling, and competition in the electricity sector.[74] The Bank promoted a model based largely on the UK approach, which moved away from a single national electric utility (a model common in many developing countries) to privatization and competition. This approach proved difficult to implement in many countries and, following the crisis in California, faced considerable resistance.[75]

In contrast, the role of the Bank as a source of policy innovation and knowledge transfer has been more successful in other less publicized areas. One has been in developing innovative schemes to extend rural electrification.[76] A program in Argentina, for example, supports competitive delivery of electricity services to isolated rural areas using renewable energy. Concessions are granted on a competitive basis, with tariffs based on those in urban areas with lower costs; the winning bid is based on the lowest subsidy required. The Clean Energy Investment Framework, discussed below, proposes a significant expansion of World Bank efforts to provide modern energy services to the rural poor and includes ambitious targets and timetables.

Another Bank-hosted program relevant to climate change is the Global Gas Flaring Reduction Partnership, initiated in 2002 with partners from the oil industry and oil-producing governments.[77] Large amounts of natural gas are flared worldwide—equivalent to about a quarter of all the gas used in the United States in a year, much of it in Africa due to the lack of local capacity to use gas associated with oil production. The World Bank is a logical host for such a program due to its technical capacity, ongoing relations with economic authorities in developing countries, credibility with industry, and in appropriate circumstances, access to financing.

The World Bank also provides important services in collecting and reporting data on infrastructure investments and related financial trends. Such data is a valuable

source of information on trends in financial flows relevant to understanding developing country financial needs.[78]

The decline in public-sector lending through the Bank was partially offset by an increase in private-sector lending through the International Finance Corporation (IFC) and the Multilateral Investment Guarantee Agency (MIGA). In the 1990s, IFC approved 57 projects with costs of $14.4 billion, versus 7 projects with costs of less than $1 billion in the previous 30 years. As of July 2006, IFC has a portfolio of $2.3 billion in power generation, distribution, and transmission. These loans typically are limited to about 25 percent of total project cost, and thus leverage a much greater amount of total investment. IFC loans, like those of export credit agencies, are sometimes more important as an assurance to other investors of likely repayment than as a source of capital. This is particularly true with respect to oil and gas projects, which often have minimal economic risk but may be in countries or regions that are politically unstable. MIGA, which provides insurance against political risks, has seen a rapid rise in power sector–related guarantees since its first in FY94; about a fifth of its liabilities are for guarantees for electric power projects. Like the Bank, IFC also provides advisory services relevant

. . . the Bank stated in March 2006 that in FY2005, its support for clean energy was nearly $750 million—more than double the amount in the previous fiscal year and 30% of total energy sector commitments.

to privatization in the energy sector. For example, IFC is advising Vietnamese authorities on how to most effectively mobilize private-sector participation in electricity generation projects.[79] The environmental and social reviews undertaken by international financial institutions also sometimes provide a legitimizing role for controversial projects such as large pipeline and hydro projects.

The World Bank Group has made a commitment to significantly increase its lending for energy efficiency and "new" renewable energy (defined to exclude hydro projects larger than 10 MW). At the June 2004 International Renewable Energies Conference in Bonn, Germany, the Bank announced it would increase its commitments for new RE and EE by at least 20% annually over the next five years (FY05– FY09), and to lead a Renewable Energy and Energy Efficiency Financing and Policy Network for developing countries. In its report on progress toward meeting this goal, the Bank stated in March 2006 that in FY 2005, its support for clean energy was nearly $750 million— more than double the amount in the previous fiscal year and 30% of total energy sector commitments.[80]

The IFC also reported a significant change in its identification, tracking and reporting of "energy efficiency" investments as a further response to the Bonn Commitment. Heretofore the Bank has historically only included projects and investments with efficiency improvements as a specific, primary purpose—e.g., a loan to banks for the purpose of energy-efficiency lending. IFC began identifying investments that made a significant contribution to energy efficiency, whatever their focus or investment objective (e.g., a significant upgrade in a pulp and paper mill). This analysis found more than $800 million in loans in FY05 that met this definition, with more than $225 million in associated IFC lending.[81]

D. The G8 Climate Change Plan of Action

At their 2005 meetings in Gleneagles, the G8 countries requested the World Bank and other IFIs to undertake a new mandate to engage with developing countries on climate change, clean energy, and sustainable development. This mandate is to result in an action plan for consideration at the 2008 G8 meetings in Japan, and may include proposals for new funding for clean energy investment. In a statement titled "Climate Change, Clean Energy and Sustainable Development," the parties recognized the importance of influencing investment in the world's energy systems as both a source of development and an opportunity to avoid substantial growth in GHG emissions. "Because decisions being taken today could lock in investment and increase emissions for decades to come, it is important to act wisely now." They further state that "tackling climate change and promoting clean technologies, while pursuing energy security and sustainable development, will require a global concerted effort over a sustained period." The World Bank was asked to "take a leadership role in creating a new investment framework for clean energy and development, including investment and financing."[82]

The implications of this broad mandate continue to unfold. In the Gleneagles Plan of Action, the World Bank and other multilateral development banks were asked to increase dialogue with borrowers on energy issues and "put forward specific proposals at their annual meetings" to:

(a) make the best use of existing resources and financing instruments to accelerate adoption of clean and more efficient energy technologies;
(b) explore opportunities to increase the volume of their investments in clean energy, consistent with their focus on poverty alleviation;
(c) work with large GHG-emitters with rapidly growing energy needs to identify less GHG-intensive growth options; and
(d) develop local commercial capacity to develop and finance cost-effective energy efficiency and low-carbon energy projects.

In response, the WB initiated a process of analysis and consultations with other banks and the private sector leading to the preparation of a paper released publicly in

April 2006, "Clean Energy and Development: Towards an Investment Framework."[83] The report provides a useful overview of the linkages between energy, development and climate change and provides an initial assessment of financial needs as the basis for the further development of proposals for possible new sources and instruments for financing clean energy and adaptation. Several new financing options are presented to accelerate investments in clean energy, power plant rehabilitation, and development and adoption of new technologies. The report notes that there are three potential sources for the incremental funds needed: voluntary expenditures on the basis of "enlightened self-interest"; public financing through national and international programs like the GEF; and "enlightened international public policy and regulatory frameworks that encourage an appropriate private sector response."[84] A process of further analysis and consultations was proposed to achieve agreement on a plan of action in time for the 2008 Japan Summit.

The World Bank prepared a second, more detailed analysis in a "Progress Report" prepared for the Board and Development Committee in September 2006.[85] The report reviews the extent to which existing financial instruments could be mobilized to meet the needs of both energy access and the transition to a low-carbon energy system in developing countries, and concludes that there is a funding gap on the order of $80 billion per year. A potential World Bank role is outlined for three areas: energy access for the poor, mitigation of GHG emissions, and adaptation to climate change. Several proposals are also included for possible new financing vehicles that could be used to mobilize resources, depending on donor interest, with costs partially offset from the value of carbon offsets generated.

E. Climate Risks to Development Projects: the Need for Increased Focus on Adaptation

The World Bank has also become increasingly concerned by the risks of climate change to development generally and its investment projects specifically. Climate disasters can set back economic growth significantly, add further risk to development projects, and create another threat to the future prospects of the world's poor. However, awareness of climate risks within development institutions remains low. A World Bank survey found that only about 2% of Bank project design documents mentioned climate risk, primarily urban flood control and land management projects where the issues are most obvious. But a review of 50 projects randomly selected from those approved in the last three fiscal years found that about half had some degree of climate risk and about a quarter could be classified as "high climate risk"—much of it from current climate, as opposed to potential climate change.[86]

The World Bank has noted that "the poorest countries and the poorest people within them are most vulnerable, having the least means to adapt." Africa is particularly exposed. During the 1990s an average of 200 million people per year from developing countries were impacted by climate-related disasters, compared with roughly one million in developed countries. The challenge is to reduce the current vulnerability of the climate-sensitive sectors, particularly agriculture and water resources, and to "climate proof" future development efforts.[87]

An initial WB estimate is that annual costs for this proposed development "climate proofing" are likely to be in the range of $10 billion to $40 billion, of which about a third will need to come from public finance. In the near term, the Bank proposes an emphasis on developing better tools for assessing climate vulnerabilities, capacity building to increase local monitoring and response capabilities, more proactive disaster preparedness, and new insurance instruments for agricultural risks. In the longer term, new sources of financing and perhaps new financial instruments will be necessary, beyond the programs currently managed by the GEF (see below).

F.   World Bank Carbon Finance Activities

The World Bank and other IFIs have become early leaders and innovators in helping to develop the emerging carbon market. As relatively public and transparent investors, their actions (even when criticized) have established useful benchmarks for others to follow. The WB role in buying carbon credits began with the establishment of the Prototype Carbon Fund with $180 million in support from six governments and 17 private donors in 1999, well before the implementation of the Kyoto Protocol.[88] These funds are primarily advanced by donor governments to the Bank carbon unit to buy credits, including the Netherlands, Italy, Spain, and Denmark; the World Bank itself is not an investor, although one objective is to integrate carbon projects with mainstream investments. The program has grown rapidly with the implementation of the Kyoto Protocol; funds under management increased from about $400 million on July 1, 2004, to over $900 million on July 1, 2005, to an expected $1.75 billion on July 1, 2006.[89] About $140 million has been committed to 30 projects. Much of this commitment has been for a single large contract for destruction of HFC 23, a greenhouse gas, in China; about 9% has been for renewables and waste management, with smaller amounts for recapture of coalbed methane, energy efficiency, and forestry projects.

With the advent of the EU ETS and significant privately based investors in the carbon market, there has been some debate about the future role for the World Bank carbon program. A paper approved by the World Bank Board in December 2005 outlines three primary objectives:

(i)   To ensure that carbon finance contributes substantially to sustainable development, beyond its contribution to global environmental efforts;

(ii) To assist in building, sustaining, and expanding the international market for carbon emission reductions and its institutional and administrative structure; and

(iii) To further strengthen the capacity of developing countries to benefit from the emerging market for emission reduction credits.

The IFC has a much smaller carbon finance program initiated in January 2002 with funding from the Netherlands. While IFC also began its program as a buyer of carbon credits on behalf of donor governments, the Corporation is now shifting toward using its own financial resources to promote private-sector investment in the market.[90] For example, IFC has invested in an agricultural company that provides waste management services to large pig farms in South America. The company provides the farms with bio-digesters to collect and flare methane, with revenues based on generating carbon credits for international sale. IFC is also developing products to address project delivery risks with the expectation that this will address some of the large difference in the value of carbon credits from CDM projects with prices in the EU ETS.

A critical issue raised by the World Bank's involvement in the carbon market has been whether projects have sustainable development benefits. While this is an issue more generally with respect to carbon trading, it is particularly important for a development institution like the World Bank; the Bank should not engage in the carbon market unless projects align with the Bank's poverty alleviation and development mission. This criticism has been made by NGOs skeptical of the Bank's efforts. One NGO argued as follows:

> An analysis of the current [WB] CDM portfolio also shows that despite the Bank's rhetoric the carbon market is bypassing the poorest countries and the poorest communities in developing countries. Investment is focused overwhelmingly on the richer developing countries, and within those countries is going not to projects that deliver sustainable development or alleviate poverty but to projects that involve reductions of gases from chemical facilities, coal mines and landfills.[91]

This accusation reflects some of the inherent tension in the CDM, which on the one hand seeks to identify the lowest-cost GHG abatement opportunities, while on the other hand includes requirements that projects also promote sustainable development, and leaving the latter determination primarily to authorities in the host government.

The Bank is also under pressure to commit more of its funds under management, which may also lead to lower cost and less complicated projects—e.g., the purchase of credits from HFC 23 destruction, which by itself has little potential for larger development impact (although funds will be applied to development as described below). The World Bank 2005 carbon finance strategy paper recognizes these concerns and, in outlining its approach to the future, states that the Bank will:

(i)   Continue to align carbon finance more closely with poverty alleviation and locally sustainable development ensuring that smaller, poorer countries benefit from carbon market development;

(ii) Expand the technology frontiers of the carbon market to ensure that carbon finance and carbon trade supports energy infrastructure and technology transfer;

(iii) Ensure that there is value-added from carbon purchase; and

(iv) Achieve greater integration of carbon finance into the mainstream of bank lending operations.

The Bank also points out that, whatever the source of GHG abatement, revenues can be applied for development purposes: "For example, the Chinese Government is establishing a facility to use 65% of the revenues from the purchase of HFC-23 emission reductions for sustainable development investments in climate-friendly projects and capacity building." Fundamentally, resolving these issues remains a highly worthwhile objective because of the potential financial flows to developing countries—an estimated $2 to $3 billion per year under the current CDM regime, and depending on future emission reduction targets and the extent of participation by industrialized countries, upwards of $100 billion per year under a post-Kyoto agreement.[92]

Another issue is the potential for integrating carbon finance with other sources of investment. With few exceptions, particularly projects to eliminate methane emissions from landfills, carbon revenues alone are insufficient to justify investments otherwise not commercially attractive. For example, carbon finance can enhance the return on a renewable energy project, but typically additional support from local policies, donors, or other sources remains necessary. There may be significant opportunities for linking the GEF and other donor aid to carbon offsets. The former may continue to assume much of the up-front risk in establishing clean energy initiatives, while the latter can provide a much-needed source of revenue for sustainability and replication.

G. The Role of the Global Environment Facility

The one international donor-funded program with a significant focus on financing the incremental costs of responses to climate change is the Global Environment Facility (GEF). The GEF is a multilateral donor fund founded in 1991 to help pay for the incremental costs of investments in developing countries that promote global environmental objectives, e.g., the added costs of renewable energy relative to fossil fuels. In

1994 the GEF was restructured by international agreement with an independent 32-country Council for governance and a CEO and Secretariat for managerial oversight. As noted above, project development and implementation is through defined implementing agencies: the World Bank, UN agencies, and four regional development banks. Since then, donors have pledged a total of about $6.5 billion, with an average of 35% to 40% allocated for clean energy projects.[93] The GEF serves as the financial mechanism for the conventions on climate change and biodiversity, and also supports activities in support of conventions on ozone depletion, desertification, and persistent organic pollutants (POPs).[94]

For the four-year period beginning July 2006, the GEF has roughly $3 billion—much less than these objectives require, but given that funding is available on a grant or highly concessional basis, still quite substantial. Between 35% and 40% of these funds are to be allocated to climate change, or up to about $300 million per year.

The priorities and eligibility criteria for GEF funding are defined in policies periodically reviewed and revised by its governing body, the GEF Council. The GEF approach to energy projects was originally outlined in an *operational strategy* and three *operational programs*.[95] These allowed for subsidies to reduce the cost of technologies with the promise of avoiding substantial GHG emissions and commercial competitiveness with increases in scale (consistent with the level of GEF resources), and measures to remove barriers to commercially competitive but underutilized efficiency and renewable energy technologies. The former rationale has been applied to solar thermal power plants, biomass gasification, and grid-connected photovoltaics; the latter has been used to justify low-interest financing, appliance labeling, and energy service companies as strategies to promote energy efficiency, and a range of demonstrations, financing for solar businesses, micro-credit, utility reforms, and other strategies for promoting solar home systems, wind energy, and to a lesser extent biogas, solar water heating, and improved cookstoves.[96] Initially the GEF had a very limited mandate to provide financing for adaptation measures, but this role has been expanded by recent decisions of the UNFCCC.

In its initial years, the GEF had more resources than eligible projects. As demand grew over time, the importance of using funds strategically increased. Further pressure on resources occurred due to political decisions to add new roles to the GEF, including projects to address land degradation and POPs, increasing the demand for resources. With experience, it became apparent that some project concepts were more successful than others, adding to the need to refine the initial funding strategies. As a starting point, the GEF concluded that resources had to be used in a more catalytic way, with greater emphasis on the sustainability and replicability of results.

One way of doing this was to put more emphasis on leverage—for example, using resources to achieve lasting policy reforms and domestic financial approaches with a lasting impact. In May 2003, two projects were included that illustrate this approach. One in Mexico will support utility policies to expand the role of renewable energy, particularly wind energy systems, as a source of grid-connected power.[97] Similar to a "reverse auction" approach used in California, a financial mechanism developed under the project will use GEF funds to augment the base tariff awarded to project developers bidding the lowest total cost level required for their projects. A second project in Eastern Europe is designed to develop a sustainable financing mechanism for geothermal energy in the region.

The program for commercializing new technologies is unique in development circles, which traditionally avoid the use of cutting-edge equipment that has not been commercially demonstrated due to its higher cost and greater risk. The GEF approach is based on investments in projects that promote learning and economies of scale. The focus is on "those technologies that have been proven or demonstrated on a commercial scale but that have not found significant application in recipient countries because of high technology transfer costs, replication costs, or commercial risks associated with the new technologies in new operational environments." Over the past decade, the GEF has committed in excess of a billion dollars—primarily in the form of grants—with the aim of accelerating the commercialization of fuel cells, concentrating solar power plants, and other climate-friendly energy technologies. Few of these projects have so far been implemented, but much has been learned, and there is some basis for expecting improved results in the future.[98]

H. Examples of GEF-Funded Clean Energy Projects

- A World Bank project in Bangladesh, Rural Electrification and Renewable Energy Development, offers an example of the integration of renewable energy technologies and capacity-building efforts. This project promotes solar energy in rural areas implemented by rural electricity cooperatives, community-based organizations, NGOs, microfinance institutions and the private sector. The project supports: a) increasing awareness of solar home systems (SHS) among consumers and providers; b) building technical and management capacity to design, implement and evaluate SHS programs; c) providing technical and business development support to implementing institutions; d) introducing standards and programs for testing and certification; and e) financing grants to buy-down capital costs and increase affordability of SHS. The project is expected to result in the installation of 65,000 solar systems, displacing fossil and traditional biomass energy in rural areas. The project budget is $38.6 million, with $8.2 million from GEF.

- In two projects focused on biomass power generation, the GEF has laid the groundwork for commercialization of power production from bagasse and other

agricultural resources in Brazil. A UNDP project with $8 million from GEF established the technical and environmental feasibility of the technology in the Brazilian market, and a $44 million World Bank/IFC project is seeking to demonstrate new technology on a commercial scale in partnership with local private interests. In the course of the two projects, technology has been developed to harvest and use locally abundant sugar cane wastes in a more efficient and environmentally beneficial manner.

- With $6.8 million from the GEF, the UN Environment Programme (UNEP) supported a Solar and Wind Energy Resource Assessment to help establish minimum baseline information needed to identify the potential for utilizing these renewable resources in developing countries.

- A new IFC project will promote the creation of a market for light-emitting diodes (LEDs) as a source of low-power, high-quality lighting for rural, off-grid consumers. The project will begin in Kenya and Ghana and has attracted significant interest from major manufacturers and others in the lighting industry worldwide.[99]

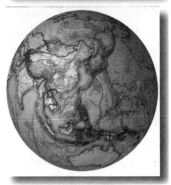

In several decisions beginning at COP 7, the UNFCCC has given guidance to the GEF to undertake additional support for adaptation measures.[100] In the past, this objective was difficult to reconcile with the GEF requirement for "global environmental benefits," as adaptation funding can be viewed as conceptually closer to compensation for damages. GEF funding for adaptation projects is possible when projects can be linked to biodiversity or other global benefits, and in addition some donors have voluntarily created two new adaptation funds under GEF management, a Least Developed Countries Fund and a Special Climate Change Fund. Approximately $150 million has been pledged for these funds to date. Much larger sums will be available through the Kyoto Protocol Adaptation Fund, to be supported by 2% of the proceeds of CDM CERs. The parties to the UNFCCC are still negotiating the question of how this new fund will be administered, with the GEF as one option. As noted in the context of World Bank climate programs, adaptation measures will need to be integrated with mainstream development activities in areas such as agriculture and water resources. Some projects have already been proposed along these lines, but bringing these diverse programs and priorities together will be a significant operational challenge.

I. GEF Experience with New Energy Technology Projects

International development agencies have historically avoided new technologies, based on the view that developing countries are difficult settings in which to do even conventional projects, and that therefore the additional technical and other risks associated with new technologies should be avoided. However, this view has been subject to reconsideration with the advent of centers of technological excellence, and especially manufacturing leadership in China and India. The widespread use of cell phones even in relatively remote countries also illustrates that new technology, even the most sophisticated, can sometimes be more appropriate and effective than conventional ones. Howard Geller explains, "As developing countries progress economically and socially, there is the potential to 'leapfrog' over the inefficient, fossil fuel–based, and polluting energy production and consumption patterns found in industrialized nations."[101] Geller gives as an example the Brazilian ethanol program, in which Brazil applied state of the art technology to produce ethanol from sugar cane with policies to facilitate its distribution and use as a substitute for petroleum.

Much of the commitment of GEF funds for new technology commercialization has gone for two technologies—concentrating solar power plants and fuel cells. Close to $60 million was proposed for fuel cell bus projects in five countries, and almost $200 million for four central solar power plant (CSP) projects.[102] These projects have struggled to achieve implementation despite the large commitment of grant funds; the majority of the projects most likely will be canceled after five or more years of negotiation. (Status reports are available at the GEF Web site.) Another proposed GEF project would support integrated coal gasification combined–cycle (IGCC) in China. This technology has generated considerable interest as it offers the potential for burning coal with greater efficiency and substantially lower emissions of conventional pollutants as well as GHG emissions, and potentially removal and sequestration of carbon to achieve close to zero net emissions. However, the promise of GEF support has so far been insufficient to overcome the myriad obstacles to developing the project. These projects were approved as commercialization efforts but arguably were mainly demonstration programs. Implementation difficulties have been underestimated in past approaches, leading to a letdown on the promise of the GEF in this area, and so far a failure to trigger large-scale impacts.

A GEF scientific advisory panel reviewed experience with these projects and concluded that they suffered from several problems related to the large capital investments required, the absence of a supporting policy environment, and the lack of a strong local champion with a substantial commitment to the project.[103] Insufficient response from international technology providers was another common problem. More conventional technologies—or at least those with costs closer to being competitive—are more appealing in the short term as they provide more immediate economic benefit at lower risk. A more general conclusion is that technology commercialization requires more than grant money, as important as that may be. Two agency reports in 2005 expand on this point. In reviewing its experience with fuel-cell bus projects, UNDP notes that its projects have several distinct functions, including convening disparate parties relevant to the process and facilitating information exchange between countries, private players, and other demonstration efforts.[104] A

WB review of its experience with CSP projects emphasizes the need for greater linkage to developments within the larger global industry.

A case study of the Chinese automobile industry highlights some of the complexities associated with the concept of leapfrogging.[105] On the one hand, foreign auto technology transferred to China beginning in 1983 resulted in modernization equivalent to skipping about 20 years of technology development. However, foreign companies have been reluctant to transfer more recent technological developments such as hybrids and fuel cells due to higher costs, lack of local capabilities for production, and potentially intellectual property concerns. The industry may also need to undertake a number of primary reforms, such as consolidation, increased emphasis on research and development, and a supportive policy environment. "By contrast, in the successful case of leapfrogging in mobile phones in China, the cost and market incentives were all strong. There was substantial consumer demand, the technology was coveted by the Chinese government, the survival of existing players was not threatened, and the revenues of existing Chinese firms were actually enhanced by leapfrogging to mobile phones."[106]

While there is merit in closer coordination with development activities in emerging economies, there is also an opportunity for more focused cooperation with private-sector innovators. The IFC has attempted to overcome these challenges through greater emphasis on partnership with private investors. An IFC-administered 1 MW grid-connected solar cell project was successfully implemented by a utility in the Philippines and three stationary fuel cell projects (each about 1 MW) for industrial applications are expected to be awarded by June 2006 and to be fully operational within roughly a year thereafter.[107] A project approved by the GEF in June 2005 authorizes up to $44.5 million for a commercial-scale pilot using new technology allowing a substantial increase in power generation from the combustion of sugar cane wastes; the project is structured in two phases so that most of the funding only becomes available if a major private investor is identified.

A series of projects administered by the IFC works with local banks to promote lending for clean energy enterprises and projects. GEF resources are used to provide loan officers with training in evaluating new risks as well as partial risk guarantees to reduce the risks in undertaking the new loan activity. IFC typically provides a parallel credit line and shares in the risks. The initial projects were in Hungary and Eastern Europe where banking was most established, but subsequent projects have extended the concept to Russia, China, and most recently the Philippines.

IV. Trans-boundary and International Adjudication Arising from Climate Change

As the regulatory regime for climate change is still at an early stage and damages attributable to anthropogenic climate change remain difficult to establish, relatively few legal actions have so far been brought, as discussed in Chapter 6. However, several legal proceedings have already been brought or threatened seeking remedies for trans-boundary or international injuries associated with climate change.

The prospect of remedies based on enforcement of public international law was until relatively recently viewed as the province of nation states as in the context of trade disputes. This view is gradually evolving with the recognition that "there are mechanisms and strategies for effective enforcement of international environmental law by civil society." From an advocacy perspective, "this function of civil society is not only crucial but essential when it is a state or group of states that are the perpetrators of environmental degradation."[108] A range of strategies have evolved in recent years:[109]

> **... several legal proceedings have already been brought or threatened seeking remedies for trans-boundary or international injuries associated with climate change.**

1. Human rights violations may be alleged for violation of the International Covenant on Civil and Political Rights, or if protection of a non-human species and its habitat are threatened, a submission to UNESCO

2. Advocating for international finance and trade institutions to enforce environmental and public health standards. For example, the North American Free Trade Agreement (NAFTA) includes a procedure for a petition before a special regional tribunal, the North American Commission on Environmental Cooperation.[110]

3. Intervention as *amicus curiae* in trade or investment disputes filed by governments or investors or any measure designed to protect species or its habitats;

4. Where provisions of a multilateral environmental agreement may be alleged to have been violated, seek to raise the issue with the Convention Secretariat and parties, where possible linked to an action before the agreement's dispute resolution process.

5. Bring a complaint in an international tribunal with relevant jurisdiction, such as the International Court of Justice, the Permanent Court on Arbitration, and the European Court of Justice.

6. Enforcing international environmental law through domestic law mechanisms, e.g., the Alien Tort Claims Act and the National Environmental Policy Act.

Several actions have already been brought or contemplated based on these diverse approaches. At least two cases have already been brought based on the alleged need to

evaluate climate change risks of federal actions to permit or finance fossil fuel–related projects. *Border Plant Working Group v. DOE and BLM,* Case No. 02-CV-513-IEG (POR) (S.D. Cal, May 2, 2003) was a challenge to a Finding of No Significant Impact by DOE and BLM in conjunction with permits and federal rights-of-way to connect an electricity substation in California with two new power plants constructed in Mexico. The court held that at least part of the planned construction was specifically attributable to one of the transmission lines and thus was an effect of the federal action. The court also held that the environmental assessment violated NEPA by failing to consider the climate change effects of the CO_2 emissions from the power plants.[111]

Friends of the Earth v. Watson, No. 02-4106, 2005 WL 2035596 (N.D. Cal. Aug. 23, 2005) was a suit brought by two environmental organizations and several municipalities against two government agencies, the Overseas Private Investment Corporation (OPIC) and the Export-Import Bank, challenging the failure to prepare an environmental impact statement on the climate change implications of their lending. The district court rejected the agencies' motion for summary judgment including challenges to plaintiffs' standing to sue, recognizing that in order to justify the procedural claims associated with impact statements, it need only be shown that the agencies' decision could be influenced.[112]

In December 2005, two environmental organizations, CIEL and Earth Justice, petitioned the Inter-American Commission on Human Rights on behalf of the Inuit, a native tribe living in the Arctic. A favorable outcome could provide the basis for a referral to the Inter-American Court of Human Rights. While the United States is not subject to the Commission's jurisdiction, the groups see some benefit in achieving formal recognition of the link between climate change and human rights. The advocacy groups also argue that a finding of a human rights violation could be the basis for a claim under the Alien Torts Claim Act.[113]

These cases illustrate the likelihood that as evidence of climate change mounts, environmental organizations and other interested parties will pursue a variety of adjudicatory forums to publicize their concerns and pursue possible remedies. "Would-be plaintiffs will no doubt refine their tactics, leaving significant emitters of greenhouse gases at risk of additional litigation."[114]

V. Conclusions

The linkages between trade, development, and climate change are co-evolving as these three closely related fields continue to undergo rapid change. Economic development and recent continued growth in trade is associated with much of the technology and financing for the rise in developing country greenhouse gas emissions. Each of these areas has its own specialized institutions, governance, and legal frameworks, and coordination among them is still at a relatively early stage. A likely source for many issues in the near future may be the evolution of carbon trading. The creation of a successful global trading system will require bringing together these divergent systems, a considerable challenge but one that could be a key step toward the next phase of the international climate change regime.

Endnotes

1. *See generally* the Web site of the WTO, www.wto.org. For a recent overview of trade and environment issues, see NATHALIE BERNASCONI-OSTERWALDER ET AL., ENVIRONMENT AND TRADE: A GUIDE TO WTO JURISPRUDENCE (2005).

2. The Doha talks came to at least a temporarily unsuccessful conclusion in July 2004 when the major parties agreed continued negotiations were unlikely to be successful. *See* Brainard, *U.S. Shares Blame for Trade Talk Collapse*, WASH. POST, July 28, 2006 (http://www.washingtonpost.com/wp-dyn/content/article/2006/07/27/AR2006072701257.html).

3. *See generally* the World Bank Web site for background information, www.worldbank.org. One of the better recent books about the World Bank is by Sebastian Mallaby, *The World's Banker: A Story of Failed States, Financial Crises, and the Wealth and Poverty of Nations* (2004). The International Monetary Fund, or IMF, is a sister organization also founded by international agreement in 1944 at Bretton Woods. The IMF monitors national economic circumstances and provides loans to governments on concessional terms in order to avoid economic crises. The IMF and World Bank are operationally and financially distinct but are linked through a Joint Ministerial Committee (www.IMF.org).

4. The IFC has a separate Web site, www.ifc.org.

5. *See* www.miga.org. The World Bank Group includes one additional institution, the International Center for Settlement of Investment Disputes, created by international agreement in 1966 to promote development by providing a forum for the settlement of investment disputes. *See generally* http://www.worldbank.org/icsid/index.html.

6. www.thegef.org.

7. www.prototypecarbonfund.com.

8. www.ifc.org/carbonfinance.

9. For a brief background and overview of the G8 process, see http://www.auswaertiges-amt.de/diplo/en/Aussenpolitik/GlobaleHerausforderungen/Institutionen/G8-Gruppe-Ziele.html.

10. Robert Watson, *A Clean Energy Pathway*, ENVTL. FINANCE, May 2006, at 16.

11. *See* Crescencia Maurer & Ruchi Bhandari, *The Climate of Export Credit Agencies*, WORLD RESOURCES INST. CLIMATE NOTES (May 2000).

12. Crescencia Maurer & Smita Nakhooda, *Financing Carbon: Export Credit Agencies and Climate Change*, WRI EARTH TREND NOTES (Dec. 2003) (on-line: http://earthtrends.wri.org/features/view_feature.php?theme=3&fid=49).

13. Gallagher, *Is NAFTA Working for Mexico?*, Env. Forum, May/June 2006, at 21-27; M. Wolf, Why Globalization Works (2004); Douglas Irwin, Free Trade Under Fire (2d ed. 2005).

14. Gallagher, *id.* at 22.

15. Grossman and Krueger made many important assumptions and adjustments in their work, including adjusting income numbers for purchasing power parity. This hypothesis has produced what Gallagher terms a "cottage industry" of academic studies. *Id.*

16. *See generally* David Stern, *The Rise and Fall of the Environmental Kuznets Curve*, 32 World Dev. 1419 (2004). *See also* J. Frankel & A. Rose, *Is Trade Good or Bad for the Environment? Sorting Out the Causality*, 87 Rev. Econ. & Stats. (2005).

17. Gallagher estimated the timing of a reduction in air pollution for Mexico based on turning points of $7,500, $10,000, and $15,000 and the associated environmental damage during the growth period. He found that Mexico would not reach the lowest turning point until 2028 and the highest until 2097, with the range of discounted damages from $79 billion to $270 billion, about one-fifth to three-fifths of the country's GDP.

18. Gallagher, *supra* note 13, at 8, 25-33 ("the marginal costs of pollution abatement in the United States are such a relatively small expense that they are not major factors" in location decisions).

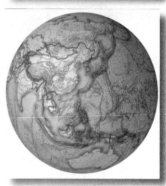

19. *Id.* at 27.

20. For a recent overview of trade and climate change issues, see Cinnamon Carlarne, *The Kyoto Protocol and the WTO: Reconciling Tensions Between Free Trade and Environmental Objectives*, 17 Colo. J. Int'l Envtl. L. & Pol'y 45 (2006).

21. Charnovitz, *Trade and Climate: Potential Conflicts and Synergies*, in Beyond Kyoto: Advancing the International Effort Against Climate Change 141 (Pew Center on Global Climate Change 2003).

22. IPCC, Climate Change 2001: Working Group III: Mitigation, Section 6.4.2.

23. Most authorities do not foresee trade issues associated with carbon trading as a "service." *See, e.g.,* Frankel; *but see* Andrew Green, *Climate Change, Regulatory Policy and the WTO: How Constraining Are Trade Rules?*, 8 J. Int'l Econ. L., 143, 145 (2005). If a host country under the CDM were to impose more stringent rules on foreign project developers than on its own nationals, a trade complaint might arise. Glen Weiser, *The Clean Development Mechanism Versus the World Trade Organization: Can Free-Market Greenhouse Gas Emissions Abatement Survive Free Trade?*, 11 Geo. Int'l Envtl. L.R. 531 (1999).

24. *See generally* Gary Sampson, Trade, Environment, and the WTO: the Post-Seattle Agenda 50-60 (2000).

25. *Id.* at 50.

26. *See* World Bank, Clean Energy for Development (2006), p. 9 Box 3 ("Subsidies") and p. 21 n.23.

27. Jeffrey Frankel, *Climate and Trade: Links Between Kyoto Protocol and WTO*, 47 Envt. 8, 13 (Sept. 2005); *see also* Charnovitz at 160 ("So far, attention to energy within the WTO has occurred mainly in negotiations for accession . . . in which governments applying for membership have been pressed to eliminate dual pricing (i.e., low domestic prices in energy-exporting countries.)").

28. STEPHEN ANDERSEN & K. SHARMA, PROTECTING THE OZONE LAYER: THE UNITED NATIONS HISTORY 353 (2002). *See also* n.39.

29. Frankel, *supra* note 27.

30. Charnovitz, *supra* note 21 at 160.

31. The current focus of trade negotiations is on reducing agricultural subsidies and trade barriers, which is expected to be of most benefit to low-income developing countries, as they have the most agriculturally dependent economies. As of the time of this writing (July 2006) it appears that these negotiations are failing, largely because major developing countries refuse to reduce their trade barriers, whereas the U.S. and EU refuse to reduce their agricultural trade barriers sufficiently. *See, e.g.*, G-20 Press Statement, June 29, 2006 ("Developing countries should not be expected to pay for the elimination of distortions that affect international trade in agricultural products. . . . This is the key to unlock current negotiations in agriculture."). The G-20 includes many of the largest agricultural-exporting developing countries as well as the largest GHG emitters, including Brazil, China, India, Indonesia, Mexico, and South Africa.

32. *See generally* Julian Newman, *Illegal Trade in Ozone-Depleting Substances, in* S. ANDERSEN & K. SARMA, PROTECTING THE OZONE LAYER 184-85 (2002), *and UNEP, Illegal Trade in Ozone Depleting Substances: Is There a Hole in the Montreal Protocol?*, OZONACTION NEWSLETTER SPECIAL SUPP. NO. 6 (2001).

33. ROBERT PERCIVAL ET AL., ENVIRONMENTAL REGULATION: LAW, SCIENCE & POLICY 1078-93 (5th ed. 2006).

34. Nathalie Bernasconi-Osterwalder, *Trade and the Environment: Where Do We Stand After Doha?*, Presentation at the Conference on WTO's Contribution to Sustainable Development Governance, Paris, Oct. 20-21, 2005 (*available at* http://www.ciel.org/Publications/IDDRIpresentation_Bernasconi_24Oct05.pdf).

35. Speech by Pascal Lamy, *quoted in* Bernasconi-Osterwalder, *id.*

36. *See generally* ozone.unep.org. Article 4 of the Montreal Protocol on Substances that Deplete the Ozone Layer regulates trade with non-parties and restricts both imports by parties from non-parties, and exports from parties to non-parties. An interesting procedure allows for treating non-parties the same as parties if they are shown to be in full compliance with the requirements of the Protocol. Provision was also made but never implemented for restrictions on imports of products made with, but not containing, restricted substances. Article 4(4). As a means of facilitating compliance, specific provision was also made for a system of licensing the import and export of controlled substances. *See* Article 4(B).

37. www.cites.org. CITES. The Convention on International Trade in Endangered Species of Wild Fauna and Flora was drafted as a result of a resolution adopted in 1963 at a meeting of members of IUCN (The World Conservation Union). The text of the Convention was agreed at a meeting of representatives of 80 countries in Washington, D.C., on March 3, 1973, and on July 1, 1975, CITES entered into force. Because the trade in wild animals and plants crosses borders between countries, the effort to regulate it requires international cooperation to safeguard certain species. CITES was conceived in the spirit of such cooperation. Today, it accords varying degrees of protection to more than 30,000 species of animals and plants, whether they are traded as live specimens, fur coats or dried herbs. Protection of species is based on technically reviewed, periodically revised lists that trigger requirements for import and export permits (see Article 3).

38. Charnovitz, *supra* note 21 at 154.

39. ANDERSEN & SARMA, *supra* note 28 at 76, 79. Sarma, a former senior UN official managing the Montreal Protocol process, has emphasized the significance of taking into account the desire for universal ratification in the design of the Protocol. Sarma, *Compliance with the Montreal Protocol, in* MAKING LAW WORK: ENVIRONMENTAL COM-

PLIANCE & SUSTAINABLE DEVELOPMENT 287-306 (D. Zaelke, D. Kaniaru & E. Kruzikova eds., 2005).

40. Article XX(b) and (g) of the GATT. With respect to its application to the Montreal Protocol, see RICHARD BENEDICK, OZONE DIPLOMACY (1991), and ANDERSEN & SARMA at 76, 79, 128, 353-54. The precise meaning of these terms is the subject of detailed parsing by numerous authorities. For a recent example, *see* BERNASCONI-OSTERWALDER ET AL., ENVIRONMENT AND TRADE: A GUIDE TO WTO JURISPRUDENCE (2005).

41. This issue is discussed at length in OFFICE OF TECHNOLOGY ASSESSMENT, TRADE AND ENVIRONMENT 46-52 (1992).

42. IPCC, *supra* note 22.

43. HUGH SADDLER, FRANK MULLER & CLARA CUEVAS, COMPETITIVENESS AND CARBON PRICING: BORDER ADJUSTMENTS FOR GREENHOUSE POLICIES (Australia Institute, April 2006).

44. Andrew Green, *Climate Change, Regulatory Policy and the WTO: How Constraining Are Trade Rules?*, 8 J. INT'L ECON. L., 143, 145 (2005). *But see* Jacob Werksman, *Greenhouse Gas Emissions Trading and the WTO*, 8 REV. EURO. CMTY. & INT'L ENVTL. L. 251 (1999) for a more optimistic assessment.

45. Carlarne; Frankel; BERNASCONI-OSTERWALDER ET AL; CHARNOVITZ; DANIEL ESTY, GREENING THE GATT: TRADE, ENVIRONMENT AND THE FUTURE (1999); Green; Gary Sampson, *WTO Rules and Climate Change: The Need for Policy Coherence, in* GLOBAL CLIMATE GOVERNANCE: A REPORT ON THE INTER-LINKAGES BETWEEN THE KYOTO PROTOCOL AND OTHER MULTILATERAL REGIMES, B. Chambers ed. (1999); Thomas Brewer, *The Trade Regime and the Climate Regime: Institutional Evolution and Adaptation*, 3 CLIMATE POLICY 329 (2003); Sanford Gaines, *International Trade, Environmental Protection and Development as a Sustainable Development Triangle*, 11 RECEIL 259 (2002).

46. HOWARD MANN & STEPHEN PORTER, THE STATE OF TRADE AND ENVIRONMENTAL LAW vii (IISD/CIEL 2003).

47. BERNASCONI-OSTERWALDER ET AL., supra note 1.

48. Andrew Green, *Climate Change, Regulatory Policy and the WTO: How Constraining Are Trade Rules?*, 8 J. INT'L ECON. L. 143, 145 (2005).

49. *E.g.*, BERNASCONI-OSTERWALDER; Esty; Robert Howse, *The WTO Dispute Settlement Mechanism: Trade, Environment and the Role of the NGOs*, 4 J. WORLD INTELL. PROP. 277 (2001).

50. The history and current status of the Millennium Development Goals is reported at a United Nations Web site, www.un.org/milleniumgoals.

51. *See, e.g.*, UNITED NATIONS, THE MILLENNIUM DEVELOPMENT GOALS REPORT 2006. The Report shows progress in some areas, particularly a reduction in global poverty, extension of primary education, reduction of child mortality, and the fight against malaria. However, sub-Saharan Africa lags behind in many areas. The baseline for the assessment of most of the MDG targets is 1990, and for most of the indicators 2004 is the latest year for which data is available. Statistical shortcomings are a problem in many developing countries, a problem recognized in the report.

52. VIJAY MODI ET AL., ENERGY SERVICES FOR THE MILLENNIUM DEVELOPMENT GOALS (2005). *See also* Christopher Flavin & Molly Hull Aeck, Energy for Development: The Potential Role of Renewable Energy in Meeting the Millennium Development Goals (paper

prepared for the REN21 Network by the Worldwatch Institute 2005, *available at* www.ren21.net).

53. *Id.* at 10-12.

54. *Id.* at 57.

55. *Id.* at Appendix II, pp. 77-85.

56. Robert Socolow & Stephen Pacala, *A Plan to Keep Carbon in Check*, Scientific Am., Sept. 2006, at 50-57.

57. Socolow, Energy Week Presentation April 2006 (citing calculations based on IEA and WEO reference scenarios), *available at* http://web.worldbank.org/WBSITE/EXTERNAL/TOPICS/EXTENERGY/0,,contentMDK:20849147~pagePK:210058~piPK:210062~theSitePK:336806,00.html?.

58. *See, e.g.*, ch. 5, *World Coal Markets*, in Energy Information Administration, International Energy Outlook 2006 (U.S. DOE 2006), *available at* http://www.eia.doe.gov/oiaf/ieo/coal.html (predicting world coal consumption in the 2006 reference case nearly doubles from 2003 to 2030, with more than 80% of this growth taking place outside the OECD).

59. *China Gains on U.S. in Emissions*, Int'l Herald Tribune, Nov. 8, 2006, at 1.

60. Martin Hoffert, *quoted in* Wayt Gibbs, *Plan B for Energy*, Scientific Am., Sept. 2006, at 103, 104.

61. *Id.*

62. Michael Klein & Tim Harford, The Market for Aid 44 (2005).

63. *Id.* Unofficial flows include numerous sources, the most important of which are foreign direct investment—increasingly in the form of equity rather than debt; migrant works' remittances (particularly important in lower-income countries); assistance from NGOs; and loans to corporations without a sovereign guarantee.

64. *Id.* at 51

65. Ada Izaguirre, *Private Infrastructure: Activity Down by 13 Percent in 2003*, Pub. Pol'y J. No. 274 (World Bank, Sept. 2004), *available at* http://ppi.worldbank.org/book/274izaguirre.pdf.

66. *See* Bradford Gentry, *Private capital flows and climate change: Maximizing private investment in developing countries under the Kyoto Protocol*, in Climate Change and Development 187-99, L. Gomez-Echeverri ed. (2000). A key point is that the investment requirements for energy infrastructure to keep pace with economic growth will be enormous with or without efforts to address climate change. For example, the projected costs for maintaining the North American gasoline economy over the next 30 years are on the order of $1.3 *trillion*, of which more than half will be invested in oil-exporting developing countries. Joan Ogden, *High Hopes for Hydrogen*, Scientific Am., Sept. 2006, at 94, 100. Another perspective is that the relative costs of carbon capture and storage are within economic feasibility if spread out over decades, but become exceedingly costly should it be necessary to absorb them in a short period. David Hawkins, Daniel Lashof & Robert Williams, *What to Do About Coal*, Scientific Am., Sept. 2006, at 68, 75 (cost of total carbon capture and storage from world electricity over next 200 years is $1.8 trillion, 0.07 percent of gross world product over the period).

67. The Intergovernmental Panel on Climate Change (IPCC), an international consensus-based review of climate change science and policy, summarizes a range of studies on the potential for low-cost or cost-saving reductions in greenhouse gas emissions in developing as well as industrialized countries. Bert Metz et al., Climate Change 2001: Mitigation (Cambridge Univ. Pr., 2001). These studies consistently show large technical possibilities for low-cost reductions relative to business-as-usual projections, e.g., negative costs to achieve an 80% reduction from the Brazilian baseline and a 36% reduction for India from the 2025 baseline. J. Hourcade & P. Shukla, lead au-

thors, GLOBAL, REGIONAL, AND NATIONAL COSTS AND ANCILLARY BENEFITS OF MITIGATION, *id*, table 8.3, p. 511. *See also* various country studies published by the Pew Center on Climate Change (www.pewclimatecenter.org).

68. IEA, TOWARD A SUSTAINABLE ENERGY FUTURE 211 (OECD/IEA).

69. *Id.* at 214.

70. UN DEVELOPMENT PROGRAMME, WORLD ENERGY ASSESSMENT 36.

71. INTERNATIONAL ENERGY AGENCY, WORLD ENERGY INVESTMENT OUTLOOK (2003). The sums involved are impressive: a total of $16 trillion, or $550 billion a year on average, to finance energy supply infrastructure worldwide between 2001 and 2030, of which about 60% is for electricity. This assumes 3% average global economic growth, and corresponding rates of 1.7% per year for energy and 1.6% for oil.

72. ENERGY SECTOR MANAGEMENT ASSISTANCE PROGRAM, ECONOMIC DEVELOPMENT, CLIMATE CHANGE, AND ENERGY SECURITY (Energy and Mining Sector Board, World Bank, 2002).

73. RAFAEL DOMINGUEZ, FERNANDO MANIBOG & STEPHAN WEGNER, POWER FOR DEVELOPMENT: A REVIEW OF THE WORLD BANK GROUP'S EXPERIENCE WITH PRIVATE PARTICIPATION IN THE ELECTRICITY SECTOR (World Bank Operations Evaluation Dept. 2003). The social consequences and governance issues created by these reforms proved challenging; the Bank evaluation report found the portfolio of these projects about "half-successful in pursuing the objectives of its reform agenda." *Id.* at 14. IFC projects, which tended to be in higher-income countries, tended to be more successful. The challenge associated with privatization of power in Georgia is the subject of a recent documentary, POWER TRIP (www.powertripthemovie. com).

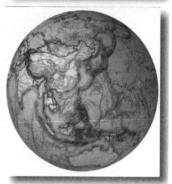

74. Xu Yi-chong, *The Myth of the Single Solution: Electricity Reforms and the World Bank*, 31 ENERGY 802 (May-June 2006); J.H. Williams & R. Ghanadan, *Electricity Reform in Developing and Transition Countries: A Reappraisal*, 31 ENERGY 815-44 (May-June 2006).

75. *See* John Besant-Jones & Bernard Tenenbaum, *Lessons from California's Power Crisis*, FINANCE & DEV., Sept. 2001, at 24-28.

76. Ray Tomkins, *Extending Rural Electrification: a Survey of Innovative Approaches, in* CONTRACTING FOR PUBLIC SERVICES: OUTPUT BASED AID AND ITS APPLICATIONS, Penelope Brook & Suzanne Smith eds. (World Bank 2001).

77. Press Release, World Bank, Reducing the Gas Flaring, June 30, 2006. *See* www.worldbank.org/ggfr.

78. World Bank Private Participation in Infrastructure Database (ppi.worldbank.org).

79. IFC, Press Release, IFC to Mobilize Private Sector Investment in Vietnam's Power Sector (2006), *available at* http://www.ifc.org/ifcext/media.nsf/Content/Vietnam_Power_Sector).

80. WORLD BANK GROUP PROGRESS ON RENEWABLE ENERGY AND ENERGY EFFICIENCY: FISCAL YEAR 2005.

81. IFC, 2005 SUSTAINABILITY REPORT 55-56 (2006).

82. G8 Gleneagles 2005, CLIMATE CHANGE, CLEAN ENERGY AND SUSTAINABLE DEVELOPMENT, paras. 5, 8 and 11.

83. WORLD BANK, CLEAN ENERGY AND DEVELOPMENT: TOWARDS AN INVESTMENT FRAMEWORK, released by the Development Committee April 5, 2006 (hereafter "Clean Energy and

Development"), *available at* http://siteresources.worldbank.org/DEVCOMMINT/Docu-mentation/20890696/DC2006-0002(E)-CleanEnergy.pdf.

84. *Id.* at 21-22.

85. WORLD BANK, AN INVESTMENT FRAMEWORK FOR CLEAN ENERGY AND DEVELOPMENT: A PROGRESS REPORT, Sept. 5, 2006 (D.C. 2006-0012) (hereafter "Progress Report").

86. WB, Clean Energy and Development, *supra* note 83, at 119-20.

87. *Id.* at 28-30.

88. *Id.* at 115-16; WORLD BANK, THE ROLE OF THE WORLD BANK IN CARBON FINANCE: AN APPROACH FOR FURTHER ENGAGEMENT (Dec. 2005), *available at* www.carbonfinance.org.

89. WB, Clean Energy and Development, *supra* note 83, at 115.

90. IFC's Carbon Finance Activities, *Information Note to the Board of Directors* (2006).

91. CDM WATCH, THE WORLD BANK AND THE CARBON MARKET: RHETORIC AND REALITY (April 2005).

92. WORLD BANK, THE ROLE OF THE WORLD BANK IN CARBON FINANCE, *supra* note 88, at 12. With a 450 ppm CO_2 cap for the period 2013-2050, annualized North to South payments are estimated to be between $27 billion and $175 billion (2005 dollars). With a 550 ppm cap, annualized payments drop to between $4 billion and $90 billion. *Id.*

93. Based on annual reports and information available at the GEF Web site, about $1.4 billion has been committed to about 140 clean energy projects with a total value in excess of $4.5 billion in more than 75 countries.

94. *See generally* www.thegef.org and description in the introductory section.

95. GEF operational policies and project documents are available at the Web site, www.thegef.org.

96. Project documents and numerous evaluation reports are available at the GEF Web site. *See also* Eric Martinot et al., *Renewable energy markets in developing countries*, 27 ANN. REV.OF ENERGY & ENVT. 309 (2002).

97. World Bank, Press Release 2006/509/LAC, Mexico: World Bank Approves $25 Million for Renewable Energy (June 29, 2006), *available at* http://web.worldbank.org/ W B S I T E / E X T E R N A L / N E W S / 0,,contentMDK:20980382~pagePK:34370~piPK:34424~theSitePK: 4607,00.html.

98. Alan Miller, *Commercializing New Energy Technologies to Reduce GHG Emissions in Developing Countries: Some Experience and Lessons Learned*, 3 ABA SECTION OF ENERGY, ENVT. & RESOURCES NEWSL. 10 (2006)

99. www.ifc.org/led.

100. WB, Clean Energy and Development, *supra* note 83, at 34; GEF, Status Report on the Climate Change Funds (GEF C.28/4/Rev.1, June 2006).

101. HOWARD GELLER, ENERGY REVOLUTION: POLICIES FOR A SUSTAINABLE FUTURE 196 (2003).

102. These projects contemplate the deployment of fields of mirrors to focus heat on a central receiver to generate steam to power a turbine. *Assessment of the World Bank / GEF Strategy for the Market Development of Concentrating Solar Thermal Power* (GEF Information Paper, GEF/C.25/Inf.11, June 2005).

103. STAP Brainstorming Session on the GEF Operational Programme on Reducing the Long-Term Costs of Low Greenhouse Gas-Emitting Energy Technologies (OP#7), March 10-11, 2003, Final Report (*available at* http://stapgef.unep.org/activities/technicalworkshops/index_html).

104. UNDP-GEF Fuel Cell Bus Programme: Update (GEF Information Paper, GEF/C.25/Inf.8, June 2005).

105. Kelly Sims Gallagher, *Limits to Leapfrogging in Energy Technologies? Evidence from the Chinese Automobile Industry*, 34 ENERGY POL'Y 383 (2004).

106. *Id.* at 391.

107. Miller, *supra* note 98.

108. Linda Malone & Scott Pasternack, *Defending the Environment: Civil Society Strategies to Enforce International Environmental Law*, in MAKING LAW WORK: ENVIRONMENTAL COMPLIANCE & SUSTAINABLE DEVELOPMENT, Vol. I, pp. 621-34, 626 (D. Zaelke, D. Kaniaru & E. Kruzikova eds., 2005).

109. *Id.* at 626-29.

110. John Knox, *Citizen Suits in International Environmental Law: the North American Experience*, in MAKING LAW WORK, *supra* note 108, at 615-20.

111. Van Ness Feldman, *Issue Alert: Recent District Court Decision Requires Greater Scrutiny of Environmental Impacts of International Power Projects* (May 9, 2003).

112. See Stephen Kass & Jean McCarroll, *Litigating Climate Change Via State Regulations, Federal Courts*, N.Y. L. J., April 28, 2006, *available at* www.clm.com/pubs/pub-6072310.html.

113. Richard Black, *Inuit Sue U.S. Over Climate Policy* (BBC News, Dec. 8, 2005) (*available at* http://news.bbc.co.uk/1/hi/sci/tech/4511556.stm); CIEL, *Inuit Case* (www.ciel.org/Climate/Climate_Inuit.html). *See also* Emily Gertz, *The Snow Must Go On*, GRIST, July 26, 2005 (http://www.grist.org/news/maindish/2005/07/26/gertz-inuit/).

114. SIDLEY AUSTIN BROWN & WOOD, ENVIRONMENTAL ADVISORY: CLIMATE CHANGE LITIGATION—RECENT DEVELOPMENTS (Oct. 2005).

Part Two

Regional, State, and Local Actions

chapter nine

Regional Initiatives to Reduce Greenhouse Gas Emissions

Eleanor Stein

I. Overview of Regional Approaches

A. Introduction

In the absence of mandatory national controls over greenhouse gas emissions, the emergence of regional initiatives engaging multiple states and, in some cases, provinces, has begun to provide the possibility of tackling the climate change problem on a grander scale than local and state programs. Since 2000, an array of regional initiatives has sought to reduce CO_2 (carbon dioxide) emissions from power plants, increase renewable energy generation, track renewable energy credits, and establish baselines for carbon sequestration.[1] The regional initiatives attempt a more comprehensive emission reduction approach than is possible state-by-state, and if mandatory plans are realized in all regions where these programs are under discussion, the sum total of the regional plans potentially covers much of the United States. In addition to widening the scope of emission reduction beyond the state level, the regional approach tracks the recent regionalization of the nation's electric power markets. Regional transmission organizations now manage much of our electric power trading, reflecting the fungible and cross-border nature of electricity, and the impossibility of either storing it or transporting it great distances economically.

These regional greenhouse gas initiatives are in part possible because of the regionalization of the nation's electric power market. Regional transmission organizations were the creation of the pro-competition policies driving the Federal Energy Regulatory Commission (FERC) in the 1980s and 1990s—policies reflecting global trends toward privatization and deregulation.[2] An unintended consequence of those federal policies is that these regional systems now provide mechanisms for an alternative energy policy that is state-based and region-by-region in form, but that may be national in scope and effect.[3]

The regional approach has attracted attention. It was noted as an alternative to federal inaction by the Inuit in their climate change petition to the Inter-American Human Rights Commission,[4] and was broached in Europe in early projects designed originally to develop and maintain greenhouse gas inventories and, more recently, to monitor Kyoto compliance.[5]

Regional programs for greenhouse gas reductions to date include the Northeast Regional Greenhouse Gas Initiative (RGGI), the New England Governors/Eastern Canadian Premiers' Climate Action Plan, Powering the Plains, the Western Governors' Association Clean and Diversified Energy Initiative, the West Coast Governors Global Warming Initiative, and the Southwest Climate Change Initiative. Under preliminary discussion, but not yet adopted, is a Midwest Regional Greenhouse Gas Registry.

To date, regional greenhouse gas emission reduction initiatives encompass the provinces of Manitoba, Newfoundland, New Brunswick/Labrador, and Quebec; and the states of Alaska, Arizona, California, Colorado, Connecticut, Hawaii, Idaho, Kansas, Maine, Massachusetts, Minnesota, Montana, Nebraska, Nevada, New Hampshire, New Jersey, New Mexico, New York, North Dakota, Oregon, Rhode Island, South Dakota, Texas, Utah, Vermont, Washington, and Wyoming, as well as American Samoa, Guam, and the Northern Mariana Islands.[6] Several states participate in more than one initiative.

Regional initiatives have brought state executives and agencies together, adopted common greenhouse gas emissions reduction targets and schedules, and commissioned staff reports on policy alternatives.[7] Most important, these initiatives have generated baseline or GHG emission inventories for their regions, essential to establish the basis for future reduction programs. To date, no mandatory regional CO_2 emission statutes or regulations have been promulgated.

Closest is the Northeast Regional Greenhouse Gas Initiative (RGGI). When participating states' regulators or legislators adopt the RGGI Model Rule and promulgate cap and trade programs, the Northeast RGGI will take effect. Signatory states are expected to seek regulatory or legislative approval in time to have the state components effective no later than December 31, 2008. The Memorandum of Under-

standing, the founding document of RGGI, commits signatories to commence its first compliance period on January 1, 2009. As of October 2006, however, no other regional initiative has adopted a schedule for binding action or mandatory emission reduction targets.

B. The Regulatory Context: the Unbundling of the Wholesale Power Market

The traditional electric utility market consisted of vertically integrated, investor-owned public utilities that generated electricity in their own power plants, transmitted it long-distance over high-voltage lines, and distributed it locally to end users. On the regulatory side, generally, the federal regulatory body governed interstate commerce in electricity and the wholesale market. State public utility commissions had traditional police power jurisdiction over the siting of generation plants and transmission lines, as well as retail sales of electricity.[8]

An electric utility was likely to own all of these facilities and use them to provide electricity directly to consumers. The vertical integration of the electric power industry allowed regulated monopoly public utilities to control the generation of electricity and the network of wires—transmission or distribution facilities—over which it was delivered.[9] Electricity was sold on a "bundled" basis, with its price incorporating the costs of these facilities. Consumers—except the largest industrial or commercial customers that could self-provide—had no choice of generation source. Until the 1990s, individual non-utility genera-

tors could obtain access to the transmission and distribution networks only through the bottleneck controlled by their competitor, the public utility generator. In 1996, pursuant to the Energy Policy Act of 1992, FERC promulgated its landmark Order No. 888,[10] which established a new architecture for the electricity network: an open access transmission regime, requiring interconnection to the transmission network for all electric generators, whether or not utility-owned, and establishing the platform for competition in the wholesale power market.[11] That order, followed by Order No. 2000, laid the basis for the creation of independent bodies—rather than utility bodies—to oversee the daily management of the transmission of electricity. What had been utility-run power pools were replaced by independent system operators and regional transmission organizations.

Today the flow of electricity to two-thirds of Americans is carried by transmission lines managed by regional transmission organizations or independent system operators.[12] These entities were created under the aegis of federal and state regulators to oversee the reliability of the bulk power system and to coordinate the sale and economic dispatch of electricity throughout a state or region.[13] Generally, the composition of the various regional greenhouse gas initiatives reflects the membership of the regional transmission organizations and independent system operators.

C. Perspective on Regional Initiatives

Regional programs can be more efficient than state-level programs, with a wider geographic reach. On its face, this approach appears more commensurate with the global harm these greenhouse gas programs are designed to remediate. However, although much of the American map is covered by states participating in these programs, the map itself is at least as striking for its holes: those states hosting many of the nation's most copious greenhouse gas emitters. For example, even full participation of all the greenhouse gas initiative regions, under mandatory programs, leaves untouched much of the generating capacity of the five power companies that alone are responsible for one-quarter of the U.S. power sector's carbon dioxide emissions, which constitute 10% of world CO_2 emissions.[14]

Regional collaboration among states has the potential to result in more consistent and predictable regulatory requirements and incentives than a state-by-state approach.

Regional collaboration among states has the potential to result in more consistent and predictable regulatory requirements and incentives than a state-by-state approach. Each of the regional plans has as a principal goal the adoption, by each state, of an identical or at least functionally identical scope, incentives, targets, and timetables. The underlying theory is that consistency across regions will facilitate market entry by renewable energy generators, who have expressed fears of disparate treatment across state lines, an array of unique energy import rules, and accounting nightmares resulting from state-based programs in an industry defined by fairly wide geographic reach.[15] Another view is that the inconsistency *among* regional plans creates additional pressure for a federal response, as industry faces a cascading set of region-wide regulations and incentives.[16]

Finally, regional greenhouse gas emission control initiatives track, and in some cases combine, the regional independent electric system operators (formerly power pools) reconfigured in part as a result of federal energy regulatory policies.[17] In 1999 the FERC also endorsed the voluntary creation of regionally operated transmission grids that, in its view, would enhance competition and efficiency and lead to lower consumer prices.[18] Although this policy is currently under reexamination,[19] its adoption was a strong force for regional market organization.

While the geographic reach of regional programs clearly comes closer to approximating the scale of the problem, programs requiring cooperation across states also risk delay, implementation obstacles, and failure, resulting from the competing political agendas of multiple participants. The coordination among states and provinces that has been achieved to date represents an extraordinary effort to devise solutions to climate change before it reaches truly catastrophic proportions, and an unprecedented new regionalism in the face of federal inaction. On the other hand, the "region" is not a meaningful entity in American law or political life, and the conflicting agendas of chief executives in participating states create obstacles to moving ahead, and even under the best of circumstances, to moving ahead expeditiously.[20]

Another potential problem with regional solutions lies in the difficulties inherent in integration of incompatible system design across state, regional, and, even more difficult, national borders. This integration may cause legal problems, but it also raises accounting and other problems, as different states and different regional power pools rely upon different protocols and standards. These inconsistencies can lead to design complications and delay. For example, the Northeast RGGI incorporates states belonging to three separate bulk power systems administered by three different independent system operators (ISOs): PJM (Pennsylvania, New Jersey, and Maryland), NYISO (New York), and ISO-NE (New England). Each of the three regions bears different load characteristics and has its own security and reliability concerns based upon its generation base. Each may have its own method of dispatching power into its market. For example, one state- or regional-based system operator may dispatch every 15 minutes, another every hour; one may reconcile power purchase transactions monthly, an-

other hourly. Each may track electricity imports and generator emissions differently, depending upon historic state regulatory policies. Overcoming these barriers to regionalizing power systems across independent system operator borders is a significant task ahead for any practicable regional greenhouse gas reduction plan.

Finally, regional plans do not substitute for a national plan. An example is the problem of "leakage": electricity imported into states that participate in a regional plan from neighboring states that do not. At issue is the potential that the plan gains will be undermined by electricity imported from states not capping emissions, whose electricity may be cheaper because of the costs of implementing the emissions cap. Thus, emissions reductions achieved in the regulated state could be negated by emissions increases occasioned by additional generation in a non-regulated state. Neither states nor regions can entirely insulate themselves from these effects, as electricity is dispatched based on cost, and attempts to burden out-of-region generators with costs or conditions are likely to be challenged on Commerce Clause grounds.

II. Regional Program Objectives and Designs
A. Common Design Goals and Characteristics

A study of the regional plans begins with a view of the objectives expressed by the governors as they enter into agreements to make commitments to work on a regional basis to meet the climate challenge. The progenitors of these plans are united in their expression of hope and expectation that the development of regional emission reduction plans will both spur the development of a national plan and serve as laboratories and models for the development of such a plan.

While regional plans with a wide range of goals and designs have been developed or are in progress, certain common characteristics appear essential to craft a meaningful greenhouse gas reduction plan on a regional basis. These include:

1. Establishment of or agreement on a source of reliable and verifiable data establishing baseline greenhouse gas emissions in the participating states and provinces;[21]
2. Agreement upon an administrative agency, independent system operator or other central data collection system for all generation plants and for any other greenhouse gas emission sources covered by the program;
3. Model rules or statutes for adoption state-by-state or province-by-province to maximize the uniformity of approach, along with plenty of room for variation among states and provinces to take local differences into account;
4. Consistency, stability and predictability of approach, in order to encourage the necessary investment;
5. Mandatory greenhouse gas emission reduction targets or goals, with a timetable to reach those targets;
6. Monitoring, evaluation, implementation and dispute resolution mechanisms;
7. Flexibility to accommodate unforeseen changes in technology, circumstance or prices of renewable energy, greenhouse gas reduction credits and fossil fuels;
8. Verifiable cost, rate, and bill impact information, taking into account effects associated with other greenhouse gas reduction incentives, including state renewable portfolio standards and energy-efficiency programs;
9. Ongoing and meaningful public involvement with and information about the program;
10. If the program involves credit trading, verification and authentication methods to protect program integrity; and
11. A compliance and enforcement structure sufficient to provide incentives and allow transparency.

This common ground emerges from examination of the wide range of regional approaches and attempts, suggesting the importance of reaching balance among the competing interests involved while maintaining credibility with the public essential for success.

B. Individual Regional Initiatives
1. Northeast Regional Greenhouse Gas Initiative

Reasoning that the federal government had yet to put in place a program to control CO_2 emissions, Northeast states committed to develop a regional plan, the Regional Greenhouse Gas Initiative (RGGI, pronounced "Reggie"). Considered as a single entity, the original signatory RGGI states emitted 577 million metric tons of CO_2 equivalent in the year 2000. This would place the RGGI states sixth in the world for volume of GHG emissions, after the United States, Japan, Germany, Canada, and the United Kingdom.

The RGGI is currently endorsed by governors of seven states (Connecticut, Delaware, Maine, New Hampshire, New Jersey, New York, and Vermont),[22] although in April 2006 Maryland legislation was enacted requiring that state to join by July 2007.[23]

In a dramatic new development, in October 2006 California Governor Arnold Schwarzenegger announced promulgation of an executive order to effectively incorporate California into the Northeast RGGI as a trading partner.[24] The executive order directs California's Air Resources Board, Secretary for Environmental Protection, and Climate Action Team to develop a comprehensive market-based compliance program that will permit trading with the European Union, the Regional Greenhouse Gas Initiative and other jurisdictions.[25]

In summary, the RGGI is an agreement to propose a coordinated cap-and-trade program to reduce CO_2 emissions: the first mandatory program of its kind in the United States. Commencing in 2009, the seven states will each cap CO_2 emissions from power plants at approximately current levels—121 million tons annually—until the year 2015. At that time, states will lower the emissions cap over four years to reach a 10% reduction by 2019.[26]

a. RGGI Objectives

December 20, 2005, saw the landmark announcement of a Memorandum of Understanding (MOU) among the seven states. The RGGI goals are to reduce global-warming pollution; maximize economic development, reliability and fuel diversity; and drive technological innovation. Participants intend to keep the attendant costs to consumers minimal. Under the MOU, the seven states are developing a cap-and-trade system, initially covering the emission of carbon dioxide (CO_2) from power plants sized at or over 25 megawatts.[27] While this first phase of the Northeast RGGI covers one greenhouse gas, emitted from one category of source—the power-generation sector—the participants have announced their intention to expand the program to include the other six greenhouse gases and other stationary sources. The most developed of the U.S.-based regional greenhouse gas programs, the Northeast RGGI's success may spur efforts in other regions and on the federal level. Northeast RGGI is on schedule to be the first regional mandatory greenhouse gas reduction program in the United States.

The MOU was followed by the issuance of a Draft Model Rule for comment. Following extensive preliminary and final comments, a final Model Rule was issued on August 15, 2006. Revisions were made to the draft in response to the comments, also requiring the execution of an amended MOU.[28] In addition, the participants released an action plan for program implementation. Each state's governor undertakes to propose regulations styled after the Model Rule for legislative or regulatory adoption no later than December 31, 2008. Implementation is state-by-state, but considerable cooperation is envisioned.

The Model Rule provides the overall basis for binding state statutory or regulatory rules. The first specific objective committed to by the signatory states is the submission of a Model Rule for their respective states' regulatory or legislative approval in time to reach the target date of January 1, 2009, to commence implementation.[29] The second is to establish a regional CO_2 "emissions budget" or cap intended to first stabilize and then reduce CO_2 emissions in those states, and finally, to implement a regional carbon allowance trading program.[30]

b. The Emissions Cap

The RGGI effort began with a process to reach agreement on a definition of the current baseline levels. The plan will commence with an initial stabilization plan capping greenhouse gas emissions at current (2005) levels, adjusted for the expected modest increase between the issuance of the Model Rule and the effective date of the program. In the later stages of RGGI, there will be a progressive lowering of the cap to lead to a reduction in total emissions.

The MOU establishes a regional emissions cap or annual CO_2 emissions budget for the region of approximately 121 million tons.[31] Within the regional cap, each state will be assigned an initial base annual CO_2 Budget Trading Program budget. From the commencement of the program in 2009 through 2014, the MOU freezes each state's base annual CO_2 budget. Commencing in 2015, the MOU commits to a reduction in the state base annual CO_2 emissions budget by 2.5% per year. By 2019, all state budgets will be 10% below the initial base annual CO_2 emissions budget.

Compliance with the cap will be measured over a three-year period to reflect energy supply and seasonal variations. An outstanding compliance concern of the RGGI drafters has been and remains "leakage": the potential problem that electricity generated in neighboring non-RGGI states may be cheaper at times than that generated in RGGI states, whether as a result of RGGI-related costs or other factors. If this energy is imported into RGGI states, it could underbid the RGGI-state, lower-emission generation and make it difficult for generators functioning under RGGI restrictions to compete effectively. Some of the solutions suggested included addressing the leakage problem by limiting or conditioning electricity imports into participating RGGI states based on the emissions profile of the out-of-region generator. These solutions bring with them Commerce Clause concerns, however, and no final approach has yet been adopted.

Some commenting parties challenged the Draft Model Rule as a departure from the spirit of the MOU. A sample of the many issues raised by these parties included concern that the Draft Model Rule relaxed the cap through exempting facilities burning 50% or more biomass and from bonus allowance award to early adopters.[32] In addition, a coalition of non-governmental organizations (NGO parties)[33] feared the Model Rule could result in emissions higher than business as usual, and would not reduce emissions until the later years of the program. Energy brokers commented that the conservative cap may fail to result in creation of a trading system at all: according to some, emissions today may already fall below the 2009 cap.[34] Proposals included expanding the sectors covered by the cap, lowering it, and accelerating the emissions reduction schedule.

> **An outstanding compliance concern of the RGGI drafters has been and remains "leakage": the potential problem that electricity generated in neighboring non-RGGI states may be cheaper at times than that generated in RGGI states . . .**

Some parties raised the spectre that the emission reduction levels would simply prove inadequate to affect the pace or direction of climate change.[35] In preliminary comments, the office of Attorney General Eliot Spitzer cautioned: "[u]nless it is superseded by an effective federal program, significant additional reductions in the regional cap will be needed. The science is clear that eventual reductions in worldwide carbon dioxide emissions of about 80% are needed to stabilize the climate. Because the United States is, and long has been, the world's largest source of carbon dioxide emissions, and power plants are the largest source of emissions within the United States, reductions of at least that magnitude in U.S. power plant emissions will ultimately be necessary."[36]

In contrast, commenters on the Draft Model Rule, such as the Business Council of New York State, Inc., joined in the view that the RGGI studies underestimated the cost impact of the program, pointing out that New York's electric rate payers are already burdened by renewable portfolio standard and system benefit charge surcharges. These parties foresaw price impacts resulting from rate-payer financing of the cost of emission allowances—however distributed—and from the expected greater dependence on natural gas to fuel electric generation.[37]

c. The Allowance Program

The RGGI plan intends on achieving these reductions through the creation of an allowance program. The plan defines an allowance as a limited authorization to emit one ton of CO_2. State regulators will initially allocate sufficient allowances to cover sources' current emissions.

Covered emission sources that exceed that portion of the cap allocated to their output may comply with RGGI by demonstrating that they have purchased sufficient allowances—permissions to emit CO_2—from other covered sources emitting below their cap to bring their total emissions minus allowances below their cap. Allowances are only provided for covered sources: that is, electric power generation plants within the RGGI participating states. According to the Model Rule, each eligible source will apply for and be given a CO_2 budget permit, including the CO_2 allowances allocated by the state regulatory agency. Generators will be accorded sufficient allowances to cover their current CO_2 emissions, in a ratio of one allowance per ton of CO_2 emitted. How the allowances were to be allocated was a disputed issue, with some parties arguing that allocation should be 100% by auction, with the proceeds to be used for public benefit. Although ultimately rate payers will finance the allocations whatever the method, the auction option was seen to allow states to earmark considerable revenues for rate relief or energy efficiency.[38] The final Model Rule provides that although allowance allocation provisions may vary from state to state, at least 25% of the state's CO_2 Budget Trading Program base budget must be allocated to a consumer benefit or strategic energy purpose set-aside account.

d. Offsets

In addition to allowances, sources can reduce their emissions footprint by the use of offsets at each stage of the program. Offset credits are available for sources to establish that they have contributed to measurable emission reductions outside the cap sector—that is, outside the electric generation sector—using methods similar to the Kyoto Protocol's international clean development mechanism. Under the Draft Model Rule, only limited forms of greenhouse gas reduction programs are available to offset a covered source's emissions. These include projects for carbon emission reduction such as landfill gas (methane) capture and combustion, afforestation, end-use efficiency for natural gas, and farm methane capture. Some parties sought to expand the availability of offsets to a wider geographical range and to broader categories of GHG reduction measures; the MOU called for further study and expansion of offset categories. In the Draft Model Rule, offset projects located inside a signatory state were awarded one allowance per ton of CO_2 reduction; outside these states, but still within the United States, only one allowance was afforded for every two tons of CO_2 reduction.[39]

The Draft Model Rule provided that up to 3.3% of emissions from a particular source may be offset by emission reduction or carbon sequestration programs outside the power generation sector. With respect to requirements for offsets, NGO parties also challenged the Model Rule's omission of MOU language requiring that offsets be "real, surplus, verifiable, permanent and enforceable," while commercial parties argued that the offset rules are too restrictive in terms of eligibility, procedures, and scope. Biotechnology interests argued to expand offset eligibility to include industrial biotechnology processes that reduce manufacturing's carbon footprint,[40] while others urged inclusion of urban trees as offsetting carbon sinks.[41] Other parties asserted the importance of price certainty and expansion of incentives, including arguing for adoption of an alternative compliance mechanism as provided in the Massachusetts Renewable Portfolio Standard and expansion of benefits for early adoption.[42]

Like the power generation sectors, business interests also sought to restrict or eliminate the limitations on offsets. In contrast, environmental parties asserted a more stringent guarantee of the verifiability and legitimacy of offsets. Under the Draft Model Rule, the regulatory agency implementing RGGI will award "CO_2 offset allowances to sponsors of offset projects that have reduced or avoided atmospheric loading of CO_2."[43] The Draft Model Rule detailed what categories of projects qualify for offsets, as well as the conditions for awarding offset allowances for the retirement of CO_2 emissions credits, including the permanent retirement of allowances or credits issued pursuant to a mandatory governmental carbon reduction program outside the United States, pursuant to the United Nations Framework Convention on Climate Change.[44]

The final Model Rule allows power plants to utilize offsets to account for up to 3.3% of their emissions, to provide generators additional flexibility in compliance with the RGGI cap. Offsets include natural gas end-use efficiency measures, landfill gas recovery, reforestation, and capture of methane from farms. Offset credits are available from projects anywhere in the United States, if regulatory agencies in non-RGGI states enter into a memorandum of understanding and oversee and validate the projects. In addition, to further constrain costs, if the allowance price rises above $7, sources may use offsets for up to 5% of emissions, and if it rises above $10, for up to 10%.

e. Procedure, Implementation and Participation

In terms of implementation of the Northeast RGGI, the formal regulatory or statutory processes are currently being commenced. Governors will choose whether to submit model legislative or regulatory rules and to propose further specifics. New York and New Jersey, for example, intend to submit model rules to regulatory bodies rather than to state legislatures. The Model Rule will serve as the basis for either regulatory adoption by state environmental agencies or public utility commissions or statutory adoption by state legislatures. Regardless of whether the rule is ultimately a regulatory or statutory one, some basic consistency across state programs and coordination of implementation is central to the success of the RGGI.

To administer the program, participating states agreed to create a regional organization (RO), governed by a board consisting of regulatory agency heads from each state. The RO board will convene in 2007 to establish rules for allowance trading and the offset program, to seek additional MOUs with other U.S. jurisdictions, and to encourage other states to join RGGI.

The Northeast RGGI Model Rule is the result of a series of stakeholder and staff processes since the inception of the program. The Northeast RGGI has been formed through a remarkably open and transparent process involving stakeholders and all participating states, including a series of well-attended public meetings and an informative and up-to-date Web site.[45] Among the ongoing efforts, the RGGI staff has convened a working group for discussions on the disputed issue of the treatment of leakage under the RGGI plan. This group is scheduled to produce a final report on this issue in December 2007.[46]

For up-to-date information and discussion of implementation, stakeholder, and regulatory processes for the Northeast RGGI as a whole and state-by-state, interested parties may subscribe to regular e-mail updates and should watch the RGGI Web site at www.rggi.org.

2. The New England Governors–Eastern Canadian Premiers' Climate Change Action Plan

This is a project of the New England Governors' (NEG) Conference, a forum for the governors of Connecticut, Rhode Island, Massachusetts, Vermont, New Hampshire, and Maine to work together to respond to regional issues. These states are also party to the Conference of New England Governors and Eastern Canadian Premiers (NEG-ECP), formed in 1973 to address regional, cross-boundary issues and including New Brunswick, Newfoundland and Labrador, Nova Scotia, Prince Edward Island, and Quebec. In 2001, the NEG-ECP developed the Climate Change Action Plan, a coordinated regional plan for reducing greenhouse gases. The plan includes a goal of achieving 1990 emission levels by 2010; reducing emissions to 10% below 1990 levels by the year 2020; and reducing regional GHG emissions by 75%-85% in the long term.

The states and provinces of the NEG-ECP are developing a variety of programs and policies consistent with the Northeast RGGI, as well as with the Canadian National Implementation Strategy for Climate Change, prepared jointly by the federal, provincial and territorial governments of Canada. The 2001 Climate Change Action Plan is based upon the recognition of the common interest of Atlantic Canadian provinces and New England states in protecting the Atlantic coastline from the expected effects of rising ocean levels, temperature increases, and intensified storm events.

The 2001 action plan includes a comprehensive and coordinated regional plan for reducing greenhouse gases; a commitment to reach specified reduction targets for the region as a whole; a commitment from each state and provincial jurisdiction to carry on its own planning for climate change gas reductions; a plan for the adaptation of the region's economic resource base and physical infrastructure to address the consequences of climate change; and education to ensure that the region's citizens continue to be educated about global warming and climate change in order to better protect the earth's natural climatic systems and natural environment.

The Canadian forecasts associated with the 2001 plan showed that, without remediation, the region would experience a 20% increase in CO_2 from 1990 to 2020. The New England forecast showed a 30% increase from 2000 to 2020, absent mitigating action. The scientific predictions of greatest concern to the region were sea-level rise, with "predictable and dramatic impacts"; stress to the common natural resources—especially in the areas of agriculture, fisheries and forestry; an increase in weather extremes; stresses on estuaries, bays, and wetlands; changes in precipitation rates impacting water supply and food production; multiple stresses on urban areas; and recreation shifts. In addition, the composition of northeastern forests was anticipated to change dramatically, affecting biodiversity and forest industries. Expected public health effects included increased heat-related illness and death and increased ground-level ozone pollution.

In August 2005, nearly halfway to the plan's target year, the regional group published a Report Card[47] to help the region's governors and premiers assess their original goals. The Report Card found wide variation among the states and provinces; generally, it found that real emission reductions were needed soon in the transportation and power generation sectors. In the transportation sector, the report urges additional state and province progress in reducing vehicle miles traveled or increasing fuel-efficient and low-emission vehicles, and the adoption of standards like the California Clean Cars Standard and tax incentives. In addition, the Report Card urges energy efficiency and promotion of public awareness. Its conclusion is that, although progress was made, the region is not yet on a trajectory to meet the plan's short-term goals. Strong executive action by the governors of the New England states, in particular, as well as the premiers, is urged to set interim goals between 2020 and 2050. The Report Card details the performance of each of the states and provinces for 2005 with respect to action items, including establishing a greenhouse gas emissions inventory; releasing a plan for reducing GHG emissions and energy conservation; promoting public awareness; leading by example;[48] and reducing GHG from the electricity and transportation sectors.

In a resolution adopted in May 2006,[49] the governors and premiers agreed to a goal of increasing new renewable generation by 10% by 2020 as well as seeking to mitigate expected future demand increase through energy efficiency and demand response.

3. Powering the Plains

Powering the Plains is a joint public- and private-sector effort of state officials, utility industry executives, agriculture representatives and renewable energy advocacy groups to develop energy and agriculture climate change initiatives while promoting regional economic development. Participants include North Dakota, South Dakota, Iowa, Minnesota, Wisconsin, and the Canadian Province of Manitoba. Powering the Plains addresses energy and agricultural issues through the development of an integrated energy strategy, policy recommendations, and demonstration projects. Participants have formed a working group meeting quarterly to develop recommendations for policy makers. Emphasizing Midwest comparative advantages, recommendations include renewable energy development (wind, biomass, and hydro); hydrogen production from renewable and carbon-neutral sources; renewable and carbon credit trading schemes; carbon sequestration in prairie soils and wetlands; and coal gasification with carbon capture and geologic sequestration.

Draft principles and objectives are being developed by participants, who have reached a consensus around the long-term objective of reducing CO_2 emissions 80% from 1990 levels by 2050. At the University of Minnesota, researchers seek options to attain this goal, incorporating efficiency, renewables, fossil fuels, nuclear and sequestration/offsets. The outcome of this research is expected to provide the basis for a regional energy transition road map to be developed by Powering the Plains participants.

A bipartisan regional Legislators Forum passed a 2005 resolution supporting the initiative, and the program is in the process of designing and implementing an Upper Midwest renewable energy tracking system as the basis for regional trading of renewable energy credits, with the goal of completing the design by the end of 2006.

Regional regulators and state legislatures have endorsed the initiatives toward renewable energy credit tracking and trading and hydrogen development.

4. Western Governors' Association Clean and Diversified Energy Initiative

Another regional initiative was announced on June 22, 2004, by the Western Governors' Association (WGA),[50] unanimously resolving to examine the feasibility and actions required to reach a goal of 30,000 megawatts of clean energy by 2015 and a 20% improvement in energy efficiency by 2020. The governors will also examine what is needed to meet the West's generation and transmission needs over the next 25 years. The resolution cites the need to protect against energy shortages and price spikes, accommodate the population's growing energy needs, position the Western energy system to respond to environmental challenges, and take advantage of new technologies that will lower the cost of renewable energy and of controlling emissions from the fossil fuel resource base. According to the resolution, the project will stress "incentive-based, non-mandatory approaches," and it will also consider federal programs that could assist in reaching the goal.

The WGA has created the Clean and Diversified Energy Advisory Committee to oversee task forces, including among their membership government, business, and the nonprofit community, to facilitate planning for the energy technologies necessary to meet this goal.[51] The WGA also issued for comment a white paper studying the role of combined heat and power in sound energy policy in the West, which concludes that the "outdated paradigm of centralized generation with large transmission and distribution investments" is unlikely to meet western load growth demands. To come is a white paper concerning the West's hydropower resources.

On June 11, 2006, the WGA governors endorsed a policy resolution based on the proposals developed by more than 250 stakeholders. The WGA issued a report entitled, "Clean Energy, a Strong Economy and a Healthy Environment." The report finds that certain climate-related goals could be met: the development of an additional 30,000 megawatts of clean energy by 2015; an increase in energy efficiency of 20% by 2020; and a guarantee of a secure and reliable transmission system for the region for the next 25 years. In addition, the WGA agreed to support the development of market-based and cost-effective national, regional and state-level policies on climate change.

The WGA identified the challenge its states face resulting from rapid growth in electricity consumption and water usage,[52] escalating fuel costs, local opposition to the siting of new transmission lines, air pollution, and growing anxiety about climate change and about the reliability of the electric system if threatened by major disasters.[53]

In addition, the Western Governors' Association identified the Mexican border region as a critical area for the development of a market-based energy-efficiency initiative, based upon forecast economic growth and constrained energy resources. In April 2004 the Association published a study recommending aggressive energy-efficiency development for the region. The study noted Mexican precedent for state-sponsored energy-efficiency programs benefiting both the public and the private sector. Recommendations include increasing program financing for developers and customers; a hospitable regulatory environment for development and delivery of energy-efficiency technology to the private sector; customer and community education concerning the value of efficiency; and tracking energy consumption data.

5. West Coast Governors Global Warming Initiative

The West Coast Governors' Global Warming Initiative was announced in September 2003 by the governors of California, Oregon, and Washington, to coordinate their states' policies to combat global warming. The governors have approved recommendations by staff from the three states collectively identifying strategies the states can pursue cooperatively and individually.

The staff report identified both the serious adverse consequences to coastal states from global warming and the economic benefits to the region in development of its ample renewable energy resources and capacity to lead in production of advanced energy-efficient technologies. A series of studies and staff reports provided the governors with data to develop specific GHG emission reduction strategies.[54] Studied were hybrid vehicle procurement, port and highway diesel emission reduction plans, development of consistent measurement and tracking mechanisms, renewable energy resources, and energy-efficiency measures.

6. Southwest Climate Change Initiative

Concerned about the potential impacts of climate change in the region, Arizona Governor Janet Napolitano and New Mexico Governor Bill Richardson signed an agreement to create the Southwest Climate Change Initiative on February 28, 2006.[55] The two states will collaborate through their respective Climate Change Advisory Groups to identify options for reducing greenhouse gas emissions and promoting climate change mitigation, energy-efficient technologies and clean energy sources. Climate change programs will be administered through the Arizona Department of Environmental Quality and the New Mexico Environment Department. The Southwest Climate Change Initiative also commits the governors to cooperate with Native American tribes and communities and to advocate for regional and national climate change remediation. No specific targets or timetables for reduction of greenhouse gas emissions have yet been established.

7. Midwest Greenhouse Gas Emission Registry: Under Discussion

Five states that make up the Lake Michigan Air Directors Consortium—Illinois, Indiana, Michigan, Ohio and Wisconsin—along with Iowa and Minnesota, are in discussions as to whether to create a voluntary greenhouse gas emission registry. The development of program guidelines is expected in August 2006.[56] Discussions among participants indicate a Midwest regional GHG registry would add to existing federal programs because it would be a public GHG registry; it would be designed to ensure credibility in accounting and reporting to participants, with a long-term view to coordination with Eastern and Western regional initiatives; and it would be designed to support a range of possible future GHG emission reduction or other policies.

8. The California-United Kingdom Collaboration

On August 31, 2006, Governor Schwarzenegger and British Prime Minister Tony Blair announced an agreement to collaborate in acting "aggressively" for energy diversity and greenhouse gas emission reduction. This transnational collaboration offers yet another model for supra-state action on climate change, and signals EU nation interest in reaching out to U.S. states individually despite the lack of interest on the part of the federal government in climate change diplomacy. The emphasis is on the nexus of climate change and economic growth, with the collaboration focused on evaluating and implementing market-based emission reduction approaches and exploring common market opportunities. Also entailed is sharing scientific and technical data, renewable generation technologies, and strategies for adaptation to a changed climate.

III. Policy and Legal Issues Raised by Regional Initiatives

A. Policy Issues Concerning Regional Initiatives

While each regional program is unique, many share certain policy and design characteristics, including either mandatory or voluntary emissions caps. Establishing a cap that is realistic but progressive is a delicate and difficult task, and the level of the cap is a matter of some dispute among regional plan participants. Too flat a cap will not realize gains and may actually delay progress, while too aggressive a cap can make compliance impossible or unacceptably costly to rate payers.

Any trading program risks setting wrong price signals: assigning or establishing market value for allowances, where the calculation includes a parameter as volatile as the price of natural gas, may build in risks to rate payers and investors when the fuel price is either underestimated or overestimated. The financial impacts of various regional plans are typically examined by consultants or staff in extensive and verifiable cost studies, open to public and industry scrutiny. These detailed cost studies may include state-by-state (or province) estimates of electricity price impacts, as well as estimated rate impacts, that take into account expected total bill savings realized from decreases in energy consumption attributable to offset energy-conservation programs. Actual rate impacts will reflect different variables: savings resulting from energy-efficiency gains including those realized through program incentives; geographic variation; and variation among industrial, commercial, and residential rate payers. If rate impacts for one or another class are unexpectedly or disproportionately high, however, equity and political considerations may make the program vulnerable. Policies under debate in regional programs center on what program design costs least. Divergence on cost studies and estimates remains. In the Northeast RGGI, for example, some parties challenge that the offset program is too complex, includes too few offset opportunities, is unnecessarily less economically valuable to a generator than an allowance, and carries too little certainty, adding to both the program's costs and the difficulty in administering it.[57]

More broadly, commentators continue to question the efficacy—and the speed and cost—of market methods. While cap-and-trade programs combine government caps, standards, or controls with market trading methods, they nonetheless rely upon market mechanisms to provide incentives for industry to participate with enthusiasm.[58] Analyses are under way as to whether market-based programs in fact are the fastest and most effective method to reduce greenhouse gas emissions. But most of the discourse concerning cap-and-trade programs concerns the difficult task of determining the level at which to cap emissions. Cap-and-trade programs holding constant the emissions levels in the early years, or indexed to 1990 levels, may chart a far more gradual emission reduction course than is called for by climate scientists today. In addition, market-based mechanisms with overly generous caps run the risk of simply redistributing the sources of greenhouse gas emissions without significant reductions. Finally, it has not been established whether it is more or less costly to rate payers to finance emission reduction through a trading program, compared to simply financing energy efficiency, renewable resource-fueled generation, and sequestration.

Of the options for reducing load and therefore cutting greenhouse gas emissions, reducing dependence on foreign energy sources, and mitigating unstable and increasing fossil fuel prices, energy efficiency is among the most valuable. Using available technology, many experts argue, is the fastest, cheapest and most effective choice.[59] While some programs already in place in participating states include energy-efficiency support, targeting these opportunities is critical for a cap-and-trade program.

Another drawback to regional plans lies in the proliferation of local, state and regional programs, a checkerboard of measures with differing targets and timetables. These plans share a reliance on the importance of attracting investment: in renewable resource-fueled electric generation, in energy-efficiency technology, in research and development of renewable alternatives to fossil fuels, and in allowances and credits. Investors consistently express concern about the lack of predictability or standardization in the regulatory picture. For those considering capital investments, investments in energy tend to be capital-intensive and need long-term stability. Investors seek certainty, which is difficult to attain without consistent national action.

Finally, it is unclear how best to translate collective state executive action into permanent rulemaking, in particular for mandatory programs. Some Northeast RGGI states, for example, intend to propose the Model Rule in regulatory rather than statutory form, and the Draft Model Rule provides for this approach. However, there have been and may continue to be disputes between the executive and legislative branch as to where it is best to house these programs and how to fund them. The

New York State Legislature has twice sought to capture the rate-payer revenues collected to fund the state's Renewable Portfolio Standard and Systems Benefit Charge; the governor has twice vetoed these measures. This dispute could present legal challenges or shake investor confidence in the program's stability. While some assert that a statutory program is more reliable, as amending or repealing a statute is a difficult and often lengthy process, others contend that a regulatory program promises far more flexibility to respond to market developments, and expert staff oversight and implementation. In addition, the collection of revenues to support these programs through utility bill assessments at least implies that the proceeds will be reserved for the purposes of the program and not merged with the state's general fund.

... it is unclear how best to translate collective state executive action into permanent rulemaking, in particular for mandatory programs.

B. Legal Issues Concerning Regional Initiatives

Regional initiatives at the instigation of state collaboration, rather than pursuant to specific authority under federal law, are new developments and are likely to face legal challenges and, once final action is taken, judicial review. These challenges are expected to arise following the adoption of mandatory carbon caps and emissions credit trading programs once these are adopted state by state. Under the terms of a memorandum of understanding, a regional organization is created as a deliberative and collective action forum, and to monitor and provide states with technical support for implementation of the program. States do not cede or delegate to it ultimate sovereignty or governmental responsibility; indeed, member states retain the ability to opt out of the RGGI at any time upon 30 days' written notice.[60] While signatory states commit to propose for legislative or regulatory approval programs "substantially as reflected in a Model Rule," this commitment appears sufficiently flexible to obviate a claim that a state has improperly contracted to delegate its authority to a regional body. However, other statutory, constitutional, and international law objections may be raised to regional action once it is finalized in the form of specific state regulation or legislation.

1. Potential Statutory Challenges

With respect to state law, the RGGI has already faced questions about its implementation strategy. In New York, for example, Governor George Pataki has expressed his intention to propose the Model Rule on a regulatory, not legislative basis. Participants have challenged whether state regulatory bodies possess the statutory authority to establish an allowance-trading program for carbon dioxide.[61] Issues have been raised as to whether the New York Department of Environmental Conservation has the statutory authority to sell or auction CO_2 allowances absent federal enabling legislation. Under Title VI of the Clean Air Act,[62] state allowance-trading programs are adopted as authorized by federal statutory mandate. Pursuing a regulatory strategy to implement RGGI leaves unanswered the question of whether regulatory agencies possess the authority to adopt such rules without specific authorizing legislation. While state public utility regulatory agencies possess broad powers to ensure safe and adequate service at just and reasonable rates with respect to the electric industry, their powers are bounded by their enabling legislation, and absent amendment, this is unlikely to encompass credit-trading programs. Parties also challenge whether state environmental protection agencies are authorized to direct the proceeds of allowances sales to lower electric prices, or to fund other consumer benefits.

For environmental agencies, the first issue is whether the authority of state environmental or public utility departments to regulate air pollution includes CO_2 under current state law. If so, the further issue is whether such regulatory authority can be interpreted to encompass the creation of an allowance-trading program outside the express authority of either the Clean Air Act or state air pollution laws. The companion issue is whether state public utility commissions have authority to institute emission allowance trading programs without independent statutory authority. In response, some states prefer to turn to statutory adoption of the final Model Rule in order to obviate this problem; however, in doing so, they may lose the flexibility attendant upon a regulatory approach; statutory energy policy can be difficult to amend or repeal in response to changing conditions.

2. Potential Constitutional and Other Challenges

Assuming the participating states successfully adopt legislation or regulations embodying the RGGI Model Rule, questions remain as to whether such state legislation or regulatory action will pass constitutional muster in the face of determined challenges. Previous attempts by various states to use indirect means to limit air pollution harming those states but resulting largely from out-of-state emissions, for example, have not survived judicial review.[63]

Constitutional challenges to regional programs differ somewhat from those potentially available to challenge state programs. With regional programs, in addition to the preemption or Supremacy Clause issues, there may be objections based upon theories that the regions are assuming the role of a quasi- or mini-federal government, without constitutional authority to do so. These claims may be based upon either a Commerce Clause or Compact Clause theory.[64] The analytical frameworks of these three constitutional doctrines overlap considerably in this area, and sometimes appear to be employed interchangeably by the courts.

a. Supremacy Clause[65] Concerns

Because Congress, in the Clean Air Act, has established a comprehensive scheme for the regulation of air pollution, the argument goes, states or regions are precluded from putting in place measures that either render the federal scheme more difficult to administer or are in conflict with it. Should courts conclude that a state scheme conflicts with a federal scheme, that state plan will be preempted.[66]

In a somewhat analogous program, in 2000 New York state enacted an Air Pollution Mitigation Law, Public Service Law § 66-k, in an effort to protect the peculiarly vulnerable Adirondack Park from acid deposition resulting from sulfur dioxide (SO_2) emissions of electric generation plants in upwind states: Delaware, Illinois, Indiana, Kentucky, Maryland, Michigan, New Jersey, North Carolina, Ohio, Pennsylvania, Tennessee, Virginia, West Virginia, and Wisconsin. The statute authorized the New York State Public Service Commission to assess an air pollution mitigation offset on New York utilities selling or trading SO_2 allowances—directly or indirectly— to any of these upwind states pursuant to the federal Clean Air Act. A coalition of generators and marketers sought to enjoin the enforcement of the law, and the U.S. District Court for the Northern District of New York agreed it violated both the Commerce and Supremacy Clauses of the U.S. Constitution.[67] On appeal, the Second Circuit concluded that the statute violated the Supremacy Clause, on the ground that the New York

law frustrated the purpose of the federal Clean Air Act; the appellate court held it unnecessary to reach the Commerce Clause issue.

The more indirect approaches planned by these regional greenhouse gas initiatives appear unlikely to so frustrate or burden federal policies as to be preempted;[68] however, as long as the federal energy policy makers decline to institute mandatory CO_2 emission controls, this possibility cannot be discounted.

b. The Commerce[69] and Compact[70] Clause Theories

Commerce Clause concerns may ultimately contribute to some of the policy choices of the Northeast RGGI and other regional programs as they move to adopt mandatory goals. Commerce Clause concerns may play a role in the final approaches adopted to address some of the difficult cross-border issues raised by the plan delineated in the Model Rule. For example, a concern of the RGGI drafters has been the issue identified as "leakage": the potential problem that electricity generated in neighboring non-RGGI states may be cheaper at times than that generated in RGGI states, whether as a result of RGGI-related costs or other factors. If this energy is imported into RGGI states, it could underbid the RGGI-state, lower-emission generation and make it difficult for generators functioning under RGGI restrictions to compete effectively. Some of the solutions suggested included addressing the leakage problem by limiting or conditioning electricity imports into participating RGGI states based on the emissions profile of the out-of-region generator.[71] However, concerns were raised that this approach would be vulnerable to Commerce Clause challenge. Regulation by states, and presumably also agreements for mandatory action by regions, is barred from undue discrimination against, or from placing burdens upon, out-of-region interstate commerce, including the generation, transmission, distribution and sale of electricity.[72] Because the regulation of the wholesale energy market is reserved for the federal government, interference—directly through the erection of import or export barriers or indirectly through conditioning imports upon voluntary compliance with a regional standard—with the terms and conditions of the wholesale trade in electricity may be vulnerable to Commerce Clause attack.

A Compact Clause challenge is also a possibility, although perhaps a more distant one, either as to whether regional plans constitute interstate compacts or international treaties. If, as has been discussed, the Northeast RGGI or other regional plans harmonize their credit- or allowance-trading system with that of the European Union or other nations, such agreements or cooperation could arguably be subject to challenge as an unconstitutional abrogation of the Constitution's Compact Clause.

Compact Clause jurisprudence has been limited to those cases in which "it is evident that the prohibition is directed to the formation of any combination tending to the increase of political power in the states, which may encroach upon or interfere with the just supremacy of the United States."[73] Commentators expect that the loose confederations represented by these regional plans are unlikely to be interpreted as an encroachment on federal power or an increase in the power of the states, and that the case law evinces no examples of similar programs falling to Compact Clause challenge.[74]

Separate Compact Clause issues are raised by those regional initiatives that link U.S. state programs with those of Canadian provinces, or by the attempts to so structure regional trading programs as to integrate them into the Kyoto Protocol or European Union greenhouse gas emission reduction schemes. While at least one regional plan—that of the New England Governors and Eastern Canadian Premiers—expresses a joint intention to reduce greenhouse gas emissions, that agreement represents "little more than expressing their mutual intent to reduce greenhouse gases."[75] Absent binding commitments, the definition of "compact" does not appear to be met. Moreover, without U.S. ratification of the Kyoto Protocol, emission reduction measures in the United States will be ineligible for trading.

A final legal question is whether regional plans may be susceptible to NAFTA challenge as impermissible discrimination against investors in electric generation in Canada or Mexico under Chapter 11, pursuant to the arbitral award in *Metalclad Corporation and United Mexican States*.[76] However, the recent arbitration decision upholding California's ban on methyl tertiary-butyl ether (MTBE) as consistent with international law standards, non-discriminatory, and not an expropriation of Methanex's investment signals that state or regional regulatory programs may survive NAFTA challenge.[77]

IV. Conclusion

In the absence of federal requirements to control greenhouse gas emissions, the emergence of regional initiatives engaging multiple states and, on occasion, provinces has begun to provide the possibility of tackling the climate change problem on a grander scale than local and state programs. While the geographic reach of the totality of regional programs resembles a national approach to the problem, much of the generation capacity and therefore greenhouse gas emission inventory has not yet been affected. Programs requiring cooperation across states, and between states and other nations, risk failure from the competing political agendas and requirements of multiple participants and may face legal challenges, but they also mobilize the political will for government to take action on climate change.

As a practical matter, the development across the board of regional GHG inventories, essential to establish baseline data for any meaningful mandatory reduction program, characterizes all the regional programs. While mandatory legislative or regulatory solutions are slow in coming, the regional impetus

is laying the basis for future action in sharing of data, establishment of public processes, and consensus on at least the urgency of long-term emission reduction objectives.

Endnotes

1. Not analyzed are programs initiated by EPA or other federal agencies to coordinate reductions region by region. For example, recognizing the possibility that large carbon sequestration projects have the potential to significantly reduce atmospheric greenhouse gas concentrations, the U.S. Department of Energy has created seven regional Carbon Sequestration Partnerships. These partnerships utilize expertise in academic institutions, state agencies, and private companies to estimate sequestration potential and develop regionally appropriate carbon sequestration strategies.

2. Existing state or multistate power pools were reconfigured as state or regional independent system operators or regional transmission organizations subject to extensive Federal Energy Regulatory Commission (FERC) proceedings.

3. Many participating states also continue collectively to pressure the federal government to take action to reduce greenhouse gas emissions. On April 27, 2006, attorneys general from 10 of these states brought suit in the U.S. Court of Appeals for the District of Columbia Circuit against the Environmental Protection Agency for

refusing to act on global warming in its revised regulations governing certain new power plants.

4. *Petition to the Inter-American Commission on Human Rights Seeking Relief From Violations Resulting from Global Warming Caused by Acts and Omissions of the United States*, p. 108, *available at* http://www.ciel.org/Publications/ICC_Petition_7Dec05.pdf.

5. For one of countless examples of the EU discussion of U.S. regional programs' potential as emissions-trading partners, *see Industry Emissions Targets Should Be Set by Brussels*, UK Institute for Public Policy Research, June 29, 2006, http://www.ippr.org.uk/pressreleases/?id=2196.

6. Not included in this list are states participating in the newly announced voluntary Midwest Greenhouse Gas Registry, which has not yet designed its program or established targets or timetables for emissions reduction.

7. *See Mitigating Global Climate Change in the United States: A Regional Approach*, 14 N.Y.U. L. J. 54 (2005).

8. The jurisdictional backdrop for the transition to competition rests in the federal authority over interstate sales of electricity, transmission, and wholesale sales of any kind: that is, sales for resale (16 U.S.C.A. § 824 (a)). FERC has jurisdiction over "all facilities for such transmission or sale of electric energy, but shall not have jurisdiction . . . over facilities used for the generation of electric energy or over facilities used in local distribution or only for the transmission of electric energy in intrastate commerce . . . ." 16 U.S.C.A. § 824(b)(2).

9. The Public Utilities Regulatory Policies Act of 1978 (PURPA) began to open up the electric generation market to competition, requiring FERC to promulgate rules mandating that utilities purchase electricity from certain cogeneration and small power production facilities. *See* FERC v. Mississippi, 456 U.S. 742, 751 (1982).

10. Promoting Wholesale Competition Through Open Access Non-Discriminatory Transmission Services by Public Utilities, Order No. 888, F.E.R.C. Stats. & Regs. ¶ 31,036, 61 Fed. Reg. 21,540, *clarified*, 76 F.E.R.C. ¶ 61,009 and 76 F.E.R.C. ¶ 61,347 (1996), *on reh'g*, Order No. 888-A, F.E.R.C. Stats. & Regs. ¶ 31,048, 62 Fed. Reg. 12,274, *clarified*,79 F.E.R.C. ¶ 61,182, *on reh'g*, Order No. 888-B, 81 F.E.R.C. ¶ 61,248, 62 Fed. Reg. 64,688 (1997), *on reh'g*, Order No. 888-C, 82 F.E.R.C. ¶ 61,046 (1998), *aff'd sub nom.* Transmission Access Policy Study Group v. FERC, 225 F.3d 667 (D.C. Cir. 2000), *aff'd sub nom.* New York v. FERC, 535 U.S. 1, 122 S. Ct. 1012, 152 L. Ed. 2d 47 (2002).

11. *See* Niagara Mohawk Power Corp. v. Fed. Energy Reg. Comm'n, __F.3d __, 2006 WL 1715639 (C.A.D.C. June 23, 2006).

12. These are the CAISO (California), Midwest ISO, ISO New England, PJM (Pennsylvania, New Jersey and Maryland), New York ISO, and SPP (Southwest Power Pool).

13. Integration of regional and state systems also may entail negotiating barriers among ISOs and RTOs: for example, different organizations have different rules for accounting for imports of power into their systems. One may keep track on a monthly basis, while another tracks imports on an hourly basis. ISOs and RTOs will also track the fuel source and other generation characteristics of their members, critical data for design of any greenhouse gas emission reduction project.

14. *See* State of Conn. v. Am. Elec. Power, 406 F. Supp. 2d 265, 268 (S.D.N.Y. 2005), *citing* State Parties' Complaint.

15. For a creative discussion of the contradiction between the geography of global warming and the locus of regulatory power, *see* Hari Osofsky, *The Geography of Climate Change Litigation: Implications for Transnational Regulatory Governance*,

WASH. U. L.Q. (forthcoming 2006) (draft on file with author).
16. For example, after the Audubon Society's efforts supporting new federal appliance efficiency standards were frustrated
by a Reagan veto, several states adopted their own standards,
each a slightly different version. Soon the National Association of Manufacturers was pressing for federal standards to
ensure consistency. Remarks of Peter Berle, at Mohawk-Hudson
Land Conservancy, May 11, 2006. *See also* Kirsten H. Engel,
*Mitigating Global Climate Change in the United States: A
Regional Approach*, 14 N.Y.U. Envtl. L.J. 54, 64 n.35 (2005).

17. FERC Order No. 888, 61 Fed. Reg. 21,540 (May 10,
1996).
18. FERC Order No. 2000, 89 Fed. Reg. 61,285, 18 C.F.R.
pt. 35 (Dec. 20, 1999).
19. FERC Notice of Proposed Rulemaking, *Preventing Undue
Discrimination and Preference in Transmission Service*, Dock-
ets Nos. RM05-25-000 and RM05-17-000 (May 19, 2006).
20. In Massachusetts, for example, Governor Mitt Romney
dropped out of the RGGI as the MOU was being finalized, as
did Rhode Island governor Donald Carcieri; the Massachusetts state legislature, however, is considering a bill to implement RGGI over his objections (INSIDE EPA, March 14, 2006).

21. Some regional efforts entail exclusively greenhouse gas
emission reporting, *e.g.*, the Eastern Climate Registry, a recent voluntary industry initiative to track greenhouse gas emission data. 117 EPA Daily Env. Rep. A-7 (6-19-06).
22. Shortly before RGGI's adoption, the governors of Massachusetts and Rhode Island withdrew, citing cost concerns. These
states continue to observe the RGGI process and may rejoin at
some future point.
23. The District of Columbia, Massachusetts, Pennsylvania,
Rhode Island, the Eastern Canadian Provinces and New
Brunswick are observers.

24. California also announced a partnership with the United Kingdom in seeking
greenhouse gas emission reductions and looking for credit-trading opportunities with
EU nations, which may be seeking U.S. state partners in the absence of federal
greenhouse gas emission reduction steps.
25. *See* http://www.pewclimate.org/what_s_being_done/in_the_states/news.cfm.
26. The RGGI signatories estimate that the program will result in an approximately 35% reduction by 2020, compared to forecast levels without the cap-and-
trade rules.
27. Maryland will join the Northeast RGGI prior to its commencement. On April
6, 2006, Maryland Governor Robert L. Ehrlich, Jr. signed into law a bill requiring
the state to join RGGI by June 30, 2007. Joining RGGI has also been under consideration in Pennsylvania.
28. Included in these is a voluntary renewable energy market set-aside of a certain
number of tons from the CO_2 Budget Trading Program annual base budget.
29. Draft Model Rule XX-1.5(c)(3).
30. MOU, p. 2. The MOU, and supporting studies and documentation, can be read
at http://www.rggi.org/agreement.htm.
31. *Id.*

32. New York State Attorney General Eliot Spitzer Draft Model Rule Comments (May 22, 2006).

33. NGO parties include Natural Resources Defense Council; Public Interest Research Groups of Rhode Island, New York, Massachusetts, Maryland, Vermont, New Jersey, Connecticut and New Hampshire; Pace University Energy Project; and Union of Concerned Scientists.

34. Preliminary Draft Model Rule Comments of Evolution Markets LLC.

35. The Draft Model Rule provisions on the emissions cap also included exemptions challenged by some parties—an exemption for large industrial power generators and for fossil fuel plants exceeding a 50% biomass input.

36. Preliminary Draft Model Rule Comments of Office of the New York Attorney General Eliot Spitzer.

37. Business Council Draft Model Rule Comments, May 22, 2006.

38. Comments of New York State Attorney General Eliot Spitzer (May 22, 2006).

39. A generator may cover up to 3.3% of reported emissions using offsets. In addition, the plan provides for expansion of the offsets depending upon the spot price for allowances.

40. Biotechnology Industry Organization Preliminary Comments.

41. Maryland Department of Natural Resources, Preliminary Comments.

42. Dominion Resources Services, Inc., Preliminary Comments.

43. DRAFT MODEL RULE XX-10.1, p. 84.

44. DRAFT MODEL RULE XX-10.3, pp. 91-93.

45. See www.RGGI.org.

46. Some parties—for example, the Independent Power Producers of New York (IPPNY)—urge that finalization of the Draft Model Rule await the results of this report.

47. *2005 Report Card on Climate Change Action*, http://www.newenglandclimate.org/files/reportcard05.pdf.

48. Vermont's governor, for example, promulgated an executive order requiring state facilities' energy usage to comply with the plan. *See* http://www.vermont.gov/governor/orders/Climate-Change-Action-Plan.html.

49. *See* http:www.negc.org/resolutions/Res_30-2_5-06.pdf.

50. The Western Governors Association includes the governors of 19 western states and three U.S.-Flag Pacific Islands: Alaska, American Samoa, Arizona, California, Colorado, Guam, Hawaii, Idaho, Kansas, Montana, Nebraska, Nevada, New Mexico, North Dakota, Northern Mariana Islands, Oklahoma, Oregon, South Dakota, Texas, Utah, Washington, and Wyoming. *See* http://www.westgov.org/wga_governors.htm.

51. http://www.westgov.org/wga/initiatives/cdeac/index.htm.

52. According to the White Paper, 39% of U.S. freshwater is consumed in power generation.

53. WGA Combined Heat and Power White Paper (January 2006), p. i.

54. The reports can be accessed in full at http://www.climatechange.ca.gov/westcoast/documents/index.html.

55. http://www.nmclimatechange.us/ewebeditpro/items/O117F8087.pdf (last consulted July 16, 2006).

56. Lake Michigan Air Directors Consortium, http://www.ladco.org/regional_greenhouse.htm (last visited July 16, 2006).

57. Northeast Utility System Draft Model Rule Comments, May 22, 2006.

58. *See, i.e*, David Driesen, *The Economic Dynamics of Environmental Law: Cost-Benefit Analysis, Emissions Trading, and Priority-Setting*, 31 B.C. ENVTL. AFF. L. REV. 501 (2004).

59. *See, i.e.,* www.oilendgame.com.

60. MOU, pp. 1, 7-8, 9 (http://www.rggi.org/agreement.htm).

61. Business Council May 23, 2006 Draft Model Rule Comments, p.2.

62. *See generally* 42 U.S.C. §§ 7401-7671q.

63. Clean Air Markets Group v. Pataki, 194 F. Supp. 2d 147 (N.D. N.Y. 2002), *aff'd,* Clean Air Markets Group v. Pataki, 338 F.3d 82 (2d Cir. 2003).

64. In contrast to these regional initiatives, the Great Lakes Basin Compact, treating the environmental health of the Great Lakes region, joins member states Illinois, Indiana, Michigan, Minnesota, New York, Ohio, Pennsylvania and Wisconsin, and associate member provinces Ontario and Quebec, bordering the Great Lakes, but with congressional consent through Public Law 90-419. *See* http://www.glc.org/about/glbc.html.

65. This Constitution, and the Laws of the United States which shall be made in Pursuance thereof; and all Treaties made, or which shall be made, under the Authority of the United States, shall be the supreme Law of the Land; and the Judges in every State shall be bound thereby, any Thing in the Constitution or Laws of any state to the Contrary notwithstanding (U.S. CONST. art. VI, § 2).

66. In a related argument, defendants in *State of Connecticut v. American Electric Power*, 406 F. Supp. 2d 265 (S.D.N.Y. 2005), moved to dismiss claiming that Congress had occupied the field of air emission regulation in the Clean Air Act, and that therefore no federal common law of public nuisance—where the asserted "nuisance" was global warming—remained. The court dismissed the complaints on political question grounds; however, the case is on appeal.

67. Clean Air Markets Group v. Pataki, 194 F. Supp. 2d 147 (N.D.N.Y. 2002), *aff'd,* Clean Air Markets Group v. Pataki, 338 F.3d 82 (2d Cir. 2003). The Second Circuit affirmed as to the Supremacy Clause,

68. *See generally* Steven Ferrey, *Sustainable Energy, Environmental Policy, and States' Rights: Discerning the Energy Future through the Eye of the Dormant Commerce Clause,* 12 N.Y.U. ENVTL. L.J. 507 (2004).

69. The Congress shall have power to lay and collect taxes, duties, imposts and excises, to pay the debts and provide for the common defense and general welfare of the United States; but all duties, imposts and excises shall be uniform throughout the United States; To borrow money on the credit of the United States; To regulate commerce with foreign nations, and among the several states, and with the Indian tribes . . . . (U.S. CONST. art. I, § 8).

70. No State shall, without the Consent of Congress, . . . enter into any Agreement or Compact with another State, or with a foreign Power . . . . (U.S. CONST. art. I, § 10).

71. Edna Sussman, *New York Addresses Climate Change with the First Mandatory U.S. Greenhouse Gas Program,* N.Y.S. B. ASS'N J., May 2006, at 47.

72. Ferrey, *supra* note 69, at 636. Generally, as Ferrey concludes, "[s]ales of power that appear to be intrastate or local in character may be considered interstate for purposes of FERC jurisdiction," and transmission of electricity in interstate commerce is defined as "electricity transmitted from one state and consumed at a point ·

outside the state. . . . However, this provision has consistently been interpreted to mean that FERC has jurisdiction when the system is interconnected " Ferrey, at 613.

73.   Virginia v. Tennessee, 148 U.S. 503, 519 (1893) (an agreement between those states affixing their border, later implicitly approved by Congress).

74.   Thomas G. Echikson & Jim Wedeking, *Compacts, Commerce and Federal Supremacy*, 2 Const. L. Task Force Newsl. 2 (ABA Section of Env't, Energy and Resources 2006).

75.   Engel, *supra* note 17, at 80.

76.   *Metalclad Corporation and The United Mexican States*, Award Before the Arbitral Tribunal constituted under Chapter 11 of the North American Free Trade Agreement (Aug. 30, 2000), *available at* http://www.worldbank.org/icsid/cases/mm-award-e.pdf (last visited July 16, 2006).

77.   *In the Matter of An International Arbitration Under Chapter 11 of the North American Free Trade Agreement and the UNCITRAL Arbitration Rules, Methanex Corp. and United States of America*, Final Award of the Tribunal on Jurisdiction and Merits (Aug. 9, 2005), *available at* http://www.state.gov/documents/organization/51052.pdf.

chapter ten

State Initiatives

David Hodas

I. Introduction

Just as "nature abhors a vacuum," so too, in human society, political actors abhor a power vacuum. In nature, air rushes in to fill the space; in society, political entities inevitably move to fill a power void. In the absence of federal leadership on global warming, state and local governments have moved into this void. The scope of state legal and policy initiatives over the past decade has been truly remarkable; it is sufficiently significant to warrant serious attention by any lawyer working in the field. In fact, for all practical purposes, since February 2001, when President Bush reversed his campaign position by rejecting participation in the Kyoto Protocol, the federal government has removed itself from mandatory action in the global warming legal and policy arena. This vacuum is being filled by the states.

As of July 2006, every state in the country has adopted some sort of law or policy to address climate change.[1] Even Alabama, Illinois, Kentucky, Oklahoma, West Virginia, and Wyoming, which had adopted statutes prohibiting state agencies from even proposing any new regulation intended to reduce greenhouse gas emissions,[2] now have climate change action plans, greenhouse gas inventories and registries, green pricing, renewable portfolio standards, other electricity sector policies, agricultural policies, and energy building codes that address global warming.[3] The news is full of new state initiatives,[4] including the efforts by treasurers of seven states and institutional investors such as California Public Employees Retirement System to push the boards of directors of ExxonMobil and other major companies to report on how the company plans to address global warming.[5]

Chapter 11 of this book presents a 50-state survey showing what every state is doing. This chapter presents an overview of these efforts.

Law and economics theory suggest that these state responses are irrational, and ought not to be happening.[6] After all, each state, as a theoretical rational actor, should be seeking to maximize the benefits from its activities that emit greenhouse gases (GHG), while sharing the costs of atmospheric disposal with the rest of the world.

Climate change presents the classic problem of externalities and the global commons. Every rational state actor would be expected to maximize its own gains from emitting GHG, and to spread the costs spatially (among the entire global population) and temporally (the effects of the increased GHG atmosphere concentrations will not be experienced today, but decades in the future). Long-term harm, discounted to present value, is easy to dismiss by present actors because, even at modest discount rates, effects 50-100 years hence have insignificant present value.

Moreover, given our nation's constitutional structure, one would not expect states to be the leaders in combating global warming, which is the cumulative result of the world's human population increasing the concentration of greenhouse gases in the atmosphere. The climate change challenge is international in scope. The Constitution prohibits states from entering into a treaty or agreement with another nation.[7] The preemption doctrine under the Supremacy Clause bars states from making foreign policy, or interfering with the President's and Congress's foreign affairs power or the so-called dormant foreign affairs power.[8] States cannot enter into regional agreements with other states without the approval of Congress.[9] States may not discriminate against interstate commerce, nor unduly burden interstate commerce,[10] although if a state acts as a market participant it is exempt from the operation of the dormant Commerce Clause (but the market participant exemption does not apply to the dormant Foreign Affairs Clause).[11]

Thus, any attempt to coordinate state efforts, absent congressional approval, must be entirely domestic, voluntary, and unenforceable by other states. Such an approach is difficult to pursue, time-consuming, and not amenable to uniform compliance. The time, effort, and resources spent by many Northeast states attempting to establish a modest CO_2 trading system, the Regional Greenhouse Gas Initiative (discussed in chapter 9), is a perfect illustration of how high, perhaps insurmountable, are the transaction costs and obstacles to coordinated voluntary action.

If, however, each state acts independently, then states may duplicate each other's efforts, a great waste of limited state resources. Each state must make its own policy and political determinations. Sharing information among states is *ad hoc*, uncoordinated, intermittent, and expensive, to the extent sharing happens at all. Each state's laws and policies emerge along their own unique time lines, within its own legislative, administrative and judicial process. Because of this state-by-state approach, the national map is becoming a complex, multi-layered, multi-patterned patchwork quilt of laws and policies, with no necessary connections, consistency, coherence, or compatibility. At best, this chaotic federalism collection of "policy laboratories" will generate ideas and innovations that might be adopted as federal law. It is a very inefficient process. Achieving consensus among states on global warming policy is a considerable challenge.[12]

Nevertheless, states have taken the lead. But why? Why are states addressing global warming? There is no single answer, although the common denominator is the vacuum formed by the absence of federal leadership. Many states are frustrated that the United States, the world's largest emitter of GHG, is not acting to reduce its emissions in any significant way.[13] Some states, taken alone, would rank high on the world list of GHG emissions by country. Texas' CO_2 emissions would rank it seventh in the world, between Germany and the United Kingdom; California would be 12th, slightly below Mexico and above France.[14] In fact, the top 33 states would rank within the top 50 CO_2 emitters in the world. Even Vermont, the lowest CO_2 emitting state in the United States, would rank 100th in the world. So, state actions to reduce GHG emissions can have a measurable impact.

> ... state per capita emissions are strikingly high compared with the rest of the developed world, let alone the developing nations; U.S. states use fossil fuels far less efficiently than their trading competition.

Just as important, state per capita emissions are strikingly high compared with the rest of the developed world, let alone the developing nations; U.S. states use fossil fuels far less efficiently than their trading competition. For instance, even the most efficient state in the nation, Vermont (10.6 tons of CO_2 per person) would still be ranked in the top 25 nations of the world in per capita CO_2 emissions, just slightly better than the Russian Federation. The 25 countries in the European Union average 8.7 tons per person, far less than the average of the 50 states, 20.0. The five most inefficient states[15] would rank one to five, above the world's least efficient nations, Qatar (39.9), Kuwait (24.8), United Arab Emirates (UAE) (24.1) and Bahrain (20.9); the United States is fifth (20.0). Twelve states would fit between Qatar and Kuwait,[16] with another two states just below Kuwait,[17] and four between Bahrain and UAE.[18] Among the states, Wyoming (130.4) tops the world's list, with per capita emissions some 3.25 times greater than Qatar, the least efficient nation in the world; North Dakota (82.9), Alaska (66.8), West Virginia (57.6) and Louisiana (41.3) would push Qatar down to sixth place. By comparison, even New York (11.0) and California (11.2), the second and third most efficient states, and whose combined total emissions would place them between Germany and the United Kingdom, would be among the 20 least efficient nations in the world, emitting more CO_2 per person than Germany (10.7), the United Kingdom (9.6), Japan (9.5), or France (6.5).

These data suggest that states face enormous opportunities to become more efficient. In 2001, California emitted about 386 million tons, a little less than the combined emissions of the five least efficient states, Wyoming, North Dakota, Alaska, West Virginia, and Louisiana (379 million tons); yet each person in the latter states emits more than three times the CO_2 of a person in California, a large state with a profound love affair with driving (in 2001, more than 310 billion vehicle miles were traveled in California).[19] Remarkably, if the U.S. average emissions per capita were the same as California's, total annual U.S. CO_2 emissions would be reduced by 45%, a 2.6 billion ton reduction. Market competition theory suggests that the inefficient states will have a competitive advantage when forced to reduce CO_2 emissions. So why are the states with the lowest emissions per capita taking the lead in addressing climate change?

Some state leaders see climate change as an environmental concern that must be addressed, if only on general ethical and moral grounds. Some states want to take early action to help themselves better prepare for a carbon-constrained future. Early plans can help the state avoid costly investment mistakes, which will consume precious capital and then could become subject to climate change regulation, making them uneconomic. States may recognize that addressing GHG emissions will be a long-term, challenging adventure. Small, early steps, compounded into the future, will lessen both the cost of change and the rate of transition. To the extent that GHG investments can be made to coincide with natural capital investment and replacement cycles, the marginal cost of reducing GHG emissions could be dramatically reduced. These savings will both benefit the state's economy by making it more efficient and benefit the general well-being of the state's citizens by reducing the stress associated with rapid transition. Moreover, given the end of the age of low-priced oil,[20] inefficient states will be hobbled with heavy economic costs.

Moreover, simply to maintain our current approach to energy use will entail huge additional investments in our frail energy infrastructure. For instance, no new oil refinery has been constructed in the United States since the late 1970s. Almost all of our refineries are located in coastal areas or along rivers, and over half of our nation's refineries are located along the Gulf of Mexico. Without new refining capacity, we are now importing more refined gasoline than ever, about 1 million barrels per day and growing.[21] As Hurricanes Katrina and Rita proved in 2005, the Gulf Coast refineries and pipelines that transport their product to much of the country are extremely vulnerable. In southeastern Florida, Hurricane Rita disrupted electric service for almost a month in many places. Without electricity, gasoline stations could not pump gas, residences could not be air conditioned, street lights could not operate, schools and businesses were closed. Sea-level rise and more intense storms associated with global warming will only put more stress on our energy infrastructure. Climate change policies that will reduce demand for fossil fuel–based energy will reduce the capital and human cost of maintaining and expanding our energy infrastructure, will help reduce the rate of warming, and will enable our economy to be more resilient in responding to the effects of global warming and other stresses. States also recognize that curtailed use of gasoline will reduce our dependence on foreign sources of oil, thereby enhancing our energy security and reducing balance of trade deficits attributable to purchasing foreign oil. Climate change initiatives by states will not solve any of these problems, but states nevertheless want to contribute to alleviating the problem by providing ideas, leadership, and symbolic statements that advance their ethical, moral, political, and policy concerns.

This chapter will review the range of state climate policies that have been adopted thus far. It will describe the nature of these policies and the shape they can take. Chapter 11 will provide specific reports on each state. More than half of the states are also engaged in at least one regional initiative. Eight northeastern and Mid-Atlantic states formed the Regional Greenhouse Gas Initiative to create a regional cap-and-trade system. These states and others have also joined together to develop a GHG registry, the Eastern Climate Registry. California, Oregon and Washington formed the West Coast Governors' Global Warming Initiative. Arizona and New Mexico formed the Southwest Climate Change Initiative in February 2006 to reduce GHG emissions and to cooperate in adapting to the effects of global warming. Eighteen states within the Western Governors' Association have instituted the WGA Clean and Diversified Energy Initiative to address global warming by increasing the use of renewable energy and energy-efficiency measures. Five

midwestern states and the Canadian province of Manitoba have formed "Powering the Plains" to promote alternative energy sources and climate-friendly agriculture. Six New England states have agreed with the premiers of several eastern Canadian provinces to pursue a climate action plan with short-term and long-term GHG emission reduction goals. Chapter 9 of this book addresses these regional projects.

II. Intersection of State Energy and Environmental Goals with Climate Change

State climate change initiatives can also produce important secondary benefits. This is particularly true with respect to CO_2 emissions from fossil fuel combustions. CO_2 emissions from motor vehicles can be reduced by making the vehicles more fuel-efficient so that, if total passenger miles remain constant, CO_2 emissions will be reduced by shifting transportation from gasoline or diesel vehicles to mass transit, walking, bicycling, or vehicles that are propelled by low or 0 GHG sources such as electricity produced from wind. One immediate by-product of these policies would be a reduction in pollution from motor vehicles. Reduced nitrogen dioxide (NO_2), volatile organic compounds (VOCs), and carbon monoxide (CO) from cars will improve urban air quality directly and by reducing ground-level ozone (O_3) and associated smog. Cleaner, more efficient diesel engines, or fewer miles driven, will reduce fine-particle diesel exhaust. These fine particles are capable of penetrating deep into our lungs, where they can promote pulmonary disease or cancer. The fine diesel particles are also extremely effective transporters of pollen and other pollutants, such as SO_2 aerosols or tiny particles of heavy metals, deep into human lungs. Ironically, global warming substantially increases pollen production, so more people are inhaling more pollen into their respiratory system. A doubling of CO_2 in the atmosphere increases the growth of the exposed ragweed by 10% but increases pollen production by 60%.[22] This may be one important factor in explaining the explosion in asthma in urban populations.[23] So reducing diesel emissions will reduce the availability of fine particles to transport pollen into our lungs, and will also reduce GHG emissions, thereby mitigating the increase in pollen-producing plants and the toxicity of the pollen. Similarly, to the extent coal-fired electricity is reduced or shifted to integrated gasification combined-cycle (IGCC) coal-burning technology, SO_2 and acid deposition should diminish, as well as NO_2 and mercury. IGCC technology is covered in Chapter 19.

Another secondary benefit of state climate change policies is the possible reduction in traffic congestion and urban sprawl. Sprawl stresses infrastructure—communities must pay for new schools, water and sewer systems, parks, roads, police and fire service to keep up, while existing systems may sit underutilized. However, as metropolitan areas across the nation experience ever more congestion on their highways, and limited resources and willingness to expand them and other municipal services, climate change policies that have the potential to alter community patterns become attractive to state policy makers. Any policy that increases average vehicle occupancy rates will diminish congestion pressures. Congress attempted to promote this idea in severe and extreme O_3 non-attainment areas in its 1990 Clean Air Act Amendments by mandating employers to institute employee trip-reduction programs;[24] however, the historically low price of gasoline, the manifest imperative of urban sprawl and the resistance of business in many areas combined to kill the idea. Congress repealed the mandate in 1995,[25] just as it was about to move into full-scale implementation. However, climate change adds an important new justification for revisiting a program that would reduce congestion and sprawl, urban pollution, fuel expense, and GHG emissions.

These transportation policies are important because simply making cars more fuel-efficient will lower the per-mile cost of commuting and thereby encourage additional sprawl and driving. More efficient cars alone will not reduce congestion or slow suburban sprawl. The vehicles people drive could be more energy-efficient, but there could still be more of them, with each one driven further than before; the net result would be an increase of GHG emissions from cars. Thus, to reduce vehicle greenhouse gas emissions, vehicles must be more efficient, and transportation and land use law must promote less driving, not more.

Climate change policies can also diversify a state's energy portfolio. Diversification enhances a state's resilience to external energy challenges. Increased efficiency adds reserve to the state's energy system in times of crisis. On a day-to-day level, diversification and efficiency can dampen price shocks in the oil market, and may even reduce total cost. Moreover, the less state residents and businesses must spend on energy, the more money remains for other uses and investments. Reduced dependence on foreign sources of fuel also lessens the impact of changes in the values of international currencies, with positive effects on trade.

The improved energy efficiency can also help reduce the energy cost burden on poor and moderate-income households. An investment in weatherizing low-income housing and in replacing old, inefficient furnaces with new efficient ones will not only improve the well-being of the resident, but will reduce future demands on state budgets to subsidize fuel during winter. And, it can dramatically reduce the GHG emitted when heating and cooling leaky, poorly insulated houses with inefficient HVAC equipment. Put in climate change terms, the low-income energy programs are not merely expenditures to help the poor in society, but are least-cost ($/ton of CO_2) measures to reduce GHG emissions—savings that will accrue to the entire state.

States can also justify GHG policies from an economic development perspective. The more energy-efficient the state, the lower the cost of living and of doing business in the state. The cost and quality of electric service in a state is now a significant factor informing location decisions of intensively computerized businesses, which now

could be almost any major business in the United States, including banks, insurance companies and other data-based companies. Installation, operation and maintenance of energy-efficient technologies and renewable energy projects generates high-wage jobs, far more than any other means of supplying energy services to a state's economy.[26] Jump-starting a market for energy efficiency and renewable energy can stimulate market opportunities for innovation and entrepreneurship. From these seeds, new, high-value-added businesses can grow, strengthening a state's economic base. Moreover, the new products, technologies and services will be in high demand elsewhere as other states and nations, such as China, invest in reducing their carbon footprints.[27]

On the flip side, failure to promote climate change policies will leave the business-as-usual deregulated energy system in place—a market system that sternly disciplines energy suppliers that reduce sales (and profits) by promoting efficiency. In fact, for a generator of electricity, reduced sales due to end-use efficiency (no matter how cost-effective the efficiency investment) is the worst possible scenario—it reduces revenue but does not reduce the generator's fixed costs. This reduced income will directly reduce the business's bottom-line profit. In contrast, innovative state climate change policies could provide market incentives to the energy industry to provide efficient energy services at a profit.[28] States that have followed this path have generated large savings (after the investment) for their economy; for instance, California, as of 2003, has reduced its electricity sales by almost 7.5%.[29] As one concrete example, California replaced almost one million lamps in traffic signals with high-efficiency light-emitting diodes and saved over 60 megawatts—enough electricity to supply 60,000 homes.[30]

These least-cost energy strategies are "win-win" policies, but need the push of climate change mitigation to overcome the structural legal barriers and the inertia of present markets that currently prevail.

III. State Initiatives

There is no common convention by which one can categorize or even identify what is a climate change initiative as distinguished from a state energy policy, economic development policy, or general environmental policy. Some state initiatives are explicitly adopted to address global warming; others are silent as to global warming but have the effect of reducing greenhouse gas emissions. Some may be categorized as just good general economic regulation seeking to make the market work more efficiently, or to promote concepts of sustainable energy[31] or sustainable development[32] within which addressing climate change is but one of many goals.[33] Moreover, state climate change initiatives address other important greenhouse gases, methane (CH_4) and nitrous oxide (N_2O), emissions of which can come from sources other than burning fossil fuels. State policies can also address CO_2 from non-energy-related sources. Thus policies range well beyond the boundaries of burning fossil fuels more efficiently or switching to renewable energy, to cover landfill gas emissions, agricultural practices, and forestry. Greenhouse gas initiatives may range from those designed to directly reduce GHG emissions, such as state GHG emission reduction legislation, to those designed to prepare a state to be ready to respond to potential future national GHG regulations (such as preparing an inventory of all sources of GHG emissions in the state), and those aimed at promoting a long-term approach to climate change (such as the litigation brought by many states against EPA requesting that EPA list CO_2 as a pollutant under the Clean Air Act).[34]

This chapter will survey those state initiatives that are designed as climate change policy, that have the potential to reduce GHG emissions, or that will help a state protect itself against the risk of future climate change regulation. The goal of the remaining discussion is to introduce lawyers to the general contours of the most commonly adopted policies. The topics to be covered include State Climate Plans, inventories, and registries; renewable energy and energy efficiency; specific carbon-based energy policies; and appliance efficiency standards, green pricing, and other market-based measures.

IV. State Climate Plans

As of June 2006, 28 states have completed some sort of climate action plan.[35] Of these, nine states (California, Connecticut, Maine, Massachusetts, New Jersey, New York, Oregon and Washington) have included emission reduction targets in their plans. Climate change plans that include an enforceable state-wide limit on GHG emissions "provide the highest certainty of significant emission reductions."[36] The climate change planning process can be a valuable tool for states to identify those "cost-effective opportunities to reduce GHG emissions that are relevant to the . . . state's economy, resource base, and political structure."[37] Because most plans are of recent vintage, it is too early to report on which are better than others in achieving their targets. However, if the plan elements are flexibly designed and produce sufficient effective feedback so lessons from past experience can be learned, they can be improved, modified, expanded or extended to other activities as future GHG restrictions warrant.

Now that a majority of states have adopted climate action plans, it is possible to discern common issues, questions and plan elements that must be faced when developing or modifying a plan. Several comprehensive reports on the climate action planning process and databases are available for any lawyer seeking more detailed information.[38] Generally, plans must address both the process of how they are developed and the substance of what is in them. Creating a useful action plan requires large amounts of good data on emissions in all sectors of the state's economy, the state's economy itself, and important demographic factors and trends. Input from the public and all stakeholders is essential from the beginning of the process through its conclusion; government and stakeholders must be committed to the process in terms of time, resources and energy. Technical expertise will be needed from the beginning. Each of these elements comes with its own set of choices.[39] To be successful, plans should not be imposed in a top-down fashion. However, plans will not "simply arise spontaneously from the bottom up. [It] is best addressed as an interactive and iterative process that includes government officials, expert analysis, and those impacted by climate change or remedial policy, which includes everyone."[40] In the end, the goal is to adopt a plan that has broad public support and can be implemented by appropriate administrative agencies that have been given the necessary power and resources. Without a strong consensus-building process, the effort will fail.

Substantive issues begin with setting goals for the plan. The planners must decide if the plan will be comprehensive, covering all economic sectors and all GHGs, or if it will be more narrow, and if so, how narrow. Planners must also consider whether the plan will overlap, compliment, or conflict with other substantive environmental and economic policies within the state; potential co-benefits of the policies must be identified. Decisions must be made on whether to set targets and timetables, and if so, what they will be and how compliance will be measured and assured, and whether requirements will be mandatory or voluntary.

States must also decide if they want to encourage business to reduce greenhouse gas emissions voluntarily before any mandatory requirement is imposed. To do this they must establish a registry that will record voluntary greenhouse gas emission reductions.[41] Early action can help businesses in the state learn how to inventory their emissions, identify reduction opportunities, design and implement GHG emission reduction projects, and measure the reductions the project produces. Many of these efforts will involve improving energy efficiency, which will help a state's economy be more productive. However, calculating emission inventories is not an easy task.[42] Early mastery of the accounting standards will help companies identify and solve accounting issues before inventory accounting becomes mandatory. California's voluntary registry (which will be mandatory shortly) has helped "business to get comfortable with emissions reporting."[43] However, to be worthwhile, the registries must be established with the view that early voluntary action to reduce greenhouse gases will be rewarded if and when mandatory reductions are required. Without such a credit, states will signal that early action will be penalized because they may be required to make future reductions from their already more efficient baseline, while laggards will be rewarded by only being required to make reductions from a higher emission baseline. In other words, registry rules must not confirm the old adage "let no good deed go unpunished." To date some 21 states have established their own or have joined a regional greenhouse gas registry.[44]

Virtually every state that has engaged in the process, even if only to the preliminary stage of establishing an inventory and database of emissions, has used 1990 as its operative baseline.[45] It is not clear why 1990 was so frequently chosen as the baseline year. Coincidental or not, 1990 is the baseline in the Kyoto Protocol and used by the EU. State targets and timetables vary. For example, California's goal is to return to 1990 emission levels by 2020 and reduce to 80% of 1990 levels by 2050. Connecticut aims for 1990 levels by 2010, 10% below 1990 levels by 2020 and, in the long term, to go 75% below 1990 levels. Maine is the same except its long-term goal is 75%–85% below 2003 levels; Massachusetts differs from Maine only by using 2004 levels as its long-term baseline. Some states set a single target: 3.5% below 1990 levels by 2005 (New Jersey, no post-2005 target has been set); 10% below 1990 levels by 2020 (New Hampshire, Rhode Island, and Vermont). Other states have different variations on the target and timetable pattern. Only the initial 1990 baseline is common. Interestingly, the Kyoto Protocol baseline is 1990 levels, the timetable for compliance is the window of 2008–2012, and the targets generally are about 7% below 1990 levels. If the United States were to agree to the Kyoto Protocol, it would have to go to 93% of its 1990 levels not later than 2012. As of 2004, for all GHGs (carbon dioxide equivalents), the United States was 15.8% above its 1990 levels.[46] So, to comply with Kyoto at this late date, the United States would need to reduce its GHG emissions about 23% by 2012.

The most comprehensive climate change action plans generally cover all major sources of GHGs and include some direct focus on one or more economic sectors. The menu of sectors and approaches from which states generally pick include[47]:

- Transportation: vehicle efficiency, low-GHG fuels, reduced travel demand
- Power generation: low-GHG supply options (e.g., renewables, advanced technology), demand-side efficiency programs
- Residential: buildings and appliances
- Commercial: buildings, equipment, and processes
- Industry: buildings, equipment, processes, and distribution
- Agriculture: waste management, production process, and soil management
- Forestry: waste management, silviculture (fire, disease, harvest), forest and soil protection
- Waste management: capture and flaring of landfill methane, waste-to-energy conversion, and recycling

State climate plans must also select the implementation methods and instruments to be used to achieve the targets and timetables. Implementation may vary within a state to address the spectrum of different GHG emitters and legal authority that exists or is needed. Some plan elements may require new statutory authority, others will already fit within the jurisdiction of existing government agencies and resources. State action plans tend to seek a diverse portfolio of approaches. A state may make some aspects of its plan mandatory, using a combination of regulations, standards, emission caps, state funding restrictions and even covenants on real estate. Other aspects of the plans may use voluntary mechanisms, utilizing financial incentives, education, and voluntary agreements to motivate emission reductions.

States must establish some sort of inventory and reporting system to track emissions and progress toward their targets. How to measure, count, and inventory GHGs is a conceptual and practical challenge of the first order. The current standard appears to be the *GHG Protocol Corporate Accounting and Reporting Standard* (rev. ed. 2004) developed by World Business Council for Sustainable Development and WRI; it is the standard currently used by the European Union, EPA Climate Leaders Program, California Climate Action Registry, the Chicago Climate Exchange, ISO 14064 – Part 1, and others.[48] Any lawyer representing a business that needs to inventory its GHG emissions must become familiar with this standard and the project standard with respect to specific projects. When emission credits are traded, these are the standards that will determine how many credits are available to trade, or to use to help finance a project.

V. Carbon-Based Energy Sector

The electric power sector of our economy uses 34% of U.S. fossil fuel energy and emits 40% of U.S. CO_2 released by burning fossil fuels.[49] GHG emissions from the electric power sector are also growing faster than emissions from other sectors. For instance, in 2005, electricity generators increased their emissions by 62.3 million tons of CO_2, a 2.7% increase in one year, whereas CO_2 emissions from the transportation sector grew only 0.2% in 2005, although prior to the oil price increases transportation CO_2 emissions had grown over 23% since 1990, about 1.4% per year.[50] Within the electricity sector, in 2004 coal accounted for 83% of all CO_2 emissions (burning 94% of all the coal used in the United States, but producing less than half of all electricity), compared to gas, 13%, and oil, 4%.[51] However, since coal contains about twice as much carbon content per Btu as natural gas, and since the new natural gas-fired plants are more efficient than coal plants, each ton of CO_2 emitted by burning natural gas generated more than twice the kilowatts as a ton of CO_2 emitted by burning coal. Both the type of fuel used to generate electricity and efficiency-based demand reduction can significantly affect the GHG profile of the sector. So, if a state can influence generators to shift from generating electricity with high CO_2 fuels to low or no- CO_2 sources of energy, it can significantly reduce its CO_2 emissions without reducing the end-use services that electricity provides. Some types of renewable energy can produce energy without emitting any GHG, as is possible for nuclear power. Improved end-use efficiency also produces the effect of reducing CO_2 emissions for the same set of energy services.

Prior to the 1990s, most electricity in the United States was generated by vertically integrated utilities that were regulated as natural monopolies by state public service commissions. Although the federal government, through the Federal Energy Regulatory Commission, had jurisdiction over wholesale sales of electricity and interstate transportation and sales of electricity, the states regulated local utilities in all other respects. States set rates, approved investments and rates of return to be earned on those investments in generating facilities, and oversaw the overall reliability, need for power, and diversity of generation of its electric utilities. However, beginning in the mid-1990s, the electric industry underwent a sea change, with essentially all generation facilities being spun out of the regulated environment into an unregulated, market-driven environment. State public utility commissions can now regulate only the rate to be charged for the distribution of electricity and the local reliability of the distribution of electricity to the retail customer; the state can regulate the fairness of the process of acquiring electricity (e.g., oversee the bidding process), but the cost of the electricity is based on unregulated market conditions. Whether this change in the legal structure of the nation's electricity sector is good or bad will not be debated here.

However, if states wish to influence the GHG emissions associated with electricity, they must develop new policy tools for the new deregulated environment. These new mechanisms that are of most importance are renewable portfolio standards, public benefit funds, net metering, green pricing, demand-side efficiency, appliance efficiency standards, carbon adders, caps and offsets, and tax and other incentives for energy conservation, renewables or improved generation technology. Each of these topics could easily fill a large book, and there are

... if states wish to influence the GHG emissions associated with electricity, they must develop new policy tools for the new deregulated environment.

many books and materials available. This chapter will attempt to provide a basic overview of each policy instrument and a road map for approaching the particulars on any program in any state.

VI. Renewable Portfolio Standards

Some renewable energy sources, primarily solar or solar-derived energy (wind, photovoltaic, solar thermal, small hydroelectric, landfill gas methane, and some cellulose-based fuels) can supply electricity without emitting any CO_2. However, facilities such as wind generators or solar technologies face a number of market barriers. Perhaps the most fundamental is that essentially the entire cost of a renewable source is paid for upfront in the capital equipment—there are no fuel costs. In comparison, the cost of a coal or natural gas-fired plant is only a portion of the cost of generating electricity. Depending on the technology and future prices, the fuel costs can exceed the initial capital investment. Financially, however, the future fuel costs of a plant with a 40-year life, discounted to present value, will be relatively small. For instance, at a 10% discount rate, the present value of $1,000 in 10 years is about $385; in 20 years it is only $148.60, and in 40 years just $22. For a wind generator, the great bulk of the cost is paid in full at the beginning (ongoing expenses can include maintenance, and land rent and taxes). The result is that from a business perspective, renewable energy will always be calculated to be more expensive. The value of the zero-GHG emissions is not included in the financial analysis because the renewable investor cannot get paid for not creating an externality.

Renewable portfolio standards (RPS) are an effective tool that states can use to boost the renewables market. RPS have been adopted around the world and have been a policy approach in the United States since 1991, when Iowa became the first state to enact one, followed by Massachusetts, Minnesota and Nevada in 1997 and then others so that by 2006, 22 states and the District of Columbia had adopted an RPS.[52] Exhibit 10-1 summarizes the key features of all these RPS. Exhibit 10-2 contains a U.S. map highlighting the states that have enacted an RPS. It provides a current, thorough summary of the design and operation of RPS across the United States.

An RPS is a requirement that a certain percentage of the electricity the utility sells to retail customers be generated from renewable energy. Generally, an RPS mandates that a specified percentage of the utility's electricity come from renewable sources. Deadlines vary, "standards range from modest to ambitious, and definitions of renewable energy vary."[53] However, as states have become more comfortable with the idea, the targets have steadily risen from Iowa's modest 1991 law (2% by 2002) or Wisconsin's 1999 law (2.2% by 2011) to California's (33% by 2020) or New York's (25% by 2013) recent enactments. The targets and deadlines are summarized in Exhibit 10-1. Exhibit 10-2 summarizes what sources will qualify as renewables for purposes of the standards. In some states the list of qualified renewables may contain sources that are controversial, such as integrated coal gasification combined-cycle, or incineration of poultry farm or municipal waste.[54] Generally, state legislatures have created the RPS via statute.

Exhibit 10-1

Qualifying Renewable Electricity Sources

State	Wind	Photo-voltaics	Solar Thermal	Biomass	Geo-thermal	Small Hydro-electric	Fuel Cells	Land Fill Gas	Tidal/Ocean	Wave/Thermal	Energy Efficiency
Arizona	✔	✔	✔	✔					✔		
California	✔	✔	✔	✔	✔		✔	✔	✔	✔	
Colorado	✔	✔		✔	✔	✔		✔	✔		
Connecticut	✔	✔	✔	✔			✔	✔	✔	✔	
Deleware	✔	✔	✔	✔	✔		✔	✔	✔	✔	
District of Columbia	✔	✔	✔	✔	✔		✔		✔	✔	
Hawaii	✔	✔	✔	✔	✔		✔	✔	✔	✔	✔
Illinois	✔	✔	✔	✔			✔		✔		
Iowa	✔	✔					✔				
Maine	✔	✔	✔	✔			✔	✔	✔	✔	
Maryland	✔	✔	✔	✔	✔		✔	✔	✔	✔	
Massachusetts	✔	✔	✔	✔				✔	✔	✔	
Minnesota	✔			✔							
Montana	✔	✔	✔	✔	✔		✔	✔	✔		
Nevada	✔	✔	✔	✔	✔		✔		✔		✔
New Jersey	✔	✔		✔	✔		✔	✔	✔	✔	
New Mexico	✔	✔	✔	✔	✔		✔	✔	✔		
New York	✔	✔		✔			✔	✔	✔	✔	
Pennsylvania	✔	✔	✔	✔	✔		✔	✔	✔		✔
Rhode Island	✔	✔		✔	✔	✔	✔	✔	✔		
Texas	✔	✔	✔	✔	✔		✔		✔	✔	
Vermont	✔	✔	✔	✔			✔	✔	✔		
Wisconsin	✔	✔	✔	✔	✔		✔	✔	✔	✔	

Source: Database of State Incentives for Renewable Energy

Source: RABE, RACE TO THE TOP: THE EXPANDING ROLE OF THE U.S. RENEWABLE PERFORMANCE STANDARDS (Pew Center on Global Climate, June 2006).

Exhibit 10-2

State Renewable Portfolio Standards — Key Design Features

State	Year Enacted	Date Revised	Governor Partisanship*	Legislature Control*	Preliminary Target	Final Target	Who's Covered	Credit Trading
Arizona	2001	2006	Rep	Split	0.2% by 2001	15% by 2025	Utility	No
California	2002	2005	Dem	Dem	13% by 2003	33% by 2020	Investor Owned Utility Municipal Utility	Yes
Colorado	2004		Rep	Rep	3% by 2007	10% by 2015	Utility Investor Owned Utility Rural Electric Cooperative	Yes
Connecticut	1999	2003	Rep	Dem	4% by 2004	10% by 2010	Utility	Yes
Delaware	2005		Dem	Split	1% by 2007	10% by 2019	Retail Electricity Supplier	Yes
District of Columbia	2005			Dem	4% by 2007	11% by 2022	Utility	Yes
Hawaii	2004		Rep	Dem	7% by 2003	20% by 2020	Utility	No
Illinois†	2005		Dem	Dem	2% by 2007	8% by 2013	Utility	No
Iowa	1991		Rep	Dem	none	105 MW	Utility	No
Maine	1999		Ind	Dem	none	30% by 2000	Utility	Yes
Maryland	2004		Rep	Dem	3.5% by 2006	7.5% by 2019	Electricity Supplier	Yes
Massachusetts	1997		Rep	Dem	1% new by 2003	4% new by 2009	Utility	Yes
Minnesota	1997		Rep	Dem	1,125 MW by 2010	1,250 MW by 2013	Xcel only	No
Montana	2005		Dem	Split**	5% by 2008	15% by 2015	Utility	Yes
Nevada	1997	2005	Rep	Split	6% by 2005	20% by 2015	Investor Owned Utility	Yes
New Jersey	2001	2004	Rep	Rep	6.5% by 2008	20% by 2020	Utility	Yes
New Mexico	2002	2004	Rep	Dem	5% by 2006	10% by 2011	Investor Owned Utility	Yes
New York	2004		Rep	Split	none	25% by 2013	Investor Owned Utility	Yes
Pennsylvania	2004		Dem	Rep	1.5% by 2007	18% by 2020	Utility	Yes
Rhode Island	2004		Rep	Dem	3% by 2007	16% by 2020	Electric Retailers	Yes
Texas	1999	2005	Rep	Rep	2,280 MW by 2007	5,880 MW by 2015	Retail Supplier	Yes
Vermont	2005		Rep	Dem	none	load growth by 2012	Retail Electricity Supplier	Yes
Wisconsin	1999	2006	Rep	Rep	none	10% by 2015	Utility	Yes

Sources: DSIRE, EIA, NGA, NCSL, Pew Center on Global Climate Change
*Political Control at time of initial enactment
**Senate was controlled by Democrats, House was split 50-50.
†Illinois implements its RPS through voluntary utility commitments.

Renewable Portfolio Standards

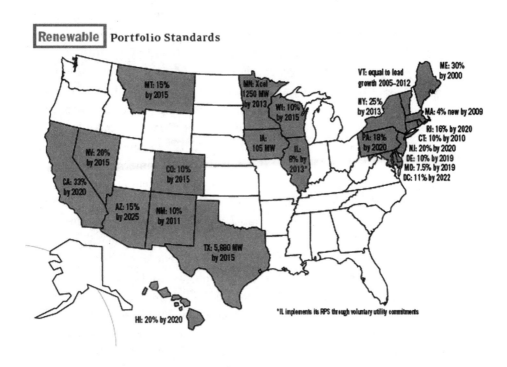

Source: RABE, RACE TO THE TOP: THE EXPANDING ROLE OF THE U.S. RENEWABLE PERFORMANCE STANDARDS (Pew Center on Global Climate, June 2006).

Design criteria for RPS are crucial, both to obtain the benefits a well-designed RPS can generate and to minimize the problems that can be associated with an RPS. A full discussion of the significant design criteria, and an analysis of how each of these design issues have been handled by 13 states, are provided by a recent Lawrence Berkeley National Laboratory Report; its Web site also provides many detailed reports on specific states and resources in the RPS context.[55] This report identifies 16 operational criteria that fall into three broad categories: 1) outcome criteria—these deal with the actual impacts of the state's RPS; 2) policy design criteria—legislative and regulatory design features that will affect the success of the RPS; and 3) market context criteria—"even a well-designed RPS may fail to have its intended effects if the market in which it is applied is not conducive to such a policy."[56] The authors then identify seven principles (with examples of best practices for each) that appear to be common among successful RPS: they are socially beneficial, cost-effective and flexible, predictable, nondiscriminatory, enforceable, consistent with market structures, and compatible with other policies.[57]

Underlying the RPS concept is a market-based mechanism designed to provide price incentives to owners of renewable energy projects. Essentially, to meet the RPS mandate, a utility must obtain sufficient renewable energy credits from qualified renewable energy sources to meet the portfolio standard target. To obtain these, the utility must either contract directly with a qualified renewable power generator to purchase the credit (along with the energy) or buy the credit from someone else in the marketplace. The credits are transferable. Hence, the price of the credit reflects the renewable electricity's premium value. For example, if a state's RPS is 5%, then a utility that sells 1 million kWh of electricity must obtain 50,000 kWh worth of renewable credits. Credits will be tracked by the various independent system operators (ISO), such as PJM,[58] so they can be traded and purchased independently from the electricity. Failure to obtain the necessary credits will result in an "alternative compliance payment" that may vary by state, but hover around $50 per MWh. In theory, a system such as this could readily be modified to fit within any GHG emission reduction credit-trading regime that might be adopted by the United States, or internationally.

GHG emission reductions may not be the primary driver behind these standards, especially in states with a political climate hostile to "global warming." An RPS may be motivated by a variety of other energy policy goals, such as deregulation of the electric utility industry, diversity of energy supply, energy independence, economic desire to use a valuable local resource, job creation or general environmental concerns. Nevertheless, renewable energy provides significant GHG emission reduction co-benefits.[59] As an example, Texas, which requires 2000 MW of new renewable generation by 2009, is ahead of schedule in meeting its goal, having brought 1322 MW of wind on line as of June 2005, with many more projects in the pipeline, and expects to exceed its 2009 target, and to do so at price competitive with fossil fuel sources.[60] These projects are expected to avoid 3.3 million tons of CO_2 emissions annually.[61] Texas has been so pleased with the success of its RPS that in 2005 the Texas legislature increased the level of renewables required and expanded it into the next decade so that "[t]he cumulative installed renewable capacity in [Texas] shall total 5,880 megawatts by January 1, 2015"; the legislature also set a non-binding target of 10,000 MW of installed renewable energy by 2025.[62]

VII. Public Benefit Funds

Public Benefit Funds (PBFs) are a pool of resources typically created by adding a small fee or surcharge on electricity rates charged to customers that can be used by states to invest in clean energy supply. Public Benefit Funds, sometimes called system benefits funds, are state programs developed as part of the electric industry restructuring process to help finance renewable energy, demand-side energy-efficiency initiatives, and low-income energy assistance. The funds are most commonly supported by a charge to all retail electric customers. The rates vary from small to tiny, with one study finding the mean to be 1.1 mills/kWh ($0.0011).[63]

> **Public Benefit Funds are a pool of resources typically created by adding a small fee or surcharge on electricity rates charged to customers that can be used by states to invest in clean energy supply.**

PBFs grew out of the deregulation of the electricity industry in the latter half of the 1990s. Prior to deregulation, many public service commissions required the utilities they regulated to invest in energy-efficiency programs. After deregulation in the 1990s, however, utilities eliminated these programs because they subsidized customers to buy less of their product, which reduced revenues and profit. Public benefit funds emerged as a means for states to continue investments in energy efficiency and renewable energy measures even under utility deregulation. Nearly every state that has passed electric industry restructuring legislation has used this method to finance some aspect of energy efficiency or renewable energy.

Although many funds help support renewable energy projects, the use of RPS is much more effective in expanding renewable energy. PBFs are much more important as a steady supporter of demand-side energy-efficiency programs. Successful energy-efficiency programs can provide durable, low-cost reductions in demand, which can translate directly into reduced GHG emissions, particularly if the electricity is coal-fired. As of 2003, electricity energy-efficiency programs funds by PBFs have saved the nation nearly 2% of total electricity (kWh). Seven states have achieved more than a 5% total energy savings. However, five states have no efficiency PBF and have not saved any energy.[64]

VIII. Carbon Adders

Because the emission of CO_2 creates a significant externality, economic theory requires that the effects be internalized. As a result, in the 1990s, just before deregulation fever set in, many PSCs turned to proxies to establish an externality value for greenhouse gases.[65] From an energy-planning perspective, the use of environmental externalities adders to internalize the external damages caused by residual emissions had been a useful educational and academic exercise,[66] but it did not have a significant impact on resource selection.[67] That is, the same results would have obtained if adders had not been used.[68] Moreover, the use of adders in new resource selection did nothing to achieve present environmental quality needs, but only helped gradually to point the utility's system toward an environmentally least-cost system.

Unlike most other air pollutants, such as particulates, SO_2, ozone, CO, or lead, whose effects tend to be relatively direct and local, or at least regional, and which survive in the atmosphere for a relatively short period of time, greenhouse gases accumulate over long periods of time in the atmosphere, with the resulting cumulative effect being a modification of climate globally and regionally. With respect to CO_2, the goal of improving the use of externalities was to minimize the *risk* of future climate change regulation in present energy decisions. In using carbon adders, commissions were seeking to create a regulatory environment in which private actors would have price-like incentives to buy real, adequate insurance against the risk of future climate change and regulatory response to climate change. However, with the advent of utility deregulation, public utility commissions no longer were regulating fully integrated utilities. Integrated resource planning, the system by which commissions would approve what kind of and how much new-generation resources would be added to the system, disappeared as a meaningful planning and analysis tool. The use of carbon adders, an exciting idea in the early 1990s, went into hibernation.

Now, as global warming is lurking as a threat to states' economies and environments, state regulators are beginning to return to the idea of incorporating global warming externalities into the electric system decision-making structure. The major problem states face is that few utilities own their own generating facilities any more, so there is little for states to regulate other than the energy supply contracts local utilities use to purchase electricity. However, many states worry about the costs of meeting future regulations limiting CO_2 emissions.

Carbon adders are policy instruments that try to account for the risk of future costs of mitigating GHG emissions in decisions about which new electric generation investments represent the lowest risk-adjusted source. Carbon adders, expressed in \$/ton of CO_2, times the tons of CO_2 the facility will emit over its anticipated future life, represent the present value (discounted over time) of the future costs of complying with future CO_2 regulations. The adoption of carbon adders is based on the assumption that the risk of GHG regulations over the next 20 years is greater than zero. The \$/ton carbon adder number represents an estimate (however uncertain) of the present value of avoiding the future costs. The present value is added to the financial cost of a wide range of potential new electricity sources such as coal-fired, natural gas-fired, renewables, and energy efficiency. The aim is to steer economically rational actors toward investments into those resources that will have the lowest lifetime costs, including the presumed cost of future CO_2 regulations.

Carbon adders are presently used only for utility-planning purposes; the cost of the adder is not actually imposed, nor is it charged to consumers. It is used instead by a PSC to assess long-term resource alternatives based on a price calculation that reflects the global warming externalities and regulatory risk associated with the option. The major difference between the previous externality approach and the present adder approach is the basis on which the value of the adder is set. The externalities approach attempted to identify, if possible, the dollar value of the damages caused by the residual emission of air pollutants. However, the early CO_2 values were not based on damages, but on the estimated cost of offsetting the emissions so that the emission did not cause any damage.[69] From the start, the CO_2 adder value was based on an economic decision to minimize the risk of future regulation on present long-term investment decisions.

In 2005, California returned to the policy instrument of externality adders as part of its larger climate change plans. The California Public Utility Commission ordered that the value of $8 per ton of CO_2 be included in the cost calculations for long-term utility planning and in the evaluation of bids for future electricity or demand-side management resources. California set

the value to address the risk of future regulation of CO_2. In its view, the probability of future regulation was greater than zero, and therefore the financial risk associated with future environmental regulation of CO_2 was greater than zero. Hence, the CPUC believed it was prudent to include a conservative estimate of the present value of future costs of offsetting or reducing CO_2 emissions in evaluating all long-term commitments. If a binding CO_2 cap is imposed in California, the CPUC will revisit its adder decision because the cap will be controlling.

In 2004, PacifiCorp, one of the major western utilities, announced that it would use adders in the range of $8–$20 per ton CO_2 in its integrated resource planning (IRP).[70] In its 2006 IRP, PacifiCorp continued to use an $8 per ton adder (in 2008 dollars); the adder will increase to $20 per ton CO_2 in 2012 and escalate at inflation thereafter, but the company intends to mitigate cost uncertainty by analyzing a range of CO_2 adder values in its IRP.[71]

Other states have adopted CO_2 adders. In 2005, the Colorado PSC approved a settlement agreement that will require its major electric utility, Xcel Energy, to add a carbon adder of $9 per ton (increasing 2.5% annually) to energy bids from sources that emit carbon dioxide; the carbon adder is to mitigate the risk of future regulatory costs of controlling greenhouse gases.[72] In 1993, the Oregon Public Utilities Commission mandated that regulated electric utilities apply a range of carbon adders from $10 to $40 (in 1990 dollars) per ton of CO_2 in their integrated resource plans.[73] In a comprehensive review of state clean energy policies, law, and best practices, EPA summarized thus:

> Vermont law requires that utilities prepare a plan for providing energy services at the lowest present-value life-cycle costs, including environmental and economic costs. Similarly, several utilities, including PacifiCorp, Idaho Power, PGE, Avista, and Xcel, incorporate an estimate of potential carbon emissions fees into their planning processes. For example, Montana requires utilities to consider environmental factors in portfolio management, but it does not require consideration of environmental externalities. These externalities, added to the cost of resources, can be used to incorporate estimates of sensitivity to risk associated with the environmental effects of plant emissions (e.g., acid rain, climate change, and other issues).[74]

IX. Net Metering

Net metering allows retail electric customers who generate their own electricity, generally from a renewable source such as solar, wind, or small hydro, to sell their excess electricity back into the grid. The meters run backward if the customer generates more electricity than the customer uses. So, when on-site production exceeds use, the customer sends surplus electricity to the grid, and when the customer's demand exceeds the customer's production, the customer uses electricity from the grid. The customer then pays the local electric provider only for the net electricity consumed. As of June 2006, 40 states and the District of Columbia have some kind of net metering program.[75]

X. Green Pricing

This is a utility service allowing customers to support a larger level of investment in renewable energy innovations by paying a premium for electricity to cover the higher incremental cost of the renewable energy. Starting in the mid-1990s, these voluntary programs now serve about 540,000 customers in 34 states. Although green pricing is a relatively small part of the U.S. energy market, it has helped finance about 2200 MW of renewable generation, and if trends continue, could help develop about 8000 MW.[76]

Because the programs are voluntary between customer and utility, states have a small role. However, states can facilitate and authorize the programs, and should insure that green power programs are consistent with RPS and system benefits requirements. States must also help insure that the certification of electricity as green is valid and reliable. Otherwise the customers will be paying a green premium for brown power. Certification is critical because customers do not actually receive the green energy from the generator. Rather, the utility contracts with the green generator for all or some of its output. The electricity is then sent to the electric grid, which must always be in exact balance between supply and demand, where it no longer can be physically tracked. The system operator credits the generator and utility based on the contract price as the energy is produced and distributed. The customer pays for "green energy" because without the contract to purchase, the utility would have met the customer's demand from some other source, probably coal-based, depending on the electricity supplier's specific fuel mix. Although the electricity generated by renewable sources is not delivered directly to the customers who pay for it, the utility certifies that renewable energy has been generated in an amount equal to the customer's purchase and delivered to the grid. EPA's Clean Energy Guide provides details and examples.

XI. State Appliance Efficiency Standards

State appliance efficiency standards set minimum energy-efficiency levels for equipment and appliances that are not covered by federal efficiency standards. Appliance efficiency standards typically prohibit the sale of less efficient models within a state. States may set standards for products covered by existing federal standards only if granted a waiver from the U.S. Department of Energy. On October 6, 2006, DOE proposed a rule that would allow states, either alone or in regional coalitions of contiguous states, to petition for a preemption waiver of a federal standard in favor of a state-based appliance efficiency standard more stringent than federal requirement. To obtain the waiver, the state's (s') petition must demonstrate "unusual and compelling state or local energy interests." DOE summarized the law:

> Federal energy conservation requirements generally supersede State laws or regulations concerning energy conservation testing, labeling, and standards. (42 U.S.C. 6297 (a)-(c)) The Department can, however, grant waivers of preemption for particular State laws or regulations, in accordance with the procedures and other provisions of section 327(d) of the Act. (42 U.S.C. 6297(d)) Specifically, States with a regulation that provides for an energy conservation standard for any type of covered product for which there is a Federal energy conservation standard may petition the Secretary for a DOE rule that allows the State regulation to become effective with respect to such covered product. The Department must prescribe a rule granting the petition if the State establishes by a preponderance of the evidence that its regulation is needed to meet "unusual and compelling State or local energy * * * interests." (42 U.S.C. 6297(d)(1)(B))[77]

DOE's notice of proposed rule explained:

> . . . that in the context of residential furnaces and boilers, where regional climatic effects can have significant impact on whether a specified energy conservation standard would be technologically feasible and economically justified in that region, such regional climatic effects will be important in DOE's assessment of whether there are "unusual and compelling State or local energy interests" for State energy conservation standards. States having higher-than-average, population-weighted heating degree days (HDDs) based on long-term National Oceanic and Atmospheric Administration data would seem to have the best prospects for demonstrating "unusual and compelling" interests to support a waiver of preemption in the particular circumstances presented here. . . . States with significantly higher heating requirements have significantly higher furnace use. This may indicate that, for those States, a State energy conservation standard which is higher than the Federal standard would be cost-effective and would provide significantly more energy savings than the Federal standard. If those States, particularly the ones most severely affected, adopted standards higher than DOE's proposed standards, and sought waivers, it could result in certain contiguous States with higher requirements, which would lessen the impact on manufacturers.[78]

As of November 2005, 10 states have set appliance efficiency standards covering 36 different appliances. Appliance efficiency standards are very effective in significantly reducing electricity load, eliminating the need for new generation: "Hundreds of power plants are not needed today because the world has invested in much more efficient refrigerators, air conditioners and motors than were available two decades ago."[79] State implementation costs are low, the process is relatively easy, and the return on investment is huge. California expects that its appliance efficiency standards will save its citizens $3 billion by 2020 and eliminate the need for three new power plants.[80] The standards help overcome market barriers to more efficient products, such as the different economic incentives of builders and homebuyers or landlords and tenants. Builders and landlords want to construct structures as inexpensively as possible; they have minimal regard for energy-efficiency investments, since the homebuyer or tenant will pay the ongoing energy costs. Similarly, to the extent that owners or tenants face an ownership or tenancy timeframe that is shorter than the time needed to recover the extra costs of energy-efficiency investments, they do not have the financial incentive to insist (to the extent they have any input) on greater efficiency. Appliance efficiency standards are also valuable because they reduce the transaction costs for customers interested in purchasing efficient appliances by insuring that the appliances meet a minimum level.

Building codes can also be used to improve the energy efficiency of new buildings. They must be adopted by legislative action; as of 2006, some form of energy code has been adopted by 42 states and the District of Columbia. They are updated periodically, but tend to lag behind the improvement curve of technical innovation. As building and lighting technology improve and become incorporated into revised codes, our new and renovated residential and commercial building stock will slowly become more efficient. These efficiency gains will provide benefits for decades. This assumes, of course, that code compliance is assured by meaningful enforcement. However, if all states adopted the most current energy codes for commercial and residential construction and manufactured housing and effectively enforced these codes, consumers would save $7 billion in energy costs and the United States could avoid the need (and expense) to construct 32 new 400-megawatt power plants.[81]

Endnotes

1. This statement is based on the author's review of a number of databases, reports, and surveys, as well as searches of Westlaw and the Internet. Among the more useful resources are the State Action Database, maps and reports available at the Pew Center on Global Climate Change, www.pewclimate.org/policy_center/ state_policy/; information provided by: the American Council for an Energy Efficient Economy (ACEEE), www.aceee.org; the Alliance to Save Energy, www.ase.org/section/_audience/ policymakers/stateinit/; the Center for Clean Air Policy, www.ccap.org; and EPA's Global Warming Web page, Actions - State, http://yosemite.epa.gov/OAR/globalwarming.nsf/content/ Actions.html. Unfortunately, the EPA site was last updated on Jan. 3, 2003.

2. ALA. CODE § 22-28A-3 (2003) ("Effective immediately, the Director of the Alabama Department of Environmental Management shall refrain from proposing or promulgating any new regulations intended in whole or in part to reduce emissions of greenhouse gases, as such gases are defined by the Kyoto Protocol, from the residential, commercial, industrial, electric utility, or transportation sectors unless such reductions are required under existing statutes."); *see also* 415 ILL. COMP. STAT. 140/15 (2003); KY. REV. STAT. ANN. § 224.20-125 (Michie 2003); OKLA. STAT. tit. 27A. § 1-1-207 (2003); W. VA. CODE § 22-23-1 (2003); WYO. STAT. ANN. § 35-11-213 (Michie 2003).

3. Pew Center on Global Climate Change, *Table of All State Initiatives*, http:// www.pewclimate.org/what_s_being_done/in_the_states/state_action_maps.cfm.(last visited June 26, 2006).

4. *Id.* at http://www.pewclimate.org/what_s_being_done/in_the_states/news.cfm.

5. *US state treasurers press ExxonMobil on climate*, ENVTL. FINANCE (May 25, 2006), *republished by* World Business Council for Sustainable Development, www.wbcsd.org/ plugins/DocSearch/details.asp?type=DocDet&ObjectID=MtkyOTg.

6. *See* Barry G. Rabe et al., *State Competition as a Source Driving Climate Change Mitigation*, 14 N.Y.U. ENVTL. L. R. 1 (2005); Kirsten H. Engel, *Mitigating Global Climate Change in the United States: A Regional Approach*, 14 N.Y.U. ENVTL. L. R. 54 (2005).

7. U.S. CONST. art. I, § 9, cl. 10, ¶ 1 ("No State shall enter into any Treaty, Alliance, or Confederation . . .").

8. *See* David R. Hodas, *State Law Responses to Global Warming: Is It Constitutional to Think Globally and Act Locally?* 21 PACE ENVTL. L.R. 53 (2003); Note, *Foreign Affairs Preemption and State Regulation of Greenhouse Gas Emissions*, 119 HARV. L.R. 1877 (2006).

9. U.S. CONST. art. I, § 9, cl. 10, ¶ 3 ("No State shall, without the Consent of Congress, . . . enter into any Agreement or Compact with another State, or with a foreign power, . . .").

10. *See* Kirsten H. Engel, *The Dormant Commerce Clause Threat to Market-Based Regulation: The Case of Electricity Deregulation*, 26 ECOLOGY L.Q. 243 (1999).

11. *See* Brian H. Potts, *Regulating Greenhouse Gas 'Leakage': How California Can Evade the Impending Constitutional Attack*, ELEC. J., June 2006, at 43.

12. *See* Tom Alkire, *Gathering of State Regulators Fails to Agree on Resolution to Address Greenhouse Gases*, BNA Daily Envt. Rpt. A-8 (Aug. 31, 2006).

13. The Bush Administration plan is to rely on voluntary private action to reduce the GHG intensity of the economy (the ton of CO_2 to $GDP ratio) about 1% per year, but not the quantity of emissions (see Chapter 3). Since the economy has historically become about 1% more efficient each year, the Bush Administration's proposal is merely that industry voluntarily continue to do business as usual. The Bush Administration has been successful in achieving this goal—we have reduced our carbon intensity slightly over the past few years, while increasing our annual GHG emissions far above our 1990 levels.

14. The ranking of CO_2 emissions and per capita emissions is based on analysis of the 2001 national and state CO_2 emission data maintained by World Resources Institute in its Climate Analysis Indicator Tool at http://cait.wri.org/.

15. Wyoming, North Dakota, Alaska, West Virginia, and Louisiana

16. Indiana, Montana, Kentucky, New Mexico, Texas, Alabama, Oklahoma, Utah, Iowa, Kansas, Nebraska, and Mississippi.

17. Missouri and Arkansas.

18. Ohio, Tennessee, Pennsylvania, and Nevada.

19. EMILY FIGDOR & ALISON CASSADY, THE CARBON BOOM: NATIONAL AND STATE TRENDS IN CARBON DIOXIDE EMISSIONS SINCE 1960 (USPIRG 2006), Appx. D (U.S. Public Interest Research Group).

20. David R. Hodas, *The Challenge of High-Priced Oil*, NATURAL RES. & ENV'T, Fall 2005, at 59.

21. Lawrence Kumins, Energy Economist, Congressional Research Service, U.S. Library of Congress, *U.S. Refining Infrastructure: An Overview* (June 9, 2006), Presentation at ABA Standing Committee on Environmental Law 34th National Spring Conference on the Environment, Baltimore, Md., June 9, 2006; *available at* http://www.abanet.org/publicserv/environmental/34th_conf_materials.shtml.

22. Peter Wayne et al., *Production of allergenic pollen by ragweed (Ambrosia artemisiifolia L.) is increased in CO_2-enriched atmosphere*, 8 ANNALS OF ALLERGY, ASTHMA, AND IMMUNOLOGY 279 (2002).

23. Interview of Dr. Paul Epstein, Director of the Center for Health and Global Environment, Harvard Medical School, by Terri Gross on *Fresh Air* (WHYY, June 26, 2006), *available at* http://www.npr.org/templates/story/story.php?storyId=5511686.

24. 42 U.S.C. § 7511(a)(d)(1)(B).

25. Pub. L. 104-73, 109 Stat. 773 (Dec. 23, 1995).

26. *See, e.g.,* MASSACHUSETTS TECHNOLOGY COLLABORATIVE RENEWABLE ENERGY TRUST, ENERGY EFFICIENCY, RENEWABLE ENERGY AND JOBS IN MASSACHUSETTS (Nov. 2005), http://masstech.org/RenewableEnergy/reports/clusterreport11405.pdf.

27. *See* JONATHAN E. STINTON ET AL., EVALUATION OF CHINA'S ENERGY STRATEGY OPTIONS (LBNL 56609, China Energy Group, Env't & Energy Technologies Div., Lawrence

Berkeley Nat'l Lab., May 2005), http://china.lbl.gov/china_pubs-policy.html.

28. *See* CHERYL HARRINGTON, CATHERINE MURRAY, LIZ BALDWIN, ENERGY EFFICIENCY POLICY TOOLKIT (REGULATORY ASSISTANCE PROJECT, May 2006), http://www.raponline.org/showpdf.asp?PDF_URL=Pubs/General/EfficiencyPolicyToolkit%2Epdf.

29. Dan York & Marty Kushler, *ACEEE's 3rd National Scorecard on Utility and Public Benefits of Energy Efficiency Programs: A National Review and Update of State-Level Activities* (Rep. #U054, American Council for an Energy-Efficient Economy, Oct. 2005), *available at* http://aceee.org/pubs/U054.htm.

30. International Energy Agency, Press Release, Saving Energy in a Hurry (June 7, 2005) (announcing publication of IEA, SAVING ENERGY IN A HURRY: DEALING WITH TEMPORARY SHORTFALLS IN ELECTRICITY SUPPLIES (Oct. 2005), http://www.iea.org/w/bookshop/add.aspx?id=201.

31. *See* UNITED NATIONS DEVELOPMENT PROGRAMME, WORLD ENERGY ASSESSMENT: ENERGY AND THE CHALLENGE OF SUSTAINABLILITY (Jose Goldenberg ed., 2000).

32. *See* ENERGY LAW AND SUSTAINABLE DEVELOPMENT (Adrian J. Bradbrook & Richard L. Ottinger eds., 2003).

33. Richard L. Ottinger & Fred Zalcman, *Legal measures to promote renewable and energy resources*, in *id.* at 79-113.

34. *See* Laura Kosloff & Mark Trexler, *State Climate Change Initiatives: Think Locally, Act Globally*, NATURAL RES. & ENV'T, Winter 2004, at 46.

35. PEW CENTER ON GLOBAL CLIMATE CHANGE, LEARNING FROM STATE ACTION ON CLIMATE CHANGE 8 (June 2006 Update).

36. *Id.*

37. *Id.*

38. *See* Thomas D. Peterson, *The Evolution of State Climate Change Policy in the United States: Lessons Learned and New Directions*, 14 WIDENER L.J. 153 (2004); Adam Rose, *Greenhouse Gas Mitigation Action Planning: An Overview*, 12 PENN. ST. ENVTL. L. REV. 153 (2004); TOM PETERSON, CLIMATE CHANGE MITIGATION: PROCESS AND POLICY OPTIONS FOR STATE GREENHOUSE GAS PLANS (Center for Clean Air Policy, Feb. 2004), www.ccap.org; EPA's global warming Web site state action page, http://yosemite.epa.gov/oar/globalwarming.nsf/content/ActionsStateActionPlans.html; and Pew Center on Global Climate Change, www.pewclimate.org (state policy and database pages).

39. *See* Peterson, *The Evolution of State Climate Change Policy, supra* note 38, at 19-30 (describing the range of choices and decisions that must be made as the process unfolds).

40. Rose, *supra* note 38, at 155.

41. Greenhouse gases covered by registries are carbon dioxide, methane, nitrous oxide, hydrofluorocarbons, perfluorocarbons, and sulfur hexafluoride.

42. World Resources Institute and World Business Council for Sustainable Development, *The Greenhouse Gas Protocol—A corporate accounting and reporting standard (revised edition)*, http://www.ghgprotocol.org/plugins/GHGDOC/details.asp?type=DocDet&ObjectId=MTM3NTc.

43. Dean Scott, *Launch of State Greenhouse Gas Registries Needed to Prepare for Mandates, Utility Says*, BNA Env't Daily A-2 (Oct. 12, 2006) (quoting Steve Kline, vice president, Corporate and Environmental Affairs, PG&E).

44. Arizona, Arkansas, California, Connecticut, Georgia, Idaho, Illinois, Indiana, Iowa, Maine, Massachusetts, Michigan, New Hampshire, New Jersey, New York, Ohio, Oregon, Rhode Island, Vermont, Wisconsin, and Wyoming. List compiled from data assembled by Pew Center on Global Climate Change, http://www.pewclimate.org/states.cfm.

45. Louisiana's inventory of GHG and sinks uses 1996 data; Mississippi's inventory uses 1992 data. Neither state has proceeded beyond the inventory stage. New Mexico set a target for future emissions using 2000 as the baseline year.

46. U.S. E.P.A., Office of Atmospheric Programs, *The U.S. Inventory of Greenhouse Gas Emissions and Sinks: Fast Facts* (April 2006), http://yosemite.epa.gov/oar/globalwarming.nsf/content/ResourceCenterPublicationsGHGEmissionsUSEmissionsInventory2006.html.

47. PETERSON, CLIMATE CHANGE MITIGATION, *supra* note 38, at 15.

48. The standard and guidelines and tools for using it are available at http://www.ghgprotocol.org/templates/GHG5/layout.asp?type=p&MenuId=ODg4&doOpen=1&ClickMenu=No. *See also* Chapter 17 of this book.

49. U.S. E.P.A., INVENTORY OF UNITED STATES GREENHOUSE GAS EMISSIONS AND SINKS 1990-2004 (Apr. 2006), ES 7-8.

50. Energy Information Agency, U.S. Dept of Energy, U.S. Carbon Emissions from Energy Sources—2005 Flash Estimate (June 2006) (based on data published in EIA, *Monthly Energy Review* (May 2006)), www.eia.doe.gov.

51. *Id.* at Table 3-3.

52. BARRY G. RABE, RACE TO THE TOP: THE EXPANDING ROLE OF THE U.S. RENEWABLE PORTFOLIO STANDARDS 3 (Pew Center on Global Climate Change, June 2006).

53. PEW CENTER ON GLOBAL CLIMATE CHANGE, RENEWABLE PORTFOLIO STANDARDS (May 2006), http://www.pewclimate.org/what_s_being_done/in_the_states/rps.cfm.

54. RABE, *supra* note 52, at 18.

55. R. WISER ET AL., EVALUATING EXPERIENCE WITH RENEWABLE PORTFOLIO STANDARDS IN THE UNITED STATES (LBNL #54439) (Lawrence Berkeley Nat'l Lab., March 2004), http://eetd.lbl.gov/ea/ems/re-pubs.html.

56. *Id.* at 11.

57. *Id.* at 25–29.

58. *See* PJM Envtl. Info. Services, Generator Attribute Tracking System, www.pjm-eis.com.

59. *See* R. WISER ET AL., *supra* note 55.

60. RABE, *supra* note 52, at 11.

61. PEW, *supra* note 53.

62. TEXAS S. B. 20, § 3a (2005), *as reported by* RABE, RENEWABLE PORTFOLIO STANDARDS, at 12.

63. For a detailed analysis of the public benefit funds in over 20 states, *see* MARTIN KUSHLER ET AL., FIVE YEARS IN: AN EXAMINATION OF THE FIRST HALF-DECADE OF PUBLIC BENEFIT ENERGY EFFICIENCY POLICIES (ACEEE Report U04, April 2004), *available at* http://www.aceee.org/store/proddetail.cfm?CFID=569382&CFTOKEN=28344766&ItemID=376&CategoryID=7.

64. DAN YORK & MARTY KUSHLER, ACEEE'S 3RD NATIONAL SCORECARD ON UTILITY AND PUBLIC BENEFITS ENERGY EFFICIENCY PROGRAMS: A NATIONAL REVIEW AND UPDATE OF STATE-LEVEL ACTIVITY (ACEEE Report U054, Oct. 2005). Summary table of every state's program can be found at http://www.aceee.org/briefs/mktabl.htm.

65. *See, e.g., In re* Quantification of Envt'l Costs, 150 P.U.R. 4th 130 (Minn. P.U.C. 1994); *In re* Calculation and Use of Cost-Effectiveness Levels for Conservation, 152 P.U.R. 4th 58 (Or. P.U.C. 1994) (noting that "costs related to . . . carbon dioxide are likely to be internalized in some form within the 20-year planning horizon"); *In re*

Central Vermont Pub. Serv. Corp., No. 5624, 1994 WL 400909 (Vt. P.S.C. June 29, 1994) (requiring the addition of a 5% allowance to base costs for "external costs of producing energy, such as contributions to . . . global warming"); and *In re* Montana Power Co., 152 P.U.R. 4th 403 (Mont. P.S.C. 1994) (ordering the utility "to include cost estimates for externalities in its next rate filing . . . although such estimates are uncertain, it is inappropriate to continue to design rates under the assumption that the value for externalities is zero. At a minimum the utility must estimate damage costs associated with carbon dioxide" and other pollutants to "reflect impacts on human health, agriculture, timber, livestock, ecosystems and biodiversity, global warming, recreation, visual and audio aesthetics, and land use (including property values)").

66. The use of environmental externality adders has been subject to criticism by some economists who prefer no values to imperfect ones; these economists urge PSCs to abandon the use of "second best" values until "improved" analysis results in accurate, site-specific damage functions. *See, e.g.,* Joskow, *Weighing Environmental Externalities: Let's Do It Right*, 5 ELEC. J. 53-67 (1992). To the extent that economic analysts devote their energies to arguing that the use of externality adders is a "bad idea," policy-makers are left to make "second best" decisions without the quantitative input of the "best or nothing at all" economists. *See* A.M. Freeman & A.J. Krupnick, *Externality Adders: A Response to Joskow*, 5 ELEC. J. 61-63 (1992) (arguing that "given reasonable assumptions about the objectives of PUCs, the use of environmental adders in utility planning is in fact necessary for improving social welfare"). More importantly, the current rigid and arbitrary methods by which the externality values are used in IRP reviews do not induce utilities to propose creative, innovative solutions to the residual emission problem.

67. Unfortunately, precise data is not readily available to evaluate the impact of using environmental externality adders. However, because the present use of externalities will only apply to new facilities, any effect will only be felt in the long term. F. Wood & R. Naill, *Externalities in Utility Planning: What Would It Cost?*, 5 ELEC. J. 35, 40 (August/September 1992). Similarly, the California PSC believes that its greenhouse externality value and risk-shifting contract clause will not affect any coal resource decisions, because other factors have already driven the price of new coal plants significantly above the cost of other options. Biennial Resource Plan Update, 132 P.U.R. 4th 200, Decision fn. 21 (Cal. P.U.C. 1992).

68. N.Y.S. ENERGY BOARD, NEW YORK STATE ENERGY PLAN VOLUME II: ISSUE REPORTS 180-83 (October 1994).

69. *See* David Hodas, *Global Warming, in* ENVIRONMENTAL COSTS OF ELECTRICITY 127-91 (Richard Ottinger et al. eds., 1990). The CO_2 value adopted by many of the public service commissions was based on reports that relied on the analysis and recommendation in that chapter. *See, e.g.,* Stephen Weil, *The New Environmental Accounting: A Status Report*, ELEC. J., Nov. 1991, at 50.

70. MARK BOLINGER & RYAN WISER, BALANCING COST & RISK: THE TREATMENT OF RENEWABLE ENERGY IN WESTERN UTILITY RESOURCE PLANS (Lawrence Berkeley Nat'l Lab., Envtl. LBNL # 58450, August 2005), *available at* http://eetd.lbl.gov/EA/EMP.

71. PacifiCorp, 2006 IRP General Meeting (April 20, 2006) http://www.pacificorp.com/File/File66699.pdf.

72. Joshua Bushinsky, *Colorado Carbon Adder*, http://www.pewclimate.org/states.cfm?ID=56.

73. *Id.*, http://www.pewclimate.org/states.cfm?ID=57.

74. U.S. E.P.A., Office of Atmospheric Programs, Climate Protection Partnership Division, Clean Energy-Environment Guide to Action: Policies, Best Practices, and Action Steps for States (EPA 430-R-06-00, April 2006), ch. 6, 6-7.

75. *See* www.dsireusa.org for information on specific state standards. http://www.dsireusa.org/library/includes/type.cfm?Type=Net&Back=regtab&CurrentPageID=7&EE=0&RE=1&Search=TableType.

76. EPA, Clean Energy, 5-59 to 5-74.

77. Proposed Rule, Energy Conservation Program for Consumer Products: Energy Conservation Standards for Residential Furnaces and Boilers, 71 Fed. Reg. 59,204-01 (October 6, 2006).

78. *Id.*

79. Robert H. Socolow & Stephen W. Pacala, *A Plan to Keep Carbon in Check*, Sci. Am., September 2006, at 52.

80. For a complete analysis of appliance efficiency programs and state-by-state, appliance-by-appliance details, *see* EPA, Clean Energy, *supra* note 74, 4-54 to 4-68. EPA also provides a list of all the federal standards and describes best practices, resources and references.

81. *Id.* at 4-37 to 4-53. These materials include detailed descriptions of the various codes and best practices, together with informational resources and references.

The State Response to Climate Change: 50-State Survey

*Pace Law School Center for Environmental Legal Studies**

This chapter compiles state legislation, rules and executive orders that specifically address climate change as of the end of September 2006. It also surveys a wide variety of state activities that may have an impact on greenhouse gases, including legislation related to energy efficiency and renewable energy. The focus of this material is to provide readers with an understanding of the range of state activity that may contribute to greenhouse gas reduction and climate change. Some types of energy efficiency, alternative fuels and renewable energy legislation (such as tax credits for hybrid vehicles) are very similar from state to state, some laws have a short duration and therefore may not be codified (such as temporary tax credits), and energy legislation is being enacted at an increasing pace. As a result, not all legislation and other activity concerning energy efficiency, alternative fuels and renewable energy in every state is included in this compilation.**

---

* This chapter was prepared by students and staff at the Pace Law School Center for Environmental Legal Studies: Paul Babchik, Naomi Galtz, Caroline Justice, Lee Paddock, Mackenzie Schoonmaker, and Megan Smith.

** The Center for Environmental Legal Studies will continue to compile legislation, rules and executive orders that relate to climate change and requests readers who have new information or information that differs from that included in this chapter to forward the information to Leslie Crincoli at lcrincoli@law.pace.edu.

The material in this chapter demonstrates how several states have taken analogous approaches to addressing climate change. For example, a growing number of states are adopting renewable portfolio standards, and many states are poised to adopt California's greenhouse gas emissions standards for motor vehicles. In addition, numerous states have formed regional initiatives to address climate change. Such actions, along with several other initiatives discussed herein, show how the states have emerged as leaders in addressing climate change.

ALABAMA

In an effort to promote energy efficiency, Alabama enacted an annual flat license fee on motor vehicles that use liquefied petroleum gas or natural gas as fuel. The fee runs from $75 to $175, depending on the class of vehicle.[1]

The Alabama Local Government Energy Loan Program, established in 1997, offers no-interest loans to small rural government agencies, including schools, for energy-efficiency equipment and building upgrades. The fund has an endowment of $2 million per year, and the maximum loan size is $150,000 per project and $300,000 per school system. In order to qualify for these loans, the facility must be in a town of no more than 20,000 people or a county with no more than 50,000 people.[2]

The Alabama STAR (Savings Through Analysis and Retrofits) Program, established in 1997, provides prevailing interest-rate loans for energy-efficiency improvements to tax-exempt, public, and nonprofit schools. Eligible improvements include lighting retrofits, HVAC equipment, load management devices, and sewage and water systems improvements, among other measures. The fund has an endowment of $4.6 million per year. Individual loans cannot exceed $2 million.[3]

The Alabama Department of Economic and Community Affairs established the Biomass Energy Program that assists businesses in installing biomass energy systems. The target audience includes industrial, commercial and institutional facilities, agricultural property owners, and city, county, and state entities. Program participants receive up to $75,000 in interest subsidy payments to help defray the interest expense on loans to install approved biomass projects. Technical assistance and feasibility studies may also be provided through the program.[4]

In addition, Alabama has developed a climate change action plan, along with a greenhouse gas emissions inventory for base-year 1990.[5]

ALASKA

In May 2006 the Alaska Legislature adopted House Concurrent Resolution 30, creating an Alaska Climate Impact Commission charged with assessing the impacts and costs of climate change to Alaska, and developing recommendations for preventive measures that can be implemented by Alaskan communities and governments. The 11-member commission is to present its preliminary report to the legislature in March 2007 and a final report in January 2008.[6]

Alaska established a fund providing loans to local utilities, local governments, regional and village corporations, village councils, nonprofit marketing cooperatives, and independent power producers for the development or upgrade of small-scale power production facilities, conservation facilities, and bulk fuel storage facilities.[7]

ARIZONA

Arizona provides numerous incentives for residences and businesses to utilize energy sources that mitigate climate change. Under the Solar Energy Credit Law, the state has since January 1995 provided taxpayers credits for installing solar or wind energy devices at their residences in Arizona.[8] The credit is 25% of the cost of a qualifying solar or wind energy device (with a $1,000 maximum allowable limit) against the taxpayer's personal income tax.[9] Devices that qualify for the credit include wind generators, wind-powered pumps, solar-powered water-heating systems, and solar-powered lighting systems.[10]

Since 1997, Arizona has offered a sales tax exemption of up to $5,000 for qualifying solar energy devices.[11] Among the power generators meeting the law's criteria are wind-powered water pumps, wind-powered electric generators, solar-powered lights, and solar-powered water-heating systems.[12] The law is set to expire on January 1, 2011.[13]

On February 11, 2005, Arizona Governor Janet Napolitano issued Executive Order 2005-05 mandating that the design and construction of every new state-funded structure derive at least 10% of its energy from a qualifying renewable resource.[14] The order also requires that Arizona's Administration and Transportation Departments, as well as the state's School Facilities Board, annually present a report to the governor's office and to the Department of Administration describing their efforts to derive energy from a renewable power source and assessing what actions are necessary to improve those efforts.[15]

On February 28, 2006, the governors of Arizona and New Mexico signed an agreement to create the Southwest Climate Change Initiative.[16] Both states now require that their Climate Change Advisory Groups work together to find methods to slow global climate change and reduce emissions of greenhouse gases.[17] In February 2006, the Arizona Corporation Commission introduced new Renewable Energy Standards that will, once adopted as a final rule, require 15% of the energy generated by regulated electric utilities to be from renewable sources by 2025. The rules will also require an increasing percentage of the state's total resource portfolio to come from distributed generation.[18] Arizona also has efficiency standards for 12 appliances.[19]

On June 21, 2006, Governor Napolitano signed into law a bill that provides solar energy tax incentives for commercial and industrial projects.[20] The law requires the state Commerce Department to establish a solar energy income tax credit.[21] It also removes the $5,000 tax exemption limit for retail and prime contracting classification and prohibits solar energy systems for on-site consumption from being added to property value.[22] The tax credit would apply retroactively to the beginning of 2006.[23]

In addition, on September 8, 2006, Governor Napolitano signed an executive order geared toward reducing greenhouse gas emissions.[24] The order establishes a statewide goal to reduce Arizona's future greenhouse gas emissions to the 2000 emissions level by the year 2020, and to 50% below the 2000 level by 2040.[25] The order also creates a Climate Change Executive Committee whose task it will be to develop a strategy to implement the recommendations in Arizona's Climate Change Action Plan[26] and to explore ways to meet Governor Napolitano's challenge of reaching the 2000 emissions level even sooner, by Arizona's Centennial in 2012.[27]

ARKANSAS

On April 19, 2001, Arkansas Governor Mike Huckabee signed into law the Arkansas Renewable Energy Development Act, which required the state's electric utilities to offer net metering for solar, wind, hydroelectric, geothermal, and biomass systems, as well as fuel cells and microturbines fueled by renewable sources.[28]

Since 2003, the Arkansas Biodiesel Incentive Act has offered a tax refund to businesses that use bio-based products, including ethanol and biodiesel.[29] The Act also provides biodiesel suppliers an income tax credit of up to 5% of the costs of the facilities and equipment used in the wholesale or retail distribution of biodiesel fuels.[30] In addition, the Act allows the Alternative Fuels Commission to provide grants for the production of biodiesel of up to $0.10 per gallon for a maximum of 5 million gallons per producer per year for a period not to exceed five years. [31]

Arkansas offers an energy technology development tax credit of up to 50% of the amount spent during the taxable year on a facility located within the state that designs, develops, or produces photovoltaic devices, electric vehicle equipment, or fuel cells.[32]

Recent legislation directs the Arkansas Office of Procurement to develop and implement a plan for all state agencies to reduce petroleum consumption of their vehicles by at least 10% by January 1, 2009, through measures that include alternative fuels and hybrid vehicles.[33] As an incentive, the Energy Office of the Arkansas Department of Economic Development offers state agencies rebates on the purchase of hybrid vehicles equal to the sales tax paid for the vehicles.[34] The rebates are funded through oil overcharge funds and are available on a first-come, first-served basis.[35]

The Arkansas Alternative Fuels Commission Act of 2003 established a seven-member alternative fuels commission to develop, coordinate, and promote the utilization of alternative motor fuels throughout the state.[36] The Commission is also in charge of providing grants and loans for research and projects supporting alternative fuels.[37]

CALIFORNIA

California passed several pieces of legislation in 2006 aimed at reducing the state's greenhouse gas emissions. On September 27, 2006, Governor Arnold Schwarzenegger signed California Global Warming Solutions Act, Assembly Bill 32.[38] The bill limits the state's global warming emissions to 1990 levels by 2020 and institutes a mandatory emissions-reporting system to monitor compliance.[39] The bill also allows for market mechanisms to provide incentives to businesses to reduce greenhouse gas emissions while safeguarding local communities.[40]

On September 29, 2006, Governor Schwarzenegger signed Senate Bill 1368.[41] The new law directs the California Energy Commission to set a greenhouse gas performance standard for electricity procured by local publicly owned utilities, whether it is generated within state borders or imported from plants in other states, and will apply to all new long-term electricity contracts.[42] Earlier in the same week, on September 26, Governor Schwarzenegger signed Senate Bill 107, which requires California's three biggest utilities—Pacific Gas & Electric, Southern Edison, and San Diego Gas & Electric—to produce at least 20% of their electricity using renewable sources by 2010.[43]

In addition to state-level efforts, on October 16, 2006, Governor Schwarzenegger and New York Governor George Pataki announced plans to link emissions trading between the carbon markets being developed for California and the states participating in the Northeastern Regional Greenhouse Gas Initiative (RGGI).[44] California and the RGGI states hope to achieve their emissions reduction targets in a more efficient manner by combining markets.[45]

On July 31, 2006, Governor Schwarzenegger and British Prime Minister Tony Blair signed a mission statement, which "commit[s both California and Britain] to urgent action to reduce greenhouse gas emissions and promote low-carbon technologies."[46] The agreement establishes a forum for California and Britain to share experiences, research efforts, and educate "the public on the need for aggressive action to address climate change and promote energy diversity."[47] It also commits both California and Britain to 1) evaluate and implement market-based mechanisms that spur innovation, 2) study the economics of climate change, 3) collaborate on technology research, and 4) enhance linkages between the scientific communities of California and Britain.[48]

In 2005, by Executive Order, California established the following milestones for reduction in all greenhouse gas emissions: by 2010, emissions reduced to 2000 levels; by 2020, reduced to 1990 levels; and by 2050, reduced to 80% below 1990 levels.[49] Executive Order S-20-04 directs state-owned buildings to reduce energy use 20% by

2015 (based on 2003 building energy use).[50] Additional legislation requires all state-run buildings and parking facilities (either existing or under construction) to install solar energy systems by 2007.[51] California first developed a climate change action plan in 1998.[52]

Commercial, residential and industrial owners are eligible for a property tax exemption of up to 100% of the value of certain types of solar energy systems.[53] Residential owners can also take tax deductions for the interest on loans for energy efficiency updates.[54]

In further support of renewable power sources, in 2002, California adopted a renewable portfolio standard program, mandating utilities to obtain 20% of their electricity from renewables by 2017.[55] The standards were later accelerated: the goal is now 20% renewables by 2010 and 33% by 2020.[56] The list of eligible sources is probably the most extensive in the nation, including biomass, solar thermal, photovoltaics, wind, geothermal, fuel cells, small hydropower, digester gas, landfill gas, ocean wave, ocean thermal, and tidal current.[57] California's energy suppliers must also disclose to all customers the mix of resources they use to generate power.[58] The disclosure forms have been standardized, and utilities are expected to deliver them four times each year.[59]

In addition, California requires all utilities to offer net metering for solar and wind systems with a capacity of up to 1 MW.[60] The state's investor-owned utilities are also required to offer net metering for biogas and fuel cell systems.[61]

Furthermore, the state's major utilities must collect revenue from their customers to support the state's Renewable Resource Trust Fund.[62] Collectively, the utilities must pay the following amounts annually: $228 million for energy efficiency and conservation activities; $135 million for renewable energy; and $62,500,000 for research, development, and demonstration.[63] In addition, California has established appliance efficiency standards for 17 products and estimates these regulations will save consumers $3 billion over 15 years.[64]

In 2005, the California Public Utility Commission ordered that the value of $8 per ton of CO_2 be included in the cost calculations for long-term utility planning and in the evaluation of bids for future electricity or demand-side management. This signifies that the Commission believed that it was prudent to address the risk of the future regulation of CO_2.[65]

In order to stimulate voluntary action toward greenhouse gas emissions reductions, California also created a climate action registry.[66] The registry is a nonprofit entity mandated to help various governmental and private actors set baselines for measuring emissions, develop reduction programs, and synchronize their programs with federal and international best practices.[67] It acts as both an informational clearinghouse and policy-making hub.[68] Its mandate is broad, encompassing, for instance, not only "traditional" sources of greenhouse gas emissions and remediation, such as fossil fuel-based power generators, but forest management practices as well.[69]

Supporting the goals of the registry, the Energy Resources Conservation and Development Commission, every two years, must make a comprehensive energy sector assessment, including forecasts for supply, production, transportation, delivery, distribution, demand, and prices.[70] These reports are meant to foster energy policies that are environmentally sound and maintain energy grid reliability.[71]

In 2002, the California legislature directed the State Air Resources Board to adopt regulations requiring the maximum feasible and cost-effective reduction of greenhouse gas emissions from motor vehicles beginning in model year 2009.[72] Chapter 5 includes a more in-depth discussion of the vehicle greenhouse gas reduction requirement.

In 1991, California mandated efficiency standards to guide the purchase of fuels, vehicles, and tires for state motor fleets.[73] Legislation in 2006 requires the formulation of alternative fuel targets for state fleets to be set for 2012, 2017, and 2022.[74] Furthermore, California integrates environmental considerations into all of its state purchasing guidelines.[75]

COLORADO

The Colorado Department of Public Health and Environment developed a climate change action plan for the state in September 1998.[76] The plan is an informational tool that contains data related to the climate change debate.[77] Colorado also has a climate change advisory group.[78]

On November 2, 2004, the citizens of Colorado voted to approve Amendment 37, establishing a renewable portfolio standard.[79] Prior to Amendment 37, the law only required Colorado's electric utilities to offer their customers dual metering—a lower rate for all electricity generated by the customer's generator but the full rate for electricity purchased from the utility.[80] In 2005, in compliance with the amendment, the Colorado Public Utilities Commission (CPUC) added rules creating additional interconnection and net metering requirements for utilities with more than 40,000 customers.[81] Net metering is now available for customers of these utilities with generators producing up to 2 megawatts of energy.[82] Furthermore, these utilities must generate 3% of their electricity from renewable power sources from 2007 to 2010; 6% from 2011 to 2014; and 10% after 2014.[83] In addition, since 1999, CPUC has required investor-owned utilities producing more than 100 megawatts to disclose their fuel mix to their customers twice yearly via mail.[84]

On June 1, 2006, Governor Bill Owens signed into law a bill that promotes low-emitting western coal-fueled electricity generation by requiring the Colorado Public

Utilities Commission to consider integrated combined-cycle electric generation (IGCC) facilities.[85] These facilities combine two technologies that use coal in a cleaner way.[86]

Colorado also offers a tax credit for hybrid vehicles.[87]

CONNECTICUT

In 1990, Connecticut passed legislation that required specific actions aimed at reducing carbon dioxide emissions.[88] The Act established a wide range of energy conservation measures, including revisions to the building code aimed at increasing energy efficiency,[89] and set goals for improving public transportation.[90] It also authorized the Connecticut Environmental Protection Commissioner to require trees or grass to be planted to offset carbon dioxide emissions associated with air discharge permits.[91]

Approximately a decade after this action, Connecticut agreed, under the auspices of the New England Governors and Eastern Canadian Premiers, to a voluntary short-term goal of reducing regional greenhouse gas emissions to 1990 levels by 2010 and by 10% below 1990 levels by 2020.[92] In order to implement this commitment, the legislature passed Connecticut Public Act 04-252 in 2004.[93] Among its many provisions, the Act charged the Governor's Steering Committee on Climate Change with developing a climate change action plan.[94] The plan, which was completed in February 2005, contains 55 recommendations for drastically reducing the state's emissions of greenhouse gases.[95]

Public Act 04-252 also required the development of a greenhouse gas inventory detailing emissions in the state.[96] To date, Connecticut has completed an inventory for the base years 1990 and 2000.[97] In addition to this legislation, Connecticut recently adopted a regulation that incorporates California's greenhouse gas emission standards for motor vehicles.[98] California's standards require that tailpipe greenhouse gas emissions from new vehicles be reduced 22% by the 2012 model year and 30% by the 2016 model year.[99]

In 1998, Connecticut passed a renewable portfolio standard that requires each electricity supplier and electric-distribution company that provides standard service, transitional standard offer or supplier-of-last-resort service to generate 4% of its retail electricity sales using renewable energy by January 1, 2004, increasing to 10% by January 1, 2010.[100] Connecticut also has appliance energy-efficiency standards in place for nine products.[101]

In terms of efforts beyond the state level, Connecticut can be credited for convening the first-ever summit on climate change for the insurance industry in the United States.[102] Connecticut is also collaborating with Northeast States for Coordinated Air Use Management (NESCAUM) to develop a voluntary greenhouse gas emission registry,[103] and is an active participant in the Northeast Regional Greenhouse Gas Initiative (RGGI).[104]

DELAWARE

Delaware developed a Climate Change Action Plan in 2000 with funding from the Delaware State Energy Office and the United States Environmental Protection Agency's State and Local Climate Change Program.[105] The Center for Energy and Environmental Policy (CEEP) at the University of Delaware researched and wrote the Action Plan with input from the Delaware Climate Change Consortium, a group comprised of representatives from government, environment, business, labor, and community organizations.[106] The CEEP had previously completed an inventory of Delaware's greenhouse gas emissions and sinks for the 1990 base year.[107] This inventory serves as a benchmark for modeling and analyzing the state's emissions in the Action Plan.[108]

Overall, the Action Plan includes a set of policy options that could reduce Delaware's greenhouse gas emissions by 7% below the state's 1990 level by 2010.[109] This would result in a decrease of almost 25% in the state's greenhouse gas emissions.[110] Delaware is also a participant in the Northeast Regional Greenhouse Gas Initiative.[111]

In July 2005, Delaware enacted a renewable portfolio standard. The standard requires the state's retail electricity suppliers to use renewable energy to generate at least 10% of the electricity they sell in Delaware by 2019.[112]

FLORIDA

Florida adopted a Renewable Energy Technologies and Energy Efficiency Act in June 2006, creating the Florida Energy Commission to advise the legislature on state energy policy based on principles of reliability, affordability, efficiency and diversity. The first report of the Commission due before December 2007 must include recommended steps and a schedule for the development of a state climate action plan. The Act provides rebates for photovoltaic and solar thermal technology installations on commercial buildings and a sales tax exemption for the purchase of energy-efficient products.[113]

Also in June 2006, Governor Jeb Bush signed a $100 million energy bill designed to diversify the state's fuel supply and promote conservation and efficiency.[114] The bill provides matching grants for research and development of alternative energy vehicles and "next generation" technologies.[115] The bill authorizes a corporate income tax credit for businesses that invest in renewable energy production.[116]

Since 1997, Florida has offered a sales and use tax exemption for solar power generators.[117] In addition, as of July 1, 2003, hybrid electric vehicles that are certified and labeled in accordance with federal regulations may be driven in high-occupancy vehicle lanes at any time, regardless of the number of passengers.[118]

GEORGIA

On April 28, 2001, Governor Roy Barnes signed into law Georgia's Cogeneration and Distributed Generation Act of 2001.[119] The Act's net metering requirement allows customer generators to be compensated at a higher than avoided cost rate[120] if the utility uses the power to supply a green pricing program.[121]

In 2004, legislators authorized the development of a Carbon Registry in Georgia.[122] Among the purposes of the registry is to encourage voluntary actions to reduce greenhouse gas emissions.[123] As directed under the law, the Georgia Forestry Commission and University of Georgia are currently working to define a Carbon Registry protocol for Georgia using Traditional Industries Program research funds.[124] A preliminary registry protocol will be developed by the spring of 2006 and implementation of the registry is expected after appropriate reviews and funding appropriations.[125]

Georgia offers an income tax credit of 10% to 20% of the cost to purchase or lease a zero or low-emission vehicle.[126] Hybrid electric vehicles will also be authorized to use high-occupancy vehicle lanes, regardless of the number of passengers, if the U.S. Congress or U.S. Department of Transportation approves such authorization through legislative or regulatory action.[127]

HAWAII

Hawaii adopted several energy-related laws in 2006. Senate Bill 2957 encourages the use of renewable energy and renewable fuels by raising the tax credit for specific renewable technologies, making the tax credit permanent and establishing a pilot financing program for residential solar hot water heating systems.[128] The legislation also supports production of biodiesel and cellulosic ethanol and establishes the Hawaii Renewable Hydrogen Program to move the state toward a renewable hydrogen economy.[129] House Bill 2175 appropriates $5 million for solar power systems for public schools and instructs state agencies to maximize energy efficiency.[130] The law also encourages green buildings by giving them priority when they apply for construction permits and sets green building standards for state buildings.[131] Finally, the legislation requires 20% of the state's new vehicles to be hybrids or alternative-fuel vehicles, with the percentage increasing over time.[132] Senate Bill 3185 establishes a public benefits fund for energy-efficiency programs and allows the Public Utilities Commission to set penalties for failing to meet the state's renewable portfolio standard.[133]

Since 1990, Hawaii has offered income tax credits to both individual residents and corporations buying and installing renewable power generators.[134] Currently, the credit is 35% of the purchase price and installation costs of a solar power generator; the credit is 20% for wind power systems.[135]

Hawaiian government agencies planning the construction or renovation of state-funded facilities after 1998 must consider the potential costs and benefits of solar-powered water-heating systems.[136]

Legislation enacted in 2001 and revised in 2004 and 2005 requires utilities in Hawaii to offer net metering to customers with renewable power systems.[137] Utilities are barred from requiring that their customers make additional payments for net metering.[138]

In 2004, Hawaii established a renewable portfolio standard requiring utilities to generate 10% of their electricity from renewable power generators by 2011 and 20% by 2021.[139] Also, the same legislation mandates that once every five years, Hawaii's Public Utilities Commission must fund a study by the University of Hawaii's Natural Energy Institute to determine whether the renewable portfolio standard should be revised.[140] Based on the study's findings, the Public Utilities Commission can revise the renewable portfolio standard.[141]

Since 2005, Hawaii has banned covenants or zoning laws restricting residents from installing solar power systems.[142] In addition, the same legislation requires homeowner associations to adopt rules providing for the installation of solar power generators.[143]

Hawaii also has completed a climate change action plan.[144]

IDAHO

In 2006 Idaho adopted a two-year moratorium on permitting new coal-fired power plants.[145] The moratorium does not apply to coal-fired power plants owned or constructed by a public utility regulated by the Idaho Public Utilities Commission or by a cooperative or municipality, nor does it apply to the operations of the Idaho National Laboratory.[146]

Idaho offers a smattering of statutes that relate, in one way or another, to greenhouse gas reduction. The state gives certified distributors a fuel tax deduction of up to 10%, based on the percentage of ethanol in a blended motor fuel, or the agricultural, animal fat, or waste products contained in biodiesel fuel.[147] It also exempts "special gaseous fuels"—including compressed natural gas (CNG) and hydrogen—from the standard 25 cents per gallon fuel excise tax when distributed for use in permitted vehicles.[148]

Regarding residential buildings, Idaho adopted the Energy Conservation Code portion of the 2003 International Code Council's (ICC) International Building Code.[149] (Local municipalities that elect to enforce building codes must also adopt the ICC standard.)[150] The code specifies minimum levels of energy efficiency for heating and cooling systems, window design, and other elements of building construction and maintenance.[151]

In 2002, Idaho formed the Carbon Sequestration Advisory Committee.[152] The Committee was established primarily to "recommend policies or programs to enhance the

ability of Idaho agricultural and non-industrial private forest landowners to participate in systems of carbon trading."[153] The Committee also seeks to promote research
and raise awareness concerning carbon sequestration in the agricultural and forestry
sectors.[154] The Committee consists of 16 members, including relevant heads of state
departments, as well as farmers; livestock producers; members of the electricity, transportation, and biofuels sectors; and one member representing an environmental protection or conservation organization.[155]

ILLINOIS

The Illinois Environmental Protection Agency in January 2006 created the Illinois
Conservation and Climate Initiative, a voluntary program that awards credits to farmers for practices that reduce greenhouse gas emissions, such as conservation tillage,
planting grasses and trees, and capturing methane from animal operations. After third-
party verification of the offsets, the credits will be sold on the Chicago Climate Exchange.[156] In 1997, Illinois developed the Renewable Energy Resources Trust Fund,
offering grants and loans supporting renewable power sources.[157] The fund is the product of mandatory contributions from public utilities and other electricity providers in
Illinois.[158] Among its many projects, the fund supports the Renewable Energy Resources
Program, which, since January 2006, has provided rebates of up to $10,000 for new
solar power generators.[159]

Another provider of renewable energy grants is the Illinois Clean Energy Community Foundation.[160] Endowed with the $250,000 settlement that the state received for
approving a utility merger, the foundation, since 1999, has offered grants to projects
designed to develop renewable power generators and improve energy efficiency.[161] In
addition, the foundation sponsors clean-energy programs for communities across Illinois.[162]

Also in 1999, Illinois enacted a law requiring utilities to list on their customers'
electric bills the percentages of different energy sources in their fuel mixes.[163] In addition, utilities must disclose the amount of carbon dioxide, nitrous oxide, and sulfur
dioxide emissions produced by their facilities.[164]

Legislation in 2001 mandated that utilities set a goal to derive 5% of the state's
electricity from renewable resources by 2010 and 15% by 2020.[165] In 2005, the Illinois
Commerce Commission issued a resolution elaborating on the 2001 law, requiring
utilities to increase their generation of renewable energy by 1% annually until 2013.[166]
The resolution also specifies that wind power must constitute 75% of each utility's
renewable energy.[167]

An executive order in 2002 required that by 2010, buildings used or owned by
state agencies controlled by the governor of Illinois must derive 5% of their power
from renewable energy sources.[168] By 2015, these buildings must depend on renewable
energy for 15% of their power needs.[169]

Illinois completed a climate change action plan in June 1994, which serves as an
informational tool for the state.[170] On October 5, 2006, Governor Blagojevich signed

Executive Order 2006-11 establishing a state Climate Change Advisory Group.[171] The Advisory Group will study a wide range of policies and actions aimed at reducing greenhouse gas emissions.[172]

INDIANA

In 2002, Indiana established the Center for Coal Technology Research to develop methods of coal use and extraction that are not detrimental to the environment.[173] Among its duties, the Center investigates methods to limit environmentally harmful emissions from coal extraction facilities.[174]

In 2004, Indiana's Utility Regulatory Commission established a set of rules requiring utilities to provide net metering to residents and schools (K-12) with renewable power systems.[175] Net-metered systems must comply with Indiana's new interconnection rules established in 2005.[176]

IOWA

In 2006 Iowa enacted a series of laws related to energy, including legislation that provides a 25 cent per gallon tax break for 85% ethanol fuel (E-85) and requiring that 25% of the petroleum used in the formulation of gasoline be replaced by biofuel by 2020;[177] a sales tax exemption for the purchase of solar power equipment;[178] and a renewable energy tax credit.[179]

Iowa provides a variety of tax incentives to promote renewable power sources. In June 2005, Iowa began offering energy providers production tax credits of 1.5 cents for every kilowatt-hour of renewable power sold to their customers.[180] Energy providers may apply the credit toward the personal income tax, sales and use tax, business tax, or financial institutions tax.[181] Iowa also exempts energy generated by wind power from the replacement generation tax.[182] Under the same law, operators of hydropower generators that produce at least 100 megawatt-hours of energy pay a reduced replacement generation tax of $0.000001847 instead of the usual $0.0006 for every kilowatt-hour.[183]

Iowa's Energy Center provides grants funding research on renewable energy and energy efficiency by colleges, nonprofit groups, and other institutions.[184] The Energy Center also administers the Alternate Energy Revolving Loan Program, providing loans to people and businesses seeking to construct renewable energy generators in Iowa.[185] The program offers half of each loan at no interest for 20 years.[186]

Since 2004, Iowa has required its electric utilities to provide their customers with annual reports on the percentage mix of fuel used in electric generation.[187] Each utility must also estimate the amount of sulfur dioxide, nitrogen oxides, and carbon dioxide emissions that its generation facilities produce.[188] Also, since 2004, Iowa has required its utilities to provide their customers with the option of contributing money to support the development of renewable power sources.[189]

In April 2005, Iowa's governor introduced Executive Order Number 41, mandating that the state's agencies rely on renewable energy for at least 10% of their power.[190] Also, the order requires the following to be achieved by 2010: (1) state agencies will reduce their energy use by 15% from the level it was in 2000; (2) all state-owned automobiles other than heavy trucks and law-enforcement vehicles will be either hybrid-electric or use alternative fuels; and (3) any bulk diesel fuel purchased by the state will be 20% renewable.[191]

Finally, the University of Iowa completed a climate change action plan for the state in December 1996.[192] The plan is built on a variety of energy-efficiency programs and renewable-energy initiatives.

KANSAS

Kansas offers two major incentives designed to promote renewable energy. First, since January 1, 1999, Kansas has provided property tax exemptions for qualifying renewable energy equipment regularly and predominantly used as electric generators.[193] Second, since July 1, 2003, the Interconnection Standards Law has permitted renewable energy sites producing power measured at 25 kilowatts (residential) or 100 kilowatts (commercial) to link with the utility grid.[194]

KENTUCKY

In 1998, with funds provided by the U.S. Environmental Protection Agency, Kentucky completed a climate change action plan.[195] In the same year, Kentucky passed a statute forbidding the state cabinet, without legislative or federal authority, from promulgating emission-reduction regulations established by the Kyoto Protocol.[196]

Most recently, in 2004, the state enacted a statute requiring all rural electric cooperatives and investor-owned utilities to provide net metering to customers with solar power generators producing at most 15 kilowatts of energy.[197]

LOUISIANA

Louisiana enacted legislation in 2006 that requires that ethanol derived from Louisiana-produced feedstock account for 2% of the total gasoline sold in the state and that 2% of the total diesel sold in the state be biodiesel once specified ethanol and biodiesel production thresholds have been reached in the state.[198]

Louisiana offers a tax exemption for solar power equipment used for buildings and swimming pools.[199] In addition, Louisiana's Department of Natural Resources offers HELP (Home Energy Loan Program), providing homeowners low-interest loans for the purchase and installation of alternative energy sources.[200]

The Louisiana Department of Natural Resources offers a state income tax credit worth 20% of the cost of converting a vehicle to operate on an alternative fuel, and

20% of the incremental cost of purchasing an Original Equipment Manufacturer alternative fuel vehicle.[201]

MAINE

On June 26, 2003, Maine established the Lead-by-Example Initiative, designed to reduce greenhouse gas emissions.[202] The initiative requires the development of a plan to reduce greenhouse gas emissions by state-owned buildings and state-funded programs to below the 1990 level by 2010.[203] Also, the law set 2006 as the deadline for Maine to establish carbon emission reduction deals with at least 50 businesses and nonprofit groups.[204]

Lead-by-Example also mandates that the government create an inventory of greenhouse gas emissions across the state.[205] The registry is designed to facilitate the following statewide greenhouse gas emission reduction goals: (1) the 1990 greenhouse gas level by 2010; (2) 10% below the 1990 level by 2020; and, in the long term, (3) a reduction "sufficient to eliminate any dangerous threat to the climate."[206] In order to meet these targets, the law mandates that the Department of Environmental Protection (DEP) develop a long-term climate action plan to reduce Maine's greenhouse gas emissions.[207] The DEP completed this plan in 2004.[208] On December 1, 2005, also in furtherance of Lead-by-Example's goals, Maine adopted California's rigorous greenhouse gas emissions standards for motor vehicles.[209]

Maine has also agreed, under the auspices of the New England Governors and Eastern Canadian Premiers, to a voluntary short-term goal of reducing regional greenhouse gas emissions to 1990 levels by 2010 and by 10% below 1990 levels by 2020.[210] Maine is a participant in the Northeast Regional Greenhouse Gas Initiative.

Finally, in September 1999, Maine's Public Utilities Commission adopted rules for the state's Renewable Resource Portfolio Requirement, requiring electric providers to supply at least 30% of their total retail electric sales in Maine using electricity generated by eligible renewable resources.[211]

MARYLAND

Since 2001, Maryland has offered the following income tax credits for owners of buildings that are green or use photovoltaic, wind, or fuel cells for power: 6-8% of the cost to construct or rehabilitate green buildings; 20-25% of the cost of photovoltaic power generators; 25% of the cost of wind turbines; and 30% of the cost of fuel cells.[212] Maryland also provides a sales tax exemption for all wood or "refuse-derived" fuel used to heat residential properties.[213] As a further incentive for the state's citizens and businesses to adopt alternative power generators, the Maryland Energy Administration, since 2005, has offered grants for solar-powered heating equipment.[214]

Since 2000, Maryland has required electricity providers to disclose fuel mix and emissions data to their customers.[215] Maryland's utilities must also provide net metering to customers with solar, wind, or biomass power generators.[216] In addition, Maryland's Renewable Energy Portfolio Standard and Credit Trading Act, enacted in 2004, requires that utilities utilize renewable power sources for a portion of the energy sold to their customers.[217] Maryland also has efficiency standards for nine appliances.[218]

The recently enacted Maryland Healthy Air Act requires the state to join the Northeast Regional Greenhouse Gas Initiative prior to June 30, 2007.[219] In addition, the Maryland Energy Administration completed a climate change action plan for the state in March 2004.[220]

MASSACHUSETTS

In August 2001, Massachusetts agreed, under the auspices of the New England Governors and Eastern Canadian Premiers, to a voluntary short-term goal of reducing regional greenhouse gas emissions to 1990 levels by 2010 and by 10% below 1990 levels by 2020.[221] As a first step to implementing this agreement, in 2004, the state released the Massachusetts Climate Protection Plan.[222] The plan contains a comprehensive set of short-term actions that can be undertaken to reduce pollution, protect the climate, and cut energy demand in the state.[223] Massachusetts had previously developed a greenhouse gas inventory detailing emissions for the 1990 base year.[224]

Massachusetts has also adopted significant climate change legislation. In 2004, the Massachusetts Department of Environmental Protection finalized a regulation that caps carbon dioxide emissions from six fossil fuel power plants at approximately 10% below 1997-1999 levels by 2006-2008.[225] In October of 2006, Massachusetts promulgated new rules that put into place a greenhouse gas emissions credit-trading system to help power plants comply with the regulation.[226] Massachusetts has also adopted California's greenhouse gas emission standards for motor vehicles.[227] California's standards require that tailpipe greenhouse gas emissions from new vehicles be reduced by 22% by the 2012 model year and 30% by the 2016 model year.[228]

Massachusetts is also collaborating with Northeast States for Coordinated Air Use Management (NESCAUM) to develop a voluntary greenhouse gas emission registry,[229] and had been an active participant in the Northeast Regional Greenhouse Gas Initiative.[230] However, Massachusetts Governor Mitt Romney declined to participate in the final version of RGGI. The RGGI rules include special provisions that would allow Massachusetts (and Rhode Island) to join RGGI if they decide to do so before January 2008.

In April 2002, Massachusetts finalized regulations for the state's renewable portfolio standard that require all retail electricity providers in the state to utilize new renewable energy sources for at least 1% of their power supply in 2003, increasing to 4% by 2009.[231]

MICHIGAN

Established in 2003, Michigan's Next Energy program promotes the research, production, and sale of alternative power generators.[232] Next Energy offers participating businesses tax credits for qualified business activities.[233] Companies in the alternative energy industry also receive tax credits for their qualified payrolls.[234] In addition, participating businesses are exempt from paying personal property taxes on alternative energy technologies.[235] The Next Energy program is set to expire in 2023.[236]

The Customer Choice and Electric Reliability Act of 2000 requires the state's electric utilities to inform their customers and Michigan's Public Service Commission biannually of the following: (1) the contents of their fuel mixes; (2) the average number of pounds per megawatt-hour of carbon dioxide, sulfur dioxide, and nitrogen oxide emissions from their facilities; and (3) the amount of high-level nuclear waste produced by their electric generators.[237]

MINNESOTA

For over a decade, Minnesota has offered tax exemptions designed to promote alternative power sources. For example, in 1992 Minnesota began offering a property tax exemption for value increases attributed to the addition of a solar electric generator.[238] Similarly, wind energy systems since 2002 have been subject only to a production tax varying by locality, but not the state's property tax.[239] Since 1998, wind power generators have also been exempt from Minnesota's sales tax.[240] Likewise, since August 2005, solar energy systems in Minnesota have been exempt from the sales tax.[241]

The Value-Added Stock Loan Participation Program has, since 1994, offered Minnesota's farmers low-interest loans to buy wind or anaerobic-digestion power generators.[242] Minnesota's Rural Finance Authority offers a low 4% interest rate for 45% of each loan provided by participating Minnesota financial institutions.[243]

Since 2004, Minnesota's Department of Commerce has offered all Minnesotans rebates of $2,000 per kilowatt for the up-front costs of grid-connected solar electric generators.[244] The rebates are available until 2008 or when the funds for the program expire.[245] As for wind power, until 2017, Minnesota will pay energy providers 1.5

cents for every kilowatt-hour of energy produced, from a minimum of 2 megawatts to a maximum of 200 megawatts.[246]

In 2001, Minnesota passed legislation requiring that the state's electric utilities provide their customers an option to buy power created by renewable energy generators.[247] The law also states a non-binding deadline of 2015 for utilities to obtain 10% of their power from renewable energy generators.[248] By 2005, 1% of energy produced by utilities should be from a renewable power source; for each subsequent year until 2015, the law expects utilities to increase their reliance on renewable energy by 1%.[249]

By order of Minnesota's Public Utilities Commission in 2002, all utilities regulated in Minnesota must twice annually disclose to their customers data on fuel mix and emissions.[250] The data must be available to customers by phone, Internet, and brochure with: (1) a pie chart of the fuel sources; (2) a bar chart of air pollutant emissions; and (3) a chart comparing the costs of different power generation systems.[251]

Minnesota requires that any plans for the construction or large renovation of any state-owned buildings must incorporate alternative energy power sources.[252] Minnesota has also adopted a mandate requiring that all diesel fuel contain 2% biodiesel.[253]

In addition to these measures, the Minnesota Pollution Control Agency developed a climate change action plan for the state in February 2003.[254]

MISSISSIPPI

Mississippi offers low-interest loans for renewable energy and energy-efficiency projects through its Energy Development Fund.[255] Eligible renewable energy technologies include biomass, solar, geothermal, and wind power generators.[256] All projects must demonstrate that they will reduce a facility's energy costs.[257] The interest rate is 3% below the prime rate, with a maximum loan term of seven years; loans range from $15,000 to $300,000.[258] This program is supported by a revolving loan fund of $7 million, established through federal oil overcharge funds.[259]

Under state law, Mississippi's Commissioner of Agriculture and Commerce is authorized to make cash payments to producers of ethanol and biodiesel in the amount of 1.5 cents for each kilowatt-hour of electricity generated using biomass in a cogeneration facility at an ethanol plant located in the state.[260]

MISSOURI

Since 1989, the Energy Center of the Missouri Department of Natural Resources has offered loans for renewable energy and energy-efficiency projects for public and government-owned buildings.[261]

Since 1997, Missouri has offered income tax credits of $5 per ton for those who process wood for fuel.[262]

Since 2003, Missouri has required utilities to offer dual metering for photovoltaic, wind, fuel cell, and biomass generators up to 100 kilowatts.[263]

Missouri has also developed a climate change action plan.[264]

MONTANA

In December of 2005, Montana Governor Brian Schweitzer directed the state Department of Environmental Quality to create a climate change advisory group to recommend strategies to reduce and sequester greenhouse gas emissions and to promote economic growth through energy efficiency and renewable energy investments. The group is also charged with developing a climate action plan by July 2007.[265]

Montana's Electric Utilities Restructuring Act establishes graduated renewable energy standards to take effect in 2008.[266] Providers of electric energy must procure 5% of retail sales from renewables for 2008 through 2009; 10% for 2010 through 2014; and 15% for 2015 and successive compliance years.[267] Requirements can be met through the purchase of energy credits or electricity output from community renewable energy projects of at least 50 MW capacity (75 MW, beginning 2015).[268] Providers who fail to meet the target for any compliance year are subject to fines of $10 for each megawatt hour of renewable energy credits they fail to procure.[269] Cooperative utilities are exempt from renewable standards, although cooperatives with more than 5,000 customers are asked to implement renewable source guidelines.[270]

The Electric Utilities Restructuring Act also authorizes the creation of pilot programs providing customer choice to small customers,[271] and it mandates net metering systems for distribution services providers.[272] Equipment and hook-up costs for net metering devolve on individual customer-generators.[273] Moreover, at the end of each 12-month billing cycle, any remaining kilowatt-hour credits revert to the utility company without compensation to the customer-generator.[274] Montana's major deregulated energy providers are required to market "green energy"—biomass, wind, solar, or geothermal—to interested consumers.[275] Under a separate provision, Montana's Public Service Commission is empowered to set the prices by which energy distributors are required to purchase from small alternative energy producers and cogeneration facilities.[276] An older provision allows utilities to gain up to 2% additions in the permitted rate of return on common equity in exchange for qualifying conservation purchases or investments.[277]

Montana provides a host of tax and other financial incentives meant to stimulate the market in renewables. Tax incentives include property tax exemptions for renewable generating facilities (structured differently for small[278] and large[279] providers); corporate tax exemptions for new or expanded providers of energy from renewables;[280] personal income tax credits for individuals installing residential geothermal systems[281] or non-fossil forms of energy generation;[282] tax credits for individual or corporate income generated by net metering on alternative energy sources;[283] exemptions from the wholesale energy transaction tax for energy generated by wind on state or reservation lands;[284] and tax credits for certified Montana venture capital companies that invest in renewables.[285]

Loans provide the other major financial incentive. These include loans to microbusinesses (including alternative energy producers);[286] to ranches and farms that introduce alternative energy production systems;[287] and to building owners who install alternative energy systems for their own use and/or net metering.[288]

Montana has also enacted a number of provisions meant to spur ethanol use. State government entities, including state post-secondary educational institutions, are required to take "all reasonable steps" to ensure that they are using ethanol-blended fuel, if available, for any mechanically suitable vehicles under their ownership/operation.[289] Ethanol production facilities receive special tax exemptions,[290] as do facilities producing alcohol from Montana agricultural products.[291] And fuel blends containing 10% or more alcohol are taxed at 85% of the rate for gasoline.[292]

NEBRASKA

On April 10, 2000, Nebraska enacted Legislative Bill 957, creating the first-of-its-kind Carbon Sequestration Advisory Committee (CSAC) to explore sequestering carbon through new agricultural policy.[293] Members of the CSAC, funded by the Nebraska Environmental Trust Fund, among other sources, include government officials and representatives from the state's agriculture and energy sectors.[294]

Nebraska also offers Dollar and Energy Savings Loans—low-interest loans first introduced in 1990—for energy-efficiency improvements on residential and commercial properties.[295] To receive the loan, the borrower must first obtain approval from a financial institution, which in turn must obtain approval from Nebraska's State Energy Office.[296] If it approves, the State Energy Office buys, without interest, half the loan, leaving the borrower to pay interest that is only half the market rate.[297]

NEVADA

Nevada has a strong renewable portfolio standard. Currently, the state's two major investor-owned utilities are required to supply 6% of retail sales through renewables.[298] This target will increase by 3% every two years, stabilizing at 20% in 2015.[299] Solar energy must comprise at least 5% of a utility's renewable portfolio.[300]

Utilities are required to send their customers regular reports disclosing their average emissions and average mix of fuel sources.[301] Utilities must also offer net metering and accept up to 1% of their cumulative peak capacity from net-metered sources.[302]

In addition to these energy-sector measures, the state has put in place incentives and mandates meant to stimulate green building markets. Municipalities are required to permit straw and other renewable sources for building construction, as well as code-compliant solar or wind energy systems for powering buildings.[303] Any state agency or unit that is planning to construct or renovate a public building larger than 20,000 square feet is required, first, to obtain an analysis of the building's life-cycle costs.[304] The analysis should include maintenance as well as construction costs, factoring in potential water and energy conservation measures, as well as potential renewable sources for energy supply.[305]

Residential, commercial, and industrial property owners are eligible for a permanent, 100% tax exemption for value added to buildings through the installation of a renewable energy system (solar, wind, geothermal, solid waste, or hydroelectric).[306] The state also offers tax abatements to commercial owners of real or personal property used to generate energy from renewable sources—50% over 10 years.[307]

Nevada has a solar-access law that prohibits local zoning provisions that would "unreasonably restrict" the implementation of solar or wind energy systems.[308] Legislation also makes void any covenants or deed restrictions that would impair solar or wind power efforts.[309] Conversely, certain provisions make it easier for private parties to enter voluntarily legally binding solar-easement contracts.[310]

NEW HAMPSHIRE

In 1998, New Hampshire established a law requiring utilities to offer net metering to customers with alternative energy power sources.[311] A year later, New Hampshire established a registry for facilities to voluntarily disclose their greenhouse gas emission reductions.[312] Three years later, New Hampshire established the Multiple Pollutant Reduction Program, which set annual upper limits or caps on emissions of CO_2, SO_2, and NO_x.[313] New Hampshire also completed a climate change action plan in December 2001.[314]

New Hampshire agreed, under the auspices of the New England Governors and Eastern Canadian Premiers, to a voluntary short-term goal of reducing regional greenhouse gas emissions to 1990 levels by 2010 and by 10% below 1990 levels by 2020.[315] New Hampshire is a participant in the Northeast Regional Greenhouse Gas Initiative.

NEW JERSEY

On June 16, 1997, New Jersey Department of Environmental Protection (NJDEP) Commissioner Robert C. Shinn, Jr. formed the New Jersey Global Change Workgroup to assist in the development of a greenhouse gas action plan for the state.[316] The next year, Commissioner Shinn issued Administrative Order 1998-09, which established a goal of achieving a 3.5% reduction in New Jersey's greenhouse gas emissions below 1990 levels by 2005.[317] Following this order, the NJDEP developed a Greenhouse Gas Action Plan, which enumerates strategies for meeting this goal.[318] In addition, the Action Plan identifies the major sources of greenhouse gases by sector and gives estimates of greenhouse gas emissions in 1990.[319]

In October 2005, Governor Richard J. Cody furthered state efforts to address climate change by classifying carbon dioxide as an air contaminant under New Jersey's air pollution control rules.[320] This action was directed toward facilitating New Jersey's engagement in the Northeast Regional Greenhouse Gas Initiative.[321] New Jersey is a participant in the initiative.

In addition, the NJDEP amended its regulations on January 17, 2006, to incorporate California's greenhouse gas standards for motor vehicles.[322] Recognizing the importance of international efforts, on June 15, 1998, the NJDEP also signed a letter of intent with the Netherlands Environmental Ministry that outlines a number of areas where the NJDEP and the Ministry plan on working together to address issues related to climate change.[323]

New Jersey's Board of Public Utilities adopted a renewable portfolio standard that requires utilities to increase the percentage of electricity produced from renewable sources from 4% in 2008 to 20% in 2020, with at least 2% derived from solar photovoltaic sources. The renewable portfolio standard allows trading of Renewable Energy Certificates for compliance purposes.[324] New Jersey also has appliance efficiency standards in place for eight products.[325]

NEW MEXICO

New Mexico has a long history of programs and legislation designed to mitigate global climate change. An early example is New Mexico's Forest Re-Leaf Program.[326] Established in 1990, Forest Re-Leaf offers grants for tree planting and related educational programs.[327] Grants have funded the planting of over 17,000 trees in over 60 communities, resulting in an annual sequestration of 139 metric tons of aboveground carbon dioxide.[328]

More recently, New Mexico enacted in 2002 (and amended in 2003 by House Bill 146) the Renewable Energy Production Tax Credit.[329] The law offers a one-cent per kilowatt-hour corporate income tax credit for businesses that produce electricity via solar, wind or biomass power.[330] The credit applies to the first 400,000 megawatt-hours of electricity that a business produces each year for 10 years.[331]

Enacted by House Bill 251 of 2004 and effective beginning July 1, 2004, New Mexico's Clean Energy Grants Program offers funds to develop renewable energy and alternative transportation fuels.[332] Grant applicants—including tribes, municipalities and state agencies—must reduce energy consumption by 5% or increase use of alternative fuels by 15%.[333] In addition, schools may receive grants for programs that advance the market demands for clean energy and clean energy technologies.[334]

The Renewable Energy Act establishes rules requiring that, by 2006, public utilities generate 5% of their energy from solar, wind, water, biomass, or geothermal power.[335] Subsequently, utilities must increase their use of alternative energy supplies by 1% each year to 10% by 2011.[336] Also, the law sets a reasonable cost threshold—a public utility need not add renewable energy sources if the cost of such sources reaches the statutory level.[337]

The Energy Efficiency and Renewable Energy Bonding Act, enacted on April 5, 2005, provides $20 million worth of tax-exempt bonds to fund renewable energy improvements to buildings owned by New Mexico and its school districts.[338] The Act also requires that the state develop an energy-efficiency plan by 2010 for maximum utility of renewable energy generators in public buildings.[339] During the same legislative session, New Mexico enacted The Efficient Use of Energy Act, which mandates that utilities research methods to lower emissions associated with electricity consumption.[340]

In June 2005, the governor's executive order created the New Mexico Climate Change Advisory Group.[341] With members having either industrial or environmental experience, the Advisory Group evaluates methods to reduce emissions of greenhouse gases to 2000 levels by 2012, 10% below those levels by 2020, and 75% below 2000 levels by 2050.[342]

New Mexico was especially active combating global climate change during February 2006. Enacted on February 15 (and set to expire on December 31, 2015), Senate Bill 269 offers New Mexico's residents 30% personal income tax credits for the purchase and installation of photovoltaic and solar thermal systems.[343] Also in February, New Mexico, along with Arizona, joined the Southwest Climate Change Initiative.[344] The states' advisory groups will collaborate on research to mitigate global warming.[345]

In 1978, New Mexico enacted the Solar Energy Rights Act.[346] The Act makes the right to use solar energy a property right and uses a prior appropriation approach to establish priority. The right is for beneficial use of the unobstructed line of sight from a solar collector to the sun.

NEW YORK

In April 2003, the Center for Clean Air Policy (CCAP), in collaboration with the New York Greenhouse Gas Task Force (Task Force), released *Recommendations to Governor Pataki for Reducing New York State Greenhouse Gas Emissions*.[347] The CCAP and Task Force recommended that New York establish a statewide target to reduce greenhouse gas emissions to 5% below 1990 levels by 2010 and 10% below 1990 levels by 2020.[348] This target was first adopted in June 2002 by the New York State

Energy Board in the State Energy Plan.[349] In addition, the Task Force and CCAP advised the state to create an annual statewide greenhouse gas emissions inventory.[350] The New York State Energy Research and Development Authority (NYSERDA) had developed greenhouse gas inventories detailing emissions levels for 1990 and 2000 prior to the report.[351] New York assumed a leading role in developing the Northeast Regional Greenhouse Gas Initiative.

In furtherance of its goal to reduce its emissions, in December 2005, New York amended its regulations to adopt California's greenhouse gas emissions standards for motor vehicles.[352]

The NYSERDA is home for a wide range of energy-efficiency and renewable-energy programs, including the New York Energy $mart Program. As of June 2006, the NYSERDA is involved in 2,700 projects in 40 funded programs. The principal source of NYSERDA funding is derived from an assessment on intrastate energy sales by the state's investor-owned utilities amounting to approximately 70 cents per residential household per year.[353] NYSERDA recently launched an Alternative-Fuel Vehicle Program, which helps various entities purchase alternative-fuel vehicles that do not emit greenhouse gases.[354] Specific alternative-fuel projects include clean-fueled bus and clean-fueled taxi initiatives.[355]

In 2004, the New York Public Service Commission adopted a renewable portfolio standard of 25% by the year 2013, up from the then-current 19% use of renewables. The Commission Order relied on two approaches to reach the standard. The first was a "central procurement approach" that would allow the state to achieve a 24% renewables rate by requiring investor-owned utilities to collect a surcharge on electric purchases by their customers and then transfer the funds to NYSERDA. NYSERDA, in turn, would provide incentives to renewable energy providers to either sell and deliver renewable energy into the wholesale market or to install renewable energy facilities "behind the meter." The remaining 1% was expected to come from a voluntary green market for renewable energy.[356] In 2005, the Public Service Commission added methane digesters to the list of qualified renewable energy facilities.[357]

New York also offers a variety of tax incentives for energy efficiency or renewable energy, including a green building corporate tax credit, a personal tax credit of up to 25% of the cost of solar electric or solar thermal systems with a maximum credit of $5,000, a personal tax credit of up to 20% for fuel cells with a maximum of $1,500, and a 100% solar tax exemption.[358] In addition, New York has appliance efficiency standards in place for many commercial and household items, such as ceiling fan and light kits; commercial washing machines; commercial refrigerators, freezers, and icemakers; and torchiere lighting fixtures.[359]

NORTH CAROLINA

In September 2005, Governor Mike Easley signed Senate Bill 1134 establishing a Legislative Commission on Global Climate Change.[360] The Commission is composed of 34 members, including 18 legislators, and the remainder from academia, environmental organizations, the state power industry, the Manufacturers and Chemical Industry Council, the North Carolina Farm Bureau, and forestry associations.[361] The commission is charged with preparing a cost-benefit analysis of various state- and federal-level greenhouse gas mitigation strategies; determining "desirable" reduction goals for North Carolina; and researching potential economic gains for the state in emerging carbon markets.[362] It is scheduled to report to the North Carolina General Assembly and the Environmental Review Commission on or before November 1, 2006.[363]

The 2002 Clean Smokestacks Act (CSA) requires North Carolina's Division of Air Quality (DAQ) to study the potential control of CO_2 emissions from coal-fired utility plants and other stationary sources of air pollution, and issue a series of reports.[364] The CSA and its mandated reports have prompted actions to develop an overall climate action plan (CAP) for the state through a formalized stakeholder process.[365] The North Carolina CAP is currently in its initial stages and will provide cost and benefit information on a wide range of greenhouse gas reduction plans for the state.[366]

NORTH DAKOTA

In April of 2005, Governor John Joeven signed into law a comprehensive package of production incentives, tax cuts, and regulatory bypasses meant to stimulate the production of wind energy, biofuels, and hydrogen power.[367] In many cases, these provisions built on prior legislation designed to spur production of alternative energy sources. As a net result, North Dakota boasts a relatively supportive legal framework for these developing markets.

Recent legislation created the North Dakota Transmission Authority to promote investment in transmission lines, with an eye to enabling wind markets in particular.[368] Owners of large wind generator facilities (defined as having at least one generation unit with a nameplate capacity of 100 kW or more) are exempt from sales and use taxes on building materials, production equipment and other tangible personal property used in construction of the facility between July 2001 and January 2011.[369] Centrally assessed property taxes have been reduced by 70% for wind power projects for which construction begins before January 2011.[370]

Ethanol and biodiesel tax, investment, and production incentives are similarly generous. Plants in operation since 1995 that produce ethanol for retail sale are eligible for direct production incentives of $.40 per gallon.[371] (Under this plan, facilities with production capacity under $15 million can receive as much as $900,000 over the 2005-2007 biennium; those with greater capacity, $450,000.)[372] The state provides additional quarterly ethanol production incentives based on an index of North Dakota corn and ethanol prices.[373] (Annual payments under this plan are capped at $1.6 million, and no facility can receive more than $10 million in total payments.)[374] At the pump, 85% ethanol fuel (E85) is taxed just $.01, as compared to the state's basic $.21 excise tax for special fuels.[375]

Biodiesel sellers are eligible for tax credits of up to 10% per year for up to five years (with a $50,000 total cap) on the direct costs of adapting or adding equipment to a facility.[376] Purchases of equipment by retail fuel facilities for the purpose of selling diesel with at least 2% biodiesel are exempt from sales tax.[377] There are also excise tax reductions for fuel containing at least 2% of biodiesel by weight.[378]

The state exempts from sales tax the sale of hydrogen for use in fuel cells or internal combustion engines.[379] It also exempts equipment purchased exclusively for the production and/or storage of hydrogen by a hydrogen generation facility.[380] One piece of Governor Joeven's 2005 legislative package authorized the Department of Commerce to provide a $25,000 grant for a wind-to-hydrogen demonstration project in a major North Dakota city.[381] Also in 2005, a House Concurrent Resolution called on North Dakota universities and research institutes to participate in a regional hydrogen and energy research and education consortium.[382]

A number of other measures provide support for the production and consumption of alternative energy sources. Recent legislation enabled the creation of a credit-trading and tracking system for renewable electricity and recycled energy[383] under the auspices of the Public Service Commission.[384] This applies to all public utilities, municipal electric utilities, and electric cooperatives.[385] Both individuals and corporations are eligible for income tax credits of 3% per year for five years for the cost of equipment and installation of geothermal, solar, or wind energy devices.[386] Solar, wind, and geothermal energy devices are also exempt from local property taxes for five years after installation.[387] Finally, the North Dakota Industrial Commission is authorized to use monies from the Oil Extraction Tax Trust Fund to sponsor studies on energy conservation programs and renewable energy sources, cogeneration systems, and waste products utilization.[388]

OHIO

In 1999, Ohio's General Assembly created the Energy Loan Fund to offer incentives for renewable energy projects.[389] For example, the Fund's renewable energy loan program offers a nearly 50% cut on the interest on loans from participating banks for the implementation of renewable power systems.[390] Administered by the Ohio Department of Development's Office of Energy Efficiency, the Fund will expire in 2011 after it has collected $100 million from utilities in the state.[391]

In 2000, Ohio's Public Utilities Commission ordered the state's power utilities to inform customers of the fuel mix and emissions data of their electric products.[392] Utilities must specifically indicate the levels of carbon dioxide, sulfur dioxide, and nitrogen oxide emissions produced by their facilities.[393] Since 2001, Ohio has also required that utilities provide net metering to customers with renewable power generators.[394]

OKLAHOMA

In April 2001, Oklahoma House Bill 1192 created a committee to explore the sequestration of carbon via new agricultural initiatives.[395] The law calls for a collaboration of government officials and representatives of the agriculture and energy sectors to devise methods to slow global warming.[396]

Since 2003, the Zero-Emissions Facilities Production Tax Credit has been available to electricity producers who utilize renewable energy via a "zero emission facility" (having a production capacity of 50 megawatts or more and producing no emissions that are harmful to the environment).[397] For electricity generated after January 1, 2004, but prior to 2007, the credit equals $0.0050 per kilowatt-hour of generated electricity; after January 1, 2007 and until 2012, the credit is $0.0025 per kilowatt-hour.[398]

Also beginning in 2003, Oklahoma briefly offered an income tax credit to manufacturers of small wind turbines.[399] The law expired on December 31, 2005.[400]

OREGON

Oregon offers a powerful example of multi-level, integrative thinking in state action toward sustainability. In 2000, then-Governor John Kitzhaber announced the ambitious goal of state-wide sustainability by 2025.[401] Toward this end, he called on state agencies to consider sustainability at every level of their decision-making; emphasized the importance of setting measurable goals; and vested leadership responsibility with the Department of Administrative Services to reshape practices within state agencies.[402] As a result of this and subsequent executive orders issued by Governor Ted Kulongowski, 20 state agencies have developed sustainability plans and monitor them in an ongoing fashion; all new state building projects are required to meet or exceed Leadership in Energy and Environmental Design (LEED) silver building standards; state agencies are beginning to factor life-cycle costs and sustainability issues into their purchasing decisions; and Oregon dedicated its first state park with sustainability as a primary objective.[403]

On the legislative front, the 2001 Oregon Sustainability Act established a comprehensive statutory framework for sustainability work.[404] Primarily, the Act authorized the creation of a Sustainability Board, vested under the governor and comprising representatives with expertise in the business and small-business sectors, as well as natural resource conservation, sustainable development, and health or economics.[405] Like the executive orders discussed above, the Sustainability Act called on state agencies to consider sustainability at every level of their work—from purchasing to facilities management.[406] Moreover, it established an Institute for Natural Resources under the supervision of Oregon State University to act as a research clearinghouse, provide information to the public, and work with state agencies striving to meet sustainability-related mandates and goals.[407]

Within this framework, and under the broad rubric of sustainability, Oregon boasts a multitude of measures specifically related to greenhouse gas emissions. Oregon's Energy Facility Siting legislation requires new facilities to limit CO_2 emissions to 17% below emissions of the most efficient and commercially viable combustion turbine natural gas–fired energy facility operated in the United States.[408] Oregon's facility-siting statutes also establish specific standards for determining compliance; a streamlined permitting process (allowing for potential conflicts with state and local ordinances to be assessed in one step); public comment periods at the outset of the review process; and the opportunity for direct appeal to the Oregon Supreme Court.[409]

Oregon also offers broad-based net metering. All types of Oregon utilities that provide commercial and residential power are mandated to provide net metering for customer-generators with up to 25kW capacity.[410] (The Public Utility Commission may increase this limit for customers of public utilities.)[411] Metering proceeds at the utilities' expense.[412] The list of qualifying alternative fuel sources includes solar power, wind power, fuel cells, hydroelectric power, landfill gas, digester gas, waste, dedicated energy crops available on a renewable basis, and nontoxic biomass based on solid organic fuels from wood, forest, or field residues.[413] At the end of the year, unused credits are either credited to the customer generator, distributed to customers enrolled in the utility's low-income assistance programs, or dedicated for other uses following notice and opportunity for public comment.[414]

In addition, in 1993, the Oregon Public Utilities Commission mandated that regulated electric utilities apply a range of carbon adders from $10 to $40 (in 1990 dollars) per ton of CO_2 in their integrated resource plans.[415]

As for vehicles and alternative fuels, Oregon offers Small-Scale Local Energy Project Loans in support of initiatives to produce or deliver alternative/low-emission fuels or conserve energy by, for instance, modifying vehicles to run on alternative fuels.[416] The Oregon Department of Energy also offers a Business Energy tax credit to businesses that invest in Alternative Fuel Vehicles (AFV), Hybrid Electrical Vehicles (HEV), or other alternative fuel or transportation-related conservation measures.[417] Eligible businesses receive a tax credit of 35% of the incremental cost of the equipment over five years.[418] Private consumers can take up to $1,500 in tax credits against their state income taxes for the purchase of qualifying AFVs or HEVs and also receive credits for the cost of conversion to an alternative fuel system.[419] Contractors can take a business tax credit of up to $750 for the construction or installation in a dwelling of a fueling station needed to operate an AFV.[420] Electric and natural-gas-driven vehicles are excluded from the requirements for certified pollution control systems.[421]

Value added to real property from installation of a qualifying renewable energy system is not included in the assessment of a property's value for tax purposes.[422] Special provisions enable renters to install alternative energy equipment (e.g., photovoltaics) without the equipment becoming a fixture and the property of the landlord.[423] Oregon also encourages solar power by allowing municipalities to enact statutes protecting access to the south face of buildings during solar heating hours (through height and setback requirements for new buildings, restrictions on type and placement of new trees, etc.).[424]

In May 2006, Governor Kulongoski established the Governor's Climate Change Integration Group[425] to continue and expand on the work of the Governor's Advisory Group on Global Warming, which prepared the *Oregon Strategy for Greenhouse Gas Reductions* in 2004.[426] The governor's charge is to develop a climate change strategy for Oregon that provides long-term sustainability for the environment, protects public health, considers social equity, creates economic opportunity, and expands public awareness.[427] Oregon's goal is to reduce greenhouse gas emissions to 1990 levels by 2010, 10% below 1990 levels by 2020, and 75% below 1990 levels by 2100.

PENNSYLVANIA

In June 2003, the Pennsylvania Department of Environmental Protection released a greenhouse gas inventory detailing emissions for Pennsylvania.[428] The inventory provides provisional estimates for two years, 1990 and 1999, as well as background data on greenhouse gas emissions.[429] In addition to these efforts, Pennsylvania is currently poised to adopt California's greenhouse emission standards for motor vehicles.[430]

Pennsylvania has established a renewable portfolio standard of 18% by 2021.[431] The state's net metering provisions were enacted in 1998.[432]

Pennsylvania operates an Alternative Fuels Incentive grant program that provides financial assistance for the use of hybrid vehicles, alternative fuel vehicles, the use of alternative fuels, and advanced vehicle technology research and development.[433] The fund is supported by 0.25 mills of the gross receipts tax levied on electric utilities.[434] Eligible applicants include schools, government agencies, and private for-profit and nonprofit organizations.[435]

RHODE ISLAND

Since 2005, Rhode Island has offered a personal tax credit of 25% for the cost of residential alternative energy systems.[436] Furthermore, for the purposes of local property tax assessments, solar-powered systems cannot be assessed at a value more than that of conventional electric generators.[437] In addition, most renewable power generators are also exempt from Rhode Island's sales-and-use tax.[438]

Also since 2005, Rhode Island has required utilities to disclose to their customers their power sources, including the percentage of energy sold from renewable energy generators.[439] In addition, utilities must charge their customers $0.0003 per kilowatt-hour of energy to be reserved for Rhode Island's Renewable Energy Fund.[440] The Renewable Energy Fund supports renewable energy projects and incentives supporting alternative power sources.[441] Finally, all utilities are bound to sell 3% of their electricity from renewable power generators before 2008, 4.5 % before 2011, and 16% before 2020.[442]

Rhode Island has also set minimum efficiency standards for 21 appliances. Some of these appliance standards are based on the voluntary U.S. EPA and DOE's Energy Star standards and California's existing appliance standards.[443]

Rhode Island agreed, under the auspices of the New England Governors and Eastern Canadian Premiers, to a voluntary short-term goal of reducing regional greenhouse gas emissions to 1990 levels by 2010 and by 10% below 1990 levels by 2020.[444] Rhode Island participated in the development of the Northeast Regional Greenhouse Gas Initiative, but the governor declined to participate in the final program, citing the impact of the initiative on the cost of electricity.[445]

SOUTH CAROLINA

The South Carolina Energy Office has developed Rebuild South Carolina Partnerships (RBSC) to help bring energy efficiency to public agencies, school districts, businesses, and industry in South Carolina.[446] The program offers energy-efficiency assistance, including energy use audits, project coordination, and energy consumption monitoring.[447] Further, a sales tax incentive in South Carolina caps the maximum tax on the sale of a manufactured home at $300 if it meets certain energy-efficiency requirements.[448]

By Executive Order in 2001, the governor announced that whenever practical and economically feasible, all state agencies operating alternative fuel vehicles are required to use alternative fuels in those vehicles, while private businesses are encouraged to increase the use of alternative fuels in the state.[449]

In June 2006, Governor Mark Sanford signed House 4312, creating a new state tax credit for individuals purchasing clean vehicles equal to 20% of the federal tax credit for these vehicles.[450] The state also recently enacted production tax credits for ethanol and biodiesel, and tax credits for solar heating and cooling equipment and for landfill gas systems.[451]

SOUTH DAKOTA

South Dakota boasts a number of production and consumption incentives for ethanol, wind and other alternative energy sources. Both 85% ethanol (E85) and 85% methanol (M85) enjoy protected excise tax status ($.10 per gallon, compared to the $.22 rate for other motor fuels).[452] Ethanol producers receive an outright $.20 per gallon production incentive for fuel that is fully produced, distilled, and blended in South Dakota.[453] Moreover, the state offers tax refunds for the construction of major new biodiesel production facilities.[454] (This includes the expansion of soybean-processing facilities to include biodiesel production.)[455]

Legislation dating from 2003 ensures that commercial wind production facilities are assessed for property taxes at the local rather than state level.[456] Commercial and residential property owners are eligible for property tax exemptions, based on the installation of solar/photovoltaic, wind, biomass, geothermal, ethanol, and landfill gas–based energy systems.[457] Residential users receive a 100% tax exemption for the entire assessed cost of systems for up to three years after installation; commercial users, a 50% tax exemption on the installed cost for up to three years. (The exemption does not apply to producers of energy for sale.)[458]

TENNESSEE

In recognition of the threat of global warming, the Biobased Products for Farmers and Rural Development Act of 2000 authorizes Tennessee's Commissioner of Agriculture to promulgate rules promoting the development of bio-based products.[459] Furthering the 2000 statute's goal of reducing greenhouse gas emissions, Tennessee, since 2003, has offered a property tax exemption of two-thirds the installation cost for wind energy generators operated by public utilities.[460] Tennessee also offers low-interest loans of up to $100,000 to small businesses seeking renewable energy technology.[461] In addition to these measures, the Energy Division of the Tennessee Department of Economic and Community Development completed a climate change action plan for the state in April 1999.[462]

TEXAS

On May 5, 1995, Texas enacted a law requiring the state to consider the economic feasibility of energy alternatives in the construction and repair of government buildings.[463] If there is a finding of economic feasibility, the use of alternative energy sources is mandatory.[464]

Effective since January 8, 2001, Texas Public Utility Commission Substantive Rules § 25.211 and § 25.212 create interconnection standards for electrical generators.[465]

The standards specify that the total capacity of a facility's on-site generation unit may exceed 10 megawatts; however, no more than 10 megawatts of a facility's capacity may be interconnected at a given time.[466]

Texas Public Utility Commission Rules § 25.475 and § 25.476, effective since June 1, 2004, require that retail electric providers offer interested customers extensive information, including lists of generators' power sources and charts showing the levels of their carbon dioxide emissions.[467]

In August 2005, the Texas legislature established the state's renewable portfolio standard at 5,880 megawatts by 2015.[468] Of those 5,880 megawatts, 500 must be from renewable energy power sources other than wind power.[469] In addition, the law sets 10,000 megawatts as the state's renewable energy capacity goal in 2025.[470]

UTAH

Utah has a mandatory net metering program applicable to all electric utilities and cooperatives.[471] Eligible sources of energy include solar, wind, hydropower, and fuel cells based on renewables.[472] The size of the program is capped at .1% of capacity at peak demand in 2001.[473]

The state also offers a number of tax credits and other provisions to enable the generation of power from solar and other alternative sources. Purchases or long-term leases of equipment used to generate energy from renewables are exempt from the state sales tax.[474] Individuals who install renewable energy systems in their homes are eligible for a tax credit of 25% of the cost of installation, up to $2,000 per system.[475] Corporate entities can claim tax credits of up to 10% of the installed cost, up to $50,000 per system.[476]

Solar energy installers are required to be licensed.[477] Municipalities are authorized to build solar access concerns into their zoning or planning.[478] The state code also contains voluntary easement provisions, which ensure that a solar easement runs with the land in perpetuity, unless otherwise stipulated.[479]

Utah also has a climate change advisory group, and the Utah Department of Natural Resources has completed a climate change action plan for the state.[480]

VERMONT

In 1998, Vermont introduced net metering laws (amended in 1999 and 2002) that allow electricity consumers to participate in a net metering program after they apply for and receive a Certificate of Public Good for Interconnected Net Metered Power Systems.[481] Currently, net metering is only available for renewable energy generators producing at most 15 kilowatts of energy (or up to 150 kilowatts for farmers).[482]

In 2002, then-Governor Howard Dean issued an executive order charging the state with developing a plan for improving efficiency and reducing greenhouse gas emissions from government sources.[483] In the same year, Vermont began offering a sales tax exemption for all renewable power systems with a capacity of up to 15 kilowatts (or up to 150 kilowatts for on-farm systems).[484]

In the following year, Governor Jim Douglas signed an executive order for state government buildings to reduce greenhouse gas emissions to 1990 levels by 2010, to 10% below 1990 levels by 2020, and, in the long term, to levels "sufficient to eliminate any dangerous threat to the climate."[485] Vermont agreed, under the auspices of the New England Governors and Eastern Canadian Premiers, to a voluntary short-term goal of reducing regional greenhouse gas emissions to 1990 levels by 2010 and to 10% below 1990 levels by 2020.[486] Vermont is a member of the Northeast Regional Greenhouse Gas Initiative and has enacted legislation incorporating its RGGI commitments into state law.[487]

More recently, in 2005 Vermont adopted California's greenhouse gas emissions standards for motor vehicles.[488] Also in 2005, Vermont set a renewable portfolio goal, which calls for the state's electric utilities to meet growth in electricity demand between 2005 and 2012 by using energy-efficiency and renewable-energy resources.[489]

In 2006, the state adopted legislation to reduce greenhouse gas emissions by 25% from 1990 levels by 2012, by 50% by 2028 and "if practical using reasonable efforts," by 75% by 2050.[490] The legislation also requires the Secretary for the Agency for Natural Resources to complete a climate action plan. Vermont Governor James Douglas also signed a bill in May 2006 that sets new energy-efficiency standards for industrial and household appliances.[491]

VIRGINIA

Since 1996, Virginia's Solar Manufacturing Incentive Grant (SMIG) Program has offered funds to encourage the construction of photovoltaic panels.[492] The program pays photovoltaic manufacturers up to $0.75 per watt (with a maximum of 6 megawatts) for every panel sold.[493]

A 2001 ruling by the Virginia State Corporation Commission (SCC) mandates the disclosure of fuel mix and emissions data by electricity providers.[494] Annually, before April 1, electric service suppliers must disclose to customers and file with the SCC their fuel mix and emissions statistics from the previous year.[495]

WASHINGTON

The Washington State Energy Office completed a climate change action plan for the state in April 1996.[496] Washington's key greenhouse gas mitigation measures appear as amendments and additions to the Washington Clean Air Act § 70.94. Such provisions:

- establish Reasonable Available Control Technology (RACT) requirements for industrial polluters;[497]
- affirm tax exemptions and credits for air pollution control facilities;[498]
- create an Abatement Account and tax incentives for manufacturers who take verifiable steps to reduce sulfur dioxide emissions;[499]
- require large employers in counties with populations over 150,000 to implement commuter trip reduction plans;[500]
- establish a ride-sharing grant program for private, public and nonprofit sector employers who offer financial incentives for employees to share rides;[501]
- create clean fuel matching grants to help local governments offset the costs of purchasing and maintaining "clean fuel" vehicles for public transportation, including school buses;[502]
- authorize New Source Review for significant sources of ambient air contaminants and require notice of proposed construction of new contaminant sources.[503]

Title 80, Public Utilities, houses a second cluster of greenhouse gas initiatives, most notably:

- Carbon Dioxide Mitigation statutes establish mandatory CO_2 mitigation strategies for new fossil-fueled thermal electric generation facilities, as well as existing facilities seeking permits to significantly increase their CO_2 emissions. Facilities are required to mitigate 20% of total emissions by one of three options: 1) payment to a third party to provide mitigation, 2) direct purchase of permanent carbon credits, or 3) investment in applicant-controlled CO_2 mitigation projects, including combined heat and power plants.[504]
- Net Metering of Electricity statutes make a net metering option available to customer-generators on a first-come, first-served basis.[505]

Washington has also established efficiency standards for 13 appliances.[506] In addition, Washington has adopted California Low Emission Vehicle (LEV) standards for passenger cars, light-duty trucks, and medium-duty passenger vehicles.[507] The legislation specifically rejects, however, the adoption of California Zero Emission Vehicle (ZEV) standards.[508] Moreover, it stipulates that emissions standards will only be effective for those model years for which the state of Oregon has adopted the California motor vehicle emission standards.[509]

WEST VIRGINIA

West Virginia provides tax benefits to wind power projects by valuing all wind turbines at salvage value for taxation.[510]

In March 1998, however, the West Virginia legislature passed a bill barring the state's Division of Environmental Protection, without legislative or federal authority, from "proposing or promulgating any new rule intended, in whole or in part, to reduce emissions of greenhouse gases from the residential, commercial, industrial, electric utility or transportation sectors in order to comply with the Kyoto Protocol."[511]

WISCONSIN

Since 1999, Wisconsin's Energy Conservation Corporation has administered a public benefits fund providing grants for renewable energy and energy-efficiency projects and services.[512] The program provides both information and technical aid for renewable energy systems to the citizens, businesses, and local governments of Wisconsin.[513] As an added incentive for the commercial, industrial, and residential sectors to purchase renewable energy generators, any value added to property from the addition of a solar or wind power system is exempt from Wisconsin's general property tax.[514]

Also in 1999, Wisconsin enacted legislation that established a renewable portfolio standard for electric utilities.[515] By 2008, 1.55% of energy generated must be from a renewable power source, such as solar power, wind power, biomass, or hydropower.[516] By 2012, 2.2% of energy must be from renewable resources.[517]

Wisconsin significantly increased its renewable portfolio standard requirements with the passage of Senate Bill 459 in 2006. The new law requires that 10% of utilities' electricity production come from renewable sources by 2015. The new legislation also increases funding to local governments for energy-efficiency projects, requires the state to support research on and development of agricultural digesters, requires the state to launch a pilot residential heating program using leftover corn plants, mandates that the state's six largest agencies purchase 20% of their energy from renewable sources by 2011, and requires the state to include higher energy-efficiency standards in building codes.[518]

In April 2006, Wisconsin Governor Jim Doyle signed an executive order requiring all state buildings to conform to "green building" standards. Applying to both new and existing buildings, the order directs the Wisconsin Department of Administration to establish standards based on the U.S. Building Council LEED certification. The order also requires overall energy use by state buildings to be reduced by 10% by 2008 and by 20% by 2010.[519]

Wisconsin has also developed a climate change action plan.[520]

WYOMING

Wyoming offers statewide net metering for solar, wind, and hydropower systems up to 25 kW.[521] Sales of equipment used to generate electricity from renewable resources are exempt from the state excise tax.[522] Ethanol producers are eligible for $.40/gallon production incentives.[523]

Endnotes

1. ALA. CODE § 40-17-160 (2006).

2. Ala. Dep't of Economic and Cmty. Affairs, Local Gov't Energy Loan Program, http://216.226.178.189/C3/Local%20Government%20Energy%20Loan%20P/default.aspx (last visited Apr. 20, 2006).

3. Ala. Dep't of Economic and Cmty. Affairs, Alabama Star Program, http://www.energyideas.uah.edu/alabama_starprog.html (last visited Apr. 20, 2006).

4. Ala. Dep't of Economic and Cmty. Affairs, Biomass Energy Program, http://www.adeca.state.al.us/txtlstvw.aspx?LstID=7d865154-617a-495b-afb8-5cf4271b56ed (last visited Apr. 20, 2006).

5. WILLIAM J. HERZ, ROBERT A. GRIFFIN & WILLIAM D. GUNTHER, POLICY PLANNING TO REDUCE GREENHOUSE GAS EMISSIONS IN ALABAMA (Dec. 1997), *available at* yosemite.epa.gov/oar%5Cglobalwarming.nsf/UniqueKeyLookup/SVDN5QRPPJ/$File/Alabama_action_plan.pdf.

6. H.C.R. 30, 24th Leg., 2d Sess. (Alaska 2006).

7. ALASKA STAT. § 42.45.010 (2006).

8. ARIZ. REV. STAT. § 43-1083 (LexisNexis 2006).

9. *Id.*

10. *Id.*

11. *Id.* §§ 42-5061, 42-5075(B)(14).

12. *Id.*

13. *Id.*

14. Ariz. Exec. Order No. 05-05 (2005).

15. *Id.*

16. Press Release, State of Arizona Executive Office, Governors Napolitano and Richardson Launch Southwest Climate Change Initiative (Feb. 28, 2006), *available at* http://www.governor.state.az.us/press/2006/0602/022806_SouthwestClimate ChangeInitiative.pdf.

17. *Id.*

18. Press Release, Arizona Corporation Commission, 15 Percent of Arizona's Energy to Come from Renewables by 2025 (Feb. 28, 2006), *available at* http://www.cc.state.az.us/news/pr02-28-06.htm.

19. H.B. 2390, 47th Leg., 1st Reg. Sess. (Ariz. 2005).

20. H.B. 2429, 47th Leg., 2d Reg. Sess. (Ariz. 2006).

21. *Id.*

22. *Id.*

23. *Id.*

24. Ariz. Exec. Order 2006-13 (2006).

25. *Id.*

26. *See* ARIZONA CLIMATE CHANGE ADVISORY GROUP, CLIMATE CHANGE ACTION PLAN (Aug. 2006), *available at* http://azgovernor.gov/dms/upload/Climate_Change_Action_Plan_final-web.pdf.

27. *Id.*

28. ARK. CODE. ANN. §§ 23-18-601 to 23-18-604 (2006).

29. *Id.* §§ 15-4-2801 to 15-4-2805.

30. *Id.*

31. *Id.*

32. *Id.* § 15-4-2104.

33. *Id.* § 19-11-217.

34. Ark. Dep't of Economic Dev., Arkansas State Agency Hybrid Vehicle Rebate Program, http://www.1800arkansas.com/energy/index.cfm?page=Hybrid_rebate (last visited Aug. 30, 2006).

35. *Id.*

36. Ark. Code. Ann. §§ 15-10-601 to 15-10-701 (2006).

37. *Id.* § 15-10-701.

38. Assemb. B. 32 (Cal. 2006).

39. *Id.*

40. *Id.*

41. S.B. 1368 (Cal. 2006).

42. *Id.*

43. S.B. 107 (Cal. 2006).

44. Press Release, State of California Office of the Governor, California, New York Agree to Explore Linking Greenhouse Gas Emission Credit Trading Markets; Gov. Schwarzenegger Tours Carbon Trading Floor (Oct. 16, 2006), *available at* http://gov.ca.gov/index.php?/press-release/4449/.

45. *Id.*

46. Press Release, State of California Office of the Governor, Gov. Schwarzenegger, Prime Minister Tony Blair Sign Historic Agreement to Collaborate on Climate Change, Clean Energy (July 31, 2006), *available at* http://gov.ca.gov/index.php/press-release/2770.

47. *Id.*

48. *Id.*

49. Cal. Exec. Order No. S-3-05 (2005).

50. Cal. Exec. Order No. S-20-04 (2004).

51. Cal. Gov't Code § 14684 (West 2006).

52. Cal. Energy Comm'n, 1997 Global Climate Change Report: Greenhouse Gas Emissions Reduction Strategies for California (Jan. 1998), *available at* http://www. climatechange.ca.gov/documents/97_report.html.

53. Cal. Rev. & Tax. Code § 73 (West 2006).

54. *Id.* § 17208.1.

55. Cal. Pub. Util. Code §§ 387, 399.11 to 399.17 (West 2006).

56. *Id.*

57. *Id.* §§ 399.11 to 399.17.

58. *Id.* §§ 398.1 to 398.5.

59. *Id.*

60. *Id.* § 2827.

61. *Id.*

62. Cal. Pub. Res. Code §§ 25740-25751 (West 2006).

63. *Id.* § 25751.

64. Cal. Energy Comm'n, Appliance Efficiency & Appliance Regulations, http://www.energy.ca.gov/efficiency/appliances/ (last visited Sept. 7, 2006).

65. This measure is discussed in more detail in Chapter 10.

66. Cal. Health & Safety Code §§ 42800-42870 (West 2006).

67. *Id.*

68. *Id.*

69. *Id.* § 42823.

70. *Id.*

71. Cal. Pub. Res. Code § 25301 (West 2006).

72. Cal. Health & Safety Code § 43018.5 (West 2006).

73. Cal. Health & Safety Code § 25000.5 (West 2006).

74. *Id.* § 43866.

75. Cal. Gov't Code § 65041 (West 2006).

76. Colo. Dep't of Pub. Health & Envt., Climate Change & Colorado, A Technical Assessment (Sept. 1998), *available at* http://www.cdphe.state.co.us/ap/down/climatechange.pdf.

77. *Id.*

78. *See* The Colorado Climate Project, http://www.rockymountainclimate.org/colorado_1.htm (last visited Oct. 26, 2006).

79. Colo. Rev. Stat. Ann. § 40-2-124 (West 2005).

80. *Id.* §§ 40-9.5-301 to 40-9.5-305.

81. 4 Colo. Code Regs. § 723-3 (2006).

82. *Id.*

83. Colo. Rev. Stat. Ann. § 40-2-124 (West 2005).

84. 4 Colo. Code Regs. § 723-3 (2006).

85. H.B. 1281, 65th General Assemb., 2d Reg. Sess. (Colo. 2006).

86. *Id.*

87. Colo. Rev. Stat. Ann. §§ 39-22-516 and 39-33-102 (West 2005).

88. 1990 Conn. Acts 219 (Reg. Sess.); U.S. Envt'l Protection Agency, Legislative Initiatives, http://yosemite.epa.gov/oar/globalwarming.nsf/content/ActionsState LegislativeInitiatives.html#RI (last updated July 2002).

89. 1990 Conn. Acts 219 § 3 (Reg. Sess.).

90. *Id.* § 16.

91. *Id.* § 6.

92. *See* New England Governors/Eastern Canadian Premiers, Climate Change Action Plan 2001 (Aug. 2001), *available at* http://www.negc.org/documents/NEG-ECP%20CCAP.PDF.

93. 2004 Conn. Acts 252 (Reg. Sess.).

94. *Id.* § 2.

95. Connecticut Climate Change, 2005 CT Climate Change Action Plan, *available at* http://www.ctclimatechange.com/StateActionPlan.html (last visited Mar. 5, 2006).

96. 2004 Conn. Acts 252 § 3 (Reg. Sess.).

97. Connecticut Greenhouse Gas Emissions and Sinks Inventory: Summary, http://yosemite.epa.gov/OAR/globalwarming.nsf/UniqueKeyLookup/RAMR6JTQS6/$File/CTInventorySummary_10-28b.pdf (last visited Mar. 5, 2006).

98. Conn. Agencies Regs. § 22a-174-36b (2005).

99. Cal. Code Regs. tit. 13, § 1961.1 (2005); Pew Center on Global Climate Change, States Poised to Require Vehicle GHG Emissions Standards, http://www.pewclimate.org/what_s_being_done/in_the_states/vehicle_ghg_standard.cfm (last updated Jan. 2006).

100. Conn. Gen. Stat. § 16-245a (2006).

101. *Id.* § 16a-48.

102. Connecticut Climate Change, Taking Action in Connecticut to Reduce Climate Change: Progress Made in 2005 (Feb. 2006), *available at* http://www.ctclimatechange.com/documents/TakingActionwithBookmarks.pdf.

103. Northeast States for Coordinated Air Use Management, Eastern Climate Registry, http://www.easternclimateregistry.org (last visited Mar. 31, 2006).

104. Regional Greenhouse Gas Initiative, http://www.rggi.org/ (last visited Aug. 30, 2006).

105. Center for Energy and Envt'l Policy, Delaware Climate Change Action Plan 1 (Jan. 2000), *available at* http://www.udel.edu/ceep/publications/energy/reports/energy_delaware_climate_change_action_plan/fullreport.pdf.

106. *Id.*

107. *Id.* at 15; *see also* U.S. Envt'l Protection Agency, Delaware Greenhouse Gas Emissions and Sinks Inventory: Summary, http://yosemite.epa.gov/oar%5Cglobal

warming.nsf/UniqueKeyLookup/JSIN5DQSUS/$File/ DESummary.pdf (last visited Apr. 6, 2006).

108. Center for Energy and Envt'l Policy, Delaware Climate Change Action Plan 16 (Jan. 2000), *available at* http:// www.udel.edu/ceep/publications/energy/reports/ energy_delaware_climate_change_action_plan/fullreport.pdf.

109. *Id.* at 1.

110. *Id.*

111. Regional Greenhouse Gas Initiative, http://www.rggi.org/ (last visited Aug. 30, 2006).

112. S.B. 74, 143d Gen. Assemb. (Del. 2005).

113. 2006 Fla. Laws ch. 2006-230.

114. S.B. 888, 108th Reg. Sess. (Fla. 2006).

115. *Id.*

116. *Id.*

117. Fla. Stat. Ann. § 212.08 (West 2006).

118. *Id.* § 316.0741.

119. Ga. Code Ann. §§ 46-3-50 to 46-3-56 (2006).

120. Avoided cost is the marginal cost for the same amount of energy acquired through another means such as through purchase from an alternate supplier.

121. Ga. Code Ann. § 46-3-56.

122. *Id.* §§ 12-6-220 to 12-6-232.

123. *Id.* § 12-6-223.

124. *Id.* § 12-6-224.

125. *Id.* § 12-6-331.

126. *Id.* § 48-7-40.16.

127. *Id.* § 32-9-4.

128. 2006 Haw. Sess. Laws 240.

129. *Id.*

130. 2006 Haw. Sess. Laws 096.

131. *Id.*

132. *Id.*

133. 2006 Haw. Sess. Laws 162.

134. Haw. Rev. Stat. Ann. § 235-12.5 (LexisNexis 2006).

135. *Id.*

136. *Id.* § 226-18.

137. *Id.* §§ 269-101 to 269-111.

138. *Id.*

139. *Id.* § 269-91 to 269-94.

140. *Id.*

141. *Id.*

142. *Id.* § 196-7.

143. *Id.*

144. *See* U.S. Envtl. Protection Agency, Action Plans, http://yosemite.epa.gov/ oar%5Cglobalwarming.nsf/content/ActionsStateActionPlans.html (last visited Sept. 7, 2006).

145. 2006 Idaho Sess. Laws ch. 367.

146. *Id.*

147. Idaho Code Ann. § 63-2407 (2006).

148. *Id.* §§ 63-2401, 63-2402. *See also id.* §§ 63-2423, 63-2434 (concerning rebates for special fuels taxes in specific categories).

149. *Id.* § 39-4109.

150. *Id.* § 39-4116.

151. *Id.* § 39-4109.

152. *Id.* §§ 22-5201 to 22-5206.

153. *Id.* § 22-5203.

154. *Id.*

155. *Id.*

156. Illinois Conservation & Climate Initiative, http://illinoisclimate.org (last visited Aug. 30, 2006).

157. 20 Ill. Comp. Stat. Ann. 687/6-4 (West 2005).

158. *Id.* 687/6-5.

159. *Id.* 687/6-3; Ill. Dep't of Commerce, Clean Energy, http://www.commerce.state.il.us/dceo/Bureaus/Energy_Recycling/Energy/Clean+Energy/RERP.htm.

160. 220 Ill. Comp. Stat. Ann. 5/16-111.1 (West 2005).

161. *Id.*

162. *Id.*

163. *Id.* 5/16-127.

164. *Id.*

165. 20 Ill. Comp. Stat. Ann. 688/5 (West 2005).

166. Response to Governor's Sustainable Energy Plan for the State of Illinois, Ill. Commerce Comm'n § 05-0437 (July 19, 2005). *See* 20 Ill. Comp. Stat. Ann. 688/5 (West 2005).

167. *Id.*

168. Ill. Exec. Order No. 6 (2002).

169. *Id.*

170. Ill. Dep't of Energy and Natural Resources, A Climate Change Action Plan for Illinois (June 1994), http://dnr.state.il.us/orep/inrin/eq/iccp/toc.htm.

171. Ill. Exec. Order No. 2006-11 (2006).

172. *Id.*

173. Ind. Code Ann. § 4-4-30 (West 2005).

174. *Id.*

175. 170 Ind. Admin. Code R. 4-4.2 (2006).

176. *Id.* R. 4-4.3.

177. H. File 2759 (Iowa 2006).

178. S. File 2398 (Iowa 2006).

179. S. File 2399 (Iowa 2006).

180. Iowa Code Ann. § 476C (West 2006).

181. *Id.*

182. *Id.* § 437A.6.

183. *Id.*

184. *Id.* § 266.39C.

185. *Id.* § 476.46.

186. *Id.*

187. Iowa Admin. Code R. 199-15.17(5) (2005).

188. *Id.*

189. Iowa Code Ann. § 476.47 (West 2006).

190. Iowa Exec. Order No. 41 (2005).

191. *Id.*

192. Iowa Dep't of Natural Resources, Iowa Greenhouse Gas Action Plan (Dec. 1996), *available at* http://atmos.cgrer.uiowa.edu/research/reports/iggap/FinalReport.pdf.

193. Kan. Stat. Ann. § 79-201(11) (2006).

194. *Id.* § 66-1,184.

195. Hugh T. Spencer, Climate Change Mitigation Strategies for Kentucky (June 30, 1998), *available at* http://yosemite.epa.gov/oar%5Cglobalwarming.nsf/UniqueKeyLookup/RAMR5ECR9B/$File/ky_2_fin.pdf.

196. Ky. Rev. Stat. Ann. § 224.20-125 (West 2006).

197. *Id.* §§ 278.465 to 278.468.

198. 2006 La. Acts 313.

199. La. Rev. Stat. Ann. § 47:1706 (2005).

200. La. Dep't of Natural Resources, HELP - Home Energy Loan Program, http://www.dnr.state.la.us/sec/execdiv/techasmt/programs/residential/help/index.htm (last updated Mar. 22, 2005). *See* La. Rev. Stat. Ann. § 36:351 (empowering the Department of Natural Resources).

201. La. Rev. Stat. Ann. §§ 47:38, 47:287.757 (2005).

202. Me. Rev. Stat. Ann. tit. 38, § 575 (2006).

203. *Id.*

204. *Id.*

205. *Id.*

206. *Id.* § 576.

207. *Id.* § 577.

208. Maine Greenhouse Gas Initiative, A Climate Action Plan for Maine 2004, *available at* http://maineghg.raabassociates.org/finalplan.asp (last visited Mar. 17, 2006).

209. Maine Dep't of Envt'l Protection, ch. 127, New Motor Vehicle Emission Standards, *available at* http://www.maine.gov/dep/air/regulations/docs/chap127%20Pavley%20FINAL%20adopted%20rule.doc (last visited Mar. 23, 2006). *See* Code Me. R. § 585-D (2006); Cal. Code Regs. tit. 13 §§ 1956.8(g),(h), 1960.1, 1961(a), 1962(a) (2006).

210. *See* New England Governors/Eastern Canadian Premiers, Climate Change Action Plan 2001 (Aug. 2001), *available at* http://www.negc.org/documents/NEG-ECP%20CCAP.PDF.

211. 65-407-311 Me. Code R. (Weil 2006).

212. Md. Code Ann., Tax-Gen. § 10-722 (2006).

213. *Id.* § 11-207.

214. Md. Code Ann., State Gov't § 9-2007 (2006).

215. Md. Code Ann., Pub. Util. Cos. § 7-505 (2006).

216. *Id.* § 7-306.

217. *Id.* § 7-703.

218. Md. Energy Admin., Energy Efficiency Standards Act, http://www.energy.state.md.us/eesa/database/index.html (last visited Sept. 7, 2006).

219. S.B. 154, 421st Gen. Assem., Reg. Sess. (Md. 2006).

220. Md. Energy Admin., GHG Emissions Reductions in Maryland (Mar. 2004), *available at* http://yosemite.epa.gov/oar%5Cglobalwarming.nsf/UniqueKeyLookup/JMSY5ZBGXC/$File/GHG%20Volume%20I%20Final.pdf.

221. *See* New England Governors/Eastern Canadian Premiers, Climate Change Action Plan 2001 (Aug. 2001), *available at* http://www.negc.org/documents/NEG-ECP%20CCAP.PDF.

222. Mass. Exec. Dept., Massachusetts Climate Protection Plan (Spring 2004), *available at* http://www.mass.gov/Eocd/docs/pdfs/maclimateprotectionplan.pdf.

223. *Id.* at 5.

224. Mass. Greenhouse Gas Emissions and Sinks Inventory: Summary, http://yosemite.epa.gov/OAR/globalwarming.nsf/UniqueKeyLookup/JSIN5DQSY8/$file/MASummary.PDF (last visited Mar. 5, 2006).

225. 310 Mass. Code Regs. 7.29 (2006).

226. Id.; 310 Mass. Code Regs. 7.00: Appx. B (2006).

227. Id. § 7.40.

228. Cal. Code Regs. tit. 13, § 1961.1 (2005); Pew Center on Global Climate Change, States Poised to Require Vehicle GHG Emissions Standards, http://www.pewclimate.org/what_s_being_done/in_the_states/vehicle_ghg_standard.cfm (last updated Jan. 2006).

229. Northeast States for Coordinated Air Use Management, Eastern Climate Registry, http://www.easternclimateregistry.org (last visited Mar. 31, 2006).

230. Regional Greenhouse Gas Initiative, http://www.rggi.org/ (last visited Aug. 30, 2006).

231. Mass. Gen. Laws ch. 25A, § 11F (2006); 225 Mass. Code Regs. 14.00 (2006).

232. Mich. Comp. Laws Ann. § 207.821 -.827 (West 2006).

233. Id. § 208.39e.

234. Id.

235. Id. § 211.9i.

236. Id. § 208.39e.

237. Id. § 460.10r.

238. Minn. Stat. Ann. § 272.02 (West 2006).

239. Id. § 272.028.

240. Id. § 297A.68.

241. Id. § 297A.67.

242. Id. § 41B.046.

243. Id.

244. Minn. Dep't of Commerce, A Tale of Two States: Small Solar Rebates—Steady Success, http://www.state.mn.us/mn/externalDocs/Commerce/Small_solar_rebate_success_013006125450_midwestsolarrebates.pdf. See Minn. Stat. Ann. § 216B.241 (West 2006) (empowering the Dep't of Commerce).

245. Id.

246. Minn. Stat. Ann. § 216C.41 (West 2006).

247. Id. § 216B.169.

248. Id.

249. Id. § 216B.1691.

250. Investigation into Disclosure of Environmental Information to Utility Customers, Minn. Pub. Util. Comm'n § E,G-999/CI-00-1343 (June 6, 2002). See Minn. Stat. Ann. § 216A, B (West 2006) (empowering the Public Utility Commission).

251. Id.

252. Minn. Stat. Ann § 16B.32 (West 2006).

253. Id. §§ 239.77, 239.771.

254. Minnesota Pollution Control Agency, Minnesota Climate Change Action Plan: A Framework for Climate Change Action (Feb. 2003), available at http://www.pca.state.mn.us/publications/reports/mnclimate-action-plan.pdf.

255. Miss. Code Ann. § 57-39-39 (2006).

256. Id.

257. Id.

258. Mississippi Development Authority, Mississippi Energy Investment Program, http://www.mississippi.org/content.aspx?url=/page/2913& (last visited Aug. 30, 2006).

259. Id.

260. Miss. Code Ann. § 69-51-5 (2006).

261. Mo. Ann. Stat. §§ 640.651-.686 (West 2006).

262. *Id.* §§ 135.300-.311.

263. *Id.* § 386.887; Mo. CODE REGS. ANN. tit. 4, § 240-20.065 (2006).

264. *See* U.S. ENVTL. PROTECTION AGENCY, ACTION PLANS, http://yosemite.epa.gov/oar%5Cglobalwarming.nsf/content/ActionsStateActionPlans.html (last visited Sept. 7, 2006).

265. Press Release, State of Montana Dep't of Envtl. Quality, First Climate Change Advisory Committee Meeting Scheduled (July 6, 2006), *available at* http://deq.mt.gov/press/pressDetail.asp?id=326.

266. MONT. CODE ANN. §§ 69-8-1001 to 69-8 -1008 (2005).

267. *Id.* §69-8-1004.

268. *Id.*

269. *Id.* § 69-8-1004(10).

270. *Id.* § 69-8-1008.

271. *Id.* § 69-8-101 to 69-8-110.

272. *Id.* § 69-8-601 to 69-8-605.

273. *Id.* § 602(2)(b).

274. *Id.* § 690-8-603(4).

275. *Id.* § 690-8-210(6).

276. *Id.* §§ 690-3-601 to 690-3-604.

277. *Id.* §§ 69-3-701 to 69-3-713.

278. *Id.* § 15-6-225.

279. *Id.* § 15-24-1401.

280. *Id.* § 15-31-124.

281. *Id.* § 15-32-115.

282. *Id.* § 15-32-201.

283. *Id.* § 15-32-401.

284. *Id.* § 15-72-104.

285. *Id.* § 90-8-101.

286. *Id.* § 17-6-401.

287. *Id.* § 80-12-201.

288. *Id.* § 75-25-101.

289. *Id.* § 2-17-414.

290. *Id.* § 15-6-201(1).

291. *Id.* § 15-70-522.

292. *Id.* § 15-70-204(3).

293. NEB. REV. STAT. § 2-5301 to 2-5306 (2005).

294. *Id.*

295. Official Nebraska Gov't Web site, Dollar and Energy Savings Loans, http://www.neo.state.ne.us/loan/index.html (last visited Aug. 30, 2006). The loans were authorized by NEB. REV. STAT. § 66-1001 to 66-1011 (2005).

296. *Id.*

297. *Id.*

298. NEV. REV. STAT. §§ 704.7801 to 704.7828 (2005). Six percent (6%) is the standard for 2005-2006. *Id.* § 704.7821.

299. *Id.* § 704.7821.

300. *Id.*

301. *Id.* § 704.763.

302. *Id.*

303. *Id.* § 278.580.

304. *Id.* § 338.190.

305. *Id.*

306. *Id.* § 361.079.

307. *Id.* § 361.0687.

308. *Id.* § 278.0208.

309. *Id.* § 111.239.

310. *Id.* §§ 111.370 to 111.380.

311. *Id.* § 362-A:1-a.

312. *Id.* § 125-L:2.

313. *Id.* § 125-O:3.

314. New Hampshire Dep't of Envtl. Servs., The Climate Change Challenge (Dec. 2001), *available at* http://www.des.state.nh.us/ard/climatechange/challenge.pdf.

315. *See* New England Governors/Eastern Canadian Premiers, Climate Change Action Plan 2001 (Aug. 2001), *available at* http://www.negc.org/documents/NEG-ECP%20CCAP.PDF.

316. New Jersey Dep't of Envtl. Protection, Sustainability Greenhouse Action Plan E3 (Dec. 1999), *available at* http://www.state.nj.us/dep/dsr/gcc/GHG02revisions.pdf.

317. *Id.* at A9-A11.

318. *Id.* at E3.

319. *Id.* at E4-E5.

320. Press Release, New Jersey Office of the Governor, Codey Takes Crucial Step to Combat Global Warming (Oct. 18, 2005), *available at* http://www.nj.gov/cgi-bin/governor/njnewsline/view_article.pl?id=2779; *see also* 37 N.J. Reg. 4415(a) (Nov. 21, 2005).

321. Press Release, *supra* note 320.

322. 38 N.J. Reg. 497(b) (2006); *see also* Cal. Code Regs. tit. 13, § 1961.1 (2005) (setting forth California's greenhouse gas exhaust emission standards and test procedures).

323. New Jersey Dep't of Envtl. Protection, Sustainability Greenhouse Action Plan E3, A11-12 (Dec. 1999), *available at* http://www.state.nj.us/dep/dsr/gcc/GHG02revisions.pdf.

324. N.J. Admin. Code tit. 14, § 8-2 (2006).

325. Assemb. B. 516, 211th Leg., 2d Reg. Sess. (N.J. 2005).

326. N.M. Stat. Ann. § 68-29-33 (Michie 2005).

327. *Id.*

328. New Mexico State Forestry Div., Forest Re-Leaf, http://www.emnrd.state.nm.us/emnrd/forestry/ReLeaf/releaf.htm (last visited Aug. 30, 2006).

329. N.M. Stat. Ann. § 7-2A-19 (LexisNexis 2005).

330. *Id.*

331. *Id.*

332. *Id.* § 71-7-6.

333. *Id.*

334. *Id.*

335. N.M. Admin. Code tit. 17, § 9.572 (2005).

336. *Id.*

337. *Id.*

338. N.M. Stat. Ann. § 6-21D-1 to 6-21D -10 (LexisNexis 2006).

339. *Id.*

340. *Id.* § 62-17-1 to 62-17-11.

341. N.M. Exec. Order No. 2005-033 (2005).

342. Press Release, Governor Bill Richardson Announces Historic Effort to Combat Climate Change (June 9, 2005), *available at* http://www.governor.state.nm.us/press/2005/june/060905_3.pdf.

343. 2006 N.M. Laws 93.

344. Press Release, Governors Napolitano and Richardson Launch Southwest Climate Change Initiative (Feb. 28, 2006), *available at* http://www.governor.state.nm.us/press.php?id=179.

345. *Id.*

346. N.M. STAT. ANN. § 47-3-1 to 47-3-5 (2005).

347. CENTER FOR CLEAN AIR POLICY, RECOMMENDATIONS TO GOVERNOR PATAKI FOR REDUCING NEW YORK STATE GREENHOUSE ACTIVITIES (Apr. 2003), *available at* http://www.ccap.org/pdf/04-2003_NYGHG_Recommendations.pdf.

348. *Id.* at ES 4.

349. NEW YORK STATE ENERGY BOARD, 2002 STATE ENERGY PLAN AND FINAL ENVIRONMENTAL IMPACT STATEMENT S-3 (June 2002), *available at* http://www.nyserda.org/sep/sepexecsummary.pdf.

350. CENTER FOR CLEAN AIR POLICY, *supra* note 347.

351. *Id.* at 19-22.

352. Press Release, N.Y. Dep't of Envtl. Conservation, State Environmental Board Approves New Vehicle Emissions Standards (Nov. 9, 2005), *available at* http://www.dec.state.ny.us/website/press/pressrel/2005/2005131.html; *see also* N.Y. COMP. CODE R. & REGS. tit. 6, §§ 218-1.2, 218-2.1(b), 218-8, 218-9, 200.9 (2005); CAL. CODE REGS. tit. 13, § 1961.1 (2005) (setting forth California's greenhouse gas exhaust emission standards and test procedures).

353. *See* N.Y.S. Energy Research and Dev. Auth., www.nyserda.org (last visited June 4, 2006).

354. N.Y.S. Energy Research and Dev. Auth., Alternative-Fuel Vehicle Program, http://www.nyserda.org/programs/transportation/AFV/default.asp (last visited Apr. 13, 2006).

355. *Id.*

356. N.Y. Pub. Serv. Comm'n, Case No. 03-E-0188 (Sept. 24, 2004).

357. N.Y. Pub. Serv. Comm'n, Case No. 03-E-0188 (Nov. 2, 2005).

358. *See* N.Y.S. Energy Research and Dev. Auth., www.nyserda.org (last visited June 4, 2006).

359. N.Y. ENERGY LAW § 16-102 (McKinney 2006).

360. 2005 N.C. Sess. Laws 442.

361. *Id.*

362. *Id.*

363. *Id.*

364. N.C. GEN. STAT. § 62-133.6 (2005).

365. N.C. Dep't of Envtl. and Natural Resources, Clean Smokestacks Reports on CO_2, NC Climate Action Plan, and other Global Warming Documents, http://www.ncair.org/news/leg/co2 (last visited Jan. 20, 2006).

366. N.C. DEP'T OF ENVTL. AND NATURAL RESOURCES, CARBON DIOXIDE (CO_2) EMISSIONS REDUCTION STRATEGIES FOR NORTH CAROLINA: FINAL REPORT (Sept. 1, 2005), *available at* http://www.ncair.org/news/leg/co2_final_09022005.pdf.

367. *See* Press Release, State of North Dakota Office of the Governor, Hoeven Signs Broad New Renewable Energy Legislation (Apr. 22, 2005), *available at* http://www.governor.state.nd.us/media/news-releases/2005/04/050422.html. As part of this package, an Office of Renewable Energy and Energy Efficiency was established "to provide secure, diverse, sustainable, and competitive renewable energy supplies and

promote the conservation of energy and the wise use of energy resources in both the public and private sectors."

368. N.D. Cent. Code § 54-44.5-09 (2005). The office also manages and distributes all production incentive payments authorized under § 4-14.1. *Id.*

369. N.D. Cent. Code §§ 49-24-01 to 49-24-10 (2005).

370. *Id.* §§ 57-39.2-04 to 57-43.2-03.

371. *Id.* § 57-02-27.3.

372. *Id.* §§ 4-14.1-07.1 to 4-14.1-10.

373. *Id.*

374. *Id.* § 4-14.1-08.

375. *Id.* § 4-14.1-09.

376. *Id.* §§ 57-43.1-01, 57-43.1-02.

377. *Id.* § 57-38-30.6.

378. *Id.* § 57-39.2-04(51).

379. *Id.* § 57-43.2-02.

380. *Id.* § 57-39.2-04(50).

381. S.B. 2018, 59th Leg. Assemb. (N.D. 2005).

382. S.B. 3011, 59th Leg. Assemb. (N.D. 2005).

383. Pursuant to N.D. Cent. Code §§ 49-02-25 (2005), recycled energy systems are systems "producing electricity from currently unused waste heat resulting from combustion or other processes into electricity and which do not use an additional combustion process." The term does not include any system whose primary purpose is the generation of electricity.

384. N.D. Cent. Code §§ 49-02-24 to 49-02-26 (2005).

385. *Id.* § 49-02-24.

386. *Id.* § 57-38-01.8.

387. *Id.* § 57-02-08(27).

388. *Id.* § 54-17-32.

389. Ohio Rev. Code Ann. §§ 4928.61 to 4928.63 (West 2006)

390. *Id.*

391. *Id.*

392. Ohio Admin. Code §§ 4901:1-10-31, 4901:1-21-09 (2006).

393. *Id.*

394. Ohio Rev. Code Ann. § 4928.67 (West 2006).

395. Okla. Stat. Ann. tit. 27A, § 3-4-101 to 3-4-105 (West 2005).

396. *Id.*

397. Okla. Stat. Ann. tit. 68, § 2357.32A (West 2005).

398. *Id.*

399. *Id.* § 2357.32B.

400. *Id.*

401. Or. Exec. Order No. 00-07 (2000).

402. *Id.*

403. Or. Exec. Order No. 06-02 (2006) (describing these and other outcomes of Or. Exec. Order No. 03-03 (2003)).

404. Or. Rev. Stat. § 184.423 (2006).

405. *Id.*

406. *Id.*

407. *Id.*

408. *Id.* § 469.501. *See also* Chapter 7, *supra.*

409. *Id.* § 469.501. *See also* Or. Admin. R. 345-020-0011 (2006) (describing requirements for a Notice of Intent).

410. Or. Rev. Stat. § 757.300 (2006).

411. *Id.*

412. *Id.*

413. *Id.*

414. *Id.*

415. Joshua Bushinksy, Oregon Carbon Adder, http://www.pewclimate.org/states.cfm?ID=56 (last visited Sept. 7, 2006).

416. *Id.* §§ 470.050 to 470.080.

417. Ore. Dep't of Energy, Business Energy Tax Credits, http://oregon.gov/ENERGY/CONS/BUS/BETC.shtml (last visited Sept. 1, 2006). *See also* Or. Rev. Stat §§ 469.040, 469.165, 469.185 (2006) (empowering the Department of Energy).

418. *Id.*

419. Or. Rev. Stat. §§ 316.116, 469.165 to 469.170 (2006).

420. *Id.* §§ 317.115, 469.165 to 469.170.

421. *Id.* §§ 815.295 to 815.300, 468A.365.

422. *Id.* § 307.175.

423. *Id.* § 90.265.

424. *Id.* §§ 227.190, 227.195, 215.044, 215.047.

425. State of Oregon Governor's Initiative on Global Warming, Climate Change Integration Group, http://www.oregon.gov/ENERGY/GBLWRM/CCIG.shtml (last visited July 7, 2006).

426. *Id.*

427. *Id.*

428. Adam Rose et al., Greenhouse Gas Emissions Inventory for Pennsylvania Phase I Report (June 2003), *available at* http://www.dep.state.pa.us/dep/deputate/pollprev/inventory.pdf.

429. *Id.*

430. 36 Pa. Bull. 715 (Feb. 11, 2006); *see also* Cal. Code Regs. tit. 13, § 1961.1 (2005) (setting forth California's greenhouse gas exhaust emission standards and test procedures).

431. 73 Pa. Stat. §§ 1648.1-.8 (2004).

432. 52 Pa. Stat. § 57.34(b)(4) (2004).

433. 2004 Pa. Laws 178.

434. *Id.*

435. *Id.*

436. S. 37, 2005 Leg., Reg. Sess. (R.I. 2005).

437. *Id.*

438. *Id.*

439. R.I. Gen. Laws § 39-26-9 (2005).

440. R.I. Gen. Laws § 39-2-1.2(b) (2005).

441. *Id.*

442. *Id.* § 39-26-1 (2005).

443. R.I. Gen. Laws § 39-27-1 (2006).

444. *See* New England Governors/Eastern Canadian Premiers, Climate Change Action Plan 2001 (Aug. 2001), *available at* http://www.negc.org/documents/NEGECP%20CCAP.PDF.

445. Conservation Law Foundation, Regional Greenhouse Gas Initiative, http://www.clf.org/programs/cases.asp?id=341 (last visited Aug. 31, 2006).

446. S.C. Energy Office, Rebuilt South Carolina, http://www.energy.sc.gov/Public/rebuildsc.htm (last visited Apr. 20, 2006).

447. *Id.*

448. S.C. Code Ann. § 12-36-2110 (2005).

449. S.C. Exec. Order No. 2001-35 (2001).

450. 2006 S.C. Acts 312.

451. 2006 S.C. Acts 386.

452. S.D. Codified Law §§ 10-47B-4, 10-47B-136 (2006).

453. *Id.* § 10-47B-162. Incentive payments to any one facility are capped at $1 million annually, $10 million cumulatively. *Id.* In order to be eligible for the incentives, facilities must begin producing qualifying ethyl alcohol by the end of the 2006 calendar year. *Id.*

454. *Id.* § 10-45B; *see also id.* § 10-45B-4.

455. *Id.*

456. *Id.* § 10-4-36 to 10-4-38.

457. *Id.* § 10-6-35.8 to 10-6-35.20.

458. *Id.*

459. Tenn. Code Ann. §§ 43-37-101 to 43-37-105 (2005).

460. *Id.* § 67-5-601.

461. *Id.* § 4-3-710.

462. Tenn. Dep't of Economic and Cmty. Dev., Energy Division, http://www.state.tn.us/ecd/energy_init.htm (last visited Sept. 7, 2006).

463. Tex. Gov't Code Ann. §§ 2166.401, 2166.403 (Vernon 2005).

464. *Id.*

465. *See* Tex. Util. Code Ann. § 14.001 (Vernon 2005) (empowering the Public Utility Commission).

466. *See id.*

467. *See id.*

468. *Id.* § 39.904.

469. *Id.*

470. *Id.*

471. Utah Code Ann. § 54-15-103 (2006).

472. *Id.* § 54-15-102.

473. *Id.* § 54-15-103.

474. *Id.* § 59-12-104(61)(a).

475. *Id.* § 59-10-134.

476. *Id.*

477. Utah Admin. Code § 156-55a-301 (2006).

478. Utah Code Ann. § 10-9a-102 (2006).

479. *Id.* §§ 57-13-1, 57-13-2.

480. Utah Dep't of Natural Resources, Greenhouse Gas Reductions in Utah: An Economic and Policy Analysis, *available at* http://yosemite.epa.gov/oar%5Cglobalwarming.nsf/UniqueKeyLookup/RAMR5ECRCK/$File/UtahActionPlan.pdf (last visited Sept. 7, 2006).

481. Vt. Stat. Ann. tit. 30, § 219a (2005).

482. *Id.*

483. Vt. Exec. Order No. 11-02 (2002).

484. Vt. Stat. Ann. tit. 32, § 9741(46) (2005).

485. Vt. Exec. Order No. 14-03 (2003).

486. *See* New England Governors/Eastern Canadian Premiers, Climate Change Action Plan 2001 (Aug. 2001), *available at* http://www.negc.org/documents/NEG-ECP%20CCAP.PDF.

487. H.B. 860, Adjourned Sess. of the 2005-2006 Biennum (Vt. 2006) (to be codified as 30 Vt. Stat. Ann. § 254).

488. 12-031-001 Vt. Code R. (2005); *see also* Cal. Code Regs. tit. 13, § 1961.1 (2005).

489. 30 V.S.A. § 8001 et seq.

490. S.B. 259, Adjourned Sess. of the 2005-2006 Biennum (Vt. 2006) (to be codified at 10 VT. STAT. ANN. 578).

491. S.B. 253, Adjourned Sess. of the 2005-2006 Biennum (Vt. 2006).

492. VA. CODE ANN. § 45.1-392 (2006).

493. *Id.*

494. *Id.* § 56-592; 20 VA. ADMIN. CODE § 5-312-70 (2006).

495. *Id.*

496. NICOLAS GARCIA, GREENHOUSE GAS MITIGATION OPTIONS FOR WASHINGTON STATE (Apr. 1996), *available at* http://yosemite.epa.gov/oar%5Cglobalwarming.nsf/UniqueKeyLookup/RAMR62FL2W/$File/WA_Action_Plan.pdf.

497. WASH. REV. CODE ANN. § 70.94.154 (West 2006).

498. *Id.* §§ 70.94.445, 82.34.01 to 82.34.901.

499. *Id.* § 70.94.630.

500. *Id.* §§ 70.94.527, 43.01.220 to 43.01.240.

501. *Id.* § 70.94.996.

502. *Id.* § 70.94.960.

503. *Id.* § 70.94.152.

504. *Id.* §§ 80.70.010 to 80.70.070. Enforcement is provided by the Energy Facility Site Evaluation Council created under *id.* § 80.50.030. This program is discussed in Chapter 7, *supra.*

505. *Id.* §§ 80.60.005 to 80.60.040.

506. *See id.* § 19.260.010.

507. *Id.* § 70.120A.010 (West 2006).

508. *Id.*

509. *Id.*

510. W. VA. CODE ANN. § 11-6A-5A (LexisNexis 2006).

511. *Id.* § 22-23-2.

512. WIS. STAT. ANN. § 16.957 (West 2005).

513. *Id.*

514. *Id.* § 70.111.

515. *Id.* § 196.378.

516. *Id.*

517. *Id.*

518. S.B. 459, 97th Leg. (Wis. 2006).

519. Wis. Exec. Order No. 145 (2006).

520. WISCONSIN CLIMATE CHANGE ACTION PLAN, http://www.dnr.state.wi.us/org/aw/air/global/WICCAP.pdf (last visited Sept. 7, 2006).

521. WYO. STAT. ANN. §§ 37-16-101 to 37-16-104 (2006).

522. *Id.* § 39-15-105(a)(viii)(N).

523. *Id.* § 39-17-109.

chapter twelve

Local Initiatives

*J. Kevin Healy**

I. The Relevance of Local Action to Greenhouse Gas Emissions

Climate change is a problem with serious and wide-ranging global implications. In fact, if the predictions of mainstream scientists are correct, the continued increase in the emission of greenhouse gases has the potential to cause environmental damage and social disruption of unprecedented dimensions, with impacts reaching into every corner of the planet. Notwithstanding the global nature of the problem, local jurisdictions play an important role in the area of climate change, representing part of the problem and offering much in the way of solutions.

Municipal activities contribute materially to the inventory of greenhouse emissions. Local governments operate and maintain sizable fleets of motor vehicles, including police cars, garbage trucks, highway service and parks maintenance vehicles, fire engines and passenger cars. Local government buildings are built to accommodate the offices and operations of municipal work forces that can range from a few employees, in smaller villages and towns, to the thousands of officials employed by the major cities around the country. Moreover, municipal landfills and sewage treatment plants contribute substantial amounts of methane to the atmosphere.

Given the scope of municipal operations around the country, it is clear that the procurement policies of local governmental entities could not just affect the level of greenhouse gas emissions, but also could foster favorable market conditions for fuel-efficient and other low-emission technologies in the United States. In light of these

---

* This chapter was prepared with the assistance of L. Margaret Barry and Alan Barker.

benefits, many municipalities are beginning to require that their existing fleets be replaced with low-emission and alternative-fuel vehicles, that municipal office buildings and other public structures be designed and equipped to be energy-efficient, and that their waste and sewage disposal operations be designed to recover methane to the extent practicable.

Moreover, although the problem of climate change may be one of global dimensions, many of the solutions to the problem can be found close to home. Indeed, much of the activity that contributes to climate change is subject to regulation under the police powers of local jurisdictions. The reason for this is that most human-induced greenhouse gas emissions result either from the burning of fossil fuels for the production of energy or from the disposal of waste. The energy that fossil fuel burning produces is used to power vehicles that serve transportation needs, provide heat and light to residential and commercial buildings, and generate the power required to drive industrial activities. Thus, local building codes, energy conservation initiatives, zoning controls and transportation policies all affect fossil fuel consumption and the associated emission of carbon.

For more than two decades, it has been well recognized that municipalities can play a pivotal role in meeting the challenge of climate change. As early as the 1980s, certain local governments were developing climate change action initiatives aimed at reducing greenhouse gas emissions from their communities and operations. The major strategies that have emerged over the years are discussed in section II of this chapter. Section III discusses the collective endeavors that municipalities have initiated over the last few years, and section IV includes a survey of specific jurisdictions that have been particularly active in the area.

II. Local Strategies to Reduce Greenhouse Gas Emissions
A. Energy-Efficient Buildings

Forty-three percent of U.S. carbon dioxide emissions come from energy use in residential, commercial and industrial buildings.[1] Accordingly, codes and regulations governing the energy efficiency of such structures have a direct bearing on the level of greenhouse gas emissions in the United States.

State and local governments first adopted requirements that address the energy efficiency of buildings in response to the fuel shortages that occurred in the 1970s. For example, San Francisco enacted the Residential Energy Conservation Ordinance (RECO) in September 1982. That local law, which remains in effect today, requires residential buildings, including one- and two-family dwellings, apartment buildings, and residential hotels, to meet certain energy-efficiency requirements addressing such measures as attic insulation, insulation of accessible heating pipes and cooling ducts, weather stripping, caulking and sealing of openings, faucet aerators, insulation of hot water heaters, low-flow showerheads, and low-flush toilets. When buildings are sold, renovated, or converted to condominium ownership, they must be inspected by the City Department of Building Inspection and certified to be in compliance with such requirements.[2]

Although, as a general rule, the seller is obligated to perform the work needed to bring nonconforming buildings into compliance, this obligation can be transferred to the buyer, so long as the buyer agrees to complete the upgrade within 180 days of the conveyance and an escrow account equal to 1% of the purchase price is established. For one- and two-family residences there is a cap on compliance costs of $1,300. As a result of RECO, the energy efficiency of the residential building stock in San Francisco is improving over time, as buildings are sold, renovated or converted to different forms of ownership. The city of Berkeley adopted a similar ordinance in 1987,[3] but other cities have not followed suit.

The main focus of municipal efforts to improve energy efficiency in buildings involves the adoption of energy codes, which establish efficiency-based specifications for insulation, heating and ventilation, and other design elements installed in new construction and substantial renovations.[4] Generally, these codes are not made from whole cloth, but are based upon models such as the Model Energy Code, which were first issued more than a decade ago, and have improved markedly over the years. The state-of-the-art model energy codes are currently the International Energy Conservation Code (IECC) and the International Residential Code. These model ordinances have been developed by the International Code Council (ICC), a nonprofit organization founded in 1994 by the Building Officials and Code Administrators International, the International Conference of Building Officials and the Southern Building Code Congress. The ICC is a substantial organization, with more than 250 staff members dedicating their efforts to the development and periodic updating, in accordance with a regular cycle, of building, fire and energy codes. The ICC first released the IECC in 1998. This version was followed by updates in 2000, 2001, 2003 and 2004, with the latest version issued in 2006. This process of regularly updating energy codes has been recognized as an important factor in addressing climate change, with one report estimating that it could result in the decrease of carbon emissions by 6 MMTC (million metric tons of carbon) annually.[5] Numerous states and municipalities across the country have adopted at least one version of the IECC.[6]

Other municipalities key their energy-efficiency requirements for residential buildings to the "Energy Star" program, a home energy rating system established pursuant to the National Home Energy Rating Technical Guidelines issued by the National Association of State Energy Officials in 1999. For example, the building code of the town of Greenburgh in Westchester County, New York, prohibits the issuance of a building permit for any one- or two-family dwelling, or multifamily dwelling of three stories or less, unless the applicant certifies that the dwelling will meet the requirements for a "New York energy star-labeled home."[7]

Building energy codes play an important role in the conservation of energy and the reduction of greenhouse gas emissions associated with building operation by improving the performance of windows, doors and skylights; increasing the efficiency of insulation in and around walls, ceilings, floors, foundations and ducts; reducing ambient air infiltration; and increasing the efficiency of lighting and equipment for heating, ventilation and air conditioning.

Local governments also have adopted energy-efficiency requirements for both existing and newly constructed public buildings. Because municipalities control these buildings in their proprietary capacity, such requirements appropriately may exceed the mandates contained in generally applicable building codes adopted under police powers. Thus, several municipalities have adopted policies requiring that public buildings be constructed or renovated as "green buildings," which meet the requirements for Leadership in Energy and Environmental Design (LEED) certification or similar criteria. The LEED Green Building Rating System was developed by members of the U.S. Green Building Council to create a common standard of measurement for "green building."[8] The LEED system awards a certain number of points in six categories (sustainable sites, water efficiency, energy and atmosphere, incorporation of local and recycled materials and resources, indoor environmental quality, and innovation in design), and buildings may attain ratings of Certified, Silver, Gold, and Platinum. Cities such as New York City, San Francisco, Portland, and Austin require new public buildings to be built to achieve a LEED Silver accreditation, while Scottsdale, Arizona, requires all new city buildings to attain the higher LEED Gold rating.[9]

Although most municipal governments that have green building requirements have tied them to the LEED system, there are other green building rating systems, such as the Model Green Home Building Guidelines and the Minnesota Sustainable Design Guide, which provide more guidance on impacts on greenhouse gas emissions.[10] Furthermore, some cities have crafted their own green building rating systems or high-performance building guidelines to take into account their own particular environmental and geographical characteristics.[11]

In addition to requiring public buildings to meet green building specifications, some municipalities are considering the extension of such requirements to buildings constructed with public financial assistance. Recently, a group named the "New Rules Project" has urged municipalities issuing tax-exempt municipal bonds for industrial development or municipal projects to adopt a resolution requiring such projects to be "climate neutral." Under the model resolution developed by this group, greenhouse gas emissions generated by municipally financed projects would have to be offset, so that there would be no net increase in emissions.[12] Cities are also using or considering the use of incentives such as expedited permit processes to encourage green building in the private sector.[13] In addition, some municipalities have introduced incentives for specific energy-efficient building features. For instance, Chicago awards grants for the

creation of green roofs, and its energy code has been modified to include standards for green and reflective roofs.[14]

B. Local Transportation Initiatives

Approximately one-third of greenhouse gas emissions in the United States comes from the transportation sector.[15] Again, municipalities are seeking to reduce such emissions through the exercise of both their "buying power" and police powers. As municipal fleets turn over, local governments around the country are replacing traditional vehicles with hybrids and low-emission, high-mileage, and even alternative-fuel vehicles. For example, the town of Amherst, Massachusetts, in 2002 passed a resolution providing that each vehicle purchased for its fleet must be the most fuel-efficient and/or lowest-emission vehicle available that is suitable for the particular municipal function.[16] Other cities, including Austin and Berkeley, have similar requirements.[17]

Numerous municipalities are also encouraging the use of bicycles as an alternative means of transportation through the addition of a system of bike lanes to transportation corridors and the development of various amenities, such as bike racks and shelters, which are designed to encourage the use of bicycles for commutation. Chicago, for instance, has created more than 100 miles of new bike paths since 1989.[18]

One major municipality, the city of New York, has recently announced a plan to dramatically increase the medallions issued by the Taxi and Limousine Commission to alternative-fuel vehicles.[19] To encourage the use of low-emission vehicles, some municipalities—including Salt Lake City, Utah; New Haven, Connecticut; Fresno, California; Albuquerque, New Mexico; and Austin, Texas—are providing parking incentives for hybrids or Ultra Low Emission Vehicles.[20]

A few municipalities have made substantial progress in reducing greenhouse gas emissions by undertaking major capital programs to improve mass transportation within their borders. For example, the per capita emissions of carbon dioxide in Portland, Oregon, recently have dropped 12.5% below 1990 levels, due in part to the construction of a new and well-utilized light rail transportation system.[21] Similarly, the Seattle Department of Transportation has designed a transit plan with goals to reduce reliance on single-occupancy vehicles and to work with other regional transportation agencies to increase the availability of public transportation to its system of "urban villages."[22] That plan includes the construction of new light rail facilities. Substantial federal and state funding has been made available for the planning, design and construction of major mass transportation projects in numerous cities around the country under the funding schemes established by the New Starts program created by the Intermodal Surface Transportation Efficiency Act of 1991 (ISTEA), the Transportation Equity Act for the 21st Century (TEA-21), and now the Safe, Accountable, Flexible, Efficient Transportation Equity Act: A Legacy for Users (SAFETEA-LU). The New Starts program funds light rail construction projects in a number of localities across the United States, including Phoenix, Arizona; Los Angeles and San Diego, California; Denver, Colorado; Baltimore, Maryland; northern New Jersey; Charlotte, North Carolina; and Seattle, Washington.[23]

C. Solid Waste Initiatives

The decomposition of organic wastes in municipal solid waste landfills results in the emission of methane, a potent greenhouse gas. Landfill gas consists of about 50% methane, with the remainder being mostly carbon dioxide. Twenty-five percent of the human-related methane emissions in the United States come from solid waste landfills, and 94% of landfill emissions are from municipal solid waste facilities.[24] It is estimated that landfills account for about 13% of the global anthropogenic methane emissions worldwide.[25] Local governments are making progress in reducing these emissions through the U.S. Environmental Protection Agency's (EPA) Landfill Methane Outreach Program (LMOP). Under this program, a municipality or county with responsibility for operating a landfill enters into a voluntary partnership with EPA through the execution of a memorandum of understanding (MOU) aimed at the development of a methane-to-energy system at the facility.[26] LMOP industry partners provide technical and financial assistance, and LMOP state partners work to reduce state and local barriers to the implementation of landfill gas energy projects. The resulting landfill gas projects offer both economic and environmental benefits, and the program is reported by EPA to be quite successful. According to the agency, as of December 2005, 490 partners had entered into MOUs for the development of cost-effective landfill gas recovery projects, and to date about 300 projects have been implemented.[27] EPA further states that the LMOP has developed detailed profiles for over 1300 candidate landfills. The reduction in greenhouse gas emissions due to the operations of all landfill gas-to-energy facilities in the United States is equivalent to removing 13 million cars from the road for a year, by EPA's estimate. Austin, Texas, and Portland, Oregon, among others, rely on power from landfill gas as part of their renewable energy portfolios.[28]

D. Zoning Initiatives and Land Use Policies

One major reason for the significant contribution of the transportation sector to greenhouse gas emissions in the United States is the inefficiency of travel patterns that results from urban sprawl. In addition, the energy efficiency of real estate developments can be affected by their density, the orientation of buildings on a site, and the nature and extent of the landscaping that is provided.

A municipality may enact zoning laws in the economic, social and environmental best interest of its citizens.[29] For example, the New York State Legislature, in

Section 261 of the Town Law, stated that "[f]or the purpose of promoting the health, safety, morals or the general welfare of the community, the Town Board [of a Town] is hereby empowered by local law or ordinance to regulate and restrict . . . the density of population and the location and use of buildings."[30] Local governments can draw on such broad powers to implement "smart growth" land use initiatives aimed at reducing the emission of greenhouse gases by decreasing vehicle miles traveled (VMT), reducing the footprint of development, and making projects more energy efficient.

The creation of mixed-use districts is an important component of smart growth programs, especially in major cities with large populations. These districts allow development of both residential and commercial uses within the same area—often within the same "mixed-use buildings."[31] This type of zoning allows for the creation of compact communities where citizens can live in close proximity to their places of employment, and where commercial needs can be met with less reliance on automobiles to get to and from essential locations.

One good example of the type of zoning ordinance municipalities have adopted to create such a district and achieve these objectives is the city of San Diego's "Urban Village Overlay Zone." This zoning law is intended to "create a mix of land uses in a compact pattern that will reduce dependency on the automobile, improve air quality and promote high quality, interactive neighborhoods."[32] Under the ordinance, each "urban village" must include a "mixed use core" component, a residential land use component and a public land use component. The mixed use core is required to be the most intensely developed portion of the urban village, and must contain commercial uses, public uses and residential uses that are centrally located in the project area.[33] Residents and employees must be "able to easily walk" to jobs, stores and service providers in the mixed use core, and pedestrian pathways must be provided to facilitate that activity.[34] Residential uses within the core area may be either in separate buildings or in mixed-use buildings above commercial uses.[35] Parks, public squares and similar sorts of open spaces must be afforded in the public use portions of the development.[36] A density bonus is provided near existing or planned rail transit stations, and parking facilities serving commercial and mixed-use buildings must be underground or to the rear or side of buildings.[37] Numerous other communities have adopted mixed-use district regulations of the sort enacted by San Diego or created mixed-use districts over the past decade, including Miami-Dade County's Downtown Kendall Urban Center District and the Pedestrian Overlay Districts of Charlotte, North Carolina.[38]

Local governments are also seeking to increase the density of residential development in areas already served by convenient mass transportation options. Thus, New York City, with its extensive 100-year-old infrastructure of rail and bus systems, has recently rezoned an extensive area of the West Side of Manhattan to allow for greatly increased residential and commercial density.[39] New York City stands as a model for such densely constructed mixed-use development, with 53% of workers over the age of 16 commuting to work by public transportation.[40] Moreover, as a result of the convenience created by mixed-use zoning and planning efforts supporting the creation of pedestrian corridors, Boston, for example, has been able to encourage 13% of its citizens to walk to work.[41]

Development fees and incentives are also an effective way of curbing urban sprawl and encouraging smart growth in cities. Planning experts have suggested that developers could be encouraged to build around existing infrastructure by forcing them to pay the real costs of creating sprawl. This would discourage developers who do not want to assume the cost for the installation of water and sewer lines, construction of schools in outlying areas, or the extension of services such as garbage collection.[42] On the positive side, municipalities could encourage smart growth by simplifying requirements relating to building restoration, offering tax incentives and expediting the permitting process for those wishing to develop existing structures or infill sites.[43] Such initiatives can be implemented in conjunction with a municipality's participation in the programs that have been adopted at the state and federal levels to redevelop "brownfields." For example, municipalities in the state of New York can enter into the Brownfields Opportunity Areas Program, under which the state provides technical and financial assistance to allow for the development of strategies to redevelop areas affected by contaminated sites.[44]

Other land use strategies that have been suggested over the years to reduce greenhouse gas emissions include the adoption of zoning ordinances allowing municipal authorities to consider energy efficiency in their review of site plans and landscaping plans for new development.[45] The correct placement of a new building on a site plan can result in significant energy savings. For example, orienting buildings to maximize southern exposure in the colder areas of the country could be particularly effective in conserving energy that would otherwise be used for heating. Similarly, landscaping new developments with evergreen trees to shield the northerly exposure of buildings in the winter and placing deciduous trees to offer shade in the summer can yield benefits in terms of energy efficiency.

The city of Portland has adopted several ordinances that support solar energy by protecting access to the sun for photovoltaics. In order to maximize solar access in lots resulting from a subdivision application, the Portland zoning code encourages variation in the width of lots to be created based on their orientation on east-west or north-south axes.[46] Portland also has established a "solar access permit program" for owners who install solar water or space-heating systems. This permit has the effect of an easement, guaranteeing solar access to owners by preventing their neighbors from shading the southerly walls of the protected building with either structures or vegetation. The permit runs with the land and notice of such a permit is attached to the deed to the adjoining landowner's property.[47] Other communities in Oregon, California and Idaho have similar ordinances to protect solar access.[48]

E. Plantings and Urban Forestry

Trees not only sequester carbon, but also reduce energy needs for both heating and air conditioning.[49] In light of these benefits, several local governments have adopted ambitious urban forestry programs. For example, the city of Chicago has several tree-planting initiatives for both the public and private sectors that have resulted in a 3% increase in tree canopy coverage since 1994, and its 2006 environmental agenda includes plans to plant more than 2,000 trees near public schools, on neighborhood streets, and near arterial roadways where there is currently little or no greenery.[50] The Los Angeles Department of Water and Power delivers free trees to Los Angeles residents who complete an online or neighborhood workshop and submit a site plan.[51]

Local forestry programs may receive substantial funding from state and federal sources. An advisory group to the state of California has recommended an "aggressive public assistance and outreach campaign to expand local urban forestry programs" and to meet a goal of planting five million trees in urban areas by 2020.[52] The U.S. Department of Agriculture also provides cost-sharing grants to organizations for the creation of programs to promote urban and community forestry.[53]

F. Renewable Energy Programs

Municipalities are also incorporating incentives designed to encourage the use of alternative energy into their tax codes and local ordinances. In addition, Austin, Texas, and Portland, Oregon, have required that a certain percentage of their energy come from renewable sources.[54] Austin gives rebates for the installation of solar power equipment, and Los Angeles has a ten-year, $150 million Solar Photovoltaic Incentive Program that runs until 2011 to help residents and businesses install solar power systems.[55] As discussed later in this chapter, City Light, the municipally owned utility in Seattle is the first utility in the country to become carbon neutral, by offsetting all of the emissions it generates in producing power. City Light has achieved this goal in part through reliance on hydroelectric and wind power.[56] San Francisco has made substantial investments in renewable energy, especially solar power.[57]

G. Procurement Strategies

As noted above, several municipalities are procuring low emission vehicles for their municipal fleets. Some municipalities—San Francisco, Santa Monica, and Jersey City, for example—have also adopted ordinances prohibiting the procurement of products containing tropical hardwoods of the types that are being over-harvested in South America and other parts of the world.[58] During the last part of the 20th century, deforestation in tropical areas resulted in substantial carbon releases.[59] Municipal tropical hardwood policies attempt to limit demand for the products of forest clearings. San Francisco's law provides for penalties such as suspension or revision of contracts, or the withholding of payments on contracts if a person provides tropical hardwood products or misrepresents the types of products provided under a contract. Santa Monica enforces its policy with fines and criminal penalties for repeated violations.

In addition, some local legislative bodies have directed that energy-efficient equipment and appliances be purchased and utilized in municipal operations. The following local governments are among those that have created such procurement programs: New York City; Portland, Oregon; Santa Monica, California; and Washington, D.C.[60] A 2001 report from the Consortium for Energy Efficiency sets forth a Model Purchasing Program for state and local governments.[61]

III. Collective Initiatives by Municipalities

While municipal governments concerned with climate change are working individually to develop localized programs, a great deal of collective activity is being pursued as well. That activity is aimed at coordinating what has become a significant grassroots effort to reduce greenhouse gases at the lowest levels of government.[62] As a result of these efforts, cities, towns and villages around the country are signing on to common emission reduction goals, committing to adopt similar strategies to meet those goals, sharing information among themselves on how to do so, and taking collective political action to urge that programs be put into place to deal with the issue at the state and federal levels. A brief description of the more significant collective local initiatives appears below.

A. U.S. Mayors Climate Protection Agreement

On February 16, 2005—the day the Kyoto Protocol went into effect in those countries that had ratified it—Greg Nickels, the mayor of Seattle, issued a statement announcing that his city would commit to reducing greenhouse gases by 7% as compared to 1990 levels (the reduction commitment that the United States would have shouldered if it had ratified the treaty) and urged other cities to do the same. That commitment was subsequently incorporated into a resolution that was adopted by the U.S. Conference of Mayors at its June 2005 meeting in Chicago.[63] After a series of recitations establishing climate change as a legitimate cause for concern, that resolution endorsed the U.S. Mayors Climate Change Agreement. Among other things, that agreement: (i) urges the federal and state governments to "enact policies and programs to meet or beat the target of reducing global warming pollution levels to 7% below 1990 levels by 2012;" (ii) urges Congress to adopt a cap and trade program, with "clear timetables and limits;" and (iii) includes a pledge from the signatories to "strive to meet or exceed Kyoto Protocol targets . . . by taking action in our own operations and communities." The agreement mentions 12 types of actions that cities may take to achieve their emissions reduction goals, as follows:

1. Inventory global warming emissions in city operations and in the community, set reduction targets and create an action plan.

2. Adopt and enforce land-use policies that reduce sprawl, preserve open space, and create compact, walkable urban communities.

3. Promote transportation options such as bicycle trails, commuter trip reduction programs, and incentives for car pooling and public transit.

4. Increase the use of clean, alternative energy by, for example, investing in "green tags," advocating for the development of renewable energy resources, recovering landfill methane for energy production, and supporting the use of waste-to-energy technology.

5. Make energy efficiency a priority through building code improvements, retrofitting city facilities with energy-efficient lighting, and urging employees to conserve energy and save money.

6. Purchase only Energy Star equipment and appliances for city use.

7. Practice and promote sustainable building practices using the U.S. Green Building Council's LEED program or a similar system.

8. Increase the average fuel efficiency of municipal fleet vehicles; reduce the number of vehicles; launch an employee education program including anti-idling messages; convert diesel vehicles to bio-diesel.

9. Evaluate opportunities to increase pump efficiency in water and wastewater systems; recover wastewater treatment methane for energy production.

10. Increase recycling rates in city operations and in the community.

11. Maintain healthy urban forests; promote tree planting to increase shading and to absorb carbon dioxide.

12. Help educate the public, schools, other jurisdictions, professional associations, business and industry about reducing global warming pollution.

It is particularly noteworthy that the agreement contemplates a process to track progress toward achieving the reduction commitments, by endorsing the creation of emission inventories, the establishment of specific targets, and the creation of an action plan by the signatories. As of October 2006, 320 mayors, representing cities located in every region of the country, had signed the agreement.[64] Signatories include the nation's largest cities such as Chicago, Los Angeles, and New York, as well as smaller communities such as Keene, New Hampshire; Durham, North Carolina; Hurst, Texas; and Moab, Utah.

B. International Council for Local Environmental Initiatives (ICLEI)

The ICLEI has organized a worldwide initiative, whereby local governments commit to, and receive technical assistance in achieving, quantified emissions reductions in greenhouse gas emissions. ICLEI runs this initiative, known as the Cities for Climate Protection campaign (CCP), on either a regional or national basis, in Australia, Canada, Europe, Japan, Latin America, Mexico, New Zealand, South Africa, Asia, and the United States.[65] Participants in CCP must adopt a resolution committing to reduce greenhouse gas emissions both in local government operations and throughout the community.[66] To accomplish this goal, a participant must commit to work toward five milestones defined by the CCP.[67] In particular, participants must pledge to:

1. Conduct a baseline emissions inventory and forecast. Based on energy consumption and waste generation, the participant is to calculate greenhouse gas emissions for a base year and for a forecast year. The inventory and forecast provide a benchmark against which the participating local government can measure progress.
2. Adopt an emissions reduction target for the forecast year.
3. Through a multi-stakeholder process, develop a "Local Action Plan" that describes the policies and measures that the local government will take to reduce greenhouse gas emissions and achieve its emissions reduction target. Plans are to include a timeline, a description of financing mechanisms, and an assignment of responsibility to departments and staff.
4. Implement policies and measures. According to ICLEI, "[t]ypical policies and measures implemented by CCP participants include energy efficiency improvements to municipal buildings and water treatment facilities, streetlight retrofits, public transit improvements, installation of renewable power applications, and methane recovery from waste management."
5. Monitor and verify results.[68]

In the United States, more than 150 municipalities and counties participate in the program. Participants in the CCP are a diverse group of small and large cities, including major cities in the Northeast (Boston, New York, Philadelphia), South (Atlanta), Pacific Northwest (Seattle, Portland), and West and Southwest (Austin, San Antonio, Denver, Tucson), as well as 30 cities and towns in California. Numerous counties also participate.[69]

Since 1993, ICLEI has organized four Municipal Leaders Summits on Climate Change, which bring together local governments from around the world. At the most recent such conference, which took place just before the United Nations Climate Change Conference in December 2005, participating mayors supported a "World Mayors and Municipal Leaders Declaration on Climate Change."[70] In this declaration, more than 300 mayors committed to emission reduction targets of 30% by 2020 and 80% by 2050 based on 1990 levels. They also committed to a variety of actions that would help to achieve these reduction goals.

C. Urban Environmental Accords

In connection with the United Nations World Environment Day on June 5, 2005, the mayor of San Francisco, California, invited more than 50 mayors from around the world to a conference on sustainability. The result of that conference, adopted unanimously by the participants, was the Urban Environmental Accords.[71] Under these accords, the participants committed to take 21 specific actions to pursue environmental sustainability. One such action requires the adoption of "a citywide greenhouse gas reduction plan that reduces the jurisdiction's emissions by twenty-five per cent by 2030, and which includes a system for accounting and auditing greenhouse gas emissions." Berkeley, Oakland, Salt Lake City, San Francisco, Santa Monica, and Seattle are all signers of the Urban Environmental Accords.

D. Chicago Climate Exchange and California Climate Action Registry

Some municipalities that have made commitments to achieve specific greenhouse gas emission reductions have done so under the aegis of programs administered by one of two noteworthy organizations, the Chicago Climate Exchange and the California Climate Action Registry. The arrangements provided by these entities are summarized briefly below.

1. Chicago Climate Exchange (CCX)

CCX is a private organization that has put together the nation's first greenhouse gas emissions credit trading system. Membership in CCX is open to corporations, institutions, municipalities, and certain other entities. Members enter into "voluntary, but legally binding" commitments to achieve specific greenhouse gas emission reductions in two phases. In the first phase, which ended in December 2006, a 4% reduction in direct emissions, as compared to average emissions in a baseline period running from 1998 to 2001, is required. In the second phase, an additional 2% reduction is called for by 2010. Members are to measure their progress in meeting these commitments against a series of interim milestones. To assist in achieving their objectives, CCX offers to members not only a registry, but an electronic trading system whereby credits can be purchased from and sold by both "members" and entities that have signed on as "participants." This platform allows for the trading of credits in six greenhouse gases, including CO_2, methane, nitrous oxide, hydrofluorocarbons, perfluorocarbons, and sulfur hexafluoride. To simplify the process, all the gases are converted to CO_2 equivalents for purposes of trading. The cities of Aspen, Colorado; Berkeley, California; Boulder, Colorado; Chicago, Illinois; and Oakland, California, have joined CCX.

2. California Climate Action Registry

The California Climate Action Registry was created by state law in 2000–2001 in order to assist businesses, institutions and municipalities in achieving and documenting greenhouse gas reductions.[72] Participants must sign a "statement of intent" to prepare and register an inventory of their direct and indirect CO_2 emissions for all operations in California for a "baseline year," which can be any year after January 1, 1990 (assuming the requisite information is available), and annually thereafter. Participants must utilize technical guidance provided by the registry, which is in the form of a detailed protocol that has been developed by the registry for calculating emissions, along with an online tool for reporting those emissions called the California Action Registry Reporting Online Tool (CARROT). The inventories submitted must be certified by pre-approved third-party technical experts. In return for these efforts, participants receive whatever protection is ultimately provided by a statutory commitment that the State of California will "use its best efforts to ensure" that reductions documented by participants "receive appropriate consideration under any future . . . regulatory scheme relating to greenhouse gases."[73] They also benefit from a great deal of support, which is offered in technical guidance documents and at conferences.

The cities of Los Angeles, Sacramento, Palo Alto, San Francisco, and Santa Monica are members of the California Climate Action Registry.

IV. Survey of the Most Active Local Governments

As noted above, numerous municipalities throughout the United States have signed on to resolutions supporting the goal of and committing to greenhouse gas emission reductions, and a substantial number of these municipalities have taken concrete actions to reduce emissions in their communities. At the forefront of local actions to combat climate change are an ever-growing number of cities that have set into motion comprehensive programs to reduce greenhouse gas emissions, often in conjunction with participation in the ICLEI's CCP. These municipalities are serving as laboratories for testing the effectiveness of various incentive and regulatory programs. Since most of their climate action plans require progress updates, with reports on emissions on a regular basis, it will be possible to monitor the success of these initiatives as the programs go forward.

The following municipalities' programs represent an array of the longest-running, most comprehensive, most effective, and most innovative municipal efforts to reduce greenhouse gas emissions. In general, the cities included in the survey have substantial populations and local governmental organizations of sufficient size to support major initiatives. The final section, however, focuses on the efforts of a small town in New York as an example of what measures can be taken on a more modest scale. While some of the cities in the survey have decades-long histories of environmental stewardship, other cities with brand-new programs are also featured. Some of the cities included in the survey have been recognized by such public agencies as the EPA as leaders on climate change issues, or by private or nonprofit organizations that have identified the cities' programs as noteworthy. The landscape of cities pursuing climate change initiatives is constantly changing, and this survey is not exhaustive—it is intended merely to provide a sampling of the broad range of activities being pursued by cities attempting to rein in greenhouse gases.[74]

A. Portland, Oregon

Portland's 1993 Carbon Dioxide Reduction Strategy[75] was the first significant plan by a local government in the United States to combat climate change.[76] Over the course of the last decade, Portland has continued to lead the way in local initiatives to counteract the negative effects of climate change. In 2000, the Energy Trust of Oregon was founded to educate businesses and private citizens about economic health and environmental benefits of reducing energy consumption, and to lend assistance in achieving such reductions. Initiatives put into place by the trust led to a total of $1.5 million in energy bill savings for over 200 Oregon businesses and 14,000 households during the first two years of operation.[77] In addition to this successful program, Portland and Multnomah County officials worked together in accordance with their commitments under ICLEI's CCP campaign in developing a comprehensive Local Action Plan on Global Warming in April of 2001. As might be expected from local governments with a long history of environmental stewardship, the goals of this plan are extremely ambitious—in some cases surpassing those of the Kyoto Protocol.[78]

The Portland Multnomah Local Action Plan focuses on five categories of actions to achieve these "quantifiable" reductions: Transportation, Energy Efficiency and Green Building, Renewable Energy Resources, Waste Reduction and Recycling, and Forestry and Carbon Offsets.[79] Within these five categories, the plan identifies the actions as either "Government Actions," which "constitute the City of Portland's and Multnomah County's green house gas-reduction plans as corporate entities," and "Community Initiatives," for which the city and county are "strategic partners, catalysts, or advocates."[80]

With 40% of Portland's greenhouse gas emissions attributable to transportation,[81] reduction targets for greenhouse gas emissions related to transportation are understandably more than twice the amount of any of the other four focus areas.[82] Portland's Government Action approach to meet this goal includes the construction of transit solutions such as a regional light rail system and the introduction of a streetcar in the city's center. In addition to the development of its mass transit system, Portland has made efficiency upgrades to the city fleet of vehicles, including putting more than 30 highly fuel-efficient hybrid vehicles into service and the conversion of diesel vehicles from an entirely petroleum-based form of diesel to a blend of 80% petroleum and 20% bio-diesel fuel (also known as B20).[83]

Portland's Transportation Options Program, a prime example of a "community outreach" approach to combating transportation-generated emissions, employs "incentive, mass marketing and grassroots" communications to convey the benefits of efficient alternatives to energy-consuming activities like single-occupancy vehicle driving. Additionally, these efforts have been used to inform citizens about the new modes of mass transit available, as well as to improve the pedestrian and bicycle infrastructure by increasing bike and walking paths throughout the city. Although the amount of greenhouse gases reduced through this type of initiative is unquantifiable, the 10% increase in travel by foot and bicycle between 1990 and 2000[84] signals an important shift in transportation patterns that may in part be due to Portland's early efforts in the 1990s to curb greenhouse gas emissions.[85]

In 1999, 55% of Portland's greenhouse gas emissions were attributable to energy consumed by buildings.[86] Continuing with the model of implementing both government actions and community initiatives, Portland plans not only to reduce the emissions produced in currently existing structures, but also to take steps to make future buildings efficient by design. In 2005,[87] Portland began requiring all public construction and renovation to meet the "Certified" level of LEED standards. Furthering these efforts, Portland's own extended LEED 2.0 Green Building Rating System™ was implemented to "identify local and state codes that go beyond LEED requirements and additional green building strategies that are regionally significant," effectively holding city development to the region's most ambitious low-emission, efficient building standards.[88] Other energy-saving measures taken by Portland include the replacement of all city traffic lights—formerly fitted with incandescent or halogen bulbs—with highly efficient LED bulbs, saving the city 5 million kilowatt-hours (kWh) and over half a million dollars each year.[89]

Portland has also taken the important first step toward weaning itself from fossil fuels by requiring the city to acquire 10% of its energy from renewable sources—a goal the city met in 2005.[90] The city achieved this objective utilizing a combination of approaches. First, the city continued to invest in an already-in-place renewable infrastructure based on hydroelectricity. Almost 3 million kWh are generated by turbines in

the city's drinking water reservoir system.[91] The turbines produce power through the movement of water between the city's two reservoirs.[92] Renewable resources are also being utilized to power the Columbia Boulevard Wastewater Treatment Plant through a combination of a 200 kW fuel cell powered by anaerobic digester gas (waste biogas consisting primarily of methane) from the plant itself and four 30 kW micro-turbines.[93] To meet remaining renewable energy needs that are not provided by the city's existing resources, Portland purchases "green tags" (also known as "renewable energy credits") from the Stateline Wind Energy Center, allowing the city to support the production of a certain amount of power from renewable sources, despite not using the power itself.[94]

With respect to the problem of solid waste, a smaller but significant source of greenhouse gas emissions, Portland again has a twofold approach aimed at curtailing the production of refuse. First, Portland has set the goal of achieving 60% recycling during 2005.[95] To support this effort Portland has joined with county officials to develop a contract to allow facilities participating in recycling to receive monthly rebates amounting to the market value of the materials.[96] The city and county also worked together in 2002 to initiate a Sustainable Purchasing Strategy, which is carried out by the Sustainable Procurement Committee, a group that advises city and county agencies on the purchase of recycled and readily recyclable materials, and also offers policy guidance on how to permanently implement

sustainable purchasing.[97] Current city requirements in place as a result of the Sustainable Procurement Committee include mandates to purchase recycled tires and petroleum products, when appropriate.[98] Additional city measures include requiring that waste disposal companies offer recycling services to all Portland residents and that businesses recycle a minimum of 50% of their waste.[99]

Finally, recognizing the importance of forests in the effort to mitigate climate change, Portland plans to restrict the amount of unsustainably harvested timber local government agencies purchase by 2010. The city also plans to continue to partner with nonprofit groups to replant large portions of its forests; to date, more than half a million trees have been planted through this program.

As a result of this multiplicity of initiatives, Portland has been able to reduce per capita greenhouse gas emissions by 12.5% between 1993 and 2005.[100] In addition, it has achieved its commitment to meet the reduction that is called for under the Kyoto Protocol.

B. The California Bay Area

San Francisco, Oakland and Berkeley have all taken extraordinary steps to reduce their greenhouse gas emissions in the Bay Area. All three are members of the ICLEI CCP campaign and have created Local (or Climate) Action Plans similar in scope to Portland's Local Action Plan. Like Portland, these three cities focus their efforts in the general areas of transportation, renewable energy, energy efficiency and solid waste reduction. While many policies and actions resemble those found in the Local Action Plans of other U.S. cities—such as replacing halogen traffic bulbs with LEDs—certain of their initiatives reach well beyond the goals of other municipal plans, and are as creative as they are ambitious.

San Francisco boasts a strong public transit system and fosters alternative modes of transportation with bicycling and walking paths, as well as providing ride-sharing alternatives for those who prefer to drive. Nonetheless, in San Francisco and Marin County it is estimated that 50% of greenhouse gas emissions are generated by private commuter automobiles.[101] In its 2004 Climate Action Plan, San Francisco announced the goal of reducing the city's greenhouse gas emissions by 20% below 1990 levels by 2012. Part of this plan includes procurement of alternative-fuel vehicles for the city fleet, even though 14% of that fleet already consists of vehicles running on lower-emission alternative fuels and includes more than 300 "zero emission" buses.[102] Berkeley's Environmentally Preferable Purchasing Policy (EPP) requires governmental managers and officials to "minimize the City's contribution to global climate change [and] consumption of resources" by prioritizing the buying of products utilizing renewable energy sources and producing lower greenhouse gas emissions.[103] With respect to transportation, this mandate requires that newly purchased city vehicles be the most fuel-efficient available, which where possible must use "renewably-derived fuels or fuels that are cleaner and less polluting than gasoline."[104] Oakland has also successfully converted 11% of its fleet to alternative-fuel vehicles[105] including 10 formerly diesel fuel-powered garbage trucks that now emit 94% less particulates and 55% less nitrogen oxides.[106] Oakland encourages bicycling as an alternative mode of transportation by providing its citizens with an abundance of bike paths and resources, such as detailed maps, to encourage their use.[107]

San Francisco officials believe that the replacement of fossil fuels with renewable energy sources will have the greatest impact on reducing greenhouse gas emissions.[108] Their belief is demonstrated by heavy investment in developing renewable projects, including wind, biomass, and solar energy. San Francisco has issued $100 million in revenue bonds to provide grants to develop solar energy solutions.[109] In fact, San Francisco has constructed the largest solar electric power system owned by any U.S. city—a system that generates 826,000 kWh per year.[110] San Francisco also funds pilot programs to test innovative ways to generate energy, and is currently working with Oakland to develop ways of harnessing tidal power in the bay and off the coast.[111] Moreover, Berkeley's program requires that, whenever practical and available, renewable energy sources are to be purchased for energy needs and states explicitly that fossil fuels, including natural gas, cannot be construed to meet this requirement.[112]

Berkeley and Oakland have also worked together to develop the Clean Energy Fund to support local efforts to reduce energy use and implement renewable solutions.[113] The fund is designed to cover the initial costs to businesses of installing solar energy and energy efficiency equipment and technology. The money borrowed from the fund is repaid by the businesses from savings realized through the reduction in energy costs resulting from the funded projects.[114] Berkeley and Oakland anticipate that the full effect of this program will save enough energy to power 4,000 households each year.[115]

Bay Area cities are also building more efficiently. San Francisco, for example, requires LEED Silver certification for all city construction projects over 5,000 square feet.[116] Berkeley also requires, as of 2006, that all city-sponsored construction or renovation of 5,000 or more total square feet meet the LEED Silver building standards and encourages all other local projects to strive to do the same.[117] Additionally, Berkeley, having found that 21% of the contents of local landfills is the result of construction and demolition projects,[118] requires that construction materials are to be reused and recycled in all instances where construction constraints allow.[119]

Berkeley,[120] Oakland and San Francisco all have met and exceeded the state's 50% waste diversion rate, and Berkeley and San Francisco have both further pledged to reduce landfilling by 75% by 2010.[121] One sign of the economic viability of these waste reduction measures is that San Francisco's Environment Department pays for a portion of its own operations through recycling revenues.[122]

C. Seattle, Washington

Since 2000, the city of Seattle has committed itself to specific reductions of greenhouse gas emissions by requiring City Light, its municipal electrical utility, to meet all growth in demand without increasing its emissions.[123] In 2001, the city adopted a goal of reducing greenhouse gas emissions to 7% to 40% below 1990 levels by 2010.[124] The city council directed the Office of Sustainability and Environment to coordinate the development of an emission inventory for 1990 and 2000, and to develop a multifaceted plan to reduce such emissions.

In November 2005, the mayor announced that City Light had reached its "zero net emissions" goal.[125] In order to do so, the utility and city participated in climate change mitigation programs that included promoting the use of a substitute for Portland cement that has a much lighter greenhouse gas footprint.[126] More recently, Seattle has developed a Climate Action Plan to attain a revised citywide emissions reduction goal of 7% below 1990 levels by 2012,[127] taking into account recommendations from a Green Ribbon Commission composed of 18 leaders from Seattle's business, labor, nonprofit, government and academic communities appointed by Seattle's mayor.[128] The Climate Action Plan proposes a continuation of City Light's efforts as well as an array of other emission-reducing programs such as increasing the availability of public transportation, expanding bicycling and pedestrian infrastructure, working with other local governments to develop and implement a road pricing system, implementing a commercial parking tax, expanding the city's smart growth policies, and working with the Port of Seattle, government agencies, and other organizations to reduce diesel emissions from freight transportation.[129]

Although its Climate Action Plan is still in its infancy, Seattle benefits from programs inaugurated before its official push to reduce greenhouse gas emissions began. According to the city's 2002 greenhouse gas emissions inventory, Seattle's emissions in 2000 would have been twice as large as they were without the recycling and energy conservation programs that already were in place.[130]

D. Austin, Texas

Austin has been a member of the CCP campaign since 1995. Its climate change actions have focused on a wide range of sectors, including energy, building and land use.

In 1999, the city council set a goal for Austin Energy, Austin's community-owned utility, to obtain 5% of its power from renewable sources by 2005,[131] and, in 2003, the city council passed a resolution to establish the even more ambitious goals of increasing the renewable energy portion of Austin Energy's portfolio to at least 20% and increasing energy efficiency by 15% by 2020.[132] Austin Energy's efficiency and renewables programs include demand-side management programs such as rebate programs for solar electric power systems and energy-efficient air conditioners.[133] Austin has created an incentive system to encourage the purchase and use of flexible-fuel plug-in hybrid vehicles (PHEVs) by Austin Energy customers.[134] Austin Energy will provide seed money for the purchase of these vehicles, and the city, county, local agencies, and businesses have made commitments to purchase PHEVs for their fleets.[135]

Austin has for many years had an extensive green building program.[136] This generally available program is mandatory for developments receiving benefits under Austin's separate affordable housing program. Thus, under the S.M.A.R.T. Housing (Safe, Mixed Income, Accessible, Reasonably Priced and Transit Oriented) Initiative, fees are waived for developments that allocate at least 10% of units to families that earn 80% or less than the Austin Area Median Family Income.[137] All residences built under the S.M.A.R.T. Housing Initiative must comply with Austin's Green Building Level One standards, the minimum level for attaining recognition under the green building program, which rates residences in six categories: energy efficiency, testing, water efficiency, materials efficiency, heath and safety, and community. In addition, Austin

has since 2000 also required that all new city buildings attain a
LEED Silver rating.[138]

E. Salt Lake City, Utah

EPA honored Salt Lake City's mayor as a Climate Protection
Award Winner in 2003.[139] In 2002, Salt Lake City committed to
a greenhouse gas emissions reduction target of 7% below 1990
levels. Since then, Salt Lake City has moved toward this goal
with the installation of 861 LED traffic signals; the conversion
to energy-efficient lighting in the City/County Building; and fuel
switching to bio-diesel for airport ground service equipment.
Salt Lake City has more ambitious plans for future actions, including the purchase of 35,000 kWh of wind power each month;
an initiative to convert the city's fleets to 100% alternative fuel
vehicles; increased recycling efforts; a landfill gas project; a
high performance buildings initiative; and an urban forestry
program.

F. San Diego, California

San Diego's city council unanimously resolved in 2002 to fulfill
the obligations of its membership in the ICLEI's CCP program
by creating a Climate Protection Action Plan (CPAP) that would
detail how the city would succeed in reducing greenhouse gas
emissions 15% below 1990 levels by 2010.[140] A stipulation of
this resolution was that an ad hoc committee of scientists be
formed to assist the city in developing programs that could ap-

propriately meet the challenge of creating material reductions in emissions. The recommendations of this committee led to a five-point plan that included proposals focusing on transportation, energy, waste, urban heat islands, and environmentally preferable purchasing.

Beginning with the goal of getting the public involved in reduction efforts, the city
is taking measures to provide energy efficiency incentives, such as free parking for
cars that meet California's Super Ultra Low Emissions Vehicle tailpipe emission standard.[141] Further efforts include requiring city departments to reduce their fuel consumption by 15% each year.[142]

San Diego's city council also resolved, in September of 2003, to add 50 megawatts
of renewable energy for city operations by 2013.[143] Avenues of renewable energy production the city plans to explore include a variety of solar solutions, such as photovoltaic panels and solar thermal water heating panels, as well as wind, hydro-electric and
geothermal energy systems. San Diego is closely monitoring the progress of its renewable energy production plans by requiring tracking and quarterly reports on compliance with the resolution.

San Diego was already using waste methane from inactive and closed landfills as a source of energy, and its CPAP supports the continuation of this practice as well as the development of some measures to combat the expansion of active landfills.[144] The city is considering bolder "incentives" to further waste-minimization efforts by proposing recycling ordinances affecting construction and demolition materials, commercial paper, and multiple-family dwellings.[145] This area of the CPAP is reviewed and revised annually.

The "urban heat island effect" results from the absorption of the sun's energy by dark-colored road and building materials, which leads to significant increases in ground-level temperatures.[146] In addition to making urban living decidedly unpleasant during the daytime, the high temperatures resulting from this phenomenon linger into the evening, and lead to the increased use of energy for air-conditioning. San Diego has attempted to address this problem by adopting a 2004 mayoral recommendation to plant 5,000 shade trees on public land each year.[147] Annual reviews and revisions may also lead to the use of alternative building and construction materials and land use requirements aimed at reducing the heat island effect in the city.

San Diego is an active participant in the U.S. Green Building Council and has committed to implementing sustainable building practices to reduce greenhouse gas emissions.[148] The city council adopted a Sustainable Building Policy in May 2003, which, among other things, commits the city to achieving LEED Silver certification in all major public building renovations and constructions of more than 5,000 square feet.[149] Additionally, to encourage the private sector to participate in its climate change mitigation policies, the city plans to provide "guidance in promoting, facilitating, and instituting such practices" for private construction and renovation projects in the city.[150]

The final element of the San Diego CPAP is an Environmentally Preferable Purchasing plan that incorporates a "triple bottom line" approach. Under this approach the city takes into account not only fiscal considerations, but also the social and environmental "bottom line" costs in its procurement activities.[151] As a result of this policy, San Diego now requires that energy-consuming products purchased by city agencies conform to the Energy Star specification for energy efficiency.[152] City employees will be instructed on how to use these products, ranging from air conditioners to computers, in the most efficient manner possible.[153]

Although San Diego's measures are rather recent compared to several of the other municipalities discussed in this survey, this municipality already has achieved more than half of its emissions reduction goals.[154] Motivated by its obligations as a member of the ICLEI's CCP campaign, the city continues to develop programs to carry it the rest of the way.

G. Town of Greenburgh, New York

The efforts made to reduce the emission of greenhouse gases by the town of Greenburgh, in Westchester County, New York, illustrate the sorts of measures that are being taken in the smaller municipalities around the country. As noted in section II of this chapter,

Greenburgh requires newly constructed one- and two-family homes, as well as multifamily structures of three stories or less, to meet certain Energy Star requirements. In addition, the town has installed solar panels on the roof of its newly converted town hall building, utilizing funds provided through a grant from the New York State Energy Research and Development Authority. Greenburgh has appointed an "energy coordinator" to develop measures to reduce carbon emissions in the town. Among other things, this official has organized a well-attended "energy fair," which offered exhibits and lectures designed to inform residents about (among other things) energy audits, solar energy, hybrid vehicles, green construction, and purchasing green power from renewable resources. She also has put together a Web site containing a wealth of information on such subjects.

Endnotes

1.   Marilyn A. Brown et al., Pew Center on Global Climate Change, Towards a Climate-Friendly Built Environment 1 (2005), http://www.pewclimate.org/docUploads/Buildings%5FFINAL%2E.pdf (citing EPA, EPA/430-R-04-003, Inventory of U.S.Greenhouse Gas Emissions and Sinks: 1990–2002, at 3-7 (2004)).

2.   San Francisco, Cal., Housing Code §§ 1201–1220 (2001).

3.   Berkeley, Cal., Mun. Code Ch. 19-16.

4.   See Brown et al., Pew Center on Global Climate Change, supra note 1, at 46–48.

5.   See id. at 59 tbl.3.

6.   See id. at 46.

7.   Town of Greenburgh, N.Y., § 100-14 (2006).

8.   U.S. Green Building Council, LEED: Leadership in Energy and Environmental Design, http://www.usgbc.org/DisplayPage.aspx?CategoryID=19& (last visited May 26, 2006).

9.   Scottsboro, Ariz., Resolution No. 6644 (Mar. 22, 2005).

10.   See Brown et al., Pew Center on Global Climate Change, supra note 2, at 13.

11.   See, e.g., Dep't of Design & Construction, New York City, High Performance Building Guidelines (1999).

12.   The New Rules Project, Model Resolution on Climate Neutral Bonding for Cities, http://www.newrules.org/de/climateneutral.html.

13.   See City of Chicago, Building Healthy, Smart and Green: Chicago's Green Building Agenda 2005, at 10 (2005).

14.   Gary Washburn, City Plan Would Pay a Bonus for "Green Roofs," Chi. Trib. (May 24, 2006). See the Web site of Chicago's Department of Environment for more information on the green roof program. Dep't of Env't, City of Chicago, Welcome to DOE, http://egov.cityofchicago.org/environment.

15.   David L. Greene & Andreas Schaefer, Pew Center on Global Climate Change, Reducing Greenhouse Gas Emissions from U.S. Transportation 3 (2003), http://www.pewclimate.org/document.cfm?documentID=212.

16. ENERGY CONSERVATION TASK FORCE, TOWN OF AMHERST, CLIMATE ACTION PLAN 27 (2005), http://www.amherstma.gov/departments/Conservation/CAP_9-27-05_FINAL-cover1.pdf.

17. *See infra* Parts IV.B and IV.D.

18. Jonathan D. Weiss, *Local Sustainability Efforts in the United States: The Progress Since Rio*, 32 Envtl. L. Rep. (Envtl. L. Inst.) 10,667, 10,675 (2002).

19. N.Y.C. ADMIN. CODE § 19-532(b).

20. *See* Brock Vergakis, *Fuel-Efficient Car Can Get You Free Parking in Salt Lake City*, CHI. SUN-TIMES, Jan. 15, 2006.

21. A Progress Report on the City of Portland and Multnomah County Local Action Plan on Global Warming 1, 4 (June 2005), http://www.sustainableportland.org/osd_pubs_global_warming_report_6-2005.pdf (hereinafter Portland Progress Report).

22. *See* SEATTLE DEP'T OF TRANSP., SEATTLE TRANSIT PLAN TO GET SEATTLE MOVING 8 (2005).

23. FED. TRANSIT ADMIN., ANNUAL REPORT ON NEW STARTS: PROPOSED ALLOCATIONS OF FUNDS FOR FISCAL YEAR 2007, app. A (2006), http://www.fta.dot.gov/18022_ENG_HTML.htm.

24. EPA, EPA 430-R-06-002, INVENTORY OF U.S. GREENHOUSE GAS EMISSIONS AND SINKS: 1990–2004, at 8-1 (2006).

25. EPA, GLOBAL MITIGATION OF NON-CO$_2$ GREENHOUSE GASES (DRAFT), at III-1 (2006), http://www.epa.gov/nonco2/econ-inv/pdfs/SectionIII_Waste.pdf; *see also* METHANE TO MARKETS, ABOUT METHANE, http://www.methanetomarkets.org/about/methane.htm (last visited May 27, 2006).

26. EPA, Landfill Methane Outreach Program (LMOP): Memorandum of Understanding for Community Partners, http://www.epa.gov/lmop/ (last visited May 27, 2006); *see also* LANDFILL METHANE OUTREACH PROGRAM, EPA, EPA 430-B-96-0004, TURNING A LIABILITY INTO AN ASSET: A LANDFILL GAS-TO-ENERGY PROJECT DEVELOPMENT HANDBOOK (1996).

27. EPA, Landfill Methane Outreach Program (LMOP): Accomplishments, http://www.epa.gov/lmop/accomplish.htm (last visited May 27, 2006).

28. *See* Portland Progress Report, *supra* note 21, at 4; City of Austin, Silver in the Mine: A Long-Term Comprehensive Energy Plan for the City of Austin (2004).

29. Village of Euclid, Ohio v. Ambler Realty Co., 272 U.S. 365 (1926). See also *Golden v. Planning Board of the Town of Ramapo*, 285 N.E.2d 291 (N.Y. 1972), and *Agins v. Tiburon*, 447 U.S. 255 (1980), for more recent development in municipal zoning and planning rights.

30. N.Y. TOWN LAW § 261.

31. *See, e.g.*, N.Y.C. DEP'T OF CITY PLANNING, ZONING HANDBOOK 79 (2006).

32. SAN DIEGO, CAL., MUN. CODE § 132.1101.

33. *Id.* § 132.1105(a).

34. *Id.* § 132.1108(c).

35. *Id.* § 132.1105(a).

36. *Id.* § 132.1105(c).

37. *Id.* §§ 132.1107(a), 132.1108(b).

38. Miami-Dade County, Fla., Ord. No. 99-166 (Dec. 16, 1999); Charlotte, N.C., Zoning Ord. §§ 10.801–10.812 (2006).

39. New York, N.Y., Special Hudson Yards District, Zoning Text Amendment, N040500(A) ZRM (Jan. 19, 2005).

40. U.S. Census Bureau, 2004 American Community Survey; Sustain Lane U.S. City Rankings: #7 New York, http://www.sustainlane.com/cityindex/citypage/newyork/1/New+York.html (last visited May 26, 2006).

41. Sustain Lane U.S. City Rankings: #12 Boston, http://www.sustainlane.com/cityindex/citypage/boston/1/Boston.html (last visited May 26, 2006).

42. Jonathan D. Weiss, *Local Sustainability Efforts in the United States: The Progress Since Rio*, 32 Envtl. L. Rep. (Envtl. L. Inst.) 10,667, 10,679 (2002).

43. *Id.*

44. *See* N.Y.S. Dep't of Envtl. Conservation, Brownfield Opportunity Areas Program, http://www.dec.state.ny.us/website/der/bfield/boa.html (last visited May 27, 2006); Div. of Coastal Resources, N.Y. Dep't of State, Brownfields Opportunity Areas Program, http://www.nyswaterfronts.com/grantopps_BOA.asp (last visited May 27, 2006).

45. *See, e.g.*, Envtl. Law Section, New York State Bar Ass'n, The Threat of Global Climate Change—What Can New Yorkers Do?: State and Local Strategies to Reduce Greenhouse Gas Emissions in New York State (Jan. 1994).

46. Portland, Ore., City Code §§ 33.639.010–33.639.100.

47. Portland, Ore., City Code §§ 3.111.030–3.111.140.

48. Ashland, Ore., Mun. Code ch. 18.70; Eugene, Ore., City Code ch. 9.

49. Robert N. Stavins & Kenneth R. Richards, Pew Center on Global Climate Change, The Cost of U.S. Forest-Based Carbon Sequestration 10 (2005), http://pewclimate.org/docUploads/Sequest%5FFinal%2Epdf.

50. City of Chicago, Environmental Action Agenda 2006: Building the Sustainable City 44, 46 (2006), http://egov.cityofchicago.org/environment.

51. Los Angeles Dep't of Water and Power, Trees for a Green LA, http://www.ladwp.com/ladwp/cms/ladwp000744.jsp (last visited May 26, 2006).

52. Cal. Envtl. Protection Agency, Climate Action Team Report to Governor Schwarzenegger and the Legislature 49–50 (2006), http://www.climatechange.ca.gov/climate_action_team/reports/2006-04-03_FINAL_CAT_REPORT.PDF.

53. *See* USDA, Release No. 0172.06, Johanns Announces More Than $790,000 in Urban and Community Forestry Grants (2006).

54. *See* text accompanying *infra* notes 89, 130–131.

55. Los Angeles Dep't of Water & Power, LADWP Proposed Solar Incentive Program Guidelines, http://www.ladwp.com/ladwp/cms/ladwp007795.jsp.

56. City of Seattle, News Advisory, City Light First in Nation to Reach Zero Net Emissions Goal (Nov. 9, 2005).

57. *See* text accompanying *infra* notes 107–110.

58. San Francisco, Cal., Env't Code §§ 800–809 (2006); Santa Monica, Cal., Mun. Code § 2.28 (2006); Jersey City, N.J., Ord. 06-035 (Mar. 23, 2006).

59. Intergovernmental Panel on Climate Change, IPCC Special Report: Land Use, Land-Use Change, and Forestry: Summary for Policymakers, § 1.5 (2000), *available at* http://www.grida.no/climate/ipcc/spmpdf/srl-e.pdf.

60. N.Y.C. Admin. Code § 6-127 (2005); Consortium for Energy Efficiency, Energy-Efficient Purchasing by State and Local Government: Triggering a Landslide Down the Slippery Slope to Market Transformation (2004).

61. Consortium for Energy Efficiency, State and Local Government Purchasing Model Program Plan: A Guide for Energy Efficiency Program Administrators (2001), http://www.cee1.org/gov/purch/MPP_Final.pdf

62. Some local entities are participating in collective efforts to reduce greenhouse gas emissions outside the municipal borders. For example, the New York City Comptroller and the New York City Employees Pension System have joined with other major institutional investors in the Investor Network for Climate Risk, which has launched a coordinated effort to induce the companies in which they invest to take action to address the issue of climate change.

63. U.S. CONFERENCE OF MAYORS, ENDORSING THE U.S. MAYORS CLIMATE PROTECTION AGREEMENT, http://usmayors.org/uscm/resolutions/73rd_conference/en_01.asp (last visited May 26, 2006).

64. U.S. Mayors Climate Agreement, Participating Mayors, http://www.seattle.gov/mayor/climate/quotes.htm#mayors (last visited Oct. 25, 2006).

65. ICLEI, Cities for Climate Protection (CCP), http://www.iclei.org/index.php?id=800.

66. A sample resolution is *available at* http://www.iclei.org/documents/USA/resolution.doc.

67. ICLEI, How It Works, http://www.iclei.org/index.php?id=810 (last visited May 26, 2006).

68. CCP Campaign is one initiative that has grown out of Local Agenda 21, which constituted Chapter 28 of Agenda 21 of the 1992 Earth Summit in Rio de Janeiro, Brazil, and the ensuing Local Action 21, which was launched in 2002 at the World Summit in Johannesburg, South Africa. *See* ICLEI, Local Action 21, http://www.iclei.org/index.php?id=802.

69. A list of participants is *available at* http://www.iclei.org/index.php?id=1121.

70. World Mayors and Municipal Leaders Declaration on Climate Change (Dec. 7, 2005), http://www.iclei.org/fileadmin/user_upload/documents/events/montreal_summit/declaration/World_Mayors_and_Municipal_Leaders_Declaration_on_Climate_Change_English.pdf.

71. Urban Environmental Accords (June 5, 2005), http://www.wed2005.org/pdfs/Accords_11x17.pdf.

72. State of California, S.B. 527 (Oct. 11, 2001); S.B. 1771 (Sept. 30, 2000).

73. CAL. HEALTH & SAFETY CODE § 42801(e).

74. The efforts of the City of Boulder, Colorado, should also be noted. In 2002, the Boulder City Council set a goal of reducing the city's greenhouse gas emissions by 7% below 1990 levels by 2012. To achieve this goal, the city has adopted a climate change action plan aimed at increasing energy efficiency, expanding renewable energy usage and reducing vehicle miles traveled. In a referendum held on November 7, 2006, the citizens of Boulder approved an energy tax, which is expected to generate revenues of approximately $1 million a year to fund implementation of the plan.

75. Portland, Ore., Resolution No. 35207 (Nov. 10, 1993). Portland's Carbon Dioxide Reduction Strategy was actually the result of GHG-conscious modification of a 1990 energy policy geared toward sustainability and cutting energy bills. Portland also claims the distinction of being the first U.S. city to have a local energy policy, beginning in 1979. *See* PORTLAND ENERGY OFFICE, 1990 ENERGY POLICY: IMPACTS AND ACHIEVEMENTS, at 1 (June 2000).

76. City of Portland and Multnomah County Office of Sustainable Development, Local Action Plan on Global Warming, at 1 (April 2001) [hereinafter Portland Local Action Plan], *available at* http://www.portlandonline.com/shared/cfm/image.cfm?id=25050.

77. The Climate Group, Portland–Municipal Government, http://www. theclimate group.rg/index.php?pid=567 (last visited May 28, 2006).

78. One example of this noted in the Local Action Plan is the goal of reducing GHG emissions 10% below 1990 levels by 2010, exceeding the Kyoto Protocols goal of 7%

below 1990 levels by a date between 2008 and 2012. See Portland Local Action Plan, *supra* note 76, at 1.

79. Portland Local Action Plan, *supra* note 76, at 5.

80. *Id.* at 7.

81. Portland Progress Report, *supra* note 21.

82. Portland Local Action Plan, *supra* note 76, at 5.

83. Portland Progress Report, *supra* note 21, at 4.

84. *Id.*

85. *See* Portland Energy Office, 1990 Energy Policy: Impacts and Achievements (June 2000).

86. Portland Local Action Plan, *supra* note 76, at 12.

87. The "City of Portland Green Building Policy" became binding law in 2005, following the passage of Resolution 36310, which essentially gave teeth to a 2002 version of the policy.

88. Office of Sustainable Development, City of Portland, G/Rated: City of Portland Supplement to the Leadership in Energy and Environmental Design (LEED) Green Building System 3 (n.d.), *available at* http://www.portlandonline.com/shared/cfm/image.cfm?id=119695 (last visited Oct. 25, 2006).

89. Portland Progress Report, *supra* note 21, at 3.

90. *Id.* at 4.

91. *Id.* at 23.

92. City of Portland, Sustainable Infrastructure Report (Dec. 2001), http://www.portland online.com/shared/cfm/image.cfm?id=82893.

93. *See* U.S. Dep't of Energy, CHP Case Studies in the Pacific Northwest: Columbia Boulevard Wastewater Treatment Plant: Environmental Services, City of Portland: 320 kW Fuel Cell Microturbine Power Plants, *available at* http://www/eere/energy.gov/de/pdfs/cs_columbia_blvd.pdf (last visited July 8, 2006).

94. Portland Progress Report, *supra* note 21, at 23.

95. *See* CHP Case Studies in the Pacific Northwest: Columbia Boulevard Wastewater Treatment Plan: Environmental Services, City of Portland: 320 kW Fuel Cell Micro turbine Power Plants, http://www/eere/energy.gov/de/pdfs/cs_columbia_blvd.pdf.

96. Portland Progress Report, *supra* note 21, at 24.

97. *Id.* at 25.

98. *Id.* Note: City Code 5.33.050 is cited in error in this document. The "Environmentally Preferable Purchasing" Code is Portland City Code 5.33.080.

99. Portland Progress Report, *supra* note 21, at 26.

100. *Id.* at 1.

101. Gregory Dicum, *Bay Area Cities Make Own Climate Policies*, SAN FRAN. GATE (Feb. 16, 2005), http://www.sfenvironment.com/articles_pr/2005/article/021605.htm (last visited May 24, 2006).

102. *Id.*; SustainLane's City Survey, sustainlane.com/cityindex/citypage/sanfrancisco/1/San+Francisco.html (last visited May 27, 2006).

103. Berkeley, Cal., Resolution 62,693-N.S (Oct. 19, 2004).

104. *Id.*

105. SustainLane U.S. City Rankings: #9 Oakland, http://sustainlane.com/cityindex/citypage/oakland/1/oakland.html (last visited May 28, 2006).

106. City of Oakland Public Works Agency, Envtl. Servs. Div., http://www.oaklandpw.com/page83.aspx (last visited May 28, 2006).

107. SustainLane U.S. City Rankings: #9 Oakland, http://sustainlane.com/cityindex/ citypage/oakland/1/oakland.html (last visited May 28, 2006).

108. San Francisco Dep't of the Env't & San Francisco Pub. Utilities Comm'n, Climate Action Plan for San Francisco: Local Actions to Reduce Greenhouse Gas Emissions, at 3-28 (Sept. 2004), http://www.sfenvironment.com/aboutus/energy/cap.pdf (hereinafter San Francisco Climate Action Plan).

109. San Francisco Climate Action Plan, *supra* note 109, at 3-28.

110. *Id.* at 3-29, 3-30.

111. http://www.sustainlane.com/cityindex/oakland/1/oakland.html; San Francisco Climate Action Plan, *supra* note 109, at 3-28.

112. Berkeley EPP 3.4.3.

113. http://www.ci.berkeley.ca.us/Mayor/PR/pressrelease2005-0511.htm. Accessed 5/ 25/2006.

114. http://www.ci.berkeley.ca.us/Mayor/PR/pressrelease2005-0511.htm. Accessed 5/25/ 2006

115. City of Berkeley. Council Study Session: Energy Project Update. April 26, 2005

116. SAN FRANCISCO, CAL., ENV'T CODE § 707.

117. City of Berkeley, Resolution No. 62,284-N.S.

118. City of Berkeley, Resolution No. 62,284-N.S.

119. Berkeley EPP 3.3.4

120. California AB939, cited in City of Berkeley Res. No. 62,849-N.S.

121. defined in The Berkeley Solid Waste Management Plan Update "all discarded material will have a beneficial use, and none will be disposed in a landfill." SWMP June 2005, Pg. S-1.

122. SustainLane's City Survey, sustainlane.com/cityindex/citypage/sanfrancisco/1/ San+Francisco.html, accessed 04/27/2006.

123. Seattle, Wash., Resolution 30144 (Apr. 10, 2000); Seattle Wash., Resolution 30256 (Oct. 16, 2000).

124. Resolution 30316 (July 23, 2001).

125. City of Seattle, News Advisory, City Light First in Nation to Reach Zero Net Emissions Goal (Nov. 9, 2005), http://www.seattle.gov/news/detail_print.asp?ID= 5656&Dept=40.

126. Seattle, Wash., Ordinance 121062 (Feb. 6, 2003).

127. CITY OF SEATTLE, CLIMATE ACTION PLAN: SEATTLE, A CLIMATE OF CHANGE: MEETING THE KYOTO CHALLENGE (September 2006), *available at* http://www.seattle.gov/climate/docs/ SeaCAP_plan.pdf (last visited Oct. 25, 2006).

128. City of Seattle, About the Green Ribbon Commission, http://www.seattle.gov/ climate/about.htm (last visited Oct. 25, 2006).

129. *See supra* note 127.

130. Office of Sustainability & Env't, City of Seattle, Inventory and Report: Seattle's Greenhouse Gas Emissions, at 4 (Sept. 2002), http://www.seattle.gov/environment/ Documents/GHG_Report.pdf.

131. Austin, Tex., Resolution No. 990211-36 (Feb. 11, 1999).

132. Austin, Tex., Resolution No. 030925-02 (Sept. 25, 2003).

133. *See* Austin Energy, Home Performance with ENERGY STAR® Rebate Program, http://www.austinenergy.com/Energy%20Efficiency/Programs/index.htm (last visited May 24, 2006).

134. Austin, Tex., Resolution No. 050301-48 (Mar. 3, 2005).

135. Austin Energy, Press Release, "Austin kicks off Plug-In Hybrid Campaign" (Aug. 22, 2005), http://www.austinenergy.com/About%20Us/Newsroom/Press%20Releases/ Press%20Release%20Archive/2005/plugInAustin.htm.

136. Austin Energy, Green Building Program: The #1 Green Building Program in

America, http://www.austinenergy.com/Energy%20Efficiency/ Programs/Green%20 Building/index.htm (last visited May 24, 2006); Austin Energy, History of the Green Building Program, http://www.austinenergy.com/Energy%20 Efficiency/Programs/ Green%20Building/About%20Us/history.htm

137. Austin Housing Finance Corporation, S.M.A.R.T. Housing as a Tool to Reduce Regulatory Barriers for Housing, as a Component of Smart Growth (Sept. 2004), http://www. ci.austin.tx.us/ahfc/downloads/barriers.pdf

138. Austin, Tex., Resolution No. 000608-43 (June 8, 2000).

139. EPA, 2003 Climate Protection Award Winners, http://www. epa.gov/cpd/awards/climatesummaries3-6-03.pdf

140. San Diego, Cal., Resolution 296074 (Jan. 29, 2002); City of San Diego, Climate Protection Action Plan 1 (2005) [hereinafter San Diego Climate Protection Action Plan], *available at* http://www.sandiego.gov/environmental-services/sustainable/ pdf/action_plan_07_05.pdf.

141. *Id.* at 4.

142. *Id.* at 4.

143. San Diego, Cal., Resolution 298412 (Sept. 25, 2003).

144. San Diego Climate Protection Action Plan, *supra* note 141, at 6.

145. *Id.*

146. *Id.*

147. *Id.* at 7; *see also* City of San Diego, Manager's Report 9–10 (2004).

148. San Diego, Cal., Council Policy 900-14 (May 20, 2003).

149. *Id.*

150. *Id.*

151. San Diego Climate Protection Action Plan, *supra* note 141, at 7–8.

152. San Diego, Cal., Council Policy 900-18 (June 19, 2001).

153. *Id.*

154. San Diego Climate Protection Action Plan, *supra* note 141, at 21.

Part Three

Corporate Actions

chapter thirteen

Disclosure Issues

Jeffrey A. Smith and
Matthew Morreale

I. Introduction

Rapid and disjointed developments in the law and the marketplace, including fragmented greenhouse gas (GHG) emission
regulatory regimes in the United States, the divide between signatories and non-signatories to the Kyoto Protocol, and prolifer-
ating GHG emission trading markets, are combining to create
substantial disclosure issues, particularly for publicly traded,
U.S.-based multinational corporations with operations and products that emit GHGs. At the same time, and on a parallel track,
stakeholder activism on climate change issues is rapidly sur-
passing that of any other environmental issue in U.S. history. Shareholders are demanding transparency, or at least substantive voluntary disclosure, on matters ranging from financial estimates of the possible consequences of the adverse effects of
climate change to a company's positioning on pending legislative initiatives and political developments. They have already achieved unprecedented success, both in the
number of reports that their demands have prompted and in gathering support, and
getting management's attention, through traditional shareholder proxy mechanisms.
On a third track, the absence, to date, of preemptive federal climate change legislation, coupled with the U.S. Environmental Protection Agency's (EPA) refusal, thus far,
to regulate CO_2 as a pollutant under the Clean Air Act in the United States, has helped
fuel several lines of litigation which may have both direct and derivative consequences
for planning and disclosure by GHG-intensive industries.

Because long-standing SEC regulations require the management of a publicly
traded company to comment both on legal proceedings that may have a material

effect and on a broader array of "known trends," the continuing rapid evolution of climate change issues and the related uncertainty surrounding them challenge management to consider how to articulate their public position and their economic prospects. For publicly traded coal-burning utilities, automobile makers and their suppliers, in particular, for which legislative or litigation outcomes will drive billions of dollars in capital expenditures and may shape their future strategic direction, and which also must abide by the demands recently imposed by Sarbanes-Oxley, meeting disclosure obligations, and making all disclosure consistent, will require increasing attention from management.

This chapter will examine the basic legal principles governing disclosure obligations and their possible application in addressing climate change. It will also examine the new, rapidly burgeoning phenomenon of voluntary disclosure and reporting, which is driven in large measure by the public's desire for data, explanations and predictions relating to climate change. It will then treat the related area of disclosure in the proxy context, where many stakeholders and companies are wrestling for the first time with the complexities of various business scenarios that could result from climate change and related regulations. Finally, it will touch briefly on the possibility of regulation, by the Federal Trade Commission or other bodies, of the growing volume of corporate speech on climate change and related topics.

II. Environmental Disclosure Requirements

A. Disclosure Obligations Under U.S. Securities Laws

The Securities Act of 1933 (the '33 Act) governs the registration and sale of securities and related disclosure requirements.[1] The Securities and Exchange Act of 1934 (the '34 Act) requires publicly traded companies to report certain information to the public periodically.[2] The mandate of these federal securities laws is to promote full and complete disclosure of material facts necessary for informed decision making by investors and potential investors.[3] The U.S. Supreme Court has often reaffirmed that the '34 act was designed to protect investors against the manipulation of stock prices by those with undisclosed, inside information.[4] Underlying the adoption of extensive disclosure requirements was a legislative philosophy articulated with axiomatic clarity: "There cannot be honest markets without honest publicity. Manipulation and dishonest practices of the market place thrive upon mystery and secrecy."[5] The Supreme Court repeatedly has described the "fundamental purpose" of the Act as implementing a "philosophy of full disclosure."[6]

The regulations promulgated under the '33 and '34 Acts by the SEC—amended, consolidated and recodified over time and now commonly referred to as Regulation S-K—further these disclosure goals.[7] Regulation S-K prescribes areas of disclosure for registration statements and periodic reporting filed under the '33 and '34 Acts.[8] In particular, Regulation S-K requires the disclosure of environmental liabilities on at least a quarterly basis, including a description of material legal proceedings (Item 103, discussed *infra*) and Management's Discussion and Analysis (MD&A) of the filing company's financial condition and results of operations (Item 303, discussed *infra*).[9] These items must be included in both the Form 10-Q, filed quarterly, and the Form 10-K, filed annually.[10] Regulation S-K also requires the disclosure of capital expenditure relating to environmental compliance (Item 101, discussed *infra*). These costs must be reported on an annual basis in Form 10-K.[11] This information also must be included in certain registration statements filed under the '33 and '34 Acts.[12]

The basic precepts of the disclosure requirements under the '33 Act and the '34 Act have neither evolved nor been amended to address specifically the demands placed on public companies by climate change and related regulation, legislative initiatives and litigation. In fact, they have not changed substantially in over 20 years. It also is noteworthy that, notwithstanding the relatively high public profile of all environmental issues during that time, there has been limited SEC guidance on critical questions of interpretation and application. Notwithstanding this relative paucity of specific SEC directives and the absence of specific amendments, the requirements of Regulation S-K, as written, clearly have potential application to climate change matters on a number of fronts. Moreover, as baseline science continues to underscore anthropogenic factors in the climate change debate and regulatory mandates continue to emerge, the SEC may come under increased pressure to speak directly on the issues.[13] If the SEC

fails to act, the marketplace may react preemptively. For example, in October 2006, a group of leading investors and other organizations, led by CERES, released a "Global Framework for Climate Risk Disclosure."[14]

1. Case Law and Guidance on "Materiality"

The concept of "materiality"—a much debated (and litigated) standard—is woven into disclosure obligations under Regulation S-K. The Supreme Court, in an oft-quoted formulation, has determined that materiality refers to something that has "significantly altered" the "total mix" of information available to an investor.[15] Material information is defined under the '34 Act as information "to which there is a substantial likelihood that a reasonable investor would attach importance in deciding to buy or sell the securities registered."[16] Accounting literature informs the "reasonable person" standard for investors, providing that, "in the light of surrounding circumstances, the magnitude of the item is such that it is probable that the judgment of a reasonable person relying upon the report would have been changed or influenced by the inclusion or correction of the item."[17] One of the purposes of this threshold is to provide a workable filter on disclosed information, allowing investors to see major trends and significant events without being blinded by a blizzard of detail. Critics of the general corporate track record of disclosure on environmental issues and other stakeholders who want greater scrutiny of disclosure of environmental risk argue, however, that traditional notions of materiality, however defined, are poorly suited to discussion of any environmental risks and should be abandoned in favor of more meaningful measurements and greater qualitative, narrative-type disclosure.[18]

Notwithstanding this criticism, it is clear that there is no bright line test of materiality. The SEC has explicitly warned issuers against using numerical formulas or rule-of-thumb percentages, such as 5% of assets,[19] and stated that in arriving at a materiality determination both "qualitative" and "quantitative" factors must be used. When the qualitative analysis called for in a materiality determination is coupled with the subjective view of trends called for in MD&A disclosure, it can fairly be argued that a company's position and prospects relating to climate change should be among the preeminent issues considered for disclosure by management of a GHG emission-intensive company.

2. Financial Statement Disclosure and Accounting Standards

Regulation S-K sets forth the form and content of and requirements for financial statements required to be filed as part of various '33 Act and '34 Act filings.[20] Regulation S-K provides the parameters of what is to be included in financial statements, but does not specify how specific items are to be accounted for and disclosed.[21] The standards governing such financial matters are established by the accounting profession, often in collaboration or consultation with the SEC's professional accounting staff.[22]

Generally Accepted Accounting Principles (GAAP) require a company to accrue and disclose environmental costs in its financial statements. As a practical matter, Financial Accounting Standards Board (FASB) No. 5, "Accounting for Contingencies," governs disclosure of most environmental liabilities, which typically are difficult to quantify, notwithstanding advances in both remedial science and environmental accounting.[23] FASB No. 5 mandates that a loss contingency be accrued by a charge to income and that the nature of the contingency be described in a footnote to the financial statement if it is probable that a loss has been incurred and the amount of the loss can be reasonably estimated.[24] If a loss contingency is only reasonably possible, or if the loss is probable but the amount cannot be reasonably estimated, then the company is not required to accrue the loss contingency, but its nature must be disclosed in a footnote.[25] That disclosure must provide an estimate of the possible loss or range of loss or state that such an estimate cannot be made.[26]

Staff Accounting Bulletin No. 92 (SAB 92), arguably the most detailed pronouncement on environmental issues from the SEC in the past 20 years, provides additional guidance on the accounting and disclosures relating to contingent environmental liabilities.[27] At the time it was issued, SAB 92 was intended to "promote timely recogni-

tion of contingent losses and to address the diversity in practice with respect to the accounting and disclosures in this area."[28] SAB 92 makes clear that contingent environmental losses must

Critics . . . argue . . . that traditional notions of materiality, however defined, are poorly suited to discussion of any environmental risks and should be abandoned in favor of more meaningful measurements and greater qualitative, narrative-type disclosure.

be accrued by a charge to income if it is probable that a liability has been incurred and the amount of the loss can be reasonably estimated.[29] SAB 92 also provides that the gross liability must be recorded in the balance sheets separately from any claim for recovery, such as expected insurance recoveries or third-party indemnification claims.[30]

More broadly, SAB 92 was intended to "elicit more meaningful information concerning environmental matters in filings."[31] In SAB 92, the SEC staff declared that the measurement of a liability be based on "currently available facts, existing technology and presently enacted laws and regulations and should take into consideration the likely effects of

inflation and other societal and economic factors."[32] Although "significant uncertainties" may exist, "management may not delay recognition of a contingent liability until only a single amount can be reasonably estimated."[33] When that amount falls within a range of reasonable likely outcomes, the registrant should recognize the minimum amount of the range.[34] Under FASB No. 5, the reporting company must disclose the range of reasonably possible outcomes that could have a material effect on its financial condition, results of operations, or liquidity.[35] Alternatively, the reporting company can disclose that the amount of reasonably possible loss in excess of the accrued amount is not material or cannot be determined, assuming that it is factually correct.[36] Companies are cautioned to avoid "boilerplate" disclosures of the possible impact of significant uncertainties.[37]

SAB 92 also states that disclosure regarding loss contingencies outside the financial statements should consider the requirements of Regulation S-K, Items 101, 103 and 303 (discussed in detail, *infra* at section II(A)(3) to (5)) and SEC's interpretative releases on these matters.[38] Disclosures should be sufficiently specific to enable a reader to understand the scope of the contingencies affecting the registrant. For example, a registrant's discussion of historical and anticipated environmental expenditures should, to the extent material, describe separately (a) recurring costs associated with managing hazardous substances and pollution in on-going operations, (b) capital expenditures to limit or monitor hazardous substances or pollutants, (c) mandated expenditures to remediate previously contaminated sites, and (d) other infrequent or nonrecurring cleanup expenditures that can be anticipated but which are not required in the present circumstances.[39]

Taken together, these accounting standards and SEC guidance have clear implications for disclosing, and reserving for, obligations arising out of legal and regulatory requirements surrounding climate change, as discussed further in the sections below. As the requirements continue to evolve, these standards will define when and to what extent related contingencies become quantifiable and disclosable. For example, at the time of this publication, the Financial Accounting Standards Board is considering a rulemaking on how electric power-generating companies and manufacturers in the United States account for trading emission allowances, in particular, "vintage year swaps," where two participants in a trading program exchange emission allowances with different vintage year designations.[40]

Whether a contingent expenditure, such as a need to install pollution control equipment at substantial cost in response to pending regulatory requirements, is probable and estimable, however, will vary by industry, company, plant and jurisdiction. Although the landscape of requirements is likely to continue to develop rapidly—particularly in industrial sectors with significant GHG emission profiles—limitations inherent in determining probability and estimability, coupled with the complexity and global nature of the questions surrounding climate change, have already resulted in a widely varied landscape of disclosure decisions. The SEC has been under continuing pressure to compel companies to sharpen their pencils further on environmental disclosure, to close perceived loopholes and ratchet down disclosure thresholds.[41] It remains to be seen, however, whether climate change will present issues that prompt SEC action similar in scope to SAB 92.

With the requisite accounting and regulatory background in place, we turn now to a more detailed examination of the requirements of Regulation S-K.

3. Item 101—Disclosure of Capital Expenditures

Under Item 101 of Regulation S-K,[42] a company must disclose any material effects that costs of environmental compliance may have on its earnings, capital expenditures and competitive position.[43] Generally, the company must also project environmental compliance costs for two years and compare these costs to those of its competitors.[44] In times of major regulatory initiatives, or when a company is responding strategically to a range of regulatory options, the resulting capital expenditures may be a company's most significant environmental disclosure.

Item 101(c)(xii) requires the disclosure of material effects that environmental matters may have on the financial condition of the registrant, including material expenditures for environmental control facilities for the remainder of the current reporting year and the succeeding year, as well as for any further periods as the registrant deems material.[45] This provision requires the disclosure of both contingent effects and those that are known or certain. Thus, in a simple case, a company may be required to disclose that it plans to spend $60 million over the next two years to retrofit the boilers in order to meet its own voluntary commitment to reduce CO_2 emissions as well as expected regional requirements for GHG emission reductions over the next seven years.

The disclosure analysis becomes more complex, however, in the developing regulatory context of GHG emissions and climate change. The SEC has stated that "to the extent any foreign [environmental] provisions may have a material impact upon the company's financial condition or business, such matters should be disclosed."[46] The SEC also has emphasized that information involving decisions and expenditures beyond the required time period may be necessary to prevent the disclosure from being misleading.[47] This is especially true when the costs expected in the traditional disclosure period are a small percentage of the expenditures that would be necessary to comply with the environmental requirements in question in their entirety and carried to their foreseeable conclusion.[48]

A brief look at a hypothetical disclosure decision tree highlights the complexities—of both timing and of substance—created by the global GHG regulatory picture. Under currently effective regulatory regimes, it is possible that a multinational company with facilities in both the United States and Europe may choose, or be compelled, to make material capital expenditures in Europe that are not currently required in the United

States. This may require disclosure under Item 101, but not on a company-wide basis, i.e., completely omitting the company's U.S. operations. Having made the cost comparison between EU emission trading credits and facility improvements in Europe, however, the company also may be considering capital commitments in the United States in anticipation of regulation that management believes is inevitable, even though it is unlikely to spend substantial money in the absence of legislative certainty. Does the issuer's analysis of the problem, taken to the brink of commitment of capital, trigger a disclosure requirement regarding its U.S. operations as well? The better view is—not yet; but circumstances could change quickly.

If a clear federal legislative or regulatory mandate governing GHG emissions emerges, for example, the company may act on its previous calculations.[49] This decision, or even the underlying regulatory requirements, may immediately trigger disclosure obligations under Item 101, in light of the SEC's stated preference for "whole picture" capital expenditure disclosure.[50] If these expenditures are going to be significant, the best posture for the company may be one in which it previously has signaled such a contingent risk to the market qualitatively, if not quantitatively. Management likely would want to avoid having complex and expensive calculations in its back pocket—and undisclosed—if the risk that the contingency will occur is more than notional, even though it may be otherwise technically compliant. The market generally reacts badly to both surprises and perceived lack of transparency. Suddenly revealing an economic or other business model that had clearly been several years in the making is an unnecessary risk in both areas.

If, however, regional rather than national regulatory regimes remain the dominant, or the sole, source of GHG emission reduction mandates, the company may reach differing conclusions concerning the economics of capital expenditure on a region-by-region basis within the United States. Disclosure under Item 101 may then be appropriate for plants in New York and California, for example, while plants in the Southwest may be unaffected and their future capital expenditure obligations appropriately undisclosed. A coal-burning power plant in the Southwest selling electricity into the California marketplace, however, may now be faced with a radically different capital expenditure horizon as the result of recent legislation.[51]

The inherent global nature of GHG emission and climate change issues, together with existing and developing regional, national, and international climate change initiatives, create similar complexities in the application of Item 101 and other disclosure obligations, when viewed across a spectrum of companies and industries. For example, while Company A, the multinational company described in the above hypothetical decision tree, may choose to signal the market about a contingent risk in the United States, nationally or regionally, Company B, a similarly situated U.S. company without significant foreign operations, either may see the math differently or be less equipped, or have less incentive, to make the calculations. This could result in different disclosure for Company A's U.S. operations, even though they are virtually identical to the U.S. operations of Company B.

The disclosure calculus also will be shaped, in part, by the emerging math of the climate change marketplace. While the EU emission trading scheme is in its infancy, has relatively limited geographical scope, and has recently experienced much publicized volatility, the effect of its existence on internal corporate capital expenditure calculations seems likely to be far-reaching and surprisingly immediate.[52] For many years, and until just recently, neither the regulatory mandates for GHG emissions nor the costs of compliance were known or knowable. Now there is a market price—not the market price or a fixed market price, but a market price nevertheless—as a benchmark against which a company can decide whether it is going to be a buyer or seller of credits or an investor in alternative, upgraded equipment to achieve any GHG emission reductions that may be required in jurisdictions in which it is doing business. For example, Sappi LTD, a South African-based international paper, fibers, and timber products company, has already incorporated such market-based calculations in its 2005 and 2006 20-F disclosures.[53] The existence of a price point may alter the timing of capital deployment, and it is almost certain to accelerate internal analyses[54] in a way that will lead to earlier, and eventually more robust, disclosure of capital expenditure programs to address climate change challenges.[55]

4. Item 103—Disclosure of Legal Proceedings

In the United States, the Clean Air Act (CAA)[56] has a long and ongoing history of litigation lending to regulation or changes to regulation.[57] This litigation has involved citizens' suits brought to compel EPA to take regulatory action, enforcement actions by the EPA against one or more individual companies, industry-wide proceedings, and both individual and industry-wide challenges to the EPA's regulatory authority and its exercise. Often the stakes in this litigation have been enormous—material, under any definition, for all the companies involved and for the affected industry as a whole. Two lines of climate change litigation are pending that are reminiscent, in their scope and potential consequences, of early threshold cases that helped shape the scope of the CAA and the EPA's authority to regulate. Depending on their outcomes, these cases may have both direct and derivative consequences for the U.S.-based operations of all companies with operation or products emitting GHGs. These cases are discussed in Chapter 5. Another case, which may yet spawn progeny, seeks to impose liability directly on a targeted set of defendants and require them to abide by guidelines and commitments that are quasi-regulatory in nature.[58] This case is discussed in detail in Chapter 6. We touch on them here to illustrate their possible effects on disclosure.

Under Item 103, a company must disclose material pending legal proceedings to which the registrant or its subsidiaries is a party or to which any of their property is subject, including such proceedings "known to be contemplated" by governmental authorities.[59] The instructions to Item 103 clarify that an administrative or judicial proceeding arising under environmental laws must be disclosed if (a) it is material to its business or financial condition; (b) it includes a claim for damages or costs in excess of 10% of current consolidated assets; or (c) a governmental authority is a party to the proceeding, or is known to be contemplating such proceedings, unless any sanctions are reasonably expected to be less than $100,000.[60] This black letter financial threshold, which is otherwise well below traditional materiality for most reporting companies, combined with the burden that the regulation places on the reporting company to prove a negative (i.e., that a pending proceeding could not lead to a fine in excess of $100,000) makes this the least understood, and most often ignored, SEC disclosure mandate.[61]

Item 103 requires the disclosure of proceedings that are pending or "known to be contemplated by governmental authorities."[62] Although Item 103 does not specifically require a company to predict the effects of litigation, it has become increasingly common to disclose whether management believes that the results of litigation will be material. In addition, aggregation of sanctions is required for purposes of Instructions

5 (A) and (B) in proceedings "which present in large degree the same issues."[63]

The absence of comprehensive federal climate change regulation, and growing political pressure surrounding the issue, has prompted numerous state attorneys general to file suits against various private parties, including several publicly held companies subject to SEC regulation. While they are unusual litigants in this posture, the attorneys general nevertheless are clearly "governmental authorities" for purposes of Item 103. To date, however, the relief that they have been seeking—a rollback of GHG emissions and a commitment to further reduce or stabilize such emissions in the future—does not appear to involve payments that have traditionally been classified as "sanctions" under SEC guidance.[64]

The July 2004 suit filed by eight state attorneys general and the city of New York in the Southern District of New York against five electric utilities (American Electric Power, Southern Company, Tennessee Valley Authority, Xcel Energy, Cinergy Corporation), the top five emitters of carbon dioxide in the United States, alleges a public nuisance resulting from their contribution to global warming,[65] and seeks a reduction in carbon dioxide emissions, not monetary damages.[66] The court dismissed the case in September 2005, holding that plaintiffs' claims involved a "non-justiciable political question."[67] Plaintiffs' appeal to the Second Circuit, in which oral arguments were heard in June 2006, was pending at the time of this publication. The suit, and the success of lead paint litigation in Rhode Island, has already inspired a similar suit in California, where the attorney general recently filed a public nuisance claim against automakers.[68] Future suits may seek relief more akin to sanctions.

Similarly, in November 2006 the U.S. Supreme Court heard oral argument in a case filed by 12 states, three cities, one U.S. territory, and several environmental groups against asserting that the CAA requires the EPA to regulate carbon dioxide and other GHGs as emissions from motor vehicles.[69] The U.S. Court of Appeals for the D.C. Circuit had dismissed the case in July 2005, after two of three judges ruled against the petitions for different reasons—one judge holding that plaintiffs lacked standing to seek judicial review and another judge holding that the EPA was permitted to choose not to regulate CO_2, even if it had the authority to do so.[70] In this matter, victory by the states might eventually lead to regulations containing sanctions for noncompliance, but any such sanctions would not flow directly or immediately from the Supreme Court's decision. In particular, if the Supreme Court sides with petitioners, the EPA will be forced to reconsider regulation of GHG emissions from motor vehicles and might be faced with other legal action to force the agency to regulate other sources of GHG emissions, such as power plants and industrial boilers.

Finally, the California Air Resources Board (CARB), which recently adopted vehicle emissions regulations for carbon dioxide and other greenhouse gases, set to take effect in 2009, is currently facing legal action from automobile manufacturers and dealership associations claiming that the California standards are preempted by the Federal Energy Policy and Conservation Act, under which federal fuel economy standards are established by the National Highway Traffic Safety Administration, and by the CAA.[71] CARB argues that the CAA gives it the authority to regulate carbon dioxide emissions.[72] A number of other states, including New York, Massachusetts, Vermont, Maine, Connecticut, Rhode Island, New Jersey and Oregon, have already adopted California's GHG standards for vehicles sold within their respective borders. Thus, should the Court uphold CARB's regulations, it would effectively establish a patchwork quilt of automobile emissions standards for GHGs.[73]

Notwithstanding the absence of direct sanctions, each of these proceedings has obvious implications for other significant GHG emitters should these or similar causes of action prove successful. They also may have indirect consequences for nondefendant but similarly situated companies, both in terms of costs and disclosure obligations. For example, a favorable holding for plaintiffs in *Connecticut v. AEP* or similar proceedings that results in regulatory requirements for GHG emitters would soon have material monetary and operational consequences for both the utility defendants and, arguably, other utilities and GHG-intensive companies. As a result, in the face of such pending proceedings, disclosure obligations may arise both for defendant and nondefendant companies as the threat of legal or regulatory consequences becomes more real or foreseeable.

With litigation over GHG emissions in its relative infancy, the litigation and regulatory maneuvering surrounding the federal new source review (NSR) program[74] may provide an analytical or tactical model for regulation of GHGs. The NSR controversy is wholly independent of other air emission issues from complex point sources, in both its genesis and in the manner in which the cases have been prosecuted and resolved. The types of capital expenditure programs, particularly at aging, coal-fired power plants, that are increasingly the subject of consent decrees or judicial orders to resolve NSR cases, however, are de facto high-stakes wagers on what may be necessary to anticipate both regulatory and economic constraints on GHG emissions from these sources. The resolution of these cases therefore may prove to be significant for climate change disclosure. In addition, even for individual companies or industry sectors that have not been directly involved in NSR controversies, the cycle of regulation, litigation, resolution and capital commitment may play out again directly in the GHG arena.

Ohio Edison's involvement in the NSR cases is illustrative. In March 2005, the company settled its NSR lawsuit by agreeing to spend over a billion dollars to reduce the air pollution at its W. H. Sammis Station in Stratton, Ohio, by 22,500 tons a year.[75] From 1999 to 2000, the Sammis plant was one of 44 power plants that received

NOVs or Compliance Orders from the EPA, alleging Clean Air Act violations.[76] The civil complaint alleged that "[d]efendant's violations, alone and in combination with similar violations at other coal-fired electric power plants, have been significant contributors to some of the most severe environmental problems facing the nation today."[77] The consent decree requires installation of pollution controls at all seven steam-generating units, as well as scrubbers and selective catalytic reduction devices on the two largest units between 2005 and 2011, so that the final emission reduction levels will be achieved by 2012.[78]

The price of compliance with the order is high, and it requires significant new technology that could steer companies—and elements of the power industry—toward new disclosure obligations. The company's 2005 10K states:

> [I]f FirstEnergy fails to install such pollution control devices, for any reason, including, but not limited to, the failure of any third-party contractor to timely meet its delivery obligations for such devices, FirstEnergy could be exposed to penalties under the settlement agreement. Capital expenditures necessary to meet those requirements are currently estimated to be $1.5 billion. . . . The settlement agreement also requires OE and Penn to spend up to $25 million toward environmentally beneficial projects, which include wind energy purchased power agreements over a 20-year term.[79]

A future regulatory environment, in which GHG emissions were constrained, would similarly require many companies to readjust their capital commitments for new, different, and expensive technology. The cost of any technical solution still depends in large measure on the degree of constraint imposed on GHG emissions by regulatory authorities. For example, Cinergy, a leading coal-fired utility, argues that compliance with so-called 3P legislation (i.e., legislation imposing limits on SO_x, NO_x and mercury, but not CO_2) requires technology different than what would be necessary to meet the demands of so-called 4P legislation, i.e., legislation imposing limits on CO_2 in addition to the other pollutants.[80] As a result, Cinergy is concerned that investments in 3P technology would only be of short-term benefit, becoming a "stranded cost" upon the implementation of CO_2 emission regulations.[81] In addition, failure to address CO_2 emissions in the current round of capital restructuring in the energy industry—whether in the context of settling NSR litigation or otherwise—might "lock in" inefficiencies and make GHG emission reduction more expensive and, thus, less attainable.[82]

Despite the daunting cost of implementing state-of-the-art scrubbers and similar technology mandated under NSR consent decrees for Ohio Edison, that cost is defined, which allows Ohio Edison to disclose the consequences to its shareholders and take comfort in knowing that the price is necessary for proper management. This certainty is increasingly sought by companies that argue for a comprehensive scheme of climate change legislation, in much the same way that industry put pressure on EPA for simplification (some say rollback) of the NSR rules. Any financial decision made in an

unregulated arena, they argue, is at risk of becoming a poor or inefficient decision once the uncertainty is resolved. For example, Cinergy states in its voluntary climate change report (a concept discussed more fully in section IV, below):

> It can take from six to 12 years to build a large base load generating station on a new site, at a cost in excess of $1 billion. . . . In an uncertain regulatory climate, these decisions must be made at the risk that they will not be optimal once the existing uncertainty is finally resolved. . . . the prompt adoption of a clear long-term federal environmental policy would benefit all.[83]

As Cinergy predicts, in the relatively near future, we will be living in a carbon-constrained—and most likely regulated—nation, and it will be prudent to manage a company in an industry facing future regulation in a manner that accepts preparation and adaptation as an immediate responsibility.[84] Yet in doing so, a company currently must act without the technological, regulatory or legal certainty afforded in the resolution of the NSR cases. This uncertainty creates a broad spectrum of possible outcomes. Although this uncertainty is increasingly being transferred into the litigation arena, the disclosure of these outcomes is best suited for, and clearly implicates, the third area of traditional SEC disclosure, discussed below.

5. Item 303—Management's Discussion and Analysis (MD&A)

To supplement the numerically driven mandates of Items 101 and 103,[85] the SEC casts a broader, more subjective net through its requirements for MD&A disclosure under Item 303. The SEC views MD&A disclosure[86] as an opportunity to give investors "a look at the company through the eyes of management."[87] In practice, this exercise generally requires the company to disclose "currently known trends, events, and uncertainties that are reasonably expected to have material effects."[88] It has been interpreted to require two distinct inquiries. First, management must determine whether an uncertainty is reasonably likely to occur.[89] Unless management can conclude that the event is not reasonably likely to occur, management must assume that it will occur.[90] Second, the trend or event must be disclosed, unless management can determine that its occurrence is not reasonably likely to have a material effect on the company.[91] Disclosure is optional when management is merely anticipating "a future trend or event, or anticipating a less predictable impact of a known trend, event or uncertainty."[92]

Item 303 requires the disclosure of "known uncertainties,"[93] an oxymoronic term that captures knowable possibilities that are less than trends but that could result in material consequences. The SEC has also stated that required disclosure is characterized by trends that are "currently known" and "reasonably expected to have material effects."[94] The predictability of the event at issue has as much significance for disclosure purposes as the size of the consequences.

For disclosure purposes, climate change is ripening from being an "uncertainty" or a "trend" to being an "event."

The instructions to Item 303 state that the information provided in the MD&A "need only include that which is available to the registrant without undue effort or expense and which does not clearly appear in the registrant's financial statements."[95] The SEC has advised that such information must be detailed "to the extent necessary to an understanding of the registrant's business as a whole."[96] Item 303(a) also states that if, in the registrant's judgment, a discussion of subdivisions of the registrant's business would be appropriate to an understanding of the business, the discussion should focus both on the subdivision and on the company as a whole.[97] Notwithstanding the latitude implicit in these requirements, in the (albeit scanty) enforcement history of this provision, the SEC has required registrants to state "the amount, or describe the nature or extent of the potential [environmental] liabilities" in their disclosure.[98] The SEC has further advised that, even when an exact calculation of potential environmental liability is not possible, the effects of such liability should be "quantified to the extent reasonably practicable."[99]

For disclosure purposes, climate change is ripening from being an "uncertainty" or a "trend" to being an "event." Just as clearly, however, it is not a single event, because its consequences, real or perceived, will register in both the commercial and financial marketplaces, as well as across geographical boundaries. Additional complexity flows from the profusion of legislative, regulatory and technical solutions that are in place or under development. For companies with operations spread throughout the EU, other non-European Kyoto Protocol ratifying countries, and the United States, for example, climate change, and the issuer's planned responses, are simultaneously a multitude of events, a trend and an uncertainty. In all such circumstances, disclosure may be warranted under Item 303.

The cutting edge of disclosure, and the tougher questions, occur when management has to determine whether the accumulation of issues related to climate change and GHG emission control are, or are likely to become, material for their company. Closely related to this determination is management's view of the level of diligence, calculation or reasonable estimation that it will have to undertake in order to make this determination in a manner that passes SEC muster.

Five years ago, a fair reading of Item 303 might have justified silence on climate change on the part of most public companies for several reasons. The scientific view, while coalescing, was far from certain and was being publicly dismissed in many quarters, and some high places, as speculative.[100] Finishing touches were being put on the Kyoto Protocol, and the long road to ratification still lay ahead. There was no established GHG emission trading marketplace. As a consequence, the effects on production, demand for products, and other business metrics translatable into financial data were unquantifiable, irrespective of the level of effort on the part of management. In fact, any disclosure involving the "math" of climate change arguably would have been misleading, in that it would have created an illusion of precision when none was possible. These uncertainties, which were palpable enough for companies immediately affected by climate change risks—utilities and automobile makers—were magnified for companies for which GHG emission risks were further attenuated, both in the marketplace and the regulatory landscape. An engine manufacturer, for example, could not make meaningful disclosure at a time when it was unclear how, if at all, the market risk of GHG emission reduction would be apportioned among GHG emission sources, such as petroleum refiners, car manufacturers, and public utilities, even though it was possible that some jurisdictions, such as California, were going to focus on auto makers as the primary source of such reductions.[101]

Today, doubts on the baseline science continue to diminish,[102] and several trading marketplaces have been established. On the regulatory front, while there are still gaping uncertainties regarding future federal regulation in the United States, a reasonably broad-based consensus for cap and trade programs is forming (irrespective of the life span of the Kyoto Protocol itself), and there are many developing regional and local variations on regulatory mandates for GHG emission reductions.[103] The market has had a chance to price, at least on a preliminary basis, the various regulatory and market-based plans to reduce

GHG emissions.[104] A few giant multinationals, for which materiality, under any available measure, is expressed in the billions of dollars, may still be justified in their view that there is no analysis that can currently be performed in any jurisdiction that would reasonably be expected to translate climate change into a material financial risk.[105]

Other companies still removed from the immediate consequences of climate change may also justifiably remain silent, because market forces creating definable economic effects of GHG emissions on their customers may remain too abstract. It is increasingly clear, however, that for publicly traded companies for which stringent regulation or unfavorable economic trade-offs in even a single country or at a major facility could translate quickly into material economic or strategic consequences, the window for well-founded silence on climate change is closing rapidly.

It is notable that companies in industries for which climate change risk is arguably accumulative, such as property and casualty insurance, which face potential material costs related to the changing weather conditions climate change may cause, also have begun to address the issue, both directly and indirectly, in their disclosure. For example, St. Paul Travelers Companies Inc., one of the ten largest U.S. insurance companies,[106] includes a discussion of climate change as a contributing element of the risk factor regarding catastrophic losses, and predicts that the severity and frequency of storms will increase in 2006.[107] Hartford Financial Services does not mention climate change directly, but in its extensive discussion of the financial effects of the hurricanes of 2005, the company states that there are "forecasts of increased frequency and severity" of catastrophic storms.[108] Eight of the top ten U.S. insurance companies disclosed the effects of the hurricanes of 2005 on their businesses,[109] with two alluding to modeling systems and other strategies used by the company to attempt to predict future losses.[110] Development of a scientific consensus that there is a causal link between global warming (already observed) and such storms (if they materialize) would quickly place climate change at the forefront of disclosure for every property and casualty company. A study recently published in the Proceedings of the National Academy of Sciences, which concludes that man-made GHG emissions are the most important factor in changes to the sea surface temperatures and a recent upsurge in hurricane activity,[111] is among several indications that such a concensus may be imminent.

B. Sarbanes-Oxley Requirements

It is now a well-recognized feature of the U.S. corporate landscape that Congress responded to high-profile accounting controversies and public outcries for corporate transparency by enacting the Sarbanes-Oxley Act in 2002.[112] Although the act does not specifically alter environmental disclosure requirements, it clearly has implications for a company's environmental disclosure protocols and practices generally, and may change a company's analysis of climate change issues in particular. The most pertinent requirement involves newly mandated "disclosure controls and procedures." Under Sarbanes-Oxley and its implementing regulations, a corporation's chief executive officer (CEO) and chief financial officer (CFO) must certify, in the company's 10-Q and 10-K reports, that the company has implemented an internal management system, including "disclosure controls and procedures," that ensures that information that must be disclosed under SEC regulations is accumulated and communicated to corporate management.[113] These controls and procedures must be evaluated periodically by the CEO and CFO. Any significant deficiencies must be reported to the company's financial auditors and to the audit committee of the company's board of directors.[114]

In addition to assuring that adequate disclosure controls and procedures have been implemented, under section 302 of the act, the CEO and CFO must sign a certification statement to be included with the company's 10-K and 10-Q. Specifically, the officers must certify that each report filed with the SEC meets all requirements of the Securities Exchange Act, and that the information contained in the report "fairly presents in all material respects" the financial condition and results of operations of the company.[115] Further, the officers must certify that (1) they have reviewed the report; (2) based on their knowledge, there are no untrue statements of material fact or omissions of material facts necessary to make the report not misleading; and (3) all significant deficiencies and material weaknesses in the design and operation of internal control over financial reporting have been disclosed.[116]

A second, and potentially more onerous, certification requirement is imposed by section 906 of the act. Under that section, the CEO and CFO must provide an additional certification with each periodic report containing financial statements filed with the SEC, stating that the report fully complies with the requirements of section 13(a) or 15(d) of the Securities Exchange Act, and that information contained in the periodic report fairly presents, in all material respects, the financial condition and results of operations of the company. Section 906 imposes criminal liability upon the certifying officers for false certifications.[117]

Another noteworthy provision of the act's implementing regulations prohibits improper influence on the conduct of the company's financial audits.[118] The regulation applies not only to corporate officers and directors, but to any person acting under their direction,[119] including, presumably, in-house and outside counsel, environmental compliance officers and plant managers, and outside environmental consultants, such as those who might be engaged to perform an analysis of GHG risk exposure. Specifically, the rule prohibits such persons from taking actions that might mislead an independent public accountant engaged in an audit of the corporation.[120]

The certifications required by Sarbanes-Oxley put ongoing pressure on management to account for and disclose, in financial statements or otherwise, any material aspect of climate change risk that can fairly be said to be quantifiable. As the regulatory picture changes, marketplaces for emission credits

develop, and the price of emissions credits fluctuates; for example, companies that place material reliance on this mechanism for meeting GHG emission reduction requirements will have to be nimble in their analyses. Similar dexterity will be required in evaluating the financial effects of rapidly evolving regulations, and in assuring investors that any litigation risk related to climate change is fairly presented in the company's financials.

In addition, existing and developing Environmental Management System protocols, which necessarily will include climate change considerations for companies facing GHG regulatory regimes, will be subject to increased scrutiny under the standards imposed by Sarbanes-Oxley. Certification requirements under Sarbanes-Oxley at the management level will, in turn, increase accountability downstream at the plant or operational level and emphasize data gathering and analysis. The responsibilities of corporate environmental compliance officers and other personnel, and their outside advisors, charged with investigating, analyzing and predicting the outcome of environmental matters, will also be scrutinized more carefully. The nature of the certifications required under the act, coupled with the potentially significant operational and monetary impact of climate change regulation, seem likely to require an increased focus on data gathering methodologies, accuracy and output, as well as third-party verification. In addition, the cross-functional decision making necessary for Sarbanes-Oxley compliance will increase the pressure to coordinate environmental data gathering and related analysis with legal, financial, human resources and public relations areas, both over the short term and the foreseeable future. All of these factors, played out against a backdrop of an uncertain regulatory climate and complex scientific and technical considerations, seem likely to increase the risk of "material deficiencies" in the climate change context.

To date, there has been no litigation or SEC enforcement on the "fairly presents" standard. It is widely believed, however, that it is a more stringent standard than the traditional 10(b)(5) materiality standard. Notwithstanding these warnings, it remains uncertain, for example, whether a fair presentation could omit discussion of a known substantial future risk, such as global warming, that was unquantifiable and arguably less than probable to occur.

C. Conclusions About Risk Disclosure

The dynamic state of GHG emission regulation clearly presents substantial, and immediate, disclosure challenges.[121] Disclosure obligations in three traditional areas of SEC regulation arguably have ripened as a result of the simultaneous onset of legislation, regulation and litigation, combined with corporate responses to each of these developments.[122]

Several new trends are already apparent. First, there are sharp divisions between seemingly similarly situated entities. Two New England power companies with plants in adjacent states (or even adjacent counties) could have vastly different disclosure obligations, depending on factors as straightforward as the regulatory requirements governing fuel feed stock or as complex as long-range corporate planning for capital improvements.[123] Similar divisions of both substance and timing are likely to play out across the industrial sectors most closely associated with GHG emission risk—principally electric utilities and automakers, and to a lesser extent steel, aluminum and pulp and paper mills—in the relatively near term. Second, management of these companies will have to contend with a timeline anomaly in disclosing their climate change responses. Capital projects that typically require expenditure over a long period, and the underlying regulatory reasons for considering such expenditures, may fall outside the range of the technical requirements of SEC disclosure rules. Because of the length and significance of the capital commitment needed to redirect a company's resources to less carbon-intensive emissions, however, which in some instances may reshape a company, for example, emphasizing production of hybrid vehicles or replacing a traditional coal-fired power plant with an IGCC plant, disclosure may be appropriate and required at the time that a strategy is chosen, rather than beginning in—and then only in—the years when the bell curve of capital expenditure peaks, or becomes material for a given year. Simply stated, materiality[124]—and the obligation to disclose—may ripen when the die is cast; for example, when procurement contracts for pollution control equipment are signed, and the company has chosen a way forward to meet emission reduction requirements or commitments.

These GHG disclosure (and related accounting) issues are maturing at a delicate time for upper-level management, which is under continuing scrutiny as a result of the certification requirements of Sarbanes-Oxley.[125] Knowing that their certifications must meet a standard of "fair presentation," which will almost certainly come to be seen in the next few years as more all-embracing than the standard of materiality, the time-honored and flexible disclosure benchmark, management will feel pressed to be inclusive in their company's disclosure, especially if the results of their medium- to long-range planning could involve material expenditures that otherwise would be substantial surprises to the marketplace.[126]

D. Business Opportunities

In addition to obligations arising from the potential capital expenditures, legal proceedings, and evolving legislative and regulatory requirements surrounding climate change, disclosure of business opportunities may also be required, and may be significantly more tempting to many companies from a public and investor relations standpoint. Participation—either directly or indirectly—in the supply chain of carbon-free power, for example, can send both an economic and political message to investors. Here the risk to the reporting company is not material omission but overstatement.

Hexcel Corporation's 2005 10-K disclosure, for example, states that, despite the fact that sales of its various other products declined, revenue from sales of the materials that it manufactures that are used to build blades of wind turbines grew more than 50% in constant currency, due mostly to the increased number of wind turbine installations.[127] Wind power, however, remains a minute fraction of the overall power generation market, and all growth claims must be put in that context or risk being misleading. Other carbon-free power options, such as solar or nuclear energy, may ultimately yield substantial revenues for a company—or an industry. Companies inclined to make optimistic disclosure to that effect, however, still need to tread carefully for many of the same reasons that make it difficult to determine what, or how, to disclose the negative aspects of climate change; the variability and unknown future of regulation, litigation, science and politics.

Methanex Corporation, a manufacturer of methanol, a chemical feedstock, provides one such cautionary tale. In its 1993 disclosure, it touted the use of MTBE, one of its derivative products, as an additive to gasoline that "reduces the amount of harmful exhaust" in gas emissions.[128] The disclosure then went on to describe the anticipated trend toward reformulated gas and stated that "MTBE is considered the oxygenate of choice by refining industry . . . ,"[129] one that "is expected to cause a fundamental shift in the marketplace as methanol evolves from a basic chemical feedstock to a primary ingredient in oxygenated and reformulated gasoline."[130] Scarcely a decade later, the MTBE story in the United States does not appear as if it will end happily for manufacturers.

A more neutral position can be seen in Ballard Power Systems Inc.'s recent disclosure regarding its proton exchange membrane (PEM) fuel cells, a building block of the highly touted hydrogen economy of the future and, as such, one potential answer to reducing GHG emissions from fossil-fuel combustion. While Ballard states that a "PEM fuel cell is an environmentally clean electrochemical device. . . ,"[131] it also cautions that, notwithstanding the current strong interest in vehicular PEM fuel cell systems due largely to environmental laws and regulations, "there is no guarantee that these laws and related policies will not change."[132]

III. Voluntary Reporting

One of the most striking disclosure developments in the past decade has been the rapid rise in volume, and a comparable improvement in the detail and quality, of voluntary environmental reports provided by many leading companies. While these developments are not exclusively linked to climate change—substantial corporate resources are being devoted both to issues not directly related to the environment, such as global labor practices, and broader issues, such as sustainable development—the high profile nature of climate change has driven much of the recent growth.

There is no single strategy behind the proliferation of these voluntary reports on climate change, nor is there a dominant template[133] or tone for their contents.[134] Some companies have offered a reflexive trade to their shareholders in lieu of fighting a protracted proxy and media campaign.[135] Others have tried to seize control of the debate early, to channel shareholders' attention and reap independent public relations rewards.[136] Still others appear to have concluded that there was no harm, and potentially some good, in being at least partially transparent with their shareholders and the public on detailed technical and strategic analyses that already were being performed for internal planning reasons. Elements of some reports also echo, or themselves constitute, part of the corporate political platform in the ongoing debate about the nature and timing of GHG emission regulation. Irrespective of the reasons that lead climate change reports to be written, the quality (and density) of these reports have typically been worlds removed from the glossy pictures and anecdotal fluff that characterized the early days of more general voluntary environmental reports, in part because of the complexity of climate change issues, and in part because of the maturation and increasing sophistication of the audience for voluntary reporting on all environmental topics.

The comparative complexity of voluntary climate change reports has also created significant subsidiary issues. As discussed in section II(B) above, it has put some companies at risk of a "data clash" with the contents of their SEC reports, particularly those fueled by the more stringent requirements of Sarbanes-Oxley certification. It has also spawned a secondary market of stakeholder engagement in the report verification process, as companies have partnered with consultants and unrelated socially responsible investing groups to add credibility to their conclusions on climate risk and the processes by which they were derived.[137]

> **One of the most striking disclosure developments in the past decade has been the rapid rise in volume, and a comparable improvement in the detail and quality, of voluntary environmental reports provided by many leading companies.**

While the voluntary reports distributed to date all address the variables of climate change in relation to their company's current and future practices, putting the individual pens to paper has produced significantly varied results. A comparison of the reports produced by Cinergy and Ford, for example, is representative of the potentially widely divergent outcomes. In its report, Ford agrees that climate change warrants "precautionary, prudent and early actions to enhance our competitiveness and protect our profitability in an increasingly carbon-constrained economy."[138] At the same time, the Ford report stops short of providing specific targets or predicting outcomes, and offers instead a general commitment to continue improving, stating, "[w]e know that many of our stakeholders expect this report to spell out specific targets and milestones for improvements in the fleet fuel efficiency of our products. It will not do that."[139] In a highly competitive industry, Ford concludes that, "there continue to be too wide a range of possible futures for technologies, markets, and regulatory frameworks for our company to set unilateral targets on the in-use performance of our products."[140]

By contrast, the Cinergy report provides detailed analysis and a specific goal "to reduce our GHG emissions to five percent below our 2000 level during the period 2010 and 2012. . . . We have committed $21 million to fund projects through the remainder of this decade. . . . "[141] Cinergy then goes on to argue in favor of market-based cap and trade reduction programs and an escalating price cap on carbon allowance prices for the first 15 to 20 years.[142] The company also urges Congress to establish national multi-emissions legislation[143] and estimates in comparative detail the cost to the company of addressing proposed regulations of SO_2, NO_x and mercury through the end of this decade.[144] In short, Cinergy elected to turn its analytical suit inside out so that the public could see the seams. Ford engaged the issues, but only on the broadest levels.

IV. Proxy Contests

In addition to disclosure requirements triggered by new issuances of securities to the public, periodic-reporting obligations and extraordinary corporate events such as a merger or sale of a business, proxy disclosure is required in connection with elections at annual shareholder meetings.[145] Under rules established by the SEC, shareholders who meet certain requirements and follow certain procedures may present proposals recommending corporate action in connection with that company's solicitation of proxies.[146]

A company can omit a shareholder proposal for any one of a number of enumerated reasons, including circumstances in which it can demonstrate[147] that the proposal:

- is not a proper subject for action by shareholders under the laws of the jurisdiction of the company's organization;
- would, if implemented, cause the company to violate any state, federal, or foreign law to which it is subject;
- is contrary to any of the SEC's proxy rules, including 17 C.F.R. § 240.14a-9, which prohibits materially false or misleading statements in proxy-soliciting materials;
- relates to operations that account for less than 5% of the company's total assets at the end of its most recent fiscal year, and for less than 5% of its net earnings and gross sales for its most recent fiscal year, and is not otherwise significantly related to the company's business;
- is beyond the company's power or authority to implement;
- deals with a matter relating to the company's ordinary business operations;
- directly conflicts with one of the company's own proposals to be submitted to shareholders at the same meeting;
- has already been substantially implemented by the company; or
- substantially duplicates another proposal previously submitted to the company by another proponent that will be included in the company's proxy materials for the same meeting.[148]

The content, source and number of proxy resolutions in recent years reveal a distinct market trend. Shareholders are not only showing a rising concern in the risk that climate change poses to a company's business, but also an interest in encouraging or compelling disclosure of the real or potential, current or future, effects of this risk in voluntary reporting. Environmental resolutions—especially those focusing on global warming—have surpassed social issues, such as fair employment, political

contributions and CEO pay/golden parachutes, which have traditionally been among the most frequent topics of corporate governance proposals.

In the first half of the 2006 proxy season,[149] 180 social and environmental shareholder resolutions were filed, compared to the 169 resolutions that were filed during the same period in 2005.[150] Of the 180 resolutions, 32 pertain to corporate policies on global warming.[151] Twelve additional global warming proposals were withdrawn after disclosure agreements were reached with management.[152] During the same period of 2005, 34 resolutions were filed, compared with 25 resolutions in 2004.[153] In addition to the growing volume of resolutions, the breadth of environmental topics is expanding as well. In the first half of 2006 there were 22 resolutions regarding toxics and pollution reductions, whereas there were 12 such resolutions in 2005.[154]

It is becoming an increasingly common occurrence for management to have to address severance payments, golden parachutes and other traditional management compensation issues at the same annual meeting where global warming is also on the agenda. In fact, this package of diverse proposals reveals another trend—the confluence of the previously distinct worlds, interests and tactics of mainstream institutional investors on the one hand, and socially concerned shareholders on the other.[155] In addition to broad-based concerns about corporate governance and transparency arguably triggered by highly publicized scandals,[156] financial markets are increasingly endorsing the proposition

that "social and environmental issues significantly impact financial performance, and that good corporate governance correlates with improved environmental, social, and financial performance."[157]

Labor pension funds, such as those of the New York City Police and Fire Departments, are beginning to serve as a bridge between social investors and the larger institutional funds. State pension and health benefit funds, always concerned with their ability to pay benefits over the long term, have increasingly translated their concerns into activism on sustainability generally and on investment issues with longer arcs of return, of which climate change is rapidly becoming the leading example. Campaign ExxonMobil, for example, was founded by faith and environmental group shareholders and works with a broader-based coalition of institutional investors, corporate governance activists and financial analysts to convince investors of certain asserted financial risks of ExxonMobil's positions as well to convince ExxonMobil to be more responsive on climate change.[158] The campaign has asked ExxonMobil to defend its position on climate change data and to report on its contributions to compliance with the Kyoto Protocol in member countries in which it is doing business. In addition to posting these resolutions on a publicly accessible Web site, the campaign also provides links to various newsletters and publications that criticize ExxonMobil's public stance on these issues.[159]

In March 2002, a group of ExxonMobil shareholders owning several million shares of common stock[160] submitted a proposal requesting the company to report on its efforts to promote renewable energy sources and incorporate such energy into its practice.[161] ExxonMobil, in return, sought permission from the SEC to exclude the proposal from the company's proxy material.[162] ExxonMobil argued that rule 14a-8(i)(3)—the clause prohibiting materially false or misleading statements—allowed the company to omit the proposal. Among other claims, ExxonMobil said the proposal's statements overstated the current status of the Kyoto Protocol, included opinions rather than fact and confused renewable energy with clean energy. The SEC allowed a small portion of the proposal to be omitted from the proxy,[163] but agreed with the shareholders on all other points raised, stating, "shareholder value will be enhanced if the Company would look beyond the next quarter and commence planning for a world in which the Kyoto Protocol is in effect almost everywhere outside of the U.S."[164] The SEC also stated "[w]hy *any* rational shareholder would be unable to understand the meaning of the term "pollution-causing fuels" is quite beyond comprehension. . . . "[165]

On the heels of the proxy fight with ExxonMobil, a coalition of shareholders seeking to force Anadarko Petroleum Corp. to disclose its greenhouse gas emissions recently withdrew the proposal after the company pledged to provide such disclosure voluntarily every year.[166] Other companies that agreed to produce similar reports voluntarily or otherwise address climate change issues, leading shareholders to withdraw their 2006 resolutions, included Alliant Energy, WPS Resources, MGE Energy, and Great Plains Energy.[167]

The substance of some of these reports, however, raises interesting political questions. For example, the Cinergy report briefly explains the history of the CAA and the difference in various emission control measures, such as "command and control" vs. "cap and trade," and defines and analyzes current and proposed legislation, including the Clear Skies Act of 2003, the Clean Air Planning Act of 2003, and the Climate Stewardship Act of 2003 [discussed in greater detail in chapter 3]. The report goes on to argue the company's position supporting Congress to act and pass a national, multi-emissions bill.[168]

Why would a company, especially one in an easily targeted or heavily impacted industry, offer up more details, estimations and proposed solutions than specifically requested by the shareholders? Clearly, there is some perceived advantage to seizing control of the debate and demonstrating to shareholders—and the general public—management's command of issues. A proactive report may also enable a company to sway the votes in the debate in a way that eventually could significantly affect its marketplace.

Outside the U.S. political theatre, U.S.-based companies also may face pressures targeted on their overseas operations, and consequently a reverse whipsaw from those operations to U.S.-based facilities that may be under no current operational constraints related to GHG emissions. Such pressures have recently been felt in areas not related to climate change, but where sustainability and long horizon investing and performance are implicated. For example, the Extractive Industries Transportation Initiative (EITI), launched by Tony Blair at the World Summit on Sustainable Development in September 2002,[169] aims to increase transparency in transactions between governments and companies within extractive industries (oil, gas and mining).[170] Nearly 20 countries have committed to EITI principles and criteria.[171] Any success of this template will be quickly transferable into the climate change arena.

In addition to these broad trends of proxy campaigns and the fight for the corporate podium on climate change issues, some companies may face specific legal risks in the context of proxy solicitation. A 1993 decision by the U.S. Court of Appeals for the Second Circuit is instructive for the way that the court analyzed the adequacy of a company's statements about its environmental performance,[172] and provides insight into a possible outcome for judicial reaction to mixed climate change disclosure messages from a major multinational company.[173] As the volume of climate change disclosure continues to build, more companies are at risk of talking themselves into the same position as International Paper; that is, telling their climate change story in their voluntary environmental reports in a manner that contrasts sharply, in substance and tone, with the story they tell to investors and the marketplace in their mandatory filings.

At issue in the *International Paper* case was a shareholder resolution calling on the company to implement the so-called Valdez Principles and to cooperate with shareholders and the public in "a continuing process to achieve a genuine and publicly trusted measure of public environmental accountability."[174] International Paper opposed the resolution on numerous grounds.[175] The company distributed copies of its own principles with the proxy statement. The company's principles, unremarkable by today's standards, declared that it was dedicated to "safe and environmentally sound products, packaging and operations"; that the company had "long standing policies on environment, health and safety" that were embodied in the principles; and that the company had a "strong environmental compliance program."[176]

The shareholder group filed suit, alleging that the proxy statement included misleading statements and omitted material facts concerning the company's environmental performance in violation of section 14(a) of the Securities Exchange Act and

Rule 14a-9. As evidence of the misleading nature of the proxy statement, the plaintiffs relied on statements made in the company's 10-K which revealed that the company had been accused of numerous environmental offenses, had pled guilty to felonies, had agreed to pay substantial fines, and had been the target of numerous administrative complaints regarding environmental matters.[177]

The company argued that, standing alone, its proxy statement was not misleading. The company also argued that, when the proxy statement was read in conjunction with the company's annual report (which was mentioned in the proxy statement and had been mailed to all shareholders), the company's 10-K (which had not been mailed to shareholders but was on file with the SEC) and various news reports concerning ongoing environmental litigation involving the company, the total mix of publicly available information was not misleading.

The trial court strongly disagreed.[178] The court found that International Paper's argument that the proxy statement itself was not misleading was "palpably without merit."[179] Comparing the company's actual experience in environmental litigation to the company's statement that it has a "strong environmental compliance program," the court found that the company's proxy statement was "to put it charitably, inconsistent with the serious and ongoing environmental challenges that the Company has endured."[180] Further, the court characterized the company's statements as "flowery corporate happy-talk" that had clearly been included for the purpose of defeating the shareholders' proposal.[181]

The facts presented by *International Paper* seem unremarkable, and the contrast between corporate rhetoric and corporate performance scarcely worthy of the judicial scorn that was heaped on it, in the view of the authors of this chapter. For a resource-intensive multinational company, International Paper had fared no better or worse with regulatory authorities and had incurred no greater costs of compliance than might be expected. Similarly, its defense of its record in response to the shareholder initiative, while clearly more confrontational than would typically occur today, was not an inherently unreasonable statement of its experience and intentions in wrestling with its environmental obligations. A similar result, and comparable discrepancies, might well be expected to develop from the complexities inherent in climate change disclosure.

The Second Circuit affirmed the lower court's decision, holding that the proxy statement, standing alone, was materially misleading on the company's environmental record.[182] According to the court, the company's self-laudatory remarks "conveyed an impression that was entirely false."[183] Agreeing with the trial court, the court also held that the annual report did not cure the misleading statements in the proxy statement, because the level of disclosure in the annual report, and the nature of the details that were omitted, were insufficient to put a reasonable shareholder on notice that the falsely "pristine picture" painted in the proxy statement was misleading.[184]

Applying the lessons of *International Paper* in practice, the corporate departments responsible for drafting a company's mandatory financial statements and SEC reports typically fall under different management supervision and may well have a different ethos from those charged with preparing voluntary annual reports on the company's environmental, sustainability or climate change performance and objectives. While corporate officers and legal counsel are often charged with preparing SEC filings and associated financial statements, environmental professionals, armed with data and anecdotes from operational staff at the plants, are generally responsible for gathering and summarizing the data included in voluntary EHS or sustainability reports. This split is compounded by the different purposes behind each report, i.e., providing investors with an accurate overview of the company's financial condition versus promoting the company's positioning on global warming, for example. Predictably, these reports often paint a different picture of the company's performance and aspirations.

The incongruity of information presented in these differing reports arguably thwarts a shareholder's ability to receive complete and accurate information on the company's performance. Following the rationale of the court in *International Paper*, for companies that fail to force convergence of their reporting systems and—at least—submit their voluntary reports to cross-checking and rigorous review by the same team that is responsible for mandatory disclosure, the door may be open for stakeholder claims that the "total mix" of information is misleading in violation of section 10(b) of the Securities Exchange Act.[185]

One can easily envision Company X preparing and distributing to shareholders a climate report describing the nature of its voluntary commitment to reduce its company-wide GHG emission footprint and its efforts at reducing emissions. The report, prepared by the company's environmental compliance officer and her staff, might include tables or graphs that clearly demonstrate annual reductions in a range of critical emissions (e.g., SO_x NO_x and CO_2) over the past five years, with a text discussion describing the company's commitment to cleaner air. In tone and text, this report would be forward-looking and positive. If, however, several of the company's facilities recently received notices of violation (NOVs) alleging that the facility's regulated emissions exceed relevant permit limits, and the NOVs sought civil penalties in excess of $100,000 (or failed to specify a penalty amount but alleged that the violation had been ongoing for a period longer than the four days likely necessary to accrue a $100,000 penalty under governing law),[186] the company's in-house counsel would correctly conclude that each NOV had to be disclosed in the company's 10-K, notwithstanding their nonmateriality.[187] Putting the two reports side-by-side after the ink had dried, the argument could be made—by any party with standing and incentive to make it—that the company's failure to mention the ongoing compliance problems renders the climate report misleading, in violation of section 10(b) and Rule 10b-5.

Suppose further that the company's shareholder relations team, unaware of pending administrative proceedings against the company, included in the discussion of compliance in the voluntary climate report a statement that the company had not received an NOV under the CAA in the past three years. Again, the general counsel, who receives service of any enforcement actions taken against the company, dutifully discloses such actions in reports to the SEC. The inconsistency is never caught, because the voluntary report, while subject to detailed wordsmithing by the shareholder relations team and the company's outside consultant, is given only cursory review by the general counsel's office. The company then distributes to stakeholders two documents containing discussions that directly contradict each other.

Assume that the company has been diligently tracking the requirements under Sarbanes-Oxley, however, and would not allow its earlier ignorance to go uncorrected. Now, the data collection process for SEC-mandated disclosure is detailed and rigorous. Matters from formerly ignored facilities are captured and, where appropriate, disclosed, either as pending enforcement proceedings or as part of management's discussion and analysis of trends—for example, in capital expenditures for pollution control equipment—that will clearly have an impact on the company's financial future. With astonishing speed, driven by the prospect of Sarbanes-Oxley sanctions, the company's mandatory environmental reporting becomes far more robust and detail-oriented. For what is likely the first time in the company's reporting history, there will be a complete matrix of data in the company's mandatory quarterly filings against which to compare the wishes, aspirations, and performance described in the voluntary climate report. A comparison must be able to withstand judicial scrutiny.

V. Corporate Image Advertising and Associated FTC Issues

A. Regulation of Commercial Speech

Outside the realm of public disclosure and voluntary reporting, many companies that see themselves at risk in the theater of public opinion due to their possible contribution to climate change have used media campaigns to reshape their corporate image and mount a preemptive defense against their critics. Such campaigns are often far more free-wheeling than communications subject to the constraints of SEC regulation. ExxonMobil's previously discussed public relations efforts, General Electric's Ecoimagination campaign, and British Petroleum's Beyond Petroleum advertisements are all examples of the trend of companies in traditionally environmentally unfriendly industries using mainstream media to emphasize a move toward "greening" their businesses and products.[188] Many of these campaigns are likely to fall under the umbrella of the vaguely defined concept of corporate speech, which is afforded less protection under the First Amendment

than noncommercial speech[189] and is subject to regulation by the Federal Trade Commission (FTC). Such oversight may create liabilities, particularly as the rhetoric of climate change escalates.

Although much of the long-running debate and jurisprudence on "commercial speech" is largely outside the scope of this chapter, certain concepts are worth highlighting in order to frame the issue in the climate change arena. For example, the U.S. Supreme Court has stated that "untruthful speech, commercial or otherwise, has never been protected for its own sake,"[190] and the Court has affirmed a state's right to regulate not only commercial speech that is false, but also that which is "deceptive or misleading."[191] Several characteristics of commercial speech have long been seen to differentiate it from other forms of speech and justify greater regulation, including the fact that commercial speech is "more easily verifiable by its disseminator"; it is intrinsically related to profit motives and thus less likely to be "chilled" by greater regulation and linked to the state's interest in regulating commercial transactions to prevent harm.[192]

Because commercial speech is afforded diminished protection under the First Amendment, the definition of commercial speech has increased importance.[193] In *Bolger v. Youngs Drug Product Corp.*, the court found that the parties' concession that informational pamphlets were "advertisements," that they contained references to a specific product, and that the speaker had an economic motivation did not, individually, necessitate a finding that there was commercial speech. The court held, however, that, taken together, these elements strongly supported a conclusion that the pamphlets were commercial speech. The court was also careful to note that while these elements together were sufficient, none is necessary.[194] In addition, speech may still be commercial if it contains "discussion of important public issues" or only refers to a product generically.[195]

Corporate campaigns in the arena of climate change may present new and difficult commercial speech issues. Such campaigns may include statements that are not advertisements on their face or in any traditional sense, but are nevertheless linked to a commercial speaker and are intended to have an effect, however indirectly, on the success of a product or the company itself. In a highly publicized case in 2003, for example, Nike, Inc. sought to overturn an appellate court ruling characterizing the company's efforts to defend allegations regarding its labor practices as commercial speech.[196] The court's ruling effectively subjected Nike's speech, including press releases, letters to newspapers, and newspaper advertisements publicizing a third-party report (prepared under a contract with Nike) on working conditions at Nike facilities, to regulation under California's False Advertising Law.[197]

To the extent they are characterized as commercial speech, modern climate change media campaigns and related efforts by a company to combat negative publicity on global warming may be subject to heightened scrutiny and regulation. This could shape the rhetoric of the debate on climate change. Many corporate contributions to the debate may be clearly recognizable as commercial speech, as they are provided within advertisements for products. For example, Ford's newspaper and television advertisements for its hybrid vehicles[198] and Entergy Nuclear Northeast's print and radio advertisements providing information about Indian Point Energy Center[199] both include statements regarding GHGs. Such traditional advertisements fall under the jurisdiction of the FTC, regardless of political statements they may contain. Increasingly sophisticated messages also include subtler and more far-reaching efforts to influence public opinion, often dealing with a company's corporate image rather than a specific product, or coming from a third party that is only tangentially linked with the company. For example, ExxonMobil recently published print advertisements touting the investments it has made in energy research and emissions-reducing technology.[200]

Corporate campaigns in the arena of climate change may present new and difficult considerations pertaining to the question of commercial speech.

The consequence of regulation of climate change campaigns as commercial speech could certainly constrain commercial interests—for example, an energy company interested in influencing public opinion about coal, or a car company attempting to demonstrate the necessity for its new hybrid. In his dissent in the *Nike* case, arguing that *cert* should have been granted by the U.S. Supreme Court, Justice Breyer addressed the possible negative consequences of leaving the debate unresolved, remarking that "uncertainty about how a court will view these, or other, statements, can easily chill a speaker's efforts to engage in public debate—particularly where a 'false advertising' law, like California's law, imposes liability based upon negligence or without fault."[201] This "chilling effect" could extend to voluntary reporting and corporate social responsibility in general, as companies may be fearful of litigation for publicizing their efforts, providing a reason for companies to remain silent in the face of criticism or attempt to hide poor environmental performance.[202]

For most large companies, the negative financial consequences of facing FTC prosecution are not material in and of themselves, and in fact are minimal compared with the damaging effects on the company's overall public image.[203] Nonetheless, in developing its own framework for defining commercial and noncommercial speech, the FTC has rendered decisions affecting a wide range of important debates on issues of public concern, arguably similar in scope to climate change.[204]

In the arena of climate change, organizations such as the Union of Concerned Scientists encourage consumers to file complaints against allegedly false and misleading ads from car and energy companies.[205] In 1999, for example, Public Citizen filed a petition with the FTC claiming that ads created by the Nuclear Energy Institute, stating that "trees aren't the only plants that are good for the atmosphere" and nuclear plants "don't pollute the air," were false and misleading.[206] The FTC issued a non-binding statement acknowledging that the advertisements were misleading, but ruling that they constituted political and not commercial speech and were therefore outside the FTC's reach.[207] In light of the significant increase over the past decade in the intensity of the debate over climate change, including corporate campaigns aimed at GHG emissions, however, the debate over commercial speech in this arena clearly will continue to evolve.

Endnotes

1. MARK A. STACH, DISCLOSING ENVIRONMENTAL LIABILITIES UNDER SECURITIES LAW 1-7 (1997) [hereinafter STACH].
2. STACH, *supra* note 1, at 1-7.
3. *See* STACH, *supra* note 1, at 1-1 and 1-7.
4. *See* Basic Inc. v. Levinson, 485 U.S. 224, 230 (1998).
5. *Basic*, 485 U.S. at 230, *quoting* H.R. REP. No. 1383, 73rd Cong. Sess., 11 (1934); *see* STACH, *supra* note 1, at 1-7.
6. *Levinson*, 485 U.S. at 230 (citations omitted).
7. *See* STACH, *supra* note 1, at 1-7.
8. STACH, *supra* note 1, at 1-7.
9. *Id.*
10. *Id.* at 1-7 to 1-8, *citing* 17 C.F.R. §§ 240.13a-13 and 240.15d-13 (concerning Form 10-K).

11. *Id.* at 1-8, *citing* 17 C.F.R. §§ 240.13a-1 and 240.15d-1 (concerning Form 10-K).
12. *Id.* at 1-8, *citing, e.g.,* Form S-3 under the 1933 Act.
13. *See, e.g.,* Ray Pospisil, *Investors press SEC on climate risk disclosure*, ENVTL. FINANCE, July-Aug. 2006, at 8.
14. *See Global Framework for Climate Risk Disclosure, A statement of investor expectations for comprehensive corporate disclosure*, October 2006, *available at* http://www.ceres.org/pub/docs/framework.pdf. (The framework focuses on the following key elements of climate disclosure: measurement of total GHG emissions, strategic analysis of climate risk management, assessment of physical risks of climate change, and analysis of emerging GHG regulations.)
15. TSC Indus. Inc. v. Northway, Inc., 426 U.S. 438, 448 (1976).
16. 17 C.F.R. § 240.12b-2 (2005) (Exchange Act); *see also* 17 C.F.R. § 230.405 (2005) (Securities Act); Securities & Exchange Commission, *Materiality*, SEC Staff Accounting Bulletin Release No. 99 (Aug. 12, 1999) [hereinafter SAB 99] (emphasizing that materiality should be measured by a "reasonable investor" standard; i.e., without reference to numerical rules of thumb).
17. Financial Accounting Standards Board, *Statement of Financial Accounting Concepts No. 2, Qualitative Characteristics of Accounting Information* (May 1980).
18. *See* PETER LEHNER, ENVIRONMENTAL AND SOCIAL DISCLOSURE AND THE SECURITIES AND EXCHANGE COMMISSION: MEETING THE INFORMATION NEEDS OF TODAY'S INVESTORS, July 10, 2003, *available at* http://www.corporatesunshine.org/sympsumm.pdf.
19. *See* SAB No. 99, 64 Fed. Reg. 45,150, 45,151:

The staff is aware that certain registrants, over time, have developed quantitative thresholds as "rules of thumb" to assist in the preparation of their financial statements, and that auditors also have used these thresholds in their evaluation of whether items might be considered material to users of a registrant's financial statements. One rule of thumb in particular suggests that the misstatement or omission of an item that falls under a 5% threshold is not material in the absence of particularly egregious circumstances, such as self-dealing or misappropriation by senior management. The staff reminds registrants and the auditors of their financial statements that exclusive reliance on this or any percentage or numerical threshold has no basis in the accounting literature or the law. The use of a percentage as a numerical threshold, such as 5%, may provide the basis for a preliminary assumption that—without considering all relevant circumstances—a deviation of less than the specified percentage with respect to a particular item on the registrant's financial statements is unlikely to be material. The staff has no objection to such a "rule of thumb" as an initial step in assessing materiality. But quantifying, in percentage terms, the magnitude of a misstatement is only the beginning of an analysis of materiality; it cannot appropriately be used as a substitute for a full analysis of all relevant considerations. Materiality concerns the significance of an item to users of a registrant's financial statements. A matter is "material" if there is a substantial likelihood that a reasonable person would consider it important.

20. 15 C.F.R. § 210.1-01(a) (2005); STACH, *supra* note 1, at 7-2.

21. STACH, *supra* note 1, at 7-2.

22. See General Revision to Regulation S-X, Release No. AS-280 (Sept. 2, 1980) [Accounting Transfer Release Binder]; Fed. Sec. L. Rep. ¶ 72, 302 (eliminating rules duplicative with GAAP); STACH, *supra* note 1 at 7-2.

23. Financial Accounting Standards Board, *Statement of Financial Accounting Standards No. 5, Accounting for Loss Contingencies* (March 1975) [hereinafter FASB No. 5].

24. FASB No. 5, § 8.

25. FASB No. 5, § 10. *See also* Jonathan S. Klavens, *Environmental Disclosure Under SEC and Accounting Requirements: Basic Requirements, Pitfalls, and Practical Tips, available at* http://www.abanet.org/environ/committees/counsel/newsletter/aug00/kla.html.

26. FASB No. 5, § 10.

27. SEC Staff Accounting Bulletin Release No. 92, 58 Fed. Reg. 32,843, 32,843 (June 14, 1993) [hereinafter SAB 92]; Richard Y. Roberts, SEC Commissioner, *SAB 92 and the SEC's Environmental Liability Disclosure Regulatory Approach*, address delivered at the University of Maryland School of Law, at 3 (April 8, 1994) [hereinafter Roberts].

28. Roberts, *supra* note 27, at 3.

29. SAB 92, *supra* note 27, at 32,843, referring to FASB No. 5; Richard M. Schwartz, Donna Mussio & Valerie Jacob, *Environmental Due Diligence for Securities Offerings*, 1489 PLI/Corp. 91 at 4 (May 2005) [hereinafter Schwartz, Mussio & Jacob].

30. SAB 92, *supra* note 27, at 32,844; Roberts, *supra* note 25, at 4; Schwartz, Mussio & Jacob, *supra* note 29, at 4.

31. Roberts, *supra* note 27, at 5.

32. SAB 92, *supra* note 27, at 32,844.

33. *Id.*

34. *Id.*

35. SAB 92, *supra* note 27, at 32,845; *see* Roberts, *supra* note 27, at 5-6. For example, in the remedial context, "[w]hile the range of costs associated with various

alternatives may be broad, the minimum clean-up cost is unlikely to be zero." SAB 92, *supra* note 27, at 32,844.

36. *See* FASB 5 at 5; Roberts, *supra* note 27, at 6.

37. Roberts, *supra* note 27, at 6. In addition to avoiding boilerplate, SEC has cautioned against leaving the reader without a clear understanding of the contingency, stating "some disclosures have so much cautionary qualifying language that they are often ambiguous. For example, a common confusing disclosure states that the ultimate amount of the liability cannot be determined, but that this amount is not expected to be material." Roberts, *supra* note 27, at 7.

38. SAB 92, *supra* note 27, at 32,845.

39. *Id.*

40. *Standards Board to Consider Project to Write Guidance on Emissions Trading,* BNA Reporter, No. 168, Aug. 30, 2006, http://www.fasb.org/project/emissions_allowances.shtml.

41. *See, e.g., Request for Rulemaking for Clarification of Material Disclosures With Respect to Financially Significant Environmental Liabilities and Compliance With Existing Material Financial Disclosure,* The Rose Foundation, revised pet., SEC File No. 4-463 (Sept. 20, 2002).

42. 17 C.F.R. § 229.101 (2005).

43. *See* Securities Act Release No. 5569, Exchange Act Release No. 11,236, 40 Fed. Reg. 7013 (Feb. 18, 1975); *see also* SAB 92, *supra* note 27, at 32,843.

44. *See* 17 C.F.R. § 229.101 (2005).

45. *See* 17 C.F.R. § 229.101 (2005).

46. 1973 WL 11973 (S.E.C. No Action Letter) (interpreting precursor to Item 101(c)(xii)).

47. *See In re* U.S. Steel Corp., Exch. Act Release No. 16,223 [1979-1980 Transfer Binder]; Fed. Sec. L. Rep. (CCH) ¶ 82,319, at 82,383 (Sept. 27, 1979) (interpreting precursor to Item 101(c)(xii)); Environmental Disclosure, Secs. Act Release No. 6130, Exch. Act Release No. 16,224 (Sept. 27, 1979).

48. U.S. Steel, Exch. Act Release No. 16,223 at 82,383.

49. For example, a decision in favor of plaintiffs in *Mass v. EPA* could result in the regulation of carbon dioxide as a pollutant under the Clean Air Act. *See* Massachusetts et al. v. Envtl. Protection Agency, 415 F.3d 50 (D.C. Cir. 2005), *cert. granted*, No. 05-1120 (U.S. June 26, 2006).

50. *See* U.S. Steel, Exch. Act Release No. 16,223 at 82,383.

51. California Global Warming Solutions Act, discussed in detail in Chapter 11.

52. For example, the European Commission reported in May 2006 that too many carbon permits had been sold to EU Members under the emissions trading scheme; e.g., the Commission reported a 2.5% surplus, with 21 states granting 44 million metric tons more carbon dioxide permits than needed, resulting in a drop in the price of carbon credits traded in Europe by nearly 60% over a two-week period. *See Concerns Over EU Carbon Trading,* BBC NEWS, May 15, 2006, *available at* http://news.bbc.co.uk/1/hi/business/4771871.stm.

53. *See* Sappi LTD Annual Report, Form 20-F, for the Fiscal Year Ended October 2, 2005, at 38 and Sappi LTD Annual Report, Form 20-F, for the Fiscal Year Ended October 1, 2006, at 35:

The countries within which we operate in Europe are all signatories of the Kyoto Protocol and we have developed a GHG strategy in line with this protocol. Our European mills have been set CO_2 emission limits of the allocation period 2005 to 2007. Based upon in-depth analysis of our mill production by a Sappi Fine Paper Europe task force, it is unlikely that Sappi will exceed their CO_2 emission limits. Consequently, in July 2005 Sappi Fine Paper Europe sold 90,000 surplus CO_2 credits to the value of $2.5 million (euro 2.0 million) on the European Climate Exchange.

54. The fact that the new market has proven to be volatile—the price of CO_2 permits fell 30% in a single day after some EU countries announced that they were emitting less CO_2 than anticipated, briefly raising the fear of systemwide overallocation of credits in the EU-ETS—seems likely to intensify the importance of such analyses. *See* Kevin Morrison, *Lower Pollution in EU Sees CO_2 Permits Fall 30%*, FINANCIAL TIMES, April 27, 2006, at 15, col. 2.

55. While the United States is not a participant in the Kyoto Protocol, there is a growing desire for a marketplace for GHG emissions trading in the U.S. The Chicago Climate Exchange (CCX) is a voluntary, GHG emissions trading scheme, created in 2003, in which account holders participate in an integrated carbon market with a linked reduction and trading system. Members include such diverse entities as Ford, IBM, Baxter Healthcare International, Bayer, Manitoba Hydro, universities, NGOs, several law firms, and the state of New Mexico. As of May 2, 2006, cumulative trading volume since December 2003 was 6.5 million metric tons of CO_2. *See* The Chicago Climate Exchange Web site, *available at* http://www.chicagoclimatex.com/, and Press Release, *Chicago Climate Exchange Announces Third Consecutive Record Trading Month* (Chicago, May 2, 2006), *available at* http://www.chicagoclimatex.com/news/press/release_20060501_ CCXAprilRecord.pdf.

56. 42 U.S.C. §§ 7401 et seq. (1970).

57. *See* JOHN-MARK STERBSVAAG ET AL., CLEAN AIR ACT 1990 AMENDMENTS: LAW AND PRACTICE 1-1, 1-4 (1991); MICHAEL B. GERRARD, ENVIRONMENTAL LAW PRACTICE GUIDE: STATE AND FEDERAL LAW, 17-1, 17.12[1][a] and 17.12[1][b] (LexisNexis 1992); Massachusetts v. U.S. Envtl. Prot. Agency, 415 F.3d 66 (D.C. Cir. 2005), *cert. granted*, 2006 U.S. LEXIS 4910 (June 26, 2006).

Most recently, nine states filed litigation on March 29, 2005, over the new mercury emission cap and trade rules promulgated under Section 112 of the CAA. *See* New Jersey v. U.S. Envtl. Prot. Agency, Civ. No. 05-1097 (D.C. Cir. 2005).

58. *See* AEP, *An Assessment of AEP's Actions to Mitigate the Economic Impacts of Emissions Policies*, Aug. 31, 2004, *available at* http://www.aep.com/environmental/reports/shareholder report/docs/ReportOnly.pdf.

59. 17 C.F.R. § 229.103 (2005).

60. 17 C.F.R. § 229.103 (Instruction No. 5) (2005).

61. *See* Envtl. Protection Agency, *Guidance on Distributing the Notice of SEC Registrants' Duty to Disclose Environmental Legal Proceedings in EPA Enforcement Actions*, Presentation to the ABA Conference on Environmental Law (Mar. 2001).

62. 17 C.F.R. § 229.103 (Instruction No. 5) (2005).

63. *Id.*

64. For example, the SEC has explicitly stated that cleanup costs under CERCLA are not "sanctions" for the purposes of Instruction 5(C) to Item 103. Thomas A. Cole, SEC No-Action Letter (Jan. 17, 1989) [1989 Transfer Binder], Fed. Sec. L. Rep. (CCH) para. 78,962, at 78,815 ("while there are many ways a PRP may become subject to potential monetary sanctions, including triggering the stipulated penalty clause in a remedial agreement, the costs entered into the normal course of negotiation with the EPA will not be recorded as "sanctions" within the meaning of Instruction 5(C)")

[hereinafter Cole No-Action Letter]; STACH, *supra* note 1, at 3-38. A broader reading of the term sanctions could result in an overwhelming amount of disclosure in the Superfund context, and would thus thwart the purpose of the $100,000 threshold to clarify disclosure of a registrant's environmental proceedings including the government. STACH, *supra* note 1, at 3-38, *citing* Cole No-Action Letter, *supra*, at 78,814. At the same time, "the SEC considers that the disclosure of fines by government authorities may be of particular importance in assessing a Registrant's environmental compliance problems [and that] . . . fines may be indicative of conduct that is illegal or against public policy." STACH, *supra* note 1, at 3-38, n.153, *citing* the Proposed Amendments to Reg. SK Item 5, Securities Act Release No. 17, 762, 22 S.E.C. Docket 946 at 951 (May 4, 1981).

65.   *See* Connecticut v. Am. Elec. Power Co., 406 F. Supp. 265 (S.D.N.Y. 2005), *appeal pending.*

66.   *Connecticut,* 406 F. Supp. 265.

67.   *Id.*

68.   *See* Sholnn Freeman, *California Sues 6 Automakers Over Global Warming,* N.Y. TIMES, Sept. 21, 2006, at C2.

69.   *See* Massachusetts v. Envtl. Protection Agency, 415 F.3d 50 (D.C. Cir. 2005), *cert. granted,* No. 05-1120 (U.S. June 26, 2006). Plaintiffs originally filed suit in the U.S. Court of Appeals for the D.C. Circuit after the EPA denied their petition for the regulation of carbon dioxide.

70.   Mass. v. EPA, 415 F.3d 50.

71.   Central Valley Chrysler-Jeep Inc. v. Witherspoon, No. CV-F-04-6663 (E.D. Cal 2005).

72.   *Witherspoon,* No. CV-F-04-6663.

73.   *See* Chapter 5, ¶ 74. 40 C.F.R. §§ 51 & 52 (2005).

75.   *Ohio Edison Signs Billion-Dollar Clean Air Settlement,* ENV'T NEWS SERV., March 18, 2005, *available at* http://www.ens-newswire.com/ens/mar2005/2005-03-18-05.asp.

76.   Ohio Edison Annual Report, Form 10-K, for the Fiscal Year Ended December 31, 2005, at 14.

77.   United States v. Ohio Edison, Civ. A. No. 99-1181 (S.D. Ohio 1999).

78.   *Ohio Edison Signs Billion-Dollar Clean Air Settlement, supra* note 75.

79.   Ohio Edison Annual Report, *supra* note 76.

80.   *See Air Issues: Report to Stakeholders,* Cinergy Corp. (2004), at 23 ("4P is typically thought of as imposed limits on SO_2, NO_x, mercury and CO_2. 3P is the same except it does not have CO_2.") [hereinafter Cinergy Report].

81.   *See* Cinergy Report, *supra* note 80, at 23.

82.   *See id.*

83.   *See id.* at 12, 23.

84.   *See id.* at 2, 23.

85.   A discussion of certain applicable accounting rules pertinent to financial statement disclosure can be found in the subsequent section of this chapter.

86.   17 C.F.R. § 229.303 (2005).

87.   Richard Y. Roberts, *Update on Environmental Disclosure,* Address at the Colorado Bar Ass'n (Sept. 28, 1991).

88.   Concept Release on Management's Discussion and Analysis of Financial Condition and Operations, Exch. Act Release No. 6211, 52 Fed. Reg. 13,715, 13,717 (Apr.

26, 1987).

89. Sec. Act Release No. 6835, 54 Fed. Reg. 22,427, 22,430 (May 4, 1989).

90. *Id.*

91. *See* Management Discussion and Analysis of Financial Condition and Results of Operations: Certain Investment Company Disclosures, Sec. Act Release No. 6835, 54 Fed. Reg. 22,427, at 22,430 (May 24, 1989).

92. *See id.* The SEC has expressly rejected as "inapposite to Item 303 disclosure" the probability/magnitude balancing test for disclosure of contingent events set forth by the Supreme Court in *Basic v. Levinson. See* Sec. Act Release No. 6835, 54 Fed. Reg. 22,427, at 22,430 n.27.

93. 17 C.F.R. § 229.303(a)(1) (2005).

94. Sec. Act Release No. 6711, Fed. Sec. L. Rep. (CCH) ¶ 84,118, at 88,624 (Apr. 20, 1987).

95. 17 C.F.R. § 229.303 (2005) (Instruction 2). *See also* Sec. Act Release No. 6835, 54 Fed. Reg. 22,427, at 22,430 (stating that MD&A requires quantification of potential liability "to the extent reasonably practicable").

96. *See* Sec. Act Release No. 6231, 20 S.E.C. Docket 1059, 1072 (Sept. 2, 1980).

97. 17 C.F.R. § 229.303(a) (2005).

98. *In re* Occidental Petroleum, 57 S.E.C. Docket 330, 571 (July 2, 1980) (discussing precursor to Item 303).

99. Sec. Act Release No. 6835, 54 Fed. Reg. 22,427, 22,430 (May 24, 1989).

100. *See* James Glanz, *The Nation: Blue Sky; Sure, It's Rocket Science, but Who Needs Scientists?*, N.Y. TIMES, June 17, 2001, at D1 (quoting various administration sources as "dismissive" of climate change science).

101. For example, both the 1999 and 2000 10-K filings for Cummins, Inc., a major manufacturer of heavy-duty diesel engines, included detailed disclosure on the impact on the company products by federal and state regulations under the CAA, but were silent on climate change issues. *See* Cummins, Inc. Annual Reports, Form 10-K, for the Fiscal Year Ended December 31, 1999, at 9-11 and the Fiscal Year Ended December 31, 2000, at 9-11.

102. The Intergovernmental Panel on Climate Change ("IPCC"), established in 1988 by the United Nations and World Meteorological Organization to assess climate change science, has released three reports, the most recent in 2001. Intergovernmental Panel on Climate Change, *Summary for Policymakers to Climate Change 2001: Synthesis Report of the IPCC Third Assessment Report*, Oct. 1, 2001, *available at* http:// www.climnet.org/resources/TAR%20synthesis%20report.pdf. (concluding that "[t]here is new and stronger evidence that most of the warming observed over the last 50 years is attributable to human activities."). The National Academy of Sciences also concluded that human activity continues to be a contributing factor to climate change. *See* National Research Council, CLIMATE CHANGE SCIENCE: AN ANALYSIS OF SOME KEY QUESTIONS (2001), *available at* http://darwin.nap.edu books/03090757/html.

103. For example, in 2004, the California state legislature passed a law requiring the California Air Resources Board ("CARB") to develop a plan to regulate and reduce the emission of GHGs from vehicles starting in 2009. The CARB regulations aim to cut exhaust emissions in cars and light trucks by 25% and in larger trucks and SUVs by 18%. Under this plan automakers would be required to use better air conditioners, more efficient transmissions and smaller engines. Automobile manufacturers and distributors are challenging these rules, principally on preemption grounds. *See* Central Valley Chrysler-Jeep, Inc. v. Witherspoon, Civ. No. F-04-6663 (E.D. Cal. 2004). *See also* Chapter 5, *infra* (discussing *Witherspoon*). In addition, under the Regional Greenhouse Gas Initiative ("RGGI") in the Northeast, Connecticut, Delaware, Maine, New Hampshire, New Jersey, New York and Vermont (with the District of Columbia, Mas-

sachusetts, Pennsylvania, Rhode Island, the Eastern Canadian Provinces and New Brunswick as observers in the process) agreed to reduce carbon dioxide emissions by developing regional strategies for controlling emissions and a multistate cap-and-trade program with a market-based emissions trading system as the cornerstone. *See* RGGI Web site, *available at* http://www.rggi.org/states.htm. Under RGGI, carbon dioxide emission levels from power plants in the region would be capped at current levels starting in 2009 and continuing through 2015, after which participating member states would reduce emissions by 10% by 2019. Similarly, in August 2006, the California legislature passed the California Global Warming Solutions Act, aimed at reducing all GHG emissions from all sources to 1990 levels by 2020. *See* Michael Gerrard, *Business Opportunities in Climate Change Mitigation*, N.Y.L.J., Sept. 9, 2006, at 3. In September, Arizona Governor Janet Napolitano signed an executive order calling a state reduction of carbon dioxide emissions, methane and other GHGs to year 2000 levels by 2020 and to 50% below that level by 2040. William H. Carlile, *Arizona to Seek 50 Percent Cut in Emissions by 2040 Under Order Signed By Governor*, BNA Reporter, No. 176, Sept. 12, 2006 at A-5.

104. *See* Paul Anderson's remarks at the *Charlotte Business Journal*'s 10th Annual Power Breakfast (April 7, 2005), *available at* http://www.duke-energy.com/news/mediainfo/viewpoint/2005/responsibility.pdf.

105. This position is represented by companies such as ExxonMobil and ChevronTexaco, both of which filed 10-K reports in 2004 that made no mention of climate change. ExxonMobil Annual Report Form 10-K for the Fiscal Year ended December 31, 2003; Chevron Texaco Annual Report Form 10-K for the Fiscal Year ended December 31, 2003. At the other end of the disclosure spectrum, SunCor, a Canadian-based company with substantial gas and reserves, calculated for its 2004 Tenth Annual Progress Report on Climate Change that Canada's ratification of the Kyoto Protocol would cost between $0.20 and $0.27 per barrel of oil in 2010. Suncor Energy, Inc., *Tenth Annual Progress Report on Climate Change* (December 2004), *available at* www.cdproject.net/download.asp?file=CDP3_suncor_10th_APReport_Climate_Change_2004_3412.pdf. Similar is the SEC's refusal to allow ExxonMobil to exclude shareholder proposals dealing with global warming. *See* Securities & Exchange Commission, No-Action Letter (Mar. 15, 2005) (dealing with the company's views on available global warming science); Securities & Exchange Commission, No-Action Letter (Mar. 23, 2005) (dealing with the company's plans for meeting GHG emission reduction targets in Kyoto-signatory countries). In both instances, the SEC staff said that it was unable to concur that exclusion was proper under Securities Exchange Act Rule 14a-8(i)(7) as dealing with a matter of ordinary business operations. In making its determination, the SEC staff also implicitly rejected the adequacy of the company's 2004 voluntary report on energy trends, GHG emissions and alternative energy.

106. SNL Financial, Ten Largest Publicly Traded Insurance Companies, Ranked by Market Value as of March 31, 2006, *available at* http://www.snl.com/insurance/vitals/top_10.asp.

107. *See* The St. Paul Travelers Companies, Inc. Annual Report, Form 10-K, for the Fiscal Year Ended December 31, 2005, at 37 ("Over the last several years, changing

climatic conditions have added to the unpredictability and frequency of natural disasters in certain parts of the world and created additional uncertainty as to future trends and exposures. It is possible that both the frequency and severity of natural and man-made catastrophic events will increase. In particular, we expect that the trend of increased severity and frequency of storms experienced in 2005 and 2004 will continue into 2006.").

108. *See* Harford Financial Services Group Inc. Annual Report, Form 10-K, for the Fiscal Year Ended December 31, 2005, at 70.

109. *See, e.g.,* Allstate Corp. Annual Report, Form 10-K, for the Fiscal Year Ended December 31, 2005; American International Group, Inc. Annual Report, Form 10-K, for the Fiscal Year Ended December 31, 2005; Berkshire Hathaway Inc. Annual Report, Form 10-K, for the Fiscal Year Ended December 31, 2005; Harford Financial Services Group Inc. Annual Report, Form 10-K, for the Fiscal Year Ended December 31, 2005; MetLife Inc. Annual Report, Form 10-K, for the Fiscal Year Ended December 31, 2005; Prudential Financial Inc. Annual Report, Form 10-K, for the Fiscal Year Ended December 31, 2005; The St. Paul Travelers Companies, Inc. Annual Report, Form 10-K, for the Fiscal Year Ended December 31, 2005; Wellpoint Inc. Annual Report, Form 10-K, for the Fiscal Year Ended December 31, 2005.

110. *See* Harford Financial Services Group Inc. Annual Report, Form 10-K, for the Fiscal Year Ended December 31, 2005, at 70; Allstate Corp. Annual Report, Form 10-K, for the Fiscal Year Ended December 31, 2005, at 110-11. In addition, in May 2006, AIG released a statement on its climate change policy and programs. *See* Alice LeBlanc, *Moving on climate change*, ENVTL. FINANCE, July-Aug. 2006, at 34.

111. *See Researchers' Models Suggest Stronger Link between Greehouse Emissions, Hurricanes*, BNA Reporter, No. 176, Sept. 12, 2006.

112. Pub. L. 107-204, 116 Stat. 745.

113. *See* 17 C.F.R. §§ 232, 240, 249 et seq. (2005).

114. *See id.*

115. *See* Pub. L. 107-204, 116 Stat. 745 § 302.

116. *See id.*

117. *See* Pub. L. 107-204, 116 Stat. 745 § 906.

118. *See* 17 C.F.R. §§ 240.13b2-1, 240.13b2-2 (2005).

119. *See id.*

120. *See id.* Other provisions of Sarbanes-Oxley that may be implicated in the broad context of GHG risk analysis include standards of conduct governing attorneys appearing and practicing before the SEC. *See* 17 C.F.R. § 205 (2005). This includes environmental attorneys preparing analyses of climate change risks for inclusion in disclosure narrative, financial statements or management presentations to substantiate Sarbanes-Oxley certifications.

121. Meaningful disclosure is, of course, a product of each company's individual situation, notwithstanding the substantial pressure that has been exerted recently on entire industries, such as the utility sector, petroleum refiners and automobile makers, to recognize and make disclosures about climate change issues.

122. It has also been argued that current SEC disclosure mechanisms are outdated and ill-suited to allow a company to communicate effectively with its investors on climate change issues. *See* CERES, *Electronic Power, Investors, and Climate Change: A Call to Action*, Sept. 2003, *available at* http://www.ceres.org. In part to gather data on this point (and the overall business implications of climate change) the Carbon Disclosure Project ("CDP"), a growing collaboration of 211 institutional investors (as of February 2006) representing more than $31 trillion in assets was launched in December 2000 and sends, each year, a greenhouse gas questionnaire to the FT500 largest com-

panies in the world, seeking disclosure of information on GHG emissions that could be relevant to investors. *See* Carbon Disclosure Project Web site, *available at* http://www.cdproject.net.
123. *See, e.g.,* Robert Repetto & James Henderson, ENVIRONMENTAL EXPOSURES IN THE U.S. ELECTRIC UTILITY INDUSTRY (2003) (arguing that different companies within the electric power sector are exposed in markedly differing degrees to future GHG legislation and related, anticipated emission restriction programs).
124. *See* discussion at Section II(A)(1), *infra*.
125. *See* Sarbanes-Oxley Act of 2002 § 404.
126. There is a strong and rapidly growing institutional audience for disclosure on climate change data, particularly among institutional investors representing public funds, and/or investors for whom social good is a valued metric and those with long-term investment horizons. For example, on February 14, 2005, the California State Public Employees Pension fund ("CalPers")—which has been active in linking its investment strategy to social responsibility and issues of environmental transparency — announced a plan to increase corporate disclosure of environmental liabilities, data and impacts, as well as improving overall transparency for shareholders. The specifics of the plan include having the companies sign on to the Carbon Disclosure Project; and supporting shareholder proposals in the auto industry, specifically for Ford and General Motors. As discussed in this chapter, Ford has reported voluntarily to shareholders on climate change issues. Ford Motor Co., *Ford Report on the Business Impact of Climate Change* (2005), *available at* http://www.ford.com/en/company/about/sustainability/default.htm. The CalPers plan also seeks to create a reporting project for the utilities industry that will standardize greenhouse gas disclosure and recognize particular companies demonstrat-

ing best practices in environmental data transparency. The office of the State Treasurer, formerly Philip Angelides, who was the unsuccessful Democratic candidate for governor in 2006, is a designated ex officio member of the Board of Administration. His active role in the governance of CalPers, through the board's overseeing of investments of funds assets and his involvement in both the Finance and Investment Committees, is emblematic of the fact that climate change issues are increasingly situated at the confluence of money, public policy and politics. Similarly, the office of the Connecticut State Treasurer, the principal fiduciary for six pension funds and eight trust funds, and the New York City Comptroller's Office, which manages over $70 billion in pension fund assets, have been increasingly active in the climate change disclosure arena. Finally, in the UK, the Universities Superannuation Scheme, a pension fund with over $30 billion in assets, has actively convened stakeholder disclosure on climate change. *See* MARK MANSLEY & ANDREW DLUGOLECKI, CLIMATE CHANGE—A RISK MANAGEMENT CHALLENGE FOR INSTITUTIONAL INVESTORS (Universities Superannuation Scheme, Ltd. 2001), *available at* http://ww.usshq.co.uk/INVMENT/climch/framclim.htm.
127. Hexcel Corporation Annual Report, Form 10-K, for the Fiscal Year Ended December 31, 2005, at 39.
128. Methanex Corporation Annual Report, Form F-10, filed with the SEC on August 16, 1993, at 41.
129. *Id.* at 42.

130. *Id.*

131. Ballard Power Systems Inc. Annual Report, Form 40-F, filed with the SEC on March 31, 2006, at 1.

132. *Id.* at 55.

133. *But see Sustainability Reporting Guidelines*, Global Reporting Initiative (2002), *available at* https//www.globalreporting.org/guidelines/2002.asp. As of June 29, 2006, 299 companies from 39 different countries have agreed to report using the GRI principles. *See* GRI Web site, *available at* http://www.globalreporting.org/governance/OS/OSlist.asp.

134. *See* the Global Reporting Initiative Web site, http://www.globalreporting.org/about/06whatWeDo.asp. *See also* the list of companies that have agreed to participate in the initiative, *available at* http://www.globalreporting.org/getInvolved/06OS.asp.

135. For example, in response to shareholder requests, companies such as Cinergy, TXU, Ford, AEP, and Southern Co. have all prepared voluntary reports on climate change. Each of these reports are available at the company's Web site. *See* Cinergy Report, *supra* note 80, *available at* http://www.duke-energy.com/environment/history/cinergy/air_issues/; *TXU Activities Regarding Actual and Potential U.S. Air Emissions and Climate Change Policies*, TXU (2004), *available at* http://www.txucorp.com/responsibility/environment/reports/Env_Study100104.pdf; *Ford Report on the Business Impact of Climate Change*, Ford Motor Co. (2005), *available at* http://media.ford.com/downloads/05_climate.pdf; *An Assessment of AEP's Actions to Mitigate the Economic Impacts of Emissions Policies*, AEP (2004), *available at* http://www.aep.com/environmental/reports/shareholderreport/docs/FullReport.pdf; *Southern Company Environmental Assessment Report to Shareholders*, Southern Co. (2005), *available at* http://www.southernco.com/planetpower/pdfs/earsall.pdf.

136. *See, e.g.,* Cinergy Report, *supra* note 80.

137. For example, Cinergy's 2004 report "acknowledged the report's value, and invited the church and Ceres, a coalition working with investors to address climate risk, to join with Cinergy management in defining the scope of the report, reviewing drafts and refining points." *See* Cinergy Report, *supra* note 80, at 4. TXU's 2004 report explains that "NERA Economic Consulting (NERA) conducted the study in collaboration with Marc Goldsmith & Associates LLC (MGA)." *See TXU Activities Regarding Actual and Potential U.S. Air Emissions and Climate Change Policies*, TXU, at iii (2004).

138. *Ford Report on the Business Impact of Climate Change*, Ford Motor Co., at 2 (2005).

139. *Id.*

140. *Id.*

141. Cinergy Report, *supra* note 80, at 2.

142. *Id.* at 9.

143. *Id.* at 16.

144. *Id.* at 21.

145. *See* Securities Exchange Act of 1934, § 14; Cynthia A. Williams, *The Securities and Exchange Commission and Corporate Social Transparency*, 112 HARV. L. REV. 1197, 1207 (1999).

146. *See* 17 C.F.R. § 240.14a-8; STACH, *supra* note 1, at 9-2 to 9-3. In order to have a proposal included in a proxy statement, the proponent must have continuously held at least 2% or $2,000 in market value of the securities entitled to be voted at the meeting for at least one year at the time the proposal is submitted, and the proponent must hold those securities through the date of the meeting. 17 C.F.R. § 240.14a-8.

147. 17 C.F.R. § 240.14a-8(g). Rule 240.14a-8(j) provides the procedures a registrant must follow if it intends to exclude a proposal.

148. 17 C.F.R. § 240.14a-8(i) (emphasis supplied); STACH, *supra* note 1, at 9-4.

149. Social Investment Forum Foundation, a national nonprofit organization of over 500 members from financial planners, banks, mutual fund companies and foundations dedicated to the concept, practice and growth of socially responsible investing, released a report in April analyzing the 2006 proxy season. *Social Investment Forum: 2006 Environmental, Social Shareholder Proxy Resolutions Up From 2005, With Emphasis on Global Warming, Toxics and Political Donations,* SOCIAL INVESTMENT FORUM, April 25, 2006, *available at* http://www.socialinvest.org/2006ShareholderProxy SeasonPreview.htm [hereinafter Social Investment Forum].

150. Dean Scott, *Report Says Environmental Concerns Led to More Shareholder Resolutions,* BNA Daily Envtl. Rep., April 26, 2006, at A:10 [hereinafter Scott].

151. Social Investment Forum, *supra* note 149.

152. *Id.*

153. *Id.; Social Shareholder Resolutions On Pace to Tie 2004 Proxy Season Record, as Push Is Launched to Get Mutual Fund Shareholders to Turn Up Heat On ExxonMobil,* Social Investment Forum, April 7, 2005, *available at* http://www.socialinvest.org/areas/news/040705.htm.

154. Social Investment Forum, *supra* note 146.

155. Bruce Herbert & Larry Dohrs, *2004 Proxy Season Review,* GreenMoneyJournal.com, *available at* http://72.12.207.104/search?q=cache:z3M52ibCs-8J:www.greenmoney journal.com/article.mpl%3Fnewsletterid=30&articleid=327 [hereinafter Herbert & Dohrs].

156. Herbert & Dohrs, *supra* note 155.

157. *Id.*

158. h t t p : / / w w w . c a m p a i g n e x x o n m o b i l . o r g / advisory_board.html.

159. The Web site provides a link to a *Wall Street Journal* article quoted as stating, "The Reputation Institute and Harris also identified companies with the worst reputations in America, including Philip Morris Cos., Exxon and Kmart Corps." There is also a link to a *PR Weekly* article next to the quote, "ExxonMobil's stubborn refusal to acknowledge the fact that burning fossil fuels has a role in global warming is creating a PR backlash against the world's biggest company." *See* Campaign ExxonMobil Web site, *available at* http://www.campaignexxonmobil.org/shareholder/EM_reputation. html.

160. *See* 2002 WL 833567 (S.E.C. No-Action Letter).

161. *See id.*

162. *See id.*

163. *See id.*

164. *See id.*

165. *See id.*

166. Scott, *supra* note 150, at A-10.

167. *Id.*

168. Cinergy Report, *supra* note 80, at 1-17 (2004).

169. *See* Extractive Industries Transparency Initiative Statement of Support, *available at* http://www.bg-group.com/cr/ki_eiti_statement.htm.

170. *See* Extractive Industries Transparency Web site, http://www.eitransparency.org/faqs.htm#What%20is%20the%20Extractive%20Industries%20Transparency%20Initiative%20(EITI)?.

171. *See* Extractive Industries Transparency Web site, http://www.eitransparency.org/countryupdates.htm.; http://www.bg-group.com/cr/ki_eiti_statement.htm.

172. *See* United Paperworkers Int'l Union v. Int'l Paper Co., 985 F.2d 1190 (2d Cir. 1993) [hereinafter *International Paper II*].

173. Although the *International Paper* decision addressed the company's environmental disclosure picture in the context of a proxy statement distribution under section 14(a) of the Securities Exchange Act, nothing in the court's decisions or subsequent case law suggests that the court's rationale is limited to the 14(a) context. Given the parallels between SEC regulations regarding proxy statements (i.e., section 14(a) and Rule 14a-9) and general corporate statements (i.e., section 10(b) and Rule 10b-5), the court's analysis might be brought to bear, and could be dispositive, in challenges under the latter section. *Cf. In re* Keystone Corp. Sec. Litig., 2003 U.S. Dist. LEXIS 20746 (E.D.N.Y. 2003) (citing *International Paper* in the context of a Section 10(b) and Rule 10b-5 complaint).

174. *International Paper II*, 985 F.2d at 1193.

175. Specifically, the company distributed a proxy statement that included the following assertions:

- The company had addressed environmental matters "in an appropriate and timely manner" and was in the "forefront" of industry on matters of environmental protection;
- The Valdez Principles were not applicable to the company's operations, would not provide "any greater protection than now exists" and would probably impose costs on shareholders which would not be justified by the environmental benefits obtained in return;
- The company had already adopted comprehensive Company Principles on environmental matters that articulated the company's "long-standing commitment to the protection of the environment" and which were more stringent and more industry-specific than the Valdez Principles;
- The company had invested hundreds of millions of dollars in pollution-control equipment and technology and regularly conducted internal audits on environmental matters;
- A committee of the Board of Directors had been established to advise the board on the effectiveness of the company's environmental programs and policies; and
- The selection of a single member of the board to represent environmental interests, as called for by the Valdez Principles, would be inappropriate, given the variety of shareholder interests and concerns.

United Paperworkers Int'l Union v. Int'l Paper Co., 801 F. Supp. 1134, 1137 (S.D.N.Y. 1992).

176. *International Paper*, 801 F. Supp. at 1137-38.

177. *Id.*

178. The lower court agreed with International Paper that the Annual Report should be considered part of the mix of information available to the public in evaluating the adequacy of the company's disclosure in its proxy statement. It also held, however, that the various press reports and the company's 10-K Report were not part of that mix. *See International Paper*, 801 F. Supp. at 1141-42.

179. *International Paper, id.* at 1140.

180. *Id.* The source of the court's information was, in part, the company's own 10-K filings, and, in part, affidavits from current and former International Paper employees.

181. *Id.* at 1144.

182. The court of appeals agreed that the 10-K report should not be considered part of the total mix, as neither the proxy statement nor the Annual Report highlighted the 10-K report, nor did either of the two documents suggest that the 10-K report was an additional source of information pertinent to the shareholders' consideration of the Valdez Resolution. Information, even if sent to shareholders, need not be considered to be part of the available mix if it is "buried" in unrelated discussions. *See International Paper II*, at 1199. Similarly, the court held that the press reports should not be included in the total mix, as such reports were "few in number, narrow in focus and remote in time." *International Paper II*, 985 F.2d at 1199.

183. *International Paper II*, 985 F.2d at 1200.

184. *Id.*

185. Section 10(b) prohibits the use of any manipulative or deceptive device or contrivance in connection with the purchase or sale of registered securities. *See* 15 U.S.C. §78j(b). SEC Rule 10b-5, which implements this section of the Securities Exchange Act, specifically makes it unlawful, in connection with the purchase or sale of any security: (a) to employ any device, scheme, or artifice to defraud; (b) to make any untrue statement of a material fact or to omit to state a material fact necessary in order to make the statements made, in the light of the circumstances under which they were made, not misleading; or (c) to engage in any act, practice, or course of business which operates or would operate as a fraud or deceit upon any person.

186. The maximum penalty for many violations of environmental laws is $27,500 per day of violation. *See* 40 C.F.R.§ 19.4.

187. *See* 17 C.F.R. § 229.103.

188. Claudia Deutsch, *It's Getting Crowded on the Environmental Bandwagon*, N.Y. TIMES, Dec. 22, 2005, at C-5, *available at* http://www.nytimes.com/2005/12/22/business/22adco.html.

189. Va. State Bd. of Pharm. v. Va. Citizens Consumer Council, Inc., 425 U.S. 748 (1975).

190. *Va. State Bd. of Pharm.*, 425 U.S. 748, at 764, 771.

191. *Va. State Bd. of Pharm.*, 425 U.S. 748, at 771.

192. *Va. State Bd. of Pharm.*, 425 U.S. at 772.

193. *Compare, e.g.*, New York Times Co. v. Sullivan, 376 U.S. 254 (1964) (rejecting the idea that mere presentation in advertising format makes a statement commercial speech) *with* Ohralik v. Ohio State Bar Assn., 436 U.S. 447, 455-456 (1978) (finding that there was a "common sense distinction between speech proposing a commercial transaction . . . and other varieties of speech.").

194. *Bolger*, 463 U.S. at 66-68.

195. *Bolger*, 463 U.S. at 68, *citing* Central Hudson Gas & Elec. Corp. v. Public Service Comm'n of New York, 447 U.S. 557, 563 (1980).

196. Nike, Inc. v. Marc Kasky, 539 U.S. 654 (2003).

197. Marc Kasky v. Nike, Inc., 27 Cal. 4th 939 (2002). The Supreme Court dismissed the case per curiam, however, stating that its original writ of certiorari had been improvidently granted. A lengthy concurring opinion authored by Justice Stevens suggested some of the reasoning behind the dismissal, but left the central question untouched. *Nike*, 539 U.S. 654.

198. *See* Ford Motor Co. Web site, http://www.ford.com/en/innovation/technology/greenerToday/default.htm.

199. "Only a few energy sources offer zero greenhouse gases and a reliable source of safe and secure power. Indian Point Energy Center is one of them . . . our baseline power is crucial to meeting our region's need for affordable, dependable clean power." *See* Entergy Nuclear Operations, Inc., advertisement, *available at* http://www.safesecurevital.org/pdf/advertisement/vital.pdf.

200. Exxon-Mobil's advertisements include statements such as "Our recent energy-saving initiatives have reduced emissions by an amount equivalent to taking well over a million cars off the road, every year." *See* Exxon-Mobil Web site, http://www.exxonmobil.com/corporate/files/corporate/ad_research.pdf, http://www.exxonmobil.com/corporate/files/corporate/ad_conservation.pdf, and http://www2.exxonmobil.com/corporate/files/corporate/campaign05/energyandenvironment.pdf.

201. *Nike*, 539 U.S. at 680.

202. David Monsma & John Buckley, *Non-Financial Corporate Performance: The Material Edges of Social and Environmental Disclosure*, 11 U. Balt. J. Envtl. L. 151, 197-98 (2004).

203. Generally, if the FTC deems an advertisement or commercial statement to be false or misleading, it will issue a consent order requiring the offending company to cease and desist. If the company chooses to dispute the FTC's decision, it may file a Petition for Review in the U.S. Court of Appeals. *See* Guide to the Federal Trade Commission, *available at* http://www.ftc.gov/bcp/pubs/general/guidetoftc.htm.

204. *See, e.g.*, In the Matter of R. J. Reynolds Tobacco Co., 1989 FTC LEXIS 68 (May 22, 1989) prosecuting a tobacco company for making deceptive statements questioning the link between cigarette smoking and coronary heart disease); FTC v. Nat'l Comm'n on Egg Nutrition, 517 F.2d 485 (7th Cir. 1975), *cert. denied*, 426 U.S. 919 49 L. Ed. 2d 372, 96 S. Ct. 2623 (1976) (issuing a cease and desist order against an egg trade association's public relations campaign that had been designed to counter anti-cholesterol attacks on eggs).

205. *See* Union of Concerned Scientists, *Fiction vs. Fact: The Auto Alliance's Ad Is Deceptive*, *available at* http://www.uscusa.org/clean_vehicles /avp/automaker-vs-the-people-usc-ad-response-to-automakers.html; Danny Hakim, *A New Automater Mantra: Emissions? What Emissions?*, N.Y. Times, March 22, 2005.

206. Kenny Bruno, *Nuclear Energy Industry: Sooo 20th Century*, CorpWatch, June 7, 2001, *available at* http://www.corpwatch.org/article.php?id=215 [hereinafter Bruno].

207. *See* Bruno, *supra* note 206.

chapter fourteen

The Fiduciary Duties of Officers and Directors

Jeffrey A. Smith and Matthew Morreale

I. Introduction

It is now almost axiomatic that recent years have seen extraordinary changes in the legal requirements for, and public expectations about, corporate governance, both in the United States and throughout the world. Corporate accounting scandals, outrage over executive pay, and, to a lesser extent, significant business failures with less nefarious causes, all have provided the courts with opportunities to revisit the basic principles of fiduciary law governing the conduct of officers and directors.[1]

While not all the results are in, early returns indicate that even conduct that is egregious and failures that are calamitous—viewed through a layman's lens—will not move courts to expand or modify significantly the basic principles of Delaware law under which directors and officers can be found personally liable for corporate acts or omissions arising in ordinary business contexts, even if the outcome for shareholders is extraordinarily bad.

Board and management response to climate change may cause the courts to test these principles in a different way, however. The complexity of the science, the uncertainty of the regulatory framework, the difficulty of predicting the reactions of the commercial and financial marketplaces, and, of course, the potential scope of the ecological consequences of global warming have already heightened the importance of knowledge and nimbleness in the boardroom. These forces may also drive a rapid evolution in expectations about management conduct, if not a change in how legal duties are framed and considered by shareholders and the courts.

This chapter begins with a brief overview of directors' fiduciary duties, including the duty of care and the duty of loyalty, as well as the developing and much-debated duty of good faith. It then briefly examines the relationship of these duties to the business judgment rule, applies some of the basic principles to decision-making scenarios in the climate change arena, and discusses the fiduciary ramifications of board inattention to climate change issues or conscious inaction on business matters with climate change implications. Finally, it examines, in greater detail and from a practical standpoint, the spectrum of business risks potentially created by climate change. Through a discussion of other significant business risks that have been faced recently by various industries, it then explores whether the risks inherent in climate change are, or should be, sui generis when analyzing directors' and officers' fiduciary obligations.

II. Directors' Fiduciary Duties

Corporate boards of directors have long been given significant powers and accorded significant discretion in their role as overseers of corporations.[2] It remains a cardinal precept of U.S. corporate governance, most notably the law of Delaware,[3] that directors, rather than shareholders, manage the business and affairs of a corporation.[4] This managerial power carries with it fundamental fiduciary obligations to both the corporation and its shareholders.[5] As corporate opportunities and challenges, particularly those of publicly traded, multinational entities, expand in an increasingly global economy, the role of directors becomes increasingly complex.[6]

Director liability for a breach of the duty to exercise appropriate attention arises in two distinct contexts. First, such liability may follow *from a board decision* that results in a loss, because that decision was ill advised or "negligent."[7] Second, liability to the corporation for a loss may arise from an *unconsidered failure of the board to act* in circumstances in which due attention would arguably have prevented the loss.[8] These settings for liability are discussed separately below. Board action is subject to review under the business judgment rule, "assuming the decision made was the product of *a process* that was *either* deliberately considered in good faith or was otherwise rational."[9]

A. The Business Judgment Rule

The business judgment rule, which generally dictates deference to informed decision making by the board, is a judicial creation that protects directors acting in their managerial capacities.[10] It creates a foundation, and a legal defense, for board action.[11] Specifically, it establishes "a presumption that in making a business decision the directors acted on an informed basis, in good faith and in the honest belief that the action taken was in the best interest of the company."[12] Absent an abuse of discretion, board judgment typically will be respected by the courts.[13]

The Delaware Supreme Court recently re-examined and repeated this proposition in the highly publicized case involving a substantial severance payment to Michael Eisner, former CEO of the Walt Disney Company. The court stated:

Directors' decisions will be respected by the courts unless the directors are interested or lack independence relative to the decision, do not act in good faith, act in a manner that cannot be attributed to any rational business purpose or reach their decision by a grossly negligent process that includes the failure to consider all material facts reasonably available.[14]

The court rejected plaintiff shareholders' contention that it should determine whether the directors had failed to exercise "substantive due care," finding that such an inquiry would be "foreign to the business judgment rule."[15] The court stated further, "Courts do not measure, weigh or quantify directors' judgments or even decide if they are reasonable in this context. Due care in the decision-making context is process due care only. Irrationality is the outer limit of the business judgment rule."[16]

Director action will be protected by the business judgment rule unless the directors fail in one of the three areas —independence, good faith, or use of a grossly negligent process that fails to consider all material facts reasonably available.[17] The presumption under the business judgment rule can be rebutted by showing a breach by the directors of a fiduciary duty. Plaintiffs bear the burden of proof for such a showing.[18]

B. Informed Decision Making and the Duty of Care

An unintelligent or unadvised judgment is not protected under the business judgment rule.[19] Rather, to benefit from the rule's protections, directors must make use of all information reasonably available before making a business decision.[20] Having so informed themselves, directors must then act with a requisite care in the discharge of their duties.[21] The presumption does not protect a fundamentally flawed process.[22] Whether a board has met its duty of care, however,

> can never appropriately be judicially determined by reference to *the content of the board decision* that leads to a corporate loss, apart from consideration of the good faith or rationality of the process employed. That is, whether a judge or jury considering the matter after the fact, believes a decision substantively wrong, or degrees of wrong extending through "stupid" to "egregious" or "irrational," provides no ground for director liability, so long as the court determines that the process employed was either rational or employed in a *good faith* effort to advance corporate interests.[23]

It seems apparent, therefore, that those seeking to use the lever of fiduciary duty to reach a specific result relating to climate change—replacement of coal-fired boilers with natural gas units, for example—face an almost insurmountable burden under well-settled principles of corporate governance. A much more intriguing avenue of inquiry goes to the manner in which decisions are made.

There is some variation at the margins of Delaware case law as to how the integrity of the decision-making process is measured or, put another way, how far the process must fall short before managerial conduct is culpable. In *Aronson*, the court found that "[w]hile the Delaware cases use a variety of terms to describe the applicable standard of care, our analysis satisfies us that under the business judgment rule director liability is predicated upon concepts of gross negligence."[24] Other courts have used a similar standard.[25] With respect to due care, gross negligence has been defined as "reckless indifference to or a deliberate disregard of the whole body of stockholders or actions which are without the bounds of reason."[26]

For reasons of managerial efficiency, however, and perhaps human capacity, the board does not have to be told everything before directors can come to a protected decision. In *Brehm*, the court stated, "[T]he standard for judging the informational component of the directors' decision making does not mean that the Board must be informed of every fact. The Board is responsible for considering only material facts that are reasonably available, not those that are immaterial or out of the Board's reach."[27] The court defined "material" as "relevant and of a magnitude to be important to directors in carrying out their fiduciary duty of care in decision-making."[28] For climate change decisions, in which the science is complex, the markets are rapidly moving, and the range of strategic options is wide, there are interesting questions of judgment posed on both operative prongs of this standard—what is (or may soon become) a material fact and what is "reasonably available" information.

These judicial constructs have a statutory corollary in Delaware corporate law in considering whether management has engaged in informed decision making. Under section 141(e) of the Delaware General Corporation Law, a director in the performance of his or her duties is:

> fully protected in relying in good faith upon . . . information, opinions, reports or statements presented to the corporation by any of the corporation's officers or employees, or committees of boards of directors, or by any other person as to matters [the director] reasonably believes are within such other person's professional or expert competence and who has been selected with reasonable care by or on behalf of the corporation.[29]

It can be fairly argued, however, that climate change decision making involves factual, scientific, political, and economic considerations that are far removed from the tightly focused, short-term business decision making that has historically been the staple of managerial discretion and has given rise to most of the judicial precedent. In deter-

mining whether a director acts on an informed or advised basis, the complexities of the underlying science of climate change, the uncertainty of regulation, and the difficulty of predicting the consequences to any particular business or industry combine to raise significant new questions about the extent to which a board must inform itself. Global warming is arguably unique in its consequences —simultaneously potent and targeted in its possible effects on a particular company or industry sector and universal in its reach.

> **Climate change also presents factors that could be fairly argued—as a matter of sound public policy—to require judging board action by a stricter standard than is used for more routine business matters.**

Under current law, those urging a board to take a specific action on a climate change issue, for example, a stance or direction with respect to GHG emission reduction, may not use disagreement with the board's position, no matter how strongly felt, as a basis for liability. Similarly, those using the term "fiduciary duty" as a synonym for "stewardship of the environment" or, more broadly, "custodians of the universal good" are pressing for a result-oriented conclusion in a manner that is contrary to existing law, because, under the business judgment rule, a court does not review the correctness of a decision, but rather the integrity of the process. Those questioning whether a board has fully informed itself before acting, or failing to act, however, may be asking the right question at the right time.

Reliance on "experts" (permitted and arguably required in some cases under section 141(e) of the Delaware General Corporate Law, discussed above) also has obvious implications in the climate change context. In most instances, directors will not possess sufficient scientific expertise on which to base their opinions. Uncertainties surrounding the science of climate change and engineering, economic and regulatory response make relying on "expert" opinion more problematic. The related questions of what constitutes "professional or expert competence" in this area and whether, in light of underlying uncertainties, it is reasonable or rational to rely on any one such opinion have yet to be resolved, or even raised, in a judicial forum.

Climate change also presents factors that could be fairly argued—as a matter of sound public policy—to require judging board action by a stricter standard than is used for more routine business matters. For instance, while corporate action may be local, the impacts of decisions, or collective decisions in an industry group, contribute to global consequences, both economically and environmentally. Board decisions in this area raise corporate social responsibility considerations more far-reaching than any other issue in the environmental arena. At the same time, however, even a cursory glance at the issue of causation—the provable relationship between one company's behavior and any aspect of global harm—reveals the complexities of judging or evaluating the consequences of a board's action. These same imponderable consequences lead us to ask whether those responsible for managing companies that contribute to the problem should be allowed to continue on with business as usual; be compelled to pay closer attention to the types of data they are already required to evaluate; look at a far deeper and broader spectrum of factors than has ever been required of them;[30] or be held accountable under a new set of rules specifically devised to meet the challenges posed by climate change.

There is limited precedent for application of stricter standards in certain traditional business contexts. For example, in *Revlon, Inc. v. MacAndrews & Forbes Holdings*,[31] in judging director actions in a takeover context, the business judgment rule was held not to protect the granting of a so-called lockup agreement when more than one bona fide bidder existed.[32] In so holding, the court found "[e]ven if the Board thought it was acting in good faith, the sale process itself was so substantially flawed that the Board's actions, considering all the facts and circumstances, were not likely to have *maximized the value of the corporation for its shareholders* and, therefore, its actions cannot be viewed as rational."[33] *Revlon* claims are rarely successful, however.[34] The decision has been construed narrowly by the Delaware Supreme Court, and the holding applies only in the sale or breakup of a company.[35]

Delaware courts also have applied enhanced scrutiny to director authorization of defensive actions intended to make it difficult for a bidder to acquire a target company.[36] In *Unocal Corp. v. Mesa Petroleum Co.*, the Delaware Supreme Court reviewed defensive measures implemented in response to an unsolicited takeover threat.[37] The court found that, where the board acts to attempt to defeat or deter an unsolicited offer, there is the "omnipresent specter that a board may be acting primarily in its own interests, rather than those of the corporation and its shareholders."[38] The court stated that, under such circumstances, the burden shifts to the board to demonstrate both that (i) it had "reasonable grounds for believing that a danger to the corporate policy and effectiveness existed" and (ii) the defensive measure adopted was "reasonable in relation to the threat posed" in order to benefit from the protection of the business judgment rule.[39]

Evaluating these limited examples of enhanced scrutiny, it is clear that courts have historically been most highly sensitized, and most skeptical of a board's conduct, when the end result might be management entrenchment. A threat from an external source, such as climate change, which may result in significant business disruption, or even substantial societal and ecological disruption, will not, and arguably should not, command the same scrutiny, no matter how grievous the consequences. Should conduct or inaction that might be characterized as corporate entrenchment against the collective good spark the same, or even more stringent, judicial demands? Nothing in the law to date suggests that it will.

C. Director Indemnification—Section 102(b)(7)

A full appreciation of the real-world consequences of actual or possible theories of liability requires that they be seen in the context of the economic realities of board membership. This relationship is particularly significant when considering an alteration or expansion of the law to address a broader social purpose or to attempt to engineer board behavior to reach a particular result, such as addressing climate change concerns through the activities of directors.

In response to the personal liability of directors following the Delaware Supreme Court's decision in *Van Gorkam*, section 102(b)(7) of the Delaware General Corporate Law was enacted to allow corporate charters to eliminate personal liability of a director for monetary damages for a breach of fiduciary duty, except:

> (i) [f]or any breach of the director's duty of loyalty to the corporation or its stockholders; (ii) acts or omissions not in good faith or which involve intentional misconduct or a knowing violation of law; (iii) under § 174 of this title; or for any transaction from which the director derived an improper personal benefit.[40]

The purpose of section 102(b)(7) was to:

> *permit shareholders*—who are entitled to rely upon directors to discharge their fiduciary duties at all times—. . . to exculpate directors from all personal liability . . . for breaches of their duty of care, but not for duty of loyalty violations, good faith violations and certain other conduct. . . .[41]

Thus liberated, directors might undertake "risky, but potentially value-maximizing, business strategies, so long as they do so in good faith."[42] The vast majority of Delaware corporations provide for exculpation to the extent permitted by section 102(b)(7) in their certificates of incorporation.[43]

Delaware courts distinguish the duty of due care from the duties of loyalty and good faith, discussed below, and provide different dispositions for matters in which the pleadings raise separate concerns.[44] Thus, in *Integrated Health Services*, for example, the court determined whether the plaintiffs' allegations amounted to "a violation of the fiduciary duty of loyalty or the fiduciary duty of care."[45] The court then stated that it would evaluate whether "fiduciary duty claims surviving that inquiry are barred by the § 102(b)(7) provision in [the company's] charter."[46]

Section 102(b)(7) protections, however, do not eliminate the fiduciary duty of care, because a court may still grant injunctive relief for violations.[47] Further, the exculpation provisions of section 102(b)(7) are "in the nature of an affirmative defense. As a result, it is the burden of the director defendants to demonstrate that they are entitled to the protections of the relevant [corporate] charter provisions."[48] With this equilibrium in mind, we turn to a brief examination of the traditional fiduciary duties.

D. The Duty of Loyalty

Corporate officers and directors owe a duty of loyalty to the corporation. As the court stated in *Guth v. Loft*:

> Corporate officers and directors are not permitted to use their position of trust and confidence to further their private interests. While technically not trustees, they stand in a fiduciary relation to the corporation and its stockholders. A public policy, existing through the years, and derived from a profound knowledge of human characteristics and motives, has established a rule that demands of a corporate officer or director...the most scrupulous observance of his duty, not only affirmatively to protect the interests of the corporation committed to his charge, but also to refrain from doing anything that would work injury to the corporation, or to deprive it of profit or advantage which his skill and ability might properly bring to it, or enable it to make in the reasonable and lawful exercise of its powers. *The rule that requires an undivided and unselfish loyalty to the corporation demands that there shall be no conflict between duty and self-interest.*[49]

Under the business judgment rule, the court will not respect board decisions when the directors lack independence in matters relating to the decision or do not act in good faith.[50]

Application of this duty to climate change seems unlikely. It is nevertheless noteworthy that recent Delaware case law makes the distinction between the duty of loyalty (or good faith) and the duty of care important in considering the protections afforded under section 102(b)(7) of the Delaware General Corporate Law. In particular, as further discussed, *infra*, at section II F., Delaware courts have found that boards have an obligation to be reasonably informed concerning the corporation, and that any failure in this area has implications for traditional director fiduciary duties, in particular the duty of good faith, as well as for protection under 102(b)(7).

E. The Duty of Good Faith

Delaware courts and scholars have historically disagreed on whether good faith constitutes an independent fiduciary duty or is part of the duty of loyalty.[51] Nevertheless, several courts have found that directors owe a duty of good faith to the corporation. The Delaware Supreme Court's recent extensive "conceptual guidance"[52] on the issue in the *Disney* case (discussed in greater detail in section II F.2, below) seems likely to enhance the chances of recognition of the independent nature of these obligations,[53] although the Supreme Court explicitly declined to address this issue in its holding.

Good faith "has been said to require an 'honesty of purpose,' and a genuine care for the fiduciary's constituents."[54] In the fiduciary context, however, the courts have recognized that it is "probably easier to define bad faith than good faith. . . . Delaware law presumes that directors act in good faith when making business judgments. Bad faith has been defined as authorizing a transaction 'for some purpose other than a genuine attempt to advance corporate welfare [when the transaction] is *known to constitute* a violation of applicable positive law'."[55] Bad faith (or a lack of good faith) is when "a director acts in a manner 'unrelated to a pursuit of the corporation's best interests'."[56] The Delaware Supreme Court stated in Disney that not every finding of a breach of the duty of good faith requires a bad faith motive (although it does require a purposeful act or intentional disregard of the corporation's interests).[57] The Delaware Chancery Court has not consistently inquired into a director's motives in finding that directors acted in bad faith.[58]

F. Director Oversight and Failure to Monitor

1. *Caremark* and Other Developments

The business judgment rule applies only when the directors act.[59] The rule has "no role where directors have either abdicated their functions, or absent a conscious decision, failed to act."[60] In addition to liability in the context of board action or decisions (discussed, *supra*, at section II(B)), liability to a corporation for a loss may arise from an "*unconsidered failure of the board* to act in circumstances in which due attention would, arguably, have prevented the loss."[61] In fact, most of the decisions that a corporation makes are not the subject of director attention, nor should they be.[62] Delaware courts, however, have also held that "a conscious decision to refrain from acting may nonetheless be a valid exercise of business judgment and enjoy the protections of the rule."[63]

Accordingly, an unconsidered failure to act may breach a director's duty, if sustained or systematic.[64] This standard raises questions about the extent, nature and process of board oversight. That is, it becomes important to determine to what extent a failure to monitor corporate developments constitutes a breach of board fiduciary duties. Much of the case law has developed from circumstances in which it was alleged that the board failed to inquire deeply or rigorously enough into conduct by management that was clearly wrong or dangerous to the company, if only the right questions had been asked in a timely way. Such a construct is useful in a case about the failure to discover corruption or wrong-doing. Whether it can or should be transferred readily to business decisions—or inaction—relating to climate change remains an open question.

In *Caremark* the court addressed the legal standard governing a board of directors' obligation to supervise or monitor corporate performance.[65] The court noted that the question of board responsibility to assure that the corporation functions within the law to achieve its purposes "has been given special importance by an increasing tendency, especially under federal law, to employ criminal law to assure corporate compliance with external legal requirements, including environmental, financial, employee and product safety as well as assorted other health and safety regulations."[66]

Caremark involved alleged violations of federal and state requirements applicable to healthcare providers, as to which Caremark ultimately agreed to pay fines and other third-party costs pursuant to a plea agreement.[67] Plaintiffs claimed that Caremark directors breached their duty of care by failing to supervise adequately the conduct of Caremark employees, or to institute corrective measures, thereby exposing Caremark to liability.[68] Plaintiffs did not allege director self-dealing or breaches of the duty of loyalty.[69] The court noted that the plaintiffs' complaint was based on "possibly the most difficult theory in corporation law upon which a plaintiff might hope to win a judgment," where directors are charged with responsibility for corporate losses for an alleged breach of care, and there is no conflict of interest or facts suggesting suspect motivation.[70]

The *Caremark* court examined the Delaware Supreme Court holding in *Graham v. Allis-Chalmers Mfg. Co.*,[71] in which plaintiffs asserted that the directors ought to have known about the behavior of subordinate employees that had resulted in liability to the corporation.[72] In *Graham*, the court stated that "absent cause for suspicion there is no duty upon the directors to install and operate a corporate system of espionage to ferret out wrongdoing which they have no reason to suspect exists."[73]

The court in *Caremark*, however, concluded that the *Graham* court could *not* have meant that "[C]orporate boards could feel free to fail to assur[e] themselves that information and reporting systems exist in the organization . . . to the board . . . timely, accurate information sufficient to allow . . . informed judgments concerning both the corporation's compliance with law and its business performance."[74] The level of information appropriate for such an information system "is a question of business judgment."[75]

Thus, the court in *Caremark* held that:

> [A] director's obligation includes a duty to attempt in good faith to assure that a corporate information and reporting system, which the board concludes is adequate, exists, and that failure to do so under some circumstances may, in theory at least, render a director liable for losses caused by non-compliance with applicable legal standards.[76]

The court described plaintiffs' claims as asserting a duty of care, a "duty satisfied in part by assurance of adequate information flows to the board."[77] In analyzing whether the directors' inattention should result in liability, however, the court spoke in terms of good faith:

> Only a sustained or systemic failure of the board to exercise oversight—such as an utter failure to attempt to assure a reasonable information and reporting system exists—will establish the lack of good faith that is a necessary condition of liability. Such a tenet of liability—lack of good faith as evidenced by sustained or systematic failure of a director to exercise reasonable oversight—is quite high. But a demanding test of liability in the oversight context is probably beneficial to corporate shareholders as a class, as it is in the board decision context, since it makes board service by qualified persons more likely, while continuing to act as a stimulus to *good faith performance of duty* by such directors.[78]

The court went on to find that the corporation information systems in question "appear to have represented a good faith attempt to be informed of relevant facts."[79]

In the aftermath of recent corporate scandals, the standards governing board oversight obligations established in *Caremark* may soon act together with new internal control requirements.[80] In the environmental context, where compliance and pollution control decisions often are made at the operational level, the possibility that this interaction of old standards and new protocols may create enhanced duties raises significant new questions about the process by which directors can, and must, inform themselves about complex technical issues. There are also related questions about the inherent limits of that process.[81]

Developments after *Caremark* underscore this trend and the concerns it raises. For example, in January 2003, the U.S. Department of Justice, in response to high profile accounting scandals, issued an internal guidance memorandum entitled "Principles of Federal Prosecution of Business Organizations."[82] The memorandum provides that the adequacy of a corporation's compliance program is a factor in determining whether to bring criminal charges against a corporation, but that the existence of such a program is not sufficient to avoid prosecution.[83] As an example of a governance mechanism to detect and prevent misconduct effectively, the memorandum, citing the *Caremark* decision, states that prosecutors should consider whether directors have:

> establish[ed] an information and reporting system in the organization reasonably designed to provide management and the board of directors with timely

and accurate information sufficient to allow them to reach an informed decision regarding the organization's compliance with law.[84]

In a related vein, revisions to the Corporate Governance Rules, adopted by the New York Stock Exchange (NYSE) and approved by the SEC in November 2003, require audit committees of listed companies to have a written charter defining the committee's purpose, which at a minimum must be to assist board oversight of the company's compliance with legal and regulatory requirements.[85]

Clearly there is a movement, expressed in several ways and emanating from several sources, toward greater internal controls, at a minimum, and proactive risk identification, at the extreme.[86] Whether this trend, which has its headwaters in crisis and began by addressing egregious but well-defined wrong-doing, will become generalized in application and used to shape board duties in the broader context of a company's participation in increasing societal risk relating to climate change will be one of the significant issues of the next decade. It must be recognized, however, that no matter how urgently one believes that climate change is a global risk, and that corporate conduct is a contributing factor, the solutions still lack the clear, moral and behavioral lines present in corporate theft and corruption cases. Stealing is wrong. Can the same thing be said about providing electricity to Boston or Beijing by building a coal-burning generation plant?

2. *Disney*

In the final Delaware Chancery Court decision in the long-running *Disney* case, which was broadly affirmed by the Delaware Supreme Court,[87] the Chancery Court held that the board's decision to hire Michael Ovitz and the compensation committee's approval of Ovitz's employment agreement were not grossly negligent or in bad faith.[88] The court discussed the implications of determining the applicable legal standards, including the concept of good faith, stating that:

> [T]he fiduciary duties owed by directors of a Delaware corporation are the duties of due care and loyalty. Of late, much discussion . . . has surrounded a so-called third fiduciary duty, that of good faith. Of primary importance in this case are the fiduciary duty of care and the duty of a director to act in good faith. Other than to the extent that the duty of loyalty is implicated by a lack of good faith, the only remaining issues to be decided herein with respect to the duty of loyalty are these relating to Ovitz's actions in connection with his own termination. . . . [I]ssues of good faith are . . . inseparably and necessarily intertwined with the duties of care and loyalty, as well as a principal reason the distinction of these duties make a difference—namely § 102(b)(7) of the Delaware General Corporation Law.[89]

The court further stated, without citation, that "the Delaware Supreme Court has been clear that outside the recognized fiduciary duties of care and loyalty (and perhaps good faith), there are no fiduciary duties."[90] The court, however, clarified that the duties overlap, stating, "[p]erhaps these categories of care and loyalty, so rigidly defined and categorized in Delaware for so many years, are really just different ways of analyzing the same issue."[91]

The Chancery Court reviewed Delaware jurisprudence on the business judgment rule and the duties of care, loyalty and good faith and found that the complaint "could be ruled to state a non-exculpated breach of fiduciary duty claim, insofar as it alleged that Disney's directors *consciously and intentionally disregarded their responsibilities,* adopting a we don't care about the risks attitude concerning a material corporate decision.'"[92] Thus, the court found that "the concept of *intentional dereliction of duty, a conscious disregard for one's responsibilities*, is an appropriate (although not the only) standard for determining whether fiduciaries have acted in good faith. Deliberate indifference and inaction *in the face of a duty to act is* . . . conduct that is clearly disloyal to the corporation. It is the epitome of faithless conduct."[93]

The Delaware Supreme Court affirmed the Chancery Court's decision on all claims. It also addressed the lack of clarity in the common law regarding the duty of good faith by elaborating on the nature of that duty and carving it out from the duty of care. The Delaware Supreme Court appeared to suggest an intermediate standard, stating that a breach of duty of good faith must involve conduct that rises above the level of gross negligence required for a breach of duty of care, but that it does not require a finding of "subjective bad faith," or "an actual intent to do harm."[94]

Other courts also have reviewed potential implications on a breach of good faith on section 102(b)(7) protections after *Caremark*. For instance, in *McCall v. Scott*,[95] the Sixth Circuit, applying Delaware law, denied defendant's motion to dismiss pursuant to the corporation's liability exculpation provision.[96] The claims in this case arose out of investigations into allegedly widespread health-care fraud at defendant's hospitals, home health agencies, and other facilities.[97] Plaintiffs alleged intentional and negligent breach of the fiduciary duty of care, and intentional breach of the fiduciary duty of loyalty by insider trading[98] and, in particular, that senior management, with board knowledge, "devised schemes to improperly increase revenues and profits, and perpetuated a management philosophy that provided strong incentives for employees to commit fraud."[99]

The court found that plaintiffs had adequately pled allegations of nonfeasance by the board (i.e., where plaintiffs alleged the directors had acted with "intentional ignorance" and "willful blindness" to illegal activities underlying plaintiffs' claims)[100] and that " '[w]here there is no conscious decision by directors to act or refrain from acting, the business judgment rule has no application'." [101] Plaintiffs maintained "that their *duty of care* claims are not barred as the [company's liability exculpation provision] excludes from protection director liability for 'acts or omissions not in good faith or which involve intentional misconduct or a knowing violation of law'." [102] Although the court refused to interpret "intentional misconduct" to include "recklessness," the court considered whether a breach of the duty of good faith could result from "reckless acts or omissions," stating that:

> Whether [§ 102(b)(7)] would protect a director against reckless acts is not altogether clear. To the extent that recklessness involves a conscious disregard of a known risk, it could be argued that such an approach is not taken in good faith and thus could not be liability exempted under [§ 102(b)(7)]. On the other hand, to the extent that the conduct alleged to be reckless is predicated solely on allegations of sustained inattention to the duty it is arguable whether such conduct is 'grossly negligent,' but not conduct amounting to bad faith. [103]

Viewed together, the leading holdings, such as those in *Disney, Caremark*, and *McCall*, simultaneously underscore traditional Delaware principles of director action and business judgment and raise critical questions, discussed in greater detail below, about the limits of the protections afforded to directors that are pertinent to board examination of climate change issues.

3. Implications for Climate Change Decision Making—Action or Inaction

Beginning with the most basic of principles, the distinction between director action and inaction has clear implications for climate change decision making. Addressing climate change may not require any affirmative board action. In fact, in the totality of the circumstances, a decision to do nothing, which in turn leads to a complete absence of short-term GHG emission constraints, may not only be defensible, but prudent or mandatory.

Informed inaction or delay on capital expenditures or corporate strategic direction as a response to regulatory uncertainty also may be both prudent and mandatory. As a result, even though a company may be reporting in depth to its stakeholders on climate change, decisive action does not necessarily follow, nor should it be required. For example, in response to shareholder resolutions on GHG strategies, Ford recently reported, after a targeted campaign by institutional investors to persuade it to issue such a report, that, while it is committed to doing its part to stabilize GHG emissions, "[i]n our highly competitive industry, there continue to be too wide a range of possible futures for technologies, markets, and regulatory frameworks for our company to set unilaterally targets on the in-use performance of our products." [104]

Varying market and consumer preferences and regulatory requirements around the world add further complexity to any decision to commit corporate resources. In the United States, they differ from state to state.[105] Not surprisingly for a company with global reach, Ford reported that its initiatives have varied by region, such as voluntarily agreeing, as part of the European Association of Automobile Manufacturers (ACEA), to reduce passenger car CO_2 emissions directly. In the United States, by contrast, it has in-

An uncertain regulatory climate also creates extraordinary risks when long-term decisions are necessary to meet future market demands.

vested in hybrid vehicle production, because of consumer demand for more fuel-efficient vehicles and innovative technologies, and bio-ethanol infrastructure, in part because of the political attractiveness of reducing dependence on foreign oil.[106]

An uncertain regulatory climate also creates extraordinary

risks when long-term decisions are necessary to meet future market demands. It can take a utility six to twelve years to site, permit and build a large base load station at a new location, at a cost of more than $1 billion.[107] It is arguably impossible to be nimble in making such long-term decisions subject to so many competing and contradictory demands.

In certain industries, there may be a substantial business disadvantage for the first mover, either strategically or in the marketplace, measured in the price of equipment, the premature expenditure of capital, or the misdirection of research and development funds. Although ignorant inaction is arguably the least protected course of managerial conduct,[108] and while regulatory and economic uncertainties alone may not excuse such inaction, they may combine to allow management to make the necessary case that, within the standards defining its fiduciary obligations, doing nothing is the prudent course.

At the other end of the commercial spectrum, a sharp analysis in a particular industry segment might reveal a substantial advantage to being the first mover in GHG efficient technology. This advantage may be strictly commercial—to seize early market share with leading technology and make it prohibitively expensive for the competition to buy it back, as may arguably be occurring with Toyota's early entry into the market with its hybrid Prius car;[109] or for reasons that, while immaterial to the balance sheet, are critical to corporate image, as is arguably occurring with British Petroleum's widely heralded (albeit recently tainted) "Beyond Petroleum" campaign and simultaneous investment in a variety of alternative energy ventures;[110] or it might be a combination of a variety of factors.

As discussed above, the traditional—and prevailing—view of the fiduciary duties of officers and directors gives broad latitude to management judgments that may not be acute or forward-looking. This is illustrated in the recent case involving the Ford board of directors on issues other than climate change (discussed *infra*). Similarly, well-settled application of the business judgment rule prohibits shareholders from asking courts to enforce a hindsight view of informed business decisions, even when the present makes the past look blatantly obvious.

Climate change, as a scientific, regulatory, and commercial phenomenon, may soon test the outer limits of these well-settled principles. The reaction of the financial and commercial marketplaces to various phenomena related to climate change also may place unprecedented strain on managerial judgment. Decisions to respond to ordinary challenges, if misguided, have ordinary bad effects. For the most part, these will occur without any remedy for stockholders under traditional fiduciary duty analyses. Miscalculation about the consequences of climate change, however, appears far more likely to have cataclysmic commercial effects. Lines of businesses, or entire businesses, that appear stable today may be uneconomical in relatively few years, or may swiftly be regulated out of existence. The CEO of the coal-burning utility, Cinergy, refers to this as the "stroke of the pen" risk.[111]

Is coal the cheap alternative fuel for the foreseeable future of the industrial world, for example, or will climate change imperatives drive it to the periphery of world markets, notwithstanding its price and increasingly sophisticated technology to burn it in a CO_2 efficient manner? When a product or a business vanishes suddenly, it will be natural for shareholders and their lawyers to ask whether the board is blameless in missing the signs saying that the bridge was out. On the up side, commercial opportunities to transform the infrastructure of the developed world and to shape the infrastructure of the developing world in a GHG-efficient way may soon prove to be as alluring as the commercial power of the Internet, and as difficult to predict.[112] Whenever big winners and big losers emerge suddenly from the scrum, shareholder discontent often leads to litigation.

G. Traditional Policy Considerations

As we have discussed above, the business judgment rule is intended to protect the full and free exercise of the managerial powers granted to directors under Delaware law.[113] It protects and promotes the board of directors as the managers of the corporation.[114] As a result, the courts have traditionally shown great forbearance in refusing to substitute their judgment for the judgment of directors.[115] The business judgment rule also provides a defense to shareholder challenges, liberating directors from the threat of disproportionate personal liability and, thus, encouraging the taking of reasonable entrepreneurial risk.[116]

It is not surprising, therefore, to see that a vast majority of the case law in which the business judgment rule has been construed arises either in the context of mergers and takeover defenses or, in more limited circumstances, when corporate corruption or scandal has substantially eroded shareholder value. These two contexts, while obviously vastly different from each other, are dramatic points of inflection for stock price, corporate direction, and institutional reputation. Like the frog that will sit contentedly in a saucepan of water if it is brought slowly to a boil, stockholders, dissidents and, just as importantly, their lawyers, have traditionally been less moved to action by slow leaks than by sudden explosions. Damages are much harder to prove when forces other than defendants' behavior have had a longer time to act on a company's fortunes and stock price. Dramatic change, or the prospect for substantial profit, are often the catalysts for litigation challenging the judgment of the people in a position to save the ship or seize the day.

Outside the boundaries of director duties in traditional corporate contexts, does the prospect of, or responsibility for, climate change implicate, or require change in, these basic principles? Do its global reach and potentially cataclysmic consequences argue for a sharper reading of the presumptions that have traditionally shielded corporate decision making, or do its diffuse causes—even among the prime suspects, such as coal-burning utilities and gasoline-burning cars—make it unjust and imprudent to hold any individual board of directors to a higher standard that has traditionally been the case?

Examining the bedrock principles of the business judgment rule in the global climate change context raises additional concerns. For example, in light of the stated risks of the consequences of climate change, including the unavailability of insurance, is it prudent or feasible to establish a rule of law that makes individuals potentially liable to shareholders under any circumstances?[117] Before exploring those questions, a brief examination of the real-world economics of a decision to impose personal liability on directors is necessary.

III. Directors' and Officers' Insurance

Even when directors or officers act, or fail to act, outside the protections of the business judgment rule they are nearly always indemnified by their companies, through directors' and officers' (D&O) liability insurance policies. Corporations have strong incentives to provide the broadest indemnification allowed under law, in order to encourage entrepreneurial risk-taking behavior that may benefit the company, and because fear of personal liability would discourage talented executives from taking board positions.[118] As a result, as a practical matter, few board members face personal, out-of-pocket liability for poor decisions.

Historically, in light of these protections, the possibility that a director who has not engaged in self-dealing or otherwise breached a duty of loyalty will face personal damages has been extremely low.[119] While there are several circumstances in which indemnification or insurance could be inadequate or prohibited under state law, there are only a few cases against board members in which these scenarios have actually played out.[120] The Delaware Supreme Court's holding in *Van Gorkam*,[121] decided prior to the enactment of section 102(b)(7),[122] represents the only instance in which a director has made out-of-pocket payments for damages awarded after a trial.[123] Since 1980, there have been twelve examples of personal payments by directors for legal expenses or settlement payments.[124] Of these, eleven cases involved claims of oversight failure related to a breach of duty of care.[125]

If indemnification is either precluded by law or unavailable due to the company's financial limitations, D&O insurance, purchased by nearly every public company,[126] provides a second shield against personal liability for directors and officers. The majority of D&O insurance policies are based on a presumption that the company will indemnify its directors to the full extent of the law,[127] because insurance carriers want companies to have a stake in any litigation and provide deep pockets for defense costs, which in turn allows the carriers to seek a higher retention, or deductible.[128] For companies incorporated in Delaware, the presumption includes the enactment of an exculpatory provision in the company's bylaws, except for breaches of the duties of loyalty or good faith.[129] As a result, in the rare event that a Delaware company has not provided for such indemnification, a director held personally liable for a breach of duty of care could pay high deductibles and receive less coverage.[130]

Some D&O insurance programs contain "Side A—Difference in Conditions" insurance, which includes coverage for potential losses that are not indemnifiable under law, such those resulting from shareholder derivative litigation, or instances in which the company cannot afford to indemnify, such as insolvency.[131] Unlike statutory indemnification of directors, D&O insurance is not precluded by a breach of duty of loyalty or good faith under Delaware law. In fact, Delaware law places no limitation at all on the terms of D&O insurance coverage.[132] The conduct exclusions in D&O policies typically bar recovery only for suits resulting from deliberate fraud or the taking of illegal profits.[133]

IV. The Principles in Practice

Keeping who is really paying the piper clearly in focus, we return to the application of basic fiduciary principles in the business decision-making context. An instructive example of how the courts might apply the fundamental duties of corporate officers and directors in the face of seemingly catastrophic business decisions dealing with both internal and external crises—mimicking the range of decisions that might be implicated in deciding issues driven by climate change—was handed down in 2002 by the District Court for the Eastern District of Michigan, applying Delaware law.[134] In a derivative suit against Ford's officers and directors, shareholders sought to impose liability for three courses of conduct that indisputably had hugely detrimental effects on Ford's financial results and arguably contributed to a significant number of deaths and injuries around the world.[135]

First, the shareholders alleged that Ford management had been slow to investigate, and flawed in its analysis of, a defective ignition switch, which, for many years, had been mounted directly onto the engine block, notwithstanding its propensity to fail and shut down the engine, sometimes at high speeds, when it became overheated.[136] Second, shareholders criticized the board's handling and oversight of Ford's long and troubled relationship with Firestone/Bridgestone Tire Company, which made the tires for most Explorer vehicles.[137] These tires caused death and injury when they lost their treads and exploded at high speeds.[138] Finally, in the more mundane arena of business economics, Ford management had designated commodity metal buyers, who were familiar with purchasing copper and steel, as their agents for trading in highly volatile precious metals, particularly palladium, which they bought high, in an unhedged position, leading to vast overstocking and ultimately a $1 billion write-off.[139]

The *Salsitz* case is instructive because it treats egregious conduct in three areas of director oversight that might be implicated in a company's climate change policy. The first is delay and alleged mismanagement of an internal investigation of a technical issue—not unlike what a utility might do in determining GHG emission reduction strategies at a generating plant. The second is an ill-fated analysis of and reaction to external forces, in this case an outside vendor who brought independent problems to the table, worsening the company's own already precarious position—arguably comparable to the complex effect of local and regional regulation on GHG emissions and the company's climate change strategy. Finally, it discusses the use of underqualified employees to assess and execute what, in retrospect, should have been a highly sophisticated metal trading strategy—similar to a company for which carbon constraint could be critical entrusting the technical assessment of its position to employees without the needed skills.

The court in *Salsitz* dismissed the complaint, because in each instance it found Ford's officers and directors blameless under well-settled principles of Delaware law.[140] With respect to the ignition switch, the District Court did not get past the business judgment rule in refusing to review the merits of the decision not to relocate the switch.[141] In fact, the court noted that there was a difference of opinion within the company about the investigation and that the board had been kept apprised of the debate.[142] The court applied the well-established principle that after-the-fact analysis of substantive decisions, even decisions that range from "stupid" to "irrational," provide no ground for director liability, as long as the decisions were made as part of a process that was done either "rationally or in a good faith effort to promote the company's best interest."[143]

With respect to the Firestone/Bridgestone tires, the court applied the same analytical construct, based on the periodic information that the board had received concerning the relationship between Ford and Firestone and the ongoing and escalating nature of the problems with the tires.[144] The board's failure to track in detail the safety record of Firestone tires was not a sufficient basis on which to hold them personally liable, according to the court.[145] Although their comparative ignorance of the issue might be "unwise" or "negligent," it fell far short of the operative standards of gross negligence or conscious disregard.[146] The court took pains to distinguish the Sixth Circuit's decision in *McCall vs. Scott*[147] and the Seventh Circuit's decision in *In Re Abbott Laboratories Derivative Shareholders Litigation*,[148] each of which had involved substantial independent criminal investigations which plainly "put the board on notice of illegal behavior."[149]

The court had the easiest time with the palladium issue.[150] It assessed the board's failure to act under the "unconsidered inaction" standard which, under settled principles of law, required "a sustained or systematic failure of the board to exercise oversight, such as an utter failure to attempt to assure a reasonable . . . reporting system exist [ed]."[151] Sending unsupervised novices into the fray did not constitute a failure of this magnitude.[152]

The case is also intriguing because, unlike most of the jurisprudence on the business judgment rule and officers' and directors' duties of good faith and due care, it involved shareholder reaction to a series of largely unrelated management decisions, each of which was damaging to Ford, both economically and reputationally, but none of which was catastrophic. In *Salsitz* the board's oversight was questioned not at a single critical juncture, but rather as their effects played out over time in a variety of different managerial contexts, ranging from appropriate use and training of corporate staff, to the management of a hazardous design defect, to flexibility in responding to the demands of third parties. For the court, applying Delaware law, where there was neglect, it was excusable; where poor choices had been made, they could not be reexamined by the court using hindsight; and where signals of substantial risk had apparently been ignored, the level of knowledge and debate at the board level, while arguably negligible to a layperson, was sufficient under established legal thresholds.

Is there now, or could there be on the immediate horizon, anything different about climate change risk so that a shareholder suit might yield a different result? A closer examination of what is, and might soon be, at stake, particularly for publicly traded companies in GHG-intensive industries, will help test these well-settled principles against potentially unprecedented challenges.

V. Climate Change Risk—Considerations for Director and Officer Behavior

While there is little scholarly work directly on point,[153] three schools of thought have emerged that arguably apply to directors' and officers' duties and responsibilities in the face of climate change challenge. First, some argue that traditional principles of

fiduciary duty, which derive from vesting corporate ownership in a limited number of shareholders and management discretion in an even more limited number of directors and officers, are antiquated, inadequate, and even dangerous, when a company contributes to a crisis with global reach.[154] At the other end of the spectrum are those who believe that any attempt to "universalize" the ownership in management of public companies, whether through proxy votes or alteration of the fundamental tenets of directors' and officers' responsibilities and duties, is an assault on the genius of the American corporation to adapt freely to market changes. They see any broadening of corporate constituencies as a raid on the boardroom, carried out by special interest groups with limited agendas, typically in the areas of corporate social responsibility, transparency in governance, and environmental issues beyond the power or duty of any single company to control.[155]

Representing the third school of thought and occupying the middle ground are those who are not convinced that, from a governance standpoint, there is anything inherently unique about climate change issues and who therefore think it is appropriate to judge management's response to the obvious internal and external business challenges presented by the prospect of climate change on an issue-by-issue basis in a traditional commercial way, using well-accepted legal precepts.[156]

The most interesting and significant question is whether the special demands of climate change will create a fourth line of analysis.[157] In this scheme, officers and directors would be less than fiduciaries for "universal owners," but more accountable, or accountable more quickly, than is currently the case under existing case law. This enhanced scrutiny would occur not because of the inherently universal nature and scope of climate change issues, but because the stresses (scientific, regulatory or other) on traditional commercial channels as the result of climate change may become so great that they demand greater vigilance, more intensive study, and far more commercial nimbleness than run-of-the-mill business issues, particularly in companies responsible for substantial GHG emissions and in subsectors of the financial marketplace, most notably insurance, for which climate change risks are accumulative.[158]

In light of the emerging understanding of, and responses to, potential consequences of climate change, the section below considers the parallel financial and regulatory developments, both real and foreseeable. Such result-oriented considerations are not fair game for judicial inquiry under traditional and current jurisprudence. Given the potential reach and impact of climate change concerns, however, they directly affect shareholder expectations and value, public perceptions, and corporate bottom lines, best practices and social responsibility and thus will have growing implications for director and officer behavior. Moreover, a board exercising its oversight responsibilities under case law following *Caremark* may be prone to liability under traditional fiduciary theories, where the ebb and flow of such obligations meet rapidly emerging financial and regulatory climate change requirements. Boards of companies with significant GHG emissions or material business prospects riding on climate change technologies may be especially prone to such risk.

A. Financial Implications

1. Revenue Opportunities

As with any trend or event that could alter existing lines of commerce and demands for products, adapting the world's economic habits and physical infrastructure to carbon constraint will almost certainly present numerous and substantial economic opportunities. Briefly tracking the promises and pitfalls of such changes through the supply chain for a single product line helps illustrate how related uncertainties may be manifested in expectations and consequences for managerial and board behavior, decision making and oversight.

> ... adapting the world's economic habits and physical infrastructure to carbon constraint will almost certainly present numerous and substantial economic opportunities.

Increasing reliance on renewable energy sources, such as wind power, for example, appears clearly to be part of a carbon-constrained future.[159] In some regions and individual states, the use of a percentage of renewable resources is already part of a legislatively mandated energy portfolio standard.[160] Wind power may well be considered as a part of such portfolios, at a minimum. At the top of the commercial supply chain, General Electric, with substantial research and development dollars and clear reputational objectives, has already made a widely publicized move into "green power" through its "ecomagination" initiative announced in May 2005.[161] GE announced it would double its investment in energy efficient and environmental technology to $1.5 billion by 2010.[162] Similarly, GE Energy Financial Services, a subsidiary of GE Energy, announced plans to triple its investments in renewable energy, to $3 billion, by 2008.[163] While the size of these initiatives is not yet material for GE, it is sufficient to drive significant follow-on investment by those hoping to be GE's suppliers of the future, as well as to garner significant public attention.

Here, the story has an unexpected interruption. Notwithstanding the seemingly forward-looking nature of this initiative, and its relative insignificance to GE's balance sheet, the company sustained an almost immediate attack via a shareholder proposal. The Free Enterprise Action Fund, an institutional GE shareholder based in Washington, D.C., presented a proposal at GE's 2005 annual shareholder meeting that, by the 2006 annual shareholder meeting, GE directors report to shareholders in

the "scientific and economic analysis relevant to GE's climate change policy," including the (i) "[s]pecific scientific data and studies relied on to formulate GE's climate change policy," (ii) "[e]xtent to which GE believes human activity will significantly alter global climate, whether such change is necessarily undesirable and whether a cost-effective strategy for integrating any undesirable change is practical," and (iii) "[e]stimates of costs and benefits to GE of its climate change policy."[164] Although, on its face, the proposal requests transparency on climate change issues,[165] supporting statements for the proposal expressed concern that GE's "lobbying for stringent global warming regulation" will have adverse economic impacts.[166] In fact, presenting the shareholder proposal, portfolio manager Steven Milloy challenged GE CEO Jeff Immelt to disclose to shareholders how GE is going to increase its earnings in a "declining economy that may result from global warming regulations."[167]

The GE board opposed the proposal, stating that ecomagination is a "business strategy to respond to the needs of GE's customers, to make the company's operations more efficient and ultimately to create and increase shareowner value." The board's opposition noted that GE has not, to date, announced a " 'climate change policy'," and argued that GE resources are not best spent articulating such a policy or reporting on the extent to which " 'human activity will significantly alter global climate change'."[168] The resolution received approximately 5.9% of the votes and qualified for inclusion in GE's 2007 proxy statement.[169]

Putting aside this early misadventure and continuing our analysis further down the supply chain, with GE as a major mover, companies whose business includes manufacturing component parts for wind turbines, including everything from rotor blades to custom support stanchions, to batteries, should arguably be readying their production capacity to meet new demand. Unfortunately, however, even the combination of regulatory requirements and a large industrial buyer does not guarantee a free flow of commerce. Wind farms have to be sited. There already have been some drawn out and spectacular public failures in attempting to garner the necessary approvals for substantial projects.[170] Any board that allows management to rest a substantial portion of its economic hopes on successful completion of such projects might soon conclude that their plans were misplaced.

Working under the traditional protections of the business judgment rule, however, and staying true to traditional readings of their fiduciary duties, the directors of such a company would be protected in this context both for failing to make the most of this opportunity and for allowing management to rely too heavily on the possibility that this opportunity would generate substantial profits.[171]

Further still down the supply chain, a well-established maker of high-strength, lightweight composite resins, which had previously marketed exclusively to the aerospace industry, might find an application for its products as a replacement for metals in the housing or blades of wind farm infrastructure.[172] While this might one day prove to be a lucrative market, subject to the limitations discussed above, the board would similarly be protected from a breach of fiduciary duty lawsuit for the lost opportunity, if the light of inspiration failed to click on, and the composites company merely continued in its traditional business lines, earning ordinary profits. For the very reason that underlies courts' traditional deference to informed board decision making, a failed investment in this market should be equally protected.

Change a few elements of this equation, however, and the dynamic by which a board's conduct might be judged could be altered by real or perceived climate change impacts. If, for example, the composites company did not have any aerospace customers, and it only achieved growth and profit through new applications; and if wind farming had become as commercially acceptable and readily siteable in the United States as it is becoming in Europe; and if management and/or the board failed to assure reasonable internal information flow, in a manner indicating a sustained and systematic ignorance of the company's position in respect of those opportunities as its business withered accordingly; then, as profits and stock price plummeted, economically injured shareholders might well mount a more credible case. Similarly, but far less likely, if Ford's management and its board were systematically uninformed as to the inroads Toyota is making into its market share through introduction of its Prius, and Ford's stock price and franchise suffered disastrous and irreversible losses, then it might push the outer limits of traditional oversight obligations to hold Ford's board harmless for its failure to act.

As follows from *Caremark* and similar holdings, a board is not culpable in these commercial contexts for a failure to act, or even for allowing management to bet wrong with all the company's chips. Although the bar for officer and director liability remains high, the board may be culpable, however, if it allows management to come to the table without due attention to what the game is or articulating how it may have changed.

The ramifications of the changes in the marketplace that may be wrought by climate change are so potentially extraordinary that they arguably place a new premium on management and board consideration of the issue. This falls far short of the board as a custodian for the common good, as urged by some in the "universal ownership" camp, but it does argue that an informed analysis of the potential commercial consequences of climate change, and the responses of government and marketplaces to all related phenomena, may emerge as a compelling component of fulfilling traditional fiduciary duties. It further suggests that the time frame for undertaking this analysis may be dramatically foreshortened by circumstances largely out of boards' control, including science, market reaction and public opinion, together with their individual and cumulative effect on stock price, which will be discussed briefly below.

2. Expense Risks

A similar dynamic plays out on the expense side of the corporate ledger. This includes accounting for the resources necessary to generate profits by competing in new marketplaces and the substantial capital expenditures that may be required to meet both regulatory requirements and self-imposed voluntary restrictions or targets; to address shareholder or other stakeholder concerns; and to respond to any adverse results of climate change litigation.[173]

The commitment of capital expenditures to respond to needs driven by climate change may be among the most significant decisions facing management in GHG emission-intensive industries. In the United States, many of the larger industries are caught in a "perfect storm" of uncertainty.[174] Instead of comprehensive federal legislation, there are a variety of competing proposals, none of which come close to being a sure bet for passage.[175] There are local, state-specific and regional initiatives to register, cap, control and/or trade CO_2 emissions, which, taken together, are an obstacle course set against any cohesive corporate planning. There are several major strands of climate change litigation pending, each of which may rewrite the rules on product formulation,[176] CO_2 regulation[177] and liability for damages

from the consequences of climate change.[178] Each of these developments is being played out against a backdrop of increasing public and stakeholder pressure for companies most closely identified with GHG emission risk—coal-burning powerplants and automobile manufacturers, in particular—to take definitive action to reduce their respective carbon footprints.

Such circumstances are tailor-made for the traditional protections afforded by the business judgment rule, which allows management and the board to focus on a complex array of choices free from fear of second-guessing and liability driven by hindsight, particularly when the expenditures are extraordinarily large, strategically determinative for the business, and functionally irreversible. For Cinergy to commit to the construction of GHG emission-efficient integrated gasification combined-cycle (IGCC) plans, for example,[179] or for Ford to divert a substantial portion of its fleet production capacity to hybrid vehicles is, in essence, to shape the future of those companies for the next generation.

In addition to strategic direction, many companies in GHG emission-intensive industries are faced with huge swings in expenditures that are dependent almost exclusively on regulatory outcomes.[180] For many utilities, the prospect of infrastructure changes or new technology to reduce CO_2 emissions or to sequester all or part of the existing emission stream are also choices about their company's future. In the current fragmented regulatory scheme, management has multiple tasks: (1) to assess the regulatory landscape and to urge the most efficient, or most favorable, result, either individually or through a trade association, on Congress or the appropriate state legislatures; (2) to assess simultaneously the economic effects of a variety of potential regulatory outcomes; (3) to prepare contingent plans for implementation of each outcome, including, in the case of public utilities, a plan to recapture from its rate-payers the costs of implementation so that a company's shareholder will not be saddled with stranded investment; and (4) to prepare detailed implementation engineering and accounting estimates for each of these contingencies.

These broad tasks are just the beginning of a much more textured and complex decision tree. As with the decision making for strategic direction, the most striking thing about this tree is that at each of the major branches there are choices, each of which involves hundreds of millions of dollars and each of which may be outcome-determinative for the company. As with decisions about strategic direction, their very complexity and the need for both minute knowledge of the business and broad perspective on trends and potential outcomes argues strongly for managerial prerogative and broad discretion on the part of the board. It is also true, however, that in this arena, perhaps even more than in questions of strategic direction, there is a heavy premium on gathering, filtering, and evaluating knowledge and information. This could soon raise the bar substantially in determining what an informed—or culpably uninformed—decision might look like.

Factored into all decision making is the commercial reality that hundreds of enterprises in the supply chain are making similar assessments of similar forces. Thus, for every public utility contemplating IGCC technology, there are dozens of suppliers deciding whether there will be sufficient demand for IGCC in the future to merit redirection of corporate resources to making component parts, just as the composite material manufacturer discussed in this section above evaluated whether a wind farm market would develop. A decision that may be strategically prudent today nevertheless may be financially imprudent in the short term because of the cost of the requisite components. Five years from now, strategy and economics may merge, as additional suppliers enter the field and prices decrease. Some industries may not be afforded this luxury of time. Once again, however, this is the traditional pulse of business—beating very quickly but pumping familiar blood, traditionally well within the purview of management to filter.

The financial marketplaces recently have become as sensitized to climate change as the commercial marketplace. This presents another multitiered set of managerial choices. On the most elemental level, those companies with access to the EU Emission Trading System (EU ETS) must determine the most financially prudent way to meet allocation limits in pertinent jurisdictions. At its inception, the choice to participate in the EU ETS was basically binary in nature: credits or controls.[181] Re-

cently, however, the market itself, together with the emission allocation scheme that was its predicate, have come under substantial pressure. Credit prices, which for the first year had been volatile only in the upward direction, tumbled precipitously in April 2006, raising fundamental questions about the accuracy of the allocation scheme.[182] Whether these developments are a momentary stumble, or will signal the beginning of a reassessment of the allocation scheme or of the trading process itself, and thus have a chilling effect on planned GHG cap-and-trade schemes in the United States,[183] remains to be seen. Most significantly, these early developments mean that one of management's obligations is to monitor the integrity of the market itself. Sustained and systematic ignorance of a company's position vis-à-vis these market conditions, followed by a loss of shareholder value attributable to this ignorance, could, in theory, give rise to a cause of action.

B. Legal Developments

Assessing and responding to litigation, legislative, and regulatory risks with direct or tangible effects on corporate well-being also has long been considered to lie within the scope of management's traditional duties.[184] As other chapters in this book make clear, both the direct and the derivative legal risks of climate change are a potent, but largely untasted cocktail. Its challenges for some industries are direct and potentially immediate. In *Witherspoon*, for example, the automobile industry has at stake the emission suit of its California vehicle fleet, together with that in any states that have adopted the California standards. In *Connecticut v. AEP*, the power industry is defending against allegations that are liability-shifting and in which the relief sought mirrors the position they might have been in had the United States adopted the Kyoto Protocol. In *Massachusetts v. EPA*, all CO_2 emitters may be required to bear the consequences of judicially mandated EPA regulation of CO_2 as a pollutant under the Clean Air Act. In the states operating under the Memorandum for Understanding published under the auspices of the Regional Greenhouse Gas Initiative,[185] the consequences also may resemble Kyoto ratification, at least in the electric utility sector.

For companies not directly involved in litigation, one or more of the major pending cases may still have derivative and equally immediate effects. Coal-burning utilities in the Southwest, for example, that are not parties to *Connecticut v. AEP* would nevertheless be affected if a court allowed the public nuisance prong of that complaint to proceed to trial. The prospect of such liability being assigned might prompt state legislatures to regulate preemptively or to embark on independent study of the issue.[186]

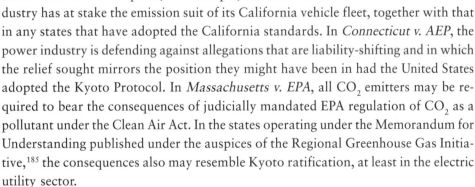

It might prompt Congress to attempt to occupy the field. To the surprise of some, the absence of certainty and the prospect of material risk have already prompted increasing numbers of prominent members of the regulated community to call for solutions, such as a carbon tax or cap-and-trade legislation, which would lead to price certainty and allow management to weigh its options in the absence of multiple litigation contingencies, each of which currently goes to a core climate change issue.[187] Similarly, success by defendants in *Witherspoon* could create a cascade of copycat state initiatives and radically change the calculus of fleet emissions requirements for automobile manufacturers for which California has not been a primary marketplace.

In short, climate change legal risk is dynamic, and moving at an unprecedented pace. It is also in a foundational stage, in that basic precepts, which, in the brief history of U.S. environmental law, have traditionally been intensely negotiated in the regulatory arena, debated in Congress and then subject to challenge in the context provided by the Administrative Procedure Act, may now be cut out of whole cloth by the courts, state and local regulatory bodies, and through ad hoc regional alliances.

In contrast to traditional litigation risk, for which specific courtroom tactics or targeted theories of liability must be assessed and strategies devised, in the climate change arena the most broad-reaching and basic issues are being decided. Although those decisions will clearly shape the future, their consequences are not necessarily direct or proportionate, however. To truly know climate change legal risk, management must know the whole picture, a scope of inquiry and obligation that is arguably unprecedented in U.S. environmental law.

By way of comparison and contrast, the closest corollary is the early days of Superfund litigation. Here, as the often-told story goes, shock over Love Canal lead a Democratic-controlled Congress to rush through ill-considered legislation in anticipation of a non-sympathetic Reagan presidency and incipient Republican control of the legislative branch.[188] Inside this legislative Trojan horse, which rumbled through the streets of corporate America at break-neck speed, was an entirely new application of strict, joint and several, retroactive liability—driven by status as a generator, .owner/operator or transporter of broadly defined hazardous materials.[189] The corporate past, and the skeletons of long-forgotten subsidiaries, quickly became fair game for a share of cleanup costs.

The first decade of Superfund litigation was particularly turbulent and included constitutional challenges to what many considered to be the fundamental rewriting of legal principles;[190] challenges clarifying the ability of potentially responsible parties to reallocate among themselves the cost of response and cleanup;[191] questions concerning the availability of traditional defenses, such as corporate form or involvement as a mere shareholder;[192] and the peculiar pains of small parties caught in the large and costly Superfund sites.[193]

Measured simply by the yardstick of frenetic legal activity, this is the beginning of a comparable time in climate change litigation. It can also be fairly argued, as early challenges did, that Superfund's operative definitions and key principles of liability

reversed settled expectations and created potential chaos in the corporate world, just as plaintiffs in *Connecticut v. AEP*, if successful, would do by grafting an ancient tort theory of recovery onto an incomplete list of defendants to compel them to alter their contributions to a global problem.

From the perspective of management's duties and obligations, however, comparability ends there. The revolutionary nature of Superfund was that it imposed liability that was both strict and retroactive. While it was a shock in many boardrooms to learn that waste disposal, legal at the time and conducted in accordance with all industry standards, could nevertheless be the source of substantial financial responsibility under a new law, and it was a further shock to know that, through the mechanism of "time of disposal," liability for the historical conduct of sold or discontinued corporate affiliates might be vested in a present day parent,[194] management's forward-looking obligations were relatively limited in scope; (i) don't buy contaminated property; and (ii) handle waste in a way that reduces the risk of creating future Superfund sites. This objective was soon reinforced by the mandates of the Resource Conservation and Recovery Act.[195] Once the details of the new scheme had been resolved, and the courts had affirmed its viability and Congress's intent, management's primary obligation was to assess potential exposure, account for it properly, and disclose it as required under SEC regulations.[196] For many this was grim arithmetic. As a boardroom matter, however, it was largely devoid of the forward-looking dynamism of climate change legal risk.

The climate change challenge for management is not simply to get the math right or to wrestle with the vagaries of estimation of remediation liability, but to understand the consequential effects of a rapidly changing legal picture; to understand how, for example, the combination of a utility's commitment to spend hundreds of millions of dollars on SO_2 and NO_x scrubbers, coupled with its new desire to reduce its CO_2 emission footprint, and its reluctance to invest in IGCC technology absent a regulatory mandate or appropriate tax incentives, might create a new market for high sulfur, but relatively efficient burning, coal.[197] Under traditional corporate governance precepts, it would be unproductive and improper to allow shareholders to second-guess management and the board for decision making in the arena. Rapid change turns foresight into hindsight very quickly. It is also true, however, that because of the depth and complexity of information material to decision making in the climate change arena, management may well be held accountable for assuring the basic channels of information flow, both as to internal compliance and external developments, required by *Caremark*. At the very least, as a best management practice, it should consider how best to position itself against these risks.

Climate change also has spurred a more direct challenge to management's authority through shareholder resolutions provided for under section 14(D) of the Securities Act of 1934.[198] Because the vast majority of resolutions to date have involved issues of corporate disclosure of climate change risk, rather than specific proposals to change corporate conduct, this subject is treated in greater detail in Chapter 13.[199] Several aspects of the climate change proxy resolution phenomenon, which is unprecedented in U.S. corporate governance, are worthy of note here, however.

First, climate change towers above all the issues of interest to shareholders and stakeholders under the broad umbrella of corporate social responsibility in the environmental arena as a lightening rod for specific shareholder requests. It has become the bellwether for management's ability and willingness to engage stakeholders on complex ecological and social issues. Second, through the SEC-mandated mechanism of 14D proxy filings, shareholders have shifted the debate from traditional SEC disclosure, required under Reg. S-K, to "voluntary" reports which, while not immune from the distractions of corporate puffery, have proven to be far more robust than any previous corporate disclosure on environmental issues.[200] These voluntary reports are often a product of negotiations with stakeholder groups and are submitted to third-party verification by respected outside agencies or consultants. Through this newly created mechanism, the management teams of companies affected by GHG issues are rapidly developing a new way to talk to constituents and the marketplace, in a verifiable manner, on the complex issues surrounding climate change. In the same vein, Carbon Disclosure Project, now sponsored by over 200 investment funds, is soliciting and analyzing significant GHG "footprint" information from major businesses throughout the world.[201] These related informational phenomena are entirely new in the last decade.

Third, the marketplace that is demanding, and beginning to receive, this information is increasingly consolidated, sophisticated, and financially significant. Ten years ago, the issue was often framed, or ignored, in boardrooms as an appeasement of fringe interest groups. Today, it is vested with the power and significance of a mainstream movement, with the backing of the substantial assets of public pension funds such as CalPers, CalSters and the five New York City pension systems (New York City Fire Department Pension Fund; New York City Police Pension Fund; New York City Employees' Retirement System; New York City Teachers' Retirement System; and New York City Board of Education Retirement System). Through these channels, awareness of, and responsiveness to, climate change issues have become a marketplace in and of itself that requires management's knowledge, attention and vigilance. Management arguably must not only ask, "Is our company in the right place on this issue?" it must also assure itself that the right financial institutions understand where the company is and approve of that direction. Failing to meet market expectations in this arena, while clearly not yet as damaging as failing to meet expectations about quarterly earnings, is nevertheless rapidly increasing in importance. Skill in managing the climate change issue is rapidly becoming, in effect, a self-fulfilling prophecy.

Taken together, the market risks and the legal risks of climate change have created strategic risks. In the short term, these risks are manifested by management's decisions on company positioning, research and development funding, deployment of capital, and the nature and quality of information given to the financial marketplace and stakeholders, for example. It is important to remember, however, that while traditional principles of fiduciary duty are broad, and often articulated in general terms, they are also highly susceptible to fact-specific analysis. The unique stresses of climate change help illustrate these differences.

The insurance sector, for example, whose ongoing viability depends on correctly calculating the magnitude of long-term risk and correctly pricing products to deal with it, [202] has, in effect, jumped a generation and articulated for the marketplace today the warning that existing financial mechanisms will be inadequate over the next 10 to 30 years to deal with property and casualty losses deriving from weather and other geophysical phenomena related to climate change.[203] For an insurance company, today's management obligations embrace aggressive assessment of forward-looking risk. Management's central task is to make continuous estimates about a likely course of events, so that products can be priced to address contingencies for customers and make profit for shareholders. For such a company, the distance to the future is dramatically foreshortened. The company's predominant interest is the continuing viability of

the financial and insurance marketplaces. This long-term interest must be articulated now if there is a definable, life-threatening storm (or too many storms) on the radar screen. The trappings of the physical infrastructure—wind power, hydrogen fuel cells, etc.—with which societies choose to operate are comparatively unimportant to them.

By contrast, an oil company with large proven reserves has a short- and medium-term interest, at least, in the continued functioning of the fossil fuel-based economy. Management of that company arguably has a corollary duty to shareholders to maximize value by selling existing products, for which the company has already incurred substantial exploration cost, into that economy for as long as possible and at the highest price. The oil company's interest in the post-fossil fuel economy is, for the moment at least, trivial by comparison. As a result, it would be imprudent, at least, for the oil company to abandon or dramatically curtail production and refining of its reserves and suddenly begin charting a new course in renewable energy. Confident that fossil fuels will be important to lifting the developing world out of poverty, and will provide the company an ongoing superior return on its investment, the company might even choose to spend all of its available research and

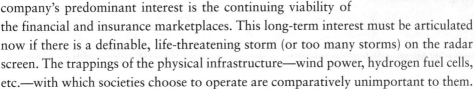

development money on seeking new oil reserves. Management might rationally conclude that the premium for being the first mover in alternative energy markets was too great, and that the sounder course would be to wait for the markets to mature and to spend more heavily later, when others stumbled over the learning curve. Each and any of these decisions, made after consideration of reasonably available material information, would be supportable under the business judgment rule. At the same time, the complexity and rapid development of these issues place additional premiums on informed management oversight.

VI. Conclusions

The complexity of possible corporate responses to climate change, including the uncertainty of the regulatory environment, the massive amounts of capital required by companies as they adapt to a carbon-constrained environment, and the long period of time over which any response to climate change must be judged, strongly suggests that any choice from a wide range of strategies may be prudent—and thus clearly defensible under the business judgment rule. In fact, even imprudent decisions, such as a utility committing prematurely to a capital expenditure program that later proves unnecessary, or waiting too long to retrofit a generating plant to reduce GHG emissions and having to pay an exorbitant premium for equipment or emission credits, would appear to be defensible under prevailing law.

While it appears unlikely that climate change issues will alter the basic precepts governing most of the managerial prerogatives of officers and directors, such as the duties of due care, loyalty and good faith, it is clear that the complexities of these issues have already added a new dimension and urgency to management's obligation to monitor corporate performance and/or to make informed decisions in light of all reasonably available material information. As a result, a prudent board of directors cannot remain systematically ignorant of, should as a best practice actively consider, and may soon be obliged to consider, five significant bodies of information: (1) emerging climate change science; (2) the relevance of scientific findings both to the industry and business that they manage and to the specific locations where they operate; (3) the public position of the company's significant stakeholders on climate change; (4) management's response to any shareholder initiatives and to any business opportunities and risks presented directly and indirectly by climate change; and (5) the consequences in the capital markets for their company of all of the issues listed above.

It is also true that, in a time of increasing scrutiny of corporate governance, the lines between corporate fiduciary duties, economic welfare and corporate social responsibility may become increasingly blurred, particularly when considering an issue perceived, correctly or not, to present irreversible global consequences. To the extent that a company's response to climate change becomes a proxy for both smart management and corporate stewardship, directors have an incentive to be increasingly vigilant in assuring that management has maximized economic opportunity, reduced economic risk, and preserved or enhanced corporate reputation. Finally, in exercising their duties of care, loyalty and (arguably) good faith owed to shareholders and effectively positioning the company in the capital markets, officers and directors must recognize that their actions will inevitably be judged against the benchmark of market and public perception of climate change, which may be as significant in the short term as scientific and commercial reality.

Endnotes

1.   At the same time, and for many of the same reasons, academic debate over issues such as "universal ownership" of public companies and the limits of social investing has rekindled, with some scholars changing sides and others retrenching. *See, e.g.*, Martin J. Lipton, *Twenty-Five Years After Takeover Bids in the Target's Boardroom: Old Battles, New Attacks and the Continuing War*, 60 Bus. Law., 1369, 1373 n.11 (2005) ("For example, Michael Jensen, formerly a vigorous proponent of 'efficient markets,' now subscribes to what he terms the 'enlightened stakeholder theory'—a proposition that, to maximize long-term market value maximization, boards must consider the perspective of all corporate stakeholders.") [hereinafter Lipton], *citing* Michael C. Jensen, *Value Maximization, Stakeholder Theory and the Corporate Objective Function*, Harv. Bus. School, Negotiation, Organization and Markets Unit, Working Paper No. 01-01 (2001).

2.   BUSINESS FOR SOCIAL RESPONSIBILITY, THE STAKEHOLDER FIDUCIARY: CSR, GOVERNANCE AND THE FUTURE OF BOARDS, April 2006, at 3, *available at* www.bsr.org (As early as the 18th century, U.S. entrepreneurs and political leaders understood the need for corporate boards to act as supervisors of corporate management.) [hereinafter The Stakeholder Fiduciary].

3.   More publicly held U.S. companies are incorporated in Delaware than any other state. As a result, the law of Delaware on the duties of directors is far more developed than in any other state and, thus, the main focus of this chapter. *See* Meredith M. Brown, *The Duties of Target Company Directors Under State Law: The Business Judgment Rule and Other Standards of Judicial Review*, 1351 PLI/Corp. 177, 185 (2003) [hereinafter Brown].

4.   *See* Aronson v. Lewis, 473 A.2d 805, 811 (Del. 1984), *overruled on other grounds by* Brehm v. Eisner, 746 A.2d 244 (Del. 2000), *citing* 8 Del. Ch. § 141(a) ("The business and affairs of a corporation organized under this chapter shall be managed by or under the direction of a board of directors except as may be otherwise provided in this chapter or in its certificate of incorporation."); Smith v. Van Gorkom, 488 A.2d 858, 872 (Del. 1985); Zapata Corp. v. Maldonado, 430 A.2d. 779, 782 (Del. 1981); *In re* Holly Farms, 1988 WL 143010, *3 (Del. Ch. 1988) ("[T]he ultimate responsibility for managing the business and affairs of a corporation falls on its board of directors."); The Stakeholder Fiduciary, *supra* note 2, at 3.

5.   *Aronson*, 473 A.2d at 811 at 13; *Van Gorkom*, 488 A.2d at 872 ("In carrying out their managerial roles, directors are charged with an unyielding fiduciary duty to the corporation and its shareholders"); *Holly Farms*, 1988 WL at *3.

6.   *See* The Stakeholder Fiduciary, *supra* note 2, at 3.

7.   *In re* Caremark Int'l Inc. Derivative Litig., 698 A.2d 959, 967 (Del. Ch. 1996).

8.   *Caremark*, 698 A.2d at 967 (emphasis in original).

9.   *Id.*; *see In re* Abbott Labs. Derivative Shareholders Litig., 325 F.3d 795, 805 (7th Cir. 2001).

10.   *Zapata*, 430 A.2d at 782; *see Aronson*, 473 A.2d at 812.

11.   *See Zapata*, 430 A.2d. at 782; *Aronson*, 473 A.2d at 812; *Van Gorkom*, 488 A.2d at 872; Lipton, *supra* note 1, at 1370.

12.   *Aronson*, 473 A.2d at 812.

13.   *Id.*

14.   Brehm v. Eisner, 746 A.2d 244, 264 n.66 (Del. 2000).

15.   *Brehm*, 746 A.2d at 264; *see* Brown, *supra* note 3, at 191.

16.   *Brehm*, 746 A.2d at 264.

17.   *Id.* at 246 n.66.

18.   *Aronson*, 473 A.2d at 812 (the burden is on the party challenging the decision to establish facts rebutting the presumption); *In re* Disney Shareholder Litig., 2005 Del. Ch. LEXIS 113, *153 (Del. Ch. 2005). In addition, while practitioners counseling directors' decisions in Delaware must focus on decisions of the Delaware courts, it is instructive to compare the American Law Institute's (ALI) summary of the general principles of the business judgment rule in its *Principles of Corporate Governance: Analysis and Recommendations*, which the ALI adopted in 1992. Brown, *supra* note 3, at 192-93. Section 4.01(a) of the *Principles of Corporate Governance* states:

> A director or officer has a duty to the corporation to perform the director's or officer's functions in good faith, in a manner that he or she reasonably believes to be in the best interest of the corporation, and with the care that an ordinarily prudent person would reasonably be expected to exercise in a like position and under similar circumstances. This Subsection (a) is subject to the provisions of Subsection (c) (the business judgment rule) where applicable.

ALI, Principles of Corporate Governance: Analysis and Recommendations, § 4.01(a) (1994). Subsections (c) and (d) describe the business judgment rule and the burden of proof for challenging its application, as follows:

> (c) A director or officer who makes a business judgment in good faith fulfills the duty under this Section if the director or officer:
> (1) is not interested in the subject of the business judgment;
> (2) is informed with respect to the subject of the business judgment to the extent the director or officer reasonably believes to be appropriate under the circumstances; and
> (3) rationally believes that the business judgment is in the best interests of the corporation.
> (d) A person challenging the conduct of a director or officer under this Section has the burden of proving a breach of the duty of care, including the inapplicability of the provisions as to the fulfillment of duty under subsection . . . (c), and in a damage action, the burden of proving that the breach was the legal cause of the damage suffered by the corporation.

Id. §§ 4.01(c) and (d).

19.   *Van Gorkom*, 488 A.2d at 858.

20.   *Aronson*, 473 A.2d at 812. Protection under the Business Judgment Rule also requires that directors be "disinterested." 473 A.2d at 813. ("From the standpoint of interest, this means that directors can neither appear on both sides of a transaction nor expect to derive any personal financial benefit from it in the sense of self-dealing, as opposed to benefit which devolves upon the corporation or all stockholders gener-

ally."); *see also Van Gorkom*, 488 A.2d at 872-873. This duty of loyalty is discussed further below. *See infra*, § II D.

21. *Aronson*, 473 A.2d at 805.

22. *In re Holly Farms*, 1988 WL at *6 (applying an enhanced level of scrutiny under *Revlon*, discussed below).

23. *Caremark*, 698 A.2d at 967 (emphasis in original).

24. *Aronson*, 473 A.2d. at 812.

25. *See, e.g., Van Gorkom*, 488 A.2d at 873 ("[G]ross negligence is . . . the proper standard for determining whether a business judgment reached by a board of directors was an informed one."); *compare* Mitchell v. Highland-Western Glass, 167 A. 831, 833 (Del. Ch. 1933) (the court posed the question as whether the board acted "so far without information that they can be said to have passed an unintelligent and unadvised judgment"); *compare also* Gimbel v. Signal Companies, Inc., 316 A.2d 599 (611), *affirmed* 316 A.2d 619 (Del. 1974) (reframing the Highland-Glass standard, "did the Signal directors act recklessly in accepting a wholly inadequate price for Signal Oil?"); Guttman v. Huang, 823 A.2d 492, 507 n.39 (Del. 2003) ("[T]he level of due care that is the litmus test of liability, absent an exculpatory charter provision [is] gross negligence. If gross negligence means something other than negligence, pleading it successfully in a case like this requires the articulation of facts that suggest a wide disparity between the process the directors used to ensure the integrity of the company's financial statement and that which would have been rational.") (emphasis supplied).

26. Tomczak v. Morton Thiokol, Inc., 1990 Del.Ch. LEXIS 47, *35 (Del. Ch. 1920), *quoting* Allaun v. Consol. Oil Co., 147 A.257, 261 (Del.Ch.1929) and *citing Gimbel*, 316 A.2d at 615; *In re* The Walt Disney Co. Derivative Litig., 2005 Del. Ch. LEXIS 113, *162, *citing Tomczak*, 1990 Del. Ch. LEXIS at *35.

27. *Brehm*, 746 A.2d at 259; Brown, *supra* note 3, at 195.

28. Brehm, 746 A.2d at 260 n.49; Brown, *supra* note 3, at 195.

29. Brown, *supra* note 3, at 195-96, *quoting* 8 DGCL 141(e); *see also* Integrated Health Services, 2004 Del. Ch. LEXIS 122, *30 n.31 (Del. Ch. 2004).

30. *Value at Risk: Climate Change and the Future of Governance*, CERES Sustainable Governance Project Report, at Forward and 1 (April 2002) ("Since climate change is arguably the world's most pressing environmental issue, it follows logically that companies' response to the threats and opportunities of climate change—or their lack of response—could have a material bearing on their financial performance and therefore on shareholder value. . . . Climate change is rapidly becoming one of the core challenges of the 21st Century for corporate directors and institutional investors . . . in the absence of preventative and adaptive measures, multibillion-dollar financial losses are distinctly possible if not probable."); *see also* Cynthia A. Williams & John M. Conley, *Is There an Emerging Duty to Consider Human Rights?*, 74 U. Cin. L. Rev. 75, 78, 79 and 95-99 (Fall 2005) [hereafter Williams & Conley].

31. Revlon, Inc. v. MacAndrews & Forbes Holdings, 506 A.2d 173 (Del. 1986).

32. *In re Holly Farms*, 1988 WL at *6 (viewing director acts under the enhanced duty imposed on a board when it adopts anti-takeover measures under *Revlon*).

33. *Id.* at *5 (emphasis supplied).

34. Williams & Conley, *supra* note 30, at 76-77, *citing* Robert B. Thompson & Randall S. Thompson, *The New Look of Shareholder Litigation: Acquisition-Ori-*

ented Class Actions, 57 VAND. L. REV. 133, 195 (2004) (finding that, in 1999 and 2000, 233 complaints in Delaware raised *Revlon* claims and none were successful).

35. Williams & Conley, *supra* note 30, at 76 (citations omitted).

36. *See* Unocal Corp. v. Mesa Petroleum Co., 493 A.2d 946 (Del. 1985); Brown, *supra* note 3, at 214.

37. *Unocal*, 493 A.2d at 949; Brown at 214.

38. Brown, *supra* note 3, at 214-15, *quoting Unocal*, 493 A.2d at 954.

39. Brown, *supra* note 3, at 215, *quoting Unocal*, 493 A.2d at 955.

40. 8 Del. Ch. § 102(b)(7). In addition to the provisions of Delaware Ch. § 102(b)(7), under Delaware Gen. Corp. Law § 145, corporations may provide indemnification for directors and officers through a company's charter for all actions except instances of breach of duty of loyalty, self-dealing, or violations of criminal law. DEL GEN. CORP. LAW § 145; Bernard Black, Brian Cheffins & Michael Klausner, *Outside Director Liability*, 58 STAN. L. REV. 1055, 1118 (2006) [hereinafter *Outside Director Liability*]. As a result of this trend, it is exceedingly rare that a director or officer would be left unprotected to face personal liability for a breach of duty of care. *Outside Director Liability* at 1093. For third-party claims, such as securities lawsuits and direct class actions brought by shareholders, this indemnification can include settlement payments, legal expenses, and damages, but in derivative litigation, indemnification is limited to legal expenses. DEL. GEN. CORP. LAW § 145(a)-(b).

41. *Emerald Partners*, 787 A.2d at 90 (emphasis in original); *see Disney*, 2005 Del. Ch. LEXIS at *166-67.

42. *Disney*, 2005 Del. Ch. LEXIS at *167, *quoting* Prod. Res. Group, LLC v. NCT Group, Inc., 863 A.2d 772, 777 (Del. Ch. 2004).

43. *Disney*, 2005 Del. Ch. LEXIS at *168.

44. *See* Matthew R. Berry, *Does Delaware's Section 102(b)(7) Protect Reckless Directors from Personal Liability? Only if Delaware Courts Act in Good Faith*, 79 WASH. L. REV. 125, 1128-29 (Nov. 2004) [hereinafter Berry].

45. *Integrated Health Services*, 2004 Del. Ch. LEXIS at *33.

46. *Id.* (citations omitted) (emphasis supplied).

47. *Disney*, 2005 Del. Ch. LEXIS at *168 (Del. Ch. 2005).

48. *Id.* (citation omitted).

49. Guth v. Loft, 5A.2d 503, 510 (Del. Ch. 1939) (emphasis supplied); *see Disney*, 2005 Del. Ch. LEXIS at *163-64.

50. *Brehm*, 746 A.2d at 264 n.66; Brown, *supra* note 3, at 196.

51. *Compare Guttman*, 823 A.2d at 506 n.34 (duty of good faith is not independent of duty of loyalty); Nagy v. Bistricer, 770 A.2d 43, 49 n.2 (Del. Ch. 2000) (a director cannot act simultaneously in bad faith and loyally toward the corporation) *with* Cede & Co. v. Technicolor, 634 A.2d 345, 361 (directors owe duties of good faith, loyalty and due care); *see also* Berry, *supra* note 43, at 1127.

52. *In re* Walt Disney Co. Derivative Litig., No. 411, 2006 Del. LEXIS 307, at *90-103 (Del. June 8, 2006).

53. *See, e.g., Cede*, 634 A.2d at 361; *see also* Berry, *supra* note 44, at 1128.

54. *Disney*, 2005 Del. Ch. LEXIS at *169.

55. *Id.* at *169-70, *quoting* Gagliardi v. TriFoods Int'l, 683 A.2d 1049 at 1051 n.2, *citing* Miller v. AT&T, 507 F.2d 759 (3d Cir. 1974) (emphasis in *Disney*).

56. *Disney*, 2005 Del. Ch. LEXIS at *170, *quoting In re* RJR Nabisco, Inc. Shareholder Litig., 1989 WL 7036, *15 (Del. Ch. 1989).

57. *Disney*, 2006 Del. LEXIS 307 at *99-103.

58. *Compare* Zirn v. VLI Corp., 681 A.2d 1050, 1061-62 (Del. 1996) (analyzing director's motives in context of breach of good faith claim); Desert Equities v. Morgan Stanley Leveraged Equity Fund II, L.P., 624 A.2d 1199, 1208 (Del. 1993) (a claim of

bad faith relies on a person's state of mind); *Van Gorkam* at 873 (Del. 1985) (director's motives were irrelevant because there were no allegations that the directors breached their duty of good faith) *with* Disney, 2005 Del. Ch. LEXIS at *170 ("it makes no difference why the director intentionally fails to pursue the best interests of the corporation."); *Caremark*, 698 A.2d at 960-962 (finding of breach of good faith without showing of bad faith motive); *See Berry* 1128-1133; *Disney*, 2005 Del. Ch. LEXIS at *173 ("It is unclear, based upon existing jurisprudence, whether motive is a necessary element for the successful claim that a director has acted in bad faith, and, if so, whether that motive must be shown explicitly or whether it can be inferred from the directors conduct.").

59. *Aronson*, 473 A.2d at 812; *Caremark*, 698 A.2d at 967.

60. *Aronson*, 473 A.2d at 813. Testing the "conscious" nature of that decision may present difficulties, however. In particular, upon what basis must a decision not to act be premised?

61. *Caremark*, 698 A.2d at 968.

62. *Id.*

63. *Id.* The court *in re* Disney Shareholder Litig., 2005 Del. Ch. LEXIS 113, *155 (Del. Ch. 2005) noted that, in *Rabkin v. Philip A. Hunt Chem. Corp.*, 1987 WL 28436 at *1-3 (Del. Ch. 1987), the court found a lower stand of liability applicable to director inaction, but that "no Delaware decision (until this one) has cited *Rabkin*" and it would appear that *In re* Caremark and other cases "have eclipsed *Rabkin* by implicitly accepting that gross negligence is the appropriate standard even in cases of alleged director inaction and lack of oversight." *Disney*, 2005 Del. Ch. LEXIS at *156.

64. *Caremark*, 698 A.2d at 971.

65. *Id.* at 961.

66. *Id.* at 969.

67. *Id.* at 965.

68. *Id.* at 964.

69. *Id.* at 967.

70. *Id.*

71. Graham v. Allis-Chalmers Mfg. Co., 188 A.2d 125 (1963).

72. 188 A.2d at 127; *Caremark*, 698 A.2d at 969.

73. 188 A.2d at 969.

74. *Caremark*, 698 A.2d at 970.

75. *Id.*

76. *Id.*

77. *Id.*

78. *Id.* at 971 (emphasis in original).

79. *Id.*

80. *See* Gregory Rogers, *Pollution Risk Oversight*, Directors Monthly, Vol. 28 No. 2 (February 2004) at 5-6 [hereinafter Rogers].

81. *See* Rogers, *supra* note 80, at 5.

82. Memorandum on "Principles of Federal Prosecution of Business Organizations," U.S. Dep't of Justice (January 20, 2003) (hereinafter DOJ Principles); Rogers, *supra* note 80, at 3.

83. DOJ Principles, *supra* note 82, at 3 and 5; Rogers, *supra* note 80, at 3.

84. DOJ Principles, *supra* note 82, at 6; Rogers, *supra* note 80, at 3.

85. NASD and NYSE Rulemaking: Relating to Corporate Governance, Securities and Exchange Commission, Release No. 34-48745 (Nov. 4, 2003). Rogers, *supra* note 80, at 4.

86. *See* Rogers, *supra* note 80, at 6.

87. *Disney*, 2005 Del. Ch. LEXIS 113. *Disney*, 2005 Del. Ch. LEXIS 113; *Disney*, 2006 Del. LEXIS 307.

88. *Disney*, 2005 Del. Ch. LEXIS at *189-227.

89. *Id.* at *148.

90. *Id.* (noting that in certain circumstances, specific applications of the duties of loyalty and care are necessary, such as the *Revlon* duties).

91. *Disney*, 2005 Del. Ch. LEXIS at *149, *citing* Sean J. Griffin, *Good Faith Business Judgment: A Theory of Rhetoric in Corporate Law Jurisprudence*, 55 DUKE L. J. (forthcoming 2005) (manuscript of May 25, 2005, at 39-42, *available at* http://papers.ssrn.com/sol/papers.cfm?abstract_id=728431) ("At first glance, the duties of care and loyalty appear quite distinct . . .").

92. *Disney*, 2005 Del. Ch. LEXIS at *174 (emphasis in original).

93. *Id.* at *175 (emphasis in original) (citations omitted).

94. *Disney*, 2006 Del. LEXIS 307 at *93, 99-100.

95. McCall v. Scott, 239 F.3d 808 (6th Cir. 2001), *amended on denial of rehearing by* 250 F.3d 997 (6th Cir. 2001).

96. 239 F.3d at 819. The liability exculpation provision in the company's charter provides:
A director of the Corporation shall not be personally liable to the Corporation or its stockholders for monetary damages for breach of fiduciary duty as a director; *provided, however,* that the foregoing shall not eliminate or limit the liability of a director (i) for any breach of the director's duty of loyalty to the Corporation or its stockholders, (ii) for acts or omissions not in good faith or which involve intentional misconduct or a knowing violation of law, (iii) under Section 174 of the General Corporation Law of Delaware, or (iv) for any transaction from which the director derived an improper personal benefit. (Emphasis supplied.)

97. 239 F.3d at 813.

98. *Id.*

99. *Id.* at 814.

100. *Id.* at 816-19; *see* Alston & Bird, Corporate Governance Advisory, July 16, 2003, at 3 [hereinafter Alston & Bird Advisory].

101. 239 F.3d at 816, *quoting* Rales v. Blasband, 634 A.2d 927, 933.

102. 239 F.3d at 818.

103. 239 F.3d at 818, *citing* BALOTTI A. FINKELSTEIN, DELAWARE LAW OF CORPORATIONS AND BUSINESS ORGANIZATION, at 4-116 to 4-116.1 (3d ed. Supp. 2000); Alston & Bird Advisory, *supra* note 96, at 3.

104. *Ford Report on the Business Impact of Climate Change*, The Ford Motor Company (undated) at 2, *available at* http://media.ford.com/downloads/05_climate.pdf [hereinafter *Ford Report*].

105. *Ford Report, supra* note 104, at 2.

106. *Id.*

107. *Air Issues Report to Stakeholders*, Cinergy Corp. at 12 (2004).

108. Aronson, 473 A.2d at 812-13; J. Kevin Healy & Jeffrey M. Tapick, Climate Change: *It's Not Just A Policy Issue for Corporate Counsel—It's a Legal Problem*, 29 COLUM. J. ENVTL. L. 89, 103-04 (2004).

109. *See With $12 Billion of Profit, Toyota has G.M. in Sight*, N.Y. TIMES, May 11, 2006, Sec. C, at 4 (citing continued popularity of the hybrid engine as a "big source of

growth" and repeating Toyota's expectation to be selling 1 million such vehicles a year by 2010).

110. *See* Terry Macalister & Eleanor Cross, *BP Rebrands on a Global Scale: Oil Group Seeks to Go Green*, THE GUARDIAN, July 25, 2000, at 24; *available at* British Petroleum Web site, http://www.bp.com/productsserviceasteaser.do?categoryId=918&contentId= 2008136, providing current examples of alternative energy ventures.

111. PEW CENTER ON GLOBAL CLIMATE CHANGE, GETTING AHEAD OF THE CURVE: CORPORATE STRATEGIES THAT ADDRESS CLIMATE CHANGE 64 (October 2006).

112. *See Visions of Ecopolis*, ECON. TECH. Q., Sept. 21, 2006.

113. *See, e.g., Van Gorkom*, 488 A.2d at 872.

114. *Zapata*, 430 A.2d. at 782.

115. *In re* Holly Farms, 1988 WL at *3 ("A court reviewing a transaction cannot substitute its judgment for a valid business judgment of a board and cannot set aside a decision of a board if a fully informed, properly motivated board has acted properly and its judgment can be attributed to any rational purpose."); Mills Acquisition Co. v. MacMillan, 559 A.2d 1261, 1279 (Del. 1989) (precludes courts from imposing themselves on the affairs of the corporation).

116. *Disney*, 2005 Del. Ch. LEXIS at *153, *citing* Gagliardi v. TriFoods Int'l, Inc., 683 A.2d 717, 720 (Del. 1971).

117. *Disney*, 2005 Del. Ch. LEXIS at *153, *citing* Graham v. Allis-Chalmers Mfg. Co., 188 A.2d 125 (Del. Ch. 1963); Kelly v. Bell, 254 A.2d 62 (Del. Ch. 1969), *aff'd*, 266 A.2d 878 (Del. 1970); Lutz v. Boas, 171 A.2d 381 (Del. Ch. 1961).

118. Susanne Mast Murray & Fred T. Podolsky, *Protecting Your Directors and Officers From Liability: Examining Indemnification Insurance*, in WHAT EVERY DIRECTOR & OFFICER SHOULD KNOW ABOUT D&O COVERAGE (Jack C. Ansitz, chair 2005), 1519 PLI/Corp. 53, 56 [hereinafter *Examining Indemnification Insurance*].

119. *See Outside Directory Liability, supra* note 40, at 1089-90.

120. *Outside Directory Liability, supra* note 40, at 1060.

121. *Van Gorkom*, 488 A.2d 872.

122. 8 DGCL 102(b)(7).

123. *Outside Directory Liability, supra* note 40, at 1060.

124. *Id.*

125. *Id.* Three of these cases included an insolvent company and sufficient D&O insurance coverage. *See id.* at 1118.

126. *Outside Directory Liability, supra* note 40, at 1085, *citing* TILLINGHAST-TOWERS PERRIN, UNDERSTANDING THE UNEXPECTED: 2004 DIRECTORS AND OFFICERS SURVEY REPORT 42 (2004).

127. *Examining Indemnification and Insurance, supra* note 118, at 58.

128. *Id.*

129. *See* 8 DGCL 102(b)(7), *supra* at Section II C.

130. *Examining Indemnification and Insurance, supra* note 118, at 59.

131. *Id.*

132. *Outside Director Liability, supra* note 40, at 1085, *citing* DEL. CODE. ANN. tit. 8 §145(g) (2005).

133. *Outside Director Liability, supra* note 40, at 1086 (citations omitted).

134. Salsitz vs. Nasser, 208 F.R.D. 589 (E.D. Mich. 2002).

135. *Salsitz*, 208 F.R.D. 589 (E.D.MI. 2002).

136. 208 F.R.D. at 590.

137. *Id.* at 596.

138. *Id.*

139. *Id.* at 599.

140. *Id.* at 591-92.

141. *Id.* at 594-95.

142. *Id.* at 595.

143. *Id.*

144. *Id.* at 597.

145. *Id.*

146. *Id.*

147. *McCall*, 239 F.3d 808.

148. *In re* Abbott Labs., 325 F.3d 795.

149. *See* discussion, *infra*, at Section II.F, as to whether the board's knowledge or desire to be informed about climate change science, for example, and the causal relationship, if any, between the company's activities and global warming might be more like the permissible ignorance of Ford's directors or the arguably culpable ignorance of the directors of Abbott Laboratories.

150. *Salsitz*, 208 F.R.D. at 599.

151. *Id.*

152. *Id.*

153. Because there is not case law directly on point, and because the scholarly debate on governance has been reenergized in the wake of global corporate governance, social and environmental issues, any new rules seem likely to emerge from this source. *See also* Williams & Conley, *supra* note 30 at 79 and 95-99 (considering whether, among other reasons, society's changing expectations of business, such as investors calling on companies to "address long-term risks such as climate change or international human rights," and changing institutional investor behavior, require a board's fiduciary duties to include consideration of international human rights).

154. *See* The Stakeholder Fiduciary, *supra* note 2 (suggesting that because corporations and their boards draw resources and capital from multiple sources, each such source is owed a duty and should be given a voice commensurate with its contribution).

155. *See, e.g.*, Martin Lipton, *supra* note 1, at 1369-70 (stating that "[s]elf-described 'reformers' of the post-Enron era are now mounting a more trenchant, multilevel and multijurisdictional attack on the ability of the board and management to manage effectively the corporation," and that resulting proposals "threaten to erode the fundamental principles that underlie the business judgment rule and that enable the board to function in an entrepreneurial manner. At the level of state common law, new theories of director liability also threaten to restrict further a board's effective exercise of its business judgment.").

156. *Cf.* The Honorable E. Norman Veasey, *A Perspective on Liability Risks to Directors in Light of Current Events*, Annual Audit Committee Issues Conference Keynote Speech, 1486 PLI/Corp. 1227, 1232-33, May 2005 ("Discussing recent events such as the Enron and Worldcom director settlements and stating, '[o]ne must take of these developments and some state law case like Caremark, Disney, Integrated Health . . . Take heed, that is. But again, don't panic! . . . Indeed, the law continues to be that conscientious directors who exercise due care, good faith and independent judgment in the honest belief that they are one acting on the best interests of the corporation and its stockholders will be protected by the courts. The time-honored business judgment rule is indeed alive and well under state law.'").

157. To the knowledge of the authors, this track has no current proponent in the climate change context. In fact, its first articulation is in these pages. It nevertheless seems to be a possible—even logical—by-product of the theoretical and commercial forces currently at work in the climate change marketplace. *See* Williams & Conley, *supra* note 30, at 78, 79 and 95-99.

158. For example, although weather-related losses make up the largest proportion of "catastrophe losses" sustained by insurers—and climate change could significantly increase the frequency and extent of such losses—fewer than one in a hundred insurance companies have sufficiently analyzed the economical implications of climate change. *See Climate Change Futures; Health, Ecological and Economic Dimensions*, The Center for Health and Global Environment, Harvard Medical School, Sponsored by Swiss Re and United Nations Development Programme (November 2005), at 92-95, *available at* http://www.climatechangefutures.org/pdf/CCF_Report_ Final_10.27.pdf.).

159. For example, "[i]n the past 10 years, the global wind energy capacity has increased tenfold—from 3.5 gigawatts (GW) in 1994 to almost 50 GW by the end of 2004. In the United States, the wind energy capacity tripled from 1600 Megawatts (MW) in 1994 to more than 6700 MW by the end of 2004. . . . Wind energy will become a major source of energy for the nation, which has only begun to tap its vast wind resources. The wind community has set a target of 100 gigawatts (GW) of wind electric capacity installed in the United States by 2020." *Federal Wind Program Highlights*, Wind Power Today, U.S. Dep't of Energy, April 2005, at 3-5, *available at* http://www1.eere.energy.gov/windandhydro/pdfs/37147.pdf.

160. See chapters 10 and 11.

161. *GE Goes Green: But Climate Change Action Cannot Be Left to Companies Alone*, Financial Times, May 11, 2005, at 18.

162. *See* GE Web site, discussing ecomagination commitment, http://www.ge.com/en/citizenship/customers/market/ecomagination.htm.

163. Ray Pospisil, *GE Finance Unit to Triple Renewable Investments*, Envtl. Finance, May 2006, at 7.

164. Shareholder Proposal No. 6–Report on Global Warming Science, GE Annual Report, Form 10-K, for the Fiscal Year Ended December 31, 2005, at 48-49.

165. *See* Action Fund Management, LLC Letter to GE Shareowners Regarding "Shareowner Proposal #6: Report on Global Warming Science," dated March 17, 2006, at 3, *available at* http://www.freeenterpriseactonifund.com/release 050206.htm [hereinafter Action Fund Management Letter].

166. Action Fund Management Letter, *supra* note 165, at 1.

167. Freedom Enterprises Action Fund Release, General Electric CEO Jeff Immelt refuses to justify lobbying for global warming regulation; Global warming shareholder resolution wins sufficient support to be voted again in 2007, May 2, 2006, *available at* http://www.freeenterpriseactionfund.com/release050206.htm [hereinafter Action Fund Release].

168. GE Annual Report, Form 10-K, for the Fiscal Year Ended December 31, 2005, at 50.

169. Action Fund Release, *supra* note 167 at 1 (May 2, 2006). GE reports that the resolution received 427,409,472 affirmative votes and 5,735,885,995 votes against,

with 575,646,737 abstaining and 2,026,269,762 non-broker votes. *See* http://ge.com/ en/company/investor/annualmeet/annual_meeting_2006.htm (last checked May 22, 2006).

170. Cape Wind Associates has proposed to build a wind farm consisting of 130 wind turbines on a 24-square-mile area of Nantucket Sound. During average winds, the project could provide three-quarters of the electricity needs of the Cape and Islands without generating pollution, yet the farm is strongly opposed by many of the local citizens as well as Governor Mitt Romney. Residents have formed the Alliance to Protect Nantucket Sound and argue the tall turbines would ruin the scenic horizon and that the project would convert a pristine setting into an industrial development. They have fought for legislation to prevent the farm under the Coast Guard and Maritime Transportation Act of 2006, to accompany H.R. 889. Stephanie Ebbert, *Cape Wind Is Dealt a Setback; Bill Would Give Romney Final Say*, BOSTON GLOBE, April 19, 2006, *available at* http://www.ebc-ne.org/index.php?id= 75&tx_ttnews%5Btt_news%5D =1&tx_ttnews%5BbackPid%5D=1&cHash=baea83656b

171. *See, e.g., Disney*, 2005 LEXIS at *6-8.

> It is easy . . . to fault a decision that ends in a failure, once hindsight makes the result of that decision plain to see. But the essence of business is risk—the application of informed belief to contingencies whose outcomes can sometimes be predicted, but never known. The decision-makers entrusted by shareholders must act out of loyalty to those shareholders. They must in good faith act to make informed decisions on behalf of the shareholders, untainted by self-interest. Where they fail to do so, this Court stands ready to remedy breaches of fiduciary duty. Even where decision-makers act as faithful servants, however, their ability and the wisdom of their judgments will vary. The redress for failures that arise from faithful management must come from the markets, through the action of shareholders and the free flow of capital, and not from this Court. Should the Court apportion liability based on the ultimate outcome of decisions taken in good faith by faithful directors or officers, those decision-makers would necessarily take decisions that minimize risk, not maximize value. The entire advantage of the risk-taking, innovative, wealth-creating engine that is the Delaware corporation would cease to exist, with disastrous results for shareholders and society alike. That is why, under our corporate law, corporate decision-makers are held strictly to their fiduciary duties, but within the boundaries of those duties are free to act as their judgment and abilities dictate, free of *post hoc* penalties from a reviewing court using perfect hindsight. Corporate decisions are made, risks are taken, the results become apparent, capital flows accordingly, and shareholder value is increased.

172. *See, e.g.,* Hexcel Corporation Annual Report, Form 10-K, for the Fiscal Year Ended December 31, 2005, at 39. ("Revenues from materials used to build the blades of wind turbine applications again showed strong growth, up over 50% in constant currency compared to 2004. The growth was driven by the increased number of global wind turbine installations and market share gains made in 2004.")

173. *See supra*, at Chapter 17.

174. For those with multinational operations, the differences between their choices in E.U. jurisdictions, for example, where CO_2 emission allocations have been made and an active credit trading market exists, and in the U.S. further complicates their position.

175. *See supra*, at Chapter 3.

176. *See* Chapter 6.

177. *See* Chapter 5.

178. *See* Chapter 6.

179. Spencer Jakab, *Utilities Consider Coal Technology to Limit Greenhouse Gases*, WALL STREET J., May 15, 2006, at C8.

180. For example, the Maryland Healthy Air Act, which was passed and then signed by Governor Robert Ehrlich in April 2006, could bring significant capital expenditures on Constellation Energy: the company already plans on installing approx. $550 million in scrubbers and bag houses at one power plant and is considering closing down another smaller power plant in Baltimore county as a more economical alternative to the cost of updating it to comply with the new legislation. Tom Pelton, *Energy Plant May Close; Constellation Says New Pollution Rules Too Costly for Balto. Co. Facility*, BALTIMORE SUN, April 15, 2006, at Section 1B.

181. *See, e.g.*, Sappi LTD, Annual and Transition Report on Foreign Private Issuers, Form 20-F, for the Fiscal Year Ending October 2, 2005 ("The countries within which we operate in Europe are all signatories of the Kyoto Protocol and we have developed a GHG strategy in line with this protocol. Our European mills have been set CO_2 emission limits for the allocation period 2005 to 2007. Based upon in-depth analysis of our mill production by a Sappi Fine Paper Europe task force, it is unlikely that Sappi will exceed their CO_2 emission limits. Consequently in July 2005 Sappi Fine Paper Europe sold 90,000 surplus CO_2 credits to the value of $2.5 million (euro 2.0 million) on the European Climate Exchange.").

182. Hyun Young Lee, *Politics & Economics: Carbon Market Braces for Report on EU Emissions*, WALL STREET J., May 15, 2006, at A8. Heath Timmons, with contributions from Katrin Bennhold, *Data Leaks Shake Up Carbon Trade*, N.Y. TIMES, May 16, 2006, Business/Financial Desk, Market Place, C Col. 1, 1.

183. For example, under the Regional Greenhouse Gas Initiative (RGGI), Connecticut, Delaware, Maine, New Hampshire, New Jersey, New York and Vermont (with the District of Columbia, Massachusetts, Pennsylvania, Rhode Island, the Eastern Canadian Provinces and New Brunswick as observers in the process) agreed to reduce carbon dioxide emissions by developing regional strategies for controlling emissions and a multistate cap-and-trade program with a market-based emissions trading system as the cornerstone. *See* RGGI Web site, http://www.rggi.org/states.htm.

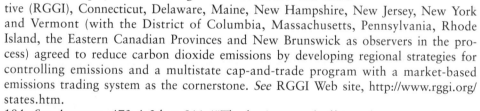

184. *See Aronson*, 473 A.2d at 811 ("The business and affairs of a corporation . . . shall be managed by or under the direction of a board of directors . . .") (emphasis in original), *quoting* 8 Del.Ch. § 141(a).

185. *See* Chapter 9.

186. *Alaska Lawmakers Approve Legislation Creating Commission on Climate Change*, DAILY ENVTL. REP., May 18, 2005 at A-7.

187. Paul Anderson, Duke Energy Corp.'s CEO, announced in Charlotte, N.C., on April 7, 2005, that his company would lobby for a tax on carbon dioxide emissions. This followed a letter accompanying the annual report he sent to shareholders, in which he vowed to be proactive in shaping a national policy on climate change. Paul Anderson, *Duke Energy CEO Proposes "Carbon Tax,"* ASSOCIATED PRESS, April 7, 2005, *available at* http://www.climateark.org/articles/reader.asp?linkid=40622.

188. *See* Frank P. Grad, TREATISE ON ENVIRONMENTAL LAW (Matthew Bender 1990), at § 4A.02 [hereinafter Grad].

189. *See* 42 U.S.C. § 9607(a)

190. United States v. Ne. Pharm. & Chemical Co., 810 F.2d 726 (8th Cir. 1986), *cert. denied*, 484 U.S. 848 (1987).

191. *See* United States v. New Castle Co., 642 F. Supp. 1258 (D.C. 1986) (discussing right of contribution under CERCLA); *see also* Grad, *supra* note 188, at § 4A.02, discussing nited States v. Chem-Dyne Corp., 572 F. Supp. 802.

192. *See* United States v. Bestfoods, 118 S. Ct. 1876 (1998); New York v. Shore Realty, 759 F.2d 1032 (2d Cir. 1985).

193. *See* Grad, *supra* note 188, at § 4A.02 ("The doctrine of strict liability, which imposes liability regardless of fault, frequently runs into objections from 'blameless' defendants who assert the injustice of assessing heavy cleanup cost liabilities on them.").

194. *See*, Grad, *supra* note 188, at § 4A.02 ("CERCLA imposes strict liability on designated PRPs, . . . including owners of sites, regardless of the time of acquisition. The owner's liability is the consequence of ownership . . .") (citations omitted).

195. 42 U.S.C. § 6921 et seq.

196. *See infra*, at Chapter 13.

197. *See* Claudia H. Deutsch, *Chemical Companies look to Coal as an Oil Substitute*, N.Y. TIMES, Bus. Section, April 18, 2006, at 1; *High-Sulfur Coal Back in Favor*, Associated Press, April 24, 2006.

198. 17 C.F.R. § 240.14(d).

199. *See, e.g.*, 2005 Resolution: ExxonMobil—Report on Kyoto Compliance, *available at* http . . . ("Shareholders request the Board undertake a comprehensive review and publish within six months of the annual meeting a report on how ExxonMobil will meet the greenhouse gas reduction target of those countries in which it operates which have adopted the Kyoto Protocol."); *Climate Change Risk and the SEC*, CERES and the Wirth Chair in Environmental and Community Development Policy at the University of Colorado for the Wirth Chair 2004 Leadership Forum, Aspen Institute, *available at* http://www.ceres.org/pub/docs/Ceres_climaterisk_SEC__100804.pdf. (There is a strong focus on improving the quality of disclosure on climate change risks versus changing the company's practices).

200. For example, see the following reports: AEP, An Assessment of AEP's Actions to Mitigate the Economic Impacts of Emissions Policies, August 31, 2004; TXU, Investing in Our World; TXU, Taking Responsible Actions for Our Texas Environment, Communities, Diversity and Safety, 2004 Corporate Citizenship Report. Also: Cinergy, Air Issues Report to Stakeholders; An Analysis of the Potential Impact of Greenhouse Gas and Other Air Emission Regulations on Cinergy Corp., December 2004.

201. *See* discussion in Chapter 13, *infra*.

202. *Cf.* Robert Muir Wood, *Adapt and Mitigate*, ENVTL. FINANCE, May 2006, at 17 (arguing that, as with the relationship between fire insurance and building codes starting in the 1600s, the insurance industry should price its products to help enforce GHG emission reductions).

203. *See* Center for Health and the Global Environment, Harvard Medical School, Sponsored by Swiss Re and the United Nations Development Programme, *Climate Change Futures: Health, Ecological and Economic Dimensions*, November 2005, at 92-107 (discussing the financial implications of climate change, including potential limits of insurability).

chapter fifteen

Insurance and Climate Change

Gary S. Guzy

I. Introduction

The insurance industry finds itself at the nexus of current concerns over global climate change for several key reasons. There is a general expectation that insurance represents a societal mechanism for reflecting, monetizing, and internalizing future risks—so that the effects on the insurance industry are seen, perhaps, as an early indicator of the economic challenges posed by global warming. It has been said that "[i]nsurers are often the messengers that change is happening, because the prices they charge, the conditions they attach to their policies, and sometimes the very availability of insurance, reflect rising or falling risks in our society."[1] Thus, the insurance industry "has a key responsibility in helping their customers and public authorities to identify how risks can be managed, reduced, and where possible averted."[2] Insurance has performed the positive societal role of driving many health and safety initiatives and prevention measures.[3]

Moreover, the insurance sector is the world's largest industry, with approximately $3.24 trillion in revenues in 2004.[4] Put another way, the industry would be the third largest economy in the world by Gross Domestic Product. So in terms of sheer economic impact alone, the effects on the industry are highly significant.

Insurance regulators, consumers, and activists harbor a growing sense of concern as the industry adjusts to the financial implications posed by increasing losses from natural catastrophes with a resultant adverse impact on the availability and affordability of essential insurance coverages. Yet there also is concern over the flip side of the coin—whether there will be adequate reserve capital to pay claims in the event of a continuation or exacerbation of the kinds of loss events seen over recent years. These areas of concern are tempered by a general respect for the industry's capabilities in understanding these risks and making such calculations, leading to an expectation that the industry will provide critical guidance on sensible risk management and avoidance in helping to identify climate change solutions. In addition, there is a growing public recognition that the insurance industry—with its expertise in risk management and risk mitigation, as well as its substantial investment authority—can provide an important and credible business voice to leverage more active climate regulatory policy in the United States, as well as globally.

II. Structure and Regulation of the Insurance Industry

The basic concept of insurance is: "to pool risks across a large and diverse population. Each individual in that population protects themselves against an uncertain loss by paying an annual premium towards the pool's expected losses. The insurer holds premiums in a fund that, along with investment income . . ., compensates those that experience losses."[5]

One of the most challenging aspects of insurance, however, is that these premiums must be set *before* the costs are actually known. The very nature of insurance depends upon the ability to make predictions about losses—including their likelihood of occurring and their extent. "Future costs, including frequency of claim events, have to be estimated in advance" to ensure adequate capital to pay for expected losses, administrative expenses, and an adequate business return.[6] Risk pooling assists in this effort, to some extent, because it provides greater statistical claims accuracy.

In order to manage this process, the industry has developed certain well-recognized "principles of insurability." These include that: (1) a loss is *random*, in other words that the insured cannot induce a claimable event; (2) it is possible within reasonable confidence limits to *assess* the frequency and severity of claimable events; (3) there is *mutuality* of interest, where the insureds believe that the terms of sharing risks with other members of the insured community are generally economically fair; and (4) the amount of payments for any event or series of events is *affordable* and can be diversified with the risk pool.[7]

These principles translate into certain strategies that the insurance industry employs to manage its overall risks. Key to these are establishing "underwriting" standards, which may entail refusing outright to cover customers who may represent an unacceptable level of risk or limiting coverage offered in particular areas.[8] These approaches help to minimize the possibility of a "moral hazard," whereby an insured is induced to take on greater risk than if it were uninsured because it has transferred the consequences of that behavior to an insurer.[9] The use of deductibles—sometimes known as attachment points—also helps to prevent this moral hazard, because it involves payment by an insured before qualifying for collecting on a loss. Reinsurance provides another tool for insurers to manage their overall risks. A reinsurer may cover a specific portion of an insurer's claims in return for a premium payment.[10]

Insurance companies are principally regulated at the state level. Congress made this approach explicit by adopting the McCarran-Ferguson Act in 1945[11] to remove the ambiguity created by the decision of the U.S. Supreme Court in *United States v. South-Eastern Underwriters Ass'n,* which found insurance to be interstate commerce within the constitutional authority of Congress to regulate.[12] States generally undertake licensing through insurance commissioners, who regulate the availability and affordability of insurance coverage, as well as the appropriateness of rates. The National Association of Insurance Commissioners (NAIC) serves as a resource to these state efforts.[13] Justifications of rate increases generally must estimate increased needs based upon a focus on past data.

There is now a robust specialized environmental insurance market that writes approximately $2 billion of premiums per year in the United States.

The insurance markets have generally become comfortable addressing a wide variety of environmental risks. There is now a robust specialized environmental insurance market that writes approximately $2 billion of premiums per year in the United States. These markets cover risks related to hazardous and toxic substances, including providing guarantees against cost overruns for site cleanups and protections against third-party harms from known and unknown chemical contamination. This market has arisen despite the fear induced by the liability provisions of the federal Superfund law, the Comprehensive Environmental Response, Compensation and Liability Act, and the unexpected payouts that many carriers were required to make for such liabilities under older comprehensive general liability policies. Superfund, combined perhaps with toxic tort liability from asbestos, however, has left the insurance industry deeply wary of the dangers of third-party litigation.

Flood insurance is generally not handled by the private markets, as the losses from flood-related events are typically very concentrated in a particular area and only those living in floodplains, who are most at risk, are likely to purchase it. The federal government, however, provides such coverage through the National Flood Insurance Program (NFIP). This program was created by Congress in 1968. It was designed to promote the wise use of floodplains through local regulation and to provide affordable flood insurance to owners of existing developed properties in areas at risk from flooding.[14] To do so, Congress authorized subsidized rates to keep premiums low enough to encourage participation. The NFIP provides flood insurance only in those communities that adopt and enforce floodplain management regulations designed to lower the risk of flooding and to assure that development will not worsen flood hazards.[15] The federal government has developed building standards for floodplain construction that provide minimum requirements for participation. Mitigation measures are explicitly linked to the price of this insurance through the Community Rating System.

Capital markets are providing new financial instruments to complement reinsurance to cover mega-losses from natural catastrophes. These are structured as catastrophe bonds, sometimes known as "cat bonds," which pay out at handsome rates in the event there is no loss but allow a reinsurance company to collect in the event losses exceed a certain threshold.[16]

III. Evolution of the Insurance Industry's Attention to Climate Change: The Particular Challenge Posed by Climate Risk

The insurance industry has gradually become sensitized to the challenges posed by climate risk. Beginning with the 1992 Earth Summit in Rio de Janeiro, several European-based insurers started to develop a framework for a sustainability focus for the industry that would establish a linkage between environmental and economic issues. In 1995, working with the United Nations Environment Programme (UNEP), they developed a Statement of Environmental Commitment by the Insurance Industry. The primary movers in this effort included General Accident, Gerling Global Re, National Provident, Storebrand, Sumitomo Marine & Fire, and Swiss Re. The essence of this commitment is a pledge to incorporate environmental considerations into internal and external business operations. These efforts developed into the UNEP Insurance Initiative.[17]

The UNEP Insurance Initiative companies became quite active in working with the Intergovernmental Panel on Climate Change (IPCC) and called for mandatory greenhouse gas emissions reductions at the international climate negotiations at Kyoto in 1997. The UNEP Insurance Initiative eventually merged with the broader Financial Institutions Initiative in 2003.

During this period, some insurance industry participants became increasingly active in United States policy as well. Swiss Re and Munich Re—two of the largest reinsurers in the world—were perhaps most involved during this period, complementing their dialogue and educational efforts with highly visible policy advocacy. Swiss Re's testimony in the fall of 2003 at hearings before the U.S. Senate Committee on Commerce, Science & Transportation was striking in its acknowledgement that "global warming is a fact" and in its call for "measures to reduce GHG emissions . . . [through] government leadership."[18] These statements echoed various public reports put out by Swiss Re claiming that the climate "has changed visibly, tangibly, measurably . . . while human intervention in the natural climatic system plays an important, if not decisive role."[19]

As the industry began to recognize an increasing pattern to its severe weather-related losses, particularly after the 2004 and 2005 hurricane seasons, a series of reports and advocacy group efforts highlighted growing concerns about the extreme economic challenges posed by climate risk. For example, a 2004 study by the Association of British Insurers (ABI) applied catastrophe models to examine the effects of extreme storms. By using more sophisticated probabilistic assessments than had ever been attempted to simulate the range of events that could unfold and weighing them by their chance of occurrence, these tools provided a more reliable picture of the potential outcomes from severe weather events. The ABI study found that hurricane losses in the United States could total $100 to $150 billion in a given season, and that Japanese typhoons and European windstorms likewise could have severe consequences. The increased losses could increase insurers' capital requirements by over 90%, leading to far greater volatility in the financial markets.[20] Indeed, the experience with Hurricane Andrew in 1992, which caused $16 billion in insured damage—an amount almost 50% larger than the premiums collected in Florida over the preceding 20 years—forced 11 insurers into receivership.

This direct loss experience was combined as well with a growing recognition that insurers' capital market investments likewise could be affected by climate risk, leading to an even greater financial impact. French insurer AXA stated, in its Carbon Disclosure Project response, that "[o]ne considers today that about 20% of the GDP is affected by climatic chances [sic] and that the climatic risk is, as a consequence, in numerous branches of industry (farm-produce industry, tourism, textile industry, energy, transport...) more important than the risk of interest rate or the foreign exchange risk."[21]

Indeed, a series of events across the globe began to highlight not only the large financial toll imposed by climate change, but the unpredictable nature of the losses as well. The 2003 European heat wave led to thousands of premature deaths, and the wildfires it spawned caused approximately $15 billion in property losses in Portugal, Spain, and France. The 2004 hurricane season in Florida was particularly devastating, with four storms hitting in rapid succession, leading to total economic losses of around $56 billion, of which $30 billion was insured. Sweden suffered a windstorm in January 2005 that caused the largest insured loss ever in that country, with severe damage to commercial forestry resources causing some $2.5 billion in losses.[22] South America saw its first-ever reported hurricane, Catarina, which caused significant damage in Brazil. Tropical Storm Vince became the most easterly and northerly tropical cyclone ever, reaching the coast of Spain in October 2005.[23] The Canary Islands witnessed their first tropical cyclone in November 2005.[24]

Not only did these recent events raise unsettling financial issues, they also demonstrated that health and life insurance coverages could be impacted, in addition to property/casualty insurance lines. These events highlighted that the challenge posed by climate change was not simply one of risk—which generally is predictable—but one of increasing levels of uncertainty.

Advocacy groups began more concentrated efforts to apply pressure to the insurance industry to be more explicit about climate-induced risks. Friends of the Earth, for example, performed an assessment of securities filing disclosures regarding climate risks and catastrophic losses for the insurance industry, among others. Only Chubb and Allstate provided explicit discussions of climate change in their discussions in Item 7 of the Form 10-K Securities and Exchange Commission filings.[25]

A. The Katrina Effect

The insurance industry, regulators, and the public were—of course—riveted by the vast scale of the devastation wrought by Hurricane Katrina. Since 2005 was the hottest year on record and had the largest number of named hurricanes in the United States since records were first kept in 1851, these combined to spur an intense focus on the management of catastrophic weather-related risks and—for many—crystallized the concerns that had slowly been gelling. For many insurers, these events highlighted concerns that losses from climate-related storms could be "highly correlated"—in other words, that many types of losses could occur together—and that there is significant uncertainty in their prediction, thus "complicating the actuarial and pricing processes that underlie well-functioning insurance markets."[26]

Insurers took careful note of the discussions in the science community of the linkage between more severe storms and rising sea surface temperatures, all correlated with increasing levels of greenhouse gases in the atmosphere.

Insurers took careful note of the discussions in the science community of the linkage between more severe storms and rising sea surface temperatures, all correlated with increasing levels of greenhouse gases in the atmosphere.[27] These studies tended to show that the unusually high levels of activity due to natural climate oscillation are "intensified" by anthropogenically induced global warming,[28] and that global warming "loaded the dice," thereby increasing the likelihood of natural disasters.[29] Insurance statistics showed a significant increase in the number of natural disasters—seven of the ten most expensive hurricanes in U.S. history occurred in 2004 or 2005,[30] and severe weather events increased from an average of 29 per year in the 1970s to 114 per year since 1990.[31]

What was perhaps most striking about Katrina was the scope of the devastation wrought by this single event. Entire state electric power systems were wiped out; 160 oil and gas platforms and 450 pipelines were damaged; 250,000 to 500,000 homes were lost; 600,000 people were put out of work; dozens of Superfund sites were inun-

dated; hundreds of drinking water and sewage systems were knocked out; some 1.4 million household or hazardous orphan waste containers just floating about were collected by the EPA; and debris was created that was estimated to fill the equivalent of between 200 and 1,000 football fields filled 50 feet high. Overall, some $60 billion in losses were incurred—consisting of some two million individual losses—in addition to the human toll of approximately 1,500 lives lost.[32] Katrina became "the costliest insured loss from a single event in U.S. history. . . . Total economic losses, including insured and uninsured property and flood damages are expected to exceed $200 billion."[33]

There were 210,000 businesses directly affected by Katrina in Louisiana and other states. The hit to the United States' economy did not stop there, however. It was felt by those needing petroleum products around the country, and by those relying on the Port of New Orleans for sending or receiving goods, for example.

The fall after Katrina also saw the release by CERES, the environmental and institutional investor coalition, of a detailed study on the availability and affordability of insurance under climate change.[34] The report noted that demographic and socioeconomic trends—like the high concentration of Americans living near a coast—compound the effects of climate-related impacts from events like floods, windstorms, thunderstorms, hail storms, ice storms, wildfires, droughts, heat waves, lightning strikes, subsidence damages, coastal erosion, and airborne allergens (e.g., mold and pollen). The end result, according to the report, has been a 15-fold increase in insured losses from catastrophic weather events in the past three decades.[35]

Changing concentrations of urbanization and increasing property values are—in addition to concerns about actual climate effects on storm frequency and severity—increasing the economic costs of risk dramatically. For example, so-called "megacities"—those with populations in excess of 10 million—have increased from just one in 1950 to nearly 25 around the world today.[36] Florida, where so many hurricanes have reached landfall, has gone from 2 million to nearly 20 million residents during this same period.[37]

Institutional investors also went on the offensive. A group of 20 public pension funds, labor pension funds, socially responsible funds, and faith-based investors—collectively representing $800 billion in assets under management—joined together to press the U.S. insurance industry on climate impacts. They directed letters to 30 publicly traded companies that are the largest in the life, health, property/casualty, and reinsurance sectors. The letters seek comprehensive disclosure from the companies on the risks they may face from direct climate-related losses, steps they are taking to prevent these risks, and any effects on their investments. The investors make the case that these losses could affect the financial performance of the companies.[38]

B. Technical Insurance Consequences and Policy Responses

For the insurance industry, one of the key effects of this event was to alter the way in which natural catastrophes would be modeled and treated. Some aspects of the industry had already changed in response to Hurricane Andrew in 1992. Florida had, for example, set up the Florida Hurricane Catastrophe Fund that operated much like a reinsurance entity, in that it was funded by a portion of insurance premiums and was managed and overseen in all the same ways. This fund was designed to act as an insurer of last resort to provide insurance when no private company was willing to underwrite disaster risks for that region. These changes are widely credited with having prevented further financial disasters for Florida's property insurance industry after Hurricane Katrina.[39]

The various loss pathways and the unpredictability of the losses from Katrina, however, suggested that a simple retrospective evaluation no longer would suffice for estimating future risks. Instead, the industry needed to evaluate scenarios "that ha[d] hitherto been considered inconceivable—we have to think the unthinkable."[40] And the industry needed to address the combination of hurricane force winds and secondary effects, such as storm surge and inland flooding.[41] The British insurance market, Lloyd's, for example, began planning for new loss scenarios involving losses of up to $100 billion.[42]

In a later report, Lloyd's recommended "a new approach to underwriting," whereby the industry would "look[] ahead and not simply bas[e] decisions on historical patterns, as has traditionally been the case."[43] Leading catastrophic modeling firms, which provide sophisticated probabilistic worst-case analyses to insurers and reinsurers for evaluating hazards, inventories, vulnerabilities, and losses,[44] brought together noted climatologists in response to the 2005 hurricane season. For the first time, they adopted new forward-looking models based upon predicting future climate activity. The consequence of these efforts was—based upon a new understanding of the activity rates of landfalling hurricanes—to recommend that the industry increase its average annual losses for quantifying insurance risk by nearly 50% in the Gulf, Florida, and Southeast and by 25% to 30% in the Mid-Atlantic and Northeast coastal regions.[45]

Reinsurers took note of these events. Warren Buffett, the founder and head of Berkshire Hathaway Inc.—one of the largest catastrophic loss providers—noted that it was an "open question" whether atmospheric, oceanic, or other factors have dramatically increased the intensity of hurricanes, but that it had to assume so and therefore significantly increased its costs of providing catastrophic coverage.[46]

Even with such changes, however, there remains a significant concern about the ability of private insurance markets to respond adequately to climate-induced risk.

The Congressional Research Service noted "the private insurance market's lack of capacity to handle the next catastrophic event should it exceed $100 billion in private insured losses."[47]

One of the more sophisticated arguments made in the CERES report was that the nature of climate-related risks and losses is eroding the insurability of catastrophic losses pursuant to the principles discussed at note 7. The CERES report cited the following "technical risks":

- "Shortening times between loss events, such as more hurricanes per season,
- Changing absolute and relative variability of losses,
- Changing structure of types of events,
- Shifting spatial distribution of events,
- Damages that increase exponentially or nonlinearly with weather intensity [citing cubing of wind damage with wind speed rise],
- Widespread geographic simultaneity of losses (e.g., From tidal surges arising from broad die-off of protective coral reefs or disease outbreaks on multiple continents),
- Increased difficulty in anticipating "hot spots" (geographic and demographic for particular hazards) [citing Seattle heat warnings],

- More single events with multiple, correlated consequences. This was well evidenced in the pan-European heat catastrophe of 2003—where temperatures were six standard deviations from the norm. Immediate or delayed impacts included extensive human morbidity and mortality, wildfire, massive crop losses, and the curtailment of electric power plants due to the temperature or lack of cooling water, and
- More hybrid events with multiple consequences (e.g., El Niño-related rain, ice storms, floods, mudslides, droughts, and wildfires)."[48]

The report also cited a range of "market-based risks" further eroding insurability:

- "Historically-based premiums that lag behind actual losses,
- Failing to foresee and keep up with changing customer needs arising from the consequences of climate change,
- Unanticipated changes in patterns of claims, and associated difficulty in adjusting pricing and reserve practices to maintain profitability,
- Responses of insurance regulators,

- Reputation risks falling on insurers who do not, in the eyes of consumers, do enough to prevent losses arising from climate change, and
- Stresses unrelated to weather but conspiring with climate change impacts to amplify the net adverse impact. These include draw-downs of capital and surplus due to earthquakes or terrorist attacks and increased competition from self-insurance or other competing methods of risk-spreading."[49]

Insurers and reinsurers echoed many of the concerns about Katrina's impact and the ability to continue to address catastrophic losses. Indeed, the staid image of the insurance industry is being replaced by a climate change-induced new brand of activism. Lloyd's argued in its Spring 2006 report, for example, that the insurance industry—given its large share of the world's financial assets—"can therefore make a difference by using their influence as investors to encourage 'climate proof' behaviour from the boards of large corporations."[50] And several insurers are complementing these statements by internally directed actions designed to demonstrate their climate leadership, such as Swiss Re's pledge to become carbon neutral over ten years.[51] American International Group (AIG)—the largest underwriter of commercial and industrial insurance in the United States—issued a climate change policy in spring of 2006, whereby it is "actively seeking to incorporate environmental and climate change considerations across its businesses."[52] And Marsh, Inc., the world's largest risk management and insurance services firm, affiliated with the Business Environmental Leadership Council of the Pew Center on Global Climate Change, pledging to provide significant information on climate risk.[53]

C. Heightened Attention from Regulators

Regulators also were spurred to further study by concerns about the effect of climate change-induced losses on the continuing availability and affordability of insurance. The National Association of Insurance Commissioners (NAIC) set up the Climate Change and Global Warming Executive Committee Task Force to evaluate and address these issues. The NAIC's first meeting to assess climate risk, ironically, was cancelled because its annual meeting was slated to have taken place in New Orleans just shortly after Katrina hit.[54] The task force plans to complete a report by its 2007 Summer National Meeting that focuses on: "the implications of climate change on health insurance and managed care; property and casualty insurance; insurer financial condition; and the availability and affordability of insurance coverages to the insurance consumer. The report shall document . . . insurers' knowledge of potential climate change impacts on their business and financial condition. . . . In its report, the Task Force shall include its recommendations with regard to steps that regulators need to take to assure that they are adequately monitoring insurer's activities with regard to managing the financial condition of insurance and the performance of insurance markets."[55]

One of the key areas of examination will be "possible interrogatories or other public disclosures that should be considered by insurance regulators," as well as "steps that insurers have taken to mitigate or manage the impact of climate changes . . . ."[56] Among the motivations for this effort is the concern that the unavailability of insurance will limit new construction or lead to loan foreclosures where there are conditions of insurance, according to task force co-chair Tim Wagner, the insurance commissioner of the state of Nebraska.[57]

The federal government effectively subsidized some of the insured Hurricane Katrina losses. The government-administered National Flood Insurance Program (NFIP) had 377,000 flood insurance policies in force in Louisiana alone when Katrina struck, providing some $52 billion in coverage.[58] Reserves under the program were inadequate, however, to respond to the losses from Katrina—suggesting that the premium rating approach was insufficient. Congress amended the NFIP in November 2005 to authorize it to borrow up to $18.5 billion.[59]

The United States Government Accountability Office has undertaken a review of insurance risks posed by a changing climate spurred by these losses. The report will be completed by March 16, 2007, and will focus on preparations being undertaken by insurers to estimate and prepare for weather-related events. The study was requested by the bipartisan combination of Senator Susan Collins (R. Maine) and Senator Joseph Lieberman (D. Conn).[60]

All of these public investigations are likely to have the effect of sharpening public focus on the increasing societal costs of volatile weather events and the cost of internalizing climate risk. Moreover, these effects may be heightened as insurers work to limit their vulnerability and their need for increasing amounts of risk capital to cover future losses. Not surprisingly, as insurance rates rise in certain at-risk areas to reflect heightened threats from climate change, these changes may well alter behavior. As *The Wall Street Journal* reported: "The insurance industry is 'going to drive commercial enterprises out of certain areas in this country,' says Bill Black, president of CDC Publishing, which has three offices in Florida. Last year, the company paid $10,000 in premiums for hurricane and business interruption coverage. This spring, the premiums went up to $120,000. Another jump of similar magnitude, Mr. Black says, could force him to consider relocating his Florida offices."[61]

These concerns are being exacerbated by the exit of some private insurers, such as Allstate, from the riskiest markets, just as more people recognize the need for high-quality insurance coverage.[62] Citizens Property Insurance Corporation, created as a safety net insurer of last resort for homeowners by the state of Florida, anticipated becoming the largest insurer of homeowners in that state by the summer of 2006.[63] Citizens had a $1.73 billion deficit from the 2005 hurricanes and received a legislative bailout of $715 million, with the remaining deficiency being charged as an assessment to policies, leading to a doubling of many premiums.[64]

Increasingly, the insurance industry is finding itself drawn into the question of which kinds of risk mitigation related to climate change it should be fostering. As Lloyd's contends, "Solutions must be found now to reverse the trend toward further increasing population concentrations in affected areas, especially coastal areas. . . . This should lead to appropriate land-use and building policies for affected areas, with construction in high risk areas discouraged, and the insurance industry creating incentives for policyholders to respond appropriately to manage risk, building these into terms and conditions of policies."[65] These considerations raise the question whether the current condition in the United States—where "54% of the U.S. population now lives in close proximity to the coast"[66]—is sustainable in view of current climate threats.

IV. Nature of the Risks Presented by Global Warming

Among the reports released after Hurricane Katrina was an assessment of the health-related impacts of global warming. The report, "Climate Change Futures: Health, Ecological and Economic Dimensions," was prepared by Harvard Medical School's Center for Health and the Global Environment, sponsored by Swiss Re and the United Nations Development Programme. It found that "[c]limate has changed faster and more unpredictably than [expected] . . . . Many of the phenomenon assumed to lie decades in the future are already well underway."[67] One of the report's principal authors noted that there have been a recent "relentless series of anomalies" and "events with non-linear impacts," leading to the conclusion that the planet is not just facing "climate change," but that it really faces "climate instability."[68]

> There is a growing perception within the insurance industry that—if anything— early science may have underestimated the pace and magnitude of climate change . . .

Many central insurance industry participants have accepted and moved beyond the concept that the climate is changing and that human activity is playing a major role.[69] There is a growing perception within the insurance industry that—if anything—early science may have underestimated the pace and magnitude of climate change and that "the latest science suggests that future climate change may take place quicker than previously anticipated."[70] Key trends cited in the *Climate Change Futures* report—such as intense and widespread storms, the extent of coral bleaching and deeper ocean warming, and the pace of glacier movement and retreat—tend to support this conclusion. Another central theme of the *Climate Change Futures* assessment was that many climate events render future scenarios simply too uncertain to predict. This only serves to heighten the nature of the risks society faces and the difficulties the insurance industry confronts in managing these risks.

The *Climate Change Futures* report further concluded that "[i]n both core businesses, as well as activities in financial services and asset management, the insurance sector is increasingly vulnerable to climate change."[71] Indeed, "[v]irtually all segments of the [insurance] industry have a degree of vulnerability to the likely impacts of climate change, including those covering damages to property (structures, automobiles, marine vessels, aircraft); crops and livestock; pollution-related liabilities; business interruptions; supply-chain disruptions, or loss of utility service; equipment breakdown arising from extreme temperature events; data loss from power surges or outages; and a spectrum of life and health consequences."[72] These widespread impacts are not surprising, given that some estimates place 25% of the United States economy as within sectors that are "sensitive to weather and climate, such as agriculture and tourism. . . ."[73]

A spring 2006 publication, *Risk Alert: Climate Change: Business Risks and Solutions,* issued by Marsh, Inc., described the practical business risks resulting from climate change that companies face: "The business risks from climate change include: the strong threat of increasingly volatile weather conditions, rising sea levels, and new health impacts; resulting impacts on insurance markets, business resources, personnel, and corporate preparedness; increasing legal and regulatory pressures; and mounting public and shareholder activism."[74]

The Marsh publication goes on to survey the physical risks to businesses:

- **Sea level rise:** Melting of the polar icecaps and a resulting rise in the sea level could be one of the most serious consequences of climate change. The potential for damage is enormous, especially as coastal areas become more developed. Companies could be affected not only through direct loss of facilities and real estate, but also through potential impacts on their workers, many of whom could be forced to move if seawaters rise significantly. Not only might some areas be submerged, but areas not previously at risk to storm surge could become so.

- **Hurricanes and typhoons:** Hurricane Katrina focused world attention on the damage a massive hurricane causes when it strikes a populated area. As with a rising sea level, coastal areas could expect to bear the brunt of the damage from increased storm activity, although tropical-storm damage from floods and wind can extend hundreds of miles inland. Asian countries dependent on monsoon season could be damaged by any change in the timing and intensity of storms.

- **Drought:** Some areas of the world may become more prone to drought; already-dry areas may find the delicate balance they now live under tilted to one of desertification. Among the potential losses are destroyed crops, loss or reduction of water resources, damage to ecosystems, and forced migration of people.
- **Wildfires:** Along with increased drought conditions comes the possibility of an increase in wildfires, both in forests and grasslands. Wildfires could threaten business facilities; tourism centers; timber, grazing, and agricultural land; wildlife habitat; private homes; and more.
- **Heat waves:** The European heat wave of 2003—widely cited as being related to climate change—caused the deaths of an estimated 22,000 people. Demand for air conditioning during periods of extreme heat could lead to massive power outages.[75]

As sweeping as this assessment claims the likely effects to be, the scale it contemplated was greatly exceeded by the review commissioned from Sir Nicholas Stern by the Chancellor of the Exchequer of the United Kingdom. The Stern Review Report on the Economics of Climate Change predicts that the consequences of inaction in addressing global warming will result in a drag on global Gross Domestic Product of between 5% and 20%—an effect on the economy similar to that caused by the Great Depression or the World Wars of the Twentieth Century.[76] These huge impacts—including on food and fresh water availability and having the greatest consequences in the developing world—could impose significant losses on the global insurance industry, and confirm the importance of insurance industry participation in the global policy debate on climate change.[77]

V. Insurance Coverage Issues Presented by Climate Change

Because businesses that sustain losses often look to insurance for potential relief, there may be a question as to whether coverage is available for damage related to climate change. At the time of this writing, there is no current policy that provides explicit coverage for the risk of "climate change." However, there are policies that cover the types of damage that might be associated with climate impacts, such as flood, wind, freezing, heat, earth movement, or collapse.

Because climate change is, arguably, at its roots an environmental issue, companies may conclude that their environmental liability policies should respond to these losses. However, at present, it appears unlikely insurers would simply accept these arguments. There are a range of potential arguments insurers could be expected to make in response to such claims. Environmental liability or pollution policies typically provide coverage for damage arising from "pollution." This is often further restricted to certain types of pollution, such as indoor-air pollution, pollution at a particular site, and/or a particular pollutant involved in an industrial process. According to Marsh's *Risk Alert* on climate change, the "term 'pollution' is often broadly defined, but is as often restricted by policy language or case law to mean industrial chemicals or substances classified as pollutants by governmental entities and environmental laws."[78] Many policies also contain the further restriction that coverage applies only to expenses incurred in response to a government order issued under authority of a relevant environmental statute, an argument that may be pertinent in states that have not adopted regulatory programs for greenhouse gases. The Supreme Court's consideration of this issue may be pertinent for interpretive purposes,[79] although insurance coverages—formed by agreement of contract—operate pursuant to various state laws, not the federal statute at issue in that case.

Insurers are also likely to argue that policy coverage would apply only where it can be shown that the particular insured's actions caused a particular and measurable harm. The scientific debate as to the causes of global climate change may present one set of issues; the arguably nonspecific nature of the effects associated with climate change presents another. Given these concerns, the above *Risk Alert* concluded that "it does not appear likely that insurers would simply agree that existing environmental liability policies provide coverage for the broad array of damages potentially associated with climate change."[80]

This is not to say that claims can never be presented under these policies. Indeed, it may be possible to argue that certain kinds of claims could trigger coverage. Litigation now developing around the concept of plaintiffs' standing to assert claims for damages from climate-related impacts (as treated in Chapter 6 of this book) may contain the seeds for some of these arguments. Similarly, any changes in statutory definitions of "pollution" to include various greenhouse gases (see Chapter 5) may also enhance the probability of success of such a claim.

There is the possibility that a general climate liability policy may be offered by insurers some time in the future. But those insurers now looking at the issue are finding that the lack of predictive certainty and actuarial data makes development and pricing of a product very difficult. Insurers are also concerned with how claims would be presented, how damages would be determined, and how compensation for alleged damage would be measured. Accordingly, it may be some time before such a specific product becomes available.

Litigation stemming from Hurricane Katrina tests some of these concepts and may provide important insights. In *Comer v. Nationwide Mutual Ins. Co.*, No. 1:05 CV 436 (S.D. Miss. filed Sept. 20, 2005), plaintiff homeowners brought an action against insurance companies, mortgage lenders, chemical, and oil and refining companies doing business in Mississippi. "Essentially, the claim against the energy and chemical companies is that their emissions of greenhouse gases contributed to global warming, which has resulted in more intense and destructive hurricanes."[81] The case against the insurers was dismissed on February 23, 2006, and an amended suit, *Comer v. Murphy Oil*, was filed in April.[82]

The increased oversight of climate risks from regulators, investors—including institutional investors in both the public and private sectors—and other public interest groups has implications for directors and officers (D&O) liability insurance. Factors treated in more detail in other chapters, such as shareholder resolutions, enhanced Securities and Exchange Commission scrutiny of general environmental disclosures, and the potential for tort or public nuisance litigation are heightening the focus on disclosure and carbon risk management as essential corporate governance issues.[83] Whether some of the risks are covered by D&O policies may depend upon the scope of the pollution exclusion which is usually written into them and whether the activities questioned are construed as "related" in any way to "pollution."[84]

Insurers are starting to take notice of all this activity, and a few have developed general questions to better assess the risk. At the time of this writing, insurers' questions during underwriting are focusing on areas such as the following: "Management accountability/responsibility: Does a company allocate responsibility for the management of climate-related risks? If so, how does it do so? Corporate governance: Is there a committee of independent board members addressing the issues? Emissions management and reporting: What progress, if any, has a company made in quantifying, disclosing, and/or reporting its emissions profile? Regulatory anticipation: How well has a company planned for future regulatory scenarios?"[85] In view of these concerns and activities surrounding corporate directors and officers, Marsh's *Risk Alert* on climate change concluded: "There may soon be an increased level of underwriting activity around climate risks."[86]

VI. New Insurance Products Responsive to Climate Change

A. New Tools for Managing the New Risks

The insurance markets are responding to climate change through the development of an array of new products.[87] A growing tool being adopted by the insurance and financial markets employs weather-based derivatives. These are financial instruments used by companies to offset financial risk and uncertainty caused by volatility in such phenomena as temperature, rain, snow, or wind. Transactions typically are structured to require a payout when a particular index (heat degree days, amount of rain or snowfall, etc.) is triggered. A ski resort, for example, may be able to use a weather derivative to smooth the financial risk from the potential for below-average snowfall. Also, power-price protection for utilities provides a means for hedging costly demands for peak power.

If climate change continues to increase the uncertainty that already surrounds extreme weather, interest in such products likely will continue to increase. "Although less than ten years old, the use of weather risk management has increased substantially in recent years, according to the Weather Risk Management Association (WRMA). For the period from April 2004 to April 2005, the face value of all weather risk management instruments increased to $8.4 billion from $4.6 billion in the year prior. The biggest users of such instruments were in the energy sector, followed by agriculture, retail, construction, transportation, and miscellaneous others."[88]

In one of the more innovative uses of these instruments, the United Nations' World Food Programme devoted its humanitarian food aid in part to purchasing an indexed insurance policy to protect crop assistance to poor farmers in Ethiopia. That policy, placed with French insurer AXA RE, would pay out in the event that severe drought—defined by pre-existing rainfall measures at agreed-upon locations—rendered the plantings unproductive.[89] Such indexed policies are likely to be far easier to administer than a traditional insurance policy, because they do not depend upon a difficult assessment of agricultural productivity for payouts, but rather a simple objective measurement that is tied to programmatic success.

The International Finance Corporation is now exploring expanding this concept through the Global Indexed Insurance Fund that would leverage private risk capital to provide developing countries with weather and catastrophe reinsurance.[90] Indeed, some particularly active insurers on the issue of climate risk have been increasingly exploring structural solutions to assist in climate change adaptation. Munich Re, for instance, launched the Munich Climate Insurance Initiative in April 2005 to explore broad-based climate insurance mechanisms that would make resources available to developing nations suffering from various catastrophic impacts related to adapting to climate change.[91]

Similar to the concept of weather derivatives are catastrophe bonds, which have been gaining greater market penetration. These are "financial contracts" that pay a significant return—sometimes up to 40%—in exchange for the loss of that return, or potentially in some situations even of the underlying capital, upon fulfillment of a trigger condition, such as a Category 4 hurricane striking the mainland United States.[92] Catastrophe bonds provide another source for risk capital for the insurance markets and may grow to a $4 billion market in 2006.[93]

B. Providing Incentives to Reduce Risks

Other insurance products are expected to emerge that reflect incentives to reduce greenhouse gas emissions or reward behaviors that lead to risk reduction. One early example is an automobile insurance policy offered by Travelers, the second largest provider in the United States of automobile and homeowners insurance through indepen-dent agents. The new policy provides a 10% discount to drivers of hybrid cars. Trav-elers reasoned that owners of such vehicles were uniquely socially conscious and tended to fall into a preferred risk category. In addition, Travelers was looking for an early differentiator to capture a share of what it perceives as a growing $227 billion market characterized as Lifestyles of Health and Sustainability.[94] Similarly, other insurers are offering preferential rates for property insurance for "green" buildings.[95]

C. Facilitating New Opportunities

One of the climate change areas with the greatest new energy and activity concerns the development and maturation of new carbon emissions finance and trading mar-kets. Carbon emissions reduction credits typically would arise in Clean Development Mechanism (CDM) or Joint Implementation (JI) projects (discussed in Chapter 2), where an entity enters into a forward-based contract that provides the promise of the future delivery of greenhouse gas emissions reductions. The allocation of non-delivery risks between buyers and sellers of carbon credits is a key commercial issue and one that impacts the price of Certified Emissions Reduction (CER) projects. Pricing categories for emissions reductions have emerged based on the risk distribution between buyers and sellers, with forward contracts for perceived high-risk, non-guaranteed emissions reductions facing significant price discounts. By employing an insurance-based credit delivery guarantee, the quality of the future credits generated and committed to may be able to—in effect—be improved so that their value more closely approximates that of an outright carbon emissions allowance.

CDM and JI projects present a wide range of risks. These include:

- design and operational risks, such as whether a new technology will be deliv-ered in time, on budget, and indeed will work;
- financial and credit risks, such as whether a project manager or technology provider will remain financially able to perform and operate the project over its projected life;
- performance risks, such as natural disasters that could inhibit the completion and operation of the project;
- political risks, stemming from the host country, including political instability, ownership interests in the project and the carbon credits generated, currency convertibility, etc.; and
- Kyoto Protocol-specific risks, such as whether a CDM project will receive ap-proval from the CDM Executive Board so that emissions reductions can be properly verified and certified.

Various insurance and reinsurance companies are willing to take on different slices of these risks and to differing degrees. As they gain experience with these projects, it is expected that they will also improve the quality and pricing of coverages available so that those who invest in projects or provide technology will have the highest quality of future credit promise possible, based upon these guarantees.

The credit delivery guarantee insurance policy generally would be designed to provide financial compensation where a covered risk affects the delivery of promised greenhouse gas emissions credits. As more risk is removed from the transaction, buyers may be prepared to pay a premium on CER prices. Importantly, such delivery guarantees can facilitate payment for CERs prior to delivery and may also help to monetize the future value of CERs, allowing them to be incorporated into project financing decisions. Where the price of securing such credit delivery guarantees is lower than the market discount for forward-based contracts of CDM- and JI-generated credits, then credit delivery guarantees may provide an effective and economic risk management tool for greenhouse gas reduction projects and may result in reduced costs of capital and improvements in overall emissions reduction project economics.

The first delivery guarantee publicly announced in the United States was placed by Swiss Re in 2006 and focused particularly on the risk of CDM Executive Board approval of a project and verification of credits. It was placed for a capital fund investing in carbon emissions credit-generating projects and is designed at a portfolio level to spread these risks across projects of different technologies and sizes, and in different locations. The coverage is limited, however, to methodologies already approved by the CDM Executive Board.[96]

Another area of likely future interest concerns approaches to hedging the efficacy of renewable energy projects. In theory, a wind-power derivative would transfer the risk of below-average energy production to a third party. The first step in structuring such a derivative is to know how much wind is likely at the site involved. This relies on data from a wind-availability study, which would have been performed by an independent source during project planning. The wind data are then combined with power-production curves for the project's wind turbines, providing an estimate of the amount of wind power that can be expected to be produced in a "normal" year.

The wind-power derivative's trigger—the point at which payments would be made to the derivative's purchaser—is entirely based on the level of power produced. For example, a derivative could be structured so that payment kicks in if low winds in a given period lead to a 10% reduction in the projected amount of power. However, if the wind is such that more power is produced, the party backing the derivative could receive—depending on the exact structure of the deal—an additional payment based on the extra revenue the energy-generating company receives. There are a number of ways to structure a wind derivative, but the bottom line is to reduce financial volatility.

The degree of financial market appetite for such coverages remains to be seen and may depend upon the relationship between future wind-power generation financial profit margins and the costs of hedges, as wind-power generation significantly increases in the United States and abroad.[97]

As a variety of new technologies are conceived of and come on line in response—in whole or in part—to global climate change, challenging insurance coverage issues may be eased if insurers can become comfortable with underwriting the engineering approaches and understanding the risks. This is playing out with carbon capture and storage, which (as discussed in chapter 19) may involve the geological sequestration of carbon dioxide through injection into underground formations. Insurance coverages may provide one means of managing the hazards posed by a rapid surface loss of carbon dioxide or by the long-term nonperformance of carbon removal from the atmosphere.

As experience with this technology grows—and as potential carbon injection sites, such as former oil and gas production facilities or salt mines, become better characterized and their geological performance better understood—such activities may become insurable. Indeed, insurance may provide a strong market advantage for project participants. The FutureGen project—a government and private industry cooperative demonstration project for clean coal technology—actually sought an indemnification, perhaps satisfied through placement of insurance coverage, for any liabilities resulting from future carbon loss from storage, to be considered as a factor in its facility siting award.[98]

Biological sequestration may be amenable to insurance solutions as well. The Model Rule promulgated by the Regional Greenhouse Gas Initiative (RGGI), the cooperative effort by Northeastern and Mid-Atlantic states to reduce carbon dioxide emissions, acknowledges the role insurance can play in making sequestration more reliable. The rule includes a 10% discount for calculating the net carbon resulting from certain offset projects that sequester carbon through the conversion of land from a nonforested to a forested condition. Yet the rule also removes that discount where a project sponsor retains approved long-term insurance that "guarantees the replacement of any lost sequestered carbon for which CO_2 offsets were issued. . . ."[99]

More generally, insurance markets are aware of climate risk issues and eager to participate in solutions to the problem. This provides an important and rare opportunity to work with the insurance industry to craft products that will provide customized solutions to these emerging issues.

Endnotes

1. Association of British Insurers, A Changing Climate for Insurance: A Summary Report for Chief Executives and Policy Makers 19 (2004), *available at* http://www.abi.org.uk/Display/File/364/SP_Climate_Change5.pdf.
2. *Id.*

3. *Id.*

4. MICHEL-KERJAN, KUNREUTHER, BRIEF OVERVIEW OF THE INSURANCE MARKET 1 (The Wharton School, April 2006).

5. ASSOCIATION OF BRITISH INSURERS, A CHANGING CLIMATE FOR INSURANCE 43 (June 2004), *available at* www.abi.org.uk/climatechange.

6. *Id.* at 41.

7. *See generally* John Coomber, *Managing Risks in an Uncertain Climate*, STATE OF THE PLANET '06 (Columbia University), *available at* www.earthinstitute.columbia.edu/sop2006/transcripts.

8. U.S. GOV'T ACCOUNTABILITY OFFICE, CATASTROPHE RISK: U.S. AND EUROPEAN APPROACHES TO INSURE NATURAL CATASTROPHE AND TERRORISM RISKS 8 (Feb. 2005 GAO-05-199).

9. *Id.*

10. *Id.*

11. 20 U.S.C. §§ 1011 et seq.

12. 322 U.S. 533 (1944).

13. *See generally* NAIC Mission Statement, www.naic.org/about/mission.htm.

14. *See generally* Taylor, *Insuring Against the Natural Catastrophe After Katrina*, 20 NAT. RES. & ENV'T 28-29 (2006).

15. 44 C.F.R. § 59.22 (2004).

16. MICHEL-KERJAN, KUNREUTHER, *supra* note 4, at 10.

17. About UNEP FI: Background, *available at* www.unepfi.org/about/background/index.html.

18. Testimony of Christopher Walker, Hearing on the Case for Climate Change Action, U.S. Sen. Cmte on Commerce, Science & Tech. (Oct. 1, 2003), *available at* http://commerce.sentate.gov/hearings/testimony.cfm??id=949&wit_id=2674.

19. SWISS RE, OPPORTUNITIES AND RISKS OF CLIMATE CHANGE (2002), at 3. *See also* SWISS RE, TACKLING CLIMATE CHANGE (2004).

20. ASS'N OF BRITISH INSURERS, A CHANGING CLIMATE FOR INSURANCE (June 2004).

21. AXA's Answer to Carbon Disclosure Project (CDP) Greenhouse Gas Emissions Questionnaire (2003), *available at* http://www.cdproject.net/response_list.asp?id=2&letter=A.

22. *Hurricanes—More intense, more frequent, more expensive*, MUNICH RE 2006 at 4, *available at* www.munichre.com.

23. *Id.* at 6, 40.

24. *Id.*

25. *Third Survey of Climate Change Disclosure in SEC Filings of Automobile, Insurance, Oil & Gas, Petrochemical, and Utilities Companies*, FRIENDS OF THE EARTH 20 (July 2004).

26. Mills, *Insurance in a Climate of Change*, 309 SCIENCE 1040, 1042 (2005).

27. Emanuel, *Increasing destructiveness of tropical cyclones over the past 30 years*, 436 NATURE 686-88 (2005).

28. *Hurricanes, supra* note 22, at 13.

29. Stott, Stone & Allen, *Human Contribution to the European Heat Wave of 2003*, 432 NATURE 610-14 (2004).

30. INSURANCE INFORMATION INSTITUTE, FACTS AND STATISTICS: HURRICANES, *available at* http://www.iii.org/media/facts/statsbyissue/hurricanes/.

31. *Climate Change Facts*, GLOBAL RISK NETWORK 3 (2006), *available at* http:// www.weforum.org/pdf/CSI/Climatechange.pdf.

32. *Id.* at 26; *see generally* MARSH, THE IMPACTS OF HURRICANES KATRINA AND RITA (2006), *available at* www.marsh.com.

33. CONG. RESEARCH SERV. REP., HURRICANE KATRINA: INSURANCE LOSSES AND NATIONAL CAPACITIES FOR FINANCING DISASTER RISK 1 (Sept. 15, 2005).

34. Mills, Roth & Lecomte, *Availability and Affordability of Insurance Under Climate Change: A Growing Challenge for the U.S.*, CERES (Dec. 2005), *available at* www.ceres.org.

35. *Id.* at 2.

36. KUNREUTHER, MICHEL-KERJAN, INSURING NATURAL DISASTERS: NEW FRONTIERS IN THE IMPACTS OF CLIMATE 7 (The Wharton School 2006).

37. *Id.*

38. CERES, News Release, Institutional Investors Urge Insurance Companies to Boost Response to Financial Risks and Opportunities from Climate Change (Dec. 1, 2005), available at www.ceres.org/new/news_item.php?nid=135.

39. CONG. RESEARCH SERV. REP., HURRICANE KATRINA: INSURANCE LOSSES AND NATIONAL CAPACITIES FOR FINANCING DISASTER RISK 6 (Sept. 15, 2005).

40. *Hurricanes – More intense, more frequent, more expensive*, MUNICH RE 2006, at 1.

41. *Id.* at 5.

42. Lloyds, News Release, Time to rethink catastrophic losses (March 23, 2006).

43. Lloyds, *Climate Change: Adapt or Bust*, 360 RISK PROJECT NO. 1: CATASTROPHE RISK 8 (2006).

44. *See* INS. INFO. INST., HOT TOPICS & ISSUES UPDATE: CATASTROPHE MODELING, *available at* www.iii.org/media/hottopics/additional/catmodeling/.

45. *U.S. and Caribbean Hurricane Activity Rates*, RISK MANAGEMENT SOLUTIONS (March 2006).

46. *Buffett links hurricane insurance to climate*, FINANCIAL TIMES (March 5, 2006).

47. CONG. RESEARCH SERV. REP., *supra* note 39, at 7.

48. Mills, Roth & Lecomte, *supra* note 34, at 12.

49. *Id.* at 12-13.

50. Lloyds, *Climate Change: Adapt or Bust*, supra note 43, at 19.

51. Swiss Re, News Release, Swiss Re implements ten-year programme to become fully greenhouse neutral (Oct. 30, 2003), *available at* www.swissre.com/INTERNET/ pwswpspr.nsf/vwallbyidkeylu/SSTK-5SRLHA.

52. AIG, AIG's POLICY AND PROGRAMS ON ENVIRONMENT AND CLIMATE CHANGE, *available at* http://media.corporate-ir.net/media_files/irol/76/76115/ aig_climate_change_updated.pdf).

53. Pew Center on Global Climate Change, Press Release, Marsh, Inc., Joins Pew Center on Global Climate Change: Leading Insurance Services Firm Raises Awareness of Global Environmental Risk (July 13, 2006), *available at* http://www.pewclimate.org/ press_room/sub_press_room/2006_releases/pr_0713_marsh.cfm.

54. *Regulators Put Climate Change on the Docket*, INS. NETWORKING NEWS (June 2, 2006), *available at* www.insurance networking.com/protected/article.cfm?articleId =4073&.

55. National Ass'n Ins. Comm'rs, Notes of Climate Change and Global Warming (EX) Task Force Meeting, Washington, D.C. (June 10, 2006), at 3.

56. *Id.*

57. *Time Bomb for Insurance Industry*, EV WORLD (May 31, 2006), *available at* www.evworld.com.

58. Mills, Roth & Lecomte, supra note 34, at 1.

59. Taylor, Insuring Against the Natural Catastrophe After Katrina, 20 Nat. Res. & Env't 26 (2006).

60. U.S. Gov't Accounting Office, Letter from John B. Stephenson, Director, Nat. Res. & Env't, to Senators Susan M. Collins and Joseph I. Lieberman (May 30, 2006).

61. *As Hurricane Season Begins, Disaster Insurance Runs Short*, Wall St. J., July 10, 2006, at A8.

62. Simons, *Risky Business*, 154 Fortune No. 6, Sept. 4, 2006, at 131.

63. *Rising Rates Push Florida Homeowners to Brink*, N.Y. Times, June 29, 2006, at A1; *see also Florida Citizens Shocked by Shifting Insurance Market* (National Public Radio, June 1, 2006), *available at* http://www.npr.org/templates/story/story.php?storyId=5443942.

64. *Id.*

65. Lloyds, *supra* note 43, at 13.

66. Preston, *Global Warming and Extreme Weather Events*, Catastrophe Risk Mgmt. 22, 23 (Spring 2005).

67. Harvard Med. School Ctr. for Health and the Global Env't, Climate Change Futures: Health, Ecological and Economic Dimensions 5 (2005).

68. Remarks of Dr. Paul Epstein, Am. Museum of Natural History, *Climate Futures* Launch (Nov. 1, 2005).

69. *See, e.g.*, Lloyds, *supra* note 43, at 3.

70. *Id.*

71. Harvard Med. School, *supra* note 67, at 11.

72. Mills, *Insurance in a Climate of Change*, 309 Science 1040.

73. Preston, *supra* note 66, at 22.

74. Marsh Inc., Risk Alert: Climate Change: Business Risks and Solutions 1 (April 2006).

75. *Id.* at 2-3.

76. Stern Review Report on the Economics of Climate Change (October 2006), *available at* http://www.hm-treasury.gov.uk/independent_reviews/stern_review_economics_ climate_change/stern_review_report.cfm.

77. *See Lloyds Releases Second "360 Report" on Climate Change*, Ins. J. (Nov. 1, 2006), *available at* http://www.insurancejournal.com/news/international/2006/11/01/73807.htm.

78. Marsh Inc., *supra* note 74, at 20.

79. Massachusetts v. EPA, No. 05-1120 (cert. granted June 26, 2006).

80. Marsh Inc., *supra* note 74, at 20.

81. Choo, *Feeling the Heat: The Growing Debate Over Climate Change Takes on Legal Overtones*, A.B.A. J. 29, 34 (July 2006).

82. *Id.*

83. *Climate Change Concerns Raise Questions on D&O: Shareholders Wary of Financial Risks*, Bus. Ins. 1 (Aug. 14, 2006).

84. *Cover May Hinge on Status of Carbon Dioxide as a Pollutant*, Bus. Ins. 28 (Aug. 14, 2006).

85. Marsh Inc., *supra* note 74, at 23-24.

86. *Id.*

87. *See* CERES, From Risk to Opportunity: How Insurers Can Proactively and Profitably Manage Climate Change (August 2006).

88. *Id.* at 24-25.

89. World Food Program, News Release, World's First Humanitarian Insurance Policy Issued (March 6, 2006), *available at* www.wfp.org.

90. *Developing country weather and cat. risk vehicle close to take-off*, ENVTL. FINANCE 4 (April 2006).

91. Munich Climate Insurance Initiative Mission Statement (2005).

92. Ass'n of British Insurers, *supra* note 20, at 14.

93. *Hedge Funds, Betting on Hurricanes, Wade in to Fund Insurers*, BLOOMBERG NEWS (July 12, 2006).

94. Press Release, Travelers Offers Hybrid Owners/Drivers in Five Additional States 10% Discount on Auto Insurance (May 1, 2006), *available at* www.hybridtravelers.com/newsroom.html.

95. CERES, *supra* note 87, AT 20.

96. *RNK Capital and Swiss Re launch 1st insurance of Kyoto CO_2 projects*, DOW JONES INT'L NEWS (June 13, 2006).

97. Marsh Inc., *supra* note 74, at 25 ("U.S. wind-power generation is growing at an estimated annual rate of 31%. In Europe . . . generation grew by 18% in 2005 to over 40,000 megawatts (MW).").

98. FutureGen Indus. Alliance, Inc., Request for Proposals for FutureGen Facility Host Site at 44 (March 2006), *available at* http://www.futuregenalliance.org/news/futuregen_siting_final_rfp_3-07-2006.pdf.

99. Regional Greenhouse Gas Initiative Model Rule, Subpart XX-10.5(c)(4)(iii)(Aug. 15, 2006).

chapter sixteen

Subsidies, Tax Policy, and Technological Innovation

Roberta Mann

I. Introduction

This chapter addresses the effect of U.S. tax policy on climate change. Tax incentives operate as subsidies by giving a better tax deal to qualifying activities than to similar nonqualifying activities. The magnitude of the subsidy, although hard to measure precisely, is approximated by the tax expenditure budget, required by Congress to be published each year by the Joint Committee on Taxation.[1] This chapter will cover federal tax incentives for renewable energy, energy conservation, and alternative fuel vehicles in sections 16.2, 16.3 and 16.4. It will also address government disincentives for carbon-reducing technology development, including federal tax incentives for fossil fuel use, utility rate structure issues, and government impact on technology diffusion in section 16.5. Finally, in section 16.6, this chapter will cover carbon tax proposals for greenhouse gas (GHG) mitigation, although none have been implemented at the federal level to date.

What is a better tax deal? Congress defined a tax expenditure by reference to a "normal" tax structure. There are four ways that an activity may benefit from a tax expenditure:

- The income from the activity may be excluded from gross income (and therefore not taxed).

- The income from the activity may be taxed at a lower rate than ordinary income (a "preferential rate").
- The expenses from the activity may be deducted more quickly than those from a comparable activity (a "deferral" of tax liability).
- The expenses from the activity may be eligible for a tax credit.

A report by the Pew Center on Global Climate Change notes that "tax credits have long been a politically popular mechanism to increase incentives for developing or deploying new technologies."[2] Political popularity, however, has not led to a coherent federal energy policy. While providing some tax incentives for renewable energy, energy conservation, and alternative fuel vehicles, the federal tax system continues to subsidize fossil fuel use. As noted in section 16.5, the United States has a long history of fossil fuel subsidies, which continues with recently implemented tax incentives. Deregulation of the electric utility industry adds to the incoherence by removing the industry's incentive to control demand, because revenues are based on units of energy sold on a competitive basis. Section 16.5.3 will explore the difference between regulated and deregulated utility markets and emerging trends such as "smart energy" systems. Changes in the regulatory climate have also affected the rate of technology diffusion. Governments can help or hinder technology diffusion, but do not always consider the issue when crafting energy policy. The federal government has so far rejected several proposals for GHG mitigation, preferring a strictly voluntary approach. Section 16.6 will examine the "carbon tax" alternative for GHG emission reductions, focusing on structure and potential economic consequences.

II. Incentives for Renewable Energy

A. Before 2005

While fossil fuels have enjoyed tax incentives since 1916, it took more than 60 years for Congress to enact tax provisions designed to encourage energy conservation and develop alternative fuels.[3] In the Energy Act of 1978, Congress enacted tax credits for investing in solar and wind energy equipment installed in a home or business.[4] The residential energy income tax credit permitted taxpayers a 30% credit for the first $2,000 spent on solar and wind energy equipment costs and a 20% credit for the next $8,000. Businesses received a 10% energy tax credit for investments in conservation or alternative fuel technologies such as solar, wind, geothermal, and ocean thermal technologies. In 1980, Congress increased the residential energy tax credit to 40% of the first $10,000 of equipment expenses.[5] Congress also increased the business energy tax credit to 15% for solar, wind, geothermal, and ocean thermal technologies, and added biomass to the list of technologies eligible for the credit. Except for the business tax credit for solar property, these credits expired by December 31, 1985. A 1986 industry study showed that the business energy tax credit had resulted in the development of over 7,000 megawatts (MW) of electricity generation.[6] The business energy tax credit for solar, geothermal, ocean thermal and biomass was extended until 1988, at varying percentages. The Joint Committee on Taxation, reviewing Department of Energy data, concluded that the business energy tax credit had resulted in substantially increased capacity for geothermal and solar generation.[7] The Energy Policy Act of 1992 created the renewable electricity production credit, which authorized a base production credit of 1.5 cents/kilowatt-hour (kWh) for electric power generated from "qualified" resources at "qualified" facilities for the first ten years of production.[8] Qualified resources included wind, closed-loop biomass and poultry waste. In 1992, Congress also made the business energy tax credit for solar and geothermal permanent at 10%.[9] However, the geothermal or solar facility had to be "placed in service" by the end of 2005. As of 2005, this 10% business energy tax credit was the last renewable energy tax incentive left standing.

B. Energy Tax Incentives Act of 2005

The Energy Tax Incentives Act of 2005, which is part of the Energy Policy Act of 2005, is the most significant federal energy legislation enacted since 1992. The 2005 Act included six new tax incentives for renewable energy:

a) the modified renewable resources electricity production credit;
b) clean renewable energy bonds;
c) the business solar investment tax credit;
d) the business fuel cell tax credit; and
e) the residential energy-efficient property credit.

The estimated cost of these incentives totaled $3.6 billion through 2015.[10] The total benefits provided by the 2005 Act, including those provided to nonrenewable energy sources, amounted to $14.5 billion. Some caveats apply to our consideration of the six renewable energy incentives. First, a renewable fuel is not necessarily a GHG free fuel. Biomass-based fuels, although renewable, do emit GHG when burned. Further, embedded in some of these incentives labeled renewable lurk benefits for fossil fuels. For example, a facility burning a combination of biomass and coal is eligible for the renewable electricity production credit.[11] A facility burning entirely coal may be eligible for the renewable electricity production credit if it burns "Indian coal."[12]

1. Renewable Electricity Production Credit[13]

The renewable resources electricity production credit applies to producers of electricity from qualified facilities, if the electricity is sold to an unrelated person. Qualified facilities include wind energy facilities, closed-loop biomass facilities, open-loop biomass facilities, geothermal energy facilities, solar energy facilities, small irrigation power facilities, landfill gas facilities and trash combustion facilities. The credit also applies to "refined" coal, although it is hard to see how that constitutes a renewable energy source. The base amount of the credit is 1.5 cents per kWh of electricity produced. The base amount varies by fuel type, and may be increased for inflation adjustments or decreased for other governmental benefits received (such as grants, tax-exempt bond revenue, subsidized energy financing, or other credits.) However, in another example of incoherence, the credit for closed-loop biomass facilities that are designed to co-fire with coal is not decreased for other governmental benefits. The amount of the credit is designed to give qualified facilities a boost when electricity prices are low. If the market price of electricity rises above a threshold level, the credit is phased out.

Although use of fuel cell technology produces little to no pollution, manufacturing hydrogen fuel is energy-intensive, requiring significant amounts of electricity.

The 2005 Act extended the availability of the credit through 2007 for all previously eligible technologies except solar facilities and refined coal facilities. Thus, facilities placed in service by December 31, 2007, are eligible for the credit. Solar facilities had to have been placed in service by December 31, 2005, so no new solar-generating facilities will be eligible for the credit. Refined coal facilities may receive the credit if placed in service before December 31, 2008. Refined coal is a qualifying liquid, gaseous, or solid synthetic fuel produced from coal. When burned, qualifying refined coal must emit 20% less nitrogen oxides and either SO_2 or mercury than the burning of comparable coal available in the marketplace. To qualify for the credit, refined coal must sell at prices at least 50% greater than that of comparable coal. The 2005 Act also added four new qualifying resources: fuel cells; hydropower; wave, current, tidal and ocean thermal energy; and Indian coal.

A fuel cell converts fuel into energy using electrochemical means. A qualifying facility must have an electricity-only generation efficiency of greater than 30%, generate at least 0.5 megawatts of electricity, and be placed in service after December 31, 2005, and before January 1, 2009 (before January 1, 2007, for commercial buildings). A variety of different fuels may be used to power a fuel cell, including hydrogen. Fuel cell technology is still in the development stage. Although use of fuel cell technology produces little to no pollution, manufacturing hydrogen fuel is energy-intensive, requiring significant amounts of electricity. Thus, the GHG impacts of fuel cells depend primarily on the fuel used to generate the electricity. In the United States, over half the electricity is derived from combustion of coal. Coal produces more GHG emissions per unit of energy than any other fossil fuel.

Hydropower is not an emerging technology. Humankind has been using water to generate power since the Middle Ages. To qualify for the credit, a hydropower facility must have installed efficiency improvements or additional electricity-generating capacity after the date of enactment, and before January 1, 2009. Only the incremental power may be used to calculate the credit.

Wave, current, tidal and ocean thermal energy generation qualify for the credit if the facility is placed in service after the date of enactment and before January 1, 2009.

Tidal power has also been used for centuries. Existing tidal power plants use turbines similar to conventional hydropower plants to convert the potential energy of water held on either side of a dam into electric energy during the tide.[14] Scientists and engineers are working on a new approach to exploitation of tidal energy, using new unconventional turbines, that does not require ocean dams. The tax credit is only available for free-flowing ocean water energy generation. Free-flowing water energy generation avoids some of the environmental problems of the dam method, as it does not have as great an impact on fish migration and sediment deposit patterns. Tidal energy is reliable and can be predicted over long periods.

Ocean thermal energy conversion (OTEC) is an energy technology that converts solar radiation to electric power. OTEC systems use the ocean's natural thermal gradient (the fact that the ocean's layers of water have different temperatures) to drive a power-producing cycle. As long as the temperature between the warm surface water and the cold deep water differs by at least 20° C (36° F), an OTEC system can produce a significant amount of power.[15]

A qualified Indian coal facility is a facility that produces coal from reserves that on June 14, 2005, were owned by a federally recognized tribe of Indians or were held in trust by the United States for a tribe or its members. The value of the credit is $1.50 per ton for the first four years of the credit, and $2.00 per ton for the last three years of the credit period. This credit, although styled a renewable energy resource credit, was evidently adopted for reasons unrelated to environmental protection or GHG mitigation.

The 2005 Act also provided that credits for all qualifying facilities (including solar) are available for ten years after the facility is placed in service, except for Indian coal. In the case of Indian coal, the credit is available for seven years.

The renewable source electricity production credit is a component of the general business credit.[16] The general business credit has 30 components. The total credit, determined by adding all the applicable components, may not exceed the taxpayer's net income tax minus 25% of the net income tax that exceeds $25,000. Thus, if the taxpayer had a net income tax liability of $25,000 and a general business credit of $25,000, barring alternative minimum tax considerations, the taxpayer would have a tax liability of zero. If the taxpayer had a net income tax liability of $125,000 and a general business credit of $125,000, the use of the general business credit would be limited to $100,000.[17] The $25,000 unused credit could be carried forward 20 years. With respect to the renewable source electricity credit, special calculations apply.[18]

2. Clean Renewable Energy Bonds

The Internal Revenue Code exempts interest received on state and local government bonds from the income of the recipient. By this exemption, the federal government reduces the cost of capital for the state and local governments, permitting them to obtain funds at a lower interest rate. State and local governments may also issue "tax credit" bonds, which provide a tax credit instead of providing a tax-exempt interest rate for the investor. Under certain circumstances, private persons may issue either tax-exempt or tax credit bonds.

The clean renewable energy bond provision of the 2005 Act creates a new category of tax credit bonds: clean renewable energy bonds (CREBs).[19] Investors receive the tax credit if a qualified issuer uses the bonds to finance a project that is eligible for the renewable energy production credit; 95% or more of the proceeds of the bonds must be used to finance capital expenditures incurred by qualified borrowers for such projects. A qualified issuer includes:

1. governmental bodies (including Indian tribal governments);
2. the Tennessee Valley Authority;
3. mutual or cooperative electric companies;
4. any not-for-profit electric utility that has received a loan or guarantee under the Rural Electrification Act; and
5. clean energy bond lenders.

A clean energy bond lender is a cooperative that is owned by, or has outstanding loans to, 100 or more cooperative electric companies, and was in existence on February 1, 2002.[20] A qualified borrower includes governmental bodies (including Indian tribal governments); the Tennessee Valley Authority; and mutual or cooperative electric companies. The overall amount available for CREBs is $800 million. The amount of proceeds used by government borrowers is limited to $500 million.

If, within a five-year period, less than 95% of the bond proceeds are used, the bonds may not qualify as CREBs. However, the five-year spending period may be extended by permission of the Secretary of the Treasury.

3. Business Solar Investment Tax Credit

The 2005 Act increases the 10% credit available under prior law to a 30% credit, which is available before January 1, 2008. The credit applies to the cost of new equipment that:

1. uses solar energy to generate electricity, to heat or cool a structure, or to provide solar process heat; or

2. is used to produce, distribute, or use energy derived from a geothermal deposit (up to the electric transmission phase).

Fiber-optic distributed sunlight to illuminate the inside of a structure qualifies as solar energy property. However, any equipment used to heat a swimming pool does not qualify as solar energy property. The business solar investment tax credit is a component of the investment tax credit, which is in turn a component of the general business credit.[21] As noted above, the general business credit has 30 components, and its use may be limited.

4. Business Fuel Cell Credit

The 2005 Act provides a new 15% credit for the purchase of qualified fuel cell power plants for business. As discussed above, although fuel cells produce energy by electrochemical means and do not produce GHG emissions, the fuel used to power the fuel cells may be created by using fossil fuels. The business fuel cell credit is a component of the investment tax credit, which is in turn a component of the general business credit.[22]

5. The Residential Energy-Efficient Property Credit

The 2005 Act modified the existing renewable electricity production credit. Under the Energy Tax Incentives Act of 2005 (new section 25D of the Internal Revenue Code), a taxpayer may get a credit for certain residential energy-efficient property installed in his or her home after December 31, 2005, and before January 1, 2008. The tax credit is the sum of three components:

1. 30% of qualifying expenditures up to a maximum credit of $2,000 to purchase qualified photovoltaic property;
2. 30% of qualifying expenditures up to a maximum credit of $2,000 to purchase qualified solar water-heating property; and
3. 30% of qualifying purchases up to $500 per 0.5 kilowatt for the purchase of qualified fuel-cell power plants.

The photovoltaic credit applies to a device that generates electricity from solar power for use in a dwelling unit. The credit is nonrefundable, and the depreciable basis of the property is reduced by the amount of the credit. Labor costs for on-site preparation, assembly, or original installation of the equipment are eligible expenditures.

The solar hot water credit only applies to a dwelling unit in the United States that is used as a residence. At least one-half of the energy used by the property must be derived from the sun. Note that the solar hot water heater must be installed in a principal residence of the taxpayer, while the qualified photovoltaic property may be installed in a "dwelling unit." Whether a residence is a principal residence is a facts-and-circumstances question.

The fuel-cell power plant must be used in a principal residence, it must convert a fuel into electricity using electrochemical means, it must have an electricity-only generation efficiency of greater than 30%, and it must generate at least 0.5 kilowatts of electricity.

III. Incentives for Conservation

Between 1978 and 1985, consumers could benefit from tax credits for investing in energy conservation products (insulation and other energy conservation components) and solar and wind energy equipment installed in a home or business.[23] About 30 million taxpayers took advantage of these credits.[24] Between 1996 and 2005, an exclusion from income for subsidies provided by public utilities for the purchase or installation of an energy conservation measure was the only conservation-oriented tax benefit.[25]

The Energy Tax Incentives Act of 2005 provided four new energy conservation tax benefits:

1. the nonbusiness energy property credit;
2. the energy-efficient commercial building deduction;
3. the energy-efficient new homes credit; and
4. the energy-efficient appliances credit.

The Joint Committee on Taxation estimates that these benefits will transfer over $1 billion over the next ten years, about 7% of the cost of the bill.

A. Nonbusiness Energy Property Credit[26]

Homeowners may benefit from the nonbusiness energy property credit. The credit is the sum of (1) 10% of the cost of qualifying energy-efficiency improvements and (2) the residential energy property expenditures. Qualified energy-efficient improvements must be made to the taxpayer's principal residence. They include (1) insulation materials or systems, (2) exterior windows and doors, and (3) metal roofs, all of which are specifically designed to reduce heat loss or gain for a dwelling. Residential energy property expenditures also must be made to the taxpayer's principal residence. They include (1) an advanced main air-circulating fan, (2) a qualified natural gas, propane, or oil furnace or hot water boiler, or (3) "other energy-efficient building property" such as a geothermal heat pump. The credit is limited to $500 in total across all taxable years, and no more than $200 of the credit may be applied to windows. As windows are "qualified energy-efficient improvements," the homeowner may spend $2,000 on energy-efficient windows and still receive the maximum $200 credit. If the homeowner pays $3,000 for energy-efficient windows, she still gets a $200 credit. Separate credit limits apply to certain residential energy property expenditures: (1) no more than $50 for an advanced main air-circulating fan; (2) no more than $150 for any qualified natural gas, propane or oil furnace or hot water boiler; and (3) no more than $300 for any item of energy-efficient building property. The credit expires after December 31, 2007. The IRS has provided additional guidance in Notice 2006-26.

B. Energy-Efficient Commercial Building Deduction[27]

The energy-efficient commercial building deduction allows businesses to deduct up to $1.80 per square foot of property for which energy-efficient commercial building property expenditures are made. Such expenditures include property (1) installed on or in any building located in the United States that meets certain defined standards, (2) which is installed as part of the interior lighting, heating, cooling, ventilation, and hot water systems, and (3) which is certified as being installed as part of a plan to reduce energy and power costs based on certain standards. The provision expires on December 31, 2007.

C. Energy-Efficient New Homes Credit[28]

The energy-efficient new homes credit allows eligible contractors to take a tax credit for the construction of a qualified new energy-efficient home. To qualify, the home must be located in the United States, completed after date of enactment, and certified under certain standards that result in either a 30% or 50% reduction in energy use. The credit is $1,000 for manufactured homes that meet the 30% test, and $2,000 for all new homes that meet the 50% test. The credit is a component of the general business credit.[29] The energy-efficient new homes credit expires after December 31, 2007. The IRS has provided additional guidance in Notice 2006-27 and Notice 2006-28 (applies to manufactured homes).

D. Energy-Efficient Appliances Credit[30]

Manufacturers of energy-efficient appliances benefit from the energy-efficient appliances credit. Dishwashers, clothes washers, and refrigerators may qualify as energy-efficient appliances, if they are manufactured in 2006 or 2007 and meet the requirements of the 2007 Energy Star program. The Energy Star Program is a voluntary program, administered by the Environmental Protection Agency (EPA), under which manufacturers that produce products that meet federal energy efficiency guidelines can market those products under the "Energy Star" label. Americans have purchased more than one billion Energy Star qualified products since the program began in 1992.[31] This credit should increase the supply of efficient appliances.

IV. Incentives for Alternative Fuel Vehicles

A. Pre-2005 Provisions

Before 2005, Congress had provided few incentives for alternative fuel-using transportation. Certain clean-fuel vehicles and clean-fuel refueling property received preferential tax treatment.[32] Qualified clean-fuel vehicles include motor vehicles that use certain clean-burning fuels such as natural gas, liquefied natural gas, liquefied petroleum gas, hydrogen, electricity and any other fuel containing at least 85% methanol, ethanol, any other alcohol or ether. For a truck or van with a gross vehicle weight between 10,000 and 26,000 pounds, the maximum deduction is $5,000. For any other motor vehicle, the maximum deduction is $2,000. Hybrid passenger vehicles like the Toyota Prius qualify for the deduction, as well as other models specifically certified by the IRS. The clean-fuel vehicle deduction will expire in 2007. Purchasers of IRS-certified cars will be able to claim a deduction of $2,000 if the vehicle was placed in service on or before December 31, 2005. No deduction will be allowed for vehicles placed in service after December 31, 2005. The one-time deduction must be taken in the year the vehicle was originally used, and the taxpayer must be the original owner. The JCT estimated that $200 million worth of clean-fuel deductions would be taken in 2004.

Up to $100,000 of the costs of clean-fuel vehicle refueling property may also be expensed in the year it is placed in service. Clean-fuel vehicle refueling property includes property for the storage or dispensing of a clean-burning fuel, if the storage or dispensing occurs where the fuel is delivered into the vehicle fuel tank. Eligible property also includes property for the on-site recharging of electric vehicles. The deduction is phased down between 2004 and 2006, and is unavailable after December 31, 2006.

The pre-2005 law also included a credit for qualified electric vehicles.[33] A qualified electric is any motor vehicle that is powered primarily by an electric motor drawing current from rechargeable batteries, fuel cells, or other portable sources of electric current. The credit for electric vehicles will be reduced by 75% in 2006 and will expire in 2007.

B. 2005 Act Provisions

A new tax law provision added by the 2005 Act replaces the clean-fuel deduction with four credits that may apply to vehicles that save fuel based on four different technologies:

1. Hybrid gas-electric;
2. Advanced lean-burn;

3. Fuel cell; and
4. Alternative fuel.

The total credit available for a hybrid motor vehicle or an advanced lean-burn vehicle is the sum of the fuel economy credit and the conservation credit. The fuel economy credit varies according to how much the fuel economy of the qualifying vehicle exceeds the base fuel economy of a comparable 2002 model year non-alternate-fuel vehicle. The conservation credit is based on estimated lifetime fuel savings over a comparable 2002 model year non-alternate-fuel vehicle, assuming a 120,000-mile vehicle life. The comparison is based on the weight of the vehicle.

The total credit available for a hybrid motor vehicle or an advanced lean-burn vehicle is the sum of the fuel economy credit and the conservation credit.

A fuel-cell motor vehicle must be propelled by power derived from one or more cells that convert chemical energy directly into electricity by combining oxygen with hydrogen fuel that is stored onboard the vehicle. An advanced lean-burn technology motor vehicle must be powered by an internal combustion engine that is designed to operate primarily using more air than is necessary for complete combustion

of the fuel and incorporates direct injection. A hybrid motor vehicle draws propulsion energy from onboard sources of stored energy providing both an internal combustion or heat engine using consumable fuel and a rechargeable energy storage system. A hybrid vehicle's rechargeable energy system must meet a maximum available power standard.

The alternative fuel motor vehicle credit only applies to vehicles that operate on compressed natural gas, liquefied natural gas, liquefied petroleum gas, hydrogen, and any liquid at least 85% of the volume of which consists of an alcohol-based fuel (e.g., ethanol). A reduced credit applies to vehicles that use those fuels mixed with petroleum-based fuels, but only if the fuel mixture is at least 75% nonpetroleum-based. The alternative fuel motor vehicle credit is based on the incremental cost of such vehicle over a comparable conventional fueled vehicle.

To qualify for any of the above credits, vehicles must be certified as meeting certain emission standards (which differ depending on the technology used and the size of the vehicle) and must be purchased or leased new from a manufacturer. Section 30B(f) limits the availability of the credit to the first 60,000 qualified vehicles sold by each manufacturer after December 31, 2005, with declining credits available for a brief grace period after the 60,000th vehicle is sold. The qualified fuel-cell motor vehicle credit expires in 2014. The other credits expire in 2010, except for medium and heavy hybrid trucks, which expire in 2009.

As of May 8, 2006, the Internal Revenue Service had acknowledged the manufacturers' certifications of the following qualified hybrid vehicles and credit amounts.[34]

Vehicle Year, Make and Model	Credit	I.R.S. News Release
2006 Ford Escape Hybrid Front WD	$2,600	IR-2006-56, April 7, 2006
2006 Ford Escape Hybrid 4WD	$1,950	IR-2006-56, April 7, 2006
2006 Mercury Mariner Hybrid 4WD	$1,950	IR-2006-56, April 7, 2006
2005 Toyota Prius	$3,150	IR-2006-57, April 7, 2006
2006 Toyota Prius	$3,150	IR-2006-57, April 7, 2006
2006 Toyota Highlander 2WD and 4WD Hybrid	$2,600	IR-2006-57, April 7, 2006
2006 Lexus RX400h 2WD and 4WD	$2,200	IR-2006-57, April 7, 2006
2007 Toyota Camry Hybrid	$2,600	IR-2006-57, April 7, 2006
2007 Lexus GS 450h	$1,550	IR-2006-57, April 7, 2006

These credits are targeted to benefit only those purchasing vehicles that meet certain standards of fuel economy and emissions. While the credit appears dauntingly complex to calculate, as noted above, the credit amount will be determined by the car manufacturers, who have their own incentives for publicizing it to their customers. Hybrid gas-electric technology can be used to create any combination of reduced gas consumption or increased performance. Early hybrids focused on fuel economy. As some newer hybrids increase performance without changing fuel economy, the provision's complexity seems justified. Purchasers' benefits will be tied to fuel economy, consistent with the energy-saving purpose of the provision.

V. Government Disincentives for Climate-Friendly Technology Development

The previous section outlines the federal government's tax incentives for renewable energy and conservation. The federal government's support for fossil fuel development reaches back to the beginning of our tax system, and still continues strongly today. This section will briefly explore that history and analyze how the traditional and continuing support for fossil fuels may impact the development and marketability of more climate-friendly technologies. Utility rate structures also impact choice of fuels and energy conservation. This section will discuss how the deregulation of the electric utility industry has affected emerging climate-change technology.

A. Federal Tax Incentives for Fossil Fuel Use

The federal government has provided tax incentives for the fossil fuel industry since 1916.[35] The fossil fuel tax incentives were designed to encourage oil and gas production and exploration during the initial stages of development by sharing the financial risks of producing oil and gas.[36] By the early 1970s, the original basis for continued tax incentives for fossil fuels had changed from supporting of an emerging industry to holding down fuel prices.[37] This section will discuss seven tax incentives that encourage fossil fuel use, from the deduction for intangible drilling and development costs first enacted in 1916, to the credit for investment in clean coal facilities enacted in 2005.

1. Intangible Drilling and Development Costs[38]

When businesses incur costs that result in assets that may last for many years, those costs must be capitalized. Capitalized costs generally may not be deducted immediately—rather, the business may only deduct an allocable portion of the cost each year over the life of the asset.[39] However, taxpayers involved in the oil industry may immediately deduct their intangible drilling and development costs (IDCs). IDCs typically include labor, fuel, hauling, power, materials, supplies, tool rental, repairs of drilling equipment and other items incident to and necessary for drilling and equipping productive wells, as well as any costs associated with a nonproductive well or "dry hole" (which make up about 80% of all wills drilled).

2. Percentage Depletion[40]

Independent oil producers and royalty owners are eligible for percentage depletion, which is another variation on cost capitalization. Unlike most businesses, which may only deduct the actual cost of developing their assets over the life of the assets, businesses that are eligible for percentage depletion may deduct a fixed percentage of the gross value of annual production. Percentage depletion is computed without regard to the taxpayer's actual investment in the property. Unlike any other investment, cumulative deductions attributable to percentage depletion deductions can exceed the taxpayer's original investment.

3. Credit for Producing Fuel from a Nonconventional Source[41]

Producers of certain qualifying fuels from nonconventional sources, including some oil and gas, may claim a tax credit equal to $3 (adjusted for inflation) per barrel or Btu oil barrel equivalent. Qualifying fuels include (1) oil produced from shale and tar sands; (2) gas produced from geopressured brine, Devonian shale, coal seams, a tight formation, or biomass; and (3) liquid, gaseous, or solid synthetic fuels produced from coal. To qualify for the credit, the fuel must be produced domestically from wells, mines or plants. For most fuels, the section 29 credit has expired, except for certain biomass gas and synthetic fuels sold before January 1, 2008.

4. Enhanced Oil Recovery Credit[42]

Oil and gas producers may claim a credit for qualified tertiary oil recovery costs incurred in the production of domestic oil and gas. The credit, part of the general business credit, is equal to 15% of costs attributable to enhanced oil recovery (EOR) projects. Qualified costs include tertiary injectant expenses, IDCs on a qualified EOR project, and amounts incurred for tangible depreciable property. A qualified EOR project must be located in the United States and involve the application of tertiary recovery methods that will likely result in "more than an insignificant increase" in the amount of recoverable oil. The credit amount is reduced if the average price of crude oil exceeds $28 (adjusted for inflation) and is phased out ratably over a $6 phase-out range.

5. Renewable Electricity Production Credit[43]

This credit, also discussed at 16.2.2.1. above, provides preferential tax treatment to certain fuel sources when used to generate electricity. Despite its "renewable" title, the credit also applies to the use of refined coal, Indian coal, and coal co-fired with biomass.

6. Clean Renewable Energy Bonds[44]

This provision, also discussed at 16.2.2.2. above, authorizes a tax credit for investors in clean renewable energy bonds (CREBs). Investors receive the tax credit if a qualified issuer uses the bonds to finance a project that is eligible for the renewable energy production credit. As refined coal, Indian coal, and coal co-fired with biomass are eligible for the credit, CREBs issued to finance projects using qualifying coal are eligible for the tax credit.

7. Credit for Investment in Clean Coal Facilities[45]

The Energy Tax Incentives Act of 2005 created this new credit to encourage use of advanced coal-based electricity-generation technologies. Typically, no more than one-third of the energy in coal actually becomes usable electricity. Integrated gasification combined-cycle (IGCC) coal generation, currently used in a few demonstration projects, may approach efficiencies of 50%. The provision allows a credit for 20% of the cost of eligible IGCC projects and a 15% credit for non-IGCC projects. The projects must be certified by the Secretary of the Treasury, in consultation with the Secretary of Energy. The Secretary of the Treasury may allocate $800 million in credits to IGCC projects and $500 million to non-IGCC projects. The provision also allows a 20% credit for certified gasification projects that convert coal, petroleum residue, biomass, or other materials into synthetic gas. The Secretary may allocate $350 million in credits to gasification projects. The clean coal facilities credit, although it does encourage use of fossil fuels, at least encourages a relatively clean use of coal. IGCC projects could be modified to also address GHG emission issues. However, the tax credit has no GHG mitigation requirements.

B. Technology Diffusion

Tax incentives for renewable energy encourage use of renewable technologies and stimulate technology diffusion. Likewise, tax incentives for energy-efficient products encourage product development and help create a market for the products, once developed. Environmentally friendly technologies face two market failures: (1) the difficulty of technology diffusion and (2) the failure of fossil fuel costs to reflect environmental pollution.[46] As taxes can correct market failure, taxes can be used to encourage technological diffusion as well as to discourage pollution. Providing perverse subsidies for continued fossil fuel use counteracts the beneficial technology-diffusing effects of the renewable and conservation subsidies, and exacerbates both market failures.

The market failure of technology diffusion is in some ways opposite from the market failure of polluting industry. In the case of polluting industry, all suffer pollution so that the industry can reap benefit. In the case of technology diffusion, the innovators bear the start-up costs of new technology and all can benefit. Thus, firms have both an economic incentive to pollute and an economic disincentive to engage in technological innovation. However, technology diffusion can also alter the economics of pollution. As technology makes pollution control more affordable, the marginal cost of achieving a unit of pollution reduction decreases.

Technological change involves two steps, both of which require investment: innovation and adoption. Technology diffusion also requires information. Researchers at Resources for the Future recently analyzed the potential impact of four types of government intervention on technology diffusion:

1. Innovation policy;
2. Adoption policy;
3. Information provisions; and
4. Command and control regulations.[47]

Tax policy may apply to each of these types of government interventions, in different ways.

1. Innovation Policy

When government policies require polluters to pay for the cost of pollution, such as through a carbon tax, that increases the demand for low-cost pollution-reduction technologies. The increased demand creates larger returns for firms developing such technologies. The government can also subsidize research activities of private firms, via direct subsidies or tax benefits. The government can directly fund research at public institutions, such as the National Energy Technology Lab. The government can run contests and award technology prizes.[48] The government could provide special protection to "green" patents.

2. Adoption Policy

Government policies can encourage the adoption of new technologies. The "clean coal" tax credits, for example, reward taxpayers that adopt certain technologies that reduce the emission of some pollutants. Adoption policy should be flexible, to prevent "technology lock-in." Governmental intervention in the form of adoption policy should be limited to the industries where private incentives for change are the lowest. Studies of adoption policies point to varying degrees of effectiveness.[49] Adoption policies can have a significant "free-rider" effect that reduces the efficiency of the subsidy. That is, firms and individuals that would have adopted the policy without the subsidy still collect the subsidy. Some studies suggest that the renewable energy tax incentives of the 1970s suffered significantly from free ridership.[50]

3. Information Provision

While education alone is unlikely to produce technology diffusion, technology diffusion is unlikely to occur without information. Government can facilitate change by funding education programs and disseminating information about energy-conserving and pollution-reducing technologies. Information provision is not generally accomplished through tax policy, although it could be. A tax credit for technology development could be made contingent on the taxpayer providing public information about the technology.

Combining an information requirement with a green patent could protect the technology developer while encouraging diffusion.[51]

4. Command and Control Regulation

Finally, classic command and control regulations, which require a certain level of pollution reduction and may mandate certain technologies, effectively drive technology diffusion, although perhaps at a higher cost than economic instruments.

C. Electric Utility Rate Structures

The legal framework governing the provision of electricity, like the collection of tax incentives that apply to energy, fundamentally shapes choice of fuel and efficiency considerations, and therefore GHG emissions. Renewable energy sources and increased energy efficiency are the primary ways of reducing GHG emissions.[52] The restructuring and deregulation of the electric utility industry have placed a greater emphasis on least-cost pricing and market choice, potentially at the expense of environmental concerns.

The early electric power industry operated in an inefficient and chaotic way. Separate companies operated in competition, using different equipment, voltages, and frequencies. Early industry leaders realized that a large centrally located power station could be operated more cheaply than numerous isolated small generating units, with the ability to serve many customers with diverse energy needs. The utility companies, finding it difficult to obtain financing, sought regulation as a means of improving reliability of service and facilitating financing. Regulation also curbed the power of the natural monopoly (a single company providing electric service, eliminating duplication of service and equipment, is naturally more economically efficient) and protected consumers.[53]

The electric power industry provides three essential services: generation, transmission, and distribution. Vertically integrated utilities supplied all three in a fully regulated industry. Deregulation of the electricity generation function facilitated the entry of renewable energy sources into the market. Under the Public Utilities Regulatory Act of 1978 (PURPA), utilities were required to buy power from "qualifying facilities" (QFs), at a price equal to the "avoided cost" of the utility.[54] QFs were independent power producers, mostly small generators, or ones using renewable energy sources. The Federal Energy Regulatory Commission (FERC) is responsible for oversight of PURPA implementation. The Energy Policy Act of 1992 extended the benefits of PURPA to all generation technologies, via orders from FERC to require open and nondiscriminatory access to transmission lines to facilitate wholesale power transactions.[55] Legislation at the state level added the potential for competition at the distribution level, providing the final move toward deregulation.[56] California, one of the first states to attempt retail competition, reversed its legislation in wake of the 2001 electricity crisis. Currently, 16 states plus the District of Columbia have retail choice.

Under most utility regulations prior to restructuring, the utility was required to develop a resource plan using both supply side and demand side measures (DSM). Demand side measures were to be used to the extent that they were cheaper than developing new capacity or even generating electricity on existing equipment.[57] In some jurisdictions, the regulators adjusted the "least cost outcome" to account for environmental externalities, thus giving a boost to renewable sourced energy and efficiency measures. In California, the legislature authorized the Public Utility Commission (PUC) to include the value of environmental costs in calculations of the cost-effectiveness of energy resources.[58] When the PUC tried to implement this by adding environmental benefits or subtracting environmental costs to calculate avoided costs for QFs, the FERC held their actions to be a violation of the law, suggesting that the state could better achieve its environmental goals through support of renewable energy and pollution taxes.[59]

Deregulation appears to have had the effect of discouraging conservation and encouraging the use of low-cost, high carbon-emitting fuel sources.

The Energy Policy Act of 2005[60] makes further changes to the electric utility industry's legal framework, although the precise consequences of those changes in terms of climate change are yet to be determined. First, the act repeals the 1935 Public Utility Holding Company Act (PUHCA) which, among other things, restricted investment by holding companies in transmission facilities and non-integrated operating utilities.[61] Second, the act confers on FERC so-called "backstop" authority to site interstate transmission facilities in "national interest electric transmission corridors" designated by the Department of Energy (DOE) as critical to uncongested and reliable transmission service.[62] To further this new federal authority, the act streamlines permitting on federal lands, and allows federal power marketing agencies to accept outside financing for transmission facilities in national interest transmission corridors. Third, it amended PURPA.[63] Where QFs have ready access to competitive markets administered by independent systems operators (a determination to be made in administrative proceedings before FERC), utilities are no longer required to purchase QF power.

In a fully competitive electricity market, absent price adjustments for environmental externalities, both higher-cost renewable technologies and energy efficiency become less attractive.[64] Not surprisingly, utility investments in DSM programs and associated energy savings fell significantly during the early years of restructuring. Between 1993 and 1999, annual utility expenditures on DSM programs fell by roughly 55%, and incremental annual energy savings fell by about 65%.[65] At the same time, coal-fired electric plants experienced increased use.[66] Trends indicate increasing sales of electricity, and even higher increases in revenue obtained by utility companies. Deregulation appears to have had the effect of discouraging conservation and encouraging the use of low-cost, high carbon-emitting fuel sources. However, it has not had the desired effect on consumer prices. The average retail price of residential use energy in 2004 increased to 8.97 cents per kilowatthour, a 3.1% increase from 2003.[67] In short, deregulation creates an incentive to minimize environmental controls in order to minimize production costs, which enables energy producers to keep their price as low as possible, allowing increased profits. When energy producers minimize environmental controls, the community's environmental costs increase.[68]

The electric utility restructuring has not eliminated all regulation. State regulators continue to have influence, even in the "deregulated" states, implementing policies like net metering and green pricing. Net metering permits a customer operating a small generator to sell excess power back to the utility at a negotiated price. The number of customers in net metering increased 132% from 2003 to 2004.[69] Residential customers dominate the net metering and green pricing participant group. Despite increases, the total number of consumers using net metering and green pricing schemes remains small, with less than 16,000 net metering customers and less than 1 million green pricing customers nationwide.[70] State legislation has also had an impact. Twenty-one states and the District of Columbia have implemented renewable portfolio standards that mandate that a certain portion of the energy used in the state come from renewable sources.[71]

VI. Carbon Tax Proposals

To date, the United States has not enacted any legislation mandating GHG mitigation. Federal tax policy has provided the carrot in the form of tax incentives, while avoiding application of the stick. Mandatory GHG mitigation could take a number of forms: tradeable allowances, carbon sequestration credits, or a carbon tax. Pollution taxes are generally considered the "gold standard" of market-based instruments.[72] Pollution taxes allow polluters the flexibility to use the most cost-effective means of reducing their emissions, in contrast with command and control regulations, which typically specify standards for the means of reducing pollution. The effect of a pollution tax is to cap the costs of abatement, while the effect of a tradable allowance is to cap the quantity of emissions. Cost restrictions, such as pollution taxes, work better than quantity restrictions when "health or environmental damages are not very sensitive to short-term emissions levels or when concerns exist about potentially high costs." [73] As the damages from GHG emissions result from cumulative exposure, short-term increases in GHG emissions cannot be traced to large environmental damages. Accordingly, for abating GHG emissions, price instruments such as carbon taxes can be expected to be more efficient and effective than quantity instruments such as tradable allowances.[74]

Other countries have successfully reduced GHG emissions using carbon taxes.[75] Estimates of the carbon tax necessary to stabilize U.S. CO_2 emissions at their 1990 level by the year 2000 ranged from under $30 per ton to over $100 per ton.[76] The carbon tax imposes a penalty for each unit of GHG emitted. The amount of the tax should be no less than the marginal cost of abatement, or else it will pay the emitter to continue business as usual.[77]

Scientific and engineering studies can predict the appropriate tax rate, which should vary based on the carbon content of the fuel used.[78] The rate may be adjusted for changing circumstances. Carbon taxes ensure the most cost-effective mitigation measures. If a carbon tax is assessed based on the carbon content of the fuel, the users get the correct price signal from the increased cost of the fuel. Thus, a carbon tax encourages several kinds of appropriate behavioral change: fuel switching, mitigation technology, increased efficiency, energy conservation, whichever is the most cost effective for the particular user. One researcher described the carbon tax as "not just a band-aid to reduce CO_2 emissions, but a program to reduce carbon-intensiveness in the economy and in individual lifestyles."[79]

Although carbon taxes may be the best policy instrument for GHG mitigation, at least two reasons argue for an alternative approach. First, the political climate in the United States is anti-tax. Accordingly, both the nomenclature and the potential for revenue enhancement (which might be viewed positively in other circumstances) reduce the likelihood of political viability.[80] Second, a carbon tax removes the stigma from polluting. Any business is free to pollute as much as it wants, as long as it pays the tax. Some environmentalists recoil at this approach.

Some might argue that equitable considerations proscribe a carbon tax. Depending on its structure, a carbon tax could fall disproportionately on low-income taxpayers, as they pay a higher percentage of their income for energy usage. Also, as low-income taxpayers tend to rent rather than own property, they would be unable to increase the energy efficiency of their dwelling units. However, recycling carbon tax revenues to offset other regressive taxes, such as the payroll tax, could ameliorate this regressive effect.

Several carbon tax proposals have been before Congress, but none has come close to enactment. One proposal would impose different rates on different types of fuels according to their carbon content.[81] Another proposal would impose a tax of $50 per ton of carbon dioxide emitted by power-generating units with a generating capacity of five or more megawatts.[82] This tax would be used to establish a Clean Air Trust Fund, which would pay for, inter alia, the development of a carbon sequestration strategy to offset growth in U.S. carbon dioxide emissions and for carrying out methods of biologically sequestering carbon dioxide. A newer version of this proposal drops the carbon dioxide tax, but imposes an excise tax of 30 cents per megawatt of power produced by fossil fuel-burning plants.[83] Carbon taxes may be more politically palatable if used in a more limited way, as a cost-limiting safety valve on a tradeable permit program.[84]

Endnotes

1.   Joint Committee on Taxation, Estimates of Federal Tax Expenditures for Fiscal Years 2006–2010, JCS-2-06 (April 25, 2006).

2.   JOHN A. ALIC, DAVID C. MOWERY & EDWARD S. RUBIN, U.S. TECHNOLOGY AND INNOVATION POLICIES: LESSONS FOR CLIMATE CHANGE 28 (Pew Center on Global Climate Change 2003).

3.   Congress first permitted the expensing of intangible drilling costs (IDCs) and dry-hole costs in 1916 to encourage oil exploration. The other early oil tax benefit,percentage depletion allowance, was first enacted in 1926. See Salvatore Lazzari, Energy Tax Policy, Cong. Res. Serv. IB100054 3 (Aug. 24, 2001).

4. Energy Tax Act of 1978, Pub. L. No. 95-618, § 301(a)(1) (1978).

5. *See* Crude Oil Windfall Profits Tax Act of 1980, Pub. L. No. 96-223 (1980).

6. James W. Moeller, *Of Credits and Quotas: Federal Tax Incentives for Renewable Resources, State Renewable Portfolio Standards, and the Evolution of Proposals for a Federal Renewable Portfolio Standard*, 15 FORDHAM ENVT'L L. REV. 69, 86 (2004).

7. Joint Committee on Taxation, Description and Analysis of Tax Provisions Expiring in 1992 86, JCS-2-92 (Jan. 27, 1992).

8. Pub. L. No. 102-486 (1992); 26 U.S.C. § 45.

9. *See* 26 U.S.C. §48 (2005). This credit applies to the cost of new equipment: (1) that uses solar energy to generate electricity, to heat or cool a structure, or to provide solar process heat; or (2) that is used to produce, distribute, or use energy derived from a geothermal deposit, but only, in the case of electricity generated by geothermal power, up to the electric transmission stage. *See* 26 U.S.C. § 48(a)(3)(A)(i) (2005).

10. Joint Committee on Taxation, Estimated Budget Effects of the Conference Agreement for Title XIII of H.R. 6, the "Energy Tax Incentives Act of 2005," JCX-59-05 (July 27, 2005).

11. 26 U.S.C. § 45(d)(2)(ii) (2005).

12. 26 U.S.C. § 45(c)(9) (2005).

13. 26 U.S.C. § 45 (2005).

14. A.M. GORLOV, TIDAL ENERGY 2955 (2001), *available at* http://freeenergynews.com/Directory/Tidal/index.html.

15. http://www.nrel.gov/otec/what.html.

16. 26 U.S.C. § 38(b)(8) (2005).

17. $125,000 net tax liability - $25,000 = $100,000 x 25% = $25,000. $125,000 credit - $25,000 = $100,000 credit available.

18. 26 U.S.C. § 38(c)(4) (2005). *See* Form 8835, Renewable Electricity Production Credit, *available at* www.irs.gov.

19. 26 U.S.C. § 54 (2005).

20. Such specific language generally indicates that Congress had a particular business in mind.

21. 26 U.S.C. §§ 38(b)(1), 46(2), 48(a)(3)(A)(i) (2005).

22. 26 U.S.C. §§ 38(b)(1), 46(2), 48(a)(3)(A)(iv) (2005).

23. Energy Tax Act of 1978, Pub. L. No. 95-618, § 301(a)(1) (1978).

24. Patrick Quinlan, Howard Geller & Steven Nadel, *Tax Incentives for Innovative Energy-Efficient Technologies* (Updated), ACEEE Rep. No. E013 2 (2001).

25. 26 U.S.C. § 136 (2005).

26. 26 U.S.C. § 25C (2005).

27. 26 U.S.C. § 179D (2005).

28. 26 U.S.C. § 45L (2005).

29. 26 U.S.C. § 38(b)(23) (2005).

30. 26 U.S.C. § 45M (2005).

31. Energy Star 2003 Annual Report at 6, *available at* www.energystar.gov.

32. 26 U.S.C. § 179A (2005).

33. 26 U.S.C. § 30 (2005).

34. *See* http://www.irs.gov/newsroom/article/0,,id=157557,00.html.

35. Salvatore Lazzari, *Energy Tax Policy* 3, CRS Report: IB10054 (Aug. 24, 2001).

36. F. J. Blaise, *What every tax man should know about percentage depletion*, Taxes–The Tax Magazine, June 1958, at 397.

37. Mona L. Hymel, The United States' Experience with Energy-Based Tax Incentives: The Evidence Supporting Tax Incentives for Renewable Energy 4, Ariz. Legal Studies Discussion Paper No. 06-21 (April 2006), *available at* http://ssrn.com/abstract=896986.

38. 26 U.S.C. § 263(a).

39. 26 U.S.C. §§ 167, 168.

40. 26 U.S.C. § 612.

41. 26 U.S.C. § 29.

42. 26 U.S.C. § 43.

43. 26 U.S.C. § 45.

44. 26 U.S.C. § 54 (2005).

45. 26 U.S.C. §§ 48A and 48B (2005).

46. Adam B. Jaffe, Richard G. Newell & Robert N. Stavins, *A Tale of Two Market Failures: Technology and Environmental Policy*, RFF DP 04-38 (October 2004).

47. *Id.*

48. Richard G. Newell & Nathan E. Wilson, *Technology Prizes for Climate Change Mitigation*, RFF DP 05-33 (June 2005); Iratu Nitta, Proposal for a Green Patent System: Implications for Sustainable Development and Climate Change, 16 Sustainable Dev. L. & Pol'y 61 (2005).

49. Jaffe et al., *supra* note 46, at 17.

50. Roberta F. Mann & Mona L. Hymel, *Getting into the Act: Enticing the Consumer to Become "Green" Through Tax Incentives*, 36 Envtl. L. Rep. 10,419, 10,422 (2006).

51. Nitta, *supra* note 48.

52. *See* Fred Sissine, Global Climate Change: The Role for Energy Efficiency (Cong. Res. Serv. Rep. No. RL30414) (2000).

53. The History of the Electric Power Industry, http://www.eei.org/industry_issues/industry_overview_and_statistics/history/index.htm%20.

54. Public Utility Regulatory Policies Act of 1978, Pub. L. No. 95-617, 92 Stat. 3117 (codified in scattered sections of 16 U.S.C.).

55. Energy Policy Act of 1992, Pub. L. No. 102-486, 106 Stat. 2776 (1992); *see also* Karen Palmer & Dallas Burtraw, *The Environmental Impacts of Electricity Restructuring: Looking Back and Looking Forward*, RFF DP 05-07 at 4 (April 2005).

56. Palmer & Burtraw, *supra* note 55, at 6.

57. Edan Rotenberg, Energy Efficiency in "Deregulated" Markets 21, Yale Law School Student Scholarship Series, *available at* http://lsr.nellco.org/yale/student/papers/14.

58. *See* Cal. Pub. Util. Code § 701.1(c).

59. *Southern Cal. Edison Co.*, 71 F.E.R.C. P61,269, at 62,080 (June 2, 1995).

60. H.R. 6, 109th Cong., 1st Sess. (2005), Pub. L. No. 109-58 (EPAct 2005).

61. Sec. 1263, EPAct 2005.

62. Sec. 1281, EPAct 2005.

63. Sec. 1253, EPAct 2005.

64. *See* Edan Rotenberg, *supra* note 57, http://lsr.nellco.org/yale/student/papers/14.

65. Palmer & Burtraw, supra note 55, at 23. *See also* EIA Electric Power Annual Report 2004 at 4 ("[N]ominal DSM expenditures have declined 43% over the last ten years, in part due to elimination of some DSM requirements when States have moved to more competitive markets.").

66. Palmer & Burtraw, supra note 55, at 15.

67. EIA Electric Power Annual Report 2004 at 4 ("Retail sales of electricity increased to 3,548 billion kilowatt-hours in 2004, a 1.7% increase from 2003 and a pace close to the historical growth rate. Revenue, however, increased to over $270 billion in 2004, a 4.5% increase from 2003 and the second straight year of strong growth.").

68. Rudy Perkins, *Electricity Deregulation, Environmental Externalities and the Limitations of Price*, 39 B.C. L. REV. 993, 1033 (1998).

69. Energy Information Administration / Green Pricing and Net Metering Programs 2004.

70. *Id.*

71. EIA, RENEWABLE ENERGY TRENDS 2004, Table 28.

72. Jonathan Baert Wiener, *Global Environmental Regulations*, 108 YALE L.J. 677, 682 (1999) (noting that "the standard analysis crowns taxes as the presumptive first choice for optimal environmental regulation").

73. RICHARD D. MORGENSTERN, REDUCING CARBON EMISSIONS AND LIMITING COSTS 3-4 (Feb. 2002), *available at* http://www.rff.org/climatechangemorganstern.pdf.

74. Roberta F. Mann, *Waiting to Exhale: Global Warming and Tax Policy*, 51 AM. UNIV. L. REV. 1135, 1209 (2002).

75. *See* MIKAEL SKOU ANDERSEN, NIELS DENGSØE & ANDERS BRANTH PEDERSEN, AN EVALUATION OF THE IMPACT OF GREEN TAXES IN THE NORDIC COUNTRIES 11 (2001); OECD, ENVIRONMENTALLY RELATED TAXES IN OECD COUNTRIES: ISSUES AND STRATEGIES 21 (2001).

76. Larry Parker, *Global Climate Change: Market-Based Strategies to Reduce Greenhouse Gases*, Cong. Res. Serv. Rep. IB7057 (April 4, 2001), *available at* http://www.cnie.org/nle/crsreports/climate/clim-5.cfm#_1_9.

77. The following chart is *available at* http://www.globalpolicy.org/socecon/glotax/carbon/carbongr.htm.

78. *See* Robert B. McKinstry, Jr., Adam Rose & Coreen Ripp, *Incentive-Based Approaches to Greenhouse Gas Mitigation in Pennsylvania: Protecting the Environment and Promoting Fiscal Reform*, 14 WIDENER L.J. 205, 215 (2004).

79. Larry Parker, *Global Climate Change: Market-Based Strategies to Reduce Greenhouse Gases* 11, Cong. Res. Serv. Issue Brief No. IB97057 (updated Nov. 18, 2004).

80. *See* Roberta Mann, *Beyond Enforcement: Top Ten Strategies for Encouraging Tax Compliance*, 111 TAX NOTES 919, 922-23 (2006).

81. *See* H.R. 1086, 102d Cong. (1991); H.R. 804, 103d Cong. (1993) (reintroducing H.R. 4805, 101st Cong. (1990) in virtually identical form).

82. S. 2636, 105th Cong. § 9 (1999).

83. *See* S. 1131, 107th Cong. § 7 (2001) (reintroducing in virtually identical form S. 1949, 106th Cong. (1999)).

84. *See* Larry Parker, *Global Climate Change: Controlling CO_2 Emissions—Cost-Limiting Safety Values*, Cong. Res. Serv. Rep. No. RS21067 (updated Dec. 22, 2004).

Part Four

Reduction Programs

chapter seventeen

Voluntary Climate Change Efforts

Tom Kerr

I. Background

While the debate continues over the science of climate change and the necessity for action to mitigate potential impacts, a growing number of companies across industry sectors have voluntarily taken action to assess and mitigate their climate change impacts. This action is sometimes taken unilaterally by the company, but often is undertaken in concert with other stakeholders, including local, state and federal government bodies, non-governmental organizations (NGOs), and other industry groups.

Companies and government policymakers have various motivations for pursuing voluntary actions to mitigate the threat of climate change. Perhaps the primary motivation is that voluntary programs allow companies and policymakers to explore solutions now, while others work to forge political and scientific consensus on the best long-term approach. However, other drivers of corporate interest in voluntary action include the chance to document "early action" in advance of regulation so that companies can receive some form of "credit" from a future regulatory scheme; the opportunity to work with governments in a collaborative manner, with an eye toward shaping policy to the company's advantage; corporate brand or image enhancement; gaining footholds in new clean energy or climate mitigation technologies and services; and the opportunity to prioritize internal efforts to enhance energy efficiency and reduce operating costs.

Voluntary corporate environmental action began in earnest in the 1980s, when corporations, reacting to growing concerns about their environmental performance, voluntarily began to track and publish information about pollution prevention and other environmental activities. In some cases, companies simply sought to enhance their reputation by publishing information about environmental good deeds. In other areas, non-governmental organizations teamed with corporations to demonstrate the viability of environmental actions that were "beyond compliance"—that is, they exceeded existing standards or reduced impacts for aspects of a company's environmental footprint that were not regulated. In the 1990s, climate change mitigation efforts fell squarely into this category, and companies began making climate change–related announcements.

Today, there is a wide variety of voluntary climate change activities. One approach is a range of government—or NGO—and industry partnerships like the World Wildlife Fund's Climate Savers or the Environmental Protection Agency's Climate Leaders that involve a single company making voluntary commitments to assess and/or mitigate its climate change impact, with the government agreeing in return to offer technical assistance and public recognition to companies that achieve milestones. Another approach involves government and industry sectors entering into agreements to set industry-wide targets and timetables for achieving goals like reduced greenhouse gas intensity. Examples in this area include the U.S. Department of Energy's Climate VISION process and the Japanese government's voluntary emissions trading scheme. Finally, there has been a proliferation of government and private-sector efforts designed to advance specific greenhouse gas mitigation technologies and/or practices, including the Chicago Climate Exchange, The Energy Star program and the World Resources Institute's Greenhouse Gas Protocol effort.

The growing field of voluntary climate change activity deserves a closer look by corporate and law firm attorneys, government policymakers and others. This chapter begins with a discussion of the common elements of corporate "Greenhouse Gas Management," which is emerging as a leading approach that companies are using to assess and mitigate their climate change impacts. It then provides an overview of the leading international, national, corporate/NGO, and state efforts aimed at spurring voluntary action to reduce the risk of climate change.

II. Voluntary Corporate Greenhouse Gas Management— Common Elements

As governments and industry have increased their reliance on voluntary efforts, shareholders, consumers and other stakeholders have required additional information and/or action to provide credibility that voluntary climate change actions are delivering promised benefits. As a result, leading firms have engaged in increasingly aggressive greenhouse gas reduction target-setting, combined with more rigorous reporting to verify their claims. There now appears to be an emerging consensus on the steps that companies can take to mitigate reputational, economic, insurance and other risks associated with climate change. These steps include performing a corporate-wide greenhouse gas (GHG) inventory, developing a management plan to ensure quality, setting a GHG reduction target that begins to mitigate a company's climate impact, and communicating results and methods to stakeholders. This section discusses these steps in more detail.

A. Elements of a GHG Management Strategy

Step One—Perform a Corporate GHG Inventory.

A first step many businesses take is creating a corporate-wide GHG inventory to identify sources of emissions, estimate risks, and identify reduction opportunities. Companies are finding that this comprehensive picture allows them to strategically and cost-effectively address climate risk. As the inventory is updated annually, it then serves as the metric for tracking the success of GHG reduction efforts. Companies are also discovering that a GHG inventory is useful in responding to requests to disclose risk from shareholder and environmental groups and the financial and insurance communities.

> **A first step many businesses take is creating a corporate-wide GHG inventory to identify sources of emissions, estimate risks, and identify reduction opportunities.**

There are various tools that companies can use to perform a corporate-wide GHG inventory, including the Greenhouse Gas Protocol,[1] the International Standard Organization's 14064 Standards for Greenhouse Gas Accounting and Verification,[2] and the Global Reporting Initiative.[3] These tools are discussed in more detail below.

Step Two—Create an Inventory Management Plan.

A second part of a corporate GHG management strategy is the creation of what has been called an "inventory management plan" (IMP). An IMP is an internal process whereby companies institutionalize the collection, calculation, and maintenance of GHG data and the completion of a high-quality inventory. This sort of management plan ensures consistency among different facilities, provides for accurate tracking over time, improves reliability of emissions and reductions estimates, and helps to ensure the credibility of the data when disclosed to interested stakeholders.

Step Three—Set a GHG Reduction Goal.

After a company understands its climate footprint, the third step is to set a near-term goal of reducing greenhouse gas emissions. Two primary decisions are required before a company adopts a target: its type and its level. The decision on what type of target to adopt can be determined by addressing target placement (the point in the product life cycle to which the target should be applied), target coverage or focus (GHG emissions or energy consumption focus), and the nature of the target (absolute or relative to indicators such as production levels and revenues). A relative (intensity-based) target allows emissions or energy use to grow, as long as emissions or energy use per unit of production does not. Absolute targets have the advantage of being consistent with international commitments, as well as with many countries' domestic policies. Absolute targets also limit total environmental impact.

The time period and target level must also be set in a "top-down" or "bottom-up" manner. In a top-down target-setting process, the level is initially set for the whole corporation. The target may then be allocated to the operating units in various ways, so that the sum of the sub-targets adds up to the corporate target. Under a "bottom-up" process, the corporate target level is based on analysis of potential reductions by individual operating units.[4]

Step Four—Communicate and Partner.

Finally, after the target is set, companies are increasingly taking steps to communicate the target and results that are achieved to stakeholders in a transparent manner. A number of private, government and non-government groups are in the business of helping companies develop a high-quality inventory, IMP, and reduction target. Partnering with one of these outside stakeholders is another strategy used to lend credibility to a company's climate efforts. This sort of reporting and transparency also allows companies to reflect long-term value to stakeholders, improves internal management systems, aids in managing risk over time, and encourages improvement and learning internally.[5]

B. GHG Accounting Tools

Accurate accounting of GHG emissions and reductions is a key component of the steps described above to mitigate the risks associated with climate change. There are three leading corporate GHG accounting tools—the World Resources Institute/World Business Council for Sustainable Development's GHG Protocol, the International Organization for Standardization (ISO)'s GHG accounting standards, and the Global Reporting Initiative (GRI).

1. GHG Protocol

The Greenhouse Gas Protocol Initiative (GHG Protocol) aims to harmonize GHG accounting and reporting standards internationally to ensure that different trading schemes and other climate-related initiatives adopt consistent approaches to GHG accounting. This broad international coalition of businesses, non-governmental organizations, government and inter-governmental organizations brings together leading experts on greenhouse gas emissions to develop internationally accepted accounting and reporting standards. The participants work in partnership to design, disseminate and promote the use of globally applicable accounting and reporting standards for corporate greenhouse gas emissions.[6] The GHG Protocol appears to be compatible with most other emerging GHG reporting schemes, including voluntary initiatives, mandatory reporting, risk management, and GHG emissions markets or trading schemes.[7]

The GHG Protocol Initiative consists of two modules: the Corporate GHG Accounting and Reporting Standard and the Project GHG Accounting and Reporting Standard. As discussed above, the Corporate GHG Accounting and Reporting Standard (Corporate Module) helps companies and other organizations to identify, calculate, and report entity-wide GHG emissions. The corporate accounting and reporting standard has been utilized and tested by over 30 companies in nine countries. The Project GHG Accounting and Reporting Standard (Project Module) aims at developing accounting and reporting standards and/or general guidance for both emission reduction and land use, land-use change and forestry projects. The Project Module also provides practical tools with additional guidance to help companies calculate their GHG emissions from various sources.[8] The Corporate GHG Accounting and Reporting Module was first published in October 2001 and a revised edition was published in 2004. The Project GHG Accounting and Reporting Module was published in November 2005.[9]

2. ISO Accounting Standards

The International Organization for Standardization (ISO) began developing voluntary corporate GHG accounting standards (known as ISO 14064) in 2002 and published the standards on March 2006. The standards provide tools for assessing and supporting greenhouse gas emission reduction and emissions trading. The standards were developed with the goal of providing industry and government a generally accepted, transparent, and credible protocol for greenhouse gas quantification, monitoring, reporting, and verification.[10] ISO 14064 includes three discrete standards, including guidance for quantifying and reporting emissions and removals at the organization level; quantifying, monitoring, and reporting emission reductions and "removal enhancement"; and verification and validation of corporate- and project-level GHG claims. These standards can be applied separately or together depending on the needs of the user.[11] ISO 14064 will be complemented by ISO 14065, which specifies requirements to accredit or otherwise recognize bodies that undertake greenhouse gas validation or verification using ISO 14064 or other relevant standards or specifications. ISO 14065 is expected to be published in early 2007.[12]

3. Global Reporting Initiative

A more comprehensive environmental reporting tool that has been used in corporate GHG reporting is the Global Reporting Initiative (GRI). GRI develops and disseminates globally applicable Sustainability Reporting Guidelines that describe why, how, and on what an organization should report, discussing the principles for sustainability reporting, and listing reporting disclosure items and performance indicators.[13] The Guidelines are voluntary and are applicable to activities, products, and services.

The Key Offerings of the GRI are the 2002 Sustainability Reporting Guidelines, Technical Protocols, and Sector Supplements. The Guidelines are applicable to any organization, regardless of sector. GRI is also developing technical protocols to address specific indicators, such as energy use, as well as Sector Supplements, so that various industries are able to address sustainability issues to a greater extent.[14]

III. Overview of Voluntary Climate Change Efforts

This section provides an overview of leading efforts that are designed to foster voluntary action to mitigate greenhouse gas emissions. The discussions below provide a description of the program's objectives, target audience, key offerings, and, where available, current program status or upcoming milestones.

A. International Initiatives

1. OECD Declaration on International Investment and Multinational Enterprises

Program Design and Objectives

The Organization for Economic Co-operation and Development (OECD) Declaration on International Investment and Multinational Enterprises was designed to improve the investment climate in OECD member countries and in countries in which companies from OECD member countries operate.[15] All 39 OECD member countries (which include the United States and most other major industrialized countries) have subscribed to the Declaration, which recognizes the social and economic contributions of multinational enterprises, and seeks to accommodate investment and operations of multinational enterprises while securing the interests of OECD member countries.[16] While the Declaration has a broader scope than climate change impacts, it offers a model for international engagement of corporations on environmental issues, including climate change.

Target Audience

The target audience of the initiative is multinational corporations and policymakers.

Key Offerings

The Declaration on International Investment and Multinational Enterprises consists of four elements: Guidelines for Multinational Enterprises, National Treatment, Conflicting Requirements, and International Investment Incentives and Disincentives.[17]

The Guidelines for Multinational Enterprises are implemented through OECD member countries' National Contact Points. National Contact Point offices provide assistance to companies, collect information on national experiences with the Guidelines, and report annually to the OECD Investment Committee. The Guidelines only recommend "responsible" behavior; they do not provide countries with measurement and reporting guidelines.[18]

Section V of the Guidelines for Multinational Enterprises calls for enterprises to establish and maintain a system of environmental management that includes collection and evaluation of information regarding the environmental, health, and safety impacts of their activities; establishment of measurable objectives and, where appropriate, targets for improved environmental performance.[19] Relevant to the climate change issue, the Guidelines state, "Where there are threats of serious damage to the environment, taking also into account human health and safety, do not use the lack of full scientific certainty as a reason for postponing cost-effective measures to prevent or minimize such damage."[20]

2. The Eco-Management and Audit Scheme

Program Design and Objectives

The Council of the European Union and the European Parliament designed EMAS, the Eco-Management and Audit Scheme, to improve companies' environmental performance. This voluntary initiative recognizes and rewards those organizations that improve environmental performance to a greater extent than the minimum level of legal compliance.[21]

Participants must regularly produce a public environmental statement that reports on their environmental performance, and the statement undergoes independent verification. Organizations must also implement an environmental management system and work on improving those aspects of their activities that need the greatest environmental improvement.[22]

Target Audience

Although the scheme was initially aimed at industrial companies, now all types of organizations can register with EMAS.[23]

Key Offerings

A number of guidance documents have been issued to assist organizations implementing the EMAS requirements. The European Commission has produced official guidance on EMAS through an official Decision and a Recommendation, which have been published in the *Official Journal*.[24]

Program Status

EMAS was launched in April of 2001 and now has 263 registered organizations, with 358 sites.[25]

3. Business Leaders' Initiative on Climate Change

Program Design and Objectives

The Business Leaders' Initiative on Climate Change (BLICC) is a program initially funded by the European Union government; it is now partially privately funded. The BLICC program aims to spur voluntary corporate action on climate change in the European Union. BLICC brings together key stakeholders, including local and national government, business, employees, civil society organizations, and the European Union, to accomplish its goals. The objectives of the BLICC are to raise the profile of the issue of climate change, to influence policymakers to create incentives for industries to make long-term, environmentally-oriented decisions, to generate dialogue between industry peers and stakeholders, and to increase transparency through better emissions monitoring and reporting.[26]

BLICC companies calculate and report direct and indirect GHG emissions using the World Resources Institute Greenhouse Gas Protocol, discussed above, and set targets for emission reductions.[27] Each year the companies in the program summarize their emission inventories.[28] Emphasis is placed on verification and accountability; BLICC reports are available to the public.[29] The long-term objectives for a company are to incorporate emission calculations into every part of the business,[30] lower greenhouse gas emissions, and reduce climatic impact.[31]

Target Audience

The target audience is companies with operations in the European Union.

Key Offerings

The BLICC program offers companies insights into methodologies for estimating GHG emissions, setting targets, and reporting.[32] Additionally, participants have opportunities to share experience across industries, collaborate with other groups,[33] and share best practice in the areas related to customer activism, renewable energy and transportation.[34] The program also provides a forum where companies can discuss the issues facing their business with regard to environmental risk management, with specific focus on greenhouse gas emissions.[35] BLICC's members have reported cost-effective energy-saving actions.[36]

Program Status

BLICC launched in 2000, and now includes approximately 30 multinational companies and an additional 20 large Swedish companies.[37]

4. Japan: Voluntary Domestic Emissions Trading Scheme

Program Design and Objectives

The objective of the Japanese Voluntary Domestic Emissions Trading Scheme is to provide incentives for additional carbon dioxide reductions outside of existing measures in Japan, gather knowledge and experience of domestic emissions trading with verification and compliance assessment, and stimulate cost-effective innovation and investment.[38,39]

There are three main schemes to the program: the voluntary scheme, the facility-based scheme and the emissions trading scheme. In the voluntary scheme, companies and facilities participate by pledging concrete emissions reduction targets. In return, they receive emissions allowances from the government.[40] Companies are allocated allowances to the amount of base-year emissions (the average of emissions of the past 3 years) minus the reduction goal.[41] As incentive to participate, the Environment Ministry subsidizes one-third of the installation cost of CO_2 emissions reduction equipment or activities. If the companies or facilities fail to achieve their target, the subsidy must be returned to the government.

In the facility-based scheme, the government selects target facilities from applicants based on the cost-effectiveness of GHG reduction activity. The government issues the tradable allowances to each facility (rather than to the company), and target facilities face the obligation to submit the same amount of emissions allowances as their actual GHG emissions to the government. Finally, in the emissions trading scheme, companies and facilities can trade allowances in order to achieve agreed-upon targets. Facilities have more flexibility in this scheme and can use Kyoto Mechanism credits (such as Certified Emissions Reductions or others) in complying with their obligations.[42]

There are two types of participants in the program: participants with pledged targets and trading participants. The 32 facilities with pledged targets receive subsidies for improving efficiency of the facilities and allowances. The eight trading participant companies open accounts in the registries and trade allowances as necessary. However, they are not eligible for subsidies.[43]

Target Audience

The target audience is facilities and companies with operations in Japan.

Key Offerings

Under the pledged target scheme, the Japanese Ministry of the Environment subsidizes one-third of the cost of GHG reduction activities. This subsidy is estimated to cost over US$23 million.[44]

Program Status

The program was launched in May, 2005; currently 34 companies and corporate groups participate.[45] The Ministry of the Environment estimates that total CO_2 emissions reductions for fiscal 2006 will be over 275,000 metric tons, 21% of average annual emissions in the base years, fiscal 2002-04. The reduction in emissions over the officially recognized service life of the subsidized equipment is calculated at about 3.7 million tons.[46] After the end of fiscal 2006, the actual CO_2 emissions during the year will be calculated and verified. The emissions quota trading system started in April, 2006.[47]

5. Australia's Greenhouse Challenge Plus Program

Program Design and Objectives

The Greenhouse Challenge Plus program is a voluntary Australian government-industry partnership. Greenhouse Challenge Plus is designed to reduce greenhouse gas emissions, accelerate the use of energy efficiency, integrate climate change issues into business decision-making, and provide more consistent reporting of greenhouse gas emissions levels.[48]

Greenhouse Challenge Plus is part of the Australian Government's comprehensive Climate Change Strategy, announced in 2004. The program is managed by the Australian Greenhouse Office (AGO) as part of the federal Department of the Environment and Heritage. Greenhouse Challenge Plus builds on the success of the Greenhouse Challenge program (established in 1995), integrates two other industry-focused measures (the Generator Efficiency Standards and Greenhouse Friendly initiative), and incorporates changes announced in the 2004 Energy White Paper *Securing Australia's Energy Future.*[49]

Companies can be involved in the program at different levels. Companies must sign an agreement whereby they agree to measure, publicly report, and independently verify their GHG emissions, and to deliver "maximum practical GHG abatement." Associate member status is offered to businesses that require additional government assistance to meet reporting obligations. Companies that distinguish themselves by using innovative methods to set and achieve greenhouse gas emissions and publicly

disclose their emissions are considered Greenhouse Challenge Plus "Leaders." "Champion" status is granted to members that have implemented highly successful greenhouse gas management programs by achieving large-scale emissions reduction or sinks enhancement and for taking an action or making an investment that has the potential to deliver substantial long-term net emissions reductions.[50]

Target Audience

The target audience includes individual companies as well as trade associations.[51]

Key Offerings

The Australian government provides recognition, administrative and technical support, and works for GHG reporting consistency/standards across agencies.[52] In addition, the AGO has developed a number of technical tools to support companies. For example, members can enter data as well as generate and submit reports online using the Online System for Challenge Activity Reporting application. AGO also assists entities in calculating greenhouse gas emissions and estimating greenhouse sinks. Companies also receive independent verification.[53] In addition, members can use the "Greenhouse Friendly" logo to market a product or service that produces zero emissions. To achieve certification, the GHG emissions associated with the production, use and disposal of the product or service need to be fully offset by approved greenhouse gas abatement.[54]

Program Status

The program was launched in July 2005; currently 780 firms from all industry sectors participate.[55] Marking a change in policy from voluntary to mandatory, the Australian government recently announced that as of July 2006, Australian companies receiving fuel excise credits of greater than $3M Australian will be required to join the program. Proponents of large energy resource development projects will also be required to participate in the program.[56]

B. U.S. Domestic Initiatives

Voluntary programs are a key part of the United States' climate change strategy. In 1992, as part of the Clinton Administration's Climate Change Action Plan, the federal government created several voluntary programs as one of the U.S. government's key policies and measures under the United Nations Framework Convention on Climate Change.[57] These programs were designed to increase energy efficiency, methane reduction, clean energy, and other greenhouse gas mitigation efforts by companies and other groups.

In 2002, the Bush Administration further elevated the profile of voluntary climate change measures by making them the centerpiece of a strategy designed to reduce U.S. greenhouse gas emissions intensity 18% between 2002 and 2012 (see Chapter 3). The White House asserts that this policy will put America on a path toward stabilizing GHG concentration in the atmosphere in the long run, while sustaining the economic growth needed to finance investments in a new, cleaner energy structure.[58]

Voluntary federal efforts fall into three categories: (1) efforts to enhance the existing U.S. Department of Energy's "1605(b)" greenhouse gas reporting scheme; (2) engaging key industry sectors to reduce their emissions intensity through the "Climate VISION" effort; and (3) challenging individual companies to reduce their GHG emissions through a suite of new and existing voluntary programs run by federal agencies.

1. The U.S. Department of Energy's Voluntary 1605(b) Greenhouse Gas Registry

Program Design and Objectives

The 1605b registry was authorized under Section 1605(b) of the Energy Policy Act of 1992.[59] The Voluntary Reporting of Greenhouse Gases Program was designed as a way for organizations or individuals to record the results of voluntary measures to reduce, avoid, or sequester greenhouse gas emissions. It is part of the Bush Administration's efforts to accelerate reductions in U.S. greenhouse gas intensity while developing the advanced technologies needed to stabilize atmospheric concentrations of greenhouse gases without impairing economic growth.[60]

In February 2002, President Bush directed the Secretary of Energy, working with the Secretaries of Commerce and Agriculture and the Administrator of the Environmental Protection Agency, to propose improvements to the current greenhouse gas registry to "enhance measurement accuracy, reliability and verifiability, working with and taking into account emerging domestic and international approaches."[61] The revised program guidelines were developed through an extensive interagency and multiyear public review process that included workshops, meetings and other opportunities to provide DOE with oral and written comment.[62]

Interim Final General Guidelines and draft Technical Guidelines were published on March 24, 2005.[63] The U.S. Department of Energy (DOE) released the final revised guidelines on April 17, 2006,[64] and they are the first revisions since the original guidelines were established under Section 1605(b) of the 1992 Energy Policy Act.[65]

Target Audience

The target audience is corporations, governments, and other organizations.[66]

Key Offerings

The revised guidelines encourage broader reporting of emissions and sequestration by utilities and industries, as well as small businesses and institutions, by introducing methods for U.S. businesses and institutions to calculate entity-wide emission reductions. The guidelines are designed for corporate GHG management efforts, as well as for estimating emissions associated with agriculture, forestry, and other sectors of the economy.[67] Participants can report emissions reductions achieved internationally and companies can bank current emissions reductions in preparation for future U.S. GHG policies.[68]

Under the registry, U.S. companies submit detailed annual reports on their emissions and reductions of greenhouse gases.[69] The information is collected in a public database.[70] The Department of Energy's (DOE) Energy Information Administration (EIA) has initiated the development of the forms and software needed to implement the revised guidelines, and EIA expects to implement the revised program in 2007. DOE's Office of Policy and International Affairs intends to review and update the guidelines approximately every three years.[71]

Program Status

In 2004, 226 U.S. companies and other organizations filed greenhouse gas reports with the registry.[72] The revised guidelines went into effect on June 1, 2006; technical guidelines are still under development.[73]

2. Climate VISION

Program Design and Objectives

Climate VISION—Voluntary Innovative Sector Initiatives: Opportunities Now—is a public-private partnership of the U.S. government and business associations representing 14 key industrial sectors and the Business Roundtable.[74] Most of the sectors are managed by the DOE, with the EPA and U.S. Department of Agriculture providing support for a small number of other sectors. Industry sectors are encouraged to accelerate the transition to practices, improved processes, and energy technologies that are cost-effective, cleaner, more efficient, and more capable of reducing, capturing, or sequestering GHGs. Program partners have issued letters of intent to meet sector targets for reducing GHG emissions intensity.[75]

Target Audience

Climate VISION partners represent a broad range of industry sectors, including oil and gas production, transportation, and refining; electricity generation; coal and mineral production and mining; manufacturing (automobiles, cement, iron and steel, magnesium, aluminum, chemicals, and semiconductors); railroads; and forestry products.[76]

Key Offerings

Participating sectors are expected to develop work plans that integrate GHG management into business plans and decisions. In return for this commitment, DOE and other participating agencies provide technical assistance, including plant-wide assessments, industrial assessment centers, standardization of software tools that identify opportunities for greater energy efficiency and consistency in calculating emissions, and training and information.[77]

Program Status

Climate VISION was launched in February 2003. Currently, business associations representing 14 industry sectors and the Business Roundtable participate. Climate VISION partners held a one-day workshop on February 2006 to hear from industry sectors on activities they have undertaken to reduce energy usage and greenhouse gas emissions intensity.[78] To date, 14 sector groups have established GHG goals.[79]

> The objective of EPA's Climate Leaders' effort is to challenge individual companies to develop long-term, comprehensive climate change strategies.

In May 2006, the Government Accountability Office (GAO) released a report that was critical of Climate VISION for not having a means of tracking trade groups' progress in completing the steps in their plans. GAO concluded that a tracking system would enable DOE to ascertain whether participants are meeting program expectations in a timely manner. GAO further stated that establishing a written policy on the consequences of not progressing as expected would allow DOE to ensure that participants are actively engaged in the programs.[80]

3. Climate Leaders

Program Design and Objectives

The objective of EPA's Climate Leaders' effort is to challenge individual companies to develop long-term, comprehensive climate change strategies. Companies implement their strategies by setting an aggressive greenhouse gas emissions reduction target and reporting on progress through submitting annual inventory data to the EPA. Companies also develop an Inventory Management Plan, which institutionalizes best practices in measuring and reporting greenhouse gas emissions. It is a voluntary industry-government partnership.[81]

Target Audience

Larger companies from a variety of sectors participate in the Climate Leaders program.[82]

Key Offerings

EPA offers Climate Leaders partners recognition, technical assistance, peer exchange opportunities, credibility, and identification as corporate environmental leaders. In

terms of recognition, Climate Leaders offers press events, articles and public service announcements in business and trade publications, speaking engagements at industry conferences, and case studies highlighting partner achievements.[83]

Companies that join the partnership receive free technical assistance in implementing the Climate Leaders GHG Inventory Guidance—including assistance defining organizational and operational boundaries, identifying emissions sources, selecting emission factors, and estimating small sources. Companies also receive technical assistance in developing a GHG management system and documenting it within an Inventory Management Plan, and setting a credible corporate-wide GHG reduction goal.[84]

Other offerings include peer exchange opportunities through a biannual partner meeting; a GHG reporting mechanism that aims to provide assurance that partners have created a high-quality GHG management process; and public recognition by EPA to partner companies as corporate environmental leaders.[85]

Program Status

Climate Leaders was launched in February 2002. The effort now includes 89 partners, 46 of whom have set greenhouse gas emissions reduction goals.[86] EPA announced that five Climate Leaders companies reached their greenhouse gas reduction goals in 2005: Baxter International Inc., General Motors Corporation, IBM Corporation, the National Renewable Energy Laboratory, and SC Johnson.

In May 2006, the GAO report mentioned earlier was also critical of Climate Leaders for the program's lack of a standardized method for moving companies along the path to set and achieve a GHG target. Although EPA tracks progress internally, GAO took issue with the fact that no policy exists describing actions taken toward companies not complying with program requirements.[87]

4. ENERGY STAR

Program Design and Objectives of Effort

The ENERGY STAR program is the crown jewel of the U.S. domestic voluntary climate change programs. A joint effort of DOE and EPA, it was launched in 1992 to reduce greenhouse gas emissions through superior energy-efficient products and practices. This voluntary program now partners with over 8,000 organizations to deliver energy-efficient solutions for consumers, businesses, industrial facilities, and non-profit organizations.

Target Audience

The target audience includes large segments of the domestic economy, including consumers, manufacturers, retailers, utilities, private businesses, building owners, industrial facilities, public-sector organizations, states, homebuilders, energy raters, and financial lenders.[88]

Key Offerings

According to surveys, the ENERGY STAR label is recognized by some 60% of the American public. The program has several key components. In one, the program selects a particular product line (such as computer equipment), identifies the brands that are the most energy-efficient, and awards those brands the ENERGY STAR label. That label, in turn, encourages consumers to buy those brands. The program works with the product manufacturers to improve the energy efficiency of the products in order to merit the ENERGY STAR label. Over 40 product lines—including appliances; office equipment; and lighting, heating and cooling equipment—contain products that have been awarded the ENERGY STAR label.[89] In another component of the program, EPA recognizes energy-efficient new homes with the ENERGY STAR label, and works with residential homeowners to implement practices to improve home energy efficiency.

For businesses and other organizations, ENERGY STAR offers an energy management strategy that helps in measuring current energy performance, setting goals, tracking savings, and rewarding improvements. The program offers tailored energy management strategies for a wide range of businesses and other organizations, including small businesses and religious congregations.

For commercial buildings, EPA provides an energy performance rating system that businesses have already used for more than 26,000 buildings across the country. EPA also recognizes top-performing buildings with the ENERGY STAR label.[90]

Program Status

There are more than 8,000 ENERGY STAR partner organizations. To date, around 2 billion ENERGY STAR qualified products have been purchased. More than 2,500 buildings have earned the ENERGY STAR label.[91] Almost 10% of the new homes constructed in 2005 earned the ENERGY STAR label.[92] In 2004, Americans, with the help of ENERGY STAR, saved over $12 billion on energy bills and reduced greenhouse gas emissions by the same amount that would result from eliminating 23 million cars. This energy savings is equivalent to 4% of total U.S. electricity demand.[93]

5. Methane Partnerships

Program Design and Objectives

EPA's methane partnerships are a suite of voluntary programs designed to reduce emissions of methane, a potent greenhouse gas. The programs aim to overcome a range of informational, technical, and institutional barriers to reducing methane emissions, while creating profitable opportunities for the coal, agriculture, natural gas, and petroleum industries. These methane partnerships include the Landfill Methane Outreach Program, Natural Gas STAR Program, AgSTAR Program, and the Coalbed Methane Outreach Program.[94]

Target Audience

The target audience includes oil and gas, agriculture, coalmining and waste management industries, state and local governments, corporations, transmission and distribution companies, and electric utilities.[95]

Key Offerings

All of the methane partnership programs follow a common approach—to provide sound technical, economic, and regulatory information on emissions reduction technologies and practices, as well as tools to help identify and implement methane reduction opportunities. Partners profit from these programs by enhancing their operational efficiency and competitive advantage and generating revenue from the recovery and use of methane as a clean energy source.[96]

The Landfill Methane Outreach Program encourages landfills across the country to capture and use their landfill gas emissions as a renewable energy source to reduce methane emissions. The program's varied tools and technical resources help landfill owners and operators overcome barriers to project development. These tools and resources include feasibility analyses, decision-making software for evaluating project economics, an on-line database of over 600 candidate landfills across the country, a project development handbook, and energy end-user analyses.[97]

Natural Gas STAR is a voluntary partnership between the EPA and the U.S. natural gas industry designed to overcome barriers to the adoption of cost-effective technologies and practices that reduce emissions of methane. The program offers tools and resources designed to help corporate partners implement management practices to reduce gas loss, including an implementation guide, a series of "lessons learned" studies, technology transfer workshops, and partner-to-partner information exchanges.[98]

The Coalbed Methane Outreach Program (CMOP) reduces methane emissions from underground coal mines by collaborating with large coal companies and small businesses, primarily independent natural gas project developers and equipment supply companies. Outreach efforts focus on providing high-quality, project-specific information. CMOP provides a range of tools and services designed to overcome the barriers to recovery and combustion of coal mine methane. These include numerous technical and economic analyses of technologies and potential projects, mine-specific project feasibility assessments, state-specific analyses of project potential, market evaluations, and guides to state, local, and federal assistance programs.[99]

The AgSTAR Program encourages the use of methane recovery (biogas) technologies at the confined animal-feeding operations that manage manure as liquids or slurries. These technologies reduce methane emissions while achieving other environmental benefits. AgSTAR provides an array of information and tools designed to assist producers in the evaluation and implementation of these systems, including conducting farm digester extension events and conferences, providing "How-To" project development tools and industry listings, conducting performance characterizations for digesters and conventional waste management systems, and providing farm recognition for voluntary environmental initiatives.[100]

Program Status

These programs were launched in the early 1990s. EPA estimates that in 2004, these voluntary partnerships, in conjunction with a regulatory program to limit air emissions from the nation's largest landfills, kept national methane emissions 10% below 1990 levels, and they are projected to remain below 1990 levels through 2012.[101]

6. High Global Warming Potential Partnerships

Program Design and Objectives

The EPA's High Global Warming Potential (High-GWP) Partnership Programs call for the reduction of High-GWP gases from industrial activities. High-GWP gases include, among others, perfluorocarbons (PFCs), hydrofluorocarbons (HFCs), and sulfur hexafluoride (SF_6). They are released as byproducts of industrial operations and are extremely potent greenhouse gases with very long atmospheric lifetimes.

Target Audience

The High-GWP Partnership Programs involve several industries, including HCFC-22 producers, primary aluminum smelters, semiconductor manufacturers, electric power companies, and magnesium smelters and die-casters.

Key Offerings

The following High-GWP Partnership Programs target particular industries and encourage them to reduce greenhouse gas emissions by developing and implementing cost-effective improvements to their industrial processes.[102]

The SF_6 Emission Reduction Partnership for Electric Power Systems is a collaborative effort between EPA and the electric power industry to identify and implement cost-effective solutions to reduce SF_6 emissions. Currently over 70 utilities participate in this voluntary program.[103]

The Voluntary Aluminum Industrial Partnership (VAIP) is a pollution prevention program developed jointly by EPA and the primary aluminum industry. Participating companies work with EPA to improve aluminum production efficiency while reducing PFCs.[104]

The SF$_6$ Emission Reduction Partnership for the Magnesium Industry is a cooperative effort between EPA and the U.S. magnesium industry to better understand and reduce emissions of SF$_6$ from magnesium production and casting processes. In February 2003, EPA's Partners and the International Magnesium Association (IMA) committed to eliminate SF$_6$ emissions by year-end 2010. EPA's voluntary partnership with the magnesium industry is facilitating progress toward eliminating SF$_6$ emissions by identifying, evaluating, and implementing cost-effective climate protection strategies and technologies, including alternative cover gases.[105]

EPA's PFC Reduction/Climate Partnership for the Semiconductor Industry supports the industry's voluntary efforts to reduce High-GWP gases by following a pollution prevention strategy. The greenhouse gas emissions of primary concern are PFCs, trifluoromethane (CHF$_3$), nitrogen trifluoride (NF$_3$), and SF$_6$. EPA's partners have committed to reduce PFC emissions 10% below their 1995 baseline by 2010.[106]

The HFC-23 Program encourages companies to develop and implement technically feasible, cost-effective processing practices or technologies to reduce HFC-23 emissions from the manufacture of HCFC-22.[107]

The goal of the Mobile Air Conditioning Climate Protection Partnership is to reduce greenhouse gas emissions from vehicle air-conditioning systems. The program will identify near-term opportunities to improve the environmental performance of mobile air conditioners and to promote cost-effective designs and improved service procedures that minimize emissions from mobile air-conditioning systems.[108]

Program Status

The Voluntary Aluminum Industry Partnership (VAIP) program was launched in 1995.[109] In 1999, EPA and the U.S. magnesium industry, with the support of the International Magnesium Association (IMA), launched a voluntary partnership.[110] PFC Reduction/Climate Partnership for the Semiconductor Industry was launched in 1996. Industry partners are expected to maintain emissions below 1990 levels beyond the year 2010, even with the potential for sizable expansion in many of these industries that would ordinarily be accompanied by higher emission levels.[111]

7. Clean Energy Partnerships

Program Design and Objectives

EPA's Clean Energy Programs are designed to help consumers improve their knowledge about their Clean Energy options by providing objective information, creating networks between the public and private sector and providing technical assistance. EPA promotes cost-effective technologies that offer improved efficiencies and lower emissions than traditional energy supply options. The initiative involves two partnership programs—the Combined Heat and Power (CHP) Partnership and the Green Power Partnership—that work with a variety of stakeholders to improve markets for renewable energy and clean, efficient CHP technologies. The CHP Partnership works with industry, state and local governments, universities, and other energy users to facilitate the development of clean, efficient combined heat and power projects. The Green Power Partnership addresses market barriers in the purchase of renewable energy electricity products—which may be termed "green power" products—and enlists businesses and organizations, primarily large electricity users, to purchase renewable energy as a portion of their power.[112]

Target Audience

The target audience for the Combined Heat and Power program is energy users, the CHP industry, state and local governments, and other stakeholders. The target audience for the Green Power Partnership is businesses and organizations interested in buying green power.

Key Offerings

The CHP Partnership provides technical assistance designed to meet CHP project needs along each step of the project development cycle in order to make investments in CHP more attractive.[113] EPA educates industry about the benefits of CHP and project development strategies, provides networking opportunities, and works with state governments to design air emissions standards and interconnection requirements that recognize the benefits of clean CHP.[114] EPA also offers recognition to leading organizations that adopt clean energy practices.[115]

The Green Power Partnership publishes information about low-cost purchasing strategies, educates partners about features of different green power products, and reduces the transaction costs for organizations interested in making green power purchases.

The Green Power Partnership publishes information about low-cost purchasing strategies, educates partners about features of different green power products, and reduces the transaction costs for organizations interested in making green power purchases. Businesses and organizations may achieve recognition as Green Power Partners by purchasing specified percentages of their power from renewable energy sources. Partners who purchase specified higher percentages achieve recognition as members of the Leadership Club. The most common method of purchasing green power is the purchase of renewable energy certificates (RECs), which are commercially available. A purchaser of a REC in effect pays a source of renewable energy—for example, a windmill farm—to generate and dispatch a specified amount of electricity into the electricity grid. That amount of electricity from

renewable sources replaces an equal amount of electricity that would have been generated by conventional (typically, fossil fuel–fired) sources.[116]

Program Status

The programs were launched in 2001. The CHP Partnership includes 185 partners, has facilitated over 800 megawatts of new CHP projects,[117] and has assisted over 160 projects representing 3460 megawatts of new CHP capacity from 2001 to 2005. On an annual basis, these projects will prevent the emissions of over 2.5 million metric tons of carbon dioxide equivalent. This is equivalent to the annual emissions of over 1.6 million cars, or the sequestration from over 2.5 million acres of forest.[118]

The Green Power Partnership has over 500 partners, including local, state, and federal governments, trade associations, universities, and *Fortune* 500 companies. The annual green power commitments of the partners in the Green Power Partnership exceed 2 million Megawatt-hours.[119]

8. Best Workplaces for Commuters

Program Design and Objectives of Effort

EPA and the U.S. Department of Transportation (DOT) jointly sponsor the Best Workplaces for Commuters (BWC) program.[120] This program encourages employers to offer employees a package of incentives to commute to work through means other

than driving alone. Participating employers achieve recognition as one of the nation's Best Workplaces for Commuters.

Target Audience

The target audience for the BWC program is employers, whether in the private sector, the public sector, or nonprofits. In addition, EPA and DOT partner with local governments and transit organizations to co-promote the program.

Key Offerings

Under the BWC program, the employer selects from a menu of options to fashion a commuter-friendly program best adapted to commuter choices in their locality. In general, the employer must offer employees a primary commuter benefit, such as mass-transit passes (which, for the employees, qualify as tax-free fringe benefits) or a significant work-at-home program, as well as three secondary benefits, such as educational programs. The package of benefits must be sufficient to encourage at least 14% of employees to get to work through means other than driving alone. The 14% figure is the national average for commuting to work other than through driving alone. An employer who qualifies as being one of the nation's Best Workplaces for Commuters generally finds that recognition helpful in employee hiring and retention.

Program Status

As of June 30, 2006, over 1,600 employers, with approximately 3.4 million employees, qualified as among the Best Workplaces for Commuters.

9. Department of Energy's Voluntary Climate Programs

The DOE undertakes a number of initiatives with the public and private sectors to promote greater research in advanced technologies and to reduce GHG emissions. DOE's Energy Strategic Goal is "to protect national and economic security by promoting a diverse supply and delivery of reliable, affordable, and environmentally sound energy." The Science Strategic Goal is "to protect national and economic security by providing world-class scientific research capacity and advancing scientific knowledge."[121] DOE's voluntary climate programs focus primarily on research and development of improved cost-effective technologies. Below is a short description of DOE program offerings.

The Motor Challenge encourages motor system manufacturers, industrial motor users, and utilities to work with states to begin an aggressive program to install the most energy-efficient motor systems in industrial applications.[122] A producer must apply to become a Motor Challenge Partner; in turn, partners receive information to help them adopt such measures.[123]

The Partnerships for Home Energy Efficiency is a joint effort of DOE, EPA, and the U.S. Department of Housing and Urban Development to improve energy efficiency in American homes by building awareness, delivering savings to those in low-income and subsidized housing, and investing in innovative research in building science technologies, practices, and policies.[124]

The FreedomCAR and Fuel Partnership is an industry-government research initiative focused on developing emissions- and petroleum-free cars and light trucks.[125]

The 21st Century Truck Partnership focuses on research and development of advanced technologies to help the nation's trucks and buses safely and cost-effectively move larger volumes of freight and greater numbers of passengers while emitting little or no pollution and dramatically reducing dependency on foreign oil.[126]

The Industrial Technologies Program (ITP) seeks to reduce the energy intensity of the U.S. industrial sector through a coordinated program of research and development, validation, and dissemination of energy-efficient technology and operating practices. ITP's Best Practices subprogram works with industry to identify plant-wide opportunities for energy savings and process efficiency. Best Practices offers many partnership opportunities through Allied Partnerships. ITP has been involved in over 1,000 projects, and more than 140 projects have reached the commercial market.[127]

The Carbon Sequestration Leadership Forum (CSLF) is an international initiative that is focused on development of improved cost-effective technologies for the separation and capture of carbon dioxide for its transport and long-term safe storage (sequestration is discussed in Chapter 19). The purpose of the CSLF is to make these technologies broadly available internationally and to identify and address wider issues relating to carbon capture and storage, including promoting the appropriate political and regulatory environments. The CSLF includes 21 member nations[128] that account for 75% of all manmade carbon dioxide emissions.[129] It is the first-ever ministerial-level sequestration forum. The CSLF charter was signed on June 25, 2003, and will stay in effect for 10 years.[130] The CSLF has "marshaled" 17 research, development, and demonstration projects. According to the program, "[s]everal of the projects mark the first involvement of developing nations in cooperative activities aimed at reducing greenhouse gases."[131]

The Industry of the Future Program works in partnership with the nation's most energy-intensive industries to find short-term solutions for greater efficiency in manufacturing and energy production processes[132] and to enhance their long-term competitiveness.[133]

10. U.S. Department of Agriculture's Voluntary Climate GHG Programs

Program Design and Objectives

In June 2003, as part of its efforts to support the President's 2002 Climate Change Strategy, the U.S. Department of Agriculture (USDA) launched a campaign to provide incentives and support voluntary actions by farmers and other private land-owners to adopt land management practices that will store carbon and reduce greenhouse gases. The USDA gives consideration to management practices that store carbon and reduce greenhouse gases in setting priorities and implementing forest and agriculture conservation programs.[134]

Key Offerings

USDA encourages GHG sequestration through the following programs, which offer financial incentives, technical assistance, demonstrations, pilot programs, education capacity building, and measurements to assess the success of these efforts.[135]

The Environmental Quality Incentives Program (EQIP) is a voluntary conservation program for farmers and ranchers. The program provides technical assistance,[136] as well as cost-sharing and incentive payments, for conservation practices on working farmlands, such as adopting greenhouse gas–mitigating technologies.[137] Through the Greenhouse Gas Pilot Projects program, the USDA aims to pursue projects in collaboration with private partners to test forest and agriculture greenhouse gas sequestration and mitigation technologies and practices. Potential partners include locally led groups, private companies, conservation groups, and farm cooperatives.[138]

The Conservation Reserve Program is a voluntary program that provides financial and technical assistance to farmers to encourage them to convert highly erodible cropland or other environmentally sensitive acreage to native grasses, wildlife plantings, trees, filterstrips, or riparian buffers.[139] The Farm Service Agency announced it would target 500,000 acres of continuous sign-up enrollment toward hardwood tree planting.[140] The program is funded through the Commodity Credit Corporation, and farmers receive annual rental payments or cost-share assistance as incentive.[141]

The Conservation Security Program (CSP) provides financial and technical assistance to promote conservation on working cropland, pasture, and range land, as well as forested land that is an incidental part of an agriculture operation.[142] Agricultural producers are rewarded for participating—both new and existing conservation practices are eligible for payments. This makes CSP the first federal conservation program that rewards farmers for the good stewardship they have already been practicing, as well as providing powerful incentives to achieve even higher levels of conservation and resource protection.[143] CSP is administered by USDA's Natural Resources Conservation Service.[144]

As mentioned earlier, the AgSTAR program is a voluntary effort jointly sponsored by EPA, USDA, and DOE. The program encourages the use of methane recovery (biogas) technologies at the confined animal feeding operations that manage manure as liquids or slurries. Livestock producers in the dairy and swine sector are attempting to show that these practices can reduce greenhouse gas emissions and achieve other pollution control benefits while increasing farm profitability.[145]

For 1605(b) reporting, USDA offers farmers and ranchers a tool called COMET-VR, which estimates soil carbon sequestration. The technical guidelines for forests include a series of detailed carbon stock default tables with guidance on applying the tables for inventory purposes, direct measurement protocols, and guidance on the use of models.[146]

C. U.S. Private Initiatives

1. The Chicago Climate Exchange

Program Design and Objectives

The Chicago Climate Exchange (CCX) is a privately sponsored, self-regulating GHG emission registry, reduction, and trading system for all six greenhouse gases.[147] The goals of CCX are to facilitate GHG emissions trading with price transparency, design excellence and environmental integrity; build the skills and institutions needed to cost-effectively manage greenhouse gas emissions; facilitate capacity-building in both the public and private sector to facilitate greenhouse gas mitigation; strengthen the intellectual framework required for cost-effective and valid greenhouse gas reduction; and help inform the public debate on managing the risk of global climate

change.[148] The program is primarily focused on emission sources and offset projects in the US, Canada, Mexico, and Brazil.[149]

Allowances and offsets became tradable on December 12, 2003, and reduction commitments and trading apply for years 2003 through 2010. There are two phases in the emissions reduction program: Phase I, which runs from 2003 to 2006, and Phase II, which extends the program into 2010. All six Kyoto gases are included. The baseline is defined as the average emissions from 1998 to 2001. For Phase I, members make a voluntary commitment to reduce GHG emissions by 4% below baseline by 2006 (1% reduction each year). For Phase II, members commit to reducing emissions by 6% below the baseline by 2010 (members make a 4.25% reduction in 2007; 4.5% reduction in 2008; and 5% reduction in 2009).[150] New members can join the Chicago Climate Exchange during Phase II and use the standard baseline or a 2000 baseline.[151] These members must also meet a 6% reduction target by 2010. All members are given Exchange Allowances equal to that of the reduction goal. The commitment is legally binding.[152]

Target Audience

The target audience is public- and private-sector companies and entities that emit greenhouse gases and make commitments to reduce emissions during Phase I. "Market participants"— providers of offsets from qualifying projects and liquidity providers—are also encouraged to participate.[153]

Key Offerings

The CCX offers a suite of tools and services to members. The CCX Trading System consists of the CCX Trading Platform, the Clearing and Settlement Platform, and the CCX Registry. Together they provide Registry Account Holders with real-time data to support trading as well as assist in managing member emissions baselines, reduction targets and compliance status. Additionally, daily and monthly statements are provided to members to assist in tracking their trading activity and holdings. CCX members register their emissions in the CCX Registry and in turn are given allowances according to their established baseline and the CCX reductions schedule. Members are also provided assistance in managing their GHG emissions and allowances.[154]

Program Status

Continuous electronic trading of GHG emission allowances and offsets began on December 12, 2003.[155] The program currently consists of 41 greenhouse gas emitter members, with 39 offset and liquidity provider participant members.

2. The World Wildlife Fund: Climate Savers

Program Design and Objectives

The Climate Savers Program is a World Wildlife Fund and the Center for Energy and Climate Solutions initiative.[156] Its mission is to work with companies to reduce GHG emissions, initially focusing on setting a multiyear carbon dioxide reduction target and strategy.[157] The program calls for independent verification of baseline and progress,[158] and the success of a company's efforts to reduce emissions is measured against companies around the world.[159]

Companies commit to conducting outreach to educate other companies and stakeholders, working with the World Wildlife Fund to improve upon existing benchmarking efforts, and participating in a yearly meeting where companies discuss successful emission reduction strategies.[160]

Target Audience

The target audience for this initiative is businesses worldwide.

Key Offerings

In return for participating, WWF provides companies with public recognition and peer exchange.[161] Companies are also given opportunities to strengthen ties with the international network of groups affiliated with the World Wildlife Fund, the chance to take part in an annual greenhouse gas mitigation event,[162] and enhanced credibility for being affiliated with the largest privately funded conservation organization worldwide.[163] Furthermore, companies may use the World Wildlife Fund panda logo with permission[164] and may use the Climate Savers logo.[165]

Program Status

The program was launched in March 2000 and has 10 participants.[166] WWF claims that by 2010 the combined commitments of the first six Climate Savers companies will result in annual emissions reductions equivalent to more than 10 million metric tons of CO_2.[167]

3. Environmental Defense: The Partnership for Climate Action

Program Design and Objectives

The Partnership for Climate Action is an Environmental Defense initiative which aims to work with companies to reduce greenhouse gases. The partnership recognizes the importance of using emissions trading to achieve its goals.[168]

Target Audience

The target audience for this initiative is larger companies.

Key Offerings

To become a member, a company must agree to measure and track greenhouse gas emissions; it must also publicly declare a greenhouse gas reduction goal and the means in which it plans to achieve its goal,[169] and report its emissions.[170] Offerings include opportunities for peer exchange, recognition, and enhanced credibility.

Program Status

The program was launched in October 2000; there are eight participants in the program.[171] British Petroleum has achieved its pledge to reduce emissions 10% below 1990 levels by 2010 without any financial loss.[172] Environmental Defense claims that targets will result in an annual reduction of 80 million metric tons of carbon dioxide equivalent by 2010.[173]

4. Pew Center: Business Environmental Leadership Council

Program Design and Objectives

The companies in the Pew Center's Business Environmental Leadership Council (BELC) set and achieve emission reductions through investments in efficient products, practices, and technologies.[174] Member companies implement strategies to achieve reduction goals, including energy supply and demand solutions; process improvements; waste management practices; transportation, carbon sequestration and offsets solutions; and emissions trading and offsets.[175]

Target Audience

The target audience for the initiative is corporations from diverse sectors.[176]

Key Offerings

Businesses gain from the expertise offered by the Pew Center on Global Climate Change, which brings together business leaders, scientists, and experts in policy and other fields.[177] BELC also brings companies together on a quarterly basis to share strategies and insight, participate in workshops and conferences, and review and offer comment on all Pew Center work.[178] The Pew Center receives no financial assistance from the companies of the BELC.[179]

Program Status

Forty companies currently participate in the BELC.[180]

5. Alliance for Climate Strategies

Program Design and Objectives

The Alliance for Climate Strategies is an advocacy coalition of industry associations set up to exemplify the principle that voluntary actions on climate are sufficient and

American ingenuity can achieve meaningful greenhouse gas reductions. Industry sectors have pledged strategies and goals to manage greenhouse gas emissions.[181]

The coalition stresses the need for consistent approaches to measure and report emissions. It emphasizes that some industries/members of the alliance are taking action to support this need by using established protocols—such as the Greenhouse Gas Protocol to develop industry-specific calculation tools. The Alliance for Climate Strategies also emphasizes the importance of reporting emissions, and recognizes the utility industry for reporting 99.9% of emissions to the EPA.[182]

Target Audience

The target audience is a variety of industry sectors.

Key Offerings

Members can use the alliance as an advocacy platform. The coalition discusses existing voluntary approaches to reduce emissions and their sufficiency, including DOE's Climate VISION and EPA's Climate Leaders.[183] The coalition lists sector-specific goals to contribute to the 18% GHG intensity reduction goal of the Climate VISION initiative.[184]

Program Status

The coalition was launched in February 2003 to coincide with President Bush's Climate Strategy and now lists eight industry associations with industry-specific goals.[185]

6. "Climate Neutral" Product/Corporate Certification

Program Design and Objectives

In addition to setting corporate GHG reduction goals and developing internal tracking and accounting strategies, the concept of developing products and enterprises with no net impact on the climate (i.e., "carbon neutral") has grown in popularity recently.[186] Utilities are offering carbon neutrality to their customers for a premium, and a variety of products and services, including carpet, wood, yogurt and rental cars, now come with carbon-neutral options. A number of organizations around the world, including the Carbon Neutral Company in the United Kingdom,[187] Carbon Neutral Australia,[188] Terrapass in the U.S. (offers carbon neutrality for corporate fleets or individual car ownership),[189] and Carbonfund.org,[190] along with at least a dozen others, offer consumers the promise of carbon neutrality.

Target Audience

The target audience for these efforts are consumers, businesses, and other organizations.

Key Offerings

The sponsoring groups have worked to establish certification and branding for products and enterprises based on design principles viewed as credible by a broad spectrum of stakeholders. These groups also commonly offer technical assistance to help

companies create new business opportunities, networking to promote climate-neutral products to corporate and institutional purchasers, and assistance with identifying and investing in offset projects.[191]

Program Status

Dozens of companies have taken steps to achieve climate-neutral certifications in the categories of products, offsets, events, and enterprise. However, observers have raised the question whether carbon neutrality is delivering real environmental benefits, saying there is a need for common offset standards that can boost consumer and business confidence in the market and reduce the current "buyer beware" nature of the market. There is also a clear need to ensure that the retail carbon-offset market accomplishes its larger potential in terms of consumer education to support future policy and in building the business case for providing consumers with carbon-neutral products and services.[192]

D. State and Local Initiatives

State and local voluntary climate change efforts supplement national or international efforts by focusing primarily on achieving reductions with state or local facilities, as well as by promoting private-sector action. State and local voluntary programs are motivated by several factors, including concerns about the potential impacts of climate change, as well as pursuit of economic development opportunities in clean energy technologies. As with the mandatory approaches described in earlier chapters, states and localities are also developing innovative voluntary approaches that are facilitating GHG reductions, accelerating markets for GHG-reducing technologies, and demonstrating ways to achieve cost-effective reductions of GHGs with multiple benefits.

1. State Actions

States are developing voluntary programs designed to promote, facilitate and provide recognition to companies and organizations that are voluntarily reducing their GHG emissions (these are discussed in more detail in Chapters 10 and 11). Some of the programs are strictly voluntary in nature, while others are designed and implemented in coordination with mandatory approaches. Voluntary state actions include establishing GHG reduction goals (e.g., New Jersey, New England Governors), GHG emission reduction registries and reporting systems (California, New Hampshire, Wisconsin, and the Eastern Climate Registry), environmental labeling and disclosure requirements for electric utilities, and negotiated settlements and permitting actions.[193] Besides participating in voluntary carbon-trading markets like the Chicago Climate Exchange (New Mexico and Illinois),[194] states are also developing mandatory requirements that help create favorable market conditions for voluntary action, such as requiring utilities to offer a green power purchase option.[195] Many state programs also include extensive education and outreach to businesses and residents about the potential impacts of climate change and steps they can take to reduce their emissions.[196]

2. Local Actions

As discussed in Chapter 12, local governments across the country are also engaged in developing voluntary climate change programs. Like state efforts, local climate change programs focus on establishing GHG reduction goals or commitments for municipal facilities and operations, and encouraging businesses and residents within their communities to take action to reduce their GHG emissions. More than 150 local governments participate in the International Council for Local Environmental Initiative's "Cities for Climate Protection Campaign," a performance-oriented campaign that offers a framework for local governments to reduce greenhouse gas emissions and improve livability within their municipalities.[197]

A few local governments (Burlington, Vermont) have established voluntary GHG reduction "challenges" for businesses and residents in their communities. Others are participating in the Chicago Climate Exchange (Portland, Oregon) and state-led efforts, such as GHG registries (San Francisco, Los Angeles and other local governments are members of the California Climate Action Registry).[198]

In June 2005, the U.S. Conference of Mayors adopted a resolution to support the Climate Protection Agreement, an initiative launched by Seattle's mayor in February 2005. The Agreement commits participating cities to meet the Kyoto Protocol's U.S. goal of reducing GHG emissions 7% below 1990 levels by 2012. Cities signing onto the Agreement also urge state and federal action to achieve the Kyoto Protocol targets. As of May 2006, 237 mayors have signed the agreement.[199]

IV. Conclusion

The long-term nature of the climate change problem, coupled with difficulties in achieving political consensus on the proper mitigation course of action, have led to a rapid increase in voluntary climate change activities at the local, state, federal and international levels. The proliferation of programs presents challenges to companies and policymakers attempting to develop consensus on the best approaches. For example, variation in the design of greenhouse gas registries and reporting protocols has been cited by more than one company as the main disincentive to voluntary climate change activity. This "patchwork quilt" of approaches may be inefficient for businesses seeking to develop a comprehensive climate change strategy, and may result in duplication of effort or incompatible program designs.

Further, while a number of programs appear to be well-designed, targeted efforts that are achieving their goals, too many voluntary efforts offer little transparent information on accomplishments or specific work plans, raising doubts about their credibility. Financial resources for voluntary programs appear to be another limitation—several programs have been launched with great expectations, only to experience reductions in funding and/or political support.

However, while voluntary approaches face a number of challenges, it is clear that these efforts offer important lessons on possible strategies for successfully mitigating climate change. The corporate goal-setting, tracking tools, accounting standards, and monitoring and verification protocols that are being developed to support these efforts offer possible models for future climate policies.

Endnotes

1. http://www.ghgprotocol.org.
2. http://www.iso.org/iso/en/commcentre/pressreleases/2006/Ref994.html.
3. http://www.globalreporting.org.
4. http://www.pewclimate.org/global-warming-in-depth/all_reports/corporate_greenhouse_targets/index.cfm.
5. *See* WBCSD (2003) Striking the Balance, *available at* http://www.wbcsd.org.
6. http://www.ghgprotocol.org/templates/GHG5layout.asp?MenuID=849.
7. http://www.ghgprotocol.org/templates/GHG5/layout.asp?type=p&MenuId=ODk0.
8. http://www.ghgprotocol.org/templates/GHG5layout. asp?MenuID=849.
9. http://www.ghgprotocol.org/templates/GHG5/layout.asp?type=p&MenuId=ODU5.
10. http://www.iso.org/iso/en/commcentre/pressreleases/2006/Ref994.html.
11. *Id.*
12. http://www.iso.org/iso/en/commcentre/pressreleases/archives/2005/Ref983.html.
13. http://www.globalreporting.org/about/OECDSynergies.pdf.
14. http://www.globalreporting.org/guidelines/framework.asp.
15. http://www.oecd.org/document/53/0,2340,en_2649_34889_1933109_1_1_1_1,00.html.
16. *Id.*
17. *Id.*
18. http://www.globalreporting.org/about/OECDSynergies.pdf.
19. *Id.*
20. *Id.*
21. http://www.emas.org.uk/aboutemas/mainframe.htm.
22. *Id.*
23. *Id.*
24. *Id.*

25. *Id.*
26. BLICC #4: Engaging in Actions.
27. *Id.*
28. *Id.*
29. *Id.*
30. Setting Examples: BLICC Impact document.
31. BLICC Report 2: Sweden: Adapting to a changing climate.
32. Setting Examples: BLICC Impact document.
33. BLICC Report 2: Sweden: Adapting to a changing climate.
34. BLICC #4: Engaging in Actions.
35. *Id.*
36. http://www.blicc.se/.
37. http://www.respecteurope.com/DesktopDefault.aspx?tabindex=102&tabid=97&parentid=1&superiorid=97&pindex=0&bindex=97.
38. http://www.iges.or.jp/en/cp/pdf/activity06/07.pdf.
39. http://www.theclimategroup.org/index.php?pid=813.
40. http://www.iges.or.jp/en/cp/pdf/activity06/07.pdf.
41. http://www.iea.org/textbase/work/2005/5ghg/japan.pdf.
42. http://www.iges.or.jp/en/cp/pdf/activity06/07.pdf.
43. *Id.*
44. http://www.greenbiz.com/news/news_third.cfm?NewsID=28866.
45. *Id.*
46. *Id.*
47. *Id.*
48. http://www.greenhouse.gov.au/challenge/members/about.html.
49. *Id.*
50. http://www.greenhouse.gov.au/challenge/members/membershiplevels.html.
51. http://www.greenhouse.gov.au/challenge/members/about.html.
52. http://www.greenhouse.gov.au/challenge/pubs/programmeframework.pdf.
53. http://www.greenhouse.gov.au/challenge/members/technicaltools.html.
54. http://www.greenhouse.gov.au/challenge/members/greenhousefriendly.html.
55. http://www.greenhouse.gov.au/challenge/pubs/list_of_challengers.pdf.
56. http://www.greenhouse.gov.au/challenge/members/about.html.
57. http://www.whitehouse.gov/news/releases/2002/02/20020214.html.
58. *Id.*
59. http://www.pi.energy.gov/pdf/library/1605BApril172006.pdf.
60. *Id.*
61. http://www.pi.energy.gov/enhancingGHGregistry/background.html.
62. http://www.pi.energy.gov/pdf/library/1605BApril172006.pdf.
63. http://www.pi.energy.gov/enhancingGHGregistry/background.html.
64. http://www.pi.energy.gov/enhancinggHGregistry/index.html.
65. http://www.pi.energy.gov/pdf/library/1605BApril172006.pdf.
66. http://www.eia.doe.gov/oiaf/1605/2nd_broc.html.
67. http://www.pi.energy.gov/pdf/library/1605BApril172006.pdf.
68. Daily Env't Rep. No. 180, at A-1, (9-19-05) (Tom's document from M. Gerard).
69. http://www.pi.energy.gov/pdf/library/1605BApril172006.pdf.
70. http://www.eia.doe.gov/oiaf/1605/2nd_broc.html.
71. http://www.pi.energy.gov/enhancinggHGregistry/index.html.
72. http://www.eia.doe.gov/oiaf/1605/vrrpt/summary/introduction.html.
73. Daily Env't Rep. No. 180, at A-1, (9-19-05) (Tom's document from M. Gerard).
74. http://www.climatevision.gov/mission.html.

75. *Id.*

76. *Id.*

77. *Id.*

78. http://www.climatevision.gov/.

79. GAO Report, *Climate Change: EPA and DOE Should Do More to Encourage Progress Under Two Voluntary Programs*, April 2006, *available at* http://frwebgate.access.gpo.gov/cgi-bin/useftp. cgi?IPaddress=162.140.64.21&filename=d0697. pdf&directory=/diskb/wais/data/gao.

80. *Id.*

81. http://www.epa.gov/climateleaders/aboutus.html.

82. *Id.*

83. *Id.*

84. http://www.epa.gov/climateleaders/resources/index.html.

85. *Id.*

86. *Id.*

87. GAO Report, *supra* note 40.

88. www.energystar.gov.

89. *Id.*

90. *Id.*

91. http://www.epa.gov/appdstar/pdf/CPPD2005.pdf.

92. www.energystar.gov.

93. *Id.*

94. http://www.epa.gov/methane/voluntary.html.

95. *Id.*

96. http://www.epa.gov/appdstar/pdf/CPPD2004.pdf.

97. http://www.epa.gov/lmop/overview.htm.

98. http://www.epa.gov/gasstar/overview.htm.

99. http://www.energystar.gov/ia/news/downloads/annual_report2004.pdf.

100. http://www.epa.gov/agstar/overview.html.

101. http://www.epa.gov/appdstar/pdf/CPPD2004.pdf.

102. http://www.epa.gov/highgwp/voluntary.html.

103. http://www.epa.gov/highgwp/electricpower-sf6/index.html.

104. http://www.epa.gov/highgwp/aluminum-pfc/index.html.

105. http://www.epa.gov/highgwp/magnesium-sf6/index.html.

106. http://www.epa.gov/highgwp/semiconductor-pfc/index.html.

107. http://www.epa.gov/cppd/mac/.

108. *Id.* ¶ 7(b). This number is to be multiplied by five for the five-year commitment period.

109. http://www.epa.gov/highgwp/aluminum-pfc/overview.html.

110. http://www.epa.gov/highgwp/magnesium-sf6/overview.html.

111. http://www.epa.gov/highgwp/voluntary.html.

112. http://www.epa.gov/cleanenergy/epaclean.htm.

113. *Id.*

114. http://www.epa.gov/chp/partner_resources.htm.

115. http://www.epa.gov/cleanenergy/epaclean.htm.

116. http://www.epa.gov/greenpower/partner_corner/partnertools.htm.

117. http://www.epa.gov/chp/chp_partners.htm.

118. http://www.epa.gov/chp/about_the_partnership.htm.

119. http://www.epa.gov/greenpower/aboutus.htm.

120. http://www.comuterchoice.gov/.
121. http://www.energy.gov/about/index.htm.
122. http://www1.eere.energy.gov/industry/bestpractices/motor_challenge_national_strategy.html.
123. http://www.greenbiz.com/reference/government_record.cfm?LinkAdvID=4738.
124. http://www.energy.gov/about/jointinitiatives.htm.
125. *Id.*
126. *Id.*
127. http://www.eere.energy.gov/industry/about/brochures.html.
128. http://www.cslforum.org/about.htm.
129. http://www.cslforum.org/documents/Delhi/press_cslf_background.pdf.
130. http://www.cslforum.org/about.htm.
131. http://www.cslforum.org/documents/Delhi/press_cslf_projects.pdf.
132. http://www.energy.gov/about/index.htm.
133. http://www.gcrio.org/CAR2002/, Chapter 4.
134. http://www.gcrio.org/OnLnDoc/pdf/usda_ghg_sequestration.pdf.
135. *Id.*
136. http://www.nrcs.usda.gov/PROGRAMS/EQIP/.
137. http://www.gcrio.org/OnLnDoc/pdf/usda_ghg_sequestration.pdf.
138. *Id.*
139. http://www.fsa.usda.gov/dafp/cepd/crp.htm.
140. http://www.nrcs.usda.gov/programs/index_alph.html.
141. http://www.fsa.usda.gov/dafp/cepd/crp.htm.
142. http://www.nrcs.usda.gov/programs/index_alph.html.
143. http://www.ucsusa.org/food_and_environment/sustainable_food/the-conservation-security-program.html.
144. http://www.nrcs.usda.gov/Programs/csp/.
145. http://www.epa.gov/agstar/.
146. http://www.usda.gov/wps/portal/!ut/p/_s.7_0_A/7_0_1OB/.cmd/ad/.ar/sa.retrievecontent/.c/6_2_1UH/.ce/7_2_5JM/.p/5_2_4TQ/.d/1/_th/J_2_9D/_s.7_0_A/7_0_1OB?PC_7_2_5JM_contentid=2006/04/0130.xml&PC_7_2_5JM_parentnav=LATEST_ RELEASES&PC_7_2_5JM_navid=NEWS_RELEASE#7_2_5JM.
147. http://www.chicagoclimatex.com/about/.
148. http://www.chicagoclimatex.com/about/program.html.
148. http://www.chicagoclimatex.com/about/features.html.
150. http://www.chicagoclimatex.com/about/program.html.
151. http://www.chicagoclimatex.com/about/faq.html.
152. http://www.chicagoclimatex.com/about/program.html.
153. http://www.chicagoclimatex.com/about/faq.html.
154. http://www.chicagoclimatex.com/trading/howItWorks.html.
155. http://www.chicagoclimatex.com/info/membershipCategories.html.
156. http://www.worldwildlife.org/climate/projects/climateSavers.cfm.
157. http://www.worldwildlife.org/climate/projects/climatesavers/faq.cfm.
158. *Id.*
159. http://www.worldwildlife.org/climate/projects/climateSavers.cfm.
160. http://www.worldwildlife.org/climate/projects/climatesavers/faq.cfm.
161. *Id.*
162. http://www.worldwildlife.org/climate/projects/climatesavers/benefits.cfm.
163. http://worldwildlife.org/about/index.cfm.
164. http://www.worldwildlife.org/climate/projects/climatesavers/faq.cfm.
165. http://www.worldwildlife.org/climate/projects/climateSavers.cfm.

166. http://www.getf.org/media/pressreleases_detail.cfm? LinkAdvID=20496.

167. http://www.energyandclimate.org/strategic.cfm.

168. http://www.environmentaldefense.org/article.cfm? ContentID=503.

169. http://www.environmentaldefense.org/subissue.cfm? subissue=3.

170. http://www.gcrio.org/CAR2002/, Chapter 4.

171. http://www.environmentaldefense.org/subissue.cfm? subissue=3.

172. *Id.*

173. http://www.environmentaldefense.org/article.cfm? ContentID=503.

174. http://www.pewclimate.org/companies_leading_the_ way_belc/.

175. http://www.pewclimate.org/companies_leading_ the_way_belc/ghg_strategies/.

176. http://www.pewclimate.org/companies_leading_ the_way_belc/.

177. http://www.pewclimate.org/policy_center/.

178. http://www.pewclimate.org/about/.

179. http://www.pewclimate.org/companies_leading_the_ way_belc/.

180. http://www.pewclimate.org/companies_leading_the_ way_belc/company_profiles/.

181. http://www.allianceforclimatestrategies.com/pdfs/ introduction.pdf.

182. *Id.*

183. http://www.allianceforclimatestrategies.com/pdfs/measur- ing. pdf.

184. http://www.allianceforclimatestrategies.com/pdfs/ acs_summary. pdf.

185. http://www.allianceforclimatestrategies.com/pdfs/voluntaryinitiatives.pdf.

186. http://www.nativeenergy.com/Trexler%20Retail_Offsets_ EnvForum_Final11. pdf.

187. http:// www.carbonneutral.com/.

188. http:// www.carbonneutral.com.au/.

189. http://www.terrapass.com.

190. http://www.carbonfund.org/site/.

191. http://www.nativeenergy.com/Trexler%20Retail_Offsets_ EnvForum_Final11. pdf.

192. http://www.nativeenergy.com/Trexler%20Retail_Offsets_EnvForum_ Final11. pdf.

193. BARRY RABE, STATEHOUSE AND GREENHOUSE: THE EMERGING POLITICS OF AMERICAN CLI-MATE CHANGE POLICY (2004), *available at* http://www.brookings.edu/press/books/ statehouseandgreenhouse.htm.

194. http://www.pewclimate.org/docUploads/states_greenhouse.pdf.

195. EPA CLEAN ENERGY-ENVIRONMENT GUIDE TO ACTION, ch. 5.5, *Fostering Green Power Markets*, *available at* http://www.epa.gov/cleanenergy/pdf/gta/guide_action_ chap5_s5.pdf.

196. http://www.easternclimateregistry.org/index.html.

197. http://www.iclei.org/fileadmin/user_upload/documents/events/montreal_summit/Media_and_Reports/InWEntReport_12Dec2005.pdf, http://www.pewclimate.org/docUploads/states_greenhouse.pdf.

198. Illinois Conservation and Climate Initiative (ICCI), http://www.illinoisclimate.org/.

199. http://www.seattle.gov/mayor/climate/quotes.htm#mayors.

chapter eighteen

Emissions Trading— Practical Aspects

Dennis Hirsch, Andrew Bergman, and Michael Heintz*

I. Introduction

Trading in greenhouse gas (GHG) emission rights has arrived. Programs exist at the global, regional, national, state and private levels, and brisk trading is under way. These programs are summarized in other chapters of this volume. Readers seeking a general introduction should consult those chapters before reading this one. The present chapter will focus on the practical knowledge that American lawyers and their clients need to navigate the various emissions trading initiatives successfully. It will go beyond the general contours and will delve into the nitty-gritty details that inform daily practice under these programs. Some of these programs are so new that the practical details have not yet fully taken shape. Where that is the case, the chapter will provide the most current knowledge available and will identify future developments to look for.

This chapter will begin by describing the program design choices and implementation rules that characterize most emission-trading programs. Having identified these concepts, the chapter will then explain how the major existing trading programs have

*   The authors would like to thank Charlotte Streck, Monique Willis, Janet Peace, Michael Walsh, and Chris James for their helpful comments on earlier drafts of this chapter. They would also like to thank Andrew Webster and Andrea Salimbene for their helpful research assistance. Any errors or omissions are solely the responsibility of the authors.

applied them. It will begin with a brief description of three U.S. trading programs: the Acid Rain trading program, the Nitrogen Oxide (NO_x) trading program, and the Offset Trading program. While these three programs focus on pollutants other than GHG, they have served as models for the emerging GHG-trading initiatives and so constitute an important part of the background needed to understand them. The chapter will turn next to the main GHG-trading programs themselves. It will explore the three Kyoto Flexibility Mechanisms (International Emissions Trading, Joint Implementation and the Clean Development Mechanism); the European Union Emissions Trading Scheme (EU ETS); the Regional Greenhouse Gas Initiative (RGGI), a trading program that a group of northeastern states in the United States recently established; and the Chicago Climate Exchange, a voluntary GHG-trading program for American companies. For each of these initiatives, the chapter will seek to explain the basic program design choices that structure the program and the program implementation rules that govern participation in it. The chapter will close with a brief discussion of the contractual issues that are likely to arise in GHG trading and strategies for handling them.

II. What Lawyers Need to Know About Emissions Trading Programs

Practicing lawyers need two main types of knowledge in order to navigate GHG emissions trading programs. First, they need to understand the broad design choices that have shaped the program in question. For example, they need to be able to quickly determine whether a given initiative is a "cap-and-trade" or a "baseline-credit" trading program (terms that we will further explain below) and what this means for the way the program will work. We will refer to this as understanding the *program design choices* that structure a given trading system. Second, lawyers need to work down from the broad design choices to the implementation rules that govern day-to-day participation in the program. Each program contains many such requirements, including rules on who can sell or buy emission rights, how emission reductions should be measured, how they should be verified, etc. We will refer to this body of knowledge as the *program implementation rules* that govern participation in a given trading initiative. Lawyers need to be able to counsel clients on such rules of the road. This section will describe, in the abstract, the key program design choices and program implementation rules that characterize most emissions trading programs. The sections that follow will apply these general principles to specific trading programs.

A. Program Design Choices

While trading programs share common features, they can also differ from each other in important ways. Counsel need to be familiar with these design features so as to be able to quickly grasp the contours of a given program and understand how it works. The main program design choices that determine the structure of emissions trading programs are as follows:

- **Economy-wide or sectoral focus?** One of the first things that the designer of an emissions trading program must decide is whether the initiative will encompass emitters throughout the economy or whether it will focus on certain industrial sectors. With respect to greenhouse gases, a trading program could focus on specific sectors such as the electricity generation industry (i.e., power plants) or the transportation sector. Alternatively, it could seek to encompass the entire economy and so include manufacturing, service businesses, residential and commercial real estate, etc., all of which emit GHG.

- **Upstream, downstream or both?** Here the choice is whether to regulate direct emitters (a "downstream" approach) or to move up the chain of production and regulate those who provided the resources needed to create the emissions (an "upstream" approach). In the GHG context, a downstream approach might regulate not only power plants but also individual automobiles, residential furnaces, facility smokestacks, etc. By contrast, an upstream approach would regulate the producers and suppliers of the fossil fuels that make such emissions possible—oil companies, petroleum refiners, coal-mining companies, natural gas pipelines, etc.

- **Cap-and-trade or baseline-credit?** Another basic division is between cap-and-trade and baseline-credit trading programs. This distinction is fundamental and is worth explaining in a bit more detail.

  - *Cap-and-trade systems* set an overall cap on the amount of a given pollutant that can be emitted during a specified period of time. They then allocate portions of that cap to the various emitters so that the sum of these allocations equals the cap. These allocations take the form of "allowances," which are essentially permits to emit a given amount of pollution. Cap-and-trade programs require that at end of a specified compliance period, each facility must hold the rights to enough allowances to cover its emissions for that period. Facilities can meet this requirement by reducing their emissions to the level of their allocation. Or, they can purchase emission permits from other sources that have reduced their emissions below their own allocation and so have excess allowances to sell. Sources that can figure out how to decrease their emissions cheaply will usually reduce to a level below their allocation so that they can sell their excess allowances for a profit. Sources that find it expensive to make reductions usually purchase allowances so that they do not have to reduce themselves. The net result is that the lower-cost reducers end up making the majority of the reductions. This enables society to achieve its emissions reduction goal (the cap) at a much lower cost than if every facility had to reduce equally.

- *Baseline-credit emissions trading programs* do not set an overall cap on emissions or allocate emissions allowances to sources. Instead, they allow sources to earn emission reduction credits by reducing their emissions below a specified baseline. Such systems identify a "baseline" emissions level for each individual source. They then assign emission reduction "credits" to those entities that reduce their emissions below their baseline. Firms that obtain such credits can transfer them to other regulated parties who can use them to meet emission limits. Baseline-credit programs give credit only for those reductions that meet specified program requirements. For example, such systems often grant credit only for those reductions that would not have occurred in the normal course of events, since only these are thought to produce an environmental benefit when judged against the status quo. From the perspective of a participating entity, baseline-credit trading systems tend to be more rule-bound than cap-and-trade arrangements.

- **Allocation or auction of allowances?** Some cap-and-trade programs allocate allowances to covered sources based on historical emissions or some other measure. Other programs auction allowances to the highest bidder and require sources to purchase a sufficient number to cover their emissions. There are also differences among allocation schemes. Some programs allocate allowances to the emitters of the pollutant. Others make allocations to consumers of electricity, providers of renewable energy or others. The performance of the program under such a system is largely the same but the distributional effects can be quite different.

- **Closed or open-market?** Closed systems limit participation to a defined set of emitters. Open-market systems do not limit themselves in this way and instead give a broader group the option of engaging in the purchasing and selling of emission rights. Hybrid systems share features of both closed and open-market programs. One form of hybrid system allows entities to "opt in" to a closed cap-and-trade scheme. Entities that voluntarily choose to opt in are assigned an initial allocation, much as if they had been one of the covered sources to begin with. Thereafter, they have to meet compliance obligations just like any other member of the closed system and are able to transfer and/or acquire allowances from others. Generally, sources opt in because they believe they will be able to reduce emissions significantly below their allocation and thereby generate surplus allowances that they can sell. Other hybrid systems allow "project-based" participation. Instead of providing an allocation to outside entities, these pro-

grams recognize and give credit for certain projects that reduce emissions below baseline. They then allow those who undertake these projects to sell the credits to entities in the closed cap-and-trade system that can employ them as permits to cover their emissions. The Kyoto Protocol's Clean Development Mechanism is a "project-based" initiative of this type.

- **Banking of excess allowances allowed?** Programs differ on whether a source that holds more permits than it needs at the end of a given compliance period can "bank" the excess permits and use them during a later period. Some initiatives provide that permits expire at the conclusion of the period in which they are issued. Others allow "banking" of the permits.

> **Lawyers also need to be familiar with the implementation rules that govern day-to-day participation in trading programs.**

B. Program Implementation Rules

Lawyers also need to be familiar with the implementation rules that govern day-to-day participation in trading programs. Entities participating in baseline-credit programs face more such rules than those engaged in cap-and-trade initiatives.

- *Measurement of emissions:* Participants in both cap-and-trade and baseline-credit programs need to be aware of any rules governing how emissions should be measured.
- *Monitoring, reporting, and recordkeeping requirements:* Participants also need to be sure that they comply with program requirements for monitoring, recordkeeping, and reporting of emissions.
- *Who can transfer and trade?* Another set of common rules govern who can transfer allowances or credits and who can trade them. To understand these rules, it is important to distinguish between a "trade" of emission rights and a "transfer" or "acquisition" of these rights.[1] When an emissions source that possesses an allowance or a credit conveys it to another covered source that uses it to meet its compliance obligations, it is said to "transfer" that allowance or credit to the other source. However, it is possible for the initial holder of the allowance or credit to first "trade" its rights to a broker or other entity before it is eventually transferred to the covered party that will ultimately benefit from it in terms of regulatory compliance. To illustrate the point, assume that Facility A possesses excess allowances under a cap-and-trade system. It trades the right to these excess allowances to Broker B, who then trades them to Broker C, who trades them to

Facility D. Facility D uses them to cover its emissions under the cap-and-trade system. The ultimate result of this transaction is that Facility A has "transferred" some of its allowances to Facility D. Along the way, Facility A "traded" the allowances to Broker B, who in turn traded them to Broker C, who traded them to Facility D. Another way of putting this is that "trading" is what happens when a source grants another entity some type of ownership right in the emissions asset, whereas "transferring" occurs when one source conveys the allowance or credit to another covered party that will employ it to comply with its regulatory obligations. Programs have rules as to who can engage in the "transfer" of allowances. Some also set rules that limit who can "trade" in allowances and how they can trade them.

- *Project eligibility:* Some baseline-credit systems set limits on the types of emission reduction projects that are eligible to generate credits under the program. These limits can be geographic, such as a requirement that the project be up-wind of the source that purchases the credit. They can also be temporal, such as a requirement that the project occur within a specified timeframe. Other limits may turn on the nature of the project. An example of this in the GHG area would be rules regarding whether parties can generate credits by expanding forests or other "carbon sinks."

- *Company or facility eligibility:* Program rules may also specify which companies or facilities are eligible to generate and/or purchase credits. For example, such rules may require that a facility be in full compliance with air pollution regulations before it will be allowed to purchase emission reduction credits.

- *Baseline calculation:* Baseline-credit programs often define how sources should go about calculating their baseline. For example, such rules may require sources to calculate their baseline in terms of actual emissions or may let them use allowable emissions. Rules may also define the time period within which baseline emissions should be measured (e.g., any consecutive 12 months within the last two years).

- *Additionality:* Many baseline-credit programs require that, in order to generate credits, reductions be "additional to" those that would have occurred in the normal course of events. Program rules structure the inquiry into which reductions are truly "additional."

- *Public participation:* Some baseline-credit initiatives require public comment on the eligibility of a given project, the additionality of reductions, and/or the validity or magnitude of reductions. Program rules may set out a process for sources to follow in seeking this public participation.

- *Certification:* Most baseline-credit systems establish a process for certifying that a given emission reduction meets program requirements such as those that have just been described. A given reduction must be certified before it can generate credits for transfer or trade.

- *Enforceability:* Programs may require sources to demonstrate that their reductions are enforceable. For example, they may require that a facility incorporate

the reductions into a permit or other enforceable legal document. They may also require a showing that the reduction is practically enforceable by the relevant authority.

III. U.S. Emissions Trading Programs

The United States developed some of the earliest and most successful emissions trading programs. While these initiatives did not directly involve the trading of GHG emission rights, they served as a model for GHG trading programs. This section will briefly describe these U.S. programs. Many of their core features will reappear in the more detailed analysis of GHG trading programs.

A. The Clean Air Act Acid Rain Trading Program

Title IV of the 1990 Amendments to the Clean Air Act sought to address the problem of acid rain through a ground-breaking, sector-based cap-and-trade system that focuses on sulfur dioxide (SO_2) emissions from electrical utilities. The program establishes a national cap on SO_2 emissions at a level of 10 million tons per year *below* 1980 levels. It then allocates to the covered utilities a number of SO_2 emission allowances, each of which permits a source to emit one ton of SO_2. The system of allocation is somewhat complex, but the upshot is that by 2000 the allocations, taken together, will add up to the cap. At the end of any given year, the program requires each utility (or other covered source)

to hold allowances equal to its emissions for that year, thereby ensuring that the cap is met. Sources pay a stiff fine for excess emissions. Non-covered sources can "opt in," in which case they receive an allocation and thereafter are treated like any other covered sources. Generally, sources choose to opt in because they believe that they have the potential to achieve reductions at low cost and so will have excess allowances to sell.

A covered source can comply by reducing its emissions to its allocation. Alternatively, it can purchase allowances from other covered sources that have allowances to spare. This encourages sources that can decrease their emissions cheaply to reduce below their allocation and then to sell the excess allowances to those that find it more expensive to reduce. Such exchanges should lower the cost of reaching pollution reduction goals. Results to date suggest that the Acid Rain Trading Program has been having just this effect. Studies place the costs of the program at $2 billion–$3 billion per year but estimate the annual benefits at $12 billion–$78 billion.[2] This success has made the Acid Rain Trading Program a model for GHG trading initiatives, including those established under the Kyoto Protocol.[3]

B. The Nitrogen Oxide (NO$_x$) Budget Trading Program

The NO$_x$ Budget Trading Program focuses on NO$_x$ emissions, a precursor to ground-level ozone. It seeks to address the NO$_x$ emissions in the northeastern and midwestern states that are transported across state lines and contribute to ozone pollution problems in neighboring states. Under a rule known as the NO$_x$ SIP Call, the U.S. EPA allocated a "NO$_x$ Budget" to each of these states and required that each achieve this cap by 2007. It allowed the states to meet the goal through participation in an interstate NO$_x$ Budget Trading Program. This program allows them to treat their NO$_x$ Budget like a statewide emissions cap and allocate emission allowances to sources within their state so that, taken together, the allocations add up to the state's NO$_x$ Budget. Thereafter, the program follows the cap-and-trade logic just described. Sources that reduce their emissions below their allocation can sell their excess allowances to those that find it more expensive to reduce, thereby driving down the overall cost of emissions reduction. Trading may take place between sources within a state or between sources in different states that are participating in the program.

C. The Offset Trading Program

The Clean Air Act's Offset Trading Program is an important example of a baseline-credit system. This program operates in regions that have not yet attained national clean air standards. Parties that wish to build a new facility or modify an existing one in such a nonattainment area, and so to increase emissions, are required to secure offsetting emission reductions. Companies can obtain emission reduction "credits" from another firm in the region that has managed to reduce its emissions below its baseline amount, and can use them to satisfy the offset requirement. To earn credits, a source must show that it has calculated its baseline in accordance with program rules. It must also demonstrate that its reductions are "creditable, quantifiable, federally enforceable, and permanent."[4] Reductions that have been certified as meeting these criteria qualify as credits. They can then be bought, sold and used to meet the offset requirement. As will be further explained below, this open-market, baseline-credit approach to emissions trading is repeated in GHG trading programs such as the Clean Development Mechanism.

In some instances, facilities located near each other have bought up a great many credits from the larger region and used them to offset their own emission increases. This has raised public concerns about emissions "hot spots" that subject the local population to a disproportionate pollution burden and can lead to troubling environmental justice issues. GHG emissions trading should not raise this issue in the same way. This is because greenhouse gases have their effects on a global, not a local, level. Thus, the emissions "hot spot" and environmental justice issues should not figure prominently in GHG trading unless the GHG emissions from facilities are accompanied by emissions of other pollutants with more localized effects.

IV. Global GHG Trading: The Kyoto Protocol Flexibility Mechanisms

Chapter 2 already introduced the UN Framework Convention on Climate Change[5] and the Kyoto Protocol[6] and described the three Kyoto Flexibility Mechanisms: International Emission Trading (Article 17), Joint Implementation (Article 6), and the Clean Development Mechanism (Article 12). This chapter will not repeat this introductory information. Instead, it will discuss how the program design choices and implementation rules listed above unfold in the context of the Kyoto Flexibility Mechanisms. The purpose here is to go beyond the general contours of these initiatives and provide the practical knowledge that will allow U.S. lawyers and their clients to navigate these complex programs.

This discussion will to refer to the various emissions assets that can be transferred (i.e., Assigned Amount Units (AAUs), Emission Reduction Units (ERUs), Certified Emission Reductions (CERs), and Removal Units (RMUs)) as "Kyoto Units." It will refer to those developed nations that are party to the UNFCCC as "Annex I nations," and will refer to those Annex I nations that have ratified the Kyoto Protocol and taken on binding GHG emission reduction commitments as "Annex I Parties." These two groups are not identical. For example, the United States and Australia are Annex I nations, but they have not ratified the Kyoto Protocol, so they are not Annex I Parties. The chapter will refer to private legal entities (corporations, nonprofits, etc.) that are domiciled in an Annex I Party as "Annex I entities." It will refer to nations that have not joined and/or ratified the Kyoto Protocol as non-Party nations, and will refer to entities in those countries as "non-Party entities."

A. International Emission Trading

The International Emission Trading (IET) Program provides the basic trading structure on which the other Kyoto Flexibility Mechanisms—the Clean Development Mechanism (CDM) and Joint Implementation (JI)—are built. This section will therefore begin with a discussion of IET before moving on to these other programs.

1. Program Design Choices

Much as the NO_x Budget Trading Program did for state governments, the Kyoto Protocol allocates a GHG emissions "budget" to certain industrialized nations (the Annex I Parties) and allows them to achieve it through an international emissions trading program. Under the IET program, a transfer increases the acquiring country's holdings of Assigned Amount Units (AAUs) and decreases that of the transferring country, thereby keeping the total allowed emissions constant. International Emission Trading is thus a closed cap-and-trade program for Annex I Parties. Features such as the Clean Development Mechanism and the ability of Annex I entities to engage in transfers of their own add some open-market qualities. These elements will be explained further below.

As in any other cap-and-trade system, each of the Annex I Parties must ultimately, at the relevant reconciliation date, hold sufficient allowances to cover all of its emissions. This means that each country must keep its actual emissions below its assigned amount, as adjusted through the IET transfers. In this respect, the IET program may be said to apply to national economies as a whole.[7] As implemented by Annex I Parties to date, the program has a downstream focus in the sense that it requires actual reductions in emissions (or enhanced removals through sinks) and not simply changes in upstream behavior, such as fossil-fuel production. Thus, IET is an economy-wide, closed, cap-and-trade program with a downstream focus.

2. Program Implementation Rules

A pure cap-and-trade program, IET does not need many of the implementation rules common to baseline-credit systems. It contains no certification requirement, no baseline calculation methods, and no additionality mandate. The key program rules focus instead on the transactions themselves—what can be transferred, when can it be transferred and, most importantly, who can transfer and trade? The following discussion will similarly focus on these points.

As to the "what" question, IET treats all Kyoto Units as fungible and allows them to be transferred among Annex I Parties. Assigned amount units (AAUs), emission reduction units (ERUs), certified emission reductions (CERs) and removal units (RMUs) can all be exchanged for one another on a one-to-one basis.[8] Annex I Parties can only formally transfer and/or acquire Kyoto Units after the first commitment period begins on January 1, 2008, and they meet other eligibility criteria. However, trading of the ownership rights to these emissions assets can commence at any time.[9] Such trades will necessarily be in the form of forward trades, i.e., commitments to transfer an asset at some time in the future.

The more interesting questions relate to who can transfer and trade Kyoto Units. The International Emissions Trading system is set up to allow Annex I Parties to transfer Kyoto Units to one another.[10] Thus, the initial answer to the question of who can transfer and acquire Kyoto Units is that the Annex I Parties can do so. Upon such a transfer, the transferring nation will experience a decrease in the Kyoto Units in its national account and the acquiring nation will experience an increase.

Upon further examination, the situation is not quite that simple. There are a number of complicating factors that lawyers practicing in this area should be familiar with. To begin with, only those Annex I Parties that meet certain eligibility requirements are authorized to transfer and acquire Kyoto Units under the IET system.[11] Specifically, a Party must:

1. Be a Party to the Kyoto Protocol. Annex I nations that have not ratified the Protocol are not eligible to engage in IET. This includes the United States and Australia. Any permits or allowances created by national GHG trading schemes in such countries will not be credited in the Kyoto system;

2. Have had its assigned amount calculated and recorded in accordance with the rules for doing so set out in Decision 19/CP.7;[12]

3. Have in place a national system for estimating anthropogenic GHG emissions and removals;

4. Have established a national registry for tracking their assigned amounts;

5. Have submitted accurate annual inventories of GHG emissions and sinks;

6. Have submitted the supplementary information on assigned amounts and made any necessary adjustments to its assigned amount.

Annex I Parties that do not meet these eligibility requirements cannot transfer or acquire Kyoto Units through the IET system. A private entity wishing to transfer Kyoto Units under the authority of an Annex I Party (see below) can only do so if the Party itself is eligible to make such a transfer.[13]

Another complicating factor is that even those Annex I Parties that are eligible to engage in the transfer of their Kyoto Units can only do so to a limited extent. The drafters of the Marrakesh Accords were concerned that some Annex I Parties would be too eager to transfer their Kyoto Units, especially if these emission rights rose in value. They worried that some Annex I Parties might transfer too many Units and be left with an insufficient number to live up to their Kyoto commitments. The Accords therefore provide that each Annex I Party hold in its national registry at least an amount of Kyoto Units equivalent to its "commitment period reserve."[14] The commitment period reserve is calculated as 90 percent of a Party's assigned amount "or 100 percent of five times its most recently reviewed inventory, whichever is the lowest."[15] Only those parties with a fully stocked commitment period reserve (and the authorized entities trading out of their national registry systems) can transfer Kyoto Units.

In addition to limiting Parties' ability to sell Kyoto Units, the Marrakesh Accords also restrict their capacity to acquire Units. The origin of this limitation stems from the concern that some Parties would rely too heavily on reductions made in other countries and would not undertake the hard work necessary to achieve emission decreases on their own. To address this concern, the Accords provide that the acquisition of

Kyoto Units through the flexibility mechanisms should be "supplemental to domestic actions" and that domestic measures and policies should "constitute a significant element of the effort" that each Annex I Party makes to meet its Kyoto commitment.[16] This has come to be known as the "supplementarity" principle, since it declares that the use of the flexibility mechanisms for compliance purposes should be supplemental to domestic actions. Annex I Parties may be hesitant to acquire Kyoto Units where doing so could be seen to go against the principle of supplementarity.

Another important issue is whether Annex I Parties can authorize private entities to transfer and/or acquire Kyoto Units on their behalf. Most Annex I Parties do not retain exclusive control over the Kyoto Units in their national accounts. Instead, they essentially create their own national cap-and-trade system (or a regional system in the case of the EU) in which a portion of their national allocation serves as a cap for covered industries (with other portions being reserved for sectors that are not part of the trading system, such as transportation). Emitters covered by the trading scheme hold their allowances, in the form of Kyoto Units, in their own accounts listed on the national registry of their home nation. They can use these allowances to meet their own obligations under the national cap-and-trade system. In addition, an Annex I Party can authorize legal entities to transfer Units through the IET system to authorized legal entities in another Annex I Party.[17] Annex I Parties must maintain a current list of those legal entities that it has authorized to engage in such activities and must make the list available to the public.[18]

When legal entities engage in such a transaction, this will affect both the holdings of the legal entities themselves and the holdings of their home nations. On one level, the transaction is a transfer between the legal entity that is selling the Units and the one that is purchasing them. The Units leave one legal entity's national registry account and enter that of the other entity. On another level, it is a transfer between nations. The Units leave the national account of the Annex I Party in which the transferring legal entity holds its registry account, and enter the national account of the Annex I Party in which the acquiring entity holds its registry account. Thus the transaction is simultaneously a transfer between legal entities and a transfer between Annex I Party nations. Given this dual nature, it can only occur if the two Annex I Parties are legally able to engage in IET trading and if these Parties both agree to and authorize the transfer and acquisition. This circumstance makes it imperative for any private entity that wants to transfer Kyoto Units to make sure that the Annex I Party that is authorizing the transfer and/or acquisition has itself complied with the eligibility and commitment period reserve requirements set out above. The UNFCCC Secretariat's list of Annex I Parties that have met the eligibility requirements should prove to be a useful resource for making this assessment.[19]

Another question of special importance to American companies is whether legal entities incorporated or domiciled in non-Party nations (such as the United States) can transfer and/or acquire Kyoto Units. On the national level, only those parties to the UNFCCC that have ratified the Kyoto Protocol can transfer and/or acquire Kyoto Units.[20]

Thus, it is quite clear that non-Party *nations* cannot engage in such transfers or acquisitions. But what of legal entities domiciled in those non-Party nations? Could an Annex I Party allow them to open an account in its national registry and employ it to acquire and/or transfer Kyoto Units? While the answer is not yet fully clear, it can be argued that Annex I Parties can open their registries to non-Party entities. The Marrakesh Accords say that Annex I Parties can authorize legal entities to trade Kyoto Units.[21] They do not distinguish between legal entities that are domiciled in an Annex I Party and those that are not. Arguably, this silence implies that an Annex I Party could authorize all such entities to open national registry accounts and to transact in Kyoto Units.[22]

Assuming that an Annex I Party had the authority to do this, would it actually do so? Some environmental groups argue against giving legal entities from non-Party nations the privilege of transferring or acquiring Kyoto Units.[23] They maintain that such firms should not benefit from participation in the Kyoto Flexibility Mechanisms because they do not face any obligations under the Protocol. It remains to be seen whether Annex I Parties will adopt this position and, as a matter of national law, deny registry accounts to companies domiciled in non-Party nations, or whether they will follow a more open policy. Current indications are that at least some of them will follow the more open approach.

Even if Annex I Parties adopt the more restrictive approach, non-Party entities may still have avenues open to engage in Kyoto Unit transactions. For example, a multinational parent corporation domiciled in a non-Party nation that has a subsidiary domiciled in an Annex I Party could use that subsidiary to transfer or acquire Kyoto Units.[24] The subsidiary could open a national registry account and use it to transfer and/or acquire Kyoto Units on behalf of its parent.[25] Nothing in the Marrakesh Accords expressly prohibits this. Moreover, the subsidiary will presumably have emission reduction obligations of its own and so will not be as susceptible to the argument that it is "free-riding" on the Kyoto Flexibility Mechanisms.[26] International trade agreements may also prevent Annex I Parties from treating such subsidiaries differently for emissions trading purposes than they treat their own companies.[27] Canada has said that it will allow subsidiary companies from non-Party States that are located in Canada to hold accounts in the Canadian National Registry on the same basis as Canadian companies.[28] Companies without a subsidiary in an Annex I Party could create one. That is, they could establish a company in an Annex I Party and use it to transfer, hold or acquire Kyoto Units.[29]

Another option would be for a legal entity from a non-Party country to develop an arrangement with a legal entity with access to a national registry account to transfer, hold or acquire rights on its behalf. [30] This would require contractual arrangements to be entered into among the cooperating parties to ensure that the Kyoto Units were transferred and/or acquired as directed. [31] The party with the national registry account would likely charge a commission for such a service. [32]

Any limits on the "transfer" of Kyoto Units would be unlikely to apply to the "trade" in such Units. [33] While the Kyoto Protocol and Marrakesh Accords expressly regulate the transferring and acquiring of Kyoto Units, they say nothing about the trading of them. [34] In theory, the doors are wide open to trading in Kyoto Units. States, private companies, brokers, and others should all be able to engage in trading of these assets regardless of their place of domicile. Moreover, trading should be able to begin at any time. Unlike IET transfers, it need not wait until the beginning of the first commitment period in 2008.

B. The Clean Development Mechanism

The second Kyoto flexibility instrument is the Clean Development Mechanism (CDM). This program is structured quite differently from IET, as reflected in its program design choices and program implementation rules.

1. Program Design Choices

The most salient feature of the CDM is that it is a baseline-credit program. It gives developing nations that are Parties to the Kyoto Protocol, and their authorized entities, credit for reducing GHG emissions below baseline levels (or removing GHG beyond baseline sink levels). It then allows them to sell these credits, known as Certified Emission Reductions (CERs), to developed Annex I Parties who can use them to comply with their Kyoto commitments or can transfer them within the IET system. The CDM is thus a baseline-credit add-on to the overall IET cap-and-trade regime.

Participation in the CDM is voluntary. [35] In addition, as will be further described below, the CDM allows a wide array of legal entities to participate as producers/transferors and/or acquirers of CERs. These attributes give the CDM features of an open-market system. Yet there are some limits on participation. The projects must be located in developing nations that are Kyoto Protocol parties. They cannot take place in the United States, since it is a developed nation and is not a party to the Protocol. While the system is quite open, it is not all-inclusive.

> CDM is a downstream system that focuses on actual GHG emission reductions and removals. It is also an economy-wide program that recognizes reductions or removals from many economic sectors and does not limit itself to one or two specific industries.

As with the IET, the CDM is a downstream system that focuses on actual GHG emission reductions and removals. It is also an economy-wide program that recognizes

reductions or removals from many economic sectors and does not limit itself to one or two specific industries. Finally, the CDM allows its credits to be banked from one Kyoto commitment period to the next, although it places some limits on this activity. Parties can only bank CERs up to an amount that equals 2.5% of the Party's assigned amount.[36]

2. Program Implementation Rules

a. *Who Can Transfer and Trade?*

The CDM is set up to allow developing countries that are not listed in Annex I of the UNFCCC but are parties to the Kyoto Protocol (non-Annex I Parties) to convey credits to Annex I Parties that have binding commitments under the Protocol.[37] Thus, as a general rule, non-Annex I Parties can carry out project activities and convey the resulting CERs, and Annex I Parties can acquire these credits. These Parties must satisfy some basic eligibility conditions before they can participate in CDM. First, they must designate a national authority to provide oversight of CDM projects.[38] Second, as was already mentioned, they must be Parties to the Kyoto Protocol.[39] Finally, Annex I Parties that seek to acquire and use CERs must meet the six eligibility requirements for participation in any of the Kyoto Mechanisms described above.[40]

Can legal entities transfer and acquire CERs? The rules here largely follow those described above in reference to IET. Where authorized by their government to do so, legal entities domiciled in an Annex I Party nation can transfer and acquire CERs[41] and can serve as "project participants" (PP), a broad term encompassing project developers, purchasers of CER rights, and project financiers.[42] However, if the authorizing Party is not itself eligible to participate in CDM, then it cannot authorize its legal entities to do so. Legal entities should accordingly make certain that the authorizing Party meets the eligibility requirements set out above.

With respect to legal entities that are not domiciled in a Kyoto Party nation (non-Party entities), the rules again largely track those discussed above in reference to IET. Both the Kyoto Protocol and the Marrakesh Accords refer only to the participation of legal entities and do not expressly refer to the domiciles of such entities.[43] Some read this as allowing Parties to authorize non-Party entities to acquire and transfer CERs and otherwise participate in CDM.[44] As described above with respect to IET, Kyoto Parties may seek to limit such participation through their national policies.[45] The experience to date suggests that this is unlikely. For example, the Netherlands has announced that it will approve entities "from the whole world" for participation in CDM projects as long as the entities meet general approval criteria.[46] The Netherlands would thus permit non-Party entities to participate directly in CDM projects. In addition, a number of American and other nonparty entities have already begun participating in CDM projects through subsidiary companies domiciled in Annex I Parties,[47] or in CDM host countries.[48] If these trends continue, domicile should not prove a barrier to participation in CDM projects.

The CDM and IET situations do differ in one significant way. The CDM Executive Board (EB) registers and certifies CDM projects (see below). There is no comparable IET requirement. Potentially, the EB could object to non-Party entity participation in CDM projects and, on this basis, refuse to register or certify such projects.[49] Yet there are reasons to believe that it will not do so. The EB will primarily be made up of representatives from developing countries who are likely to favor broader participation in CDM.[50] Moreover, participation by a non-Party entity presupposes that an Annex I Party has authorized this participation. The EB is unlikely to override the wishes of such a Party.[51] These factors accordingly suggest that the EB is unlikely to pose a significant obstacle to non-Party entity participation.[52] Practitioners should watch for future EB actions and decisions on this topic.

b. Project Eligibility

The Kyoto Protocol provides for a "prompt start" to CDM[53] that allows some CDM projects to begin to accrue CERs beginning in 2000 and to apply them to the first commitment period.[54] In this respect, they differ from Joint Implementation projects, which generally cannot begin to generate emission reduction units until the beginning of the first commitment period in 2008.[55] Thus, the CDM is quite expansive when it comes to project timing. The program does place a few limits on the types of projects that can qualify for CERs. To begin with, the Preamble to the Marrakesh Accords decision on CDM provides that "Annex I Parties are to refrain from using CERs generated from nuclear facilities to meet their commitments under Article 3.1."[56] This language will bar most such projects, but may allow those that the host country believes to be essential to sustainable development.[57] Secondly, the CDM places some limits on the use of carbon sinks to generate CERs and meet Kyoto commitments. It grants units only for afforestation and reforestation activities and does not award them for maintenance of existing forests or other sinks.[58] Moreover, it caps at 1% of base-year emissions the amount of sinks-based CERs that a Party can use to meet its obligations during the first commitment period.[59] It does not place such a cap on the use of sinks-based CERs for future commitment periods, leaving this as a subject for future negotiations.[60]

c. Baseline-Credit Rules

Like other baseline-credit programs, CDM has rules for assessing and certifying project-based reductions and removals. As was explained in Chapter 2, CDM relies on a private/public partnership between Designated Operational Entities (DOE) and the CDM Executive Board to carry out these functions. The CDM process can be boiled down to seven basic steps: (1) the Project Participants (PP) submit a Project Design Document (PDD) to the DOE; 2) the DOE assesses this document in accordance with existing protocols and policies and, if it passes muster, "validates" it; (3) the EB reviews the validation and, if it approves, "registers" the project; (4) the PPs carry out the project; (5) based on reports submitted by the PPs, and in accordance with the monitoring plan set out in the PDD, the DOE "verifies" the project's GHG reductions or removals; (6) the EB reviews the verification and, if it approves, "certifies" the reductions and/or removals; and (7) the EB issues CERs corresponding to the amount of certified reductions or removals.

d. Public Participation

The rules make provision for public input at various stages in this process. The Project Participant must show in the PDD that it gave members of the public an opportunity to comment on the document and that it took "due account" of these comments.[61] The DOE must give the public an opportunity to comment on how the validation requirements apply to the project, make these comments publicly available, and take them "into account" in determining whether the project should be validated.[62] It must also make its validation and verification reports publicly available.[63]

Project Design Document. In the Project Design Document, the Project Participant sets out the core information about a proposed CDM project. This document then serves as the basis for the DOE's evaluation and possible validation of the project design. The PDD must follow the specific format set out in the Marrakesh Accords in Appendix B of Decision 17/CP.7.[64] The Accords further specify the criteria under which the DOE should assess the PDD.[65] Specifically, DOE must evaluate whether:

- The governments that are authorizing the project are themselves eligible to participate in CDM;
- The PPs have properly invited local stakeholders to comment on the PDD, have provided a summary of comments received, and have explained how they intend to respond to such comments;
- The PPs have documented their analysis of the project's environmental impacts and, if these impacts are significant, have undertaken an environmental impact assessment in accordance with the host nation's procedures for such assessments;
- The project is going to result in GHG reductions or removals that are "additional" to those that would otherwise be achieved;

- The methodologies for calculating the baseline and for monitoring reductions and removals are in accordance with those that the EB has previously approved or have themselves been approved by the Board;
- The provisions for monitoring, verification and reporting are in accordance with the Marrakesh Accords Decision 17/CP.7, its Annex and the relevant decisions of the Conference of the Parties serving as the meeting of the Parties (COP/MOP); and
- The project activity conforms to all other requirements contained in Decision 17/CP.7, its Annex and the relevant decisions of the COP/MOP.

The Executive Board has published a model Project Design Document as well as guidance explaining how such a document should be prepared. This useful information is available at the CDM Web site at http://cdm.unfccc.int/Reference/Documents.

e. Baseline Calculation

A Project Participant must include a baseline calculation in its Project Design Document. The Marrakesh Accords define a "bottom-up" approach to the development of baselines.[66] They call on Project Participants, working through the DOEs, to either propose a new baseline calculation methodology to the EB or to adopt a methodology that the Board has previously approved. The Accords provide some instructions to PPs, and to the Board, on the development of these methodologies.[67] To begin with, they define the baseline scenario as that which "would occur in the absence of the proposed project activity."[68] They further specify that a valid baseline calculation:

- must be transparent and conservative and should take uncertainty into account;
- must be established on a project-specific basis;
- must take into account relevant national and/or sectoral policies and circumstances;[69]
- may include scenarios where GHG emissions are projected to rise above current levels;[70] and
- must be defined in a way that does not allow CERs to be earned for decreases in activity levels outside the project activity itself, or due to *force majeure*.[71]

In addition to this list of requirements, the Accords require project participants to choose from among three possible approaches to baseline calculation: (1) existing actual or historical emissions; (2) emissions given installation of economically attractive technology, taking into account barriers to investment; and (3) "the average emissions of similar project activities undertaken in the previous five years, in similar . . . circumstances, and whose performance is among the top 20 percent of their category."[72]

The Marrakesh Accords instruct the Executive Board to develop further guidance on the calculation of baselines.[73] Pursuant to this mandate, the EB has established a CDM Methodologies Panel that has begun to publish accepted methodologies. Project participants can adopt these methodologies and incorporate them into their PDD. Alternatively, they can propose new methodologies to the EB for approval. The approved methodologies, recently proposed methodologies, and instructions for proposing a methodology are available at http://cdm.unfccc.int/methodologies/PAmethodologies. The CDM Methodologies Panel also fields questions from DOEs regarding the application of approved methodologies and publishes its responses to these queries. These documents constitute regulatory guidance on how to utilize the methodologies. They are available at http://cdm.unfccc.int/methodologies/PAmethodologies/Clarifications. For additional guidance on methodologies and other CDM-related matters, see http://cdm.unfccc.int/Reference/Guidclarif. These and other materials make the CDM Web site, http://cdm.unfccc.int/, an important resource for attorneys working in this evolving area.

f. Monitoring

The Project Design Document must also include a monitoring plan.[74] This plan sets out the methods for collecting and archiving the data and for carrying out the calculations needed to determine whether project activities are leading to GHG reductions or removals beyond baseline conditions.[75] As with the baseline calculation, Project Participants can either adopt an approved monitoring methodology or propose a new one to the EB.[76] The EB publishes approved monitoring methodologies much as it does baseline methodologies[77] and issues clarifying guidance in response to queries from DOEs.[78]

The Marrakesh Accords set forth the basic parameters for a monitoring plan.[79] Such plans must provide for:

- The collection and archiving of all data necessary to estimate GHG emissions within the project boundary during the crediting period;
- The collection and archiving of all data necessary to determine the baseline GHG emissions within the project boundary;
- The collection and archiving of data on the extent to which project activities will cause sources outside the project boundary to increase their GHG emissions (i.e., leakage);
- The collection and archiving of information related to the assessment of the project's environmental impacts, including transboundary impacts;
- Quality assurance and control procedures for the monitoring process;
- Procedures for the periodic calculation of GHG emission reductions and of leakage effects; and

- Documentation of all steps in all calculations used in developing the above information.

g. *Additionality*

The Kyoto Protocol requires CDM projects to achieve emission reductions "that are additional to any that would occur in the absence of the certified project activity."[80] Projects that cannot demonstrate additionality will not receive credit and will not produce CERs. The CDM program thus resembles the Offset Trading Program[81] and many other baseline-credit systems in requiring that reductions be additional to those that would otherwise have occurred.

The Marrakesh Accords provide a general definition of additionality for the purposes of CDM, stating that "[a] CDM project activity is additional if anthropogenic emissions of greenhouse gases by sources are reduced below those that would have occurred in the absence of the registered CDM project activity."[82] This straightforward definition requires the DOE to assess what GHG emissions would have been in the absence of the project and compare them to the emissions level achieved with the project in place. The CDM Executive Board, in its sixteenth meeting, fleshed out this definition in a document titled "Tool for the Demonstration and Assessment of Additionality."[83] In this document, the EB sets out a step-by-step approach to assessing additionality that includes the following:

- Identification of realistic and credible alternative scenarios that Project Participants might otherwise engage in and that provide similar outputs or services (e.g., electricity, cement, etc.) as those provided by the CDM project activity;[84]
- An "investment analysis" that determines whether, absent the revenue from the sale of CERs, the proposed project activity would actually be less economically or financially attractive than other comparable alternatives;[85]
- A "barrier analysis" that examines whether the proposed project faces barriers that prevent the implementation of the project activity but do not prevent the implementation of at least one of the alternatives;[86]
- A "common practice analysis" that examines whether the project activity already represents common practice in the relevant sector or region. This part of the assessment is intended as a check on the investment and barrier analyses;[87]
- An explanation of how the benefits and incentives associated with the CDM will alleviate the economic and financial hurdles or other identified barriers that would otherwise prevent the project activity from being undertaken.[88]

h. *Leakage*

As mentioned previously, the CDM monitoring plan must measure the extent to which project activities result in emissions of GHG outside the project boundary.[89] This requirement seeks to address the issue of "leakage" where efforts designed to decrease GHG emissions in one setting result in increased emissions elsewhere (e.g.,

enhanced energy efficiency at an electrical utility leads to greater demand at a less efficient, and hence cheaper, utility; or, restrictions on timber removal from a forest serving as a carbon sink lead to increased demand for timber from other nearby forests not included within the project). The Accords define leakage as "the net change in anthropogenic emissions by sources of greenhouse gases which occurs outside the project boundary, and which is measurable and attributable to the CDM activity."[90] They require that the emission reductions claimed with respect to a given project be adjusted to account for any increased emissions caused by leakage.[91]

C. Joint Implementation

Joint Implementation allows one Annex I Party to invest in an emission reduction or sequestration project located in another Annex I Party, and then to use the resulting credits (known as Emission Reduction Units or ERUs) to meet its own Kyoto Protocol commitments.[92] In this way, it allows two Annex I Parties to "jointly" pursue meeting their GHG reduction obligations. Chapter 2 of this volume introduced this program. This chapter will describe the program design choices and program implementation rules.

1. Program Design Choices

While IET is a pure cap-and-trade program and CDM a baseline-credit initiative, JI blends aspects of both. Under JI, Annex I Parties that wish to transfer ERUs must reduce their emissions below a baseline amount (or sequester GHG beyond baseline conditions) and must certify these reductions to produce credits. In these respects, the program resembles a project-based, baseline-credit system much like CDM.[93] Yet when it comes time for a Party that has reduced project-based emissions to transfer the resulting ERU, the process resembles a cap-and-trade system. As described in Chapter 2,[94] the selling nation decrements its national account by one AAU for every ERU that it transfers, and the purchaser adds one AAU for every ERU that it acquires. At the end of the day, the selling nation is essentially transferring an AAU to the purchasing nation, much as it would in a cap-and-trade system. Joint Implementation thus resembles a baseline-credit system in its generation of credits, and a cap-and-trade system in its transfer of these units. This combination of features strongly influences the program rules.

The Kyoto Protocol states that the JI program allows "any Party" that has undertaken an emission reduction "commitment[]" under the Kyoto Protocol (i.e., Annex I Parties) to transfer or acquire ERUs.[95] This language limits the program to Annex I

Parties and expressly excludes those Parties to the UNFCCC, such as the United States, that did not ratify the Protocol and do not have a binding commitment. In this regard, JI is a "closed" system that limits participation to a specified group of participants. Yet the Protocol goes on to state that a Party "may authorize legal entities to participate, under its responsibility, in actions leading to the generation, transfer or acquisition" of ERUs. In practice, this opens the door to participation by private and public legal entities as long as they do so in cooperation with, and with authorization from, the Annex I Parties involved in the ultimate transfer of ERUs.

Other program design choices are more clear-cut. Joint Implementation is an economy-wide program that allows ERUs to be generated from many sectors and does not narrow its focus to one or two industries. The program has a downstream focus in that it requires the projects to reduce or sequester GHG and does not generally grant ERUs for reductions in upstream activity (such as reductions in fossil fuel production). Finally, the JI program places important limits on the banking of ERUs. Under the Marrakesh Accords, Parties may "bank" ERUs acquired in one commitment period and carry them into the next. However, they may only do so in an amount equal to 2.5% of their initial assigned amount.[96]

2. Program Implementation Rules

The JI program's implementation rules reflect its dual nature as both a cap-and-trade and baseline-credit initiative. Due to JI's cap-and-trade element, rules on who can transfer, hold and acquire units are relevant. Given its baseline-credit dimension, rules on the determination of baselines, additionality and certification also play an important role, much as they do in the Clean Development Mechanism.

a. Who Can Transfer and Trade?

As stated above, Annex I Parties are generally authorized to transfer, hold and acquire ERUs.[97] However, the JI program does limit these activities. First, as is true in both the IET and CDM programs, Annex I Parties that wish to transfer and/or acquire ERUs must meet the eligibility requirements set forth in the Marrakesh Accords[98] and described above.[99] Parties can initiate JI projects prior to fulfilling all of these eligibility requirements, but they must meet them in order to ultimately transfer any ERUs that are generated.[100] Second, as with transfers of AAUs, a Party's use of ERUs for compliance purposes should be supplemental to its domestic actions to reduce GHG emissions.[101] Other than these limits, Annex I Parties are generally free to transfer and/or acquire ERUs. Legal entities can hold and transfer ERUs only as long as they do so with the approval of the Annex I Party in whose nation they hold a registry account.[102] Moreover, the JI Project will only come to fruition—in terms of an actual transfer of ERUs—if that Annex I Party is eligible to participate in JI.[103]

One issue of relevance for American lawyers is whether non-Party entities such as a U.S. company can gain entry as a JI project sponsor, organizer, financier or other "participant." As with the IET and CDM programs, the Kyoto Protocol prohibits non-

Party *nations* from participating in JI[104] but does not expressly address the domicile of the legal entities that can participate in the program.[105] This would appear to leave the door open to participation by non-Party entities. As was mentioned above, any entity seeking to acquire or transfer ERUs will need the approval of the Annex I Party in whose nation it seeks to hold a registry account. Thus, national policies will be important to participation of this type.[106]

A related issue is whether non-Party entities can "trade" in the ERUs that are generated by others. For example, could such an entity serve as a "broker" that holds rights to ERUs generated by one Annex I Party and trades these rights to another Annex I Party that ultimately acquires the ERUs? Nothing in the Protocol or Marrakesh Accords prohibits this. It may accordingly be argued that both documents implicitly accept such arrangements.

b. Project Eligibility

One important difference between JI and CDM is that, whereas CDM allows CERs to be generated beginning in 2000,[107] JI allows Annex I Parties to issue ERUs only for reductions or removals achieved after the first commitment period begins in 2008.[108] As with CDM, participants in the JI program are supposed to refrain from using nuclear projects to generate ERUs.[109] The JI program expressly recognizes GHG removals achieved through sinks projects.[110] The Marrakesh Accords confirmed this and specified that such sinks projects must conform to the rules set out in Article 3 of the Kyoto Protocol.[111]

c. Baseline-Credit Rules

JI has rules governing baselines, additionality, certification and other such elements of the baseline-credit approach. However, JI differs from other baseline-credit systems (such as CDM) in that it creates two separate "tracks" for evaluating whether a given project meets these requirements and establishes different sets of rules for each. Track 1 is for JI projects in which the host (transferring) Party meets all six eligibility criteria for participating in the Kyoto Flexibility Mechanisms.[112] In such situations, the host Party is thought to be in a position to evaluate its own transactions. It is accordingly allowed to establish its own policies for setting baselines, monitoring reductions and assessing additionality. It is also authorized to verify that these policies have been complied with and, once it has done so, to issue the ERUs all without international oversight. As mentioned above, upon transfer of the ERUs, the corresponding number of AAUs will be subtracted from the host Party's national account and will be added to that of the acquiring Party. This fact, combined with the host Party's need to have sufficient AAUs to cover its emissions at the end of the commitment period, are thought to provide a sufficient check on the system.

The Track 2 procedure applies where the host Party does not meet all six eligibility criteria.[113] In these situations host Parties are not authorized to verify their own reductions. Instead, as is explained in Chapter 2, the JI program sets up a verification procedure similar to that found in CDM.[114] A third-party verifier—known as an Independent Entity (IE)—reviews the Project Design Document (PDD) and "determines" whether it is consistent with the JI program policies and procedures.[115] After the project has been implemented, and upon receiving a monitoring report from the Project Participant, the IE determines whether the project has actually resulted in the GHG reductions and/or removals.[116] Each of these determinations is to be made publicly available.[117] An international body—the JI Supervisory Committee—establishes protocols for determining baselines, monitoring, etc., serves as the accrediting body for the IEs,[118] and reviews the IE's determinations.[119]

Given that JI will not formally begin to produce ERUs until 2008, Track 2 JI is not as developed as CDM. The JI Supervisory Committee has not yet fleshed out the policy framework to the extent that the CDM Executive Board has, although it has made some progress.[120] At present, the best sources of guidance on baseline calculation, monitoring and additionality requirements in the JI program are the Marrakesh Accords themselves.[121]

d. Project Design Document

With respect to the first determination—the evaluation of the PDD—the Marrakesh Accords[122] instruct the IE to assess whether:

- The parties involved have approved the project.
- The project would result in GHG reductions or removals that are "additional to any that would otherwise occur."
- The project has an appropriate baseline and monitoring plan that is in accordance with JI policies.
- The Project Participants have analyzed the project's environmental impacts and, if they are significant, have conducted an environmental impact assessment.

e. Baseline Calculation

The Marrakesh Accords[123] specify that a JI project baseline is to be established:

- On a project-specific basis and/or using a multiproject emission factor.
- In a transparent manner.
- In a way that takes into account relevant national and/or sectoral policies and circumstances.
- In such a way that decreases in activity levels outside the project itself or due to *force majeure* cannot lead to the generation of ERUs.

- Using conservative assumptions and taking uncertainties into account.

f. Monitoring Plan

The Marrakesh Accords[124] also spell out the basic contours of the Monitoring Plan that each Project Participant will have to build into the PDD. Such a plan must provide for:

- The collection and archiving of the data necessary to estimate project-based GHG reductions and removals during the crediting period.
- The collection and archiving of the data necessary to determine emission and sink baseline levels.
- Identification of the ways in which the project could lead to increased emissions or reduced removals outside the project boundaries (i.e., leakage).
- The collection of information on the project's environmental impacts.
- Quality assurance and control procedures for the monitoring process.
- Procedures for the periodic calculation of emission reductions and sink removals attributable to the project and of any leakage effects.
- Documentation of all steps involved in these calculations.

g. Additionality

Like CDM, the JI program requires that GHG reductions and removals be "additional to any that would otherwise occur."[125] In their PDD, Project Participants must demonstrate that their reductions and/or removals are in fact additional. The IE will assess this as part of determining that the PDD meets program requirements.

V. Implementation of the European Union Emissions Trading Scheme

This section will address the trading aspects, protocols, and implementation issues as they exist in the European Union (EU) Emissions trading Scheme (ETS) and the impacts on potential traders from the United States. In the context of the ETS, it is important to remember that while the EU governing bodies create laws for member states to follow, individual member nations are left to develop the necessary details to implement those laws.[126] While all member states may be operating under the same overarching set of rules, each nation's individual program will have differences in the details of implementation.

The members of the EU, as a group, agreed to take on the requirements of the Kyoto Protocol and share the burdens among its members. As such, the amount of greenhouse gas (GHG) reduction across the EU is different between member states. While some nations, such as Germany and the United Kingdom, must reduce their GHG emissions, other countries, such as Spain and Portugal, can actually increase their GHG emissions under the burden-sharing agreement.[127] Such an arrangement allows member states who are developing their economic and manufacturing base some flexibility in becoming "developed" nations.[128]

A. Program Design Choices

1. Cap-and-Trade and Baseline-Credit Aspects

In looking more closely at the ETS, one sees that it is, at its heart, a cap-and-trade program, with influences of baseline-credit systems. While member states commit to a percent total reduction from 1990 levels, each nation has flexibility to disperse individual allowances as it sees fit as long as it adheres to the Directive creating the ETS.[129] Each participant's emissions are then limited to the number of European Union Allowances (EUAs) it receives or purchases on the market—the standard cap-and-trade program.[130] However, with the inclusion of both the Joint Implementation (JI) and Clean Development Mechanism (CDM) portions of Kyoto in the EU ETS, an aspect of baseline-credit appears.[131] The Linking Directive ensures that the JI and CDM will be available to EU trading participants like any other Kyoto signatory.[132] The remaining portions of this section will discuss the specific implementation concerns of the EU ETS, with an analysis of the opportunities presented to non-EU entities for trading within the system as an investment tool.

2. Scope, Reach, and Allocation of Allowances

While each EU member state determines the details of its own national trading plan, there are commonalities as dictated by the ETS and Linking Directives. Remember that the EU determines the scope and overall design of the ETS, but that each member state enacts local laws to implement the directives set forth by the EU.[133] Three primary concepts are present, although treated differently, throughout the EU. First, implementation of the full ETS is accomplished as an economy-wide program, which regulates downstream emitters in a mostly open-market system.[134] Consequently, allowances are divided among the different industries before assigning to individual emitters, but other entities and individuals can enter the trading system after initial allocations are made to the emitters or "participants."[135] Most of the National Allocation Plans (NAPs) address the same points, but there are other slight differences in the implementation by member states. Because each member state sets individual terms for implementation of the ETS through the NAPs, it is important to be aware of differences between them.

3. National Allocation Plans

Second, the NAPs set the framework of the member state's trading scheme within the confines of the ETS as directed by the EU.[136] They are developed using the criteria in the ETS Directive Annex and must be approved by the EU Commission before taking effect. A major part of this undertaking is the allocation of EUAs to regulated participants. The Kyoto Protocol and burden-sharing agreement determine the amount of reduction imposed upon each member state from 1990 levels, but then each individual nation determines the amount of EUAs to assign to each economic sector and then to each participant.[137] The obligation placed upon the member states is to achieve the percent reduction assigned to each nation as a part of the burden-sharing arrangement and report back to the Commission.[138] Most member states elect to distribute allowances on a proportional share to emitters based on the amount of carbon each releases, while also holding a certain percentage of EUAs in reserve for new entrants.[139]

4. Banking

Finally, a related issue to allowance allocation is banking, or holding allowances in the current phase for use in future phases.[140] While the ETS permits banking,[141] most EU member-nations will not allow emitters to bank EUAs into the first Kyoto commitment period, or second ETS phase.[142] Banking EUAs into the first Kyoto trading phase would make achieving Kyoto emission reduction goals more difficult due to the increased total available allowances during that first Kyoto commitment period.[143] Banking could also lead to the flow of Kyoto allowances to other nations from the EU member states, given the potential surplus in Europe.[145] This would further damage the Kyoto system at its earliest stages of development. However, the EU is leaving the door open for member states to replace certain voided allowances based on the wording of the ETS Directive.[145] Given recent developments, this appears unlikely; but based on the current wording of the ETS Directive, it is still technically possible. Regardless of future banking, it is again important to read the specific governing NAP carefully to determine if it permits banking in the registry in question.

B. ETS Program Implementation Rules

1. Who Can Transfer, Trade, and Hold Registry Accounts

Very plainly, the ETS Directive assures that "Member States shall ensure that allowances can be transferred between: (a) persons within the community; [and] (b) persons within the Community and persons in third countries, where such allowances are recognized in accordance with the procedure referred to in Article 25 [Kyoto Annex I Parties] without restrictions other than those contained in, or adopted pursuant to, this Directive."[146] However, the ETS Directive is properly limited to only EU citizens and institutions. Under the European Constitution and various treaties, as well as the Vienna Convention on the Law of Treaties, only EU citizens have rights and obligations pursuant to the laws of the EU.[147] Consequently, a "person" in the EU is a "natural or legal person" of an EU member state.[148] While individuals and companies alike may partake in ETS trading, they must first be a "person" in the EU to create a registry account. Consequently, most NAPs are silent on the issue of who may engage in trading given the preemption of the ETS Directive.[149]

> In order to accomplish transfers between member states and to keep track of all EUAs, the Commission created a higher-level EU system to approve all transfers.

Once determined to be a "person" in the EU, potential traders may enter the ETS trading system by registering for one of two accounts.[150] These accounts are electronic and managed in registries created by member states. Individual traders and interested parties register using "person trading accounts," while participants use "operator accounts."[151] The only difference between these two accounts is that only operator accounts may generally receive allowances upon the initial allocation at the beginning of the trading phase.[152] Despite that difference, anyone who holds a registry account may participate in trading in the ETS. Creating one of these accounts is quite simple, and generally involves only the completion of forms found at the registry's Web site.

2. Conducting Transfers and Trades

In order to accomplish transfers between member states and to keep track of all EUAs, the Commission created a higher-level EU system to approve all transfers.[153] The Community Independent Transaction Log (CITL) serves as a clearinghouse for transfers within the ETS. The CITL does not analyze the underlying agreement that addresses the exchange of money and, as explained below, is only a check on the transfer of valid allowances.[154] The member state registries, on the other hand, act as electronic bank accounts that are overseen and checked for errors by the CITL, while the agreements setting out the terms of the transfer are handled outside the bounds of the ETS.[155]

To complete a transfer, registrants must complete the following steps, regardless of whether the transfer happens within a member-nation or between member-nations. First, the buyer and seller must agree on a price and amount of allowances at issue.[156]

Generally, the price is set by the market, and such information is easily available from market watchers such as the European Climate Exchange, Evolution Markets, and Ecosystem Marketplace.[157] Once terms are agreed to, the seller initiates the transfer at its registry site by informing the registry of the buyer's account information, the number of shares to be transferred, and the seller's account information. Next, the seller's registry then checks the account information to ensure that the required allowances are owned by the seller and that the seller is authorized to conduct such a transfer. Then, the transaction information is sent to the CITL for further checks to ensure that the allowances are available and the buyer and seller are authorized to conduct the transaction. The CITL must respond to transfer requests within 24 hours with an "accepted" or "rejected" designation. Should the CITL not respond within 24 hours, the transaction is cancelled, and consequently stopped. Upon approval of the transaction by the CITL, permission to conduct the transfer is provided to the seller's registry and executed through the CITL. The buyer's and seller's registries are only linked through the CITL; hence, all transfers must go through that central clearinghouse. Finally, the purchased allowances are debited from the seller's account and credited into the buyer's account in the buyer's registry. At this point, ownership is transferred and the buyer may use the allowances as it wishes, regardless of whether the buyer has paid. The transfer of monetary funds occurs outside the scope of, and without oversight

by, the registry system.[158] Upon the start of the first Kyoto trading period, 2008–2012, the above process will change to add one layer of oversight. In order to allow all the national registries in the Kyoto system to communicate equally with the Kyoto clearinghouse, the UNFCCC International Transaction Log (ITL), all transactions will be routed to the ITL before going to the CITL for approval. The CITL will then route approval back to the ITL for continuation of the transaction. In essence, this change will add some time necessary to complete the transaction and prevent member state registries from communicating directly with the CITL.[159]

As can be expected with this arrangement, while legal persons involved in ETS trading must be "persons" as defined by the EU, either real people or corporations, such trading can, in reality, include traders from outside the EU. The ETS Directive defines the terms and conditions for trading within the ETS.[160] Consequently, to the extent allowed by member-nation laws, non-EU citizens may create EU corporate interests with the goal of entering into the ETS trading process.

C. Ownership of Allowances

This then raises the question of ownership rights and who may lawfully transfer or trade in the ETS. The ETS Directive explicitly states, "[a]ny person may hold allowances," but only citizens of the EU may hold registry accounts and engage in ETS transfers or trades.[161] However, because of the free-market nature of the European Union, there are opportunities for non-EU traders in a market worth approximately $12.4 billion in 2005 and expected to triple in 2006.[162]

1. *Who May Own an Allowance*

First, allowances may be transferred to any registrant within the EU regardless of "participant" status.[163] While non-participants are permitted to engage in EUA transferring, they are generally not eligible to receive the initial allocation of allowances provided for under most NAPs.[164] However, once initial allocations are made to emitters, any EU "natural person" with a registry account may engage in transferring allowances through the market system in place.[165] Second, the legal aspects of the EU are such that individual member-states cannot limit another member-state's ability to transfer.[166] In fact, the EU specifically allowed any person to open an account in order to increase participation and liquidity in the system. Consequently, anyone who establishes themselves as a "person" and creates a registry account in any EU member state may engage in ETS transfers Union-wide.

2. *Participation by Non-EU Actors*

The most obvious option for participation is through the brokers that have appeared to do business in this arena. Exchanges such as the European Climate Exchange and brokers such as Evolution Markets have easy access to ETS buyers and sellers and will conduct initial contacts on behalf of clients.[167] While establishment as an EU citizen (see below) is still needed in order to transfer, brokers help connect buyers and sellers quickly to accomplish transfers. Additionally, it is possible brokers could conduct trades and hold EUAs in trust on behalf of non-EU actors, but brokers generally do not seem to be engaging in this behavior. Risks associated with using brokers include the increased cost of using a broker, less direct contact with transaction partners, and potentially missed opportunities depending on the focus of an individual broker. Of course, becoming an established "person" in the EU is necessary, leading to the second avenue for EUA transfers.

The next option is for a non-EU person or company to establish themselves as a "natural person" in the EU and conduct transfers without the assistance of a broker. While there are limitations and additional steps to this option, it avoids the "middleman" aspect of the brokers and could be more cost-effective. As indicated above, entering the ETS is a simple matter of completing registration forms upon establishment as an EU person. Once the registry account is created, the owner may fully participate in the ETS. Particularly for corporations, this option may be more attractive if a subsidiary company can be easily established in an EU member-state. Risks associated with this option include national restrictions on "shell" companies and

increased difficulty in finding transfer partners and executing transactions, but it gives direct access to the ETS system and potential partners.

The final option for non-EU entities to engage in the ETS is through the Clean Development Mechanism or Joint Implementation programs.[168] As explained earlier, CDM and JI projects are those aimed at reducing emissions in a country other than the one sponsoring the project.[169] The Linking Directive serves to bridge the gap between the ETS Directive and the CDM and JI programs. The ETS Directive did not clearly address CDM and JI programs as part of the EU ETS, hence the need for the Linking Directive. Through these programs, non-EU entities may engage in relevant projects either on behalf of EU entities or through selling generated credits to EU entities, with the approval of an Annex I Party.[170] Based on current trends, it appears likely that non-Party entities will be able to participate in CDM and JI programs.[171] However, there is nothing to indicate that a corporation or other legal entity that is an EU "natural person" cannot take advantage of CDM or JI projects.[172] As such, an EU "shell" company could engage in either CDM or JI projects, and once those credits are certified under Kyoto, may openly and freely sell them on the EU market. Of course, risks such as those outlined earlier in the chapter addressing recognition of CDM and JI credits are present with this option. In addition, while there is the advantage of not needing to be an EU "person" to engage in CDM and JI projects, by instead working

directly with the country that houses the project, there is the practical consideration of whether an EU/Annex I Party will approve such projects by non-Party companies without attempting to have its own citizens perform the work.

There are several routes for ETS involvement. While most options involve establishing an EU "person," possible trading with brokers and involvement in JI or projects present less restrictive, if not more speculative, options for entry into the system.

D. Looking Ahead

While the first stage of ETS trading is currently under way, the EU is already looking to the next phase of trading beginning in 2008.[173] Revised versions of the NAPs were due to the EU Commission on or before June 30, 2006,[174] with the review and approval process extending from there.[175] Further, the EU Commission is in the process of reviewing the ETS to make changes to the scheme. Any amendments made to the ETS are not expected until sometime in 2008, and will consequently only be applicable for the 2013-18 trading phase. Anticipated changes to the ETS include the narrowing of participation by outside entities, as well as changed methods of initial EUA allocation, increased harmonization between member states concerning installations required to participate, revised criteria for NAP creation, and addressing member states' planned purchases of Kyoto allowances to help fulfill national goals.[176] In addition, there has been some discussion about regulating gases other than carbon dioxide in the second phase; however, no final decision has been made. Additionally, it is unclear how prices will fluctuate in the future in light of the European Commission's recent report stating that "increased trading is necessary to meet the Kyoto targets cost-effectively."[177] As a result, there are opportunities at present for involvement. However, those opportunities may narrow or disappear entirely with the anticipated, and as yet unknown, revisions to the ETS. Entities wishing to work with the system need to stay aware of those changes as they develop through subsequent program revisions.

In addition to the potential changes addressed above, recent market fluctuations may cause additional modifications. In May 2006, Ecosystem Marketplace reported a dramatic drop in EUA prices, raising concerns over the viability and future of the ETS.[178] This report noted that EUA prices unexpectedly dropped by 50% on April 28, 2006,[179] resulting from two member states, France and Spain, announcing that the amount of carbon each emitted was surprisingly low.[180] This, in turn, caused future demand for EUAs to drop.[181] The report explained that, given their volatile nature, environmental markets require the ability to adapt immediately, and specifically, the ETS does not have the needed ability to respond to new information to the market "on the fly."[182] The numbers released by France and Spain were not the result of decreased emissions, as envisioned by the ETS, but rather of industry's ability to obtain more allowances than needed.[183] The ETS cannot adjust the allowance cap in a manner to keep the market from becoming saturated, resulting in drastically lowered prices.[184] This information was confirmed on May 15, 2006, when 21 of the 25 EU member states released verified emission reports. These reports indicated that 99% of installations covered by the ETS met required emission caps, with allowances remaining available on the market.[185] Consequently, allowance trading slowed even further. No one predicts a total collapse of the ETS, but short-term, spot, or speculative investors should remain acutely aware of events that could shape a sudden correction in the market.[186] In addition, potential investors should remain aware of changes implemented for subsequent phases as revised NAPs are approved, and as the ETS moves into operation in conjunction with the first commitment period under Kyoto.

While the current phase was designed as a time to "work the bugs" out of the system, this phase is a useful exercise as the EU looks towards Kyoto implementation. It is premature to determine the learning curve associated with this initial trading, and most issues will not be identified until revised NAPs are issued in June 2006 and subsequently approved. Anyone intending to enter the EU trading scheme should be aware of possible changes to outside participation rules as well as mechanical changes based on lessons learned from the first trading phase.

VI. Regional Greenhouse Gas Initiative

As discussed in Chapter 9, the Regional Greenhouse Gas Initiative (RGGI) is a greenhouse gas trading system established by seven states in the Northeast and Mid-Atlantic regions of the country.[187] After much research and discussion, the RGGI states released a Memorandum of Understanding (MOU) on December 20, 2005 (as amended on August 8, 2006), signed by all seven governors that describes the essential elements of the trading system.[188] Based on the MOU, RGGI's Staff Working Group issued a final Model Rule on August 15, 2006.[189] Each participating state must promulgate its own rule to implement RGGI, and the Model Rule is meant to be the foundation for the individual state rulemakings. This chapter describes the structure of the RGGI based on the MOU and the Model Rule.

A. Program Design Choices

RGGI is a cap-and-trade system, with aspects of a baseline-credit program based on the generation of credits from CO_2 mitigation projects. It establishes a regional emissions cap for the years 2009 to 2018, and regulates CO_2 emissions from fossil fuel-fired electricity-generating units having a rated capacity of 25 megawatts (MW) or more, referred to as "CO_2 budget units."[190] Thus the program has a downstream structure specific to the electricity generation industrial sector. Each state is given an annual base budget of a certain number of tons of CO_2 for each of the years from 2009 to 2014 based on its share of the regional cap

of 121.3 million short tons of CO_2, which is approximately equivalent to 1990 CO_2 emissions. This approach of capping a state's allowable emissions at an emissions baseline that is based on historical experience (commonly referred to as a "budget") and then allowing the state to set up a system for allocating the budget closely resembles the NO_x Budget Trading Program discussed earlier.

For the years 2015-2018, the state's annual base budget is calculated by a certain reduction in the earlier baseline. Beginning with the annual allocations for the year 2015, each state's base annual CO_2 emissions budget will decline by 2.5% per year so that each state's base annual emissions budget for 2018 will be 10% below its initial base annual CO_2 emissions budget.[191]

Each state decides how to allocate allowances from its CO_2 emissions budget to a CO_2 budget unit based on the unit's emissions. Each entity that includes one or more CO_2 budget units, referred to as a "CO_2 budget source," maintains its allowances in a compliance account and must obtain a permit that contains all the CO_2 Budget Trading Program requirements that apply to that source.[192] In addition to allocating allowances to CO_2 budget sources based on the source's emissions, a state may also award

Early Reduction CO_2 Allowances (ERAs) to a source for reductions in the source's CO_2 emissions that are achieved during the period from 2006 to 2008. The state will calculate the number of ERAs to be awarded to a source based on a methodology that reflects the extent that CO_2 emissions in the baseline period (2003 to 2005) exceed CO_2 emissions in the early reduction period.[193] ERAs thus will be issued for actions taken at a CO_2 budget unit that improves efficiency of the unit and reduces emissions.

Every state must also reserve at least 25% of the base budget to the Consumer Benefit or Strategic Energy Purpose Account. Allowances will be sold or distributed from this account to provide funds to promote energy-efficiency measures, mitigate electricity ratepayer impacts attributable to the implementation of the CO_2 trading program, promote renewable or noncarbon-emitting energy technologies, or stimulate or reward investment in developing innovative carbon emissions abatement technologies with significant carbon reduction potential. The state may auction allowances as the method for distributing allowances from this account.[194]

A CO_2 budget unit is not the only entity that can hold an account to transfer allowances. Any person can establish a general account for the purpose of holding and transferring CO_2 allowances—for instance, to hold CO_2 offset allowances generated from CO_2 emissions offset projects or CO_2 emissions credit retirements. RGGI thus is structured as a hybrid closed-open market system.

The general account must designate a CO_2 authorized account representative who can legally bind each person with an ownership interest with respect to CO_2 allowances held in the general account and all matters pertaining to the CO_2 budget trading program. Each submission concerning the general account must be submitted, signed and certified by the CO_2 authorized account representative.[195]

B. Program Implementation Rules

RGGI's Model Rule has detailed implementation rules to guide states in setting up a system that complies with the Memorandum of Understanding. A state can put its own regulatory gloss on the system as it integrates RGGI into its regulatory scheme, but the basic elements must apply to all the participatory states for RGGI to function effectively.

1. Compliance

Each state will establish one compliance account for each CO_2 budget source. By January 1, 2009, the state's regulatory agency will record CO_2 allowances for the allocation years of 2009-2012 in each CO_2 budget source's compliance account. After the initial allocation, the state will record CO_2 allowances in the compliance account for the year after the last year for which CO_2 allowances were previously allocated to the compliance account on an annual basis.

The state deducts available CO_2 allowances for compliance until the number of CO_2 allowances that are deducted equals the number of tons of total CO_2 emissions, less any CO_2 emissions attributable to the burning of biomass, from all CO_2 budget

units at the CO_2 budget source for the control period. A control period is a three-year period, unless extended by one year due to a "stage-two trigger event" defined later, thus allowing for weather-related sharp increases in emissions to be smoothed over a longer averaging period. Each source must cover its emissions with CO_2 allowances at the allowance transfer deadline, which falls on March 1 after the control period ends. Also on March 1 of every year, the CO_2 authorized account representative must submit a compliance certificate report that certifies compliance with all emissions limitations, monitoring, and reporting requirements.

The state can account for excess emissions by deducting from the CO_2 budget source's compliance account a number of CO_2 allowances, allocated for allocation years that occur after the control period in which the source has excess emissions, equal to three times the number of the source's excess emissions. In other words, if the source has excess emissions, it can use future allowances to achieve compliance, but only by forfeiting some number of allowances at a 3-to-1 penalty. No CO_2 offset allowances may be deducted to account for the source's excess emissions. The CO_2 budget source may also be assessed fines or penalties under the applicable state law for excess emissions, which states that each day the source has excess emissions constitutes a day in violation and each ton of excess emissions constitute, a separate violation.[196]

2. Banking and Transferring CO_2 Allowances

RGGI establishes a regime for banking and transferring CO_2 allowances. Each CO_2 allowance that is held in a compliance account or general account can be banked by remaining in an account until the CO_2 allowance is deducted or transferred. The CO_2 authorized account representative seeking to record a CO_2 allowance transfer must submit the transfer to the state agency and include: 1) numbers identifying both the transferor and transferee accounts, 2) a specification by serial number of each CO_2 allowance to be transferred, 3) printed name and signature of the CO_2 authorized account representative of the transferor account and date signed, 4) the date of the completion of the last sale or purchase transaction for the allowance if any, and 5) the purchase or sale price of the allowance that is subject to the transaction. Within five days of receiving a CO_2 allowance transfer, the agency will record a CO_2 allowance transfer by moving each CO_2 allowance from the transferor to the transferee account as specified by the request. Within five business days of recordation of a CO_2 allowance transfer, the agency will notify each party to the transfer. Although RGGI does not explicitly establish a trading regime, presumably CO_2 allowance transfers could be made through trading by market brokers.[197]

3. Monitoring, Recordkeeping, and Reporting

Each CO_2 budget unit must comply with the monitoring, recordkeeping, and reporting requirements under the applicable sections of 40 C.F.R. Part 75. 40 C.F.R. Part 75 is the U.S. Environmental Protection Agency regulation that includes specific requirements for monitoring, recordkeeping, and reporting CO_2 emissions (as well as SO_2 and NO_X emissions as required under the acid rain provisions of the Clean Air Act). Each CO_2 budget unit must install and operate monitoring systems and successfully complete all certification tests and record quality assurance data by following 40 C.F.R. Part 75. For example, each CO_2 budget unit must install all monitoring systems required for monitoring CO_2 mass emissions, including those systems used to monitor CO_2 concentration, stack gas flow rate, O_2 concentration, heat input, and fuel flow rate in accordance with 40 C.F.R. 75.13, 72.71, and 75.72 and all portions of 40 C.F.R. Part 75 appendix G, except for equation G-1.

The CO_2 authorized account representative must submit quarterly reports that report the CO_2 mass emission data and heat input data for each CO_2 budget unit, along with a compliance certification supporting each quarterly report based on a reasonable inquiry by those persons with a primary responsibility for ensuring that all the units' emissions are correctly monitored.[198] These certifications shall state that (1) the monitoring data meets 40 C.F.R. Part 75 quality assurance procedures and specifications, (2) any add-on emission controls are operating within the range of parameters listed in the quality assurance/quality control program under 40 C.F.R. Part 75, and (3) any CO_2 concentration values substituted for missing data under 40 C.F.R. Part 75 do not systematically underestimate CO_2 emissions.[199]

4. Baseline-Credit Program Rules

Baseline-credit programs grant credit for reducing emissions below a specific baseline. RGGI incorporates a modified baseline-credit program within its cap-and-trade program by awarding CO_2 allowances for CO_2 emissions offset projects or CO_2 emissions credit retirements that have reduced or avoided atmospheric loading of CO_2 (or CO_2 equivalent) or sequestered carbon, thereby reducing emissions below where they would have been without the project. The Model Rule seeks to ensure that the CO_2 equivalent emission reductions or carbon sequestration that can result in offset allowances are "real, additional, verifiable, enforceable, and permanent within the framework of a standards-based approach."[200] The resulting CO_2 offset allowances can be used for compliance or transfer, although the use of CO_2 offset allowances is limited.

a. Project Eligibility

The state may award CO_2 offset allowances to the sponsor of any of the following types of CO_2 emissions offset projects:

- landfill methane capture and destruction
- reduction in emissions of sulfur hexafluoride (SF_6)

- sequestration of carbon due to afforestation
- reduction or avoidance of CO_2 emissions from natural gas, oil or propane end-use combustion due to end-use energy efficiency
- avoidance of methane emissions from agricultural manure management operations

The state may also award CO_2 offset allowances to the sponsor of a CO_2 emissions credit retirement, which include the permanent retirement of greenhouse gas emissions reduction credits issued pursuant to any governmental mandatory carbon-constraining program outside the United States that places a specific tonnage limit on greenhouse gas emissions, or issued pursuant to the United Nations Framework Convention on Climate Change (UNFCCC) or protocols adopted through the UNFCCC process. In this way, RGGI acknowledges that protocols acceptable to RGGI are consistent with those used in the EU ETS. To receive a CO_2 emissions credit retirement, the sponsor must demonstrate that the credit issued through the UNFCCC process is equivalent to an RGGI CO_2 allowance and has been permanently and irrevocably retired. As will be discussed later, awarding CO_2 offset allowances for a CO_2 emissions credit retirement is strictly limited.

b. Project Implementation Rules

The state may award CO_2 offset allowances only for CO_2 emissions offset projects that are initially commenced on or after December 20, 2005. The offset project sponsor must submit a consistency application that contains the following information: the project sponsor's identification information, a project description, a demonstration that the project meets all applicable requirements, the emissions baseline determination, and an explanation of how the projected reduction or avoidance of atmospheric loading of CO_2 (or CO_2 equivalent) or the sequestration of carbon is to be quantified, monitored, and verified. The project sponsor also must include a verification report and certification statement drafted and signed by an independent verifier that expresses that the independent verifier has reviewed the application and evaluated the adequacy and validity of the information supplied by the project sponsor and the adequacy of the monitoring and verification plan to demonstrate that the project meets the applicable eligibility requirements.

RGGI includes an additionality requirement such that CO_2 offset allowances will not be awarded to a project or CO_2 emissions credit retirement that is required pursuant to any local, state or federal law, regulation, administrative or judicial order. Projects also may not be awarded credits or allowances under any other mandatory or voluntary GHG program or market.[201]

i. Landfill Methane Capture and Destruction

These are projects that capture and destroy methane from landfills that are not municipal solid waste landfills subject to New Source Performance Standards, 40 C.F.R. Part 60, Subparts Cc and WWW. The emissions baseline is determined by measuring the potential fugitive landfill emissions of methane as represented by the methane collected and metered for thermal destruction as part of the project. Emissions reductions are determined based on potential fugitive methane emissions that would have occurred at the landfill if the metered methane was not collected and destroyed.[202]

ii. Reduction in Emissions of Sulfur Hexafluoride (SF$_6$)

These are projects that prevent emissions of SF$_6$ to the atmosphere from an electric utility's transmission or distribution equipment through capture and storage, recycling or destruction. Baseline SF$_6$ emissions are determined based on annual entity-wide reporting of SF$_6$ emissions for the calendar year immediately proceeding the calendar year in which the project application is filed. Emissions reductions shall represent the annual entity-wide emissions reductions of SF$_6$ for the reporting entity, relative to emissions in the baseline year.[203]

iii. Sequestration of Carbon Due to Afforestation

These are projects that sequester carbon through the conversion of land from nonforested to forested conditions, provided that the land has been in a nonforested state for at least 10 years. The existing sequestered carbon within the project boundary must be calculated prior to the commencement of the project. CO$_2$ emissions offsets can be issued based on the amount of net additional carbon sequestered within the project boundary during each reporting period. The project must meet the requirement to address permanence of sequestered carbon by placing the land within the project boundary under a legally binding permanent conservation easement that requires the land to be maintained in a forested state in perpetuity, and that carbon density be maintained.[204]

iv. Reduction or Avoidance of Co$_2$ Emissions from Natural Gas, Oil, or Propane End-use Combustion Due to End-use Energy Efficiency

These are projects that reduce CO$_2$ emissions by reducing on-site combustion of natural gas, oil or propane in an existing or new commercial or residential building by improving the energy efficiency of fuel usage and/or the energy-efficient delivery of energy services. The emissions baseline is determined based on energy usage by fuel type for each energy conservation measure, and emissions reduction is determined based upon annual energy savings by fuel type for each energy conservation measure.[205]

v. Avoided Methane Emissions from Agricultural Manure Management Operations

These are projects that capture and destroy methane from animal manure using anaerobic digesters. The emission baseline shall represent the potential emissions of the methane that would have been produced in a baseline under uncontrolled anaerobic storage conditions and released directly into the atmosphere in the absence of the offset project, with emissions reductions determined based on these same potential emissions of the methane that would have been produced in the absence of the offset project.[206]

c. *Award and Use of CO_2 Offset Allowances for CO_2 Offset Projects and CO_2 Emissions Credit Retirements*

The award of quantities of CO_2 offset allowances to a project sponsor for CO_2 offset projects or CO_2 emissions credit retirements is strictly limited and is based on whether the agency has declared a "stage-one trigger event" or a "stage-two trigger event." A "stage-one trigger event" essentially is when the 12-month rolling average spot price for CO_2 allowances is $7 or more. A "stage-two trigger event" essentially is when the 12 month rolling average spot price for CO_2 allowances is $10 or more.[207]

If the project sponsor filed the monitoring and verification report prior to the declaration of either a stage-one trigger event or stage-two trigger event during the current control period, then one CO_2 offset allowance will be awarded for each ton of demonstrated reduction in CO_2 emissions (or CO_2 equivalent) or sequestration of CO_2 from a CO_2 emissions offset project that was undertaken within a RGGI participating state, and one CO_2 offset allowance will be awarded for two tons of demonstrated reductions or sequestration that was undertaken within any state that is not a participating state. Thus offset projects in states other than the RGGI participating states are eligible for allowances but at a discounted amount. Offset projects in non-RGGI states may be eligible for allowances only if the non-RGGI state has entered into a memorandum of understanding with an RGGI state to carry out certain obligations to ensure the credibility of offset allowances, such as performing audits of offset project sites.

If the project sponsor filed the monitoring and verification report on or after the declaration of a stage-one or -two trigger event during the current control period, then one CO_2 offset allowance will be awarded for each ton of demonstrated reduction in CO_2 emissions (or CO_2 equivalent) or sequestration of CO_2 from the CO_2 emissions offset project that was undertaken within any state, Mexico or Canada. In this way, CO_2 offset allowances can be more readily generated from projects throughout North America when the CO_2 offset allowance exceeds a certain price, thereby increasing the supply of CO_2 offset allowances and consequently using a market mechanism to reduce the price.

A project sponsor can file for a CO_2 emissions credit retirement only after the occurrence of a stage-two trigger event during the current control period, at which time one CO_2 offset allowance will be awarded for each ton of reduction or sequestration represented by the relevant credits or allowances recognized under the CO_2 emissions credit retirement requirements.

The total number of CO_2 offset allowances that may be deducted for compliance is also strictly limited, but more may be used for compliance as the price of CO_2 allowances increases. Although CO_2 offset allowances are generally limited to the number of tons representing 3.3% of the CO_2 budget source's CO_2 emissions, the availability of CO_2 offset allowances can be increased to represent 5% of CO_2 emissions if a stage-one trigger event occurs, and 10% if a stage-two trigger event occurs.   RGGI is the first mandatory CO_2 mitigation system in the United States. As such, it had to develop a trading system essentially out of whole cloth. The result is a thoroughly detailed system that has incorporated all the aspects needed for a workable emissions trading system as described earlier in this chapter. RGGI can be considered a model for any future U.S. mandatory GHG emissions trading system. In fact, the Memorandum of Understanding anticipates the possibility that a federal mandatory system will be established, and commits to transitioning RGGI into the federal program if it is deemed comparable to RGGI.

VII. Chicago Climate Exchange

As discussed in Chapter 17, the Chicago Climate Exchange (CCX) is a self-regulatory organization that administers a voluntary, legally binding greenhouse gas reduction and trading program involving multiple industrial sectors. An entity can affiliate with CCX either (1) as a member who commits to GHG emission mitigation from facilities in the United States, Canada and Mexico (with inclusion of facilities in Canada and Mexico being optional),[208] (2) as an associate member who has little or no direct GHG emissions but still commits to offset its GHG emissions from its business-related activities, (3) as a participant member who provides offset projects or liquidity in the trading market, or (4) as an exchange participant who establishes an account to acquire and retire CCX allowances or credits. These affiliated entities are referred to collectively as CCX Registry Account Holders.

CCX has established a fully developed trading program that incorporates the basic emissions trading elements described earlier in this chapter. This section will describe CCX's design and implementation based in part on The Chicago Accord, a description of the details that lay out the foundation of CCX's trading program.[209]

A. Program Design Choices

CCX is a cap-and-trade program that seeks to reduce all six GHGs: CO_2, methane, nitrous oxide, hydrofluorocarbons, perfluorocarbons, and sulfur hexafluoride.[210] CCX issues Exchange Allowances (XAs) in declining amounts based on the emissions baseline

for each of its members but also provides for additional tradable credits to be generated as a result of GHG mitigation projects termed Exchange Offsets (XOs). XAs and XOs are collectively referred to as Carbon Financial Instruments (CFIs). CCX also provides for credits to be generated by early GHG mitigation projects, which yield instruments termed Certified Early Action Credits (CEACs). Each CFI and CEAC represents 100 metric tons of CO_2 equivalent emissions. Thus, CCX incorporates aspects of a baseline-credit program within the cap-and-trade system framework.

... the Chicago Climate Exchange (CCX) is a self-regulatory organization that administers a voluntary, legally binding greenhouse gas reduction and trading program involving multiple industrial sectors.

Each CCX member's emission baseline is the annual average emissions from covered facilities over the years 1998 through 2001 or over the year 2000. CCX rules determine which facilities a CCX member must include in determining the member's emission baseline, usually the member's main emission sources, with the option of including electricity purchases and small sources. Those CCX members primarily engaged in electric power production must include CO_2 emissions from all power generation facilities having a rated capacity of 25 MW or larger, and can opt-in emissions from facilities having a rated capacity of less than 25 MW as long as all such facilities are included. The emissions baseline does not include the use of renewable fuels such as wood fuels, agricultural residues, and landfill methane, which are treated as zero-carbon sources.

CCX was initiated in 2003, and the first phase of emission reductions covered 2003 through 2006. By the end of this phase (December 2006), CCX members are to have reduced emissions 4% below the emissions baseline. The next phase covers 2007 through 2010, with the ultimate goal of 6% below emissions baseline by 2010. These emission reductions are accomplished by each CCX member receiving CFIs in their CCX Registry Account in an amount equal to declining emission targets reflected in the following CCX emissions reduction schedule:

Phase I	CCX Emission Reduction Target
2003	1% below member's baseline
2004	2% below member's baseline
2005	3% below member's baseline
2006	4% below member's baseline
Phase II	**CCX Emission Reduction Target**
2007	4.25% below member's baseline
2008	4.5% below member's baseline
2009	5% below member's baseline
2010	6% below member's baseline

For new Phase II members (those joining in 2006), the Phase II target limit by 2010 is the same but is based on a different reduction schedule:

Phase II	CCX Emissions Reduction Target
2006	1.2% below member's baseline
2007	2.4% below member's baseline
2008	3.6% below member's baseline
2009	4.8% below member's baseline
2010	6% below member's baseline

B. Program Implementation Rules

1. Compliance

Subsequent to the compliance year, each CCX member must surrender any combination of CFIs in an amount equal to the CO_2 equivalent emissions released from that member's facilities during the compliance year as part of the process referred to as the "annual true-up." However, CCX effectively limits the number of CFIs that a member can use to meet its commitment by establishing an Economic Growth Provision (EGP), which is the maximum increase in CO_2 equivalent emissions that have to be accounted for when determining the annual true-up. The EGP is expressed as a certain percent above the CCX member's baseline emission level during a particular year. For example, the EGP was 3% above a member's baseline emission level during 2005 and 2006. When combined with the emission reduction schedule, then, the EGP allows for the maximum amount of net purchases of CFIs required for compliance to be 6% of each CCX member's emission baseline during 2005 and 7% of its baseline during 2006. In essence, the EGP limits the overall reduction requirements imposed on CCX members because, as a member's emissions increase due to increased output, the maximum reduction a member is required to make is only a certain limited percent over the original reduction schedule.

CCX has allowed European Union Allowances (EUAs) to be used to comply with CCX commitments in calendar year 2005, thus linking CCX with the EU ETS. A CCX member was able to transfer batches of 100 EUAs from its EU allowance account into an account CCX established in an EU registry; the EU allowances were then retired, and CCX issued one CFI for each batch of 100 retired EUAs into the member's CCX Registry Account.

2. Transferring and Trading CFIs

Any CCX member can transfer a CFI to another member or trade through a CCX participant. Each member holds CFIs in a CCX Registry Account that is integrated with the CCX Trading Platform, which is designed to allow a registered user to interact and trade with all other users in a fully electronic format that does not require intervention or assistance from brokers. CCX thus is set up to facilitate trading at low transaction costs. However, CCX imposes some market constraints on the sale and banking of CFIs to ensure that emission mitigation occurs across CCX member facilities and offset system projects, and to prevent market instability and price congestion.

a. Single-Firm Sales Limit

Net sales of CFIs by any single CCX member are limited to a certain percent of the program-wide emissions baseline, apportioned over a period of time according to a schedule established by CCX. This percent can be increased if program-wide emissions rise above baseline levels.

b. Limitation on Banking

Each CCX member is allowed to sell or bank the quantity of CFIs that is the lesser of the quantities determined by the EGP and the single-firm sales limit. CCX members may also bank the amount by which the quantity determined by the EGP exceeds the single-firm sales limit.

3. Monitoring, Recordkeeping, and Reporting

CCX power sector members monitor CO_2 emissions at their electric power–generating units by using CO_2 emissions data from continuous emission monitors (CEMs) as reported to U.S. EPA under 40 C.F.R. Part 75. If CEMs data is not available, those members can quantify CO_2 emissions by using the fuel consumption methods contained in 40 C.F.R. Part 75. CCX electric power sector members may also opt-in SF_6 emissions from electric power transmission equipment, quantified by using protocols provided by U.S. Environmental Protection Agency, and may also opt-in emissions from vehicles they own and operate or lease by using protocols for mobile sources developed by the World Resources Institute/World Business Council for Sustainable Development (WRI/WBCSD) Initiative.

Those CCX members not primarily engaged in electric power production can report GHG emissions as follows:

- CO_2 emissions from stationary source fossil fuel combustion as quantified using the applicable WRI/WBCSD protocols.
- Process emissions as quantified using the applicable WRI/WBCSD protocols.
- Vehicle emissions as quantified using the applicable WRI/WBCSD protocols. (CO_2 emissions from vehicles must be included in a member's commitment if these emissions are greater than 5% of the total entity-wide emissions and represent an integral part of the member's operations. Otherwise, CCX members have the option to include such emissions from vehicles.)
- CCX members in the forest product sector that have wood-harvesting operations quantify and report net changes in carbon stocks (expressed in metric tons of CO_2 equivalent) held in aboveground biomass on land owned by the member or on land for which the member owns carbon sequestration rights. Net declines in carbon stocks will require the member to surrender CFIs in the corresponding amount.

As noted, CCX members can use WRI/WBCSD protocols to evaluate GHG emissions. The WRI/WBCSD established the Greenhouse Gas Protocol Initiative in 1998. The Initiative's mission is to develop internationally accepted GHG accounting and reporting standards and/or protocols. The Initiative has produced two manuals: the *GHG Protocol Corporate Accounting and Reporting Standard (Corporate Standard)*, revised edition published in March 2004, and the *GHG Protocol for Project Accounting (Project Protocol)*, published in November 2005. The Corporate Standard is designed to help companies prepare a GHG inventory that represents an accurate account of their emissions through the use of standardized approaches and principles, and to increase consistency and transparency in GHG accounting and reporting among various GHG programs. The Project Protocol provides specific principles, concepts, and methods for quantifying and reporting GHG reductions from climate change mitigation projects. Both the Corporate Standard and Project Protocol can be reviewed to understand the type of protocols used by CCX to account for and report GHG emissions.[211] For example, CCX uses the WRI/WBCSD GHG Emissions Calculator referenced in the Corporate Standard and found on the GHG Protocol Initiative Web site to measure emissions.[212]

CCX members must submit annual emission reports. Emissions and offset project reports data is subject to verification and audits undertaken by entities approved by CCX.

4. Baseline-Credit Program Rules

CCX allows for CFIs to be generated from projects that mitigate GHGs. As such, it incorporates elements of a baseline-credit program into its cap-and-trade system.

a. Project Eligibility

Eligible GHG mitigation projects will be recorded in the CCX Registry and will be issued CFIs on the basis of how much CO_2 equivalent is mitigated. In general, projects in the specified categories will qualify if they were placed into operation on or after January 1, 1999 (with the exception of forestry projects, which will be eligible if undertaken on or after January 1, 1990). Some offset projects undertaken by CCX members prior to 1999 will be eligible for CEACs under CEAC provisions.

The categories of eligible offset projects already approved by CCX are:

- landfill methane destruction;
- agricultural methane destruction;
- carbon sequestration in forestry projects;
- carbon sequestration in agricultural soils in specified areas of the United States and Canada;
- fuel-switching landfill methane destruction, renewable energy and forestry projects in Brazil;
- renewable energy projects; and
- clean development mechanism projects.

The CCX Standing Committee on Offsets can recommend additions to the list of eligible offset project types and locations.

b. Project Implementation Rules

The CCX eligible projects have set rules that cover how they are to be managed in order to be eligible for CEOs. These rules can be found in specific project eligibility, project baseline, quantification, monitoring and verification protocols, some of which are set forth in the project overviews published on the CCX Web site.[213] CCX relies substantially on CCX-approved verifiers to certify project eligibility and effectiveness by providing an independent third-party review of project reports, maintenance of project activity, and data accuracy.

i. Certified Landfill Offsets (CLOs)

CLOs will be issued to owners of GHG emission reductions achieved by landfill methane collection and combustion systems that are not required to comply with U.S. EPA's new source performance standards. Information required to be submitted includes records of methane content of the recovered gas, the methane destruction efficiency in the control device, total gas flows or total electricity generation, and engine manufacturer's efficiency rating. CLOs will be issued on the basis of tons of methane destroyed, net of CO_2 released upon combustion, at a net rate of 18.25 tons CO_2 for each ton of methane combusted. Under certain conditions, landfill electricity production equipment may earn CLOs on the basis of displaced emissions on the grid.

ii. Certified Agricultural Methane Offsets (CAMOs)

CAMOs will be issued to owners of GHG emission reductions achieved by methane collection and combustion systems such as covered anaerobic digesters, complete-mix and plug-flow digesters. CAMOs will be issued on the basis of tons of methane destroyed, net of CO_2 released upon combustion, at a net rate of 18.25 tons CO_2 for each ton of methane combusted. CAMOs are often managed through an Offset Aggregator who is a CCX-registered entity that serves as an administrative and trading representative on behalf of multiple individual participants.

iii. Certified Forestry Offsets (CFOs)

CFOs will be issued to owners of GHG emission mitigation achieved by qualifying forestry sequestration projects, such as forestation and forest enrichment, combined forestation and forest conservation, and urban tree planting. Forest owners need to provide evidence that all their forest holdings are sustainably managed in the form of certification from CCX-approved third-party verification programs. CFOs will be issued on the basis of increases in tons of CO_2 equivalent carbon storage. CFO projects commit to long-term maintenance of forest carbon stocks, including options such as establishing long-term conservation easements or legal protection through transfer of ownership to recognized conservation entities. A quantity of offsets equal to 20% of all CFOs is held in a CCX forest carbon reserve pool to account for any future catastrophic losses in forest carbon stocks.

iv. Certified Soil Offsets (CSOs)

CSOs originally were only issued to owners of GHG emission mitigation produced by agricultural soil carbon sequestration activities in designated states, counties and parishes in the Midwest, and in Mississippi Delta regions of the United States, but CCX has expanded the range of geographic coverage to additional parts of the United States and Canada. Projects include conservation tillage and grass-planting activities, with a minimum commitment of four years of continuous no-till or low-till practices. In the central United States, farmers who commit to continuous no-till practices will be is-

sued CSOs at a rate of 0.5 metric tons CO_2 per acre per year, and farmers who commit to maintain soil carbon storage realized as a result of grass cover plantings will be issued CSOs at a rate of 0.75 metric tons CO_2 per acre per year. CSOs are often managed through an Offset Aggregator who is a CCX-registered entity that serves as an administrative and trading representative on behalf of multiple individual participants.

v. Certified Emission Reductions in Brazil (CERs)

CERs will be issued to owners of GHG mitigation produced by qualifying projects undertaken in Brazil. Qualifying projects will include:

- reforestation and/or forest regeneration;
- avoided deforestation together with reforestation and/or assisted forest regeneration;
- fuel switching;
- landfill methane destruction; and
- renewable energy generation.

vi. Renewable Energy Projects

Certain renewable energy systems such as wind, solar, hydropower, and biofuel can be awarded CFI offsets on the basis of displacing CO_2 emissions from grid-supplied power. For systems that displace electricity, CFIs are issued at a rate of 0.40 metric tons of CO_2 per megawatt hour. To be eligible for CFI offsets, the environmental attributes associated with the renew-

able energy system cannot be used to meet any state or local obligations, such as renewable portfolio standards; the energy generated by the renewable energy system cannot be sold as "green"; and any renewable energy credits generated by the renewable energy system must be retired by CCX.

vii. Clean Development Mechanism Projects

CCX will accept as CFI offsets any Certified Emission Reductions generated under the Clean Development Mechanism system established under the Kyoto Protocol.

c. Certified Early Action Credits

CEACs will be issued to certain projects undertaken from 1995 to 1998. To qualify, reductions must be:

- off system,
- originally undertaken or financed by CCX members,
- direct emissions reductions or involve sequestration,

- clearly owned by the CCX member,
- measured and verifiable, and
- registered in 1605b,[214] USIJI[215] or an equivalent registry system.

CEACs can be used for compliance only by the CCX member that originally owned them. CEACs will be given to project types that meet the eligibility criteria, such as reforestation, afforestation and avoided deforestation, landfill methane destruction in the United States, fuel switching, and other energy-related USIJI projects.

d. Limits on Use of XOs and CEACs

Use of XOs and CEACs for compliance are allowed in an amount equal to a certain percentage of the total program-wide baseline emissions apportioned over a certain time period as determined by CCX rules. The total program-wide quantity of CEACs used for compliance over a certain time period will not exceed 50% of the total quantity of XOs plus CEACs used for compliance. Use of XOs and CEACs for compliance can be escalated if program-wide emissions rise above program-wide baseline emission levels. In addition, CCX limits the amount of XOs that a CCX member can use for compliance at its own facility.

VIII. Eligibility of U.S. Companies Participating in U.S. Emissions Trading Programs for Kyoto Protocol CERs or ERUs

The Kyoto Protocol only recognizes emission allowances and credits created pursuant to its provisions, and does not allow Kyoto Protocol parties to use non-Kyoto Protocol credits to comply with their emission targets. Because the United States is not a party to the Kyoto Protocol, emission reductions by U.S. companies that have been certified and verified under a U.S.-based emissions trading program such as RGGI or CCX are not a recognized commodity under the Protocol, and thus those companies cannot receive CERs or ERUs for the emission reductions. If the United States were to adopt a formal emissions trading program and join the Kyoto Protocol as a party, the credits a company received for participating in RGGI or CCX could someday be considered CERs or ERUs (or the functional equivalent) as a type of early reduction credit. However, for U.S. companies to receive Kyoto Protocol credit now for reducing emissions pursuant to a regional or voluntary U.S. emissions trading program, Kyoto Protocol parties would have to amend the Protocol. Such an amendment would likely require the U.S. trading systems to be generally compatible with the Kyoto Protocol.

Thus, although participating in a trading system such as RGGI and CCX will not currently allow the company to receive CERs or ERUs, it is conceivable that credits generated under RGGI or CCX could be recognized under the Kyoto Protocol in the future. The best way for a U.S. company to maximize the likelihood that emission reductions now will someday be certifiable under the Kyoto Protocol would be to use accounting and reporting protocols recognized by international trading systems. Good examples of generally accepted protocols are those set out in the WRI/WBCSD Greenhouse Gas Protocol Initiative. In fact, the Initiative's Corporate Standard is specifically designed to enable a company to participate in mandatory GHG-reporting programs, to participate in GHG markets, and to have early voluntary emission reductions accounted for and recognized. The Initiative's Project Protocol is specifically designed to enable a company to undertake a GHG project to generate officially recognized reduction credits for use in meeting mandatory emission targets and obtain recognition for GHG reductions under voluntary programs. As discussed earlier, some Initiative protocols such as measuring GHG emissions have already been adopted by CCX, and the Initiative has been broadly adopted and accepted around the world by businesses, governments and nongovernmental organizations. Using the Initiative's protocols would be a good way for a company to attempt to integrate its participation in a U.S. regional or voluntary emissions trading system with the Kyoto Protocol.

IX. Contracting Transactions in GHG Credit Trading

The nature of a free market trading system inherently raises issues of how parties arrange for and accomplish trades and transfers. While working through a broker or buying and selling commodities on an exchange is comparatively easier than direct trading or transferring without assistance, traders must be able to interact in order to form a transaction. Hence, contracting, like in any other sale of goods transaction, is a useful tool in accomplishing the goals of emissions trading. While there is no set structure to a greenhouse gas-trading contract, there are several items that are common to most. Because many of the transactions are international in scope, special attention must be given to the intricacies of such deals. This final portion of the chapter will provide some basic information in drafting and executing emission-trading contracts. While not designed to be an exhaustive source, it will point out the scope and common terms of trading contracts as well as point to locations of model contracts for further investigation.

A. The Necessity of Contracting in GHG Deals

As addressed at the beginning of this chapter, there are two types of emission-trading systems within a free-market scheme. Both baseline-credit and cap-and-trade programs have their own advantages and disadvantages. But, because of the nature of credit creation and ultimate sale into the market, the issue of contracting is better suited to baseline-credit. However, given the possible involvement of third parties who are not signatories to a cap-and-trade system, contracting may still play a role in those transactions as well.

Contracting is already under way in the United States for the sulfur dioxide (SO_2) and nitrogen oxide (NO_x) trading programs. While not widespread, the Clean Air Act allows for trading, and some emitters in the United States are beginning to take advantage of the system. While operating on a smaller scale than global GHG emissions and trading, these domestic traders use contracting to establish the bounds of the transactions. And in fact, current prices of SO_2 and NO_x indicate a more robust, if not widespread, market than GHG counterparts. For comparison, on November 12, 2006, as reported by Evolution Markets and the Chicago Climate Exchange, prices for one ton of SO_2, NO_x, and CO_2 were trading at approximately \$490, \$1,000, and \$4.00 per ton, respectively.[216]

As with most other transactions, contracts for emission credits or allowances can take several forms depending on the needs of the parties. In GHG trading specifically, two forms of contracts operate in overlapping and dependent forms. First, the "derivative contract" is the standard credit or allowance for a set price arrangement.[217] These contracts are commonly used to hedge against higher future costs of carbon and to manage future economic expectations, such as increased costs of electricity. Derivative contracts can be for future transactions (obligations to conduct a future transaction at a set price) or "spot trades" (transactions that occur within 3-5 days), and can include option terms (where a buyer pays a premium for the option, but not the obligation, to conduct a future trade or transfer) to address market volatility.[218] Other avenues for delivery or price terms include "forward settlements," which assure continuing streams of allowances or credits over the course of time as well as options on a futures contract,[219] which are available only through an organized futures exchange in conjunction with a broker.[220] Hybrid arrangements are also available, and are commonly used when addressing emission reduction credits generated from CDM or JI projects.[221]

Second, "master agreements" are being developed to streamline the process for negotiating derivative agreements.[222] Master agreements, created under individual GHG-trading systems, set forth the legal relationships between parties to derivative agreements, define common terms to the specific trading scheme at issue, and are useful for increasing transaction efficiency.[223] Master agreements generally include the governed derivative agreements as attachments to create a better connection between the two.[224] As such, potential traders should be aware of any master agreement that may exist in the market in question. After selecting the basic form of the contract, parties must agree to the individual terms. A brief discussion of the common terms and clauses in GHG contracts follows.

B. Contracting Terms and Conditions

While there is no single uniform contract in GHG trading, a few trade groups created model contracts through which several commonalities can be drawn.[225]

In many ways, GHG contracts are very similar to common goods and services contracts that are prevalent throughout any market. Of note, the following provisions are included in most, if not all, model emissions trading contracts:

- *Key actions to take under the contract.* These terms set forth the timeline for actions to be taken under the contract as well as timing for performance and payment. Key actions include price terms, delivery dates, credit or allowance amounts, and delivery methods, as well as other actions and commitments required under the agreement.

Master agreements . . . set forth the legal relationships between parties to derivative agreements, define common terms to the specific trading scheme at issue, and are useful for increasing transaction efficiency.

- *Key defined terms.* Because emissions trading is a field that involves unique terms or cross-border agreements, a lengthy definition section is generally included to avoid confusion later in the transaction. These sections are particularly important in international transactions, and key terms may have different meanings depending on the country or culture. Examples of the types of unique terms common throughout emissions contracting include: call options, collars, strangle, and strike price. Furthermore, contracts may also set forth the terms that would normally be expected in more traditional contracts, including the allowance or credit to be transferred or traded, the currency the agreement is operating under, events constituting default, baseline terms for CDM and JI agreements, and the valid GHGs that may be traded under the agreement.

- *Dispute resolution/choice of laws.* While more important in cross-border trading, dispute resolution and choice of laws clauses, like in any contract, can serve to avoid costly litigation should the transaction break down. Dispute resolution can include negotiation and arbitration either between the parties or through neutral third parties. Choice of laws provisions help to resolve confusion concerning the governing jurisdiction in advance of any dispute that may arise. As might be expected, the selection of one jurisdiction's law to govern the agreement over another could impact the structure or terms throughout the contract. For international transactions especially, it is important to become familiar with the legal structure surrounding contracts and emissions trading from both nations to avoid any unnecessary legal complications at both the negotiation and execution stages. It is also important to know if a nation has a treaty in place for enforcing foreign judgments. Without such an agreement in place between nations, a nation is under no obligation to enforce a judgment against one of its citizens from a foreign court.

- *Certification provisions.* Especially with Joint Implementation or Clean Development Mechanism projects, certification of the produced GHG credits is essential to marketability. The speculative nature of CERs and ERUs call for increased protection against events such as the credit not being certified or not being produced. As such, traders may want to condition the sale of any CDM or JI credits on certification or adjust price terms appropriately.

- *Force majeure and warranties.* Clauses covering *force majeure* account for unanticipated events, legal impossibilities, and changed circumstances that may put an otherwise valid transaction in jeopardy. These terms are standard throughout many goods and service contracts in the United States, and inclusion of these sections should not be an unexpected occurrence. Additionally, warranty clauses help to define the expectations and authority each party brings to the agreement. Like choice of laws provisions, these warranties will help to shape the structure of the contract and the expectations of the parties, as well as more substantive terms such as price and quantity.

- *Telephone confirmation and recording phone calls.* While not necessary to the nature of trading GHG credits and allowances per se, many model contracts include provisions on confirmation and recording in order to simplify the negotiation process, especially for international/long-distance transactions. And, in some cases, telephone confirmation conditions are necessary due to provisions in the governing master agreement setting forth time limits for responses and counteroffers during negotiations.[226]

- *Other transactional considerations.* Various trade groups identify additional terms that are worth considering when contracting for emissions credits and allowances. Examples of these terms include nonstandard transfers and payment considerations (i.e., payment before or after delivery of the credits or allowances, rather than at delivery), terms defining default, and recourse in the event of default.

As can be seen, emissions trading contracts have the potential to be exceedingly long and complex. However, with proper planning and clear communication, a well-drafted contract will avoid unnecessary disagreements further along in the transaction.

C. Brokers[227]

As mentioned above, the other option associated with contracting is the use of brokers to facilitate the trades. Brokers are simply "middlemen" to parties looking to buy and sell emission credits and allowances, and simplify the process by bridging the gap between traders. They are directly involved with the trading systems at issue and, while they do not always conduct transactions on behalf of clients, they use their resources and experience to simplify transactions, especially for new or infrequent

traders. In this way, emission brokers act much like commercial traders in the United States. And while each broker has its own set of rules as to who may make trades, most are generally open to involvement by anyone. However, like other types of brokers, there are fees and commissions associated with emission-trading brokers. Additionally, there is less opportunity for direct market access by the party who hired the broker. Consequently, there may be less opportunity to control the specifics of a transaction. A potential trader must evaluate the specific advantages and disadvantages in determining whether to use a broker.

When entering the realm of emissions trading, care must be taken to avoid unnecessary complications in completing the transactions. Especially given the high propensity for international involvement, traders must have familiarity with both contracting terms and local laws governing the transactions. For those who plan on entering the systems available, an understanding of the contracting structure associated with trading is essential.

X. Conclusion

The practicing environmental lawyer can draw several conclusions from the above review of existing GHG emission-trading programs. First, GHG trading is an up-and-running part of the environmental regulatory structure that creates important opportunities and risks for clients. American environmental lawyers need to understand this area today, not at some distant time in the future. Second, the GHG-trading area is not all that different from other parts of environmental regulatory practice. Each GHG-trading program has its own terminology and is governed by its own set of rules and procedures. Each promises to create its own regulatory framework and body of regulatory guidance. Environmental attorneys have work to do in understanding these rules and interpreting them for private, governmental and NGO clients. Finally, the programs profiled here each provide opportunities for businesses and other emitters to think creatively about how to reduce their GHG footprint. Participation in GHG-trading initiatives should lower the cost of achieving meaningful GHG reductions and so has the potential to contribute to climate stabilization.

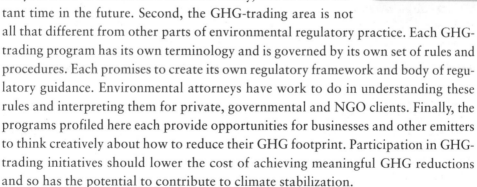

Endnotes

1.   *See generally* Rutger de Witt Wijnen, *Emissions Trading Under Article 17 of the Kyoto Protocol*, *in* LEGAL ASPECTS OF IMPLEMENTING THE KYOTO PROTOCOL MECHANISMS: MAKING KYOTO WORK (David Freestone & Charlotte Streck eds., 2005) (helpful book chapter elaborating on this distinction).
2.   ROBERT V. PERCIVAL, CHRISTOPHER H. SCHROEDER, ALAN S. MILLER & JAMES P. LEAPE, ENVIRONMENTAL REGULATION: LAW, SCIENCE AND POLICY 544 (4th ed., 2003).

3.   *Id.* at 546.

4.   U.S. EPA Office of Air Quality Planning and Standards, *New Source Review Workshop Manual* G.6 (October 1990); *accord* ROY S. BELDEN, CLEAN AIR ACT 52 (2001); U.S. EPA, *Emissions Trading Policy*, 51 Fed. Reg. 43,814, 43,831 (1986).

5.   UN Framework Convention on Climate Change, May 9, 1992, S. TREATY DOC. No. 102-38 (1992), 1771 UNTS 108, *reprinted in* 31 ILM 849 (1992) [hereinafter UNFCCC]. The UNFCCC, the Kyoto Protocol and many of the other UNFCC documents discussed in this chapter are available online *at* http://unfccc.int.

6.   Kyoto Protocol to the UN Framework Convention on Climate Change, Dec. 10, 1997, UN DOC. FCCC/CP/1997/7/Add.2, *reprinted in* 37 ILM 22 (1998) [hereinafter Kyoto Protocol].

7.   An individual nation could decide to focus its emission reduction obligations on one or more industrial sectors, effectively turning this economy-wide system into a sector-based one. Given that the EU ETS is based on meeting Kyoto Protocol Targets, and that it does this by assigning obligations to specific, covered sectors, it might be said to represent a sector-based approach.

8.   *See* Report of the Conference of the Parties on Its Seventh Session, Held at Marrakesh from 29 October to 10 November 2001, U.N. Framework Convention on Climate Change, 7th Sess., Add., Vol. II, Dec. 15/CP.7, Draft Decision, ¶ 6 [hereinafter Marrakesh Accords].

9.   Wijnen, *supra* note 1, at 410.

10.   Kyoto Protocol, *supra* note 6, Art. 17.

11.   Marrakesh Accords, *supra* note 8, Dec. 18/CP.7, Annex, ¶ 2 (IET).

12.   *Id.,* Dec. 19/CP.7.

13.   *Id.,* Dec. 18/CP.7, Annex ¶ 5.

14.   *Id.,* Dec. 18/CP.7, Annex, ¶¶ 6, 7.

15.   *Id.* ¶ 6.

16.   Marrakesh Accords, *supra* note 8, Dec. 15/CP.7, Draft Decision, ¶ 1.

17.   *Id.,* Dec. 18/CP.7, Annex, ¶ 5.

18.   *Id.*

19.   *Id.,* Dec. 18/CP.7, ¶ 4.

20.   *See, e.g.,* Kyoto Protocol, *supra* note 6, Art. 17 (limiting IET to "Parties included in Annex I"); Marrakesh Accords, *supra* note 8, Dec. 18/CP.7, Annex, ¶ 2 (same).

21.   Marrakesh Accords, *supra* note 8, Dec. 18/CP.7, Annex, ¶ 5.

22.   *See, e.g.,* Martijn Wilder, *Can Companies or Entities from a Non-Party to the Kyoto Protocol Participate in the Flexible Mechanisms?, in* Freestone & Streck, *supra* note 1 at 249, 252 (useful book chapter covering this topic in some depth); Wijnen, *supra* note 1, at 412.

23.   Wilder, *supra* note 22, at 255.

24.   *Id.* at 250.

25.   *Id.* at 258.

26.   *Id.*

27.   *Id.* at 254.

28.   *Id.* at 255, *citing* Paul Fauteaux, Director General, Climate Change Bureau Environment Canada, *Party/Non-Party Emissions Trading: Compatibility Now, Convergence Later?* (Notes for a presentation), http://www.ieta.org/About_IETA/IETA_Activities/SBTA16/Fauteux.doc.

29.   Wilder, *supra* note 22, at 250.

30.   *Id.* at 258.

31.   *Id.* at 260-61.

32.   *Id.* at 261.

33. For the distinction between the "transfer" and the "trade" of Kyoto Units, *see supra* note 1 and accompanying text.

34. Wijnen, *supra* note 1, at 410.

35. Marrakesh Accords, *supra* note 8, Dec. 17/CP.7, Annex, ¶ 30.

36. Marrakesh Accords, *supra* note 8, Dec. 19/CP.7, Annex, ¶ 15.

37. Kyoto Protocol, *supra* note 6, Art. 12(2), (3); Marrakesh Accords, *supra* note 8, Dec. 17/CP.7, Annex, ¶¶ 30, 31.

38. *Id.*, Dec. 17/CP.7, Annex, ¶ 29; FARHANA YAMIN & JOANNA DEPLEDGE, THE INTERNATIONAL CLIMATE CHANGE REGIME, A GUIDE TO RULES, INSTITUTIONS AND PROCEDURES 150 (2004) (helpful and comprehensive treatise).

39. Marrakesh Accords, *supra* note 8, Dec. 17/CP.7, Annex, ¶ 30; YAMIN & DEPLEDGE, *supra* note 38, at 149.

40. *See supra* notes 11-12 and accompanying text; Marrakesh Accords, *supra* note 8, Dec. 17/CP.7, Annex, ¶ 31.

41. *Id.*, Dec. 17/CP.7, ¶ 33.

42. CDM Executive Board Glossary (defining "project participants" as "either a Party involved or . . . a private and/or public entity authorized by a Party to participate, under the Party's responsibility, in CDM project activities").

43. Kyoto Protocol, *supra* note 6, Art. 12(9); Marrakesh Accords, *supra* note 8, Dec. 17/CP.7, ¶ 33.

44. Wilder, *supra* note 22, at 252.

45. *See supra* note 23 and accompanying text; Wilder, *supra* note 22.

46. Netherlands Ministry of Housing, Spatial Planning and Development, Clean Development Mechanism Approval Criteria, *available at* http://www2.vrom.nl/pagina.html?id=9716 (last visited Oct. 25, 2006).

47. *See* Foreign Affairs Canada, Environmental and Sustainable Development Affairs Bureau, Letter of Approval of Voluntary Participation in a CDM Project (May 5, 2005) (approving AgCert Canada, a subsidiary of an American company, for participation in a CDM project).

48. *See, e.g.,* Pacific Hydro Limited, Press Release: Pacific Hydro Negotiates Bank-Intermediated Carbon Credit Contract (June 6, 2005), *available at* http://www.pacifichydro.com.au/docs/0505_CER_trade_releas.pdf (describing generation and transfer of CERs by Fijian company of which Australian firm is a co-owner).

49. Wilder, *supra* note 22, at 254.

50. *Id.;* Marrakesh Accords, *supra* note 9, Dec. 17/CP.7, Annex, ¶ 7.

51. Wilder, *supra* note 22, at 254.

52. *Id.*

53. Marrakesh Accords, *supra* note 8, Dec. 17/CP.7, ¶ 1.

54. Kyoto Protocol, Art. 12(10).

55. Discussed below at notes 93-126 and accompanying text.

56. Marrakesh Accords, *supra* note 8, Preamble to Decision 17/CP.7; YAMIN & DEPLEDGE, *supra* note 38, at 175.

57. *Id.*

58. Marrakesh Accords, *supra* note 8, Dec. 17/CP.7, ¶ 7(a).

59. *Id.* ¶ 7(b). This number is to be multiplied by five for the five-year commitment period.

60. *Id. ¶* 7(c).

61. Marrakesh Accords, *supra* note 8, Dec. 17/CP.7, Annex, ¶ 37(b).

62. *Id.* ¶¶ 40(b)-(d).

63. *Id.* ¶¶ 40(g), 62(h).

64. Marrakesh Accords, *supra* note 8, Dec. 17/CP.7, Appx. B.

65. *See id*, Annex, ¶ 37 (setting out these standards).

66. YAMIN & DEPLEDGE, *supra* note 38, at 177.

67. Marrakesh Accords, *supra* note 8, Dec. 17/CP.7, Annex, ¶¶ 44-48.

68. *Id.* ¶ 44.

69. *Id.* ¶ 45.

70. *Id.* ¶ 46.

71. *Id.* ¶ 47.

72. *Id.* ¶ 48.

73. *Id.*, Appx. C.

74. Marrakesh Accords, *supra* note 8, Dec. 17/CP.7, Annex, ¶ 53.

75. *Id.*

76. *Id.* ¶ 54.

77. *See* http://cdm.unfccc.int/methodologies/PAmethodologies (visited May 24, 2006).

78. http://cdm.unfccc.int/methodologies/PAmethodologies/Clarifications (visited May 24, 2006).

79. Marrakesh Accords, *supra* note 8, Dec. 17/CP.7, Annex, ¶ 53.

80. Kyoto Protocol, *supra* note 6, Art. 12(5)(c).

81. *See supra* note 4 and accompanying text.

82. Marrakesh Accords, *supra* note 8, Dec. 17/CP.7, Annex, ¶ 43.

83. CDM Executive Board, *Tool for the Demonstration and Assessment of Additionality* (version 2) (Nov. 28, 2005), *available at* http://cdm.unfccc.int/methodologies/ PAmethodologies/approved.html.

84. *Id.* at 2.

85. *Id.* at 3.

86. *Id.* at 5.

87. *Id.* at 6.

88. *Id.* at 7.

89. Marrakesh Accords, *supra* note 8, Dec. 17/CP.7, Annex, ¶ 53(c).

90. *Id. ¶* 51.

91. *Id.* ¶¶ 50, 59, 62(f).

92. Kyoto Protocol, *supra* note 6, Arts. 6(1), 3(1), (11); *see generally* Charlotte Streck, *Joint Implementation: History, Requirements, and Challenges, in* LEGAL ASPECTS OF IMPLEMENTING THE KYOTO PROTOCOL MECHANISMS: MAKING KYOTO WORK 107-26 (David Freestone & Charlotte Streck eds., 2005) (useful chapter describing JI program).

93. *See supra* notes 35-36 and accompanying text.

94. *See* Chapter 2, *supra*.

95. Kyoto Protocol, *supra* note 6, Art. 6(1).

96. Marrakesh Accords, *supra* note 8, Dec. 19/CP.7, ¶ 15(a).

97. Kyoto Protocol, *supra* note 6, Arts. 3(1), (11) & 6(1).

98. Marrakesh Accords, *supra* note 8, Dec. 16/CP.7, Annex, ¶ 21 (setting forth these requirements in reference to the JI program).

99. *See supra* notes 11-12 and accompanying text.

100. DEBORAH STOWELL, CLIMATE TRADING: DEVELOPMENT OF GREENHOUSE GAS MARKETS 60 (2005). The only exception to this is the Track II JI mechanism (discussed below) under which Annex I Parties can transfer ERU even if they only meet some of the eligibility requirements so long as there is proper international supervision. *See* YAMIN & DEPLEDGE, *supra* note 38, at 194.

101. Kyoto Protocol, *supra* note 6, Art. 6(1)(d).

102. Marrakesh Accords, *supra* note 8, Dec. 16/CP.7, Annex, ¶¶ 29, 33(a).

103. *See supra* notes 11-12 and accompanying text.

104. Kyoto Protocol, *supra* note 6, Art 6(1).

105. *Id.,* Art. 6(3).

106. Wilder, *supra* note 22, at 250.

107. *See supra* note 53 and accompanying text.

108. Marrakesh Accords, *supra* note 8, Dec. 16/CP.7, Draft Decision -/CMP.1, ¶ 5. This limitation poses an obstacle for those JI projects that would not be sufficiently profitable if they had to wait until 2008 to begin generating ERU. This has led some parties to experiment with "early crediting" in which a host nation with surplus AAUs transfers some of them through the IET system to cover emission reductions generated before 2008 by a potential JI project in their country. After 2008, the project begins to generate ERU and these are transferred instead. Streck, *supra* note 92, at 121.

109. Yamin & Depledge, *supra* note 38, at 196.

110. Kyoto Protocol, *supra* note 6, Art. 6(1) (emission reduction units result from "enhancing anthropogenic removals by sinks").

111. Marrakesh Accords, *supra* note 8, Dec. 16/CP.7, Draft decision -/CMP.1, ¶ 4. For additional information on the rules governing sinks projects, see the decisions reached at COP-9, which defined the modalities for incorporating such projects into the Kyoto Flexibility Mechanisms.

112. To meet these requirements, they must be a party to the Protocol, have properly calculated and recorded their assigned amounts, have in place national system for the estimation of GHG emissions and removals, have in place a national registry, have submitted accurate annual inventories of GHG emissions and sinks, and have submitted the supplementary information on assigned amounts and made any necessary adjustments to its assigned amounts. *See* Marrakesh Accords, *supra* note 8, Dec. 16/CP.7, Annex, ¶21; Conference of the Parties serving as the meeting of the Parties under the Kyoto Protocol (COP/MOP), Guidelines for the Implementation of Article 6 of the Kyoto Protocol, Annex, ¶¶ 21, 23 [hereinafter Article 6 Guidelines, Annex].

113. Marrakesh Accords, *supra* note 8, Dec. 16/CP.7, Annex, ¶ 24. Before it can transfer ERU, however, the host party must at least meet three core eligibility criteria: it must be a party to the Protocol, have a properly calculated and recorded assigned amount, and have a national registry in place. *Id.* ¶ 24. Host parties that meet all six eligibility criteria may still elect to use the Track 2 verification procedure. *Id.* ¶ 25. They may do so because they believe that ERU that have gone through this more rigorous verification process will have greater market value.

114. *Id.,* Dec. 16/CP.7, Annex, Section E (describing verification procedure).

115. *Id.* ¶ 33.

116. *Id.* ¶ 37.

117. *Id.* ¶¶ 34 (first determination), 38 (second determination).

118. For the accreditation standards and procedures *see id.,* Appx. A.

119. *Id.,* Section C (describing makeup and functions of the Supervisory Committee), ¶ 35 (review of first determination), ¶ 39 (review of second determination).

120. At its first meeting, the JI Supervisory Committee agreed to open a call for public input with regard to the development of guidance on the criteria for baseline setting and monitoring. The initial deadline for such input was March 1, 2006. Information on this and other actions of the Supervisory Committee is available at the UNFCCC's JI homepage, http://ji.unfccc.int/.

121. Those looking for early insight into how the JI program is likely to develop should be able to draw some lessons from the CDM Executive Board Methodologies Panel's guidance on baselines and monitoring. Streck, *supra* note 92, at 116. In fact, the Marrakesh Accords instruct the JI Supervisory Committee to "giv[e] consideration" to the work of the CDM Executive Board (CDM EB) when setting criteria for baselines and monitoring. Marrakesh Accords, *supra* note 8, Dec. 16/CP.7, Annex, ¶ 3(d). The CDM EB's work is therefore likely to influence the JI Supervisory Committee's efforts in these areas. As was mentioned above, *see supra* notes 73-74 and accompanying text, the CDM Executive Board has set up a Methodologies Panel to assess and approve baseline and monitoring methodologies. Information on these assessments can be found at the Panel's Web site, http://cdm.unfcc.int/EB/Panels/meth.

122. Marrakesh Accords, *supra* note 8, Dec. 16/CP.7, Annex, ¶ 33.

123. *Id.* Appx. B, ¶ 2.

124. *Id.* Appx. B, ¶ 4.

125. Kyoto Protocol, *supra* note 6, Art. 6(1)(b); Marrakesh Accords, *supra* note 8, Dec. 16/CP.7, Annex, ¶ 31(b).

126. Council Directive 2003/87/EC, establishing a scheme for greenhouse gas emission allowance trading within the Community and amending Council Directive 96/61/EC.

127. EU COMMISSION, EU ACTION AGAINST CLIMATE CHANGE: EU EMISSIONS TRADING—AN OPEN SCHEME PROMOTING GLOBAL INNOVATION (2005). The EU is committed to reducing GHG emissions community-wide from 1990 levels by 8% by 2012. By way of illustration, Germany and the United Kingdom must reduce their GHG emissions by 21% and 12.5%, respectively, from 1990 levels, while Spain and Portugal can increase their GHG emissions by as much as 15% and 27%, respectively. *Id.*

128. JOHN GRUMMER & ROBERT MORELAND, THE EUROPEAN UNION & GLOBAL CLIMATE CHANGE: A REVIEW OF FIVE NATIONAL PROGRAMMES (2000).

129. Council Directive 2003/87/EC, establishing a scheme for greenhouse gas emission allowance trading within the Community and amending Council Directive 96/61/EC (hereinafter ETS Directive); *see also* Chapter 2, *supra*.

130. *Supra* beginning of chapter.

131. *Supra* beginning of chapter; Council Directive 2004/101/EC, amending Directive 2003/87/EC, establishing a scheme for greenhouse gas emission allowance trading within the Community, in respect of Kyoto Protocol's project mechanisms (hereinafter Linking Directive).

132. *Id.* Some narrowing of JI and CDM occurs through Linking Directive. For example, land use and forestry projects are not permitted for use as JI or CDM projects in the ETS. *Id.* However, a recent meeting among EU member states indicates that forestry projects may be viable sources for CDM projects in the next trading period. While no formal action has been taken by the EU, countries including the United Kingdom, France, the Netherlands, and Spain are actively discussing such options. The group ClimateFocus has also proposed an amendment to the Linking Directive to reflect forestry projects for use in CDM projects. *See* Ecosystem Marketplace Opinion, *Using Forest Carbon Credits in the EU ETS*, http://ecosystemmarketplace.com/pages/article.opinion.php? component_id=4271&component_version_id=6141&language_id=12 (last visited 4/26/2006); ClimateFocus, *Amendments to the EU ETS to Recognize LULUCF*, http://www.ecosystemmarketplace.com/documents/word/CharlotteStreckDownload.doc (last visited 4/26/2006).

133. It is important to note that in the first allocation period, only CO_2 is regulated by the ETS.

134. See Freestone & Streck, *supra* note 1, at 419-20.

135. Council Directive 2003/87/EC, establishing a scheme for greenhouse gas emission allowance trading within the Community and amending Council Directive 96/61/EC.

136. *Id.*

137. *See, e.g.,* DEP'T FOR ENVIRONMENT, FOOD, AND RURAL AFFAIRS (United Kingdom), *EU Emissions Trading Scheme: Approved National Allocation Plan 2005-2007* (2005). "Participants" are those actors that emit greenhouse gases and must receive allowances in order to meet emissions requirements. *See* ETS Directive *supra* note 129.

138. ETS Directive, *supra* note 129.

139. DEP'T FOR ENVIRONMENT, FOOD, AND RURAL AFFAIRS, *supra* note 137.

140. FEDERAL MINISTRY FOR THE ENVIRONMENT, NATURE CONSERVATION AND NUCLEAR SAFETY, NATIONAL ALLOCATION PLAN FOR THE FEDERAL REPUBLIC OF GERMANY 2005-2007 (2004). The term "phase" is commonly used throughout the ETS to refer to the trading period at issue. There are two phases currently envisioned under the ETS system. The first phase is ongoing, and is designed to be a "learning curve" for emissions trading. The second phase coincides with the first Kyoto commitment period.

141. ETS Directive *supra* note 129.

142. *See, e.g., id.*

143. *Id.* Furthermore, given May 2006 developments, there is concern over the number of allowances available now and going forward. See *infra* note 178 and accompanying text.

144. *Id.*

145. *Id.* (stating, "Member States may issues allowances to persons for the current period to replace any allowances held by them which are cancelled [under the rules of the Directive].").

146. ETS Directive, *supra* note 129.

147. European Union, *EU Citizenship*, http://europa.eu.int/youreurope/nav/en/citizens/factsheets/eu/eucitizenship/eucitizenship/en.html (last visited 4/26/2006); *see* Streck, *supra* note 1; Treaty of Maastricht 1992, Title II (G)(2)(8).

148. ETS Directive, *supra* note 129 ("person" means "any natural or legal person").

149. Most NAPs are silent or provide no participation limitations, but some, such as the Netherlands and Ireland, expressly allow for "non-participants," i.e., those not obligated to join the ETS, to engage in trading. *See Allocation plan for CO_2 emissions allowances 2005-2007: Dutch national allocation plan regarding the allocation of greenhouse gas emission allowances to companies* (2004); Environmental Protection Agency, *Ireland's National Allocation Plan 2005-2007: 2nd Public Consultation* (2004).

150. Commission Regulation (EC) No. 2216/2004 for a standardized and secured system of registries pursuant to Directive 2003/87/EC of the European Parliament and of the Council and Decisions No. 280/2004/EC of the European Parliament and the Council (hereinafter Registry Regulation). There are, in reality, more than these two accounts; however, for the purposes of day-to-day transfer concepts, the person holding the account and operator account are the most important. For further information concerning the party account, retirement account, and cancellation account, see *id.*

151. Registry Regulation, *supra* note 150.

152. *See, e.g., Terms and Conditions for the Information System of the Registry for Greenhouse Gas Emission Allowance Trading* (Slovakia) (2005). There are some exceptions, including in Denmark, where non-emitters may purchase allocations at the initial allowances auction. Ministry of the Environment, *Danish National Allocation Plan* (2004).

153. Emission Certificate Registry, Austria, *Guidelines for the Use of the Registry 2005 to 2007* (unknown).

154. European Commission, *EU Action Against Climate Change* (2005).

155. *Id.*

156. Emission Certificate Registry, Austria, *Guidelines for the Use of the Registry 2005 to 2007* (unknown).

157. For further information on these organizations, *see* www.europeanclimateexchange.com, www.evomarkets.com, and www.ecosystemmarketplace.com.

158. Emission Certificate Registry, Austria, *Guidelines for the Use of the Registry 2005 to 2007* (unknown).

159. International Emissions Trading Ass'n, *Greenhouse Gas Market 2004: ready for take-off* (unknown).

160. ETS Directive, *supra* note 129, at Arts. 11 and 19.

161. ETS Directive, *supra* note 130.

162. *Cleaning up; Carbon trading*, THE ECONOMIST (May 6, 2006), *available at* http://www6.lexisnexis.com/publisher/EndUser?Action=UserDisplayFullDocument&orgId=1925&topicId=100002042&docId=l:382446644&start=2 (last visited May 10, 2006). However, see below on recent market developments.

163. *Allocation plan for CO$_2$ emissions allowances 2005-2007: Dutch national allocation plan regarding the allocation of greenhouse gas emission allowances to companies (*2004) (stating "Anyone may participate in emissions trading, even persons and companies who are not obliged to comply with the emission standard.").

164. There are some exceptions, including in Denmark, where non-emitters may purchase allocations at the initial allowances auction. Ministry of the Environment, *Danish National Allocation Plan* (2004).

165. Linking Directive, *supra* note 131.

166. PAUL CRAIG & GRAINNE DE BURCA, EU LAW TEXT, CASES, AND MATERIALS (2d ed. 1998). *See also* footnote 134 et seq., *supra*.

167. *See* http://www.europeanclimateexchange.com/ and http://www.evomarkets.com/ for more information on these two brokers.

168. Linking Directive, *supra* note 131.

169. *Supra* earlier in chapter.

170. Council Directive 2004/101/EC, amending Directive 2003/87/EC, establishing a scheme for greenhouse gas emission allowance trading within the Community in respect of Kyoto Protocol's project mechanisms (defining an acceptable CDM or JI project as only those "approved by one or more Annex I parties.").

171. See *supra* notes 43-48 and accompanying text.

172. Linking Directive, *supra* note 131.

173. European Commission, Directorate General for the Environment, *Further Guidance on allocation plans for the 2008 to 2012 trading period of the EU Emissions Trading Scheme, in* REVIEW OF EU EMISSIONS TRADING SCHEME: SURVEY HIGHLIGHTS (2005).

174. However, as of November 12, 2006, seven EU member states had not submitted their revised NAPs to the European Commission, although efforts are ongoing. It is expected that some NAPs may not receive Commission approval until possibly February 2006. *EU Unlikely to Sue States Over CO$_2$ Plans*, PLANETARK WORLD ENV'T NEWS (Aug. 3, 2006), *available at* http://www.planetark.org/avantgo/dailynewsstroy.cfm?newsid=37503 (last visited on Aug. 10, 2006); *National Allocation Plans for 2008*

to 2012 notified to the Commission, available at http://ec.europa.eu/environment/climat/2nd_phase_ep.htm (last visited on Nov. 12, 2006).

175. European Commission, *Questions and Answers on national allocation plans for 2008-2012* (Jan. 9, 2006), http://europa.eu.int/rapid/pressReleasesAction.do?reference=MEMO/0 6 / 2&format=HTML&aged=0&language=EN&guiLanguage=en (last visited on April 20, 2006).

176. *Further Guidance on allocation plans for the 2008 to 2012 trading period of the EU Emissions Trading Scheme, supra* note 173.

177. http://www.ecosystemmarketplace.com; European Commission, *Further Guidance on allocation plans for the 2008 to 2012 trading period of the EU Emissions Trading Scheme* at Annex 4 (2005).

178. Ecosystem Marketplace, *1 V-Carbon News: Carbon beyond Kyoto . . . Carbon for the rest of us* 7 (May 8, 2006) (*hereinafter* Ecosystem).

179. Ecosystem, *supra* note 178.

180. *Cleaning up; Carbon trading*, The Economist (May 6, 2006), *at* http://www6.lexisnexis.com/publisher/EndUser?Action=User DisplayFullDocument&orgId=1925&topicId=100002042 &docId=l:382446644&start=2 (last visited May 10, 2006) (*hereinafter* Economist).

181. Economist, *supra* note 180.

182. Ecosystem, *supra* note 178.

183. Economist, *supra* note 180. However, the cause of this excess seems to be that the governments involved allocated too many allowances to certain sectors. It is not known if there will be a similar surplus in the second phase of trading until revised NAPs are submitted, approved, and implemented.

184. Ecosystem, *supra* note 178.

185. European Climate Exchange, *Press Release EC Verification Data 2005*, http://www.europeanclimateexchange.com/pages/page555.php (last visited May 15, 2006).

186. Ecosystem, *supra* note 178.

187. In addition to the seven original states of Connecticut, Delaware, Maine, New Hampshire, New Jersey, New York, and Vermont, the state of Maryland is obligated under state law to become a full participating member of RGGI by June 30, 2007. Also, the governor of California signed Executive Order S-20-06 on October 18, 2006, that commits California to develop a market-based climate change program that permits trading with RGGI.

188. The MOU can be found at www.rggi.org/docs/mou_12_20_05.pdf. The Amendment to the MOU can be found at www.rggi.org/docs/mou_8_8_06.pdf.

189. The Model Rule can be found at www.rggi.org/docs/model_rule_8_15_06.pdf.

190. Some 25 MW EGUs may be exempted from coverage, such as those that burn biomass as the majority fuel or that sell less than 10% of the electricity they generate to the grid.

191. The regional and state emissions caps and schedule for future reductions in the caps can be found at Memorandum of Understanding § 2(B), (C) and (D).

192. Permitting requirements can be found at Model Rule subparts XX-1.5(a) and XX-3.

193. The discussion of ERAs, including the methodology for calculating ERAs, can be found at MODEL RULE subpart XX-5.3(c).

194. The Consumer Benefit or Strategic Energy Purpose Account is discussed at MODEL RULE subparts XX-1.2(ad) and XX-5.3(b). The Model Rule describes an optional method for a state to set up a voluntary renewable energy set-aside allocation to meet its Consumer Benefit or Strategic Energy Purpose allocation at subpart XX-5.3(d).

195. The discussion of general accounts can be found at MODEL RULE subpart XX-6.2(b).

196. Compliance is discussed at MODEL RULE subparts XX-1.5(c) and (d), XX-4, and XX-6.5.

197. Transferring CO2 allowances is discussed at MODEL RULE subpart XX-7.

198. CO_2 budget units that co-fire biomass have additional reporting requirements found at MODEL RULE subpart XX-8.7.

199. Monitoring, reporting and recordkeeping is discussed at MODEL RULE subparts XX-1.5(b) and (e), and XX-8.

200. MODEL RULE subpart XX-10.1. The requirements for CO_2 offset projects can be found generally in MODEL RULE subpart XX-10.

201. Additionally, project application requirements, the accreditation of independent certifiers, and the contents of monitoring and verification reports are discussed at MODEL RULE subparts XX-10.3(d), XX-10.4, XX-10.6, and XX-10.7(c).

202. Eligibility standards, baseline and emissions reduction calculations, and monitoring and verification requirements for landfill projects can be found at MODEL RULE subpart XX-10.5(a).

203. Eligibility standards, baseline and emissions reduction calculations, and monitoring and verification requirements for SF6 reduction projects can be found at Model Rule subpart XX-10.5(b).

204. Eligibility standards, baseline and emissions reduction calculations, and monitoring and verification requirements for afforestation projects can be found at Model Rule subpart XX-10.5(c).

205. Eligibility standards, baseline and emissions reduction calculations, and monitoring and verification requirements for energy efficiency projects can be found at MODEL RULE subpart XX-10.5(d).

206. Eligibility standards, baseline and emissions reduction calculations, and monitoring and verification requirements for agricultural management projects can be found at MODEL RULE subpart XX-10.5(e).

207. The definition of a stage-one trigger event and stage-two trigger event and the complete formula for calculating the stage one and stage two threshold prices can be found at MODEL RULE subpart XX-1.2(bb), (bc), (bd) and (be).

208. CCX membership recently has been geographically expanded to allow entities in Brazil and other locations to adopt standardized baseline and reduction commitments.

209. The Chicago Accord can be found *at* www.chicagoclimatex.com/about/pdf/ChicagoAccord_050623.pdf. Other details about CCX can be found more generally at www.chicagoclimatex.com.

210. All GHGs are converted to CO_2 equivalent using the 100-year global warming potential values established by the Intergovernmental Panel on Climate Change.

211. The Corporate Standard can be found *at* http://pdf.wri.org/ghg_protocol_2004.pdf and the Project Protocol can be found *at* http://pdf.wri.org/ghg_project_accounting.pdf.

212. The GHG Protocol Initiative calculation tools can be found *at* www.ghgprotocol.org/templates/GHG5/layout.asp?type=p& MenuID=OTAx.

213. Project overviews can be found *at* www.chicagoclimatex/environment/offsets/offset_project_types.html.

214. The Department of Energy's Voluntary Reporting of Greenhouse Gases Program. *See* final guidelines published at 71 Fed. Reg. 20,784 (2006) for more information on the section 1605(b) program.

215. The U.S. Initiative on Joint Implementation, a flexible nonregulatory program that encourages U.S. participants to engage in GHG-reducing projects overseas.

216. *See* www.evolutionmarkets.com and www.chicagoclimatex.com.

217. *See* Stowell, *supra* note 100. The "derivative contract" is named as such because the value of these agreements is "derived" from the underlying product, in this case, the emissions allowance. *Id.*

218. *Id.*

219. *Id.*

220. *Id.*

221. *Id.*

222. *Id.*

223. *Id.*

224. *Id.*

225. The model contracts used as the sources for this section, in their entireties, can be found at the following locations: *IETA CDM Emissions Reductions Purchase Agreement v. 2.0 2004, at* http://www.ieta.org/ieta/www/pages/getfile.php?docID=311 (last visited May 11, 2006); *Emissions Marketing Association Master Agreement for the Purchase and Sale of Emissions Products, at* http://www.emissions.org/publications/emissions_trader/model_so2/download.html (last visited May 11, 2006); *Emissions Marketing Association Contract Language for SO₂ and NOₓ Allowance Financial Trading, at* http://www.emissions.org/docs/contract_template/ (last visited May 11, 2006); *Evolution Markets Standard Agreement for the Purchase and Sale of SO₂ Allowances, at* http://www.evomarkets.com/assets/tk-so2/Standard_SO2_Immediate_Settlement_Areement.pdf (last visited May 11, 2006).

226. *See* Stowell, *supra* note 100.

227. See information and Web sites on specific brokers in carbon trading, *supra* this chapter.

chapter nineteen

Carbon Sequestration

David J. Hayes and Joel C. Beauvais

Most policymakers concerned about climate change have focused their attention on reducing emissions of carbon dioxide and other greenhouse gases (GHGs) at their sources—by shifting away from carbon-intensive fuels to renewables and other lower-emitting energy sources, by improving energy efficiency and thereby reducing GHG emissions, and the like. While this focus on direct reductions in GHG emissions is appropriate, and must be the centerpiece of any serious effort to reduce overall atmospheric loadings of GHGs, the capture or "sequestration" of carbon provides an additional tool for netting out GHG emissions. As discussed in this chapter, pursuing carbon sequestration strategies can significantly reduce the level of GHGs available in the atmosphere for warming, while providing important co-benefits to the environment and, in the case of physical sequestration, providing an important option for continued reliance on coal and other carbon-heavy fuels.

Carbon sequestration measures divide into two basic categories: biological sequestration and physical sequestration (commonly referred to as carbon capture and storage). Biological sequestration strategies rely on the natural function of forests and other terrestrial ecosystems as carbon "sinks."[1] Plants take up CO_2 through photosynthesis, and a portion of the carbon is then stored—often for very long time periods—in plant biomass and soil organic matter. The amount of CO_2 that natural systems take up and store can be increased through a broad range of land-use practices, including improved forest conservation and management, reforestation, and agricultural practices that boost levels of soil organic matter.

Carbon capture and storage (CCS) uses engineered systems to capture carbon emissions at their source *before* they are released into the atmosphere, and then to inject the captured carbon into reservoirs for long-term storage. One storage option that is receiving significant attention involves the injection of carbon in underground geologic formations where it potentially can play a role in enhancing oil and gas recovery from such formations. Captured carbon also can potentially be stored in the oceans by injecting it into the water column at or above the ocean floor, but this approach has generated considerably less interest because of potential environmental risks and potential legal obstacles.

Both biological sequestration and CCS strategies are likely to play a significant role in U.S. and global efforts to mitigate climate change. These strategies can be implemented using currently available technology and can achieve substantial reductions in atmospheric CO_2 loading without requiring drastic changes in how we generate or use energy. Sequestration techniques also are attractive because they may provide relatively low-cost ways to reduce carbon loadings; they expand the constituencies that have an economic interest in reducing overall carbon emissions—including foresters, farmers and ranchers; and they can provide significant side benefits. More specifically, biological sequestration measures can yield non-climate environmental dividends by helping to conserve biodiversity and to enhance environmental quality. CCS technologies, for their part, may enable continued reliance on important fossil fuels (most notably coal) that would otherwise have a significant negative impact on climate change, and, as noted above, underground storage of carbon can be combined with enhanced oil and gas recovery to expand reserves. Thus, while carbon sequestration is no silver bullet, many believe that it can help to buy time as we seek to move to a less carbon-intensive economy.[2]

For all of its promise, carbon sequestration is not without controversy. Biological sequestration, in particular, has attracted opposition from some countries and environmental groups due to skepticism about whether we can accurately measure sequestration in complex natural systems and the risk that stored carbon will be released back into the atmosphere through land-use change, fires, and so forth. There is real concern that biological sequestration will not perform as advertised, and that relying on false or temporary sinks to offset emissions will result in higher overall emissions. In addition, projects aimed at enhancing biological carbon sequestration can have negative environmental and social effects if not carefully designed and implemented. For CCS, there are uncertainties regarding potential environmental and safety risks of geological, and especially ocean, storage. Finally, both strategies have been criticized on the ground that they distract from the necessary hard work of reducing emissions and transitioning away from reliance on fossil fuels.

Despite these concerns, policy makers and private actors are actively pursuing biological sequestration and CCS initiatives in the United States and abroad. Under

the Kyoto Protocol, Annex I (developed) countries must account for GHG emissions and sequestration from at least some land-use activities in determining compliance with mandatory emissions limits, thereby bringing biological sequestration issues into play. Moreover, at least some types of biological sequestration projects are eligible to generate tradable credits under the Kyoto regime's flexibility mechanisms (Joint Implementation and the Clean Development Mechanism). In the United States, meanwhile, companies and nongovernmental organizations are investing in reforestation and other sequestration projects intended to offset GHG emissions from major sources—despite the absence of any mandatory national limits on such emissions. Some states have adopted policies to encourage such offset projects, and the Chicago Climate Exchange now provides a forum for registration and trading of offset credits from forestry and agricultural soils projects. At the federal level, farm and forestry subsidy programs have been adjusted to encourage biological sequestration, and virtually every major piece of climate change legislation proposed in recent years would allow offsets from biological sequestration projects. On the CCS front, governments and private firms in the United States and abroad are investing heavily in research and development, and a growing number of underground geologic storage pilot projects are now under way. In short, carbon sequestration has arrived and is likely to play a substantial role in future efforts to mitigate climate change.

In this chapter, we provide a broad overview of each of the two major strategies for carbon sequestration, focusing on (1) the relevant scientific and technical background; (2) potential benefits and costs; and (3) current and emerging initiatives and policies and related accounting, regulatory, and legal issues. We focus on U.S. experiences wherever possible, but we also give considerable attention to the treatment of carbon sequestration under the Kyoto regime, as this framework provides a valuable perspective on issues of relevance to U.S. policy.

I. Biological Sequestration in Terrestrial Ecosystems
A. Scientific Background and Land Use Strategies

Terrestrial ecosystems provide both a massive reservoir of stored carbon and a major buffer against increasing anthropogenic emissions of GHGs. Forests, which have very large stocks of standing biomass, are by far the largest component of terrestrial carbon stocks—accounting for roughly 1,146 billion tons (gigatons or Gt). Grasslands, savannas and croplands are estimated to store around 765 Gt, and wetlands account for another 240 Gt.[3] At present, terrestrial ecosystems act as a net carbon sink, taking up somewhere in the range of 1-1.5 Gt of carbon each year—equivalent to roughly 15% to 20% of current annual emissions from combustion of fossil fuels and cement production.[4]

The driving force behind this sink is photosynthesis, through which plants convert atmospheric CO_2 (along with water and solar energy) into carbohydrates—which in turn are used either to form new plant tissues or as fuel for cellular respiration. Plant growth is basically the difference between the amount of carbon fixed through photosynthesis and the amount released through the plant's respiration. Almost all of the carbon fixed through plant growth is eventually released back into the atmosphere as CO_2 through either decomposition or fires. Carbon absorbed by plants is deposited on or in the ground in the form of detritus, and a portion is ultimately incorporated into the soil as soil organic matter. Detritus generally has a comparatively short turnover time (less than 10 years), while soil organic matter decomposes over a period of decades or even centuries.[5]

Human land use has had dramatic impacts on the natural terrestrial carbon cycle, and land-use change is responsible for 10% to 30% of current anthropogenic CO_2 emissions.

Human land use has had dramatic impacts on the natural terrestrial carbon cycle, and land-use change is responsible for 10% to 30% of current anthropogenic CO_2 emissions.[6] Most significantly, deforestation has caused massive releases of carbon stored in vegetation biomass and in soil organic matter. Deforestation has reduced global forest area by 20% since 1850, and is responsible for almost 90% of the estimated CO_2 emissions due to land-use change during that period.[7] While net deforestation in the United States peaked around 1920 and has reversed since then,[8] deforestation in the tropics continues at an astonishing pace—roughly 45,000 square kilometers per year in Brazil and Indonesia alone.[9] In addition, conversion of natural systems to arable lands results in major reductions in vegetative biomass and soil organic carbon, and draining of wetlands also speeds decomposition and release of large reservoirs of stored organic carbon.[10]

While terrestrial ecosystems' carbon stocks are continually turning over, the amount of carbon stored by a system at any given time is essentially a function of how much biomass and soil organic matter they contain. Biological sequestration strategies seek to increase the magnitude and/or duration of carbon storage in plant biomass and soils through land-use conversion or land management practices. The most well-established strategies focus on conserving existing forests and planting new ones, but strategies focusing on the management of agricultural lands, grasslands, and wetlands are receiving increasing attention.

Preventing deforestation serves both to preserve forests' role as active carbon sinks and to avoid the release of their massive carbon stocks. While the rate of sequestration in most natural systems decreases over time, even old-growth forests continue to accumulate carbon at significant rates.[11] Avoiding deforestation is critically important because deforestation releases significantly more carbon into the atmosphere on a per-area basis than can be sequestered through reforestation (i.e., replanting trees on recently harvested or burned forest lands) or afforestation (planting trees on lands that have not recently been forested) on a discounted basis.[12] It can take over 200 years for a newly reforested area to attain the carbon storage capacity of an old-growth forest, and even at maturity, regenerated forests generally store less carbon than natural forests.[13] Finally, reducing deforestation can avoid major emissions of nitrous oxide (N_2O)—a GHG that is more than 300 times more powerful than CO_2—because (at least in the tropics, where most deforestation occurs) much of the biomass removed through deforestation is burned.[14]

Because forests generally store more carbon per area for a longer time than other natural systems, afforestation or reforestation can significantly enhance carbon sequestration. In addition, a variety of management practices can increase the rate of carbon sequestration in existing forests.[15] For example, lengthening harvest rotations and adopting low-impact logging practices can reduce the amount of carbon released as a result of harvesting.[16] Fire management practices can also increase carbon retention rates by introducing more frequent, limited, and natural fires in forests, and avoiding the larger catastrophic fires that are associated with the unnatural buildup of fuel loadings in improperly managed forests.[17]

Carbon storage in agricultural lands can be increased through practices that conserve soil organic matter, such as no-till farming techniques. Conventional tillage (plowing) exposes soil organic matter and breaks down soil macroaggregates, speeding decomposition of organic matter and the release of carbon back into the atmosphere. By reducing soil disturbance and leaving more crop residue on the surface, conservation tillage can significantly reduce the loss of soil carbon.[18] Techniques that increase crop yields—e.g., effective fertilizer use, higher-yield crops, or irrigation—can also increase soil carbon in croplands.[19] Soil carbon in grazing lands can be augmented through a number of practices, including reducing grazing intensity and introducing new plant species such as legumes or deep-rooted grasses.[20] Finally, retiring marginal agricultural lands from production or converting croplands to grasslands or agroforestry systems can increase carbon storage in soils and vegetation biomass.[21]

Conserving or creating wetlands also can play a role in carbon mitigation.[22] Wetlands are major carbon reservoirs. By some estimates, northern peatlands alone store 270 to 370 Gt of carbon—representing about one-third of the total global soil carbon pool.[23] On the other hand, the wetlands picture is made more complicated by the fact that some types of wetlands produce methane—a powerful GHG.[24]

B. Policy Issues—The Promise and Challenge of Biological Sequestration

All indications are that biological sequestration measures can achieve major reductions in atmospheric loading of CO_2. The Intergovernmental Panel on Climate Change (IPCC), for example, has estimated that land use, land-use change, and forestry measures could conserve or sequester up to 100 Gt of carbon in forests and agricultural soils by 2050. That is equivalent to 10% to 20% of business-as-usual fossil fuel emissions during that same period.[25] Even excluding reforestation and afforestation, the IPCC has estimated that improved land management and land-use change could increase carbon sequestration by over 1 Gt of carbon per year in 2010—which could offset nearly 15% of current annual anthropogenic emissions.[26]

In addition to being a potentially significant overall factor in the carbon balance, it appears that most biological sequestration measures compare favorably in terms of cost with direct emissions reductions. One recent study conducted for the Pew Center on Global Climate Change analyzed a large number of surveys on the per-ton cost of reducing carbon through the use of biological sequestration techniques. The Pew Center study estimated that a forest-based sequestration program in the United States that would sequester up to 300 million tons of carbon per year would cost between $7.50 and $22.50 per ton of CO_2 equivalent.[27] The authors concluded that these costs are "not very far above typical cost estimates for emissions abatement through fuel switching and energy efficiency improvements," and that a domestic carbon sequestration program "ought to be included in a cost-effective portfolio of compliance strategies if and when the United States chooses to implement a domestic GHG reduction program."[28] Another recent study concluded that agricultural soil sequestration and forest-based measures in the United States could yield over 200 million tons of CO_2 equivalent mitigation per year at a cost of $5/ton.[29]

Costs are projected to be lower for sequestration projects undertaken in the developing world, where land is cheaper and plant productivity is higher.[30] The World Bank's BioCarbon Fund, for example, expects that its investments in developing world host countries will sequester carbon at a cost of $3 to $4 per ton of CO_2 equivalent.[31] Other cost estimates for biological sequestration projects in tropical countries range from $0.10 to $20 per ton of carbon (roughly $0.36 to $73 per ton of CO_2 equivalent)—although the methods of financial accounting are not comparable and the low-end estimates are likely biased downward.[32]

In addition to mitigating climate change, biological sequestration measures can yield substantial nonclimate environmental and social dividends.[33] Prevention of deforestation and wetlands conservation in particular provide important side benefits in terms of habitat and biodiversity conservation and environmental quality. Primary tropical forests, for example, are estimated to contain 50% to 70% of all terrestrial species, and tropical deforestation is a major cause of biodiversity loss.[34] And although tree plantations typically have lower biodiversity than natural forests, afforestation and reforestation measures can provide habitat and biodiversity benefits if properly designed.[35] In addition, many sequestration-enhancing measures—including forest con-

servation, carbon-conserving forest management, afforestation, reforestation, conservation tillage, retirement of marginal croplands, and preservation or regeneration of wetlands—can help to prevent soil erosion, protect water quality, and prevent flooding.[36]

Policies designed to encourage sequestration-enhancing land-use practices—for example, subsidies, tax incentives, or the award of emissions offset credits—also can help to channel resources to rural communities and developing countries.[37] In the United States, such policies might provide a more legitimate basis for cash payments to farmers than the current U.S. practice of providing direct farm subsidies—a practice that arguably runs afoul of international trade principles. And because the greatest potential for biological carbon sequestration lies in the developing world, policies to promote sequestration could support sustainable development by compensating developing countries and their citizens for conserving tropical forests and undertaking climate-friendly land-use measures.[38]

As discussed at greater length in the following section, governments and private parties in the United States and abroad are already investing substantial resources in biological carbon sequestration projects, and it is likely that these efforts will expand in the future. The bulk of these initiatives involve the generation of credits that can be used to offset GHG emissions—the premise being that sequestration offers a lower-cost alternative to reducing emissions directly. To be effective, however, these regimes must ensure that offset credits do not overstate the real reductions in atmospheric CO_2 loading achieved by sequestration projects. Otherwise, they could have the perverse effect of *increasing* CO_2 loading by providing cover for uncompensated emissions increases. Ensuring the environmental integrity of offset credit programs will require policy makers to confront a number of challenging accounting and regulatory concerns.

Measurement and Scientific Uncertainty. The measurement of carbon sequestration in natural systems—particularly forests—is inherently more complicated than measuring GHG emissions from engineered sources. While considerable strides have been made in this area, the continuing development of accurate, precise, verifiable, and cost-effective measurement methodologies remains an important concern for future policies.[39]

There also are still significant areas of scientific uncertainty regarding the interaction of terrestrial ecosystems and climate change. For example, recent studies suggest that tropical forests are a significant source of methane, which exerts a warming effect on the atmosphere that is more than 20 times more powerful (by volume) than that of

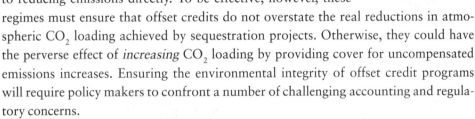

CO_2.[40] Most observers do not believe that this phenomenon comes close to netting out the beneficial impacts that forests play in absorbing CO_2 from the atmosphere, but it illustrates the challenges of quantifying biological sequestration benefits, and it also highlights the evolving nature of our understanding of natural systems.[41]

Adding to the complexity of the measurement issue, climate change impacts may have significant effects on terrestrial ecosystems' capacity to sequester carbon. For example, increasing atmospheric concentrations of CO_2 can have a "fertilization" effect on plants, resulting in increased carbon fixation.[42] The magnitude and duration of this effect is unclear, however, in part because the availability of key nutrients is likely to limit growth in many ecosystems.[43] On the other side of the ledger, rising global temperatures may increase the rate at which detritus and soil organic matter decompose, thus hastening the release of carbon into the atmosphere—but, again, the magnitude of this effect is unknown.[44] In some regions, warmer temperatures and longer growing seasons may increase productivity, whereas in others drought or increased vulnerability to fire and pests may cause die-back.[45]

Non-permanence. The non-permanence of biological carbon sequestration presents another major challenge in accounting for the benefits of sequestration practices. When some GHG emissions are avoided—for example, through increased fuel efficiency—they are avoided forever. As explained above, however, carbon sequestered in plant biomass and soils will eventually be released into the atmosphere through respiration, decomposition, or combustion. The risk of fires, hurricanes, or forest disease outbreaks also can have a significant impact on the benefits of carbon sequestration measures, and the difficulty of controlling future land-use decisions that could result in release of stored carbon further complicates the picture.

The non-permanence issue makes it more difficult to accurately account for biological carbon sequestration, but it is not an insuperable problem, and several potential solutions have been proposed.[46] For example, it is possible to provide credit for carbon sequestration on a temporary basis, for example, by awarding expiring credits that can be renewed only if the stored carbon is retained. This is the approach used under the Kyoto Protocol's Clean Development Mechanism, discussed below. Similarly, in a subsidy program, the party seeking to purchase emissions offsets can "rent" or "lease" the carbon sequestration provided by the project rather than "buying" it outright. Alternatively, the project sponsor or the credit purchaser can be required to insure against future releases by holding some credits in reserve. Finally, the risk of future release (to the extent it can accurately be quantified) can be incorporated into the original accounting of the sequestration project—for example, by discounting the credit awarded based on the likelihood of release over a predetermined timeframe.

Because most observers agree that short- and medium-term reductions in overall carbon loadings—of the type potentially delivered through biological sequestration measures—are a key component in any climate change strategy, all of these approaches are potentially attractive. That is, because it will take many decades to transition to major new, lower-GHG-emitting energy sources, biological sequestration may provide important transitional benefits in reducing reducing atmospheric loadings of GHGs.

Additionality, Baselines, and Leakage. Biological sequestration projects also face a number of other issues germane to all offset projects. First, to determine what net impact a particular land-use measure has on carbon sequestration—and thus the amount of offset credits that it should generate—one has to determine the relevant baseline (or "business-as-usual") scenario. This is a critically important exercise because providing offset credits for a project that would have gone forward in the absence of carbon-based incentives—and which therefore should be in the business-as-usual baseline—would have the effect of masking an increase in emissions, insofar as the credits would allow another GHG source to emit more than it otherwise could. Estimating baselines, and the corollary exercise of determining whether a project satisfies an "additionality" test (i.e., it is additional to, and not part of, the expected baseline) can be challenging, as it requires prediction both of how the natural system is expected to evolve and how economic and social factors are likely to shape future land-use decisions. The balance is a difficult one to strike because a too-loose additionality test could provide a false reading of overall reductions, while a too-strict additionality test could create perverse disincentives to engage in sound land-use management practices. How does one account for the fact, for example, that tree plantations were already being established in the year 2000 at a rate of 1.9 million hectares per year in tropical countries? [47] Should new plantations receive no offset credits in a carbon-constrained system? The presumed answer is that some should and some should not, depending on whether, in light of relevant market conditions, they would have been established absent the incentive provided by the offset credits.

A final accounting issue that can bedevil biological sequestration projects (and other types of carbon offset projects) is whether there is "leakage" outside the scope of the immediate projects that should discount the otherwise-applicable credit. For example, a project that reforests agricultural land may succeed in sequestering carbon on the relevant parcel, but if the landowner simply clears land elsewhere to accommodate the displaced activity, "leakage" has occurred and the project should not receive credit in a carbon-constrained system. To ensure the environmental integrity of the crediting system, leakage must either be avoided through project design or it must be fully accounted for.

Collateral Environmental and Social Costs. While sequestration policies can provide substantial environmental and social side benefits, they also can have adverse environmental and social effects if not carefully designed and implemented. Replace-

OZONE
FRIENDLY

CONTAINS **NO** CHLOROFLUORO **C A R B O N** PROPELLANT ALLEGED TO DAMAGE THE **OZONE** LAYER

ment of natural forests, wetlands, or grasslands with tree plantations—even if this yields net gains in sequestration rates—can adversely affect habitat and biodiversity.[48] Afforestation also may not be appropriate for some areas.[49] And practices that enhance carbon sequestration by intensifying agricultural production may have negative environmental impacts.[50] On the social side, carbon sequestration activities can have negative impacts on local economies and livelihoods by limiting, for example, land that is available for agricultural use or by reducing access to forest subsistence products.[51] These concerns can be mitigated by requiring proposed projects to meet mandatory environmental and social standards in order to receive credits or subsidies.

> **A number of major environmental organizations have undertaken tropical forest conservation and reforestation projects intended to maintain and enhance carbon sequestration.**

C. Domestic and International Initiatives and Policies

Notwithstanding the challenges posed by biological sequestration, governments, firms, and nongovernmental organizations in the United States and abroad are pressing forward with biological sequestration projects and policies throughout the world. This section provides an overview of these efforts, focusing on three general categories of activity: (1) private voluntary initiatives; (2) U.S. government policies directed at carbon sequestration, at both the federal and state levels; and (3) treatment of carbon sequestration under the Kyoto regime.

1. Private Voluntary Initiatives

Well before the Kyoto Protocol was negotiated or came into force, companies and nongovernmental organizations had begun to invest in biological carbon sequestration projects. The earliest major international project was initiated in 1988, when an American power company established a project to plant 52 million trees on deforested lands in Guatemala with the objective of making a new power station "carbon neutral."[52] Since then dozens of carbon sequestration offset projects have been undertaken in the United States and overseas.[53] U.S. power companies have taken the lead in subsidizing such projects, both on an individual basis and through joint efforts such as the UtiliTree Carbon Company and the PowerTree Carbon Company.[54] Carbon sequestration projects increasingly involve partnerships between private firms, conservation organizations, and government agencies.[55]

A number of major environmental organizations have undertaken tropical forest conservation and reforestation projects intended to maintain and enhance carbon sequestration. The Nature Conservancy, for example, has established a project in Noel Kempff Mercado Park in Bolivia—with funding from American Electric Power, PacifiCorp, and BP—that is expected to result in a net reduction of up to 17.8 million tons of CO_2 emissions over the next 30 years.[56] Domestically, conservation organizations such as the Conservation Fund and Ducks Unlimited have developed programs to approve and market credits for carbon sequestered through conservation practices on private lands.[57] In addition, a growing number of private companies are beginning to market carbon offsets generated through biological sequestration projects. Firms and individuals seeking to label their operations, facilities, and events—even a single plane trip—"carbon neutral" can purchase offsets from such companies.[58]

Since 2003, the Chicago Climate Exchange (CCX) has provided a forum for trading of approved offset credits from qualified biological sequestration projects. CCX, which is discussed in greater detail in Chapters 17 and 18 of this book, is a voluntary, legally binding GHG reduction trading program for emission sources and offset projects in North America and offset projects in Brazil. Members adopt emissions reduction targets and can purchase offset credits to satisfy their obligations. Offset credits can be generated through several categories of sequestration projects, including forestry and agricultural soils projects in the United States and forestry projects in Brazil.[59] Medium- and large-scale forestry projects must be verified by an independent CCX-approved verifier, while agricultural soils projects are merely "subject to" independent verification.[60] The minimum trading unit on the CCX is equal to 100 tons of CO_2 equivalent, but a CCX-registered "aggregator" can act as an intermediary that registers and bundles eligible offset projects for trading.[61] The Iowa Farm Bureau, for example, acts as an offset aggregator for agricultural soils projects and has enrolled over 330,000 acres of farmland in Iowa, Kansas, and Nebraska.[62]

While much of this activity is laudable, the absence of generally accepted standards for offsets in the voluntary context of current U.S. policy has created opportunities for the recognition of some dubious sequestration credits or offsets due to serious baseline, additionality, leakage, and/or measurement issues. The lack of recognized, transparent conventions for creating offsets has had the unfortunate effect of increasing concerns in some quarters about the appropriate place that sequestration credits should have as part of an overall strategy to reduce carbon emissions.

2. Government Policies in the United States

The United States has long been a major proponent of biological sequestration as a carbon mitigation strategy, both because of its vast forests and agricultural lands and in part because of the anticipated cost advantages of biological sequestration. While the United States has yet to adopt any comprehensive policy addressing GHG emissions, it has established a number of programs that promote biological sequestration in the forestry and agricultural sectors.

First, the National Voluntary Reporting of Greenhouse Gases Program, established by Section 1605(b) of the Energy Policy Act of 1992, permits entities to voluntarily report GHG emissions and reductions.[63] The Section 1605(b) program since its inception has encouraged reporting of sequestration data from the agriculture and forestry sectors, and the revised program guidelines issued in April 2006 are expected to enhance such reporting.[64]

The federal government also has taken steps to tailor federal farm and forest subsidy programs to encourage carbon sequestration. In 2003, the U.S. Department of Agriculture announced that it would take carbon sequestration benefits into account in evaluating applications for technical and financial assistance under the Conservation Reserve Program (CRP), the Environmental Quality Incentive Program (EQIP), and the Forest Lands Enhancement Program (FLEP).[65] The CRP subsidizes removal of environmentally sensitive lands from agricultural production and is estimated to provide carbon sequestration benefits of upwards of 15 million tons of carbon per year.[66] EQIP provides technical and financial assistance to farmers for planning and implementation of soil and water conservation practices and is estimated to provide carbon sequestration benefits of roughly 12 million tons of carbon per year.[67] The FLEP provides technical assistance and subsidies (on a cost-sharing basis) to non-industrial private forest landowners to support the implementation of sustainable forest management practices.[68] In addition, the Healthy Forests Restoration Act of 2003 authorized the acquisition of short- and long-term agreements and easements from owners of private forest lands to adopt practices that enhance carbon sequestration.[69]

On the international front, the United States provides debt relief to support tropical forest conservation programs under the Tropical Forest Conservation Act (TFCA).[70] Six countries (Bangladesh, Belize, El Salvador, Panama, Peru, and the Philippines) currently have TFCA "debt-for-nature" agreements in place, and the Bush Administration has touted the program's carbon sequestration benefits.[71]

Finally, legislators have introduced a substantial and growing number of proposals in recent years to expand subsidies, tax credits, and other incentives for domestic and international carbon sequestration programs on agricultural and forest lands.[72]

If and when the United States adopts legislation imposing mandatory limits on GHG emissions, biological sequestration is likely to play a substantial role. The availability of offset credits for biological sequestration has been a prominent feature of every major climate change-related legislative proposal put forward in recent years. The Climate Change Stewardship Act of 2005 sponsored by Senators McCain and Lieberman, for example, caps GHG emissions from certain economic sectors and allows regulated sources to offset up to 15% of their emissions through sequestration projects—which can include "agricultural and conservation practices," reforestation, and forest preservation.[73] Senator Bingaman's draft Climate and Economy Insurance Act of 2005 would allocate a portion of GHG emissions allowances to offsets generated through domestic or international carbon sequestration projects.[74] And legislation introduced by Senator Feinstein would allow unlimited offsets through agricultural sequestration and afforestation projects.[75]

Biological sequestration already plays a role in current and forthcoming climate change initiatives at the state level.[76] Oregon, for example, has enacted legislation requiring new power plants to meet CO_2 emissions standards and allowing such plants to offset some emissions through carbon mitigation projects.[77] Regulated plants can meet a portion of their obligations by contributing on a per ton CO_2 rate to the Oregon Climate Trust, which generates offset credits through reforestation and other carbon mitigation projects.[78] Similarly, Washington state requires new power plants rated 25 MW or greater to offset 20% of their CO_2 emissions over 30 years of operation, and permits regulated plants to pay a state-approved third party at a fixed per-ton rate for offset projects.[79]

Several states have nonregulatory programs to encourage biological carbon sequestration projects. For example, the Oregon Forest Resource Trust (a state entity) subsidizes forest restoration efforts on private lands, and requires that the landowner cede to the Trust any carbon sequestration credits generated by such efforts. Minnesota's ReLeaf program provides matching grants for tree-planting and tree management projects to sequester CO_2. And Hawaii has established a fee-based pollution fund intended in part to subsidize carbon offset and forestry projects.[80] In addition, the governor of California has issued an executive order establishing statewide targets of reducing GHG emissions to 2000 levels by 2010, to 1990 levels by 2020, and to 80% below 1990 levels by 2050.[81] It is expected that biological sequestration activities in the forestry and agricultural sectors will play an important role in meeting those targets.[82] Finally, several midwestern states have established advisory committees to examine the potential for in-state agricultural carbon sequestration initiatives.[83]

OZONE
FRIENDLY

CONTAINS **NO** CHLOROFLUORO C A R B O N PROPELLANT ALLEGED TO DAMAGE THE **OZONE** LAYER

3. The Kyoto Protocol

The Kyoto Protocol to the United Nations Framework Convention on Climate Change (UNFCCC) provides a useful case study of a regime incorporating mandatory limits on GHG emissions with tradable offset credits available for biological sequestration activities. (The UNFCCC and the Kyoto Protocol are discussed in more detail in Chapter 2.) Biological sequestration plays a role in three key aspects of the Kyoto regime: (i) accounting for GHG emissions and sequestration from land use, land-use change, and forestry activities in determining whether Annex I countries have met their emissions reduction commitments; (ii) the Clean Development Mechanism; and (iii) Joint Implementation.

a. Biological Sequestration in Annex I Countries

The Kyoto Protocol requires the countries listed in both Annex I to the UNFCC and Annex B to the Protocol (the so-called "Annex I" countries) to limit their GHG emissions during the first commitment period (2008 to 2012) to "assigned amounts" that will, in the aggregate, reduce their emissions to roughly 5% below 1990 levels. Under Article 3.3 of the Protocol, Annex I countries must account for the "net changes in greenhouse gas emissions by sources and removals by sinks resulting from . . . afforestation, reforestation and deforestation since 1990" in determining whether they have complied with their emissions limits during the first commitment period (2008 to 2012).[84]

In addition, pursuant to Article 3.4 of the Protocol, the parties have decided that Annex I countries are permitted (but not required) to account for GHG emissions by sources and removals by sinks resulting from "forest management," "cropland management," "grazing land management," and "revegetation" activities during the first commitment period.[85] Each party can elect which, if any, of these activities it wants to count during the first commitment period, although certain limitations are placed on accounting for forest management activities.[86] Under Article 3.4, emissions and removals from all of the these activities must be taken into account during the second and subsequent commitment periods (post-2012).[87]

The use of land use and forestry sinks and sources in determining whether Annex I countries have met their quantitative emissions limits should provide these countries with incentives to invest in domestic biological sequestration programs. For example, although the United States has not ratified the Kyoto Protocol, some commentators believe that biological sequestration potentially could have accounted for up to half of the U.S.'s annual reduction obligations.[88] Of course, each country will have to determine independently what combination of domestic policies (subsidies, offset credits, fees and taxes, management of public lands, or command-and-control regulation) can maximize its biological sequestration of carbon for purposes of meeting overall quantitative limits.[89]

b. The Clean Development Mechanism

The Kyoto Protocol also provides some incentives for investment in biological sequestration projects in developing countries through the Clean Development Mechanism (CDM). The CDM allows non-Annex I parties (mostly developing countries) to generate tradable certified emissions reduction credits (CERs) through projects that reduce net emissions of GHGs.[90] CERs can be generated only for "[r]eductions in emissions that are additional to any that would occur in the absence of the certified project activity."[91] CERs are equivalent to the tradable "assigned amount units" allocated to Annex I countries in connection with their emissions commitments, and Annex I countries can acquire CERs and add them to their assigned amounts for purposes of complying with those commitments.[92]

The Kyoto parties have imposed fairly strict limits on the generation of CERs from biological sequestration projects during the first commitment period.[93] First, within the category of land use, land-use change, and forestry (LULUCF) activities, only reforestation and afforestation projects are eligible to generate CERs during the first commitment period.[94] That is much narrower than the set of LULUCF activities that can be taken into account in determining Annex I countries' compliance with emissions commitments. The decision not to award CDM credits for the avoidance of deforestation is especially noteworthy, as it eliminates a major potential funding source for tropical forest conservation. In addition, the Kyoto parties have limited Annex I countries' use of LULUCF-based CERs during the first five-year commitment period to 1% of the country's 1990 emissions times five.[95] These limitations reflect continuing concern about the types of scientific uncertainties and accounting issues discussed above.

The parties have agreed that the treatment of LULUCF activities under the CDM in future commitment periods (i.e., post-2012) will be determined as part of the negotiations for the second commitment period, but they have agreed that any revisions will not affect afforestation and reforestation CDM projects that were registered prior to the end of the first commitment period.[96] It is possible (and, indeed, likely), therefore, that the parties will opt to broaden the LULUCF activities that can generate CERs and/or relax the restriction on the use of LULUCF-based CERs. The parties have already agreed, at the request of several tropical countries, to reconsider the exclusion of avoided deforestation from the list of activities eligible to generate CERs.

The parties have developed fairly detailed "modalities" to govern the issuance of CERs for LULUCF projects.[97] These modalities present one real-world approach to addressing the baseline, additionality, leakage, nonpermanence, and collateral effects issues discussed above. Under the Kyoto regime, the CDM Executive Board is responsible for approving CDM projects and issuing CERs. Project proponents must submit a proposal (known as a Project Design Document) that addresses additionality and leakage issues and explains the methodology for calculating the project baseline.[98] The proponent can use a baseline methodology already approved by the Executive Board if there is one, or it can seek the Board's approval of a new methodology.[99] To date, the Executive Board has approved only one afforestation and reforestation methodology, and no afforestation or reforestation project has yet been registered with the Board. The Project Design Document must also document the environmental and socio-economic impacts of the project, although no minimum standards are specified.[100]

An approved "designated operational entity" (DOE) must independently evaluate and validate the project before it can be submitted to the Executive Board for registration. Credits are issued by the Board only after the DOE has verified and certified the net GHG removals achieved by the project. Verification and certification must be repeated every five years.[101]

The guidelines address the nonpermanence issue through a temporary crediting system. The crediting period for sinks projects is either a 30-year nonrenewable period or a 20-year period that can be renewed twice (up to 60 years). The guidelines provide for two types of temporary credits for sinks projects: tCERs (temporary CERs) and lCERs (long-term CERs). In both cases, a DOE must confirm every five years that the project has sequestered enough carbon to cover the credits issued. The main difference between the two credit types is that a tCER expires at the end of the commitment period after the one in which it was issued (e.g., in 2017 for a tCER generated in the 2008-2012 commitment period), whereas lCERs expire at the end of the crediting period for the relevant project (20 or 30 years). The upshot is that tCERs expire every five years and can be reissued only upon certification that the sequestered carbon remains sequestered; thus (five-yearly) certification and reissuance automatically corrects for any carbon losses from the project over time. For lCERs, carbon losses between two (five-yearly) certification reports must be replaced by other credits. At the end of the agreed crediting period, all tCERs and lCERs must be replaced by credits from other projects.[102]

c. *Joint Implementation*

Article 6 of the Kyoto Protocol establishes a mechanism referred to as Joint Implementation (JI), which allows Annex I countries to trade (between themselves) emission reduction units (ERUs) "resulting from projects aimed at reducing anthropogenic emissions by sources or enhancing anthropogenic removals by sinks of greenhouse gases in any sector of the economy . . . ."[103] Acquisition of ERUs generated through JI allows a country to increase its assigned amount (i.e., its emissions cap) commensurately, while the transferring country subtracts the ERUs from its assigned amount.[104] As a result, Annex I parties can use biological sequestration projects to generate emissions credits that can then be sold to other Annex I parties to offset the latter's emissions. One significant distinction between JI and the CDM is that projects involving the whole range of LULUCF activities—not just afforestation and reforestation—should be eligible to generate credits under JI. Nevertheless, there has been comparatively little discussion of the role of LULUCF projects in the JI context, and the parties have not yet developed specific guidance in this area.

d. *The World Bank BioCarbon Fund*

The World Bank is seeking to boost investment in biological sequestration projects through the establishment of the BioCarbon Fund. Established in 2002, the BioCarbon Fund is a $100 million public/private partnership that provides financing to mitigate GHG emissions through conservation and biological sequestration projects. The Fund has two "windows." The first invests in projects eligible to generate credits under the

CDM (afforestation and reforestation) or JI (the range of LULUCF activities). The second window invests in projects in developing countries that involve activities that are not eligible for crediting under the CDM during the first commitment period, such as restoration of degraded forests and grazing lands and improved forest management. The objective is to gain experience with such projects and to demonstrate their feasibility. Participants in the Fund will contribute monies in exchange for a pro rata share of the emissions credits generated through investments in carbon sequestration projects.[105] This approach should encourage biological sequestration projects by pooling investor risk and allowing the fund to accumulate experience with financing, approval, and implementation of such projects.

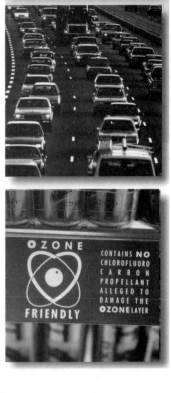

II. Physical Sequestration—Carbon Capture and Storage

Carbon capture and storage is a relative newcomer to climate change policy discussions, but it has quickly attained a very prominent role.[106] Underground geologic storage in particular is looking increasingly feasible in the near term—technically, economically, and environmentally. And although CCS does not have the secondary environmental and social benefits associated with biological sequestration, it has many advantages. The technology for capturing, transporting, and storing CO_2 underground is already being used in commercial applications. CCS does not present major measurement or accounting issues, and evidence is mounting that CO_2 can be stored in geologic reservoirs with minimal risk of leakage. The costs of CCS (especially capture technologies) remain somewhat high, but are likely to decline with broader application. In the meantime, combining CCS with enhanced oil and gas recovery potentially can significantly defray costs while expanding existing fossil fuel production. In light of these factors, it is likely that geologic sequestration of CO_2 will be a significant element of any future U.S. climate change regime.

A. Capture and Transport Technologies

Capture Technologies. In order to physically sequester anthropogenic emissions of CO_2, the CO_2 must first be "captured" and then compressed for transport to a storage site. At present, CCS is suitable only for emissions from large point sources. Although dispersed sources such as vehicles and buildings account for roughly 38% of CO_2 emissions, application of capture and transport technology to these sources is at present too costly and difficult.[107] Most attention to date has focused on power plants, but capture technologies can also be applied to other large, energy-intensive, CO_2-emitting industries, including cement manufacture, oil refining, ammonia production, and iron and steel manufacture.[108] The number of large point sources is projected to increase in the future, and 20% to 40% of global CO_2 emissions from fossil fuel combustion could be technically suitable for capture by 2050—including 30% to 60% of emissions from electricity generation and 30% to 40% of those from industrial sources.[109]

There are three basic approaches to capturing carbon from fossil fuels—pre-combustion, post-combustion, and oxy-fuel combustion. (Similar technologies can be applied to capture potential emissions from a range of industrial processes.)[110] The primary method of pre-combustion capture of CO_2 involves processing the primary fuel (coal or natural gas, for example) in a reactor with steam or air prior to combustion to produce a mixture consisting principally of carbon monoxide and hydrogen known as "synthesis gas" or "syngas." The carbon monoxide is then mixed with steam in a second reactor—a "shift reactor"—to produce CO_2 and more hydrogen. The hydrogen becomes a carbon-free fuel to power the plant, while the CO_2 can be compressed for transport and ultimate storage.

Although pre-combustion CO_2 capture technology can be applied to natural gas- or oil-fired plants, most attention has focused on the use of integrated gasification combined-cycle (IGCC) technology in coal-fired power plants. In an IGCC plant, the hydrogen fuel generated through gasification of coal is used to power a turbine and the excess heat is used to power a secondary steam generator.[111] There are only four coal-fired IGCC facilities in the world today, including two in the United States—the Tampa Electric facility in Florida and the Wabash River Coal Gasification Repowering Project in Indiana—but, as explained below, a number of others are currently planned.

IGCC has generated intense interest in the United States because of its potential to dramatically reduce the climate change impacts of coal-fired power generation.[112] The United States has the largest known coal reserves in the world (enough to satisfy current demand for over 200 years), and coal fuels over 51% of U.S. electricity generation.[113] Coal also provides a very large and growing proportion of electricity generation in fast-growing countries such as China (79%) and India (68%).[114] Despite its dominance, coal has been a problematic energy source because it generates high emissions rates for many pollutants, including mercury, NO_x, SO_x, particulate matter, and, of course, CO_2. But coal-fired plants using IGCC technology are relatively clean, and IGCC is well-suited to CO_2 capture for geological storage.

Post-combustion capture systems generally use a solvent or a membrane to separate CO_2 from the flue gases produced by combustion of the fuel in air. CO_2 is usually a relatively small fraction of these gases, depending on the fuel used—around 3% by volume for a natural gas combined-cycle plant to 15% by volume for a coal-fired plant.[115] For a modern pulverized coal power plant or a natural gas combined-cycle (NGCC) power plant, projected post-combustion capture systems would use an organic solvent such as monoethanolamine to separate out CO_2.[116] Post-combustion capture technologies are already commercially available and are used, for example, to capture CO_2 from coal and gas-fired plants for use in the food and beverage and chemical-production industries. They would have to be scaled up significantly from current applications to be used in large

IGCC has generated intense interest in the United States because of its potential to dramatically reduce the climate change impacts of coal-fired power generation.

(500 MW) power plants, but this appears feasible.[117] Indeed, the European CO_2 Capture and Storage project (CASTOR)—a consortium funded in part by the European Commission—has recently initiated a pilot project that uses post-combustion technology to capture a ton of CO_2 per hour from a 420 MW coal-fired plant—a rate described as large-scale enough to

ensure reliable industrial exploitation. CASTOR also will invest in research and development for post-combustion capture technologies.[118]

Oxy-fuel combustion eliminates nitrogen from exhaust gases by burning the fuel in pure oxygen or a mixture of pure oxygen and CO_2-rich recycled flue gas. The main emissions from this process are CO_2 and water, and after cooling to remove water vapor, the exhaust stream contains about 80%–98% CO_2. Once compressed, dried, and purified, this CO_2 is ready for transport and storage.[119] Oxy-fuel combustion is the most advanced of the carbon capture methods described here, and although the key elements of this technology are currently in commercial use, it has not yet been deployed for CO_2 capture on a commercial scale.[120]

Both pre- and post-combustion systems are capable of capturing 80%–90% of CO_2 emissions from power plants.[121] Some conventional coal plants can be "re-powered" with IGCC technology to permit pre-combustion capture—and the resulting cost of energy may, at least in some cases, be lower than it would be to retrofit the plant with post-combustion capture technology.[122] Installation of CO_2 capture and compression technology increases capital costs and can also increase plant energy requirements by 10%–40%.[123] This translates into higher per-unit electricity costs, but it is expected that broad deployment will reduce capital costs and that emerging technologies could, in time, significantly reduce the energy penalties for CO_2 capture.[124]

Capture is the most expensive aspect of CCS. Whether power plants and other major sources implement capture technologies in the near term may depend in significant part on whether the government provides requirements or incentives to do so through mandatory limits on CO_2 emissions, subsidies, tax breaks, or regulatory mandates.[125] In that regard, the federal government has taken some initial steps to promote capture technologies. The Energy Policy Act of 2005 provided for a 20% investment tax credit for the construction of IGCC plants, federal loan guarantees for new IGCC plants, and subsidies for research on clean coal technologies including IGCC.[126] In addition, the Bush Administration has promised to provide 75% of the funding for the $1 billion FutureGen project—the centerpiece of which is a 275 MW "zero-emissions" coal-fired IGCC plant. The plant—slated for completion by 2012—is expected to be used both to generate electricity and to produce hydrogen to power fuel cells. The carbon content of the fuel will be captured for underground geologic storage.[127]

A number of other initiatives are also under way. Subsidiaries of BP and Edison International recently announced plans to build a $1 billion oil-residue-fired power plant near Los Angeles that would use gasification to capture carbon for underground injection in conjunction with enhanced oil recovery operations.[128] In March 2006, German electricity producer RWG announced plans to build a $1.2 billion coal-fired, 450 MW IGCC plant using geological sequestration of captured carbon.[129] The same month, Shell and Statoil announced plans for a $1.5 billion project involving construction of an 860 MW gas-fired power plant with a carbon capture system and a pipeline to transport captured carbon for offshore underground geologic storage in combination with enhanced oil recovery.[130] Elsewhere in Europe, some governments are moving toward mandating the inclusion of capture technology in new facilities.[131]

Transport. Once carbon is captured at major point sources, it must be transported to wherever it is to be stored—predominantly in underground geological reservoirs. Pipelines are expected to provide the primary means of transport. After CO_2 is captured and compressed, it then must be dried and purified of hydrogen sulfide before pipeline transport in order to avoid corrosion. Pipeline transport of CO_2 is not new; there are over 2500 km of CO_2 pipelines in the western United States that transport roughly 40 megatons of CO_2 per year, primarily for use in enhanced oil recovery projects (discussed at greater length below).[132] While the CO_2 pipeline network would have to be expanded to implement a large-scale CCS program, the technology is proven and pipeline transport presents no novel regulatory issues.[133] Like natural gas, CO_2 also can be transported in liquefied form by ship. But shipping is unlikely to play much of a role in transport for underground storage (including offshore) because of its comparatively high costs and the relative proximity of storage sites to sources. Shipping could be required for some methods of direct injection of CO_2 into the ocean (discussed below), and may be less costly than pipeline transportation provided the distance from shore is sufficiently great.

B. Underground Geologic Storage

Underground geologic storage of CO_2 was suggested as a possible way to mitigate global warming as early as the 1970s, but it received little attention until the 1990s.[134] It is now front and center in climate change policy discussions.

Underground injection of CO_2 has been used since the early 1970s as part of enhanced oil recovery (EOR) projects—the injected CO_2 dissolves into residual oil and increases its viscosity, making extraction easier. About 30 megatons of non-anthropogenic CO_2 are injected annually, mostly in west Texas, for EOR projects. In addition, there are at least three major commercial projects that now inject captured CO_2 for underground storage. Statoil's Sleipner project in the North Sea separates CO_2 from natural gas at an offshore processing facility. To avoid paying Norway's hefty carbon tax (lowered from \$200/t to \$140/t in 2000), Statoil injects the captured CO_2 into a saline formation deep beneath the sea floor for storage. At the In-Salah gas field in Algeria, CO_2 is stripped from natural gas and injected underground. And the Weyburn project in Saskatchewan, Canada, uses CO_2 that is captured 200 miles away at a coal synfuel plant in North Dakota for injection in conjunction with EOR activities. A number of other projects are under development, and, as noted above, there are now several major proposals involving geologic sequestration of CO_2 captured from new power plants.[135]

Technical background. Before it can be stored underground, CO_2 must be compressed into a dense fluid (supercritical) state. It can then be pumped through an injection well into porous geological formations—typically over 800 meters below the surface (the depth at which CO_2 will remain in a supercritical state under normal geological and pressure gradients). The key to underground geologic storage of CO_2 is to identify reservoirs that will keep injected CO_2 from escaping. The main strategy is to use a permeable formation located below a layer of impermeable caprock, which acts as a physical seal preventing the CO_2 from escaping upwards. In addition, CO_2 can be trapped by dissolution into water located in deep formations—and, over very long time frames, through partial conversion into stable carbonate minerals.[136]

Three types of geologic formations are well-suited to long-term storage of injected CO_2: depleted oil and gas fields, saline formations, and deep coal seams. Depleted oil and gas reservoirs are ideal because the same geological characteristics that allowed long-term storage of oil and gas—typically permeable rock formations overlain by caprock—are likely to permit long-term storage of CO_2. The safety and reliability of these reservoirs has been proven, and they have already been the subject of extensive geological study. One concern with use of depleted oil and gas fields for CO_2 storage is that many are already perforated by numerous old wells, which could permit the escape of stored CO_2. Research on risks and possible mitigation strategies is now under way.[137]

Storage of CO_2 in oil and gas fields is particularly attractive where it can be combined with EOR to tap "stranded" reserves. Conventional primary production generally extracts only 5% to 40% of the oil in a given field. Injection of CO_2 can increase production by an average of around 13%, and the economic returns from this increased production can be used to defray CO_2 capture and storage costs.[138] The U.S.

Department of Energy has recently reported that new technologies using CO_2 for EOR have the potential to quadruple U.S. oil reserves.[139]

Saline formations are deep sedimentary formations saturated with waters or brines that contain high concentrations of dissolved salts, and often are overlain by caprock. Although saline formations contain vast quantities of water, the high salt concentration makes this water unsuited for consumption or irrigation. The Sleipner project is the leading example of use of a saline formation as a CO_2 reservoir.[140]

Unminable, deep coal seams contain fractures that make them at least somewhat permeable, and solid coal has micropores into which CO_2 and other gas molecules can be absorbed. Although the suitability of coal seams for trapping CO_2 in its supercritical state is not yet well understood, CO_2 has successfully been injected into coal seams at depths corresponding to the supercritical state. Because injected CO_2 can displace methane located in coal beds, there is significant interest in coupling CO_2 storage with coal bed recovery of methane—the cleanest of fossil fuels. Like EOR, coal bed methane recovery could generate returns that would permit recovery of at least some of the costs of CO_2 capture, transport, and storage.[141]

Capacity and Cost. Surveys indicate that the capacity of reservoirs suitable for underground CO_2 storage is potentially vast. Oil and gas fields have an estimated global storage capacity of 675 to 900 Gt of CO_2, while saline formations could store anywhere from 1000 to as much as 10,000 Gt. Unminable coal seams potentially could store another 5 to 200 Gt.[142] Even the low-end estimate of 1680 Gt of global capacity is equivalent to over 70 years of emissions from global fossil fuel combustion at current levels, while the high-end capacity estimate would be over six times greater. The U.S. Department of Energy projects that U.S. domestic geologic formations "have at least enough capacity to store several centuries' worth of point source emissions" from the United States.[143]

Of course, it will not be economically feasible to exploit all technically available capacity. The IPCC estimates that it will likely be cost-effective (in light of the cost of CO_2 emissions reductions or other mitigation options) to capture and store underground somewhere between 200 and 2000 Gt of CO_2 over the course of the next century. That represents 15%–55% of anticipated global mitigation effort needed during this period.[144] It is virtually certain that there is at least 200 Gt of available capacity, and it is likely that there is at least 2000 Gt of capacity.[145] In addition, there appears to be a good correlation between major emissions sources and geological basins likely to be suitable for underground CO_2 storage. Many major source areas lie directly over or within a couple hundred miles of prospective storage areas.[146]

The costs of geologic storage are relatively modest in comparison with those of CO_2 capture. Estimates of costs for CO_2 storage and monitoring in depleted oil and gas fields or saline formations range from $0.60 to $8.30 per ton of CO_2 stored. If storage is combined with enhanced oil or gas recovery, CO_2 storage could generate significant positive income, depending upon the price of oil and gas.[147]

Risks. The main concern with underground geological storage is that CO_2 will leak into groundwater or escape into the atmosphere. CO_2 could escape from geological storage reservoirs through the pore system in caprock if capillary pressure were high enough; through openings, fractures or faults in the caprock; or through anthropogenic openings, such as abandoned or improperly sealed wells. The primary risk is that stored CO_2 will simply end up back in the atmosphere, undoing (at least partially) the climate change mitigation benefits of sequestration. The only substantial direct risk to human health from a leak would be if people were exposed to elevated CO_2 concentrations in ambient air—for example, from a sudden, large-scale release at the surface. Such exposure could have negative effects on the respiratory systems and, if the concentration were high enough, it could lead to unconsciousness and even death. In addition, migration of CO_2 into shallow groundwater used for drinking or agriculture could negatively affect water quality. Dissolved CO_2 forms carbonic acid, which could affect water quality by potentially mobilizing metals, sulfate, or chloride. Finally, underground injection of CO_2 at high pressures potentially could induce seismic activity, which could lead to release of CO_2 from the reservoir and even earthquakes.[148]

The risks of escape are considered minimal, however, for appropriately selected and monitored reservoirs. Retention times of over 10 million years are found in many natural reservoirs, and data derived from experience with underground natural gas storage indicates that the risk of release from properly selected storage sites is quite low. Studies also indicate that the risk of induced seismic activity is quite low. Methods exist to assess and control the risk of seismic activity, and the extensive experience with CO_2 injection for EOR suggests that risks are minimal with proper site selection, monitoring, and regulatory oversight. Based on this evidence, the IPCC estimates that appropriately selected and managed geological reservoirs would retain over 99% of stored CO_2 over 1,000 years.[149]

Government Support for Geologic Storage. Underground geologic storage has received substantial and growing attention from policy makers in the United States and abroad. The FutureGen project, discussed above, is expected to demonstrate the feasibility of using geologic sequestration to store CO_2 emissions from a large-scale power plant. In addition, the Department of Energy has established the Carbon Sequestration Regional Partnership program, which involves collaboration with seven regional partnerships of state government agencies, universities, private firms, and nongovernmental organizations. This program provides funding for research and demonstration projects, including geologic sequestration.[150] The Energy Policy Act of 2005 also pro-

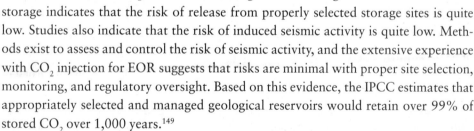

vided a number of incentives for increased investment in CO_2 injection in connection with enhanced oil and gas recovery.[151] In response to this legislation, the Bureau of Land Management and the Minerals Management Service recently initiated a rulemaking process to "provide for royalty relief incentives to promote the capture, transportation, and injection of produced carbon dioxide (CO_2), natural CO_2, and other appropriate gases or other matter for injection into oil and gas fields . . . ."[152]

Other countries also are looking toward geologic sequestration. The EU and China recently announced an agreement to jointly study the feasibility of CCS,[153] and the EU-funded CASTOR project will develop case studies of underground storage sites representative of geologic sites across Europe.[154] Finally, as noted above, a number of European firms have recently unveiled plans to build large-scale "zero-emissions" power plants using geological sequestration of CO_2.[155]

C. Ocean Storage

Oceans are the largest global carbon reservoir, containing roughly 50 times the quantity of carbon currently contained in the atmosphere and roughly 20 times the carbon currently stored in plants and soils.[156] Oceans are also a major carbon sink, taking up an average of 7 Gt CO_2 per year in recent decades. Indeed, oceans are estimated to have absorbed well over a third of anthropogenic CO_2 emissions over the past 200 years.[157]

The basic mechanism for the net uptake of CO_2 in oceans is the dissolution of atmospheric CO_2 into ocean water at the air-sea interface. At present, increased concentrations of dissolved CO_2 are observable only in the upper ocean (to about 1000 meters of depth) because of the slow rate of exchange between deep ocean and surface waters. Over time, much of this dissolved inorganic carbon will be carried by cold downwelling currents to the deep ocean, where it will reside for centuries. Some inorganic carbon will be converted to organic carbon by phytoplankton; after passing up the food chain, some of this carbon will sink to deeper waters in the form of detritus or dead organisms, where (again) it will remain for centuries. Eventually, upwelling will return dissolved carbon to the surface, where at least some portion will be returned to the atmosphere through outgassing.[158]

A number of methods have been proposed whereby captured CO_2 could be physically injected into the ocean water column for long-term storage.[159] These methods anticipate that injected CO_2 will either dissolve into ocean water at depth or collect on the ocean floor so as to avoid a rapid return to the surface—and thus provide a longer storage period. One proposed method involves injection at depths of 1000 to 1500 meters from a fixed pipeline or a pipeline towed by a ship, which would create a rising plume of CO_2 that would be absorbed into the surrounding waters. A second method would involve injection at shallower depths of a mixture of dense seawater and absorbed CO_2, which would then sink into the deeper ocean, especially if aided by a natural sinking current. Finally, because CO_2 is denser than seawater at depths of over 3000 meters, CO_2 injected at such depths would sink to the ocean floor to form a stable

"lake." Injection of CO_2 in seawater has been tested only in the laboratory, in small-scale *in situ* experiments, and through mod-

A number of methods have been proposed whereby captured CO_2 could be physically injected into the ocean water column for long-term storage.

els. Vigorous public opposition has derailed attempts to stage ocean tests—including, for example, the CO_2 Ocean Sequestration Field Experiment that was planned off the Kona coast of Hawaii in 2001.[160]

The environmental impacts of ocean storage of CO_2 are not well understood, but could be significant. For example, increased CO_2 concentrations may have adverse effects on marine organisms.[161] Observed effects include increased mortality and reduced rates of reproduction, growth, and mobility.[162] Increased CO_2 concentrations and acidity in the deep ocean could make it more difficult for deep-sea organisms and ecosystems to adapt.[163] Localized impacts of CO_2 injection near the injection site may be of greater concern. If CO_2 were sufficiently dispersed—for example, by injecting CO_2 using a deeply towed pipeline—impacts on marine organisms might be minimized, but injection from a fixed source would likely create a large zone of water with elevated CO_2 concentrations and acidity.[164] The intentional creation of highly concentrated CO_2 "lakes" on the sea floor could confine acute impacts to the zone of the lake, but would likely kill most marine organisms that could not escape from that zone.[165]

Because of the scientific uncertainties concerning the potential environmental risks, and in part because of potential legal obstacles (discussed below), physical injection of CO_2 into the oceans for storage has received comparatively little support from policy makers.

In addition to physical injection strategies, some consideration has been given to the possibility of marine biological sequestration through "fertilization" of the oceans. It is hypothesized that introduction of key limiting nutrients (e.g., iron) in certain marine regions would cause phytoplankton blooms that would sequester large amounts of carbon, some portion of which would be transported to the deep ocean for long-term storage in the form of dead organic matter. This approach has gained little support, however, because of major uncertainties regarding its practical feasibility and potential environmental impacts.[166]

D. Legal, Regulatory, and Accounting Issues

1. U.S. Legal and Regulatory Issues Relating to Underground Storage

Underground geological storage of CO_2 implicates a number of legal and regulatory issues related to selection and management of storage sites, environmental and safety standards, property rights in storage sites and stored CO_2, and potential liability for releases of stored CO_2.

a. *Regulation of Underground Injection and Storage*

The United States has a regulatory framework in place at both the federal and state levels to address underground injection and storage issues. As noted above, the United States has decades of experience with the underground injection of CO_2 in connection with EOR operations. In addition, there is significant experience through underground injection of "acid gas," a mixture of CO_2 and hydrogen sulfide separated from natural gas in the course of "sweetening" the gas for market. Finally, the United States has considerable experience with injection of natural gas into underground reservoirs for storage purposes.[167] Large-scale injection and storage of CO_2 for non-EOR purposes undoubtedly will present some new concerns, but these are likely to be addressed through adaptation of existing regulatory regimes.

Underground injection is regulated at the federal level through EPA's Underground Injection Control (UIC) Program, promulgated under the Safe Drinking Water Act (SDWA). The SDWA directs EPA to establish minimum requirements for state regulatory programs to protect drinking water sources from contamination by underground injection.[168] EPA is authorized to delegate primary enforcement authority (primacy) to any state or tribe that has adopted a regulatory program for underground injection that meets the requirements of EPA's UIC regulations. If a state or tribe fails to submit an application showing that it has a satisfactory program, EPA is to administer the program for that jurisdiction.[169] To date, 34 states have assumed primacy, six have assumed primacy for one or more but not all classes of injection wells, and EPA retains full authority in the 10 remaining states.[170]

The UIC Program is codified at 40 C.F.R. Parts 144 through 148.[171] As relevant here, the UIC regulations prohibit injection activities that would "allow the movement of fluid containing any contaminant into underground sources of drinking water" if such contamination may cause a violation of any primary drinking water quality regulation under 40 C.F.R. Part 142 (including stringent maximum contaminant levels) or may "otherwise adversely affect the health of persons."[172] Congress in 1980 amended the SDWA to exempt "underground injection of natural gas for purposes of storage" from the coverage of the UIC program.[173]

The UIC regulations separate injection wells into five separate classes, each subject to different regulatory requirements.[174]

- Class I wells are used to inject hazardous, industrial, or municipal waste beneath the lowermost formation containing, within one quarter mile of the well bore, an underground source of drinking water.
- Class II wells are used to inject fluids (a) that are brought to the surface in connection with natural gas storage or conventional oil and natural gas production, (b) that are used for enhanced oil or gas recovery, or (c) for storage of hydrocarbons that are liquid at standard temperature and pressure.
- Class III wells are used to inject fluids for the extraction of minerals.
- Class IV wells are used to inject hazardous or radioactive waste into or above a formation containing, within one quarter mile of the well, an underground source of drinking water.
- Class V is a catch-all category for injection wells not included in Class I, II, III, or IV. Class V wells are usually shallow wells used to place fluids directly below the land surface (such as for storm water drainage or large septic systems), although deep wells can fall into this category as well.[175]

Injection of CO_2 in connection with EOR is covered under regulations relating to Class II wells, but the UIC regulations do not address CO_2 injection outside this context. Texas reportedly has applied Class V regulations—together with additional requirements drawn from the Class I regulations to bolster environmental safeguards—for permitting non-EOR CO_2 injection projects.[176] EPA is presently considering how to address CO_2 injection projects under the UIC Program, and ultimately must decide whether to allow or require CO_2 injection and storage to be regulated under existing well classifications or to develop a new classification for this purpose.[177] Alternatively, Congress could opt to enact new legislation to address the issue—by exempting CO_2 injection from regulation under the SDWA and the UIC Program and/or by establishing a new regulatory framework.

In addition to the UIC regime, many states have independent regulatory programs governing the storage of natural gas in underground geologic reservoirs and injection and storage of acid gas. These regimes address many of the regulatory concerns relevant to CO_2 storage—reservoir selection, injection and withdrawal parameters, well and equipment operational requirements, unauthorized releases of stored gas, and pressure limitations. The Interstate Oil and Gas Compact Commission (IOGCC) has concluded that existing natural gas storage and acid gas injection regimes can and should be adapted to CO_2 storage projects outside the EOR context.[178] Existing regimes may need to be adjusted to ensure that reservoir, well, and equipment standards take adequate account of the unique properties of CO_2, and to ensure that procedures for release and leakage mitigation and operational plans to address public health and safety concerns are adequate. In addition, existing regulations may not include adequate monitoring and verification requirements to ensure that injected CO_2 is accounted for.[179] This last point is particularly important because concerns about CO_2 release are not directed solely to health, safety, and environmental risks, but also to the integrity of underground storage as a dependable climate change mitigation measure.

b. Post-Injection Liability

Long-term geologic storage of CO_2 presents two basic types of liability issues associated with the risk of release. The first—which can be termed "climate liability"—concerns liability for the effects of release on credits that were issued based on the assumption that no release will occur.[180] As discussed below in the context of accounting for nonpermanence, a tradable credit regime could adopt a number of strategies to address this possibility, including, for example, discounting, temporary expiring credits, or self-insurance. A second type of liability—which could be called *in situ* liability—relates to the risk of direct damages from CO_2 release or migration. These risks include harm to human health or the environment from CO_2 release at the surface, contamination of groundwater from subsurface CO_2 migration, and the possibility of "trespass" of injected CO_2 into underground areas for which property rights have not been acquired.

During a CO_2 storage project's operational phase, the owner of the CO_2 and/or the operator of the storage facility presumably will bear responsibility for operational standards, release, and leakage mitigation. Responsibility and liability can, of course, be allocated through contractual, credit, and insurance arrangements. Over the long-term, however, the prospect that responsible parties will cease to exist or to be financially liquid presents significant questions about who will monitor the storage facility, be responsible for preventing and mitigating release, and be held liable for any releases that do occur.

The IOGCC has concluded that existing regimes do not adequately address these issues and that a new framework will need to be established to address post-injection and storage issues, including long-term liability for releases.[181] A number of options for assuring financial responsibility for CO_2 underground storage projects have been discussed, including the establishment of surety bonds, insurance funds, government trust funds, or public, private or semi-private partnerships.[182] Both the Resource Conservation and Recovery Act (RCRA) and the UIC regulations for Class I hazardous injections wells, for example, require that owner/operators meet certain financial assurance requirements to ensure long-term responsibility. Concerns have arisen in recent years, however, as to whether these requirements are adequate.[183] In most oil and gas producing states, the state assumes ultimate responsibility for orphaned oil and natural gas sites. Similar "backstop" assurances will likely be necessary for long-term underground storage of CO_2—particularly given the millennial length of projected storage periods. Such assurances could be supported through federally guaranteed and industry-funded abandonment programs.[184]

c. Property Rights

Underground geologic storage of CO_2 raises a number of property issues as well—principally relating to rights to geologic storage sites, rights to the stored CO_2 itself, and the legal effects of CO_2 migration outside of storage sites.

With regard to the ownership of geologic storage reservoirs, three separate interests are relevant: surface interests, mineral (subsurface) interests, and interests in groundwater. Property rights in the United States are primarily a matter of state law, and rules for allocating rights in these various interests may vary significantly from state to state. The default rule in the majority of American states is that the owner of the surface owns the subsurface, but subsurface rights can be severed from surface rights for purposes of separate conveyance.[185] The operator of a CO_2 storage facility must acquire whatever surface interests are needed to establish transport and injection facilities. These facilities will occupy a significantly smaller footprint than the underground geologic reservoir, however, so storage facility operators will likely try to acquire subsurface rights separately.[186] Where the operator seeks to store CO_2 in a saline formation, it may be necessary to acquire separate rights in the groundwater.[187]

Development of large-scale CO_2 storage projects will likely require the adoption of eminent domain legislation to authorize the condemnation of surface and subsurface interests for storage facilities. The Natural Gas Act of 1938 authorizes condemnation of property for natural gas storage, and several states also have enacted eminent domain statutes for acquiring underground natural gas storage rights.[188] Based on existing statutes, the IOGCC has drafted a conceptual framework for a CO_2 geological storage statute that would authorize any certified storage facility operator to "appropriate for its use for the geologic storage of CO_2 any subsurface stratum or formation in any land which the [oil and gas conservation commission] shall have found to be suitable and in the public interest for the geologic storage of CO_2, and in connection therewith [to] appropriate other interests in property as may be required adequately to examine, prepare, maintain, and operate geologic storage facilities."[189]

Virtually all states now follow the "ownership theory" of injected gas, which provides that title to gas is not lost upon injection into an underground reservoir for storage purposes.[190] A similar rule makes sense in the context of CO_2 storage, both because CO_2 has some commodity value and because of the potential liability issues discussed above. The IOGCC framework provides that ownership of injected CO_2 remains the property of the injector and (absent a final judgment of willful abandonment rendered by a court of competent jurisdiction) shall not be deemed the property of the surface or mineral owner.[191] The IOGCC framework also provides that if injected CO_2 migrates to adjoining subsurface property that has not been acquired, the owner of the adjoining property is entitled to compensation for use of or damage to the subsurface formation.[192]

> **Virtually all states now follow the "ownership theory" of injected gas, which provides that title to gas is not lost upon injection into an underground reservoir for storage purposes.**

2. Legal Issues Relating to Offshore Geological and Ocean Storage

Injection of CO_2 into offshore geological reservoirs or into the ocean itself implicates a number of international treaties and U.S. laws. While a comprehensive analysis of these regimes is beyond the scope of this chapter, a brief overview of relevant law and legal issues follows.

a. United Nations Convention on the Law of the Sea

The United Nations Convention on the Law of the Sea (UNCLOS) is an international treaty ratified by 149 countries (not including the United States) which, as relevant here, allocates jurisdiction over offshore activities. UNCLOS assigns coastal states "sovereign rights for the purpose of exploiting, conserving and managing the natural resources, whether living or non-living, of the waters superjacent to the seabed and of the seabed and its subsoil" within a 200-mile exclusive economic zone.[193] Rights to exploit non-living natural resources could be read to include the right to use the water column or offshore geological reservoirs for the storage of CO_2. In addition, UNCLOS gives coastal states exclusive sovereign rights over the continental shelf and its "natural resources"—which consists of "the mineral and other non-living resources of the seabed and subsoil together with living organisms belonging to sedentary species . . . ."[194] Here, again, "non-living resources" potentially could be interpreted as including geological storage capacity, and indeed, there are some situations in which countries have taken the position that they have sovereign rights over the use of offshore geological storage sites located on the continental shelf.[195] Within their exclusive economic zone and on the continental shelf, coastal states have exclusive authority to authorize and construct installations and structures for purposes of exploiting the sea and the seabed, which presumably would include facilities related to offshore CO_2 storage.[196]

On the high seas outside the 200-mile exclusive economic zone, UNCLOS provides that all states may exercise certain freedoms—including, as relevant to carbon storage activities, the freedom to construct "installations permitted under international law" and to engage in scientific research.[197] These freedoms must, however, be exercised "with due regard for the interests of other States in their exercise of the freedom of the high seas."[198] UNCLOS designates the portion of the ocean floor that is beyond national jurisdiction (referred to as the Area) "the common heritage of mankind." The treaty requires that activities in the Area be carried out for the common benefit of mankind—including "equitable sharing of financial and other benefits from activities in the Area" among states.[199] Although it is unlikely that offshore geological storage would be practicable beyond the continental shelf, sea floor storage of CO_2 in "lakes" might conceivably fall within the UNCLOS provisions governing the Area.

Finally, UNCLOS imposes a number of broad prescriptions regarding protection of the marine environment and control of ocean pollution—all of which could bear on offshore geological or ocean storage of CO_2. Specifically, the treaty requires states to take "such measures for their respective nationals as may be necessary for the conservation of living resources of the high seas";[200] directs the International Seabed Authority to ensure effective protection of the marine environment with respect to activities in the Area, including through adoption of rules to prevent, reduce or control pollution;[201] and requires states to adopt laws and regulations to prevent, reduce, and control pollution of the marine environment from land-based sources, seabed activities subject to national jurisdiction, dumping, and vessels.[202]

b. The London Convention and the London Protocol[203]

Offshore geologic and ocean storage of CO_2 are more directly and specifically affected by the Convention on the Prevention of Marine Pollution By Dumping of Wastes and Other Matter (the London Convention), which came into force in 1975 and has been ratified by over 80 states, including the United States and all major OECD countries. The London Convention prohibits the "dumping" of "industrial waste," which is defined in relevant part as "waste materials generated by manufacturing or processing operations."[204] The parties to the Convention have not yet reached consensus as to whether CO_2 captured from point sources falls within this definition, but there is certainly a strong argument to be made that it does.[205] Even if captured CO_2 did not constitute "industrial waste," it could be "dumped" only if a permit were obtained from the national party with jurisdiction over the activity.[206]

"Dumping" is defined under the Convention as "any deliberate disposal at sea of wastes or other matter from vessels, aircraft, platforms or other man-made structures at sea," but it does not include "placement of matter for a purpose other than mere disposal thereof, provided that such placement is not contrary to the aims of th[e] Convention."[207] This definition poses a number of potential issues for offshore geologic and ocean storage of CO_2. First, the question of whether disposal under the seabed constitutes disposal "at sea" remains unresolved, despite extensive debate in the context of disputes over seabed disposal of radioactive waste. Second, the limitation to disposal "from vessels, aircraft, platforms, or other man-made structures" suggests that disposal directly from land—e.g., via pipeline into the ocean or into an offshore geological storage site—may not be subject to the Convention's requirements. Finally, the exemption for placement "for a purpose other than mere disposal" may cover injection of CO_2 for enhanced hydrocarbon recovery, provided that such activity is not contrary to the aims of the Convention—which are broadly "to prevent marine pollution caused by dumping."[208]

The 1996 London Protocol to the London Convention came into force in March 2006 and supersedes the Convention for the contracting parties to the Protocol. There are presently 26 such parties, including many European countries, Australia, Canada, and Mexico—but not the United States, which remains bound by the London Convention. Although the 1996 Protocol does not specifically address CO_2 storage, it resolves at least some of the issues raised under the London Convention. First, the disposal of CO_2 falls within the Protocol's general prohibition against the "dumping" of any unlisted wastes (CO_2 is not on the list).[209] Second, the Protocol defines "dumping" to include "disposal into the sea of wastes or other matter from vessels, aircraft, platforms, or other man-made structures at sea" *and* "any storage of wastes or other matter in the seabed and the subsoil thereof from vessels, aircraft, platforms or other man-made structures at sea."[210] Thus, geological storage of CO_2 under the seabed is clearly covered, provided that disposal is from a vessel, platform, or structure at sea. The exception for placement "for a purpose other than mere disposal" is maintained, such that enhanced hydrocarbon recovery activities may be exempted.[211]

c. U.S. Law—The Ocean Dumping Act and the Clean Water Act

In the United States, two federal statutes bear on offshore geologic or ocean storage of CO_2: the Marine Protection, Research and Sanctuaries Act of 1972 (also known as the Ocean Dumping Act) and the Clean Water Act.

The Ocean Dumping Act—which is intended to effectuate the United States' obligations under the London Convention—prohibits any person from "dumping" "industrial waste" "into ocean waters."[212] "Dumping" is defined broadly to mean any "disposition of material" (except effluent outfalls regulated under the Clean Water Act, the Rivers and Harbors Act, or the Atomic Energy Act).[213] The statute does not define "industrial waste," but waste CO_2 captured from power generation, industrial, or gas-processing facilities potentially could qualify. If it does, the statute would forbid the direct disposal of captured CO_2 "into ocean waters," although it might permit injection into offshore geological storage sites if release could be prevented.

In addition, the Ocean Dumping Act requires an EPA permit in order to (1) transport "any material" from the United States for the purposes of dumping it into ocean waters, or (2) dump "any material" transported from outside of the United States into the United States' 12-mile territorial sea or the contiguous zone (the 12-mile band located seaward of the territorial sea).[214] Thus, even if captured CO_2 did not qualify as "industrial waste," it could not be disposed of directly into ocean waters without a permit. And EPA can issue a permit only if the Agency determines that the proposed dumping "will not unreasonably degrade or endanger human health, welfare, or amenities, or the marine environment, ecological systems, or economic potentialities."[215] In reaching that determination, EPA must consider, among other things, the need for the proposed dumping and its effect on human health and welfare, fisheries resources, and marine ecosystems.[216] EPA regulations provide that a need for ocean dumping has been demonstrated when the agency determines that "[t]here are no practicable alternative locations and methods of disposal or recycling available . . . which have less adverse environmental impact or potential risk to other parts of the environment than ocean dumping."[217] Unless amended, these requirements may foreclose ocean storage of CO_2 given the risk of environmental impacts and the practical availability of less risky methods of disposal.

The Clean Water Act prohibits the "discharge of any pollutant" from "any point source" into the waters of the United States (including the 12-mile territorial sea), or from "any point source other than a vessel or other floating craft" into ocean waters located beyond the territorial sea, without a permit issued under the National Pollutant Discharge Elimination System (NPDES).[218] The CWA defines "pollutant" to include "industrial . . . waste discharged into water," which could include CO_2 captured from power generation, industrial, or natural gas-processing facilities.[219] However, the definition of pollutant expressly exempts "water, gas, or other material injected into a well to facilitate production of oil or gas," meaning CO_2 injection for enhanced oil or gas recovery is not covered by the statute.[220]

Section 403 of the CWA provides that an NPDES permit may be issued for a discharge into the territorial sea, the contiguous zone (the 12-mile band beyond the territorial sea), or the oceans (i.e., the seas beyond the contiguous zone) only if it complies with EPA's ocean discharge guidelines.[221] Under the EPA guidelines, an NPDES permit can be issued only if the agency determines that the discharge will not cause "unreasonable degradation of the marine environment."[222] If the agency has insufficient information to determine whether the "no unreasonable degradation" standard can be met, it can issue a permit only if it finds, among other things, that the discharge will not cause "irreparable harm to the marine environment" and that there are "no reasonable alternatives to the on-site disposal" of the materials.[223]

The upshot of these provisions is that the CWA does not cover CO_2 injection for offshore enhanced oil and gas recovery projects, but it may cover the offshore discharge of CO_2 in other circumstances. If CO_2 qualifies as an "industrial waste," direct injection into the water column would certainly be covered, but it is not clear whether injection into an offshore geological reservoir would be covered. Ship-based discharge of CO_2 would be covered only within the 12-mile territorial sea, while discharge from other point sources would be covered beyond the limits of the territorial sea. Given the limits of current scientific knowledge about CO_2 disposal in ocean waters, and the likelihood that underground geological storage may provide a reasonable alternative to ocean storage, an applicant may have difficulty in securing an NPDES permit for ocean storage.

3. Accounting Issues

Carbon capture and storage (CCS) does not present the complex measurement and uncertainty concerns associated with biological sequestration, but it nonetheless will require policy makers to address a number of tricky accounting issues if CCS is to be used for offset credits.

a. Nonpermanence

As with biological sequestration projects, regulatory systems must account for the possibility of future release of CO_2 from storage. As discussed above, the likelihood of release from properly selected and managed underground storage sites is low. The IPCC estimates that it is likely that such sites will retain over 99% of stored CO_2 for over 1,000 years, which would represent a loss on the order of 0.001% per year. However, if the release rate were one order of magnitude greater than that—0.01% per year—and the volume of CO_2 stored were sufficiently great, future releases from underground storage could account for a significant proportion of acceptable future emissions budgets.[224] While the first line of defense against release is to select, monitor, and manage sites appropriately, it may also be important to account for the risk of future releases in determining compliance with emissions caps or awarding offset credits.

Potential methods for addressing the risks of nonpermanent storage are similar to those discussed above in the context of biological sequestration. In principle, it is possible to apply an ex ante discount rate to the award of offset credits based on the probability of future releases over the crediting period, and this rate could be calibrated to the predicted integrity of the storage site.[225] However, limited knowledge about the likelihood of future releases from a given site may make it difficult to set credible rates.[226] Alternatively, it is possible to create rules that account for actual releases over time, provided that accurate, long-term monitoring is in place. For example, the project sponsor could be required to self-insure by holding reserve credits as a hedge against future releases, or to adopt some form of temporary but renewable credits such as those currently used for afforestation and reforestation projects under the CDM.[227]

b. Baselines and Additionality

As with biological sequestration, any regulatory regime that seeks to give credit for the effects of CCS projects must address the question of baselines and additionality. In CCS retrofit projects, the baseline typically is defined by the emissions profile of the facility before retrofitting.[228] For new (or so-called "greenfield") projects, the analysis is more complicated. One approach would be to establish the baseline based on the demand for the product (e.g., increased electricity generation) and the technology that—in light of market and regulatory conditions—would likely be used to supply that product in the absence of the capture and storage element of the proposed project.

Additionality is unlikely to be an issue for most CCS projects, because the lack of economic return from capture and storage means that, almost by definition, any CCS project is "additional" to baseline conditions. The main exceptions, of course, are projects involving enhanced hydrocarbon (oil, gas, or coal-bed methane) recovery—where there may be an independent economic incentive for the project.

c. Project Boundaries and "Leakage"

Another concern for CCS projects is the complete accounting of emissions. Simple measurement of the amount of carbon captured would overstate the actual net benefit of the capture and storage system (i.e., the amount of carbon emissions *avoided*). The most important reason for this is the energy penalty (and resulting additional emissions) imposed by the capture and storage system. As noted above, the energy penalty can range from 10% to 40% in coal- and gas-fired power plants, and since capture systems typically capture only 80% to 90% of CO_2 emissions, any increase in fuel combustion results in increased emissions. In addition, transport of CO_2 may result in fugitive emissions of captured CO_2. Use of captured CO_2 in enhanced hydrocarbon recovery is likely to result in further fugitive emissions, as some CO_2 is released into the atmosphere in the course of separation from the recovered oil, gas, or methane. Furthermore, any later releases from the reservoir itself must also be accounted for to obtain a clear picture of the project's net benefits.

Finally, effects outside the boundary of the capture-transport-storage system itself ("leakage" in the economic sense) also must be taken into account. For instance, a project that combines CCS with enhanced hydrocarbon recovery will bring more fossil fuels to market than would otherwise be produced, which likely will result in additional downstream CO_2 emissions.

4. Kyoto Protocol Flexibility Mechanisms

The Kyoto parties have not yet determined how CCS will be accounted for within Annex I countries or whether CCS projects will be eligible to generate emissions credits under the CDM or the JI. The CDM Executive Board has received proposals for capture and geological storage projects in non-Annex I countries,[229] and at the Montreal meeting of the Kyoto parties in 2005, the parties agreed to address the issue of eligibility of CCS projects under the CDM and solicited submissions on this subject.[230]

In addition to the generic accounting issues discussed above, capture and storage projects raise a number of other issues under the JI and CDM, including what methods of storage will be eligible to generate credits, given environmental concerns and potential international legal barriers that have been raised with regard to ocean storage, for example. Also in question are requirements for selection, management, and monitoring of storage sites that the CDM Executive Board or the JI Supervisory Board could require.

Cross-border projects, where carbon is captured in one country and stored in another, raise a host of additional accounting and liability issues under the Kyoto Protocol. In the case of two Annex I countries with emissions caps, the issue is likely to be comparatively straightforward. The party from which emissions were captured would account for the capture as a source reduction or removal, and the party hosting the storage facility would be accountable for any future releases for purposes of complying with its Kyoto obligations.[231] The parties presumably could enter an agreement allocating liability for future releases and responsibility for monitoring and verification of storage.[232]

Projects involving storage in non-Annex I countries raise more complex issues, because such countries have no direct liability under the Protocol for future releases. Default rules would likely need to be adopted to govern liability for such releases. In a cross-border project involving two non-Annex I countries, the buyer of CDM credits presumably would bear some potential liability for future releases (for example, through a discount and/or a temporary credit regime).[233] Where an Annex I country captures CO_2 for storage in a non-Annex I country, the former presumably would be required to account for any future releases in its national inventory unless the CERs purchaser accepted liability via a discount, temporary credit, or the like.[234]

Another wrinkle would be added where carbon captured in a number of separate countries is stored in a single facility. Future releases from storage could not be assigned to any individual contributor, and some mechanism for allocation of liability might have to be adopted. A different set of concerns would arise in the case of CO_2 storage at an offshore site located in international waters. Here again, the parties would likely have to settle on at least a default rule regarding liability for future releases—for example, by assigning liability to the party that captured the CO_2 (or some contribution-based allocation formula in the case of multiparty storage sites). The parties also may be able to contract around this default rule through agreements reallocating liability.[235]

III. Conclusion

Policy makers are showing increasing interest in carbon sequestration as a potentially important arrow in the quiver of measures to mitigate global climate change in the near term. Both biological and physical sequestration strategies show promise, and both are likely to play a significant role in any future U.S. climate change regime. As the foregoing discussion makes clear, large-scale implementation of these strategies will require sustained engagement with a host of interesting and challenging legal and policy issues.

Endnotes

1.   Scientists also have examined the possibility of enhancing biological sequestration in marine ecosystems by fertilizing the oceans with iron or other nutrients to induce phytoplankton blooms. The idea is that phytoplankton would act as biological "pumps," sequestering carbon, which ultimately would be deposited on the ocean floor in the form of dead organic matter. However, this approach has not gained traction because of major uncertainties regarding its practical feasibility and potential environmental risks. *See* Intergovernmental Panel on Climate Change, Climate Change 2001: Mitigation 332-33 (2001) [hereinafter "IPCC Mitigation"]; Karen N. Scott, *The Day After Tomorrow: Ocean CO2. Sequestration and the Future of Climate Change*, 18 Geo. Int'l Envtl. L. Rev. 57, 93-96 (2005); Alexander Gillespie, *Sinks and the Climate Change Regime: The State of Play*, 13 Duke Envt'l L. & Pol'y F. 279, 280-81 (2003). Because marine biological sequestration has not played any significant role in recent policy discussions and initiatives, the discussion in this chapter focuses primarily on land-based strategies.

2.   *See* S. Pacala & R. Socolow, *Stabilization Wedges: Solving the Climate Problem for the Next 50 Years with Current Technologies*, 305 Science 968 (2004).

3.   IPCC Mitigation, *supra* note 1, at 307.

4.   *See* Intergovernmental Panel on Climate Change, Land Use, Land-Use Change, and Forestry 30 (2000) [hereinafter "IPCC LULUCF Report"]; Pacala & Socolow, *supra* note 2, at 398 (estimating current emissions at roughly 7 GtC/year); Robert T. Watson & Ian R. Noble, *The Global Imperative and Policy for Carbon Sequestration*, in The Carbon Balance of Forest Biomes 1, 3-4 (H. Griffiths & P. Jarvis eds., 2005) (providing estimates of carbon sinks and sources).

5.   *See* Intergovernmental Panel on Climate Change, Climate Change 2001: The Scientific Basis 191-92 (2001) [hereinafter "IPCC Scientific Basis"].

6.   *Id.* at 204; *see also* Marcio Santilli, et al., *Tropical Deforestation and the Kyoto Protocol*, 71 Climate Change 267, 267 (2005).

7.   IPCC, Scientific Basis, *supra* note 5, at 193.

8.   *See, e.g.,* Herman Shugart et al., Forests & Global Climate Change: Potential Impacts on U.S. Forest Resources 1 (Pew Center on Global Climate Change, Feb. 2003).

9.   *See, e.g.,* Santilli, *supra* note 6, at 267-68.

10.   IPCC LULUCF Report, *supra* note 4, at 198.

11. *See, e.g.*, United Nations Environmental Program, Secretariat of the Convention on Biological Diversity, Interlinkages Between Biological Diversity and Climate Change, CBD Tech. Series No. 10, at 54 (Oct. 2003) [hereinafter "UNEP"].

12. ROBERT N. STAVINS & KENNETH R. RICHARDS, THE COST OF U.S. FOREST-BASED CARBON SEQUESTRATION 18 (Pew Center for Global Climate Change Jan. 2005).

13. U.S. ENVIRONMENTAL PROTECTION AGENCY, GREENHOUSE GAS MITIGATION POTENTIAL IN U.S. FORESTRY AND AGRICULTURE, EPA 430-R-05-006, at 2-5 (Nov. 2005) [hereinafter "EPA GHG Mitigation Potential"]; IPCC Scientific Basis, *supra* note 5, at 193.

14. Sandra Brown et al., *Changes in the Use and Management of Forests for Abating Carbon Emissions: Issues and Challenges Under the Kyoto Protocol*, in CAPTURING CARBON AND CONSERVING BIODIVERSITY: THE MARKET APPROACH, 42, 46 (Ian R. Swingland ed. 2002).

15. *See, e.g.*, IPCC LULUCF Report, *supra* note 4, at 214-27; IPCC Mitigation, *supra* note 1, at 316.

16. EPA, GHG Mitigation Potential, *supra* note 13, at 2-4; IPCC LULUCF Report, *supra* note 4, at 216-17.

17. IPCC LULUCF Report, *supra* note 4, at 216.

18. EPA, GHG Mitigation Potential, *supra* note 13, at 2-5; IPCC LULUCF Report, *supra* note 4, at 202.

19. IPCC LULUCF Report, *supra* note 4, at 202; IPCC Mitigation, *supra* note 1, at 324, 327.

20. IPCC LULUCF Report, *supra* note 4, at 204-08; IPCC Mitigation, *supra* note 1, at 325.

21. IPCC Mitigation, *supra* note 1, at 325; EPA GHG Mitigation, *supra* note 13, at 2-5.

22. IPCC Mitigation, *supra* note 1, at 324.

23. UNEP, *supra* note 11, at 60-61.

24. IPCC LULUCF Report, *supra* note 4, at 217-18.

25. IPCC Mitigation, *supra* note 1, at 8, 303.

26. IPCC LULUCF Report, *supra* note 4, at 14 (Table 4); *see also* Pacala & Socolow, *supra* note 2, at 968 (estimating anthropogenic emissions at roughly 7 Gt of carbon per year).

27. Unless otherwise noted, we use the term "ton" to mean metric ton and all mass measurements are in metric units. A short ton is 2000 lbs, equal to 0.9 metric tons.

28. STAVINS & RICHARDS, *supra* note 12, at 32-33. For studies modeling the likely extent and mix of carbon sequestration activities in the United States for different prices per ton of CO_2, *see generally, e.g.*, EPA GHG Mitigation, *supra* note 13, and Ruben N. Lubowski et al., *Land-Use Change and Carbon Sinks: Econometric Estimation of the Carbon Sequestration Supply Function*, RESOURCES FOR THE FUTURE DISCUSSION PAPER 05-04 (Jan. 2005).

29. *See* Brian C. Murray, *Overview of Agricultural and Forestry GHG Offsets on the U.S. Landscape*, CHOICES, Fall 2004, at 13.

30. *See, e.g.*, Gillespie, *supra* note 1, at 282-83.

31. WORLD BANK, BIOCARBON FUND BROCHURE, *available at* http://carbonfinance.org/Router.cfm?Page=BioCF&ItemID= 9708&FID= 9708.

32. IPCC Mitigation, *supra* note 1, at 8; *see also id.* at 318-19 (Table 4.3), 321 (Table 4.5).

33. *See generally* IPCC LULUCF Report, *supra* note 4, at 106-09.

34. *See, e.g.*, UNEP, *supra* note 11, at 63.

35. *See, e.g.*, IPCC Mitigation, *supra* note 1, at 326; UNEP, *supra* note 11, at 58-60.

36. *See, e.g.*, IPCC Mitigation, *supra* note 1, at 326-27; UNEP, *supra* note 11, at 67-68.

37. *See generally* Pew Center on Global Climate Change, *Agriculture's Role in Addressing Climate Change*, In Brief, No. 2; Tanveer A. Butt & Bruce A. McCarl, *Farm and Forest Carbon Sequestration: Can Producers Employ it to Make Some Money?*, Choices, Fall 2004, at 27.

38. *See, e.g.*, Sebastian Scholz & Ian Noble, Generation of Sequestration Credits Under the CDM, in Legal Aspects of Implementing the Kyoto Protocol Mechanisms: Making Kyoto Work 265, 278 (David Freestone & Charlotte Streck eds., 2005) [hereinafter "Making Kyoto Work"]; John O. Niles, *Potential Carbon Mitigation and Income in Developing Countries From Changes in Use and Management of Agricultural and Forest Lands, in* Capturing Carbon and Conserving Biodiversity, *supra* note 14, at 70.

39. *See* Gillespie, *supra* note 1, at 291-92; *see also* IPCC LULUCF Report, *supra* note 4, at 11 (discussing measurement methods on a landscape level); Kelly Conelly Gary, *Managing Carbon in a World Economy: The Role of American Agriculture*, 9 Great Plains Nat. Resources J. 18, 23 (2005) (discussing new technologies for measuring soil carbon); Timothy Pearson et al., Sourcebook for Land Use, Land-Use Change and Forestry Projects 11-30 (2005) (discussing measurement methods at the project level).

40. *See* Frank Keppler, *Methane Emissions From Terrestrial Plants Under Aerobic Conditions*, 439 Nature 187 (2006); David C. Lowe, *Global Change: A Green Source of Surprise*, 439 Nature 148 (2006).

41. *See Do Recent Scientific Findings Undermine the Climate Benefits of Carbon Sequestration in Forests?: An Expert Review of Recent Studies on Methane Emissions and Water Tradeoffs* 4-6 (April 2006), *available at* http://www.env.duke.edu/institute/methanewater.pdf.

42. IPCC Scientific Basis, *supra* note 5, at 195.

43. *See, e.g.*, Peter B. Reich, et al., *Nitrogen Limitation Constrains Sustainability of Ecosystem Response to CO2*, 440 Nature 922 (2006); Kees-Jan van Groenigen, et al., *Element Interactions Limit Soil Carbon Storage*, 103 Proc. Nat'l Acad. Sci. 6571 (2006); IPCC LULUCF Report, *supra* note 4, at 314.

44. IPCC Mitigation, *supra* note 1, at 314; IPCC LULUCF Report, *supra* note 4, at 41.

45. *See* IPCC LULUCF Report, *supra* note 4, at 42; *see also, e.g.*, Doug Struck, *"Rapid Warming" Spreads Havoc in Canada's Forests*, Wash. Post, Mar. 1, 2006, at A-1 (reporting attribution of pine beetle outbreak in Canadian Rockies, and accompanying forest die-off, to rapid warming).

46. *See, e.g.*, EPA GHG Mitigation Potential, *supra* note 13, at 6-4.

47. Niles et al., *supra* note 38, at 73.

48. *See, e.g.*, IPCC LULUCF Report, *supra* note 4, at 106; Gillespie, *supra* note 1, at 295-96; Michael Totten et al., *Biodiversity, Climate, and the Kyoto Protocol*, 1 Frontiers in Ecol. & Env't 261 (2003).

49. *See, e.g.*, IPCC Mitigation, *supra* note 1, at 326; IPCC LULUCF Report, *supra* note 4, at 108-09; Robert B. Jackson et al., *Trading Water for Carbon With Biological Carbon Sequestration*, 310 Science 1944 (2005).

50. *See, e.g.*, UNEP, *supra* note 11, at 66-67.

51. *See, e.g.,* IPCC Mitigation, *supra* note 1, at 326; IPCC LULUCF Report, *supra* note 4, at 111-12.

52. *See* Gillespie, *supra* note 1, at 283.

53. *Id.* at 283-84; *see also* United Nations Food and Agriculture Organization, A Review of Carbon Sequestration Projects, AGL/MISC/37/2004 (2004) (cataloguing over 30 bilateral carbon sequestration projects), *available at* http://www.fao.org/AG/AGL/agll/carbonsequestration/documents.stm.

54. UtiliTree is a nonprofit corporation established in 1994 by a group of 40 North American utility companies through the leadership of the Edison Electric Institute. UtiliTree's members raised $3 million for 10 carbon sequestration projects involving tree planting, forest preservation, and forest management both in the United States and abroad. These projects are projected to sequester 3 million tons of CO_2 equivalent over 40-70 years. *See* National Carbon Offset Coalition, Carbon Sequestration: A Handbook, Version 2.1, at 32 (Dec. 2005) ["NCOS Handbook"]. PowerTree is a consortium of 25 U.S. electric power companies organized by the Edison Electric Institute that are partnering with conservation organizations and federal agencies in bottomland hardwood reforestation projects in the lower Mississippi Alluvial Valley. The project is expected to sequester more than 1.6 million tons of CO_2 and to provide critical habitat. *See id.* at 32-33. For further information, visit PowerTree's Web site at http://www.powertreecarboncompany.com. For an overview of business involvement in voluntary sequestration projects, see the page maintained by the Pew Center for Global Climate Change at http://www.pewclimate.org/what_s_being_done/in_the_business_community/sequestration.cfm.

55. *See* Melissa Chan & Sarah Forbes, Carbon Sequestration Role in State and Local Actions, DOE/NETL-2005/1212, at 13-14 (Jan. 2005) (summarizing projects). PowerTree, for example, involves partnerships with a number of conservation groups and the U.S. Fish & Wildlife Service. *See* NCOS Handbook, *supra* note 54, at 33. In 2002, Entergy Corp.—with financial support from the Conservation Fund—provided 600 acres of fallow agricultural lands along Louisiana's Red River to the federal government as the first tract of the Red River National Wildlife Refuge near Sheveport. Entergy will receive credit for reforestation efforts on the land if future caps on greenhouse gas emissions are adopted. In 2001, American Electric Power, the Conservation Fund, and the Fish & Wildlife Service collaborated in acquiring, protecting, and restoring over 18,000 acres of bottomland hardwood forest near Catahoula Lake in Louisiana. *See* Eryn Gable, *Entergy Donates La. Land for Refuge in Effort to Reduce CO_2,* Land Letter, Sept. 5, 2002, *available at* http://www.eenews.net/LandLetter/Backissues/090502ll.htm.

56. *See* The Nature Conservancy, Climate Action Project: Noel Kempff Mercado National Park, Bolivia, *at* http://www.nature.org/initiatives/climatechange/work/art4253.html.

57. *See* Ducks Unlimited's Carbon Sequestration Program, *at* http://www.ducks.org/conservation/CarbonSequestration.asp.

58. Examples include the Carbon Neutral Company (www.carbonneutral.com) and 500 ppm (www.500ppm.com/en).

59. *See, e.g.,* Chicago Climate Exchange, The Chicago Accord (2004), *available at* http://www.chicagoclimatex.com/about/pdf/ChicagoAccord_050623.pdf. For an overview of eligible forestry and agricultural soils projects, *see* Chicago Climate Exchange, CCX Forestry Carbon Emission Offsets, at http://www.chicagoclimatex.com/news/publications/pdf/CCX_Forest_Offsets.pdf (last visited May 4, 2006), and Chicago Climate Exchange, CCX Agricultural Soil Carbon Offsets, at http://www.chicagoclimatex.com/news/publications/pdf/CCX_Soil_Offsets.pdf (last visited May 4, 2006). For some further discussion of CCX rules applicable to forestry projects,

see NCOS Handbook, *supra* note 54, at 24-25.

60.   *See* CCX Forestry Carbon Emission Offsets and CCX Agricultural Soil Carbon Offsets, *supra* note 59.

61.   *See* NCOS Handbook, *supra* note 54, at 24; CCX Agricultural Soil Carbon Offsets, *supra* note 59.

62.   Jerry Perkins, *Program Pays Farmers to Try Greener Methods*, DES MOINES REGISTER, Mar. 5, 2006.

63.   *See* 42 U.S.C. § 13385(b).

64.   *See* Guidelines for Voluntary Greenhouse Gas Reporting, 71 Fed. Reg. 20,784 (April 21, 2006); NCOS Handbook, *supra* note 54, at 35.

65.   *See* Kelly Connelly Garry, *Managing Carbon in a World Economy: The Role of American Agriculture*, 9 GREAT PLAINS NAT. RESOURCES J. 18, 24-25 (2005); Brian Stempeck, *Land Management: Farmers to get credit for carbon sinks – USDA*, LAND LETTER, June 12, 2003, *at* http://www.eenews.net/Landletter/print/2003/06/12/9.

66.   *See* CLIMATE CHANGE POLICY BOOK, *available at* http://www.whitehouse.gov/news/releases/2002/02/climatechange.html (visited April 21, 2006).

67.   *See id.*

68.   *See* Forest Land Enhancement Program; Interim Final Rule, 68 Fed. Reg. 34,309 (June 9, 2003).

69.   Pub. L. 108-148, 117 Stat. 1887 (2003), codified at scattered sections of Title 16 of the U.S. Code.

70.   Pub. L. 107-26, 115 Stat. 206 (2001), codified at 22 U.S.C. § 2431 *et seq.*.

71.   CLIMATE CHANGE POLICY BOOK, *supra* note 66; *see also* U.S. State Dep't, Tropical Forest Conservation Act, *at* http://www.state.gov/g/oes/rls/fs/2003/22973.htm.

72.   *See* David J. Hayes & Nicholas Gertler, *The Role of Carbon Sequestration in the U.S. Response to Climate Change—Challenges and Opportunities*, 32 ENVT'L L. REP. 11,350, 11,352 (2002); *see also, e.g., Climate Change: Brownback introduces carbon sequestration bills*, ENV'T & ENERGY DAILY, Apr. 25, 2001 (reporting introduction of legislation promoting domestic and international carbon sequestration programs). For a comprehensive listing of carbon-sequestration legislation introduced in recent Congresses, see the "On the Hill" Web page maintained by the Pew Center for Global Climate Change *at* http://www.pewclimate.org/policy_center/congressional/.

73.   S.342, § 302(b)(2); *see also id.* § 3(16) (defining sequestration).

74.   *See* Pew Center on Global Climate Change, Summary of Bingaman Climate and Economy Insurance Act of 2005, *available at* http://www.pewclimate.org/policy_center/analyses/bingaman_summary.cfm.

75.   Press Release, Senator Feinstein Outlines New Legislation to Curb Global Warming, Keep Economy Strong (Mar. 20, 2006), *available at* http://feinstein.senate.gov/06releases/r-global-warm320.htm.

76.   *See generally* Chan & Forbes, *supra* note 55; Kenneth L. Rosenbaum et al., FAO Forestry Paper 144, Climate Change and the Forest Sector: Possible National and Subnational Legislation 22-23 (2004); Pew Center on Global Climate Change, Climate Change Activities in the United States: 2004 Update, at 11-12 (2004), *available at* http://www.pewclimate.org/docUploads/74241_US%20Activities%20Report_040604_075445.pdf.

77. *See* Oregon Carbon Dioxide Emissions Standards for New Energy Facilities, *available at* http://www.oregon.gov/ENERGY/SITING/docs/ccnewst.pdf.

78. *See* Climate Trust, Oregon Power Plant Offset Program, *at* http://www.climatetrust.org/programs_powerplant.php.

79. Chan & Forbes, *supra* note 55, at 5.

80. *See id.* at 6-7.

81. Executive Order S-3-05 (June 1, 2005); *see also* Chan & Forbes, *supra* note 55, at 5.

82. *See* California Climate Action Team, Climate Action Team Report to Governor Schwarzenegger and the California Legislature 47-50 (Mar. 2006).

83. *See* Pew Center on Global Climate Change, Learning from State Action on Climate Change, March 2006 Update, at 8, *available at* http://www.pewclimate.org/policy_center/policy_reports_and_analysis/state/index.cfm; Chan & Forbes, *supra* note 55, at 5-6.

84. Kyoto Protocol to the United Nations Framework Convention on Climate Change, Dec. 10, 1997, art. 3.3, 37 I.L.M. 22, 33 [herinafter "Kyoto Protocol"]. The Kyoto parties have settled on the following definitions: "'Afforestation' is the direct human-induced conversion of land that has not been forested for a period of at least 50 years to forested land through planting, seeding, and/or the human-induced promotion of natural seed sources." Decision 16/CMP.1, Annex ¶ 1(b), U.N. Doc. FCCC/KP/CMP/2005/8/Add.3, at 3 (Mar. 30, 2006) [hereinafter "Decision 16/CMP.1"]. "'Reforestation' is the direct human-induced conversion of non-forested land to forested land through planting, seeding and/or the human-induced promotion of natural seed sources, on land that was forested but that has been converted to non-forested land. For the first commitment period, reforestation activities will be limited to reforestation occurring on those lands that did not contain forest on 31 December 1989." *Id.* ¶ 1(c) "'Deforestation' is the direct human-induced conversion of forested land to non-forested land." *Id.* ¶ 1(d).

The focus on afforestation, reforestation, and deforestation has required significant attention to the definition of "forest." As one observer explains, "If a high [canopy cover] threshold was set (e.g., over 70% canopy cover), then many areas of sparse forest and woodland could be cleared or planted and the resultant carbon losses or gains would not be accounted in determining forest emissions/sequestration under the Protocol. If a low threshold was set (e.g., 10% canopy cover), then dense forest could be heavily degraded and significant amounts of carbon released, without the actions being registered as 'deforestation.'" Gillespie, *supra* note 1, at 297. The Kyoto parties settled on a definition derived from the Food and Agricultural Organization definition, which focuses primarily on crown density. *See* Decision 16/CMP.1, Annex ¶ 1(a).

85. *See* Decision 16/CPM.1, *supra* note 84, Annex ¶ 6. Definitions of revegetation, forest management, cropland management, and grazing land management can be found at Decision 16/CMP.1, Annex ¶ 1(e) through (h). This decision was taken in accord with Article 3.4 of the Protocol, which directs the parties to "decide upon modalities, rules and guidelines as to how, and which, additional human-induced activities related to changes in greenhouse gas emissions by sources and removals by sinks in the agricultural soils and the land-use change and forestry categories shall be added to, or subtracted from, the assigned amounts for" Annex I parties.

86. *See* Decision 16/CPM.1, *supra* note 84, Annex ¶¶ 7, 10, 11.

87. *See* Kyoto Protocol, *supra* note 84, art. 3.4 (The Conference of the Parties' decision on modalities, rules, and guidelines for accounting for additional activities "shall apply in the second and subsequent commitment periods.").

88. *See* Gillespie, *supra* note 1, at 288.

89. *See, e.g.,* Masahiro Amano & Roger A. Sedjo, Forest Carbon Sinks: European Union, Japanese, and Canadian Approaches (Resources for the Future Disc. Paper 03-41) (Oct. 2003).

90. Kyoto Protocol, *supra* note 24, art. 12(2).

91. *Id.* art. 12(5)(c).

92. *Id.* art. 12(3)(b), art. 3(12).

93. It bears mentioning that Article 12 is silent as to whether and to what extent CERs can be generated from biological sequestration projects. Indeed, the additionality provision's reference to "reductions in emissions" but not to enhancement of removals by sinks (in contrast to Articles 3 and 6, for example) might be read to suggest that CERs cannot be generated based on sequestration projects at all.

94. Decision 16/CMP.1, *supra* note 84, Annex ¶ 13; *see also* Decision 17/CP.7, ¶ 7(a), U.N. Doc. FCCC/CP/2001/13/Add. 2, at 20 (Jan. 21, 2002) [hereinafter "Decision 17/CP.7"].

95. Decision 16/CMP.1, Annex ¶ 14; *see also* Decision 17/CP.7, *supra* note 94, ¶ 7(b).

96. Decision 5/CMP.1, ¶ 3, U.N. Doc. FCCC/KP/CMP/2005/8/Add. 1, at 61 (Mar. 30, 2006) [hereinafter Decision 5/CMP/1"]; Decision 16/CMP.1, *supra* note 84, Annex ¶ 15.

97. *See* Decision 5/CMP.1, *supra* note 96, Annex.

98. *See generally* Scholz & Noble, *supra* note 38, at 268-77.

99. Decision 5/CMP.1, *supra* note 96, Annex ¶ 20; *see also* Decision 19/CP.9 Annex ¶¶ 12-13, U.N. Doc. FCCC/CP/2003/6/Add. 2, at 13 (Mar. 30, 2004). For LULUCF projects, proponents must select from three general approaches to calculating the baseline: (a) existing or historical changes in carbon stocks in the pools within the project boundary; (b) changes in carbon stocks within the project boundary from a land use that represents an economically attractive course of action; or (c) changes in carbon stocks in the pools within the project boundary from the most likely land use at the time the project starts. Decision 5/CMP.1, *supra* note 96, Annex ¶ 22.

100. *See* Decision 5/CMP.1, *supra* note 96, Annex ¶ 12(c) and Appendix B ¶ 2(j), (k); *see also* Scholz & Noble, *supra* note 38, at 275-77.

101. *See* 5/CMP.1, *supra* note 96, Annex ¶¶ 10-37.

102. *See* 5/CMP.1, *supra* note 96, Annex ¶¶ 38-50; *see generally* Scholz & Noble, *supra* note 38, at 269-72.

103. Kyoto Protocol, *supra* note 84, art. 6.1.

104. *Id.* art. 3.10, 3.11.

105. *See* World Bank, BioCarbon Fund Brochure, *available at* http:// carbonfinance.org/ Router.cfm?Page=BioCF&ItemID=9708&FID=9708.

106. *See, e.g., Senior DOE Official Says Carbon Sequestration Gains Global Support,* Inside EPA, Nov. 17, 2005 (describing the "sea change" in the global view of CCS over the past few years).

107. Intergovernmental Panel on Climate Change, Special Report on Carbon Dioxide Capture and Storage 60 (Bert Metz et al. eds., 2005) [hereinafter "IPCC CCS Report"].

108. *Id.* at 112-13.

109. *Id.* at 9.

110. *Id.* at 111-13.

111. *E.g., id.* at 133.

112. *See, e.g.*, Kevin Coughlin, *King Coal Comes Clean*, SUNDAY STAR-LEDGER, Mar. 6, 2005, at 41.

113. WORLD BANK, LITTLE GREEN DATA BOOK 2006, at 221 (2006).

114. *Id.* at 64, 109.

115. IPCC CCS Report, *supra* note 107, at 114.

116. *Id.* at 25. A number of other technologies for post-combustion capture are also now emerging, including those using adsorption, membranes, and solid sorbents. *See id.* at 119-21.

117. *Id.* at 121.

118. Marcus Hov, *EU-Backed Carbon Sequestration Project Goes Online at Power Plant in Denmark*, 29 BNA Int'l Envt Rep. 187 (Mar. 23, 2006). For more information, visit CASTOR's Web site: http://www.co2castor.com.

119. IPCC CCS Report, *supra* note 107, at 122.

120. *Id.* at 122.

121. *See, e.g., id.* at 150, 157, 169 (Table 3.15).

122. *Id.* at 158.

123. *Id.* at 61. For a survey of capital costs and energy-efficiency costs associated with capture technologies for various types of new power plants, see *id.* at 169 (Table 3.15).

124. *Id.* at 140-41.

125. *See, e.g.*, Ram C. Sekar et al., *Future Carbon Regulations and Current Investments in Alternative Coal-Fired Power Plant Designs*, MIT Joint Program on Science and Policy of Global Change, Rep. No. 129 (Dec. 2005); Soren Anderson & Richard Newell, *Prospects for Carbon Capture and Storage, Resources for the Future Discussion Paper* 02-68, at 34-46 (Jan. 2003).

126. Pub. L. 109-58, § 1307, 119 Stat. 58 (2005).

127. *See* Darren Samuelsohn, *Lure of $1B FutureGen Project Energizes Mining States*, GREENWIRE, Nov. 8, 2005; *see also* U.S. DEP'T OF ENERGY, FUTUREGEN – TOMORROW'S POLLUTION-FREE POWER PLANT, *at* http://www.fossil.energy.gov/programs/powersystems/futuregen/.

128. Matthew L. Wald, *Power Plant Would Reuse Carbon Dioxide*, N.Y. TIMES, Feb. 11, 2006.

129. *Electric Company Plans Coal-Fired Plant With Carbon Sequestration in Germany*, 29 BNA Int'l Env't Rep. 270, 270 (Apr. 19, 2006).

130. Marcus Hov, *Shell, Norway's Statoil Announce Project to Use Captured Carbon to Extract More Oil*, 29 BNA Int'l Env't Rep. 187, 187 (Mar. 22, 2006).

131. Norway requires inclusion of carbon-capture technology as a precondition for the award of new gas power licenses. Marcus Hov, *supra* note 130 at 187, 188 (Mar. 23, 2006). In the United Kingdom, a recent Parliament report recommends requiring that all new power and industrial plants be fitted with equipment to make them "capture-ready." Tom Blass, U.K. *Parliamentary Report Urges Steps to Promote Carbon Capture, Storage*, 29 BNA Int'l Env't Rep. 114 (Feb. 22, 2006).

132. IPCC CCS Report, *supra* note 107, at 181.

133. The U.S. Department of Transportation's Office of Pipeline Safety administers pipeline construction and safety regulations. *See* 49 C.F.R. Parts 190-99. The Interstate Oil and Gas Compact Commission recently concluded that, "given the large body of experience in pipeline operation, including CO_2 pipelines, well-established regulatory frameworks, and well-established materials and construction standards, there is little necessity for additional state regulations." INTERSTATE OIL AND GAS COMPACT COMMISSION, CARBON CAPTURE AND STORAGE: A REGULATORY FRAMEWORK FOR STATES 44-45 (2005).

134. IPCC CCS Report, *supra* note 107, at 199.

135. *See generally id.* at 200-04; Anderson & Newell, *supra* note 125, at 6-7.

136. *See* IPCC CCS Report, *supra* note 107, at 208.

137. *See, e.g., id.* at 244; Jan M. Nordbotten et al., *Semianalytical Solution for CO₂ Leakage Through an Abandoned Well*, 39 ENVTL. SCI. & TECH. 602 (2005).

138. IPCC CCS Report, *supra* note 107, at 215-16.

139. Ben Geman, *New Carbon Technologies Could Quadruple U.S. Reserves – DOE*, GREENWIRE, Mar. 6, 2006.

140. *See* IPCC CCS Report, *supra* note 107, at 217.

141. *Id.* at 217-19; Anderson & Newell, *supra* note 125, at 28.

142. IPCC CCS Report, *supra* note 107, at 221-24.

143. U.S. DEP'T OF ENERGY, CARBON SEQUESTRATION TECHNOLOGY ROADMAP AND PROGRAM PLAN 2005, at 4 (May 2005).

144. IPCC CCS Report, *supra* note 107, at 12.

145. *Id.* at 33.

146. *Id.* at 23.

147. *Id.* at 36-37.

148. *Id.* at 246-50.

149. *Id.* at 244-46.

150. *See* U.S. Dep't of Energy, Carbon Sequestration Regional Partnerships, *at* http://www.fe.doe.gov/programs/sequestration/partnerships/index.html

151. *See, e.g.*, Energy Policy Act of 2005, Pub. L. 109-58, § 354, 119 Stat. 594 (2005) (Enhanced Oil and Natural Gas Production Through Carbon Dioxide Injection).

152. Advance Notice of Proposed Rulemaking, Enhanced Oil and Natural Gas Production Through Carbon Dioxide Injection, 71 Fed. Reg. 11,557, 11,557 (Mar. 8, 2006).

153. *China, European Union Sign Agreement to Jointly Study Feasibility of Sequestration*, BNA Daily Env't Rep., Feb. 28, 2006.

154. Marcus Hov, *EU-Backed Carbon Sequestration Project Goes Online at Power Plant in Denmark*, 29 BNA Int'l Env't Rep. 187, 187 (Mar. 22, 2006); *see also* http://www.co2castor.com.

155. *See supra* notes 129-30 and accompanying text.

156. IPCC CCS Report, *supra* note 107, at 281.

157. *Id.* at 281.

158. *See* IPCC Scientific Basis, *supra* note 5, at 197-200; Scott, *supra* note 1, at 58 & n.8.

159. For a more in-depth discussion of these methods, *see, e.g.*, IPCC CCS Report, *supra* note 107, at 295-98; Anderson & Newell, *supra* note 125, at 29-30.

160. *See* IPCC CCS Report, *supra* note 107, at 285.

161. *See id.* at 298-306; Anderson & Newell, *supra* note 125, at 30-31.

162. IPCC CCS Report, *supra* note 107, at 38, 303; Anderson & Newell, *supra* note 125, at 31.

163. *See* IPCC CCS Report, *supra* note 107, at 298.

164. *Id.* at 306; Anderson & Newell, *supra* note 125, at 31.

165. IPCC CCS Report, *supra* note 107, at 307.

166. *See supra* note 1.

167. *See* INTERSTATE OIL AND GAS COMPACT COMMISSION, CARBON CAPTURE AND STORAGE: A REGULATORY FRAMEWORK FOR STATES 8-10, 28-35 (2005) [hereinafter "IOGCC"].

168. 42 U.S.C. § 300h.

169. 42 U.S.C. § 300h-1. The regulations governing state and tribal assumption of primacy are found in 40 C.F.R. Part 145. The applicable UIC programs for each state are set forth in 40 C.F.R. Part 147. The requirements for the EPA-administered programs are found in 40 C.F.R. Parts 144 and 146.

170. U.S. Environmental Protection Agency, State UIC Programs, at http://www.epa/gov/safewater/primacy.html (last updated Feb. 28, 2006) (visited May 1, 2006).

171. For an overview of the program, see, e.g., U.S. Environmental Protection Agency, Technical Program Overview: Underground Injection Control Regulations, EPA 816-R-02-025 (July 2001), available at http://www.epa.gov/safewater/uic/pdfs/uic_techovrview.pdf.

172. 40 C.F.R. § 144.12(a). "Underground sources of drinking water" is defined broadly so as to include aquifers not currently being used as drinking water sources and those that could not be used without some form of water treatment. See U.S. Environmental Protection Agency, Technical Program Overview: Underground Injection Control Regulations, EPA 816-R-02-025, at 5 (July 2001); 40 C.F.R. § 144.3 (regulatory definition). This broad definition is consistent with 42 U.S.C. § 300h(d)(2), which provides that "[u]nderground injection endangers drinking water sources if such injection may result in the presence in underground water which supplies *or can reasonably be expected to supply* any public water system of any contaminant, and if the presence of such contaminant may result in such system's not complying with any national primary drinking water regulation or may otherwise adversely affect the health of persons." (Emphasis added.)

173. See 42 U.S.C. § 300h(d)(1).

174. For definitions of the various well classes, see 40 C.F.R. § 144.6. Construction or operation of new Class IV wells is prohibited except in limited circumstances. 40 C.F.R. § 144.13. Regulations for the other well classes are set forth in 40 C.F.R. Part 146. For a discussion of the number and types of wells falling within the various classes, see, e.g., MARK A. DE FIGUEIREDO, THE UNDERGROUND INJECTION OF CONTROL OF CARBON DIOXIDE 8-15 (Special Report to the MIT Carbon Sequestration Initiative) (Feb. 2005).

175. 40 C.F.R. §§ 144.80, 144.81; see also de Figuereido, supra note 174, at 14.

176. *EPA Developing Policy on CO_2 Storage, But Faces Long-Term Questions*, INSIDE EPA, Mar. 15, 2006; see also DE FIGUEIREDO, supra note 174, at 19 (reporting that "[s]cientists affiliated with the Gulf Coast Carbon Center received a Class V permit from Texas regulators for an experiment injecting carbon dioxide into the Frio brine formation in Texas").

177. *See id.* Some commentators have argued that CO_2 injection and storage should be regulated under a Class I regime because CO_2 is likely to be stored for long time periods at depths greater than those where most underground drinking water sources are found. See de Figueiredo, supra note 174, at 17-18. Only the regulations for Class I hazardous wells authorize mandatory monitoring of fluid movement in an injection zone, monitoring leakage in overlying zones, and monitoring water quality in nearby drinking water aquifers. See 40 C.F.R. § 146.68; DE FIGUEIREDO, supra note 174, at 19. Other commentators have suggested that if the UIC regime is to be applied to underground injection and storage of CO_2, it must be adapted to focus on realistic performance-based standards, such as maximum leakage rates. See David Keith et al., *Regulating the Underground Injection of CO2*, ENVTL. SCI. & TECH., Dec. 15, 2005, at 499A, 504A.

178. IOGCC, supra note 167, at 51-53.

179. *Id.* at 53.

180. The terms "climate liability" and "*in situ* liability" are from M.A. de Figueiredo et al., *Framing the Long-Term* In Situ *Liability Issue for Geologic Carbon Storage in*

the United States, 10 MITIGATION AND ADAPTATION STRATEGIES FOR
GLOBAL CHANGE 647, 648 (2005).

181. IOGCC, *supra* note 167, at 54-56.

182. *Id.* at 55; de Figueiredo et al., *supra* note 180, at 653.

183. De Figueiredo, *supra* note 180, at 653-54.

184. IOGCC, *supra* note 167, at 55-56.

185. MARK A. DE FIGUEIREDO, PROPERTY INTERESTS AND LIABILITY OF
GEOLOGIC CARBON DIOXIDE STORAGE 5-7 (Special Report to the MIT
Carbon Sequestration Initiative) (Sept. 2005).

186. DE FIGUEIREDO, *supra* note 185, at 6.

187. *Id.* at 8-9. Rules for allocating groundwater rights vary
greatly from state to state: In broad strokes, the "absolute dominion" rule assigns the owner of surface interests rights over
underlying groundwater; the "reasonable use" rule provides that
groundwater can be taken as long as it is used in a reasonable
and beneficial manner; the "correlative rights" rule allocates
groundwater rights proportionally to surface ownership; and
the "prior appropriation" rule assigns rights on a first-come,
first-served basis. *Id.* at 9-11.

188. *Id.* at 12-13, 21-22; *see also* 15 U.S.C. § 717f(h) (eminent
domain provision of Natural Gas Act); Columbia Gas Transmission Corp. v. An Exclusive Gas Storage Easement, 776 F.2d
125, 128 (6th Cir. 1985) (holding that Natural Gas Act's eminent domain provision authorized condemnation of an underground natural gas storage facility); Schneidewind v. ANR Pipeline Co., 485 U.S. 293, 295 n.1 (1988) (endorsing this interpretation in dicta).

189. IOGCC, *supra* note 167, at Appx. 6.

190. DE FIGUEIREDO, *supra* note 185, at 17-18.

191. IOGCC, *supra* note 167, at Appx. 6, Part II, § 1.

192. *Id.* at Appx. 6, Part II, § 3.

193. United Nations Convention on the Law of the Sea, opened
for signature Dec. 10, 1982, art. 56.1(a), 21 I.L.M. 1261 [hereinafter "UNCLOS"].

194. *Id.* art. 77.1, 77.4.

195. Scott, *supra* note 1, at 66.

196. UNCLOS, *supra* note 193, art. 60, 80.

197. *Id.* art. 87.1.

198. *Id.* art. 87.2.

199. *Id.* art. 136, 140.

200. *Id.* art. 117.

201. *Id.* art. 145.

202. *Id.* art. 207, 208, 209, 210, 211.

203. In addition to the London Convention and the London Protocol, extensive attention has been devoted to treatment of offshore CO_2 storage under OSPAR Convention—a treaty between 15 European states and the European Union establishing a
regional regime governing marine pollution in the northeast Atlantic. *See generally*
Convention for the Protection of the Marine Environment of the North-East Atlantic,
Sept. 22, 1992, 32 I.L.M. 1072 (entered into force Mar. 25, 1998). Although the OSPAR
Convention does not implicate the United States and therefore is beyond the scope of
this book, it provides a useful perspective on international and regional approaches to
offshore storage issues. For discussion of CO_2 storage issues under the OSPAR Convention, *see* OSPAR COMMISSION, REPORT FROM THE GROUP OF JURISTS AND LINGUISTS ON PLACE-

MENT OF CARBON DIOXIDE IN THE OSPAR MARITIME AREA, in Summary Record OSPAR 2004, OSPAR 04/23/1-E, Annex 12 (2004), *available at* http://www.ospar.org/eng/ html/meetings; Scott, *supra* note 1, at 79-85;

204. Convention on the Prevention of Marine Pollution by Dumping of Wastes and Other Matter, Nov. 13, 1972, 11 I.L.M. 1291 (entered into force 1975), Art. IV.1(a), Annex I, ¶ 11 [hereinafter "London Convention"].

205. *See* Scott, *supra* note 1, at 77; Jason Heinrich, Legal Implications of CO_2 Ocean Storage 3 (Mass. Inst. Tech. Laboratory for Energy and the Envt. Working Paper, July 2002).

206. London Convention, *supra* note 204, art. IV.1(c); *see also id.* art. III.4 (defining "waste" broadly as "material and substance of any kind, form or description").

207. *Id.* art. III(1)(a)(i), (b)(ii).

208. *See id.* art. II.

209. 1996 Protocol to the Convention on the Prevention of Marine Pollution by Dumping of Wastes and Other Matter, Nov. 8, 1996, 36 I.L.M. 1 (entered into force Mar. 24, 2006) [hereinafter "London Protocol"], Art. 4.1.1, Annex I.

210. *Id.* art. 1, § 4.1.

211. *Id.* art. 1, § 4.2.2.

212. 33 U.S.C. § 1414b(a)(1)(B).

213. 33 U.S.C. § 1402(f).

214. 33 U.S.C. § 1411.

215. 33 U.S.C. § 1412(a).

216. 33 U.S.C. § 1412(a). EPA has promulgated regulations governing ocean dumping, which are codified at 40 C.F.R. parts 220 through 229. Part 227 sets forth EPA's criteria for evaluation of permit applications.

217. 40 C.F.R. § 227.16(a)(2).

218. 33 U.S.C. §§ 1311(a), 1342; *see also* 33 U.S.C. § 1362(12) (defining "discharge of a pollutant").

219. 33 U.S.C. § 1362(6).

220. *See* 33 U.S.C. § 1362(6).

221. 33 U.S.C. § 1343(a).

222. 40 C.F.R. § 125.123(a), (b). "Unreasonable degradation of the marine environment" means "(1) Significant adverse changes in ecosystem diversity, productivity and stability of the biological community within the area of discharge and surrounding biological communities, (2) Threat to human health through direct exposure to pollutants or through consumption of exposed aquatic organisms, or (3) Loss of esthetic, recreational, scientific or economic values which is unreasonable in relation to the benefit derived from the discharge." 40 C.F.R. § 125.121(e).

223. 40 C.F.R. § 125.123(c); *see also* 40 C.F.R. § 125.121(d) (defining "no unreasonable alternatives").

224. *See* Sven Bode & Martina Jung, On the Integration of Carbon Capture and Storage into the International Climate Regime 9-10 (HWWA Discussion Paper 303) (2004).

225. *See, e.g.*, Susanne Haefeli et al., Carbon Dioxide Capture and Storage Issues— Accounting and Baselines Under the United Nations Framework Convention on Climate Change (UNFCCC) 29 (Int'l Energy Ass'n Information Paper 2004).

226. Sven Bode & Martina Jung, Carbon Dioxide Capture and Storage (CCS)—Liability For Non-Permanence Under the UNFCCC 8-9 (HWWA Discussion Paper 325).

227. Bode & Jung, *supra* note 224, at 20-22.

228. *See* Haefeli et al., *supra* note 225, at 25-26.

229. At the time of this writing, the CDM Executive Board has already received two proposals for carbon capture and storage projects, one to use CO_2 captured from NGCC plants for enhanced oil recovery in Vietnam and a second to capture CO_2 from

liquefied natural gas processing and inject it into an aquifer in Malaysia. The Board has deferred consideration of these projects until the parties have taken action regarding the eligibility and guidelines for capture and storage projects.

230. Decision 7/CMP.1, *supra* note 185. The submissions of the parties are available on the UNFCCC Web site.

231. Bode & Jung, *supra* note 226, at 10.

232. *See* Haefeli et al., *supra* note 225, at 21.

233. Bode & Jung, *supra* note 226, at 10.

234. *Id.*; Haefeli et al., *supra* note 225, at 21.

235. *See* Haefeli et al., *supra* note 225, at 22.

Index

A

additionality 651
Aguinda v. Texaco 230
Alexander v. Sandoval 220
alternative fuel vehicles, incentives for
    574–76
    2005 Act provisions 574–76
    pre-2005 provisions 574
Army Corps of Engineers 65
Asia-Pacific Partnership on Clean
    Development and Climate 56

B

*Border Plant Working Group v. DOE and
    BLM* 303
*Border Power Plant Working Group v.
    Dep't of Energy* 217
Byrd-Hagel Resolution of 1997 21

C

carbon sequestration 685–721
    biological sequestration in terrestrial
        ecosystems 693–707
        government policies in the United
            States 702
        Kyoto Protocol 704
        land use strategies 693–96
        policy issues 696–700
        private voluntary initiatives 700–
            01
        scientific background 693–96
    capture and storage 707–27
        accounting issues 724–26
        capture and transport technologies
            708–11
        Kyoto Protocol flexibility mecha-
            nisms 726
        legal issues and offshore geological
            and ocean storage 720
        ocean storage 714–16
        U.S. legal/regulatory issues and
            underground storage 716–20

underground geologic storage
    711–14
Center for International Environmental
    Law 150
Citizens for Better Forestry v. U.S.D.A.
    194
City of Los Angeles v. NHTSA 187–
    89, 216
*City of Milwaukee v. Illinois (Milwaukee
    II)* 209
civil remedies 181–237
    Alien Tort Statute 224–37
        Aguinda v. Texaco 230
        Amlon Metals, Inc. v. FMC Corp.
            230
        Beanal v. Freeport-McMoRan, Inc.
            232
        environmental claims 230–58
        Erie Railroad Co. v. Tompkins
            228
        Federal Tort Claims Act 227
        Filarartiga v. Pena-Irala 225–26
        Flores v. Southern Peru Copper
            235
        future environmental human rights
            claims 236–58
        private versus state actors 229
        Sarei v. Rio Tinto PLC 233
        Sosa v. Alvarez-Machain 227–28
    causation 200–08
        Comer v. Murphy Oil 201–04
        equitable defense of unclean hands
            208–09
        generic and specific 200–04
        liability for and apportionment of
            damages 207
        potential types of defendants 206–
            07
        proximate causation and substanti-
            ality requirement 204–06
    Endangered Species Act 219
    environmental justice 220–21
        Alexander v. Sandoval 220
    human rights claims 221–24

M

Massachusetts v. EPA 191–93, 523
McCall v. Scott 509
McCarran-Ferguson Act 543
*Mid States Coalition for Progress v.
   Surface Transportation Board* 218
Montreal Protocol 73, 269
   ban on hydrofluorocarbons 269
motor vehicle emissions 20–21
   Corporate Average Fuel Economy 20
Multilateral Investment Guarantee
   Agency 291

N

National Academy of Sciences 73
National Academy of Sciences Report,
   2001 73
National Aeronautics and Space Admin-
   istration, 80
National Climate Program Act 75–76
National Commission on Energy Policy
   82
National Environmental Policy Act 21,
   186, 213–14, 270
National Highway Traffic Safety
   Administration 187
National Oceanic and Atmospheric
   Administration 80
National Research Council 3–5, 77, 81
Natural Resources Defense Council
   187–89
*Natural Resources Defense Council v.
   EPA* 193–94
New England Legal Foundation v. Costle
   209
new source construction
   consideration of Greenhouse gases in
      PSD and NNSR
         academic literature 150
new source construction
   consideration of greenhouse gases in
      prevention of significant deteriora-
      tion and nonattainment new source
      review 147–55
         additional case law 153–55
         environmental appeals board
            decisions 151

new electric utility construction
   149–50
*Northwest Environmental Defense
   Center v. Owens Corp.* 148
Page letter 151–53
new source performance standards
   challenge 145
      attorneys general citizen suits
         146–47
      Integrated Gasification Combined
         Cycle 146
      Our Children's Earth Foundation
         145
      Sierra Club 145
*Northwest Environmental Defense Center
   v. Owens Corp.* 148

O

Organization of the Petroleum Exporting
   Countries 69
   oil embargo 69

P

Public Utilities Regulatory Act of 1978
   581
Public Utility Holding Company Act
   582

R

Regional Greenhouse Gas Initiative 22
regional greenhouse gas initiatives
   318–42, 659–66
   California-United Kingdom Collabora-
      tion 331
   emissions trading 659–66
   individual regional initiatives 321–31
   legal issues 333–42
      Commerce Clause theories 335–42
      Compact Clause theories 335–42
      potential constitutional and other
         challenges 334–42
      potential statutory challenges
         333–34
      Supremacy Clause concerns 335
Midwest Greenhouse Gas Emission
   Registry 330